DATE DUE

			PRINTED IN U.S.A.

CLASSICAL
AND MEDIEVAL
LITERATURE
CRITICISM

Guide to Gale Literary Criticism Series

For criticism on	Consult these Gale series
Authors now living or who died after December 31, 1959	*CONTEMPORARY LITERARY CRITICISM (CLC)*
Authors who died between 1900 and 1959	*TWENTIETH-CENTURY LITERARY CRITICISM (TCLC)*
Authors who died between 1800 and 1899	*NINETEENTH-CENTURY LITERATURE CRITICISM (NCLC)*
Authors who died between 1400 and 1799	*LITERATURE CRITICISM FROM 1400 TO 1800 (LC)* *SHAKESPEAREAN CRITICISM (SC)*
Authors who died before 1400	*CLASSICAL AND MEDIEVAL LITERATURE CRITICISM (CMLC)*
Black writers of the past two hundred years	*BLACK LITERATURE CRITICISM (BLC)*
Authors of books for children and young adults	*CHILDREN'S LITERATURE REVIEW (CLR)*
Dramatists	*DRAMA CRITICISM (DC)*
Hispanic writers of the late nineteenth and twentieth centuries	*HISPANIC LITERATURE CRITICISM (HLC)*
Native North American writers and orators of the eighteenth, nineteenth, and twentieth centuries	*NATIVE NORTH AMERICAN LITERATURE (NNAL)*
Poets	*POETRY CRITICISM (PC)*
Short story writers	*SHORT STORY CRITICISM (SSC)*
Major authors from the Renaissance to the present	*WORLD LITERATURE CRITICISM, 1500 TO THE PRESENT (WLC)*

ISSN 0896-0011

Volume 17

CLASSICAL AND MEDIEVAL LITERATURE CRITICISM

Excerpts from Criticism of the Works of World
Authors from Classical Antiquity through the
Fourteenth Century, from the First Appraisals
to Current Evaluations

Jelena O. Krstović
Mary L. Onorato
Editors

GALE

STAFF

Jelena Krstović, *Editor*

Mary L. Onorato, *Contributing Editor*
Ondine Le Blanc, *Assistant Editor*

Susan Trosky, *Managing Editor*

Marlene S. Hurst, *Permissions Manager*
Margaret A. Chamberlain, Maria Franklin, *Permissions Specialists*
Diane Cooper,
Michele Lonoconus, Maureen Puhl, Susan Salas, Shalice Shah,
Kimberly F. Smilay, Barbara A. Wallace, *Permissions Associates*
Sarah Chesney, Edna Hedblad, Margaret McAvoy-Amato, Tyra Y. Phillips, Lori Schoenenberger, Rita Velazquez,
Permissions Assistants

Victoria B. Cariappa, *Research Manager*
Alicia Noel Biggers, Tamara C. Nott, Michele P. Pica, Tracie A. Richardson, *Research Associates*
Julia Daniel, Michelle Lee, Cheryl Warnock, *Research Assistants*

Mary Beth Trimper, *Production Director*
Deborah Milliken, *Production Assistant*

Barbara J. Yarrow, *Graphic Services Manager*
Sherrell Hobbs, *Macintosh Artist*
Pamela A. Hayes, *Photography Coordinator*
Randy Bassett, *Image Database Supervisor*
Robert Duncan, *Imaging Specialist*

This book is printed on acid-free paper that meets the minimum requirements of American National Standard for Information Sciences—Permanence Paper for Printed Library Materials, ANSI Z39.48-1984.

Library of Congress Catalog Card Number 88-658021
ISBN 0-8103-9301-8
ISSN 0896-0011
Printed in the United States of America

10 9 8 7 6 5 4 3 2 1

Contents

Preface   vii

Acknowledgments   xi

Preface

Since its inception in 1988, *Classical and Medieval Literature Criticism* has been a valuable resource for students and librarians seeking critical commentary on the writers and works of these periods in world history. Major reviewing sources have assessed *CMLC* as "useful" and "extremely convenient," noting that it "adds to our understanding of the rich legacy left by the ancient period and the Middle Ages," and praising its "general excellence in the presentation of an inherently interesting subject." No other single reference source has surveyed the critical reaction to classical and medieval literature as thoroughly as *CMLC*.

Scope of the Series

CMLC is designed to serve as an introduction for students and advanced readers of the works and authors of antiquity through the fourteenth century. The great poets, prose writers, dramatists, and philosophers of this period form the basis of most humanities curricula, so that virtually every student will encounter many of these works during the course of a high school and college education. By organizing and reprinting an enormous amount of commentary written on classical and medieval authors and works, *CMLC* helps students develop valuable insight into literary history, promotes a better understanding of the texts, and sparks ideas for papers and assignments. Each entry in *CMLC* presents a comprehensive survey of an author's career, an individual work of literature, or a literary topic, and provides the user with a multiplicity of interpretations and assessments. Such variety allows students to pursue their own interests; furthermore, it fosters an awareness that literature is dynamic and responsive to many different opinions.

CMLC continues the survey of criticism of world literature begun by Gale's *Contemporary Literary Criticism (CLC)*, *Twentieth-Century Literary Criticism (TCLC)*, *Nineteenth-Century Literature Criticism (NCLC)*, *Literature Criticism from 1400 to 1800 (LC)*, and *Shakespearean Criticism (SC)*. For additional information about these and Gale's other criticism series, users should consult the Guide to Gale Literary Criticism Series preceding the title page in this volume.

Coverage

Each volume of *CMLC* is carefully compiled to present:

- criticism of authors and works which represent a variety of genres, time periods, and nationalities

- both major and lesser-known writers and works of the period (such as non-Western authors and literature, increasingly read by today's students)

- 4-6 authors or works per volume

- individual entries that survey the critical response to each author, work, or topic, including early criticism, later criticism (to represent any rise or decline in the author's reputation), and current retrospective analyses. The length of each author or work entry also indicates relative importance, reflecting the amount of critical attention the author, work, or topic has received from critics writing in English, and from foreign criticism in translation.

An author may appear more than once in the series if his or her writings have been the subject of a substantial amount of criticism; in these instances, specific works or groups of works by the author will be covered in separate entries. For example, Homer will be represented by three entries, one devoted to the *Iliad,* one to the *Odyssey,* and one to the Homeric Hymns.

Starting with Volume 10, *CMLC* will also occasionally include entries devoted to literary topics. For example, *CMLC*-10 focuses on Arthurian Legend and includes general criticism on that subject as well as individual entries on writers or works central to that topic—Chrétien de Troyes, Gottfried von Strassburg, Layamon, and the Alliterative *Morte Arthure.*

Organization of the Book

An author entry consists of the following elements: author heading, biographical and critical introduction, principal English translations or editions, excerpts of criticism (each preceded by a bibliographic citation and an annotation), and a bibliography of further reading.

- The **Author Heading** consists of the author's most commonly used name, followed by birth and death dates. If the entry is devoted to a work, the heading will consist of the most common form of the title in English translation (if applicable), and the original date of composition. Located at the beginning of the introduction are any name or title variations.

- A **Portrait** of the author is included when available. Many entries also feature illustrations of materials pertinent to the author or work, including manuscript pages, book illustrations, and representations of people, places, and events important to a study of the author or work.

- The **Biographical and Critical Introduction** contains background information that concisely introduces the reader to the author, work, or topic.

- The list of **Principal Works** and **English Translations** or **Editions** is chronological by date of first publication and is included as an aid to the student seeking translated versions or editions of these works for study. The list will focus primarily on twentieth-century translations, selecting those works most commonly considered the best by critics.

- **Criticism** is arranged chronologically in each entry to provide a useful perspective on changes in critical evaluation over the years. All titles by the author featured in the critical entry are printed in boldface type to enable the user to ascertain without difficulty the works being discussed. Also for purposes of easier identification, the critic's name and the publication date of the essay are given at the beginning of each piece of criticism. Anonymous criticism is preceded by the title of the journal in which it appeared. Publication information (such as publisher names and book prices) and parenthetical numerical references (such as footnotes or page and line references to specific editions of works) have been deleted at the editors' discretion to provide smoother reading of the text. Many critical entries in *CMLC* also contain translations to aid the users.

- A complete **Bibliographic Citation** designed to facilitate the location of the original essay or book precedes each piece of criticism.

- Critical excerpts are also prefaced by **Annotations** providing the reader with information about both the critic and the criticism, the scope of the excerpt, the growth of critical controversy, or changes in critical trends regarding an author or work. In some cases, these notes include cross-references to excerpts by critics who discuss each other's commentary. Dates in parentheses within the annotation refer to a book publication date when they follow a book title, and to an essay date when they follow a critic's name.

- An annotated bibliography of **Further Reading** appears at the end of each entry and lists additional secondary sources on the author or work. In some cases it includes essays for which the editors could not obtain reprint rights. When applicable, the Further Reading is followed by references to additional entries on the author in other literary reference series published by Gale.

Topic Entries are subdivided into several thematic rubrics in which criticism appears in order of descending scope.

Cumulative Indexes

Each volume of *CMLC* includes a cumulative **author index** listing all authors who have appeared in Gale's Literary Criticism Series, along with cross references to such biographical series as *Contemporary Authors* and *Dictionary of Literary Biography*. For readers' convenience, a complete list of Gale titles included appears on the page prior to the author index. Useful for locating an author within the various series, this index is particularly valuable for those authors who are identified with a certain period but who, because of their death date, are placed in another, or for those authors whose careers span two periods. For example, Geoffrey Chaucer, who is usually considered a medieval author, is found in *Literature Criticism from 1400 to 1800* because he died after 1399.

Beginning with the tenth volume, *CMLC* includes a cumulative index listing all topic entries that have appeared in the Gale Literary Criticism Series *Classical and Medieval Literature Criticism, Contemporary Literary Criticism, Literature Criticism from 1400 to 1800, Nineteenth-Century Literature Criticism,* and *Twentieth-Century Literary Criticism.*

Beginning with the second volume, *CMLC* also includes a cumulative nationality index. Authors and/or works are grouped by nationality, and the volume in which criticism on them may be found is indicated.

Title Index

Each volume of *CMLC* also includes an index listing the titles of all literary works discussed in the series. Foreign language titles that have been translated are followed by the titles of the translations—for example, *Slovo o polku Igorove (The Song of Igor's Campaign)*. Page numbers following these translated titles refer to all pages on which any form of the title, either foreign language or translated, appears. Titles of novels, dramas, nonfiction books, and poetry, short story, or essay collections are printed in italics, while those of all individual poems, short stories, and essays are printed in roman type within quotation marks. In cases where the same title is used by different authors, the author's name or surname is given in parentheses after the title, e.g. *Collected Poems* (Horace) and *Collected Poems* (Sappho).

Critic Index

An index to critics, which cumulates with the second volume, is another useful feature of *CMLC*. Under each critic's name are listed the authors and/or works on whom the critic has written and the volume and page number where criticism may be found.

A Note to the Reader

When writing papers, students who quote directly from any volume in the Literary Criticism Series may use the following general forms to footnote reprinted criticism. The first example pertains to material drawn from a periodical, the second to material reprinted from books.

Rollo May, "The Therapist and the Journey into Hell," *Michigan Quarterly Review,* XXV, No. 4 (Fall 1986), 629-41; excerpted and reprinted in *Classical and Medieval Literature Criticism,* Vol. 3, ed. Jelena O. Krstović (Detroit: Gale Research, 1989), pp. 154-58.

Dana Ferrin Sutton, *Self and Society in Aristophanes* (University of Press of America, 1980); excerpted and reprinted in *Classical and Medieval Literature Criticism,* Vol. 4, ed. Jelena O. Krstović (Detroit: Gale Research, 1990), pp. 162-69.

Suggestions Are Welcome

Readers who wish to make suggestions for future volumes, or who have other comments regarding the series, are cordially invited to write or call the editors.

Acknowledgments

The editor wishes to thank the copyright holders of the excerpted criticism included in this volume, the permissions managers of many book and magazine publishing companies for assisting us in securing reprint rights, and Anthony Bogucki for assistance with copyright research. The editor is also grateful to the staffs of the Detroit Public Library, Wayne State University Purdy/Kresge Library Complex, and the University of Michigan Libraries for making their resources available. Following is a list of the copyright holders who have granted permission to reprint material in this volume of *CMLC*. Every effort has been made to trace copyright, but if omissions have been made, please let the editor know.

COPYRIGHTED EXCERPTS IN *CMLC*, VOLUME 17, WERE REPRINTED FROM THE FOLLOWING PERIODICALS:

Classical Antiquity, v. 9, October, 1990 for "Deceptions and Delusions in Herodotus" by Donald Lateiner. © 1990 by The Regents of the University of California. Reprinted by permission of the publisher and the author.— *Greek Roman and Byzantine Studies*, v. 26, Autumn, 1985. Reprinted by permission of the publisher.—*History and Theory*, v. XVII, 1978. Copyright © 1978 Wesleyan University. Reprinted by permission of the publisher.— *The Classical Quarterly*, v. XXII, November, 1972; v. XXXIX, 1989. © Oxford University Press 1972, 1989. Both reprinted by permission of the publisher.

COPYRIGHTED EXCERPTS IN *CMLC*, VOLUME 17, WERE REPRINTED FROM THE FOLLOWING BOOKS:

Adcock, F. E. From *Thucydides and His History*. Cambridge at the University Press, 1963. © Cambridge University Press 1963. Reprinted with the permission of the publisher and the author.— Anderson, J. K. From *Xenophon*. Charles Scribner's Sons, 1974. Copyright © 1974 J. K. Anderson. All rights reserved. Reprinted with the permission of Gerald R. Duckworth & Company, Ltd.—Cochrane, Charles Norris. From *Thucydides and the Science of History*. Oxford University Press, 1929. Reprinted by permission of Oxford University Press.—Collingwood, R. G. From *The Idea of History*. Oxford at the Clarendon Press, 1946. Reprinted by permission of Oxford University Press.—Connor, W. Robert. From "Narrative Discourse in Thucydides," in *The Greek Historians: Literature and History*. Anma Libri, 1985. © 1985 by Anma Libri & Co. All rights reserved. Reprinted by permission of the publisher and the author.—de Selincourt, Aubrey. From *The World of Herodotus*. Little, Brown and Company, 1962. Copyright © 1962 by Aubrey de Selincourt. All rights reserved. Reprinted by permission of Harold Ober Associates.—den Boer, W. From *Progress in the Greece of Thucydides*. Royal Netherlands Academy of Arts and Sciences, 1977. Reprinted by permission of the publisher.—Dionysius. From *Dionysius of Halicarnassus: On Thucydides*. Translated by W. Kendrick Pritchett. University of California Press, 1975. Copyright © 1975, by The Regents of the University of California. Reprinted by permission of the publisher and the translator.—Evans, J. A. S. From *Herodotus*. Twayne Publishers, 1982. Copyright © 1982 by G. K. Hall & Company. Reprinted with the permission of Twayne Publishers, an imprint of Simon & Schuster, Inc.—Evans, J. A. S. From *Herodotus, Explorer of the Past: Three Essays*. Princeton University Press, 1991. Copyright © 1991 by Princeton University Press. All rights reserved. Reprinted by permission of the Princeton University Press.—Finley, M. I. From *The Use and Abuse of History*. The Viking Press, 1975. Copyright © 1971, 1975 by M. I. Finley. All rights reserved. Used by permission of Viking Penguin, a division of Penguin Books USA Inc.—Finley, M. I. From *The Greek Historians: The Essence of Herodotus, Thucydides, Xenophon, Polybius*. Edited by M. I. Finley. Viking Press, 1959. Copyright © 1959 by The Viking Press, Inc. Used by permission of Viking Penguin, a division of Penguin Books USA Inc.—Finley, John H. From *Thucydides*. Cambridge, Mass.: Harvard University Press, 1942. Copyright 1942 by the President and Fellows of Harvard College. Renewed 1970. Excerpted by permission of the publishers and the author.—Fornara, Charles W. From *Herodotus: An*

Greek Historiography

INTRODUCTION

Scholars have traced the beginnings of Greek historiography, or the writing of history, to the body of mythical tales, first transmitted orally in Greek culture, that made up its earliest literature. One of the main purposes of Greek myths, in fact, was to create a sense of the past and to make that past intelligible to the average citizen. Greeks first learned something about their origin as a people through Homeric poetry, some of which is now known to have a basis in fact and some of which was wholly imaginative. In some ways, as critics have observed, the events of the distant past became more real than the present, as stories of the gods and such mythical heroes as Odysseus and Agamemnon took hold of the national psyche. The *Theogony*, a work dating to the eighth century B.C. and generally attributed to Hesiod also supported this tradition by presenting the story of the beginning of the world based on legends of the Greek gods; the *Works and Days*, likewise attributed to Hesiod, related a kind of history of civilization by describing the various "ages" of the world. Early Greek poetry recited by bards at festivals and in private homes presented a past that was customarily viewed as at least partly factual; it also certainly kept alive an interest, albeit highly ethnocentric, as scholars have pointed out, in the idea of history.

The Greek worldview began to expand, however, in the mid-sixth century B.C., when Anaximander of Miletus began writing prose accounts about geography and eventually went on to construct a map of the known world. These two strands—mythical history and observational geography—helped to provide the impetus for what is often referred to as the Ionian intellectual revolution of the fifth century B.C. The chief two characteristics of this revolution were a new spirit of scepticism toward received myths and an interest in inquiry *(historia)* into matters concerning man and his world. During this period Greece was ruled first by Lydian overlords who controlled lands from Asia Minor to Sardis, and later by the Persians. Apparently inspired to find out more about their occupiers and about the other people with whom they came into contact through trade and travel, prose writers known as logographers, writing in the Ionian dialect of Greek, composed numerous accounts dealing with ethnology and anthropology, and preserving in writing many legends, folktales, traditions, and myths. The writings of the logographers have not survived, but they are thought to have played a key role in the development of Greek

historiography, since, combined with later prose such as chronicles, genealogies, and reports of journeys, they constitute among the earliest of historical accounts. The culmination of this phase of historiography came in two works by Hecataeus of Miletus, *Journey round the World* and *Genealogies*—the first a geography interspersed with commentary, and the second a chronological generational scheme probably based on the Spartan king-list. As Michael Grant has observed, these two works "did not reject the [traditional] myths, but modified them here and there on commonsense, rationalistic grounds, examining them on their supposed merits in the light of [Hecataeus's] own judgment so as to make them more sane and credible." From there it was a relatively short leap to the historical approach of Herodotus, Thucydides, Xenophon, and, later, Polybius.

Scholars often point out that, in discussing Greek historians, it is important to remember that they were not all Greek and not all historians. Herodotus came from bilingual Helleno-Carian Halicarnassus, Thucydides was of partly Thracian descent, Josephus was a Jew, and Procopius a Philistine. Further, they were influenced and inspired by contact with other cultures—the Syro-Iranian in the case of Herodotus, and Roman Italian in the case of Polybius. Many were voluntary or forced exiles from their country (for example, Diodorus of Sicily and Dionysius of Halicarnassus, first century B.C. Greek immigrants in Rome), and all did not even compose their works in the Greek language. Finally, they were in no sense "professional" historians, for many also composed poetry, philosophy, romance, anthropological works, and studies in physical science. Yet they all shared, to various extents, the basic Greek attitude toward history.

According to the prevailing view in Greek metaphysics, it ought to be impossible to know history: the Greeks believed that only certain unchangeable things and concepts can be understood and known and that anything changeable cannot be grasped by the mind. R. G. Collingwood has noted in this context how truly remarkable it is that the early Greek historians attempted to write history at all. As a result, Greek historians tended to concentrate on contemporary history—on what they witnessed in their own time. Another characteristic of the Greek attitude toward history is the belief that any written history must be treated simply as a collection of facts, without any causation necessarily implied, yet with the inherent possibility of clarifying future events. As Collingwood has written, "history has a value; its teachings are useful for human life; simply because the rhythm of its changes is likely to repeat itself, similar antecedents leading to similar consequents; the history of notable events is worth remembering in order to serve as a basis for prognostic judgments, not demonstrable but probable, laying down not what will happen but what is likely to happen, indicating the points of danger in rhythms now going on." History, then can teach; but ancient writers continued to consider poetry superior to history because, while history presented man with facts, poetry presented timeless truths. In the words of Aristotle in *The Poetics*, "Poetry. . .is a more philosophical and higher thing than history: for poetry tends to express the universal, history the particular." Scholars traditionally credit Thucydides with being the best of the Greek historians in terms of style and narration. Herodotus and Thucydides both used eyewitness accounts as evidence for their narratives, indicating that they carefully screened eyewitnesses by cross-examining them to ensure the truthfulness of their testimony. At the same time, however, they felt free to embellish their narratives with at least some measure of the fictional, as in the speeches attributed to historical personages in their histories.

Scholarship on Greek historiography has concerned itself with various questions, but chief among the topics studied have been the limitations of and the problem of the continuity of Greek historical writing, the investigation of the competency of the ancient historians, and inquiry into the influence and reception of their ideas. One of the main problems of studying Greek historiography is that so little of it survives: Herodotus, Thucydides, Xenophon, and Polybius are the only Greek historians whose work has reached us in anything but fragments. Based on the available texts, critics have identified the fundamental problems inherent in the Greek view of history as being its small scope (the idea that history should only be written about events in living memory), the lack of choice with which the historian is presented (because contemporary subjects are deemed most suitable for study), and the fact that no comprehensive history can ever be written under the Greek model, since only a limited view of events is afforded each historian. For these and other reasons, scholars have concluded that, compared to other kinds of texts, Greek literature is comparatively poor in historical writing. They have explored some of the factors responsible for the break in the continuity of Greek historiography—or the question of why Herodotus's lead was not followed—and have cited such factors as Herodotus's unique ability to see his subject as part of a larger process, his interest in Egyptian and Asian "barbarian" cultures, and his unusually literary prose as partly responsible. As Arnaldo Momigliano has pointed out, "The fact is that Greek historiography never replaced philosophy or religion and was never wholeheartedly accepted by either. The status of historiography was never clearly settled among the Greeks." In fact, it seems more unusual that a figure like Herodotus ever emerged from the Greek tradition than that he was not the start of a new way of thinking about history. The validity of the historians' techniques and the question of disentangling the strands and degree of myth in their writings has long been a topic of debate. The statement made by the English historian Thomas Babington Macaulay in the nineteenth century still holds true: "The fictions [in Greek historical writing] are so much like the facts, and the facts so much like the fictions, that, with respect to many most interesting particulars, our belief is neither given nor withheld, but remains in an uneasy and interminable state of abeyance. We know that there is truth, but we cannot exactly decide where it lies."

Greek historiography has greatly influenced the later course of western historical writing as a discipline and has even made contributions to the growth of related genres such as biography, ethnography, geography, travel narratives, and romance. Momigliano has written that "Modern history-writing has been by choice a continuous confrontation with the Greek originals and with what the Romans made of their models." The major characteristics of Greek historical writing shaped the way that historians approached their work through the Roman and early Christian periods. The idea of using texts as evidence, concentrating on contemporary events, the notion of the historian as a witness and recorder of events, and the need to explain rather than merely enumerate events remained vital hallmarks of early historical thinking. The question, too, of the balance between instructing and giving pleasure to the reader of a given historical narrative, first debated by the ancient historians, still remains a point under discussion in modern times.

CRITICISM

Thomas Babington Macaulay (essay date 1828)

SOURCE: "History and Literature: Thomas Babington Macaulay," in *The Varieties of History: From Voltaire to the Present,* revised edition, edited by Fritz Stern, Macmillan and Co., 1970, pp. 71-89.

[Macaulay was a respected English writer and statesman whose best-known work is The History of England *(1848-61), covering the reigns of James II and William III. In the following excerpt from his essay "History," first published in the* Edinburgh Review *in 1828, he comments on Herodotus and Thucydides in the context of separating truth from fiction in historical writing.]*

To write history respectably—that is, to abbreviate despatches, and make extracts from speeches, to intersperse in due proportion epithets of praise and abhorrence, to draw up antithetical characters of great men, setting forth how many contradictory virtues and vices they united, and abounding in *withs* and *withouts*—all this is very easy. But to be a really great historian is perhaps the rarest of intellectual distinctions. Many scientific works are, in their kind, absolutely perfect. There are poems which we should be inclined to designate as faultless, or as disfigured only by blemishes which pass unnoticed in the general blaze of excellence. There are speeches, some speeches of Demosthenes particularly, in which it would be impossible to alter a word without altering it for the worse. But we are acquainted with no history which approaches to our notion of what a history ought to be—with no history which does not widely depart, either on the right hand or on the left, from the exact line.

The cause may easily be assigned. This province of literature is a debatable land. It lies on the confines of two distinct territories. It is under the jurisdiction of two hostile powers; and, like other districts similarly situated, it is ill defined, ill cultivated, and ill regulated. Instead of being equally shared between its two rulers, the Reason and the Imagination, it falls alternately under the sole and absolute dominion of each. It is sometimes fiction; it is sometimes theory.

History, it has been said, is philosophy teaching by examples. Unhappily, what the philosophy gains in soundness and depth the examples generally lose in vividness. A perfect historian must possess an imagination sufficiently powerful to make his narrative affecting and picturesque. Yet he must control it so absolutely as to content himself with the materials which he finds, and to refrain from supplying deficiencies by additions of his own. He must be a profound and ingenious reasoner. Yet he must possess sufficient self-command to abstain from casting his facts in the mould of his hypothesis. Those who can justly estimate these almost insuperable difficulties will not think it strange that every writer should have failed, either in the narrative or in the speculative department of history.

It may be laid down as a general rule, though subject to considerable qualifications and exceptions, that history begins in novel and ends in essay. Of the romantic historians Herodotus is the earliest and the best. His animation, his simple-hearted tenderness, his wonderful talent for description and dialogue, and the pure sweet flow of his language, place him at the head of narrators. He reminds us of a delightful child. There is a grace beyond the reach of affectation in his awkwardness, a malice in his innocence, an intelligence in his nonsense, an insinuating eloquence in his lisp. We know of no writer who makes such interest for himself and his book in the heart of the reader. At the distance of three-and-twenty centuries, we feel for him the same sort of pitying fondness which Fontaine and Gay are said to have inspired in society. He has written an incomparable book. He has written something better, perhaps, than the best history; but he has not written a good history; he is, from the first to the last chapter, an inventor. We do not here refer merely to those gross fictions with which he has been reproached by the critics of later times. We speak of that colouring which is equally diffused over his whole narrative, and which perpetually leaves the most sagacious reader in doubt what to reject and what to receive. The most authentic parts of his work bear the same relation to his wildest legends which *Henry the Fifth* bears to the *Tempest*. There was an expedition undertaken by Xerxes against Greece, and there was an invasion of France. There was a battle at Platæa, and there was a battle at Agincourt. Cambridge and Exeter, the Constable and the Dauphin, were persons as real as Demaratus and Pausanias. The harangue of the Archbishop on the Salic Law and the Book of Numbers differs much less from the orations which have in all ages proceeded from the right reverend bench than the speeches of Mardonius and Artabanus from those which were delivered at the council-board of Susa. Shakspeare gives us enumerations of armies, and returns of killed and wounded, which are not, we suspect, much less accurate than those of Herodotus. There are passages in Herodotus nearly as long as acts of Shakspeare, in which everything is told dramatically, and in which the narrative serves only the purpose of stage-directions. It is possible, no doubt, that the substance of some real conversations may have been reported to the historian. But events which, if they ever happened, happened in ages and nations so remote that the particulars could never have been known to him, are related with the greatest minuteness of detail. We have all that Candaules said to Gyges, and all that passed between Astyages and Harpagus. We are, therefore, unable to judge whether, in the account which he gives of transactions respecting which he might possibly have been well informed, we can trust to anything beyond the naked outline; whether, for example, the answer of Gelon to the ambassadors of the Grecian confederacy, or the expressions which passed between Aristides and Themistocles at their famous interview, have been correctly transmitted to us. The great events are, no doubt, faithfully related. So, probably, are many of the slighter circumstances; but which of them it is impossible to ascertain. The fictions are so much like the facts, and the facts so much like the fictions, that, with respect to many most interesting particulars, our belief is neither given nor withheld, but remains in an uneasy and interminable state of abeyance. We know that there is truth, but we cannot exactly decide where it lies.

The faults of Herodotus are the faults of a simple and imaginative mind. Children and servants are remarkably Herodotean in their style of narration. They tell everything dramatically. Their *says hes* and *says shes* are proverbial. Every person who has had to settle their disputes knows that, even when they have no intention to deceive, their reports of conversation always require to be carefully sifted. If an educated man were giving an account of the late change of administration, he would say—"Lord Goderich resigned; and the King, in consequence, sent for the Duke of Wellington." A porter tells the story as if he had been hid behind the curtains of the royal bed at Windsor: "So Lord Goderich says, 'I cannot manage this business; I must go out.' So the King says—says he, 'Well, then, I must send for the Duke of Wellington—that's all.'" This is in the very manner of the father of history. . . .

The history of Thucydides differs from that of Herodotus as a portrait differs from the representation of an imaginary scene; as the Burke or Fox of Reynolds differs from his Ugolino or his Beaufort. In the former case the archetype is given, in the latter it is created. The faculties which are required for the latter purpose are of a higher and rarer order than those which suffice for the former, and, indeed, necessarily comprise them. He who is able to paint what he sees with the eye of the mind will surely be able to paint what he sees with the eye of the body. He who can invent a story, and tell it well, will also be able to tell, in an interesting manner, a story which he has not invented. If, in practice, some of the best writers of fiction have been among the worst writers of history, it has been because one of their talents had merged in another so completely that it could not be severed; because, having long been habituated to invent and narrate at the same time, they found it impossible to narrate without inventing.

Some capricious and discontented artists have affected to consider portrait-painting as unworthy of a man of genius. Some critics have spoken in the same contemptuous manner of history. Johnson puts the case thus: The historian tells either what is false or what is true: in the former case he is no historian; in the latter he has no opportunity for displaying his abilities: for truth is one; and all who tell the truth must tell it alike.

It is not difficult to elude both the horns of this dilemma. We will recur to the analogous art of portrait-painting. Any man with eyes and hands may be taught to take a likeness. The process, up to a certain point, is merely mechanical. If this were all, a man of talents might justly despise the occupation. But we could mention portraits which are resemblances—but not mere resemblances; faithful—but much more than faithful; portraits which condense into one point of time, and exhibit at a single glance the whole history of turbid and eventful lives—in which the eye seems to scrutinise us, and the mouth to command us—in which the brow menaces, and the lip almost quivers with scorn—in which every wrinkle is a comment on some important transaction. The account which Thucydides has given of the retreat from Syracuse is, among narratives, what Vandyck's Lord Strafford is among paintings.

Diversity, it is said, implies error: truth is one, and admits of no degrees. We answer that this principle holds good only in abstract reasonings. When we talk of the truth of imitation in the fine arts, we mean an imperfect and a graduated truth. No picture is exactly like the original; nor is a picture good in proportion as it is like the original. When Sir Thomas Lawrence paints a handsome peeress, he does not contemplate her through a powerful microscope, and transfer to the canvas the pores of the skin, the blood-vessels of the eye, and all the other beauties which Gulliver discovered in the Brobdingnagian maids of honour. If he were to do this, the effect would not merely be unpleasant, but, unless the scale of the picture were proportionably enlarged, would be absolutely *false*. And, after all, a microscope of greater power than that which he had employed would convict him of innumerable omissions. The same may be said of history. Perfectly and absolutely true it cannot be; for, to be perfectly and absolutely true, it ought to record *all* the slightest particulars of the slightest transactions—all the things done and all the words uttered during the time of which it treats. The omission of any circumstance, however insignificant, would be a defect. If history were written thus, the Bodleian library would not contain the occurrences of a week. What is told in the fullest and most accurate annals bears an infinitely small proportion to what is suppressed. The difference between the copious work of Clarendon and the account of the civil wars in the abridgment of Goldsmith vanishes when compared with the immense mass of facts respecting which both are equally silent.

No picture, then, and no history, can present us with the whole truth: but those are the best pictures and the best histories which exhibit such parts of the truth as most nearly produce the effect of the whole. He who is deficient in the art of selection may, by showing nothing but the truth, produce all the effect of the grossest falsehood. It perpetually happens that one writer tells less truth than another, merely because he tells more truths. In the imitative arts we constantly see this. There are lines in the human face, and objects in landscape, which stand in such relations to each other that they ought either to be all introduced into a painting together or all omitted together. A sketch into which none of them enters may be excellent; but, if some are given and others left out, though there are more points of likeness, there is less likeness. An outline scrawled with a pen, which seizes the marked features of a countenance, will give a much stronger idea of it than a bad painting in oils. Yet the worst painting in oils that ever hung at Somerset House resembles the original in many more particulars. A bust of white marble may give an excellent idea of a blooming face.

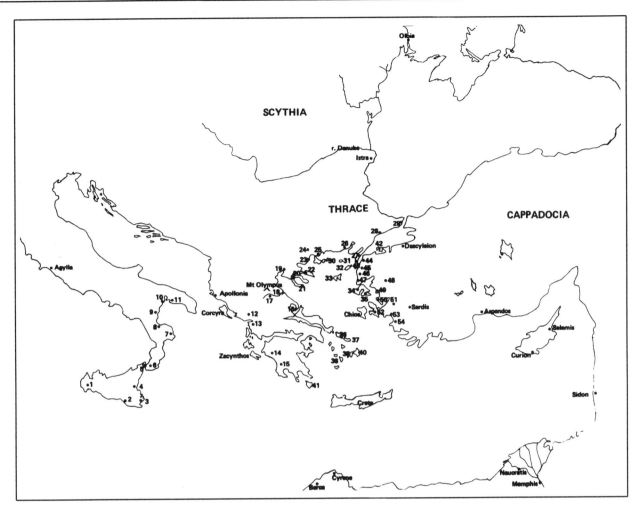

The Greek world.

Colour the lips and cheeks of the bust, leaving the hair and eyes unaltered, and the similarity, instead of being more striking, will be less so.

History has its foreground and its background; and it is principally in the management of its perspective that one artist differs from another. Some events must be represented on a large scale, others diminished; the great majority will be lost in the dimness of the horizon; and a general idea of their joint effect will be given by a few slight touches.

In this respect no writer has ever equalled Thucydides. He was a perfect master of the art of gradual diminution. His history is sometimes as concise as a chronological chart; yet it is always perspicuous. It is sometimes as minute as one of Lovelace's letters; yet it is never prolix. He never fails to contract and to expand it in the right place.

Thucydides borrowed from Herodotus the practice of putting speeches of his own into the mouths of his characters. In Herodotus this usage is scarcely censurable. It is of a piece with his whole manner. But it is altogether incongruous in the work of his successor, and violates, not only the accuracy of history, but the decencies of fiction. When once we enter into the spirit of Herodotus, we find no inconsistency. The conventional probability of his drama is preserved from the beginning to the end. The deliberate orations and the familiar dialogues are in strict keeping with each other. But the speeches of Thucydides are neither preceded nor followed by anything with which they harmonise. They give to the whole book something of the grotesque character of those Chinese pleasure-grounds in which perpendicular rocks of granite start up in the midst of a soft green plain. Invention is shocking where truth is in such close juxtaposition with it.

Thucydides honestly tells us that some of these discourses are purely fictitious. He may have reported the substance of others correctly. But it is clear from the internal evidence that he has preserved no more than the substance. His own peculiar habits of thought and expression are everywhere discernible. Individual and national peculiarities are seldom to be traced in the sentiments, and never in the diction. The oratory of the Corinthians and Thebans is not less Attic, either in matter or in manner, than that of the Athenians. The style of Cleon is as pure, as austere, as terse, and as significant as that of Pericles.

In spite of this great fault, it must be allowed that Thucydides has surpassed all his rivals in the art of historical narration, in the art of producing an effect on the imagination, by skilful selection and disposition, without indulging in the licence of invention. But narration, though an important part of the business of a historian, is not the whole. To append a moral to a work of fiction is either useless or superfluous. A fiction may give a more impressive effect to what is already known, but it can teach nothing new. If it presents to us characters and trains of events to which our experience furnishes us with nothing similar, instead of deriving instruction from it, we pronounce it unnatural. We do not form our opinions from it, but we try it by our preconceived opinions. Fiction, therefore, is essentially imitative. Its merit consists in its resemblance to a model with which we are already familiar, or to which at least we can instantly refer. Hence it is that the anecdotes which interest us most strongly in authentic narrative are offensive when introduced into novels; that what is called the romantic part of history is in fact the least romantic. It is delightful as history, because it contradicts our previous notions of human nature, and of the connection of causes and effects. It is, on that very account, shocking and incongruous in fiction. In fiction, the principles are given, to find the facts: in history, the facts are given, to find the principles; and the writer who does not explain the phenomena as well as state them performs only one half of his office. Facts are the mere dross of history. It is from the abstract truth which interpenetrates them, and lies latent among them like gold in the ore, that the mass derives its whole value: and the precious particles are generally combined with the baser in such a manner that the separation is a task of the utmost difficulty. . . .

Arnold J. Toynbee (essay date 1924)

SOURCE: An introduction to Greek Historical Thought, from Homer to the Age of Heraclius, translated by Arnorld J. Toynbee, 1924. Reprint by The Beacon Press, 1950, pp. v-xxviii.

[*Toynbee was an eminent English sociologist and economist. In the following excerpt from his work on Greek historians, he argues that the writers included in this category were neither, by and large, solely Greek, nor only historians, because they also contributed to other genres.*]

Ancient Greek or Hellenic historical thought began at the moment when the first rudiments of the poetry of Homer shaped themselves in Greek minds. It came to an end when Homer yielded precedence to the Bible as the sacred book of a Greek-speaking and Greek-writing *intelligentzia*. In the series of historical authors the latter event occurred between the dates at which Theophylactus Simocatta and George of Pisidia produced their respective works. . . . A historical process, however, seldom takes place abruptly, and the transition from Hellenic to Byzantine civilisation (of which this literary revolution was one sympton among many) occupied from first to last a period of fully three centuries. This becomes evident as soon as we bring other aspects of life into our field of vision. Paulus, for example, an Imperial Groom of the Bedchamber and a *confrère* of his contemporary the historian Agathias in the art of minor poetry, was still able in the sixth century after Christ to write with ease in the language and metre of Mimnermus; but the subject of his longest and most celebrated poem is the Church of Agia Sofia—the masterpiece of an architecture antithetical in almost every feature to any Hellenic monument of Colophon or Ephesus or Athens. The change declares itself simultaneously in the field of Religion. The creed, at once primitive and profound, of Pride, Doom and the Envy of the Gods is characteristic of the Hellenic outlook upon life. It appears already articulated in the earliest strata of Homer. . . . The spirit of this specifically Hellenic religion is unmistakable in all the literature which it pervades; but an examination of the passage entitled "Agnosticism" which has been translated from Agathias's immediate predecessor Procopius reveals the fact that by the middle of the sixth century after Christ Hellenic religion was extinct—even in the hearts of men who had been educated in the Hellenic literary tradition and who still paid lip-service to the Hellenic gods. In a rather pedantic reminiscence of a Herodotean mannerism, Procopius refrains from discussing the *arcana* of contemporary Christian controversy on the ground that the subjects professedly in dispute are by their nature incomprehensible to the human reason, and incidentally he propounds what to his mind are the bare axiomatic facts regarding the character of God. Yet anybody who has caught . . . the real religious outlook of Hellenism will see at once that Procopius's axioms would have appeared to Herodotus or Thucydides or Polybius to beg the fundamental questions of good and evil. Poor Procopius! How deeply he would have been mortified could he have realised that, in the estimation of his classical literary ensamples, his intellectual superciliousness would have stood him in no stead whatsoever, and that they would have classed him remorselessly with their reverences Hypatius and Demetrius, and with His Sacred Majesty Justinian himself, as a *type croyant* characteristic of his soft-headed age.

The Envy of the Gods was a serious matter to the

Hellenes because they preferred to lay up their treasure where moth and rust doth corrupt and where thieves break through and steal. Their kingdom was emphatically a kingdom of this world. Pericles exhorted his countrymen to let the greatness of Athens "fill," not "pass," their understanding; the "salvation" debated at Melos meant bodily escape from massacre or enslavement and not the release of the soul from guilt or perdition; the "Saviour" *par excellence* in the Hellenic tradition was Ptolemy, son of Lagus, who successfully abstracted that title from Zeus until he forfeited it to a proletarian descendant of his Oriental subjects; and the "sin" over which Polybius declined to draw a veil was the political folly by which Diaeus and his colleagues brought the Achaean Confederacy to ruin. In other words, the world of Hellenism (and herein lies its supreme interest for us) was a world like that in which we live to-day, by contrast with the Christian dispensation which in the chronological sense intervenes between us, or with that religion, yet unborn, which will undoubtedly lay up a new treasure in a new heaven as our world sinks, to founder at last like its predecessors in "the abyss where all things are incommensurable."

There is no space within the limits of this introduction to offer anything like a biographical index, however summary, of the historical authors whose works are represented in the text of the book; but one or two general observations may be an aid to interpretation. In the first place, the Hellenic historians (especially the greatest of them) were by no means purely Hellenic in race. Herodotus came from the bilingual Helleno-Carian community of Halicarnassus; Thucydides, although Athenian born and possessed (until his exile) of Athenian citizenship, had Thracian blood in his veins; Josephus was a Jew, Procopius a Philistine—though, from the age of Alexander onwards, it goes without saying that Hellenic historians were drawn from all the peoples among whom the Gospel of Hellenism was successively propagated. In this phase historical writing of the Hellenic school did not even confine itself to the vehicle of the Greek language. . . . The unparalleled political aggrandisement of Rome enabled Roman historians to group the world's affairs round the destinies of their own city-state; and therefore, as Dionysius of Halicarnassus pointed out, they tended to cultivate a particular branch of Hellenic historical literature: the local chronicle. From this point of view the Roman historians, like the Roman adaptors of the Athenian Comedy of Manners, offered us almost our only material for reconstructing a lost branch of Hellenic literature, until the recent discovery of the Aristotelian *Constitution of Athens* restored to us, in epitome, the local chronicle of the most interesting city-state in Hellas Proper. Thus, in history as in other spheres, the influence of Hellenism radiated far more widely than the Greek language or the Greek race; and that is one of the principal testimonies to its greatness.

At the same time, it is equally true that some of the most profound and most illuminating creations of Hellenic historical thought were inspired by contact with non-Hellenic societies. Herodotus's eyes were opened by his study of the Syro-Iranian civilisation embodied in the universal state of the Achaemenids, which in his time had attempted, and failed, to assimilate the Hellenic world. Polybius was similarly stimulated by the revelation of Roman Italy (with its broadening hinterland in the West) at a moment when Rome was achieving, in the military sense, what Persia had failed to do, while in every other department of life the victor was being carried captive by Hellenism. Polybius, who came from Megalopolis in the depths of Arcadia, was the only one of the three great historical geniuses of Hellenism who was a pure Hellene in the comparatively unimportant zoological sense of the word; but a civilisation, at any given moment of its existence, is never a mere product of physical transmission or local environment. It is a communion of saints (and of sinners) compassed about by that great and ever-increasing cloud of witnesses that have already joined the majority of mankind; and membership in it is therefore a matter of spiritual rather than of material affiliations. It is conceivable, for instance, that the fifteenth-century Athenian historian Laonīcus Chalcocondyles, who, in excellent classical Greek and in a style carefully modelled upon Herodotus and Thucydides, has recorded the rise of the Ottoman Empire, could have traced his genealogy to Erechtheus or Deucalion on both sides of the family more plausibly than Thucydides himself, or that he would have been found, if examined by a trained anthropologist, to exhibit a "more Hellenic" pigmentation, cephalic index and facial angle. Yet, for all that, Thucydides would retain his unchallenged supremacy as the greatest Hellenic historian, while Chalcocondyles would remain the ornament that he is to Byzantine—but not to Hellenic—civilisation. It would have been idle for Chalcocondyles and his Byzantine contemporaries of the Renaissance to protest that they had Deucalion to their father, when, two thousand years before, the Heavenly Muse had already raised up children to Deucalion out of the stones of Thrace and Caria.

It is a second characteristic of Hellenic historical thought that it was by no means exclusively the creation of professional historians. The poetry of different ages, as well as the philosophy of Plato and the medical literature of the Hippocratean School, have been laid under contribution in this book because they happen to have expressed certain fundamental Hellenic historical ideas more clearly than any work of history in the technical sense. Conversely, the historians have made many contributions to Romance, Genealogy, Anthropology and Physical Science. . . . Perhaps as much (to hazard a guess) as four-fifths of the total body of Hellenic historical writing that has reached us is occupied by detailed accounts of military operations—a curious fact, considering how intellectual, and speculatively intellectual, was the public for whom most works of Hellenic history were written. . . .

The features just mentioned are possibly not peculiar to Hellenic historical writing. It is more characteristic that, even when we narrow down our range of vision to the professional historians themselves, we find that the vast majority of them were men of the world. Thucydides, Xenophon, Polybius and Josephus (four out of the five greatest figures) were all rising men of action with broken careers, who only turned their energies into a literary channel when the Envy of the Gods had deprived them of the opportunity to hold offices of state, to carry public business through political assemblies, or to command fleets or armies in the field. The private life of Herodotus, the fifth great figure, is hardly known to us. His Voltairean turn of mind suggests a born observer and critic rather than an instinctive participant in affairs; yet his intellectual work was always a living and a humane activity, because he studied contemporary history and sociology, and studied them from nature, in an extensive and adventurous series of travels. In other words, he took his observations with the eyes of Odysseus and not through the lenses of Ranke, and this is a distinctive note of the Hellenic Historical School. Polybius, again, travelled as extensively in the north-western as Herodotus had done in the south-eastern hinterland of the Hellenic world of his time; and Diodorus, whose work sometimes smells pungently of the lamp, was not content (as he tells us himself) to sit in libraries at Agyrium or even at Rome. In the case of historians who were fortunate enough to live during the Time of Growth or the Time of Troubles, this salutary intimacy with the active life of their society is not really surprising, unless by contrast with the phenomena of other civilisations. It is remarkable, however, to find that this feature did not disappear during the third and last phase, during which the Hellenic world lay more or less passive under the pall of the *Pax Romana*. In that age, at least, the academic historian might be expected to predominate; yet, even from the period of the Roman Empire, Dionysius and Eunapius are the only undoubted examples of the type who have found their way into the present volume. Arrian and Dio were soldiers and statesmen with as varied an experience of public life and of practical responsibilities as had ever fallen to the lot of a Xenophon or a Polybius. Herodian was probably a civil servant; Appian was either a civil servant or a member of the local aristocracy of Alexandria, which in his time still carried on the municipal administration; Marcus Diaconus was a practical (and on occasions exceedingly drastic) missionary; Priscus was a barrister, and so likewise were Procopius, Agathias and Menander, the three notable figures from the sixth century after Christ. The Bar was the last liberal profession that held out against the disintegration of Hellenic society; and, although Agathias might complain that it left him too little leisure for his historical studies, we may feel less sorry for him when we contemplate the use to which unchastened leisure was put by his successor Simocatta.

After this brief discussion of the Hellenic historians and of the world in which they lived, it may be well to close with a word upon methods of translation. In the present translator's view, the capital and almost irreparable error to be avoided by a modern Western mind in approaching any branch of Hellenic literature is to allow itself to be dominated by the thought that all this was done and felt and written between two and three thousand years ago—as though chronological antiquity implied, in this case, any corresponding *naïveté* or poverty of experience. The fact is that the relation in which we consciously stand to our own Western predecessors of three or six or twelve centuries ago has hardly any analogy to our relations with members of other civilisations, even though the life-history of those civilisations may in the chronological sense be previous to ours. In spite of such chronological priority, the remote past embodied in foreign civilisations may be subjectively nearer to the life of our own day than is the recent past out of which our life has arisen. In other words, chronological priority and posteriority have little or no subjective significance except within the single span of a given civilisation, while, in comparing the histories of different civilisations, the direct chronological relation between them is an almost irrelevant, and therefore usually misleading, factor. In the philosophical sense, all civilisations have been and are and will continue to be contemporaneous with one another. They are all the offspring of the same family in the same generation, and the differences of age between them are infinitesimal in comparison with the immense period during which the human family had existed before any civilisation was born. Therefore, in attempting to find an equation between two independent civilisations (and that is what translation from Ancient Greek into Modern English ultimately means) it may be a not unprofitable exercise of the fancy to date in some approximate and conventional way their respective starting-points, measure the chronological interval between these, and then subtract the amount of that interval in order to discover the century in the chronologically earlier civilisation to which any given century in the later civilisation corresponds from this point of view. For example, if we take 1125 B.C. as a conventional year for Hellenism, in which Hellenic civilisation began to emerge out of the wreckage of the shattered Minoan world, and A.D. 675 as a conventional year of a similar kind for the West, in which Western civilisation began to emerge out of the wreckage of Hellenism (in its Roman extension), we shall estimate at something like 1800 years the chronological interval between Hellenic and Western history which has always to be eliminated in order to find their correspondence, at any given stage, as measured from their respective starting-points. It is hardly necessary to say that this is not intended as a historical dogma, but merely as a suggestion for arriving at a method of comparative study. By the aid of this fanciful measuring-rod we can ascertain which Hellenic and which Western generations were "contemporary" with one another in the sense that they were separated from their respective starting-points by an equal period of time, and therefore possessed at any rate a quantitatively (though by no means necessarily a qualitatively) equal fund of traditional experience or social heritage in the various fields of economics, politics, literature, art, religion and the rest. With this magic wand in our hands, we may amuse ourselves by translating (say) Plutarch himself, and not merely Plutarch's writings, from the Hellenic world into ours; and if we do so, we shall find that Plutarch would have been born in 1846 and would be destined to die in 1925 as a last grand survivor of the Victorians! If there is any significance at all in this, we cannot expect to appreciate Plutarch so long as we insist upon reading him in Langhorne's translation, or to reproduce him to our own satisfaction so long as we interlard our modern translation with Elizabethan tags until we have compounded a hotch-potch of "translationese" unlike any living piece of literature of our own age or any other. *A fortiori,* we cannot defend such false archaism in the case of authors who, if magically translated in person into our own world, would at this moment be either still unborn or in their early infancy. Marcus Aurelius, for example, would be not yet four years old, and would be able to look forward to living until 1980. May the Envy of the Gods spare our own children born into this Western World in 1921 from so melancholy a view of human life as their great Hellenic contemporary's!

What is the bearing of this suggested parallelism upon the translation of literature? At first sight it might appear as though we ought to translate Marcus and Plutarch into the literary English (or French or German or Italian or whatever our particular Western vernacular may be) that is being written in our own generation, and then clothe their predecessors, phase by phase, in the corresponding styles of our own literary background—maintaining the same interval of approximately eighteen centuries throughout the process. As soon, however, as we attempt to think this programme out, the obstacles become apparent. In the first place, the "curves" of Western and Hellenic history do not correspond. In Hellenic the highest peak was reached (and never again equalled) during the two centuries between the years 525 and 325 B.C., which were contemporaneous (on our fanciful scheme of measurement) with the two centuries between A.D. 1275 and 1475 in the West. In our case, however, that period, though it marked a secondary peak in the life of Northern and Central Italy, was far from being the zenith in the entire life-history of the whole society. The West, as a whole, rose to greater heights of self-expression (or, as Peri-

cles might have put it, "raised more imperishable monuments of its presence for good or evil") between about the year 1775 and the European War; while, in contrast, the equivalent period of Hellenic history (25 B.C.-A.D. 114) fell wholly within the latest phase of Hellenic life, during which a world stricken to death by four centuries of troubles was attempting a final rally before its inevitable dissolution. We who are still young in 1924 do not yet pretend to know whether the West has just (though only just) begun to descend on its long journey *ad tartara leti,* whereas Plutarch in his old age must have known for certain, deep down in his heart (though he may never have admitted it with his intellect), that Hellas was already far advanced upon the downward road. Therefore we, with several more chapters of progress and several fewer of decline behind us than were present to Plutarch's consciousness, are bound to look back upon our predecessors with different eyes. The Hellenic mediaeval world of the fifth and fourth centuries B.C. was not only more mature and more triumphant in actual fact than the Western mediaeval world of the fourteenth and fifteenth centuries of our era, but its proportions were inevitably exaggerated in the eyes of Plutarch's generation by contrast with their own lassitude and timidity. To our modern mental vision, on the contrary, the fourteenth and fifteenth centuries (even as embodied in their Italian representatives) bear the stamp of what we either disparage as "immature" or praise as "primitive." There are elements in them, and noble elements, of which we may feel and regret the absence in ourselves; but as a whole we cannot take them quite seriously or treat their children, our predecessors, as men quite on a mental level with ourselves. We cannot even affect to do so without a certain consciousness of insincerity. Contrast with this the attitude of Plutarch and Dionysius towards Herodotus and Thucydides respectively. First, they approached their mediaeval predecessors in an attitude of adoration, as exponents of no longer attainable and almost lost ideals; and then, in the second place, they were cruelly dazzled at close quarters by the clouds of glory with which these Titans had been transfigured by their Olympian visions. "And when he came down from the mount, Moses wist not that the skin of his face shone while he talked with him. And when Aaron and all the children of Israel saw Moses, behold, the skin of his face shone, and they were afraid to come nigh him." Did Moses's punier countrymen resent as well as fear the light which repelled them? Dionysius and Plutarch, in the same situation, were utterly unable to conceal the aversion and dismay with which the "hard gem-like flame" of a Herodotus or a Thucydides inspired them. Devoted as they and all their finest contemporaries were to nursing the old age of Hellas, smoothing the ever-recurring wrinkles from her brow, stilling her fevered movements, checking her delirium and directing her thoughts (when living thoughts still flitted across her brain) away from the formidable future towards a golden or a gilded past, they could no longer bear to meet face to face the strong men armed who had loved Hellas and laughed with her and seen her as she was and beheld that she was both very good and very evil, and therefore altogether human, in the irrevocable years when Hellas and her sons were still young together. No, the Hellenes of the Empire could not face the Hellenes of the Fifty Years, with their fearless intellectual curiosity, their instinctive and effortless faculty for looking truth in the face, and their consciousness of superfluous strength which gave them the heart to be humorous or sardonic in due season. That is the pathos of all archaism. It is flustered and put out of countenance whenever it ventures to look its professed models in the face.

This means that the translation of each Hellenic phase of thought and style into an equivalent Western phase would be an historical impossibility, even to a scholar endowed with a very much finer sense of language than is possessed by the present translator. Nor, if the impossible could be achieved, should we unquestionably profit by the result; for in so far as we succeeded in translating the past of Hellenic literature into the past of our own, we should be almost wantonly putting it out of focus for our modern vision. Our Western literary heritage is, in fact, the one domain of literature which is essentially "untranslatable" into the Western style of to-day. The moment that we attempt to modernise a sixteenth- or seventeenth-century work of English literary art, the charm of sentiment and association, and therewith most of the beauty, vanishes as if by magic; while, on the other hand, when we try to yield our fancies up to the undesecrated original, we are often conscious that other elements in the essence escape us, and that the very iridescence of "Elizabethan" quaintness and age (like the colours on Roman glass) spreads a fog of obscurity between our minds and the minds by whom and for whom the original truth and beauty was created. It was created in a living present by living men, into whose appreciation of it no tinge of archaism entered at the creative moment; and for this reason it is virtually impossible to establish a perfect spiritual communion between us and them. It would therefore surely be mistaken from a practical point of view, even if it were possible, to translate the work of other civilisations into a form so elusive to our own powers of apprehension, while theoretically, likewise, it might well be wrong. After all, are any products of Hellenic literature immature or primitive or naïve or archaic when regarded as they really are, without the qualifying and distorting consciousness that they were brought into existence so many hundreds of years ago? The vague notion of Herodotus among modern Western readers as a simple-minded "Father of History" would have filled a Dionysius or a Plutarch with amazement. The traditional title of honour ought to be a sufficient warning in itself against the conception of its bearer with which it is usually associated

among ourselves, for creation and innovation are achievements not of simple but of subtle and ruthless minds; and the subtlety and ruthlessness of Herodotus, presented in their nakedness, would undoubtedly shock many Western readers of to-day as deeply as they shocked the Hellenic public of the Empire. Nor, again, is *naïveté* characteristic of any stratum in Homer. . . .

Aristotle on the distinction between poets and historians (c. 4th century B.C.):

[It] is not the function of the poet to relate what has happened, but what may happen,—what is possible according to the law of probability or necessity. The poet and the historian differ not by writing in verse or in prose. The work of Herodotus might be put into verse, and it would still be a species of history, with metre no less than without it. The true difference is that one relates what has happened, the other what may happen. Poetry, therefore, is a more philosophical and a higher thing than history: for poetry tends to express the universal, history the particular. By the universal I mean how a person of a certain type will on occasion speak or act, according to the law of probability or necessity; and it is this universality at which poetry aims in the names she attaches to the personages. The particular is—for example—what Alcibiades did or suffered. . . .

Aristotle, in The Poetics of Aristotle, *edited and translated by S. H. Butcher, Macmillan, 1911.*

R. G. Collingwood (essay date 1946)

SOURCE: "Greco-Roman Historiography," in *The Idea of History*, 1946. Reprint by Oxford University Press, 1963, pp. 14-45.

[*In the following excerpt, Collingwood analyzes some of the mental predispositions of Greek historians that influenced their view of history, historical writing, and the role of the historian.*]

. . . I should like to point out how remarkable a thing is [the] creation of scientific history by Herodotus, for he was an ancient Greek, and ancient Greek thought as a whole has a very definite prevailing tendency not only uncongenial to the growth of historical thought but actually based, one might say, on a rigorously anti-historical metaphysics. History is a science of human action: what the historian puts before himself is things that men have done in the past, and these belong to a world of change, a world where things come to be and cease to be. Such things, according to the prevalent Greek metaphysical view, ought not to be knowable, and therefore history ought to be impossible.

For the Greeks, the same difficulty arose with the world

of nature since it too was a world of this kind. If everything in the world changes, they asked, what is there in such a world for the mind to grasp? They were quite sure that anything which can be an object of genuine knowledge must be permanent; for it must have some definite character of its own, and therefore cannot contain in itself the seeds of its own destruction. If it is to be knowable it must be determinate; if it is determinate, it must be so completely and exclusively what it is that no internal change and no external force can ever set about making it into something else. Greek thought achieved its first triumph when it discovered in the objects of mathematical knowledge something that satisfied these conditions. A straight bar of iron may be bent into a curve, a flat surface of water may be broken into waves, but the straight line and the plane surface, as the mathematician thinks of them, are eternal objects that cannot change their characteristics.

Following the line of argument thus opened up, Greek thought worked out a distinction between two types of thought, knowledge proper . . . and what we translate by 'opinion'. . . . Opinion is the empirical semi-knowledge we have of matters of fact, which are always changing. It is our fleeting acquaintance with the fleeting actualities of the world; it thus only holds good for its own proper duration, for the here and now; and it is immediate, ungrounded in reasons, incapable of demonstration. True knowledge, on the contrary, holds good not only here and now but everywhere and always, and it is based on demonstrative reasoning and thus capable of meeting and overthrowing error by the weapon of dialectical criticism.

Thus, for the Greeks, process could be known only so far as it was perceived, and the knowledge of it could never be demonstrative. An exaggerated statement of this view, as we get it in the Eleatics, would misuse the weapon of dialectic, which is really valid only against error in the sphere of knowledge strictly so called, to prove that change does not exist and that the 'opinions' we have about the changing are really not even opinions but sheer illusions. Plato rejects that doctrine and sees in the world of change something not indeed intelligible but real to the extent of being perceptible, something intermediate between the nullity with which the Eleatics had identified it and the complete reality and intelligibility of the eternal. On such a theory, history ought to be impossible. For history must have these two characteristics: first it must be about what is transitory, and secondly it must be scientific or demonstrative. But on this theory what is transitory cannot be demonstratively known; it cannot be the object of science; it can only be a matter of . . . perception, whereby human sensibility catches the fleeting moment as it flies. And it is essential to the Greek point of view that this momentary sensuous perception of momentary changing things cannot be a science or the basis of a science.

The ardour with which the Greeks pursued the ideal of an unchanging and eternal object of knowledge might easily mislead us as to their historical interests. It might, if we read them carelessly, make us think them uninterested in history, somewhat as Plato's attack on the poets might make an unintelligent reader fancy that Plato cared little for poetry. In order to interpret such things correctly we must remember that no competent thinker or writer wastes his time attacking a man of straw. An intense polemic against a certain doctrine is an infallible sign that the doctrine in question figures largely in the writer's environment and even has a strong attraction for himself. The Greek pursuit of the eternal was as eager as it was, precisely because the Greeks themselves had an unusually vivid sense of the temporal. They lived in a time when history was moving with extraordinary rapidity, and in a country where earthquake and erosion change the face of the land with a violence hardly to be seen elsewhere. They saw all nature as a spectacle of incessant change, and human life as changing more violently than anything else. Unlike the Chinese, or the medieval civilization of Europe, whose conception of human society was anchored in the hope of retaining the chief features of its structure unchanged, they made it their first aim to face and reconcile themselves to the fact that such permanence is impossible. This recognition of the necessity of change in human affairs gave to the Greeks a peculiar sensitiveness to history.

Knowing that nothing in life can persist unchanged, they came habitually to ask themselves what exactly the changes had been which, they knew, must have come about in order to bring the present into existence. Their historical consciousness was thus not a consciousness of agelong tradition moulding the life of one generation after another into a uniform pattern; it was a consciousness of . . . catastrophic changes from one state of things to its opposite, from smallness to greatness, from pride to abasement, from happiness to misery. This was how they interpreted the general character of human life in their dramas, and this was how they narrated the particular parts of it in their history. The only thing that a shrewd and critical Greek like Herodotus would say about the divine power that ordains the course of history is that it . . . rejoices in upsetting and disturbing things. He was only repeating (i. 32) what every Greek knew: that the power of Zeus is manifested in the thunderbolt, that of Poseidon in the earthquake, that of Apollo in the pestilence, and that of Aphrodite in the passion that destroyed at once the pride of Phaedra and the chastity of Hippolytus.

It is true that these catastrophic changes in the condition of human life, which to the Greeks were the proper theme of history, were unintelligible. There could be . . . no demonstrative scientific knowledge [of them].

But all the same history had for the Greeks a definite value. Plato himself laid it down [in *Meno*] that right opinion (which is the sort of pseudo-knowledge that perception gives us of what changes) was no less useful for the conduct of life than scientific knowledge, and the poets maintained their traditional place in Greek life as the teachers of sound principles by showing that in the general pattern of these changes certain antecedents normally led to certain consequents. Notably, an excess in any one direction led to a violent change into its own opposite. Why this was so they could not tell; but they thought it a matter of observation that it was so; that people who became extremely rich or extremely powerful were thereby brought into special danger of being reduced to a condition of extreme poverty or weakness. There is here no theory of causation; the thought does not resemble that of seventeenth-century inductive science with its metaphysical basis in the axiom of cause and effect; the riches of Croesus are not the cause of his downfall, they are merely a symptom, to the intelligent observer, that something is happening in the rhythm of his life which is likely to lead to a downfall. Still less is the downfall a punishment for anything that, in an intelligible moral sense, could be called wrongdoing. When Amasis in Herodotus (iii. 43) broke off his alliance with Polycrates, he did it simply on the ground that Polycrates was too prosperous: the pendulum had swung too far one way and was likely to swing as far in the other. Such examples have their value to the person who can make use of them; for he can use his own will to arrest these rhythms in his life before they reach the danger-point, and check the thirst for power and wealth instead of allowing it to drive him to excess. Thus history has a value; its teachings are useful for human life; simply because the rhythm of its changes is likely to repeat itself, similar antecedents leading to similar consequents; the history of notable events is worth remembering in order to serve as a basis for prognostic judgements, not demonstrable but probable, laying down not what will happen but what is likely to happen, indicating the points of danger in rhythms now going on.

This conception of history was the very opposite of deterministic, because the Greeks regarded the course of history as flexible and open to salutary modification by the well-instructed human will. Nothing that happens is inevitable. The person who is about to be involved in a tragedy is actually overwhelmed by it only because he is too blind to see his danger. If he saw it, he could guard against it. Thus the Greeks had a lively and indeed a naïve sense of the power of man to control his own destiny, and thought of this power as limited only by the limitations of his knowledge. The fate that broods over human life is, from this Greek point of view, a destructive power only because man is blind to its workings. Granted that he cannot understand these workings, he can yet have right opinions about them, and in so far as he acquires such opinions he becomes able to put himself in a position where the blows of fate will miss him.

On the other hand, valuable as the teachings of history are, their value is limited by the unintelligibility of its subject-matter; and that is why Aristotle said [in *Politics*] that poetry is more scientific than history, for history is a mere collection of empirical facts, whereas poetry extracts from such facts a universal judgment. History tells us that Croesus fell and that Polycrates fell; poetry, according to Aristotle's idea of it, makes not these singular judgements but the universal judgement that very rich men, as such, fall. Even this is, in Aristotle's view, only a partially scientific judgement, for no one can see why rich men should fall; the universal cannot be syllogistically demonstrated; but it approaches the status of a true universal because we can use it as the major premiss for a new syllogism applying this generalization to fresh cases. Thus poetry is for Aristotle the distilled essence of the teaching of history. In poetry the lessons of history do not become any more intelligible and they remain undemonstrated and therefore merely probable, but they become more compendious and therefore more useful.

Such was the way in which the Greeks conceived the nature and value of history. They could not, consistently with their general philosophical attitude, regard it as scientific. They had to consider it as, at bottom, not a science but a mere aggregate of perceptions. What, then, was their conception of historical evidence? The answer is that, conformably with this view, they identified historical evidence with the reports of facts given by eyewitnesses of those facts. Evidence consists of eyewitnesses' narratives, and historical method consists of eliciting these.

Quite clearly, it was in this way that Herodotus conceived of evidence and method. This does not mean that he uncritically believed whatever eyewitnesses told him. On the contrary, he is in practice highly critical of their narratives. And here again he is typically Greek. The Greeks as a whole were skilled in the practice of the law courts, and a Greek would find no difficulty in applying to historical testimony the same kind of criticism which he was accustomed to direct upon witnesses in court. The work of Herodotus or Thucydides depends in the main on the testimony of eyewitnesses with whom the historian had personal contact. And his skill as a researcher consisted in the fact that he must have cross-questioned an eyewitness of past events until he had called up in the informant's own mind an historical picture of those events far fuller and more coherent than any he could have volunteered for himself. The result of this process was to create in the informant's mind for the first time a genuine knowledge of the past events which he had perceived. . . .

This conception of the way in which a Greek historian

collected his material makes it a very different thing from the way in which a modern historian may use printed memoirs. Instead of the easy-going belief on the informant's part that his prima facie recollection was adequate to the facts, there could grow up in his mind a chastened and criticized recollection which had stood the fire of such questions as 'Are you quite sure that you remember it just like that? Have you not now contradicted what you were saying yesterday? How do you reconcile your account of that event with the very different account given by so-and-so?' This method of using the testimony of eyewitnesses is undoubtedly the method which underlies the extraordinary solidity and consistency of the narratives which Herodotus and Thucydides finally wrote about fifth-century Greece.

No other method deserving the name scientific was available to the fifth-century historians, but it had three limitations:

First, it inevitably imposed on its users a shortness of historical perspective. The modern historian knows that if only he had the capacity he could become the interpreter of the whole past of mankind; but whatever Greek historians might have thought of Plato's description of the philosopher as the spectator of all time, they would never have ventured to claim Plato's words as a description of themselves. Their method tied them on a tether whose length was the length of living memory: the only source they could criticize was an eyewitness with whom they could converse face to face. It is true that they relate events from a remoter past, but as soon as Greek historical writing tries to go beyond its tether, it becomes a far weaker and more precarious thing. For instance, we must not deceive ourselves into thinking that any scientific value attaches to what Herodotus tells us about the sixth century or to what Thucydides tells us about events before the Pentecontaetia. From our twentieth-century point of view, these early stories in Herodotus and Thucydides are very interesting, but they are mere logography and not scientific. They are traditions which the author who hands them down to us has not been able to raise to the level of history because he has not been able to pass them through the crucible of the only critical method he knew. Nevertheless, this contrast in Herodotus and Thucydides between the unreliability of everything farther back than living memory and the critical precision of what comes within living memory is a mark not of the failure of fifth-century historiography but of its success. The point about Herodotus and Thucydides is not that the remote past is for them still outside the scope of scientific history but that the recent past is within that scope. Scientific history has been invented. Its field is still narrow; but within that field it is secure. Moreover, this narrowness of field did not matter much to the Greeks, because the extreme rapidity with which their own civilization was developing and changing afforded plenty of first-class historical material

within the confines set by their method, and for the same reason they could produce first-rate historical work without developing what in fact they never did develop, any lively curiosity concerning the remote past.

Secondly, the Greek historian's method precludes him from choosing his subject. He cannot, like Gibbon, begin by wishing to write a great historical work and go on to ask himself what he shall write about. The only thing he can write about is the events which have happened within living memory to people with whom he can have personal contact. Instead of the historian choosing the subject, the subject chooses the historian; I mean that history is written only because memorable things have happened which call for a chronicler among the contemporaries of the people who have seen them. One might almost say that in ancient Greece there were no historians in the sense in which there were artists and philosophers; there were no people who devoted their lives to the study of history; the historian was only the autobiographer of his generation and autobiography is not a profession.

Thirdly, Greek historical method made it impossible for the various particular histories to be gathered up into one all-embracing history. Nowadays we think of monographs on various subjects as ideally forming parts of a universal history, so that if their subjects are carefully chosen and their scale and treatment carefully controlled they might serve as chapters in a single historical work; and this is the way in which a writer like Grote actually treated Herodotus' account of the Persian War and Thucydides' of the Peloponnesian. But if any given history is the autobiography of a generation, it cannot be rewritten when that generation has passed away because the evidence on which it was based will have perished. The work that a contemporary based on that evidence can thus never be improved upon or criticized, and it can never be absorbed into a large whole, because it is like a work of art, something having the uniqueness and individuality of a statue or a poem. . . . [The works of Herodotus and Thucydides were] written to rescue glorious deeds from the oblivion of time, precisely because when their generation was dead and gone the work could never be done again. The rewriting of their histories, or their incorporation into the history of a period, would have seemed to them an absurdity. To the Greek historians, therefore, there could never be any such thing as a history of Greece. There could be a history of a fairly extensive complex of events, like the Persian War or the Peloponnesian War; but only on two conditions. First, this complex of events must be complete in itself: it must have a beginning, a middle, and an end, like the plot of an Aristotelian tragedy. Secondly, it must be . . . like an Aristotelian city-state. As Aristotle thought that no community of civilized men under a single government could exceed in size the number of citizens that could be within earshot of a single herald, the dimensions of the political organism being thus limited by a purely physical fact, so the Greek theory of history implies that no historical narrative could exceed in length the years of a man's lifetime, within which alone the critical methods at its disposal could be applied.

M. I. Finley (essay date 1959)

SOURCE: An introduction to *The Greek Historians: The Essence of Herodotus, Thucydides, Xenophon, Polybius,* edited by M. I. Finley, The Viking Press, 1959, pp. 1-21.

[*In the excerpt below, Finley explores the evolution of Greek historical thought, noting significant milestones in the shaping of the historians' worldview, and concluding that "In the end, its intense political orientation, which was the great force behind the histories of Herodotus and Thucydides, was the fatal flaw in Greek historical writing."*]

History in its root sense means *inquiry*. For a considerable time before it took on the specific, narrower meaning the word now has, and even long thereafter—we still say "natural history"—the stress was on the inquiry as such, regardless of subject matter, on the search for explanation and understanding. Man is a rational being: if he asks rational questions, he can, by the unaided efforts of his intellect, discover rational answers. But first he must discover that about himself. The Greeks did, in the seventh century B.C. (insofar as so abstract a notion can be dated at all), and thereby they established the greatest of their claims to immortality. Significantly, the inquiry was first directed to the most universal matters, the nature of being and the cosmos. Only later was it extended to man himself, his social relations and his past.

It was no accident that this profound intellectual revolution took place in the region the Greeks called Ionia (the west coast of Turkey). There they were in closest touch with the older cultures of the ancient Near East. Greek-speaking peoples first migrated into the lower Balkans by 2000 or 1900 B.C. and eventually spread eastward across the Aegean Sea (and later west to Sicily and southern Italy). Like all invaders, they adopted and adapted a variety of ideas and institutions from their new neighbours. How much they borrowed we are only beginning to appreciate, as one after another the lost languages of the area are recovered, most recently Mycenaean Greek itself. In the course of centuries religious ideas, gods, myths and rituals, scientific and technological information found their way from Babylonians, Hittites, Hurrites, and other peoples of the Near East and were embodied in Greek ways of life and thought on a scale undreamed of by historians fifty or a hundred years ago.

Paradoxically, the more we learn about this process of diffusion and adaptation, the more astonishing is the originality of the Greeks. One need only read their earliest poetry or look at their archaic statues and vases to catch some of the genius. Then one turns to the Ionian intellectual revolution for another side of it, the spirit of rational inquiry. Without Babylonian mathematics and astronomy and metallurgy there could have been no Thales or Anaximander. But it was the Ionian Greeks, not their Babylonian forerunners, who first asked the *critical* questions about the earth and the stars and metals and matter. And so, too, with man himself and his past. The older civilizations had their records and their chronicles, but the essential element of inquiry, of history, was lacking. The writers of these accounts, the late R. G. Collingwood pointed out [in *The Idea of History*, 1946], were "not writing history," they were "writing religion"; they were not inquiring, they were recording "known facts for the information of persons to whom they are not known, but who, as worshippers of the god in question, ought to know the deeds whereby he has made himself manifest." It was the Ionians, again, who first thought to ask questions in a systematic way about the supposedly known facts, in particular about their meaning in rational, human terms.

The magnitude and boldness of this innovation must not be underestimated. Today we too easily assume, without giving it much thought, that a concern with history is a natural human activity. All men have memories and "live in the past" to a greater or less extent. Is it not natural that they should be interested in their ancestors and the past of their community, people, nation? Yes, but such an interest is not necessarily the same thing as history. It can be satisfied entirely by myth, and, in fact, that is how most of mankind has customarily dealt with the past (and, in a very real sense, still does). Myth serves admirably to provide the necessary continuity of life, not only with the past but with nature and the gods as well. It is rich and vivid, it is concrete and yet full of symbolic meanings and associations, it explains institutions and rites and feelings, it is instructive—above all, it is real and true and immediately comprehensible. It served the early Greeks perfectly.

When myth was finally challenged, by the Ionian enlightenment, the attack was directed not to the events and the stories, such as the details of the Trojan War, but to the mythic view of life and the cosmos, to its theogony and divine interventions. "Homer and Hesiod have attributed to the gods everything that is disgraceful and blameworthy among men: theft, adultery, and deceit." So runs the famous protest by Xenophanes of Colophon, who was born about 570 B.C. Such criticism helped bring about a new cosmology and a new ethics; it did not, of itself, lead to the study of history. The skeptics stripped the traditional accounts of irrational elements and contradictions, but they neither doubted the remaining hard core nor tried to extend it by research of their own. They historicized myth, they did not write history. A remarkable example will be found in the first fifteen chapters of Thucydides. Here is a rapid review of the evolution of Greek society in which not a single trace of the mythic conception survives: the gods have disappeared completely, and with them fate and fortune and every other extra-human agency. In their place Thucydides put common-sense human causes and impulses, and the result looks so much like history that many people today, even historians who should know better, praise it as a great piece of historical writing. In fact what Thucydides did was to take the common Greek traditions, divest them of what he considered to be their false trappings, and reformulate them in a brilliantly coherent picture by thinking hard about them, using as his sole tools what he knew about the world of his own day, its institutions and its psychology.

It takes more than skepticism about old traditions to produce historical investigation. A positive stimulus is needed, and again Ionia provided the starting point. That part of the Greek world was not only in closest contact with other peoples, eventually it was also subjected to them, first to the Lydians and then to the Persians. The Greeks thought it was important to know something about their overlords, and so they investigated the subject and wrote books putting together the geography, antiquities, customs, and bits of history of the nations with whom they were concerned. Significantly, this had never been done before: the prevailing view, as any reader of the Old Testament must realize, was totally ethnocentric. Nations other than one's own had no intrinsic interest. Significantly, too, the Greek innovation was for a long time a restricted one: they were not attracted to ethnography as such, or history as such, but to the manners and institutions of the two nations with whom their lives were now closely bound. The Greeks had no myths to account for the past of the Lydians and Persians. That is why their first steps toward historical writing—for these works were not histories in any proper sense—were about foreign nations, not about themselves.

None of this writing survives apart from scattered quotations. Its general character, however, is clear enough from the first half of Herodotus' book. Herodotus, born early in the fifth century B.C. in the city of Halicarnassus in Asia Minor, planned a *periodos* on an unprecedented scale. Stimulated no doubt by the Persian Wars, which demonstrated that thinking Greeks must widen their horizons, Herodotus decided to extend the inquiry to more peoples and places. He proposed to investigate as much as he could personally, to confront and cross-question a variety of expert witnesses, and to report faithfully and accurately what he learned, distinguishing for his audience between first-

and second-hand information, between probable and improbable (or impossible) accounts, between what he believed to be true and what he disbelieved but repeated because it had significance nonetheless. Every reader can judge for himself how successfully Herodotus carried out his program. But, had he done no more, it is unlikely that we should now have this opportunity: in the end, his writings would have disappeared like those of Hecataeus and the others, and Herodotus would be just another name today, the author of a few surviving fragments of books called *Lydiaca, Aegyptiaca, Scythica,* and so on.

We know virtually nothing about the life of Herodotus, and therefore we can only infer when and why he made a radical shift in his program. It seems most likely that this happened in Athens, toward the middle of the century. There Herodotus began a new inquiry, one utterly unlike any which had been attempted before. He determined to reconstruct, by personal investigation, the generation of the Persian Wars. In the process, he assembled much material about still earlier generations of Greek history, and he tied his account to the mythical tradition, which he rationalized and historicized as well as he could. The final product is an amalgam, for Herodotus did not abandon his earlier work. The *Aegyptiaca* and *Scythica* appear as long digressions; the Lydians and Persians have their story woven in with Greek affairs, but they are also given space for customs and manners; and the Greeks themselves appear in semi-mythical form at times (with unmistakable influences from epic and tragedy). Yet the work as a whole is surely a history.

No twentieth-century reader can really visualize Herodotus at work, under conditions which make both his effort and the final result a miracle of human enterprise. Written records did not exist, for all practical purposes, and few men who had any direct knowledge of the Persian Wars (let alone the still earlier years) could have been alive when he began this part of his study. Everything—the politics and the battles and the ravaging of cities and the intrigues—had to be rescued from oral tradition, as it was preserved and transmitted among the great families of Athens or the priests of Delphi or the kings of Sparta. These traditions were fragmentary, unreliable, self-serving, and often contradictory. That he nevertheless undertook so difficult and unprecedented a task implies some overpowering impulse, and I have little doubt that it was a political one, in the broadest sense of that term. Democratic Athens, under Pericles, was asserting itself with more and more pressure in the Greek world, offering leadership and military security, but at the same time demanding, and if necessary compelling, tribute and a measure of dependence. Difficult problems were raised—political problems which were, as always, at heart moral questions. Discussion was lively and often heated; out of it the sophists, and later Socrates, created the new discipline of ethics and, as a subdivision, political theory. Herodotus was no philosopher, he was not even a systematic thinker; but he was no less sensitive than the sophists and the tragedians to the great moral issues, and he made a unique contribution to the discussion. He found a moral justification for Athenian dominance in the role she had played in the Persian Wars, and he sought to capture that story and fix it before its memory was lost.

Herodotus had a most subtle mind, and the story he told was complex, full of shadings and paradoxes and qualifications. In traditional religion, for example, he stood somewhere between outright skepticism and the murky piety of Aeschylus. His political vision was Athenian and democratic, but it lacked any trace of chauvinism. He was committed, but not for one moment did that release him from the high obligation of understanding. His great discovery was that one could uncover moral problems and moral truths in history, in the concrete data of experience, in a discourse which was neither freely imaginative like that of the poets nor abstract like that of the philosophers. That is what history meant to Herodotus; nothing could be more wrong-headed than the persistent and seemingly indestructible legend of Herodotus the charmingly naïve storyteller.

It did not follow as a self-evident and automatic consequence that the new discovery was at once welcomed or that histories and historians arose on all sides to advance the new discipline. The Athenians appreciated Herodotus, obviously, and yet a full generation was to elapse before anyone thought it a good idea to write a complete history of Athens, and even then the step was taken by a foreigner, Hellanicus of Lesbos, and he was an annalist, a chronicler, not a historian, and he continued to repeat the traditional myths alongside more recent, verifiable history. Other Greeks naturally resented the phil-Athenianism of Herodotus and his version of their role in the Persian Wars, but they did not rush to reply by writing their own histories. They objected and they challenged a detail here and there, and they eventually pinned the label "Father of Lies" to him, a late echo of which can still be read in Plutarch's essay *On the Malice of Herodotus*. The new discipline, in short, remained highly problematic. In all honesty men could doubt whether it was possible to know the past, and whether the effort to find out was worth the trouble.

One man who read Herodotus carefully and fully appreciated his achievement (and the inherent difficulties) was Thucydides. He was probably in his late twenties when the second decisive struggle in Greek history broke out in 431 B.C., the war between Athens and Sparta, and he decided immediately that he would be its historian. Apart from the acute prognostic sense which Thucydides revealed thereby, his decision was

a critical one for the future of Greek historical writing in general. There could be no more complete turning of one's back on the past than this, the idea of writing a history of an event which lay in the future. The war lasted twenty-seven years and Thucydides survived it, possibly by five years. All through it he worked away at his book with a remarkable singleness of purpose, collecting evidence, sifting, checking and double-checking, writing and revising, and all the time thinking hard about the problems: about the war itself, its causes and issues, about Pericles, about the Athenian Empire, about politics and man's behaviour as a political animal.

The book was not finished: that is obvious at a glance, and the way it breaks off more than six years before the end of the war leaves us with something of a puzzle. Possibly Thucydides found himself in a bitter impasse, unable to resolve to his own satisfaction either the general problems of politics, which concerned him more and more as the war continued, or the more technical questions of how to present to the public what he thought and what he had learned. The book is filled with tension, not merely the external tensions inevitable in so long and difficult a war, but also the inner conflicts of the author, as he tried to fight through the mass of facts and the complex moral issues which became obsessive with him, to a basic understanding of politics and ethics. He certainly did not abandon his life work in the year in which the manuscript suddenly stops. There are things in the earliest portions which could not have been said until after the end of the war in 404 B.C. There are unmistakable evidences of rethinking and rewriting. Very probably the Funeral Oration and Pericles' last speech were among the latest sections Thucydides wrote, and they (together with the so-called Melian Dialogue at the end of the fifth book) sum up the whole generation as Thucydides saw it at the end of his life.

From the standpoint of the history of historical writing, Thucydides' political ideas are perhaps not so interesting as his technique. To begin with, he set out consciously to overcome certain weaknesses in Herodotus: hence the insistence on careful checking of eyewitness testimony, on precise chronology, on the total elimination of "romance" from his work, on a rational analysis which has no patience with oracles and supernatural interventions and divine punishments. His account of the great plague in Athens, for example, is a model of reporting; Thucydides even equipped himself with the most advanced medical knowledge, and his technical language and accuracy on this subject are unparalleled among lay writers in the whole of antiquity. All this is so impressive and has such an aura of earnestness and sincerity that, even though we have no independent evidence for virtually anything Thucydides tells us, we believe him without hesitation. The same cannot be said of any other historian in the ancient world.

It is no underestimation of these remarkable qualities in Thucydides to say that none of this—whatever its worth *sub specie aeternitatis*—locates him in the development of Greek historiography. Our admiration, however warranted, tends to divert attention from the crucial fact that his subject was contemporary, that he was writing about things which were happening under his eyes, or in sight of others whom he could cross-examine, not about events of the literally dead past. Therefore in his very explicit statement of his working methods and principles there is not one word about research into documents or traditions; there are only the rules to be followed in eliciting accurate information from eyewitnesses. When Thucydides did make a brief excursion into earlier times, as in the first fifteen chapters or in the sketch of developments from the point at which Herodotus' history breaks off to the beginning of the account of the Peloponnesian War, his motives were either to justify his own work or to provide certain necessary background materials, nothing more. They were not history, either in Thucydides' sense or in ours; they were introductory to his proper subject. Only contemporary history could be really known and grasped; if one worked hard enough and with sufficient intelligence and honesty, one could know and write the history of one's own age: that, we may say, was Thucydides' answer to the doubters, to the men who challenged Herodotus and the validity of his enterprise.

But what about the past? If one is interested in it, then what? In a famous and unique disgression, Thucydides set out at some length to prove that, contrary to the common and official view, Harmodius and Aristogeiton, who had assassinated Hipparchus near the end of the previous century, were not the liberators of Athens from tyranny, because it was Hippias who was the elder son of Pisistratus, and therefore he (and not his brother Hipparchus) was the reigning tyrant at that time. There has been much speculation about Thucydides' reasons for this digression, which adds nothing to his story, and the most likely explanation is that he inserted it, at a late date, in reply to something—perhaps the publication of Hellanicus' chronicle of Athens—which annoyed him. His proof, which is perfectly sound, rested on two dedicatory inscriptions. This is an astonishing performance precisely because of its irrelevance, for it is one of the very few instances in which he quoted a document of any kind. Nothing else in the work shows so decisively what a great historian of the past Thucydides could have been. Here, he seems to be saying in contemptuous anger, is the way to go about writing the history of the past, if you think it is worth the bother.

Thucydides himself emphatically did not think it was. He shared the firm conviction, general among Greek thinkers, that mere knowledge of facts for their own sake was pointless (and sometimes harmful). Curiosity, a desire to know, had to lead to understanding, virtue, action. Of course, it is impossible to guess just what the young Thucydides had in mind when he decided, in 431 B.C., to become the war's historian. Perhaps he had no clear idea himself. But the time came—and I believe very quickly—when he set himself the goal of uncovering, through the story of his own generation, the essentials of man's behaviour, his political behaviour. That would be the "possession for all time" he would give to the world. And that, I suggest, is why Thucydides abandoned the past for the present. Human nature and human behaviour were for him essentially fixed qualities, the same in one century as in another. The good and the bad, the rational and the passionate and irrational, the moral and the immoral, the attractions and excesses of power—these were always present and operative, in various combinations. Therefore they could best be brought to light, where they could be studied and known, in the contemporary world rather than in the bygone generations which one could never really know. For Thucydides the choice was made even simpler and more obvious by the Peloponnesian War, which, he took pains to demonstrate in his introduction, was the greatest power struggle in Greek history.

By moving from history, in its narrower sense of a narrative of the war, to the basic political questions, Thucydides set himself an unattainable goal. It was difficult enough for him to reach the depth of understanding he desired. There remained the equally difficult problem of finding ways to communicate to his readers what he had learned. Merely to write the history of the Peloponnesian War, no matter how accurately and completely, would not do: that would add up to nothing more than a succession of concrete events, and how could the general ideas emerge from this mass of facts, each a particular and unique datum? To be sure, there is no explicit statement by Thucydides to say that he thought in those terms; nevertheless, the book he wrote seems to me to suffer no other explanation.

To begin with, there is the question of his selection of materials. All historical writing, like any form of rational discourse, must choose the relevant and discard the rest, must group and organize data, establish connections and patterns. But very often Thucydides' exclusions transcend the limits of the permissible by any definition of history that the modern world would recognize. For example, he wrote a long analysis of the civil disturbance (*stasis*) in Corcyra and thereafter he ignored this major factor of fifth-century Greek history almost completely, to the extent of not mentioning a number of other occurrences at all, not even those which had a demonstrably important bearing on the war. The balance is equally lopsided with the men in the war: instead of the expected proportions, according to Thucydides' judgement of the significance of the various generals and politicians, the method tends to be all or nothing. Of the popular leaders in Athens after the death of Pericles, only Cleon is given a role; the others receive no attention and are sometimes not even named. This cannot be dismissed as carelessness. Thucydides was too intelligent and serious a writer; we must assume that a principle of selection was at work, and I find it in his search for general ideas. Having demonstrated the nature and meaning of *stasis,* or the character and function of the demagogue, he saw no necessity to report other instances of the same general phenomenon. One good example was sufficient for his purposes; the rest would be useless repetition.

It is to be noticed, further, how the ideal demagogue is portrayed, in the shape of Cleon. Although Cleon was the decisive personality in Athens for at least five years, among the most crucial in the war, he is allowed but three full-dress appearances, much like the character in a play. Thucydides required no more in order to fix the image of Cleon completely, and he left everything else out. We are not told anything about Cleon's rise to power, or about his financial measures, or about his program in any proper sense. And characteristically, one of the three appearances is in the Mitylene debate, in which Cleon was outvoted in the assembly. Speeches, often in antithetical pairs, were Thucydides' favorite device, and his most problematical one. Despite his explicit statement about his method with respect to speeches, they have preplexed and upset commentators from antiquity to our own day. It is simply undeniable that all the speeches are in the same style, Thucydides' own, and that some of the remarks could not have been made by the speakers in question. Worse still, in the Mitylene debate, whether Cleon and Diodotus are accurately reported in substance or not, the whole tone is false. From what Thucydides himself said in introducing the two speeches, his choice of these two out of the many which were actually delivered that day in the assembly distorted the actual issues, and distorted them badly. Thucydides was surely not unaware of the effect he was creating—that would be too stupid—and therefore we have still another instance of how his interest in general ideas prevailed over mere reporting, and, in that sense, over historical accuracy. When it comes, finally, to the Melian Dialogue, . . . history goes by the boards altogether. For whatever reason, Thucydides chose that point in his story to write a little sophistical piece, thinly disguised as a secret discussion between two groups of unnamed negotiators, in which he played with abstract ideas of justice and empire, right and might, freedom and slavery.

In the end we are confronted with two different, and almost unrelated, kinds of writing brought together under one cover as Thucydides' "history" of the Peloponnesian War. On the one hand there is the painstaking, precise, almost impersonal reporting, filled with minor details arranged in strict chronology. And on the other hand there are the many attempts, varied in form and tone, to get beneath and behind the facts, to uncover and bring into clear focus the realities of politics, the psychology of political behaviour, the rights and wrongs of power. These are, by and large, much the more interesting and enduring sections of the work, and the most personal (though rarely in the naïve dress of outright editorializing). They are the most dramatic, in form more than in content; they are the freest, in their portrayal of a few men and events and their exclusion of many others, in their accent, and even, I may say, in their preaching. They represent the Thucydides who restricted Cleon to three appearances; the other is the historian who solemnly put down the names and patronymics of endless obscure commanders and ship captains.

None of this is said in criticism of Thucydides. Few historians have goaded and whipped themselves so mercilessly for the better part of a lifetime to achieve complete accuracy and at the same time to discover and communicate those truths which would give value to, which would justify, their effort. I do not believe Thucydides ever came to the point of being satisfied that he had found the answers, either to the great questions of political life or to the more philosophical one of moving from the concrete and particular event to the general truth. Increasingly, however, he seemed to feel himself impelled away from narrow historical presentation. The paradox is that to give meaning to history he tended to abandon history. If the historian, by definition, concentrates on the concrete event, then Thucydides, for all his advance over his predecessor in techniques of investigation and checking, was a poorer historian, or at least less a historian, than Herodotus. It is plain that he could have been a greater one—I do not speak of charm and elegance of style—but he chose otherwise. And his reasons, which I have indicated, were beyond reproach.

No Greek again undertook a task so difficult and unrewarding. The surviving histories after Thucydides number less than a dozen, but we know the names of nearly a thousand writers of history, of one sort or another, and all the evidence leaves no doubt that not one of them approached Thucydides in intellectual rigour or insight. At least five men in the middle or second half of the fourth century wrote continuations of Thucydides' history. One work survives, Xenophon's *Hellenica,* and it is very unreliable, tendentious, dishonest, dreary to read, and rarely illuminating on broader issues. Such talents as Xenophon had lay elsewhere. . . .

Probably some, and perhaps all four, of the continuators of Thucydides were better historians than Xenophon. That is to say, they were more accurate, more penetrating in their analysis of events, and more skilful in combining and relating movements in various parts of the Greek world. But no more. We have no reason to believe that they appreciated the real problems of historiography which Thucydides saw, or that they really understood what troubled Thucydides and drove him to re-examine his ideas and his methods over and over again. Nor did the so-called Atthidographers, the six men more or less contemporary with them who wrote—compiled, rather—lengthy chronicles of Athens, year by year, in which the mythological age received the same attention, on the same level and in the same tone, as the historical era proper. Thucydides saw in the study of contemporary history a road to understanding. Those who came after generally lowered their sights to far lesser goals: local patriotism, object lessons for politicians, elementary moralizing, and, above all, entertainment, high or low. The quality of their work, even at its best, was no better than their purposes deserved.

From Xenophon in the middle of the fourth century B.C. to Polybius two hundred years later, nothing survives. Our knowledge of these two centuries has suffered much as a result, but it is hardly conceivable that the art (or science) of history has lost anything of value. It is perhaps curious that the career of Alexander the Great failed to stimulate anything better than it did, memoirs written by several men closely associated with him and a large and constantly growing body of legend. But then, neither did Napoleon; his campaigns produced great novels, not great histories. After the fifth century Greek politics lacked the epic element which nourished Herodotus and Thucydides, and it was Rome which in the end provided the stimulus for the only Greek historian who was in any sense a worthy successor. Polybius also obeyed an impulse which was political, in his case stated much more explicitly. How did Rome succeed in conquering and dominating the world in so short a time? To answer that he produced a huge work, nothing less than a history of the "world," that is to say, of both Greek and Roman affairs, from the middle of the third century on.

Polybius was a good historian in many ways. If he was not of the calibre of Thucydides, I attribute that as much to his time as to his personal capacities. His expressed intentions and methods of work were sound, but his performance is often slovenly and inaccurate, his political analysis is very shallow, he is flagrantly partisan, and he repeatedly descends to the rhetorical tricks and sensationalism which he does not hesitate to censure severely in his predecessors. Nevertheless, he belongs to the great tradition of Greek historians because he, too, insisted that history must be instructive and that politics is its proper and serious subject, with the stress on the contemporary (it is noteworthy that his excuse for going back several generations is essentially aesthetic: every story must have a beginning, a middle, and an end); and because, within his limitations, he felt the danger of submerging the central

problems and issues in the mass of concrete events. He editorialized all the time, so that no reader could possibly miss his points, and he digressed at length in one pivotal book, the sixth, in which he described the Roman constitution, explained and exemplified the theory of the cycle of governmental forms, and, with understandable caution, suggested that Rome would not escape this inevitable movement. Once again history failed a Greek historian. In order to demonstrate the cycles, which, if they are anything, are a historical phenomenon, Polybius made not the slightest attempt to write history. Instead, he gave a purely speculative account, of a kind long familiar to Greek philosophers from whom he borrowed it, into which he worked a number of comparative illustrations, inadequate, inconsistent, and all floating in the air, without historical context or concreteness.

Historians continued to write in Greek for centuries after Polybius. A few of them are not without interest—Diodorus, who used scissors and paste to compose a universal history; Dionysius of Halicarnassus, who, at the end of the first century B.C., wrote a voluminous *Roman Antiquities;* Arrian; and Dio Cassius—but they belong essentially to Roman history, and, for all their effort and their knowledge of the past, they did not advance the art of history one bit. Nothing new will be learned from them about this subject. Only Plutarch was genuinely creative and original, and his kind of biographical writing brushes history very lightly. His interests were ethical and psychological. His selection of events, his organization of the material he chose, and his assessments—in short, his portraits— often came out of history (but often, too, from myth). They are live, real, profound, moral; but they remain abstractions from the past, not the history of a period or a career, not even biographies, in the historian's sense. There is a simple test: one need only try to recreate either fourth-century Athenian politics or Demosthenes' role in it from Plutarch's life of Demosthenes.

The second half of the fifth century B.C. has been called the Greek age of enlightenment. The parallel is tempting, not least in the view of history: there are the same dissatisfaction with the prevailing mythical accounts of the past, the same insistence on a strictly rational explanation of events, the same feeling that a proper study of history could be illuminating. But the eighteenth-century enlightenment was followed, at once, by the emergence of modern historiography, with its technical refinements, its demand for absolute accuracy, its unflagging search for more and more evidence, its vast scale of investigation and interests. History became a discipline and its study a profession. Not so in ancient Greece. In biology, mathematics, and astronomy, in grammar and rhetoric, great work of systematic investigation and classification still lay ahead of the Greeks when the fifth century came to an end. Herodotus and Thucydides, however, led nowhere.

What came after them was less systematic, less accurate, less serious, less professional. The fathers of history produced a stunted, sickly stock, weaker in each successive generation apart from a rare sport like Polybius.

It is not easy to explain the different outcomes of the two enlightenments; it is altogether impossible until we rid ourselves of the assumption that the study of history is a natural, inherent, inevitable kind of human activity. That few Greeks, if any, took this for granted is immediately apparent from the regularity with which most historians opened their works by justifying themselves, their efforts, and the particular subjects they chose. Utility or pleasure: that was how they customarily posed the alternative. Those who aimed at the latter were defeated before they began. Poetry was too deeply entrenched in Greek life, and, when the highest forms were epic and tragedy, both "historical," there was no chance for history unless it could demonstrate its value in other than aesthetic terms. How could Xenophon or Ephorus or Phylarchus compete with Homer, from whom every literate Greek learned his ABCs? Many tried, by rhetoric and sensationalism, by writing "tragic history" as Polybius contemptuously called it, and they failed on all scores: they still gave less pleasure than the poets and in the process their history became pseudo-history.

As for utility, somehow the essential intellectual and social conditions were lacking, at least in sufficient strength. One obstacle was the Greek passion for general principles. History, Aristotle said in a famous passage dismissing the subject, tells us only "what Alcibiades did and what he suffered." And any Greek who was serious enough to inquire about such matters wanted to know not what happened, but why, and by what fixed principles, in human affairs as in the phenomena of nature. Not even Thucydides could find the solution in his historical work, and surely none of his successors, all lesser men. Poetry and philosophy gave the answers, and they valued the immutable and universal qualities far more than the individual and transient. There was no idea of progress—here the parallel with the modern enlightenment and its aftermath breaks down completely—and therefore there was no reason to look to the past for a process of continuing growth. What one found instead was either a cyclical movement, an endless coming-to-be and passing-away; or a decline from a golden age. Either way the objective was to discover the great absolute truths and then to seek their realization in life, through education and legislation. History, as the nineteenth century with its geneticism and its fact-mindedness understood the study, was obviously not the answer to the needs which the Greeks felt for themselves.

The presence or absence of the idea of progress (on a significant scale) is not just an intellectual phenomenon. It is not merely a matter of someone's having thought the idea up, and then of its being widely accepted (or not) simply because it appealed to aesthetic sensibilities or emotions or logic. In the nineteenth century such an idea seemed self-evident: material progress was visible everywhere. In ancient Greece, after the emergence of the classical civilization of the fifth century, it was not visible at all. Everyone knew, of course, that there had been an earlier stage in Greek society and that non-Greeks, barbarians, lived quite differently, some of them (such as the Thracians or Scythians) being what we would call more "primitive." This rudimentary conception fell short of the modern idea of progress in at least two respects, each fundamental and critical. In the first place, whatever advances were conceded were chiefly moral and institutional rather than material. Second, the Greeks of the fifth and fourth centuries B.C. were unanimous (insofar as any people can ever be) in thinking that the city-state was the only correct political structure, in rejecting territorial expansion and growth in the size of the political organism as a road to social and moral improvement, and in ignoring completely the possibility of further technological and material progress (or the notion that this could have anything to do with the good life or a better life).

The differences which were observed were explained partly by differences in the quality of the men—as between Greeks and barbarians above all; and partly by differences in institutions. The former obviously invites no significant historical investigation. The latter might, but to them it rarely did, thanks to their *idée fixe* that current political institutions could be explained sufficiently by the genius of an original "lawgiver" and the subsequent moral behaviour of the community. That is why so much writing about Sparta gravitated around the largely legendary Lycurgus; or of Athens around Solon, who was a real person to be sure, but who by the middle of the fifth century B.C. had been mythicized beyond recognition. This kind of writing may, at its best as in Plutarch, have the air of history, but in fact it is not much more historical than the *Iliad* or the *Odyssey* or Sophocles' *Oedipus Rex*. And at its worst, it became a wild farrago about divine ancestors, their feuds, philanderings, and settlements. The great national rivalries of the nineteenth century stimulated serious historical study; the sharp Greek intercity competition led to little more than a continual re-historicizing of myth to meet the shifting requirements of prestige and power. The one sought to explain and justify current politics by historical development, the other by a foundation myth and ethical claims.

In the end, its intense political orientation, which was the great force behind the histories of Herodotus and Thucydides, was the fatal flaw in Greek historical writing. Politicians have always created the history they needed, and Greek politicians were no exception. Those

Greek thinkers who were able to raise themselves above the immediate needs of their particular cities turned to philosophy for wisdom. And after Alexander the Great, Greek politics became too parochial and paltry to stimulate serious political thought of any kind. Then men turned entirely to nonpolitical questions, or they turned to Rome and Roman political problems, or they remained within the small compass that was left in the Greek city-state, its cult and legends and ancient glories. Of all the lines of inquiry which the Greek initiated, history was the most abortive. The wonder is not so much that it was, as that, in its short and fruitless life, its two best exponents still stand with the greatest the world has seen.

Aubrey de Sélincourt (essay date 1962)

SOURCE: "The Greek Feeling for History," in *The World of Herodotus,* Little, Brown and Company, 1962, pp. 21-27.

[*Here, de Sélincourt enumerates some of the main reasons why Greek tradition is comparatively poor in the area of history.*]

Greek literature, the richest in the world after our own, Is comparatively poor in the department of history. Only two Greek historians have a title to greatness: Herodotus, first in time and incomparably the greater, and Thucydides. Xenophon, who continued the story of Greece where Thucydides left it, was a second-rate historian; he did indeed write one good book, his account—a splendid piece of first-hand reporting—of the expedition of a Greek mercenary army deep into the interior of Asia on a wild adventure in the service of the Persian prince, Cyrus; and he left some amiable tracts, in the manner of a country gentleman, on hunting and the management of an estate; but his major historical work few nowadays can bring themselves to read. Polybius, the fourth and last, was a writer of eminence, but though his long work included much Greek history, he was primarily a historian of Rome, telling the eventful story of her wars with Carthage. These four—unless we include Arrian, who wrote in the second century of our era a pious and competent history of Alexander the Great—complete the list of the Greek historians whose work has survived in anything but a fragmentary state and has quality above the mediocre.

Survival, indeed, is not a proof of quality, but it is some indication at least, and we can be pretty sure that neither accident nor time nor the judgement of the old Alexandrian scholars, has deprived us of any Greek histories of first-rate importance. Chroniclers of second—or fourth-rate-importance, and laborious compilers of historical facts and fictions, such as Diodorus the Sicilian who wrote a work in 144 books on world history from the Trojan War to the death of Julius Caesar, can be reckoned in hundreds; but to us these men themselves are not even names, and even of the hundreds I mentioned . . . , the great majority are little more than names. For the fact is that the brilliant lead of Herodotus and Thucydides was not followed. Herodotus, the Father of History, had an undistinguished family. This makes his own achievement only the more remarkable, as all the evidence forces us to the conclusion that historical writing of a high order was, unlike poetry, philosophy and the visual arts, in some way alien to the subtle and inventive genius of the Greeks. Poetry was in their blood: they were born poets, seeing what they saw with passion and immediacy, never, in the great early centuries before their decline, misting it with sentiment or wrapping it in rhetoric. They were born philosophers, too, with their devotion to first principles and insatiable curiosity about the workings of the sensible universe, of man in society and of their own minds; but they were not, it seems, by temperament or inclination, historians. Thus Herodotus, a native of Caria, part of that region on the Eastern shores of the Aegean where the first great impulse towards free speculation began in the sixth century before Christ—though a Greek of the Greeks in his habitual attitudes, and representative of much that was wisest and most civilised in that brilliant people whose civilisation was yet never separated by anything but the thinnest wall from savagery and barbarism, was nevertheless, in one important respect, untypical of his race. Homer (as we now believe) wrote the first great poem, and from that fount of poetry flowed innumerable streams. Men like Thales and Anaximander broke through the age-long darkness of superstition and the universal tyranny of myth to use their wits and their senses upon the fundamental problems of science and cosmology ('where does the visible universe come from, and how was it made?') and were followed throughout the six centuries of Greek intellectual pre-eminence by a succession of thinkers and speculators who built upon that priceless foundation of the freedom of thought; but Herodotus, who wrote the first great History in Greek, wrote also the last; Thucydides indeed, his younger contemporary, wrote a history which is still very much alive today and thus justifies its author's claim to make it a 'possession for ever'; but compared with Herodotus, Thucydides' book is tendentious in matter, parochial in scope, and difficult to read from the violences it does to the beautiful and perspicuous Greek language.

Homer, then, and the earliest Ionian thinkers, did what other Greeks with a similar intellectual endowment were potentially capable of doing, once they had been shown the way; Herodotus, on the contrary, did what others of his countrymen could never learn to do, or never wished to do. He was able (surely the first quality of a good historian) to see his subject as part of a larger process and to be constantly aware of the threads which linked his country with the vast and mysterious lands of Egypt and Asia. He was able to keep before his reader the sense that Greece, the centre of his interest, was still only one country in an immense and diverse world which it was yet to dominate by virtue of certain qualities which that world lacked, above all by that passion for independence and self-determination which was both her glory and her bane; to be aware of the past, not only the immediate but the most remote, as a living element in the present; and to find—unlike, in this, most historians writing today—a continuing moral pattern in the vicissitudes of human fortune all the world over. That pattern was simple enough: too simple for modern criticism, which tends to reject moral causes in tracing changes in the power-patterns of human society. It was formed from the belief that men, as men, are subject to certain limitations imposed by a Power—call it Fate or God—which they cannot fully comprehend, and that any attempt to transcend those limitations is met by inevitable punishment. In the search for a principle one might, after all, go farther and fare worse; such as it is, it has, in one form or another, lived on beside our newer notions. We still believe I suppose, that men are bound by the necessity of obedience. The only point of debate is obedience *to what?*

Perhaps I have suggested that the fact that Herodotus had no worthy successors during the period of Greek intellectual supremacy is a matter for surprise. This is not so. It is Herodotus himself who is surprising; for the study of history, in Herodotus' sense and in our own, was alien to the whole temper and circumstances of the ancient world. The priests in Egypt kept records stretching back to the remotest antiquity; but records are not history. Even the book of Thucydides, in many ways a noble one, is only an essay in history, dealing as it does, except for an introductory sketch, the validity of which has lately been called into question, only with contemporary events, and attempting the delineation, memorable indeed, of the contemporary political behaviour of men under the stresses of a civil war. But free and far-ranging inquiry into the past, either for its own intrinsic interest or in the search for a fuller understanding of the present, is an activity more natural to the modern than to the ancient world. Nor is this a question merely of techniques, which for Herodotus were almost totally non-existent; it is also, and predominantly, a question of the different direction of interest fostered by a comparatively primitive and a highly complex and artificial civilisation. The Greeks, most inquisitive of peoples, were not, on the whole, much interested in the past simply because they were too intensely occupied with the present. A civilisation like our own, though it liberates a man from many of the pressures of living, at the same time softens the impact of the basic realities. Perforce nowadays we live largely at second hand, not knowing, or wishing to know, the processes which supply our needs, and

not understanding, or wishing to understand, even if we could, the evidence upon which most of our current beliefs rest. The enormous amount which we take on trust must be obvious to anyone. The ancient Greek world was a small world, in which a man counted for something: he counted for something even if the tiny community in which he lived was governed by a despot; for there was always the hope that an opportunity might arise to stick a knife into the despot and have a revolution. And because it was a small world, what went on in it came home to a man's business and bosom in a way which is hardly possible for us today. Moreover it was not afflicted with the curse, unavoidable in modern conditions, of departmentalism. Every man had his public duties to perform, at least in the democratic communities, as politician and soldier. The Greeks had a word for those who avoided these duties: the word was 'idiot'. To all this we can add the extreme uncertainty amongst the ancients of the physical bases of life, the imminence of death by hunger, disease or violence, and the continual internecine feuds between neighbouring communities and between rival political parties within the same community, the whole sunlit scene shading off into a spirit-haunted darkness and a horror of the unknown—conditions of living which the Greeks seem to have accepted sometimes with a fierce joy, sometimes with a gloomy resignation to life's inevitable ills. It is not hard to see why they had little inclination to bother themselves with the past. The present filled them, and, if they did look to the past, it was through legend and myth, mainly local and particular, by which a community might connect its origin with a divine founder or a family with a divine ancestor.

Another reason why the Greeks were comparatively poor in historical writing is that they had no sense of the general march or development of human society. This difference between the Greeks and ourselves is important, and not easy to grasp. Time, for us, has been enormously extended by modern accretions of knowledge; our ability by means of geology, anthropology and other sciences to see, however dimly, into its dark backward and abysm, has necessarily affected our views of the development of man during the comparatively brief period he has been upon this earth. Evolution, in one form or another, is a part of our common mental furniture, and even the notion of progress, so fervently entertained in the hopeful years of the later 19th century, is not yet dead. At any rate we still believe that humanity is moving somewhere, even if not towards a better state. The odd identification of progress with material improvement has had, no doubt, to be seriously questioned recently; but we still know that our species is on the march, and that is progress of a kind; for one cannot but march forward even when the road leads back. The Greeks, when they looked back at all, looked back to a mythical Golden Age, since when they had steadily declined; nor did they fancy that Golden Age as very different in essentials from their own, except that men then were, so to put it, better at being men. The heroes who so splendidly walked the earth, sometimes in company with the gods, were but heightened images of themselves—better fighters, lustier lovers, bigger eaters and drinkers able to consume whole chines of beef and swallow honey-sweet wine by the barrelful, cunninger thieves, like the god Hermes, more ingenious tricksters in love or war. In short, they were fine fellows compared with their degenerate children. But any conception of a movement of humanity from primitive savagery to civilisation was absent from Greek thought, and when they looked at the future the Greeks saw it in the same terms as the present. In the political thought of the classical period, the City-state, for instance, had come to stay; and stay it did, till Alexander the Great left it in ruins. It is amusing to remember that Aristotle, who was Alexander's tutor, and whose reputation as a philosopher is still, I suppose, as high as most, laid it down in his *Politics* that no state should ever consist of more than 100,000 people; elsewhere, I believe, he said that a really satisfactory community should be small enough to allow everyone to know everyone else by name. That lesson, at any rate, his young pupil did not learn.

Lastly, the Greeks in general were not very much interested in countries and civilisations other than their own. They were aware, indeed, that the world was full of men, but the men were of two kinds only: Greeks and barbarians. The word 'barbarian' is itself a measure of their lack of interest: it means people whose unintelligible lingo sounds to a Greek ear like *bar-bar-bar*—or to borrow a more agreeable and imaginative comparison from Herodotus, like the twittering of birds. Unlike the Romans, who spoke Greek familiarly, the Greeks never seem to have bothered to learn a foreign language.

Herodotus overcame the disabilities imposed by time and place with astonishing success. Anyone can read his book with pleasure and profit, but the magnitude of his achievement can be grasped only by an imaginative reconstruction of the circumstances in which it was written. He was the first European historian and remains, in many respects, amongst the greatest; he was also—an achievement hardly less important—the first European writer to use prose as an artistic medium. The *art* of Greek prose was Herodotus' invention. English literature began, fully grown, with Chaucer; but Herodotus' achievement was greater than Chaucer's, because, unlike the Englishman who built his work on the solid foundation of the already long tradition of European literature, Herodotus had nothing to build upon at all. Prose had indeed been written before his time, and by others contemporary with him, 'logographers', as they were called—chroniclers, that is, of collections of facts in history and geography, the

best known of whom were Hecataeus of Miletus, whom Herodotus often quotes, and Hellanicus; but the work of these men, only fragments of which survive, had no literary pretension. They were pioneers, seeking a form which would express what could not be satisfactorily expressed in poetry, and what they did was valuable; but it was left for Herodotus to take the strange, new medium of language freed from the lilt and melody of verse—verse, which is so easily memorised, so well adapted to recitation which, in those days when solitary reading was seldom, if ever, indulged in, was the only form of 'publication'—and to mould it into an instrument of the subtlest and most delicate art. Herodotus' prose has the flexibility, ease and grace of a man superbly talking, and it is the easiest Greek, with the possible exception of Homer's, for anyone with modest pretensions to scholarship to understand. That it should have the grace of heightened and superb speech is, moreover, no accident, for Herodotus, like the poets, wrote his book to be read aloud, not to be perused in the privacy of a man's study.

Stephen Usher   (essay date 1970)

SOURCE: "Some Minor Historians," in *The Historians of Greece and Rome,* Taplinger Publishing Company, 1970, pp. 235-57.

[*In the following excerpt, Usher presents an overview of two minor Greek historians-Diodorus of Sicily and Dionysius of Halicarnassus-who were émigrés living and working in Rome during the latter part of the first century* B.C.]

Beginning with Diodorus of Sicily, we encounter history in its broadest conception. He inherited the idea of universal history from Ephorus, divested it of its Greek orientation, and included the whole of the inhabited world in a compendious *Library of History.* No less a Greek than Ephorus, he was convinced by two things of the obsoleteness of his 'Hellenocentric' view of the civilized world: he lived, like Polybius, under Roman rule; and, more significantly, he was influenced by a Stoic doctrine which radically affected his attitude to history, that of the brotherhood of man. The placing of his date of birth in the region of the year 90 B.C., probably at Agyrium in Sicily, makes it possible that he acquainted himself with the current teaching of the Stoic philosopher and historian Posidonius on that subject. Like several other Hellenistic historians, he made Rome his centre of study, but he travelled abroad at least as far as Egypt. He probably survived into the Augustan era. There is no evidence that he did anything of note except to write; and the length of his *Library* (forty books, of which fifteen survive in unabridged form) disposes us to doubt whether much time was left for any other creative writing.

The title itself arouses a curiosity which is to some extent satisfied in the eloquent introduction. Here Diodorus engagingly disclaims deep intelligence or insight, and admits the second-hand nature of his material. From other personal utterances it becomes plain that his main interest lies not in creative historiography but in the presentation, in a convenient and readable form, of a comprehensive history of the human race. To further increase understanding of his intentions we may most usefully turn to his application of Stoic doctrine. Two main concepts are involved. The first affirmed that mankind, though separate in space, arc brothers in blood, and that this conceptually united world is harmonized and ruled by divine providence. The universal historian becomes the servant of this providence, and will attempt to relate the apparently confused and disconnected events of world history to a central divine plan. Diodorus falls far short of realizing this ideal, and does not seem to have fully grasped the difficulties inherent in it. On the concept of human brotherhood, however, he is frequently articulate, often expressing pity at the sufferings of men at one another's hands. More specifically, the evil of slavery, of which he may have become conscious through his childhood experiences in Sicily, the scene of two servile revolts in living memory (135-132 and 104-102 B.C., moved Diodorus to write two notable passages describing conditions in gold mines in Spain and Egypt.

Another aspect of Stoic doctrine which affected the form of Diodorus's history is the concept of the utility of history as a medium of education and general benefit. Linked with the universal concept, this finds its logical form in Diodorus's concentration upon imparting information in a simple, straight-forward (and, it should be said, often dull) style, but with particular emphasis upon the deeds and memorable utterances of important men, which illustrate good or evil in human endeavour. Most of Diodorus's own personal comments are upon such actions. This interest in individuals and in moral instruction affects his choice of material, a fact which is best illustrated by comparison with the parallel narrative of another author—Xenophon—whose interests lie in a somewhat similar direction. True to his universal conception, Diodorus gives the broader coverage of events outside the immediate theatre of the Ionian War. On the other hand, Xenophon's accounts of battles, though by no means entirely satisfactory, are clearer than those of Diodorus, who too readily resorts to rhetoric. Xenophon also usually scores when it comes to the disclosure of motives and strategy, and is correspondingly less lavish with censure and praise. When we come to the period of Theban dominance, however, Diodorus's pro-Athenian bias, which he derives from his source Ephorus, proves less mischievous than Xenophon's adulation for Agesilaus, and it is mainly from his account that we are able to estimate the genius of Epaminondas. Before the period of the Peloponnesian War Diodorus is scarcely less useful,

devoting a whole book to the *Pentekontaetia,* which is scant coverage by other standards, but since Thucydides summarizes these years in thirty chapters it is the fullest continuous account we have. And again, after the more detailed Xenophontine account breaks off in 362 B.C., Diodorus, using Ephorus as his main source, once more furnishes the only consecutive account of these years, while for the period 323 to 302 B.C. he is the main literary authority. Sicilian episodes, which understandably occur frequently, and for which he is indebted chiefly to Timaeus, provide modern historians with much of their knowledge of the early history of that island.

The foregoing facts concerning the scope and value of Diodorus's narrative being undeniable, criticism of his work has been directed mainly against two faults: his superficiality, which from his own terms of reference and the brevity of the human span is inevitable; and his lack of originality. The latter needs definition. Distinction must be made between content and form. He has been called, among other things, a 'scissors and paste historian', and the fact that he depended upon others for his material has led to the wide assumption that he had no style of his own, but copied his sources verbatim. Such assertions are, in the absence of more than a few fragments of some of the original sources, very difficult to prove. On the other hand, recent work on the style of Diodorus, including statistical examination of his sentence structure and vocabulary, has tended to show uniformity, and to lead to the conclusion that he tried, not without success, to forge a style of his own and to create a work of independent merit.

. . . . .

Another émigré Greek historian who took up residence in Rome during the latter part of the first century B.C. was Dionysius of Halicarnassus. He tells us that he arrived in Rome in the middle of the 187th Olympiad (30 B.C.). From other indirect sources it can be deduced that he was in his late twenties at this time, and that he probably had considerable resources or influence to have been able to make the journey from Halicarnassus to Rome at that troubled time. Once ensconced in the great city, Dionysius was allowed to enter into its cultural life and became the leading member of an active circle of *literati.* Both Greeks and Romans comprised this coterie, but they shared a common interest in the purification and promotion of Greek as a literary language, and turned for their models to the orators of fourth-century Athens. Of these the most admired was Demosthenes, who was considered to embody all the major oratorical virtues. But due attention was also paid to the peculiar qualities of his lesser brethren—the smooth periodic virtuosity of Isocrates; the plain, pellucid simplicity of Lysias, which concealed his artistry; and the vehement and exhaustive argumentation of Isaeus, from which Demosthenes learned so much. Dionysius wrote essays on these and other authors, including Thucydides, part of whose introduction (in Book I) he has the temerity to rewrite, omitting chapters 2 to 20 as irrelevant. However, this essay also contains more mature criticism, and is of some interest on the grounds that it explores the possibilities of adapting the best Attic oratorical usages and techniques to the medium of historiography.

Dionysius's choice of history as the medium for his single excursion into creative, as distinct from critical, literature was to a large extent conditioned by time and circumstances. Roman oratory had attained to a brilliant virtuosity in the hands of Cicero (whom Dionysius never mentions in his writings), Caesar and their contemporaries under the free republic, whereas Greek oratory had languished since the fall of democracy in the motherland. Under Augustus, any form of free speech was subject to certain restrictions, and there was no longer any scope for impassioned political harangues. But oratory now became a form of mass entertainment, an alternative, for the more gentle or the more squeamish, to the blood-sports of the Colosseum. The language used in this stage-oratory was Latin, the language of the Roman populace. But in history Greek maintained its continuity, largely because it retained a reading public of intellectuals like the circle of Dionysius. Therefore, in electing to devote his creative talents to the writing of history, Dionysius was choosing the most acceptable medium through which to promote his crusade for the revival of Attic Greek. By further choosing the early history of Rome down to the First Punic War as his subject, he discharged an obligation to his hosts. In his preface he expresses his gratitude to them for their cordial hospitality and offers his work as a token of this gratitude. But he intended it to be much more than this. In his rhetorical writings he had expressed the view that the first duty of the historian was to select a worthy subject. What worthier than the rise to supremacy of the mightiest power of his day? But in the same passage he unwittingly reveals the danger inherent in such a choice. How is a 'great subject' to be defined? Dionysius criticizes Thucydides for choosing a subject inferior to that chosen by Herodotus, since the latter embraces a cosmic war, while the former is concerned with a parochial affair among Greeks. Such a shallow criterion of great historiography raises serious doubts concerning Dionysius's own competence as a historian, whatever his pretensions. And in spite of a considerable measure of solid achievement, these doubts are never wholly dispelled.

His *Early History of Rome* (*Antiquitates Romanae*) consisted of twenty books, of which the first ten are preserved complete, together with most of the eleventh. In order to study native sources Dionysius acquainted himself with the Latin language (the influence of which is curiously perceptible in the word-

order of his Greek). He also shows a commendable appetite for precise information, and is responsible for the preservation of the Servian Census. He had also read Thucydides and Polybius (whom he disliked on stylistic grounds) on the subject of historical causes, understood the distinctions they made and tried to apply them. He paid careful attention to chronology, and is not entirely to blame for the errors which arise from the confusion between the Greek and Roman calendars. In the matter of bias, his obvious admiration for Rome did not prevent him from censuring her politicians when this seemed appropriate. He scrupulously compares his sources in the best Hellenistic manner, and in much the same critical spirit as that which he applies to his learned literary discussions of the authenticity of the speeches of Dinarchus and others. And finally, his preconceived 'programme'—to represent Rome's achievement as a continuation of a glorious Greek past by showing that the founders of Rome were Greek in origin—was not in itself an impediment to the truthful presentation of subsequent Roman history.

But these virtues are to some extent cancelled out by the author's preoccupation with form at the expense of content. As a leading rhetorician, he conceived his *magnum opus* in a rhetorical spirit, which in the context of his own day meant that it was designed, like the public declamations, to make the maximum emotional impact on a listening public. An obvious means of achieving this effect in a work of history is to include a high proportion of live speech; and this Dionysius does. After the first two books, orations become frequent, forming about a third of the whole text. In the shadowy context of early Roman history, where little was known for certain of personalities and motives, or in some cases even the existence of some of the leaders named by tradition, the assignment of arguments and characterization could not be made with any serious claim to authenticity. On this view the speeches in the early books of Livy are open to the same criticism as those of Dionysius. But at least Livy's speeches were written in Latin, whereas those of Dionysius take unreality a stage further by having all the signs of their author's reverence for the canon of Attic orators, for Herodotus, Thucydides and Xenophon, from whose pages he has culled many sentiments and verbal expressions. Sometimes whole speeches appear to be modelled on classical originals, like that of Coriolanus advising the Volscians, the model for which is Thucydides's speech of Alcibiades to the Spartans. Often it seems probable that the existence of a classical model to fit the situation, rather than the knowledge that a speech was actually made, has led to the insertion of a speech.

Another aspect of rhetorical technique, amplification, is very much in evidence, and often destroys the historical perspective. Dionysius's narrative of the story of Coriolanus once more provides an excellent example, especially when compared with that of Livy. Dionysius needs forty-eight chapters to deal with it and assigns fifteen speeches to the protagonists: Livy dismisses the episode in half a chapter. It is a story full of tragedy, pathos and torn loyalties, and as such contains rich material for rhetorical display. Livy and Dionysius had access to the same sources, and yet treated the same episode very differently. It might be objected that Livy's reticence may be due in part to embarrassment at the treason of a prominent countryman; but he is elsewhere as ready as Dionysius to censure bad generalship or statesmanship with impartiality. The difference between the two historians is further illustrated by later divergences. The Samnite Wars, a protracted and dreary series of campaigns which lacked the definition of time and space (an essential quality for successful rhetorical treatment) that characterized the Coriolanian episode, were nevertheless probably more fully documented, and were certainly more important for the survival of Rome and the growth of her power. They cover six books in Livy, whereas Dionysius accords them less than four. Altogether it is not unfair to say that it is only when historical importance and rhetorical or dramatic qualities coincide in an event that one can be sure it receives from him the attention it deserves.

Perhaps Dionysius's most original contribution to ancient historical thought is his attempt, in the first two books, to combine within a single narrative the work of many different authorities for the legend of the Greek origins of Rome. Even this, however, is not without its weaknesses, for the more successful his synthesis is, the more completely is early Rome deprived of its native primitive elements—elements whose existence has been firmly established by modern archaeological discoveries. Thus deprived of the credit for experiment and innovation, the early Romans lose much of their vigour and individuality. Nevertheless Dionysius is one of those minor historians we should least want to be without, since his scholarly diligence has enabled us to fill many of the gaps in Livy's account.

M. I. Finley (essay date 1975)

SOURCE: "Myth, Memory, and History," in *The Use and Abuse of History,* The Viking Press, 1975, pp. 11-33.

[*In the excerpt below, Finley examines the interaction between myth, memory, and history in Greek culture and writing, and posits that, because of certain methodological and metaphysical limitations, after the time of Herodotus and Thucydides, "serious Greek historical writing was about contemporary history" only.*]

The Fathers of History were Greeks. Historians of antiquity are very proud of that, so much so that they prefer not to remember that some of the best minds in antiquity were not all impressed by this achievement. History as a discipline has always been a great favourite with the coiners of *bons mots*—it is false, it is dangerous, it is bunk. Historians can comfortably ignore the jibes and doubts of Walpole or Henry Ford, or even Goethe, but Aristotle is another matter; Aristotle, after all, founded a number of sciences and made all the others his own, too, in one fashion or another—except history and economics. He did not jibe at history, he rejected it, in the famous dictum in the ninth chapter of his *Poetics*:

> Poetry is more philosophical and more weighty than history, for poetry speaks rather of the universal, history of the particular. By the universal I mean that such or such a kind of man will say or do such or such things from probability or necessity; that is the aim of poetry, adding proper names to the characters. By the particular I mean what Alcibiades did and what he suffered.

No wonder the ninth chapter has been perhaps the worst victim of all in the familiar 'grousing about what are thought to be Aristotle's omissions' in the *Poetics*. It has been called 'inadequate'; it has been explained away by clever exegesis, as if Aristotle were one of the pre-Socratic philosophers of whom only a few cryptic sentences survive, which can be made to fit a thousand different theories; or it has been politely dismissed as not dealing with history at all. This last argument has a dangerous element of truth in it. It is not only chapter nine which does not deal with history; Aristotle never does. Apart from two incidental references in the *Poetics,* and a recommendation in the *Rhetoric* (1360a33-37) that political leaders should widen their experience by reading books of travel and history, he fails to mention the subject again in all the vast corpus of his extant works. Nothing could speak more emphatically than that massive silence. Evidence from the past, the past as a source of paradigms, is one thing; history as a systematic study, as a discipline, is another. It is not weighty enough, not philosophical enough, not even in comparison with poetry. It cannot be analysed, reduced to principles, systematized. It tells us merely what Alcibiades did or suffered. It establishes no truths. It has no serious function.

One can go much further. All Greek philosophers, to the last of the neo-Platonists, were evidently agreed in their indifference to history (as discipline). At least that is what their silence suggests, a silence broken only by the most fleeting of whispers. Aristotle's pupil Theophrastus is reported to have written a work called *On History,* and so, too, the latter's younger friend Praxiphanes, another Peripatetic. Beyond their titles, nothing is known of either work. Speculation about their content is idle. We must simply record the total disappearance of both works, the fact that they are never quoted by Diogenes Laertius in his *Lives of the Philosophers,* for example, or by the commentators on Aristotle.

Polybius, criticizing Phylarchus, contrasts historical with imaginative writing (c. 200 B.C. - 118 B.C.):

In his eagerness to arouse the pity and attention of his readers he treats us to a picture of clinging women with their hair disheveled and their breasts bare, or again of crowds of both sexes together with their children and aged parents weeping and lamenting as they are led away to slavery. This sort of thing he keeps up throughout his history, always trying to bring horrors vividly before our eyes. Leaving aside the ignoble and womanish character of such a treatment of his subject, let us consider how far it is proper or serviceable to history. A historical author should not try to thrill his readers by such exaggerated pictures, nor should he, like a tragic poet, try to imagine the probable utterances of his characters or reckon up all the consequences probably incidental to the occurrences with which he deals, but simply record what really happened and what really was said, however commonplace. For the object of tragedy is not the same as that of history but quite the opposite. The tragic poet should thrill and charm his audience for the moment by the verisimilitude of the words he puts into his characters' mouths, but it is the task of the historian to instruct and convince for all time serious students by the truth of the facts and the speeches he narrates, since in the one case it is the probable that takes precedence, even if it be untrue, the purpose being to create illusion in spectators, in the other it is the truth, the purpose being to confer benefit on learners.

Polybius quoted in Ancilla to Classical Reading, *by Moses Hadas, Columbia University Press, 1954.*

What philosophy would not have, rhetoric took possession of. It is a sobering thought that the only ancient work to have come down to us which pretends to be a systematic essay on historiography is Lucian's *How to Write History,* written soon after A.D. 165. And that is nothing but a concoction of the rules and maxims which had become the commonplaces of a rhetorical education, a shallow and essentially worthless pot-boiler. Its one point of interest for us is that five hundred years after Aristotle, Lucian was still setting history against poetry. Historians themselves had long since accepted the need to compete for favour with poetry—by surrendering and writing works which Polybius dismissed with the sneering label, 'tragic history'. Not every historian, but too many, and, what is crucial, even the stoutest of the resisters failed to break down either the indifference of the philosophers or the taste of the ordinary readers.

Why poetry? The answer, of course, is that by poetry Aristotle and the others meant epic poetry, late lyric poetry such as Pindar's, and tragedy, which portrayed the great figures and the great events of the past. The issue was not whether or not, or to what extent, such poetry was historically reliable, in the sense in which we ask that kind of question of the ancient epics today, but the deeper question of universality, of truth about life in general. The issue, in short, was that between myth and history. By 'myth' I mean what is commonly meant, in ordinary usage, by both 'myth' and 'legend', and not the more metaphorical senses, as in the phrase, 'the racist myth', or in the well-known extensions of the term by such modern thinkers as Sorel or Cassirer. I mean such myths as that of Prometheus and Heracles and the Trojan War.

The atmosphere in which the Fathers of History set to work was saturated with myth. Without myth, indeed, they could never have begun their work. The past is an intractable, incomprehensible mass of uncounted and uncountable data. It can be rendered intelligible only if some selection is made, around some focus or foci. In all the endless debate that has been generated by Ranke's *wie es eigentlich gewesen* ('how things really were'), a first question is often neglected: what 'things' merit or require consideration in order to establish how they 'really were'? Long before anyone dreamed of history, myth gave an answer. That was its function, or rather one of its functions; to make the past intelligible and meaningful by selection, by focusing on a few bits of the past which thereby acquired permanence, relevance, universal significance.

When Herodotus was in his prime, the distant past was very much alive in men's consciousness, more so than the recent centuries or generations: Oedipus and Agamemnon and Theseus were more real to fifth-century Athenians than any pre-fifth-century historical figure save Solon, and he was elevated to their ranks by being transformed into a mythical figure. Annually the mythical heroes re-appeared at the great religious festivals in tragedy and choral ode, and they re-created for their audiences the unbroken web of all life, stretching back over the generations of men to the gods; for the heroes of the past, and even many heroes of the present, were divinely descended. All this was serious and true, literally true. It was the basis of their religion, for example. There is a fine passage by Robertson Smith [*Lectures on the Religion of the Semites,* 1907] which sums the picture up:

> In ancient Greece . . . certain things were done at a temple, and people were agreed that it would be impious not to do them. But if you had asked why they were done, you would probably have had several mutually contradictory explanations from different persons, and no one would have thought it a matter of the least religious importance which of these you chose to adopt. Indeed, the explanations

offered would not have been of a kind to stir any strong feeling; for in most cases they would have been merely different stories as to the circumstances under which the rite first came to be established, by the command or by the direct example of the god. The rite, in short, was connected not with a dogma but with a myth.

Greeks did not love epic and tragedy, however, solely because they needed to be reminded about the origins of their rites, important as that function was for the individual—and even more for the community, which was rooted in divine patronage and ancestry. Myth was their great teacher in all matters of the spirit. There they learned morality and conduct; the virtues of nobility and the golden mean or the menace of *hybris;* and they learned about race and culture and even politics. Were not both Solon and Pisistratus accused of falsifying the text of the *Iliad,* interpolating two lines in order to have Homeric authority for the seizure of Salamis from the Megarians?

With this background it is not surprising that history should have been discussed and judged in antiquity, should have been measured, against poetry. Fundamentally, one kind of retelling of the past was being measured against another. For there must be no misunderstanding about one thing: everyone accepted the epic tradition as grounded in hard fact. Even Thucydides. He tells us that right off, as soon as he finishes introducing himself. The Peloponnesian War, he argues, is more worthy of narration than any which preceded, 'for it was the greatest movement thus far among the Hellenes and among a portion of the barbarian world', greater, specifically, than even the Trojan War. He argues this at some length, and among the 'historical' personages whom he introduces in his opening pages there appear Hellen son of Deucalion (the eponymous ancestor of the Hellenes), Minos, king of Crete, and Agamemnon and Pelops. Details are uncertain, he says, both about the remote past and about the period before the Peloponnesian War—a most significant coupling— but the general outlines are clear and reliable. Homer exaggerated, because he was a poet and properly employed a poet's licence, and Thucydides, unlike the vulgar majority, allowed for this in his introduction. Thucydides himself, we remember, warns his readers that his own work will not cater to the demand for exaggeration and poetic adornment; it will relate the facts free from romance. But neither Thucydides nor Plato nor Aristotle nor anyone else proceeded to outright scepticism about what a modern writer might call the historical kernel in the epic, and surely not to outright denial.

Yet, whatever else it may have been, the epic was *not history*. It was narrative, detailed and precise, with minute descriptions of fighting and sailing and feasting and burials and sacrifices, all very real and very vivid; it may even contain, buried away, some kernels of historical fact—but it was not history. Like all myth, it was timeless. Dates and a coherent dating scheme are as essential to history as exact measurement is to physics. Myth also presented concrete facts, but these facts were completely detached: they were linked neither with what went before nor with what came after. The *Iliad* begins with the wrath of Achilles over an affront to his honour and ends with the death of Hector. The *Odyssey,* as background to the travels of Odysseus, mentions the ending of the Trojan War and the return of some of the heroes. But it all happened 'once upon a time', flowing out of nothing (for the rape of Helen is merely another isolated fact, totally unhistorical in any significant sense) and leading to nothing. Even within the narrative the account is fundamentally timeless, despite the many fixed numbers (of days or years). 'These numbers, most of them typical numbers which recur for all possible quantities, are in general not binding; they are not the bases for calculations or synchronizations. They merely indicate, broadly, magnitude or scale, and in their stylized pseudo-precision they symbolize long duration. To all intents and purposes there is no interest in chronology, whether relative or absolute.' Many years later the Greek tragedians maintained the same indifference: Oedipus, Iphigenia, Orestes all did things or suffered things which were believed to be historical facts, but what occurred floated dimly in the far-away past, unconnected by time or pattern with other events.

Timelessness is reflected in still another way, in the individual characters. Death is one main topic of their lives (along with honour from which it is inseparable), and fate is often the chief propelling power. In that sense they live in time, but in no other way. It ought not escape any reader of the *Odyssey* that when the hero returns after twenty years, he and Penelope are exactly what they were half a generation earlier. It escaped Samuel Butler, to be sure, when he wrote: 'There is no love-business in the *Odyssey* except the return of a bald elderly married man to his elderly wife and grown-up son after an absence of twenty years, and furious at having been robbed of so much money in the meantime. But this can hardly be called love-business; it is at the utmost domesticity.'

The poet does not say that Odysseus was bald and elderly; Butler says it, and this is presumably what he called reading the Homeric lines 'intelligently' by reading 'between them'. It goes against common sense and 'intelligence' for Odysseus not to be bald and elderly by the time of his return. The flaw—and Samuel Butler is only a convenient whipping-boy for a frequent practice—is to apply modern historical thinking in the guise of common sense to a mythical, non-historical tale. Historical husbands and wives grow old, but the plain fact is that neither Odysseus nor Penelope has changed one bit; they have neither developed nor deteriorated, nor does anyone else in the epic. Such men and women cannot be figures in history: they are too simple, too self-enclosed, too rigid and stable, too detached from their backgrounds. They are as timeless as the story itself.

Perhaps the most decisive example comes not from Homer but from his near contemporary Hesiod. The opening of the *Works and Days* contains one of the most famous of all primitivistic tales, the account of man's decline from a golden age of the past in several stages, each symbolized by another metal: after gold comes silver, then bronze or copper, and finally iron (the present age). But Hesiod's vision is not one of progressive deterioration, of evolution in reverse. Each race of men (Hesiod speaks of races, *genê,* not of ages) does not evolve into the next; it is destroyed and re-placed by a new creation. Each race exists neither in time nor in place. The races of man are as timeless as the Trojan War: for the future as well as the past. And so Hesiod can lament: 'would that I were not among the men of the fifth generation, but either had died before *or been born afterwards*' (lines 174-75).

It is possible that the myth of the four metallic ages or races was an eastern one in origin, Hellenized by Hesiod. But there was also a fifth age or race, and that was surely Greek through and through, the age of heroes injected between the bronze and the iron. 'But when earth had covered this [bronze] generation also, Zeus the son of Cronos made yet another, the fourth, upon the fruitful earth, which was nobler and more righ-teous, a god-like race of hero-men who are called demi-gods, the race before our own, throughout the bound-less earth.' This is patchwork, unavoidable because the myths of the heroes were too deeply fixed in the mind, too indispensable to be passed by. Patchwork is the rule in myth, and it gives no trouble. Only the histor-ically minded see the rough stitches and the faulty joins and are bothered by them, as is abundantly evi-dent in Herodotus. But Hesiod was not historically minded. Here on the one hand were the four races and here on the other hand was the race of heroes. They were data, and his task was to assemble them. He did it in the easiest way possible, thanks to the total ab-sence of the time element. There were no chronolog-ical problems, no dates to be synchronized, no devel-opment to trace or explain. The race of heroes had no beginning in history: it was simply made by Zeus. And it had no ending, no transition to the next, contempo-rary stage. Some of the heroes were destroyed before the gates of Thebes and in the Trojan War. 'But to the others father Zeus the son of Cronos gave a living and an abode apart from men, and made them dwell at the ends of the earth. And they live untouched by sorrow in the islands of the blessed along the shore of deep swirling Ocean.'

There is a sense, of course, in which the myth of the ages is not a proper myth. It is too abstract. Hesiod's poem deals, in its first part, with the problem of evil, and no more despairing indictment of the injustice of the world has ever been written. Why, he asks, why is the world so full of evil? His first answer is mythical in its most traditional sense; he tells the story of Prometheus and Pandora: that is the answer, a typical-ly mythical answer, the kind of answer Greeks contin-ued to give to explain rites and beliefs all through their history. But now, he continues without pause, I will tell you another tale, and his second one, the alterna-tive to the Pandora myth, is the account of the races of man. Clearly there is a new kind of thinking here, inchoate, poetic and not systematic, not followed through and not even properly linked with the rest of the long poem, but nonetheless pointing to an entirely new line of intellectual endeavour and pointing away from myth and epic. 'What was at the beginning?' a historian of Greek philosophy wrote of Hesiod, 'is the question of history precisely at the point where it turns into philosophy. . . . The question Hesiod poses is no longer about the historical past, but about the begin-ning of what exists, the question of philosophical or-igins. . . .' But 'history' is wholly out of place here. Hesiod is foreshadowing the step from *mythos* to *logos,* and that step was not mediated by history. It bypassed history altogether. It moved from the timelessness of myth to the timelessness of metaphysics.

More than two centuries went by before the (more recent) past was bound into any sort of chronology. That was the work of Herodotus. Writing in the third quarter of the fifth century, Herodotus conjectured that Homer lived four hundred years earlier (about 850 B.C.) and that the Trojan War took place another four hun-dred years before that (about 1250 B.C.). Many events were known to have occurred during that long interval, such as the return of the Heraclids to Sparta, the var-ious (and chronologically incompatible) deeds of The-seus, or the legislation of Lycurgus. These Herodotus was totally unable to fit into his chronological scheme. The fault was not his, but a consequence of the fact that the data were timeless, and therefore unhistorical. The measure of his genius lies in the simple point that he appreciated these limitations (if not to the extent of disbelief in the 'fact' of Orestes and Theseus and the rest) and therefore he made no effort to assign dates to the undatable myths. Herodotus' historical chronolo-gy, in so far as there is one, is more accurate than has usually been allowed, equally so in his refusal to ruin it by incorporating the mythical events. The latter fre-quently recur in his work, but as something detached, as something which happened once upon a time, un-like, say, the career of Solon or the reign of Polycrates in Samos. Polycrates, says Herodotus (3.122), seems to have been the first Greek to think of a maritime empire, 'leaving aside Minos' and others like him, the first, in other words, 'in what is called the time of men'—which we should express as the first in historical, as distinct from mythical, times. What Herodotus was able to do was to establish some kind of time-sequence for perhaps two centuries of the past, roughly from the middle of the seventh century B.C. on. All that came before remained as it had been when he began his work, epic tales and myths believed to be true, at least in essence, but incorrigibly timeless.

The plain fact is that the classical Greeks knew little about their history before 650 B.C. (or even 550 B.C.), and that what they thought they knew was a jumble of fact and fiction, some miscellaneous facts and much fiction about the essentials and about most of the details. One need only consider Thucydides' introduction, which I have already mentioned, in which he justified his own effort by offering in twenty-one chapters (a dozen pages) a most remarkable interpretation of early Greek history. From chapter fourteen he was on pretty firm ground, established by Herodotus (whose book he had studied with great care) with the indispensable help of Egyptian, Persian and other Near Eastern records. But in the first part he had nothing to go on other than Homer and other 'old poets', tradition, contemporary evidence, and a very powerful and disciplined mind. The result is a sweeping theory, namely, that Hellenic power and greatness emerged only in consequence of the systematic development of navigation and commerce, which were followed by an accumulation of resources, stable community organization, imperialism (to use an anachronistic word), and finally the greatest of all Greek power struggles, the Peloponnesian War. This theory may be right, in whole or in part, or it may be wrong—I am not concerned with that question here. What is crucial is that it is a theory derived from prolonged meditation about the world in which Thucydides lived, not from a study of history. True, there is something here which is history in a conceptual sense: Thucydides has made the bold suggestion that there was a continuity and a development in Greece from the most ancient (mythical) times to his own. I do not underestimate this new conception, but its actual working out by Thucydides in his opening pages is not history in any meaningful sense of that word. Instead he has given us what amounts to a general sociological theory, a theory about power and progress, applied retrospectively to the past, and applied, one must add, with caution and hesitation, for, as Thucydides explains at the outset, one cannot achieve certainty about ancient times, one can merely say that this is what all the 'signs' point to.

Among the signs are astonishingly few concrete events: the first thalassocracy 'known to tradition' (that of King Minos), the Trojan War, a few migrations, change in habits of dress and in the practice of carrying arms, the extension from Sparta to the Olympic games of the practice of competing entirely naked in athletics, and a few other scraps—until the age of tyrants and Persian annals. There are only four dates: the migration of

the Boeotians to Boeotia sixty years after the Trojan War and of the Dorians into the Peloponnese twenty years after that; the construction of four triremes (an important new invention) by the Corinthian Ameinocles for the Samians three hundred years before the end of the Peloponnesian War (i.e., about 700 B.C.); and forty years later the first recorded naval battle, between Corinth and Corcyra. Thucydides does not date the Trojan War, but if he accepted Herodotus' chronology, then he has no dated event between 1170 and 700 B.C., a period equal in length to that between the accession of Henry VII and our own day. Everything that fell between could only be fixed as 'later' or 'much later'. Moreover, we have no independent check on his two late dates, and we can dismiss his two early ones as still in the realm of myth, whatever the truth about the movements of Boeotians and Dorians.

But we do have some control over the general picture of material progress and migration, and the result is negative (quite apart from the possible validity of the sea-power theory itself). Twice in this section Thucydides argues explicitly from what we should call archaeological evidence, once from the ruins of Mycenae and the other time from the bones and artifacts uncovered when Delos was purified in 426/5 B.C. (in Thucydides' own lifetime) by opening all the graves and transferring their contents to the adjacent island of Rhenaea. The arguments are clever and cogent, but are they valid? On the contrary, they reveal a gross ignorance and misunderstanding of the past on several points of major significance. Thucydides was clearly unaware (as were all other Greek writers, so far as we know) of the catastrophic destruction of Mycenaean civilization near the end of the second millennium B.C. and of the profound discontinuity between Mycenaean civilization and Greek civilization proper; he 'did not recognise Geometric . . . pottery as being particularly Greek and dated it at least three hundred years too early'; he 'either did not know of what we call the Bronze Age or else dated its end too early'. In sum, in his view, 'Agamemnon's Mycenae and fifth-century Mycenae could be thought of as one city, repaired and casually rebuilt but essentially the same'.

These mistakes, coupled with the absence of all dates and of virtually all fixed events between 1170 and 700, destroy any possibility of a proper history of early Greece. I do not mean that Thucydides tried to write one, even in capsule form, and failed: on the contrary, he did not try because he did not believe it possible or necessary. I mean, rather, that from such a start no Greek could write one, and the proof is in the pathetic failure of those men in later centuries who tried to write annals and universal histories from the Trojan War (or from the creation of the world) to their own day. They lacked the information, and there was no way they could get it. Of this we can be confident, as we can confidently correct Thucydides' mistakes about the fall of Mycenae or the origin and date of Geometric vases. More than that, we know much more (and much more accurately) about the political trends and the growth of cities and the development of trade and money and so on through the whole list of institutional and social phenomena. And yet, we too are wholly incapable of writing a history of this period. That is our inescapable heritage from the Greeks. We can, for example, discourse with considerable subtlety and sophistication—and with inherent probability—about the decline of monarchy and the rise of the aristocratic *polis,* but we cannot narrate that story, not even in fragmentary fashion, for any single community; we are gradually assembling much information about the physical appearance of early Ionian cities and we can date their development to close limits, but we have no significant knowledge about the political life within them; we can lay out the vases in most elaborate series, but we know nothing about the potters or the pottery industry. And we never shall. In short, like Thucydides, we can formulate sociological theories, and unlike him, we can write art history (largely restricted to pure externals). But we, too, cannot write a history of early Greece.

The reason is very simple: there are no documents, nothing which records events or reports who did things, what things, and why. Before the year 700 B.C. (a round number which I use as a signpost, not as a precise date) such documents never existed, not even in the most transient form, on papyrus or wax. After 700 a body of Greek writing began to emerge, steadily increasing in volume and variety as the classical world of the fifth and fourth centuries B.C. drew nearer. Little survives, some quotations in later writers and fragmentary collections recovered in the present century on Egyptian papyri of Hellenistic and Roman times. It is not beyond hope that more will be found in the future which will add to our stock of information, much as the new fragments of the poet Alcaeus have taught us things about the political struggles within the aristocracy of Lesbos round the year 600, and about the tyranny of Pittacus which had been as mysterious in its details as it was famous in legend. Were every lost line written between 700 and 500 to be recovered, including the texts of laws and decrees as well as poems and philosophical writings, a generation of historians would be kept busy sorting and organizing and interpreting the new material—and we should still be unable to write a history of these two centuries, let alone of the earlier centuries.

That gloomy prediction follows inevitably from the nature of the material. For complicated reasons—which I do not believe we are in a position to formulate fully—the composition of epic poetry came to a rather abrupt end. Poets turned their backs on the past, both on the literary forms of the past and on the past as subject-matter, and they began to write about themselves and their friends, their loves and hates, their feelings, their joys and their pleasures. For two centuries all the poetry was personal; it might be flippant or anacreontic, it might be amatory (Sapphic or otherwise), or it might be serious, moralistic and philosophical—but always it dealt with personal problems and with generalities, not with narration nor with politics or society in their concrete institutional expressions.

> I hate the lanky officer, stiff-standing, legs
>   apart,
> Whose cut of hair and whisker is his principal
>   renown;
> I prefer the little fellow with his bigness in
>   his heart,
> And let his legs be bandy, if they never let
>   him down.

These lines of Archilochus reveal a new, un-heroic, un-Homeric set of values. Others offer biographical bits—'We, the down-and-outs of Hellas, flocked to Thasos in a troop'—often with important social implications (in this instance, the appearance of the mercenary soldier). They are precious bits, given the sparseness of our knowledge of these centuries, but they cannot be converted, not even if they were counted in the tens of thousands, into a consistent and continuous story of how the Greek cities emerged, grew, took shape, struggled and lived. Nor do the philosophical writers add another dimension. And that is all there was.

No one before the fifth century tried to organize, either for his own time or for earlier generations, the essential stuff of history. There were lists—of the kings of Sparta and the archons of Athens and the victors in the various games. They could provide a chronology, if we knew what happened in the archonship of X or the reign of Y; but we do not know, except in a few isolated instances about a few isolated events. Law codes and individual rulings were recorded somehow, but there were no proper archives, and they soon disappeared from sight for the most part. This combination of negatives—the absence of annals (like those of the kings of Assyria), the indifference of poets and philosophers, and the loss of public documents—is irrevocable. Unless a generation is captured on paper and the framework of its history fixed, either contemporaneously or soon thereafter, the future historian is for ever blocked. He can reinterpret, shift the emphases, add and deduct data, but he cannot create the framework *e nihilo*. That is why we can write the history of the Persian wars, thanks to Herodotus, and the history of the Peloponnesian War, thanks to Thucydides, but not the history of the intervening fifty years, not for all the writers of tragedy and comedy and all the inscriptions and material objects unearthed by modern archaeologists.

Contemporary archaeology is a highly refined, highly

professional and technical procedure. Carbon-14 dating and similar techniques will one day produce firm evidence undreamed of in the world of Thucydides. Yet it would be a great mistake to explain our superior knowledge of Mycenae solely by reference to scientific advances. Technically, Schliemann and Sir Arthur Evans had little at their disposal which was not available to fifth-century Athenians. The ancient Greeks already possessed the skills and the manpower with which to discover the shaft-graves of Mycenae and the palace of Cnossus, and they had the intelligence to link the buried stones—had they dug them up—with the myths of Agamemnon and Minos, respectively. What they lacked was the interest: that is where the enormous gap lies between their civilization and ours, between their view of the past and ours. A reverse example comes from their use of literary evidence. Thucydides and his contemporaries knew the full corpus of lyric and elegiac poetry, but they made less use, and less skilful use, of this material for historical analysis than we make of the few scraps which have survived in our time. Again neither technique nor intelligence is a useful criterion; only interest will explain the difference.

Some kind of interest in the past is, of course, universal. That statement helps very little, however, though it is repeated often enough in books about history and the writing of history, as if it were an important point worth making. In so far as it is not just a tautology—man by nature has memory, including memory of things told to him by older generations, and therefore he has an 'interest' in the past—it has no meaning which is not either wrong or confusing. Interest in the sense of curiosity or desire for knowledge is, in ordinary usage, a term of individual psychology, descriptive of a state of mind or feeling, not sufficient as an explanation of individual behaviour, totally useless when extended to a society. Interest must itself be defined and accounted for: what part of the past and how much of it? Interest to what purpose, to fulfil what function? The past has been studied didactically and morally, as an exemplar of man's essential sinfulness, for example, or as a guide to future political action; it has performed the social-psychological function of giving a society cohesion and purpose, of strengthening morale and encouraging patriotism; it can be and has been put to romantic uses. And so on. Each of these interests requires a different kind of approach and a different kind of study (within limits)—in short, a different kind of knowledge.

None of the interests I have just enumerated requires a systematic account of the past. The question which is implicit in so much modern writing on the history of history—how could the Greeks (or anyone else) remain content with a past which was filled with so many blank spaces and which was, essentially, timeless?—rests on a false conception of time in human psychology. We are in thrall to the highly sophisticated, highly abstract scientific conception of time as a measurable continuum, a conception which is largely meaningless for ordinary human purposes. Time past consists of a number of individual events (including biological transformations and sensual satisfactions); time future consists of anticipated events or satisfactions. Duration of time, if it is a consideration at all, which is not always the case, is not experienced as a measurable quantity but as an associative or emotional quality: time drags, for example. Individual memory illustrates this exactly. We do not recall a past event, whether we are consciously searching our memories for one or one comes to mind without deliberation, by working our way from the present through the past. Memory leaps instantaneously to the desired point and it then dates by association. There is a certain consciousness of duration, to be sure, but that is satisfied by 'long ago' or 'the other day', or by an association which implies 'long ago', for example, 'when I was still a schoolboy'.

This is familiar and obvious, and it is as true of group experience as of personal experience. Claud Cockburn records a revealing meeting with three Ladino-speaking Jews in Sofia shortly after the Second World War. He had approached the three men in the railway station, not knowing who or what they were. After attempting conversation in several languages without success, he tried Spanish.

'They understood, and replied in what was certainly intelligible as a form of Spanish—though a very strange form. . . . I remarked that it was rather odd to find Spanish here [in Sofia]. They explained. They were not Spaniards, but, one of them said, "Our family used to live in Spain before they moved to Turkey. Now we are moving to Bulgaria." Thinking that perhaps they had been "displaced" from Spain by the upheaval of the civil war, I asked how long it had been since their family lived there. He said it was approximately five hundred years. . . . He spoke of these events as though they had occurred a couple of years ago.'

Essentially the 'historical' references of these Ladino-speaking Jews were like the 'mythical' references of most Greeks, with one difference the significance of which is more potential than actual. When pressed, the former translated 'our family used to live in Spain' into 'it was approximately five hundred years ago'. They were able to do that thanks to the modern calendar, with its dating by years from a fixed initial point. The Greeks eventually acquired that technique, too, when dating by Olympiads was introduced, but that remained for them an artificial convention, invented and used by a small number of antiquarian-minded intellectuals, never introduced into daily life. And that brings us back to the matter of interest. The only people in antiquity who were somehow 'modern' in this respect were the Hebrews, and the interest which lay behind, and which provoked, their detailed account of the past as a continuum was, of course, a religious one, the story of the unfolding of God's will from the Creation to the final triumph in the future. The Greeks had no such interest, religious or otherwise; whatever the function in the present of Agamemnon, it did not require locating him along a time continuum; it did not matter whether he lived two hundred years ago or four hundred or a thousand.

Effectively, Greek thinking divided the past into two parts, two compartments, the heroic age and the post-heroic (or the time of the gods and the time of men). The first was the part fixed, defined and described by the myth-makers, who worked in the centuries which are, to us, prehistoric in the strict sense. They created and transmitted myths orally, bringing together purely cult material (the origins of which can be speculated about, but not documented), genuine historical events (including personal details about the noble families), and much purely imaginary material. Their orientation was towards the past; at first, presumably, towards the more recent past, but, as time went on, increasingly—and to a considerable extent, deliberately—to more remote times. The interest, however, was not historical in the sense of an objective inquiry into the facts of the Trojan War (or any other period of history). That is obvious, but it needs saying. Even when we put aside aesthetic considerations, the pleasures evoked by the beauty of the lines and the chanting, or the not inconsiderable satisfactions aroused by a story simply because it is a good story, the remaining interests lay far outside the realm of inquiry and science. Pan-Hellenic or regional consciousness and pride, aristocratic rule, and especially their right to rule, their pre-eminent qualifications and virtues, an understanding of the gods, the meaning of cult practices—these and other, comparable, ends were served by the continual repetition of the old tales. And by their constant re-working, for new conditions were always intruding.

In this first phase, then, when oral tradition was built up and kept alive, the product was a mythical past created out of disparate elements, differing in their character and their (factual) accuracy, and having their (factual) origin in widely scattered periods of time. 'Tradition' did not merely transmit the past, it created it. In a shape which sometimes looks like history, and has been widely accepted as history both by the Greeks and (with qualifications) by many modern students, the bards fashioned a timeless mythology. Then a new phase set in, symbolized by the eventual writing down of the epics and other mythological documents. In a world which lacked any kind of central authority, political or ecclesiastical, and which was filled with separate and often clashing political and regional interests, this step helped fixed the texts of the tales, creating an authoritative version. Important as that was, however, it need not, by itself, have been decisive.

The myth-making process did not stop in the eighth century; it never wholly stopped. Apart from the myth-icizing of men like Solon, myth-making continued because Greek religion continued to develop new rites, introduce new gods, and combine old elements into new forms, each step requiring an appropriate adjustment in the inherited mythology. Likewise, the great dispersion of Greeks from about 750 to about 600 B.C., carrying them to southern Italy, Sicily, and to many other places along the Mediterranean and Black Sea shores, demanded further changes to suit new political alignments between cities and regions and to incorporate traditions of the (non-Greek) peoples among whom they settled. All this later myth-making activity, however, was secondary: the 'mythical charter' of Hellenic self-consciousness was now fully fashioned. Interests moved in new directions.

The second phase was therefore one in which interest in the distant, and important, past, though fully alive, expressed itself in retention and repetition of the mythical charter. Along with the writing down of the epics went the disappearance of the bards as a class. They were replaced by rhapsodes, men like Plato's Ion who were professionals too, but reciters—actors—not creators. The creative intellects, as I have already said, turned to entirely new fields, to personal and contemporary poetry and to philosophy. The heroic past needed no further attention, other than the passive one of seeing to it that everyone was reminded of it, in the accepted version, on all appropriate occasions, and that each succeeding generation retained this knowledge and made use of it in the same ways.

How and by whom, we must then ask, were traditions about the post-heroic centuries preserved and transmitted? How, for example, did the memory survive of the sea-battle between Corinth and Corcyra or of the construction by a Corinthian of four warships for the Samians, which Thucydides reports and to which he even assigns precise dates? Thucydides himself could have read about these things in Herodotus or in some other writer. But someone put them down on paper for a first time two hundred or more years after the event (and there were many other traditional facts of a still earlier date, requiring oral transmission for still more centuries). The first man to write them down (and in some instances that may well have been someone as late as Thucydides) had no documents or archives to draw on—that cannot be stressed too often. He had to capture something which had been transmitted orally.

Oral tradition is an old favourite in books dealing with distant ages, or even with fairly recent ages, for which there are few (or no) written records. And there are few notions which historians of the Greek Dark Age are less prepared to examine critically enough, enveloping themselves in the warm glow thrown off by the word 'tradition'. Now there is the tradition which shapes a large part of our lives, perpetuating customs, habits of behaviour, rites, ethical norms and beliefs. There is nothing mysterious about tradition in this sense; it is transmitted from one generation to the next, partly by the ordinary process of living in society, without any conscious effort on anyone's part, partly by men whose function it is to do so: priests, schoolmasters, parents, judges, party leaders, censors, neighbours. There is also nothing reliable about this sort of tradition; that is to say, its explanations and narrations are, as anyone can judge by a minimum of observation, rarely quite accurate, and sometimes altogether false. Reliability is, of course, irrelevant; so long as the tradition is accepted, it works, and it must work if the society is not to fall apart.

But 'tradition' detached from living practices and institutions—a tradition about a war two hundred years back, for example—is not the same thing at all; only a semantic confusion seems to place it in the same category. Wherever tradition can be studied among living people, the evidence is not only that it does not exist apart from a connection with a practice or belief, but also that other kinds of memory, irrelevant memories, so to speak, are short-lived, going back to the third generation, to the grandfather's generation, and, with the rarest of exceptions, no further. This is true even of genealogies, unless they are recorded in writing; it may be taken as a rule that orally transmitted genealogies, unless some very powerful interest intervenes (such as charismatic kingship), are often distorted, disputed or wholly fictitious beyond the fourth generation, and often even beyond the third. There is a nice Greek illustration: the Homeric heroes recite their genealogies frequently and in detail, and without exception a few steps take them from human ancestors to gods or goddesses.

The analogy with individual memory is again useful. It, too, normally stops at the third generation, with things told by grandparents, by parents about their parents, by elderly nurses. It, too, is controlled by relevance. All memory is selective, and though the reason why something remains (apart from something actively and deliberately learned, like a school lesson) more often than not escapes us, that is a defect in our knowledge, not a manifestation of random, purposeless behaviour. But then the analogy breaks down, for 'group memory' is never subconsciously motivated in the sense of being, or seeming to be, automatic and uncontrolled, unsought for as personal memory so often appears. Group memory, after all, is no more than the transmittal to many people of the memory of one man or a few men, repeated many times over; and the act of transmittal, of communication and therefore of preservation of the memory, is not spontaneous and unconscious but deliberate, intended to serve a purpose known to the man who performs it. He may misjudge his motives, he may not formulate them clear-

ly, he probably does not go through a long prior process of reflection, but invariably he is acting, doing something, bringing about an effect he desires or wills. Unless such conscious, deliberate activity occurs, eventually the memory of any event will die; whereas individual memories can lie dormant for decades and then come to life without warning or conscious action.

Oral tradition, therefore, is not a tool the historian can count on 'in the nature of things'. He must always ask *Cui bono?* In my judgment, for the post-heroic period well into the fifth century, the survival of the sort of tradition I have been discussing must be credited largely to the noble families in the various communities, including royal families where they existed, and, what amounts to the same thing in a special variation, to the priests of such shrines as Delphi, Eleusis and Delos. They alone, in most circumstances at least, had both the interest to 'remember' events and incidents which mattered to them (for whatever reason), and the status to impress that memory, whether true or false, so as to convert it into a public tradition. It goes without saying that neither the interest nor the process was historical—perhaps I should say 'historiographical'—in any significant sense. The objective was an immediate and practical one, whether it was fully conscious or not, and that was the enhancement of prestige or the warranty of power or the justification of an institution.

Several conclusions follow. In the first place, the losses, the numbers of facts which were completely and irrevocably forgotten by everyone, were enormous, in a never ending process. Much depended on the fortunes of the individual families, as to whether their particular memories became public memories, and then as to the duration and purity of the tradition in succeeding generations.

Second, the surviving material has the appearance of a random scatter. For example, Thucydides writes (1.13.2) that the 'Corinthians, they say, were the first to pursue the naval art in a modern sort of way, and Corinth was the first place in Greece where triremes were constructed'. No names are mentioned, but in the following sentence Thucydides adds the irrelevant fact that a Corinthian named Ameinocles built four triremes for Samos, presumably the first on that island. Why this curious choice? As far as our evidence goes, no name of the inventor of triremes had come down in the tradition, but Ameinocles did (no doubt among the Samians). We cannot possibly explain this particular survival pattern, nor can we in most of the other instances, for the explanation rests in contemporary circumstances about which we know absolutely nothing. That is why I speak of the *appearance* of a random scatter, of a large number of individual facts most of which bear no visible connection with one another, as if pure chance, the throw of dice, determined whether they were to be remembered or not. They did not even have a close chronological connection until one was imposed upon them. Thucydides' dates for Ameinocles and for the battle between Corinth and Corcyra are his own calculation, not the tradition as he received it. And, though we cannot check either date, there are strong reasons for believing that they are much too early, assuming that the two events are facts, not fictions. Given the paucity and the scatter of the tradition, it would be sheer luck if he or anyone else were able to construct an accurate chronological relationship.

Third, individual elements of the tradition were conflated, modified and sometimes invented. Family rivalries, conflicts between communities and regions, changes in power relationships, new values and beliefs—all these historical developments shaped tradition. They had a relatively free hand with what was happening currently, but often they could not afford to ignore traditions they themselves had inherited. Where a vital interest was affected, it was imperative that corrections be made. Even in a world which makes considerable use of writing, this process is not too difficult; for example, falsification of archaic Athenian political developments was characteristic of the political pamphleteering and party conflict in Athens in the last years of the Peloponnesian War and the next two or three decades. So effective was this falsification that neither fourth-century Athenians nor modern historians have been able to unscramble the pictures which were drawn. And when tradition is entirely oral, conflation and falsification are that much simpler to bring about. They cannot, indeed, be prevented.

Truth, however, as I have already said, truth in the Rankean sense of 'how things really were', was neither an important consideration nor a claim one could substantiate. Acceptance and belief were what counted, and the Greeks had all the knowledge of the past they needed without the help of historians. The poets took care of the heroic past; for the rest, specific traditions, largely oral, were sufficient. In Athens, the Solonic codification, the tyrannicides, Marathon were the stock allusions of political orators and pamphleteers, and everyone knew all that anyone needed to know about them. Occasional efforts by historians to correct factual errors in the tradition met with no response, as Thucydides' angry remarks about the tyrannicides reveal. Harmodius and Aristogeiton were essential to the Athenian mythical charter, which the truth would have damaged and weakened. Even in the fourth century, after Herodotus and Thucydides, Athenian orators still clung to their traditional myths and their popular history, utterly indifferent to the new knowledge and the new conceptions. Demosthenes could be as precise as anyone about current affairs, citing customs house records and treaties and court proceedings to support his facts and figures, but about the past he was as ignorant, perhaps deliberately so, as his hearers, restricting himself to the same commonplace references—and inaccuracies—as his opponents, and his audience.

It is both an intellectualist and a modernist fallacy to think that this is what requires explanation. On the contrary, the difficult question is why anyone—specifically, why Herodotus and Thucydides—broke so radically from the customary attitudes and 'invented' the idea of history. The conventional answer begins with the Ionian philosophers and their scepticism, and that contains a half-truth. The Ionians and their successors provided two necessary conditions, their scepticism about the myths and their notion of 'inquiry'. These were, however, not a sufficient reason, as I have already said in discussing Hesiod. Scepticism about myth led the Ionians to inquiry about the cosmos, to metaphysics, not to historiography. We must still ask why Herodotus applied the word *historia,* which simply means 'inquiry', to an inquiry into the past. His own answer is given right at the beginning of his work: to preserve the fame of the great and wonderful actions of the Greeks and barbarians and to inquire into the reasons why they fought each other.

The reasons why they fought each other: that is not a new question. After all, myth gave the reasons why the Greeks and Trojans fought each other, and reasons why many other events occurred. What is new in Herodotus is not only the systematic inquiry he pursued in seeking answers, which produced an historical narrative, but the extent to which his explanations are human and secular, and, in particular, political. In the next generation Thucydides then carried those novelties very much further, as he insisted on continuous narrative with a strict chronology, on a rigorously secular analysis, and on an equally rigorous emphasis on political behaviour. The new impulse came from the classical *polis,* and in particular the Athenian *polis,* which for the first time, at least in western history, introduced politics as a human activity and then elevated it to the most fundamental social activity. A new look at the past was required. That is to say, not that no other impetus could have produced the idea of history, but that among the Greeks this was the decisive condition (in combination with the scepticism and habit of inquiry already mentioned).

The new look had to be secular, non-mythical, and political—but did it have to be historical in the sense of a survey over a long period of continuous time? More precisely, for how long a period, for how much of the past? If one considers the histories of Herodotus and Thucydides without prejudice, the obvious—though not the most familiar—answer is that not much of the past was really relevant. Herodotus wandered about a great deal in the past, the mythical as well as the historical, the Egyptian as well as the Greek, but for reasons which were more often than not irrelevant to that part of his inquiry which was properly historical. Thucydides rejected that kind of digression, that 'romancing', so completely that his work contains no continuous past history at all. When Thucydides decided in 431 B.C. that the Greek world was entering the greatest war ever and that he would devote his life to recording it, that war was still in the future. Ultimately, he wrote an introduction, drawing some generalizations about the Trojan War and the emergence of the classical world, and filling a little of the gap between Herodotus' narrative and the onset of the Peloponnesian War. But that was no more than an introduction, conceptually historical, as I have already said, but not history. Everything else was contemporary.

Thereafter serious Greek historical writing was about contemporary history. In a brilliantly phrased paragraph, Collingwood said [in *The Idea of History,* 1946]: The Greek historian

> cannot, like Gibbon, begin by wishing to write a great historical work and go on to ask himself what he shall write about. . . . Instead of the historian choosing the subject, the subject chooses the historian; I mean that history is written only because memorable things have happened which call for a chronicler among the contemporaries of the people who have seen them. One might almost say that in ancient Greece there were no historians in the sense in which there were artists and philosophers; there were no people who devoted their lives to the study of history; the historian was only the autobiographer of his generation and autobiography is not a profession.

This may be too simple, too one-sided; it is not simply false. Thucydides found himself caught up in contradictory pulls, which he was never able to resolve. He accepted the need to narrate events in sequence, but on the other hand he wished to extract from the events the essence of politics and political behaviour, the nature and consequences of power. That, if he could achieve it, would be a 'possession for ever', among other reasons because human nature is a constant and therefore recurrence is the pattern. But if so, what is the point to a linear account over long periods of time? One can really know only one's own time, and that is sufficient anyway. The past can yield nothing more than paradigmatic support for the conclusions one has drawn from the present; the past, in other words, may still be treated in the timeless fashion of myth. There is a relevant passage in Sir Isaiah Berline's *The Hedgehog and the Fox,* which is about Tolstoy but in which one could substitute the name of Thucydides and go a long way (though not the whole way) without sacrificing accuracy.

> Tolstoy's interest in history began early in his life. It seems to have arisen not from interest in the past as such, but from the desire to penetrate to first causes, to understand how and why things happen as they do and not otherwise . . . from a tendency to doubt and place under suspicion and, if need be, reject whatever does not fully answer the question, to go to the root of every matter, at whatever cost. . . . And with this went an incurable love of the concrete, the empirical, the verifiable, and an instinctive distrust of the abstract, the impalpable, the supernatural—in short an early tendency to a scientific and positivist approach, unfriendly to romanticism, abstract formulations, metaphysics. Always and in every situation he looked for "hard" facts. . . . He was tormented by the ultimate problems which face young men in every generation . . . but the answers provided by theologians and metaphysicians struck him as absurd. . . . History, only history, only the sum of the concrete events in time and space . . . this alone contained the truth, the material out of which genuine answers . . . might be constructed.

So one wrote *War and Peace,* the other the *Peloponnesian War*. I am not being frivolous when I put it that way. History 'contained the truth', and for Thucydides that meant that it was unnecessary to invent as the poets did. But it was also impossible merely to record what had happened. It was necessary to compose speeches which would lay bare the appropriate arguments (appropriate in Thucydides' judgment) on both sides of an issue. It was even necessary to write a sophistical treatise on might and right, the Melian Dialogue. The narrative alone proved a failure in the end: it told only what Alcibiades did and what he suffered. Those were facts, not truths.

After Thucydides every serious historian wrestled with the same difficulties, and usually preferred to wrestle with them in the field of contemporary history. The idea of a historical narrative, of a continuum of events in time, had come to stay. But what purpose was it to serve? That question was never answered satisfactorily. The idea had arisen, and had been nurtured, that society was bound to its past, and up to a point could be understood from its past, in ways which differed from the old ways of myth. That idea was thwarted, however, by the absence of an idea of progress, by the idealization of the eternal and immutable against the changing and transient ('a rigorously anti-historical metaphysics' in Collingwood's phrase), by cyclical views of history, by primitivistic doctrines. On the intellectual level everything was against the idea of history. Only the Tolstoyan types struggled on, stimulated by each extraordinary situation or development to try again: Timaeus and the fierce struggles in Sicily over tyranny, Polybius and the establishment of Rome's world-empire; or, among the Romans, Sallust and the disintegration of the Roman Republic, Tacitus and the emergence of despotic absolutism. Like Thucydides, each of these men was ultimately seeking to understand and explain his own, contemporary world.

Their appeal and influence are hard to measure. It is significant, however, how quickly historians abandoned the austerity of Thucydides for the emotional appeals of the poets, how history became 'tragic history', even in Polybius who denied it so vehemently. It is also significant that the philosophers rejected the whole enterprise. As for the people at large, there is no reason to think that they ever moved beyond the old myths and the occasional bits of mythologized history. Why should they have, after all? As Hans Meyerhoff said [in *Time in Literature*] in a different, but somewhat related, context: 'Previous generations *knew* much less about the past than we do, but perhaps *felt* a much greater sense of identity and continuity with it. . . . ' Myth achieved that, and there was nothing in the society which required its abandonment or replacement. Perhaps that was a flaw in the *polis*—but that is a different subject.

Arnaldo Momigliano (essay date 1978)

SOURCE: "Greek Historiography," in *History and Theory,* Vol. XVII, No. 1, 1978, pp. 1-28.

[*Below, Momigliano, a notable Italian historian, discusses the nature, transmission, and reception of Greek historical models and methods, noting that, even given its limitations for the modern historian, the significance of Greek historiography lies in the fact that it "spread among non-Greeks and became an international form of communication."*]

I

Like the ancient Romans we are conscious of having inherited "history" . . . [*istoria*] from the Greeks. Herodotus is to us the "father of history," as he was to Cicero. We are also conscious that history has come to us as part of a greater legacy which includes the most important intellectual activities (such as philosophy, mathematics, astronomy, natural history, figurative arts), in which we are still involved—and more particularly the most prestigious literary genres (epic, lyric, eloquence, tragedy, comedy, novel, idyll), by which we still satisfy our needs for verbal expression.

We know, however, that, properly speaking, we ought not to use the word "inheritance" in the case of history or indeed for any other aspect of Greek culture. Since the humanists of the fourteenth and fifteenth centuries made it their business to restore the validity of the ancient models after medieval deviations, it has been a question not so much of legacy as of conscious choice. Modern history-writing has been by choice a continuous confrontation with the Greek originals and with what the Romans made of their models. Consequently there was in the Renaissance a revival and further elaboration of the theories (sketched rather than developed)

which in ancient Greece defined the characteristics of history and its legitimate forms: the sophistic invention of "antiquities," the Isocratean-Ciceronian notion of history as a rhetorical genre, the Polybian attribution of strictly utilitarian purposes to historiography, and finally the separation between biography and history, which is stated, for instance, by Plutarch (*Alexander* 1, 2).

Fundamental questions are involved in the reception of Greek historiography. Of these we are perhaps more aware than the historians of previous generations. We may ask how far Greek historiography is compatible with the Biblical vision of the world; and how far it can express our modern views of the world. The former question had already been recognized by those Fathers of the Church who created ecclesiastical history (and perhaps even more radically by those rabbis who simply did not write history). The second question is at least implicit in the recent creation of the social sciences, for which there is no clear precedent even in the most "modern" of Greek writers, Thucydides and Aristotle.

II

A new branch of intellectual activity always poses problems of origins: it would be a true paradox if we had been spared the problems of the historical genesis of Greek historical writing.

As the Greeks had a long tradition of epic poetry before they began to write historical prose, it is tempting to take Homer as a predecessor of the historians and to add the poets of the "cycle" and the writers of poems on the foundations of Greek cities (Semonides, Xenophanes). Herodotus may seem to encourage us in this direction. But the Greeks themselves, and the Romans, knew that there were two differences between history and epic poetry: history was written in prose, and was meant to separate facts from fancies about the past. Homer was too much of an authority not to be used by historians as evidence for specific facts. The use of a text as evidence was precisely one of the characteristic operations which distinguished Greek history-writing from epic poetry.

More attention has to be given to a statement by Dionysius of Halicarnassus (*On Thucydides,* 5) which seems to reflect the opinion of previous Hellenistic scholars but would not lose its interest if it had been inspired by Dionysius' acquaintance with Roman historiography. Dionysius thought that Greek historical writing had begun in the form of histories of cities or regions based on local evidence—whether sacred or profane. A priori this sounds likely enough because city and temple chronicles existed not only in Rome but in some of those Eastern civilizations with which the Greeks had contacts. It is very doubtful, however, whether Dionysius knew of any history earlier than the fifth century B.C. Herodotus and Thucydides do not show any awareness of such archaic histories, though they were by no means disinclined to quarrel with their predecessors. Thucydides does not tell us in I, 13 where he found his information about naval history. After 500 B.C. local chroniclers were just one—and not the most important—group among the writers who created the new climate of historical research. We hear of writers of biographical and autobiographical accounts (Scylax of Caryanda, Ion of Chios), of students of chronology (Hippias of Elis), or researchers in literary history (Theagenes of Rhegium, Damastcs of Sigeum), and, of course, of local and regional historians (Charon of Lampsacus, Antiochus of Syracuse). Above all there were writers who, like Herodotus and probably before him, tried to inform the Greeks about the Persian Empire or some of its parts. The oldest (about 460 B.C.?) is apparently the shadowy Dionysius of Miletus, who is said to have composed both a book on "Persian affairs" (*Persika*) and a book on "after Darius." More famous was Xanthus, the author of a history of Lydia, a hellenized native who tried to combine some of his national traditions with Greek stories for the benefit of the Greeks—a phenomenon which was to become characteristic of later, Hellenistic, historiography. Two works on "Greek affairs" (*Hellenika*) by Charon of Lampsacus and Damastes of Sigeum may have already been inspired by Thucydides. It is significant that the majority of the earliest writers in Greek on historical subjects, including Herodotus, came from Asia or from the Aegean islands. This does not necessarily support the opinion of Dionysius of Halicarnassus on the original types of Greek historical works, but raises the more general question, easier to ask than to answer, whether contacts with Oriental nations and life under the Persian rulers gave an impulse to Greek historiography.

Herodotus (who wrote about 445-425 B.C. clearly treats Hecataeus of Miletus as his only authoritative predecessor. Hecataeus, a principal figure in the Ionian rebellion of about 500 B.C., had tried to put order and "rationality" into the mythical genealogies of the Greeks (whom he considered capable of transmitting "many and ridiculous stories") and had written a model travelogue (*periodos*) in which geography and ethnography were mixed. In his turn Thucydides intimated disapproval of two contemporaries. One was Herodotus himself; the other was Hellanicus, a learned man from the island of Lesbos, who wrote many books of local history, mythography, and geography, among them a chronicle of Attica made public after 406 B.C.

The novelty of Herodotus, in comparison with his predecessors and contemporaries, seems to have been twofold. He seems to have been the first to produce an analytical description of a war, the Persian War. Furthermore he was probably the first to use ethnographi-

cal and constitutional studies in order to explain the war itself and to account for its outcome. The very word "historia" in the sense in which we are using it is a tribute to Herodotus as the inventor or perfector of a new literary genre. Herodotus used "historia" in his ethnographic sections as a generic name for "inquiry," but in the fourth century B.C. "historia" was taken to mean what Herodotus had done—namely, specific research on past events.

The three components of the Herodotean inquiry—ethnography, constitutional research, and war history—did not remain indissolubly united. The combination was most usually restricted to two elements: either ethnography and constitutions, or ethnography and wars, or constitutions and wars. Thucydides is the most obvious example of the almost total elimination of ethnography, though he preserved the close integration of war with constitutional history. Constitutional problems were indeed discussed independently, without reference to historical research, as we can see in the "Constitution of Athens" attributed to Xenophon, but written about 440-420 B.C. Yet the reciprocal relevance of customs, institutions, and wars which Herodotus had discovered remained inherent in historical research— with the consequence that one series of facts was implicitly or explicitly treated as the explanation of another series (a better constitution explained a victory, but a defeat might result in changes of customs and institutions). To go one step further, it was Herodotus who made it a rule for historians to explain the events they told.

Explanation took the form of search for causes, especially of wars and revolutions. At least since Thucydides a distinction had been made between immediate and remote causes—or between causes and pretexts. The causal analysis of constitutional changes often went deeper than the analysis of causes of wars because the Greeks took the existence of hostility between independent states for granted, whereas they did not regard internal political conflicts as inevitable. Greek historians therefore gave the impression of being more mature in their descriptions of revolutions than in their phenomenology of war. Even Thucydides and Polybius are no exceptions.

The search for causes, understandably enough, was less prominent or at least took more devious forms in the case of ethnographic research. Occasionally geographic factors were adduced as causes of somatic and psychic peculiarities: love of liberty was connected with a temperate climate. But the most famous of these explanations is to be found, not in an historian, but in the author of the Hippocratic treatise on "Airs, Waters, and Places." Ethnography was based on the consciousness of the distinction between Greeks and Barbarians, and this distinction seemed to be in itself sufficient explanation. Research was further limited by the disinclination of the Greeks to learn foreign languages. Greek ethnographic research contributed extremely little to the knowledge of non-Hellenic tongues. Whatever acquaintance it had with foreign texts was secondhand and garbled. Thus Greek ethnography was fed by the peculiarities of Greek national consciousness and in turn fed them. From this point of view there was little inducement to do ethnographic research on individual regions of Greece. What curiosity existed about Greek regions was better satisfied by research on specific topics, such as cults and monuments and, indeed, dialects. It was naturally connected with local political history. Particularly in the Hellenistic period authors of local chronicles are also local antiquarians. Greece as a whole became of ethnographical interest to the Greeks only in the Hellenistic and Roman periods—and even then not very often.

III

From Herodotus came the example of a near contemporary subject (the Persian Wars) as the most suitable for an historian. This involved a specific perception of the structure of historical research as founded upon evidence which had to be tested. As the simplest way of knowing the facts is to see them, it is not surprising that Herodotus rated direct visual observation best, and next to it the collection of reports from reliable witnesses. In fifth century B.C. Greece, written evidence was not abundant, and the documents which had been transmitted from previous centuries raised problems of interpretation and reliability which were beyond Herodotus' powers. Thus a subject near in time became preferable, though the exploration of more remote events was not excluded, as Herodotus himself made clear. Thucydides basically did nothing more than reinforce the strictness and coherence of Herodotus' criteria by preferring contemporary to near-contemporary history and by refusing to tell anything which he did not consider absolutely reliable, whereas Herodotus had considered it legitimate to report with a warning what he could not vouch for directly. Thucydides was able to transcribe some written evidence (letters, inscriptions, and treaties) which came within his criteria of reliability, but it is remarkable that he did not depart from the Herodotean rule of preferring oral to written evidence. He definitely left his successors with the impression that direct observation and oral reports by witnesses were altogether preferable to written evidence. Insofar as he suppressed what he did not consider trustworthy, there was a dangerous implication in his rigor. But he introduced a note of austerity which became part of the historian's ethos (if not of the historian's praxis). And though he did not consider possible a reconstruction in detail of the remote past, he produced a memorable sample of how one could reach *some* conclusions about archaic Greece.

With Herodotus and even more with Thucydides, the historian established himself as a witness and a recorder of changes—especially of recent changes—which in his judgment were important enough to be transmitted to posterity. In his choice he took into account, and even reflected, the prevailing interests of the community to which he belonged. Military and political events emerged as the main themes of Greek historiography.

It was also the example of Herodotus, and after him of Thucydides, that made the Greeks unwilling to accord the full dignity of history to mere narratives of local events. The Athenian local chronicle (Atthidography), though involving leading personalities and important constitutional changes, was never put on the same level as the history of the Peloponnesian War with its panhellenic horizon. The canon of the Great Greek Historians constructed in the Hellenistic age reflects this opinion in its exclusion of local historians. The community about which and for which the "good" historians spoke was not that of the individual city. Greece as a whole was their most obvious term of reference. Granted the difference between Greece and any barbarian land (as Herodotus had exemplarily shown), the historian had of course to recognize the conflicts between Greek States and inside Greek States (as Thucydides had exemplarily shown).

In the same perspective it was difficult to attribute the quality of full history to the study of genealogies, foundations of cities, festivals, rituals, laws, customs, words, chronological systems, and the like. Research on such topics remained in a limbo to which Hippias apparently gave the name of "archaeology" (Plato, *The Greater Hippias* 285 D.). According to the same Hippias anything "archaeological" had a special appeal for the Spartans. This denomination, however, was not generally accepted in the Graeco-Roman world. It was left to the Renaissance to collect under the name of "antiquities"—inherited from Varro—all the historical subjects which did not correspond to the Herodotean-Thucydidean notion of history centered on politics and war. For the same reason biographical accounts were not history, though proper history could contain short biographical sketches. Xenophon wrote twice on Agesilaus from a biographical and from an historical point of view. That biography first appeared in the form of eulogy of an individual contributed to its separation from history. It was another implicit feature of the Herodotean-Thucydidean approach that history, aiming as it did at truth, should refrain from excesses of praise and blame. It is probable that local history, too, suffered from this suspicion of bias. The Greeks knew themselves: they appreciated the power of their local loyalties. "Real" history was above local feuds.

IV

Herodotus' creation and the Thucydidean developments are rooted in the intellectual revolution of the fifth century and derive their full significance from it. This was the time in which tragedy, comedy, medicine, philosophy, and eloquence were either created or transformed. Even if we did not know that Sophocles was a friend of Herodotus, we would perceive the latter's connections with the former in moral, religious, and political feelings. Thucydides, Hippocrates, and Euripides recall each other irresistibly. One of the inventions of Thucydides—the use of fictitious speeches to report currents of public opinion and to reconstruct the motivations of political leaders—is unthinkable without the formalization of public eloquence which happened in the late fifth century in and outside Athens. In other civilizations written accounts of events were inspired by contemporary figurative arts, or at least can easily be illustrated by contemporary figurative arts. Ancient oriental historiography has been said (not without exaggeration) to have its origins in narrative paintings and reliefs. Medieval historical accounts call to mind contemporary painting and, as a matter of fact, were often illustrated by illuminations. Greek historical accounts were hardly influenced by contemporary art. The "pedimental style" attributed to Herodotus is not very convincing even as a metaphor. The style of Greek history was essentially regulated by rules of prose-writing and by its differentiation from other literary genres.

History in the Herodotean and Thucydidean form not only learns from other branches of knowledge and contributes to them (the reciprocal influence is especially evident in the case of philosophy), but presupposes them. It is not for history to give the ultimate sense of things or to measure in full the relevance of gods to men, or indeed to explore systematically the nature (*physis*) of man: for this there are other sciences. The direction given by Herodotus and even more by Thucydides to history-writing certainly presupposes—and helps to reinforce—the assumption that the intervention of gods in human affairs is neither constant nor too patent. But this is an implicit acceptance, or exploitation, of the general trend of Greek thought in the fifth century rather than a programmatic aim. Even in later centuries the marginal importance of gods in historical narrative presupposes, rather than expresses, Greek lack of interest in theological speculations. History had a limited purpose with a varied and by no means scholastically rigorous culture. It was meant to preserve a reliable record of past events and therefore had to establish criteria of reliability. It was meant to pay special attention to wars and political revolutions, because they produced consequential changes. It was bound to give an explanation of the events insofar as this was compatible with the use of evidence. Metaphysical explanations were, as a rule, either avoided or only briefly hinted at. Later in the Hellenistic period some historians (the most important of whom was Polybius) used with special relish the notion of *Tyche* (fortune) which represented an elegant way of avoid-

ing any serious religious or philosophical commitment.

Though historians seemed to be prepared to pay homage to philosophy and some philosophers (such as Plato in the *Laws* and Aristotle) derived much instruction from research on historical facts, Greek philosophy as a whole was not kind to history. History seemed to philosophers to be rooted in that transient world of ambitions and passions from which philosophy was supposed to liberate man. A philosopher directly involved in history-writing and obviously enjoying it, like Posidonius in the first century B.C., is sufficiently exceptional to become mysterious. The pressure of philosophy on historians induced some of them to turn historical books into philosophical novels. Xenophon supplied in the *Cyropaedia* the model of the paedagogic pseudo-biography. Two generations later Onesicritus turned the life of Alexander into a quasi-cynic novel. His contemporaries Hecataeus of Abdera and even more Euhemerus presented their own speculations in the form of ethnography.

Since historians were free to introduce into their accounts any philosophical or religious reflection they fancied, it is possible to ascribe specific philosophical or religious opinions to individual historians. But it remains to be proved that any of them based their accounts on philosophic or religious notions. Many tedious discussions on the circularity of time in Greek historiography could have been spared if it had been observed that the span of time with which Greek historians normally operate is too short to be defined either as linear or as circular. Characteristically, Polybius theorized the cycle of constitutional forms, but reported ordinary military and political events without reference to any such circularity. It has been possible for later civilizations (notably the Arabic) to absorb Greek philosophic and scientific thought without being deeply affected by Greek historical thought.

V

The historian's account was supposed to give some sort of pleasure to his readers. At the same time it could hardly justify its existence if it were not also useful. But the precise relation between pleasure and usefulness, and the form both of pleasure and use, had been matters of dispute and of personal preference at least since Thucydides accused Herodotus of putting delectation before instruction. The care with which Thucydides wrote his prose shows, however, that even he did not overlook the pleasurable side of his exposition. We must of course distinguish between the techniques actually adopted by individual historians to produce pleasure and the theories about the proper forms of giving pleasure. In the fourth century B.C. Ephorus and Theopompus used the rhetorical techniques they had learnt in Isocarates' school to enliven their expositions. Clitarchus and other historians of Alexander the Great became notorious for their propensity to amuse the reader. In the third and second centuries B.C. a technique of "pathetic" over-dramatizations of events was in favor with some historians, such as Phylarchus (whom we know mainly through his critic Polybius) and the author of the *II Maccabees*. What remains unclear is the relation between this "pathetic" technique and the theory of historiography as "imitation" (*mimesis*) which seems to have been propounded or supported by Duris in order to save political historiography from the strictures of Aristotle. Polybius reacted by condemning any appeal to emotions and by emphasizing the importance of sober political experience and of geographical knowledge for the historian.

The most visible weakness of the Greek historians was their approach to the evidence (that is, their criteria for establishing the facts). The lack of precise rules about collecting and choosing data created confusion in the minds both of the authors and their readers. Herodotus could be treated by turn as the father of history and as a liar, because nobody was in a position to check the stories he had told. His younger rival Ctesias was believed when he accused Herodotus of lying, though he too was known as a liar. Only modern Orientalist research has been able to show that Herodotus was a truthful reporter (within the limits of his information), whereas Ctesias was unscrupulous. Rhetorical rules of composition further complicated matters by offering reasons or excuses for departing from the truth even when it was unmistakably known. The selection of topics for history corresponded so closely to the primary interests of Greek political life as to be imprisoned by them. Both spiritual and economic life remained marginal (and hardly identified) themes for historians. This in turn conditioned the principles of explanation. Other limitations in the analysis and therefore in the explanation were inherent in the absolute preference given to the narrative form for political history, whereas biography and antiquarian research frequently took a descriptive form which permitted better analytical work. Some remedy was found in digressions and excursuses in which Greek historians often said what mattered most to them, but digressions leave the main line of the interpretation unaffected (as is obvious, for instance, to the readers of Thucydides' chapters on the fifty years before the Peloponnesian War and of Polybius' theory on the cycle of constitutions).

To the Greeks, therefore, history was not one of the sciences with clear methods which create a body of undisputed knowledge. As it was not included in ordinary education, except as a provider of rhetorical examples, it was also a basically non-professional activity. Though it was in the nature of things that a good historian should find a continuator, the continuator could come from anywhere, without any implication of a school. We do not know why Xenophon, Theo-

pompus, and the author (sometimes identified with Cratippus) of the historical fragment known as *Hellenica Oxyrhynchia* chose to continue Thucydides—or why Posidonius and Strabo connected their histories with those of Polybius. The work done in Aristotle's school on constitutional antiquities, and perhaps on biography, is the major exception to the individual, unscholastic character of Greek historiography as a whole; this work was not done on ordinary political history and was intended to prepare the ground for philosophical theory.

It has repeatedly been noticed that historians were often voluntarily or compulsorily exiles from their own city. The list of distinguished historians who wrote abroad includes Herodotus, Thucydides, Xenophon, Ctesias, Theopompus, Philistus, Timaeus, Polybius, Dionysius of Halicarnassus, and, in a sense, Posidonius, who wrote as a Rhodian citizen but was born in Syria. This may even suggest that historiography, unless it was local history written to satisfy local patriotism, had an ambiguous status in Greek society. It was certainly easier to get proper information for a large subject and to be impartial if one had the mobility of an exile.

If the historian, as a rule, operated alone, he was not necessarily left alone after he had operated. The temptation to please and flatter was constant, especially when historiography was centered on recent events. States knew how to reward popular historians; even Herodotus got a big prize from Athens, according to a story which seems to have a documentary basis. Alexander the Great made the experiment of having an historian on his staff, Callisthenes—and killed him. Later, Hellenistic kings and Roman emperors had the power both to honor and to persecute historians. Not being supported by institutions (and therefore never exactly speaking on behalf of institutions), the historians had to rely on their personal inspiration and integrity.

Notwithstanding all these difficulties, the Greek historians after Thucydides showed great capacity for experiment and adaptation to new circumstances. Their vitality can be measured in two ways: by considering how many new forms of historical writing they created and transmitted to us and by observing how after Alexander Greek historiography spread among non-Greeks and became an international form of communication. The point of departure of all these developments is of course represented by Herodotus and Thucydides. But their successors reshaped and simplified the highly individual Herodotean and Thucydidean models—or created new types. Even in the Renaissance and later, Herodotus and Thucydides were seldom closely imitated. They provided a stimulus rather than a rigid model. The idealization of Thucydides as the perfect historian in the nineteenth century marks the point in which modern historiography really began to create types of historical research unknown to the classical world (such as economic history, history of religions, and beyond certain limits cultural history).

VI

Greek culture was fiercely introvert in the fourth century B.C., and the continuation of Herodotus' work in ethnography was confined to cheap information on Persia (Ctesias and, for the little that is known of him, Dinon). The Thucydidean monograph on war and politics suited the age. It provided the model not only for accounts of individual wars, but for books on "Hellenic affairs" (*Hellenika*), one of which, written by Xenophon, has come down to us. The main external divergence from Thucydides was the abandonment (gradual in Xenophon) of the annalistic scheme. Theopompus, who in his youth had competed with Xenophon by writing *Hellenika* of his own, realized that the intervention of Philip of Macedon in Greek affairs introduced a strong personal element into Greek politics. He transformed the *Hellenika* into *Philippika,* "Philip's affairs." The change would not have been possible without contemporary developments in the art of biography, but the essential elements of the Thucydidean monograph were preserved. On the other hand Philistus, a Sicilian historian, applied Thucydidean methods to the history of his island, which had been treated in a Herodotean way by his predecessor Antiochus of Syracuse.

The Thucydidean model was never forgotten by Hellenistic, Roman, and Byzantine historians. Sometimes only its style and its liberal use of speeches were imitated, but normally the co-ordination of political and military analysis survived the changes. It proved to be a satisfactory instrument for recording a limited period of wars complicated by internal agitations or revolutions: Sallust, for all his personal traits, shows this. But already in the fourth century B.C. there is a tendency to turn the Thucydidean monograph into a comprehensive Greek history from the earliest times. Ephorus of Cyme (followed by Anaximenes of Lampsacus?) conceived this extension. Thucydides had, of course, pointed this way by his introductory chapters on archaic Greek history; and local histories started from the beginnings of a city or of a regional unit. Ephorus' ambition was to produce, not antiquarian details, but a full account of past political and military events for the whole of Greece. A history of this scope had to define its own limits in relation to the mythical age and was bound to involve an account of foreign nations (of "barbarians") in their political conflicts and cultural contrasts with the Greeks. Polybius considered Ephorus his predecessor in writing universal history, but one has to add that Polybius himself had a narrow view of universal history. Ephorus was rather the founder of national history and already displayed (if we can trust what survives of him in later sources, such as Diodorus) that fatal

characteristic of national history, patriotic prejudice. When Plutarch condemned Herodotus as philobarbarian, he accepted the set of values introduced by Ephorus. In Ephorus, universality existed only in the form of excursuses subordinated to Greek history. Roman annalists substantially accepted the type of Greek national history with some accommodation to local habits of registering events (a legacy of the old pontifical chronicle, though Roman historians did not care much for it). In the Ephorean (and Roman) type of narration the exploitation of pre-existing historical work was conspicuous, and perhaps inevitable. Ephorus therefore started the fashion which has lasted into our day of "books made of books," that is, of compilation. Not by chance does the genre of historical epitome—or summary—make its first appearance with Ephorus' contemporary Theopompus, who abbreviated Herodotus to two books. Compilations did not require much "historia" in the Herodotean sense. Polybius, for instance, was conscious of this; nevertheless with Ephorus compilation had become an accepted practice in historiography.

Meanwhile Xenophon, who played so large a part in transmitting the Thucydidean model, created or contributed to the creation of new models by his personal memoir as a general in the retreat of the Ten Thousand (*Anabasis*) and by the encomiastic biography of King Agesilaus (in which he was preceded by Isocrates' encomium of King Euagoras). His "Recollections" (*Memorabilia*) of Socrates and his "Education of Cyrus" were also potentially historiographical types and operated as such in later times, though it is unlikely that Xenophon himself attributed any value to them as factual records.

Books on the education (or on the youth) of great men existed in ancient times and came into favor again with the Renaissance; their status between history and novel remained ambiguous. Collections of sayings of great men multiplied after Xenophon and have been used ever since to fill up the biographies of philosophers, saints, and even kings. The personal memoir of a general became a popular genre when after Alexander generals controlled the known world; it is still in our repertoire. The memoirs of two generals, Ptolemy (King Ptolemy I of Egypt) and Hieronymus of Cardia, were the principal sources for the history of Alexander and his successors. Caesar contributed his prestige and his stylistic skill to the genre. In the second century A.D. the Roman provincial governor and Greek historian Arrian used the memoirs of Ptolemy together with those of a minor companion of Alexander, Aristobulus, to compile what the chance of survival has made for us the most authoritative account of Alexander's campaigns. He also wrote a memoir of his own campaign against the Alans. It would be pedantry to try to separate in such memoirs—in which the author normally speaks in the third person, even if he is a protagonist—

the biographical, the autobiographical, and the "historical" elements. Polybius knew very well that a biography of a general is something different from a history of the events in which a general was involved, but how the distinction was preserved in practice is another matter. With the collapse of the city state and the rise of monarchies, first in the Hellenistic East and then in Rome, the period of the rule of a sovereign became the natural unit for political history: history became increasingly biographical.

Altogether biography flourished in the Hellenistic and Roman periods when writers extended biographical treatment to all sorts of people as representatives of certain forms of life (theoretical, practical, voluptuous, and the like). Biography of intellectuals produced its own problems of method: often very little was known about their lives, except what could be inferred from their works. Even for authors of the fourth century and later for whom some biographical tradition existed, the question of how far the works reflected the character of the man remained. The ease and arbitrariness with which biographers inferred from the life the works and vice versa seem to us appalling. There was certainly a marked inability to appreciate the jokes of old comedy: they were often converted into facts. Little survives of Hellenistic biography in its original form (we had to wait for a papyrus to give us Satyrus' life of Euripides), but the masters of Greek and Latin biography of the imperial age worked on Hellenistic models and in their turn became the models for later ages. The Latin Cornelius Nepos and more conspicuously the Greek Plutarch idealized the Greek and Roman past and compared Greek "heroes" with Roman "heroes." In the third and fourth centuries, from Philostratus to Eunapius, biography was used to defend Paganism, while the Christians also produced their exemplary lives of bishops, monks, and martyrs.

The pagan biographical models of the early second century A.D., Plutarch and Suetonius, survived into the Middle Ages, notwithstanding the introduction of new Christian themes and modes. The chronologically organized account of a life (such as we have it in Plutarch) is to be distinguished from the systematic description of an individual as we have it in the "Caesars" of Suetonius and in the lives of philosophers by Diogenes Laertius (third century A.D.?). Both types have their roots in Hellenistic biography and ultimately go back to the two sections (on "life" and "virtues") of Xenophon's *Agesilaus*. After having variously found favor in post-classical times, the two types of biography are even now reflected in the distinction between the "life" and the "character sketch" or "profile."

Since the fourth century B.C. there have also been biographical or autobiographical letters, one of the most ancient and famous of which comes from or is attributed to the pen of Plato. Autobiography, whether in the form of letters or otherwise, contained possibilities of development toward the genres of soliloquy and confessions. The models for us are Marcus Aurelius' *Meditations* and St. Augustine's *Confessions,* but the origins of both genres are obscure.

VII

Alexander's conquests gave new scope to Herodotean ethnography. As the regions described by Herodotus were now for the greater part under Greco-Macedonian control, one could expect better information—and to a certain extent it was forthcoming. Some names of ethnographers became famous in the third and second centuries B.C.: Hecataeus of Abdera for Egypt, Megasthenes for India, and Agatharchides in general for Asia and Europe. The little we know of them is mainly secondhand. Agatharchides still appears to have been a very humane observer of ordinary life. More typical was Hecataeus of Abdera as the author of a philosophic Utopia rather than an authentic historian of Egypt. It is difficult to escape the conclusion that the Greek intellectuals of the early Hellenistic period took more interest in problems of physical geography and in astronomy (Eratosthenes) then in knowledge about the nations among whom they moved as masters. They did not learn the languages of the natives. Menander of Ephesus was the exception, if he was a Greek and really studied Phoenician and other foreign records, as Flavius Josephus states (*Against Apion* 1, 116). The greatest work done by an early Hellenistic historian concerns not the East, but the unconquered West. It was the individual effort of a Sicilian exile in Athens, Timaeus, and reflected his isolation in contemporary society. As he was the first to include Rome in the horizon of Greek history, the Romans repaid him by much attention and probably learned a great deal from him in their first attempts to absorb the Greek art of historiography. Polybius, therefore, attacked him as his most dangerous rival.

Isolated in his own day, Timaeus pointed to the future. When the Romans began to conquer East and West, Greek students of ethnography—such as Polybius, Artemidorus of Ephesus, Apollodorus of Artemita, and Posidonius—hastened to describe Spain, Gaul, and Parthia. One great savant, who was imported into Rome as a slave, Alexander Polyhistor (about 70 B.C.), specialized in providing his masters with the ethnographical knowledge they needed to rule, or at least to enjoy the world they ruled. One of his books, on the Jews, was sufficiently good to provide the Fathers of the Church with some of their most recondite quotations from Jewish writers. It is this late Hellenistic learning under Roman hegemony rather than early Hellenistic doctrine which is summarized in the geography of Strabo—itself a product of Greek erudition inspired by the ideals and interests of Roman imperialism. Chance made Strabo (first century

A.D.) the main transmitter of ancient ethnography to later times: we have inherited from him our notion of "historical geography."

Also Hellenistic is our notion of a historico-geographical guide for visiting places of interest, in one's own country or outside it. Polemon of Ilium, who in the second century B.C. wrote on his own city, on the acropolis of Athens, on "inscriptions city by city," on Samothrace and even on Carthage, is a good early example of a mixture of Greek and non-Greek tourist interests. But Pausanias, who in the second century A.D. confined himself to Greece, became the prototype of this genre for Renaissance scholars—through the mere fact of having survived.

Though the transformation of Greek erudition from a local to a national one is especially noticeable in the Roman period, Dicaearchus had already written under the Macedonians in the third century B.C. an antiquarian and nostalgic "life of Greece" (a remarkable title). He does not seem to have had many followers in this comprehensive and exacting genre, but he inspired Varro to do the same for Rome. Besides writing a "life of the Roman people" on the lines provided by Dicaearchus, Varro went beyond his model in the gigantic *Roman Antiquities* (divided into "divine" and "human") which dominated Roman erudition until St. Augustine. Varro's work did not survive the early Middle Ages, but what St. Augustine said about it moved Flavio Biondo to attempt a revival of the genre and ultimately to create the type of Renaissance and modern "Antiquities."

The Greeks did more than provide the Romans with materials for mapping their empire and with models of erudition. They tried to understand and recount Roman history in a way which might satisfy both Romans and Greeks. Some may even have tried to oppose the Greek to the Roman point of view in writing Roman history. The evidence is not clear. The famous debate, still echoed by Livy, Justin, Plutarch, and even Ammianus on the part played by mere luck in the Roman successes, seems to have originated in the heat of war propaganda before penetrating into historical works. Questions of erudition about Roman origins offered opportunities for pin-pricking Roman vanity which were less dangerous and required less thought. Dionysius of Halicarnassus refers with disapproval to some of these criticisms of Roman traditions. "Real" historians, who had read their Thucydides and Ephorus, tried to explain the Roman Empire in forms acceptable to both nations. It is always difficult to produce consistent opposition history when there is no hope of shaking off foreign rule.

Polybius remains the unique expression of the moment in which the Greeks for the first time in their history recognized their complete loss of indepen-

dence. The Macedonian-Greek symbiosis of previous centuries had not compelled, or even prepared them for, such a catastrophic admission. Polybius was a time-server of genius. He adapted Thucydidean historiography to the new situation by writing a history of the contemporary world with the scrupulous regard for factual truth, the political and military competence, the direct observation, and the care for speeches which Thucydides had prescribed. In the organization of a universal history, though limited to the last fifty years, Polybius was helped by the example of Ephorus, whom he respected, and of Timaeus, whom he affected to despise. But the plan of his exposition was his own. His own, too, was the emphasis on the practical use of history with which the skillful presentation of Roman victory as inevitable and lasting was connected. Polybius inspired Posidonius, guided Livy (as far as Livy was guidable), and in later days moved the pagan Zosimus (early sixth century) to tackle the decline of Rome as he, Polybius, had tackled her rise. Anthologized and therefore mutilated in Byzantium to provide examples for military operations and diplomatic missions, Polybius returned to Western Europe in the early fifteenth century. First admired in Florence (by Machiavelli among others), by the middle of the sixteenth century Polybius had risen to the position of the master of military and diplomatic history for the whole of Europe. He remained the most authoritative Greek historian until the French Revolution, when he was replaced by Thucydides.

After Polybius the question of how Roman history stood in relation to universal history was always present. Posidonius saw deeply into the social unrest of the period between 145 and about 63 B.C. He painted both the degeneration of the Hellenistic monarchies and the rapacity of the Roman capitalists. When he lovingly described the tribal life of Gaul and Spain, he was probably aware that the Romans were bound to transform it. The influence of Oriental, especially Jewish, speculations on the succession of empires combined with research by Greek historians. In the universal histories written in Greek in the first century B.C. by Diodorus and Nicolas of Damascus (the latter preserved only in fragments) Hellenic presuppositions prevail. Diodorus has in fact great difficulty in connecting Roman and Greek history. The mixture of Hellenic and Oriental elements is more deeply embedded in the structure of the universal history written in Latin by the Gallo-Roman Trogus Pompeius, which belongs to the same period and has been transmitted to us only in the summary by Justin (second century A.D.). It is an open question whether Trogus was guided by a Greek source. Whoever first mixed Oriental speculations with Greek-Latin historiography prepared the way for the Late-Antique summaries of universal history of which the one compiled in Latin by Orosius (early fifth century) was read in the Middle Ages even in an Arabic translation.

By modifying Greek forms to write Roman history, other Greek historians created influential prototypes. Dionysius of Halicarnassus used the basic ingredients of local Greek history to construct a monumental Roman archaic history or "Roman Antiquities." He read both Roman antiquarians and Roman annalists. The result was imitated by Flavius Josephus in his *Jewish Antiquities* (where "antiquities" is used again in the sense of ancient or archaic history). Too much is lost of the historiography of the Roman Empire to allow safe guesses as to the origins of the historiography of Barbarian nations which emerged in the sixth and seventh centuries. Where Cassiodorus, Gregory of Tours, and Bede found their models is not yet clear. But Dionysius' and Josephus' *Antiquities* belong to this story.

In the second century A.D. Appian used Greek regional history and Greek ethnography to encompass the expansion of the Romans. He divided their wars according to regions, with the consequence that he had to create a special section outside this geographic order for "civil wars." Appian (from Egypt) was expressing the new second-century feeling about the Roman Empire as an association of various regions. The feeling did not last long, and therefore Appian did not find immediate imitators, but his notion of the "history of the civil wars" and his example of parallel histories of regional wars regained prestige in the Renaissance and after. Not only in Davila and Clarendon but also in Ranke there is still more than a touch of Appian. In the third century A.D. the fusion of Greek and Roman historical traditions was such that the Greek historian and Roman senator Dio Cassius compiled a Roman history in eighty books according to the Roman annalistic scheme, yet in a style inspired mainly by Thucydides. Dio taught the Byzantines (through the summaries of his work rather than the original text) most of what they knew about Roman history. But as a model the Byzantines preferred Herodian, who wrote c. A.D. 240 about events from the death of Marcus Aurelius to A.D. 238. They transmitted him to the early humanists, who shared their admiration. Both took seriously Heriodian's professions of truthfulness which more rigorous tests have shown to be nearly empty. Dexippus, who really tried hard to follow Thucydides' example in his *Scythian Histories,* a story of the Gothic wars of the third century, was allowed to disappear.

VIII

One of the technical factors which made universal history possible in the Hellenistic period was the development of chronological studies. The results were ultimately tabulated, and we have some of these tabulations in Christian chronographers (Eusebius). But the jump from the creators of scientific chronology in the third century B.C. (Eratosthenes) to the Christian canons is a wide one. We know the latter better than the former; and it was from the latter that Scaliger took his start in the late Renaissance. Yet we have enough of the original Hellenic texts—such as the fragments of the "Marmor Parium" (a chronicle engraved in an inscription found at Paros) and of Apollodorus' Chronicle—to know what books of Hellenistic chronography looked like: one wonders whether Apollodorus wrote in verse in order to be memorized.

For the other types of Hellenistic antiquarian research we are in a worse position. Only seldom do we get a taste of the genuine product. A few good fragments have been recovered in papyri (for instance a fragment of Didymus' notes on Demosthenes). A work by Dionysius of Halicarnassus on Dinarchus deals with the chronology and authenticity of texts in the best manner of Alexandrian philology. The same Dionysius and later Plutarch and Lucian present samples of literary discussions affecting historiography: they deal with both form and contents. The outlines of the interesting theory on history by Asclepiades of Myrleia (first century B.C.) are preserved by Sextus Empiricus. But the great works of Alexandrian and Pergamene philology—beginning with Callimachus' bio-bibliographical repertory or "tablets" (*pinakes*)—are lost, and their results are known only from later scholia, epitomes, lexica, and similar compilations. We have none of the Hellenistic critical editions, commentaries on texts, collections of inscriptions, examinations of customs and rituals, or treatises on "discoveries" and "inventions" (one of the earliest of which was by Ephorus). Nor have we any of the local chronicles, with the exception of the temple chronicle of Lindus (99 B.C.) discovered in an inscription and a partial summary of the chronicle of Heraclea Pontica by Memmon preserved in Photius' *Bibliotheca*. We would have quite a different notion of the variety and intensity of Greek historical research if works of Hellenistic erudition and of local history had been representatively preserved.

Renaissance antiquarian erudition, except for chronography and lexicography, had few Greek models to use. It had to depend mainly on the Roman equivalents; and there is a real question in many cases how far these Roman models reflected Greek prototypes. We do not know, for instance, the Greek predecessor of the *Attic Nights* by Aulus Gellius (second century A.D.), a book which was read in the Middle Ages and which through the mediation of Politian's *Miscellanea* became the model for short discussions of texts and antiquarian questions. No doubt the Hellenistic antiquarians were as original as the Greek political historians in relation to Eastern predecessors. They corrected, though they did not eliminate, the unilateralism of the Herodotean-Thucydidean historiography. This is not to underrate the stark fact that such research was seldom recognized and classified as history.

IX

The other criterion we suggested for an evaluation of Greek historiography, its spread among non-Greeks, can be dealt with more briefly because it is partly implicit in what was said about the reception of Greek historiographical forms in Rome. Greek historiography was accepted in several countries during the third and second centuries B.C. as a way in which native intellectuals could explain in Greek to the Greeks and to themselves what their local traditions were. The ambition to look Hellenized can hardly be separated from the effort to defend ethnic tradition against the inroads of Hellenization. The Egyptian Manetho, the Babylonian Berossus, the Jew Demetrius, and the Roman Fabius Pictor, who in the third century B.C. wrote in Greek about their own countries, did not all write under the same conditions and with the same purpose. A Babylonian or Egyptian historiography of the Greek type in the vernacular seems never to have developed. The Romans soon passed from writing history in Greek to writing history in Latin. They branched out from Greek forms with variations of their own. We know of no exact Greek parallel to Cato's *Origines,* the first historical work written in Latin under Greek influence. If it was inspired by Greek books on "foundations of cities," it soon became something else which corresponded to the realities of second-century Italy. Even Cicero's scattered theoretical opinions about historiography are not necessarily simple adaptations from the Greek.

The Jews were in a peculiar position insofar as they had powerful historiographical models of their own in the Bible. On the other hand, the majority of the Jews who migrated to Egypt, Asia Minor, and Italy lost the knowledge of Hebrew and Aramaic and replaced it by Greek. They had to have the Bible translated into Greek. Thus the challenge of Greek historiography produced among Jews various results which the First and the Second Book of the Maccabees can exemplify. Book I was originally written in Hebrew and was later translated into Greek. It is a dynastic history of the Biblical type in Biblical language but with many technical details (including the semi-ethnographical chapter on Rome) suggested by Greek historiography. Book II is, characteristically, an epitome of a larger history in Greek written by the Jew Jason of Cyrene. The techniques of this book are very much those of the more popular Greek historiography with its abuse of miracles and of pathetic episodes. At the same time, either the epitomist or Jason himself was acquainted with the Biblical Book of Judges and presents Judas Maccabaeus in the splendid isolation of the Judges of old. The episodes of martyrdom indicate a new religious outlook which is of Jewish rather than Greek origin. Furthermore, the historical account serves to recommend to the Egyptian Jews the celebration of a new festival. The Greeks gave historical explanations of festivals (Callimachus, followed by Ovid), but do not seem ever to have written historical books to recommend the celebration of festivals. The Jewish author tries to improve on the Book of Esther, which was the prototype of the Jewish festal book. By comparison Flavius Josephus stands much more in the direct line of pure Greek historiography, notwithstanding his extensive use of the Bible and his early attempt to write history in Aramaic (about which we know almost nothing). Besides modelling his *'Jewish Antiquities'* on Dionysius of Halicarnassus, he wrote three other works in the Greek style—a history of a war (the Jewish War of A.D. 66-70), an erudite polemical work *(Against Apion),* and an autobiography.

The style of Greek historians affected their native imitators even in their use of evidence in the vernacular. The wealth of official chronicles and documents in the Near East had already been emphasized by Greek historians such as Ctesias and became an occasion for the nationalistic boasts of Manetho, Berossus, and Josephus. But they never made extensive searches for documents. In the main they followed the Greek practice of reporting readily accessible traditions, whether written or oral.

The ease with which foreigners could use the Greek models for a variety of purposes goes together with the ease with which Greeks became historians of foreign nations and potentates. Greeks wrote on behalf of Hannibal, almost as his official historians; and Polybius was fortunate enough to discover that not only the Roman version of the first Punic war (by Fabius Pictor) but also the Carthaginian one (by the Sicilian Philinus) had been written in Greek. There probably were Carthaginian (and Etruscan?) histories in the Greek style but in the vernacular which we shall never read. One of these may be mentioned in Sallust *(Jugurthine War,* 17). The national history which the Greeks wrote only partially and spasmodically for themselves they managed to write easily enough for other nations. The type of national history the Italian humanists conceived for the benefit of the new national states of Europe (from England and France to Hungary and Poland) was a mixture of Livy and of Late Antique models. Humanistic national historiography corresponds in form, function, and ethos to the work done by Greeks (and later by Romans) in writing the history of other nations. This was always a history which, after paying due homage to legends of origins, gave pride of place to wars. It particularly suited the Romans, but even the Jews used Greek historiography mainly to narrate their own wars.

X

The Greek historians were clearly not prepared for the Christian message either in the form communicated by Jesus and his immediate disciples or in the form which was elaborated by the Church of the first two centuries. The History of Salvation was not a Greek type of historiography in pagan days. Nor were the historical books of the Bible of much use as models to the Christians, because they told the story of an existing nation in its obedience or disobedience to God during its periods of organized political life. No Jew apparently ever thought of chronicling the Babylonian exile (or the period after the destruction of the Second Temple). The Christians were a new nation, and Jesus was the beginning of a new history. The nation was created by baptism, that is by individual choice. Yet it was also a nation *ab aeterno,* and destined to dissolve the other nations.

The historical works which expressed this new view, with its implication of eternity, had to be new creations. Even for Luke and Acts, written by a man familiar with Greek historians and anxious to follow their tradition, it is impossible to find a parallel in the extant Greek historians: in fact, Luke had Mark as his main model. What the Gospels—either canonical or apocryphal—and Acts presented was the beginning of a new earth and a new heaven: no continuation of the story was expected (except perhaps in apocalyptic terms). For about two centuries there was no further Christian historiography concerned with Christendom as a whole. The Acts of the Martyrs can be compared with some chapters of *II* and *IV Maccabees* and with the Greek and Roman literature on the death of illustrious men. Behind all there is the account of Socrates' death, though the Jewish texts are perhaps independent of it.

When Constantine made Christianity socially acceptable, an historical subject emerged which was amenable to at least some of the traditional practices of Greek historiography: the spreading of the true Apostolic Church and its consolidation, against heresies and persecutions, culminating in its recognition and official toleration by the Roman State. The Gospels tell how the message of salvation had been revealed and spread. The new "ecclesiastical" history as invented by Eusebius is the account of the development of the Church within definite limits of time and space, in its victorious struggles against heretics and persecutors. The new history was provided with documentation which would have been inconceivable in ordinary political history, but was not unheard of in antiquarian, polemical, and biographical works. The example of Alexander Polyhistor, famous as a diligent excerptor of texts about the Jews, was probably of special relevance to Eusebius. In Eusebius' continuators in the next two centuries (from Socrates, Sozomenus, Theodoretus, and Philostorgius to Euagrius) ecclesiastical history became the story of dogmatic controversies and of the relations between Emperors and Church. For reasons which we can perceive only faintly, ecclesiastical history lost its ecumenical meaning at the begin-

ning of the seventh century. In the West the fragmentation of the Roman Empire worked against a literary genre which presupposed one State facing one Church and many heresies. In the East, where the Roman Empire survived, it became perhaps difficult to separate the affairs of the Church from the affairs of the State. However, there were attempts in the West to produce regional ecclesiastical histories, but, as the example of Bede is enough to show, it was impossible even within restricted boundaries to separate what was sacred from what was secular. An independent history of the Universal Church did not make sense again until the Reformation and the Counter-Reformation. Ecclesiastical history thrived in times of dogmatic controversies.

Ecclesiastical history was never meant to be and never was a substitute for political history. The Christians Procopius and Agathias wrote Thucydidean histories of wars long after Eusebius had produced his new type of history. The dualism between sacred and profane history, between history of the State and history of the Church—which for opposite reasons neither the Greeks nor the Jews had even known—was born with Eusebius. This dualism was hard to defend against the complications of ordinary life. After Eusebius, ecclesiastical history proved to be an unstable compromise. It was written with a considerable contribution from Hellenic expertise. But it was very different from all the previous histories the Greeks had ever written. It presupposed Revelation and judged history according to Revelation.

XI

Before Christianity, Greek historians never offered more than interpretations of limited human transactions. They operated according to evidence and graded evidence according to probability. From this point of view the main question to ask is the one we have already asked: how competent were the Greek historians in their evaluation of evidence? The question, if rigorously asked, involves the interference of rhetoric with historical research.

But the value which we are now prepared to attribute to Greek historiography largely depends on what we expect from historical research. It is certain that historiography is more important to us than it was to the Greeks. This is mainly due to four factors. As Judaism, Christianity, and Islam are religions whose validity depends on the authenticity of certain traditions, historical research has a decisive importance in evaluating their claims (which was not the case with classical paganism). Secondly, the increasing rapidity and dimension of social and intellectual changes provoked a corresponding increase in the demand for historical research to explain and evaluate the changes. Thirdly, in the last two centuries history has been asked to provide community identity for the nations which have established themselves at a rate unknown in previous centuries. Finally, the physical and biological sciences have themselves developed an historical side, especially in theories about the evolution of the cosmos and of the species, and have encouraged the notion or the hope of an all-embracing historical explanation of reality.

Hellenic pre-Christian historiography was not meant to reveal the destiny of man. It is therefore also alien to any notion of development of the Hegelian variety, in which the events are both the progressive self-revelation of truth and the criterion of value. But the notion of an historical continuum from the beginning of the world, which is characteristic of the Old Testament in comparison with the New, does not seem to be ultimately incompatible with the empirical methods of Greek historiography: it becomes a question of evidence. Hints of a general evolution of human society are of course to be found in Greek thought, and the similarity continues insofar as both Greeks and Jews shared the illusion of an initial Golden Age. Nor does there seem to be logical incompatibility between the methods of Herodotus and Thucydides and the creation of a general empirical science of society. Aristotle, after all, operated with the data collected by previous historians or by his own school in order to create the sciences of politics and ethics. The limitations of historical research among the Greeks would turn out to be fatal only if we were satisfied that there is no way of unifying what the Greeks treated as real history and what they classified as biography, philology, antiquities, and so forth. But the unification of political history with other branches of research on the past is now a reality; and if anything is desirable, it is to avoid the delusion that there was never good reason for making some distinction between the different branches.

The most serious objection against the Greek approach to history would seem to be that it can never assess achievement except by reference to success and therefore can never teach more than prudence. The objection cannot be answered merely by mentioning those cases in which Greek historians show appreciation of generosity or forgiveness or sacrifice. One would have to show that there was a real place for such values in Greek historiography. The demonstration would not be easy. Hence the devaluation of history not only in ancient, but in modern moral theories, even in Kant; hence the nostalgia for the Hebrew prophets, who knew little history, but at least knew what was right. The fact is that Greek historiography never replaced philosophy or religion and was never wholeheartedly accepted by either. The status of historiography was never clearly settled among the Greeks. Choosing Greek historiographical models, even in modernized versions, therefore implies involvement in the difficulties of the use of such models when they are confronted by religion or philosophy.

FURTHER READING

Barnes, Harry Elmer. *A History of Historical Writing,* second revised edition. New York: Dover Publications, 1962, 450 p.
> Survey of the history of historical writing from the earliest times to the modern era. This work was first published in 1937.

Brown, Truesdell S. *The Greek Historians.* Lexington, Mass. and Toronto: D. C. Heath and Co., 1973, 208 p.
> Overview that is "an attempt to indicate some of the important changes that took place in the writing of history from the old logographers down to the period of Roman supremacy."

Bury, J. B. *The Ancient Greek Historians.* 1908. Reprint. New York: Dover Publications, 1958, 281 p.
> Historical survey of Greek historiography (up to the first century B.C.) that traces "the principles, governing ideas, and the methods of the Greek historians, and [relates] them to the general movements of Greek thought and Greek history."

Butterfield, Herbert. "The Rise of Classical Historiography." In *The Origins of History,* edited by Adam Watson, pp, 118-37. New York: Basic Books, 1981.
> Overview of the beginnings of Greek historical writing, focusing on attitudes toward the passage of time.

Gomme, Arnold Wycombe. *More Essays in Greek History and Literature.* Edited by David A. Campbell. Oxford: Basil Blackwell, 1962, 229 p.
> Examines various aspects of Greek historiography, asserting that, in ancient Greece, "freedom, never, probably, precisely formulated nor philosophically defended, is the individual freedom of the citizen in relation to the state."

Grant, Michael. "Introduction." In *The Ancient Historians,* pp. 3-20. New York: Charles Scribner's Sons, 1970.
> Excellent introductory overview.

Griffith, G. T. "The Greek Historians." In *Fifty Years (and Twelve) of Classical Scholarship,* edited by Maurice Platnauer, pp. 182-241. New York: Barnes & Noble, 1968.
> Concise summary of key studies and trends in Greek historiography up to 1968.

Levick, Barbara. *The Ancient Historian and His Materials: Essays in Honour of C. E. Stevens on His Seventieth Birthday.* Westmead, England: Gregg International, 1975, 251 p.

Collection of essays on various topics related to ancient history, touching on Aristophanes, Aristotle, Xenophon, Octavian, Tacitus, and others.

Mahaffy, J. P. *A History of Classical Literature, Vol. II.* New York: Harper & Brothers, 1880, 458 p.

Treats historical writing in the context of early Greek prose, with sections on Herodotus, Thucydides, Xenophon, and others.

Momigliano, Arnaldo. *Studies in Historiography.* London: Weidenfeld and Nicolson, 1966, 263 p.

Essays on scholars, trends, and influences on ancient history and historians by one of the foremost scholars in the field.

————. *Essays in Ancient and Modern Historiography.* Middletown, Conn.: Wesleyan University Press, 1977, 387 p.

Wide-ranging essays on topics in ancient history.

Shotwell, James T. "Greek History." In *An Introduction to the History of History,* pp. 128-210. New York: Columbia University Press, 1922.

Overview of Greek historical writing from Homer to Polybius and some later historians.

Herodotus

c.484 B.C.-c.429/425 B.C.

Greek historian.

INTRODUCTION

Called the "father of history" by the Roman philosopher Marcus Tullius Cicero, Herodotus is best known for his long and compelling prose account of life in Greece, Asia Minor, and Egypt which focuses on the causes and events of the Greco-Persian Wars. For Herodotus, history (*historiai*) meant "inquiry," and his attentions in the *History* are devoted not just to epic moments in the past, but also to geography, ethnology, and myth. Herodotus combines religious belief with secular knowledge; he took seriously the pronouncements of oracles but also travelled to see distant places for himself and to gather eyewitness accounts from others. While critics have rejected his work as too often anecdotal, accusing Herodotus of naive credulity, his informal style and omnivorous appetite for interesting and sometimes fantastic historical narratives have made the *History* an enduring fixture in the classical literary canon.

Biographical Information

Herodotus reveals little in the *History* about his own life and many of its details remain obscure or disputed. He was born in Helicarnassus (now Bodrum) in Caria, Asia Minor, the son of Lyxes and Dryo, and the nephew of the epic poet Panyassis. With the advent of civil war in 461 B.C., Herodotus was exiled to the island of Samos, where he began to write his *History* in the literary Ionic language. He subsequently returned to Helicarnassus and was instrumental in the downfall of the tyrant Lydgamis, who had been responsible for the death of Panyassis. From 454 B.C. to 443 B.C. Herodotus travelled widely, observing and interviewing informants for the *History*. His long itinerary included India, Babylon, Scythia, Egypt, Thrace, and Magna Graecia, and he noted both the physical geography and the customs and myths of each region. Much of Herodotus's information on the Persian Wars was collected toward the close of this period from 444 B.C. to 443 B.C. Herodotus then returned to Athens, where his pro-Athenian stance was popular and where his skill as a public speaker was recognized and financially rewarded. He was not permitted to become a citizen of Athens, so he joined the colony of Thurii (now Taranto) in southern Italy, where he continued to work on the *History* until his death. Scholars have suggested that the growing civil strife accompanying the Peleponnesian War provided special motivation for Herodotus to tell his story of former Greek unity. Herodotus died at age sixty and was probably buried in Thurii, although other accounts suggest burial in Athens or at Pella, in Macedonia.

Major Works

Although Herodotus makes reference to a projected history of Assyria, his only known work is the *History*. This early prose work combines personal inquiry into the geography, ethnology, and myths of Asia Minor with an attempt, in Herodotus's own words, to record "those great and wonderful deeds, manifested by both Greeks and barbarians" and to find the cause of the Greco-Persian struggle. Much of the geographical and ethnographical description in the *History* is the result of Herodotus's own travels; but he also draws extensively and trustingly on the fabulous accounts of storytellers. Divided into nine books, the *History* is written in an open, anecdotal style with many entertaining digressions. In Book I Herodotus begins his search for the causes of the Persian Wars: the Persian conquest of Lydia, the story of Croesus and Cyrus, and the wars between Cyrus and the Assyrians and Massagetae. Book II is devoted to Egypt; in part one Herodotus provides a detailed description of the Nile valley, and in part two a history of the Egyptian kings. In Book III he describes the Persian King Cambyses and the Persian invasion of Egypt. Book IV, while very digressive, focuses on Scythian and Libyan geography and history, including an account of the Persian King Darius's military expeditions to Thrace, Scythia and Libya. In Book V Herodotus describes numerous military campaigns in the Ionian Revolt against Darius, and Book VI incorporates an account of the Athenian victory over the Persians in the battle of Marathon. The last three books are less digressive, focusing more fully on the course and conclusion of the Persian Wars. In Book VII Herodotus deals with the accession of Xerxes I, his preparations for war and his invasion of Greece in 480 B.C. Here Herodotus narrates the capture of Persian ships at Artemisium, the land battle at Thermopylae, and the death of Leonidas. In Book VIII Herodotus describes further naval warfare between the Greeks and the Persians, including the Greek victory in the battle of Salamis, and the return of Xerxes to Persia. Book IX recounts the battle of Plataea and the defeat of the Persian commander Mardonius, including the destruction of the Persian naval force at Mycale and the liberation of the Hellespont. Despite the military conclusion and the invocation of Cyrus in the epilogue, many scholars believe that the *History* remained unfinished at Herodotus's death.

Textual History

Herodotus is thought to have written much of the *History* during the later years of his life while resident in Thurii. The division of the *History* into nine books and the naming of the books after the Muses was carried out by a scholar in Alexandria, long after Herodotus's death. Five key manuscript collections form the basis of textual scholarship on the *History*: a tenth-century Codex Florentinus or Mediceus in the Laurentian Library at Florence, an eleventh-century Codex Florentinus, and a Codex Romanus, also dating from the eleventh century. Two other important manuscripts are the thirteenth-century Codex Parsinus and a fourteenth-century Codex Romanus. The *History* was translated into Latin by Laurentius Valla in 1474, and the first Greek edition was published by Aldus Manutius at Venice in 1502. The first English translation (of Books I and II only) was published in 1584 and has been attributed to Barnaby Rich. There have been many more translations into English, notable among them Isaac Littlebury's of 1709, George Rawlinson's of 1858-60, A.D. Godley's 1920-25 Loeb Classical Library translation, Aubrey de Sélincourt's popular Penguin edition of 1954, and David Grene's of 1987.

Critical Reception

Herodotus made his living from lecturing, and his entertaining and vivid readings from the *History* found receptive audiences, especially at Athens. Plutarch has suggested that Herodotus's appeal for the Athenians lay only in his flattering accounts of Athenian exploits, but ever since Aristotle's favorable comment in the *Rhetoric*, Herodotus's disarming literary style, his personal charm, and his ear for a good story have made the *History* both popular and instructive. Among Herodotus's early detractors, Thucydides was scornful of his method, making veiled references to the superficial and momentary attractions of Herodotus's storytelling but claiming greater longevity for his own historical writing. Without mentioning Herodotus by name, Thucydides criticized his predecessor's unreliability, pointedly correcting Herodotus's facts in his own work and insisting that history must rely on autopsy, not hearsay. The entertaining and literary qualities of the *History* have long battled such demands for historical truth. Herodotus's account of the Egyptian kings, for example, was refuted by the Egyptian priest Manetho of Sebennytus, who in the third century B.C. provided a list of Egyptian kings wholly at variance with that of Herodotus. Plutarch's notorious attack on Herodotus, accusing him of deliberate falsehood, was widely condemned by critics as an exercise in polemic

not worthy of its author. However, Herodotus's reputation as a liar does not end with Plutarch; many subsequent critics have accused Herodotus of passing on to his readers as history the fantastic inventions of his informants. Despite such criticism, the broad scope of the *History*, its epic literary power, and its even-handed treatment of the Persian Wars have won it fresh generations of readers. New editions of the *History* appeared frequently throughout the Renaissance, and in the eighteenth century, François Marie Arouet Voltaire, echoing Cicero, devoted a chapter of his *Le Pyrrhonisme en histoire* (1768) to Herodotus, calling him "the model of historians." Archaeological excavations carried out in the nineteenth century only enhanced Herodotus's reputation, confirming many of his ethnological and geographical claims. Twentieth- century critics have continued to praise Herodotus as a prose stylist and raconteur, while nonetheless refuting as literary embellishment many of his historical claims.

PRINCIPAL ENGLISH TRANSLATIONS

The famous hystory of Herodotus (Books I and II) (translation attributed to Barnaby Rich) 1584
The history of Herodotus (translated by Isaac Littlebury) 1709
The history of Herodotus (translated by W. Beloe) 1791
Herodotus (translated by Isaac Taylor) 1829
Herodotus, a new and literal version from the text of Baehr (translated by Henry Cary, absed on the 1830 edition of J. C. E. Bähr) 1847
The History of Herodotus (translated by George Rawlinson) 1858-60
The History of Herodotus (translated by G.C. Macaulay) 1890
Herodotus (translated by A.D. Godley) 1920-25
The History of Herodotus (translated by Aubrey de Sélincourt) 1954
The History (translated by David Grene) 1987

CRITICISM

Plutarch (essay date c.105-c.115)

SOURCE: "Is Herodotus Malicious?" in *Greek Historical Thought: From Homer to the Age of Heraclitus*, translated by Arnold J. Toynbee, The Beacon Press, 1950, pp. 229-36.

[*Plutarch was a Greek biographer and essayist on morals whose works achieved their greatest influence during the Renaissance. Here, he takes strong exception to Herodotus, warning his readers to be wary of the superficial appeal and "charm" of Herodotus' historical writing, which, Plutarch claims, is rife with malicious "slanders" and "grotesquely false ideas." This essay is believed to have been written between the years 105 and 115.*]

Many readers of Herodotus are taken in by his plain, unlaboured, flowing style, and still more by his character. If Plato is right in saying that the last refinement of immorality is the false appearance of probity, it is equally true that the consummate achievement of malice is the assumption of such good-nature and simplicity as to defy detection. The malice of Herodotus is mostly directed (though he spares nobody) against the Boeotians and Corinthians, and I therefore feel called upon to defend truth and my ancestors in the same breath by exposing this part of his work in particular. If a critic were to deal with all his falsehoods and fictions, he might fill many volumes. However, to quote Sophocles, "Persuasion hath a cunning countenance," and especially when she resides in writings so full of charm and so masterly in concealing not merely this or that eccentricity but the whole character of the author. When the Hellenes revolted from Philip V. and joined Titus Flamininus, the king remarked that the collar into which they had put their necks was smoother but thicker. Now the malice of Herodotus is certainly smoother and softer than that of Theopompus, but it is also more penetrating and more wounding, just as draughts blowing slily through a crack are more injurious than the winds of heaven. . . .

Take his treatment of Io the daughter of Inachus at the very outset of his story. It is the general opinion in Hellas that this famous heroine has received divine honours from the Orientals and has bequeathed her name to many seas and to the principal straits of the world, and that she is the ancestress of the most distinguished royal houses. But what does our chivalrous historian say of her? That she threw herself at the heads of some Phoenician merchant-seamen, because she had been seduced (though not against her will) by the captain and was afraid that her pregnancy would be detected. This pretty story he libellously attributes to the Phoenicians; cites Persian historians as evidence that the Phoenicians had kidnapped Io and other women; and proceeds to enunciate the opinion that the Trojan War—the greatest and most splendid achievement of Hellas—was fought out of stupidity for the sake of a worthless woman. "It is evident," he remarks, "that they would not have been kidnapped if they had not been willing victims." In that case, we must call the Gods stupid for visiting the violation of the daughters of Leuctrus upon the Lacedaemonians or for punishing Ajax for outraging Cassandra. According to Herodotus, at any rate, it is clear that they would not have been outraged if they had not been willing victims. Yet Herodotus himself states that Cleomenes was taken alive by the Lacedaemonians, and the same fate

afterwards befell the Achaean general Philopoemen, while Regulus the Roman consul was captured by the Carthaginians. We would like to hear of braver fighters or better soldiers than these were. But there is nothing extraordinary in their experiences, considering that leopards and tigers are taken alive by human beings. All the same, Herodotus denounces women who have been violated and whitewashes the men who have raped them. . . .

When he comes to the Seven Sages (he calls them "uplifters"), he traces the family of Thales to a Phoenician, or in other words to a non-Hellenic origin; and he impersonates Solon in order to insult the Gods as follows: "Sire, I know for a fact that the Godhead is invariably envious and destructive, and then you question me regarding human life!" This is his own opinion about the Gods, and in palming it off upon Solon he adds malice to blasphemy. . . .

Now let us examine his account of the sequel to the battle [of Marathon]. "The Orientals," he writes, "pushed off in their remaining ships, picked up the slaves from Eretria at the island on which they had left them, and started to sail round Sunium, intending to reach the city [of Athens] before the Athenians themselves. At Athens it was alleged that this stratagem had been suggested to them by the Alcmaeonidae, who were supposed to have displayed a shield as a signal to them after they were once more on board. So the Persians started to sail round Sunium." A reader might pass over his reference to the Eretrians as slaves, although they had shown as gallant a spirit as any other Hellenes and had suffered a fate unworthy of their character. Nor does it so much matter that he has slandered the house of the Alcmaeonidae, with all the great families and distinguished individuals belonging to it. But it is unpardonable to have spoilt the greatness of the victory and to have made the world-famous achievement of Marathon end in nothing. Obviously there can have been no battle or action of any consequence, but only a brief "scrap" with an enemy landing-party (as detractors and belittlers maintain), if after the battle, instead of their cutting their cables, taking to flight and abandoning themselves to whatever breeze would carry them furthest from Attica, they received a treacherous signal by the display of a shield, bent their sails for Athens in the hope of capturing the city, rounded Sunium at their ease and lay to off Phalerum, while the most prominent and distinguished Athenians were betraying Athens in despair of her salvation. Later, he does acquit the Alcmaeonidae, but only to attribute the treachery to others. "A shield undoubtedly was displayed," writes our eye-witness, "and there is no getting over the fact." What an extraordinary occurrence, when the Athenians had just won a smashing victory! But even if it had occurred, it would not have been observed by the enemy, who were being driven headlong into their ships under close pressure with heavy

A double bust of Herodotus and Thucydides.

casualties, and were leaving the field as fast as each individual soldier could manage. Again, in affecting to defend the Alcmaeonidae against charges which he was the first to bring against them, he writes: "To my mind, the supposition that the Alcmaeonidae would ever have displayed a shield as a signal to the Persians, with the intention of bringing Athens under the yoke of Hippias, is too incredible to be accepted." But this merely reminds me of the nursery-rhyme:

Stay where you are, Mr. Crab.

When I've caught you, I'll soon let you go.

Why so eager to catch him, if you are going to let him go again? And so you, sir, first accuse and then defend. You indict slanders against famous men and then erase them. We must infer that you distrust your own evidence, for you heard from nobody but yourself that the Alcmaeonidae displayed a shield to the enemy when they were defeated and in flight. . . .

Then there are the Argives. Everybody knows that they did not refuse to help the other Hellenes, but only insisted that they should not be under the permanent command of the Lacedaemonians, their bitterest enemies. These being the facts, he insinuates a most malicious accusation, writing that, when the Hellenes asked the Argives to join them, the latter knew that the Lacedaemonians would not share the command with them and therefore laid down this condition, in order to have an excuse for remaining neutral. He adds that Artaxerxes, when subsequently reminded of this incident by Argive ambassadors who had made the journey to Susa, declared that there was no state which he regarded as a more friendly power than Argos. Then, characteristically, our author takes refuge in innuendoes, declaring that he has no exact information on this point but that he knows very well that nobody is immaculate and that the Argives are not the worst sinners in History. "My personal duty," he comments, "is to reproduce what is related, but I am under no obligation whatever to believe it—a principle which applies, incidentally, to all my work. *A propos* of this, there is a further story to the effect that it was the Argives who called in the Persian against Hellas, because they had done badly in war against the Lacedaemonians and felt anything to be preferable to their present humiliation." The reader is reminded of Herodotus's own story in which he records the Aethiopian's dictum regarding the scents and dyed-stuffs: "The ointments and the clothes of the Persians are equally deceitful!" What a motto for our author! "The phrases and artifices of Herodotus are equally deceitful!"— "They twist and turn, all roundabout, and naught's straightforward." Painters throw their lights into relief by their shadows. Herodotus intensifies his slanders by his denials of them, and heightens the effect of his insinuations by equivocation. Of course it is undeni-

able that the Argives did decline to join the Hellenes and that they left the palm of valour to the Lacedaemonians owing to their objection to leaving them the command. To that extent, they disgraced the noble lineage of Heracles; for it would have been better to fight for the freedom of Hellas under the command of Siphnians or Cythnians than to lose their share in those great and glorious struggles by disputing the command with the Lacedaemonians. But if it was they who invited the Persian into Hellas because they had done badly in war against the Lacedaemonians, why did they not openly take sides with him when he arrived? Short of joining forces with the King, they might have stayed behind and devastated Laconia, made a fresh attempt on Thyrea, or embarrassed the Lacedaemonians by some other form of intervention. By preventing them from sending so large an expeditionary force to Plataea, they could have dealt a great blow to the Hellenic cause.

But at least he has magnified the Athenians in this part of his work and has proclaimed them the saviours of Hellas? Very right and proper, if his praises were not interspersed with so much vituperation. These are his words: "The Lacedaemonians would have been deserted by the other Hellenes and would have died a glorious death after performing magnificent exploits in their hour of isolation—unless they had detected that the other Hellenes were going over to the Persian side in time to come to terms with Xerxes themselves." In this passage his real object is obviously not to praise the Athenians. On the contrary, he only praises them in order to abuse the others. The reader can hardly any longer resent the torrents of bitter insults which he discharges upon the Thebans and Phocians, when he convicts those who risked their lives for Hellas of treachery which did *not* occur in fact though it might have occurred in his opinion under hypothetical conditions. He even casts an incidental aspersion upon the Lacedaemonians by making it an open question whether they would have died on the field of honour or have capitulated, the account of themselves which they had given at Thermopylae being doubtless too insignificant to impress him! . . .

Having to describe four battles against the Orientals, what does he do? From Artemisium he makes the Hellenes run away; at Thermopylae, when their king and commander was risking his life for them, he makes them stay at home and think of nothing except the celebration of the Olympian and Carnean festivals; when he comes to Salamis, he devotes more space to Queen Artemisia than to the whole battle; and finally, at Plataea, he declares that the Hellenes stayed in camp and were unaware of the engagement until it was over. Presumably those who went into action agreed to fight in silence in order not to attract the others' attention, like the scene in the burlesque epic of *The Battle of Frogs and Mice,* written as a joke by Artemisia's son Pigres. He also makes out that the Lacedaemonians were no braver than the Orientals and only defeated them because of the disparity in equipment. Remember that when Xerxes himself had been present at Thermopylae, they had had to be driven forward with whips before they would advance against the Hellenes; and now, apparently, at Plataea, they had become reformed characters and "were not inferior in *moral* or physical strength. Their weak point was their equipment, which included no body-armour, so that they had to fight exposed against troops under cover." It effectively disposes of any glory attaching to the Hellenes on account of these battles, if the Lacedaemonians were fighting unarmed men, if the rest were unaware that a battle was taking place in their vicinity, if the cemeteries of the Glorious Dead contain no corpses, if the inscriptions with which the war memorials are covered are lies, and if nobody knows the truth except Herodotus, while every other human being who has taken an interest in Hellas and believes that her achievements in the Persian War were superhuman, has been taken in by a legend. Is it not more likely that our author, with his picturesque and entrancing style, his charm and wit and grace, has been telling us "old wives' tales, with all the poet's skill," and not merely with the poet's polish and sweetness? No doubt everybody finds him attractive and enchanting, but evil-speaking and slander lurk among his smooth, pretty phrases like sting-ing-flies among roses. Be on your guard, or he will poison your minds with grotesquely false ideas of the noblest and greatest countries and men of Hellas!

Thomas De Quincey (essay date 1842)

SOURCE: "Philosophy of Herodotus," in *Blackwood's Edinburgh Magazine,* Vol. LI, No. CCCXV, January, 1842, pp. 1-21.

[*An English critic and essayist, De Quincey used his own life as the subject of his best-known work,* Confessions of an English Opium Eater *(1822), in which he chronicled his addiction to opium. He contributed reviews to a number of London journals and earned a reputation as an insightful if occasionally longwinded literary critic. At the time of De Quincey's death, his critical expertise was underestimated, though his talent as a prose writer had long been acknowledged. In the twentieth century, some critics still disdain the digressive qualities of De Quincey's writing, yet others find that his essays display an acute psychological awareness. In the following excerpt, De Quincey tries to rectify what he sees as a false and narrow view of Herodotus. He argues that Herodotus is much more than a historian and compares him to the French Encyclopedists, calling Herodotus "the first great parent of discovery."*]

Few, even amongst literary people, are aware of the true place occupied by Herodotus in universal literature; secondly, scarce here and there a scholar up and

down a century is led to reflect upon the *multiplicity* of his relations to the whole range of civilization. We endeavour in these words to catch, as in a net, the gross prominent faults of his appreciation; on which account, first, we say pointedly, *universal* literature, not Grecian—since the primary error is, to regard Herodotus merely in relation to the literature of Greece; secondly, on which account we notice the circuit, the numerical amount; of his collisions with science—because the second and greater error is, to regard him exclusively as an historian. But now, under a juster allocation of his rank, as the general father of prose composition, Herodotus is nearly related to all literature whatsoever, modern not less than ancient; and as the father of what may be called ethnographical geography, as a man who speculated most ably on all the *humanities* of science—that is, on all the scientific questions which naturally interest our human sensibilities in this great temple which we look up to, the pavilion of the sky, the sun, the moon, the atmosphere, with its climates and its winds; or in this home which we inherit, the earth, with its hills and rivers—Herodotus ought least of all to be classed amongst historians: that is but a secondary title for *him*; he deserves to be rated as the leader amongst philosophical poly-histors, which is the nearest designation to that of encyclopædist current in the Greek literature. And yet is not this word *encyclopædist* much lower than his ancient name—*father of history?* Doubtless it is no great distinction *at present* to be an encyclopædist, which is often but another name for bookmaker, crafts-man, mechanic, journeyman, in his meanest degeneration; yet in those early days, when the timid muse of science had scarcely ventured sandal deep into waters so unfathomable, it seems to us a great thing indeed, that one young man should have founded an entire encyclopædia for his countrymen, upon those difficult problems which challenged their primary attention, because starting forward from the very roof—the walls—the floor of that beautiful theatre which they tenanted. The habitable world, was now . . . daily becoming better known to the human race; but how? Chiefly through Herodotus. There are amusing evidenc-es extant, of the profound ignorance in which nations the most enlightened had hitherto lived, as to all lands beyond their own and its frontier adjacencies. But within the single generation (or the single half centu-ry) previous to the birth of Herodotus, vast changes had taken place. The mere revolutions consequent upon the foundation of the Persian empire had approximated the whole world of civilization. First came the con-quest of Egypt by the second of the new emperors. This event, had it stood alone, was immeasurable in its effects for meeting curiosity, and in its immediate excitement for prompting it. It brought the whole vast chain of Persian dependencies, from the river Indus eastwards to the Nile westwards, or even through Cyrene to the gates of Carthage, under the unity of a single sceptre. The world was open. Jealous interdicts, inhospitable laws, national hostilities, always in *procinctu,* no longer fettered the feet of the merchant, or neutralized the exploring instincts of the philosophic traveller. Next came the restoration of the Jewish people. Judea, no longer weeping by the Euphrates, was again sitting for another half millennium of divine probation under her ancient palm-tree. Next after that came the convulsions of Greece, earthquake upon earthquake; the trampling myriads of Darius, but six years before the birth of Herodotus; the river-draining millions of Xerxes in the fifth year of his wondering infancy. Whilst the swell from this great storm was yet angry, and hardly subsiding, (a metaphor used by Herodotus himself, . . .) whilst the scars of Greece were yet raw from the Persian scymitar, her towns and temples to the east of the Corinthian isthmus smouldering ruins yet reeking from the Persian torch, the young Herodotus had wandered forth in a rapture of impassioned curiosity, to see, to touch, to measure, all those great objects, whose names had been recently so rife in men's mouths. The luxurious Sardis, the nation of Babylon, the Nile, the oldest of rivers, Memphis, and Thebes the hundred-gated, that were but amongst his youngest daughters, with the pyramids inscrutable as the heavens—all these he had visited. As far up the Nile as Elephantine he had *personally* pushed his enquiries; and far beyond *that,* by his obstinate questions from all men presumably equal to the answers. Tyre, even, he made a separate voyage to explore. Palestine he had trodden with Grecian feet; the mysterious Jerusalem he had visited, and had computed her proportions. Finally, as to Greece continental, thought not otherwise connected with it himself than by the bond of language, and as the home of his Ionian ancestors, (in which view he often calls it by the great moral name of *Hellas,* regions that geographically belong to Asia and even to Africa,) he seems by mere casual notices, now prompted by an historical incident, now for the purpose of an illustrative comparison, to have known so familiarly, that Pausanias in after ages does not describe more minutely the local features to which he had dedicated a life, than this extraordinary traveller, for whom they did but point a period or circumstantiate a parenthesis. As a geographer, often as a hydrographer—witness his soundings thirty miles off the mouths of the Nile—Herodotus was the first great parent of discovery, as between nation and nation he was the author of mutual revelation; whatsoever any one nation knew of its own little ring fence, through daily use and experience, or had received by ancestral tradition, *that* he published to all other nations. He was the first central interpreter, the common dragoman to the general college of civilization that now belted the Mediterranean, holding up, in a language *already laying the foundations of universality,* one comprehensive mirror, reflecting to them all the separate chorography, habits, institutions, and religious systems of each. Nor was it in the facts merely, that he retraced the portraits of all leading states; whatsoever in these facts was

mysterious, for that he had a self-originated solution; whatsoever was perplexing by equiponderant counter-assumptions, for that he brought a determining impulse to the one side or the other; whatsoever seemed contradictory, for that he brought a reconciling hypothesis. Were it the annual rise of a river, were it the formation of a famous kingdom by alluvial depositions, were it the unexpected event of a battle, or the apparently capricious migration of a people—for all alike Herodotus had such resources of knowledge as took the sting out of the marvellous, or such resources of ability as at least suggested the plausible. Antiquities or mythology, martial institutions or pastoral, the secret motives to a falsehood which he exposes, or the hidden nature of some truth which he deciphers—all alike lay within the searching dissection of this astonishing intellect, the most powerful lens by far that has ever been brought to bear upon the mixed objects of a speculative traveller.

To have classed this man as a mere fabling annalist, or even if it should be said on better thoughts—no, not as a fabling annalist but as a great scenical historian—is so monstrous an oversight, so mere a neglect of the proportions maintained amongst the topics treated by Herodotus, that we do not conceive any apology requisite for revising, in this place or at this time, the general estimate on a subject *always* interesting. What is everybody's business, the proverb instructs us to view as nobody's by duty; but under the same rule it is *any* body's by right; and what belongs to all hours alike, may for that reason belong without blame to January of the year 1842. Yet, if any man obstinate in demanding for all acts a "sufficient reason" to speak *Leibniticé*] demurs to our revision, as having no special invitation at this immediate moment, then we are happy to tell him that Mr Hermann Bobrik has furnished us with such an invitation by a recent review of Herodotus as a geographer, and thus furnished even a technical plea for calling up the great man before our bar.

We have already said something towards reconsidering the thoughtless classification of a writer whose works do actually, in their major proportion, not essentially concern that subject to which, by their *translated* title, they are exclusively referred; for even that part which *is* historical, often moves by mere anecdotes or personal sketches. And the uniform object of these is not the history, but the political condition, of the particular state or province. But we now feel disposed to press this rectification a little more keenly by asking—what was the reason for this apparently wilful error? The reason is palpable: it was the ignorance of irreflectiveness.

I. For with respect to the first oversight on the claim of Herodotus, as an earliest archetype of composition, so much is evident—that, if prose were simply the negation of verse, were it the fact that prose had no separate laws of its own, but that to be a composer in prose meant only his privilege of being inartificial—his dispensation from the restraints of metre—then indeed it would be a slight nominal honour to have been the Father of Prose. But this is ignorance, though a pretty common ignorance. To walk well, it is not enough that a man abstains from dancing. Walking has rules of its own, the more difficult to perceive or to practise as they are less broadly *prononcés*. To forbear singing is not therefore to speak well or to read well: each of which offices rests upon a separate art of its own. Numerous laws of transition, connexion, preparation, are different for a writer in verse and a writer in prose. Each mode of composition is a great art; well executed, is the highest and most difficult of arts. And we are satisfied that, one century before the age of Herodotus, the effort must have been greater to wean the feelings from a key of poetic composition to which all minds had long been attuned and prepared, than at present it would be for any paragraphist in the newspapers to make the inverse revolution by *suddenly* renouncing the modesty of prose for the impassioned forms of lyrical poetry. It was a great thing to be the leader of prose composition; great even, as we all can see at other times, to be absolutely first in any one subdivision of composition: how much more in one whole bisection of literature! And, if it is objected that Herodotus was *not* the eldest of prose writers, doubtless in an absolute sense no man was. There must always have been short public inscriptions not admitting of metre, as where numbers—quantities—dimensions were concerned. It is enough that all feeble tentative explorers of the art had been too meagre in matter, too rude in manner, like Fabius Pietor amongst the Romans, to captivate the ears of men, and *thus* to ensure their own propagation. Without annoying the reader by the cheap erudition of parading defunct names before him, it is certain that Seylax, an author still surviving, was nearly contemporary with Herodotus; and not very wide of him by his subject. In *his* case it is probable that the mere practical benefits of his book to the navigators of the Mediterranean in that early period, had multiplied his book so as eventually to preserve it. Yet, as Major Rennell remarks, . . . "Seylax must be regarded as a *seaman or pilot,* and the author of a coasting directory"; as a mechanic artizan, ranking with Hamilton, Moore, or Gunter, not as a great liberal artist—an *intellectual* potentate like Herodotus. Such now upon the scale of intellectual claims as was this geographical rival by comparison with Herodotus, such doubtless were his rivals or predecessors in history, in antiquities, and in the other provinces which he occupied. And generally the fragments of these authors, surviving in Pagan as well as Christian collections, show that they were such. So that, in a high virtual sense, Herodotus was to prose composition what Homer 600 years earlier had been to verse.

II. But whence arose the other mistake about Herodotus—the fancy that his great work was exclusively (or even chiefly) a history. It arose simply from a mistranslation, which subsists every where to this day. We remember that Kant, in one of his miscellaneous essays, finding a necessity for explaining the term *Histoire,* [why we cannot say, since the Germans have the self-grown word *Geschichte* for that idea,] deduces it of course from the Greek [Istoria] . . . This brings him to an occasion for defining the term. And how? It is laughable to imagine the anxious reader bending his ear to catch the Kantean whisper, and finally, solemnly hearing that [Istoria] . . . means—History. Really, Professor Kant, we should almost have guessed as much. But such derivations teach no more than the ample circuit of Bardolph's definition—"*accommodated*—that whereby a man is, or may be thought to be"— what? *"accommodated."* Kant was an excellent Latin scholar, but an indifferent Grezian. And spite of the old traditional "*Historiarum* Libri No vem," which stands upon all Latin title-pages of Herodotus, we need scarcely remind a Greek scholar that . . the noun [Istoria], *never* . . . bears in this writer the latter sense of recording and memorializing. The substantive is a word frequently employed by Herodotus: often in the plural number; and uniformly it means *enquiries* or *investigations,* so that the proper English version of the title-page would be—"Of the *researches* made by Herodotus, Nine Books." And in reality that is the very meaning, and the secret drift, the conservation running over-head through these nine sections to the nine muses. Had the work been designed as chiefly historical, it would have been placed under the patronage of the one sole muse presiding over History. But because the very opening sentence tells us that it is *not* chiefly historical, that it is so partially, that it rehearses the acts of men, . . . together with the monumental structures of human labour, . . . and other things beside, . . . because in short not any limited annals, because the mighty revelation of the world to its scattered inhabitants, . . . therefore it was that a running title or superscription so extensive and so aspiring had at some time been adopted. *Every* muse, and not one only, is presumed to be interested in the work; and, in simple truth, this legend of dedication is but an expansion or variety more impressively conveyed of what had been already notified in the inaugural sentence; whilst both this sentence and that dedication were designed to meet the very misconception which has since notwithstanding prevailed.

These rectifications ought to have some effect in elevating—first, the rank of Herodotus; secondly, his present attractions. Most certain we are that few readers are aware of the *various* amusement conveyed from all sources then existing, by this most splendid of travellers. Dr Johnson has expressed in print, (and not merely in the strife of conversation,) the following extravagant idea—that to Homer, as its original author, may be traced back, at least in outline, *every* tale or complication of incidents now moving in modern poems, romances, or novels. Now, it is not necessary to denounce such an assertion as false, because, upon two separate reasons, it shows itself to be impossible. In the first place, the motive to such an assertion was— to emblazon the inventive faculty of Homer; but it happens that Homer could not invent any thing, small or great, under the very principles of Grecian art. To be a fiction, as to matters of *action,* (for in embellishments the rule might be otherwise,) was to be ridiculous and unmeaning in Grecian eyes. We may illustrate the Grecian feeling on this point (however little known to critics) by our own dolorous disappointment when we opened the *Alhambra* of Mr Washington Irving. We had supposed it to be some real Spanish or Moorish legend connected with that romantic edifice; and, behold! it was a mere Sadler's Wells travesty, (we speak of its plan, not of its execution,) applied to some slender fragments from past days. Such, but far stronger, would have been the disappointment to Grecian feelings, in finding any poetic (*à fortiori,* any prose) legend to be a fiction of the writer's—words cannot measure the reaction of disgust. And thence it was that no tragic poet of Athens ever took for his theme any tale or fable not already pre existing in *some* version, though now and then it might be the least popular version. It was *capital* as an offence of the intellect, it was lunatic to do otherwise. This is a most important characteristic of ancient taste; and most interesting in its philosophic value for any comparative estimate of modern art, as against ancient. In particular, no just commentary can ever be written on the poeties of Aristotle, which leaves it out of sight. Secondly, it is evident that the whole character, the very principle of movement, in many modern stories, depends upon sentiments derived remotely from Christianity; and others upon usages or manners peculiar to modern civilization; so as in either case to involve a moral anachronism if viewed as Pagan. Not the colouring only of the fable, but the very incidents, one and all, and the situations, and the perplexities, are constantly the product of something characteristically modern in the circumstances, sometimes for instance in the climate; *for the ancients had no experimental knowledge of severe climates.* With these double impossibilities before us, of any absolute fictions in a Pagan author that could be generally fitted to anticipate modern tales, we shall not transfer to Herodotus the impracticable compliment paid by Dr Johnson to Homer. But it is certain that the very best collection of stories furnished by Pagan funds, lies dispersed through his great work. One of the best of the *Arabian Nights,* the very best as regards the structure of the plot—viz. the tale of *Ali Baba and the Forty Thieves*—is evidently derived from an incident in that remarkable Egyptian legend, connected with the treasure house of Rhampsinitus. This, except two of his Persian legends, (Cyrus and Darius,) is the longest tale in Herodotus; and by much the best in an artist's sense, indeed, its own remarkable merit, as a fable in which the incidents *successively generate each other,* caused it to be

transplanted by the Greeks to their own country. Vossius, in his work on the Greek historians, and a hundred years later, Valekenaer, with many other scholars, had pointed out the singular conformity of this memorable Egyptian story with several that afterwards circulated in Greece. The eldest of these transfers was undoubtedly the Bæotian tale (but in cays before the name Bæotia existed) of Agamedes and Trophonius, architects, and sons to the King of Orehomenos, who built a treasure-house at Hyria, (noticed by Homer in his ship catalogue,) followed by tragical circumstances, the very same as those recorded by Herodotus. It is true that the latter incidents, according to the Egyptian version—the monstrous device of Rhampsinitus for discovering the robber at the price of his daughter's honour, and the final reward of the robber for his petty ingenuity, (which, after all, belonged chiefly to the deceased architect,) ruin the tale as a whole. But these latter incidents are obviously forgeries of another age; "*angeschlossen*" fastened on by fraud, *"an den ersten aelteren theil,"* to the first and elder part, as Mueller rightly observes, . . . of his *Orchomenos.* And even here it is pleasing to notice the incredulity of Herodotus, who was not, like so many of his Christian commentators, sceptical upon previous system and by wholesale, but equally prone to believe wherever his heart (naturally reverential) suggested an interference of superior natures, and to doubt wherever his excellent judgment detected marks of incoherency. He records the entire series of incidents as . . . reports of events which had reached him by hearsay, . . . "but to me," he says pointedly, "not credible."

In this view, as a *thesaurus fabularum,* a great repository of anecdotes and legends, tragic or romantic, Herodotus is so far beyond all Pagan competition, that we are thrown upon Christian literatures for any corresponding form of merit. The case has often been imagined playfully, that a man were restricted to one book; and, supposing all books so solemn as those of a religious interest to be laid out of the question, many are the answers which have been pronounced, according to the difference of men's minds. Rousseau, as is well known, on such an assumption made his election for Plutarch. But shall we tell the reader *why*? It was not altogether his taste, or his judicious choice, which decided him; for choice there can be none amongst elements unexamined—it was his limited reading. Except a few papers in the French *Encyclopédie* during his maturer years, and some dozen of works presented to him by their authors, his own friends, Rousseau had read little or nothing beyond Plutarch's Lives in a bad French translation, and Montaigne. Though not a Frenchman, having had an education if such one can call it) thoroughly French, he had the usual puerile French craze about Roman virtue, and republican simplicity, and Cato, and "all that." So that *his* decision goes for little. And even he, had he read Herodotus, would have thought twice before he made up his mind.

The truth is, that in such a case, suppose, for example, Robinson Crusoe empowered to import one book and no more into his insular hermitage, the most powerful of human books must be unavoidably excluded, and for the following reason: that in the direct ratio of its profundity will be the unity of any fictitious interest; a Paradise Lost, or a King Lear, could not agitate or possess the mind as they do, if they were at leisure to "amuse" us. So far from relying on its unity, the work which should aim at the *maximum* of amusement, ought to rely on the *maximum* of variety. And in that view it is that we urge the paramount pretensions of Herodotus; since not only are his topics separately of primary interest, each for itself, but they are collectively the most varied in the quality of that interest, and they are touched with the most flying and least lingering pen; for, of all writers, Herodotus is the most cautious not to trespass on his reader's patience: his transitions are the most fluent whilst they are the most endless, justifying themselves to the understanding as much as they recommend themselves to the spirit of hurrying curiosity; and his narrations or descriptions are the most animated by the generality of their abstractions, whilst they are the most faithfully individual by the felicity of their minute circumstances.

Once, and in a public situation, we ourselves denominated Herodotus the Froissart of antiquity. But we were then speaking of him exclusively as an historian; and even so, we did him injustice. Thus far it is true the two men agree, that both are less political, or reflecting, or moralizing, as historians, than they are scenical and splendidly picturesque. But Froissart is little else than an historian. Whereas Herodotus is the counterpart of some ideal Pandora, by the universality of his accomplishments. He is a traveller of discovery, like Captain Cooke or Park. He is a naturalist, the earliest that existed. He is a mythologist, and a speculator on the origin, as well as value, of religious rites. He is a political economist by instinct of genius, before the science of economy had a name or a conscious function; and by two great records, he has put us up to the level of *all* that can excite our curiosity at that great era of moving civilization:—first, as respects Persia, by the elaborate review of the various satrapies or great lieutenancies of the empire—that vast empire which had absorbed the Assyrian, Median, Babylonian, Little Syrian, and Egyptian kingdoms, registering against each separate viceroyalty, from Algiers to Lahore beyond the Indus, what was the amount of its annual tribute to the gorgeous exchequer of Susa; and secondly, as respects Greece, by his review of the numerous little Grecian states, and their several contingents in ships, or in soldiers, or in both, (according as their position happened to be inland or maritime,) towards the universal armament against the second and greatest of the Persian invasions. Two such documents, such archives of political economy, do not exist elsewhere in history. Egypt had now ceased, and we may say that (according to the Scriptural prophecy) it had ceased for ever to be an independent realm. Persia had now for seventy years had her foot upon the neck of this unhappy land; and, in one century beyond the death of Herodotus, the two-horned hegoat of Macedon was destined to butt it down into hopeless prostration. But so far as Egypt, from her vast antiquity, or from her great resources, was entitled to a more circumstantial notice than any other satrapy of the great empire, such a notice it has; and we do not scruple to say, though it may seem a bold word, that, from the many scattered features of Egyptian habits or usages incidentally indicated by Herodotus, a better portrait of Egyptian life, and a better abstract of Egyptian political economy, might even yet be gathered, than from all the writers of Greece for the cities of their native land.

But take him as an exploratory traveller and as a naturalist, who had to break ground for the earliest entrenchments in these new functions of knowledge; we do not scruple to say that, *mutatis mutandis,* and *concessis concedendis,* Herodotus has the separate qualifications of the two men whom we would select by preference as the most distinguished amongst Christian traveller-naturalists; he has the universality of the Prussian Humboldt; and he has the picturesque fidelity to nature of the English Dampier—of whom the last was a simple self-educated seaman, but strong-minded by nature, austerely accurate through his moral reverence for truth, and zealous in pursuit of knowledge, to an excess which raises him to a level with the noble Greek. Dampier, when in the last stage of exhaustion from a malignant dysentery, unable to stand upright, and surrounded by perils in a land of infidel fanatics, crawled on his hands and feet to verify some fact of natural history, under the blazing forenoon of the tropics; and Herodotus, having no motive but his own inexhaustible thirst of knowledge, embarked on a separate voyage, fraught with hardships, towards a chance of clearing up what seemed a difficulty of some importance in deducing the religious mythology of his country.

But it is in those characters by which he is best known to the world—viz. as an historian and a geographer—that Herodotus levies the heaviest tribute on our reverence; and precisely in those characters it is that he now claims the amplest atonement, having formerly sustained the grossest outrages of insult and slander on the peculiar merits attached to each of those characters. Credulous he was supposed to be, in a degree transcending the privilege of old garrulous nurses; hyperbolically extravagant beyond Sir John Mandeville; and lastly, as if he had been a Mendez Pinto or a Munchausen, he was saluted as the "father of lies." Now, on these calumnies, it is pleasant to know that his most fervent admirer no longer feels it requisite to utter one word in the way of complaint or vindication. Time has carried him round to the diametrical counterpole of estimation. Examination and more learned study have justified every iota of those statements *to which he pledged his own private authority*. His chronology is better to this day than any single system opposed to it. His dimensions and distances are so far superior to those of later travellers, whose hands were strengthened by all the powers of military command and regal autocracy, that Major Rennell, upon a deliberate retrospect of his works, preferred his authority to that of those who came after him as conquerors and rulers of the kingdoms which he had described as a simple traveller; nay, to the late authority of those who had conquered those conquerors. It is gratifying that a judge, so just and thoughtful as the Major, should declare the reports of Alexander's officers on the distances and stations in the Asiatic part of his empire, less trustworthy by much than the reports of Herodotus: yet, who was more liberally devoted to science than Alexander? or what were the humble powers of the foot traveller in comparison with those of the mighty earthshaker, for whom prophecy had been on the watch for centuries? It is gratifying, that a judge like the Major should find the same advantage on the side of Herodotus, as to the distances in the Egyptian and Lybian part of this empire, on a comparison with the most accomplished of Romans, Pliny, Strabo, Ptolemy, (for all are Romans who benefited by any Roman machinery,) coming five and six centuries later. We indeed hold the accuracy of Herodotus to be all but marvellous, considering the wretched apparatus which he could then command in the popular measures. The *stadium,* it is true, was more accurate, because less equivocal in those Grecian days, than afterwards, when it inter-oscillated with the Roman *stadium;* but all the multiples of that stadium, such as the *schœnus,* the Persian *parasang,* or the military *stathmus,* were only less vague than the *coss* of Hindostan in their ideal standards, and as fluctuating *practically* as are all computed distances at all times and places. The close approximations of Herodotus to the returns of distances upon caravan routes of 500 miles by the most vigilant of modern travellers, checked by the caravan controllers, is a bitter retort upon his calumniators. And, as to the consummation of the insults against him in the charge of wilful falsehood, we explain it out of hasty reading and slight acquaintance with Greek. The sensibility of Herodotus to his own future character in this respect, under a deep consciousness of his upright forbearance on the one side, and of the extreme liability on the other side to uncharitable construction for any man moving amongst Egyptian thaumaturgical traditions, comes forward continually in his anxious distinctions between what he gives on his own ocular experience . . . what upon his own enquiries, or combination of enquiries with previous knowledge . . . —what upon hear-say . . . —what upon current tradition . . . . And the evidences are multiplied over and above these distinctions, of the irritation which besieged his mind as to the future wrongs he might sustain from the careless and the unprincipled. Had truth been less precious in his eyes, was it tolerable to

be supposed a liar for so vulgar an object as that of creating a stare by wonder-making? The high-minded Grecian, justly proud of his superb intellectual resources for taking captive the imaginations of his half-polished countrymen, disdained such base artifices, which belong more properly to an effeminate and over-stimulated stage of civilization. And, once for all, he had announced at an early point as the *principle* of his work, as what ran along the whole line of his statements by way of basis or subsumption . . . that he wrote upon the faith of hearsay from the Egyptians severally: meaning by "severally," . . . —that he did not adopt any chance hearsay, but such as was guaranteed by the men who presided over each several department of Egyptian official or ceremonial life. . . .

Frank Byron Jevons (essay date 1900)

SOURCE: "Herodotus," in *A History of Greek Literature: From the Earliest Period to the Death of Demosthenes,* Charles Scribner's Sons, 1900, pp. 306-27.

[*In the following essay, Jevons provides a general introduction to the* History, *addressing Herodotus's rhetorical methods and beliefs and considering his credibility as a travel narrator.*]

Halicarnassus, the birthplace of Herodotus, was situated on the south-west coast of Asia Minor, and was originally occupied by Carians. Dorian emigrants from Troezene then settled there, and for some time the place belonged to a confederation consisting of six Dorian cities, but eventually was excluded or withdrew from the alliance. Like the other Greek colonies on the coast of Asia Minor, Halicarnassus became subject first to the Lydian power, and then, when Cyrus conquered the Lydian kingdom, to the Persian empire. In pursuance of the policy which they employed elsewhere, the Persians did not directly govern Halicarnassus, but established or confirmed the rule of a native Tyrant, who was a vassal of the great king, and was responsible for the payment to the local satrap of a fixed tribute, and for raising troops when required. During the boyhood of Herodotus, Halicarnassus was ruled by a queen, Artemisia, who took, as Herodotus tells us with evident pride, high position for her courage and sagacity in the counsels and esteem of Xerxes during the second Persian invasion.

The best evidence that we have of the date of Herodotus is afforded by the historian himself when he tells us that he had a conversation with Thersander of Orchomenus, who had been present at a banquet given by Mardonius during the second Persian war, and to whom on that occasion a Persian had confided his presentiment—destined to be fulfilled—that shortly the Persian host would be destroyed, and but few would survive. This is good though indefinite evidence. It shows that Herodotus was not old enough to tell the tale of the Persian wars from his own experience, but yet was old enough to meet people who had taken part in them. Thus, although we cannot regard Pamphila's statement, which would make Herodotus to have been born B.C. 484, as anything more than a conjecture, we may take it as approximately correct, for the supposition that he was born some time between the first and the second Persian wars (*i.e.* between B.C. 490 and 480) accords with tradition, and with what little we know of his life.

According to Suidas, Herodotus belonged to a good Halicarnassian family. His most distinguished relative was Panyasis, a literary man, who must be supposed to have exercised some influence on his literary and mental development. Herodotus was doubtless by nature inclined to put much belief in omens, portents, and prodigies of all kinds; and an acquaintance with the epic poets was part of the education of his time; but it could not have been wholly without effect upon Herodotus that Panyasis applied the method of observation to portents, &c., and obtained some distinction as an epic writer. We know, further, that Panyasis wrote a poem on the adventures of Heracles, a Heracleiad; and Herodotus himself took so much interest in the myths connected with Heracles, that he voyaged to Tyre solely in order to investigate one of them. Finally, we find that Herodotus' taste for the antiquities of history, and probably to some extent his knowledge of the subject, were forestalled in a work by Panyasis on the colonisation of Ionia.

Of the life of Herodotus, all that we know practically is, that he undertook extensive travels over all the world then known. The result of these travels was the *History* of Herodotus which we now possess, divided by the grammarians of Alexandria into nine books, named after the nine Muses. Whether Herodotus from the beginning of his explorations entertained the design of writing the history of the long struggle between the Greeks and the barbarians which resulted in the Persian wars, there is no direct evidence to show. There is, however, nothing improbable in making the assumption, and the whole tone of the work is much more in harmony with the feelings which animated Hellas in the time of Herodotus' youth, than with those which were rife when, in his declining years, he was reducing to form at Thurii the materials which he had laboriously collected. The history of Herodotus is throughout national. It is the story, not of the struggle and success of some one Greek state, but of *all* the Hellenes against the barbarians; and this sentiment belongs to the time of the Persian wars and the time which immediately succeeded them—the period of Herodotus' youth—rather than to the time when the feeling of national unity had yielded before the divisions produced by the great struggle between Athens and Sparta in the Peloponnesian war. Further, the defeat of the barbarians is treated of by Herodotus as an his-

torical verification of the religious theory that no mortal power can become exceeding great without incurring the disfavour of the gods, and eventually meeting destruction from them. This sentiment, again, is one which was much more dominant in the early than the late years of Herodotus, and was likely to influence his conception of his History from the time when he first thought of writing it, and not to have grown up during the writing of it. Finally, the history of his own native place, which, as we have already seen, went through every phase of the national conflict with the barbarian, was the thread round which all his later knowledge crystallised, and naturally determined the way in which he would regard the Persian wars, *i.e.* as the result of a long series of collisions between the Greek and the barbarian worlds. In other words, the view which Herodotus takes is that of the Greeks who lived on the eastern side of the Ægæan. This view he learned in his youth before he left Halicarnassus, not when he settled in Thurii; and it was this view which determined the information he would collect, not the information which he collected that determined his point of view.

Herodotus begins his *History* by declaring that his purpose is to tell the causes of the wars between the Greeks and the barbarians. The wrongs and reprisals on both sides, which belong to the domain of myth, he sets aside without giving an opinion on them; he prefers to begin with what he knows, and the first thing he can vouch for is, that Cræsus, the king of Lydia, attacked and subjugated the Greek cities on the coast of Asia Minor. This leads him to give a history of the Lydian kings—including the wonderful story of Gyges and his magical ring, and the famous interview of Solon with Cræsus—and a description of the country of Lydia and its most noteworthy sights. The wrong Cræsus did to the Asiatic Greeks and the excessive wealth which he acquired brought down on him the wrath of Heaven, and he was overthrown by the Persian Cyrus. Then follows an account of the Medes and their history to the time of Astyages, of the birth and exposure of his grandson Cyrus, and of the way in which Cyrus at the head of the Persians overthrew the Median kingdom. We are thus brought into the domain of Persian history, and the growth of the Persian kingdom until it collided with Greece is the main subject of the first six books of Herodotus. He describes the customs of the Persians, their conquest under Cyrus of the Asiatic Greeks, of Babylon, and of the Massagetæ—in each case giving a description of the country and an account of the history of the conquered people. Cyrus was succeeded by Cambyses, who undertook the invasion of Egypt, and this gives Herodotus an opportunity for introducing his wonderful description of the land of Egypt, of the strange customs of its peoples, of its marvellous history and its astounding monuments. This fills the whole of the Second book, which is to us, as it was to the Greeks, the most enthralling of all the nine books.

In the Third book, he returns to the invasion of Egypt and its conquest by Cambyses. The death of Cambyses was followed by the appearance of a pretender to the throne, the pseudo-Smerdis. Herodotus relates his dethronement and the trick by which Darius contrived to obtain the crown for himself. At this point Herodotus introduces the history of the celebrated tyrant of Samos, Polycrates; the tale of his unsuccessful attempt to avert the Nemesis of the gods which his over-great prosperity was doomed to bring upon his head, and his fall. Darius organised the government of the now vast kingdom of Persia with a broad statesmanship and minute attention to detail which stamp him as the greatest of the Persian monarchs; and the review of the Persian kingdom and its resources thus introduced serves to impress the reader with the magnitude of the danger threatening Greece, and to heighten the interest of Herodotus' tale.

The Fourth book is occupied by Darius' attempt against the Scyths, which was unsuccessful, and by an account of their country and the countries bordering on it. The history of Cyrene is also introduced in this book, on the ground, which we may doubt, that Darius meditated an invasion in this direction also. But the plea serves as an excuse for the development of all the information about the tribes on the north coast of Africa between Cyrene and Egypt, which Herodotus had picked up from the traders along that coast. The invasion of Scythia, though unsuccessful, and all but the destruction of Darius and his army, paved the way for the invasion of Greece under Xerxes, inasmuch as it incidentally resulted in the conquest of the south of Thrace, through which Xerxes' army eventually marched. Accordingly the Fifth book opens with a description of Thrace; and then we come to the proximate causes of the first Persian invasion of Greece.

Histiæus, the tyrant of Miletus, who had once saved Darius, but was regarded by that monarch as too clever to be allowed entire liberty, was nominally a guest, and really an honoured prisoner at the Persian court. Growing weary of this, he secretly instigated the Ionian cities to revolt, in order that he might be sent to quell the insurrection and thus gain his liberty. In this revolt the Ionians were supported by the Athenians, but not by the Spartans, to whom they first applied for help. The revolt failed, and the attention of Darius was drawn to the necessity of crushing Greece. The first expedition which he sent for this purpose failed, and the second resulted in the glorious Athenian victory at Marathon, a victory which owes not a little of its immortal fame to the *History* of Herodotus. This closes the Sixth book.

The Seventh book opens with the preparations of Darius to take condign vengeance on Athens, and the opportune revolt of Egypt, which, by delaying the invasion of Greece until the death of Darius, left it in the hands of his unworthy successor, Xerxes, and thus probably saved Greece. The inception of the second Persian war is conceived by Herodotus in an epic spirit. Xerxes is loth to undertake the invasion of Greece, but the time is come for the wrath of the gods, provoked by the overweening greatness of the Persians, to descend upon this mighty empire, and false dreams are sent to Xerxes to drive him on destruction. War once resolved on, preparations of astounding magnitude were made. Magazines were prepared along the route in advance, and the neighbouring peoples engaged for months in filling them with stores. A canal was driven through Athos, that the fleet might escape the dangerous necessity of rounding this dangerous point. Bridges were built across the Hellespont, and all the many nations comprised in the Persian empire called upon to furnish contingents of troops. The dress and arms of all these peoples are described in the pages of Herodotus, and the advance of this army, numbering, according to Herodotus, over five million altogether, and probably the greatest the world has ever seen, traced from Sardis on. This prepares the reader to realise the dismay of the Greeks, the despair of their very oracles, which Herodotus pictures, and the valour of the handful of Greeks who, under Leonidas, waited for death and glory at Thermopylæ. The main incidents of the Eighth book are the battle of Salamis and the flight of Xerxes, as are the battle of Platæa and the flight of the Persian army of the Ninth book.

Herodotus is such simple and delightful reading, he is so unaffected and entertaining, his story flows so naturally and with such ease, that we have a difficulty in bearing in mind that, over and above the hard writing which goes to make easy reading, there is a perpetual marvel in the work of Herodotus. It is the first artistic work in prose that Greek literature produced. This prose work, which for pure literary merit no subsequent work has surpassed, than which later generations, after using the pen for centuries, have produced no prose more easy or more readable, this was the first of histories and of literary prose.

Without attempting to analyse the literary merit of Herodotus, it will be enough here to point out one or two of its constituent elements, a comprehension of which will throw light on the development of Greek literature and the position of Herodotus in that development. In the contemplation of any work of art, after the first period of enjoyment, the thought usually travels with reverence to the artist—what manner of man was he to whom it was granted to conceive and execute this? And whereas a picture or a statue conveys but little definite information about the artist as a man, and the imagination has to draw on its own stores for a likeness which may have but little resemblance to the original, it is the privilege of literature to convey information much more definite in kind and more extensive in range. The extent to which we thus become acquainted with the man through his writing may vary, from the marked and deliberate way in which Thucydides withdraws himself and his own views from the reader's gaze, to the delightful intimacy which in reading Charles Lamb we come to feel with the man. But even with Thucydides we come to be acquainted, for his very withdrawal from us gives us the man's character. Herodotus, however, belongs to the type, not of Thucydides, but of Charles Lamb. Even if the tale of how the Greeks fought well for liberty, and thus bequeathed to us the heritage of their art and literature, were not of interest to us, we still should read it for the sake of making the acquaintance of Herodotus, by listening to him as he tells the tale. Or again, if, forgetting the sack of Sardis, Herodotus says that the Athenians at Marathon were the first Greeks who dared to look the Persians in the face, or makes the total of Xerxes' army too great by a million, or some other conjectural sum, this lessens our affection for Herodotus as little as it lessens our admiration for the Greeks. They fought well, and he tells the tale well, and we are the better for the fight and for the tale. *Dulce et decorum est.* The charm of Herodotus is, then, that in him we are listening to one who has seen many cities and known many men, and is not writing a book, but telling in his fresh old age the brave deeds that were done in the days before him, and describing the marvels of the strange lands which in his youth he had himself seen. That Herodotus' narrative has the characteristics of a tale told rather than of a book written is no accident, nor is it to be explained solely by reference to the temper of the man. It is due to the fact that Herodotus wrote his work for oral delivery, and not for a reading public. The Greeks of his time were not in the habit of perusing literature, each man in the privacy of his own home. Epic poetry they were accustomed to hear recited in public. Lyric poetry they became acquainted with either by hearing choruses perform it at some sacred festival, or—as in the case of triumphal odes—on some public occasion, or by listening to some friend reciting an ode of Alcæus or Theognis after a banquet. Dramatic literature reached the Greek not in the form of books, but by being performed before him on the stage. A reading public can scarcely be said to have existed at this time; for although some public libraries were to be found, Euripides was the first private man who possessed a library. It was not, therefore, by spreading written copies of his work that an author could hope to gain much publicity. The prose writer at first naturally adopted the same means as the poet for bringing his work before the notice of the public; that is, he sought for some opportunity when large numbers of his fellow-countrymen were gathered together, and he would be able to read to them his productions. Such an opportunity was found in such a festival as the Panathenæa at Athens, or the national games of Greece. At the latter we know prose works were regularly read, and special provision made for their recitation. This, then, was the way in which Herodotus had to gain the ear of the public. The idea is so alien to the notions of the present day, with its printing-press, that at first we are inclined to doubt the possibility of any considerable portion of a prose work—to say nothing of the whole of Herodotus—being thus recited. But when we reflect that a speech such as that of Demosthenes *On the Crown,* or that *On the Embassy,* is longer than the longest book of Herodotus, and that the Greeks (like the Japanese of the present day) were accustomed to listen for a whole day to the performance of play after play, we shall have little difficulty in believing that Herodotus might easily read at a sitting, say, the whole of the Second book, describing the land, the manners and customs, and the history of Egypt. More than this we are not called upon to believe, for what evidence there is on the point seems to indicate that these recitations of lectures of Herodotus extended not to the whole, but only to parts of his work.

The well-known story that Thucydides, as a boy, being present at one of these recitations, burst into tears, and that Herodotus thereupon declared the boy's nature was ripening towards learning, has the appearance of being an invention due to the desire of grammarians to bring the two great historians into connection with each other, and, further, is hard to believe because of the chronological difficulties. If we suppose that the recitation took place when Thucydides was fifteen years old, B.C. 456, Herodotus can scarcely have been thirty years of age then, had probably not yet visited Egypt, and could hardly have composed any of his work. But although we may reject this story, there is no reason to doubt that Lucian is right in saying that Herodotus gave recitations at the Olympia, in Athens, Corinth, Argos, and Sparta. As far as Athens is concerned, the testimony of Lucian is amply confirmed by Eusebius, and by the author of the attack on Herodotus (*De Malignitate Herodoti*) which goes under the name of Plutarch. The latter (c. 26) states that the Athenians decreed a gift of ten talents to Herodotus, and the former states that Herodotus was "honoured" by the Boulê of the Athenians for reciting his works to them. These statements may be regarded as referring to the same circumstance, and as proving a recitation at Athens at least.

Taking it as proved that Herodotus did give readings of his **History,** we shall see that the work is not complete, and that therefore his readings were probably of selections from, and not the whole of his history. In the first place, the last chapter of the last book was presumably not meant to conclude the work. It contains no indication that it is the last chapter, does not sum up the work, nor does it present anything corresponding to the introduction at the beginning of the history. In the next place, the **History** does not comprise the last phases of the struggle between the Greeks and the barbarians, the battles at the Eurymedon and Salamis in Cyprus. It thus seems that Herodotus must have contemplated continuing his work down to a later date than it reaches as we have it. If, in objection to this, it is alleged that the division of the work into nine books, named after the Muses, excludes the possibility of a tenth having been added, it is only necessary to point out that there is no evidence in the work itself of any such division. When Herodotus wishes in any passage to refer to some other passage, he does not refer to the number of the book, as Josephus, for instance, does, but says "in the former" or "the latter part of my *History*." The first author who knows the division into books is Diodorus Siculus, and the first who knows them by the names of the Muses is Lucian. From this we may infer that it was by the Alexandrine grammarians that the names of the Muses were given to the books.

Not only does Herodotus seem to have broken off without bringing his *History* down to its proper termination, but he also seems not to have finished that which he did write. Thus he promises to say more about Ephialtes (who betrayed the Greeks at Thermopylæ) in a later part of the *History,* but never does say anything more. He also promises to give an account of the capture of Nineveh by the Medes, but he never redeems his promise. Again, he promises to say more about the Babylonian kings in his "Assyrian History," but we have no Assyrian history. Whether Herodotus ever wrote the Assyrian history which he promises, and whether, if he wrote it, he intended to publish it separately or as part of the work we have, are questions which do not seem to admit of being settled. Aristotle alludes to an account of the siege of Nineveh—by Herodotus according to some MSS., by Hesiod according to most MSS. It is difficult to imagine how Hesiod could come to be writing of the siege of Nineveh, and this difficulty, together with the fact that Herodotus, as we have seen, certainly intended, at least, to give an account of the siege, incline us rather to think that Herodotus did write his Assyrian history. In this case, it was not incorporated with the work which we possess, as Herodotus seems to have intended, and this is a fresh indication that the work is incomplete. Thus, although Herodotus gave various readings from his work before he finally settled down in Thurii, and evidently wrote or revised many passages of the last four books during his stay at Thurii, he yet neither brought the work to a conclusion nor completed his revision.

Unfinished though the work is, it is so far from being left in a disorderly state, that one of its charms, and of its points of superiority over previous prose, is its unity. This unity is due to its simplicity of conception. Herodotus' one theme is the conflict between the Greeks and the barbarians, and with this theme all the episodes have a direct connection. To this simple conception Herodotus was led by the sentiment of nationality, which nerved the better-minded Greeks to their successful resistance, but unfortunately was disappearing rapidly in the later years of Herodotus' own life. The

Hellas of Herodotus includes Miletus and Cyrene, Sicily and Rhodes. He evidently has great sympathy with that state which made the greatest sacrifices for the national good in the Persian wars—Athens; and with a boldness which, in view of the envy and hatred that was rife against Athens at the time he wrote, deserves credit, he does not hesitate to show it. Thus he properly calls attention to the patriotism of the Athenians in resigning the command of the fleet to the Spartans (though, as they contributed the largest contingent, they had the best claim to take the maritime lead), rather than cause dissension among the allied Greeks; and he rather goes out of his way to declare that, however unpopular the opinion may be, he is convinced that the Athenians, when they abandoned Athens and took to their "wooden walls" in accordance with the oracle, saved Hellas. The democratic government of Athens also pleased him. He disapproved of tyranny and of oligarchy, and believed in equality; and he ascribes the rise of Athens to her escape from tyranny. But this liking for Athens does not make him a blind partisan. He has praise for Athens' great rival, Sparta, and even for the courage of the Bæotians, although they were traitors, and for the Corinthians.

Herodotus' breadth of view and his sentiment of nationality is due in part to his extensive travels, which tended to make him cosmopolitan, and feel his kinship with all Hellenes wheresoever planted; but it is still more due to his being an Asiatic Greek. The natural boundary of the Persian kingdom towards the west was the Ægæan, and farther than this Persian statesmen would have had little temptation to extend their rule but for the Greeks on the coast of Asia Minor. The relation of Greece to the Persian empire was in the time of Darius much like that of Britain to the Roman empire. The Channel might have remained the boundary of Roman rule but for the fact that the tribes of Gaul found a perpetual refuge and an everready assistance from their kinsfolk in Britain, and therefore peace could not be lasting in Gaul until Britain also was subdued. The Greek cities in Asia Minor, in the same way, could not be expected to become contented subjects of the great king so long as their brethren across the Ægæan remained free. It was to the Greeks in Greece, without distinction, that the Greeks in Asia Minor looked for assistance in their struggles against the barbarians, whether Persian or Lydian, and this of itself served to make the Asiatic Greeks think little of minor divisions and much of their common nationality.

A strong national feeling, then, running all through Herodotus' work, is one thing which gives unity to his *History.* Another is the predominance of the religious feeling of Nemesis, a theory which the overthrow of the enormous power of Persia by a handful of Greeks is regarded by Herodotus as verifying. Nemesis, the visitation which lights from heaven on over-great prosperity, as the lightning strikes the tallest trees and the loftiest houses, does not appear in Homer, but is to be found in Hesiod, in Pindar, Æschylus, Sophocles, and Euripides. The workings of Nemesis are seen by Herodotus not only in the defeat of Persia, but in the fall of Cræsus and of Apries, and in the tales of Polycrates, Orætes, Aryandes, Pheretime, Cleomenes, Talthybrus, and the death of Mardonius; in the result of Cyrus' expedition against the Massagetæ, that of Cambyses against the Ethiopians, and of Darius against the Scyths. Nemesis is incurred by conspicuous prosperity, but the absence of such prosperity is no safeguard, for no one may escape from the "envy" or "jealousy" of the gods. Short as life is, Herodotus says, there never yet was or will be a man who does not wish more than once that he were dead: Heaven gives man a taste, but grudges him more of the pleasure of life. Thus Nemesis and jealousy, together covering the whole of human experience, afford a universally applicable explanation of the vicissitudes through which individuals and countries go; and these vicissitudes it is the business of the historian to record. This is Herodotus' philosophy of history.

His God is not only a jealous God, but one who visits the sins of the fathers on the children. That Heaven punished offenders in their own persons and rewarded the righteous, Herodotus firmly believed, and he records many instances in which this happened. But there remained cases which Herodotus, like Solon and Æschylus, seemed to think found a satisfactory explanation in ancestral guilt. Thus Cræsus paid the penalty for Gyges' crime.

Polytheism Herodotus practically abandons. He prefers not to commit himself, and, though he tells many stories of the gods, is careful not to guarantee them, when he does not deny them. In the spirit of toleration he allows that the effects of an earthquake might be regarded as the work of Poseidon. Strange to say, he speaks of the sun as a god. Perhaps this is a mere and natural inconsistency, or he may have deliberately used the expression to guard himself from the charge of atheism, which a denial of the sun's divinity brought on Anaxagoras, with whom he may have been, and with whose works he probably was, acquainted. But, although not a polytheist, Herodotus was not an atheist. He believes in a God and in fate. From fate neither man nor even god can escape. It is thus that many things, otherwise hard to understand, are to be explained; and Herodotus is never weary of pointing out how everything was ordained by Providence. Consistently with this belief in fate, Herodotus believes in oracles as a means of finding out what is fated. Instances of non-fulfilment of an oracle are, of course, explained away; either the inquirer was guilty in some way, or the oracle was a forgery, or due to bribery. It further harmonises with this belief in fate and oracles that Herodotus believed also in omens.

The belief of Herodotus in Nemesis and fate gives unity to his work, for the history which he relates is regarded by him as but the working out of a divine plan preordained from all time. But a theory is dangerous for a historian, who may unconsciously be drawn into adapting facts to suit his theory, and it thus becomes necessary to examine the credibility of Herodotus. The credibility of a writer depends on his capacity, his honesty, and his means of information. Under the head of capacity we have to distinguish between the capacity of a writer for stating the results of his own observation and his capacity for estimating the evidence of others: and in the case of Herodotus it is the more necessary to observe this distinction, because, in conformity with the custom of logographers, he regarded it quite as much part of his task to describe the land, monuments, habits, and customs of the peoples whose history he was writing, as to write their history. The historical events which Herodotus recorded happened before his time, and came to him from the lips of others; but the descriptions of countries and peoples are, to a great extent, the result of his own travels. With regard, then, to his capacity for this portion of his work, the essential conditions are that he should have been an accurate observer, and that he should be able to distinguish in his statements between what he himself observed and what he was told by others. But in forming our opinion we should be on our guard against applying the standard of modern times to an ancient author. Thus, naturalists of the present day—owing partly to the modern taste for sport and to modern weapons of precision—are accustomed to much closer study, both of specimens and of the habits of the living animal, than any Greek naturalists. We are not, therefore, surprised to find that the acquaintance of Herodotus with crocodiles and hippopotami was a distant one; that he has no accurate measurements of the latter, and little knowledge of the conformation of the jaws of the former; that he is apt to confound the poisonous asp with the equally venomous horned viper; that he makes mistakes about pisciculture; and accepts without close investigation what he was told by the natives. In this branch of knowledge, Herodotus falls below the modern, but not below the ancient, standard, and will compare favourably with Aristotle, who wrote on zoology. If we set aside this special department of inquiry, and consider him not as a naturalist, but as a general observer, we find, in the first place, that he recognises the difference between the evidence of his own eyes and hearsay, and that he is generally careful to inform us to which kind of testimony a statement belongs. In the next place, it is generally admitted that "what he saw himself he may be supposed to describe with fair accuracy." Everything, of course, he did not observe. He does not state, for instance, that the Egyptians used gold and glass as well as bronze for drinking vessels; that they ate wheaten as well as other bread; that women as well as men plied the loom in Egypt, and that they drove the woof upwards as well as downwards. But, nevertheless, he gives us a picture of Egypt as he saw it, the charm of which is indisputable, and which is as valuable as it is charming.

As an observer, then, Herodotus may be credited with capacity. In the historical portions of his work we must look for other qualities to establish his capacity. To begin with, he has the first great quality of a historian: he distinguishes between facts and his inferences from them. What was told to him he tells to us, and gives us his authority: he draws his own inferences, but also gives his reader the opportunity to draw other inferences. Further, he does not present us with that version alone of an event which he considers most likely, but lays before the reader all the versions with which he is acquainted, choosing one himself, but also leaving the reader liberty of choice. Again, he is free from the error of infallibility; if he cannot test the truth of a story, he admits his ignorance.

As Herodotus is so careful to distinguish between what he has heard and what he infers therefrom, and to give his authorities, his capacity for estimating evidence becomes a matter of less consequence. But he is fully aware of the importance of getting evidence at first hand, if possible, and naturally prefers that version of an event which has the best evidence to support it. It is, however, at this point that his theory of Nemesis and fate affects his credibility as a historian. When the evidence for two versions of an event was about equal, Herodotus cannot be blamed for choosing that version which accords with his theory. In such a case it is perfectly legitimate to take into account the tendency of a general law, and to give weight to general considerations. What is not legitimate is for the historian to imagine that conformity with his theory dispenses him from the necessity of further investigation: and there can be little doubt that his theory frequently led Herodotus into taking a superficial view of history, accepting fate as a sufficient explanation of an event, about the causes of which he might have found out and told us more. On the other hand, there is not the least reason to believe that he ever rejected the better-attested version because it did *not* harmonise with his theory. He believed his theory to be well enough established to dispense with such props, and has no hesitation in rejecting an application of the doctrine of Nemesis when the facts do not support it. Nor does his appetite for the marvellous—although it occasionally led him to record, if not to believe, some very extraordinary tales told him in the East, as, *e.g.* that about the cats in Egypt—prevent him from exercising a perpetual criticism on what he was told or from frequently rejecting the stories he heard.

Herodotus' capacity as a historical writer is marred by his tendency to overlook general causes and to see only personal motives, to substitute occasions for causes. Thus, he ascribes the revolt of the Persians from the Medes to personal motives on the part of Harpagus and Cyrus; the conquest of Egypt by Cambyses to an eye-doctor's desire for revenge; Darius' design of invading Greece to the intrigues of Democedes, the enslaved physician, who longed to return to Greece; the Ionian revolt to the pecuniary difficulties of Aristagoras; the Persian invasion of Samos under Darius to the monarch's gratitude to Syloson; and the effeminacy of the Lydians to Croesus' suggestion to Cyrus that they should be compelled to live luxuriously. But here, again, Herodotus is no worse than the greatest philosophers of Greece, who imagined, for instance, that the unnatural camplife of the Spartans was, not the result of hostile pressure from without, exerted for centuries, but due to the fiat of a single lawgiver, and also believed that a similar state of things could be brought about elsewhere by the mere command of a philosophical king.

Another defect which Herodotus shared in common with other Greek writers, and which, though in a different way, marred the philosophy as well as the history of Greek writers, was ignorance of foreign languages. In the course of his travels he picked up about a score of foreign words; but when he says that Persian proper names express always some bodily or mental excellence, and that they invariably end in *s,* he betrays his ignorance of the language. So, too, his remark that the language of the Troglodytes, of the Egyptians, and of foreigners generally was like the chirping of birds, shows that he had learnt no language but his own.

The result of this ignorance of foreign languages was that Herodotus had to depend for much of his information about the foreign countries he visited on interpreters; and this brings us to the second point we have to consider in connection with the credibility of Herodotus—his means of information. In the case of public monuments or documents, of which there existed authentic translations from the original into Greek, Herodotus' linguistic ignorance would not vitiate his statements, and it is probable that it was on such translations that his accounts of Darius' cadastral system, the itinerary to Sardis, and the description of Xerxes' army rested. But in the case of inscriptions which he had to get translated by his interpreter, *e.g.* the inscriptions about the amount of onions consumed during the building of a pyramid, or about the method of building a pyramid, or the pillars in Palestine commemorating the conquests, whether of Sesostris or Rameses III. or the Hittites, obviously the translation depended on the capacity of the translator, not of Herodotus, and is of uncertain value. Considerations of this sort apply to the whole of Herodotus' Persian and Egyptian history. He depended entirely on his interpreter or dragoman, and the result is that we have rather folk-lore than history, the tale of Rhampsinitus, and not the real history of the Egyptian dynasties; and we are the gainers. The monuments will reveal to us in course of time the history of the kings of

Egypt, but Herodotus has given us what the monuments cannot reveal, and what would have otherwise utterly perished—a faithful and charming version of the popular stories current in the streets of Memphis in his day.

With Herodotus' Greek history the case is different. Some of the inscriptions which he consulted were undoubtedly forgeries, *e.g.* the Cadmeian inscriptions at Thebes, and were known by himself to be forgeries, *e.g.* the offerings of Croesus at Delphi falsely inscribed as offerings from Sparta. But many were genuine and valuable, *e.g.* those on the field of Thermopylae, the list at Delphi of the Greeks at Salamis and Plataeae. and that of Mandrocles in the temple of Here at Samos. The value of his accounts of the various ancient works of art which he saw is less than that of the inscriptions. Thus what Herodotus tells us of Croesus, Alyattes, and Gyges may possibly have been the tales which clung to the offerings sent by those rulers to Delphi. But the myth which was told about Arion in connection with the erection on Taenarum, and that about Ladike and her offering at Cyrene, suffice to show that little confidence can be placed in this kind of evidence.

By far the larger part of Herodotus' information, however, was necessarily drawn from the lips of the people with whom he became acquainted. The history of the Persian wars had not been committed to writing, and Herodotus had, therefore, to rely on oral testimony. This is for the purposes of history generally inferior evidence, but its value is materially affected by the number of persons through whom it is transmitted. Next to the evidence of eye-witnesses, that of contemporaries ranks, and Herodotus could and did get information from both classes. This guarantees the substantial truth of his history, but does not allow us to put much faith in his statistics, or in any point in which minute accuracy is needed.

But although Herodotus depends mainly on oral testimony, he is not unacquainted with the literature of his country. He not only, being an educated man, possesses familiarity with the poets, *e.g.* Archilochus, the Cyclic poems, Sappho, Æschylus, Hesiod, Pindar, Olen, Alcæus, Solon, Simonides, and Phrynichus; but he has references to Pythagoras, Anaxagoras, and possibly Anaximander. Whether Herodotus was acquainted with the logographers is hard to say, because we know so little of them. Hellanicus was later than, and therefore unknown to Herodotus, as was Damastes, the pupil of Hellanicus. Bion, Deiochus, Hippyas, Eugeon, Eudemus, Democles, Melesagoras, and Xenomedes are mere names to us, and there is no hint to be found anywhere that Herodotus either used or knew their works. The few fragments that go under the name of Dionysius are probably spurious, and the celebrated voyager Scylax probably did not write any account of his travels, certainly was not known as an author to Herodotus. What little we know about Charon seems to show that Herodotus was unacquainted with his works. Xanthus was said by the historian Ephorus to have given Herodotus the starting-point, but the few fragments left of Xanthus throw no light on the meaning of this statement. With Cadmus, Acusilaus, and Pherecydes, Herodotus may have been acquainted, but there is nothing to show that he was. With Hecatæus the case is different. We have the best of authority—that of Herodotus himself—for believing that he knew the works of Hecatæus. In two places he refers to him by name, and quotes his genealogies. Elsewhere he refers, in all probability, to him, but does not mention his name; as when he ridicules people who draw maps of the world and put a mathematically circular Oceanus round it, without knowing anything about it; or when he condemns the theory of the Nile flowing out of the Oceanus, as having no basis in facts. From these passages it seems clear that Herodotus had only a poor opinion of Hecatæus. But according to Porphyry, Herodotus was indebted to Hecatæus for a good deal of his book on Egypt; and this leads us to the third point which we have to consider in connection with the credibility of Herodotus—his honesty.

If Herodotus borrowed without acknowledgment from Hecatæus, he was, according to modern notions, guilty of literary dishonesty; and if he tried to pass off the matter thus borrowed as the result of his own observation or inquiry, he is an untrustworthy historian. The passages specified by Porphyry as borrowed are those about the phœnix, the hippopotamus, and the method of hunting crocodiles. These passages apparently are intended by Herodotus to be regarded as the result of his own observation and of his own inquiries from the natives; as therefore, we have not a single fragment by Hecatæus bearing on these passages, and as Porphyry is our only authority—and we do not even know him at first hand—for this plagiarism, it becomes necessary to inquire what Porphyry could know about it. We learn from Eusebius that Porphyry, in discussing the question of plagiarism, accused Herodotus, along with Menander, Hyperides, Ephorus, Theopompous, Hellanicus, and others, and quoted in support of his accusation a work on the "thefts" of Herodotus by a certain Pollio. Now Porphyry himself is of very late date; he flourished about A.D. 270, and Pollio probably was very little earlier than Porphyry. In the next place, in the time of Athenæus, about A.D. 180, and of Arrian, about A.D. 100, there were spurious works in circulation under the name of Hecatæus. Further, we learn from Athenæus that in the time of Callimachus, about B.C. 250, these spurious works were already in circulation. It becomes therefore probable that Pollio, like Arrian and Athenæus, had the spurious works of Hecatæus before him, and we may suppose that between Herodotus and the spurious Hecatæus there was sufficient resemblance to make it probable that the later author copied from his predecessor; but we have no ground for believing that the spurious Hecatæus is the earlier author. On the contrary, it seems more probable that the spurious

Hecatæus was partly made out of materials taken from Herodotus. We may, therefore, reasonably on the whole say, although there is no certainty to be attained either way, Porphyry's charge of plagiarism rests on unsatisfactory testimony.

The speeches, *e.g.* those of Artabanus and Xerxes, or of the Persian conspirators, are not historically true; but no one would think of accusing Herodotus *therefore* of dishonesty in inserting them. It was natural to the Greek to throw into the lively form of dialogue or debate the considerations which moved, or were supposed to have moved, the agents in historical events; and it was as unnecessary for the historian to warn his fellow-Greeks that the speeches were his own inferences from what facts he knew, as it is for a modern historian to give a similar warning as to the motives which—in the confidence of knowledge—he feels justified in ascribing, though they are but inferences, to historical personages. And when Herodotus repeats with asseveration that the speech he ascribed to Otanes was, whatever some Greeks might think, actually delivered, he means that the grounds he has for inferring the delivery of some such speech were quite convincing to his mind. In one or two places in the book on Egypt, Herodotus says that he went to Thebes, and even as far as Elephantine. But it seems quite clear that in reality he never went to either place. As, therefore, in one passage the MS. authority for the statement in question is doubtful, and in the other the statement seems to have little connection with the context; and as both statements are in ludicrous contradiction to what Herodotus himself says, we seem justified in following Professor Sayce in striking them out.

To sum up, then, the argument for the credibility of Herodotus: his impartiality and honesty in the matter of Greek history seem beyond doubt. With regard to his journeys, a suspicion has been cast upon him, but not successfully, that he was more than liable to the infirmity which is often imputed to travellers when telling their tales. In capacity he was rather above than below the standard of his age. But his means of information were poor. In the case of his Greek history, his information, though the best at his command, was only oral testimony. In the case of his Oriental history, even when he met trustworthy informants, as the priest of Neith at Sais, or Zopyrus the son of Megabyzus, he was entirely at the mercy of his interpreter, and his Oriental history therefore is that of the dragoman, not of the monuments.

T.R. Glover (essay date 1924)

SOURCE: "The Story and the Book," in *Herodotus*, University of California Press, 1924, pp. 37-75.

[*In the following essay, Glover provides an overview* of the History, *discussing the development of Herodotus's methods, his goals as an historian, and his use of written and oral sources.*]

I

It is not often we are in a position to know how the impulse came to a great artist to produce what has proved to be his masterpiece. Probably, as a rule it comes after long preparation, which has been less conscious than instinctive. The subject drew him; he thought much upon it; then one day he saw it in a new way, and wondered, and then perhaps suddenly realized how intensely it suited him, how much of his work was done already; he would finish it. But in working it out, he found he had only begun his work, and it must all be done again; new views broke in upon him, he saw fresh implications, deeper significance; and his task grew under his hand. And then he had to re-learn how to handle it, to experiment with method and approach, to discover or to develop the one style in which he could make all tell—the "inevitable" style. One imagines that somehow so Herodotus came to write his masterpiece. We have seen already how much there was in his situation, his environment and life at Halicarnassus to lead him on to his great theme and to enable him to see it in its true setting of the world. He "wished to know," he "wondered"; and he became a historian.

A parallel may illustrate his case. "The surprising nature of the events which I have undertaken to relate," says a later Greek historian,

> is in itself sufficient to challenge and stimulate the attention of every one, old or young, to the study of my work. Can any one be so trifling or idle as not to care to know by what means and under what kind of polity, almost the whole inhabited world was conquered and brought under the dominion of the single city of Rome, and that within a period of not quite fifty-three years. . . . It will be a useful and worthy task to discover why it is that the Romans conquer and carry off the palm from their enemies in all the operations of war, that we may not put it all down to Fortune and congratulate them on their good luck, as vulgar minds would, but may know the true causes.

So writes Polybius of a story as wonderful if not so romantic as the Persian War. He too has wondered and wished to know, but he wrote at a later day, and with an older mind than the ever young Herodotus. It is one of the greatest losses in *History* that it was so, and that the great gifts and powerful mind of Polybius lacked the supreme gift of charm. Still the parallel will serve.

Landward or seaward, whichever way he looked, there lay the region of wonder for Herodotus. The seamen about the harbour, the traders in the agora, all spoke of strange lands over the hills and far away, of strange men and animals, and other manners and customs, of great deeds and splendid adventures. Story-telling ran in the family blood, and Herodotus was a *logopoios* from the cradle; he told the tales again to his brother Theodorus; to his mother and father, to his schoolfellows, and went again to the haven and the market for more stories. He was one of the world's great listeners, and the best of them turn story-tellers; the bright eyes flashed as the point came, and the story-teller at Halicarnassus talked more and more to the boy. "You Greeks are always young; you are always boys at heart," said the Egyptian priest to Solon in Plato's tale; and it was true. It was autobiography in Plato; and it is confirmed by the great story-tellers, Homer, Herodotus, Walter Scott, Dumas, the tellers of tales "without psychology," as the old Englishwoman said of Shakespeare, great, big, genial natures too full of zest and vitality to analyse, but with the boy's quick instinct for life.

Over the hills and far away! What would Alexander have attempted but for that fever at Babylon? To add Europe to Asia? the British Isles to Europe? "I cannot really conjecture," writes Arrian, "and I do not care to guess. One thing I think I can be sure of; it would have been nothing small or mean, nor would Alexander have rested quiet, but would have pressed on, onward into the unknown." "There were many great things," says Herodotus in much the same vein of Cyrus, "that uplifted him and drove him forward; first of all, it was born in him."

It was born in that Greek race to want to know, to wonder, and to range the world. There lay Cos full in view, two hours' sail away, and all the Cyclades were out beyond it, each with a tale to tell, and the mainland of Greece. Farther off lay the lands of wonder, Scythia where feathers fell from the sky, and away beyond it were eaters of men and men with goat's feet and men who slept for six months—tales which travel might lead a man to doubt, "credible to another, to me not"; and southward lay Egypt, true enough, where the one river overflowed instead of drying up, and the lizards grew to the size of nightmares; and eastward "all the fairest things are in the ends of the earth." "If there were such darling things as old Chaucer sings," wrote Charles Lamb to a great Cambridge explorer, "I would up behind you on the Horse of Brass, and frisk off for Prester John's country. But these are all tales." "I wanted to know," and when Lygdamis was gone and the Halicarnassians showed no wish to keep their patriot at home, he sailed away to learn. And probably, quite apart from the wonders of the world, the greatest of all stories was calling him. Some have fancied that considerable parts of his book were originally meant to be a part of a geography, and were afterwards incorporated in his history. So critics will conjecture, forgetting Homer's ways and the aptness of Geography to Tragedy which Aeschylus saw, forgetting Herodotus

himself, one thinks, who was an artist all through, and left it to Diodorus and Suidas to "incorporate," and, whatever digressions his story sought saw to it that nothing was in it but what belonged to it. No! Sooner or later, he realized that all the calls were one call—the call of the greatest story in the world. Homer had heard the same call, though it was a different story.

II

"What Herodotus of Halicarnassus [some manuscripts read "of Thurii"] has learnt by inquiry is here set forth," so his **History** begins, "in order that so the memory of the past may not be blotted out from among men by time, and that great and marvellous deeds done by Greeks and barbarians may not lack fame, least of all the cause for which they warred with one another." After a page or two of tales told by Persians, he says, and by Phoenicians to explain the ancient feud of East and West, "for my own part," he continues

> I will not say that it befel so or otherwise; but him whom I know myself to have begun wrong deeds against the Greeks, him I will name and then go on with my story speaking of cities of men [a Homeric phrase from the very beginning of the Odyssey] small and great alike. For many cities which of old were great have become small, and those that were great in my time were in other days small. I know that human prosperity never continues steadfast, so I will make mention alike of both.

Then he starts with Croesus, initiator of evil deeds against the Greeks, and his very good friend long before he says his last word to Cambyses.

He wants to know how the war arose and how they fought it through. He was not a practical soldier, he had had no personal experience of war, Mr. Grundy tells us, and was eminently unmilitary. The struggle with Lygdamis was fought out in the streets of what we should call a little country town, a smaller affair than the revolutions of Paris; and to hold a barricade or storm a little palace is a different thing from managing an army and a navy acting together. The hugeness of the task that Xerxes imposed upon his admirals and generals in the main escaped Herodotus; he misreads his sources, he does not take in naval language, and in manoeuvres ashore he misses the object of tactics, he fails to see the real strategy, and once he drops two whole days out of his story of a big movement. Yet he took pains to talk with men who had fought the actions; Mr. Grundy holds that he drew his stories of Artemisium and Plataea from men who had been present, but who did not know the plans of the commanders. He travelled over the ground of the great march and of the famous actions, and Mr. Grundy once and again remarks his great accuracy in description; at Thermopylae, at Plataea,—"there can be no real question that he visited both places, and, not merely that, but that his examination of them was extremely careful." It is true that he slews the pass of Thermopylae round through a quarter of the compass, speaking of the east end of it as the south end, but at all events it was the Greek end and he did not confuse it with the Persian. He missed the point of the combined work of fleet and army on both sides in the movement from the north to the south end of the Euripus, as probably many of the hoplites themselves did, and many perhaps of the sailors. But important as actions are, the history of a war is more than the story of its battles, even when they are as important and tremendous as Thermopylae, Salamis, and Plataea.

"My story was looking for additions," he says; and his real interest comes out in them. Aeschylus does not precisely explain his purpose in writing his *Persians;* he lets the play tell the spectator or reader, who may miss it or hit it. Herodotus does not unfold his design and discuss his own outlooks with the length of a Polybius,—to whom be no disrespect! for his mind has a real affinity with Polybius, though he is a greater artist and conceals his art better. Can any one be so trifling or so idle as not to care to know how Greece and Persia came to fight, the politics, the natures, and the minds that brought about the conflict or were involved in it? He does not theorize offhand in our modern way and call it all inevitable; the Athenians perhaps need not have been "humbugged" by Aristagoras into sending those twenty ships which "were a beginning of evils for Greeks and for barbarians." Nor will he call it all fortune; the hand of God was in it, as we shall see later on. Was it all avoidable? Was it all inevitable? It will, at all events, be a useful task to discover who and what manner of people the combatants were, and how they looked at life; and life, as one looks into it, proves very complex, very manifold, and if you want to understand it, you must know it very well and know it all round; and the story grows in depth and breadth. He goes to see the countries as well as the spots concerned, and there are no marked lines to be drawn on the Mediterranean, and even mountain ranges are not very definite or difficult lines on the land, however abrupt they may look on a map. One land involves another land; one people more means other tribes on its frontiers; his intellectual curiosity is as compelling and as universal as Alexander's; and it is all relevant to his story. "He did not look on history as formed in a vacuum."

Nor did he look upon it, in our modern way, as chiefly composed of abstract nouns: of tendencies, and popular opinions, and economic pressures, and the circumstances of the time. Lygdamis was not driven out by circumstances, though circumstances did help Athens to get rid of Hippias; no, in both cases some man had to get comrades and do it, an "Archibald Bell-the-Cat." It was Themistocles who precipitated the fight at Salamis; all the circumstances were against it, and if it had been left to tendency or, in English, drift, that battle would not have been fought. In heroes of one kind and another, in men, Herodotus is as much interested as Carlyle; and, heroes or villains, he loves to watch men. What sort of men, then, did Greece and Persia produce? And the answer is, all sorts of men; Persia, grandees who could jump overboard and drown to save their King, and Greece, commanders who could vote to a man, every one of them, that Themistocles was second best among them. These types the races produced and all the variety that makes a world.

Students of Thucydides have remarked how he will deliberately sum up a situation in a speech, gathering up the ideas that were generally in the air and the things that would be said,—"putting into the mouth of each speaker the sentiments proper to the occasion, expressed as I thought he would be likely to express them, while I endeavoured, as nearly as I could, to give the general purport of what was actually said." What Thucydides did upon reflection, we may possibly say that Herodotus did by instinct. Where in Thucydides' pages some Athenians, who were present for other business, came forward on invitation and spoke, in the story of Herodotus we are more behind the scenes and in the counsels of the men who put the things through; and of course there was no reporter present, no maker of *précis;* but Herodotus, a born story-teller, like Elia uses the first person, and dialogue with him is neither deception nor art but nature. Ancient and modern alike have found the speeches he gives easier to read than those of Thucydides. In a modern historian his method, the method of either of them, unless the modern turned Thucydides' speeches steadily into a series of vague third persons, would be intolerable. The daily press stands between us and the real agents in any political or international transaction. "Current opinion in France is that the Germans' attitude, etc." is the language of today, and in huge nations the real forces operate only in this muffled way. In a small Greek town it was different; . . . there was talk indeed and anonymous rumour enough in the agora, but when the decisive thing was done, it was the speech or act of some very definite person whom everybody knew. In a despotism like Persia, the circle in which policies were decided was a small one, too; and shrewd observers, and there were plenty among the Persians, could know, or pretty certainly guess, where the responsibility lay for one act and another of the Great King.

Men and women are always talking, intriguing, reflecting, in the books of Herodotus, and to mingle with them as they talk is one way of understanding History. To understand Canada and Arabia there are two ways open to the modern: one is to amass histories and other books, and Board of Trade returns, statistics of lunacy, illiteracy, wheat production, railroads; another is to ride on the trains or the camels, as may be, and live as

Doughty did in Arabia or Martin Allerdale Grainger in lumber camps, and assimilate the people unconsciously. It is well to know how many miles of railroad a country has, it is well for democrats to reflect that 94 per cent of the population of India is illiterate, and the percentage far higher among Hindus than among Christians; but to know how the mind of Greek or Persian, of Scot or Irishman, will instinctively react to circumstances, is a higher and more valuable knowledge. But will not a novel, or a series of novels, tell you this as well? It might, if written by a man of genius. In the case before us, happily, the man of genius wanted to know, not what might happen, but what did happen, and was anxious that great deeds that stirred wonder should never be blotted out by time. He immersed himself in the actual as far as he could get it. Men did not always tell him the truth; men are horribly careless, as Thucydides grumbled, they do not discriminate, they are too ready to accept old traditions or inaccurate statements of the present and to pass them on, to form wrong opinions as to the greatness of the war that absorbs them, to lack historical perspective, to see one side of a question, one facet of an event and forget all else. Herodotus is not so incisive in his criticism of his informants and predecessors, but in his long travels, or perhaps earlier, he grew aware of the human weaknesses that Thucydides pillories. "The task was a laborious one" says Thucydides. "I wanted to know, so I went to Tyre" says Herodotus.

Herodotus travelled further afield than Thucydides—far further. His subject was a larger one, and involved the whole world. A man who will try to get the whole world on to his canvas will make mistakes of his own and fail at times to see where he is deceived. But, broadly, mistakes in detail do not matter much. Herodotus might have been more accurate about the votes of the Spartan kings, but there are two much more fundamental questions to ask about his picture of Sparta. Are those sketches of her kings, of Cleomenes, of Demaratus, of Leonidas true, are they individual, are they alive? Only one answer to that question is likely. They are intensely alive; they are individual; they have every appearance of being as true as a foreigner not contemporary with them could hope to get them. And the second question is this: Is he drawing the real Sparta? Certain things are plain here; he is not idealizing Sparta as Plutarch did; he is not attacking Sparta as Isocrates did; the Sparta which he draws is substantially the Sparta drawn by Thucydides and by Xenophon, and his picture is confirmed by Isocrates and by Plutarch, the critic and the panegyrist. In short, he got the kings alive on to his pages and he gives you the Sparta that was really there,—fighting her way to Tegea, conquering the Thyreatis, jealous of Argos, well-disciplined, invincible, mother of men, and just a little slow.

Let us take two more illustrations. A great deal of criticism, ancient and modern, has been directed to Herodotus' accounts of Persia and Egypt; we shall have to return to these, but for the moment, let us note that Adolf Erman the Egyptologist calls Herodotus "an indefatigable and careful observer," who "observed exactly those things which are of special interest to us." Spiegel says at once that his account of Persia as it stands no one will take for historical, but it cannot be denied that it has historical traits; taken as a whole it is of high value, for of all the legendary accounts that the ancients have preserved from the time of the Persian Empire, none is so thoroughly Iranian as his. It will be remembered that for centuries the story of the Achaemenids virtually rested on the statements of Herodotus alone, and that in 1837 his narrative received startling confirmation from Darius' hand upon the Rock of Behistun deciphered by Henry Rawlinson. With the judgment of a later Rawlinson we may leave this phase of our subject. "On the whole," writes H. G. Rawlinson, "the account given by Herodotus of the Indian satrapy is careful and accurate. It is no doubt drawn from the lost narrative of Skylax; or from first-hand evidence—probably from accounts given by Persian officials who had served in India."

Burke could not, he said, draw an indictment against a nation, and national portraits are as hard to draw. Mrs. Trollope and Charles Dickens and Münsterberg have not altogether satisfied Americans, nor perhaps even Lord Bryce and Goldwin Smith. It is not criticism to ask the miraculous of a human writer, to expect the impossible. If it can be shown that he used to the full, that he transcended, the means and opportunities that lay to his hand, that by some inspired combination of hard work and intuition he can re-create the foreign or the ancient scene and give it you with the people talking, planning, thinking, and emphatically alive all the time; if, in addition, his honesty is such as to enable you to check his statements and sometimes from his data to seize a truer interpretation of his reported facts than he has given; if throughout he is human and makes humanity mean more and more to you as you live with him; then he has surely some strong claim to be called a historian.

III

How he was able to achieve so great a triumph is our next inquiry. It has been of late a favourite exercise with scholars of a certain type to try to discover how great books came to be organic wholes. We are told on ancient authority that Virgil drafted his *Aeneid* and then wrote here and there as fancy led him, trusting at last to give two or three years' revision to the whole and so to remove inconsistencies and temporary passages that served as scaffolding; then can we trace his movements in his half-revised poem? Or can we decide what Thucydides in each case means by "this war,"—the whole of the Peloponnesian War or the so-called "Archidamian War," its first ten years; did he write "this war" and then that war in Sicily, and then join them somehow with book v and prolong them with book viii? If he did, he had the whole under his hand all along, says Eduard Meyer, and is surely right in saying so. A strong attempt has been made to prove that Herodotus began with the expedition of Xerxes and wrote what are now his seventh, eighth and ninth books, and then expanded gradually his design to include the world and last of all Egypt. A contrast is drawn between the piety of the ninth book and the tone of religious speculation in the second, which seems to some critics to imply psychologically that the second book is later. Psychology might surely be used equally well to imply the opposite. If one man inquires more freely in religion as he grows older, another is more impressed with the hand of God in human affairs. To this we shall have to return, but we may remark that the second book shows greater caution in its references to the gods than is sometimes noticed. There are other suggestions as to evidence upon the order of writing, but perhaps the inquiry is not one to give very certain results nor one that is supremely interesting. That his conception of his theme grew as he handled it, that what he eventually left us is a book of far larger design and vastly richer content than what he perhaps planned at first, we can readily believe; "my tale sought additions from the start." The real wonder is that any man was able to gather so much, and to give so much, without losing his thread; and the wonder grows as we consider the means at his disposal.

Later Greek historians drew largely upon the books of their predecessors, and it is clear enough that Herodotus used written sources. The list of Persian satrapies, for instance, in his third book must evidently have come from some document; that is generally agreed, and perhaps the Royal Road did too. We know, for he tells us, that there were great collections of oracles; perhaps they were copied out together; and it seems highly likely that Herodotus had access to something of the sort, quite probably at Delphi. Lists of priests and of archons were publicly kept, we know, and events were dated by them; and there may have been books of genealogies, though this is perhaps doubtful. There were also geographers, or at least there was Hecataeus, for Herodotus quotes him now and then by name and is supposed to refer to him when he uses the anonymous plural "the Ionians." He also mentions Skylax, as we saw; and other names of men who wrote books at or about his date are known. Charon of Lampsacus wrote a history of Persia down to 492 B.C., which may have been published after 465-4 B.C. Dionysius of Miletus wrote another down to Marathon and the death of Darius. Dionysius of Halicarnassus, centuries later, indicates that their style was somewhat bare if clear and concise. Professor Bury traces their work to the impulse of Hecataeus. There was also a Greek history of Lydia by a Lydian Xanthus. "In any case," says Professor Sayce,

there must have been Greek translations of Persian and Phoenician books as well as of official documents from which Herodotus derived his statements; and the fact that they were translations may explain why he always speaks of his Oriental authorities in the plural. . . . His chief aim was to use their [his predecessors'] materials without letting the fact be known. We must not forget that although there were no publishers or printing-presses in the age of Herodotus, public libraries were not altogether unknown; as the library of Pisistratus at Athens and that of Polycrates at Samos. Pericles at Athens was surrounded by literary men, and books were at any rate cheaper than travelling. He pilfered freely and without acknowledgement; he assumed a knowledge he did not possess; he professed to derive information from personal experience and eye witnesses which really came from the very sources he seeks to disparage and supersede.

It would be difficult to parallel such a tissue of absurdities and false assumptions, all so unworthy of a scholar. For the library of Pisistratus at Athens, the rather confused story of some connexion of the tyrant with the standard text of Homer, and Herodotus' account of Hippias' collection of oracles, are the only warrants. Greek poets came to that court and to Polycrates, but that does not warrant the assertion of public libraries. Pericles was indeed surrounded by men of letters, but that proves nothing as to Charon and Xanthus and the rest. It is a pure assumption to say that books were cheaper than travel; yes, if they are in the shop down the street in quantity, but it might today be cheaper to go to Mexico than to buy Lord Kingsborough's volumes. To say there must have been translations is to beg the question. Greeks did not care for such works; they neglected Latin literature very largely in later days, and Manetho and Berossus were apparently dull, flimsy, and inaccurate, and wrote long after Herodotus. Can any one name a Persian or Phoenician author, unless it be Zeno or some Stoic disciple? The one point on which any evidence at all can be brought is the relation of Herodotus to Hecataeus.

As to Hecataeus the evidence is of two sorts. Herodotus knew the work of Hecataeus and alluded to him, so much is certain. That he used him, but rejected his theories, may be inferred from Herodotus' pages, but it is an inference. That Herodotus took verbally from Hecataeus his descriptions of the crocodile hunt and the hippopotamus, without acknowledgment but with all the errors, is a statement that rests on the assumption that those who first made it knew for a fact that it was the genuine Hecataeus which they held in their hands. It is quoted by Eusebius from Porphyry. The authority of Porphyry is not high, and it is conjectured that he used a book bearing the name of Hecataeus, which other ancient authorities knew and doubted. "So," writes Athenaeus, "so says Hecataeus of Miletus in his Description of Asia, if the book is the genuine work of the historian; for Callimachus entitles it that of the Islander; whoever made the book then, this is what he says." The Islander seems not very easy to identify. Arrian, the historian of Alexander, remarks that "both Herodotus and Hecataeus the *logopoios* (or whoever wrote the book about Egypt whether it was some one else or Hecataeus) both of them call Egypt the gift of the river." Eratosthenes, the rival of Callimachus and his successor in the great library of Alexandria, took the book to be genuine. But it is interesting to note that for the great libraries of Ptolemy and of the Attalids (as well as for prophetic purposes) lost books were found. Galen, the great physician, says: "In the time of the Attalids and Ptolemies when they were rivals for the possession of books, the forging of titles and matter began among people who for money offered the kings the writings of famous men." Elsewhere he repeats his statement, "when men who brought them writings of some ancient writer began to get money, then indeed they brought them in great numbers with false inscriptions." It may be, as Müller suggests, that part of the volume was genuine and the rest of it fake; and that Porphyry made or borrowed his statement on the strength of a book on Egypt, partly composed of Herodotus' own material. Milton was once convicted of plagiarism in a similar way, on the evidence of passages taken from a Latin translation of *Paradise Lost* and attributed (with some slight adjustment) to earlier poets. Aristotle at any rate quoted the passages supposed to be stolen without allusion to the theft. At all events in the 380 fragments attributed to Hecataeus there is not the least allusion to the Persian wars properly so called, or the Ionian revolt. Many of them are mere names of places quoted from him by lexicographers. Professor Bury counts him one of the founders of geographical science and associated with the birth of history and, in a sense, of rationalism—a bold assertion in view of the scanty evidence. One cannot but recall the question of Aphrodite in the Greek epigram,

Pray, how did Praxiteles see what he shows?

But, in all this as in many other things, the line of sense is taken by Eduard Meyer. Herodotus, he says, knew and used his predecessors; not to have done so would have been a reproach, and indeed unthinkable. If Xanthus' *Lydiaca* or Hellanicus' earlier works were already published (which can neither be proved nor refuted), why should Herodotus trouble about works of detail when for years past he had collected material himself and had achieved a complete picture of history? How anybody can speak of his plagiarizing from Hecataeus, Dr. Meyer does not understand. One is tempted to add that the habit, at one time, spread among scholars, like an infectious disease, of attributing everything possible, whoever the writer, to a neglected and lost predecessor to whom should be the praise; and the evidence of the casual reader in antiquity was often accepted, without inquiry as to his capacity or right to form an opinion.

Herodotus probably had occasional opportunities to consult collections of legends and myths, of traditions about migration and colonization, the settlement and foundation of cities, of pedigrees and oracles (as we saw), perhaps even of *bons mots*. When Dr. Macan adds army and navy lists, one may hesitate without disrespect, and concede Simonides' epigrams and the *Persians* of Aeschylus with some readiness, and, with a little uncertainty, memoirs. Nehemiah and Ion of Chios were writing memoirs in his day, but memoirs of the previous generation have to be proved, and the attempt to saddle Dicaios with memoirs is not generally counted successful. Thus, broadly speaking, all the literature (the poets excepted) which he may have seen—for in that age still more than in our own postwar days no one can well dogmatize about the speedy circulation or availableness of any book, a fact sometimes forgotten—all the accessible literature was probably on the whole rather dull; and Herodotus is not often called dull by good judges. So we may take it that, whatever he found in books, he brought something of his own, as Shakespeare is allowed to have added something to the Hamlet of Saxo Grammaticus. One question may be asked here but hardly answered: What system or method had he for making all he read (and all he heard, we shall add) available? Did he take interminable notes, in an age before paper? Then, how did he carry them about with him? What library can he have taken from Naucratis to Tyre, from the Black Sea to Italy? Weight and bulk have to be considered as factors in the question of his literary indebtedness. Little doubt he read everything he could; we have already seen something of his acquaintance with Greek literature. The problem of the notebooks remains if we limit him to oral sources. In any case his memory must have been a remarkable one, full of minute detail, and amazingly orderly.

But before we go further, we have to recall the monuments of which he speaks,—the fetters which the Spartans took to Tegea and wore there, which "in my time" were hung around the temple of Athene Alea in Tegea; the pillars of Darius, with Assyrian and Greek inscriptions, which the Byzantines used to build the altar of Artemis Orthosia; the picture hung in the Heraeum at Samos which Mandrocles, the architect, had made for himself of the bridge of boats he built for Darius; the offerings innumerable at Delphi, its works of art, and other gifts "worth seeing." "I myself saw" pillars set up by Sesostris in Syria;

also there are in Ionia two figures of this man carven in rock, one on the road from Ephesus to Phocaea, and the other on that from Sardis to Smyrna. In both places there is a man of a height of five ells and a half cut in relief, with a spear in his right hand and a bow in his left, and the rest of his equipment answering thereto; for it is both Egyptian and Ethiopian; and right across the breast from one shoulder to the other there is carven a writing in the

Egyptian sacred character, saying: I myself won this land with the might of my shoulders. There is nothing here to show who he is and whence he comes, but it is shown elsewhere.

Professor Garstang accepts the Hittite origin of the monuments on the pass of Kara Bel, and it is generally conceded today; the conical cap and the high boots turning up at the toe and other features connect them with similar figures at Boghaz-Keui. Herodotus puts spear and bow in the wrong hands, and could not, Dr. Garstang holds, himself have seen the monuments: "there is just enough general accuracy in his account to identify the monuments, and enough discrepancy to make it apparent that he had not visited them himself." It will be noted that he does not claim to have seen them. His theory of an Egyptian origin is proof of limits to his knowledge of seventh and eighth century Asia, limits which our own knowledge only very recently surmounted.

But probably the great mass of his information was gathered from living men. Three he names—three only—Archias, the Spartan of Pitane, who told him of the siege of Samos; Tymnes, the deputy for Ariapeithes, who gave him information as to the pedigree of Anacharsis; and Thersander of Orchomenos, who told the tale of the banquet which Attaginos gave to Mardonius and the Persians, and how the Persian who shared his couch told him in Greek his ill forebodings for the battle of Plataea and the doom from God that no man could avert. The last is the best, and illustrative of much, of the mind of Herodotus, and of the difficulty of language overcome as a rule by the foreigner and not by the Greek. Herodotus, it has been said, was "at his weakest as linguist." He discovered, he says with pride, what the Persians had not noticed—that their names ("which are of a piece with their persons and their magnificence") all end in the letter S. They did in Greek, but the King whom Greeks and others tried to write down as Xerxes and Ahasuerus, was in Persia called Khshayârshâ—sibilant enough but fatal for Herodotus' rule. He also connected Artaxerxes with Xerxes, which the Persians did not, for they called it Artakhshathra. Wherever Herodotus went, the foreigner had to talk Greek, and he seems to have been very glad to do it, with such a listener.

A good deal of interesting research has been done as to the Persian friends of Herodotus. He was evidently highly satisfied as to the value of his Persian information, which was very various and not always, as he says, consistent, but which was far too much to be due to a single source. Three distinct groups have been noted. When Herodotus tells of the capture of Babylon by the aid of Zopyrus "son of that Megabyzus who was one of the seven destroyers of the Magian," who mutilated himself and was received as a deserter by the Babylonians, he ends his story with a little more about the family: "son of this

Zopyrus was Megabyzus who commanded in Egypt against the Athenians and their allies; and son of this Megabyzus was Zopyrus who deserted to Athens from the Persians." The family was one of high distinction and of independent habits. Megabyzus the second himself revolted from Artaxerxes, was reconciled, banished and restored, and he appears in spite of the great blow he dealt to Athens in Egypt to have been head of the Hellenizing party in Persia. Hence the flight of Zopyrus the second was not a freak, but an act not out of tune with his family's spirit. The date of the desertion may have been in 440 B.C. when the war party in Persia was in the ascendant, and it is easy to think that Zopyrus and the historian met. At all events Herodotus is able to tell us that Megabyzus the first, when the Magian was slain, stood for oligarchy. He knows the history of the house for four generations, and it may be to them that he owes his knowledge of what the Persians say "who do not desire to make a fine tale of Cyrus"; Cyrus, whom alone, in Darius' opinion, Zopyrus did not surpass for his service to the Persians.

There was another Persian house which Herodotus evidently knew, a house as significant or more so in Greek history. He tells us a rather surprising number of things about Artabazus, son of Pharnaces, and his part in Xerxes' expedition—his capture of Olynthos, his shrewd advice to the king to bribe the Greek leaders, his dislike of Mardonius being left to command in Greece and his forecast of Plataea, and his adroit escape from Thessaly after the disaster. From Thucydides we learn of the later history of this man, who was given the satrapy of Daskyleion to promote the intrigues of King Pausanias. He was succeeded in turn by his son Pharnabazus I and his grandson Pharnaces II; and Xenophon draws a pleasant picture of the fifth generation, Pharnabazus II, a lover of hunting and gardens, a great gentleman, certainly a man, perhaps something of a great man.

The third Persian noble family was originally Greek. In or about 491 B.C. King Demaratus was exiled from Sparta. Ninety years later Xenophon alludes to his descendant, with the old Herakleid name of Procles, and a brother Eurysthenes, more than once intervening in the fortunes of the Ten Thousand. King Darius gave Demaratus land and cities, and Xenophon found the family established near the Dardanelles and in possession of Pergamon, Teuthrania, and Halisarna. It is natural to suppose that they had been there throughout, and the abundance of reference in the pages of Herodotus to Demaratus suggests that Herodotus knew them, and knew them well. The full tale of the exile and his generous reception, of his acute suggestion to Xerxes at the critical time of his succession, of his frequent talks with the Great King whom he very frankly informed as to Spartan character, correctly predicting in the face of Xerxes' incredulity that the Spartans would fight at Thermopylae, of his advice to Xerxes as to how the Greek fleet might be broken up at once and safely—advice not taken, and the king's defence of him against Persian criticism; where else could all this have been so familiar and so interesting as in his own family? Who but his own kin could have known, or cared to invent, the story of Demaratus' part in the palace intrigues on Darius' death?

Now let us try to translate all this into life—three noble houses and a guest from Halicarnassus—and the words of Callimachus the poet come back, when he speaks of his friend from that old city: "I remembered how often we two saw the sun set as we talked, O Halicarnassian guest; and yet thy nightingale-notes live, nor shall death that plunders all lay hand on them." Herodotus was not, like Heraclitus, a poet, of course; but who can doubt of the rest? The bright-eyed traveller, with a boy's zest and a man's quick mind, full of travel, full of tales, and always at leisure to hear old legends and old family traditions, anything and everything that bore on his great themes, the old War and the eternal nature of man—who would not be glad to know him and talk with him, and tell so eager a listener the best there was to tell? How else did he ever amass the boundless store from which he chooses what to give us? Think of the memory, the interest, the perennial freshness of the mind that gathered not alone the traditions of three noble houses but of all Persia and all the world, and remembered and fitted new detail into its right place as he got it. Take the story of the physician Democedes; where did he get it? All in a piece in the west, seventy years after Democedes' day, or some of it in Italy, some in Samos, and some in Persia? Who in Croton would know, as he knew, the influence of Queen Atossa? For queens live and die, and distant democracies will know little of them, and little of eastern palace etiquette. Who told him of the Persian registers, who gave up leisure to inform him of Persian life and thought, politics, history and religion, the spread of Persia eastward to the Panjāb, north into Scythia, to the Aegaean, to Egypt and Cyrene? Not three noble houses alone; his informants and friends must have been legion, all over the world; and what one said in Heliopolis tallied or clashed with what he had heard in Babylon or Byzantion, and he noticed it, as minds of that sort do, without recourse to notes. A little discreet use of the imagination, with a map marked to show the points Herodotus reached, will do much toward a real sense of his achievement and of the powers it implies.

To some such friendly discussion with a Persian, Professor Bury refers those early chapters of the first book of Herodotus, which strike a modern reader so oddly. What have Europa and Helen to do with the Persian war? "As for Europe," he says elsewhere,

> it is not clear who gave the name, unless we are to say that the land took its name from the Tyrian Europa and before that was nameless as the other

lands. But she is plainly of Asian origin and never came to this land which the Greeks now call Europe, but only from Phoenice to Crete and from Crete to Lycia. Now that so much is said, let it suffice; we will use the ordinary names.

Similarly, as we have already seen, after recording this exchange of alleged precedents, he turns off from what Persian and Phoenician talk to tell what he knows.

IV

Now to sum up what we have reached. We saw him started on his travels and his inquiries by the call of the greatest story in the world, and we have seen how the whole world is gradually taken up into its greatest story, how race after race is involved, and how, like others who inquire and research, he finds his outlook grow and his views change. Whatever his earlier feelings as to Persian power, in the days when he hated Lygdamis and his rule—and it must be noted again that he does not tell his own story and that his reticence extends to his contemporaries and to things familiar to them—he saw more to admire in the Persians as he knew them better and he found them more and more interesting. "No writer," says Mr. Sikes, "is more free from prejudice." He wrote avowedly that the great and marvellous deeds of barbarians—not "Greek victories and barbarian defeats," as Lucian re-modelled it—might never be lost. He obviously felt the fascination of Egypt; but where did he not find interest and friendship? What does it mean, this charm that one finds in race after race? An ancient writer, if we except Polybius and his kind, does not analyse his own work for the reader, but we may recognize throughout Herodotus his response to the challenge of the foreigner, an appeal that many good patriots never feel. Plutarch called him in angry criticism "a lover of barbarians." The world is not all Greek; a great deal of the best of it is not Greek at all, nor even Anglo-Saxon, and Herodotus' work is largely a study of the history of civilization, the contact and collision of the progressive types that go to develope the mind of the world. Long before Freeman he realizes the unity of history. At a later point we shall return to his study of the foreigner and his customs good and bad,—generally interesting, rarely called bad,—his political and religious ideas, his myths and legends.

Side by side there rises the greater challenge the full effect of which we reach only in the Stoics, the challenge of nature. Men were already noting and speculating upon soils and climates and their effect on animal and human life. River and sea and desert, natural phaenomena and their causes, were growing in interest. It was perhaps a side-product of the sophistic movement. Herodotus was, as we have seen, a keen student of topography. Sometimes it bore immediately and visibly upon ordinary history, like the ebb at

Potidaea and the currents of the Propontis, or gave a local bias to industry and trade, like the swift stream of the Euphrates. But often great problems in physical geography are raised by him, as in the case of the Nile and its summer overflow. It made Egypt; that was evident about the busy river; but why should it reverse the ordinary habits of rivers and be fuller in the time of heat? What problems of wind or snow, or what not, did it involve? An unpractical problem, but to a Greek mind fascinating. We shall have later on to linger over the outer edges of the world.

But in this world most of us will agree with what Herodotus does not say but surely thinks: that Greeks are really in their variety, their restlessness, and their impossibility, the most interesting of all peoples. We shall find that of all their wonderful discoveries the most wonderful—and that puts it far beyond anything that barbarians have achieved—is the discovery of Freedom and its positive value in making men real and adding dignity and stability to political life. We must return to this, and watch with him the rise of the Greeks, and their discovery and development of Freedom; and so we shall reach the central theme of the whole book, the conflict in which this supreme achievement of Hellas was put to the test. Would it, could it, survive the attack of the best organized monarchy that the world had ever seen, would it prove equal to the strain upon it, or would it break down into anarchy and be lost? Was Law in Liberty to prove master?

These are great themes, and the parallel of Polybius has suggested to us that a great theme of unequalled interest may, like the heroes before Agamemnon, lack the inspired touch that shall bring it into every man's business and bosom. There is perhaps in every day's issue of *The Times* as much variety of old and new, near and distant, as in Herodotus; certainly no encyclopaedia but has it. Herodotus brought something more to his work than the widest range of knowledge then available of all the world, more than accuracy and the alert inquiring intellect. He was one of the great artists of Greece, so great that his instinctive art conceals itself till you look for it, and perhaps even then. One may read him over and over again, and note with surprise how much one has missed. He is an incomparable "source," as historians say. But his art is more wonderful even than his range of knowledge, and his mind and personality than his art. He is the Greek world in person, he is ancient humanity, yes! and he is Herodotus of Halicarnassus.

His avowed object in writing we have already discussed and the great purpose of his work. From time to time he speaks of his method and his plans, generally when he is conscious of some possible challenge or criticism. He will omit the native chieftains who commanded their tribes in Xerxes' levy; he is not obliged to give them, he says, his story does not re-

quire it; they were not persons who deserve mention and there were so many of them in each nation. That his story was on the lookout for additions, we have seen; and he adds accordingly a curious fact about mules in Elis, and elsewhere he says his account of Rhegians and Tarentines is an inset. He will give two or three variants of a story. He contrasts the Corinthian and the Athenian statements as to the services of Corinth at Salamis; and the former is supported by the general voice of Greece, says the historian, who is supposed to dislike Corinth and to glorify Athens. He knows more than one variant of Cyrus' early adventures and confines himself to one, or he gives a story both ways and his readers may decide which to believe. He will not tell them what they know already; Greeks are familiar with the general look of the camel, so he only adds one detail "not generally known," but admitted, it is said, by modern naturalists. Again and again he is careful to state that he does not exactly know, he could not exactly learn; he thinks, or he is of opinion; he cannot convince himself, but at any rate this is what he has heard—and sometimes this is what people say and others may believe it, he cannot himself; or he offers no opinion, his business is simply to record what he is told—though he will add "yet all things are possible," the sensible comment of the much-travelled man who has seen a good many things that clever people who stay at home would recognize at once as impossible. "How, I cannot for my part conceive," he says again, "but everything is possible in long ages." Once he says definitely that he will not mention something which he knows, being well aware that people who have not themselves visited Babylonia will not believe it. Such passages are surely overlooked by some critics of his credulity,—generally people who have not travelled and do not realize that it is often folly *not* to believe what you are told in a strange land. On the other hand, when he says categorically, as he now and then does, that he *knows,* he should surely have the credit that his general caution seems to warrant.

Otherwise, he does not discuss method or art. But it is abundantly evident that he based himself on long thought and practice; he had told tales for years before he wrote his book, and he has the tale-teller's art. He watches his listeners and (in the Greek sense) he *economizes,* he manages his tale, he cuts things out, he makes circuits, he amplifies, he digresses; and by each movement the tale is richer in colour and life, more full of feeling and intensity, or in some subtle way the humour is heightened. But he has his eyes on his audience throughout and he never loses them. Yet it may be better to say no more at this point, but to let the Greeks who came after him give us their impressions and criticisms.

V

Thucydides said he was inaccurate. He never mentions

Herodotus by name, but he makes it quite plain to whom he refers. "There are many other matters," he says,

> not obscured by time but contemporary, about which the other Hellenes are equally mistaken. For example, they imagine that the kings of Sparta in their council have not one but two votes each and that in the army of the Spartans there is a division called the Pitanate; whereas they never had anything of the sort. So little trouble do men take in the search after truth; so readily do they accept whatever comes first to hand.

He knows that Greek readers will remember that Herodotus made both of these unlucky statements, and others as bad. When Thucydides speaks of Cylon's conspiracy and its failure, he says the nine Archons were in charge, and he adds severely: "for in those days public affairs were chiefly administered by the nine Archons." The guilty Herodotus had said "the prytaneis of the naukraries" were responsible. A little before 431 B.C., he says "the island of Delos had been shaken by an earthquake for the first time within the memory of Hellenes." Herodotus had said that the Delians had reported to him that the one earthquake in their history was when Datis sailed on from them to Euboea in 490 B.C.; there had never been another before nor since that one "down to my own time." Herodotus had talked of Mnesiphilus suggesting ideas to Themistocles; but Themistocles was equal to divining the right plan by sheer force of nature, without assistance, says Thucydides. There are some other corrections of the same austere kind. But his most caustic criticism is in his most famous phrase. "Very likely the strictly historical (literally: the non-mythical) character of my narrative may be disappointing to the ear. My history is a possession for ever, not a prize composition which is heard and forgotten." "The ear"—"heard and forgotten"—and the suggestion of a show performance; is there truth then in the story that Herodotus read his history or part of it aloud in Athens, and that Anytos, whose name at least recalls the accuser of Socrates, moved for an award of ten talents to him? Plutarch quotes the story as from Diyllos, a fourth century Athenian historian. Thucydides' language would lose its sting if there had been no recitation, and he disliked carelessness, as he says. A date about 446-445 B.C. is given by Jerome for the recitation and scholars consider it possible enough. Thucydides was of age to follow the whole course of the Peloponnesian war which began in 431, and he died about 399 B.C. It would not have been a specially long life, if he was twenty or so when the recitation took place, if it did take place; and yet there are legends that he wept for emulation.

The *History* of Herodotus lasted better than Thucydides predicted. Isocrates in his *Panegyric* (which he was writing for a good while and published in 380

B.C.) wished to emphasize a sort of natural hatred between Athens and Persia, and amongst other signs of it he noted that "even where stories are concerned we linger with most pleasure over the Trojan and Persian wars, in which we can learn of their disasters. . . . I think that even Homer's poetry has greater glory, because he praised right well those who fought the barbarians." We may accept the fact both as to Homer and Herodotus, and perhaps guess other reasons. Later on, Strabo speaks contemptuously of Herodotus' geography as less reliable than Homer's; some of it, as we shall see, was very wrong, but at least once the older writer was correct against Strabo.

But the most famous of ancient attacks on Herodotus was made by Plutarch who wrote a tract on his *Malignity*. Herodotus, we are told, uses hard names when he might use kinder; he loves to introduce ill reports against peoples in wanton zest of abuse, and conversely to omit what is good about them; he prefers the worse account where there are several, and the worst explanation where the real reason is obscure; he damns with faint praise; he takes away the character of Io; he is a lover of barbarians and suggests that Greeks learnt their religion from them; he first makes Croesus a fool and then a sage; he accuses Cleisthenes of bribing the Delphian priestess; he calls the burning of Sardis the beginning of trouble, when it was a stroke for freedom; he muddles the full moon at Marathon and throws the day and the story into confusion; his style is "all twists, and nothing sound, but all about"; he bitterly slanders Thebes; Aristophanes the Boeotian says it was because he asked and failed to get money from the Thebans; in short, like his own Hippocleides he dances away the truth, and "Herodotus don't care"; "he can write and his story is pleasant, there is grace and cleverness and bloom upon his tales, . . . he charms and seduces everybody." The general verdict seems to be that Plutarch this time has written himself down an ass (unless the tract be spurious, which plea is rejected,) and that the whole thing is "a monument of critical incompetence," based on an absurd patriotism—and a false conception of history.

Halicarnassus produced after some four centuries a second historian, who, besides writing on early Italy at some length, wrote a number of essays (or letters) on Style. Dionysius deals with his townsman and commends him as against Thucydides. Herodotus chose a more attractive subject, victory rather than defeat; he showed more judgment in knowing where to begin and where to leave off, and what to put in and what to omit; he chose to vary his story in the Homeric way, copying Homer, and indeed, "if we take his book we like it to the last syllable and always wish for more," while Thucydides rarely attempts variety; and Dionysius finds Thucydides' chronology boring. Then Herodotus has the kindlier disposition, while Thucydides had a grudge against his country. Both are great writers, Herodotus the superior in character drawing and natural writing, Thucydides in pathos and a clever style; the beauty of Herodotus is bright and happy, that of Thucydides terrible.

"He chose to vary his story in the Homeric way." So also hints Longinus, a far surer and stronger critic— "Herodotus most Homeric" is his phrase. It is not the common eulogy of a historian, but let us look at it, first recalling Matthew Arnold's four notes of Homer's style: he is simple in thought, simple in language, rapid, and noble. If these terms be given the meaning that Arnold intended, they are not far from a true description of the style and mind of Herodotus. He is so simple in narrative, so easy and plain, that many readers wholly miss the clarity, with which he takes an idea, and with which he judges it. Arnold found in Homer some traits, not all, of Voltaire. Herodotus had seen more of the world than Voltaire and was less dogmatic; he was kindlier-natured; but was he really less clear? Do not the kindlier nature, the larger sympathies, the "human catholic" quality, which we all feel in him, the leisure for all mankind, the quick keen interest, suggest that the parallel with Homer is not idle? He has not Homer's zest for battle, he had seen little of fighting, except in the town streets of his home; and he did not wish to be classed with poets. Homer or some older poet invented, he supposes, the name Oceanus and brought it into his poetry, but he carried his tale into the unknown, where proof or disproof is impossible. He dismisses Greeks who have dealt in poetry and made play with forecasts; Aristeas of Proconnesus, "making poetry and possessed by Phoebus" does not convince him as to the One-Eyed; and elsewhere he gives us a caution about "trusting the Epic poets." But candour is not un-Homeric.

He writes a "book of good faith," and he can be read and known in every page of it; and that is Homeric. He takes a large canvas and he fills it, and every paragraph contributes to the general theme, as it does in the *Odyssey*. He is said to digress; but in Homer and in Herodotus every digression is centripetal; and there are historians and poets of whom that cannot be said. He loves variety and he loves a good story—and he tells a good story—as Homer does; and these are not superficial resemblances, for they rest on something fundamental, love of man and love of this world and its wonder. Both find a fascination in seafaring,—not

> the foam
> Of perilous seas, in faery lands forlorn—

No! but the real sea and the lands beyond; both are honestly charmed with Geography—word of prose for thing of poetry! They both knew the joy of the explorer better than we do, in spite of La Salle and Livingstone, heroes more fit for Homer and Herodotus than for our day. Herodotus has the Homeric impulse to

make men realize the wonder of the world he lives in, and achieves it;—to make men see the characters that he watches, and they speak their own words and go their own way in his pages as in Homer's; and you listen to them and watch them, and you like them as you read; you are won for a larger humanity, whether it is Homer who wins you or Herodotus. He loves, as Homer loves, a pageant, the marshalling of men, in all that variety of gear that expresses the variety of life and land and climate. Like Homer he rejoices in the skill of the craftsman who weaves the rich web, who works dead metal into life, who catches colour and keeps it. He loves the scene, the movement, be it scandalous as the Spartan king sitting on the glove of money, or noble as the other Spartan king in the pass, preparing to die. He is not afraid of wickedness; he saw plenty of it; and, though he never leaves you in doubt as to his mind on it, he cannot hate the sinner any more than Homer could. Are there two writers in Greek literature who stand nearer together than these two, in knowledge of men, or in that love of men which makes it their master-aim to interpret men, or in the power they have to make one proud of one's race and glad to be a man? Longinus was assuredly right in calling Herodotus "most Homeric."

E. M. W. Tillyard (essay date 1954)

SOURCE: "The Greek Historians: Herodotus," in *The English Epic and Its Background,* Oxford University Press, 1954, pp. 41-51.

[*Tillyard was a scholar of English literature best known for his work on Shakespeare and the English Renaissance. In the following essay, Tillyard provides a concise overview of the* History, *addressing the epic character of Herodotus's writing, and calling him "the authentic voice of the Greek world in its expansive phase."*]

> *For someone intending to treat history philosophically the study of Herodotus is sufficient. There he will find everything that has gone into the making of all subsequent world history: the activity, the foolishness, the suffering, and the fate of the human race.* (Schopenhauer)

Herodotus was akin to Homer in more ways than one. He was a native of the Asia Minor coast, and, though citizen of a Dorian city, the vehicle of Ionian culture. Like Homer he used the Ionic dialect, and like him a form of it not tied to any one city but a conflation. Like him he used an early form of syntax, with many main verbs and few periods. But above all Herodotus, as a narrative writer, showed himself to be in the Homeric tradition. It could hardly have been otherwise. He was eminently an artist, and what writers of prose history had preceded him were list-makers; they could not help him. For a supporting tradition he had to turn to the poets; and of these the best was to the point, being both a teller of stories and, as was then thought, the recorder of actual events. Herodotus was born between the two Persian Wars, after Marathon and before Salamis. His ears, from the first, must have been full of talk about them; and when he decided to write their history, he could not have failed to bear in mind the writer of the only other war in the Greek world that could match the Persian Wars in significance. This kinship of Herodotus with Homer was recognised in antiquity. Dionysius of Halicarnassus (late first century B.C.) said that in rivalry with Homer he wished to give variety to his history. A recent historian of Greek literature wrote that the breadth of Herodotus's theme was epic and the treatment no less so. There is therefore a good initial case for considering Herodotus as a writer of prose epic, no more disqualified as such for being a historian than Aeschylus as tragedian for writing a tragedy on the second Persian War.

At the outset there is the question of literary skill. Does Herodotus command a style capable of compassing the epic breadth?

In antiquity it became the custom to contrast the two historians, acknowledged superior to all others, Herodotus and Thucydides. Herodotus was considered more varied and charming and graceful, Thucydides narrower but more intense and more powerful. But Herodotus's grace was allowed to be equal to a wide range of subjects. To a modern reader acquainted with even a little Greek the charm of Herodotus's style makes itself quickly felt; as quickly as does the weight of Dante's *terza rima* on a reader who knows only a little Italian. But there is the accompanying danger that such a reader may be content with the quickly won and the obvious, and seek no further. And the danger takes two forms. First, it is hard to allow depth to the pellucid and to convince oneself, as one should, that Herodotus's grace was the result of much labour, of long experiment with prose rhythms, of a technique that weighed every syllable in a manner nearer to verse than to most prose writing. Secondly, we are tempted to read Herodotus for the parts and not for the whole. We get a particularly quick return from his separable details: his anecdotes and his reports of the marvels men told him on his travels. His style was so suited to making these charming that we can easily be blind to the other uses to which he could put it. The risk, in fact, is to treat his history as if it were the Greek equivalent of Mandeville's *Travels*. As that equivalent, as the most enchanting of travel-books, it is hard to give it the chance of rising to the height of its nominal argument: the crucial war between East and West.

It is hard for a reader with no Greek to be just to Herodotus, for he is peculiarly untranslatable. Rawlinson's version runs well and is readable, but his com-

petent Victorian periods are distant from Herodotus's harmonious and elegant and subtle sequences of short sentences. B. R.'s version of the first two books (1584) is in agreeable Elizabethan prose, but is full of mistranslations and is too euphuistic to be near the original's simplicity. The *kind* of English prose nearest to Herodotus is the late medieval narrative prose. The syntax of Mandeville and Malory is not unlike; but Mandeville is a much smaller writer, and Malory's nostalgia and tragic spirit are alien to Herodotus's love of his subject and warmth of treatment. If a union of Malory's genius with Mandeville's geniality could be imagined, a glimmering of Herodotus's style might appear. But my main point is that Herodotus's simple prose, like Homer's syntactically simple verse, is capable of many kinds of effect.

Coming to the question whether Herodotus did indeed produce many kinds of effect, I am compelled to answer it in a way I do not usually follow in this book. The ***History*** of Herodotus is so little known to the general reader that it is only by giving an account of its scope that I can hope to convey any sense of its nature, whether of content or of structure. But before I give this account, there are two points to be made. First, Herodotus's theme provided in itself a scope ample enough for epic requirements. He had the world to range over and from which to draw his illustrations; and his action, the clash of East and West, was a human action of very high significance and was transacted by men of very varied and very forceful natures. Secondly, whatever the quality of the structure, Herodotus in composing his ***History*** made the great choice of risking everything on one great work and showed a very powerful will in carrying it through. This conclusion of course depends on the quality of Herodotus's style. If, indeed, his prose is concentrated in the manner of very good verse, then only a strong will could have sustained it so long.

The first great unit of Herodotus's ***History*** ends with the hundred and thirtieth chapter of the first book, when Cyrus by the overthrow of Croesus, King of Lydia, has become master of the whole of Asia Minor. What does that unit accomplish and what does it lead us to expect? The answer to these questions should go a long way towards settling the problem of structure.

In his beginning Herodotus tells us that his theme is the great actions of the Greeks and barbarians; and there is nothing in his first unit that contradicts this profession. Further, he leaves no doubt where his centre of interest is; and for structural coherence a centre is essential. His centre is Greece, and he shows the highest artistry in developing his theme *from* Greece. He could easily have begun from the Persian side and then recounted the defeat of Croesus and the fall of Sardis; but Croesus and his Lydians were closer to the Greeks geographically, Lydia was the first country to

Scythian warrior.

bring under its sway the hitherto free Greek colonies on the Asiatic coast, and Solon the Athenian was supposed to have visited Croesus. By beginning with Lydia, which has so many relations with Greece, Herodotus maintains the sense of Greece being still central. And lastly the sobering words of Solon the Athenian to Croesus about the gods' jealousy of excessive power and wealth and their proneness to bring down the greatest men look forward to the culminating event in the Persian Wars, the Battle of Salamis, won mainly by Athenian steadfastness and resourcefulness. Unlike Thucydides and like Homer, Herodotus upsets the strict time sequence. He refuses to interrupt the story of Croesus's fall, and only when that is known do we hear the early history of Cyrus, his overthrower. That being completed, he adds, in conclusion of his first unit: 'It was after these events that he was wantonly attacked by Croesus and overthrew him, as I related before. And by overthrowing him, he became master of all Asia.' This conclusion is brilliant. Herodotus had told Croesus's overthrow with perfect narrative tact and timing and diversified it with delightful contributory stories. But he postponed comment on its *significance* till he got to his overthrower, Cyrus. This delay both heightens its significance—for the statement of that significance comes suddenly and with all the emphasis of brevity—and places it where it is most due, namely in Cyrus, symbol of the astonishing rise to power of Persian imperialism. From being a fascinating and exemplary human tale about a great king (neighbour to the Greeks), the career of Croesus becomes a turning-point in the affairs of a vast empire; a turning-point as fateful ultimately to the Greeks as to the Persians themselves. Herodotus, whether through Homer's example or by native genius, both shows himself a master of the novelist's art and promises a tight control of his main theme. Could he have continued thus, his epic grasp would have been sure.

The rest of the first book is interesting enough. Herodotus is at the height of his narrative powers in describing Persian customs, the fall of Babylon, and the Persian war with the Massagetae, its fluctuating fortunes, Cyrus's total defeat and death, and finally Tomyris's outrage on his body, but our attention does not spread beyond the business in hand. Any hesitation to believe that Herodotus was deserting his main theme is settled by the second book, which, because Cyrus's son Cambyses was destined to conquer Egypt, concerns the geography and customs of that country. The curiosity of Herodotus the traveller, admirable in itself and highly entertaining in its results, is indulged so freely that the original epic purpose is quite lost. Herodotus never loses his artistry; in itself the description of Egypt is admirable: but he had forgotten the lesson of Hesiod that the half is greater than the whole. The same criticism applies roughly to the next two books, which deal with Persian campaigns in various parts of the world and with the manners of various nations. I say roughly, because the theme of Greece does begin faintly to make itself felt in these books. In the third book we hear of Polycrates, tyrant of Samos, of his wealth and his correspondence with Amasis, King of Egypt. The Spartans, supporting some disaffected Samians, made unsuccessful war on him; and Herodotus makes the significant comment that this was the first expedition into Asia of the Dorians from Sparta. He shows that he still has in mind his main theme of wars between East and West. Polycrates, like other very wealthy and fortunate rulers in Herodotus, came to an evil end. He was succeeded by two more tyrants, and Herodotus remarks that the Samians appeared just not to wish to be free, thus insinuating the theme, so dominant later, of Greek freedom and oriental tyranny. After the main business of Polycrates, Herodotus recounts the plot to get rid of Cambyses, now a maniac in his excesses and cruelties, and the choice of Darius as

king from among the conspirators, after their plot succeeded. Before this choice Herodotus puts into the mouths of three of the conspirators an extremely Greek debate on the comparative merits of democracy, oligarchy, and monarchy, thus strengthening the Greek theme.

In the fifth book the campaigns of Darius bring him much closer to the Greek world. The Persians enter Thrace, and the Ionians revolt. Herodotus very aptly narrates the early history of Athens and repeats what he ultimately makes clear is one of his main themes: the excellence of political independence and free institutions. These are his comments on Athenian prosperity after the tyrants had been expelled:

> So the Athenians grew in power. And it is clear not from one only but from many instances, that equality before the law is a fine thing. While the Athenians in the times of the tyrants prospered no better in war than the peoples around them, as soon as they were quit of the tyrants they became pre-eminent; which proves that while they were kept under they let themselves be beaten because they were working for a taskmaster, but when they were freed each man was eager to give the best account of himself he could.

The sixth book tells how the Persians suppressed the Ionian Revolt and invaded Greece for the first time. It ends with the Battle of Marathon. Herodotus introduces very clearly another master-theme: the need for the Greeks to unite. His picture of Greek dissension before the invading Persians is very vivid. But the Battle of Marathon is described with no special spirit. Herodotus does indeed hint its significance when he says that the Athenians were the first Greeks to charge the enemy at a run and to face the Medes resolutely, the Medes whose very name had been a terror to the Greeks. In spite of vivid or pertinent details, the sixth book resembles its predecessors in the slowness of its pace.

The change comes in the seventh book with the accession of Xerxes and his preparations for a second invasion of Greece. The spirit of the hundred and thirty opening chapters of the first book reappears; events are set in time with a powerful sense of cause and effect. The hints of large themes, scattered through the earlier books, are resumed and made explicit. It thus happens that Herodotus now not only intensifies and vivifies his narrative of actual events but universalises them by making them illustrate great moral laws. The changed tone, the new solemnity, appear in the council scene when Xerxes declares his intention to invade Greece and invites comment. That this scene has no historical verity but was Herodotus's invention does not make it weigh less as a part of the book. Xerxes tells his council that he aspires to nothing less than world-dominion, and in highly passionate language. He will make the Persian land co-extensive with God's heaven, for once he has broken the Greeks there will be no more resistance in the world. Mardonius, who had been pushing Xerxes into the Greek campaign, supports him, saying that the Greeks may not even dare to fight. Then, after a silence, for the Persians were too timid to say what they thought, Artabanus, Xerxes's uncle and therefore better able to speak his mind in safety, opposed the expedition. His grounds are familiar but not the less impressive in the context. The gods are jealous of any abnormal power or height; a principle seen in the natural world, where God's lightning strikes the large animals, the highest houses, and the tallest trees, sparing the lowly. And he reproves Xerxes's excess by saying that God allows no one but himself to have high thoughts. The scene is entirely successful in giving cosmic importance to the events to be narrated. Xerxes, though little characterised, is kept from being a merely symbolic figure by thinking over Artabanus's warning and ending in doubt about his plan.

Xerxes, now fixed in our minds as a man both of passionate moods and of reflective power, is capable of presenting the kind of general thought Herodotus wants the reader to have. In pride he scourged the Hellespont for breaking his bridge, and in pride he ascended the citadel of Priam in Troy, thinking of himself as reversing the fate of the king who died at the hand of invaders from Europe. When he reviews his forces, military and naval, at Abydos, he grows reflective and laments that after a hundred years not one of his millions will be alive. Then, still apprehensive about the outcome of his expedition, he asks Artabanus his opinion. Artabanus, now resembling one of the Hebrew prophets in his authority, replies that two of the greatest things are against him, sea and land: the first because it has not harbours enough to offer, the second because it cannot yield food enough for the invaders' hosts. Xerxes, as well he may be, is awed by the warning, and ceasing to speak in character, comments chorically on the reasons why great deeds are attempted at all. Artabanus, he says, may be right, but always to be cautious is never to act. It is better to be bold and incur evil than to be ever fearing what may happen. Great empires can be acquired only by great risks. Here Herodotus shows the great gift, so powerful in creating the epic effect, of being on both sides. He knows that the great expeditions of the oriental conquerors are lamentable displays of human pride and cruelty; and he also knows that without the willingness to accept the risks these great expeditions must incur human nature would be the poorer. Not only is the scene at Abydos great and tragic in itself, it is perfectly timed on the brink of the *History*'s culminating enterprise and perfectly sited in the last patch of Asia near the bridge to Europe.

The last piece of staging (on the Persian side) is the conversation between Xerxes and the exiled Spartan King Demaratus, now at his court, and it serves to bring out the contrast, already hinted at, between oriental tyranny and Greek freedom. Demaratus assures Xerxes that the Spartans, however few, will resist the Persians, however many. Xerxes is incredulous and says that if like his troops they had one master, their fear of him might cause them to do desperate things or the whip might urge them to face a superior foe, but left to themselves and their own choice how could they? Demaratus replies that though the Spartans are free from a despot, they are not altogether free, for they are bound by a custom which they fear more than his subjects fear Xerxes; and that custom forbids them to run away in battle, however many the enemy, and requires them to stand firm and either to conquer or to die.

In this way Herodotus prepared for the Battle of Thermopylae, from the Persian side. He now turns to the Greeks. Though Xerxes aimed his expedition against the Athenians in revenge of Marathon, the Greeks knew that he really included them all, and each state had to decide how to act. How the Spartans would act we have learnt from Demaratus; and Herodotus tells us—he says he is forced to tell us although the opinion will not be popular—that the Athenians were in the key-position: without their sea-power Spartan valour would be useless. Then, and the timing is perfect, he introduces Themistocles, the true hero of the war, the man who above all others achieved just that measure of unity among a number of small states necessary to repel the Persians. It is the timing and not any direct statement that tells us that Themistocles is the hero.

From now on Herodotus recounts the different stages of the war. He is not particularly strong in battle-narrative, but in the events and the human motives leading up to the decisive engagements he is masterly. Each move has the separate significance and the logic of a perfect game of chess. Herodotus invests his narrative of world events with the kind of clarity Homer attains in domestic. The seventh book ends with the classic Spartan glory at Thermopylae; classic as Plataea could never be, because the special Spartan talent was surpassing valour against overwhelming odds. But Thermopylae in itself did no more than delay the crisis; and the eighth book begins by recounting that crisis at Salamis. The issue, Herodotus knows, was not whether the Greeks were a match for the Persians—that had been proved already—but whether they would hold together. And it was the Athenians, and Themistocles especially, who knew this and acted on their knowledge; and they are the heroes of this critical portion of the *History*. Their master-stroke of policy and magnanimity was to allow a Spartan to command the united fleet, though they were far the strongest naval power. And Herodotus praises them for having the salvation of Greece at heart and knowing that it could never be achieved if there were quarrels about the command, for, he says . . . , civil strife is as much worse than international war as war is than peace.

Herodotus had staged his preliminaries with impeccable tact and emphasis; what of the crisis itself? It was both an event of the first world-significance and one which hung on the trivialities of human temperaments, on the decision of a small group of Greek commanders deeply perplexed and quite divided about the right course of action. And the right course was followed only because Themistocles had the wit to act secretly and send an envoy to the Persians. This happening was perfect material for the author of a heroic poem, proving that history, in spite of Aristotle, could on one occasion at least be as philosophical as poetry. The combined Greek fleet was anchored in the bay of Salamis, and it had become clear that there would be a majority among the commanders for quitting. Themistocles knew rightly that if they did, the fleet would disintegrate. The message he sent to the Persians had the artistic advantage of being ironical: it was mainly true, but it was misunderstood. He informed the Persians that the Greeks were preparing flight and that if they wanted to destroy the Greek fleet they must immediately cut it off. Xerxes acted on Themistocles's advice, and thus forced on the Greek commanders a unity they would otherwise have lacked. Herodotus's intense simplicity of style proved equal to his difficult task at this culminating point. Every detail stands out sharp, and yet contributes to a single great end: that of symbolising all the other great balancing points in history, when little things became enormous in deciding which of two scales is to kick the beam. Once again Herodotus is on two sides, or rather is both near and far: near, in being quite sunk in the actuality of his supremely thrilling narrative: far, in mastering a whole philosophy of history. The eighth book ends strongly with the episode of Alexander of Macedon seeking on behalf of Mardonius, now in command of the Persians, to persuade the Athenians to change sides. The Spartans, getting wind of this, in great alarm send envoys to Athens. The Athenians, after rejecting the Persian offer, solemnly rebuke the Spartans for their fears.

The ninth book, dealing with the battles of Plataea and Mycale, shows no slackening of grip. That the preliminaries to the battle of Plataea were, as a matter of history, less exciting and more petty than those to Salamis was a gain, for it spared Herodotus the temptation of trying to contrive a second climax. Instead, he advances the theme of Greek moderation and seemliness contrasted with Persian excess and insolence. The *History* ends with the capture of Sestos by the Athenians: Sestos the chief fortress on the Dardanelles and near the bridge which Xerxes constructed from Asia to Europe. They find the bridge already broken up, while the capture of Sestos made any renewal of invasion unlikely. Xerxes's expedition was indeed ended.

It should have become clear, granted high distinction of execution, that Herodotus succeeds partially as an epic writer. He had a theme, belonging it is true to recent history, but sufficiently momentous and typical, sufficiently apt to call forth strong human feelings, to be universal as well as specific. But after a splendid beginning he allowed his consuming curiosity about the world at large to distract him from his real theme and to establish a new and incompatible centre of interest. The world at large ceased to be background and became a second theme. Herodotus should of course have written two books: the greatest of guide-books, and the epic history of the wars between the Greeks and Persians. Not that the dichotomy is so stark in the actual *History* as this sentence suggests. It takes the reader some time to notice the shift of balance, while Herodotus the truant never quite forgets the business he has forsaken. Nor is the guide-book all loss for the epic. It does add weight; it does establish the amplitude of the writer's brain. But it does so at a quite excessive expense; and in the end the dichotomy, for all its mitigations, has to be admitted.

In claiming parts of Herodotus to be epic, I do not mean to say that they are of Homeric quality. Herodotus has less sense of tragedy and of religion. He knows a great deal about human nature, but he creates no characters whose sufferings or ruminations go beyond the present issues and imply the basic problems of man's destiny. His religion, though sincere, is conventional. His cast of mind is primarily comic, and his criterion is the heart of man at its most observant and reasonable and tolerant, or, to vary the expression, the way of the best possible world. Granted that cast of mind, Herodotus achieves a very high order of originality. His passion of observation is all his own, his tolerance a powerful moral principle. This is his comment on the ignoble part borne by the Argives in the Persian War (the Argives who led Greece against Troy):

> Suppose all men to bring their own evil deeds to a common place, in the hope of exchanging them with their neighbours; when they had had a good look at those lying near them, they would be glad to carry their own back again. So the Argives should not be thought to have acted with exceptional baseness.

Rawlinson thinks these sentences show over-tenderness to a guilty nation. More likely Herodotus had in mind the later crimes of the men who acted best in the Persian Wars, the Athenians; and meant that tolerance in judging sins must go with the knowledge that no nation can be morally self-satisfied.

This primarily comic temper does not mean that Herodotus was not serious or that he thereby lacked epic breadth or that he could not cope with his great general themes. It is not by possessing the comic temper but by not possessing the tragic in addition that he falls short of Homer. Here it may be helpful to think of Chaucer. Chaucer, indeed, could never have taken the ultimate risk of putting everything in one great venture. But his most mature verse, that of the least conventional of the *Canterbury Tales,* of the *Miller's* or *Nun's Priest's Tales,* resembles Herodotus's prose in its comic temper. The essentially comic way in which Chaucer recounts the murder story in the *Nun's Priest's Tale* is close to Herodotus's way of recounting the more violent tales in his **History,** while Chaucer's treatment of the marvellous in the *Squire's Tale,* so cool and so fresh, reminds us of Herodotus in Egypt. But the resemblance must not be pressed too far. As Chaucer was not good at finishing things and lacked the epic staying power, so he avoids the more tremendous political themes. Though beginning from the comic side, Herodotus in coping with the great events of the Persian War reaches an epic eminence where merely to have arrived is enough and where the route followed is irrelevant.

Last, does Herodotus speak for a large body of men? Very emphatically yes. But he looks back rather than forward. Writing when the sophists in Athens were revolutionising (or making explicit an already revolutionary) thought, Herodotus interprets an earlier and simple and highly extroverted world. This world is much like Homer's: generally Greek and not confined to this or that city. The notion that Herodotus wrote as a Periclean Athenian with a partisan bias in favour of the Athenian share in the Persian War has no warrant from his text as a whole and could only have been conceived by an unfair concentration on selected parts. Herodotus is the authentic voice of the Greek world in its expansive phase: in its phase as coloniser and pioneer explorer of external nature. As Wells says, he is 'the crown of the intellectual greatness of the Asiatic-Greek sea-board, driven by Persian conquest into exile, and developed in new fields, and on new lines by the enterprising life of the Greek world in the West'. And Wells sees that Herodotus is not only a historian but that he includes all knowledge and that in so doing he 'continues the old tradition of Ionia, where the Philosophers took all knowledge for their province.

To call Herodotus archaic because he looked back would not be fair. The great critical and introspective trend which began in the second half of the fifth century, and of which the sophists were the worse and Socrates the better representatives, was a local Athenian trend and took years to make itself generally felt. To have come under its influence would have been to forgo all possibility of epic breadth. Though the Greek world for which Herodotus spoke was actually past its prime, it was to persist in some of its parts for many years to come and it was the only world offering an adequate scope to a Greek writer of the highest aspirations.

Richmond Lattimore (essay date 1958)

SOURCE: "The Composition of the *History* of Herodotus," in *Classical Philology,* Vol. LII, No. 1, January, 1958, pp. 9-19.

[*In the following essay, Lattimore, a noted classicist, explores a series of textual and structural problems in the* History. *He provides a detailed analysis of Herodotus's compositional methods and considers the constraints on writing and historical research that Herodotus faced.*]

The *general problem.* Concerning the composition of the **History** of Herodotus, one must choose between two general propositions. Either Herodotus wrote his book so that the parts always stood substantially in the order in which we now have them; or he did not. If we believe he did, we shall be more persuasive if we can show that this was, a priori, the more likely way for him to compose his work, and if we can present internal evidence in favor of a continuous forward process. If we believe that the parts of the work originally stood in an order different from what we now have, then we believe in transpositions of written material, or in insertions, or in deletions, or other or all sorts of revision; and we should be able to point to passages which we consider indicative of such processes, and show how they force us to believe in changes made by the author.

I believe that the text of Herodotus as we have it is a continuous piece of writing which Herodotus set down from beginning to end in the *order* in which we now have it; that the sentence at the opening of the work is a true statement of the author's intention at the time when he wrote it, and that it was written down before any of the subsequent text was written down; and that the whole **History** is, substantially at least, a first draft which was never revised, nor meant to be, because the first draft was always meant to be the final draft.

Practical considerations. Such a method of writing—to begin at the beginning and write straight on to the end, never working backward—was, I believe, the natural way to write at the time when Herodotus was writing. It was, I believe, the method followed by the predecessors of Herodotus in the fields of narrative and exposition, by Homer, Hesiod, and the elegiac poets; also, I believe, probably by the logographers, philosophers, and tragic and lyric poets as well. There are two good reasons for this. There is the fact that composed literature comes first and writing comes second; that the written piece is not for the reader to read to himself but for the writer, or his representative, to read from to others; that the writer therefore naturally thinks of himself as a speaker who, when he has contradicted himself or got his parts in the wrong order, cannot go back to correct or transpose, but must make the correction as he goes forward. There is also the fact that writing straight ahead is mechanically the easier way to write. In the time of Herodotus, writing at its easiest could not have been easy. We do not know exactly what writing materials he had, but we certainly know some of the writing materials he did *not* have. He did not have what we would call good paper, good ink, good scissors, or a good eraser. He did not have a set of identical sheets of paper and so he could not, if he found something objectionable on page 8, take it out and write a new page, number it 8, and put it in the stack where it belonged. He could not, in case he needed to add to page 8, make a new page called *8a,* and insert it. It was probably very bothersome to erase. To be more particular: he could not write about Cambyses first, and then about the topography and anthropology and early history of the pharaohs, and then switch them around—not, at least, without some surgery. To insert the Athenian and Lacedaemonian excursuses (1. 59-69 or whatever you think the insert is) *into* an *already written* sequence would have been no simple process but a bitterly difficult one. What has been gained to justify the labor and time spent? It was hard enough to write the ***History*** anyway. Further, Herodotus had at no stage, as we have, a printed text of his ***History,*** conveniently if arbitrarily divided into books, chapters, and subchapters, and supplemented by Powell's admirable Index. It was far harder for him to find his way from place to place in his own work than it is for us to find our way in it. Finally, if he composed a finished piece from notes, those notes were laborious to make and unwieldy to handle when made.

The natural way for a writer to compose a large work under these circumstances would be to use what might be called a forward, or point to point, or progressive style; one subject to irrelevancy and contradiction, but controlled to some extent by being thought out in advance, and capable, for short or simple pieces, of producing a perfectly articulate work; still, because of the necessity to shape material in transit, assuming the superficial appearance of a number of independently made parts which have been rather badly assembled.

Cases of the progressive style: Correction-in-stride. "This is what the Persians and the Phoenicians say, but as for me, I shall not go on to say whether it happened thus or otherwise, but I shall indicate the first man who to my own knowledge was responsible for wrong acts against the Greeks, and when I have indicated him I shall go on ahead with my account . . . Croesus was a Lydian born, and he was the son of Alyattes . . . this Croesus was the first barbarian we know of who overthrew some of the Greeks and made them pay tribute to him, and he did also take some of the other Greeks as friends . . . Before Croesus ruled, all the Greeks were free . . . The kingship, which had belonged to the Heracleidae, came around to the line (Mermnad) of which Croesus was born, in the following way. Candaules . . . was lord of Sardis . . . and as Candaules was going to bed Gyges came out of hiding and killed him, and held his queen

and his kingship. . . . Gyges also, once he was king, led an army into Greek territory, against Miletus and Smyrna, and he took the city of Colophon. . . . I will mention Ardys the son of Gyges who was king after Gyges. He captured Priene . . ."

The contradiction is evident. It can be explained but not explained away. The great achievements of Greeks and barbarians, above all, how they fought each other. Who began it? Stories are told from the heroic age, but that is not a time we have real knowledge about. When we look for the first real historical character who wronged the Greeks, and so caused the wars, we light on Croesus. An exception immediately occurs, the Cimmerians but the Cimmerians merely raided and ran. Exception dismissed. But who was Croesus and why was he on the throne? The question takes us back to the succession of Gyges, and from Gyges we can pass on down through the known succession of Mermnad kings until we shall come to Croesus once more. But immediately there is a slight embarrassment. The *erga* of Gyges included attacks, patently unprovoked, on Greek cities, and Gyges came before Croesus. We might say Herodotus, who has not yet wasted much work, should scrap his beginning and start all over again, with Gyges. But he has by now achieved his beginning, an immense gain, for Croesus leads to Cyrus, and Cyrus to the grand Persian progress which will be a frame to help support the main story and all its attached excursuses. And besides, there was a sense in which Croesus, who let the Persians loose on the Greeks, was far more responsible for the ensuing trouble than Gyges. Herodotus was right, but he did not choose the right language. Gyges actually had attacked them too. . . .

Herodotus has now *made* his correction and acknowledged the error. The reader who goes on reading, the listener who goes on listening, has no right to complain that he has been misled, because he has been set right. So we can get on with the *logos.*

We can trace the same method elsewhere. "Alyattes . . . had other achievements to show for his rule, notably this. He fought the Milesians, this being a war he took over from his father. For he [antecedent not stated] invaded that territory and besieged Miletus in the following way . . . In this way he [antecedent again not stated] fought them for eleven years . . . Now for six of the eleven years it was Sadyattes, still ruling the Lydians, who kept leading these expeditions into Milesian territory, for it was he, Sadyattes, who had started the war; but for the five years that followed the six it was Alyattes the son of Sadyattes. . . ." Here it would have taken only a minor operation to restore the first six years to Sadyattes, who has been dealt with immediately above, and then go on with Alyattes. Failure to do this makes a rather messy and self-conscious progress for a page or so. Herodotus did not cancel or erase. Did it ever occur to him to do so? He goes straight on writing, but does not leave the subject until he has left the reader with the right facts: six years for Sadyattes, who started it, and five years for Alyattes, who finished it.

"Besides, if Heracles was alone, and besides that, if he was only a mortal man, as they say he was, how could it be within nature for him to have killed many tens of thousands? Now that we have said as much as we have said, I hope neither the gods nor the heroes will be angry with us." This is a sort of overpass quite in the manner of Pindar. The trouble-some thing said is un-said not by cancellation but by apology which follows on the saying.

"The Libyan nomads make sacrifice as follows . . . They sacrifice to the Sun and Moon and to them only. All Libyans sacrifice to these gods; but those who range . . . around the Lagoon of Tritonis sacrifice to Athene chiefly, and after her to Triton and Poseidon." The antecedent of "they" (Libyans or nomad Libyans?) is uncertain, nor is it clear whether the Libyans of Tritonis are included among the nomad Libyans or not. . . . It seems pretty plain that the sacrifice to Athene and the others was not in the mind when the phrase about sacrificing to Sun and Moon *only* was written; the exception occurred to Herodotus immediately and he set it down.

" . . . Aristagoras made an expedition against Sardis. Now he himself did not go on the expedition but stayed in Miletus." The first phrase by itself . . . would naturally imply that he did go, so this is a correction-in-stride.

"These nations all have cavalry, except on this occasion they did not provide cavalry, but only the following ones did." There is no real contradiction, but Herodotus writes as if he were correcting himself. The word "except" . . . shows that.

" . . . the biggest single national group he [Mardonius] selected was the Persian force, men who wear necklaces and bracelets: the next largest was the Medes; actually there were as many Medes as there were Persians, but they were not such strong men." We can now see that this is a classic example of correction-in-stride.

Dislocated additions. In the above cases, the sign of progressive style is the acknowledged or at least recognized contradiction and the means taken to prevent such contradiction from leaving the reader or listener falsely informed. There are also unrecognized contradictions, often noted, but these are only what we should expect to find in an early work of this magnitude, in whatever way the parts were composed, and whether or not the entire draft was revised. Correction-in-stride, on the other hand, cannot well indicate revision in the modern manner, for there is no point to it.

Alteration of content in the process of composition is also, I think, betrayed when an addition to the text is put, not where it logically belongs, but apparently at the point the author had reached when the thought of adding occurred to him.

"Next came a thousand spearmen, who were also a force picked out of the entire army. They carried their spears with the points held down toward the ground (7. 40. 2) . . . Immediately behind Xerxes came a thousand spearmen, the bravest and highest born of the Persians. They carried their spears in the normal position. After these came another picked force of a thousand cavalry. After the cavalry came ten thousand men chosen out of the Persian forces. This was an infantry force. A thousand of these had golden pomegranates instead of spikes on the butts of their spears, and these were formed so as to enclose the rest of the force; and the other nine thousand who were thus enclosed had silver pomegranates. Those who carried their spears with the points held down toward the ground also had golden pomegranates on their spears, and those who immediately followed Xerxes had apples" (7. 41. 1-2). This is obviously akin to the correction-in-stride, and might be called an addition-in-stride. A systematic revision made later than the original draft might better have put this information in the place (so near!) where it belonged.

"Croesus was dissatisfied with the size of his army, for the force he had used in the battle was far smaller than that of Cyrus; and being thus dissatisfied, when the next day came and Cyrus made no move to attack him, he marched back to Sardis. He had it in mind to call up the Egyptian forces in accordance with their sworn agreement (for he had made an alliance with Amasis, king of Egypt, before he made one with the Lacedaemonians), and to call for the Babylonians too (for he had an alliance made with them also, and the ruler of the Babylonians at this time was Labynetus), and to request the Lacedaemonians to be there at a stated time. . . . (1. 77. 1-3)." The narrative struggles through a series of after-thoughts hung on *gar*-clauses. They *could* be marginal corrections, but if so why are they here? The note on numbers belongs just back at the account of the battle (76. 3 or 4); and the alliances should come at 53. 3 or somewhere in 69-70, where alliances are under consideration. From analogies observed, it is more likely that the Egyptian and Babylonian alliances were hitherto forced from Herodotus' attention by the interest inherent in the Lacedaemonian alliance, and recalled to mind only by the context of Croesus' proposed winter withdrawal. (As for Croesus, he seems from this to have fought in pretty much the same way Herodotus wrote, meeting the occasion as it came along. *Ce n'est pas la guerre.* Croesus did not win.)

"As the Lacedaemonians say, they made the expedition not so much because they wanted to help the

Samians in their need as because they wished to avenge themselves for the theft of the mixing bowl which they had tried to convey to Croesus, and for the corselet, which Amasis the King of Egypt sent them as a gift. For the Samians had stolen the corselet too, the year before they stole the mixing bowl . . . There is another one like it which Amasis dedicated to Athene in Lindos" (3. 47). The story of the mixing bowl has been explicitly told at 1. 70; and the language in this passage makes it pretty clear that Herodotus remembers dealing with it, whether or not he had his finger on that place in his own manuscript. The technique of "Schlußredaktion" would have shifted 1. 70 (in an adapted version) to the Samian passage or (less happily) 3. 47 to the Croesus passage; the technique used is that of oral discourse, and the thought is something like: "you remember the mixing bowl lost by robbery on its way to Croesus; well, they stole a corselet too."

This type of addition with *gar*-clause may thus, I think, be taken as supplementary evidence, less cogent than the true correction-in-stride, for a process of composition which worked always forward. The passages have been taken in isolation and in part as negative check cases against revision, but this keeps us from seeing how the progressive manner builds a positive style, which is to be seen only in an extended sequence. One aspect of this is a tendency to follow out the implications carried in single words, so that we can pick out guide words that direct the progress for extended duration.

Consider, for instance, the stretch from 3. 4. 3–3. 9. 4. When Cambyses was resolved to conquer Egypt, he was puzzled by the problem of crossing the *waterless* stretch on the way. Phanes of Halicarnassus advised him to win safe conduct from the King of the Arabians, through whose domain lay Cambyses' only *entrance* to Egypt. This *entrance* is then indicated, and the account closes with a note that a part of the route, "no small distance but three days' journeying," is dangerously *waterless*. This leads to a description of the system by which the Persians now keep this area watered; but the system was not in operation until the Persians came, and now Cambyses must acquire the good offices of the Arabian king by giving and taking *pledges*. The Arabian ceremony for *pledges* is then described. It involves a ritual of bloodletting, and the invocation of *Dionysus* and *Ourania*. "These are the only gods whose existence they believe in, and they say that their way of *cutting their hair* short is after the way *Dionysus has his hair cut*. They *cut it* so that it is round on top like a wheel, shaving up to the level of the temples. Their name for *Dionysus* is Orotalt and for *Ourania,* Alialat." We return to the measures taken by the Arab after the *pledges* were given and taken, and end with an appendix devoted to a "less easily believed version"; and can now (3. 10) resume the account of the war.

This passage has been called the Arabian Logos; and if there is any such thing as an Arabian Logos, this must be it. But it is no organized, potentially free-standing anthropology of Arabia or the Arabians, rather a sequence of notices which grows organically out of its place of occurrence in the Persian progress. The information given—and doubtless more information about Arabia and Arabs as well—was held in the magnificent memory of Herodotus, until the waterless stretch that faced Cambyses led, on the guide words given above, as far as Orotalt and Alilat, and no further.

The body of material which grows out of the watering problem comes to medium length. Analogous sequences can be found, not different in kind, which range in bulk from the single-sentence gloss parenthetically put or hung on a *gar*-clause, which is generated direct from an idea or single word such as a spoken aside in the forward progress of live speech, to really extensive stretches of complex narrative which have not been fixed on the sustaining frame of a definite journal. Examples of the former are altogether too numerous to be worth listing; an example, at random, would be 5. 119. 2: "Those [Carians] who escaped were presently trapped at Labraunda in the sanctuary of Zeus Stratios, which is a large and hallowed grove of plane trees. The Carians are the only people we know of who make sacrifices to Zeus Stratios. When they found themselves trapped in this place, they made plans . . ." The long form might be shown if we enter the text at 5. 38. 2, where Aristagoras arrives at Sparta; and we are thus transported from the main line of the narrative, which has reached Miletus and the Ionian Revolt, and then pick our way forward, following the guide words and phrases until we come back to the Revolt at 5. 97. 3. We shall by then have been told how Cleomenes, not Dorieus, was then King of Sparta, and of the adventures of disappointed Dorieus (39–48); of the interview of Aristagoras and Cleomenes, with the use of that "map of the world displayed on a board which he carried around with him" (49–51); of the royal road (52–54); of Aristagoras in Athens (55. 1); and thereto the story of how the Athenians, who when last extensively mentioned had been in bondage to the tyrants or scattered abroad to escape them (1. 65. 1), had by now got rid of their tyranny, escaped the designs of Cleomenes, beaten the Boeotians and Chalcidians and been involved in hostilities with Aegina; further how a movement to restore Hippias was foiled by Socleēs of Corinth with the story of Cypselus and Periander (55–59); and finally, of the effort of the Athenians to stop Persia from supporting Hippias, their failure and consequent state of mind, as a result of which they let Aristagoras persuade them to send help to the Ionians (96–97).

After the Persian progress toward ultimate collision with Greece has struggled along a far from open course through Scythia, Libya, and Thrace, Herodotus has almost formally announced a new phase of the war-making (5. 28. 1) and moved forward in a businesslike manner until Aristagoras in Greece embarks him on the diversions indicated above. One might say that throughout he keeps a firm hold on the leitmotiv, as indicated at 49-51, 55. 1, and perhaps 96. 1; but I cannot think that the excursus was meant to be so long or so complex. Rather, the first of it grows out of a *gar*-clause to elaborate "not through being more of a man but through birth" (39. 1); and after returning at least close to the matter of the Ionian Revolt, Herodotus enters on the Athenian account by "Athens, now free of tyrants, *thus*" (55. 1). Further, there are excursuses within excursuses, as for instance when the reforms of Cleisthenes in Athens suggest the reforms of the elder Cleisthenes in Sicyon (*gar*-clause transition) and take us as far from Persia, Ionia, and 500 B.C. as the legendary base of the cult of Melanippus in Sicyon; or as when Socle s' speech against restoring Hippias brings us to the circle of Corinthian conspirators who pass the laughing baby tyrant from hand to hand and none has the heart to smash him on the ground.

Revision or addition under the circumstances in which Herodotus wrote could hardly have achieved this Chinese-puzzle pattern of minor parts within parts. It is rather what we should expect from a composition in the progressive style in which—subject to a guiding plan and a main line of narrative—the details are to some extent permitted to generate themselves.

Parallels in early composition. It is now generally conceded that there can be literature before there is writing. Grant that; then grant also that, even *after* writing becomes available to the composers of literature, there will still be a period in which the composer writes his work, or causes it to be written, but is not yet familiar or easy enough in the process to be able to think in terms of writing. The oral method of composition will carry over for some time; and for some time, too, the composition will be communicated by recitation or by reading aloud, not by silent reading to oneself with eye and mind alone.

Although the Homeric poems were undoubtedly Herodotus' chief model for composition on the scale and scope of the **History,** I can make little use of these for parallels in the progressive style of composition. The unity of composition for the *Iliad* and *Odyssey,* even the authority for any given text, is still in dispute; and even if we grant that our text (approximately) of the *Iliad* is the authentic work of one author, various considerations, particularly the traditional nature of Homer's material, disturb the analogy. We may, however, cite a few cases of the misplaced addition or explanation, mostly having to do with the larger progress of the campaign at Troy; for instance, the non-heroic armor and weapons of the Locrians (13. 712-22), the peculiar

arrangement of the Achaean ships (14. 29-36), the presence of such specialists as steersmen and supply-corps personnel in the Achaean army (19. 42-45), come into the poem late, as if thought of late and then immediately set down. In general, Homer can best be used to interpret Herodotus by referring from specific passages in Herodotus back to Homer.

Archaic poetry contains several cases which seem to make it clear that the author in question composed and wrote down his piece straightforward without working back. Solon in his elegy addressed to the Muses prays for prosperity to be got honestly, since criminal action immediately draws down the punishment of the gods; it is immediately seen that this is not true; God may wait, even past the lifetime of the wrongdoer, and strike his innocent descendants or fellow citizens. The rejected proposition is left in the text, being in fact *used* to further the progress of the poem. Pindar can mention the horrible story of Pelops in the stewpot or of Heracles thrashing major divinities, reject or at least deprecate the allusion, but leave it standing in the text. This is contradiction and correction-in-stride. Unpremeditated excursus, another sign of oral thinking in composition, also appears. Theognis starts an elegy with the reflection that there is only one "virtue" which does people any good, and that is "having money." He is of course parodying Tyrtaeus 9 and could, like his original, progress to the end and repeat his point, clinging firmly to the familiar frame of the catalogue; but when he has progressed from Rhadamanthys to Sisyphus, he allows the clue of that name to lead him down with Sisyphus to Hades and Persephone, whence no mortal ever returned except Sisyphus, before he returns to his catalogue and finishes his poem. Elsewhere he simply drifts and winds up talking about something quite different from what he began with.

Such passages as the above do not perhaps *prove* that systematic rewriting and revision were unknown to Greek literature until a relatively late period. They are, however, what we should expect to find in the work of gifted writers who rejected, or did not know of, that kind of revision. If we remember the difficulties of practicing such revision on any sizable scale with the materials available at the time, perhaps we should not ask whether Herodotus and his predecessors wrote in a continuous forward sequence, but whether they could have written in any other way. If they could not, we should hardly be surprised to find the sorts of anomaly and irrelevance noted above.

The composition of Herodotus: The major scheme. But the complexity, the sheer size of the work of Herodotus, is prodigious compared with that of all predecessors except Homer. Beyond the contradictions and the sometimes wayward excursions we have noted and paralleled, we ought to find, in a forward-written first draft, faults in the major scheme, cases of material which he should have presented, or has implied he will present, and has not presented.

Squeeze-out. We do find such cases. Sometimes the material in question ultimately finds its way into the text; at other times it is lost for good. After the capture of Thasos, Darius "sent various heralds directed to various parts of Greece, with orders to claim earth and water for the King" (6. 48. 2). Other heralds went to his own seaboard cities to order a shipbuilding program. "When the heralds arrived in Greece many of the mainlanders gave them what the Persian demanded, and all the islanders to whom they came with their demands did so. Now with the rest of the islanders giving earth and water to Darius, the Aeginetans also did so; and when they did, the Athenians immediately, etc." (6. 49. 1-2). The Athenian action leads into a long excursus on affairs in the Greek homeland involving an account of the Spartan kingship and the Spartan kings, with a part of the career of Cleomenes and his death, and returns to the main narrative at 6. 94. The heralds marked the point of entry from the Persian Journal to the excursus; we do not hear of their fate at Athens and in Sparta until 7. 133, but there they do make their delayed appearance. But the *men-de* clause of the text involves "many of the mainlanders" and "all the islanders to whom they came with their demands." We are not to know *what* mainlanders, for the *men*-clause is left, the *de*-clause (islanders) developed. But even these are developed by the figure of *all s-te-kai,* so that the Aeginetans exclude "the rest of the islanders" and of these, too, we hear no more. This type of squeeze-out may be noted elsewhere, as in the exclusion of "the other big cities of Assyria"; the loss of the subsequent fate of the Paeonians around Pangaeum and Lake Prasias "who were not conquered *at first* by Megabazus"; the failure to narrate the Persian annexation of Macedonia, for which 5. 21 is inadequate; the failure to record the fortunes of the Carians between their great victory at Pedasus and their ultimate submission; the disappearance of the 4000 Athenian cleruchs from Chalcis; the failure to note the message for help sent to the Plataeans; the disappearance from the narrative of the Persian land force which marched on the Peloponnese; of the "many other renowned Persians and Medes" besides Ariabignes lost at Salamis; and of the Corinthian group at Plataea; Exclusion may be deliberate, as at 7. 99. 1: "I shall not give the names of the other taxiarchs, since I am not forced to do so, but I shall speak of Artemisia . . ." Mostly, examination of the text will show that the squeezing out is a result of the style, where in a clause of the *men*-de type the second member is carried forward and the first thus lost in transit.

Unfulfilled promises. These differ from the foregoing cases mainly in that Herodotus has assured us that he means to deal with the material excluded. The cases, well-known and much discussed, include the promise

to deal with other kings of Babylon "where I shall be dealing with the Assyrians" (1. 184; *polloi alloi* and *men-de* construction; exclusion by interest in queens, and Nitocris and her wall?); the promise to give an account of the capture of Nineveh; the promise to give the reason why Athenades killed Epialtes "to be told in a later part of my story"). If these unfulfilments of promise rise, like the organic squeeze-out, out of the circumstances of writing, we should only be surprised not to find more of them. But Herodotus, though a writer, was able to control enormous masses of material in his head. He had been exposed to only the first phases of the sickness of Thoth, and the art of writing had not destroyed his memory or even impaired it much.

The problem and ideas of order. He might, indeed, have done even better if he had been able to work out more completely in advance a framework which would help to fix the order of his *History*. If the view I have been detailing is right and the first sentence in the *History* is rightly placed and represents the true beginning of the composition, Herodotus was faced with an unprecedented problem: to write the history of the Persian attack on Greece and the Greek resistance, with full notes on the peoples, barbarian and Greek, involved. The main line must be an orderly chronicle of the Persian progress, the only part of the complex which could be viewed as a continuous narrative. But barbarian attacks on Greece began with Lydia. From Croesus he found his way back to Gyges, as we have seen, and from Gyges forward again to Croesus through a chronicle of the Lydian kings dominated by the idea of recording their dealings with Greek cities. Then Croesus faces Cyrus and goes down, and from Cyrus Herodotus works, again, back to the beginning of Median power, thence forward via Median chronicle to Cyrus. From Cyrus, the main line is secured by the succession of Persian kings. Follow them, and you will finally come to the great invasion.

This was the main frame. To it adheres, in the first line, the succession of notices concerning peoples little known (or, Herodotus would say, inaccurately reported) to Greek audiences; and also a succession of notices concerning Greek states which can be joined directly to the main line of the *History* or joined to other notices which join to other notices—this procedure can be continued indefinitely. For these two types of major excursus no orderly over-all frame was available. The first would demand a written *periodos gēs;* the second, a history of Greece. Supposing Herodotus could have written either or both, he would have had three works on his hands instead of one. Instead, the inclusion of both types of excursus depends on finding a point of departure in the body of the Persian progress. But there is a difference once inclusion has been started. The barbarian notices can be organized into subdivisions treating of geography, ethnography and, if practicable, history. For the Greek, there is no such organization possible, and we depend far more on the comparatively casual guideword and generated series.

Thus it happens that no real "Greek Journal" is worked out until the time of the great invasion, when the Greeks acted more as a single group than ever before. The method is rather one of "keeping up with the Greeks" as they make contact with the Persian progress. Occasionally we find a summarizing sentence, which seems to show consciousness that the whole *History* could be more thoroughly organized under a series of headings. "Thus Ionia was enslaved for the second time" and "thus the Ionians were enslaved for the third time, for they had been enslaved first by the Lydians and twice, now, by the Persians"; such statements suggest a schematic control of material. But it is not followed out, merely noted down as it occurred in the process of writing; for the first such note comes at 1. 92. 1 (following the fall of Croesus) not at 1. 27. 1 (conquest by Lydians) and reads: "Thus it was with the reign of Croesus and the first overthrow of Ionia." There are also rudimentary signs of recognition that a systematic chronology, and even synchronization of events or biographies (1. 12. 1; 1. 23), would be helpful. Two years are logged for the interval between the death of Atys and the preparations to attack Cyrus (1. 46. 1); an attempt to keep firm hold on the chronology is evident in the sequence following the fall of Miletus, but it is considerably disturbed by the cutback to the former career of Miltiades; an annalistic approach is indicated at 9. 121: "and during that year nothing further happened," but by now the work is all but concluded. Had the work proceeded from this point, an annalistic scheme might (in theory) have been followed, from thence forward; but an annalistic scheme would have been alien to the methods of Herodotus. There is a feeling of time, but no scheme; some time notices are afterthoughts with *gar*-clause or as parenthesis.

The progress of the History. In view of all the above considerations, and in view of the physical difficulties of composition and the still greater difficulty of revising composition, I think it best to regard the *History* as a document set down as it was composed and composed in substantially the same order in which we now have it. This does not mean that there could have been *no* deletions or marginalia whatever, it does mean that to posit such functions of revision is neither a valid nor a practicable approach to the study of the *History*. If the foregoing is right, we may draw some conclusions about the time and place of writing.

Born probably between 490 and 480 B.C., Herodotus set out from Athens to Thurii, probably about 443 B.C. It is not certain that he ever returned to Greece proper, though he may have done so. Between these two (tentative!) dates, he apparently participated in the expulsion of the tyrant Lygdamis from Halicarnassus, but subsequently left his own city for good; spent some time in Samos, traveled extensively, with visits to Egypt, Libya, the Black Sea and the coast of Scythia, and many parts of the Greekspeaking world including Macedonia and the coast of Thrace.

Thucydides comments negatively on Herodotus's reliability as a historian:

The way that most men deal with traditions, even traditions of their own country, is to receive them all alike as they are delivered, without applying any critical test whatever. [Thucydides then instances the story of Harmodius and Aristogiton as told in Herodotus, but without naming him.] So little pains do the vulgar take in the investigation of truth. . . . I have written my work not as an essay to win the applause of the moment, but as a possession for all time.

Thucydides, Quoted in Ancilla to Classical Reading, *by Moses Hadas, Columbia University Press, 1954.*

It seems most likely that he began to write the *History* at some time during the period of 450-444, and that he did so in Greece, probably in Athens (he would have set out from there for Thurii), at a time when his great period of traveling was behind him. Certainly he had been at Delphi before he wrote 1. 14. 2-3, which shows absolute familiarity with the offerings there. How long the idea had been in his mind before he began to write is something we can only guess at. The work was still in progress when he left, and had probably not progressed beyond or much beyond the first three books; for the early extant plays of Sophocles, *Aiax* and *Antigone,* show the influence of Herodotus strongly, but definite parallels can be established only with Books 1 and 3. He is also said to have given readings at Olympia, and to have read aloud to the Athenians, and been rewarded for it, in 445/4. The readings would then have been from the first part of his work; or else they were not readings, but lectures from memory.

There is no conclusive evidence that Herodotus ever returned from the west to Athens or any other place in mainland Greece. The latest event which is absolutely datable and referred to in his work is the seizure and execution of Aristeas and other ambassadors in 430 B.C. He died, therefore, at some time after this date; but if my view about composition is right, he lived long enough after it to complete 7. 138-9. 122, which was therefore *composed after 430* and probably composed at Thurii or elsewhere in the Greek West.

When we use Herodotus as our main source for the reconstruction of Xerxes' invasion and the great battles of 480-479, it may therefore be helpful if we bear in mind (always granting the correctness of the foregoing) that his accounts were set down at least twelve or thirteen years after most of the material was collected and the sites visited, when and if they were visited at all; that they were probably set down from memory, without adequate notes, certainly without those topographical maps which modern scholarship requires; that they were subject to all the vicissitudes of omission and diversion involved in the process of composition indicated above; and finally, that they are the work of a historian who, as far as we know, had never seen a fullscale battle, who had more epic schooling than military imagination, and who was setting forth to write history before history was history. All this we must keep before our eyes as we study Herodotus the historian of the Persian Wars.

Aubrey de Sélincourt (essay date 1962)

SOURCE: "Scepticism and Credulity in Herodotus," in *The World of Herodotus,* Little, Brown and Company, 1962, pp. 53-67.

[*In the following essay, de Sélincourt provides a sketch of religious thought in the time of Herodotus and discusses the Greek concepts of fate, pride, and guilt. De Sélincourt notes Herodotus's religious credulity, but also detects in the* History *a sceptical intelligence.*]

One way in which the artist differs from the rest of us is that he knows better than we do what to leave out. A sculptor, knowing which bits of stone are irrelevant to his purpose, chips them away. Knowledge of what to leave out makes the difference between a good talker or a successful raconteur and a bore; between a good book and a ragbag of information or gossip. A good book may deal with all sorts of peripheral matters, but the reader perceives, or comes in the end to perceive, that the line they follow is indeed a periphery—the circumference of a circle which, by the nature of things, has a centre.

The Greeks possessed this knowledge in a high degree. We commonly call it a sense of form, which is as good a term as any. It was the sense which led their first philosophers to seek a single principle underlying the bewildering multiplicity of the visible world; it was the cause of their delight in the beautiful shapeliness of mathematics—NO ONE ADMITTED, said the notice over the door of Plato's Academy, WHO HAS NOT STUDIED GEOMETRY. It was one cause, also, and not the least important, of the excellence of their best literature. The best Greek writers did not over-elaborate or fluff; they said what they wanted to say, clearly and directly, and left it at that, assuming that readers would take their point. The assumption would perhaps be a rasher one today than it was then, for modern readers are jaded and need artificial, or artful, stimulus to keep them awake. They too often want what might be called emotional rhetoric, as well as verbal rhetoric: it is not

always safe for a modern writer, if he hopes to hold attention, to leave things alone. He is tempted to make mountains out of what for a Greek would have been a molehill, a spiced dish for what would have been a plain Greek loaf. This leads some modern readers to fancy that Greek literature is cold—a great mistake. It has a cool surface, but that is a very different thing. The molten earth has a cool surface too.

> *The moon is down*
> *And the Pleiades;*
> > *It is midnight and the hour had passed;*
> > *Yet I sleep alone.*

In that lyric of Sappho's the irrelevant bits of stone have been chipped away indeed. A single image suffices: moon-set—hope-set.

Herodotus, as I have already said, had no literary guides to follow, and the scope and contents of his book, containing, as it does, such a mass of miscellaneous information on any subject likely to interest an inquiring mind, would tend to make it formless, at any rate in the hands of a less competent artist. All the more remarkable is the skill with which he has succeeded in subduing this heterogeneous material to the service of his central theme. His sun, so to speak, has sufficient power of attraction to keep his unruly planets in orbit. The opening sentence announces his theme: 'In this book, the result of my inquiries into history, I hope to do two things: to preserve the memory of the past by putting on record the astonishing achievements both of our own and of the Asiatic peoples; secondly, and more particularly, to show how the two races came into conflict.' That sentence, though it stands at the beginning, was certainly not the first to be written; for there can be little doubt as I have said that Herodotus began by intending to amplify the work of the logographers and to produce separate accounts of the various countries which he included in his travels. But suddenly, it seems, perhaps when much was already written, by a flash of inspiration, or simply by that innate Greek sense of form and shapeliness which in Herodotus was as vigorous as in any other Greek writer or artist, he saw his work as an organised whole. The unruly planets began in his mind to circle obediently about their sun.

The scheme of the book is very simple. Herodotus begins with an account of Lydia, the first foreign power to come into direct contact with the Asiatic Greeks; the defeat of Croesus, the last King of Lydia, by Cyrus the Great of Persia brings him on to the road which leads straight to the climax of his story—the triumphant struggle of little and divided Greece against the vast resources of the Persian empire under Darius and Xerxes. The description of the rapid growth of Persian power serves a double purpose: first historical, as it enables the historian to tell what he knows of the various countries—Egypt, Babylonia, Scythia (portions of southern Russia), North Africa, the more easterly of the Aegean islands—which were invaded or subdued by the successive Persian Kings; and, secondly, dramatic, as by building up stage by stage in the reader's mind a sense of the sheer physical magnitude of this Empire which controlled half the known world, it thereby increases the impact of the climax of the story, which is the successful resistance to it of the tiny country of Greece. This, the 'more particular' theme of the history, the account, namely, of how the two great civilisations of the East and of the West came into conflict, is worked out in a narrative of beautiful clarity and balance, and at the same time flexible enough to admit subsidiary matter of almost infinite variety and degree of interest. Digression, with Herodotus, is not a vice but a virtue: 'I need not apologise for it,' he says, 'it has been my plan throughout this book to put down odd bits of information not directly connected with my main subject.' Any reader will agree that he had no need to apologise; the 'odd bits of information' may not, indeed, be directly connected with Herodotus' main subject, but—and a reader who fails to see this has not been reading Herodotus as he ought to be read—they form an essential part of the self-revelation which lies behind all truly imaginative writing—behind 'books of power' (to repeat De Quincey's distinction) as opposed to 'books of knowledge.' What a man sees is determined not by his eyes only but by the quality of his mind, and Herodotus' mind was a very subtle as well as a very capacious one. Like all great writers, behind and beyond his ostensible theme, he was writing indirectly of himself, and it is that self—warm, humorous, humane; rational and credulous by turns; curious and kindly, daringly speculative, undismayed by the brutality and beastliness of men, and always *on the side of life*—which gives Herodotus' book its other—its personal—unity. Ultimately this is a question of style. Few writers less resemble Herodotus than the seventeenth century Bishop Burnet; but I am reminded of the bishop because of what Charles Lamb once said in connection with him, when he compared his sort of history favourably with that of Gibbon: 'None,' wrote Lamb to his friend Manning, 'of the cursed philosophical Humeian indifference, so cold, and unnatural, and inhuman! None of the cursed Gibbonian fine writing, so fine and composite!' There is no cursed Gibbonian fine writing in Herodotus either. Herodotus' changes of mood are as subtle as his perceptions of men; with his beautiful bare narrative he can tickle the fancy, inflame the imagination, or touch the heart.

Underlying Herodotus' delight in the kaleidoscope of human life is the characteristic Greek pessimism. Only in Homer, of all Greek writers, is this fundamental pessimism not discernible, though even in him the life of men in the sunlit world gets half its brilliance from the sense of its brevity and the ever-present darkness of death. In Homer's world, full though it was of death, violence and blood, men had no speculative burdens; in it there is an innocence of thought almost childlike. The gods have been almost wholly humanised. Immortal and powerful, they nevertheless act from motives precisely like those which move ourselves, and a Homeric hero, to get or keep a god on his side, had to treat him precisely as he would treat a friend or enemy: he had to pay him the honour that was his due, in word, or in the giving of a gift, or in acceptable sacrifice. Homer's fighting chieftains could, one feels, have got on perfectly well without any gods at all; but, as old tales told them that there were, indeed, such beings, they re-formed them in fancy to suit their own ardent unspeculative lives. The Homeric religion, if it can be called a religion, seems, in its complete divorce from morality, divine justice and a sense of sin, to have sprung, unlike all other religions, from a transitory morning of self-confidence and self-sufficiency, and not at all from the almost universal consciousness of the mysterious and inexplicable powers which, for good or ill, menace or sustain the little life of men.

But the morning passed; we see it passing in the poems of dour old Hesiod; and what I called the characteristic Greek pessimism took its place. The Greeks were a religious people and carried religious observance into the commonest acts of daily life to a degree hardly imaginable by a modern man. Families and states looked for protection to their special and peculiar gods, called by local names and often fragmentations, as it were, of the official Olympian hierarchy. But the Greeks had no established priesthood and no sacred book, and hence no body of religious teaching. Their religious observances tended always to be more in the nature of propitiation than of worship, except perhaps in the mystery cults of which few details are available to us. Fear of God was universal; of the love of God they knew nothing. The notion of a benevolent and all-powerful deity, the sense found in Judaism and Christianity of the 'everlasting arms', was utterly foreign to Greek thought. Hence their pessimism. Life, for a Greek, was to be enjoyed or endured—if the gods would let him. Orphism, indeed, taught a kind of immortality; but for the Greeks in general death was the end. The recurrent image for death in Greek poetry is the loss of the sunlight—to see the sun no more, to go down into the dark. It is strange that the Greeks with their philosophic passion for first principles did not move more quickly towards monotheism. There is a groping after it in the tragic poet Aeschylus, Herodotus' elder contemporary—'Zeus, power unknown . . . when I weigh all things, I can guess at nothing but Zeus, if the burden of vanity is to be cast off from my soul . . .'—but Aeschylus' one God, even if his guess is right, is still a harsh and malevolent power, forcing men to learn the truth by pain. It was Plato, early in the fourth century, who with his rejection of the sensible world and his pursuit of the ideal—of 'beauty absolute, separate, simple and everlasting, without diminution or increase or change'—who marked the end of the old classical Greece and offered much which could later be absorbed into Christian theology.

In Herodotus there is nothing of all this, though the religious colouring of his mind is, like everything else in him, full of delicate shades. In religious matters he is at once curious and credulous. Everyone, he says, naturally—and rightly—thinks that the beliefs and observances in which he has been brought up are the best. He himself was no exception, though it should be noted that this very way of putting it suggests a broad tolerance and a refusal to claim absolute validity for any one system of belief, even his own. The gods, in Herodotus' view and in that of his time generally, were not all-powerful; like men they were subject to a mysterious something called Fate—the Greek word, *moira,* means 'the dealer-out of portions'—or to the same thing under another name, Necessity. The power of Fate was unsearchable, though a certain pattern in its operations upon human affairs could be seen. It was Fate, not the Gods, which brought retribution, and the crime which more than any other called retribution down was Pride—that self-exaltation which led a man in the moment of success to 'think more than mortal thoughts'. The idea was deeply characteristic of the Greeks, and sprang, obviously enough, from the insecurity of life in the ancient world, an insecurity more immediate, insistent and universal than any that has until recently menaced the world today, and, at the same time, from the passion which was innate in the Greek character for personal distinction and power. The Greeks knew that they wanted inordinate things—and knew at the same time that such things were dangerous: Fate would see to it that the too prosperous man would one day lose his prosperity. The gods were jealous gods: hence the insistence upon (combined with the very rare practice of) the virtue of 'moderation'—on the necessity for *sophrosyne,* or 'saving thoughts', the kind of thoughts which do not let a man step out of the sphere which is proper to him. If he does, Fate, the Sharer-out, will give him sooner or later what he deserves.

Herodotus' book is full of this sense of Fate, of the watchful and jealous power of this Necessity, which broods like a shadow over the struggles, toils, triumphs and adventures of men and cities. It gives an added depth to the brilliant and varied scene played out on the human stage, linking it with a mystery beyond itself. The whole story of Croesus, one of the most moving and beautiful in the book, is heavy with it—'count no man happy until he is dead.' With a different effect, almost with a touch of implied irony, it is the hinge upon which turns the well-known story of Polycrates of Samos and the ring, his dearest possession, which he proved unable to lose. 'Not God himself,' said the priestess at Delphi, 'can escape Destiny'; and no man, however great, can escape punishment for pride.

Fate, too, is more than the punisher: it is the ultimate power which determines the course of human events; it sets the bounds within which a man can act. A man is free to act, or seems to be free, but the end of his action is ordained. The pattern of life belongs to Fate. 'Now I know,' said the Persian King Cambyses when he was near his miserable end, 'that it is not in human power to avert what is to be.' Yet, with a touch of inconsistency perhaps, we are constantly shown how this same Necessity is prepared to give poor mortals a chance by sending them warnings of coming disaster in the shape of dreams, or portents, or whatever it may be. 'There is nearly always,' Herodotus writes, 'a warning of some kind when disaster is about to overtake a city or a nation'; and he goes on to relate how, before the island of Chios fell to Histiaeus and the Persians, the people of the island had sent a choir of a hundred young men to Delphi, and that all but two of them had died of the plague, while at almost the same time, in the island's chief town, the roof of a school had fallen in and killed all but one of the hundred and twenty children who were learning their letters there. Both these events, Herodotus adds, were acts of God to forewarn the people of Chios. But what could they have done about it, had they taken the warning? The question comes to mind, but it is an idle one, for we are not dealing here with anything like a systematic or philosophical scheme of belief, but only with an inherited and ancient *sense* of things, with a kind of primitive awe which is the stuff out of which theologies come to be made, with a recognition, instinctive rather than reasoned, of the dependence of men upon a shaping power the nature of which is beyond their understanding. It is one of the charms of Greek-literature and of Herodotus in particular that it is the work of men whose religious beliefs have not hardened into dogma: of men with quick minds and quicker senses who do not pretend to understand the incomprehensible: who, filled with awe by the invisible, with delight by the visible, can still turn upon human destiny a speculative and wondering eye.

Retribution and the fear of retribution is a recurring idea in Greek literature. Often the retribution is delayed; but punishment for sin, hobbling on its lame foot after its victim, catches him at last, even in the third or fourth generation. The theme of inherited guilt, of the family curse, is frequent in Greek tragic drama; it is a symbol, no doubt, and a powerful one, of what must in the dawn of things have been the disturbing discovery that no fact or act ever is, or can be, isolated; a deed is a pebble dropped into a pond, and the concentric rings spread wide. Croesus was a good man and a good King, friendly on the whole towards Greece; but he came to grief and was dethroned. Why?—because, Herodotus says, he had to expiate in the fifth generation the crime of his ancestor Gyges, a mere soldier in the royal bodyguard, who, tempted by a woman's treachery, murdered his master and stole the crown to which he had no claim. Gyges had long been dead, but his guilt lived after him. Again, in his account of Egypt, Herodotus relates how he heard from certain Egyptian priests a different story from the one which Homer told about the abduction of Helen: according to them, when the Greeks landed in the Troad and sent envoys to King Priam to demand the restoration of Helen, they were assured that she was not in Troy at all but had gone to Egypt. Thinking this to be a merely frivolous answer, the Greeks laid siege to the town and ultimately sacked it. But the story was true none the less, and 'I do not hesitate to declare,' Herodotus wrote, 'that the refusal of the Greeks to believe it was inspired by providence, in order that their utter destruction might plainly prove to mankind that sin is always visited by condign punishment at the hands of God. That, at least, is my own belief.'

The word 'sin' in the last sentence needs some comment. 'Sin' has no word in Greek which exactly corresponds to it. Greek has many words of reproach to express the things which they felt a man should not do, but those things were not by any means in every case what we should describe as sinful. Of the seven deadly sins of Christian doctrine—Pride, Envy, Wrath, Sloth, Avarice, Gluttony, Lust—six, in the Greek view, would have been called *hamartiae*—errors, or 'bad shots'—worthy, perhaps, of reproof from a teacher of virtue, but even so mainly because indulgence in them might spoil the proper balance and satisfaction of a man's life. The only one which a Greek would have recognised as 'sinful' in anything like our sense of the word is Pride—and even that must be understood in a somewhat different sense from ours. The Greeks called it *hubris,* and it meant, as I have already suggested, a failure of that proper subordination, a breaking of that due order of things, upon which life in this world is, and must be, founded. The act of presumption may be against other men, or against the gods: in each case it brings certain punishment.

'Revenge and wrong,' wrote Aeschylus (the translation is Shelley's) 'bring forth their kind

> The foul cubs like their parents are;
> Their den is in the guilty mind,
> And conscience feeds them with despair.'

When Pheron was on the throne of Egypt, it so happened that the Nile, one year, rose too high, and the excessive floods, accompanied by gales, did much damage. In sudden rage Pheron seized a spear and hurled it into the swirling waters—the sacred waters, for all rivers were in part divine. For the act of presumption the Pharaoh lost his sight. Herodotus' book is full of such stories of the perils of pride—pride of wealth, pride of power, pride of success, and, deadliest of all, the pride which leads a man to forget that he is a nothing in the sight of the gods. This is Herodotus'

fundamental morality, and it is not ignoble. Incidentally though the Greeks took to most vices (except gluttony) as a duck takes to water, of *accidie,* at any rate, I do not think any Greek before the fourth century would have been capable.

In all this Herodotus was a man of his time, as he also was in his belief in oracles and in the significance of dreams and omens. In a general way, that is: for one can never be sure with Herodotus whether or not, when one is listening to him telling some tale, one is going to catch at the end of it a hint of half-subdued yet mocking laughter. Popular legend comes in for much amused and rational criticism; there is, for instance, his pleasant comment on the supposed origin of the oracle of Zeus at Dodona. The three priestesses—and Herodotus duly records their names—who served the temple told him that two black doves, long ago, flew away from Thebes in Egypt and that one of them alighted at Dodona, the other in Libya. The former, perched on an oak, and speaking with a human voice, told whoever was there to hear that on that spot there should be an oracle of Zeus. The mystic words were understood to be a command from heaven, and were at once obeyed. Similarly the dove which flew to Libya told the Libyans to found the oracle of Zeus Ammon in the Libyan desert. So much for the legend. Herodotus, however, had previously heard from certain Egyptian priests that a party of Phoenician marauders had, in the distant past, carried off two women from the temple of the Theban Zeus; these they sold, one in Libya, the other in Greece, and it was these women who founded the two oracles. Putting the two stories together, Herodotus goes on to suggest that if there is any truth in the Egyptian version, then the woman who was sold in Greece must have been sold to the Thesprotians, in whose territory Dodona lies; later, while she was working as a slave in that part of the country, she built, under an oak which happened to be growing there, a shrine to Zeus, remembering in her exile the god she had served in her native Thebes. Subsequently, when she had learnt to speak Greek, she established an oracle there. As for the doves, Herodotus adds, 'the story came, I should say, from the fact that the women were foreigners, whose language sounded to the local inhabitants like the twittering of birds; later on the dove spoke with a human voice, because by that time the woman had stopped twittering and learned to speak intelligibly. That at least is how I should explain the obvious impossibility of a dove using the language of men.'

It has always to be remembered that ancient Greek legends and myths, like the legends and myths of all ancient peoples, were not fairy stories. They were believed as historically true, and it is precisely this universal popular acceptance of them as historical fact which throws into relief, for us, the first beginnings of a rational criticism of them. To call Herodotus a rationalist would be untrue and absurd; he shared much too deeply in the general temper of his times. Nevertheless, he asked questions; and, as I have said, one never quite knows what direction his questions will take, and the fact that he can keep us in this uncertainty is not the least interesting aspect of his wide-ranging and many-shaded mind. Does he, or does he not, believe in the significance of dreams? I have suggested that he does; and there are plenty of passages in his book where he gravely tells of some dream whose warning was all too true—the very odd dream, for instance, which Astyages dreamed of his daughter Mandane. Suddenly, however, he will appear to take another look at the whole business, and to smile at his own credulity. In the splendid passage of the seventh Book, recording the conversation between Xerxes and Artabanus before Xerxes had decided upon the invasion of Greece, we are told of the King's ominous dream and how, in doubt and fear, he went to Artabanus, his uncle, for advice upon its meaning. In the course of his reply the old man assured him that dreams do not, as men imagine, come from God. 'I, who am older than you by many years, will tell you what these visions are that float before our eyes in sleep: nearly always these drifting phantoms are the shadows of what we have been thinking about during the day; and during the days before your dream we were, you know, very much occupied with this campaign. Nevertheless it is possible that your dream cannot be explained as I have explained it: perhaps there is, indeed, something divine in it . . .'

Those were two Persians, not two Greeks, talking together; but the thoughts are Herodotus' thoughts. It is true, indeed, that the story goes on to tell how Artabanus, persuaded to sleep that night in the king's bed, himself dreamed a dream of similar import and was thereby convinced of its divine provenance. Nevertheless, the question has been slipped quietly in.

Another instance is Herodotus' comment on a popular belief of the Egyptians, a belief quite consonant with ordinary Greek feeling. Cambyses the Persian king after his conquest of Egypt, committed in that country numerous acts of outrageous cruelty and beastliness, which culminated in his wantonly sticking a dagger into the thigh of the sacred bull, Apis. The wound festered, the bull died, and Cambyses went mad. According to the Egyptians his madness was a divine punishment for his impious act, and, says Herodotus, perhaps it was; 'nevertheless,' he adds, 'it may have been the result of any one of the many maladies which afflict mankind, and there is, in fact, a story that Cambyses suffered from birth from a serious complaint, epilepsy; there would then be nothing strange in the fact that a serious physical malady should have affected his brain.' Again and again we hear Herodotus quietly putting forward the proposition—sometimes with a smile, sometimes with a hint of irony, most often with the sheer pleasure of intelligent curiosity—that there are, indeed, 'more things in heaven and earth

. . .'—and especially, perhaps, on earth, as for him at any rate it was the more interesting place of the two. Is it not, he seems to ask, at least possible, in attempting to account for such or such a phenomenon, to leave the gods out of it for once, and to find, perhaps, some cause in human psychology or in the forces of nature? The case of Thessaly, for instance, which was once a vast lake ringed round by mountains, but is now a plain, good for horses, and drained by the River Peneus flowing out through the gorge of Tempe—*was* it Poseidon, Shaker of Earth, who, as men say, split asunder those enclosing hills? Or could it have been an earthquake?

Herodotus would not at all have approved of the remarks of Xenophanes about the gods; he was happy enough in the religion of his race, though he used to the full the opportunities of incidental comment and criticism which a religion like the Greek, lacking as it did any sacred scripture or body of doctrine, rendered available to whoever chose to use them. The nature and accent of these comments, flickering like summer lightning over a mind fundamentally reverential and steeped in tradition, is one of the things which constitute the incalculable originality of Herodotus' book.

Herodotus has been taken to task for his credulity about oracles, and there is some justice in the charge. It is important, however, to clear away a very common misconception about the nature and function of the Greek oracles, especially of Apollo's oracle at Delphi which was the most generally respected. Contrary to what many people suppose, the least important function of the oracle was to foretell the future, or to exercise any sort of magical or superhuman power of prevision. Its responses were, indeed, given by the God, through the mouth of his Priestess inspired by him—or perhaps, at Delphi, inspired by certain gases which are said to have arisen through a cleft in the mountain, or even by some sort of self-induced frenzy aided by the ancient and numinous associations of the place; and they were usually delivered in archaic, and often ambiguous, terms, couched in hexameter verse, all of which no doubt added something to their apparent weight and solemnity. But—and this is the point—behind the imposing façade erected by a very ancient tradition and kept in being by a continuing sense of religious awe, there was, in fact, a highly competent, and wholly human, organisation. The Delphic oracle acted as a kind of Central Information Bureau for the whole of Greece, and even beyond—for we hear of Asiatic princes, Gyges, for instance, and Alyattes and Croesus, sending gifts to adorn the temple at Delphi and asking Apollo for advice. The organisation seems on the whole to have been most efficient, and information on political and other matters from all parts of the civilised world was carefully collected. Precisely how it was collected we do not know; but there were numerous oracles both in Greece and in Asia Minor (Apollo alone had twenty-two), and it seems pretty certain that the officials who served them were in constant touch with each other. The commonest type of question put to the God was not 'What will happen?' but 'What, in the present circumstances, is the best, or safest, course to take?' To consult the oracle meant not so much to ask for a revelation as to seek advice. No colony, or new settlement, for instance, was ever sent out by the parent city until the oracle had been consulted about the suitability of the proposed site; for the 'oracle-service'—if one may use so irreverent a term—was much more likely to have useful and accurate information about conditions in a distant part of the world, say in the far West or on the Black Sea coast or in North Africa, than any of the people at home who had travelled little, if at all. Information of this kind was, quite obviously, of solid value. The oracle was also asked for its advice on procedure in all sorts of tricky situations, both public and private; and in these cases its answer was not dependent upon a body of carefully collected and perfectly genuine factual knowledge, but upon the general acumen and knowledge of the world of its functionaries. Politically the oracle tended to have a stabilising effect—if anything could be called stable in the Greek world—and its influence was normally used to support the existing order. At Delphi it was under the supervision of a group of distinguished Delphian families, and this fact led, naturally enough, to a certain political bias in favour of the Dorian states, of which Delphi was one. In early centuries this was probably harmless enough, but during the struggle between Athens and Sparta, which occupied the last thirty years of the fifth century, the bias became so marked—Sparta being the leading Dorian state—that by the rest of Greece the oracle's authority was no longer taken seriously and fell into general disrepute. In its religious aspect the influence of the oracle was undoubtedly good: it was believed to give its answers to anyone who came to consult it with a pure heart, and no one was supposed, if he had guilt on his conscience, to get a reply until he had made atonement.

On the whole, then, the oracle was a useful institution, and its service was performed efficiently and intelligently. Naturally it made mistakes; and frequently it was forced to express its judgements darkly and ambiguously, in order that the error, if error there was, might be laid to the interpretation of its answer, not to its own failure in knowledge. There was the well-known response, for instance, which was given to the Athenians when the Persian armies were approaching from the north with Xerxes:

> 'the wooden wall only shall not fail, but help you and your children.
> Divine Salamis, you will bring death to women's sons
> When the corn is scattered, or the harvest gathered in.'

What was the wooden wall? The wall of the Acropo-

lis, or the ships of the Athenian navy? Fortunately for Athens, Themistocles guessed right, but not before he had overcome strong opposition from other Athenian leaders, even from those who accepted the interpretation that the wooden wall meant the fleet—for whose sons did Apollo mean were to die at Salamis? Was Athens to fight a naval action in the straits, and be beaten? No, said Themistocles; had Apollo meant that, he would surely not have called Salamis 'divine'. And most people, if they have read Herodotus or not, will be familiar with the classic ambiguity of the Delphic oracle's advice to Croesus, who wanted to know—poor man—if it would be wise for him to make war upon Cyrus of Persia. This was indeed a tricky question, for the abilities of Cyrus had not yet by any means been fully proved. 'Fight him,' said the oracle, 'and you will destroy a mighty empire.' So Croesus did so—and destroyed his own.

I have not met with any remarks of Xenophanes about the oracle, so I do not know if he included it in his general scepticism about the Olympian religion. There is no doubt, however, that belief in the value—and divine authority—of its responses was all but universal in the Greek world, at least until the fifth century was drawing toward its close. Herodotus was no exception, and he cannot, I think, be charged with credulity when one considers the very real services which the oracle performed; on the other hand, the charge cannot be wholly suspended, because he, like most of his contemporaries, was prepared to accept its occasional silliness-es as well as its more habitual wisdom. Herodotus *liked* oracles; and he quotes a large number of them in his book, uncritically and with evident pleasure. He doesn't turn a hair at the absurd story of how Croesus tested the veracity of the various oracles before deciding which one to consult upon his major problem—how he sent envoys to each with instructions to inquire what, exactly, he was doing at a particular pre-arranged moment on a particular day. Several of the oracles, Herodotus tells us, including Delphi, answered that Croesus was boiling a tortoise in a bronze cauldron: and, strange to say, they were right. Second-sight of this sort is not, I suppose, inexplicable, granted a little collusion and hanky-panky, with perhaps the passing of a coin or two; but for Herodotus, apparently, it was second-sight indeed.

Greek religion was based not upon doctrine but upon observances and ceremonial hallowed by ancient tradition. In these matters all Greeks, with the exception of a few philosophers and free-thinkers, were traditionalists. Herodotus himself was a traditionalist, but with a difference. He treasured the tradition, but allowed himself at the same time to question it.

Charles W. Fornara (essay date 1971)

SOURCE: "Herodotus' Perspective," in *Herodotus: An*

Interpretative Essay, Oxford University Press, 1971, pp. 59-74.

[*In the following essay, Fornara contrasts Herodotus with Thucydides, suggesting that while Thucydides wrote for posterity, Herodotus's* History *addresses chiefly his own generation. Defending Herodotus against scholars who have found the* History *inconsistent and unscientific, Fornara calls him "essentially an artist" who mixes historical narrative with drama.*]

Thucydides believed and claimed that he had written . . . a possession for all time. The boast may have struck his contemporaries as arrogant and rhetorical. To the modern world it is a truism. Our consciousness of the perfect justification of these words, however, deprives them of impact and robs them of all but superficial meaning. Yet their value is inestimable. They tell us, if we needed to be told, what stance he had adopted, what perspective he had taken, in writing his history. These words explain the principle of his selection and inclusion of material. Thinking of future generations more than of his immediate audience, his task as he defined it was to create a history of the Peloponnesian War that would be self-explanatory; no special knowledge beyond his own history would be required to secure perfect comprehension of the important and universally relevant issues. He neither played upon the knowledge of his contemporaries nor allowed that knowledge to deflect him from his course. He would not be constrained to include matter which his audience might well expect to find—gossip about Pericles, intra-political strife, etc. Thus he divorced his account as much as he could from what he considered intrinsically irrelevant, whatever the expectations of his audience may have been, and he included material which they hardly needed to be told in order to make the picture clear to future generations lacking the specific knowledge of contemporaries. Thucydides' sense of the future is one of the most remarkable aspects of his genius. It dominates his history and justifies his boast. For this reason he is to us not only the most brilliant of historians but also, from our point of view, one of the most satisfactory. Although we miss a good deal by not seeing the world he described through the eyes of his contemporaries, and although we may question whether in certain cases he may not have omitted data important for our comprehension of the war, nevertheless, his conception of history or, rather, of the audience for which he was writing, guarantees that his history of the Peloponnesian War leaves nothing he considered relevant taken for granted.

The same sentence in which Thucydides proclaims the eternal relevance of his work ends by contrasting it with a 'declamation intended for a momentary display'. . . . The reference is to Herodotus; only his predecessor can here be intended. Thucydides is alluding to an historical work literally comparable to his own, one

which was written . . . in a highly wrought and artistic fashion. That is enough to exclude the more austere and even scholarly works of Herodotus' predecessors and such later contemporaries as Hellanicus of Lesbos. The disapprobation contained in Thucydides' remark is hardly malicious or spiteful. Rather is it a consequence of what, in Thucydides' view, history should be and what Herodotus failed to make it. It reflects Thucydides' belief that Herodotus' perspective was wrong, that his great work was directed to a particular audience at a particular moment in time. In a word, Thucydides wrote for the future, Herodotus for his contemporaries. And in doing so, Herodotus, as Thucydides was very much aware, was incomplete and misleading or would eventually become so through the passage of time. That is probably one of the reasons Thucydides was moved to supplement his predecessor in several important details, as we shall see. It is enough to say here, however, that their difference in perspective, in their conception of the audience to which they were speaking, is of the greatest importance in attaining a just estimation of Herodotus' intent and method. For judged by our accustomed standards, Herodotus' technique is distinctly unusual. We have misconstrued him because automatically we read him in the same way that we read other historians such as Thucydides, who set the standard for all who follow. Although Thucydides wrote a work with an eye to later generations and attempted to present his material as scientifically as possible, Herodotus directed himself exclusively to his own generation. Only by reading him as if we were his contemporaries can his intentions be fully understood.

One further contrast between Herodotus and Thucydides, which is the corollary of that already mentioned, relates to the manner in which each of them present their material. If Thucydides is eminently 'scientific', Herodotus is essentially an artist. Herodotus' work, especially the last three books, is neither narrative nor 'drama', but something of both. He owed much to the *Iliad* and the *Odyssey,* as frequently has been pointed out. In spirit, however, and in general effect, his work is most like to the Athenian drama. Herodotus' reticence, his reliance on understatement, is the reticence of the dramatist who expresses his opinion through the characters of his creation. Though Herodotus could comment in his own person about whatever he wished, and does so frequently enough, this 'Ionic' and pedagogical strain in his work recedes in proportion as his work becomes dramatic. In VII-IX, for instance, he separates himself carefully from those scenes of greatest dramatic impact. Precisely as the audiences of Aeschylus and Sophocles were intended to form their conclusions without the explicit aid of the playwright, so does Herodotus demand or expect an involved audience participating in and judging what is evoked before them. Herodotus' artistic method is to lead the hearer by what he does not say as much as by what he does. Irony, pathos, paradox, and tragedy develop from his tacit dialogue with his audience. But it is a contemporary audience, whose expectations he could predict, not some future generation with different expectations, for which he was writing.

The truth of these contentions should become apparent from the examination of two test cases. His treatment of Pausanias and Themistocles has frequently been considered problematical or at least surprising. Both are excellent examples of his method and his standpoint.

Herodotus portrays Pausanias, the Regent of Sparta, as if he were the epitome of the knight *sans peur et sans reproche*. The picture he paints is one of the most detailed in the **Histories**—a companion piece to that of Themistocles. Unquestionably he expended the greatest care and thought in the elaboration of the picture, which is consistent and obtrusive. He tells us emphatically that at Plataea Pausanias 'won the finest victory of any man of whom we know,' and Pausanias is told substantially the same thing by a noble Aeginetan, Lampon son of Pytheus. 'O son of Cleombrotus, you have accomplished a great and splendid feat. God has granted you, since you have saved Greece, to lay up in store the greatest glory of any Greek of whom we know.' Shortly thereafter, Pausanias, whose attempt to keep the spoil secure is noted, is granted a tenth of it. Herodotus then relates that extraordinary story which has Pausanias look upon Xerxes' oriental luxury, that equipage which he gave over to Mardonius when he fled from Greece. Pausanias orders the servants to prepare the kind of dinner they were accustomed to serve to Mardonius. 'They did as they were bid and then Pausanias, after he saw the richly covered couches of gold and silver, and the gold and silver tables, and the dazzling display of the dinner, was thunderstruck by the good things set before him. He ordered his own servants to prepare a Laconian feast for the humour of it. After the dinner was prepared Pausanias laughed since the difference was great. He summoned the Greek generals and when they came Pausanias said, pointing to the display of each of the dinners, "I have assembled you because I want to show you the folly of the Mede. With a way of life such as this he came to take away from us our miserable fare." This it is said that Pausanias remarked to the generals.' In IX. 88, Pausanias shows compassion and charity to the children of men guilty of treachery. One further anecdote concerns Pausanias' solicitous and lofty treatment of a misused woman.

Herodotus' description of the Regent is surprising on two counts. In the first place, the dramatic acknowledgement of his personal contribution is unusual and surprisingly emphatic. Herodotus' interest is frankly biographical: the man interests him as much as his achievement. His account is also surprising in view of

Pausanias' subsequent career and lamentable end. The question of his intent in depicting Pausanias as he has done, in sparing no effort to portray him as an extraordinarily noble and fortunate figure, naturally suggests itself. The question cannot be skirted by invoking a source hypothetically concerned to magnify Pausanias' role in 479 B.C. That the recollection of Pausanias' greatness managed to survive the obloquy cast upon his name is not to be believed—he was not another Nero, with people setting flowers on his grave. In any event, Herodotus' presentation must be the mirror of his own attitude and that presentation reveals a uniform conception of the Spartan Regent. For this reason, some have concluded that Herodotus' account of Pausanias is governed by scepticism about his guilt, that a natural implication of Herodotus' sketch is that he did not consider Pausanias to be the scoundrel others supposed.

Nothing could be farther from the truth. What surprises us is precisely what Herodotus was counting on but what we do not expect because this is a 'historical work'. It is almost as if we assume that Herodotus intended to write a competing version. When 'historians' are good to villainous characters they are setting the record straight, combating an erroneous tradition, repeating an apologetic source. We are so accustomed to completing Herodotus' account of Pausanias by adding to it as a matter of course the final chapters as recorded by Thucydides that we have forgotten that Herodotus could not know that Thucydides would tell of Pausanias' end. When we realize that he thought in no such terms, that he was confronting his audience independently and alone, the conclusion is as revealing as it is startling. If *we* had only Herodotus on the subject of Pausanias, the son of Cleombrotus would indeed 'have laid up the greatest store of glory of any Greek'. It certainly did not occur to Herodotus that he could mislead anyone in this fashion. There is not the slightest reason to suppose that he could have wished to. It follows inescapably that Herodotus took for granted the knowledge of Pausanias' fall. Herodotus' intention was to build upon that knowledge; the reflections of his contemporaries are the precondition of his narrative. They believed, and Herodotus knew they believed, that Pausanias was a traitor. Herodotus' dramatic treatment of Pausanias takes its departure and acquires its significance from the common knowledge of his time. His portrait of Pausanias is in the light of that knowledge a masterpiece of irony and a harbinger of tragedy. Lampon's words have a double meaning. 'God has granted you to lay up in store the greatest glory of any Greek.' What God granted Pausanias threw away. The implicit lesson is not the less immediate because Herodotus studiously avoided any allusion to Pausanias' later *hybris*. On the contrary, it is the more impressive because of it. Herodotus has characterized the finest hour of a man whose degeneration provides a striking example of Herodotus' law of history, of the

Herodotus crowned by muses; from J. Gronovius's 1715 edition.

instability of good fortune . . . That is why his treatment of Pausanias is so carefully done and so eminent a feature of the ninth book.

Herodotus' method is artistic, not historical. He has created a drama to which the audience, as the 'dramatist' well knows, and indeed demands, will bring a level of comprehension that altogether changes its point. What appear to be mere anecdotes without direction are in reality magnificent and richly allusive passages. From the point of view of the audience, that fascination of Pausanias with the luxury of the Persians will have been only too clear. The vision proved too much for him. Herodotus, in depicting the scene, foreshadowed that later disaster and presupposed the knowledge of it. As a final example of his method, one so rich in irony that it needs no comment, let us consider the brave speech Pausanias delivers in refusing to maltreat the corpse of Mardonius, as was suggested by the same Lampon. 'O friend from Aegina, I am delighted by your good feeling and solicitude. Nevertheless you have strayed from sound judgement. For having raised me high in respect to fatherland and deed, you bring me down to nothing by urging me to do injury to the dead, saying that if I do this my fame will be greater. This is a thing a barbarian may suitably do and not a Greek. And them we despise. In this matter, therefore, I would neither desire to please the Aeginetans nor anyone else who desires it. It is enough for me to please the Spartans by acting piously and by speaking piously. And I say that Leonidas, whom you urge me to honour, has been honoured greatly. He and the rest of the dead at Thermopylae are honoured by the numberless wraiths of these men here. Do not you then approach me or advise me if you remain in the same opinion but be thankful that you go off unharmed.'

It is a magnificently ironic and tragic picture. One thinks of Oedipus damning himself, condemning what will prove to be his own tragic flaw. But this picture could be misleading; it depends on knowledge that is taken for granted. Perhaps that explains Thucydides' supplementary account. He may have felt obliged to provide it in order to keep the historical record unambiguous and free from what easily could become a deceptive tradition. Thucydides certainly was capable of such prognosis. It is also, I think, a superb example of what Thucydides had in mind when he spoke of the 'prize composition for the moment'. For Herodotus' concern was with the minds and emotions of his listeners, not with the inferences of later generations or the requirements of 'scientific' history. His account of Pausanias was an imaginative recreation calculated to achieve maximum psychological effect. His contemporaries unquestionably responded as he expected.

No person is depicted by Herodotus with more care and more skill than Themistocles. It is therefore illustrative of the manner in which Herodotus has been studied, of the presuppositions which we bring to our reading of his work, that his portrait of Themistocles has been held up as an example of Herodotus' malignity and incomprehension. Ivo Bruns, in his excellent study of biography, helped to formulate this prevalent view. In speaking of Herodotus' Themistocles he claimed that Herodotus, unlike Thucydides, lacked a clear conception 'of the nature of his characters and stood helplessly before the most contradictory traditions'. That opinion is misconceived. Far from lacking a conception of Themistocles' personality, Herodotus is responsible for having created it. He presents us with a person whose distinguishing characteristics are cleverness and foresight on the one hand and greed and unscrupulousness on the other. The problem has not been that Herodotus lacks a self-consistent idea of Themistocles but that we evidently would prefer a different conception. And that preference has facilitated the view that Herodotus was either unaccountably malicious or that he mechanically reproduced 'hostile traditions' without clearly knowing what he was doing. It is ironic that an author who is supposed to have written an encomium of Athens is suspected of malignancy towards that state's greatest hero and is regarded as incapable of distinguishing a 'hostile' tradition from a favourable one.

Herodotus' 'intent' deserves clearer analysis than it has received. When, for example, Themistocles is described essentially as the sort of man 'openly filling his pockets at every opportunity', is Herodotus malignant or uncomprehending because Themistocles was actually known to have been honest? The charge of cupidity levelled against him is an ancient one. Was Herodotus hostile, then, because it is a mark of hostility not to have suppressed this objectionable trait? Herodotus assuredly did not write his history in order to present Themistocles as if he were the hero of a nineteenth-century novel. The important consideration for judging Herodotus' historical perception is that he recognized Themistocles' genius and resource and, more important, that the picture he paints of Themistocles is one which permits *us* to recognize his greatness. For Themistocles is the dominant figure in his account of Xerxes' War.

Again, I suggest, the cardinal assumption has been that Herodotus was writing 'scientific' history—that he intended his sketch of Themistocles to be a straightforward 'historical' portrayal like that of Thucydides. Thucydides, from his perspective, wanted future generations to realize that the intelligence and the foresight of Themistocles were crucial factors in the development of the Athenian state. His moral character and even the question of whether he became treasonable are irrelevant to that concern—not, by any means, that his own opinion of Themistocles' character is noticeably different from Herodotus'. Thucydides' emphasis is different. Herodotus, though he provides us with the material permitting us to form a proper estimate of Themistocles' intellectual capacity, was concerned to present a dramatic portrait of this figure which would be credible to his contemporaries. He was dealing with the expectations of his audience. Merely consider, for instance, that oft-discussed and unappreciated first mention of Themistocles made by Herodotus in VII. 143. 'Now there was a certain Athenian man who recently had stepped up to the forefront whose name was Themistocles and who was called the son of Neocles' . . .

Most commentators consider this introduction a slap. Would his audience have thought so on hearing it? Herodotus has just finished describing very dramatically the plight of Athens, the fact that 'authority' was against any attempt to fight a sea-battle at Salamis (which the audience well knew was crucial). Dark was the moment; 'but there was a certain Athenian man who had recently stepped to the forefront'. The first two words . . . are enough to show a rift in the clouds. And then, deliberately, the name is withheld until the sentence runs to its end. Expectation, suspense and understatement: Herodotus has given Themistocles a drumroll. The formula is an excellent one with which to start an important episode. Homer used it to introduce Dolon (*Iliad* X. 314). The tone of such an introduction is nicely indicated by Xenophon in *Anabasis* III. I. 4. At a critical moment, when the Greek mercenaries faced crisis, Xenophon introduced the hero with these words: 'Now there was a certain man in the army, Xenophon the Athenian,' . . . We seem to expect that Herodotus should have provided us with some reference to Themistocles' earlier career (assuming he had knowledge of it) or have made some weighty historical judgement when actually his own concern was dramatic.

Let us therefore consider Herodotus' Themistocles from the point of view of his audience. The artistic and dramatic problems which the expectations of his audience would have created for him, if his account was to be successful, were considerable. Whatever his contemporaries may have known of Themistocles' contributions in 480-79 B.C. and however they viewed his epochal work in making Athens a sea-power, we may assume that he was chiefly pre-eminent as the personification of wiliness. The popular conception of this great man undoubtedly centred on his suppleness and craft. He had been condemned to death for treason and after a sensational flight to Persia had gained an extraordinary reception from the Great King. Themistocles' life was the kind to make people marvel; the final chapter of it would have been as notable and even more inciteful of speculation about the man and anecdotes about his nature than the earlier ones. His greatness may have been proved by his leadership in 480-79 B.C.; but to a later generation removed from that era the amazing dexterity and capacity to look after himself signalled by his final Asiatic venture will have been the most remarkable and most notorious of all.

That final chapter must, for Herodotus, have been the starting point in his attempt to fathom the character of that remarkable man. The challenge to his skill was to create a believable character who was capable of being at once the saviour of the Greeks in Xerxes' War and the presumed traitor of not very long after. Herodotus married the known unscrupulous but invariably successful figure who died in Persia with the man who in 479 B.C. was proclaimed 'the wisest man in Greece.'

As in the case of Pausanias, Herodotus expected his audience to superimpose its knowledge of the sensational downfall of Themistocles on to his description of that character. Where we are apt to make him an abstraction, Herodotus gave him verisimilitude. An admirable instance of his technique is provided by his narration in VIII. 108ff. of Themistocles' famous message to Xerxes after the battle of Salamis. The Greeks, having reached Andros in pursuit of Xerxes, halted for a council of war. Themistocles as usual hit upon the most effective means to wound the enemy and advanced the proposal that the Greeks race to the Hellespont and dismantle the bridges. We are reminded of former occasions when the others are hostile to his bold and successful measures. However, though Herodotus could attribute the resolve to Themistocles, the nature of the case forbade him from presenting us here with the successful operation of his powers or his craft. The plan was not attempted. Yet Themistocles' defeat is but temporary, for he is able to capitalize even on that. 'When he understood that he would not persuade the many, at any rate, he changed course with the Athenians. For they were especially grieved at the thought of the Persians escaping, and were eager to sail to the Hellespont even if the others did not want to and even if they must act alone.' Themistocles then dissuades them with an effective speech and Herodotus resumes: 'This he said intending to lay up store with the Persian in order that he might have some place of refuge if by some chance a disaster should come upon him from the Athenians. And this was the very thing that happened. Themistocles deceived them in his speech and the Athenians were persuaded' to give up the venture. Sicinnus was thereupon sent by Themistocles to tell Xerxes that 'Themistocles, desiring to do Xerxes a service, *stopped the Greeks* when they wished to pursue his ships and break down the bridges at the Hellespont.'

Eduard Meyer excoriated Herodotus for this story. He believed that Herodotus intended to make Themistocles responsible for 'the betrayal of the Greek cause'. Macan and Stein assume the phrase 'intending to lay up store of credit with Xerxes' 'shows how much prejudiced Herodotus is . . . even in a case where not a shadow of suspicion falls on him.' How, in his note to VIII. 110, writes that Herodotus is 'evidently here under the influence of traditions hostile to Themistocles. There is no special reason to suspect him of double dealing in this case.' Surely these scholars have studied the passage with the wrong lens. Herodotus' intent was to show Themistocles' great capacity for the clever ruse. Deceit, to be sure, is part of the nature Herodotus, like Thucydides, supposed him to possess. That, after all, was the key to his strategic genius. But the purpose of the anecdote is not to show some treasonable intent on Themistocles' part. Herodotus went to considerable length to make that clear; one half of the episode should not be separated from the other. Themistocles was forestalled by his colleagues from inflicting the crushing blow that he had himself conceived of. If Herodotus had intended to make Themistocles a *traitor,* he would have presented the story differently. Themistocles did not deceive the Greeks; he fooled Xerxes. His allegation that he had stopped the Greeks from racing to the Hellespont was the reverse of the truth. But Xerxes did not know it and so Themistocles laid up store of credit with the King.

What is worthy of especial note in Herodotus' narrative is the care he has taken *not* to suggest that Themistocles was already marching down the path of treason. Herodotus has attributed to Themistocles a remarkable instance of his famous foresight. But he put Themistocles' prevision in the most general terms—'If possibly . . . some evil fall upon him from the Athenians.' His Themistocles viewed the possibility of a dangerous turn in his career very hypothetically. Herodotus has separated the actual treason everyone thinks of from Themistocles' own prognostication. It is a splendid example of Herodotus having it both ways, and intentionally so.

What we, in an overprotective way, have taken to be an anecdote derogatory of Themistocles would to his audience have appeared to be the ultimate example of Themistocles' capacity to look after himself. Herodotus did not intend to suggest that Themistocles was a traitor to the Greek cause. But he very definitely permitted that conception of Themistocles to illuminate his account. His purpose is artistic. He was attempting neither to blacken Themistocles' reputation nor to whitewash it. He was recreating Themistocles' character for the sake of his story, not for the 'historical record'. If we do not like this fifth-century Odysseus, it is perhaps because we are apt to glorify our heroes in more conventional terms and because we are unaccustomed to finding this kind of dramatization in a history. That was not the opinion of Cicero or, one suspects, of Thucydides. The Greeks were not so prim in their younger days. They could admire cleverness and dexterity for their own sake. We have only to think of Themistocles' predecessor and his protector's attitude to *him:*

> Athena began to smile;
> She caressed him, her form now that of a
>   woman,
> Beautiful, tall, skilled at weaving fine things.

She spoke to him in winged words:
> 'Cunning and thievish the man who could beat
>   you
> In all your tricks, even if some god were to
>   try it.
> You devil! You schemer! Fraud! You never
>   cease,
> Not even at home, from the cheats
> And lying words that are your nature.
> But we'll say no more: we're both
>   Alike.'

Herodotus' treatment of Themistocles, like that of Pausanias, is directed to contemporaries well aware of what he leaves unsaid. The impact derives from his reliance on the response of his audience, from what he knows his hearers will conclude. His procedure is not substantially different from that of the tragedians. The basics were known, the end result predictable. What mattered was the presentation of the detail in such a way as to keep the audience involved and make the pattern explicable. This is the essence of Herodotus' art and the key to his technique. The instances already discussed provide what are perhaps the most remarkable examples of this technique because of Herodotus' subtlety and because his imaginative recreation was so daring. But it is the same with Xerxes. No Greek was unaware that this splendid figure would fall heavily and Herodotus, in presenting Xerxes to his audience, made him the more splendid so that the fall would be more dramatic. In this case, to be sure, our own presuppositions coincide with those of Herodotus' contemporaries. What I have tried to suggest, however, is that this is not inevitably so, as the usual interpretation of his treatment of Pausanias and Themistocles should show. When our expectations do not jibe with contemporary expectations, it is easy to misconstrue Herodotus' intentions as being to 'exculpate' Pausanias or to 'vilify' Themistocles. We expect him to 'tell the truth' where he expected his contemporaries to use 'the truth' as the touchstone of his account. How different might our interpretation of Herodotus' portraits of Pausanias and Themistocles have been if we realized that in both cases Herodotus expected his audience to be thinking primarily of the fall of each man. Instead we have assumed that these final stages of each man's career were unimportant for Herodotus or, rather, that Pausanias' was unimportant. For in the instance of Themistocles, it is we who dissociate that final chapter from the earlier and virtually condemn Herodotus for remembering it. The difference between Herodotus and Thucydides, between the *Histories* and 'history', is at once subtle and profound.

We must therefore think away the predisposition to approach Herodotus as if he were speaking to us directly, and understand him, as best we can, as his contemporaries would have done. There are fundamental but unspoken connections he relied on his audience to make. In this respect, also, we must abandon that general willingness to judge events from a perspective favourable to Athens, to assume that everyone shared it. The projection of that attitude into Herodotus has made his sympathies seem a chaos of inconsistency. Herodotus did not write his history for the partisans of the Athenian democracy. He directed his work to the Greek world in general and more particularly to a class which he, like Thucydides considered hostile to the state of Athens. Finally, since it is Herodotus' technique to mesh his narrative with the predictable thoughts of his contemporaries, we must remind ourselves constantly that the people for whom he was writing were living during the outbreak of the Archidamian War.

Oswyn Murray (essay date 1972)

SOURCE: "Herodotus and Hellenistic Culture," in *The Classical Quarterly,* Vol. XXII, No. 2, November, 1972, pp. 200-13.

[*In the following essay, Murray traces the influence of Herodotus on early Hellenistic historiography and ethnography, detecting evidence of familiarity with Herodotus in the works of Hecataeus of Abdera, Nearchus, and Megasthenes. Accepting that Herodotus's influence had declined by the late Hellenistic period, Murray nonetheless contends that the* History *had a broad and lasting impact on Hellenistic understanding of the world.*]

Our understanding of the world is not static; it can both expand and contract, and it can also stagnate. In history the expansion of the known universe has come about from various causes, from scientific advance, the slow processes of trade and exploration, from colonization, and especially from conquest. Periods of expansion produce often a re-evaluation of the external world, both that which was already known and that which was previously unknown, or on the fringes of the known. But no one is wholly capable of a direct response to reality: reality as soon as it is experienced is perceived, organized: 'Die Weltist die Gesamtheit der Tatsachen nicht der Dinge' (the world is the totality of facts, not of things). To the understanding of experience, new as well as old, everyone comes with the preconceptions and prejudices of his own environment, and seeks to explain the unknown in relation to it, in terms of marvels, opposites, or contrasts ('The Egyptians in most of their manners and customs exactly reverse the ordinary practices of mankind') in terms of theoretical preconceptions of the noble savage, or the ideal state, or some notion of the structure behind all societies: or in terms of what has been established by previous observers as the proper way of dealing with the unknown, a process which often involves the re-evaluation of those previous observers. And to these periods of expansion there correspond periods when the vision of the world stagnates, when it is viewed in terms of a set of stereotypes which were once part of a fresh and intelligent response to the new situation, but are now the stale clichés of a generation too traditional to think for itself.

These statements may be illustrated from many periods of history. The great Arab expansion was followed in the ninth to eleventh centuries by a period in which Arab writers tried to grapple with the new horizons of knowledge. They produced a literature based in part on their own observations (the importance of travel was emphasized), on official records, and on written or oral accounts of the travels of others by land and sea. The old world of the Koran was no longer adequate; it even became uncertain whether Mecca was the centre of the world. The theoretical basis of these Arab geographers and ethnographers was not, however, empirical. It was derived from earlier Pahlavi and Greek writings, and especially from the works of Ptolemy and Marinus, now translated into Arabic. Often there was a conflict between these theoretical structures and the empirical facts gathered by travel and observation; but this conflict was a necessary one. The complexities of the construction of a great geographical literature can be seen for instance in the work of Ibn Khurradādhbih (published in two editions of 846 and 885), a director of posts and intelligence under the Abbāsid caliphs, who wrote at the desire of the Caliph, but was also a scholar, a translator of Ptolemy; or in the Arab Herodotus, al-Masʿūdī, who died in 956, traveller, geographer, historian, who believed that geography was a part of history, and wrote his geographical account as an introduction to and an integral part of his history. Then from the twelfth century onwards there was a period of consolidation, compilation, and decline, in which the old geographers were used to propagate a view of the world which the West had rejected by the sixteenth century, but which in the East lasted till the nineteenth. Here we can see too the effect of the transfer of the spirit of exploration from the Arabs to the Portuguese, and so to other western nations.

In literary terms, the re-evaluation of previous writers is well illustrated, as Professor Momigliano has shown, by the effect of the reports of European travellers in the sixteenth century, the accounts of the discovery and exploration of America. Fifteenth-century scholars had accepted the view that Herodotus was the father of history perhaps, but also the father of lies. A hundred years later Stephanus in his *Apologia pro Herodoto* (1566) could point to the comparative study of native customs as showing that Herodotus was basically reliable. The influence was reciprocal; Alonso de Zorita in his *Relation of the Lords of New Spain* (written before 1570) could discuss the problems of barbarism and civilization in terms of the Greek and Roman response; and Bartolomé de Las Casas in his *Apologéti-*

ca Historia (written in the 1550s) could analyse and compare Indian culture, society, and religion with those of ancient peoples, and according to the categories of Aristotle.

In the ancient world these same phenomena can be observed. During and immediately after the periods of expansion there is a new awareness, a new flexibility of response, to the variety of human cultures. It is no accident that the great writers of cultural history appear in or just after such periods—the first age of colonization and of contact with the East, the conquests of Alexander, and those of the middle and late Roman Republic in the West. Ancient writers knew this well: Polybius expresses best this interrelationship of conquest and geographical knowledge, the importance of travel, the difficulties of autopsy, and the effect of Alexander and the Romans in a passage too long to quote. These periods of expansion are followed by periods when the new vision becomes another stereotype to imprison the imagination. But also, in such periods of change, there is continuity; the writers who grappled with these new worlds tried to understand them in relation to their own preconceptions, and their predecessors. It is my design in this preliminary study to show something of the influence of Herodotus on the most sudden and dramatic extension of the frontiers of the known world which ever faced antiquity, the conquests of Alexander.

I

For a long time the accepted modern view was that Herodotus was not read widely in the Hellenistic world; his style was out of favour, and his reputation was that of a liar, or a *muthologos,* a teller of charming stories. He had nothing to teach the new scientific ethnography of the Hellenistic period, which mentioned him only in disparagement or for ridicule; and the ordinary reader, finding his delight in the pleasures of the moment, works written . . . in romantic stories of distant places, was now better served by the wilder shores of prose romance or utopian travelogues.

Nowadays it is usual to dismiss this 'old view'; we know, it is said, that Herodotus continued to be read in the Hellenistic world. But usually this admission is immediately qualified: he was read for his style, but despised as a historian; he was an author for the schools of rhetoric, not a man read by the true seeker after knowledge; he was of course read, but his influence was slight compared with that of Thucydides—it is Thucydides who dominates the historiography of the Hellenistic world.

In the face of this attitude, I must begin by offering in general terms some indications of the popularity of Herodotus as an author; for such grudging admissions scarcely do justice to the central position of Herodotus

as one of the most widely read authors throughout antiquity. And it is against this general background, in which it must be assumed that almost every educated man had read Herodotus, and quite as many as had read Thucydides, that we must consider what difference this acquaintance with Herodotus made to the vision of the world created in the early Hellenistic period.

First, a general numerical argument. From the provincial capitals of Graeco-Roman Egypt have come, according to the last count, no less than twenty-one papyrus fragments of Herodotus; he stands fifteenth in the top twenty authors, and sixth among prose writers, after Demosthenes, Plato, Isocrates, Thucydides, and Xenophon. The fragility of such calculations is shown by the fact that in a volume of the Oxyrhynchus Papyri series soon to appear, fragments of at least eleven new manuscripts on papyrus will be published, which would raise Herodotus from fifteenth to ninth in order of popularity, roughly equal with Thucydides, and above Xenophon. Moreover, Xenophon was for the Graeco-Roman world a philosopher as much as a historian: in terms of his historical works alone he falls far behind Herodotus. This popularity of Herodotus might be explained by local factors, by the Egyptian Greek's interest in his own country; but the Egyptian section of Herodotus' work, book 2, is no more heavily represented than any other part. Of course it is true that such calculations fail to distinguish between the Ptolemaic and Roman periods; but I can see no reason why the reading habits of the bourgeoisie of Oxyrhynchus should have radically changed *towards* rather than away from Herodotus under Roman rule. And if none of the papyrus fragments of Herodotus are Ptolemaic, the same is almost true of Thucydides: against the one third-century B.C. fragment of Thucydides we can set the far more significant evidence, also from a papyrus, that Aristarchus the great Alexandrian scholar of the early second century wrote a commentary on Herodotus—the earliest known commentary on a prose author, and the only known one before Didymus wrote on the orators. Nor was Aristarchus the only Alexandrian to interest himself in Herodotus; Aristophanes of Byzantium used him for his *Lexeis;* and Aristarchus' great rival Hellanicus the grammarian lectured on Herodotus.

From the papyri then we may perhaps surmise that the two most popular historians in Graeco-Roman Egypt were Herodotus and Thucydides together; or that at least there is no support in the evidence for the view that there was a period when one eclipsed the other. Both were standard authors to be read for pleasure or instruction; and Herodotus at least was the victim of learned Alexandrian discussion and lectures, philological study, and textual criticism.

The general popularity of Herodotus is also well shown by the poetry of the period. Herodotus is of course of all historians . . . likely to appeal to poets, whereas one can scarcely imagine Thucydides, the political historian of small Greek cities, appealing to the court poets of Alexandria; so the poetic popularity of the two can hardly be compared. But at least the positive conclusion emerges again, that Herodotus was used extensively by Hellenistic poets. His influence has been detected on Callimachus, and there are clear echoes of him in Apollonius Rhodius. Perhaps the most interesting example is Apollonius' account of the Argonauts on Lake Tritonis, and the prophecy of the clod of earth which was to symbolize future colonization in Libya. Here Apollonius does not just use the obvious poetic model; for the story is told in Pindar's *Fourth Pythian*. He also uses the variant account in Herodotus book 4, deliberately combining the two in a composite story.

The list of poets who read and appreciated Herodotus could be extended, with the help of the local epic poets and the Greek anthology; but, for the sake of being controversial, I will add only one more writer. There could scarcely be a greater tribute paid to a historian by a poet than the versification of his narrative. I refer of course to the faithful transmutation into tragedy of the Herodotean story of Gyges of Lydia by some unknown writer of the Hellenistic age.

This affection and respect for the first Greek historian also found expression in honorific statues. That might be expected of Halicarnassus, which in florid Asianic style proclaimed (on a statue base which has survived): 'Nineveh was not allotted the furrow of mankind nor was the self-sown shoot of the Muses reared in India, nor did primeval Babylon bring forth the sweet lips of Herodotus and Panyassis beloved of Hera, but the rocky soil of Halicarnassus; through whose songs she has found great glory among the cities of the Greeks.' We possess also the base of the portrait of Herodotus which stood in the library of the kings of Pergamon, the most famous library of the Hellenistic world after that of Alexandria.

Such evidence is perhaps enough to show that the appreciation of Herodotus was not confined to natives of Halicarnassus like Dionysius, who tried to place Herodotus above Thucydides on stylistic grounds; rather Herodotus was read widely by educated people. If we ask how he was read, the answer is one which will emerge more clearly later on. But the poets at least, like the philosophers, read him for information. And Aristarchus' comments (or those that survive in the miserable fragment of excerpts, perhaps also partly in epitome) are surprisingly wide. He does the things we would expect of a grammarian, explaining difficult words, offering parallels (not of obvious relevance), discussing variant readings. But he is also concerned with the factual information in Herodotus; he appears to add to it, he offers modern parallels, and in discussing his variant reading he supports it by comparative

factual material. This is not a purely linguistic, stylistic, and textual commentary.

II

My present purpose is however more specific; I wish to show the influence of Herodotus on the conception which the Hellenistic age had of the world around it. And especially I wish to argue that it is this influence which lies at the basis of the whole tradition of Hellenistic historical ethnography. The easiest way to demonstrate this is perhaps to investigate those prose authors of the early Hellenistic period who interpreted for the new rulers of the world the alien cultures which now belonged to them; for this small group of writers created a view of foreign civilizations which lasted at least until the differently oriented Roman conquests produced a Poseidonius.

Already in the fourth century B.C. the influence of Herodotus on the writing of history had been strong, especially on Ephorus, whose history used Herodotus as one of its main sources, and also shows many Herodotean elements. The historians of the court of Philip of Macedon seem to have been particularly interested in Herodotus—a specific instance perhaps of the growing interest in the Persian empire as an area of expansion. Theopompus wrote an epitome of Herodotus in two books (the first known epitome), and his histories were noted for his Herodotean digressions: he seems to have offered a defence of this addition of *poikilotēs* to history, for Strabo records him as saying that 'he would write stories in his histories more marvellous than Herodotus and Ctesias and Hellanicus and those who write on India.' Callisthenes too is known to have followed Herodotus almost word for word on occasions.

But it is the early Hellenistic writers who seem most heavily indebted to Herodotus. They never tire of denouncing him, and declaring his information to be unreliable. That was of course necessary in order to assert (often falsely) their own independence of his narrative, and their allegedly better sources of information: it was a game which had been played with equal dishonesty by Ctesias earlier. Thus Hecataeus, writing the standard account of Egypt under Ptolemy Soter, can say: 'Now as for the stories invented by Herodotus and certain other writers on Egyptian matters, who deliberately preferred to the truth the telling of marvellous tales and the insertion of myths to please their readers, these we shall omit, and give only what appears in the written records of the priests of Egypt and has passed our careful scrutiny.' References to the unreliability of Herodotus and his love of stories . . . are numerous; as Josephus says, other writers may attack each other, 'but everyone accuses Herodotus of lying.' Indeed I know of only one author to have said anything respectful about Herodotus; Agatharchides calls him 'a tireless investigator if ever there was one, and with much experience of history'—a significant tribute, for Agatharchides goes on to discuss and refute Herodotus' theory of the rising of the Nile.

In one sense all the attacks on Herodotus by professional historians and ethnographers help to show that he was widely read, and all the contradictions of his detailed information similarly show how carefully he was studied by the very authors who denounce him. But my aim is to go further still, to suggest that for all their denunciations the early Hellenistic writers saw the world through Herodotean eyes, modelled large sections of their works on him, indeed that their achievement in so successfully describing the new world they saw was made possible only with the help of their great predecessor.

The earliest work I wish to discuss is that written by Alexander's admiral and companion in India, Nearchus. Here there is no need to sort out in detail the work of Nearchus from the accounts of India in Arrian and Strabo. My point is a simple one. Nearchus is a reasonably trustworthy and reliable writer, who reports largely what he saw, without romantic exaggeration. This is the account of an honest and perceptive soldier, not an intellectual. And yet we know that Nearchus took Herodotus' account of India very seriously, and we can still see traces of its influence, both in detail and in general conception—all this despite the fact that his own experiences must have shown Nearchus how unreliable the account of India in Herodotus was. Nearchus saw India not wholly as the innocent traveller, but through Herodotean eyes; he may very well have travelled with a copy of Herodotus. At least when he came to write his account of India and of his travels some time before 312, he wrote with Herodotus in mind; and there is good reason to suspect that he even wrote in Ionic in order to emphasize this connection. He was prepared to go a long way in his trust of Herodotus; thus Nearchus was interested in the gold-digging ants of enormous size which are perhaps Herodotus' most fabulous animals; he said that though he never saw any of these strange creatures, their skins were brought in large numbers to the Macedonian camp, and they looked like panther skins. Now the Herodotean story is presumably a combination of genuine Indian myth with a trade in skins and gold; but the interesting fact is that Nearchus (and perhaps others on Alexander's expedition) knew of the Herodotean story, and did not disbelieve it, but rather sought to verify it. Again we find Nearchus echoing Herodotus' account of Indian dress, and in F 17 quoting and generalizing Herodotus' famous description of Egypt as the gift of the Nile, to cover other alluvial plains—in connection of course with the great river plains of North India. The parallelism with Egypt is indeed an underlying theme of Nearchus' work: he discussed the flooding of the Indus valley in relation to the Nile floods,

and attributed both to summer rains; he described the flora and fauna of the same area against the background of Egypt. This comparison between the Indian plains and Egypt is on one level the reaction of an intelligent observer, who saw how similar the natural forces were in both countries. But it is also the observation of a man whose eyes have been adjusted to a river valley environment through the reading of Herodotus; Nearchus' account of India looks not only to Herodotus' short section on the country, but also to the full-scale description of Egypt in book 2. And the Herodotean sections on Arabia and Ethiopia, which occur directly after the account of India, have been used by Nearchus as a model for his description of the desert country and its inhabitants on his voyage to the Persian Gulf.

And yet Nearchus is perhaps closer to Herodotus in spirit than other Hellenistic writers are; for he still retains something of the innocent eye of the traveller without preconceptions. That innocent eye was lost in the work of the writer who influenced most decisively Hellenistic history and ethnography, Hecataeus of Abdera, the first author to write for and under the patronage of one of the Diadochoi. His work on Egypt, largely preserved in book 1 of Diodorus, was written very early in Ptolemy Soter's control over Egypt, probably between 320 and 315, before the essential character of the Ptolemaic state apparatus had been established, and when native Egyptian attitudes were more respected; its purpose was primarily to glorify the land of Egypt, to present it as the source of all civilization, and the ideal philosophical state. Hecataeus' work transformed the writing of ethnography. It was arranged on logical principles, carried out for the first time with total consistency. Firstly the *archaeologia,* prehistory or *theologoumena*—the mythical period (theology and mythology being in typical Greek fashion equated, and explained as a reflection of early history). Then perhaps a geographical section, though this could be disputed. After the mythical period, the historical; finally a systematic description of the customs of Egypt. Hecataeus' account is based on his own investigations and information gathered from Egyptian priests, to be sure: he is insistent on his access to the written archives of Egypt, and on the new standards of accuracy he has imported. But it is also clear that he used previous Greek writers; and of these writers he used most extensively Herodotus. Before he embarks on his description of the customs of Egypt, he delivers the explicit attack on Herodotus as an unreliable source, quoted above. But the whole section on the history of Egypt, just before that, is in fact for the most part taken with only the smallest alterations from Herodotus. Again Hecataeus' rationalistic attitude to Egyptian religion and its relation to Greek is modelled on that of Herodotus; and even in the section on customs, where he is so insistent on his own superiority, it is clear that he has used Herodotus extensively.

Hecataeus may have known of the lost fourth-century works on Egypt; but it is obvious that he regarded his greatest predecessor as Herodotus. He thought that he was superseding Herodotus because Herodotus was too credulous for the modern taste, and because he was insufficiently 'scientific' in his approach; instead of organizing his material, he wrote as caught his fancy. Hecataeus imported structure into his account, a structure based on philosophical theories—theories of the ideal state which for Hecataeus was exemplified in old Egypt, and theories of the nature of ethnographic description. This marriage of the Herodotean innocent eye with genuine local tradition on the one hand and on the other with Greek philosophy, set a standard and a pattern for the writers of the next two centuries: it was the renewal of the Herodotean approach adapted to a more sophisticated age.

Hecataeus' work provoked immediate competition from the other successor kingdoms. Megasthenes was on several occasions the ambassador of Seleucus to the court of Chandragupta in India. The work he wrote in the first decade of the third century on the basis of his experiences was a direct reply to Hecataeus, and modelled on the method, form, and content of his book—a systematic account of Indian culture with geography, flora, fauna, and the people (book 1), the system of government and *nomoi* (book 2), society and philosophy (book 3), archaeology, mythology, and history (book 4). This work is the source of Diodorus' section on India, as of much of Strabo and Arrian. Megasthenes was a well-read man; and, like Hecataeus, he aimed to write a definitive account. He relied on his own travels and the information he had carefully gathered from Indians, but also on the accounts of previous Greek writers; it was perhaps unfortunate that their stories were so unreliable. But he knew at least on general grounds that he should prefer Herodotus to Ctesias. Apart from Megasthenes' debt to other writers on India, the work contains a large number of obvious reflections of Hecataeus, for it is an attempt to show that India is an even better land than Hecataeus' Egypt, a Platonic ideal state with a rigid caste system and philosophers on top, and that all civilization springs from India not Egypt. The book also looks back through Hecataeus and Nearchus to Herodotus' great set piece of ethnographic description, the land of Egypt.

The other great early Seleucid writer is in a rather different situation. Berossus was a bilingual priest of Baal, whose *Babyloniaka* was addressed to Antiochus I. As the work of a non-Greek it is not surprising that his book shows no direct acquaintance with Herodotus. But it still belongs within the same tradition, for it too is arranged according to the principles established by Hecataeus, and can be seen as yet another reply, complied perhaps under direct Seleucid patronage, to the court historian of the Ptolemies. Its three books described the land of Babylon, the origins of civiliza-

tion, and Babylonian mythology in book 1, the ten mythical kings of Babylon in book 2, and the history in book 3. Berossus is of course a good deal more accurate than either Hecataeus or Megasthenes, because he knew the Babylonian records, and kept closely to their form. But the arrangement of his material and his explanations of it fit the pattern established by Hecataeus. Berossus writes as a Babylonian trying to provide his Greek masters with an explanation of his culture in accordance with their preconceptions. One vital section is however missing, that on the customs of Babylonia: a native perhaps could not distance himself enough to be able to describe his culture from the outside, as a foreigner would see it.

Berossus was in turn followed by Manetho, the Egyptian high priest of Heliopolis; he is so confidently placed after Berossus that it may be that he specifically referred to Berossus in his works. His attitude at least is very similar. His work was probably produced under royal patronage, and may well have been addressed to Ptolemy. Even more than Berossus, he was a product of the fusion of Greek and native cultures, as is shown best by his collaboration with Timotheus, of the Athenian priestly family of the Eumolpidae, in creating a theology and cult of the new Graeco-Egyptian ersatz god, Sarapis; Josephus calls him 'a man well acquainted with Greek culture'. His history shows more strongly the same limitations as that of Berossus: it is based directly on the sacred books of Egypt; writing thus, Manetho sought to correct the mistakes of Greek writers who had access to these records only indirectly. His work is therefore primarily concerned with what appeared in those records—the history of the kings of Egypt; and Manetho's account is so accurate that it is still the foundation of Egyptian chronology. Manetho does not seem to have written a complete Hecataean ethnography, but merely to have covered the same ground as his historical section, and (both in his history, and more especially in other works) to have discussed the theology of Egyptian religion. Within these limits it is still clear that Manetho followed the Hecataean structure, the threefold division of the early kings of Egypt into gods (identified with physical elements), divine kings, and human kings; and he accepted the rationalistic physical explanation of the Egyptian gods provided by Hecataeus. But despite these signs of Hecataeus' influence, that author is not named in the extant fragments. Rather we hear that Manetho's history was ostensibly directed to the correction of Herodotus: according to Josephus, 'he convicted Herodotus of making many mistakes about Egyptian affairs because of ignorance.' Manetho may even have written an independent work *Against Herodotus,* though this may rather be a characterization of his main work. But it is perhaps worth noting that Herodotus is accused not of falsehood, but of ignorance. . . . Why Manetho sought to correct Herodotus rather than Hecataeus I do not know; perhaps he did not wish to attack the respected protégé of the Ptolemies: perhaps he recognized that Hecataeus' historical section was so derivative on Herodotus that it was better to concentrate on the mistakes of the original. For some reason at least, he felt that Herodotus was still worth attacking, despite the existence of a more modern account equally open to criticism.

It was not just ethnographers and cultural historians who used Herodotus. One of the greatest of the early Hellenistic political historians, Hieronymus of Cardia, wrote the standard account of the Diadochoi—pure political and military history. And yet, for instance, his account of the expedition of Antigonus against the Nabataean Arabs in 312 is organized and arranged like a Herodotean *logos,* with a detailed description of the habits and customs of the Arabs before the account of the actual fighting.

With Berossus and Manetho we begin to see the development, the branching out of different tendencies which can be traced back through Hecataeus to Herodotus. The analysis of this Herodotean tradition could be extended to the later Hellenistic writers, to Timaeus (the Herodotus of the west), to Agatharchides (who admired Herodotus), to Eratosthenes (who was always quoting him), and to Poseidonius. But this will be enough to show how the Herodotean legacy affected the world view of the Hellenistic period, and how important he is for an understanding of Hellenistic historiography. It would hardly be too much to say that the early Hellenistic period saw the new world of Alexander through Herodotean eyes, and sought to give the Herodotean tradition a more systematic basis. But without the example of Herodotus the achievement of the writers under the Successor kingdoms in recording and understanding the *oikoumene* would have been very different, and more difficult.

Only in the late Hellenistic period does Herodotus seem to have suffered a slight eclipse as a serious writer to be studied. Dionysius of Halicarnassus might praise his literary merits; but Diodorus did not use him; and the great majority of the references to Herodotus in Strabo come not from his own reading but through earlier writers, like Eratosthenes.

How does this sketch which I have given of one of the most important areas of Hellenistic historiography fit into the standard modern accounts? It shows, I believe, that modern attempts to write the history of historiography in this period are seriously distorted and inadequate. So far interest has concentrated on Polybius, on his theoretical statements about the writing of history, and on his polemic against his predecessors. But, as F. W. Walbank has shown, this polemic is remarkably selective, and often selective on grounds which have nothing to do with the writing of history, but rather with the discrediting of rivals to Polybius' own repu-

tation, like Timaeus and Pytheas of Massalia, or with historians who belonged to the wrong states or held the wrong political views for Polybius. One type of history, however, Polybius does attack with some justification, a type which has been called by modern scholars 'tragic history'. The discussion of this genre of tragic history, its existence or nonexistence, its importance, its origins, has dominated the study of Hellenistic historiography for seventy years, since Eduard Schwartz first raised the problem. The central idea in this type of history is that of *mimesis*; the reader must feel the emotions which the actors themselves felt—it is a sort of psychological version of the theory of Croce and Collingwood, that all true history is contemporary history, the re-enactment of past experience, relevant to the modern age. Now many political historians of the Hellenistic period did aim for such effects; and if there is also a theory of history behind this practical aim, it may well be an application of the Aristotelian theory of tragedy to history. And Polybius was at least right to object to such tendencies when they were allowed to obscure the search after truth. But my point here is that tragic history is essentially a form of political history; it is concerned with the sufferings and actions of men and peoples at war, emotions in a night battle or at the sacking of a city. To set up the theory of mimetic history as central to the Hellenistic period is to accept the limitations of Polybius' polemic in an even more important way than Walbank has pointed out. For Polybius was a political historian, in the tradition of Thucydides: he is not particularly interested in other types of history, though he could of course achieve remarkable standards of cultural history with his description of the Roman constitution or his geographical sections, especially we may suppose in book 34. But since Polybius is primarily a political historian, his polemic is directed against political historians for the most part (and also against professional geographers): it simply ignores a whole area of Hellenistic historiography. Among the great and famous authors whom Polybius loves to attack, one name is wholly absent. In all the work of Polybius, there is no reference at all to Herodotus.

H. Strasburger, in an important article called *Die Wesensbestimmung der Geschichte durch die antike Geschichtsschreibung,* has pointed to a basic dichotomy in ancient historiography, indeed in all historiography: between 'kinetic history', the history of battles, events, political decisions on the one hand, and on the other 'static history', the history of culture, of civilization, and of areas at peace. Of the former Thucydides stands as the archetype, of the latter Herodotus—at least in the early books, for Herodotus really fused the two. This distinction is I think useful. But Strasburger goes on to accept the traditional account of Hellenistic historiography: there Thucydides, kinetic history, was supreme, and was exemplified in two schools, the mimetic and its opposite, the factual Polybian approach.

Static history was forgotten until the tradition of Herodotus revived with Agatharchides (a curious choice), and especially Poseidonius, who united again for the first time the two strands. For all its attempts at balance, this analysis seems to me to accept the traditional myths of the importance of mimetic history and the neglect of Herodotus in the Hellenistic world. Certainly Polybius is the greatest surviving political historian of the period, and our accounts will always to some extent be biased towards his preoccupations. But anyone who has read Diodorus, and reflected on the remarkably homogeneous school of Hellenistic philosophical histories which he used as his sources, will see that it is possible to avoid excessive concentration on Polybius.

The only full-length work to discuss this period of history-writing is indeed S. Mazzarino's stimulating and perverse *Il pensiero storico classico*. In volume ii of that work, he chooses as his models for part of that area of Hellenistic history which I have been discussing, not Herodotus, but two fourth-century historians of Persia, Deinon (father of the historian Cleitarchus), about whom we know little more than that his work was romantic but reasonably reliable and covered both Persian history and Persian customs, and Deinon's predecessor, the notoriously unreliable Ctesias. Certainly Ctesias was widely read and had considerable influence on Hellenistic prose, but on historical romances rather than on serious history. It would not be possible to gather for Ctesias the great mass of references and allusions in serious historians which can be offered for Herodotus. Moreover Ctesias and Deinon are themselves romantic and unworthy representatives of the Herodotean tradition; and they covered only one area of the new Hellenistic *oikoumene*. It seems unnecessary to set up these two as the source of a type of Hellenistic history, when their predecessor Herodotus is such a much more obvious candidate.

In 1909 Felix Jacoby wrote a famous article giving the theoretical justification of the structure of his proposed 'Fragments of the Greek Historians'. This was to include virtually all forms of non-fiction prose writing, not just what we should narrowly call history, but also mythography, ethnography, chronography, biography, literary history, and geography. His reason for this wide sweep was that Greek history-writing in its origins did not distinguish between these different types; and the various developed forms sprang from a complex interaction between the conflicting interests of these undifferentiated attitudes of mind. When Jacoby died exactly fifty years later, his work, the greatest philological work of this century and the greatest work on Greek history for all time, was only three-quarters finished, and there seems no sign of anyone taking up the task. To many, his work has seemed marred by a principle of organization which was unnecessarily complicated and with little point. Yet I believe that Jacoby was right in his central insight. It is impossible to consider Greek historiography and its development unless ethnography, geography, and so on are included. And this is not just because the early Ionian writers failed to distinguish these genres. It is because one of the central strands of Greek historiography remained this Ionian tradition, a tradition which dominated cultural history, as Thucydides dominated political history, and did so as a direct consequence of the continuing influence of Herodotus. No satisfactory history of Hellenistic historiography will be written until this dual legacy is recognized, and each side given its proper prominence. Nor can the Hellenistic world view be understood without appreciating the importance of Herodotus.

J.A.S. Evans (essay date 1982)

SOURCE: "The Sources: The Evidence for Written Sources," in his *Herodotus,* Twayne Publishers, 1982, pp. 142-53.

[*Evans is professor of classics at the University of British Columbia, Canada. In the following excerpt, he finds little clear evidence that Herodotus relied on written sources. He describes Herodotus instead as an original researcher and interviewer whose History synthesizes the claims of a variety of mostly oral informants, including the guardians of official oral traditions, keepers of family genealogy, and individual storytellers.*]

Some four centuries after Herodotus, another historian from Halicarnassus, Dionysius, briefly described the beginnings of historical research: "Before the Peloponnesian War [431-404 B.C.] there were many early historians in many places. Among them were Eugeon of Samos, Deiochus of Proconnesus, Eudemos of Paros, Democles of Phygele, Hecataeus of Miletus, Acusilaus of Argos, Charon of Lampsacus, and Amelesagoras of Chalcedon. A second group was born a little before the Peloponnesian War and were Thucydides' early contemporaries; these were Hellanicus of Lesbos, Damastes of Sigeum, Xenomedes of Ceos, Xanthus of Lydia, and many others." All of these wrote histories of individual tribes or cities, using records from temples or secular archives, and telling myths and folktales which, remarked Dionysius, who lived in the society that produced the emperor Augustus, "seem silly to present-day men." Herodotus, however, enlarged the historian's scope. "He chose not to write down the history of a single city or nation, but to put together many, varied events of Europe and Asia in a single comprehensive work."

This is a well-worn passage. Taken at face value, it indicates that before Herodotus there was a clutch of shadowy writers who wrote local histories. Herodotus himself mentions only one of them, Hecataeus of Miletus, who wrote a work in two books on historical geography (*Periegesis*), accompanied by a map that showed the world as a disc edged by Ocean, and another work on genealogies. He lived through the Ionian Revolt, and twice gave the rebels advice that they rejected. Herodotus says nothing pejorative about him, though once he tells a tale that has been taken as ridicule. In Egypt, Hecataeus gave the priests of Amon his own pedigree, beginning with a god and descending through sixteen generations, whereupon the priests showed him the series of statues of their high-priests, three hundred and forty-five in all, each representing a generation of men. The story illustrated the antiquity of Egypt, and it is not clear that Herodotus meant it as a joke at Hecataeus's expense, as some commentators have thought. In any case, the tale probably derived from Hecataeus's own *Periegesis,* and the joke, if joke it is, was told by the victim himself.

Herodotus had absorbed what Hecataeus wrote about Egypt, but too little survives to be sure how dependent Herodotus was. The description of the phoenix, the hippopotamus, and the hunting of the crocodile had parallels in Hecataeus. Hecataeus called Egypt "the gift of the Nile," and Herodotus approves of the description without mentioning its source. At Buto, Herodotus viewed the floating island of Chemmis, reported that he saw no sign that it floated, and was skeptical about floating islands in any case. However, a fragment of Hecataeus states that Chemmis, which he spelled "Chembis," floated.

All this indicates familiarity with Hecataeus but not dependence. Outside Egypt, Herodotus quotes Hecataeus only once, for a variant version of how Athens expelled the aborigine Pelasgians from Attica. Perhaps he found in Hecataeus his list of Persian satrapies and the myth of Scythian descent from a union between Heracles and a woman who was half snake. His disapproval of the Ionian Revolt may have come in part from him, for Hecataeus thought it was foolish, and so did Herodotus. But Hecataeus was a friend of Artaphrenes, the satrap at Sardis during the revolt, and his attitude can have been no secret. For that matter Hecataeus and Herodotus belonged to the same social class, and may have had more in common than an interest in historical geography. But Herodotus had progressive ideas about cartography, and was contemptuous of maps that showed the earth circular, with a Europe and Asia of equal size and all surrounded by Ocean. Hecataeus's famous map shared this disdain but not alone, for he was part of an Ionian tradition of cartography, and the concept of the circumambient Ocean went back to Homer.

Hecataeus is the most solid of Herodotus's predecessors, although evidence is lacking to substantiate theories of widespread borrowing. There is less to say about the other writers mentioned by Dionysius (and

some he did not mention), and they are harder to date. Charon of Lampsacus is credited with a number of works, including one on Persia, two on Lampsacus, and a chronicle of the kings and ephors of the Lacedaemonians, based on Spartan sources. We cannot show that Herodotus read him, but it is at least possible, for though Jacoby, a generation ago, dated him to the last decades of the fifth century, too late for Herodotus, more recent scholarship is inclined to make him earlier. His *Persika* [On Persia] took up only two books; other than that, we can say only that it included an account of Mardonius's expedition into northern Greece in 492 B.C. Charon's scope was narrower than that of Herodotus.

Xanthus of Lydia wrote a work *On Lydia* which Herodotus may have used; in the next century, the historian Ephorus claimed that Herodotus got his "starting-points" (*aphormai*) from him, but his meaning is obscure. The **History** does begin with Lydia, and in that sense Xanthus may have provided Herodotus with a starting point. But surviving fragments show no parallels with Herodotus. He borrowed nothing from Xanthus that we can identify.

Even more shadowy is Dionysius of Miletus, who wrote a work on Persia down to Darius's death, and then followed it with a sequel. The one morsel of information that we know about his works reveals that he described the revolt of the *magi,* and named Smerdis's brother Panxouthes rather than Patizeithes, as Herodotus does. Dionysius of Halicarnassus overlooks him, which is a tribute to his obscurity. However, the king lists of Lydia and of Media in Herodotus do not synchronize, which has given grounds for suspecting that he took his lists from two separate sources, and *faute de mieux,* Dionysius of Miletus is a candidate for one of them. As for Acusilaos of Argos, a fragment has turned up in an Oxyrhynchus papyrus; it gives a straightforward account of the myth of the Lapith king Caeneus who was changed from a man into a woman. It reads like an entry in a mythology handbook: the sort of material purveyed by the *logioi,* or prosewriters, whose imaginary debate on the causes of the Persian War begins the **History**. Herodotus's researches were a different sort of thing.

Hellanicus of Lesbos was a prolific writer who was still working in the last decade of the fifth century, but a *Persika* by him could have antedated the **History,** although we cannot show that Herodotus used it. However, he demonstrates the availability of chronological sources, for three of his works betray a fascination with dates. One was a local history of Athens dated by archon years. A second was on the victors at the Cernean Festival in Sparta, and the third was on the priestesses of Hera in Argos, who held office for life; Hellanicus reckoned their tenure by years, thus producing a chronological framework. Another writer whom Herodotus may have used was Pherekydes of Athens, who wrote a work containing much information about the Philaids, the family to which Miltiades belonged, but what Herodotus has to say about Miltiades' ancestors might as well have been obtained from any well-informed member of the clan. We are far from being able to demonstrate Herodotus's dependence. Moreover, his failure to mention any prose writer except Hecataeus is remarkable, for he frequently cites poets, not merely Homer and Hesiod, but even one as *récherché* as Aristeas of Proconnesus, the author of the *Arimaspeia*. In part, this is because familiarity with the poets was the mark of an educated Greek, but that cannot be the whole reason. Herodotus, it is clear, regarded himself as an independent researcher whose analysis of the Persian War was an original achievement.

What is evident is that Herodotus did not conduct his researches in a vacuum. The fifth century was a period when records and genealogies were being ferreted out, and what may have been left to memory in the past was put in writing. Herodotus maintained the persona of an oral historian working with oral sources. He put down the stories that people told him, even when he did not accept their truth, and he would not impose his own critical judgment so far as to suppress variant versions— as Hecataeus did, for in his proem he made a claim for accuracy. All versions were evidence for Herodotus, and he would not neglect evidence in his research.

The Sources Cited

Halfway through the Egyptian *logos,* Herodotus announces that what he has written so far is based on observation (*opsis*), judgment (*gnome*), and interrogation (*historie*), but from that point on he will relate stories of Egypt, some told by the Egyptians themselves, and some by other nations about Egypt. Elsewhere, he prefaces various reports with phrases such as "the Greeks say," "the Lacedaemonians say," "the people living around Thermopylae say," to give only a few examples. Not infrequently he contrasts the reliability of these sources: the priests of Ptah in Egypt told how Psammetichus discovered that the Phrygians were the world's most ancient people; the Greeks, he adds, related silly stories about his experiment. Or at times he is precise about his limitations: he describes the golden statue of Marduk-Ba'al at Babylon, but he had not seen it himself, for Xerxes had removed it; he could only tell what the Chaldaeans said. Four times only he mentions informants by name, but all of these gave him private information. The sources designated as "Greeks," "Carians," "Scythians," and the like seem to purvey information which, if not official, was shared widely among the peoples named. It was part of the body of tradition that they preserved.

Can we take this view seriously? When Herodotus says of the Nile Delta that "the Ionians say" it is Egypt, and that its coast stretches from the so-called watchtower of Perseus to the salt marshes of Pelusium, can we believe that this was an oral tradition widespread in Ionia? It may be argued that behind many of these references to oral traditions there lies a literary source: Hecataeus took Egypt as the Delta, and so we can read "the Ionians say" as "Hecataeus writes." But Hecataeus's geographical notions, like his map, belonged to a school of Ionian *savants*. Herodotus was strictly accurate when he wrote "the Ionians say."

Or was the persona of an oral historian purely conventional, in which case we must treat these interjections as literary fictions? This is not to accuse Herodotus of dishonesty, but simply to suggest that he was not merely the father of history, but also of the literary conventions that affect historiography. Herodotus was capable of literary convention. But before we weigh his claim to be an oral historian, we must look at what oral history consists of.

The nature of oral tradition

The boundary between a literate and a nonliterate culture is notoriously difficult to define, and if it would be incorrect to denominate the Greece of Herodotus as nonliterate, neither would it be right to think that the elements of oral culture were dead. Oral history is transmitted by what we may visualize as a long series of interlocking conversations continuing from generation to generation, and each generation makes its own adjustments to the tradition. What is of social relevance is remembered and subjected to interpretation; what ceases to be relevant is forgotten.

Let us look first at problems of chronology. In Africa south of the Sahara, where the elements of oral culture are still alive, the sources of history for the precolonial period are generally professional storytellers and official keepers of state traditions, and usually they have at best a hazy notion of absolute chronology. However, they can, by means of genealogy, establish an area of time within which an event took place. In nearly every state headed by kings or chiefs, the custodians of traditions possess king lists, in what is supposed to be chronological order, and when these states came into contact with writing, such lists were often the first morsels of history to be written down. In them, kings generally appear as consecutive rulers, even when their reigns in fact overlapped. The Behistun inscription provides an example of this, for there Darius names nine ancestors who were kings before him, without indicating that, in part, they ruled in parallel lines of the Achaemenid house. The same sort of distortion affects Herodotus's dating of the fall of Media and the rise of Cyrus, for by his reckoning Cyrus became king in 558 B.C., and the act by which he secured the throne was the overthrow of the king of Media, Astyages, whose fall, therefore, belonged to the same year. The two are made to rule consecutively. In fact, Cyrus first succeeded his father, Cambyses I, as vassal king of Anshan, and only later, in 550, did he unseat Astyages.

However, some regnal lists can assign a sum of years to a reign with great accuracy, for statistics of that sort could be preserved with great care, sometimes by means of mnemonic devices. It follows that when we find a reign measured precisely in oral tradition, we should pay attention, for the statistic may depend on a reliable method of time reckoning. Herodotus provides an example: he assigns thirty-six years to the Pisistratid tyranny before its expulsion from Athens. If Herodotus knew the date of the expulsion—Thucydides gives 510 B.C.—then he knew that Pisistratus routed his opponents at Pallene and became tyrant in 546: a troublesome date, for Herodotus puts Cyrus's first conquest, his overthrow of Croesus, just after Pallene. Yet we must not discard the thirty-six years, for oral tradition tends to be exact about such things.

At the same time, genealogies are subject to adjustment, sometimes due to social considerations, sometimes from structural amnesia, a process that streamlines tradition by forgetting irrelevant details. Generations tend to lengthen with time, and genealogies preserved in oral traditions now, may list no more names than they did a century ago, though there are a hundred more years to account for. Herodotus's rule of thumb for a generation was three to a century, but when he listed the pedigrees of the two Spartan royal houses, he traced both back to Heracles, whom he placed nine hundred years before his time, and at three generations to a century the pedigrees cannot stretch so far. Consequently these generations must be calculated at forty years. Structural amnesia, combined with a determination to make Heracles the progenitor of the Spartan kings, has resulted in a generation too long to be probable.

It must ultimately have been the Spartans themselves—specifically the Spartan kings—who stretched these generations, for the royal houses derived prestige from descent from Heracles. Herodotus probably got these pedigrees in Sparta, for, as Plato noted, the Spartans had an extraordinary appetite for genealogies. There is no compelling reason to think that he got them through an intermediary, such as Hecataeus. But there is no such thing as a standard generation in Herodotus. His three generations to a century is a rule of thumb, and usually he follows the practice of the oral historian who deals with areas of time rather than precise years.

The methods of transmission

Oral traditions found in African states generally fall into two categories: official and private. The first category represents the "truth" about the past as the state recognizes it, and it is common to find professionals charged with its preservation. The Yoruba town of Ketu in Nigeria, for instance, had an hereditary official known as the *baba elegum* who knew the town history by heart. Rwanda, a kingdom until 1961, had an assortment of officials: genealogists who remembered pedigrees, memorialists who knew the important events of reigns, rhapsodists who preserved panegyrics on the kings, and the *abiiru* who kept the secrets of the dynasty. There are exceptions: Burundi, which ceased to be a monarchy in 1966, had no official traditions as such, but history was transmitted by songs, tales, and proverbs. But, in general, organized states had both official traditions and specialists who were charged with preserving them.

Private traditions are those transmitted by individual groups, such as families and clans, which may have a official status within the clan, but as far as the outside world is concerned, they are private, and are handed down with less care, though at the same time there is less motive to distort. However, oral traditions are never transmitted purely for the love of objective knowledge. Private traditions may be put to political and social uses less blatantly than official ones, but there is still the wish to put the clan's ancestors in a good light.

When Herodotus cites ethnic groups as sources, such as "the Carians" or "the Spartans," *inter alia,* the implication is that he is giving their official traditions. Thus the Cretans could say that the Carians once inhabited islands under Minoan suzerainty, but Carian tradition differed, and Sparta, Thera, and Cyrene all had traditions about the founding of Thera and Cyrene. More than once Herodotus notes the Spartan version of a morsel of Spartan history differed from that held by the rest of Greece. He saw himself as a reporter of traditions such as these, but he declined to vouch for their accuracy. Yet, the question arises: if Herodotus could draw on oral traditions, were there specialists in archaic Greece who preserved them, as there have been, and are, in other parts of the world?

The evidence is meager, but tantalizing. Aristotle names among the officials necessary for a city various registrars called "temple-remembrancers, archive keepers, and remembrances." The "remembrancer" (*mnemon*) was a registrar of property, but the name seems to indicate an official who relied simply on his memory at one time, before literacy became common. From Crete we have an inscription that sets forth the rights of one Spensithios, who was to be *poinikastes* (specialist in Phoenician letters) and *mnemon* of a Cretan city, and his descendants after him. Slight as it is, the evidence suggests that Herodotus found keepers of tradition in various cities and temples, and that these specialists could expound history. At Delphi, a *hieromnemon* could have told him of Croesus's dedications and other memorials—the *erga* ("works") of famous men—and would give official answers to queries about oracles that Delphi had given, although this need not imply that the oracles were kept on file. Temple memorialists could elucidate difficult inscriptions or describe important mementoes; one in the Theban temple of Ismenian Apollo may have given Herodotus a hand with "Cadmean letters" he found on some tripods dedicated there, and another at the Samian Heraeum may have expounded upon the picture of the bridge built by the engineer Mandrocles over the Bosphorus, and dedicated to Hera by Mandrocles himself.

In one instance we find Herodotus interviewing an official such as this. At Sais, in Egypt, he approached the temple of Neith to inquire about the source of the Nile. His interlocutor was the temple scribe, and if we may infer from evidence for Egyptian temples in the Hellenistic period, he was the keeper of traditions. The scribe of Neith purveyed myth, but he was performing his proper function of expounding priestly wisdom.

He was, however, a scribe rather than a "sacred remembrancer" (*hieromemnon*), for Egypt had long used writing, and literacy was a qualification for the priesthood. In contemporary Greece, too, many memorialists must have used writing, but they still acted as spokesmen for an undifferentiated group, such as the priests of Dodona, whose spokesman told Herodotus that the Pelasgians had no names for their gods until they got them from Egypt. Only occasionally did he single out an individual as a source, because his information was unique, or because—as in the case of the scribe of Neith—Herodotus did not believe him.

There were also private family traditions, usually favorable to the family in the sense that forgetfulness obscured what cast aspersions on its past, but less prone to official bias. The family status was what concerned such traditions. Thus, when Herodotus indicates that both the great political families of Athens of the fifth century, the Philaids and the Alkmaeonids, had been hostile to the Pisistratid tyrants, he is reflecting the traditions of the two families, which forgot that they had ever cooperated with the tyrants. Yet, family traditions could not be distorted outrageously without provoking disbelief; they had to compete with other family traditions, and with official tradition as well, which it was difficult to impose upon. Alkmaeonid and Philaid tradition notwithstanding, the archon list that was inscribed and set up in the marketplace of Athens about 425 B.C. bore evidence that both families had cooperated with the tyrants. A better case is the competition between the two versions of how Athens was freed from her tyranny. The story with a degree of official sanction gave credit to the tyrannicides, Harmodius and Aristogeiton: a statue-group of the pair was erected in the *agora,* and their descendants received special honors. The competing tradition, for which both Herodotus and Thucydides vouched, claimed that the tyrannicides were motivated by a pri-

vate quarrel, that they killed the wrong man, and that Athens was delivered from the tyrant four years later through the efforts of the Alkmaeonids. We may safely assign this tradition to the Alkmaeonid family. Yet, in spite of this family's prominence, and the authority of Herodotus and Thucydides, it did not displace the official version, for the descendants of the tyrannicides continued to receive honors into the fourth century.

There are a number of instances in the *History* where Herodotus has clearly drawn upon family traditions. He knew what the Gephyraean clan, to which the tyrannicides belonged, said about its antecedents, and his defense of the Alkmaeonids against the charge of medism at the battle of Marathon belonged to Alkmaeonid tradition. His slighting references to king Cleomenes of Sparta must derive from the traditions of the house to which he belonged, for Cleomenes' heirs belonged to another branch that had no reason to cherish his memory. He may have dealt kindly with Artabazus, who fled ingloriously from Plataea, because one of his sources was Artabazus's family. The descendants of Demaratus, who governed three towns in the Caicus valley as Persian vassals, were probably the source for the tale of Demaratus's friend, Dicaeus, who had seen a foreboding vision prior to Salamis. The grandson of Zopyrus who won Babylon for Darius came to Athens as an exile and may have had tales to tell there. Family traditions were kept with less care than their official counterparts and faded badly after three generations, but they probably had much color, some of it political, and they were strong on genealogy.

Finally there were the legends of storytellers. Who knows what Herodotus learned at Halicarnassus, where the Oriental world marched with the Greek? As we have seen, he may have heard there about the turncoat Phanes, and the story of the Magian Revolt could have been based on one of the versions of the Behistun inscription that reached Ionia; fragments of an Aramaic version have turned up in Egypt. Herodotus made a point of disdaining idle tales, but a discriminating listener must have found a good many that were not idle.

Archives

In 403 B.C., Athens organized a central archive in the Metroon, the temple of the Mother of the Gods. Before that time, our information about her archives is scanty, though a late source states that they date back to the sixth century B.C. Outside Athens, our evidence is even scantier, but no doubt temples kept archives: inventories, for the most part, including lists of priests, but perhaps secular records too. A fair amount of archival material was preserved.

How accessible these records would be to the curious researcher, however, is another question. Unless a document was published, Herodotus would have been at the mercy of *mnemones* and *hieromnemones,* and as we suspect, many of these were still working within an oral tradition. Publication meant inscribing a document and setting it up in a public place. Herodotus cites twenty-four inscriptions, half of them Greek, and half non-Greek. Some he copied, for he gives the texts, but one at least, an inscription on the Great Pyramid at Gizeh, he paraphrased from memory. On the whole, he does not seem to have valued documentary evidence highly, though the reason may have been, not that it was unavailable, but that it was inaccessible.

Conclusion

We must conjecture, but we can be brief. Herodotus was gathering his source material at a time when a minor explosion of historical research was taking place, but he was in the vanguard. It is likely that he was widely read; he was not isolated from the intellectual milieu of his time, but we can *prove* that he read only one predecessor, Hecataeus, and we cannot demonstrate real dependence even on him. It is futile to conjure up shadowy predecessors whose works he may have copied.

Yet, he lived at a time when oral traditions were still preserved with care, and he probably gleaned much of his information from oral sources: from *mnemones, hieromnemones,* family traditions, and individuals with tales to tell. Even without the structures intended to preserve oral traditions, memories can remain fairly green for three generations. The Persian Wars were still within the three-generation span when Herodotus did his research, and indeed, there were still men alive who had witnessed the great invasion firsthand. The persona of an oral historian that Herodotus assumed must be taken seriously.

David Grene (essay date 1987)

SOURCE: An introduction to *The History: Herodotus,* translated by David Grene, University of Chicago Press, 1987, pp.1-32.

[*In the following essay, Grene focuses on the dramatic and literary artistry in the* History. *Contrasting Herodotus with Thucydides, he contends that Herodotus's genius lies in his imaginative interpretation of past events.*]

Herodotus' only slightly younger contemporary, Thucydides, rejects the historical account of remote events in very telling terms; he does so at about the date of Herodotus' probable death. Thucydides says that even such a careful (and barely sketched) account as he is forced to give of an earlier Greece, as background for his own times, is only moderately satisfactory. "For," he says, "most of the events of the past, through lapse of time, have fought their way, past credence, into the country of myth" (perhaps the Greek *epi to muthōdes eknenikēkota* in Thucydides 1.21.8 is fairly translated as this). Thucydides conceived of acts and even words and thoughts as existent at a given moment and ideally recapturable in that form. They will, if allowed to do so by the lapse of time, become transfigured and so be useless to history. The word *eknikan*—"fight its way through completely"—implies that there is a natural tendency in the event so to do, and the perfect participle looks at the finished product: "they have got to the country of myth and there they stay."

Thucydides' preference for contemporary history as the only likely true history is to be followed, with few exceptions, for centuries by Western historians, as is also his conception that only military and political events constitute true history. In both respects, Herodotus runs against the current. Herodotus certainly also thought that acts and words fought their way through into the country of myth if you left them enough time. Indeed, he thought that the country of myth for acts and words was just around the corner from them the moment they were done or uttered. But he was very far from thinking that this rendered them valueless for history. He had chosen for his subject the enmity of the Greeks and the barbarians—by "barbarians" meaning the peoples of Asia Minor—which culminated in the great battles of Herodotus' childhood, Salamis and Artemisium and Plataea, in 480 and 479 B.C. But the beginning of the story, the origins of the enmity, as he saw it, stretched all the way back, almost to what was known as the beginning of the civilized world. To this vast area of the past Herodotus had no key, or almost none, other than oral tradition; for there were few written records and, for such as existed, he almost certainly lacked the necessary languages to understand them. Probably most of his informants as to myths and folklore were either Greeks settled in Asia or native inhabitants, probably a considerably number, who spoke Greek. This oral tradition constituted for him the imaginative record of the past as it mattered to the present.

Herodotus is the writer of Greek history who comes between Homer the epic poet, some four hundred years before him (as he himself thought), and Thucydides, the till now almost "modern" historian, who died perhaps twenty-five years after Herodotus. Herodotus, no less than Thucydides, thought of his **History** as a thing different from epic poetry—as much more bound by the necessity of covering the actual great events truly. For instance, he says that he believes (with some good evidence) that Homer knew that Helen had gone to Egypt and had in fact been there all through the Trojan War. But, says Herodotus, because Homer found the other version of the story (Helen's stay in Troy) more suitable for his poetry, he chose it. Herodotus certainly sees his ***History*** as something not so malleable as this. Thucydides certainly knew Herodotus' ***History*** and regarded him as a very loose kind of historian. When in recommending his own work as "a possession for ever" he couples this with the remark that "it has not been composed for the pleasure of the hearers of the moment", it is not difficult to identify the rival historian and his audience of listeners, especially when Thucydides follows his remark by criticizing two so-called "errors" in Herodotus' **History**.

Of course, there are facts given him by his informants that Herodotus rejects almost in the Thucydidean way. He corrects what he regards as false geographical statements by some of his predecessors. He expresses total disbelief in the existence of goat-footed men to the north of Scythia while accepting (one supposes correctly) the other physical oddity, snub-nosed bald-headed men. He stakes his reputation on his account of the course of the Nile, telling us how far he had checked this personally. He denies the possibility of the sacrifice of Heracles on the grounds that the Egyptians never practiced human sacrifice.

But all these rejections are criticisms of single facts. It is when Herodotus is giving us folklore and myths that his opponents say he is uncritical. He does, in fact, never criticize the skeletons of his mythical stories. He accepts a story based on some historical act but conforming to a widely known psychological pattern, which is certainly not singular. It does not strike him that he ought to ask: Did this happen on this occasion, or is it the *kind of thing* that people describe on many such occasions? It is exactly because he does *not* ask that question that he is interesting and important as the unique kind of historian he is. I want to discuss in detail two such stories. The first concerns the birth of Cyrus, perhaps the greatest of the Great Kings of Persia and the founder of the Persian Empire.

Cyrus' birth was heralded by a prophecy that he would displace his grandfather, Astyages, King of Media, from the throne of Media. Astyages promptly married his daughter to a nobleman of the then socially inferior race of the Persians in the hope that this would render such a succession improbable. Moreover, when the child was born, he ordered it to be exposed, to become a prey to wild beasts. Through a breakdown in the chain of command, this order failed, and Cyrus survived through the kindness of a herdsman, who had been told to destroy him, and through the love and care of the herdsman's wife.

Herodotus very probably accepted the imaginative core of this story as something *real* when describing the survival of the royal child—a child, moreover, with a great destiny inside the setting of the court of the Great King, who was, in the minds of his subjects, a being unique and set apart. The herdsman's wife, "as God would somehow have it so, . . . gave birth when her husband had gone to the city", and her child was born

dead. This stillborn child is to be the necessary link in the survival of Cyrus, and, in the phrase "as God would somehow have it so," Herodotus indicates that he in some sense accepts the Persian story at face value. At least he certainly does not see the tale of Cyrus' survival, *de haut en bas,* as a trick practiced on a superstitious population. By contrast, that is exactly how he describes the pageant of the political agents who brought back Pisistratus, the tyrant of Athens, from exile. The tyrant was reintroduced to his state by a huge woman dressed up to look like Athena, and Herodotus comments on the silliness of this stratagem and its most unlikely success, which it all the same achieved. For these were Greeks, to whom a belief in the sanctity of rulers was entirely alien, and therefore the deception was all the more remarkable. The story of Cyrus lived among the Persians. Herodotus knows that the deepest sentiment of sacredness on the part of a people can actually alter the relationship of king and subjects on both sides. Herodotus bears testimony to this for the Great King throughout his **History**. He cannot be born like other people (Cyrus); he cannot die without portents and elaborate coincidences (Cambyses). Most striking of all, when the royal family becomes extinct and, in defect of hereditary claim, a new Great King must be *chosen,* the elevation of Darius is preceded by a unique debate among the nobles of Persia on the merits of monarchy, aristocracy, and democracy. Herodotus tells us that the Greeks do not believe this debate took place but that he knows it did. The authenticity of this great moment is vouched for by him personally. I think that for Herodotus the Persian monarchy in its typical form, the essential antagonist of Greece in his story, has the very quality of Fate in it. Its individual kings are strangely protected or deluded by the gods. But there is human choice in the matter of the monarchy, too; for it is guided to a majestic and terrible end, as when, much later than this, the dream of Xerxes, on the eve of his invasion of Greece, drives him on to the tragic conclusion of that expedition. As I read it, this earlier scene of the choosing of Darius is of a similar kind. The Persian nobles, delivered from the hereditary claims on their religious sentiment by murders and deaths within the royal family, deliberately choose autocracy and absolutism under Darius after a prolonged debate as to the merits of the other systems, aristocracy and democracy. Of course, we do not know what special evidence Herodotus may have had for the existence of the debate. But it is certainly of the order of events he believed in, which necessarily included the significant shape of history in tragic terms, the powers (whatever they are) outside of man, the choices men themselves make, and the conjunction and interaction of all these as an uneasy blend in the making of destiny.

In the story of Cyrus' birth and survival Herodotus is playing with our sense of wonder or potential miracle, now almost guaranteeing our right to credulity, now drawing us back. He is also flavoring our sense of the meaningful with his sense of the meaningful by supplying realistic detail of his own invention for the tremendousness of the archaic myth.

The herdsman had been summoned unexpectedly to the palace. His wife was heavy with child and near her time. They were both much in each other's thoughts, the man thinking of the forthcoming birth, the woman of the reason for the surprise summons of her husband to the palace. Herodotus describes the scene when the herdsman returns. He had gone to the palace and been amazed to receive orders to expose a child, which he found all decked out in gold and embroidered clothes. To his terror, he learned from the palace servants that the child was royal, the son of Mandane, daughter of his own lord, Astyages, king of Media. He received his orders, of course, through an intermediary, Harpagus, a great noble of the court. The herdsman comes home, much troubled in his mind, with the future Cyrus in a box, dressed in all his glory.

> When his wife saw the child so big and beautiful, she burst into tears, and taking her man by the knees she besought him by no means to expose it. He said he could not do otherwise. . . . [Then the woman said:] "I too have given birth, and the baby I bore was dead. Take then the dead boy and expose it, and let us bring up as our own this child of Astyages' daughter. So you will not be detected in cheating our masters. . . . The dead child will have a royal burial, and the survivor will not lose his life." . . . [So the herdsman took up] his own child that was dead and placed [him] in the box wherein he had brought the other. He put on the dead body all the ornaments of that other child and bore it off to the loneliest part of the hills and left it there.

Of course, the details, so skillfully, so evocatively, inserted, come from Herodotus the artist. They have no place in the *History* if, by history, we mean verifiable facts. They are there as additions to the myth pattern, made by Herodotus as he feels himself inside its reality and leads us to the moment of belief.

But in this story Herodotus appears also as the omniscient and seemingly common-sense intermediary between us and his informants and explains *away* another aspect of the traditional account, apparently one commonly given. Herodotus says that the true parents of the child, the royal parents, in order for their own ends to make the birth seem even more miraculous, set afoot the rumor that the child, when exposed, had been suckled by a bitch and so had survived. This, he thinks, was suggested to them by the name of the herdsman's wife, the foster mother, to whom the boy repeatedly referred. Her name was Cyno, which is vaguely like the Greek word for dog (*kuōn*).

It is customary to regard such aspects of Herodotus'

treatment as his "rationalizing tendency." This misses the point. For Herodotus, the basic elements of the myth attract to themselves other explanations, other aspects of the ordinary or the marvelous; one overlies the other. It is his job to report them all so that the nature of the belief and rejection that attend the myth comes before us in all its fullness. This, I think, is why he so often disowns responsibility for the truth or accuracy of a statement. It is its being thought or voiced that counts in the end, as it comes down from the past to us. The original facts, whatever they were, have taken to themselves a supervening shape—universal, cultural, or, in the deepest sense, religious. It is then that Herodotus thinks they have assumed their closest relation to reality, which is not for him conterminous with what happened in the physical world but rather what was released by the act into the world of thought and feeling and continued thereafter.

I doubt if Herodotus made an effective distinction—except about particular, singular facts, such as the course of the Nile or the sacrifice of Heracles—between the reality of verifiable truth and imaginative reality. He is a man who probably lived easily with myths. He certainly lived easily with the rationalized trappings that his age found conventional as the clothing of myth, much as Elizabethans and Jacobeans found Renaissance costumes natural for the representation of classical heroes and indeed for the kings and noblemen of any age or time. But I see no evidence that such rationalizing is designed by him to diminish the intrinsically incredible quality of the myth and make it into something nearer credibility. The credibility comes from something shared by him and his informants, the depth of meaning in the myth. The sheer unlikelihood—in many cases the sheer impossibility—of stories like that of Cyrus' exposure and survival is in no sense disarmed by the excision of the seemingly supernatural element. The degree of magic or the want of it, the direct intervention of the divine or its aloofness from the particular event, renders the story modish or the reverse for his informants, for himself, and for the audience who listened to his readings. It is the myth itself that reaches down through the impossible stretching of probability and guarantees its own truth. This and some of the other stories belong to the *dreams* of mankind, impossible, delightful, or in other cases fantastic and horrible. In their rationalized form (to borrow the nomenclature), they are being represented in their special costume of a given moment in history, as belonging to it, as part of what it finds "natural."

My second story comes from Herodotus 1.8, which deals with Candaules, the last member of the family of the Mermnadae, which lost the Lydian throne to Gyges, who was the ancestor of Croesus. Croesus is a very important monarch in Herodotus, for he is the man who (according to Herodotus) first began unjust actions against the Greeks. His ancestor, Gyges, is a very important man in Herodotus, for he is the one whose guilt in stealing his master's, the king's, wife and murdering the king, Candaules, was finally punished in the fourth generation—that of Croesus. Croesus pays for the sin of his ancestor and himself and is displaced by Cyrus. So it is Cyrus and the Persians who finally take the lead of the "barbarians" (Asiatics) against the Greeks when they come to invade Europe. Croesus therefore stands at the very front of the theme in Herodotus: he is the first man to molest the Greeks, the decisive figure whose displacement brought the Persians to Greece, and the first and great example of the downfall of a king through the action of fate based on past offenses. The way Herodotus tells of the primal sin is as follows:

> This Candaules fell in love with his own wife; and because he was so in love, he thought he had in her far the most beautiful of women. So he thought. Now, he had a bodyguard named Gyges, the son of Dascylus, who was his chief favorite among them. Candaules used to confide all his most serious concerns to this Gyges, and of course he was forever overpraising the beauty of his wife's body to him. Some time thereafter—for it was fated that Candaules should end ill—he spoke to Gyges thus: "Gyges, I do not think that you credit me when I tell you about the beauty of my wife; for indeed men's ears are duller agents of belief than their eyes. Contrive, then, that you see her naked."

The bodyguard protested, and Herodotus includes his evidence of how shameful it is among the barbarians for even a man, much less a woman, to be seen naked. But despite Gyges' objections, Candaules arranges that he should be hidden behind the open door of the bedroom when the queen undressed. Inevitably the lady spotted him when, departing, he slipped from behind the door; but despite her outrage she kept silent until the next day, when she offered Gyges the unpleasant alternative of killing the king and winning the queen or being killed himself. "So," says Herodotus, "he chose his own survival." Hence the destruction of the dynasty of the Mermnadae, who were the descendants of Heracles, and the fulfillment of the oracle declared at Delphi, that retribution would come for this offense upon the Lydian king Croesus in the fourth generation after Gyges.

We know another version of this myth in Plato, and it is instructive to compare the two. In Plato, Gyges is a shepherd who one day, straying in the hills, comes upon a cave with a dead man in it and, on the dead man's hand, a ring. Gyges steals this. Later, accidentally turning it on his finger, he discovers that it renders him invisible. By this power he contrives to lie with the queen and afterwards to murder the king and take both queen and throne. In the *Republic,* where the story occurs, it is cited by the interlocutors of Socrates, who request him to take Gyges as the extreme case for justice that they want to make. Assuming that

the just man had the ring of Gyges and his invisibility, would he persist in justice, as the true health of the soul, and ignore the potentiality of scatheless villainy?

There can be no doubt that these are two versions of the same story. The significant common mythic element would seem to be the relation of invisibility to guilt or guiltness. This has shrunk in Herodotus from the magical ring to spying from behind the door and accepting the connivance of the husband. There is also, in both, the fantastic crime-stained rise to supreme power by someone who has no claim to it. There is, as bedrock in Herodotus' version, the murder of the king-father and the incest with the mother in a wholly paternalistic eastern monarchy. There is also in Herodotus the certainty that the crime will later be paid for as a crime, though not in the person of the criminal who committed it. I suggest that these are indeed the deep mythical elements, and, again in this instance, the absence of the magical ring does not affect the appeal of the fantasy in which it is rooted, nor does it diminish significantly the area of improbability or unreasonableness of the story. What we may guess is that the difference between the two stories lies in the disinclination of Herodotus' informants for overt magic. The magic is dropped out exactly in order to admit the entry of fantasy, which at that time balked at the vocabulary of magic. We are made to see the princes and kings of the distant days of the East as people like ourselves, in their most private human moments, in their most denationalized, declassed reality. But it is not as our ordinary selves that we see them; we seem them, rather, the way we see David against Goliath, or Cinderella in the Cinderella story. What is being rejected for Herodotus' contemporaries is not only the remoteness and impersonality of the potentates but also their assimilation into a fairy-story world like that of the enchantresses of the *Odyssey,* Circe and Calypso. Admittedly, it is sometimes hard to see why Herodotus rejects a specifically magical form—for instance, of animal intervention—in one case and not in another. For Arion is rescued by a dolphin, who carries him home on its back. True, this is classified as a "wonder," the greatest that befell Periander during his reign. Herodotus is, of course, also recollecting the representation of the scene on a coin. But "wonder" though it is, Herodotus does not support disbelief in this instance as he does in that of the suckling bitch. The key is certainly in what his informants felt to be the proper dress of the myth. But perhaps we can go further. Plato's tyrant, as he arises in the democratic state, is someone who transfers into the daylight his dream fantasies. But scarcely literally. He did not go around sleeping with his mother or having sexual relations with beasts and gods. Perhaps the current form of the myth, as in the Herodotean Gyges story, is a bridge between an earlier form, nearer to the literal expression of the fantasy, and the daylight implementation, as Herodotus' informants and contemporaries saw it.

For this particular myth also presents in its mythical elements a funny and undignified reality that may, paradoxically, coincide (in its origin, at least—in the psychology of the action) with something that once happened. Today we are no longer completely convinced, like the more solemn academic historians of the nineteenth century, that history is invariably made by strategy and economics. It is conceivable that crowns have been lost by something as frivolous as Candaules' peculiar voyeurism. Totally improbable though it is, this tale may strike as deep in presenting a general human truth as does the tragedy of another destroyed king Herodotus tells us of, one who knew that the greatest suffering was too great for tears—that tears belonged to the next-lowest grade of sorrow. For in the story of Candaules, as in only a few of the myths, the very tone of the myth strikes home. This one convinces and illuminates as much by the humorousness of its suggestions *as to cause* as it does in stating the causes themselves.

There are two very terrible stories in book I of men being made to eat, unknowingly, human flesh—in one instance, the flesh of the man's own child. They are then confronted with the truth. One of these "feasts" was the revenge taken of King Cyaxares of Media by some nomad Scythians he had hired as huntsmen and who, after a dispute with him, kidnapped one of his pages, killed and cooked him, and served him up to Cyaxares. The other involved the revenge that Astyages (the king who tried to expose the infant Cyrus in the story I have recounted) took on his servant, the nobleman Harpagus, who was indirectly responsible for Cyrus' survival. Herodotus reports each of these instances in detail.

Let us again recall Plato, who affords us a generalized psychological insight into these horrors. He says, in his account of the tyrant in the corrupt states, that the tyrant is one who enacts in daytime with delighted license the fantasies that alternately tempt and terrify ordinary men in sleep, when the rational part of them is not in control. One part of this dreamworld, according to Plato, is "abstaining from *no* sort of food." This license goes on the list along with incest and miscegenation. Apparently, the temptation to cannibalism had this fantastic bent in the Greek mind of the time, for we also know, from Aeschylus and others, of Thyestes' feast, where again a father in ignorance is made to eat the flesh of his children. Clearly, this fantasy had currency enough to figure in great plays written for public exhibition in fifth-century Greece.

Herodotus' informants reported both instances of cannibalism in book I as events that actually happened. Herodotus is probably indifferent to the Thucydidean question "But *did* they happen?" because, like Plato, he knew very well that men's fantasies and deeds live terribly close to each other and often move interchange-

ably. Besides, for Herodotus it is what the Greeks and barbarians *believed* had happened that counts, rather than anything so unique as to depend on Herodotus' personal verification.

All of this explains the preponderance of myth patterns in the first four books of the *History,* where the mental background of the Asiatics is being covered. For this background is one half of the *why* of the enmity between Greeks and barbarians, and that is one reason why Herodotus tells us at such length of the political climate of the court of the great Asiatic despots, the implicit obedience of their subjects, and the submerged but ever-threatening hatred of possible rivals for power.

Clearly, one big question mark is how right Herodotus is to transfer the fantasies current among fifth-century Greeks to Asiatics living two and three centuries earlier. To answer that, one can say only that Herodotus certainly believed in the universal characteristics of the human imagination and hence in the inevitability of certain patterns in human dreams and fantasies. Strong as he is on the side of the importance of local customs, and interested as he is in the eccentricities of men's beliefs and practices, he is sure of a certain common core where men think and feel alike. For instance, he says that all men "in my opinion" know equally about the gods. (Their differences of belief affect only the applicability of this knowledge to names and places and customs.) It is this attitude of his that would constitute his defense (if he thought of making one) for using, as authentic evidence for Asiatic folklore, what his Greek-speaking informants tell him. Nor would he be without additional support for this defense in *our* terms, such as the fact that most of the peoples from whom the folktales are derived are Indo-Europeans, so that what is drawn on may well be a common Indo-European mythology. Moreover, these peoples lived in a relatively small area of the earth's surface and had been in constant cultural contact for a long, long time. But, in the end, whether we think Herodotus is a significant historian or not depends on our acceptance or rejection of his thesis that in logic or illogic the mental and passionate structure of the human mind is the same, though separated and superficially diversified in time or place.

It is overwhelmingly evident that Herodotus makes no effective discrimination in his *History* between the skeletal act—for instance, the murder of Candaules by Gyges, which is "historical"—and the imaginative reality toward which the story reaches. His *History* is that of a storyteller who is never quite out of the frame of the narrative and never quite within it. The broad lines of the *History* are shaped like those of a Greek tragedy. But it is never an acknowledged artistic fiction; it is never an artistic fiction, completely, at all. It has another dimension, this creation of his. It lies in a threefold relation to reality: reality as ordinarily perceived, reality as coming to a special meaningful pattern in myth, and reality as expressed in the original creation of a tragic writer. For the author who builds the story of the Persian attack on Greece under the shadow of the text "It is always the greatest houses and the tallest trees that the god hurls his [lightning] bolts upon" is a Greek tragic writer. It is a new art form, a kind of history. We dare say that, now that military and political history is no longer looked on as the sole lifeline by which to connect ourselves to great events of the past. But it is a history that nearly always suggests the observer within the framework. No doubt Herodotus actually checked the course of the Nile as he says he did. He certainly took notice of and recorded the customs of the Lydians and the Egyptians and all the peoples he visited. Such matters as these are the givens on which he rests the superstructure. This superstructure is the creation of his own dramatic imagination and partly consists of materials that are *imaginatively* dramatic in man's *remembrance,* man's myths and folklore, where the understanding is deepest and most explosive and least committed to the singular fact. These myths were certainly there for him in the mouths of his informants. Think, for example, of the miraculous birth and survival of the baby Cyrus and the vengeance taken by the cowgod upon the impious Cambyses, who mortally wounded her with his dagger but then himself perished through an injury in the selfsame part of the body where he had struck the god he sneered at as mortal.

The older editors, such as Sayce, respond to what they constantly refer to as the charm of Herodotus' stories, but they are far from seeing in what the charm consists. They regard the myths and folklore in the **History** as something removed from the very nature of reality, as the food of the child's mind before he grasps the conditions of the mature world. They understand nothing of the compelling pattern of the imagination to which the child and the adult alike respond. So they fail to grasp the magnitude of Herodotus' achievement. He has written a history of the greater part of the then known world, and backwards and forwards in man's then known span of civilization, with guidelines set by the archetypes of joy and sorrow, truth and falsehood, strength and feebleness as these live in *narrative form,* in the great primary stories. He supports this structure by scenes he himself has witnessed and by accounts of customs and places that are undeniably personally observed. There is thus a continuum from the palpable and checkable to the familiarity of the fantastic—familiar because it is the fantasy of all of us revisited. The **History** of Herodotus in its use of the human imagination is perhaps the solidest historical structure ever written. But the solidity is not that of reconstructed and verifiable fact but of the interaction between experience and dreams—between the uncommitted personal eyewitness and the generalized committedness of the patterns of fantasy and dreaming.

This is his famous introductory statement of purpose in book I:

> I, Herodotus of Halicarnassus, am here setting forth my history, that time may not draw the color from what man has brought into being, nor those great and wonderful deeds, manifested by both Greeks and barbarians, fail of their report, and, together with all this, the reason why they fought one another.

Two points in this statement should be noted. The first is that Herodotus sets himself against the power of time. Time is the destroyer, Herodotus is the preserver, of what man has created. This involves "saving," to some extent, monuments and moments of entire civilizations ("What has come into being through men"). It shows us a Herodotus keenly aware of the huge remnants of a civilization, such as the Babylonian, among which he has to potter in the hope of finding the key to its significance and power. As a subject of the Persian Empire and a great traveler, at a time when records and archeological research were almost nonexistent, he sees nakedly the possibility of obliteration of whole systems of life and their accompanying buildings, customs, languages. Second, what he is bent on presenting in his fight with time, as it concerns the hostility between the Greeks and barbarians, is the *kleos,* what men say and hear about the subject. In Homer, *kleos* means the glory that the hero's great deeds have attracted to themselves, and it remains for his descendants to enjoy as the quintessence of their ancestor. However, in the history of the Greek language, the word has a broader application than "glory" as we understand it. It is nearer "report," which is the way I have translated it here. It is connected with words that mean to "call out" and "to be heard." It is a misconception, I think, to render, as some translators do, "that such deeds may not fail of their meed of glory"; for what is involved is not only the glory (in our sense) of the story of the Greek-Asiatic hostilities and the gallantry shown on both sides in the battles but what men tell and hear about the typical acts (or what they regard as typical acts) of both sides—and this is very often *not* what we see as glory, particularly when it deals with deeds of the enemy. King Xerxes, having been entertained by the richest of his subjects, tells the man he can ask for any boon and he will grant it. The man asks for his eldest son to be left behind when the Persian army marches to Greece. Xerxes complies by cutting the boy's body in two and marching his army away between the two parts. This deed belongs to the report of the Persians as the Greeks received it. It is the monstrousness of the act that counted, the arbitrariness and savagery of the Eastern despot and the submissiveness of his subjects. This is a most important aspect of the way the Greeks saw the conflict between the two political systems, if one can call them that, and certainly between the two "nations," the Greeks and the barbarians, where our nomenclature is on much safer ground.

Probably no Greek writer makes so strong an impression of talking directly to us as Herodotus. Certainly, no Greek historian does. Undoubtedly, this is related to the known fact that most of his "publishing" was done by public readings from his text. It is intensely exciting to hear the echoes of his voice still and the conscious appeal to us as we listen. In speaking of his book on Egypt, he distinguishes among several kinds of materials. "So far it is my eyes, my judgment, and my searching that speak these words to you; from this on it is the accounts of the Egyptians that I will tell to you as I heard them." The Greek for "my eyes etc. that are speaking" is as strong and grammatically unusual as the English makes it appear direct and almost colloquial. Nor is the personality addressing us a matter even principally of style. There is the extreme boldness of many of the defining sentences themselves. He tells us about the people of Haliopolis, who "are the greatest chroniclers among the Egyptians." "Now, the part of their account that deals with the divine, and to which I listened, I am not anxious to set forth, save only the matter of the gods' names; for I think that all men know equally about the gods. When I do mention the gods, it will be because my history forces me to do so."

Perhaps the most startling of all his statements on how his **History** is constructed runs as follows (he has been commenting on the various stories of the Persians and Phoenicians about the traditional hostility between Greeks and barbarians):

> For my part I am not going to say about these matters that they happened thus or thus, but I will set my mark upon that man that I myself know began unjust acts against the Greeks, and, having so marked him, I will go forward in my account, covering alike the small and great cities of mankind. For of those that were great in earlier times most have now become small, and those that were great in my time were small in the time before. Since, then, I know that man's good fortune never abides in the same place, I will make mention of both alike.

These sentences correspond exactly to the manner of a very brilliant speaker, whose aphorism sticks in one's mind and forces one to wonder whether one has grasped all the implications of what one has heard. These are not the forms in which an expositor declares the nature of his argument or makes clear the grounding of his evidence. They sometimes look like this, but they are not. What they build is an illusion of a discussion between a storytelling friend and his listeners. The "I" who thinks divine stories uninteresting or dangerous in comparison with the human is accepted as a person like ourselves, only a little more surprising in attitude, more paradoxical in expression. (Is he saying all men know "equally much" or "equally little" about the gods?) As he stood before his audience, he comes

before us on the page, invisibly watching us, presenting himself as clever, whimsical, at times naive and impulsive, at times reflective and tragic in emphasis. This history is designed to give the feeling of a personal appearance on the scene, to mediate between the great events and the audience. Sometimes the personal appearance is indeed personal; sometimes it is highly formalized. Herodotus is sometimes rather like the reader in Thornton Wilder's *Our Town* or the actor-commentator in Tennessee Williams' *Glass Menagerie*. He is introducing us to his great theme—the achievements in war of Greeks and Persians at one another's expense and the cause of their quarrel, together with all the more general features of the civilizations of the world of his day—as a thing which, with all its hugeness, can be seen as a unity and expressed as the vision of one man who, as a child, was a contemporary of the last of the great acts in this universal drama. Here is the man in front of us, seizing the myths, the folklore of the countries involved, the relevant bits of his own (the chronicler's) history, weaving them all together and constantly even appearing himself, to explain that he has checked this but not that. Paradoxically but very naturally, he does not account for his knowledge of such things as the conversation between Croesus and Cyrus when Croesus is upon the pyre and, at the last minute, the words he utters induce Cyrus to take him down and spare his life, nor does he tell us how he came to know the thoughts in the mind of the shepherd's wife, who exchanged her own dead child for the royal baby Cyrus. What one has here is the writer, akin to Homer, who exists throughout the work, acknowledged, but with no formal attribution.

This personality, then, formalized as speaker, commentator, intermediary, is integrated into the *kleos*, the report that attends on all the events and through which they live for future times. Some of the *kleos* that goes to create the artistic effect are the echoes of the human voice, the undress of personal interest, the glory of rhetoric, the joking comment.

The *kleos* itself is multifarious, as the different people who contribute to it bring in their different hopes and antagonisms, all of which are utilized for the total effect. This past carries with it the multiple hopes and thoughts men have invested in it. Moreover, Herodotus himself has a ranging mind and an incorrigible sense of distant relevancies, which further extend the relation of everything to everything else and can only very hardly be controlled within any crabbed confines of immediate applicability. He has often enough been taken to task for this by serious critics, of which he himself is the first. "This history of mine," he says somewhat ruefully, "has from the beginning sought out the supplementary to the main argument."

But the extraordinary farrago of motifs, stories, geographical excursus, and reported observations of artistic objects, strange customs, and miraculous events has a deeper and, it seems to me, more serious reason for being what it is than comes out in any of the explanations I have given so far. Herodotus is in a very strong degree an uncommitted observer even as he creates his *kleos* of the past, and he is so for reasons that are startling and perhaps, in the end, convincing. Here is an illuminating comment on the theories of the Egyptians on various religious practices and also on the transmigration of souls: "As for the stories told by the Egyptians, let whoever finds them credible use them. Throughout the entire history it is my underlying principle that it is what people have said to me, and what I have heard, that I must write down." It is impossible to be sure what he means by "use" here. Because it is linked to what is persuasive, I should think it must mean something like "adopt as true for him." What is certain is that Herodotus is divorcing himself from the capacity or will to declare that one thing is true and another false, as beliefs go. One overlies another for the *use* of the different observers. This is exactly what is implied in his remark about the gorge in Thessaly: it is the result of an earthquake or the work of Poseidon—if you think that earthquakes are the work of Poseidon. It is the job of the historian, in Herodotus' terms, to identify objects, events, and thoughts in various ways, offending as few people as possible by strictness in psychological dogmatism. But there is always some fundamental matter that is thus being variously identified, and one cannot tell which system of nomenclature is most useful or especially will be so in the days to come. The passage on the transmigration of souls is not in the narrative as a probing of the nature of man's soul and its pilgrimage. Herodotus wants us to realize that in it we have one more important addition to the way man saw his cosmos. How this belief affected the Egyptians in dealing with the Great King he does not say and perhaps does not know. In short, it is beliefs and traditions and practices in their totality that characterize each national unit in his story. This belief about the soul is clearly relevant, probably important, and so in it goes.

I am convinced that this is what underlies the oddest statement of this kind in the whole lot—the one in 1.5 that I have already quoted on the principle of all-inclusiveness in his treatment of cities, without concern for stricter differences of importance.

For Herodotus there is a real truth, that is, a line of true causation, involving many causes. Because the threads of this true causation lie in the hands of some supernatural power or some nonhuman order of the world that embraces all its multiplicity, Herodotus thinks it cannot be understood by men in its altogetherness. But there is at least a sequence of events that constitutes a unity (that may be a unity even within the gods' range of meaning), an episode framed of events that match one another in some system of counter-

poise. At some point a significant conclusion can be drawn about success or the reverse, about happiness or the reverse, as far as man is concerned. (It is remarkable how much of Herodotus' presentation of history openly deals with its illustrative or even pedagogic value for human happiness or its failure.) But the verdict of importance on what actually *has happened,* made at too early a moment, is very fallible. The great towns of Herodotus' own day had many of them come to greatness from an earlier era of insignificance. Many of those now insignificant will one day be great. In that day the story he is now telling will not only look different but *be* different. The backward glance from the place of vantage the intervening years have given affords more evidence of what was taking place that made the previously great cities unimportant and vice versa. The principle on which all this operates is that it is impossible for human *well-being* to remain, established in one environment. The historian must then watch for its shifting, and how it shifts, and try to survey the conceivable factors, and conceivable possibilities, barely understood at an earlier moment, that were the potential major occasions for change. Herodotus' *kleos,* to be any good, must contain as many as possible of the seeds of the importance and *real* meaning of events—that is, their final consummation in time. For the present, it tries to show us a reasonable estimate of such a truth. But, as to the future, Herodotus is always hedging his bets. With Sardis and Susa, Babylon and Athens, and Sparta, the great centers of power, to the fore, he tries to retain in the picture some of the little towns: the rejection of emigration by the Ionians, the migrations to Italy. Some day, he implies, these may prove to have been the definitive places and the definitive events of the *History*. In the same willful jettisoning of simpler and more sharply defined standards of importance, he includes in his account of Periander of Corinth "the greatest wonder in all his life," the dolphin's rescue of Arion, the minstrel, by carrying him home, over the sea, on its back. A "wonder" means for Herodotus a disturbance of the psychic atmosphere. Who knows what this portends? Or even what it *does* to the world? Really to meet Herodotus is to realize how expansible the connections between events and thoughts can be when these connections are surveyed by the mind of a genius.

The famous meeting of Solon and Croesus (which, historically, probably never took place) has a crucial meaning for the *History,* occurring right at its beginning. It is at this meeting that Croesus learned from Solon, the Greek statesman and poet, to look on death, the last event of man's life, as the one necessarily overwhelming piece of evidence for the success or failure of that life. Because, says Solon, man's life, set at seventy years, contains so many months, days, etc., and because no day ever brings anything like any of its fellows, man is altogether what happens to him (*sumphorē*). Death, since it stops the process, allows one to look on the life as an intelligible unit or at least as one that can be reckoned up. The life of a man or a city or a nation is composed of strips of reality. Each has its *telos,* which does not here mean, as it does in Aristotle, a perfection or crowning point but the end from which the unit as a whole makes sense. What Herodotus was doubtful of and sought for constantly and widely was this definition of the *telos* or end of the unit that was larger than the single unit—namely, the city or nation. In the service of this, he is surveying the interaction of the cities or nations in the history of the world. He looks at the past and builds a formidable list of contributions to his sense of the total reality of man in his world. Thus in his huge narrative he glances, in the past, at the oldest language spoken, the beginning of Greek religion, the oldest people, the youngest people, the potentially most powerful nation, the cleverest people, the stupidest people those in the lands by the Euxine Pontus, except for the Scythians), the truest way of life in a community the Ethiopians), and so on. All of these conditions, fully realized only in man's hopes or thoughts, lie on a continuum of existence, and that existence endlessly accommodates itself to the total span of reality. Hence the ambiguity of the importance of big cities as opposed to small ones, which will one day be big, and vice versa. Hence the inclusion of particolored elements in wonders and miracles and what men believe and the stories they tell of their wonders and beliefs. In the end, these elements of the total scene, which a narrower mind would neglect or subordinate, may have a bearing on the result out of all proportion to what the common sense of Herodotus' contemporaries would afford them. So Herodotus has a duty to these antiquities and to his own intuition in discovering them. The reality that the stories and the myths reveal, both those in the early accounts of Asia Minor and later, in the account of the invasion itself, is hardly, finally, the regular series of victories and defeats and the rise and fall of thrones. These indeed constitute the set of actions through which Herodotus works, dealing with our sense of wonder and its arousal of excitement and joy. What the ***History*** is really about lies behind this: man, giant-sized, seen against the background of the entire world, universalized in his conflict with destiny, the gods, and the cosmic order. The medium that is most fertile in showing the true nature of reality is the human mind, remembering, reflective, and fertile most of all when its memory and reflection are put at the service of its dreaming and fantastic side.

When Herodotus examined man in a historical setting, he apparently thought of human nature as possessed of a number of logical choices that are differently exploited. What determined the choice that was made was sometimes a series of unsought challenges that explored these potentialities; for instance, the Scythians developed a peculiar but effective way of protecting themselves as a result of their climate and their empty, new country and because of the course of their rivers. More often, however, one course of action supersedes or is preferred over another by the decision of one man or by the voluntary choice of a people referred to as "they." Cyrus, as a result of Croesus' advice, once Croesus was his captive, changed the entire way of life of the Lydians; they became pliable victims of their conquerors. At 5.3 we learn that "the nation of the Thracians is the biggest of all mankind, except for the Indians. If they were under a single ruler or could be of a single mind, none could fight them down, and they would, in my judgment, be far the mightiest of all the people on earth. But such agreement is quite impossible for them; no means can bring it about, and this is the respect in which their weakness lies."

His is a kind of universal history; that is, it is the record of all the logical possibilities, political and human, that coexist in the human world. The *kleos* is the tale that makes one understand and admire this; that obtrudes itself between one's bewilderment at the diversity of experience and one's inner single moral certainty of man's nature; that harmonizes what one knows is true of man, because he is oneself writ large, and the excitement of the vision of men and events greater than anyone, without Herodotus' aid, could easily conceive of. The moral stories are another form of this aid; for example, the king who wept for sorrows suitable for tears but was silent before those that were too great for weeping; the enormity of the army of Xerxes, drinking rivers dry on its march to Greece; Xerxes who wept at the review of his huge army when he reflected that in a hundred years not a one of them would be alive; and the story of the crafty Artemisia at Salamis.

The great innovative rulers also come before us in the *kleos.* There are Cyrus and Darius, founders of dynasties, with whom, on the whole, all goes well, who are decisive and will also listen to advice at the right moments, and whom, all the same, destruction finally overtakes when they disregard good advice, Cyrus in facing the Massagetae, Darius the Scythians. And Cambyses and Xerxes, who are their sons and their exact opposites. And, to set the whole in perspective, we have the king of Ethiopia, who rejected and banished the spies of Cambyses with a denunciation of the clothes, money, and imperialism of his contemporary world as decisively as did the king of Brobdingnag in dealing with Gulliver; he stands for an entirely different and elementary way of life. And in ways of life, the bottom of the scale is held by the cannibals: "The Man-Eaters have the most savage manner of life of all men; they believe in no justice nor use any law."

We have here, within the scope of Herodotus' history, the entire gamut of human possibilities, in social, political, and, in a way, moral terms. When I say this, I do not want to do away with the difference between Herodotus and Homer, between the historian and the poet. Herodotus did not invent the peoples; they and the personalities were actually there or nearly always there, in his historical scene, to bear the weight he assigns them. But he did assign them this weight. And the range and the significance are matters of obvious selection, so that the **History** becomes a pattern, itself a kind of myth. Inside, of course, there are massive passages of detail that are the result of eyewitness work and of the careful balancing of one aspect of probability against another. Yet these are built into a framework that is poetic. Man lives on a continuum of intellectual and moral possibilities. The king of Ethiopia may be right, may indeed be righter than Cambyses' spies or the contemporary powerful Persian and Greek politicians. It is always within the power of any ruler, or perhaps within that of any community, to opt out of modernity and choose a different road. It is possible, and may be desirable, to choose a different moral scheme for oneself and one's country. This is as different a view of history as possible from that expressed by the Corinthians, at the Lacedaemonian Congress before the beginning of the Peloponnesian War, in the pages of Thucydides. They lecture the Spartans on the grounds that their institutions are "old-fashioned" (*archaiotropa*). They say that advances in technology have their corollary in general human political institutions; the more advanced phases overcome the older. But in Herodotus the king of Ethiopia is the political equivalent of Solon when the latter lectures Croesus on the superiority of the life of the private man to that of the Eastern despot. One may choose a national (and international) position that willingly disregards power politics, increase in money, technical development. Indeed, one of the main emphases borne by the Persians in Herodotus' narrative is the disastrous disappearance of the private sphere within the distorted unity of their community.

So the *kleos,* the tale of glory, to be true to its *natural* function in man's report of past events, and to be true to Herodotus' artistic handling of it, must show all the facts and aspirations of human life that are present on this great continuum, stretching from King Cambyses to the cannibals, and this involves also individuals such as Cyrus and Darius along with Prexaspes.

Of course, Herodotus has his preferences in forms of life and political organization. Bias of Priene was *right* to advise as he did when he urged the Ionians to move away and form in Sardinia an empire of their own. Herodotus himself does not want to live like the Scythians. But he has an overwhelming sense of the diversity of man, of his fertile gift for innovations, at times his reseeking of elementary patterns in resistance to the trend of a time, or the supersession of one form of political theory by another that is temporarily superior.

Thucydides, in the passages of his **History** where he is clearly criticizing his predecessor, speaks, as I noted near the start of this introduction, of the contrast between his own work, which he intended to be "a possession for ever," and the other (by implication, Herodotus') as aimed at the delight of the immediate hearer. In the main, I think Thucydides is right about the immediate delight of the ear. Herodotus can be felt as a living voice fairly often. Listen to the end of the story of Adrastus, the man who killed his brother; whom Croesus then purified of bloodguilt; and who was assigned as bodyguard to Croesus' son, whom he then accidentally killed:

> So Croesus buried his son as was right. But Adrastus, the son of Gordias, the son of Midas, he who was the slayer of his own brother and had become the slayer of his purifier, who was, moreover, aware within himself that he was of all men he had ever known the heaviest-stricken by calamity, when there was a silence about the tomb and none was there, cut his throat over the grave.

This is indeed as though we saw the figure before us on the stage, and we would do well to remember the bitterness of Thucydides' phrase—"I have not composed my work as a competition piece for the delight of the moment"—where "competition piece" agōnisma is certainly a reference to the theater or to the rhapsodes' or actors' competitions. But we would do well also to remember the line in the *Odyssey* where Odysseus is praising the minstrel at the court of Alcinous and speaks of the supreme power of the singer in rendering a subject "as though you were there yourself." It is *as though*—not as a real onlooker. The *artifice* of Herodotus' *kleos* is very important. Its purpose is to give artistic substance to a moment or an event; thus there is an object that draws men's *natural* pleasure in the great moment or great deed to a single concentration of delight and meaning. The *kleos* will then, in the process of time and recollection, become part of the future of that moment or event. As the *kleos* deals with the natural possibilities of man's memory in their most significant form, the natural enemy is time and forgetfulness. And the most potent opponent of time and forgetfulness is the creation of the things that, in Helen's phrase, are "subjects of song for men of future days."

The listening audience is certainly the target of much of Herodotus' shaping of the narrative. In the later books, one thinks of the presentation of Xerxes' dream and the intervention of Artabanus and the obviously readable and actable conversation between the evil spirit of the dream and Artabanus. And of the ringing eloquence of the Athenian answer to the timid address of the Spartans when King Alexander of Macedon, in the name of the Great King, tried to tempt the Athenians to desert the Greek alliance: "There is our common Greekness: we are one in blood and one in language; those shrines of the gods belong to us all in common, and the sacrifices in common, and there are our habits, bred of a common upbringing." The element of the theatrical, Thucydides' *agōnisma,* is plain in many places throughout the history. Often the parts are intricately fitted together but designed for a series of dramatic climaxes. There is the naturally supreme moment when Xerxes in his agony weeps at the thought that of all his magnificent army none would be alive in a hundred years, but the listing of the peoples and the description of their colorful uniforms are meticulously shaped to draw the historical detail into the moment of Xerxes' agony.

There are two worlds of meaning that are constantly in Herodotus' head. The one is that of human calculation, reason, cleverness, passion, happiness. There one knows what is happening and, more or less, who is the agent of cause. The other is the will of Gods, or fate, or the intervention of daimons. Herodotus did not, I think, have very clear notions of theology, at least as Christianity came to understand it. He does not feel sure of the identity of particular Gods, as intervening at particular moments, except on the rarest occasions. He gives as a glimpse of an Apollo who wished to save Croesus and couldn't, of a difference between the will of *one* God and Fate. Indeed, the oracle (or the priests) at Delphi document this by saying that even a God cannot cheat the Fates, who are personalized for this occasion. This is indeed the same dilemma we see in the *Iliad* when Zeus fails to save Sarpedon and, later, Hector, "long since condemned by fate." But in Herodotus, generally, any special God, or the Gods, or Fate; or (very commonly) The Divine (*to theion* or *to daimonion*) are all one. They all mean the power that controls the world of man. And this power's relation to man is bound up with a maddening relation between man's reason and understanding and such "signs" as the Divine has allowed us to have of its future or past intervention. Herodotus is quite definite on two points: that the Divinity is altogether "jealous" and prone to trouble us and that "there is, somehow, some warning given in advance [*prosēmainein*] when great evils are about to fall on either city-state or nation [*ethnos*]." He also affirms his belief in oracles in general, although, like a sensible man, he can detect many occasions when one has a right to distrust a particular oracle.

A very great deal of the ***History*** is necessarily concerned with men's attempts to read these signs. The Egyptians, we are told, have the most complete set of records on wonders and their outcome, and, except for oracles, this is the only system that can lead to results. But, from first to last, man is dogged by the mysterious nature of the Divine purpose (if purpose it should be called) and its relation to his human understanding. For the outcome of a "sign" may accord in name and in some peculiar symmetry of form or meaning but, in the value and significance of the event, be quite altered. The Magi at the court of King Astyages had predicted that from his daughter he would have a grand-

child who would take the crown from him. After the usual ineffectual effort to destroy the child by exposing it (an episode I have discussed above, in another context), the boy—Cyrus—reappears. He tells a story of how in the village, where his shepherd foster father lived, some children had in play chosen him king. Astyages now wanted to know from the Magi whether this fulfilled the oracle or whether further harm was to be feared for himself and his crown. The answer was as follows: "If indeed the boy survives and has become king with no connivance, be of good cheer and good heart: he will not come to rule a second time. Some, even of our prophecies, issue in very small matters, and in all that pertains to dreams the fulfillment is often in something trifling." This story is all the more significant because, after all, the event proved that the Magi had been right the *first* time. The "real" meaning can be established only by hindsight. But this "real" meaning is what counts for human beings, and men have no indication whether the Divine recognizes any distinction between it and other outcomes that in some fashion bear the same name or the same shape.

At times the jealousy of the Gods, to which Herodotus refers, makes it look as though the *intention* of the God or Gods had been to deceive and maliciously to mock. It is hard to acquit of malice the utterance of Apollo given to Croesus ("if he made war on the Persians he would destroy a mighty empire." Yet it does look as though the Delphic priests, in Herodotus' report at any rate, thought they had saved the God's reputation; for Croesus should, he was told, have asked "*what* empire" (as he now agrees), and the priests cite Apollo's undoubted aid to him when he was on the burning pyre (the deliverance through the rainstorm) and the benefit they claimed the God rendered in extending his period of success. On the whole, I think that Herodotus believes that the Divine is altogether jealous and prone to trouble us because it controls a world in terms that we cannot understand and that distort the outcome we would want; but it is not necessary that we believe that the Gods have personal vindictiveness against those who are destroyed. What is decisive is the impersonal hinge of fate. Particular Gods may at times be represented as the unwilling assistants as the hinge of fate turns. But fate in its compulsive patterns depends on the potency of single events or blocks of events. Croesus, we are told, was expiating the fault of his ancestor, Gyges. Also involved, though not always, is some personal act or attitude on the part of the person who suffers punishment. Croesus, we learn, suffered, "one may guess . . . because he thought he was of all mankind the most blessed." And in the case of Apries, "since it was fated that he should end ill, something now caused it to happen, which I will [later] tell at greater length." Yet such apparent causes or even superficial occasions are mainly *signs* to the human world; they do not correspond to the effective power of causation. This seems entirely due to a matching of acts from past to future. In such matching acts, however, moral wrongs seem to have a place. For instance, Herodotus speaks out as to his own conviction on the question of the cause of the Trojan War: "The reason of this, if I may declare my opinion, was that the Divine was laying his plans that, as the Trojans perished in utter destruction, they might make this thing manifest to all the world: that for great wrong-doings, great also are the punishments from the gods." Again, about the Queen Pheretime: "But neither did Pheretime end her life well. For straightway after her vengeance on the Barcans she went back home to Egypt and there died very foully. For when yet living she bred of herself a mass of worms, so that mankind may see that violent vengeance earns the gods' grudges." Yet it sometimes seems that it is the act that calls for the appropriate response, and only incidentally and occasionally the actor. Mycerinus, for example, was severely punished by the shortening of his life and reign because he did not understand that he was the third in a necessary sequence of three *bad* kings; his regrettable lapse into virtue necessitated his removal. And Xerxes, who clearly would have preferred to follow Artabanus' advice *not* to invade Greece, was forced on his evil course by a dream. Of course, we do not know what the antecedent events were, in the case of either Mycerinus or Xerxes, that constituted the impersonal pattern of Divine planning. Some such, we may conjecture, there must have been, given the evidence of the Divine urging. In such a system the choice of the individual man himself, his preference for virtue or vice, is valid only as it harmonizes with fate. Indeed, the individual man, saint or sinner, is hardly more important than the individual animal. For example, "There is a divine providence, with a kind of wisdom to it, as one might guess, according to which whatever is cowardly of spirit and edible should be prolific in progeny so that, with all the eating of them, they should not fail to exist; while things that are savage and inflict pain are infertile." This certainly pictures a world of design, as far as Divine providence is concerned, since the fertility and infertility of the animals turn on the balance between eaters and eaten. But if one puts this together with the exclusive emphasis elsewhere on the sin and not the sinner, one comes out, I believe, with the conviction that great sins are punished because some order of the universe is maintained by divine punishment. But this simply does not reach down to the moral choice of the individual man any more than the general laws about fertility and infertility in the animal kingdom concern the fate of the individual rabbit or elephant.

Piety there is in Herodotus, but, interestingly enough, it concerns mostly not what you feel about the Gods but what you feel about your fellow men's feelings about the Gods or what the Gods feel about you. King Cambyses was crazy, said Herodotus, or he would never have outraged the feeling of the Egyptians by injuring their sacred cow. Illustrating this is the story of the wise Darius, the story of *nomos*. Darius asked his Greek and his Indian subjects about their burial customs and jokingly inquired of each what they would take to break with their ancestral customs, the one by eating, the other by burning, their ancestors. He is greeted with horror by both. From Herodotus' point of view, Darius is not only the wise but the pious ruler. Herodotus on the same model has tried to write as a pious and sensible historian, offending no one's religious susceptibilities and recording all religious accounts. There are, it is true, certain attitudes or acts that seem to directly provoke the Gods' wrath on human beings. God does not suffer anyone to "think high" but himself, says Herodotus. But such high thoughts nearly always appear only as the *apparent* cause (*prophasis*); the offense of Apries is an example. The weight of causation seems to lie solidly on an antecedent series of events. In a famous passage of Aeschylus' *Agamemnon,* the chorus says that theirs is a special and unusual belief, that they think that punishment does not come from the gods simply on the high and mighty in itself but on sin. It is quite possible that Herodotus would agree with the poet. But for him it would not be the sin of the individual, or at least not necessarily so, but a sin that, for some special reason (unknown), constitutes for the Divine the beginning of a significant sequence.

Piety also figures in Herodotus' book—in terms of a direct relation to the Gods—in his cautious avoidance of denying the existence of any daimon or God who can conceivably have done the things that people say he has done. Thus Herodotus severely questions the divinity of the Thracian daimon Salmoxis, but, when he passes to another subject, he has hardly denied the divinity explicitly. And when he tells us that the Egyptians do not believe in heroes at all and is concerned to disprove the Greek stories about Heracles in Egypt, he concludes with this hope: "May both gods and heroes view me kindly!"

In speaking of animals in Egypt and their relation to religious practices, he says the following: "But if I were to say why it is that the animals are dedicated as sacred, my argument would drive me into talking of matters divine, and the declaration of these is what I would particularly shun. To the degree that I have spoken of them, it was with but a touch, and under the stress of necessity, that I have spoken." Yet of course, since the gods or fate or the divine or the daimonic control the world, one is forced, even in history, to mention them, even with "but a touch."

Since all men know equally about the divine, it is only the names of gods, the customs of their worship, and the accounts and rituals that differentiate our notions of religion. It may be, and sometimes is, the historian's work to concern himself with these but only very rarely with the basic religious concepts underlying them all. It is the differences between peoples on which, to adapt Yeats's phrase in another context, history keeps house. That the Divinity is always jealous and prone to trouble us, as Solon tells Croesus, is perhaps a universal religious perception; that God allows no one but himself to think high is another. What these sentences mean is that two important aspects of the divine are caught by statements that are, strictly speaking, analogical. God can be understood *as if* he were a jealous and troublesome despot; he permits no one to be haughty but himself. This is one way of *speaking* about the inner knowledge that all men have of the Divine. It is the way of speaking when what is drawn on is the aspect of God that appears to man personal. God alone is free of danger or vulnerability. He therefore alone can "think high." Man never can and should never dare to. On the other side are the many references to an impersonal balance of fate, which is often shown as being independent of God's control and *a fortiori* of man's control or even his reasoned comprehension. The balance of fate can sometimes be traced to past events. Otherwise one can only hazard guesses, sometimes assisted by the Gods, sometimes by the semiscientific examination of similar cases and their outcomes. The basic religious "truths" thus analogically expressed underlie all the historical narrative, perhaps even give it its characteristic flavor and very form. But they are really not in need of comment; they are too basic and too general. But that the Persians approach their God not in human form but as the natural elements and therefore worship on the tops of mountains; that the Egyptians see Apis as a calf; that Homer and Hesiod had furnished the Greeks with an appropriate gallery of deities, with forms and honors assigned them; that the Indians' sense of the sacred commits them to eating their dead parents—these are all of concern to the historian because, in their multiplicity, they extend the range of our understanding of man's condition in the world, the world that is ultimately entirely controlled by a power not his own. The human notion of fate as an evening-out of the balance—upset by some monstrous sin, such as Pheretime's punishment of the people of Barca—is a human metaphor for an observed religious truth that cannot be otherwise communicated. But granted the evening-out, the human observer is often at a loss to find the first and the last of the series of responsive events. Unlike the varying customs and rituals, the truth implied in the metaphor of balance is commonplace and universal, but its application to particulars is difficult and unsatisfactory. It is therefore sometimes communicated by Herodotus or commented on, but comparatively rarely.

This is a mystery, this relation between the two worlds, that of divine control and that of the human beings on the receiving end. And, I think, Herodotus would avoid, as far as he can, the world of divine control, not only because of the risk to himself as observer and recorder. There is in him a deep admiration and delight in the human, and this, in his terms, implies a certain neglect of the divine and a wish to leave it, if possible, out of

consideration. "That time may not draw the color from what man has brought into being"; time is the destroying agent against which you erect the *kleos*. Against the Gods there is nothing to be done. The world of humanity, controlled by finally incomprehensible powers, is a tragic world. At best, the Divine meaning mocks the other. If one is to be great and glorious as man or nation or city, one is the more likely to fall into the traps of the supernatural. The most sensible course is to choose the private life; but the purpose of Herodotus' *History* is to chronicle the great men, great cities, and great deeds. So as a writer he is almost committed to a world of tragedy, where good or great intentions have but little to do with what happens. Still, the *kleos* remains, not, I think, as a moral warning nor yet as a national eulogy. Perhaps Herodotus saw himself as securing for the great deeds of the Persian War the only permanence in this world of relative values, the permanence of memory.

. . . . .

The English in which Herodotus comes before us should be direct, powerful, and clear but also, I think, a little odd. His Ionic is a literary dialect; it links him with Homer, the main share of whose language is Ionic. This bond with Homer was intended to be very suggestive. Herodotus' *History* is to be the story of another great war, that of the Persians against the Greeks, as Homer's was that of the Greeks against the Trojans. But it was to be something new—prose history, not poetry, and history that would concern itself not only with the glories of the great deeds in battle but with reasons why the war and its great deeds had come about. It is this combination of tradition and innovation that is at the heart of Herodotus' work. The English in which he now speaks to us must have a flavor, at least, that is as traditional and literary and a little archaic as Homer sounded for the fifth-century Greek.

Of course, it is quite possible, and some would consider it desirable, to disregard any special quality of the original Greek style. Rather concentrate, these critics might say, on a forceful English version without bothering to render the peculiar character of the Greek by some sought-out quirk in the English. But though this seems a bold and telling attitude, it misrepresents the Greek that faces the translator. It is indeed what makes de Selincourt's version in the Penguin edition much less satisfactory than it otherwise might be. His English is racy, it reads well, and it is sharp and to the point, but it entirely fails to convey any part of the conscious mask of Herodotus: his use of an inherited way of talking (from Homer) while treating of something new. The Penguin Herodotus sounds exactly as though new-minted by a twentieth-century journalist. There are keen strokes and very little nuance, which is quite false to the Greek style and to the strange man who is himself so preeminently the style. Herodotus must sound somewhat literary and whimsical. Still, he must, even more importantly, be powerful and direct, because the history is largely designed for public reading. Very many of his greatest stories are folklore that must have come straight from the mouths of local inhabitants and were to find their artistic form of publication in the mouth of the public reader and for an audience. If there is one feature an English Herodotus must pass on to us, it is an air of straightforward impact, especially in the conversations and speeches. But, paradoxically, it is exactly at those places that the literary background of Homer is most heavily laid under contribution. In reminiscences, interventions, and personal notes, the contribution of the writer must again appear direct, almost involuntarily so. One of the chief objections to the other current Herodotean translation, the older version of Rawlinson, is that it is dull and prolix. No one could read it, or listen to it, with surprise or enjoyment.

What I was looking for, then, was an English Herodotus who speaks not altogether with his own tongue but with echoes of the tongues of older writers; a powerful eccentric who has made even the traditional his own, so that we feel that no man but himself could have originated the phrase, the sentence, the cadence, which is so often a blend of Homer and himself. . . .

Donald Lateiner (essay date 1990)

SOURCE: "Deceptions and Delusions in Herodotus," *Classical Antiquity,* Vol. 9, No. 2, October, 1990, pp. 230-46.

[*In the following excerpt, Lateiner focuses on the question of credulity and deception in the* History. *Lateiner notes Herodotus's admiration for ingenious trickery, but also considers, by appeal to the case of Salmoxis, his skeptical and cautious treatment of religious charlatanism.*]

Not every self-interested charlatan is condemned in any society that values ingenuity. The Hellenes admired the lies of shrewd Odysseus, worshipped Hermes, patron of thieves and sharp entrepreneurs, and found admirable the hedgehog deceits and shams of Aristophanes' comic heroes.

Greek epic, tragedy, and comedy describe cheats and their dupes. After the development of history, philosophy, biography, and the later genres of the novel and hagiography at times would explore popular delusions and false prophets. History proper, from Herodotus on, supplies examples, large and small, of political, religious, and other entrepreneurs who hatch schemes at the expense of the credulous. Frauds require a knowing agent, usually one who works for his own profit or advance.

On another hand, we have unplanned delusions, as when groups share a belief in a natural or supernatural event without anyone's being the richer for it. Individual or mass delusions and panics enrich the fabric of historiography and implicitly provide lessons for the attentive audience. Herodotus certainly plays to his Greek audience's pleasure in descriptions of deception and delusion, allowing the listener's or reader's amused perception of a different reality. The responsible historian tried to separate fact from fiction, sham from truth, charlatan from dupe and clearheaded exposer of deceit.

Herodotus prizes artful deception and quick-thinking acts that promote self-preservation. Particularly when the otherwise defenseless individual outwits the powerful autocrat, or the group to be victimized outthinks the armed and threatening aggressor, Herodotus recounts in detail the survival of the (mentally) fittest. The phenomenon represents the Odyssean facet of Homeric Herodotus, indeed, but also such glorification of cleverness, moral *and* amoral, permeates not only Greek literature but Greek life, so far as we can reconstruct its reality as well as the response to literary representations.

In the other, but related category of popular delusions and beliefs about the supernatural, any historian can only know what he or she has been told and should refrain from quick condemnation or even condescension. Classical literature represents generally the elite's view of mass spiritual phenomena, with all the prejudices that such a situation implies. Nonempirical phenomena seemed dubious matters to Herodotus, so his accounts of gods on earth, spiritualists, and oraclemongers are critical, or at least distanced from authorial credence. Nevertheless, he includes many accounts of Greek and barbarian popular spiritual movements, and he often recounts them without recourse to explicit condemnation. Here the admired deceivers will be treated first.

THE VIRTUES OF DECEIT

Herodotus clearly admired conspicuous exemplars of human wit and presumed that Hellenic audiences would enjoy hearing tales of both ordinary and prominent men deluded, especially when their motives were ignoble and the upshot produced a form of poetic justice. . . . Oral informants then and now emphasize the roles of individuals, their self-serving motives, and foibles, mercenary and sexual. In an age of tyrants and despots, the whims and delusions of the mighty and the desperate maneuvers of subjects can be significant historical factors. We turn to case histories.

The Milesian adventurer Histiaeus and the Athenian politician Themistocles are prominent in any list of celebrated Herodotean swindlers. Both wily devisers of their own remarkable success are presented as con-men who can inveigle their fellow Greeks *and* the Persian king into complying with their self-serving schemes. Other adventurers, both petty and great, also gain their ends after promising the king easy profits or conquests. Themistocles' superiority to the competition lies in his ability to make a personal profit from a Euboean bribe or to secure his enemy's good will while actually promoting the national interests of his Athenian and Hellenic countrymen. He had a natural genius for estimating the perceived self-interest of his audiences and "to improvise what the situation at hand needed". Herodotus likes to note the good consequences of apparently immoral, impolitic, or otherwise unwise actions.

Other figures exhibit single or multiple instances of their aptitude for survival through fraud. Democedes the Crotoniate physician concocted lies for himself and a charade for Atossa that gained him freedom from Persian house arrest and eventually return to southern Italy and a rich marriage. Herodotus's amusement at the wily Italian's schemes is conveyed by the vocabulary of deceit . . . , Democedes' persiflage, and elements of folk-tale comedy such as the request for a single boon and a battle over a runaway slave. In other narratives, Spartan wives disguise their Minyan spouses as women to save their lives; Macedonian men disguise themselves as women to kill the lecherous ambassadors of Persia. The motives in these cases of cross-dressing deceptions are self-preservation and protecting honor. Artemisia's extraordinary skill in exploiting a lucky ruse at Salamis, whereby she escaped Greek attack and sank the ship of an ally, won Xerxes' commendation and *a fortiori* Herodotus's. She is acclaimed for both her strategic perception and clever impromptu survival skills. The Samians assisted Periander's three hundred eunuchs-to-be by first instructing them to take refuge from their transporters in Artemis's sanctuary and then fabricating an "ancient festival" with dances and dancers to provide the suppliants with sufficient food to prevent starvation at the hands of the furious Corinthian armed guards. The cultic evasion succeeded. *Dolos* is entirely appropriate to conserve lives, honor, and the deceiver's *oikos,* or to gain revenge. Herodotus approves, and an audience would be likely to share the Hellenocentric assumptions of his tales of deception.

There are less savory, some less justifiable traps laid, however, which also deserve mention. Political treachery . . . traps or attempts to trap Tomyris, the Scythian king Ariapeithes, sundry Ionian tyrants, and the entire Persian nation in the case of the Magi.

Various military deceits are admired for their effectiveness or intellectual ingenuity, for example, the way the Persian military commander Amasis trapped and captured the Barcaeans by a legal quibble and the way Thrasybulus fooled Alyattes. Herodotus dwells on the complex means by which Themistocles kept his Hellenic allies at Salamis and lured the Persians into the narrows. The Elean *mantis* Tellias devised a tactical ruse with a pretense of the supernatural. He had the Phocian troops near Thermopylae, his employers at the time, whiten their faces for a night attack. His fraud frightened their Thessalian foes, who fled in panic. The enemy troops thought that ghosts, . . . were coming against them.

Xerxes king of Persia is reported to have attempted a ruse to raise the confidence and morale of his Greek sailors after his expensive victory at Thermopylae. Trying to present the military engagement that had delayed his advance as a triumph, he dressed up many Asiatic corpses to look like Lacedaemonians, buried many others of his own (of the twenty thousand reported dead, only a thousand were left above the ground), and invited his nearby Greek naval allies to visit and view the contrived fate of his opponents. Many came, eager to sightsee; no boats were left to ferry other remaining hopefuls. However, no one was deceived by Xerxes' fraud, and in fact its clumsiness was laughed at by the perceptive Greeks. Xerxes had left the thousand Oriental troops strewn about Thermopylae, but he had had four thousand supposedly Spartan (and Thespian?) corpses heaped up in one spot (the number is suspiciously large even for this fabrication). A whole day was given up to the illusory pageant but the deceit was transparent. The improbable Greek tale reported by Herodotus served to bring Xerxes into contempt and asserts the limit of Greek gullibility, at least in the face of Persian military-political propaganda. The barbarian fraud is seen as such at once.

The Aeginetans and other Greeks, in an attempt to fool future generations about their patriotic devotion to the Hellenic cause, constructed false memorials for their allegedly nonexistent dead warriors at Plataea. . . . This other incident of bogus fallen warriors attests to anxiety for the historical record in the generation that fought the Persian War, and to Herodotus's noteworthy belief that the men of the Great War would bother to try to impose a false belief on future Hellenes about their accomplishments. It marks an epoch in popular historical consciousness. The historian seems obliged to discover and report falsifications of the past. . . .

FANTASTIC BEINGS

Herodotus denounces many accounts of meeting the unnatural or supernatural. He faults them for lack of probability, for internal illogic, or excess of logic, and twits other reporters for excessive credulity. He addresses on occasion problems of data, method, verification, and falsification. At the same time, he is reluctant to discard reports of surprising and fascinating phenomena that may be true or even seem certainly false, or to reject without record even obviously overrationalized versions of biased informants. Part of his task seems to be the preservation of local accounts and explanations that he or his sources explicitly describe as fabricated fictions, jokes, impostures, or unbelievable tall tales. Often enough he leaves the reader unsettled, without the crutch of the author's judgment. Almost always, he distances himself from reports of phantoms and miracles by identifying the responsible source or by reporting recorded *logoi* in indirect discourse.

Some supernatural appearances and disappearances are reported almost as if they were ordinary, because the people who related these events to Herodotus accepted their possibility. Those who first heard or read him retelling these stories of the fantastic may have enjoyed the human experience of condescending to other people's gullibility. Furthermore, Herodotus likes to recount—on the authority of others—popular stories, floating fictions that remind him of the human will to believe and foiled selfish self-interest. A huge apparition . . . allegedly fought opposite Epizelus the Athenian hoplite at Marathon, and another phantom, this time a female voice, was reported to have urged on the whole Hellenic fleet at Salamis. Demaratus's mother is said to have told him she had been inseminated by a phantom, the hero Astrabacus himself. Periander was reported to have successfully consulted by proxy the ghost of his wife Melissa at the Thesprotian oracle of the dead on the Acheron River.

Herodotus himself does not believe that flesh-and-blood people vanish, but he reports that Mardonius's corpse was not discovered at Plataea in 479. His reason for mentioning this fact was to record a certified fraud repeatedly perpetrated on a Persian grandee. The act of sepulture of Mardonius after the battle was fraudulently claimed by many people from various nations who obtained rich rewards from his son Artontes. . . .

BOGUS GODS, FALSE PRIESTS, AND SHAM MESSENGERS OF
THE DIVINE

A catalogue and discussion of reputed religious fakers and charlatans in Herodotus illuminates the historian's special interest in theatrics of the supernatural and cultic pretenses. In some cases, his informants may have been even more skeptical than the historian, who is open to diverse beliefs and practices in his sources. All these stories are somehow attached to the ethnographic or historical progress, but in most of these tales of supernatural entrepreneurial enterprise, human cleverness and fallibility in private life attract Herodotus's attention rather than historical acts of political importance. The human condition with its uncertainties gains the historian's compassion and indulgence, but—no less—his amusement. Personal-interest stories elbow out national strategic concerns, at least for the moment, although some of these dramatic pretenses had long-term public consequences.

His predecessor Hecataeus of Miletus and his contemporary Hellanicus of Mytilene seem to have been shaped primarily by critical tendencies of the Ionian Enlightenment and the Sophistic Movement. These writers recorded, synthesized, and debunked accounts of geography, myth, heroic genealogy, and traditional chronologies. Neither occupied himself with the detailed description of recent major events and their causes. Therefore their subjects, largely distant in time, required them to be descriptive and then deconstructive, for instance, when "logically" separating the "historical" from the legendary Heracles or King Codrus of Athens. Hellanicus uncritically recorded various chronological lists and tried, by various compromises, to coordinate them plausibly. He also attempted to explain Attic customs by mythical precedents and etymologies. These two pre- or parahistorians had not developed a method equal to their ambition, the deconstruction of implausible tales of the distant past and the reconstruction of a reliable record. It is not clear from the scattered fragments of their books how they treated beings with spiritual pretensions, such as "Apollo-controlled" Aristeas (clearly a source for both), Pythagoras, or Salmoxis, but their intellectual orientation would not lead us to expect sympathetic accounts of supernatural claims, foreign gods, and parareligious prophets.

Those of Herodotus's narratives that are based on myth necessarily suffer from the same analytic incapacity of the Greeks to separate fully myth from history in *any specific instance*. His methodological advance in this area was to isolate (by various narratological devices) such interruptions of myth from the narrative of recent events and to focus on what living memory could reasonably reconstruct. Unlike Hecataeus and Hellanicus with their rationalizations, Herodotus thinks it wiser to acknowledge the possibility of some surprising coincidences and reports of the otherwise unknown than to cut every historical mystery down to common-sense proportions.

The result may be less consistent (as we shall see in his bifurcated account of Salmoxis) but more satisfactory for extracting historical sense from misunderstood or garbled accounts. In the incidents mentioned above and below, which involve supernatural claims, Herodotus the enlightened skeptic struggles with Herodotus the patient recorder of belief, practice, and memory as encountered around the world he explored.

Early in the *Histories,* we hear that Pisistratus and his cronies cunningly contrived . . . to have him escorted back to Athens by the outsized but gorgeous woman Phye from the Paeanian deme. She was outfitted and posed in glamorous disguise as the goddess Athena in epiphany. Either Athena appeared to honor her servant and promoter Pisistratus as he processed to the capital of Attica, or he piously escorted the patroness of Athens to her home on the Acropolis. Herodotus calls this sham Athena the silliest scheme by far ever . . . and it was successfully practiced on the usually percipient Athenians, who at this moment adored a merely human female. Herodotus points out that what separates Hellenes from barbarians is the former's superior cleverness and the absence of credulous imbecility, but he mentions this distinction here at the beginning of his *History* in a context where it is plainly unjustified, false, clearly undercut. He adds that the Athenians were then supposed to be supreme in cleverness even among the Hellenes, but they were completely swindled by the tyrant and his impostor. This is one of several notices that chortle at Athenian victimization.

Other explanations of this dramatic event than the one Herodotus chooses to purvey are possible, even probable. Pisistratus was a master of political propaganda, including the use of myth and religion in promoting his political interests. "Con-men" and "victims" may be prejudicial or even wrong labels for this and similar relatively small and tightly knit religious communities. Pisistratus's version of Athena may have been recognized by her peers in the fields as symbolic rather than a real goddess. The enemies of the Pisistratids and later generations may have misguidedly or, more likely, maliciously reported her to have been a successful hoax. Whatever the original event, in Herodotus's day, after more than one hundred years, such manipulation of religious ideas was deemed a real possibility. That is, religious fraud was a perceived reality.

Religious con-men and deceivers hold a venerable position of distrust in Greek literature, as Homer can show. Herodotus reports with amusement stories of the faked epiphany of Phye, the alleged ascetic and pilgrim Abaris, the reputed journey of Rhampsinitus to the land of the dead, the allegedly faked death and resurrection of Salmoxis, falsified Delphic oracles, fake Phocian ghosts, and an allegation that Deïphonus was a pretender prophet. The skeptical empiricist usually shows little sympathy for belief in supernatural interference in earthly affairs.

Barbarians and Hellenes both fall for hocus-pocus and religious sham. Amasis shows the Egyptians that the golden idol they duly revere had once been his golden pisspot; the pharaoh serves his nation as a Sophist exposing religious impositions. Amasis refused to stay locked away always in royal pomp and to swell his dignity before his subjects, as his advisers urged, unlike the Median usurper Deïoces, who appreciated the need to solemnize all his person and acts in order to impress his people. Amasis also ignored oracular shrines that he observed to have been wrong in attempts to predict the future.

Perialla the suborned Pythia, at the bidding of a Delphian dynast, delivers the fabricated anti-Demaratan oracles that Cleomenes wants. Later both Delphians were caught and punished. The Alcmaeonid Cleisthenes had also successfully bribed the Pythia. Barbarian Croesus accused Apollo at Delphi, *the* oracular god of the Greeks, of defrauding his benefactors.

The Athenian oraclemonger Onomacritus exemplifies either real life masquerading as Aristophanic comedy or, more likely, hostile Athenian oral tradition assimilating a few historical facts to the chresmologue's enemies' contemporary political fiction. According to Herodotus, in his fraudulent audacity this prophet had "edited" Musaeu's collection of oracles and inserted forged verses. Lasus, the agent of Pisistratus's sons, caught him in the act, and Hipparchus expelled him from Athens. Later in Susa the Pisistratids rediscovered his supernatural powers and praised his awesome abilities while the sham himself sang out rosy predictions for Xerxes, who was still reluctant to invade Europe. Onomacritus now prudently omitted any prophecies that boded ill for the Persian venture. The doctored prophecies persuaded Xerxes, who initially had no relish for attacking Greece, to change his mind (one of the many too many explanations that Herodotus gives for the overdetermined main event of his *Histories*). Flexible oral tradition and Herodotus's account utilize the skepticism of the Age of the Sophists to defame the tactics of the exiled tyrants.

In Book 4, three northerners whom Meuli, Carpenter, Dodds, and others have connected with Asiatic shamanism come into Herodotus's ken: Abaris, Aristeas, and Salmoxis. The alleged Hyperborean Abaris obtains a single parenthesis. He was reported to have gone on a long journey, to have lived without eating for long periods, and to have carried an arrow everywhere. The legend is contemptuously dismissed between Herodotus's skeptical impatience toward Delian tales of long-distance travel from the inaccessible north and toward improbable Ionian cartography with its perfect circle of Ocean, bilateral symmetry, and continental equalities too schematized for the real world.

The Greek missionary of Apollo, Aristeas, a northern nobleman of Proconnesus in the Propontis, was believed to have written an epic poem *Arimaspeia* about his travels to the lands of the Black Sea. Herodotus cautions the quickly credulous that the author himself of this work called himself "inspired" . . . and the poem was largely based on hearsay from Issedonian Scyths and made up in large part. The poet reported one-eyed Arimaspians, a nation of gold-filchers, and gold-guarding griffins, also Hyperboreans on the Northern Ocean, but did not claim eyewitness information. Herodotus acknowledges only the existence of the gold and discards the fabulous creatures, if not the rest of Aristeas's bizarre report.

Herodotus devotes more attention to a *logos* that he heard in Proconnesus and Cyzicus about the apparent sudden death of the same Aristeas in a fuller's shop in Proconnesus. The reported story relates that he simultaneously appeared elsewhere (shamanistic "bilocation") and conversed on the road with a Cyzicene traveling toward Proconessus. The resulting dispute, when the Cyzicene reached Proconnesus, as to whether Aristeas was alive or dead and where he then could be found, was to be settled when the family came to the locked fuller's shop to collect and prepare the corpse for burial. No Aristeas, living or dead, in one place or the other, was found, the story related.

Seven years later, Herodotus's sources continued, Aristeas the man reappeared in his home town, wrote his poem about the marvelous Arimaspians, and disappeared a second time. The Metapontines in Italy told Herodotus that he subsequently reappeared as a man in their city. Aristeas . . . at this time ordered them to build a statue of Aristeas and an altar to Apollo, who once had visited their city alone of all in Italy. Aristeas alleged that he had accompanied the god on that earlier journey . . . in the form of a raven (indeed, an avatar of Apollo). Then he disappeared a third and last time. In Italy they called him a phantom. Delphi endorsed the phantom's Apolline wishes, of course. The dedication was built as ordered and yet stood in Herodotus's day.

Aristeas's embellished legends clearly exhibit characteristics of Asiatic shamanism. The ability to bilocate, psychic excursion, appearance and disappearance at will, metamorphosis into a soul-bird, materializing of the immaterial, connections with the northern god Apollo, northern Milesian colonies, and northern travels, a lifespan of centuries and the capacity for metempsychosis, all connect Aristeas with genuine aspects of Siberian "medicine men" or ecstatic prophets, not to mention isomorphic figures of Greek legend such as Pythagoras and adjacent peoples' reincarnation myths.

Herodotus in this account collates ethnic traditions, calculates probable dates, but keeps some distance from this *Wunderleben* by citing his sources, keeping the tales in *oratio obliqua,* and dismissing without prejudice the farrago at the end . . . Ecstatic trances were not the material he would dwell on. Incidents that appeared more suitable to supernatural fable than fact were not entirely to be eliminated because: (a) obviously partial or inadequate sources are not thereby false; (b) Herodotus wants to report instructive stories that he does not believe to be historical; (c) spiritual reality does sometimes oddly resemble suspicious fiction.

REPUTED GOD AND DISPUTED PROPHET: THE CURIOUS CASE
OF SALMOXIS

Herodotus repeatedly reminds the reader that he appreciated the historiographical difficulties of reporting religious phenomena in an objective manner. He begins his detailed account of Egyptian gods, myth, rit-

ual, and dogma with a disclaimer and a caveat. Nevertheless his vision, . . . requires attention to the views of the supernatural that his subjects hold. A palmary example of his open approach is found in the account of the disputed divinity of Thracian Salmoxis.

Herodotus approaches Salmoxis in two ways. The first approach is the cool anthropologist's narration, free of polemical references to sources or personal expressions, describing the ethnology of the Getae of Thrace, "the immortalizers," men who "believe they have a recipe for escaping death.". . . They believe in personal immortality and that they join their Creator when they vanish from earth. They also believe in Salmoxis's own original reincarnation. Their Getic cult includes weather magic: shooting arrows at thunder and lightning. They also had a peculiar technique, reported only by Herodotus, for sending emissaries for assistance to Salmoxis now dwelling in the Great Beyond. Periodically and by lot a messenger is chosen. Some men point their spears upward; others whip the elect high up into the air by his limbs. If, when he falls on the spears, he dies, Salmoxis is deemed propitious. If the messenger lives, he himself is judged unacceptable and roundly abused. Then they try to send another winner of the Getic lottery to the Beyond. Herodotus adds at the end—parenthetically and with evident amusement—that they put in their requests for divine aid before the heavenly heave-ho, while the messenger is still alive.

More relevant material for students of charlatans is the second, cynical and garbled version of Salmoxis's story purveyed by the Hellenes of the Propontis and Pontus, "Euhemerists before Euhemerus." They said that Salmoxis was no more than a Thracian slave of Pythagoras in Samos, that he became civilized in Hellenic ways and a learned student of that very wise man's lore. He subsequently won his freedom, got rich, and went home to bring the refined Ionic way of life . . . to the local yokels, his poor, savage, and witless countrymen . . . .

Salmoxis, the story continued, after his return built a clubhouse retreat among the Getae, in which he entertained the Getan elite with ritual banquets and persuaded them . . . that neither he nor they and their offspring ever after would have to die, but they would come to such a place where he and the congregation would live forever and enjoy all life's good things after this mundane existence.

While carrying on his preaching, Salmoxis built an underground apartment, believing that Pythagoras's message required some validation of a supernatural sort, as the unsympathetic Greeks explained. When the hideout had been completed, Salmoxis disappeared for three years, descending into the underground dwelling . . . His companions missed and mourned him . . . They behaved as if he had died, but in the fourth year he reappeared and thus proved (without perfect logic, it may be said) the truth of his dogma . . . To Herodotus's Greek informants, the disappearance was a fraud practiced to gain the respect of credulous savages.

Herodotus opens and closes both the native Getic account and the reported Hellenic account that demeans the god to a slave and a hoax with distancing and disclaiming source references . . . . At the end, he adds a sound objection to the derisory Greek version: he believes Salmoxis lived, if he lived, long before the Samian "sophist" Pythagoras. As to Salmoxis's underground retreat, he personally does not disbelieve or believe it "a whole lot." . . . Whether a man Salmoxis ever existed or whether he is a local Getic daemon, Herodotus here dismisses the whole matter, presumably as a question beyond the scope of his historiography. He maintains his unique openness, equally rejecting Greek positivist reductiveness and Thracian certainties about the inhabitants of the divine realm.

The Greek account of Salmoxis is a travesty of Asiatic shamanism, however, an *interpretatio Graeca* of an alien religion in which Pythagoras's strangeness is used to "read" Salmoxism as it had been used by Herodotus to read Egyptian belief in 2.37 and 81 [Herodotus asserts that Greek Pythagoreanism falsely claims to have originated doctrines of metempsychosis that are really Egyption (2.123). In other words, he sooner credits the long-memoried and civilzed Egyptions than the nomadic and uneducated (4.46.1) northerners. In fact, the southeastern Europeans did hold such beliefs, and Egypt religion held no such doctrine (Eliade *passim*, Guthrie. J. Bremmer, *The Early Greek Concept of the Soul* (Princeton, 1983) 24-49, disconnects Aristea's and Abaris's ecstasy and soul-wandering from Central Asiatic shamanism]. Among the characteristics of shamanism, observe the long sleep, often the mimicry of an underworld journey; occultation or sudden disappearance and reappearance, usually the shaman's novitiate; the uncertainty of status as mortal or immortal being; the attempt to reestablish communication with the spirit world; the description of an everlasting life of bliss. This garbled Greek information ties the chapter to genuine characteristics of Dacian and Scythian religion.

Salmoxis's chief doctrine, once correction is allowed for the misunderstandings of Herodotus's Greek sources, was "a blissful postexistence," a state that required initiatory rites performed by a medium who can journey to the "other world." This symbolic death of the prophet in the Greek version marks a point of agreement with the purportedly real but beneficial death of the messengers to the beyond in the Getan version. Both accounts hold that the life beyond this one will be better and can only be reached by a special rite.

Salmoxis inaugurates a new era for Getic believers by his revelation. The occultation and return "prove" his special knowledge. Historians of religion see him as a brother god of Dionysus or a prototype for shamans. In either case Salmoxis has occult knowledge of death and special powers "peculiar especially to the Thracians and the related Balkan and Carpatho-Danubian peoples." Parallels with Pythagorean beliefs and practices are evident. Herodotus's chronological objection is sound, since the scattered and late evidence for Pythagoras's life points to a relatively late date, *fl.* ca. 530.

The communal banquets, the emphasis on dining, the teaching about a better reward and immortal life after death, the descent to the world of the dead or a pretense of such, show the Greek version of Salmoxis reported to Herodotus to be clearly no more than a plagiarism of Pythagoreanism, no matter what the genuine nature of the Getic cult was. These activities make an alien ritual and belief derivative from a known, docketed Greek phenomenon. The Greeks analogized alien practices, then recognized and criticized the "hoax." The Greeks found Pythagoras's doctrines and his sect already improbable, but his Ionian-Italian school's ideas and doctrines were already recognizable, by now domesticated eccentricities. The Greeks did not realize or care that the Pythagoreans' life and practices reflect various cultic acts of Greek mystery religions such as those of Eleusis, and many shamanistic features brought to the Aegean by travelers to the north.

The idiosyncratic historian Herodotus "sometimes writes for children, sometimes for philosophers," but sometimes, too, for the prudent historian. He exposes palpable frauds, mercenary, political, spiritual, and cultic, while leaving the decision on other disputable instances open [Herodotus's audience: E. Gibbon, *The History of the Decline and Fall of the Roman Empire*, (New York, 1845), ed. H. H. Milman, Vol. II, p. 57, n. 52 = ch. 24, n. 54 (Bury)]. Paranormal phenomena, Olympian epiphanies, and savage messiahs evoke his doubt, on empirical principle; but on another, quintessential principle, to wit, understanding alien and not-so-alien peoples by honestly recording their versions of the past and of eternal verities, he preserves his informants' accounts. The result, to take an example from geography and history, for the Phoenician circumnavigation of Africa was the precious preservation of a startling historical achievement in exploration. The result for Salmoxis was the precious preservation of both genuine Getic cult practices and hostile Hellenic ethnocentric responses. Both the skeptical and the respectful strains in Herodotus were necessary for the difficult achievement of inventing a reliable way of doing history, preserving the fragile traces of the past.

J. A. S. Evans (essay date 1991)

SOURCE: "The Imperialist Impulse," in *Herodotus, Explorer of the Past: Three Essays,* Princeton University Press, 1991, pp. 9-40.

[*In the following essay, Evans discusses Herodotus's treatment of the causes of the Persian invasion of Greece, focusing on the imperialist motives of Xerxes, the fall of Croesus, and the concepts of nomos, aitia and fate that colored Herodotus's account of the Persian Wars.*]

Nine years after their defeat at Marathon, the Persians were ready once again to invade Greece. The Greeks owed a debt of gratitude to Egypt for the delay. For three years after the defeat, Darius had prepared a new assault to wipe out the disgrace, but then Egypt had risen in revolt, and in 486 *b.c.*, Darius died; Xerxes succeeded him and the rebellion was not crushed until 484. Then Xerxes called a synod of the Persian magnates. It was a congress that Herodotus recreated with imaginative skill, but there may be a solid morsel of tradition behind it: in the romance of Esther, King Ahasuerus (Xerxes) summoned his nobles to a great festival in the third year of his reign, but in the Hebrew tradition these festivities were merely a backdrop for the fall of Vashti and the elevation of the Jewish heroine Esther in her place. For Herodotus, the feasting and the pageantry that must have accompanied a congress of this sort were of no importance: the synod is treated merely as a bit of theater for a remarkable exposition of the motive force behind Persian imperialism. Herodotus has undertaken to explain the reasons why Xerxes chose to invade Greece.

Persian despots were not given to parliamentary procedures. Herodotus reported in another context that the Persians debated questions drunk, and reconsidered them sober, or vice versa, as the case may be, but he portrayed no councils of the sort for his readers. He made short shrift of the debate that took place before Darius' Scythian expedition. "While Darius was making ready his invasion of Scythia and dispatching messengers round about with orders to some to raise troops, to others to supply ships and still others to build a bridge over the Thracian Bosporus, Artabanus, son of Hysptaspes, Darius' brother, urged him strongly not to make the expedition against the Scyths, on the ground that Scythia was a difficult objective. But good as his advice was, he failed to convince and he ceased." So much for the counsel that Darius was willing to accept before he set out against the Scyths. Cyrus did better before he advanced across the river Araxes against the Massagetae: he called a council of his "first men," and all but one advised him to allow the queen of the Massagetae to move into Persian territory and fight a decisive battle there. The exception was Croesus, who had lost the throne of Lydia and taken over the persona of a wise adviser instead. He argued that to advance was both safer and more appropriate for a Persian king: therefore Cyrus should move forward into the queen's territory and use trickery to defeat the Massagetae on their soil. The result of this strategy was, first, the capture and suicide of the queen's son, and then the death of Cyrus himself in battle. There is

nothing approaching the cut-and-thrust of a full-scale debate here, but only a *topos* that provided an opening for a wise adviser to make a point, and for the hero of the tale, Cyrus, to make an existential choice.

In fact, if we except the famous debate of the Persian grandees on the question of the proper constitution for Persia, which is more influenced by the sophists (particularly Protagoras) than anything in the Persian tradition, there is only one other assembly in the **Histories** which is comparable. That is the council at Phaleron before the battle of Salamis. There the king took his seat; then the various princelings and squadron commanders took theirs in order of rank: the king of Sidon first, next the king of Tyre, and so on in order. Mardonius went around to each to put the question whether or not to fight. All voted for battle, except the irrepressible Artemisia, the only commander in the Persian force with an intelligence comparable to Themistocles', who delivered a brief address to Mardonius, and he in turn reported it to Xerxes. Dissent was handled with courtesy and decorum, and then dismissed: a stark contrast with the councils of the Greek admirals before Salamis. Xerxes accepted a majority verdict which, not surprisingly, agreed with his own inclination, and chose the wrong course of action, whereas the Greeks did otherwise.

This Persian council was the inverse counterpart of the conclaves of the Greek admirals, and it was hardly more than a little showcase that Herodotus used to parade the might-have-beens of history before his readers' eyes. He chose as his mouthpiece Artemisia, a woman, and therefore an outsider in this masculine assembly. But the speeches of Xerxes, Mardonius, and Artabanus before the Persian magnates at the king's levee are intended to reveal something of the substance of Persian imperialism as Herodotus understood it.

The king at first had not possessed any great wish to invade Greece. He did not initially feel the weight of Persia's imperial tradition, or the obligation to expand the frontiers of the empire. The chief instigator of the war was Mardonius, son of Gobryas, who had taken command of Persia's Aegean front in 494 B.C.; Herodotus implied that he owed his elevation then, at a young age, to his "recent" marriage to Artazostra, Darius' daughter. He had advanced into Europe as far as Mt. Athos, where he had lost three hundred ships and twenty thousand men in a tempest, and was wounded himself in a night attack on his camp by a local tribe, the Brygoi. Not a glorious achievement overall.

But Mardonius had not returned home before conquering the Brygoi, his wound notwithstanding, and his influence with the new king was paramount. Convinced of Persian superiority, and quite without any comprehension of the Greeks, he was to be the spokesman for aggressive imperialism, who still believed that no Greek would dare "look without flinching at Persian dress and the men who wore it," to take a phrase from Herodotus, who wrote that, before the battle of Marathon, a Greek would not have summoned the courage to do any such thing. "Indeed my lord, who will oppose you and offer war, when you bring with you the host of Asia and all your ships?" he asked.

Events are to change his mind not one iota. In his last speech before his death, he was to gloat that the retreat of the Spartans on the battlefield of Plataea demonstrated their inferiority. He pressed his advice upon the new king. Athens, he argued, had committed great crimes, and had to be punished. She had helped the king's Ionian subjects to rebel, and then at Marathon, she had humiliated Datis and Artaphrenes. Vengeance was necessary for the sake of security: Athens had to be punished so that no one in the future would dare invade the Great King's dominions.

But that was not all. Europe was beautiful: a fertile land with trees of every kind. Mardonius stood the truth as the Greeks perceived it on its head, for the contrast between Persian wealth and Greek poverty was commonplace in classical Greece. Pausanias, son of Cleombrotus, staged a tableau to illustrate this after the victory at Plataea, and at the end of the century, Xenophon was to tell his ten thousand mercenaries that they must get back to Greece to tell their friends and relatives that they were poor by their own choice, for if they migrated to Persia, they could live in luxury. Mardonius reversed the polarity that the Greeks accepted as conventional wisdom. But Mardonius also harbored an ulterior motive: he wanted to be governor of Greece himself.

He had assistance in this endeavor. The pro-Persian Aleuad family, dynasts of Larissa in Thessaly, seconded his efforts; in 479 B.C., after the defeat at Salamis, they were still to urge the Persians on to their ultimate defeat at Plataea. The deposed Pisistratid tyrant Hippias had guided the Persians to Marathon in 490 B.C., and died soon thereafter; who the new pretenders were, we do not know, but Herodotus considered the Pisistratid lobby still effective at the Persian court, and it included a *kresmologos,* Onomakritos, a collector and editor of oracles who provided a selection of prophecies predicting Persian success. Xerxes let himself be persuaded by a team made up of an ambitious courtier, self-interested Thessalian aristocrats, and the lobby for a discredited dynastic family driven from Athens three decades before.

Thus far, the new king of Persia had appeared in the **Histories** as a shallow prince, the victim of his own naivety, but no great imperialist. He was, in fact, in his mid-thirties when he came to the throne, and he had already shown himself to be more ruthless and bigoted than his father, but his portrayal by Herodotus is otherwise. Yet his speech to the Persian magnates presents a new dimension, for he proceeded to enunciate the principles of imperialism that actuated the empire which he had inherited.

First, expansionism was a Persian *nomos,* and not a new one. "I learn from our elders that we have never remained inactive since we took over this sovereign power from the Medes, when Cyrus deposed Astyages." It was a *nomos* sanctioned by Heaven, and it brought Persia greatness and prosperity. Second, there was the example of Xerxes' predecessors who had followed this *nomos.* Cyrus, Cambyses, and Darius had added to the empire, and so must Xerxes too. Greece still remained outside it, and, echoing Mardonius' misrepresentation of the truth, Xerxes pronounced Greece as large and as rich as Persia itself: the intended victim of Persian aggression was Persia's equal. Last, there was the motive of revenge. Athens should be punished for the wrongs she had inflicted on Persia. Yet vengeance seems a secondary cause, for Xerxes' ambitions went far beyond Athens. If Europe and Asia were yoked, Xerxes could make them one country. The world would have one monarch. There would be no limits to the realm of the Great King, and hence, we may note, no boundaries left to transgress. Thus, said Xerxes, downgrading the guilt of Athens as a motive, those who were *aitioi* and those who were not would both be enslaved. With that, Xerxes invited debate.

The dialectic that follows is uneven. Mardonius was outclassed by the king's uncle, Artabanus, whose role as a wise adviser urging caution has already been foreshadowed: he had tried similarly to dissuade Darius from his Scythian expedition. Mardonius has less to say; his points are comments on the king's speech, and his purpose was to soften its rough edges. The Ionians living in Europe could not be allowed to make fools of the Persians: the outrages committed at Sardis and Marathon had to be avenged. Yet, Mardonius pointed out that vengeance had played no role in Persia's expansion thus far. Persia's previous victims had done her no wrong. But that made the argument for invading Greece all the stronger, for now that Persia did have a just cause for war, it would be extraordinary if she failed to exploit it. In any case, the Greeks were poor fighters and their knowledge of military tactics puerile. They would not resist, but if they did, they would discover that the Persians were the best soldiers in the world. With that, Mardonius concluded with a wry note of irony: he gave Xerxes the conventional warning against overconfidence.

One of these arguments we have met before. Aristagoras of Miletus, who was also a fomenter of war, had tried the inverse of it on the Spartans: the Persians, he said, were not valiant men, and their weapons and armor were inadequate. It was a war hawk's standard argument. Herodotus himself, on the first point, granted the Persians valor equal to the Greeks, but on the second point, he agreed with Aristagoras.

Yet a new overtone has emerged. Herodotus' judgment on the Ionians was unflattering, though we should not overemphasize, for he makes exceptions. Yet his general assessment is explicit. Of all the Hellenes, the Ionians were the weakest. Their only city of importance was Athens, and she did not like to be called "Ionian." Cleisthenes, whose reforms had started the growth of Athens to power, had established new tribes that had no counterpart among the Ionians out of contempt for them. The reason for Herodotus' assessment is another story; here we should note merely that the Persian miscalculation of the Greek will to resist was founded on their familiarity with those Greeks under Persian dominion. This included not merely the Ionians but the Dorians and Aeolians as well, though to the Persians they were all *Yauna,* nor did Herodotus himself think it always necessary to differentiate. They were a quarrelsome lot: those benefitting from Persian rule had been forced after the Ionian Revolt to settle their differences by arbitration rather than war, but the free Greeks settled theirs by choosing a level parcel of ground and fighting it out. In any event, Xerxes had no fears that the Ionians would be anything but obedient subjects until his defeat at Salamis, after which it occurred to him that they might instigate the Greek fleet to sail to the Hellespont and destroy the bridges there. The stature of the Ionians led the Persians to underestimate all the Greeks. In any assessment of the causes of Xerxes' invasion, the poor reputation of the Ionians had something to answer for.

Only one Persian dared to present the opposing view: the king's uncle, Artabanus. He is a dramatic figure whose ultimate archetype is Cassandra. More than a wise adviser, he is almost a seer whose accurate vision of the future introduced a note of dramatic irony. The Greeks were valorous, he said, shifting the gaze of the magnates from the subject Ionians to Athens: at Marathon, the Athenians alone had vanquished the great army of Datis and Artaphrenes. Suppose the Greeks defeated the Persians on sea and then destroyed the bridge over the Hellespont? He cited Darius' Scythian expedition as a parallel: when Darius was forced to retreat, all that stood between him and disaster was the resolve of one Greek, Histiaeus of Miletus: for a few hours, the future of Persia had rested upon the shoulders of this one man. Therefore Xerxes should not act rashly; he should reflect at leisure, and Artabanus seemed confident that reflection would result in inaction.

He went on, developing an argument that Solon had put to Croesus at the height of his power. "My lord Croesus," Solon had said, "I know that all Heaven is jealous, and loves to create mischief and *you* ask me about the fortunes of men!" Heaven loved to smite the great, warned Artabanus, unconsciously drawing the parallel with the Lydian king, and God endured presumption in no one but Himself. He concluded with nothing less than a confident wager on a Persian defeat: let him and Mardonius both stake their children's

lives on the outcome of the expedition! If it was a success, Artabanus' line would be wiped out.

The king replied wrathfully, full of dynastic pride. The war was a necessity; vengeance *had* to be exacted from the Athenians. "I know well that if we remain at peace, they will not; they are sure to invade our country!" The expedition had become a preemptive strike: Persia must attack or herself be attacked. There was still, of course, the example of the past, though Xerxes dredged Greek mythology for a specious parallel: if Pelops the Phrygian could conquer Greece, could not the Great King too, who counted the Phrygians among his slaves?

The story is quickly concluded. At night, Xerxes did rethink, and decided that Artabanus was right. His anger, as he was to explain to the Persian council the next day, was the hot temper of youth. Then Xerxes was visited twice in dreams by a phantom: a tall, handsome man, who also visited Artabanus. The message was always the same: Xerxes would countermand the expedition at his peril. The penalty for remaining at peace would be the loss of his royal status. "Be, then, very sure of this," said the phantom, on its second visit, "if you do not launch your war at once, this shall be the outcome: just as a brief span of time raised you to be great and mighty, so shall you speedily become humble again." The reader may note that the apparition failed to promise victory, though even Artabanus imagined that a successful outcome was implied. But the message was unavoidable: Xerxes had to invade Greece or face an unpleasant alternative.

Years ago, Macan remarked that the analogy between Xerxes' dream and the deceitful dream sent to Agamemnon in the *Iliad* has "often been pointed out." But though Herodotus has borrowed the literary device, he has shifted the emphasis. The dream in the *Iliad* is a simple case of a mischievous god playing with the overconfident Agamemnon, exploiting a weak point in his character by promising him victory without Achilles' help. The dream of Xerxes was not explicitly deceitful, for it did not presage a Greek defeat, though it left that impression. Instead it emphasized the danger of trying to reverse what was destined to be. It was Xerxes' position as king of Persia, the descendant of a line of Achaememid imperialists who had increased the size of the empire during their several reigns, that circumscribed his freedom of action. All the reasons Mardonius had given for invading Greece and Artabanus' rebuttals did not matter. Xerxes seems to be caught, all unknowing, in a dilemma of fate and free will, quite as much as the protagonist of Sophocles' *Oedipus Tyrannus*. Xerxes was intended to invade Greece, and the dream intervened when he seemed on the point of falling short of what Bernard Knox, in his study of Oedipus, calls "the divine intention." But it is fair to ask why there should be any such "divine intention" at all. What forces were there at work that forestalled Xerxes' impulse to draw back from disaster?

THE NECESSITY OF REVENGE

One thinks naturally of vengeance and retribution. The concept appears frequently in the ***Histories***. Retribution (*tisis*) was a way of evening up the score, or paying off someone to whom an obligation was due, and it served the function of enforcing a kind of equilibrium in a macrocosm of contrapositions. Its near synonym, *timoria,* could mean "assistance" as well; in the Hippocratic writings, it might mean simply "medical aid." Xerxes told the assembled magnates that *tisis* and *timoria* were among the by-products of his expedition; the mention is casual, but as he went on, he elaborated. The vengeance-motive centered around the twenty ships that Athens sent to help the Ionians in their revolt against Persia; Herodotus calls them the "beginnings of evils for the Greeks and the barbarians." The phrase has the Homeric echo that Herodotus liked to evoke, but it was almost a cliché, and we should not give it undue significance: the aid that Athens and Eretria sent the rebels was a provocation which re-awakened Persia's aggressive instincts, but it was not the real cause of her expansionism. Mardonius referred to the vengeance motive, but with a cynical twist: Persian imperialism had developed and progressed thus far without it, he said, for the various peoples whom the Persians conquered had done Persia no wrong; but now, when the Persians did possess a vengeance motive, it would be too bad if they failed to exploit it! Vengeance was a good reason for imperial expansion if there were grounds for it, but if there were not, the impulse that drove imperial aggression could make do without it.

As an *alleged* cause of action, the importance of vengeance in the ***Histories*** cannot be denied. It could hardly be otherwise. Retribution was part of the moral and intellectual baggage that Herodotus had inherited from the epic and the whole tradition of Greek mythopoeia. "Famine and blight do not beset the just," wrote Hesiod. Zeus exacted great penalties from proud men who worked evil. On the level of popular theology, Herodotus was not far removed from that view. He recorded that, in the general opinion of the Greeks, Cleomenes, king of Sparta, went mad as retribution for sacrilege (the Spartans were the exception: they attributed his madness to heavy drinking). But Herodotus himself thought his insanity was retribution for his unjust treatment of Demaratus. Talthybius exacted retribution for the Persian heralds whom the Spartans killed in 491 B.C., and the whole story of the Trojan War, reflected Herodotus, as he compared the Egyptian account of it with Greek legend, was a revelation of how the gods exacted great penalties for great wrongdoing.

This theological mindset left its mark in the world of

diplomacy as well. "You started this war," the Spartans told the Athenians in the spring of 479 *b.c.*, when Mardonius tried to entice them into a separate peace, "and we had no wish for it. The struggle began as a war for your territory and now it involves all Greece." In the Spartan view of things, the Athenian intervention in the Ionian Revolt began the war. It was a starting point, which led directly to Xerxes' invasion. But nowhere does Herodotus suggest that Persian aggression would never have taken place if the Athenian contingent of twenty ships had not set sail for Ionia in the first year of the revolt!

Alleged causes might serve very well as justifications, but they were not necessarily real causes. Darius remembered the Athenian part in the Ionian Revolt: he assigned a slave the task of reminding him of it, but Herodotus labels it a *prophasis:* a prior injury that can be put forward to justify revenge. It was only his ostensible motive for the dispatch of Datis and Artaphrenes to Marathon; his real intention was to conquer all of Greece that had not surrendered to him by giving earth and water. And finally, Herodotus states his own view of the matter, which by implication rejects vengeance for the twenty ships as the cause of the war. The expedition of Xerxes, he says, was nominally against Athens, but in fact its objective was to subjugate all of Greece. The Athenian intervention was never more than a provocation, and when such provocations were available, Persian imperialism might exploit them as pretexts, but when they were not, it continued on its course equally well without them. Herodotus does not display the cynicism about allegations of prior wrongs used to justify aggression that Thucydides evinces, but he seems merely to have included them among the tactics of war.

Darius' Scythian expedition is a case in point, which illustrates how useful a tactic the *prophasis* of vengeance could be. Darius' motive for the expedition against Scythia was revenge for an ancient wrong, but in the same breath Herodotus adds the economic argument for expansion: Asia was full of wealth and population: hence the time was ripe to put this casus belli to practical use. The Scyths, faced with the invasion, sent envoys to their neighbors to seek help. They argued that the Persian motive for aggression was not revenge but simple appetite for conquest: otherwise the attack would have been directed against the Scyths alone, and Darius would have ignored the Getae and the Thracians whom he swept up along the way. The reply was mixed: some agreed to help but more rejected the Scythian argument, replying that the Persians were really reacting to an unprovoked wrong, the Scythian conquest of Asia that had lasted twenty-eight years. A god had presided over the Scythian rule of Persia as long as he had ordained it, and now the same god presided over the interaction of vengeance and countervengeance. These neutrals felt confident that they would suffer no harm from Darius if they did him none. "However," they added, "if he enters our land and starts doing us wrong, we shall not put up with it."

This exchange is close to a parody of the diplomatic efforts that the Hellenic League made to find allies against Xerxes, and on one point it twists historical accuracy. It was the Medes, not the Persians, whom the Scyths had conquered. Herodotus pretends that the neutrals saw Darius' attack within the larger context of chronic strife between Europe and Asia, a premise that makes the parallel between the Scythian expedition and Xerxes' invasion all the closer. And in the answer of the neutrals to the appeal of the Scyths for help, there is an echo of the debate in Greece over the responsibility for the Persian attack. Darius could allege vengeance, though he had to delve back into history and distort it a bit to find a wrong that merited retribution, but this vengeance motive served well enough to justify his attack that it partially aborted the Scythian effort to form an alliance against him.

But it is affluence that Herodotus puts forward as the premier cause. "For, as Asia was at its flower in numbers of men, and great wealth was coming in, Darius conceived the desire to take vengeance on the Scyths." This is not Herodotus speaking as a modern economic historian, nor is it an example of a tragic pattern, where *koros* leads to blindness, and blindness to a fall. Darius returned safely from Scythia, having established Persian authority in the north Aegean area. Rather, Herodotus is stating simply that the possession of power, measured in population and revenue, is a stimulus to imperial expansion. The Scythian act of aggression that Darius decided to avenge was not pure fiction: alleged causes rarely are. Their purpose is to shift the blame away from the perpetrator of the aggressive act, and they would serve it poorly if they were patently false. But they mask the true reason.

Miltiades, after the victory of Marathon, led an attack on Paros, and he had a well-founded *prophasis:* Paros had contributed a trireme to the fleet of Datis and Artaphrenes. But he also had a private motive, which Herodotus is careful to point out. Aryandes, satrap of Egypt, dispatched an expedition against Cyrene, and his pretext was vengeance for the murder of Arcesilaus. Yet Herodotus considered it merely an excuse to conquer Libya, for it was full of tribes and most of them paid Darius no attention.

Vengeance, therefore, was a respectable justification for aggression, and Heaven deemed it satisfactory, as the neutral neighbors of the Scyths reminded them. It was equally acceptable in the Athenian law courts, where the strict relevance of what was being avenged was not required. But ostensible causes were not to be confused with real ones. Xerxes might retort wrathfully to Artabanus that Persia must attack or be attacked,

but he forgot the point once his anger had cooled. The dream that visited Xerxes did not tell him that he *had* to avenge wrongs inflicted by the Athenians on the Persians; it stressed instead the consequences if he did not. Xerxes' mission went beyond vengeance. As he told his magnates, he wanted to subdue both the *aitioi* and *anaitioi* to slavery.

This conclusion, that on the level of international politics, vengeance served more as an alleged cause than as a real one, is all the more remarkable because in two other spheres Herodotus did regard vengeance as a causal agent. On the divine level, he believed that the gods exacted retribution. The Persians under Artabazus' command who were drowned by an unusually high tide as they assaulted Potidaea, suffered retribution for desecrating Poseidon's temple. So the Potidaeans said, and Herodotus agreed. The Aeginetans who put down the uprising of Nicodromus and killed the rebels who sought asylum in the temple of Demeter, suffered vengeance before they could obtain divine mercy: they were driven from their homes in the first year of the Peloponnesian War. Divine vengeance fell also upon the Pelasgians for murdering and raping Athenian concubines.

But this was popular theology that was generally accepted, and Herodotus did not dispute it, for it made sense out of what would otherwise be irrational. In instances such as the madness of King Cleomenes of Sparta, there might be a difference of opinion about the particular sin for which the sinner suffered retribution, but Herodotus had no doubt that his madness *was* retribution from the gods. But vengeance on this level fell within the province of Heaven, and could be recognized clearly only after it had taken place. Then men might look back and discern (or think they discern) the offense for which the gods had meted out condign punishment. But the reasons why men acted as they did, and the motives that impelled them, belonged to the human space.

The other level, where Herodotus recognized the working of vengeance, is what we may call the realm of natural science, which had engrossed the Presocratics. The winged snakes of Arabia that guarded the frankincense bushes would have overwhelmed mankind but for the design of divine providence. The female killed the male after he had impregnated her, and suffered retribution for it, for her offspring avenged their sire by chewing their way out of her womb, thus killing her. In this way, divine providence prevented the snakes from growing too numerous and overwhelming their enemy, mankind. This is vengeance operating as a natural force to maintain balance within the sphere of biology, and to our eyes, it seems completely amoral; but perhaps not to Herodotus or his contemporaries, for whom the universe itself was a moral construct, and thus we cannot make a sharp distinction between natural science and the divine. The vengeance that controlled the population growth of the winged snakes seems to be the same sort of retribution to which Heraclitus referred when he said that the sun would not overstep its measures, for if it did, the Furies would find it out, and before Heraclitus, Anaximander of Miletus had seen the same force as a law of nature. The earliest, and perhaps the most lasting influence upon Herodotus was the thought-world of Ionia, and when Xerxes crossed the Hellespont, the reader of the *Histories* must sense that the natural boundary between Europe and Asia that was defined by the *logioi* of the proem has been overstepped. For Herodotus, even the geographical space within which human action occurs is commensurate and balanced, evidently reflecting in some way the mandate of justice. But did some inexorable law of nature demand that Xerxes avenge the outrages that Persia had suffered at Sardis and Marathon, thereby making him overstep the natural limits of Asia and opening him in turn to retribution?

Herodotus avoided any such conclusion. The dream of Xerxes merely warned him of the consequences that he would suffer if he canceled his expedition. It was Artabanus who thought it promised success: he had imagined that Xerxes would have a happy reign if he remained inactive, but "since there is some divine impulse, and some destruction sent from Heaven has fallen upon the Greeks, I of myself change my mind and abandon my view." But Artabanus assumed more than the dream told him. The divine message was simply that Xerxes could not turn aside from what had to be.

The restricted choice of Xerxes resembles the choices that Sophocles allows Oedipus, but is the force that restricts it an iron law that demanded vengeance upon the Greeks? The evidence seems to point in another direction: whatever the directing power of vengeance might be in the dark workings of fate and destiny, on the human level of everyday international affairs, it was neither a natural force nor a divine law. Rather, it was a debating point: a justification for a policy that recommended itself for other reasons.

This was the conclusion of a shrewd observer of his own times, who saw the contemporary world without illusions. Vengeance as justification for imperialism was a leitmotiv of the fifth century. Revenge on the Medes was the advertised purpose of the Delian League: for that we have Thucydides as witness, though Herodotus, following another tradition that fitted his detached cynicism better, attributed Athenian imperialism to an innate desire for hegemony that antedated Xerxes' invasion. An outside observer might have seen a chain of vengeance and countervengeance continuing from the Ionian Revolt right down to the date of publication of the *Histories,* following a kind of Hegelian dialectic that saw the opposition between the Persian Empire and the Hellenic League replaced by one between the cen-

ters of power in Greece itself. In public discussion retribution served as a respectable motive for aggression; thus, in the winter of 432-431, Sparta put together a list of grievances perpetrated by the Athenians to justify the Peloponnesian War. But it was not the guiding force of imperialism. When Cyrus undertook to extend his empire to annex the Massagetae, his motives did not include revenge. Rather, Herodotus suggests two: first, his birth, which made him superhuman in men's eyes, and second, his success in war. The first had to do with the psychology of kings, and the second with the psychology of empire: the reputation of Persia as a successful imperialist power, which Cyrus had created and which now drove him forward. The satrap Oroetes killed Polycrates of Samos out of wounded pride: his fellow satrap Mitrobates had taunted him with failing to bring Samos into the Empire. Polycrates had done Oroetes no wrong, and Oroetes sought no vengeance. He slew Polycrates to prove himself a worthy expansionist of the empire in the Persian tradition.

It is instructive to make a comparison with Thucydides. The Athenian envoys in Sparta who addressed the assembly of the Peloponnesian League in 432 B.C. made an attempt to state the reasons for Athenian imperialism. "We did nothing surprising nor contrary to human custom," they said, "if we accepted the rule (*arche*) that was given to us, and do not let it go, for we are conquered by overwhelming motives: honor, fear and profit." The persona of the Persian king did not admit fear, but what of profit? Thucydides assumed that imperial exploitation for gain was a fact of nature. But Greece was poor, and in Greek eyes, Pausanias, the son of Cleombrotus, made the defintive judgment on the profit motive: Xerxes' passion to add what few possessions Greece had to the wealth of Persia was proof of his utter lack of sense. The Persians had well-developed acquisitive instincts. Atossa told Darius that she wanted to add women from the leading states of Greece to her attendants, and Mardonius extolled the fertility of Greece, and its variety of trees. But both really acted from personal motives.

For the most part, Herodotus saw the economic causes of expansionism working in a different way. For him, the increasing resources of the imperialist power itself, resulting from growth of population, prompted it to look beyond its borders, and the wealth of the people it proposed to subjugate was unimportant, to the extent that Pausanias could make no sense out of it. Thus, power grew avid for more power, and in Herodotus' view, the profit motive seems to play only a small role in Persian expansionism. But the third motive—honor—was a different matter.

The king's pride and honor were constant factors, along with the requirement that he appear a restless and ambitious man of energy. This was the reputation of Cyrus and of the Medes before him. They would not keep still. "It is not proper, my lord, for the Athenians, who have done the Persians many wrongs, not to pay retribution for their deeds," said Mardonius, urging his *logos timoros* upon the still-reluctant Xerxes. But he developed his argument with a point that deserves particular attention. "Invade Athens, so that you may have a good reputation among men, and anyone in the future will have a care before he makes war upon your land." The king had to maintain his reputation. "I formed the opinion," said Artabanus, admitting his error to the king, "that if you kept still, in the eyes of all men you would be happiest." But Xerxes could not be a lesser man than his predecessors, for he had to maintain the integrity of the Great King's persona as a competent ruler who could not be challenged with impunity. Contempt of a ruler led to rebellion, as Aristotle was to point out: the dignity and reputation of Xerxes defended both his empire and his own position as king, and both might suffer if he allowed a wrong to go unavenged. To that extent, Xerxes was governed by the vengeance motive, but this was no iron law of retribution that directed his actions: rather, it was a simple axiom of statecraft. A king had to sustain his prestige if he was to maintain his status.

NOMOS AS EXPLANATION

Xerxes began his speech to the Persian magnates with a significant statement: "Men of Persia, this *nomos* I set before you is not one that I am the first to put forward; it is because it has been handed down to me that I make use of it." For Thucydides, imperialism was part of human nature; it was natural for the strong to exploit the weak. For Herodotus, expansionism was a *nomos,* and therefore, if we want to understand it, we should look at an empire's *nomoi.* Imperialism, therefore, fell within the field of ethnology, which was Herodotus' initial interest.

Nomoi, which Havelock once translated correctly, if somewhat awkwardly, as "custom-laws," bulk large in the **Histories,** and we should define what we mean by the word. First, what it is not: it is not the antithesis of *physis.* In one instance, Herodotus could couple the two concepts in one breath: those Greeks were ignorant, he states, who accepted the silly myth that told how Heracles, upon his arrival in Egypt, was led out to be sacrificed, and at the altar turned on his captors and slew them in vast numbers. The purveyors of this tale knew nothing of the *physis* and *nomos* of the Egyptians, and anyway, it was contrary to nature (*physis*) for a single mortal to kill such great numbers. It was not that Herodotus thought of *physis* and *nomos* as synonyms; rather, the *nomoi* of a nation were the outgrowth of its *physis.* A report could not be authentic if it failed to conform to the *nomoi* of the people it purported to portray, for their *nomoi* were rooted in their nature, and thus possessed an integrity that could not be disregarded.

Physis was in no sense a technical word: it might refer to the appearance of the hippopotamus, the life cycle of the crocodile, or the physical stature of man—all qualities over which man (or the crocodile or hippopotamus, as the case might be) has no control. There is also such an entity as human *physis:* the "nature of man," which defined human competence, as Cambyses discovered to his cost. He slew his brother Smerdis because, in a dream, he saw a messenger come from Persia to tell him that Smerdis was on the throne, and then he learned of the revolt of the *magos* by the same name, and realized that he had acted with greater haste than wisdom, "for it is not in the *physis* of mankind to turn aside what is going to be." The natural condition of mankind was constrained by limits that were beyond the power of even kings to change.

Yet those limits did not rule out choice. Before the battle of Salamis, Themistocles told his sailors that in the nature and constitution of men (*physis* and *katastasis*), there were some qualities that were better and some that were worse, and he urged them to choose the better. What Themistocles wanted his men to choose was the quality that would drive them forward into battle, and that quality might be expressed as a *nomos.* At least we may conclude as much from the discourse of Xerxes with the exiled king of Sparta, Demaratus, who equated the *nomos* that required the Spartans to take up arms with the royal power that compelled the Persian troops to fight.

Thus, though men might not alter their *physis,* within the limits it set, they could make choices, and their *nomoi* were based on a choice, or a series of choices that they, or their ancestors had made. Herodotus has broken almost completely with the ancient view that *nomoi* were ordained by Heaven. To be sure, he reported the tradition that Lycurgus took the Spartan *nomoi* from Delphi, but the Spartans themselves said that he borrowed them from Crete, and there is the implication that the Spartans were the weightier authority. Gyges explained the origin of *nomoi* to Candaules: mankind had found out in the past by trial and error what was lawful and unlawful. In much the same way, Hippocrates explained how primitive man discovered by trial and error what was good to eat and what was not: he experimented with all sorts of foods, raw and cooked, and learned to avoid those that made him ill. In like manner, the Lydians had discovered that viewing another man's wife naked was not lawful, and Gyges begged Candaules not to insist that he do it. But Candaules was bound by an evil destiny. And when Cambyses in Egypt laughed at Egyptian *nomoi,* Herodotus saw it as a symptom of madness.

For *nomoi* possessed authority. Every people preferred its own, and if given a chance to choose, would not exchange them for those of another people. Yet it was a mark of wisdom to respect alien *nomoi,* and recognize their authority. Herodotus quotes a gobbet of Pindar which is later quoted more fully by Plato. *"Nomos* is king of everything," but quite out of context. Pindar spoke of *nomos* as justification for the right of the powerful to use violence against those who were weaker. Callicles in the *Gorgias* used the quotation to support the argument that Xerxes acted in accordance with the *nomos* based on nature that allowed the strong to seize the possessions of the weak. But Herodotus wanted only to show that *nomoi* exercised quasi-despotic power. Xerxes, bedazzled by the sheer bulk of his host, summoned Demaratus and asked if the Greeks would dare resist. Demaratus would speak only for the Spartans whom he knew, but they at least would fight, even though they had no despot to force them. "For though they are free," he said, "they are not free in everything, for *nomos* is over them as master, which they fear in their hearts more than your people fear you." Xerxes, like Cambyses, laughed.

There is a degree of irony to the failure of Xerxes to understand the import of what Demaratus had to say, for the Persian borrowed alien customs most readily of all men, and yet their kings failed to comprehend the authority of *nomoi*. Cambyses' reaction was laughter, while Xerxes dismissed Demaratus with tolerant amusement. At Marathon, the Persians thought the Greeks were mad when they charged them; at Thermopylae Xerxes was angered by their impudence and suicidal folly; and at Artemisium, the Persian captains considered the Greeks demented. Before Salamis, Xerxes had come to realize that his great host had failed to live up to his expectations, but he believed the reason was that he himself had not been present to inspire his men. This failure of the Persians to comprehend the *nomos* that commanded the Greeks to resist is a leitmotiv which continues as far as their defeat at Plataea, where Mardonius led his men in a disorderly pursuit of the Spartans, imagining that they were running away!

Yet the Persians themselves were actuated by a *nomos* too—one that forbade them to remain inactive. "Men of Persia," Xerxes said to the assembled Persian notables, "I am not myself setting up this *nomos* among you to follow, but it is one I have inherited, and I shall use it. I learn from our elders that we have never remained inactive since we took over this sovereign power from the Medes, when Cyrus dethroned Astyages. It is a god who leads us on." An imperial regime never remained still; it was always stirring with ambition. Nitocris had recognized this quality in the Medes, the Babylonians recognized it in Cyrus, and years later, on the eve of the Peloponnesian War, the Corinthians are to point it out as the disposition of imperial Athens. An ancestral *nomos* directed the Persians always to push on and maintain the momentum of expansion. Xerxes thought that they were led by a god, but he was wrong: *nomoi* in the *Histories* evolve on the human, not the divine level, and the *nomos* that brought Persia her empire was based on deliberate choice quite as

much as any other custom. Xerxes' conviction that the *nomos* of expansionism had divine sanction was myopic. It was a symptom of blindness.

There are two pertinent stories in the *Histories* that make clear how the Persians acquired and maintained their *nomos* of imperialism. The first tells how Cyrus persuaded the Persians to revolt from the Medes. He summoned an assembly of Persians and set them to work clearing a parcel of land overgrown with weeds. The next day, he gave them a sumptuous banquet. Then he asked which they preferred: the toil that was the lot of a subject, or the good life of a ruler. They chose the latter.

The second story concludes the *Histories*. The Persians have made their choice, and have acquired the *nomos* of imperialism and an empire to go along with it. A Persian noble named Artembares suggested to Cyrus that the Persians leave their own rocky and infertile native land, and choose another from among their dominions, where life would be easier. Cyrus allowed his Persians a choice. But first he taught them a percept borrowed from the Hippocratic school of medicine: soft lands breed soft men, better fitted to be subjects than rulers. The Persians chose to rule, and remained where they were. This *nomos* of imperialism was a harsh master, and the story of Cyrus that ends the *Histories* has palpably ironic overtones, for by the fifth century, the Persians had long since abandoned the hard life, but the *nomos* of imperialism still drove them forward.

After the defeat at Salamis, Mardonius, the war hawk at the meeting of the magnates, continued to remain faithful to this *nomos*. He carried on where Xerxes left off, all the more determined because he had urged the expedition upon a disinclined Xerxes in the first place, and hence would have to bear some responsibility for its failure, if it should come to that. He was by no means pessimistic: "his judgement actually inclined him to think that he would subdue Greece," to quote Grene's translation of Herodotus' cautious, ironic Greek. At Plataea, he was still eager to push forward and start the fight: in the council before the battle, he was uncompromising, urging his commanders to pay no attention to the negative omens produced by their sacrifices made according to Greek rites, but instead to abide simply by the Persian *nomos* and attack.

His last words were charged with irony. He was full of overconfidence: the Spartans had seemingly fled and he would make them pay for the wrongs they had committed. The Persian *nomos* of never keeping still but always pushing forward led him in the end to disaster. He was already a marked man; Xerxes had appointed him to make amends for Leonidas' death (which Delphi had demanded), and at Plataea the ironic purport of that appointment becomes clear: it was Mardonius, not the Spartans, who had to pay for the wrongs that had been done.

Some two decades ago, I wrote an article which examined the connection between the role of *nomos* and causation in the *Histories*. In his proem, Herodotus states a two-fold purpose: he had the praise-poets' concern to impart renown to the exploits of the warriors in both camps, and the philosopher's concern to find the reason for the conflict. I concluded that the reason (for which Herodotus uses the equivocal word *aitia*) could not be discovered among Persian *nomoi,* but that the *nomoi* of a people did expalin their course of action, and consequently understanding *nomoi* was a mark of wisdom. In any given situation, one might expect a people to behave according to its *nomoi.* I have not abandoned that view, for *nomos* does serve as an explanatory principle, but I gave insufficient weight to *nomos* as a governing force. The *nomos* of ambition and restlessness that Xerxes inherited from his forebears exercised a directing influence over his policies which is akin to the "divine intention" in the *Oedipus Tyrannus.* It did, therefore, supply a reason why he had to attack Greece.

Perhaps Xerxes might have paid no attention to this *nomos* of expansionism, and adhered to the decision he had reached upon reconsideration. But the weight of tradition was against him: it was appropriate for a Persian king who was young and master of great wealth to achieve something worth notice, as Queen Atossa had told Darius in a bedroom conversation that led to Persia's first expedition to Europe. The cost of refusing to invade Greece would have been great. The apparition that appeared to Xerxes threatened him with loss of this throne. It did not promise victory, although Xerxes and Artabanus inferred it. Rather, its message was that there was a high price to be paid if Xerxes failed to follow this *nomos* of imperialism which the Persians had chosen years before, when Cyrus had given them a choice—and *then* it had been a free choice. Herodotus did not treat imperialism itself as an expression of human nature, as Thucydides did, but rather as a *nomos* that is elected freely, but once chosen, cannot be abandoned without cost. The Persians had followed their chosen *nomos* with good fortune thus far, and now Xerxes was governed by it.

The Greeks were equally directed by *nomos.* Wisdom and *nomos* were the basis of the courage with which they resisted both poverty and despotism. Demaratus' attempt to explain this to Xerxes proved futile, and yet the *nomos* that directed the Greeks to fight possessed as much authority as the Great King himself. But Xerxes could not understand. The power and glory of Persia's monarchy had brought her kings to the point where they found the *nomoi* of other people at best amusing. This incomprehension was a kind of blindness, and, as the outcome of the Persian Wars was to prove, it was a dangerous state of mind.

THE CONCEPT OF GUILT

Any reader of the first sentence of Herodotus' proem must wonder what part he assigned to war guilt as a factor working its way through the strands of history, for he concludes with a statement that he was looking for the *aitia* of the conflict. The word *aitia,* or in the Ionian Greek of Herodotus, *aitie,* occurs fifty-one times in the *Histories.* Twenty-two times, the meaning is fault, blame, or the sort of charge a plaintiff might launch in a court of law, and an equal number of times it can be translated simply as "cause," though the cause can imply a degree of blame. There are a few remaining instances, but they do not help to resolve the ambiguity. What, for instance, can we make of Herodotus' tale of the bond that existed between Cleomenes of Sparta and Cleisthenes' rival, Isagoras? "*Aitia* had Cleomenes going into (i.e., having sexual intercourse with) the wife of Isagoras." *Aitia* here is an accusatory morsel of gossip, not, to be sure, without moral connotations, which people suggested as the reason for the claim Isagoras had upon Cleomenes.

Or let us take another example: the *aitia* of Cambyses' attack on Egypt. "Cambyses, son of Cyrus, made an expedition against Amasis . . . for an *aitia* of such a kind as this." *Aitia* here, Powell assures us, means "the reason why." Then follows the story of how Cambyses demanded Amasis' daughter as wife, which he did at the instance of an Egyptian eye doctor whom Cyrus had demanded from Egypt. The verb "to demand" is *aitein,* and there may be a play of words here between the *aitia* that means "the reason why," and the demands that brought about this reason: the *aitia* of the Persian invasion was the response of the pharaoh to Cambyses' demand, and hence by reciprocation this demand develops into a cause. Yet at the same time, the *aitia* was a charge that Cambyses brought against the pharaoh.

Finally, there is the use of the word in the proem. It carries the suggestion that someone was to blame for the war, and the debate of the *logioi* develops upon that assumption. Yet, at the same time, it looks forward to the common usage of *aitia* among the philosophers of the fourth century B.C., where it is the synonym of the Latin *causa,* meaning "reason," "motive," or "inducement."

Guilt is closely tied to vengeance, and it may be argued that the two concepts should not be separated. But in a Greek court, guilt had to be established before punishment could be applied, and, to quote Arthur Adkins, "In Greek there can be no *phonos* (violent death) without someone being *aitios phonou* (guilty of murder). The same should be true of the supreme act of violence, war. Some person or thing should be guilty of it, and ordinarily the guilty party should be the one that initiated the war. Thus, as I have argued, it was to shift guilt to the targets of aggression that invaders alleged retribution.

Given the opening sentence of the *Histories,* we might be excused for imagining that the concept of war guilt bulked large in his thought. But this was not so. Herodotus gives first a Persian story of how strife between Europe and Asia began, and this story is marked by a pronounced distinction between being "guilty" and "greatly guilty." The Phoenicians incurred guilt first by kidnapping Io, but the Greeks were guilty to the second power by mounting a military expedition, the Trojan War. The Phoenicians have a gloss to add to the story, but that is all. Then Herodotus dismisses this speculation and the logic that went along with it, and chooses his own starting point: the imperialist action of the king of Lydia, Croesus.

His existence was solid enough: there were his dedications at Delphi to attest it. He was more than a mere aggressor. Earlier Mermnads had attacked the Greeks, but Croesus established a polity that exacted tribute from them, thus fitting the definition of empire. Upon succeeding his father to the throne, Croesus moved first against Ephesus, and then against the other Ionian and Aeolian cities one by one, putting forward various *aitiai,* the best he could find, though some of them were trivial indeed. Nevertheless, Herodotus imagined that Croesus sought to assign some guilt to the Greek cities to justify his aggression: "He brought different *aitiai* against various cities: important ones when he could find them, but against others he brought *aitiai* that were truly slight." These *aitiai* were accusations: hardly more than stratagems to shift the burden of guilt, and they did nothing to explain the real motive of Lydian imperialism. Herodotus himself preferred to present Croesus within a tragic framework: he was a great king whose imperialism was the outgrowth of his wealth and prosperity: his consequent power and affluence resulted in blindness, which in turn allowed him to blunder into fatal error. He attacked a people toughened by a hard life, whose poverty could add little to his wealth even if he were victorious. Herodotus has sunk his teeth into a traditional tale here, but it sets a pattern, and his aim in telling it is moral as much as it is historical.

The story of Croesus seems to present the rise and fall of empire *in parvo*: a sort of paradigm of imperial development that suggests comparison with the career of Xerxes. But it leaves us little wiser about the *aitia* of the Persian Wars. The reason for Croesus' fall, according to Delphi, was bound up with *moira;* Croesus was expiating Gyges' sin after five generations, which was the portion of time allotted to his dynasty. According to Herodotus, whose view does not quite tally with Delphi's, "great *nemesis* overtook Croesus, as one would guess, because he thought himself the most blessed of all men." So Croesus had fallen for two reasons: *moira,* because he had reached the end of an allotted span established before he was born, and *nemesis,* for which he bore some guilt himself: he considered himself more fortunate than a mortal should.

These are two separate concepts that are uneasily coupled here. Just how uneasy the coupling is, becomes apparent in another instance: the men of Paros consulted Delphi on the proper punishment for the priestess Timo, who had attempted to betray them to Miltiades, and received the reply from the Pythia that she was blameless, for Miltiades was doomed to a bad end, and Timo was only the instrument of his fate. Similarly, Apollo did not accept any blame for Croesus' fall. Indeed, he went so far as to argue that Croesus himself was blameworthy. The oracle had warned him that he would destroy a great empire if he attacked Cyrus, but he had failed to ask which empire was meant. Croesus had taken care to test the reliability of the oracles, but when it came to the central issue, his astuteness was clouded by his egocentrism and overconfidence. So much for Delphi's view of Croesus' guilt.

At whose feet, then, should the guilt for the Persian Wars be laid? I have already argued that the motive of revenge did not account for Persian imperialism. Their conquests took place equally well with or without it. Herodotus was as skeptical of Persia's *aitiai* as he was of those that Croesus put forward. But the conventional wisdom which no *logios* could ignore without provoking comment from his audience had it that Athens had incurred guilt by intervening in the Ionian Revolt, thus committing an unprovoked wrong. Given the Greek concept of guilt, followed (when proven) by retribution, it was arguable that Athenian guilt caused the Persian attack. Quite unfairly, punishment that should have fallen on Athens alone involved all Greece. That, at least, was how the Spartans viewed the matter: they were innocent bystanders, whereas Athens had stirred up the war.

Herodotus thought that Darius, angry as he was with the Athenians for their part in burning Sardis, nonetheless used their intervention in the revolt only as a pretext, and the war hawk Mardonius refers almost cynically to the guilt of the Greeks as he develops his case for Xerxes' invasion. Yet on the actual question of guilt, Herodotus seems to lean toward conventional wisdom. The twenty ships that Athens sent to help the Ionians were the beginning of evil in the sense that they started a fresh chain of events which led directly to Xerxes' invasion. Herodotus found it quite possible to accept that point of view, and at the same time, recognize that they were not the real reason for the onslaught. The Ionian Revolt deserved faint praise, and the Athenian decision to intervene showed how easily a democracy could be gulled by an adventurer like Aristagoras. But as Herodotus saw it, the troubles (which began with Naxos and Miletus, and expanded into a revolt thanks to Aristagoras and Histiaeus) served to revive the restless expansionism of Persia, and the twenty ships that Athens sent to help the rebels channeled it in the direction of Greece. To that extent, Athens was *aitios.* She made Greece an immediate objective of Persia's imperialism. Thus, Herodotus did not altogether reject the Spartan view of the matter even though he was at pains to point out that Xerxes' expedition was only ostensibly directed against Athens; in fact, its object was all Greece.

The search for who or what was to blame for the war, which Herodotus announced in his proem, runs to ground. To take him literally, the primal *aitia* for which he could vouch, belonged to Croesus, who was the first to wrong the Greeks by making them tributary, which was the mark of empire. But Croesus' legacy was taken over by Persia, which followed its own imperative, and whatever interlinked chain of causes Croesus started, it mattered little as a reason why Xerxes invaded Greece. His aim was to subdue guilty and guiltless alike, and although Athens might be guilty in the limited sense that she attracted the attention of a king who had already expanded into Europe, the expedition of Xerxes was within the tradition of Persian expansionism.

There was, therefore, little purpose in asking who was to blame for the war. Blame might serve as a debating point or as a gambit in diplomacy, or as a satisfactory notion to give point to a story illustrating a historical pattern, but it did not explain the motive force behind Persian imperialism. A keeper of tradition might assign guilt for the war to this party or that, sometimes with a degree of justification, but guilt did nothing to explain the motive force behind Persian imperialism.

I suspect that this was a verdict which Herodotus reached not without hesitation, first because a good portion of Greece thought otherwise, and second because Herodotus shared the Greek attraction to tragic patterns in history. His story of Croesus is a case in point. The primal *aitia* was Candaules' wayward resolve to display his wife, naked, to Gyges, and from this *aitia* a chain of cause and effect led to Croesus' final expiation of an ancestors' forgotten wrong. Yet the causes and effects did not become apparent until *after* Croesus' fall, when the underlying pattern at last became clear. This was the sort of moral template that Herodotus' listeners expected him to use in his reconstruction of what happened when Persia expanded into Europe: an act of violence, in this case war, implied a guilty party that was to blame for it. The Greeks were familiar with the pattern, both in the theater and in the lawcourts. One feels that Herodotus would have been not unhappy if he had found some such design in Persian history. It would have provided easy explanations. But in fact, Herodotus made no consistent effort to discover who was guilty of causing the war, in spite of his announced intention in his proem, for it had no bearing upon the fundamental cause of Persian expansionism.

THE FATE OF THE PERSIAN EMPIRE

Finally, there is the question of fate. To what extent was Persian imperialism and its consequences governed by fate? It needs little imagination to discover tragic patterns in the *Histories* that compare with those we find in *Oedipus Tyrannus* or the *Antigone,* and cross-fertilization is more than possible: the friendship of the two men is documented well enough. Herodotus makes more than the occasional obeisance to the dark workings of necessity. Candaules commanded his bodyguard Gyges to view his wife naked, because it was necessary for things to turn out badly for him. Candaules was a foolish king; yet it was necessity that decreed his false step. It was not merely the consequence of his own lack of wisdom. At the end of the *Histories,* Herodotus said very much the same about a royal scion as unwise as Candaules, Xerxes' daughter-in-law, and niece, Artaynte. Things were bound to turn out badly for her and her house. She acted foolishly, but her action conformed to a foreordained pattern.

There are other examples scattered throughout the *Histories*. The Naxian expedition that served as prologue to the Ionian Revolt was a failure because Naxos was not fated to fall to the Persians at that point in time. It fell later to Datis without a blow because the Naxians remembered the futility of their earlier resistance! Fate accomplished the dethronement of Demaratus, king of Sparta. Skylas, the Scythian king who was initiated into the Dionysiac rites, was fated to end badly. His adoption of Greek rites was a *prophasis* that served to explain why the Scyths revolted from him; but at a deeper level, fate directed events. The pharaoh Apries, whose subjects rebelled after his defeat in Cyrene, was also a casualty of fate: the disastrous attack which he launched against Cyrene, took place so that fate could work itself out. Miltiades, the victor at Marathon, was destined to come to a bad end. Finally, Herodotus appears to make an explicit acknowledgment of the omnipotence of fate. He related a story told by Thersander of Orchomenos, who attended a banquet given by the Theban medizer, Attaginus, for Mardonius and fifty Persian nobles before the battle of Plataea. The Persian who shared Thersander's couch told him in tears that few of the banqueters would survive. Men could not turn aside what God had decreed. Many of the Persians—so said Thersander's companion—knew what the outcome would be, but they were bound by necessity. "Thus, out of the darkness, the hand of divine superiority guides the destinies of humanity, the will and behaviour of men, according to its own purposes."

The quotation comes from Erwin Rohde's *Psyche,* and refers to the fates of Deianeira in the *Trachiniae* and Oedipus in *Oedipus Tyrannus.* Fate as inexorable as any that dogged Oedipus seems to close in upon Mardonius at the end of the Histories, so much so that Sir John Myres once argued that it is he who should be seen as the tragic hero of the last three books. Herodotus, who professed trust in oracles, used them skillfully to show how Mardonius was trapped by necessity. He discovered an oracle which predicted that the Persians would plunder Delphi and then perish; therefore the Persians would not plunder Delphi, and nothing would prevent their victory. But Mardonius had misunderstood; the oracle did not refer to the Persians at all. However, the oracles had not been silent, for there were prophecies of Bacis and Musaeus that Mardonius overlooked, which did foretell the Persian defeat. Mardonius, who more than any other Persian embodied Persia's imperialist impulse, could not for all his acumen escape his destiny.

Finally, we return to the dream of Xerxes. He assumed that he was free to launch an invasion of Greece or not, as he saw fit. Then, out of the dark, of night, he was told that he was not a free agent, and even Artabanus, after seeing the vision, withdrew his objection, imagining that some *daimonie horme* awaited the Greeks. Was there a "hand of divine superiority" behind the imperialist thrust of Persia?

The question is fair to ask, and the answer cannot be an easy one. Herodotus, who disagreed with the creeping cynicism of his day about oracles that we find in Thucydides, held up a prophecy of Bacis as an example of oracular accuracy. This oracle attributed the Persian defeat to "divine Dike" which quenches Koros, the son of Hybris. There is a close parallel in the second stasimon of the *Oedipus Tyrannus:* there Hybris begets Koros, and the result is disaster. Sophocles' chorus here portrays the traditional unrighteous man who is the victim of Hybris, Koros, and Ate. Guilt which is described in this Aeschylean fashion does not sound like the involuntary guilt of a man who has acted in ignorance. The oracle of Bacis which Herodotus quotes does not suggest any such thing, and since Herodotus held up this oracle as an example of divine prescience, I do not think he saw it that way either. At some point, the Persians had made a choice.

In fact, what must impress the reader of the *Histories* is the number of times that individuals are presented with choices that they must make. The clearest of these are placed in the *Histories* before the battles of Marathon and Salamis, and they are introduced with the same words. "It lies in your hands, Callimachus, whether to enslave Athens or keep her free," said Miltiades before Marathon; and before Salamis, Themistocles put the choice equally sharply to Eurybiades: "It lies in your hands to save Greece." In both instances, men who deserved the label "makers of history" approached relative nonentities and told them that the choice was theirs. They could decide whether or not Greece would be free. But these are only the most dramatic choices. The Ionians who guarded the Danube bridge for Darius on his Scythian expedition had a choice to make, and they could make it freely without incurring guilt, for they had done their duty and remained at their post

for as long as they had pledged. Their leaders debated the question, first supporting Miltiades and then switching their support to Histiaeus, after he had pointed out to them where their own interests lay. Thus, the Ionians chose servitude.

Once again, before the battle of Lade, the Ionians faced a similar choice. Dionysius of Phocaea put it to them with a flourish borrowed from Homer: "Our affairs are on the razor's edge." The consequence of the choice was important: there could be no doubt of it, and the Ionians repeated the response they had made at the Danube bridge. They rallied at first to the cause of freedom and then they changed their minds.

Before Cyrus launched his Persians on the path to empire, he showed them the advantages both of servitude and imperial power, and let them choose. They chose imperialism. Even Gyges, who brought a curse upon the Mermnads that destroyed Croesus' empire after five generations, was given a choice. The queen summoned him and laid before him the alternatives. "There are two roads before you, Gyges, and I give you your choice which you will travel." It was a grim choice: Gyges might kill his king and usurp the throne, thereby incurring guilt, or die himself. But it was a choice nonetheless, and Gyges chose to survive and become king.

These situations where men are faced with alternatives are analogous to the tragic choices of Aeschylus: Pelasgus in the *Suppliants* faced such a choice, and the plot of the *Agamemnon* hung upon a choice made by Agamemnon at Aulis ten years before the story represented by the play began. "In Aeschylus," writes Bruno Snell, "the hero's choice becomes a problem whose solution is contingent on nothing but his own insight, but which is nevertheless regarded as a matter of compelling necessity." The choice once made might be hard to unmake, or it might not. Athens judged it natural enough that Sparta should fear that she might accede to the overtures which Mardonius made her in the spring of 479 B.C., but the Athenians themselves believed there was only one answer they could give. Yet in all these cases, the act of decision seems to be entirely within the human sphere of action.

The situation in which Xerxes found himself when he chose to invade Greece appears to differ. He first announced his resolve to undertake the expedition, confident that he could choose to make it or not as he pleased, and Artabanus gave his counsel in the belief that Xerxes could countermand it. Then an apparition in a dream warned Xerxes that his choice was limited, and when the same apparition visited Artabanus, it threatened him with punishment for trying to turn aside "what had to be." Similarly, before the battle of Plataea, Mardonius appears to have a choice: he may have urged his officers to attack, following the Persian *no-*

mos, but he had the option of yielding to the counsel of Artabazus and the Thebans, and withdrawing to Thebes, a plan that seemed more sensible to Herodotus. Yet Mardonius too was moving toward a predestined end. He was to render *dike* for the murder of Leonidas, as the oracle had predicted.

We need not expect from Herodotus any solution to the dilemma of predestination and free will. They exist in uneasy partnership throughout the classical world and the problem passes into Christian theology unresolved. But here we are looking at the narrower question of why Xerxes' freedom to choose between an imperialist policy and a nonaggressive one was so restricted. If Dionysius of Phocaea, Miltiades, and Themistocles could all propose free choices, why should Xerxes have been deprived of one before he took the fateful step of invading Greece? For though he was not left *absolutely* without choice, the apparition made it clear that the penalty attached to countermanding the expedition was such that no Persian could endure it and survive.

We may find part of the answer in Sophocles. To what extent were Oedipus and Antigone free agents? They made free choices, but when the pattern of events was finally revealed, their choices appear to have directed them to an end that was determined before they were born. They were unwittingly working out the ancient curse of the Labdacids. In the case of Xerxes, it was not an ancient curse that directed his decisions; instead, he was governed by a choice that Cyrus had put to the Persians before he was born. The Persians had elected the *nomos* of imperialism when they chose for themselves the life of masters rather than subjects, and the choice that they had made freely under Cyrus so restricted the options of Xerxes four generations later that, for practical purposes, he had to invade Greece. The alternative involved penalties that he could not contemplate.

Xerxes was not the only player in the *Histories* who was governed by an ancient choice. Lycurgus chose laws for the Spartans, and as Demaratus was to tell Xerxes, their law ruled them as firmly as the Persian king ruled his subjects. The Medes, gathered in an assembly, chose Deioces as king; thereafter they were constrained by their choice and lived under a monarchy with all its trappings. Gyges chose to kill Candaules, and Croesus' fate was governed by that ancient choice made five generations before his time.

The Persians had chosen the *nomos* of imperialism under Cyrus, and by the time of Xerxes it had attained the status of ancestral law. Time had increased its insistence on obedience. Cyrus attacked the Massagetae because he set his heart on conquering them. Darius invaded Scythia because Asia was overflowing with population and wealth. Both kings conformed to policies that were in line with the *nomos* of imperialism,

and hence no conflict arose. Yet there is no hint that they acted under compulsion. But Xerxes wavered between what Thucydides might have called *apragmosyne* and *polypragmosyne,* and discovered that there was a penalty he must pay if he transgressed this *nomos.* He was in the grip of a dark, ambivalent force that was driving him on to overstep the natural boundaries of his empire, and that force obtained its power from a free choice which the Persians had made long before Xerxes was born: their decision to be rulers rather than subjects, and to possess the good things of an imperial people rather than the toil and sweat of servitude. It was a choice with consequences quite as much as the choice that Agamemnon made at the bay of Aulis, and they reach their consummation with Xerxes. Cyrus might have restrained his hunger for more subjects before he attacked the Massagetae, and Darius might perhaps have held back before he invaded Scythia, but under Xerxes the empire was at such a pitch of wealth and extent that obedience to the *nomos* of expansionism had to take him beyond the natural boundaries of Asia.

THE IMPERIALIST IMPULSE

During the years that Herodotus researched his **Histories,** the Persian Empire, grown soft and luxurious, was in decline and another empire, that of Athens (which, like Persia, exacted tribute), had come to dominate the Aegean world, and showed the same restless ambition that marked the Persians under Cyrus. It was a remarkable peripeteia, which seemed to corroborate Herodotus' dictum that in the course of time, great cities became small and small ones became great, and good fortune is forever inconstant. Persian expansionism seemed to have ceased. It was time to ask what had been the nature of the impulse behind it?

Joseph Schumpeter once remarked that the Hellenic world found the reason for Xerxes' campaign utterly baffling. Schumpeter himself explained Persian expansionism as the manifestation of a warrior nation's essence: the Persians had acquired a warlike disposition, and the social organization that went along with it, before their energies could be absorbed by the peaceful exploitation of the land they had settled. They undertook conquest as a manifestation of their ethos, and they introduced imperialism into the Greek world, although Herodotus thought that Croesus had taken the first step. Before the Persian Wars, warfare had been a common state of affairs in Greece; but wars to acquire empires were not—not even the Trojan War, which was a constant comparison. Achaemenid Persia's effort to make Greece a tribute-paying province was the first attempt at empire in the Greek experience, and after Persia, Athens had taken up her legacy.

The conventional wisdom in the Greek world judged the causes of war in terms of provocation, guilt, and vengeance, and behind them all, the working of fate. Herodotus, who had an audience to consider (unlike Thucydides), chose not to ignore conventional wisdom. Thucydides may have been cranky and unjust to refer to the **Histories** as a prize essay designed for the taste of the immediate public—almost certainly he had Herodotus in mind—but nonetheless Herodotus knew the sort of reasoning with which his audience was familiar. He knew what they would expect. The search for who or what was to blame for the wars was the stock-in-trade of the *logioi*: the oral chroniclers whom Herodotus in his proem imagines in a debate on the cause of the Persian War. Aristophanes ridicules their logic, but is nevertheless witness to the popularity of this sort of reasoning: retribution fell upon the *aitioi,* or at least it should in a just world.

Herodotus puts a modicum of distance between himself and all that sort of speculation; instead, he will proceed dealing equally with cities great and small, for the world was changing ceaselessly. For individual changes there might be individual causes, some of which could entail guilt, and in retrospect, the past might disclose tragic motifs, such as tales of divine jealousy following upon great success, and calamity falling upon the overconfident. Foretime was a vast deposit of tragic themes and motifs for poets to mine. But flux was the underlying condition of mankind. For Herodotus, human fortune was by nature inconstant. But the specific problem for which he sought an answer was: why did the Persians choose to attack Greece? For that, tragic story patterns did not supply an answer.

In the end, his explanation was not far removed from Schumpeter's. Imperialism was a *nomos:* the word embraces Schumpeter's "disposition," but it meant more than that. It was a law that required obedience. However, the Persians had chosen it freely. Cyrus allowed them to taste both the hardships that subjects endured and the good life of a ruling people, and though ancient imperial conquests were not generally motivated by economic concerns, Herodotus imagined the Persians making their choice out of self-interest, but their decision was taken with deliberate intent and it was binding. It took a tough people of the sort which a hard land produced to acquire and maintain an empire, and yet the luxuries that an empire provided its rulers made them soft and eventually unfitted to rule. There was an internal dynamic to the rise and fall of empires that forced them to conform to the ebb and flow of history.

Under Xerxes, Persian expansion reached its zenith. He had inherited the *nomos* of imperialism. Chosen freely under Cyrus, it had become an expression of Persian nature by the time Xerxes reached the throne. Xerxes could not transgress it with letting go his power. The apparition that came to him in his dream warned him rightly of the consequences of his refusal to invade Greece: he would lose his throne. The abandonment of imperialism would have meant changing the nature of the Persian Empire, and the king himself could not expect to survive so fundamental an innovation.

FURTHER READING

Bernardete, Seth. *Herodotean Inquiries.* The Hague: Martinus Nijhoff, 1969, 213 p.

　　Addresses Herodotus's status as an historian, and provides an introductory overview of the *History.*

Drews, Robert. *The Greek Accounts of Eastern History.* Cambridge: Harvard University Press, 1973, 220 p.

　　General study of Greek historical accounts of the East. Includes a chapter on Herodotus's treatment of Lydia, Babylon, and Egypt.

Fehling, Detlev. *Herodotus and His Sources: Citation, Invention, and Narrative Art.* Translated by J.G.Howie. Leeds: Francis Cairns, 1989, 277 p.

　　Questions the veracity of Herodotus's sources and discusses his historical methods. This work was originally published as *Die Quellengaben bei Herodot* in 1971.

Flory, Stewart. "The Personality of Herodotus." *Arion: A Journal of Humanities and the Classics* 8, No. 1, (Spring, 1969): 99-109.

　　Notes the anecdotal character of the *History* and the appeal of Herodotus's personal "charm" as a storyteller.

Gomme, A. W. "Herodotos" and "Herodotos and Aeschylus." In *The Greek Attitude to Poetry and History,* pp. 73-94, 95-115. Berkeley: University of California Press, 1954.

　　Discusses Herodotus in historical and social context, focusing on received ideas about history.

Gould, John. *Herodotus.* London: Weidenfield and Nicolson, 1989, 164 p.

　　Introductory monograph which addresses Herodotus's background and sources, historiographical methods, and world view.

Grant, Michael. *The Ancient Historians.* New York: Charles Scribner's Sons, 1970, 486 p.

　　Places Herodotus in the context of early Greek and Roman historiography.

Gray, Vivienne. "Herodotus and the Rhetoric of Otherness." *American Journal of Philology* 116, No. 2 (Summer, 1995): 185-211.

　　Explores "the validity of current readings of certain

stories in Herodotus in terms of the rhetoric of male / female otherness" and "the presentation of women in terms of the otherness of the royal barbarian."

Hart, John. *Herodotus and Greek History.* London: Croom Helm, 1982, 226 p.
Focuses on Herodotus's treatment of Greece.

Hartog, François. *The Mirror of Herodotus: The Representation of the Other in the Writing of History.* Translated by Janet Lloyd. Berkeley: University of California Press, 1988, 386 p.
Explores Herodotus's representation of non-Greeks, especially the Scythians, and examines his rhetorical strategies.

How, W. W. and Wells, J. *A Commentary on Herodotus.* 2 vols. Rev. ed. Oxford at the Clarendon Press: Oxford, 1936.
Scholarly commentary on the *History,* including explanatory introduction, appendices, and maps.

Immerwahr, Henry R. *Form and Thought in Herodotus.* Cleveland: Press of Western Reserve University, 1966, 374 p.
Provides a general survey and discusses problems of structure and historiography in the *History.*

Lateiner, Donald. *The Historical Method of Herodotus.* Toronto: University of Toronto Press, 1989, 319 p.
Examines Herodotus's historical and research methods, and discusses his interpretation of past events.

Lattimore, Richmond. "The Wise Adviser in Herodotus." *Classical Philology* XXXIV, No. 1, (January, 1939): 24-35.
Identifies and discusses a recurring figure in the *History.*

Mahaffy, J. P. "Herodotus and the Contemorary Ionic Prose Writers." In *A History of Classical Greek Literature, Vol. II,* pp. 16-52. New York: Harper Brothers, 1880.
Detailed examination of Herodotus's writings, style, use of rhetoric, dialect, and historical sources.

Moles, J.L. "Truth and Untruth in Herodotus and Thucydides." In *Lies and Fiction in the Ancient World,* edited by Christopher Gill and T.P. Wiseman, pp.88-121. Austin: University of Texas Press, 1993.
Addresses the tension between factual reportage and literary invention in Herodotus and Thucydides.

Myres, John L. *Herodotus: Father of History.* Oxford at the Clarendon Press, 1953, 315 p.
Examines numerous aspects of Herodotus's work and the claim that Herodotus was "the man who first formulated ... [the] aims and method [of history], and implemented this conception in his own writings."

Spengler, Joseph J. "Herodotus on the Subject Matter of Economics." *Scientific Monthly,* 81, No. 6 (December, 1955): 276-85.
Focuses on Herodotus's treatment of economics, but finds no consistent economic theory in the *History.*

Waters, Kenneth H. *Herodotus on Tyrants and Despots: A Study in Objectivity.* Wiesbaden: Franz Steiner Verlag, 1971, 100 p.
Examines Herodotus's treatment of Greek and Persian despotic rulers and addresses the problem of objectivity in the *History.*

Wood, Henry. *The Histories of Herodotus: An Analysis of the Formal Structure.* The Hague: Mouton, 1972, 201 p.
Detailed discussion of Herodotus's historiographical method.

Polybius

c. 200 B.C. - c. 118 B.C.

Greek historian.

INTRODUCTION

A Greek historian of the second century B.C. whose *Histories* provides the most detailed contemporary account of the rise of the Roman empire, Polybius is credited with being the first historian to formulate a methodology of history. Writing during a period when the entire Mediterranean basin was quickly falling under the domination of a single power—Rome—Polybius was also the first to postulate and practice the need for a "universal" history emphasizing concurrent events and their interrelationships throughout the known world. His ideas about the superiority of mixed constitutions influenced seventeenth- and eighteenth-century political philosophers and are a source of the system of checks and balances in the United States Constitution, while echoes of his theory of the cyclical nature of history can be found in Marxist thought and in the works of twentieth-century historians Oswald Spengler and Arnold Toynbee.

Biographical Information

Born in Megalopolis in Arcadia, central southern Greece, around 201 B.C., Polybius was the son of Lycortas, a prominentpolitician of the Achaean League, which united most of the city-states of the Peloponnesian peninsula. Although nominally allied with Rome, the League offered only tepid support to the Roman army in its campaign against the Kingdom of Macedonia. When Rome crushed the Macedonian forces at Pydna in 168 B.C., the League was punished for its lack of enthusiasm by seeing a thousand of its young upper-class men deported to Italy. Among them was Polybius, who had served as an Achaean cavalry officer during the Macedonian war. Despite his unenviable status as a foreign internee, Polybius thrived in Rome, becoming friend and mentor to young Scipio Aemilianus (later known as Scipio Africanus Minor), whose father had commanded the Roman forces at Pydna. Allowed to remain in Rome while most of the other detainees were sent to remote areas of Italy, he circulated freely among the members of Rome's ruling class; scholars believe that he may even have been allowed to travel outside Italy before the official release of the Achaean detainees in 150 B.C. It was apparently during his first years in Rome, around 167 B.C., that he began writing his *Histories*, drawing in-

formation from Roman archives as well as from his personal experiences and his contacts with Roman political and military leaders. He accompanied Scipio as a military advisor during the siege of Carthage during the Third Punic War and was present at the destruction of the city in 146 B.C. When a revolt by the Achaean League led to its being crushed and disbanded by Roman forces in that same year, Polybius was dispatched to aid in the political reorganization of the Peloponnese. Although the exact dates of his trips are not known, information in his *Histories* indicates that he travelled extensively throughout the Mediterranean and also took part in an exploration of the Atlantic coast of northern Africa and Portugal. Polybius died in Megalopolis, tradition has it, of a fall from his horse at the age of 82, in about 119 B.C.

Major Writings

By his own account, before leaving Greece in 168 B.C. Polybius had written a biography of the Achaean leader Philopoemen, but no trace of this work remains. He also appears to have written several monographs (also lost) during the course of his lifetime, including one on military tactics and others on the Numantine War and on the habitability of the equatorial regions. The work for which he is now best known is his forty-volume *Histories*, of which only fragments have survived. This massive study describes the events in the Mediterranean basin from the middle of the third century B.C. to 146 B.C. Polybius began writing the *Histories* in about 167 B.C. as an account of the expansion of Roman rule to encompass virtually the entire known world. He originally intended the work to cover the period up to 167 B.C., but later decided to extend the period covered to include the destruction of the cities of Corinth and Carthage in 146 B.C., and he appears to have continued to revise and add to the *Histories* until his death. The stated purpose of the work was to determine the value of Roman policies as well as to provide present and future statesmen with practical instruction in military and political matters. Of the surviving sections the best known and most widely studied is Book VI, in which the historian provides a theoretical account of the development of society and government. He saw the history of government as falling into a recurring cycle by which kingship inevitably gave way to successive stages of tyranny, aristocracy, oligarchy, democracy, and anarchy, at which point a strong leader would emerge and establish himself as king, thus starting the cycle over again. The only hope of breaking the cycle, Polybius maintained, lay in a "mixed" government on the Roman model, which combined elements of kingship, aristocratic rule, and democratic representation.

Textual History

With the exception of the first five books, which have survived intact, Polybius's *Histories* have come down to us in a fragmentary state. Scholars still debate the correct order of some of the fragments and the extent to which they are representative of the entire work. Parts of the missing thirty-five volumes have been pieced together from an abridged version of books six to eighteen prepared in the tenth century A.D. or earlier (the *Excerpta Antiqua*) and from a collection of excerpts copied by the order of the tenth-century Byzantine emperor Constantine VII Porphyrogenitus. Italian bishop Niccolò Perotti translated Books I-V into Latin in 1455 and published them in 1473. A Greek edition of the first five books appeared in 1530, followed by French and Italian translations in the mid-seventeenth century and the first English translation, of Book I, in

1568. A Latin translation and commentary prepared by Johannes Schweighaeuser and published in Leipzig from 1789 to 1795 formed the basis for subsequent Latin editions by F. Hultsch (1870-92) and Theodorus Buettner-Wobst (1889-1905). English translations of the complete extant *Histories* have been carried out by Evelyn S. Shuckburgh (1889) and W. R. Paton (1922-27); Shuckburgh's translation, based on Hultsch, is considered more accurate, but it does not reflect subsequent conclusions about the correct order of the fragments.

Critical Reception

While the historical methodology of Polybius is inadequate by modern historiographical standards, his *Histories* continue to be valued by historians for their detailed and insightful treatment of the period they cover. His thoughts on politics and on the writing of history have been a recurring focus of critical attention throughout the centuries since his death. Later Roman writers criticized his writing as stuffy and pedantic, but nonetheless used him extensively as a source; the statesman and philosopher Cicero was influenced by his theory of mixed constitutions, and the historian Livy derived much of his material about the rise of Rome from the *Histories*. According to Wesley E. Thompson, the selection of excerpts preserved under Byzantine emperors indicates an acute interest in his accounts of Roman military strategy. After several centuries of neglect, interest in Polybius revived during the Italian Renaissance, when Niccolò Machiavelli and other political theorists mined the surviving volumes of the *Histories* for historical information as well as for the historian's thoughts on political and military matters. Polybius's preference for mixed constitutions was taken up by the English philosopher John Locke and the French philosopher Montesquieu. The German historian Barthold Niebuhr, considered the founder of modern historiography, relied on Polybius extensively as a source and praised his emphasis on personal experience and eyewitness accounts in the writing of history. As Polybius remains the major source of historical information about the rise of the Roman empire, he continues to invite critical commentary and analysis. Historians still debate his attitudes towards the events he recounts as well as the exact nature and acuity of his views on the purpose and methodology of history. F. W. Walbank, a British professor considered the leading modern authority on Polybius, has published a detailed three-volume commentary on the *Histories* as well as a more general book-length study and numerous shorter articles. Arthur M. Eckstein has also published extensively on Polybius, with much of his work focusing on the political and personal context of the historian's views and on his attitude toward the role of ethics in statecraft.

PRINCIPAL WORKS

Life of Philopoemen
A Treatise on Tactics
History of the Numantine War
On the Habitability of the Tropics
Histories. 40 vols.

PRINCIPAL ENGLISH TRANSLATIONS

Book I (translated by Christopher Watson) 1568

The Histories of Polybius (translated by Evelyn S. Shuckburgh) 1889.

Polybius. The Histories (translated by W. R. Paton) 1922-27

Polybius. The Histories (translated by Mortimer Chambers) 1966

Polybius. The Rise of the Roman Empire (partial translation by Ian Scott-Kilvert) 1979

CRITICISM

J. L. Strachan-Davidson (essay date 1879)

SOURCE: "Polybius and His Times," in *The Quarterly Review,* Vol. 148, No. 295, July, 1879, pp. 186-222.

[*In the following excerpt from an originally unsigned article on the Roman Republic, Strachan-Davidson briefly reviews Polybius's life and work, praising his "strict integrity" and "sound practical intelligence."*]

In the centuries when the knowledge of the classical writings slumbered, the tradition of ancient politics was summed up in the memory of the Roman Cæsar. The idea of law and order concentrated in the person of a universal monarch, and sanctified by the name of Rome, had impressed itself deeply on the imagination of the world; and this idea meets us throughout the middle ages, crossing the turbulent freedom of barbaric tribes and the license of petty local rulers, and surviving amidst all the changing forms which conquest and migration gave to the actual structure of medieval society. Cæsarism and its works alone remained of all the institutions of antiquity, to tell the younger nations of the political life of their predecessors. That such should be the result of the ancient system, and such the last word which it was destined to leave to posterity, would have seemed a grievous failure and disappointment to the statesmen and philosophers of Greece and Rome. For them the free self-governed Republic is the home of civilisation and the indispensable condition of political life. The City, not the Empire, is the subject of the ideal politics of Aristotle and Plato. The civic Republic is the cause for which Demosthenes and

Cicero struggled in vain, and the object of the pathetic regrets of Tacitus. How are we to account for this fantastic dissimilarity of parent and offspring? How was it that the liberty of the ancient world brought forth bondage?

The doctrine of self-governing freedom and rational obedience to law, first worked out and systematized in these ancient Republics, is a great step in advance in the domain of politics, then and there achieved by the human race. But the advantage gained was limited by the impossible requirements, which the ancient world attached to the conception of political freedom. Liberty staked its existence on the success of one particular form of its manifestation, and, when this form became obsolete, liberty itself suffered an eclipse of centuries. The shock of great events disturbed the conditions under which alone healthy civic Republics could exist. The conquests of Alexander began, and the conquests of Rome completed the destruction of freedom, except in the narrow circle of a single Republic: that Republic found itself incapable of combining self-government and empire: and so we pass into an age, in which the world is compelled to turn away its eyes from the higher gifts of political life and energy, and has to content itself with the material prosperity, the shallow though wide-spread culture, the mediocre abilities, and the passive virtues, which alone can find a place under the cold shade of a despotism.

Disappointing as is the result, and disheartening as is the spectacle of brilliant hopes and grand aspirations frustrated, and mighty possibilities dwarfed or become abortive, still there is hardly any topic suggested by ancient history more interesting and more instructive than that of the failure of the earliest form of the free State. One of the most important epochs, in this process of transition from civic Republicanism to universal monarchy, is the period of the absorption of Greece into the Roman Empire; and of this period we happily possess an accurate and interesting account, preserved to us in the works of the contemporary historian Polybius. It is the purpose of this article to present a picture, drawn for the most part after Polybius, of the two great historical peoples, the Greeks and the Romans, in this time of struggle and transition.

We must first say a few words concerning the historian who is to be our guide. The person of Polybius, like his book, occupies a middle place between the Greek world of independent states, and the Roman world of subjects dominated by the Sovereign Republic. In his boyhood he was the pupil of Philopœmen, 'the last of the Greeks'; in his later life the chosen friend of Scipio Æmilianus, the destroyer of Carthage. In early manhood a magistrate of the Achæan League, then for long years a prisoner in Italy, Polybius found himself at last in the position of mediator between his conquered countrymen and the Romans. He was selected by the victors for the painful but honourable task of settling the internal affairs of the Greek states after the conquest, and of accommodating their local institutions to the regulations which their new masters had ordained. Throughout an eventful and chequered life, he appears as a stateman of strict integrity and of sound practical intelligence. While there was yet a hope for the freedom of Greece, he strove hard to enable her to tread safely in the slippery path to which she was called. When the last chance was absolutely and irretrievably lost, he did not seek to lead a forlorn hope or to bury himself beneath the ruins of his country, but set himself hard to work to make the subjection of the Greeks as mild and as tolerable as possible, and he urged upon them both by precept and example submission to the inevitable. To Polybius, as a Greek statesman, the breaking up of the Achæan League, and the subjection of every Greek state to Rome, was inexpressibly bitter. Sometimes, though very seldom, the suppressed sorrow finds a pathetic utterance. After being present in company with his friend Scipio at the destruction of Carthage, Polybius hurried back to his native land in time to look on the yet smoking ruins of Corinth, and to see the Roman soldiers playing dice on the choicest pictures of Greece. The comparison which rose before his mind is expressed in the following passage:—

> Though the fate of Carthage might seem to be the greatest of all possible calamities, yet one may well regard that which then befel Greece as not less but even in some respects greater. For the former their end is their plea with posterity; but the latter have left not so much as a plausible excuse for those who would fain plead their cause. The Carthaginians at the moment of their fall perished from off the face of the earth, and were thenceforth insensible of their misfortunes; but the Greeks look on at their own calamities, and hand down their losses as an inheritance to their children's children; and just as we count those who live on under torture more wretched than those who expire under their torments, so we should esteem the fate of the Greeks yet more pitiable than that which befel the Carthaginians.

But Polybius feels that it is not for him to waste time over vain regrets for the past. He will strive to record it faithfully for a warning, and then devote his powers to making the best of any materials for well-being, which have survived the general wreck.

> At the time of these disasters it was my part, as a Greek for the Greeks, to give them my aid in all ways, defending them, palliating their faults, deprecating the anger of the conquerors; and this I did then and there with all sincerity. But I here record for posterity the memory of the events, not seeking to please for the moment the ears of my readers, but to edify their minds and save them from committing the same faults again. And so I leave this subject.

The writings of Polybius, like his life, have little in them of splendid or heroic, but much patient research, much clear intelligent appreciation, and above all unswerving honesty and truthfulness. Never did a writer strive more earnestly to purge his mind from every prejudice and from every hallucination, and to look with unclouded eyes on actual realities. He bends all the powers of his mind to lay before his readers the exact facts of his time, pleasant or disagreeable, without exaggeration and without extenuation.

In the task before us it is much to have the guidance of an author who has so well conceived the ideal at which a historian should aim. We find in him ample materials for reconstructing the image of the times in which he lived and of which he wrote, materials which can be arranged in their true perspective by aid of the light which subsequent events throw on the main lines of the picture. Much in ancient history which was hidden from the wisest of contemporary observers cannot but now be clear. With the result to inform us, we can distinguish the essential from the accidental, the growing force from the declining, the silent tendency from the obvious and external manifestation: institutions and practices, still in their embryo stage, appear to us, as we look back on them, already invested with the characteristics of their developed forms: often we can correct the judgment of the contemporary writer, often we can catch the true significance of that which he casually records. There is ample room within these limits for the labours of modern students, but the value of their work must in every case depend on the fulness and trustworthiness of their ancient authorities. For the period with which we propose to deal, almost our sole sources of information are Polybius himself and Livy, who draws mainly from Polybius. Of the forty books, in which our author originally composed his history, five and a half remain entire, and the rest are known to us by the copious and well-chosen extracts of Byzantine compilers. The work as preserved is sufficient to make the age with which it deals more intimately accessible to us than any other period of ancient history, excepting only the time of Thucydides and Aristophanes, and the time of Cicero. While we follow Polybius, we feel that we are on safe ground. There is no room here for that vexatious though often necessary form of historical criticism, which has to occupy itself with weighing and testing authorities, subject always to the chance of having its verdict set aside by the next generation of scholars. Polybius may not only be followed implicitly in matters of fact, but his wide and accurate knowledge of men enabled him to present us with a faithful picture of the thoughts and the feelings, the fears and the hopes, the social conditions and the moral aspects, of the contemporary world. The very diffuseness and love of digression, which spoil the artistic beauty of his history, open out rich veins of information, and provide abundant material of all kinds for those who would write after him. . . .

Mountstuart E. Grant Duff (essay date 1897)

SOURCE: "Presidential Address," in *Transactions of the Royal Historical Society, New Series, Vol. XI*, 1897. Reprint by Kraus, 1971, pp. 1-17.

[*In the following excerpt, Duff cites passages from the writings of Polybius to demonstrate the timeliness of his political ideas and to advocate a wider study of his works.*]

In previous Addresses I have spoken of Thucydides, Tacitus, Herodotus, and Aristotle, with special reference to the amount of light to be gained from their writings by the modern statesman. To-day I propose to take for my subject a far less famous personage, but one who should certainly not be passed over without some notice, by anybody who is interested in the contributions made by the ancient world to political thought.

Polybius—for it is to him that I allude—has been in several respects very unfortunate. In the first place, of his large and carefully ordered work only five books have come down in a complete or pretty complete form; while large portions of it have been preserved in the shape of fragments, to be pieced together by able editors as best they can. It might have been better in some ways for his fame, if only the five books had been preserved; for although his work was, as I have said, *carefully* ordered, it was not exactly *well ordered*. His elaborately thought-out plan was not a very happy one, but lent itself to a certain amount of confusion; which confusion, thanks to the fragmentary state in which many of his writings have been transmitted to us, has become confusion worse confounded. In the second place, his style is by no means brilliant. He says what he has got to say in a straight-forward, soldierly fashion, but his style is lumbering and has assuredly no charm. He knew this himself, and said (Book xvi. chapter 17):

> To my mind it is quite right to take great care and pay great attention to the presentation of one's facts in correct and adequate language, for this contributes in no small degree to the effectiveness of history; still I do not think that serious writers should regard it as their primary and most important object. Far from it. Quite other are the parts of his history on which a practical politician should rather pride himself.

In the third place, many of the subjects which he treats are profoundly uninteresting to the modern reader. The virtues of the Arcadians, the vices of the Ætolians leave me at least entirely unmoved; and I feel very little interest in any of his narratives, save those which relate to the conquering march of Rome.

In the fourth place, he is not unfrequently too didactic, too determined that the reader shall not only taste, but devour and digest every morsel of the moral which he presents for his consumption.

These are, I think, the chief reservations which we must enumerate, if we wish to do neither more nor less than justice to Polybius. These made, however, we may, I think, say that he was a very worthy and a very wise man.

It should be remembered, too, that although Polybius is little read now, he has had great influence at different periods of the world's history. Cicero had evidently studied him with great care, and it is very probable that if Polybius had not led the way, neither what has been described as the golden observations of Machiavelli upon Livy, nor Montesquieu's study of the greatness and decadence of the Romans would ever have been written. . . .

The first thing which strikes a reader of Polybius is his curious modernness. His mind was assuredly not a more powerful one than that of Thucydides; but there was endless discussion about history and its uses, between the days of the older and the younger author. The world had immensely widened on his view. His horizon was not bounded by the narrow limits of Greece and her colonies; but extended over all the three basins of the middle sea, far into Asia, and over wide regions both of Europe and Africa with which Greece and Greek civilisation had but little or nothing to do. On many subjects he took a much more sensible view than was at all common until quite recent times—nay, a more sensible view than that which we often hear, even from the mouths of fairly intelligent persons amongst our contemporaries.

Thus in Book iv. chapter 74, speaking of the people of Elis, he says:

'For peace is a thing we all desire, and are willing to submit to anything to obtain; it is the only one of our so-called blessings that no one questions'; and in the same Book, chapter 31, speaking of the Messenians, he supplies just what is wanted to qualify the rather too sweeping language of that passage:

> I admit, indeed, that war is a terrible thing; but it is less terrible than to submit to anything whatever in order to avoid it. For what is the meaning of our fine talk about equality of rights, freedom of speech, and liberty if the one important thing is peace? We have no good word for the Thebans, because they shrank from fighting for Greece and chose from fear to side with the Persians—nor indeed for Pindar, who supported their inaction in the verses—
>
> A quiet haven for the ship of state
>   Should be the patriot's aim,

And smiling peace, to small and great
    That brings no shame.

For though his advice was for the moment acceptable, it was not long before it became manifest that his opinion was as mischievous as it was dishonourable. For peace, with justice and honour, is the noblest and most advantageous thing in the world; when joined with disgrace and contemptible cowardice, it is the basest and most disastrous.

In short, we may, I think, set down Polybius not as a peace-at-any-price man, nor as a man who acquiesced in or even welcomed war on account of the incidental advantages which it sometimes brings, but as a peace-almost-at-any-price man, which is what I consider everyone ought to be.

Observe in the last passage the phrase 'Peace with honour,' which became so famous in our own times, and was, I daresay, believed by many to have been invented by the eminent person who used it; just as was the case with his almost equally famous *'Sanitas sanitatum, omnia sanitas,'* which is to be found in 'Menagiana,' a book of the seventeenth century. . . .

Now let us turn to some of his views about history. In Book ii. chap. 56 he says:

> Surely an historian's object should not be to amaze his readers by a series of thrilling anecdotes; nor should he aim at producing speeches which might have been delivered, nor study dramatic propriety in details, like a writer of tragedy; but his function is above all to record with fidelity what was actually said or done, however commonplace it may be. . . .

    . . . . .

[Yet] he was very far from thinking that a bare statement, even of true facts—let alone of imaginary ones—was enough; for in Book iii. chap. 31 he says:

> Neither the writer nor the reader of history, therefore, should confine his attention to a bare statement of facts; he must take into account all that preceded or followed them. For if you take from history all explanation of cause, principle, and motive, and of the adaptation of the means to the end, what is left is a mere panorama without being instructive; and, though it may please for the moment, has no abiding value.

And again, in Book vi. chap. I, he adds:

> What is really educational and beneficial to students of history is the clear view of the causes of events, and the consequent power of choosing the better policy in a particular case.

Could Professor Seeley have put it better?

Here again is a passage, in which he anticipates the views of a well-known modern historian (I mean Mr. Buckle):

> For we mortals have an irresistible tendency to yield to climatic influences; and to this cause, and no other, may be traced the great distinctions which prevail amongst us in character, physical formation, and complexion, as well as in most of our habits, varying with nationality or wide local separation.'

Polybius had no sympathy with the habit, consecrated by the practice of many illustrious persons, of inventing speeches. In Book xii. chap. 25 he says:

> The historian therefore who omits the words actually used, as well as all statement of the determining circumstances, and gives us instead conjectures and mere fancy compositions, destroys the special use of history. In this respect Timæus is an eminent offender, for we all know that his books are full of such writing.

He deserves the greatest possible credit for having seen more clearly than most writers, ancient or modern, the immense importance of Geography. We may compare him in this respect with Dr. Arnold in our times, or with his pupil Dean Stanley.

I am afraid that Dr. Arnold would not have considered this observation very complimentary; for he disparages Polybius, as a geographer, in his 'History of Rome.' I am sure, however, that Polybius had the root of the matter in him, and that if he had had anything like the same facilities as those which his critic enjoyed from books, maps, plans, and opportunities of travel, he would have shown himself at least the equal of his successor.

'The science of genuine history,' he remarks, 'is three-fold: first, the dealing with written documents and the arrangement of the material thus obtained. Second, topography, the appearance of cities and localities, the description of rivers and harbours, and, speaking generally, the peculiar features of seas and countries and their relative distances. Thirdly, political affairs.' . . .

On one point Polybius has very directly and very powerfully influenced the modern world, for it was he, to the best of my belief, who first set forth, in detail and with reasons, the importance of Constantinople. His views on this subject are given in Book iv. chapter 38 and the following chapters. He begins by saying that:—

> As far as the sea is concerned, Byzantium occupies a position the most secure and in every way the most advantageous of any town in our quarter of the world: while in regard to the land, its situation is in both respects the most unfavourable.

He then points out that Byzantium so completely commands the entrance to the Pontus, that no merchant can sail in or out against its will; adding that, the Pontus being rich in what all the rest of the world requires for the staff of life, the Byzantines are absolute masters of all such things—as for instance cattle, slaves, honey, wax, and salt fish; in exchange for which the Greeks sent them oil and wine, while they sometimes exported corn, and sometimes imported it.

Next follows a long account of the Pontus, and a curious prophecy (which has been falsified by events) that it would be gradually filled up by the alluvium of the Danube and other rivers. This is succeeded by a description of the currents which 'lash and lave Europe and Asia,' ending thus:—

> A current runs from the place on the Asiatic side called the Cow, the place on which the myth declares Io to have first stood after swimming the channel. From there it runs right up to Byzantium, and, dividing into two streams on either side of the city, the lesser part of it forms the gulf called the Horn, while the greater part swerves once more across. But it has no longer sufficient way on it to reach the opposite shore on which Calchedon stands; for, after its several counter-blows, the current, finding at this point a wider channel, slackens; and no longer makes short rebounds at right angles from one shore to the other, but more and more at an obtuse angle, and accordingly, falling short of Calchedon, runs down the middle of the channel.

> What then makes Byzantium a most excellent site, and Calchedon the reverse, is just this; and although at first sight both positions seem equally convenient, the practical fact is that it is difficult to sail up to the latter, even if you wish to do so; while the current carries you to the former, whether you will or no, as I have just now shown.

Steam has long since destroyed the importance of the currents on which Polybius so much dwells, and the Thracians plus the Gauls, whose near neighbourhood made, in his view, its position so unfavourable by land, have long since vanished into space; but we are still constantly occupied with thoughts about its admirable maritime position and its relation to various neighbours at least as dangerous as ever was Gaul or Thracian.

How much of our preoccupations are reasonable, and how much merely inherited, I will not now inquire; but surely Polybius did much to turn men's thoughts in this direction.

He not only came to wise conclusions about the world around him, and about past events; he looked forward with very clear eyes into the future. Devoted as he was to the Roman Constitution, personally attached as he was to many Romans of distinction—more especially

to the family of the Scipios—he had no illusions about the seeds of mischief in the Great Republic. He foresaw the days of Marius and Sulla, nay he even had the vision of the Cæsarian power, under which the terrified and distracted citizens would eventually have to take refuge.

He has been accused by some of not being impartial. I should say that, considering all things, he was *very* impartial—quite as impartial as most historians who have a real interest in the subject about which they write. One might as soon have expected a French soldier, who had fought through Napoleon's campaigns, to write impartially of the conduct of England during the great war, as to find Polybius speaking well of the mortal foes of his native Arcadia and of the Achæan league. That such a lover of Rome should be so fair to Hannibal is infinitely to his credit. He is often severe in censuring other historians, but they probably richly deserved the censure; and he was quite willing to be censured for faults similar to those which he reproves in them. There is an interesting passage in Book xvi. chapter 20, which shows his way of looking at honest criticism—not the mere criticism of private spite:

> When Zeno received my letter, and found that it was impossible to make the correction, because his history was already published, he was much vexed but could do nothing. He, however, put the most friendly interpretation on my proceeding; and in regard to this point, I would beg my own readers, whether of my own or future generations, if I am ever detected in making a deliberate misstatement, and disregarding truth in any part of my history, to criticise me unmercifully, but if I do so from lack of information, to make allowances; and I ask it for myself more than others, owing to the size of my history and the extent of ground covered by its transactions.

I might quote a great many more passages illustrating my point, but I think I have quoted enough to show that Polybius deserves more attention than he receives. . . . When everyone gets their rights, I think a little of Polybius will be insisted on, and that those who read some well-chosen passages of his works will, if the accidents of life give them the management of public affairs, have not unfrequently occasion to remember judicious observations made or wise counsels given by him.

J. B. Bury   (lecture date 1909)

SOURCE: "Polybius and Poseidonius," in *The Ancient Greek Historians,* 1909. Reprint by Dover Publications, 1958, pp. 191-223.

[In the following excerpt, Bury provides an overview of Polybius's philosophy of history, emphasizing his

views on the purpose of historical study, the role of Fortune, and the significance of the individual.]

The life of Polybius covered about the first eighty years of the second century B.C. (c. 198-117 B.C.)—the period of the great political process which linked together the destinies of Greece and Rome. He was born in the Hellenistic world, a noble representative of its civilisation, to become the herald of the new Graeco-Roman world into which he witnessed the Hellenistic system passing. You will remember that having played a public part in the politics of the Achaean League of which his father Lycortas was then the leading statesman, and having served as a commander of cavalry, he had been taken with other hostages, after the battle of Pydna (168 B.C.), to Rome, where he was placed in the house of the victorious general Aemilius Paullus. There he enjoyed the intimate society of Scipio Aemilianus, and had exceptionally good opportunities of gaining a first-hand knowledge of Roman affairs and of studying the character of the governing class and the working of the constitution. There he became reconciled to the fate of his country. He lived sixteen years at Rome before he was allowed to return to Greece, and during that time he conceived the idea of his work and wrote a considerable part of it (at least fifteen Books). His original design was to relate the history of the advance of Roman conquest, through a period of fifty-three years from the eve of the Second Punic war (220 B.C.) to the Roman conquest of Macedonia (168 B.C.). He explains very fully why he chose his starting-point. There broke out almost at the same moment three great conflicts: the war of Rome with Carthage, the war of the Leagues in Greece (in which the Achaeans and Philip were ranged against the Aetolians), and the war in the East between Antiochus and Ptolemy Philopator. Up to that epoch, events happening in the various quarters of the world were unconnected and did not bear upon each other either in their purposes or in their issues. But from this time Italian and African affairs begin to come into relation with Asiatic and Greek affairs, and history begins to assume the form, not of strewn *disiecta membra,* but of a single organic body. . . .

But, while Polybius marks this date as the proper beginning of his work, he goes back farther in a long introduction, filling two Books, in which he sketches the earlier history of the relations of Rome with Carthage, including the First Punic war and the previous history of the Achaean League. Thus, so far as the lands of the Western Mediterranean are concerned, his history began where Timaeus had left off, as he expressly notes.

He signalises the *motif* of his work in imposing phrases. "Our own times have witnessed a miracle, and it consists in this. Fortune moved almost all the affairs of the world towards one quarter and constrained all things to tend to one and the same goal. And so it is the special note of my work to bring under one purview for my readers the means and the manipulations which fortune employed for this end. This idea was my principal motive and stimulus. It was an additional reason that in our time no one had attempted a universal history."

Subsequent events, the fall of Carthage and the annexation of Greece in 146 B.C., led Polybius to extend his plan and fix this later year as the term of his history. In its augmented form it reached the considerable bulk of forty Books, of which only the first five have been preserved completely, though of many of the others we possess long excerpts. He seems to have finished the composition of the whole work about the year 134, but he continued to insert many additions and corrections up to 120 B.C. These supplements are often in contradiction with other passages, for he died without submitting the book to a systematic revision. Indeed, he had allowed the original introduction, which expounded the first scheme of his history, to remain unchanged, and simply inserted a statement of his revised plan. Of the later additions the most interesting are those which were suggested by the author's visit to Spain about 133 B.C., and those which allude to the revolutionary movement of the Gracchi. . . .

Polybius is not less express than Thucydides in asserting the principle that accurate representation of facts was the fundamental duty of the historian. He lays down that three things are requisite for performing such a task as his: the study and criticism of sources; autopsy, that is, personal knowledge of lands and places; and thirdly, political experience. He was himself a man of action, and had acquired political and military experience before he became a historian, so that he fulfilled the third condition; and he was most conscientious in endeavouring to satisfy the two other self-imposed requirements. He possessed a wide acquaintance with historical literature, and criticized the authorities whom he used with fearless independence of judgment. He was not taken in by "authority," and he declined to render unreserved credit to a writer on the ground that he was a contemporary or a man of character. For instance, he criticizes the views of the Roman historian Fabius on the causes of the Punic war. "There are some," he observes, "who think that because he lived at the time and was a Roman senator he should be believed without more ado. Whereas I consider his authority high, but not absolute or such as to dispense the reader from forming his own judgment on the facts themselves."

Polybius was also a traveller, and he travelled for the purpose of historical investigation in accordance with his belief that topographical autopsy was a primary qualification for writing history. He passes severe criticisms on Timaeus, who, he says, always "lived in one place," and on Zeno of Rhodes, for the blunders they committed through ignorance of geography. He was intimately acquainted with Greece itself; his description of the battle of Sellasia was censured by Delbrück, but has been successfully defended by Kromayer. He travelled in Italy and Sicily; he visited Africa in an official capacity; he went with Scipio to Spain, and explored the coast of the Atlantic, returning to Italy by Sourthern Gaul and the Alps.

The historians of whom Polybius seems to have most highly approved were Ephorus and Aratus. The Memoirs of the Achaean statesman naturally appealed to him as an Achaean politician, but also because they satisfied his doctrine that history is a practical and not an antiquarian study. Written by a man of action, whose interests were directly practical, they gave the kind of instruction which it was the main function of history, in the esteem of Polybius, to give. On the other hand, Ephorus appealed to him as a universal historian, "the first and only writer who undertook to write universal history." Thus Aratus and Ephorus displayed severally the two great features of the work of Polybius, on which he constantly insists. His view of history is *pragmatical* and it is *universal*. The word pragmatical . . . has been sometimes misunderstood. By a pragmatical man he means a practical politician, and by pragmatical history he means history which bears on political actualities and furnishes practical instruction. In an interesting passage he says that this kind of history has always been useful, but is more than ever opportune now, "because in our times science and art . . . have made such great advances that theoretical students can deal, as it were on methodical principles, with the situations that occur." He insisted very strongly on the point that, in order to serve such pragmatical uses, a mere narrative of events is inadequate, and the historian must investigate and explain the causes and the inter-connexions. The whole value of history, he said, lies in a knowledge of causes. Some exponents of Polybius have applied the term "pragmatism" to his work, in the particular sense that he investigated the causal nexus of events. This is a misuse of the word, and is not countenanced by his language. "Apodeictic" is the term which he uses of his history in so far as it traces causes. His history is pragmatical, and because it is pragmatical, it is also apodeictic.

Now, what does Polybius understand by causes? He is careful to enlarge on the distinction between cause and beginning . . . , and he illustrates it by examples. For instance, while the beginning of the Persian war of Alexander the Great was his crossing over into Asia, the causes are sought by Polybius as far back as the expedition of Cyrus and the wars of Agesilaus. But it cannot be said that he goes very deep into the question of historical causes. He conceives causation in an external and mechanical way, and he does not proceed beyond the idea of simple one-sided causation to the idea of reciprocity, or of action and reaction, which is often required to express adequately the relations of historical phenomena.

The view of Polybius on causation in general is more interesting than his applications of it to particular cases. Until he was well on in years and had virtually completed his work, he shared the popular belief that, apart from the regularly operating natural and human causes, a superhuman power, which men call Tyche, exerts a control over events and diverts them in unexpected ways. This popular view had been presented in a quasi-philosophical dress by Demetrius2Some time will of Phaleron. . . . The event of 167, the fall of the Macedonian monarchy, the new step in the resistless advance of the western world-power, in whose chariot wheels Polybius himself and his country were caught up, might well seem a powerful confirmation of the theories of the wise man of Phaleron. Though Polybius traces the causes of the success of Rome to its history and constitution, he writes as follows in the preface to the original plan of his work: "Fortune has caused the whole world and its history to tend towards one purpose—the empire of Rome. She continually exercises her power in the lives of men and brings about many changes, yet never before did she achieve such a labour as she has wrought within our memory." Thus the Roman conquests produced upon Polybius the same impression which the Macedonian conquests had produced upon Demetrius. Elsewhere Polybius quotes the very words which Demetrius had used. "Fortune, who exhibits her power in compassing the unexpected, is even now, I think, displaying it to the world, having made the Macedonians the inheritors of Persian prosperity. She has lent them these blessings, till she forms a new resolution on their destiny." In many other places, too, Polybius recognises the active operation of Fortune, and comments on her instability, her paradoxes, her caprices, quite in the tone of Demetrius.

But there are other passages in which Polybius sounds a very different note. Thus he finds fault with writers who ascribe public calamities or private misfortunes to Fortune and Fate, and only allows that when it is impossible or difficult for man to discover causes, as in the case of storms or droughts, he may in his embarrassment refer them to God or Fortune, "but when you can discover the cause of an event it is not, in my opinion, admissible to impute it to God." Before you pray for rain, it is wise to look at the barometer. Again, he deprecates the practice of ascribing to fortune or the gods what is due to a man's ability and prudence. These and other similar observations are not perhaps ultimately inconsistent with the doctrine of Demetrius, but the note is different; they show a desire to restrict the operation of the external power within as narrow limits as possible. But there are other assertions which are directly opposed to that doctrine. When he inquires into the causes of the power and eminence attained by the Achaeans, a people who were not numerous and lived in a small country, "it is clear," he says, "that it would be quite unsuitable to speak of Fortune; that is a cheap explanation; we must rather seek the cause. Without a cause nothing can be brought about, whether normal or apparently abnormal." When he wrote this, he had reached a point of view diametrically opposed to that which he had learned from Demetrius. Further, he applied his new doctrine to the empire of Rome. If, in the words which I quoted a few moments ago, he had claimed Rome's successes as a supreme illustration of the mysterious dealings of Fortune, he now, with equal confidence, repudiated the theory that Fortune had anything to do with the making of Rome's greatness. "It was not by fortune, as some of the Greeks think, nor causelessly, that the Romans succeeded; their success was quite natural; it was due to their training and discipline; they aimed at the hegemony and government of the world, and they attained their purpose."

Thus it appears that Polybius, having originally started with the conception of an extra-natural power, directing the world and diverting the course of events from its natural path, was led by wider experience of life and deeper study of history to reduce within narrower and narrower bounds the intervention of this *deus ex machina,* until he finally reached the view that it was superfluous for the pragmatical historian. But it would be rash to assert that he ultimately embraced a theory of pure naturalism. All we can say is that he came to entertain the view that nothing happens without a natural cause, and the operation of Tyche or chance is, in general, an invalid assumption.

It is probable that Stoicism had something to do with his change of view. It is certain that he came under the influence of the new school of liberal Stoics, through intercourse with Panaetius, who, like himself, was an inmate of the house of Scipio at Rome. "I remember," says a speaker in Cicero's *De Republica,* "that you, Scipio, often conversed with Panaetius in the presence of Polybius, two Greeks the most deeply versed in politics" (*rerum civilium*). Polybius did not become a Stoic, but he assimilated some Stoic ideas, as in his earlier life he had been influenced by the Peripatetics.

In his actual treatment and presentation of historical events, the fluctuation in his views on this question probably did not make much difference. A change in his views as to the freedom of the will would have affected his treatment far more deeply. I know for myself that on days when I am a determinist I look on history in one way, and on days when I am an indeterminist, in quite another. Polybius was an indeterminist, like most Greeks; he believed in free-will. The particular Stoic influences to which he submitted did not touch this doctrine. For Panaetius did not share the doctrine of Chrysippus and older Stoics, that the world is governed by laws of iron necessity which exclude free-will.

We can see the results of his contact with Stoicism in the account which Polybius gives of the rise and fall of political constitutions [in Book VI]. He adopts the newer Stoic version of the theory of a cyclic succession of forms of government. When the human race is swept away (this has happened, and may be expected to happen again) through deluges, plagues, or famines, and a new race takes its place, the work of civilisation has to begin afresh; monarchy is the first form in which society constitutes itself; this passes through successive corruptions and revolutions (tyranny, aristocracy, oligarchy, democracy) into an anarchical democracy which Polybius calls *cheirocracy,* the rule of might; from which a dissolving society can only be rescued by a return to monarchy, and then the cycle begins again. In the interval between two cataclysms there may be any number of such cycles. Polybius accepts catastrophic occurrences not as a mere ancient tradition or philosophical speculation, but as a proved scientific fact.

The theory of a recurring cycle of political constitutions which comes from Plato and the Stoics is an application of the cyclical theory of the world-process which was propounded by early philosophers. Such a theory is more or less implied by Anaximander and Heracleitus, but it was clearly formulated, in very definite terms, by the Pythagorean school. You remember the passage in Virgil's Fourth Eclogue where a new Argonautic expedition is contemplated and a second Trojan war:—

atque iterum ad Troiam magnus mittetur Achilles.

That is the cyclical doctrine, and logically it applied to small things as well as great. I may illustrate it in the vivid manner of the philosopher Eudemus. According to the Pythagorean theory, some day I shall again with this manuscript in my hand stand here in this hall and lecture on Polybius, and you each and all will be sitting there just as you are this evening; and everything else in the world will be just as it is at this moment. In other words, the cosmical process consists of exactly recurring cycles, in which the minutest occurrences are punctually repeated. We do not remember them— if we did, they would not be the same.

But the cyclical doctrine was not, perhaps, generally taught in this extreme form. Polybius does not appear at first to have held even the universal validity of the law of growth, bloom, and decay. He considered that it holds good of simple constitutions, pure monarchy, for instance, or pure democracy, but he thought that the setting in of decay could be evaded by a judicious mixture of constitutional principles. He has submitted to a minute analysis the Spartan and the Roman systems of government, as eminent examples of the union of the three principles of monarchy, aristocracy, and democracy, compounded in such a way that they balanced one another and mutually counteracted the separate tendencies of each to degenerate. The Spartans owed the idea of their mixed constitution to the happy divination of the genius Lycurgus, the Romans attained to theirs through the school of experience. In other words, the Spartan constitution was an invention, the Roman was a growth. From these premises, which are largely untrue, Polybius deduced the exceptional permanence of the institutions of Sparta and Rome, and evidently thought that they defied the law of degeneration. It may be noticed that the superiority of a mixed constitution was not a new idea.

In other passages, however, Polybius speaks in a different tone. He sacrifices the theory that Rome owed everything to her mixed constitution, by admitting that her government was aristocratic when she reached her greatness in the time of the Second Punic war. It was a mechanical and wholly inadequate theory, even if the facts on which it was based had been correct— even if Rome *had* possessed a constitution in which the equilibrium of the three constitutional principles was maintained. In abandoning it Polybius was forced to recognise that the secret of life did not lie in a mechanical adjustment of the parts of the state, and to admit that there was no guarantee that Rome herself would not decline. But what induced him to abandon it? Undoubtedly his observation of the revolutionary movements in the time of the Gracchi. These movements came as a great surprise to him; nothing could have seemed to enjoy a more secure stability than the fabric of the Roman state in the days when he began writing his book. But the Gracchan revolution opened his eyes. Its significance was brought home to the friend of Scipio by Scipio's assassination. These stormy years flashed a lurid light on the past, and Polybius could now look back with illuminated vision and see in the agrarian law of Flaminius (232 B.C.) the beginning of the degeneration of the people. Without touching what he had written before, he introduced into his work new paragraphs which meant the surrender of his former belief in the permanence of the constitution. He now recognised that Rome, too, was destined to decline, and he could consequently accept unreservedly the principle of anacyclosis. Stoic teaching may have gradually prepared him for this change of theory; and Scipio assuredly had not been blind to the signs of the times. The revolutionary outbreak illustrated the melancholy prediction which he heard from the lips of his friend on the ruined site of Carthage:—

> . . . . Some time will come the day
> Of doom for Troy divine and Priam's sway,
> And Priam and his folk shall pass away.

More than an epitaph on Carthage, it was a prophecy on Rome.

Both Polybius and Thucydides, as I have already observed, held with equal conviction that the first obligation of a historian is to discover and relate facts as they actually occurred, and herein they both represented a reaction against the history which held the field. Each alike feels that the purpose of his work is to be instructive and not to be entertaining. Polybius is fully aware that for the majority of the reading public his work will have no attractions; it is intended for statesmen, not for antiquarians or people who want to be amused. Just as Thucydides is conscious that his conception of how history should be written is opposed to that of Herodotus, so Polybius repudiates the fashion of historiography which was in vogue, and denounces the rhetorical effects or exciting sensations of the works which were most popular, such as those of Timaeus and Duris. He is severe upon Phylarchus for introducing into history effects which are appropriate to tragedy. Phylarchus was always "forcing the note." He was ever attempting to arouse the pity and sympathy of the readers by pictures of despairing men and dishevelled women, children and aged parents, embracing, weeping and making loud lamentation, in the extremity of woe. Tragedy and history, says Polybius severely, have different objects. The aim of tragedy is to move the soul; but the aim of history is to instruct the mind. Again, just as Thucydides ignores all the gossiping anecdotes which memoir-writers like Ion and Stesimbrotus collected, so Polybius condemns writers of a later day for retailing what he calls the "vulgar babble of a barber's shop"— what we should call the gossip of the clubs, or the canards of the daily press.

Polybius then represents a return, though not a conscious return, to the principles of Thucydides and a reaction against some of the most conspicuous tendencies which had marked historiography in the interval. But Thucydides exercised no direct influence upon him, and the extant parts of his work indicate that he was not one of the historians with whom he was familiar. Polybius has been affected by the speculations in political science and by the schools of philosophy, no less than by the changes in the political world which had come to pass since the lifetime of Thucydides. Any one who turns from one to the other is struck by the salient contrasts between their methods of treatment. Thucydides is an artist, Polybius is a teacher. Thucydides, as we saw, employs the objective treatment of a dramatist, and rarely comes forward himself to address directly to the reader brief criticisms or explanations. Polybius on the contrary is entirely subjective. He is always on the stage himself, criticizing, expounding, emphasizing, making points, dotting the *i*'s and crossing the *t*'s, propounding and defending his personal views. Thucydides did all his constructive work beforehand, and presents to the reader only the syntheses and results. Polybius takes the reader fully into his confidence, and performs all the processes of analysis in his presence. Thucydides states in a few sentences the plan of his work, indicates in a few lines his principles of historiography; and his rare criticisms on other historians are confined to a word or two. Polybius devotes pages to an exposition of the scheme of his history, at the outset, and reiterates it in another place. At the end of his work he gave a chronological scheme of the whole plan. He had commenced with the intention of supplying an epitome of contents at the beginning of each Book, but afterwards preferred to place at the beginning of each Olympiad a summary of the events which occurred in it. He thus showed a kindly solicitude that the reader should fully understand the construction of his work. He goes, at length, into the proper principles and methods of history, frequently returning to the subject, and he digresses into elaborate criticisms of other historians, such as Timaeus and Phylarchus, Ephorus and Theopompus. He is unsparingly didactic and his diffuse explanations are often wearisome. This feature, as to which he stands in marked contrast to the early historians, may partly be set down to the influence of popular philosophy, which tended to promote a didactic style. We might indeed say that the history of Polybius contains the material for a handbook of historical method; and this adds greatly to its value for us.

Like Thucydides and the ancients in general, Polybius believed in the eminent significance of the individual in history. He reiterates the platitude that one mind is more efficacious than a mass of men, quoting the saying of Euripides, "One wise plan prevails over many hands." He takes a deep interest in the characters of the men who appear on his scene. On the other hand, he sees that there are potent forces at work besides great men. A student of the history of Rome, which had won her supreme position, unsteered by single men of transcendent powers, could not be blind to this. Polybius recognises the importance of national character. He considers the influence of climate upon it, and finds a key to a nation's character in its institutions and political life. We have seen the importance which he ascribed to the mechanism of political constitutions. But he had no idea of history as a continuous progress, no eye for what we call historical tendencies, no notion of the way in which historical changes are brought about by the innumerable and almost invisible activities of thousands and thousands of nameless people. He possessed a knowledge of the facts and conditions of his own age, and of the men of his own age, to which we could not attain even if we had his whole work in our hands. Yet, fragmentary as our knowledge is, we can say with some confidence that we have a deeper insight than he into the tendencies of his time, and of the time

immediately preceding, and a clearer comprehension of the change through which the Roman state was then passing and of the causes at work. He never discerned how the new circumstances of Rome in the latter half of the third century were altering her commercial and economic condition, and were already modifying the character of the state. We owe our power of divining this to the enlarged experience of the human race.

To return to his treatment of individuals. While Thucydides leaves us to form our own impressions from their public acts and from the words which he makes them say, Polybius, in accordance with his method, analyses and discusses their qualities. But it is important to observe that he does not, like Xenophon in the *Anabasis,* and nearly all modern historians, attempt to draw complete portraits of Philip or Hannibal or Scipio, or any of the leading persons of his history, but condemns on principle such a mode of treatment. For, he says, men are inconsistent: they constantly act in a manner which belies and contradicts their real nature, sometimes under the pressure of friends, at others on account of the peculiar complexion of the circumstances. It is therefore misleading to characterize a man when he first appears on the stage, or to infer his whole character from particular acts. The right method is to criticize his actions as they occur. The same man must be praised as well as blamed; he is changed by vicissitudes of affairs; his conduct, for instance, may become better or worse. Characters such as that of Philip III. of Macedon, which seems to have specially attracted him as a problem, impressed him with the necessity of adopting this principle; and in the treatment both of Philip and of Hannibal we must admire the conscientious fairness of Polybius in endeavouring to understand and estimate their characters.

Psychology indeed was a subject on which Polybius seems to have reflected much. We can see his interest in it, for example, in the account which he gives of the mental process of learning to read; in his observation that in fighting those have an advantage who have a stronger will to conquer, so that a battle is in a certain measure a contest of wills; in his insistence on the importance of personal experience . . . ; or in such a remark as that change from one kind of activity to another is a relief. His psychological ideas have furnished material for a treatise to a German scholar. One principle must specially be noticed because he applies it to his own work: the importance of connecting the unknown and remote with the known and familiar. For instance, he considers it useless to mention the names of strange places, which are mere sound conveying no meaning, unless they are brought into relation with the geographical knowledge which is familiar to the reader. He does not omit to make observations on the psychology of the masses. Their chief characteristics he considers to be ignorance and cowardice; and therefore religious feeling is important for them, because they cannot endure surprises or face dangers without hope from the gods. The only use of mythology is to preserve the religion of the multitude. Polybius does not hold that religious belief has any value for the educated person; it would be superfluous in a state consisting exclusively of wise men. But he certainly did not underrate its importance in actual societies. He designates religion as the keystone of the Roman state.

> Polybius . . . stands out among the few ancient writers who understood the meaning and recognised the obligation of historical truth and impartiality.
>
> — *J. B. Bury*

In general, it may be said that Polybius is large-minded in his judgments and aims at scrupulous fairness. While he applies ethical standards to the conduct of public men, his broad study of human nature inclines him generally to the more indulgent view of their acts. Perhaps no ancient writer was more impartial in temper than he, and the prejudices which we can detect are exceptions to the rule. These prejudices are chiefly to be discovered where he deals with the affairs of Greece. Here his patriotism has unquestionably coloured his account of Achaean politics, and he is distinctly unjust to the Aetolians. The danger of such partiality did not escape him. "A good man," he says, "should be fond of his friends and of his country, he must share in the hates and affections of his friends. But when he undertakes to write history, he must forget these attachments, he must often bestow the highest praises on enemies when facts require it, and, on the other hand, censure severely his most intimate friends when their errors demand such censure." Elsewhere, in censuring two Rhodian historians (Zeno and Antisthenes) for twisting facts to the credit of their country, he discusses the question whether a historian should allow himself to be influenced by patriotic feelings. "Admitting," he says, "that historians should lean to their countries, I deny that they should make assertions inconsistent with facts. We writers must unavoidably fall into many errors through ignorance, but if we write what is false, for our country's sake or to please our friends or to win favour, and measure truth by utility, we shall discredit the authority of our works and be no better than politicians." The indefeasible claim of historical truth cannot be more explicitly expressed or emphatically enforced; and the significance of these passages lies in the challenge which was thrown down to the prevailing practice of the rhetorical school of history. But Polybius has not absolutely adhered himself to his admirable doctrine. He is disposed to make their attitude to the Achaean League the measure for judging other Greek states. On the other hand, he is impartial towards Rome. The justification of Roman dominion is the *motif* of his work, and the practical lesson for his fellow-Greeks was acquiescence in that dominion. But if he fully recognised the great qualities of the Romans, his Greek sympathies secured him from being blind to their faults.

Polybius, then, stands out among the few ancient writers who understood the meaning and recognised the obligation of historical truth and impartiality. Belonging to no school, he opposed the tendencies of the current historiography of the day. But while he protests against straining after pathetic effects and such bids for popularity, he shows occasionally that he possessed the art of telling a moving tale, as in his description of Hannibal's passage of the Alps, and he can display powers of realism in describing an insurrection at Alexandria or the Mercenary war of the Carthaginians. But there is no attempt at striking word-pictures or purple passages; when he is effective, he succeeds, like Herodotus, by the simplest means. He followed the received usage of inserting speeches, and laid stress upon their importance. But he held that they should reproduce the tenor of what was actually said, and he censures Timaeus severely for having invented orations entirely out of his own imagination. Some of the speeches have a Polybian flavour, but we are bound to believe him that he had always evidence to work upon in their construction. . . .

Kurt von Fritz (essay date 1954)

SOURCE: "Polybius's Principles of Historiography and His Theory of the Origin of the State," in *The Theory of the Mixed Constitution in Antiquity: A Critical Analysis of Polybius's Political Ideas*, Columbia University Press, 1954, pp. 40-59.

[In the following excerpt, von Fritz compares elements of Polybius's political thought with the ideas of Aristotle, Plato, and the Stoics.]

It was Polybius who coined the expression "pragmatic history" or "the pragmatic method of historiography," yet the meaning of "pragmatic," as Polybius uses it, is not quite identical with, though it is closely related to, the meaning which the term has acquired in modern times. In coining the new term Polybius wished to set off his own method against other methods of which he disapproved, and the full meaning of the term as he uses it is, therefore, to some extent determined by this contrast to other prevailing trends in the historiography of Polybius' own time and of the preceding century.

Polybius was strongly opposed to the dramatizing type of historiography which had developed especially since the time of Alexander the Great, though its less pronounced beginnings can be traced back to the early fourth century. This type of historiography fulfilled to some extent the functions of the novel in modern literature. It catered to a public which demanded from history entertainment at least as much as enlightenment. In its later phases this type of historiography was apparently also influenced by Aristotle's famous statement, made in connection with his discussion of tragedy, that poetry is more philosophical than history. By dramatizing history many historians of the Hellenistic age believed that they could raise history to the level of poetry. They also believed, though in varying degrees, that by tampering occasionally with factual, but purely accidental, truth, they could attain that higher and timeless truth which, in Aristotle's opinion, is the domain of poetry.

To all this Polybius was most strongly opposed. History, in his opinion, had above all to tell the truth, the important truth to be sure—Polybius would probably have shaken his head over a modern pragmatist like Cornford, who asserts that to the true historian any ascertainable fact must be equally important as any other ascertainable fact—but important factual truth and nothing but what is true. But if Polybius was opposed to the dramatizing type of historiography, he also despised the scholarly historian who derived all his knowledge exclusively from books and documents, who had never had any personal political experience, and who would not even take the trouble to interrogate the real actors on the political scene, to cross-examine eyewitnesses, to obtain firsthand knowledge of the practical working of political bodies such as the Senate in Rome, or to visit the places in which the historical events about which he wrote had taken place. "Plato," he writes,

> has said that human affairs will be well attended when either the kings become philosophers or philosophers become kings, but I would say that everything will be well with history when practical statesmen turn to writing history, and not, as they do now, as an avocation but all through their lives with undivided intention and in the conviction that this is one of the most necessary and noble things they can do, or if those who wish to become historians consider a practical political training a prerequisite for their work.

Thus history, in the opinion of Polybius, should be written by practical statesmen, but it should also be written *for* men who are or wish to become political or military leaders; if other historians have written for entertainment, he wishes above all to write to serve this higher practical purpose. The range of what can be learned from history, he believes, is very wide. Of Jacob Burckhardt's famous dictum concerning the

purpose of history, "Wir wollen nicht klüger werden für ein ander Mal, sondern weise für alle Zeiten," Polybius would have emphatically accepted the second and positive part, but violently disagreed with the first and negative one. When a man sees that he cannot change the course of events, then he will draw consolation and fortitude from his knowledge of the past, which has taught him that similar misfortunes have always befallen men. This is the wisdom for all times that a man can learn from history: to brace himself against the sudden onslaughts of fortune, in the knowledge that much is happening in this world that even the keenest and best-trained mind cannot foresee or avert. This is also the reason why Tyche, or Fortune, plays such an extraordinarily large part throughout Polybius' work, and for the same reason it is unthinkable that he should ever have intended to exclude this concept entirely from his philosophy of history.

But Polybius also and most emphatically believes that history should make the statesman "wiser for another time" by teaching him to avoid the mistakes that others have made in the past. If such lessons are to be learned from history, it is necessary to be aware of what causes, controllable by human beings, produce what effects. This is why Polybius sometimes inveighs against those who explain everything by Tyche, or Fortune. That the statesman should learn from history to brace himself against the unpredictable but also to predict the predictable and to control it whenever this is possible sums up his fundamental philosophy on this problem, though Polybius nowhere expressed it exactly in this way.

The lessons of this second kind that can be learned from history are again manifold and cover a very wide range. They begin with purely technical matters, as for instance in the field of military engineering, where one can learn that a surprise attack on a city may fail simply because the ladders prepared for climbing the walls are not long enough. The lessons extend to military tactics and strategy, a subject on which Polybius has much to say whenever he deals with wars and battles, as well as to discussions on the advantages and disadvantages of citizen armies and armies of mercenaries, and, finally, to the highest problems of sound policy. Not everything, however, is either entirely unpredictable or subject to direct human control. Often the statesman, trained by history, will be able to predict that certain causes will have certain effects, but cannot change the causes. In such cases his ability to foresee the future will enable him to adapt himself to inevitable changes and to avoid catastrophes that would otherwise befall him. In making it possible to predict changes of this kind, history, in Polybius' opinion, has made the greatest progress, "so that those who are eager to learn from history are now able to deal methodically with almost any contingency that may arise."

The historian, therefore, must not be content with presenting the facts truthfully; he must also, and primarily, inquire into causes. In discussing the causes of the Second Punic War, Polybius makes a threefold distinction, which, he believes, every historian ought to make, and which, in fact, historians have very widely accepted. The distinctions are: first, the real and underlying causes of an event, which often may precede the actual event by many years or even decades; second, the reasons or pretexts given by the statesmen or political leaders for their decisions, which, however, are but rarely identical with their real motives, much less with the deeper causes of an event; and, finally the beginning of a great event, that is, those happenings and actions which precede an event directly and which to a superficial observer may appear to be its causes—as for instance, in case of a war, the breach of a treaty, a quarrel over certain rights, or the violation of a boundary. In dealing with the first type of cause, which is of course by far the most important one, Polybius makes a further distinction between what may be called the active or driving motive (as, in the case of the Second Punic War, the dissatisfaction of Hamilcar after the First Punic War and the Carthaginians' indignation over Roman encroachments in Sardinia) and the circumstances which caused the driving motive to result in action at a given moment (as the belief of the Carthaginians that their power had increased sufficiently to give them a chance of success in a renewed war with the Romans).

The relation, then, between Polybius' theory of historical causation and his political theory is quite clear. One of the most important types of primary causes in history, in his opinion, consists in the power constellations existing at any given moment. These power constellations in their turn are greatly influenced by the stability or instability of the internal political structure of the states involved. The degree of stability can be largely determined on the basis of general political theory. Such a theory therefore will benefit the practical statesman in various ways. Polybius believes that, under certain favorable circumstances, a good constitution can be created by a wise statesman; when the opportunity occurs, political theory will then provide such a statesman with a sound theoretical foundation. But political theory will also enable a statesman to evaluate the stability or instability of states in which he has no influence. In fact, it will even make it possible for him, within certain limits, to predict in what way the constitution of a given state may develop in the future and to take his own measures in accordance with this foreknowledge.

Political theory derived from historical experience is thus a very essential part of "pragmatic history," as defined by Polybius, and deserves a central part in any historical work. Polybius expounds his general political philosophy in connection with a detailed analysis of the Roman constitution at the time of the battle of Cannae. Rome at this time appears to him to be the most perfect example of a well-balanced and stable political system that had yet been evolved in history. He inserted this discussion of the Roman constitution immediately after his narrative of the battle because he believed that it was chiefly due to the excellence of the constitution of their republic that the Romans were able to recover so quickly from this crushing defeat and to conquer the greater part of the inhabited world within hardly more than fifty years after Cannae.

Polybius begins the exposition of his political theory by taking issue with those teachers of political science who speak only of three types of constitutions: monarchy, or one-man rule; oligarchy, or minority rule; and democracy, or majority rule. In each of these three cases, he believes, a further distinction should be made between government by consent and according to law on the one side and arbitrary or lawless rule on the other. By making this distinction one arrives at a sixfold division: kingship and its counterpart, tyranny; aristocracy and its counterpart, oligarchy; democracy and its counterpart, ochlocracy or mob rule.

In fact, this sixfold division was not altogether new. All its essential features can be found in Plato's dialog *Politicus,* which was written about 360 B.C., with the one exception that Plato states that arbitrary and lawless majority rule and democracy based on laws are called by the same name, while Polybius uses the term ochlocracy for the depraved form and democracy for the legal form. Since "ochlocracy" is not found in Greek literature before Polybius now extant, it is quite possible that he invented the term himself, though he may equally well have picked it up from discussions current in his time. It is of course futile to attempt to identify those "teachers of political theory" who, according to Polybius, were satisfied with the distinction between monarchy, oligarchy, and democracy, since these simple terms had been widely used in a general and vague sense ever since the fifth century B.C. at the latest, just as they continue to be used up to the present day. The point that Polybius wants to make in connection with his sixfold division is that, though kingship, aristocracy, and democracy, in contrast to tyranny, oligarchy, and ochlocracy, are all in a way good constitutions, or rather good types of government, they are all necessarily unstable, since each of them easily and even inevitably degenerates into a depraved type. Hence, the problem is to find a type of government which is free from this weakness of all simple forms of rule; the solution is a system which combines all the three fundamental types, that is, a mixed constitution.

To prove his point Polybius has first to demonstrate why the simple forms of political rule are necessarily unstable, and this leads him to the problem of the origin of the state. In order to solve this problem he imagines, as Plato for similar reasons had done in his *Laws,* that a great catastrophe had destroyed all human communities and only a few scattered individuals had survived. Then he asks the question: What agent in such circumstances would make these individuals seek out one another to form a community, and what form of government would they be likely to adopt? His answer is that the agent is the weakness . . . of the individual when left to his own devices, and he points out that this same agent makes many animals which are impotent and defenseless as individuals live together in herds. He uses this analogy to draw the conclusion that just as animals in a flock or a herd take the strongest and bravest animal among them as their leader, so human individuals, when they first formed a community to defend themselves against wild beasts and against aggression on the part of individuals or groups of their own kind, undoubtedly flocked around the strongest and bravest of their group, seeking protection in his leadership. The first and original form of some kind of human political community, therefore, is the rule of the strongest, or a kind of monarchy.

It is interesting to compare Polybius' theory with the theories of his most famous predecessors. Both Plato and Aristotle had asked the question: What agent makes human beings live together in political communities? Both had given an answer somewhat different from the one given by Polybius. They found the fundamental motive not in weakness . . . but in a lack of self-sufficiency. . . . This lack of self-sufficiency includes, of course, physical weakness as one of its aspects, but not the most important one. . . .

There can be no doubt that Polybius was familiar with Plato's *Republic.* The extent of his knowledge of Aristotle's latest and most mature political thought is less certain. It is most improbable that he knew his *Politics,* though he probably knew the works of some of Aristotle's disciples on political theory. But it is sufficient to be sure that he must have been acquainted with the theory that the lack of [self-sufficiency] in the individual human being was the cause and origin of human society in order to ask why Polybius not only replaced this theory by the assertion that the origin of the state is to be found in weakness rather than in a lack of self-sufficiency, but does not even so much as mention the earlier theory.

In fact, Polybius and his predecessors differ not only in the answer which they give, but to some extent also in the question which they ask. Both, to be sure, wish to explain the "origin" of the "community" in which human beings are accustomed to live. But Plato and Aristotle wish to explain, above all, the "origin" of the differentiated society in which we, as individuals, have

different functions, and which enables us through this arrangement to become and to be human beings in the fullest sense, while Polybius wishes to explain why we live in a community in which there exist certain definite power relations among the individuals.

In these different contexts the word "origin" also assumes somewhat different meanings. Plato in the first part of his discussion describes a simple and "primitive" society, so primitive indeed in its spiritual needs, or rather in its lack of spiritual needs, that Glaucon in the dialog says that he finds it difficult to see in what way this society differs from "a pigs' state." Yet this society, with its weavers, tailors, shoemakers, toolmakers, metalworkers, architects, export-import traders, and shopkeepers, is much more differentiated than the most primitive societies of which we know, and in this sense "more advanced" in its material culture. Plato can hardly have been unaware of this fact. Thus, when he asks "What is the 'origin' . . . of human society?", he obviously does not mean to ask the "historical" question, "For what reasons did human beings *first* band together?" but rather, "What is the fundamental or primary agent that makes them live together as they now do?" In other words, he aims at an analytical rather than a historical construction. It is different with Polybius. He too, in discussing the "origin" of the human community, does not relate ascertainable facts, but his is a historical construction, an attempted answer to the question "What made human beings *first* band together?" and in this context the answer "weakness" is not inappropriate. Nor is his reconstruction of the most primitive form of "political power" inappropriate. In very primitive societies physical prowess and distinguished bravery in combat are still indispensable qualities of a chieftain or a ruler. Even in the *Iliad* or the old Slavic or Germanic epics the physical strength and the daily demonstrated bravery of all leaders and rulers played a very great role.

What Polybius tries to reconstruct is a state much more archaic and primitive than the society described in the Homeric or similar epics. In terms of Aristotle's philosophy one might say that Polybius tries to reconstruct that phase in an evolutionary process when human society "comes into existence for the sake of bare physical survival," while both Plato and Aristotle try to lay bare the foundations of a human society that "exists for the sake of the good life." This difference has rather far-reaching implications.

Greek political terminology does not clearly distinguish between what we call society and what we call the state. The word "polis," which Plato and Aristotle use in the context discussed, means primarily the city community, in its wider sense any political community, or to use the modern terminology, the state *together* with its social foundation or understructure, while the word "politeia," which Polybius uses, designates the political structure of such a community, or, more specifically, the distribution of competences and powers in such a community. It is evident that when Plato in the *Republic* and Aristotle in his *Politics* speak of the *origin* of the polis, they are thinking primarily of human society and only at a much later point in their discussions come those problems which concern what we would call the state. But does Polybius speak of the "state," if we assume that a *state* presupposes an administrative machinery and the existence of more or less fixed institutions regulating the power relations between the different elements of the body politic? Since, in contrast to Plato and Aristotle, he thinks from the beginning in terms of power relations, one may say that Polybius speaks of the germ from which the state was ultimately to develop, but not of a state in the full sense of the word.

Closely related to this is the further difference that Plato and Aristotle, when they discuss the origin of society, begin with the question of "happiness" and "the good life," and only at a much later stage arrive at the problem of the stability, internal strength, and external success of different types of states, while Polybius begins at once with this latter question. In modern times Plato and Aristotle have often been characterized as idealists, and Polybius has sometimes been contrasted with them as the first "realist" among political philosophers. Polybius himself would certainly have agreed with this estimate. The term "pragmatic," which he coined for his historiographical method, though of a somewhat wider meaning, includes what we mean by the term "realistic." Polybius refused to consider Plato's ideal state on the same level with states that had had a concrete historical existence, and his own concept of the best state or the best constitution was not a construction of something that had never existed and may never exist, but was directly derived from actually existing states such as Sparta and Rome.

Yet this distinction between the idealists Plato and Aristotle and the realist Polybius is rather superficial. In the last phase of the development of Aristotle's political philosophy the question of the best state, though not completely abandoned, recedes rather into the background and is largely replaced by a more empirical study of the means of improving existing constitutions under various historical circumstances and of making them more stable. Yet it is exactly in this same and latest phase of Aristotle's development as a political thinker that the inquiry into the social or "societal" foundations of the state, and with it the question of "the good life," play a fundamental role in his whole political theory. In fact, it is not difficult to see that the necessity of inquiring first into the general anthropological foundations of human society in order to arrive at a complete and sound theory of the state is quite independent from the search for an "ideal" state.

One may ask, therefore, whether a political theory that concentrates exclusively on the power relations existing in a state, and this in terms of more or less clearly defined competences, can be really quite realistic, or, more precisely, whether a theory conceived in such narrow terms can even correctly evaluate the power relations themselves and the stability of the system to which they belong. This question can be answered only in much later stages of the present inquiry and on the basis of the historical evidence provided by the history of the Roman constitution.

The second step in the original development of the state, according to Polybius, is the transition from the rule of the strongest and bravest to true kingship, which is based on the administration of justice. This is at the same time a transition from a condition that is common to human beings and other gregarious animals to a type of community which only human beings are capable of organizing. Such a transition becomes possible because man, unlike other animals, lives not only in the present but also in the future. His ability to reason from the present to the future is the source from which the notion of a moral good ultimately springs, and with it the possibility of a human community or state based on and devoted to the preservation of justice. The growth of this state out of the notion of justice is described in the following fashion.

When, for instance, adult human beings see that children who have been brought up with great care and pains by their parents do not show gratitude and do not take care of their parents when they have grown old, then even those who are not directly concerned will be indignant over the children's behavior. They will be indignant because they realize that if children in general behave this way, then they themselves will not be taken care of in their old age. Thus they are aware that it is in the interest of everybody that children be punished if they do not pay back the debt of gratitude they owe their parents. Similarly, if a man harms a person from whom he has formerly received help and support, there will be general indignation because everybody applies the case to himself. Thus, the notion of gratitude as a socially desirable attitude or a "moral good" is formed, and such is generally the origin of all moral concepts.

Once the moral concepts have become firmly established in a community they will have a profound influence on the form of the state and of the government. If the man who, because of his strength and his bravery in fighting the enemies of the community, has become the leader and the ruler of the human herd always supports the general sentiment in questions of "justice" and decent behavior and uses his strength to force the recalcitrant and "unjust" members of the community to live according to rules derived from these concepts or sentiments, then the majority of the people will retain him as ruler; they will even support him by their combined strength after he has grown old and has lost that physical strength and power through which, in the beginning, he had obtained the first place in the human herd. It is in this way that the primitive monarchy of the strongest is gradually replaced by the kingship of the just. This kingship tends to become hereditary, because people expect the children of a just and wise father to develop the same qualities and so be fit to become kings. So far Polybius' theory.

The notion of the just and wise judge as the natural ruler was widespread in the ancient Orient; it appears for the first time in Greek literature in the guise of an Oriental story. This story, as told by Herodotus, differs in some respects from Polybius' version. When the Medes, so the story goes, had freed themselves from Assyrian domination, they lived for some time in complete liberty. But this liberty led also to much lawlessness. A man by the name of Deiokes, who was hungry for power and wished to become a tyrant, realized that he could use this situation for the attainment of his aspirations. Within a lawless world he decided to be straightforward and just and to work for justice within his village. After some time his fellow townsmen made him their judge, and as the fame of his justice spread, more and more people from distant places came to ask him to act as arbitrator in their quarrels with one another. After this had gone on for some time and he had become famous all over the country, he suddenly declared that he could not continue to neglect his own affairs in order to serve as arbitrator for others. When the lack of his former services was severely felt everywhere, the Medes came together and decided to make him king, since under his rule there would be law and order in the country. Deiokes accepted on the condition that they would build him a strongly fortified place and grant him a military force under his exclusive command. This granted, he built himself an extremely strong fortress, introduced a very strict court ceremonial, and withdrew from all direct contact with the people. He had his supervisors and his spies everywhere in the country and was very harsh in enforcing a rule of strict justice.

There is an interesting difference between Polybius' historical construction and Herodotus' story, which is, of course, also a historical construction, in the guise of a story. In the first case the chieftain, who owes his chieftainship originally to his physical strength and bravery, *retains* his power when his strength is gone because he has used it to defend justice, while in the second case power not possessed previously is *acquired* through the administration of justice. But the idea which is common to both reconstructions, namely, that a renown for justice may give power, is not altogether lacking in sound historical sense.

Still more important, however, is Polybius' theory of the origin of human morality and of the notion of justice. According to Polybius the notion of justice originates from the ability of human beings to reason and to realize in advance that the harm which is done to another human being may also be done to themselves if such conduct is generally acknowledged as unobjectionable by everybody. It is very widely assumed that Polybius took over this theory of the origin of morality and of the notion of justice from the Stoic philosopher Panaetius of Rhodes, who like Polybius himself was a friend of the younger Scipio and with whom Polybius may have been well acquainted in his later years, though this cannot be proved. The reason for this assumption lies in the fact that the passage in which Polybius develops his theory about the origin of the notion of justice has a close parallel in a passage in Cicero's treatise *De officiis,* which, according to Cicero's own testimony, is based on a work of Panaetius.

It is, however, characteristic of Polybius that he derives morality and the notion of justice, together with the emergence of a society in which the principle of justice is enforced, *exclusively* from enlightened self-interest and the ability to reason by analogy about the future. In consequence of this ability men are indignant when they see that children do not pay back the debt of gratitude they owe their parents. The question of why the parents have done so much for their children in the first place remains undiscussed, but since Polybius does not mention any principle except enlightened self-interest, one would have to assume that they do it in order to have someone who will take care of them in their old age. This, however, is no longer in agreement with Cicero-Panaetius, who continues in the very next sentence with the assertion that "nature" has made human beings in such a way that they love not only themselves but also their offspring, their wives, their family, and generally their fellow human beings with whom they have to live. Here, then, the egotistic principle of enlightened self-interest is clearly supplemented, though not completely replaced, by the altruistic principle of a natural love of various degrees for other human beings, without which genuine gratitude could not even come into existence. For if the parents take care of their children only in order to have someone take care of them in their old age, the children may still keep this bargain because they, in their turn, wish to be taken care of by their children. But in such a bargain there is hardly more room for a feeling of personal gratitude than in the relation of a man to his life insurance.

The one-sided application of one of Panaetius' principles to the exclusion of the other is neither Panaetian nor Stoic. In fact, if one looks for an explanation of the origin of the state as a guarantor of justice purely on the basis of enlightened self-interest, it is to be found in Epicurean rather than in Stoic philosophy; it is an Epicurean doctrine that natural justice must be derived from an agreement concerning that which is useful or advantageous for everybody, namely, agreement not to harm others on the condition of not being harmed by them. Nobody, as far as I know, has yet claimed that Polybius was an Epicurean, and this for very good reasons. For much in Polybius' philosophy of life, especially his positive evaluation of the active life, the life of the practical statesman, and his notion of honor, which has found expression in many parts of his work, are absolutely irreconcilable with Epicurean philosophy.

If, then, a strong agreement with Epicurean doctrines in his theory of the origin of a society which protects justice does not make Polybius an Epicurean, it is no more permissible to regard him as a Stoic or a Panaetian because of the agreement of one of his statements made in the context of his theory of the origin of the notion of justice with a statement that in all likelihood goes back to Panaetius. The relation of Polybius to Stoic philosophy, to be sure, is somewhat stronger than his relation to Epicureanism and deserves somewhat closer attention since it is characteristic of his relation to philosophical theories and systems in general. Polybius uses a great many terms that play a central role in the philosophy of Panaetius and of his Stoic predecessors. But he uses such terms with a meaning frequently quite different from the meaning which they have in Stoic philosophy. . . .

Two basic concepts in Stoic ethics are the notions of "the beautiful" . . . and "the useful" or "the expedient". . . . The concept of "the beautiful" has a wider meaning in Greek, and especially in Greek philosophy, than in most modern languages. It means everything that calls forth spontaneous and disinterested admiration. It can therefore also be applied to the moral field, where it designates any action that evokes spontaneous and disinterested approval, as in someone risking his life to save someone else's, but also outstanding honesty in all matters. Thus, "the beautiful" in this sense can be equated with what we would call "the moral good." Its opposite is "the ugly" or "the shameful" . . . , that which calls forth spontaneous disapproval. It is, then, one of the most fundamental tenets of Stoic moral philosophy that what is morally bad or shameful can never be really useful or expedient, since the harm that such action does to the soul of its perpetrator is much greater than any profit that he can derive from it. In fact, the older and sterner school of Stoics contended that such external goods or profits, even if acquired honestly, are no goods at all, but indifferent. . . .

Though Panaetius deviated from old Stoic orthodoxy in several respects, there can be no doubt whatever that he retained its doctrine according to which there can be no real clash between the morally good or

beautiful and the useful or expedient, since nothing can be expedient that is not at the same time morally good. This is proved by the fact that Panaetius, according to Cicero, intended to write a book in three parts, the first on the morally good or beautiful, the second on the useful or expedient, and the third on the apparent conflict between the morally good and the seemingly expedient. This last section (which was not completed) was to show that there could be only an apparent, not a real, conflict between what is good in itself and what is good or expedient for an individual or for a group.

The manner in which Polybius uses these Stoic terms is then most significant. When speaking of Philopoemen he says that

> the morally beautiful and the expedient come very rarely together, and there are few people who can bring them into harmony with one another. For we all know that most of the time the morally good is far removed from immediate expediency and vice versa. But Philopoemen made this his aim [that is, to bring them into harmony] and he actually achieved it, for to bring back [to Sparta, their home country] the exiles who had been captured by the enemy was a most beautiful deed, and to weaken or subdue that Lacedaemonian city was most expedient [for the Achaean League].

This whole paragraph, with the exception of the last sentence, might well have been written by a Stoic, though it does not follow the strictest Stoic terminology. A Stoic like Panaetius might very well have said that it is most difficult for an ordinary man to bring the morally good and the expedient into harmony because it is not easy to realize that the seemingly expedient is not expedient if it is not morally good. But when we come to the last sentence we are suddenly in an entirely different world. True, it was one and the same action of Philopoemen, which resulted in the weakening of Sparta, an event most expedient from the Achaean point of view, and which at the same time made it possible for Philopoemen to do "a fine thing" by bringing the Spartan exiles back into their home country. But these two results are merely incidental to one another; and this kind of reconciliation of the "morally good" with the politically expedient is certainly often excellent policy, but it has no more to do with Stoic than with Christian ethics.

All this is most characteristic of Polybius' relation to Stoic philosophy and to Greek philosophy in general, with which, as a further analysis will show, he was very familiar. He uses the concepts, terms, and theories of the philosophers as his intellectual tools with which to describe and, so to speak, to dissect reality as he sees it. But fundamentally his viewpoint remains that of a historian and of a practical statesman whose guiding principle is "good realistic common sense," and not absolute logical consistency. It is quite possible that he was not conscious of the fact that he used the Stoic theory concerning the relation between the morally beautiful and the expedient in such a way as to reveal himself to be miles away from true Stoic doctrine.

There is, however, another point that requires further elucidation, and this will lead back to Polybius' theory of the origin of the notion of the moral good and of the state as a guarantor of justice. The rationalism of Polybius' attempt to derive the moral notions exclusively from enlightened self-interest and the ability of calculating from the present to the future agrees perfectly with the rationalism of his theory of religion. If all human beings had enough of that calculating ability there would be no need for religion, since everybody would behave decently out of enlightened self-interest. But since this is not so, it is good that the common crowd should believe in the gods and in divine punishment, and the wise man therefore will consider religion one of the greatest supports of the state, even though he is not a believer himself. This is his opinion where he deals with the question ex officio, so to speak, and on a purely theoretical level. But reading his whole work one discovers that on some occasions he makes concessions to the belief in divine powers, though in a somewhat skeptical and tentative fashion, while on still other occasions he shows a spontaneous indignation over violations of sacred objects that does not seem to be quite in agreement with his theoretical convictions.

The same inconsistency can also be seen in the moral field, where the moral *indignation,* which he ascribes to the men who first observed ingratitude in children and which in his history he himself often expresses over many things, does not seem to agree completely with his assumption that the moral concepts are derived from purely rational calculations. But these are not the only cases in which a certain discrepancy between his purely rationalistic opinions and his somewhat less rationalistic convictions or sentiments can be observed. There is another instance in which Polybius uses the Stoic concepts of the "beautiful" and the "expedient" in a not quite Stoic fashion, though in this case the deviation from true Stoicism is in a different direction. When he speaks of the fate of Carthage and Greece in the fateful year 146 B.C., he says that one should consider the fate of the Greeks, who (through their own folly) came under the domination of Rome after a crushing defeat but survived, more pitiful than the fate of the Carthaginians (who were completely exterminated), unless one pays no attention to what is befitting and "beautiful" and bases his judgment merely on what is "useful." Here, once more, the Stoic terms appear, and in an entirely different context. Yet again they are not used entirely in the Stoic sense, for the "beautiful" here has rather the meaning of tradi-tional honor; this is not quite what this concept meant to the Stoics, though they approved even of suicide if a man could no longer live in agreement with Stoic principles. But this would hardly have applied to the Greeks in general after 146 B.C.

Thus, while the use of the term "the beautiful" in this passage deviates to some extent from genuinely Stoic usage, it nevertheless, through the notion of "the beautiful" in the sense of the glorious, the noble, the honorable, also brings in an element that is foreign to the rationalistic theory of the origin of morality and justice which Polybius expounds in the sixth book. This theory is built exclusively on the notion of the "useful" or the "expedient," that is, on the same criterion which in the passage on Carthage and Greece appears as so much lower than the criterion of "the noble."

This shows again conclusively that on the purely theoretical level Polybius has a strong tendency to think exclusively in terms of power relations, of political expediency and political success, and of enlightened self-interest, but that this absolutely pure rationalism is sometimes alloyed with other elements that have their origin partly in traditional notions of honor and the like, partly in very genuine but less rationalistic feelings. The introduction to his third book shows that in his later period the "beneficial" became a criterion along with success. But this is hardly sufficient reason to explain all the apparent and real discrepancies in Polybius' moral philosophy as evidence of different phases in his development; and it will be seen that in the political theory expounded in the sixth book there is but very little evidence of the viewpoint which Polybius, according to his own testimony, adopted when he set out to write the last ten books of his work.

F. W. Walbank (essay date 1957)

SOURCE: In *A Historical Commentary on Polybius, Vol. 1,* Oxford at the Clarendon Press, 1957, pp. 1-37.

[*A British Professor of ancient history and classical archeology, Walbank is the twentieth century's most noted authority on Polybius. In the following excerpt, Walbank provides an introduction to the life and works of Polybius, focusing in particular on his view of history and his use of the concept of* Tyche *(Fortune).*]

1. *Polybius' Life and Journeys*

Born about the end of the third century at Megalopolis, Polybius spent his first thirty years acquiring the military and political experience of an Achaean statesman. His father Lycortas was an eminent politician, a follower, though hardly (as has been suggested) a relative, of Philopoemen. In 182 the young Polybius was selected to carry the ashes of Philopoemen to burial, and some time later he wrote his life. The boy's up-bringing was shaped by the family's position as rich landowners. His interest in military matters is shown by his lost book on *Tactics,* and by many digressions in the *Histories;* he was also much given to riding and hunting. His knowledge of literature was not extensive; the occasional quotations from the poets frequently suggest the use of a commonplace-book rather than first-hand acquaintance, and his philosophical studies too were of a limited character. Despite . . . references to Heracleitus, Plato, Aristotle, Demetrius of Phalerum, and Strato of Lampsacus, he shows little evidence of deep study of any of these writers; and the philosophical background in book vi seems to lie mainly in recent or contemporary popular writers rather than in the original minds of the fourth and third centuries. On the other hand, he had obviously read closely and critically the historians of his own and preceding generations, such as Timaeus, Phylarchus, Theopompus, and Ephorus.

Of Polybius' career between Philopoemen's death and the Third Macedonan War only a little is known. In 181/0 the Achaean Confederation designated him one of three ambassadors to visit Ptolemy V Epiphanes in Egypt, . . . but the trip was cancelled when the king suddenly died, and he next appears as Hipparch of the Confederation for the year 170/69. This was a critical moment in his country's history. Involved in an irksome war with Perseus of Macedonia, the Romans were carefully watching all Greek states for signs of disloyalty. Polybius has left a detailed defence of his behaviour; but his family tradition was one of maintaining an independent, if friendly, attitude towards Rome, and in 170 independence among Greeks was a quality little respected by the Senate. In the purge which followed the downfall of Perseus Polybius found himself one of a thousand eminent Achaeans who were summoned to Rome, ostensibly for examination, and subsequently detained there without any pretence of justice.

Once at Rome, Polybius was more fortunate than most of his colleagues. Soon after his internment began, and while he was still in the city, he had the good fortune to attract the attention of the 18-year-old Scipio Aemilianus. The acquaintance, which took its origin 'in the loan of some books and conversation about them', quickly ripened into friendship, and when shortly afterwards the other internees were distributed into custody among the municipal towns of Italy, Polybius received permission to stay on in Rome, where he became Scipio's mentor and close friend. His position was now highly ambiguous. Technically a foreign internee, he enjoyed friendship on equal terms with men like Aemilianus, his brother Q. Fabius, and the whole of their brilliant circle. In this company he made the acquaintance of the Seleucid prince Demetrius, and did not hesitate to encourage and support his plans to escape from Italy. Cuntz has argued that until the rem-

nant of the internes was amnestied in 150, Polybius will have been restricted to Latium under pain of death; but there was all the difference in the world between allowing him to return to Greece, where he could exercise political influence, and letting him leave the boundaries of Latium and even Italy in responsible company in order to make journeys in the west.

It seems in fact probable (though it is a hypothesis not susceptible of complete proof) that the journeys which Polybius made 'through Africa, Spain, Gaul, and on the ocean that lies beyond', are to be dated in part before his release from internment. The evidence . . . suggests that Polybius accompanied Scipio to Spain in 151, when he acted as legatus to the consul Lucullus, that during his stay in Spain he went with Scipio to Africa, where he met Masinissa, and that he crossed the Alps on his way back to Italy. In 150, thanks to the influence of Scipio and the acquiescence of Cato, the internes were released, or at least the three hundred of them who still survived. Polybius had barely had time to reach Arcadia when a request arrived from the consul for 149, M'. Manilius, to proceed to Lilybaeum . . . ; he readily obeyed, but when at Corcyra he received reports which suggested that the Carthaginians had accepted the Roman terms, he returned home. After the war again flared up, however, he joined Scipio at Carthage and was present at its fall. It was probably in 146, shortly afterwards, that he undertook the voyage of exploration in the Atlantic, which carried him both down the African coast and some way up that of Portugal. . . . He is known to have been at Corinth shortly after its destruction; but this event cannot be dated with accuracy, and an Atlantic voyage may have been a welcome distraction from the embarrassment of being in Achaea at the headquarters of a Roman general operating against the Confederation.

The *Histories* enable us to follow Polybius' movements for the next two years. He spent the rest of 146 and part of 145 working to secure as favourable a settlement as possible in Greece, and he visited Rome once more in the course of these negotiations. After that it becomes impossible to attach dates to his journeys. He was at Alexandria sometime during the reign of Ptolemy Euergetes II (Physcon), but whether in the company of Scipio or not cannot be determined. At some equally uncertain date he was at Sardes, where he met the Galatian Chiomara, and he may have visited Rhodes. During these years he undoubtedly spent some time in the company of Scipio. Cicero makes Laelius say that Scipio, Polybius, and Panaetius had frequently discussed together problems of the Roman constitution; but when such conversations are to be dated—whether at Carthage or on some subsequent occasion, such as Scipio's eastern embassy—remains quite obscure. It is often assumed that Polybius accompanied Scipio to Numantia; but his personal acquaintance with New Carthage, and Scipio's inquiries in Gaul (probably incited by Polybius), can equally well date to the earlier Spanish journey of 151/0, for the composition of a monograph on the Numantine War is no evidence that Polybius himself took part in it, when approximately seventy years old. . . .

Polybius died, according to the author of the *Macrobioi*, from a fall off a horse at the age of 82; the authority is not impeccable, but the statement would fit reasonably well into the other data on Polybius' life, and may be accepted.

2. *Polybius' Views on History*

At the outset of his work Polybius indicates its double purpose: it is to provide useful training and experience for the practical politician, and at the same time to teach the reader how to bear the vicissitudes of Fortune, by describing those that have befallen others. Throughout the **Histories** both aspects are repeatedly stressed. The discussion in book iii on the distinction between causes, pretexts, and beginnings is specifically directed towards the statesman, and it is as something essential for statesmen as well as students that he includes his account of the Carthaginian treaties. The description of the Gallic invasions of Italy is designed especially to teach those who direct the fortunes of the Greeks how to cope with such attacks. It is, in particular, statesmen who can correct their own conduct by a study of the change in character displayed by Philip V, and statesmen (as well as students) who will profit from the account of the Roman constitution. . . .

In several places Polybius expatiates upon the superior merits of universal history. None of his contemporaries and virtually none of his predecessors had attempted history of this sort. Yet it is only from universal history that one can gain a proper notion of cause and effect and estimate the real importance of events, and so understand and appreciate the work of *Tyche*. It is true that universal history acquires a special significance from the hundred and fortieth olympiad, since from that date events themselves had taken on a universal character, and the history of the various parts of the inhabited world had coalesced into an organic whole; but Siegfried is hardly right in thinking that universal history is proper only to the period with which Polybius is concerned. . . . The position is rather that universal history, while always preferable, had now become the only form capable of treating the period which opened in 220. . . .

In the course of his work Polybius succeeds in conveying a fairly comprehensive picture of what he regarded as the prerequisites for the writing of [political history]. In an elaborate comparison between the career of medicine and that of the historian, he defines the latter's task as the study and collation of memoirs and other documents, acquaintance with cities, districts, rivers, harbours, and geographical features generally, and finally experience of political activity; and of these the last two are essential, for one can no more become an historian by studying documents than one can become a painter by looking at works of former masters. The essential thing is to see the sites, so that one can, for example, test out the account of a battle on the spot, and as far as possible to interview those who actually took part in important events . . . . Equally, no one can write about fighting and politics who has not had some experience as a soldier and as a practical politician. It is on personal experience that Polybius lays his main emphasis . . . and above all on personal inquiry. . . . 'It will be well with history', he writes, adapting Plato's famous words 'either when statesmen undertake to write history . . . or when those proposing to become authors regard a training in practical politics as essential to the writing of history.' He could put forward this thesis with the greater confidence because he had himself made many voyages, and played an active part as a politician and a general.

The object behind this programme of restless activity was to get at the truth. 'Truth is to history', Polybius writes, 'what eyesight is to the living creature.' If history is deprived of truth, all that remains is an idle tale. . . . One of the main objections to the sensational history of such writers as Phylarchus is that it obscures the truth and so prevents the reader from benefiting by what he reads; and it is a great fault in Timaeus that he puts out false statements. What would be permissible in panegyric is quite out of place in history; and Polybius contrasts his own treatment of Philopoemen in his encomium on the hero with that in the **Histories,** where he has tried to apportion praise and blame impartially. In general, only absolute truth is to be tolerated in history; and the problem of securing it Polybius sees partly as one of scale. As the writer of a 'universal history' he is critical of those who work on a smaller canvas. The fault of the special study, the monograph, is that it puts things out of perspective, and does not allow the reader to see events in their proper proportions, and so to appreciate the continuous nexus of cause and effect; it is also an incentive to its author to exaggerate the importance of his own topic and material. On the other hand, the very magnitude of his task perhaps renders the universal historian more liable to the occasional factual slip or misstatement; if this should unfortunately happen, it is excusable, and such errors should be treated, not with the bitterness and virulence displayed by Timaeus in his attacks on Ephorus, Theopompus, and Aristotle, but with the kind of charitable good nature which led Polybius himself to write to Zeno pointing out his errors . . . unfortunately after the book was already published and so too late for Zeno to correct them.

In two situations Polybius was prepared to allow exceptions to his general rule. Certain historians had reported miraculous happenings in connexion with the statue of Artemis Cindyas at Bargylia and the temple of Zeus in Arcadia. 'To believe things which are beyond the limits of possibility', comments Polybius, 'reveals a childish simplicity, and is the mark of a blunted intelligence.' On the other hand, such statements may contribute towards sustaining a feeling of piety towards the gods . . . and if so they are excusable, provided they do not go too far. . . . This admission may seem shocking, but it hardly affects Polybius as an historian, since he was little concerned with miracles and not in any case writing for the common people. More dangerous is his concession to patriotism. 'I would admit', he writes, 'that authors should show partiality towards their own country . . . but they should not make statements about it which are contrary to the facts.' The concession is carefully hedged about; but it is clear that Polybius availed himself of it in his own work. The extent of his bias can easily be exaggerated. It has, for example, been alleged [by Edson, in *AHR,* 1942] that Polybius' picture of Philip V is distorted in order 'to motivate and thus to excuse the Achaean League's declaration of war on Philip in 198 B.C.'; and the fragment 'on traitors and treachery' (xviii. 13-15) has been quoted as evidence for the violent controversy which surrounded the Achaean decision. The digression on treachery was, however, evoked by the handing over of Argos by Philip to Nabis of Sparta in the winter of 198/7. Certainly there is a hint at Aristaenus' decision to have the Achaean League declare war on Macedon: Polybius wishes to make it quite clear that this was not treachery according to his definition. But there is no evidence for a storm of controversy. Polybius needed to provide no elaborate *apologia* for the Achaeans, since only an insignificant minority queried the wisdom of the official policy.

It is much more in the hostile treatment he accords to opponents of the Achaean League that Polybius' [partialities] appear. His venom towards Aetolia has long been noted and needs no illustration; and if the hostile picture of Cleomenes of Sparta and the distorted account of Aetolian machinations in the decade before the Social War go back to Aratus' *Memoirs,* Polybius must shoulder the responsibility for swallowing his version uncritically, as well as for many anti-Aetolian *obiter dicta.* Recently it has been demonstrated that political prejudice has also produced a completely false picture of conditions in third-century Boeotia; the account of social decadence in xx. 5-7 can be refuted from the evidence of contemporary coins and inscriptions, and is to be interpreted as a reflection of Achaean hostility. Frequently, too, Polybius' assessment of a situation is determined by the attitude of those concerned in it towards Achaea or Rome. How far in all these instances the bias is consciously applied it is difficult to say; but Polybius' willingness to grant something to patriotic prejudice probably rendered him less alert to the risks he was running.

Another field in which practice fell short of theory was in the speeches which, following Greek tradition, Polybius included at intervals throughout his *Histories;* some thirty-seven survive, and several times Polybius makes it clear that such speeches should represent the actual words of the speaker. It was the custom of Hellenistic historians to set rhetorical compositions in the mouths of their characters, and Polybius condemns this wholeheartedly in Timaeus. 'A writer who passes over in silence the speeches made and the reason (sc. for their success or failure) and in their place introduces false rhetorical exercises and discursive speeches, destroys the peculiar virtue of history.' Similarly Phylarchus tries 'to imagine the probable utterances of his characters' instead of 'simply recording what was said, however commonplace'; and both Chaereas and Sosylus are roundly condemned for setting down versions of rival speeches made in the Senate on the question of war with Carthage, when they had no access to a reliable source. There is certainly a proper place in historical composition for speeches 'which, as it were, sum up events and hold the whole history together'; but they must give what was actually said. . . . In fact Polybius does not always come up to the standard he sets. The long report of the speeches delivered by Flamininus, Philip V, and the other participants in the conference held in Locris in the winter of 198 has all the marks of being derived from a verbatim account of the meeting, and may be accepted as authentic. But once he went outside the scope of Achaean and Roman records, Polybius is unlikely to have had access to much reliable material for speeches, and must have drawn largely on earlier literary accounts or the uncertainties of an oral tradition; this probably helps to explain why many of his speeches, and especially such pairs as those of Hannibal and Scipio before Zama, read like a series of commonplaces. But he never concedes to the historian the right to improvise, and it would be unjust to assume that he consciously composed rhetorical exercises for inclusion in his *Histories.* Set occasions *are* apt to produce commonplaces, and people's speeches, like their actions, are often governed by prevalent attitudes and traditions. Polybius is therefore entitled to our confidence that he made a determined effort to discover what was actually said . . . and that any failure here and there is due to practical shortcomings rather than a deliberate betrayal of principle.

There is, however, another field in which Polybius sometimes appears to fall short of the standards implied in his criticisms of others. His attacks on various of his predecessors—Timaeus, Phylarchus, and others—for a style of presentation that is inaccurate, sensational, and full of expressions of wonder, has already been mentioned. But it was so deeply rooted a feature of historical writing in the Hellenistic period that Polybius allows it to influence his own presentation to a greater degree than his professions would suggest. . . .

A slight concession (in principle) to politic piety and (in practice) to local patriotism, a limited success in retailing the real contents of some of his reported speeches, a readiness to embrace the terminology (but not the emotional attitudes) of 'tragic' history in the interest of . . . moral edification—these probably represent the sum of what a critic of Polybius' truthfulness can assemble. They amount in total to very little, and leave the overwhelming impression of a reliable and conscientious writer, with a serious theme and a determination that at all costs his readers shall comprehend and profit by it.

3. *Tyche*

The role in history which Polybius assigned to *Tyche* is notoriously hard to define. He regarded the study of the past as essentially a means of attaining practical ends by learning lessons; but the value of such lessons is seriously reduced if the sequence of cause and effect is at the whim of some incalculable and capricious power. On the other hand, the lessons of history were moral as well as political, and one important moral lesson lay in learning how to meet those vicissitudes which demonstrably occurred in every man's life. To have left these out of his **Histories** would have falsified the observed course of human events. It would also have deprived Polybius of much of his purpose in writing at all. Unfortunately in discussing these vicissitudes he made use of a word familiar to his contemporaries, but to us (and probably to them too) exceptionally ambiguous because of the variety of its meanings and the difficulty of deciding which is present in any particular passage.

It is clear that in many places the word *Tyche* is used quite loosely. . . . When, for instance, the Mamertines took possession of the wives and families of the men of Messana . . . the sense is simply 'as they happened upon them'. Such examples can be neglected; they reflect current colloquial usage, and have no special significance. Elsewhere, however, the introduction of *Tyche* seems to mean something rather more, and fortunately a passage survives in which Polybius discusses the occasions when *Tyche* may properly be invoked. 'In the case of things of which it is difficult or impossible for mortal men to grasp the causes,' he writes, 'one may justifiably refer them, in one's difficulty [to Fortune]; such things are heavy and persistent rain, drought destroying the crops, outbreaks of plague, in short what would today be termed 'acts of God'. But in general one should not be prompt to ascribe to *Tyche* events for which a cause can be found.

This passage reserves for the workings of *Tyche* the area which lies completely outside human control and those events of which the causes are not easy to detect or for which there are apparently no rational causes at all. Clearly 'acts of God' and irrational or fortuitous acts of men are not identical; but they have this in common, that they stand outside the sphere of rational analysis. . . .

It is well known that Polybius' concept of cause and effect is somewhat one-sided, and fails to allow adequately for the interaction of events and the dynamic and dialectical character of almost any train of causation. This may help to explain why happenings which are external to the particular sequence of cause and effect with which he is concerned are often attributed to *Tyche,* though there may be a perfectly rational explanation of them in their own context. . . .

Within the field thus assigned to *Tyche* it might logically seem that events of any kind might be regarded as her handiwork; but in practice she is restricted to certain contexts. In particular, events of a sensational and capricious character are attributed to her. Often she will decide great issues by a narrow margin; thus the Illyrian invasion which compelled Antigonus Doson to march north came just too late to save Cleomenes. Or a great general, Epaminondas or Philopoemen, having risen to success on his merits, may be defeated through no fault of his own. . . . In such cases, *Tyche* may justly be censured. Her caprice is especially liable to precipitate a sudden reversal of men's lot. Thus *Tyche* caused Hannibal to be crucified on the very cross on which Spendius had died, apparently for the sake of ironical contrast. At Medion the Aetolians debated in whose name they should dedicate the spoil they were going to win; but *Tyche* showed her power inasmuch as they were themselves obliged to concede spoils to the Medionians. Sometimes this reversal of fortune is vividly illustrated, as on the occasion when Callicrates' portraits were carried away into the darkness on the same day that those of Lycortas were brought out, so that people observed that 'it is the characteristic function of *Tyche* to bring to bear in turn on the lawgivers themselves the very laws they originated and passed'. This capricious and irrational force allows no one to prosper indefinitely; and recognizing this Demetrius of Phalerum was able to foretell the downfall of Macedon, a prophecy which greatly impressed Polybius, who witnessed its fulfilment.

One of Polybius' main moral lessons is the need for moderation in success, in the light of this instability of fortune, and the certainty that no prosperity can last. The events at Medion, the fate of Achaeus or Perseus, the contrast of the pictures of Lycortas and Callicrates, and the fate of Hasdrubal at Carthage evoke the same trite homily with monotonous regularity; sometimes it comes from Polybius' own mouth, sometimes in the words or behaviour of some historical figure—Antiochus weeping at the downfall of Achaeus, remembering the inconstancy of *Tyche* (just as Scipio Aemilianus was to weep over the sight of burning Carthage, and for the same reason), Scipio himself pointing to the wretched Hasdrubal exactly as his father Aemilius Paullus had moralized over the vanquished Perseus, the Punic envoys before Zama urging moderation on the Romans. . . . It is the mark of a great man to have learnt this lesson; both Scipio and Hannibal came up to this test, whereas Philip V, and the Spartans after the Peloponnesian War, failed.

Polybius implies that the reversal which is bound to follow upon prosperity will come because that is the way things happen, the way of *Tyche,* regardless of any steps we may take. It is in the nature of prosperity that it does not last; and the reason for behaving moderately is not to avert the blow, but simply that moderate conduct is more fitting to a man and may help to secure mitigation of one's lot when misfortune comes. . . . It is the instability of fortune which he makes his theme; and indeed it was morally more edifying to have men behave with moderation in prosperity because it could not in any case last, than to have them moderate because they were afraid lest arrogance might precipitate disaster.

Slightly different is the concept of *Tyche* as a power which punishes wrongdoing. For example, she punished the Boeotians for the unhealthy state of their public affairs. . . . The Spartan ephors, who had been bribed to make Lycurgus king, were murdered by Cheilon. . . . [This concept] is also used of Philip and Antiochus, who after their nefarious plot against the dominions of the infant Ptolemy, were led on by *Tyche* to attack the Romans, and so met ruin and defeat; their dynasties perished, while that of Ptolemy was revived. The action of *Tyche* against Philip is developed at length. As if to punish him, she sends against him a host of furies, which lead him into a succession of acts culminating in the destruction of his own son, a sign of divine wrath. Here *Tyche* takes on a purposive character, which is also evident when the sacrilege committed by Antiochus Epiphanes and Prusias meets speedy vengeance in the form of death or disaster.

Close in attitude to this are several passages in which *Tyche* seems to approximate to something like Fate or Providence. *'Tyche',* writes Polybius, 'is for ever producing something new . . . and for ever playing a part . . . in the lives of men, but in no single instance has she ever put on such a show-piece as in our own times', with the rise of Rome to world-dominion in fifty-three years. [This] passage, as Warde Fowler observed, . . . suggests that *Tyche* is here conceived as a power working to a definite goal, the domination of Rome. . . . It does, of course, create a difficulty, on Polybius' definition of *Tyche* as a power which restricted its activity to that sphere which is not amenable to reason; for the whole of his history is based on the assumption that Roman success can be explained in rational terms. 'By schooling themselves in vast and perilous enterprises',

he writes, 'it is perfectly natural that they not only gained the courage to aim at universal dominion, but executed their purpose'; and the sixth book is written mainly in order to analyse the role which the Roman constitution played in Roman success. . . .

Consequently, in attributing Roman success both to calculation and rational causes and, simultaneously, to the overriding power of a *Tyche* which comes close to 'providence', Polybius raises a problem which has stirred up much debate and evoked many attempts at a solution. One answer has been to postulate a development in his beliefs: beginning as a believer in the capricious *Tyche* of Demetrius of Phalerum, he later came round to the view that [Tyche] was merely a convenient label to cover a gap in our knowledge, and, in Cuntz's opinion, ended up a complete rationalist who would allow nothing to be without its cause; alternatively, he began by attributing Roman success to prowess, but subsequently came to believe in a *Tyche* which meant rather different things at the different stages of the ideological development which this theory postulates. The fatal objection to such views is that they not only build up a preconceived system by an arbitrary division of passages, but that in each case they are obliged to separate passages which despite apparent contradictions can be shown to be closely linked together. For example, the ideas of *Tyche* as a capricious, and as a just, retributive power are fundamentally contradictory. But Polybius can write without any feeling of awkwardness: 'Who of those who reasonably find fault with *Tyche* for her conduct of human affairs, will not be reconciled to her when he learns how she later imposed on Philip and Antiochus the fitting penalty, and exhibited to those who came after, as a warning for their edification, the exemplary punishment which she inflicted on the above-named kings?' Clearly it is the same *Tyche* which is now just and now capricious; and it is consistent with this that the metaphor of *Tyche* as the play-producer is applied both in contexts where mere change and sensational incident are uppermost, and in those where the concept is that of providential design. . . .

This absence of well-marked divisions between the various uses of a word which, by its very history, had become singularly ill-adapted to the conveying of clear and precise thoughts is against any theory which would assign these different usages to different periods of Polybius' mental development. It is equally against the theory of Siegfried, who sees Polybius as a man 'with two souls in his breast', switching easily and without inner conflict from a scientific, rational, view of a universe subject to the law of cause and effect, to a religious attitude which sees history as the working out of a plan by an external power of *Tyche*. This bisection is not plausible as a psychological account of Polybius, as one comes to know him in his work; nor is it adequate as a treatment of the evidence, for the contradictions in Polybius' account of *Tyche* are not one but several. The various conceptions merge one into another; and it often appears as if the particular aspect of *Tyche* which Polybius invokes in any instance, no less than the extent to which he allows *Tyche* to be introduced into the situation at all, depends in part at least upon his own sympathies in the matter, and upon how far he is removed from the incidents he is describing. When, for example, the Macedonians rallied behind Andriscus with such will and vigour that they even defeated the Romans, their perversity placed them outside the range of comprehensible conduct, and Polybius dismisses it as what might be called a heaven-sent infatuation. . . .

To a large extent, therefore, the personality with which Polybius invests *Tyche* is a matter of verbal elaboration, helped by current Hellenistic usage, which habitually spoke of *Tyche* as a goddess; and this helps to explain many of the inconsistencies, for consistency is not essential to a rhetorical flourish. With regard to his main theme, however—the work of *Tyche* in making Rome mistress of the world in fifty-three years—one must allow for at least the possibility that as he looked back on this startling and unparalleled process Polybius jumped the step in logic between what had happened and what had had to happen, and so in a somewhat muddled way invested the rise of Rome to world power with a teleological character; in so doing he probably fell a victim to the words he used and to his constant personification of what began as a mere hiatus in knowledge. Certainly the use of teleological expressions in i. 4. 1-3 points in that direction. But if this is so, it remains equally true that Polybius had neither the clarity in philosophical thought nor a sufficiently fine sense of language to enable him to isolate the contradiction in his ideas. The word *'Tyche'* was already corrupted when he adopted it; as Erkell observes, it covered all the gradations in sense between a sharply defined philosophical concept and a hazy, outworn cliché, and Polybius was not the man to find a lonely way across the morass. Consequently, to the question whether he believed in an objective power directing human affairs, the answer cannot be an unqualified 'No'; but in so far as it is a qualified 'Yes', his belief was neither sufficiently strong nor sufficiently clear for him to recognize any inconsistency with his normal, rational formulation of the character of *Tyche*.

This is perhaps unsatisfactory; but Polybius' lack of clarity can be paralleled in other writers. Shorey quotes the hesitations of Plato, who in the *Laws* attributes a great role to *Tyche* yet insists on the control extended by Providence over the minutest details, of Julian the Apostate, of Dante, and of Renan, all of whom at times admitted Fortune illogically into their philosophical schemes. This discussion may conveniently close with an extract from a contemporary historian [Chester Wilmot, in *The Struggle for Europe,* 1952], 'The putsch would have succeeded if Hitler had not been saved by what can only be regarded as a miracle. It was mere chance that on 20 July the midday conference should have been held in a flimsy wooden hut, and not in the usual concrete bunker, where the explosion would have been deadly.' The author of this passage was habitually a clear and factual writer. The equivocal and contradictory terms in which he comments on an incident sensational in itself and fraught with fatal consequences are perhaps not without relevance to the problem of *Tyche* in Polybius.

4. *Polybius' Sources*

The vast literature which exists on Polybius' sources is perhaps disproportionate to the results it has achieved; and the chief reason for this is that for the main part of his work Polybius has used a great variety of material, much of it no longer identifiable, and has woven it into a close and homogeneous fabric in which the separate threads are not now distinguishable. Both the character of this material and Polybius' method of dealing with it are alike described in the course of his work with complete and typical frankness. In a passage in book xii, already quoted, the preparation of the historian is defined as the study and collation of written sources, acquaintance with relevant sites, and political experience; but in the same book Polybius explains that the most important activity, at any rate for recent and contemporary history, is the questioning of as many as possible of those who participated in the events. . . . From this it follows that the introductory books i and ii must necessarily fall into a different category from the *Histories* proper. They are admittedly derivative, and based wholly on written authorities. Here, to an extent unnecessary for the later books, Polybius finds it important to discuss the merits of these authorities and to explain what amount of confidence he places in them. On the other hand, neither his inclination nor ancient historical practice led him to indicate how closely he followed them nor the points at which he passed from one to another.

Four historians receive special mention in books i and ii. They are Aratus and Phylarchus on Greek events, and Fabius Pictor and Philinus for the First Punic War. Aratus is explicitly given as the source for the Cleomenean War, though Polybius does not conceal the omissions which are to be found in his *Memoirs;* the rejection of Phylarchus is justified at length, but he appears nevertheless to have been used occasionally in default of other evidence. In contrasting Fabius and Philinus, Polybius' sympathies are less closely engaged; he recognized both to be honourable men, and uses their accounts to check each other. That Philinus was also his source for the Carthaginian Mercenary War is improbable; but Fabius is likely to have been used for the account of the Gallic Wars in book ii as well as for later events. These four writers, however, cover neither the whole of the contents of the introductory books nor yet the many digressions in the main part of the work which draw on incidents taken from earlier periods in Greek history. For the preliminaries of the First Punic War, including the rise of Hiero of Syracuse, Polybius probably followed Timaeus; and Timaeus was very probably his source for the digression on the Pythagoreans in south Italy as well. This is not rendered less likely by the violent and even malevolent attacks on Timaeus in book xii and elsewhere, for criticism of an author by Polybius did not exclude use of his works. Callisthenes, for instance, is severely attacked in book xii, but Polybius uses him for a digression on early Messenian history, and probably for references to the Spartan seizure of the Cadmea in 382 and the peace of Antalcidas. Ephorus too was both criticized and used. Though he is the object of polemic in several parts of book xii, he is mentioned with approval on various occasions, and Polybius may have used him in book iv for the passage dealing with the wealth and neutrality of Elis. Theopompus is also criticized, but there is no evidence that Polybius used him as a source.

These are in general the authorities to which Polybius turned for his account of events before 220. When he comes to his main narrative in book iii, written sources are still very important, though here—and no doubt increasingly in the later books—they are supplemented by other material. For the Hannibalic War Fabius continues to be used. But it seems reasonable to assume that in addition Polybius read as widely as possible among writers on both the Roman and the Carthaginian sides. Of these he mentions two, as usual censoriously; they are Chaereas, and Sosylus of Lacedaemon, who retail 'the gossip of the barber's shop'. But there were others, too, writing about the Hannibalic War in Greek, and mainly from the Carthaginian side: Silenus of Caleacte, who like Sosylus accompanied Hannibal on his expedition, and may well be Polybius' source for the Carthaginian campaigns in Spain before Hannibal set out for Italy, Eumachus of Naples, and Xenophon. The latter two are no more than names; and from such references as iii. 47. 6 it is apparent that there will have been others, of whom not even names now survive. On the Roman side we are rather more fully informed. L. Cincius Alimentus, who was praetor in Sicily in 210/9, and was taken prisoner by Hannibal, wrote a history of Rome from the earliest times which helped to fix the senatorial tradition for the Hannibalic War; like that of Fabius it was in Greek. He will hardly have been overlooked by Polybius. The histories (also in Greek) of C. Acilius will perhaps have been used for the later part of the Hannibalic War; but if they were published about 142, as seems likely, they must have appeared too late for Polybius to use them for the years down to Cannae. Also available, and equally certain to have been read by Polybius, was [a work by] A. Postumius Albinus, the consul of 151, whom he censures sharply for his vanity, loquaciousness, indifferent Greek, and love of pleasure. There is, however, no indication in the text of how Polybius used these or other Roman historians writing in Greek; nor is it clear whether he drew on Cato's *Origines,* for, as De Sanctis points out, if books i to xv were written before 146, he will scarcely have been able to utilize for this part of his work Cato's later books, which were in all probability published after their author's death. Another possible Latin source is L. Cassius Hemina, who may have published his first three books before 150; but almost nothing is known about him or the contents of his work. Ennius Polybius may have read—*Annales* ix and x dealt with the Second Punic War—but there is no evidence for use of him in the ***Histories***.

For his account of the Greek East, Polybius' written sources are even more obscure. For events round about the end of the third century he quotes the Rhodian historians Antisthenes and Zeno as typical of writers of 'particular histories' covering that period, and deserving special regard because they were Rhodian statesmen. Zeno was the author of a history of Rhodes, but this probably contained wider material used by Polybius; he is likely to be the source for the events in Crete and Sinope in book iv, and for the chapters on the earthquake of 225 in book v. Polybius criticizes his accounts of the battles of Chios and Lade, of Nabis' attempt on Messene, and of the siege of Gaza and the battle of Panium, and relates with satisfaction his own letter to Zeno correcting them. But for other names one has to fall back on conjecture. There were, for example, writers of monographs on Philip and Perseus and their wars with Rome; they included a certain Strato, and the Poseidonius mentioned by Plutarch in his *Life* of Aemilius Paulus. As Mioni observes, there were many local historians, whom Polybius' general contempt will not necessarily have precluded him from using. The writers on Hieronymus who are criticized at vii. 7. 1 may have included Baton of Sinope, who was probably his contemporary. . . . Polybius mentions the public career of Ptolemy of Megalopolis; he may have made a limited use of his anecdotal and scandalous history of Ptolemy Philopator for Egyptian events, including the death of Cleomenes. But the complicated picture of the use of sources which seems to emerge from a comparison between the treatment of the events associated with Cleomenes' death in Polybius and in Plutarch shows how little can be ascertained about the literary sources for the greater part of the ***Histories***.

Moreover, Polybius' written sources were not limited to published histories. He is the more ready to criticize historians of Scipio Africanus' achievements in Spain and Africa, who attribute his success to Fortune and the gods, because he had had the advantage of drawing directly on the evidence of his friend and close companion C. Laelius—though whether C. Laelius composed memoirs on the subject or merely talked to Polybius is conjectural. Still more valuable, he had at his disposal a letter sent by Africanus himself to Philip V of Macedon, in which he apparently dealt with his Spanish campaign and in particular his capture of New Carthage. . . . Such material as this, similar in genre to Aratus' *Memoirs,* and leading on to the memoirs and commentaries of the first century, may have been available to a wider extent than can be ascertained. It will have been supplemented by published speeches, such as that of Astymedes of Rhodes, which Polybius appears to have read, or Cato's famous speech on the Rhodians, which he inserted in the fifth book of the *Origines*.

Written material was also to be had in official archives, and Polybius made some use of these. He supports his polemic against Zeno and Antisthenes, who represented Lade as a Rhodian victory, by an appeal to the dispatch sent by the Rhodian admiral to the Council and Prytaneis 'which is still preserved in the Rhodian Prytaneum'. This may imply that he consulted the document himself; on the other hand, he does not say so, and it is equally possible that Zeno quoted it, but tried to draw from it conclusions unacceptable to Polybius. Schulte discusses a number of passages for which he is inclined, in the main following Ullrich, to see a source in the Rhodian record office. There is not one of these, however, which could not equally well have drawn on some other source, such as Zeno, and a direct use by Polybius of the Rhodian records has yet to be proved. For the Achaean records at Aegium the case is altogether stronger and more likely. It is conceivable that Polybius owes to a memorandum kept here his detailed account of the conference between Philip and Flamininus in Locris in 198. But it is no longer possible to assign passages to sources deriving from the Achaean record office with any degree of certainty. A similar use of Aetolian and Macedonian royal records has been alleged; neither source seems very likely. Indeed Polybius' main access to public records was at Rome, where there would be official accounts available of embassies sent or received by the Senate. Whether he himself consulted the Carthaginian treaties in the 'treasury of the aediles' or merely saw a version privately circulated is uncertain. But such passages as those giving the *senatus consultum* relative to the peace with Philip, or the terms of the peace with the Aetolians or Antiochus clearly go back to a documentary source, for which a Roman origin seems plausible. Another official source available at Rome was the *annales* of the pontifex maximus. It now seems established that the *annales maximi* were first published by P. Mucius Scaevola, who was pontifex maximus from 131/0 to a date between 123 and 114; but the material then published will have been available in

the form of inscriptions on the original wooden boards in the regia at an earlier date for any historian who wished to consult it, including Polybius. It seems doubtful, however, if the records of magistrates, elections, and commands, and the sacerdotal details which made up the contents of the *annales* will have been of great interest to him. Finally, mention should be made of the inscription on a bronze tablet, which Polybius himself discovered on the Lacinian Promontory, giving full details left by Hannibal of his numbers and troop formations. The use which he made of this shows that not too much attention need be attached to his gibes at Timaeus for his discovery of 'inscriptions at the back of buildings and lists of proxeni on the jambs of temples'.

Literary sources, official documents, and archives provide the framework of Polybius' history; but, as the passages quoted above make clear, the real business came in the questioning of eyewitnesses. It seems fair to assume that Polybius' insistence on this is not mere talk, and that he had in fact mastered and habitually used this specialized technique in order to ascertain what he wanted to know; indeed on occasion he appears to have enlisted his friends to make inquiries for him. Of the hundreds of informants who must in this way have contributed to Polybius' material and share the anonymous responsibility for a fact here and a mark of emphasis there few can still be identified. If C. Laelius gave Polybius his information orally, he was not the only representative of an older generation to be questioned. Whether the men 'present at the occasion' . . . of Hannibal's crossing of the Alps were Gauls, Greeks, or Carthaginians, we cannot say; but if Polybius met them after he came to Italy, they must already have been men of 70. He certainly talked to Carthaginians who had known Hannibal, and supplemented his information from Masinissa, who (probably in 151/0) discoursed on Hannibal's avarice as a particular illustration of a fault common to Carthaginians in general. Masinissa's son Gulusa is also mentioned as an informant, specifically on the use in parts of Africa of elephants' tusks as door-posts and palings, but almost certainly also for events connected with the Third Punic War.

Polybius' detention at Rome was no handicap in carrying out his interrogations. It was if anything an advantage; for, apart from the great concourse of internees and resident Greeks, there was a constant stream of ambassadors and other visitors from all parts of the Mediterranean, to whom it cannot have been difficult for Polybius to gain access. Thus he mentions Perseus' friends as informants on the negotiations between Perseus and Eumenes, which broke down through the avarice of the two kings; one of these was probably Pantauchus, the son of Balacrus, . . . who played an important role in the approach to Genthius. Both he and Hippias surrendered to the Romans after Pydna, and it seems certain that they and many other eminent Macedonians will have been brought to Rome. It was no doubt to some member of this group that Polybius owed intimate knowledge of affairs at the Macedonian court during the last years of Philip's reign. Besides Macedonians, there were assembled in Italy internees from most of the states of Greece. Since the thousand Achaeans fell in number to three hundred in sixteen years, they were evidently for the most part elderly men in 167, and so valuable informants on earlier events. Aetolians, too, like Nicander of Trichonium, could supplement the Achaean version from the opposite camp. Von Scala has many suggestions on informants both in Rome and elsewhere—Praxo of Delphi, Menyllus of Alabanda, Stratius the doctor of Eumenes, and a source for the affairs of Athamania and Zacynthus dependent on the close connexion between Amynander and Philip of Megalopolis; the case for some is plausible, but more often von Scala presses the details in a way which testifies only to his own fertile imagination. In any case a list of names is without significance. One has only to consider the multitude of highly placed informants who will have found themselves in Rome at some time or other during the years 167 to 150, and the host of others whom Polybius will have met and talked to during the years 145 to his death, when we know virtually nothing of his movements, to realize that the identification of half a dozen names means next to nothing. Faced with the anonymity of almost all his informants, Polybius' readers can only take on trust his facts and the exercising of his critical judgment in selecting them. . . .

Michael Grant (essay date 1970)

SOURCE: "Polybius," in *The Ancient Historians,* Charles Scribner's Sons, 1970, pp. 144-64.

[*A highly respected British classical scholar, Grant has published numerous books on ancient history for the general public as well as many scholarly works. In the following excerpt, he traces Polybius's role in political and military events of his time and briefly reviews the strengths and weaknesses of his political thought.*]

Polybius of Megalopolis in Arcadia (*c.* 200-118 BC) wrote a **Universal History** in his native Greek. We are told of the stages by which Rome had gained its dominion over the whole civilised world, achieving supremacy first over the western and then the eastern Mediterranean during the fifty-three years 220-168 BC. Polybius then goes on to describe the aftermath of those events, down to 144. The work is divided, by himself, into forty books. Of these, five have been preserved in their entirely. From the rest, we have excerpts of varying size, including a large part of Book VI, substantial

portions of VII-XVI, and smaller extracts and fragments from most of the others. Nearly a third of the whole history has survived.

The first book begins with an explanation of the supreme significance of the subject. There follows a sketch of the first Roman interventions among the Greek city-states of south Italy during the early third century BC. Some of these states appealed to the Carthaginians, who were Rome's competitors for the control of the western Mediterranean. This situation led to the First Punic War (264-241), which is spite of terrible losses was finally won by the Romans. Book II tells of the subsequent rivalry in Spain between the Romans and Carthaginians, who were led first by Hamilcar (d. 229/8) and then by his son-in-law Hasdrubal, followed after his death (221) by Hannibal who was Hamilcar's son.

The third book describes the outbreak of the Second Punic War, the most serious war in which Rome had ever been engaged. An account is given of Hannibal's crossing of the Alps into Italy, followed by his victories over the Romans at the rivers Ticinus and Trebia and then at Lake Trasimene and Cannae (218-216). Book IV is mainly concerned with Greek affairs, and contains a long geographical digression on the advantages of the site of Byzantium (Constantinople). The next book describes how King Philip V of Macedonia (238-179 BC) concluded a treaty with Hannibal which led him into hostilities against the Romans and thus helped to bring about their subsequent intervention in eastern affairs. The sixth book breaks off the story to discuss state constitutions and their relative merits. Polybius explains why he believes that the Roman constitution is the best, and why it comprised a major cause of Rome's greatness. The military system of the Romans is also analysed.

In Book VII the year 215 marked the beginning of an annalistic treatment. Henceforth events in east and west are described year by year, with deviations when necessary. Usually a whole or half Olympiad (four-year period) fills each book. Books VII-XV continued the Second Punic War to the climactic victory at Zama by Scipio the elder. The account is interrupted, in Book XII, by the prolonged attack on the historian Timaeus, which gives Polybius an opportunity to explain his own views about historical writing. Thus XII, like VI, marks a break which represents a division of the first part of the work into groups of six books, though later the groups vary in length.

Book XVI starts to recount the Second Macedonian War (200-197), and two books later there is a description of a confrontation in 198 between Philip v and Flamininus, the Roman general who subsequently defeated the monarch and announced the unreal 'liberation' of Greece. The work then went on to describe

Rome's decisive rebuff to the Seleucid imperialist Antiochus III at Magnesia in Asia Minor (190), followed in Book XXVI by the equally conclusive victory at Pydna over Perseus, King of Macedonia, Philip's son (168).

Polybius then carried out his supplementary plan, and described the events of the twenty-four years subsequent to Pydna. Books XXX-XXXV deal with the events of the next few years, and surviving excerpts include, in XXXI, a full portrait of Scipio Africanus the younger (Scipio Aemilianus). There was a geographical interlude in the lost Book XXXIV. The final books gave an account of Scipio's conquest of Carthage in the Third Punic War, and the sack of Corinth and destruction of the Achaean League by the Romans in the same year 146. The work concluded with the events of the two following years, and culminated in a sort of chronological recapitulation or index.

Polybius' birthplace the 'Great City', *Megale Polis* or as the Romans called it Megalopolis, had been founded between 370 and 362 under the influence of the Theban Epaminondas. Standing in a splendid setting on a plain ringed by mountains, it was designed to be the centre of an Arcadian League which should serve as a counterweight against Spartan influence in the Peloponnese. Forty villages were absorbed into the new foundation and most of the people of Arcadia became its citizens. Then, in 235/4, Megalopolis joined the much larger Achaean League, at that time controlled by its first great leader Aratus, and was made the meeting-place of the federal Senate and Assembly. Destroyed by the Spartans, the city was restored by the second Achaean hero, Philopoemen of Megalopolis, who abolished the military power of Sparta (188). Three centuries later the place was already a heap of ruins. The fragments which still survive include traces of the senate-house, and the remains of the largest theatre in Greece.

Polybius, himself the son of a politician of the Achaean League, was chosen as a youth to carry the ashes of Philopoemen to their grave (183). Shortly afterwards he wrote the life of the dead statesman, and carried on his policy of insistence that the Achaeans should be as independent as possible of their Roman protectors, and should take every possible step to retain a predominant position in the Peloponnese. In 169-168 Polybius held the federal post of Cavalry Commander, the second most important office in the League.

However, during the war which ended in the conquest of Macedonia by the Romans (168), his party had shown Macedonian sympathies. Consequently, he and a thousand other Greeks were ordered to Rome. Ostensibly they were summoned for examination, but they were detained for many years without trial. Polybius himself, however, was protected by the famous

Lucius Aemilius Paullus, conqueror of Macedonia, and by his son Scipio Aemilianus with whom he formed a close friendship. Although Polybius was able to travel within Italy, we do not know whether he could temporarily go outside the country or not. At any rate, an application to permit him to go back and live in Greece was turned down. It was not until 152 BC that the 300 survivors of the 1000 internees were allowed to go home. Polybius would have been able to go with them; but he refrained from doing so. Instead, he almost certainly accompanied Scipio Aemilianus to Spain in 151-150 when the latter served against the Celtiberians (centred on Numantia) whose final downfall Scipio was to encompass eighteen years later. Then, after a brief visit to Greece, Polybius was with Scipio again in north Africa, and witnessed his destruction of Carthage.

Meanwhile the Achaean League, egged on by the returned deportees who were given a free hand by a pro-Roman leader's death, had incurred the wrath of Rome, with fatal results. Destroying its principal member-city Corinth, an action which marked a terrible and decisive stage in their relations with Greece, Rome also abolished the League itself. Polybius, by now a man of some importance in the eyes of the Romans, was requested by them to supervise the extensive administrative changes that such a step required. These changes involved the establishment of a direct, separate relationship between the Roman government and the individual cities which had formerly belonged to the League. Polybius regarded this difficult and delicate task as the finest achievement of his career.

He outlived these events by a quarter of a century, writing and adding greatly to the travels he had already undertaken. The extensive journeys of his long life included a crossing of the Alps, visits to Alexandria and Sardis and Numidia and Gaul and perhaps Spain, and an exploration of the African coast which took him out into the Atlantic Ocean and up the west coast of Portugal (146). He was very proud of these journeys, and there was some justification for his epitaph at Megalopolis which declared that he 'had wandered over every land and sea'. He was killed, so it was said, by a fall from his horse at the age of eighty-two.

Polybius' *History,* in the form in which we possess it, is the fruit of his enforced leisure at Rome. Some of his material on Achaean affairs may already have been more or less prepared before he arrived in Italy. But that is doubtful, and in any case he appears to have got to work on the major part of the book soon after his internment began. References to Roman events suggested that he had published the first four or possibly five books before 150, and Book XI, relating to constitutional matters, probably came out with them. By that time he may have written as far as the end of the

Second Punic War (202 BC; up to XVI, except perhaps XII), appropriately publishing this material while the Third and last war of the series was being fought (147-146).

His original intention had been to terminate his work with the victory over the Macedonians (168, Book XXVI) which placed the whole of the eastern Mediterranean under Roman control. But then the almost simultaneous destructions of Carthage and Corinth (146) made him decide to carry on the story to those epoch-making events and what came immediately after them, 'because of the scale of the operations therein and the dramatic nature of what happened, and above all because I was not only a witness to most of the events but took part in some and administered others'. That observation, like certain others, was inserted in books that had already been written, in order to explain the new plan and add further emphasis to the general theme of Rome's rise to supremacy. But the revisions were not systematic, since there still remain a number of passages which presuppose that Carthage was still in existence. The thorough revision of an ancient book presented practical difficulties, and in any case, as Ernst Badian remarks, 'perhaps rightly, he saw no need to eliminate or amend, as a modern scholar might, any reference or part of his discussion that no longer reflected topical reality'. All the same, Polybius apparently continued, throughout his life, to insert additions and corrections here and there. A sort of obituary note in the last narrative book (just before the final summing up) suggests that the whole work, incorporating these amendments, was published after his death.

He gives powerful reasons for selecting as his principal theme the expansion of Roman power over the whole Mediterranean world (220-168 BC):

> There is, I trust, no one so sluggish and dull as not to be curious how, and because of what qualities in Roman government, practically the whole inhabited world in less than 53 years fell completely under the control of Rome—the like of which, it will be found, has never happened before.

These events were of unprecedented significance because the whole huge territory of the Mediterranean and middle east—the whole inhabited world as he calls it, or at least almost the whole civilised Western world—had become one. 'The wider the circle is,' said Edward Meyer, 'over which the effects of a historical event extend, the more important it is.' By this standard Polybius' subject, as he declares, was exceptional and unique.

In this situation the only serious kind of history that could be written seemed to be the universal synoptic kind, because this alone corresponded objectively with the actual situation which had come into being in the contemporary world. Evidently the claim to write this sort of history had been advanced before, because Polybius refers to such endeavours—though only to discuss them as flimsy and insufficiently comprehensive. It is true that he praises a predecessor, Ephorus, for making a similar attempt when dealing with a period before the Roman unification, and indeed he praises him rather more than he deserves. Nevertheless, Polybius claims that he himself is a pioneer in the enterprise he is undertaking.

> No one in my time has essayed a systematic world history; had anyone else done so, I should have been much less ambitious to undertake this task. . . . I have set my hand to write, not narrowly limited affairs as my predecessors did—for instance, the affairs of Greece or Persia—but rather those occurring everywhere in the known parts of the inhabited world.

This, says Polybius, was a form of historical activity infinitely superior to the mere construction of narrow specialised studies—which inspire in him a decided animosity.

> Those who think that they can gain a sound view of history as a whole from historical monographs seem to me to make the same mistake as would those who gazed on the dissected limbs of some body that was once animate and beautiful, and fancied that this was as good as seeing the life-force and beauty of the creature itself. . . .
>
> To the degree that learning surpasses mere listening, to that same degree I consider my history to surpass the total contribution of all the separate monographs.

For detailed theses of that kind put things out of perspective, obscure causes and effects, and encourage exaggerations and sensationalisms which a wide canvas makes it easier to avoid. Consequently, Polybius feels nothing but contempt for specialised works on genealogies, foundations and kinship ties. He considers them fit only for antiquarians—whose differentiation from serious historians, a very influential distinction in later Europe, had already become canonical. For narrow efforts of that kind do not really get one anywhere, he says. It is only a truly universal history, such as he was trying to write himself, that can give a correct idea of the all-important causes and effects which are essential if one is going to try to assess the true significance of events.

The possibility of taking this broader view had been created by the completely new state of affairs brought about by Rome. The Romans had seized the opportunities that history and geography had combined to provide, and Polybius proposes to give us a rational account of how this came about. 'It was not by an act of chance, as some of the Greeks suppose, nor by spontaneous action, but through quite reasonable causes that the Romans . . . achieved their aim.' At the same time, however, the historian advises us that he is going to adopt an objective attitude to the Roman phenomenon: he is not disposed to regard success as the sole criterion of history. 'Judgments about the victors or the vanquished cannot be final when they are based simply on their achievements alone. . . . For obviously, evidence of what happened afterwards will make it clear whether the dominion of the Romans is to be shunned or, on the contrary, welcomed.' As a result of this unbiased attitude, his judgment of Rome was finely balanced. He greatly admired the old Roman spirit which had triumphed by 'the discipline of many struggles and troubles, and the continual choice of the best in the light of experience gained in disaster'. Moreover, even in his own day, he was still enormously impressed by the best representatives of Rome, men such as Scipio Aemilianus and other eminent personages who, like Scipio, had given him their friendship. Polybius thought the traditional immunity of Romans to bribes was a wonderful thing.

He also felt a great admiration for the Roman constitution, and devotes an entire book (VI) to explaining why. Extending his 'science' of prognostication to this field, he is clearly very pleased with the result. In the first place, he strongly shares the Greek conviction, based on the moral and educational value of laws, that national constitutions are all-important; the fate of states is completely bound up with them. And so he decided that the constitution of the Romans, too, was the key to their successes. He knew it was the product of many struggles and experiments. Yet he scarcely appreciated that what had really made Rome powerful was its flexibility and capacity for growth. Instead he regarded the Roman constitution as the decisive factor which had raised the country to supremacy.

He believed that this constitution had achieved such a special degree of excellence because it incorporated a perfect balance between the various elements of political life.

> From a date 32 years after Xerxes' invasion of Greece, the Roman constitution was one of those that are continually being further improved in detail; it reached its best and perfected form at the time of the war with Hannibal. . . . Not even a native citizen could declare with certainty whether the state, taken as a whole, was aristocratic or democratic or monarchic.

In fact, however, this alleged balance was not so evenly poised as Polybius maintained. For the Roman system inevitably favoured conservatism. Indeed, all these 'mixed constitutions' are more oligarchic than anything else. And it is therefore no accident that Polybius approved of them: because what really impressed him

was the oligarchic and stable element in the Roman State—the majesty of the Senate.

His admiration of the Roman constitution is so great that he compares it favourably to other alleged mixed systems, including those of Carthage and the Dorian city-states of Crete, and, on the Greek mainland, particularly Dorian Sparta. The 'mixed' formula had already been applied to Sparta by Greek thinkers, and at Rome the same idea had recently been developed by Cato the elder, again, it appears, with a Roman as well as a Carthaginian comparison. Such analogies are not very valuable, because the classification seems too schematic to fit even one individual state, let alone several. But one is left with the strong suspicion that what Polybius privately has in mind, as an example of a mixed constitution, is his own Achaean League. Indeed, he seems to be thinking of it as a *model* for contemporary Rome, though he does not mention this conception explicitly, since it would have been tactless to do so after the Romans had forcibly dissolved the League.

It would be of importance to discover what Polybius felt about the future prospects of Rome's constitution, since this ought to show where this acute observer really thought Roman imperialism was leading. But the answer that we get is somewhat equivocal. His survey has not survived in all its complexity, but enough has remained to indicate that its argument is contradictory and puzzling. In spite of its great influence on subsequent European thought, this analysis shows him not, as he supposed, at his best but at his worst. The various traditional Greek ideas which he introduces, 'mixed constitution', cycle of constitutions, and natural law of decline are uneasy and indigestible in combination. The main interest of Polybius' treatment lies in his application of these ideas to the vast phenomenon of Rome. It had often been maintained that a natural process of retribution makes decline and catastrophe the inevitable destiny of every mortal thing, and it was easy to infer from this that all phenomena proceed in cycles. If that is so, the cyclical formula is applicable to constitutions: they are bound ultimately to fall. Yet the Romans, according to Polybius, had obtained exemption or at least a moratorium from this doom, since the emergence of their mixed constitution in the fifth century BC had enabled them to arrest and suspend the downward cyclical process, 'owing to the principle of equivalence of forces'.

As long as this balance lasted, there was no reason why the suspension should not persist. But would the balance last? Did Polybius, that is to say, believe that Rome would continue to escape from the law of decline? His answer is rather confused and confusing. Being less interested to develop the cyclical theory than to stress Roman longevity and the self-correcting tendencies which had, at least for the present, applied the desirable brake, he is able to refrain discreetly from giving an unambiguous verdict. We know too little, he says, about Rome's earlier institutions to be able to deduce from them with any confidence what is going to happen in the future. Most of his own observations about the early Romans are lost. Nevertheless, he does make it pretty clear that he felt that even Rome must succumb in the end to the mob-regime which upsets such balances and produces collapse. For he repeatedly and emphatically quotes the rule that this is what happens to states, and Rome is not to be an exception. In his eyes it was not destined for eternity.

Polybius was, by nature, inclined to favour this pessimistic sort of view, because he believed the old Roman excellence to be already, to some extent, a thing of the past. Like later writers, he saw the eastern wars of the second century BC as the causes of this moral decline. When he had been a young man, he and his friends adopted a detached or critical attitude towards current Roman policy. This earned him and them deportation, and his exile began with 'utter loss of spirit and paralysis of mind' which was unlikely to make him love the Romans so much that he wanted to throw all historical rules overboard in their favour.

As a result, he treats Hannibal, for example, with a fairness notably deficient in the Roman tradition: 'When a man takes on the character of a historian, he will often have to praise and glorify his enemies in the highest terms, when their actions demand it, and often criticise and blame his dearest friends in harsh language, when the errors in their conduct indicate it.' Although Polybius did not approve of making history into biography, he inherited a measure of the biographical preoccupations that had developed over the past three centuries. Consequently he could not help taking an interest in the strength of personality which had been so manifest in Hannibal. His admiration for this quality helped him to put into practice the general principle of balance enunciated above, and thus to attain an unfamiliar degree of objectivity. In accordance with the same principle, his remarks about Roman policy in the 160s and 150s modify their generally favourable verdict by a good many censorious remarks. From then onwards, it is true, his sympathies are increasingly with Rome. Nevertheless, just as he had been willing in the Second Punic War to see the good side of Hannibal, so again before the Third Punic War he openly sets out the arguments put forward by the Carthaginians.

The hostility which the Achaeans were now showing towards the Romans was the product of League policies which Polybius now deplored. Nevertheless, Rome's destruction of the entire federal entity must have come as a terrible shock to him. No doubt this was partly assuaged, human nature being what it is,

by the fact that he personally was called in by the Romans to organise the subsequent settlement. By agreeing to do so, he became an early exponent of the type of Greco-Roman literary man who chose to collaborate with the conqueror—interpreting Rome to Greece, explaining that the Empire had come to stay and could not be resisted, and indicating that this was such a vast historical design that it absolved his own compatriots from any slur of failure or importence. Another Greek friend of Scipio Aemilianus, who again sought to reconcile his countrymen to Roman rule, was the Stoic philosopher Panaetius of Rhodes (c. 185-95 BC). The founder of Stoicism, Zeno of Citium in Cyprus (c. 300 BC), had concluded that since every man possesses a share of divine spark we are all brothers, and are therefore bound by a moral imperative to treat one another decently. Panaetius adjusted these ideas of human brotherhood to the requirements of the Roman aristocracy, and declared that the Empire was beneficial to rulers and ruled alike. And he was followed by Posidonius of Apamea, who actually declared that the Roman Empire and the ideal Stoic world-state were identical.

> Those who have read their Polybius are supposed to be equipped with the means of coping scientifically with any emergency that may arise, improving themselves by studying other people's calamities rather than experiencing them in person, and resisting and counteracting the natural tendency of all things to deteriorate.
>
> —*Michael Grant*

Polybius, true to his reserved attitude towards success stories, was not prepared to go to quite those lengths. Nor could he, like Thucydides, bring himself to conclude or imply that self-interest and aggression are inevitable and therefore acceptable. On the contrary, he clearly indicates that ethical standards, and moderate ways of behaving, must be maintained. They are morally desirable; they also pay good dividends. And one of the reasons why he admired Rome so much was because he believed this was the code it had followed in the past.

All the same, Polybius never forgot he was a Greek. He even, explicitly, reserved the right (which other historians have assumed surreptitiously) to show partiality to his own fellow-countrymen—provided, he adds a little perplexingly, that nothing is said contrary to the facts. Certainly he appreciates the faults of the Greeks very clearly, blaming the depopulation of their land on their own selfish exploitation, and comparing their honesty very unfavourably with that of the Romans. Nevertheless, his work contains many signs of attachment to his own region and locality. His decision to follow Timaeus and base his chronology on Olympiads and Olympic Years was a direct consequence of his Peloponnesian origin (though this procedure bisected the campaigning-seasons and had to be modified, in the interests of comprehensibility, by Roman and other systems).

But, above all, he shows a strong patriotic bias towards his native Arcadia and towards the Achaean League and his own party within the League. These attitudes powerfully influence his views about earlier historians. Achaean politicians, too, who had opposed his father and himself are naturally deplored; though, after the dissolution of the League, he refused to accept the property of one of these opponents when it was offered to him. When speaking of the admired Achaean leader Philopoemen, he makes a conscious and explicit attempt to be impartial, pointing out again that history is not the same thing as panegyric. On the other hand, his pro-Achaean alignment makes him deeply hostile to the rival Aetolian League, and he hates King Cleomenes III of Sparta who seized Megalopolis. Here the memoirs of the Achaean statesman Aratus are uncritically accepted. Achaea, in return, recognised the sympathy and practical services of Polybius by numerous statues and monuments in his honour.

Thucydides had indicated that his work was intended as a permanent possession which would be of value to those who studied it. Polybius echoed the claim, adding more explicitly that his own work is designed to provide instruction. He asserts over and over again that history, in the way that he has written it, can be useful. 'Even if our current affairs are prospering, no sensible person could reasonably be certain about the future by inferring from the present. It is on this basis that I declare an understanding of the past to be not only pleasant but actually necessary.' This utility may recently have been reasserted by Cato, but clearly it was not regarded as self-evident, for Polybius labours the point. His history is not merely intended to be a general guide. It is actually designed as a sort of manual, which will help public figures to act rightly. To predict it, and also to deal with it. Those who have read their Polybius are supposed to be equipped with the means of coping scientifically with any emergency that may arise, improving themselves by studying other people's calamities rather than experiencing them in person, and resisting and counteracting the natural tendency of all things to deteriorate. He felt that his own achievement in settling Achaea after 146 had proved this point. Even in almost hopeless conditions, men in public life can find the right course if they work on the right assumptions, based on historical experience. And

he is continually astonished and annoyed at people's failure to learn from history.

The lessons are concrete, practical ones. Interest in the past for its own sake, or as the subject-matter of pure scholarship, is conspicuous by its absence. Moreover, the claim to timeless universality is overlaid by a good deal of direct advice to contemporaries. In spite of the deliberate echo of Thucydides, this unsparing, rather hectoring didacticism, with its numerous personal and subjective interventions, presents a great contrast to the older historian's indirect, artistic and dramatic approach. Polybius' work, more than any other ancient writing that has survived, is deliberately and openly a case-book for politicians, rather as the Chinese history which came into being a generation or two later was intended to train civil servants.

Because of this overriding and constantly expressed instructive aim, even the relatively limited portions of Polybius that have survived are hard to get through. It is true that, in citing the conventional contrast between the pleasurable and the useful, he says he wants his work to be the former as well as the latter, recognising that a literary work ought to be attractive. And indeed, when he wants to tell a good story, he can do so, especially when lessons are out of the way and he is content to use simple and straightforward methods. For example, his account of the escape of the Syrian prince Demetrius from Rome (162), an adventure in which he himself personally assisted, is vivid and authentic. Moreover, he shows artistic skill in devising his over-all structure, breaking off, for example, to talk of Roman institutions just at the time when readers, shocked by the setbacks in the Second Punic War and excited by Rome's determination to resist, are ready and eager to learn what the city and people were like in those days.

There is also some evidence of a progressive attention to grammar and style. On the whole, however, his language has the flat and prosy verbosity of a government department. Unlike almost any other notable literary product of antiquity, it is actually improved by a good translation. After all, Polybius himself said that the aim should always be commensurate with the effort. He may have been theoretically aware that one must write attractively, but he was really out not to amuse but to teach. So evidently he did not exert himself to the utmost to write good Greek. But here his skill, or his psychology, was deficient; if he had written better he would have been a better teacher. He himself is uncomfortably aware that the length of his work makes it tough reading, though he declares it to be wrong that people should take this view—because it is he, and not the writers of shorter books, who is giving the true causes of events.

For causes are the essence of his history and the basis of its value. Descriptions of events which do not take them into account are not enough. For what is the good of a statesman who cannot reckon how, and why, and from what source each event has originated? Polybius' own claim to discern and demonstrate such causes is based on 'science and art', that is to say on the efficiency of his own, modern type of history, assisted by the speeches inserted in his work, which were designed to clarify causation. His method is explicitly stated to depend upon the adoption of a scientific and technical point of view. Like Thucydides, he is inspired by the achievements of science, and consciously revives the analogy of medicine; and he has the advantage over Thucydides that further centuries of rich historical experience have now gone by.

His consciousness of this long and enigmatic past warned Polybius that the historian's power to reconstruct causes is subject to profound limitations. This modest attitude, which agreeably conflicts with some of his more priggish assertions about other matters, is summed up by repeated appeals to the concept of Chance. He uses the term incessantly, to denote everything in his theme that is imponderable, irrational and uncontrollable. In his first three books alone, the word 'unexpected' appears on no less than fifty-one occasions.

As in other ancient writers, Chance is interpreted in various ways. But Polybius believes it to merit particularly serious treatment in an instructive work such as his own, because its identification as an operative factor will teach the reader how to bear the vicissitudes of his own life with a more philosophical endurance. Half-personified, Chance is occasionally just a punisher of wrongdoing; but innocent people are equally likely to get hurt. It is as much a part of man's endowment as his looks or mental gifts. It produces, even seems to delight in, coincidences, contrasts, reversals. And reversals mean downfalls, because success cannot last. Here again, as in Thucydides, is the language of tragic drama, retained by a man whose ways of thinking were alien from those of the dramatists.

These seemed good reason to ascribe the Romans' seizure of power to Chance. Nevertheless, there are also perfectly rational, identifiable causes for their emergence. So there are, indeed, for every other phenomenon as well. Indeed, the identifiable causes are precisely what produce the unexpected developments grouped under the general heading of Chance. To attribute to Fortune what is really the product of human action is a mistake. Yet the two sorts of cause are frequently interconnected, and the best thing, therefore, is to cite rational causation and Chance at one and the same time. Chance is the producer of the play, but inside the grand production man can control the sub-plots and scenes. And Polybius goes on to add, in the spirit of the Stoics, that man is also in a position to control his own inward temper with which he faces events.

Sometimes Chance may be merely another way of saying Providence. True, when you can discover the material reason for something, you are not entitled to introduce any supernatural agency. All the same, a transformation on the scale of the rise of Rome must be providential—a comfort for the humiliated Greeks.

You are warranted, that is to say, in ascribing inexplicable developments and events to the gods. You can ascribe to them also the human states of mind that are the springs of action. But myths are to be avoided by historians, and miracles do not happen. Stories of such things, however, are permissible so long as they do not go too far. And indeed the whole paraphernalia of religion is justifiable, because the masses are so unstable that they need it. This doctrine, with its anticipation of the Marxist 'opiate of the people', was coming into vogue in official Roman circles. Or rather, it had long prevailed there, and was now receiving articulate expression.

Causation, then, is the product of analysable events modified by a strong unpredictable element. This is an elaboration of the rationalism of Thucydides. And Polybius chose to take the analogy with his great predecessor further still. Thucydides had devoted his full talent for the investigation of causes to his main subject, the encounter between Athens and Sparta. Central to Polybius' theme, also, is a war—the Second Punic War, in which the Romans finally defeated Hannibal.

Thucydides had distinguished between the immediate and ultimate causes of hostilities. Polybius borrows this distinction, but adds a third element, the 'first overt act' (*arche*). Speaking with characteristic acidity about writers who fail to distinguish this additional factor, he goes on to make a triple diagnosis on these lines he has indicated, both of Alexander's Persian war and of Rome's war against the Seleucid Antiochus III. His analyses are a little far-fetched; Xenophon's eastern expedition, for example, had a certain significance, but it is strange to find it actually described as a 'first cause' of Alexander's war. The formulations are meticulous but they simplify and schematise, and they do not go deep. The improvement on Thucydides is just not there. Polybius' ideas of causes are rather crude and dogmatic, showing a certain lack of insight into the historical process. He is not, for example, concerned with the degree to which the Romans were, or were not, aggressive imperialists, or interested to know what drove them on. Nor has he got the imagination to penetrate to Thucydides' profound levels of humanity.

Moreover, the older historian could never have descended to the anticlimaxes and banalities which recur from time to time in Polybius' work.

Just as he likes to elaborate on Thucydides' theories of cause and effect, so he also repeats, again at increased length, his forerunner's emphasis on the truth. What Polybius aims at is 'pragmatic' history—serious, systematic, interpretative treatment of matters of fact. If history is to teach efficiently and reliably, the first essential is that the account should be true. Indeed, 'just as a living creature is completely useless if deprived of its eyes, so if you take truth from history, what is left but an unprofitable tale?' Though minor errors are excusable—especially in an extensive work—the deliberate failure to make oneself into a competent historian is unforgivable. And so is deliberate distortion.

Polybius specifically extends this doctrine to speeches, of which about fifty appear in the surviving portions of his work. Their purpose is to illustrate causes and effects, 'summing up events', as F. W. Walbank points out, 'and holding the whole history together'. The historian, Polybius declares, must record what was really said, however commonplace. There is a new stringency in this statement of what speeches ought to do. More clearly than any previous writer, Polybius was making an explicit stand for truthfulness in regard to this vital element in ancient historical writing. He did so all the more sharply because some of his predecessors had allowed themselves an almost complete abandonment of any such criterion, one of them, Callisthenes, even pronouncing, in the spirit of 'the appropriate' stressed by his uncle Aristotle, that what a speech in a history had to do was to hit off the character—to match the oratory to the person and the situation.

Having stated the ideal, however, Polybius fails to live up to it. On certain occasions he admits he has selected and abbreviated. Besides, his most elaborate speeches, those intended to possess special significance, are worked over and worked up—to say the least: for sometimes whole orations, notably those of Hannibal and the consul Publius Scipio in 218, are obviously fictitious from beginning to end. What Polybius really wanted to achieve by such speeches was to provide the sort of arguments which converted people from one cause to another. This seemed to him a good way of illustrating the dynamic interactions between one individual, or one group of individuals, and another. 'A single well-timed speech by a trustworthy person often turns men from the worst courses and incites them to the best.' Exact fidelity, then, was less important than psychological cogency.

And yet, there are those unprecedentedly sharp statements about truthfulness. Like his explanation of the causes of the war, they represent an extension, or a more emphatic assertion, of Thucydidean doctrines. And the attention to Thucydides is carried further still.

First, Polybius agrees with him that the only history is contemporary or near-contemporary history, The historian must be able to consult actual participants. It is no more possible to become a historian by studying documents than to become a painter by looking at the works of earlier artists. The analogy between the two sorts of activity is a false one, since a historian does not read books as models but as sources. But the pronouncement in favour of contemporary history was not out of line with most historical thinking, both of his own and of earlier times. As to the definition of what 'contemporary' means, Polybius chose 220 BC as the beginning of his main period because eyewitnesses could not be examined for any happenings before that time. He had many opportunities, while at Rome, of meeting the stream of envoys and hostages that came to Italy, and he went to great lengths to interview men who had taken part in important events.

But this was not nearly enough for him. The eye, he said, is far more accurate than the ear, and he regarded it as essential that the historian should have participated personally in the circumstances he described. That is what Thucydides had done, and Polybius, too, played an active role in the happenings of his times. The failure to do likewise, he believed, was what had made his predecessor Timaeus so futile. To be a historian it is necessary to have been a politician and military commander oneself. As one would expect from Polybius who was the author of a tactical handbook (now lost), this meant in his case that his battle-pieces are generally clear. Moreover, he adds a prolonged account of the Roman army. This contains a description of camp layouts which is, admittedly, tantalisingly inadequate. But the account is supplemented by an explanation of Roman signalling that is actually based on inventions of his own.

Not only must historians have occupied leading positions in public events, but Polybius regards his other sort of personal experience as equally indispensable—that is to say, his travelling. In this respect, he is the heir of Herodotus even more than of Thucydides, and it was an achievement to have blended the two traditions. To Polybius, the elements in historical research are three. Political experience is one, and written documentation is another; and the third 'consists in inspection of various cities and places, rivers, lakes, and generally the particular features and distances on land and sea'. He had a sharp eye for the lie of the ground, and always insisted on the importance of accurate geography to the historian. Like an eighteenth-century *savant,* he was conscious that the opening up of the world had provided new opportunities for getting at the truth. He wrote a work—probably a separate essay—*On the Habitability of the Equatorial Region*. And he obtained great satisfaction from his own travels, especially his voyage of discovery into the Atlantic. So keen was he to be regarded as the second Odysseus that the geographer Pytheas is fiercely attacked (*c.* 310-306): there must be no western explorations other than his own. Consequently, his work offers many digressions on geography. And there was even a whole book on the subject, the lost XXXIV, including detailed accounts of his journey in Spain. Polybius' knowledge of geography is not, in fact, up to recent Alexandrian standards. But he was very insistent on comprehensibility. Just as chronology has to be clear and understandable, so, also, the geographical digressions strike a further blow for the same cause of popularisation: it is useless, he rightly says, to mention strange places unless these are brought into relation with the knowledge of the reader.

Political experience, then, and geographical observation are two of the elements which Polybius requires in a historian. His third requirement is the utilisation of written records. He employed archives and documents wherever he could get access to them, chiefly in Rome but also elsewhere. In this field his greatest success, of which he was very proud, was the discovery on the south Italian promontory of Lacinium of a bronze tablet listing Hannibal's army. He seems to suggest that no historian had ever seen the inscription before.

As regards his literary sources, our information is extremely deficient. Because of the vastness of his project, he clearly had to use written evidence throughout. Yet he does not seem to have been very well read. With regard to philosophy, for example, he is capable of using the word 'unphilosophical' as a term of abuse, and yet his own studies in the subject were evidently slight. Indeed, the way in which he refers to earlier authors, in whatever field, makes it probable that he drew upon one of the books of collected quotations that were available for this purpose.

At one point he adopts an appreciative and indeed deferential attitude to his forerunners: 'We should not find fault with writers for their omissions and mistakes, but should praise and admire them, considering the times they lived in, for having ascertained something on the subject and advanced our knowledge.' This, however, proves to have been a very strange pronouncement for Polybius to have offered, since, as we have seen at some length, he conspicuously fails to act in accordance with it. Historians customarily criticised their predecessors, but the attitude adopted by Polybius is remarkably and unpleasantly sharp. Perhaps this tone would not have seemed so unusual if more works by Hellenistic historians had survived. For this was a time when criticism was violent. Standards of truthfulness were unsteady—and productive of furious disputes. Like others who engaged in these quarrels, Polybius accepted the convention that they were part of the game. But his ferocity was not purely conventional, for he felt very strongly on the subject and wanted to defend his views. Consequently his claims to intellectual tolerance were cancelled out by an equally marked tendency to indulge in resentful abuse and self-justification. This duality sometimes appears in a schizophrenic form when the same author is disagreeably attacked at one point, and courteously praised at another. Polybius is prepared to admit that many things prevent writers from expressing themselves quite frankly. He appreciated that this was true even of his hero Aratus. All the same, he claimed to regard it as a public duty to correct other historians. Thucydides lies outside the range of his censure. This is partly because he was too remote in date to attack jealousy or provide a suitable target. Besides, although Polybius knew so much about his historical principles, it seems doubtful whether he had actually gone to the length of *reading* him. The passages with which he was familiar could well have been culled from intermediaries. But in any case it would not have been proper to criticise Thucydides, because Polybius knew himself to be affected by his attitude and approach, and believed that the two of them stood for the same historical ideas and ideals. For both desired to impart instruction, and both directly participated in events.

However, a great period of time, nearly three eventful centuries, had passed since Thucydides; and Polybius, not unnaturally, felt greater concern about writers of more recent date. Of Xenophon little need be said, since although Polybius mentions him (and indicates a disagreement) there is no important debt or clash to record. Since then, however, a great many people had written histories, although they are all now lost. For one thing, there had been a large outcrop of the specialist monographs to which Polybius objected so strongly. But there had also been quite important, indeed major, historians since Thucydides and Xenophon. Polybius made great use of their writings, but largely conceals this fact by telling us how little he thought of them, and particularly of Timaeus.

As we have seen, his reasons for this depreciation fall into two main categories. First, there were partisan reasons. He took marked exception to critical comments about his native Arcadia, or his Achaean League, or its admired leader Aratus. But there was also a second and more objective reason for his disapproval of the fourth-and third-century historians. It seemed to him that Timaeus and Phylarchus and the rest had degraded history into mere sensational, quasi-historical romance.

Polybius obviously does not quite do them justice. Their way of writing, for example, must often have been much more attractive than his own. And yet, as far as we can tell, there was a good deal to be said for his view. His nagging manner, however—which led him, for example, to write to contemporary historians explaining where they had gone wrong—inspires irritation. Nor was he always free from partiality or untruthfulness. Yet in such an enormous pioneer work the imperfections to which humanity is liable are hard to avoid. Polybius did avoid the worst of them: a lot of the snares into which one after another of his predecessors since Thucydides had fallen were safely shunned.

Even if he could not always reach the heights, his eyes were always fixed in that direction. In spite of all hindrances, he possessed a genuine and indeed passionate admiration for the truth. He was diligent and shrewd. He could see most things in proportion, and except when he embarked on fields which did not suit him (such as studies of constitutions), he was well able to comprehend what he saw. 'In history', said Theodor Mommsen, 'his books are like the sun.' Their contrast to the preceding and following darkness is, in part, due to the accident which has preserved large portions of his work, but not more than fragments of any other historian for nearly three centuries before him and a century afterwards. But the contrast is also an objective matter: because it can confidently be surmised that, even if all these writers had survived, Polybius would still have been outstanding among them.

Arnaldo Momigliano (lecture date 1973)

SOURCE: "Polybius's Reappearance in Western Europe," in *Essays in Ancient and Modern Historiography,* Wesleyan University Press, 1977, pp. 79-98.

[*An Italian scholar, Momigliano (1908-1987) was widely known as one of the most learned historians of his time. In the following excerpt from a lecture originally delivered in 1973, he traces the rediscovery of Polybius's writings in Western Europe during the Renaissance and discusses his significance for the development of Western historical, political, and military theory.*]

I

Polybius arrived twice in Italy, the first time in 167 B.C., the second time at an uncertain date about A.D. 1415. In both cases he had some difficulty in establishing his credentials. He was born too late to be a classic, too early to be a classicist. Furthermore, he had committed the unpardonable sin of having underrated Sparta and Athens, the two pillars of classicism. There was also the suspicion, never definitely dispelled, that he was something of a bore. Only Dionysius of Halicarnassus (*Comp.,* 30) was courageous enough to list him among the authors one does not read to the

end, but the silence of Quintilian was even more deadly. Yet Cato the Elder respected him; Sempronius Asellio learnt from him what pragmatic history was about; Varro, Nepos and Cicero—that is, the greatest authorities of the Caesarian age—recognized his worth. Livy praised and plundered him. Pliny the Elder quoted him twelve times on geographic matters, and presented him as a great traveller (*Nat. H.,* V, 9). Ammianus Marcellinus shows that Julian the Apostate was acquainted with Polybius (XXIV, 2, 16) and St Jerome repeated Porphyry's opinion that Polybius was one of the authors necessary for the understanding of the last part of the Book of Daniel (*In Dan.,* in *PL,* XXV, 494A), and Orosius quoted him twice, once very prominently (*Hist.,* IV, 20, 6; V, 3, 3).

For the reputation of Polybius in the Renaissance not all these testimonials were of equal value. Cicero's praise in *De republica* was wasted on an age *de libris quidem rei publicae iam desperans,* to repeat Petrarch's words (*Sen.,* 16, 1). This, however, made the same Cicero's definition of Polybius as *bonus auctor in primis* in *De officiis* (III, 32, 113) all the more valuable. Again, the reference to Polybius in Livy, XLV, 44, 19, became known only in 1527, but since Petrarch had put together Livy's first, third and fourth decades in the present cod. Harleianus 2493—that is by A.D. 1329—humanists were aware that for Livy Polybius was *haudquaquam spernendus auctor* (XXX, 45, 5); *non incertum auctorem cum omnium Romanarum rerum tum praecipue in Graecia gestarum* (XXXIII, 10, 10). With the spread of Plutarch in the Quattrocento nothing could be more impressive than the knowledge that Brutus had been hard at work on an epitome of Polybius on the eve of the battle of Pharsalus. . . . The rediscovery of Pausanias added new elements to Polybius' posthumous glory. But we must remember that, if the *editio princeps* of Pausanias by Marcus Masurus goes back to 1516, what counts are the two Latin translations by Romulus Amasaeus and Abramus Loescher which appeared respectively in 1547 and 1550. Scholars of the second part of the sixteenth century could not fail to be touched by the decree of the Megalopolitans which praised their fellow-citizen Polybius as one who 'roamed over every land and sea, became an ally of the Romans, and stayed their wrath against the Greeks'. Indeed (Pausanias went on to report) 'whenever the Romans obeyed the advice of Polybius things went well with them, but whenever they would not listen to his instructions they made mistakes' (VIII, 30, 8-9). From Pausanias scholars learnt furthermore that in the temple of the Despoina near Arakesion an inscription roundly declared that 'Greece would not have fallen at all, if she had obeyed Polybius in everything, and when she met disaster, her only help came from him' (VIII, 37, 2). Here one found a historian *magister vitae*.

I am not aware of any quotation of Polybius in the Latin writers of Antiquity after St Jerome and Orosius.

When Petrarch wrote his letter to Livy he asked him to convey his greetings to 'Polybius and Quintus Claudius and Valerius Antias and all those whose glory thine own greater light has dimmed' (*Fam.,* XXIV, 8): he had in mind Orosius, *Hist.,* V, 3, 3, where Polybius is found together with Claudius and Antias. To Petrarch all these gentlemen were mere names. What, so far, remains obscure is the extent of the knowledge and reputation of Polybius in his own Greek world between the fifth and the fifteenth centuries. This obscurity also conditions our appreciation of the reappearance of Polybius in the West at the beginning of the fifteenth century.

Leaving Zosimus aside, I am insufficiently informed about what Polybius meant to Byzantine historians. Imitations of individual passages have been identified in Procopius and Agathias. It would be surprising if Procopius' notion of Tyche and his emphasis on the technical factors in warfare had not been affected by Polybius. He may have thought of the comparison between the Macedonian phalanx and the Roman legion in Polybius XVIII 28 ff. when in the prœmium to the *Persian War* he compared the bowmen of his time with the archers of the past: but I do not find Polybius' influence self-evident. The stylistic models of Procopius and Agathias are Herodotus, Thucydides, Xenophon, Diodorus, Arrian and even Appian, but not Polybius. Photius, strangely enough, took no notice of Polybius. In the tenth century Constantine VII Porphyrogenitus redistributed Polybius' history among his collections of excerpts—that is, he reduced the history to the function of *exempla*. Somebody else, not later than the tenth century, made excerpts of a less systematic nature from Books I-XVI and XVIII: which we now call the *Excerpta antiqua*. Book XVII may already by then have been lost. It is pleasant to remember that Casaubon did not think it impossible that the *Excerpta antiqua* went back to the epitome of Polybius by Brutus! The influence of Polybius has been noticed in the biographies of Theophanes Continuatus, in Anna Comnena, in Byzantine treatises on fortifications and, no doubt, in many other places. In the late eleventh century Xiphilinus preferred Polybius to Dio Cassius because he was less inclined to report portents (LI, p. 506 Boiss.). Xiphilinus obviously knew what sort of historian Polybius was. Polybius' status in the history of Byzantine thought—and especially in Byzantine historiography—still needs to be clarified by an expert.

To all appearances, Polybius was not one of the Greek authors most prominently exhibited by Byzantine scholars when they came to the West either as ambassadors or as refugees, or both. The first Byzantine scholar to produce an edition and translation of Polybius (a partial text of Book VI), Janus Lascaris in 1529, did so in response to the increasing interest by Italian scholars and politicians in this author. How the MSS. of Polybius reached Italy is only partially known. John M. Moore has done much in recent years to reclassify *The Manuscript Tradition of Polybius* (Cambridge 1965) but we need a Billanovich to tell the true story of Polybius' reception. The most important codex for Books I-V, A, *Vaticanus Gr.* 124—written in A.D. 947 by Ephraim the Monk—was almost certainly in the Vatican Library in 1455 under Pope Nicholas V. Moore believes that B—*Londiniensis, Mus. Brit., Add.* MS. 11728—was directly copied from A. If so, there are some interesting inferences to be made for both B and A. B was copied by a monk, Stephanus, in the monastery of John the Baptist in Constantinople in 1416: the same MS. was in the Badia of the Benedictines in Florence by 1437; and it came to the Badia from the library of Antonio Corbinelli, who had died in 1425. It follows that A was still in Constantinople in 1416, and that B reached Florence between 1416 and 1425. Indeed B was transferred to Siena in 1435, when Antonius Athenaeus made a copy of it for Francesco Filelfo, the present *Mediceus Laurentianus Plut,* 69, 9, or B3. From B3 descended B4 and B5, both now in the Marciana, one as *Marcianus Gr.* 371, the other as *Marcianus Gr.* 369, both belonging to the library of Cardinal Bessarion: the subscription of B5 makes it clear that it was copied at Bessarion's command, and this is also probable for B4. The name of Filelfo is particularly interesting. He had been trying hard to get hold of manuscripts of Polybius. In a letter of 1428 to Traversari, after his return from Constantinople, he said that he had (or was expecting) a MS. of Polybius. But Filelfo, not to speak of Bessarion, had apparently begun to take an interest in Polybius only when his reputation had already been solidly re-established in Florence.

The location of Polybius' rediscovery is not in any doubt: Florence. The discoverer does not seem to be in doubt either: Leonardo Bruni Aretino. The date was about 1418-19—when Bruni wrote his history of the first Punic War and of the subsequent Illyrian and Gallic Wars, a free translation from Polybius, I-II, 35.

J. E. Sandys—a name one always utters with respect—thought he had found some evidence that about 1403 Pier Paolo Vergerio had chosen Polybius as an example of a Greek historian who knew Roman history better than the Romans (or at least than the Italians) themselves. But Vergerio's speech *De ingenuis moribus* has no definite allusion to Polybius and may allude, for instance, to Plutarch: *Et est eo deventum ut Latinae quoque historiae et cognitionem et fidem a Graecis auctoribus exigamus.* The name of Vergerio may be left out of the story. We still do not yet know where and how Bruni found a manuscript of Polybius with an account of the first Punic and of the Illyrian and Gallic Wars. I am not aware of any evidence suggesting that when his teacher Manuel Chrysoloras came to Florence in 1397 he brought with him a manuscript of

Polybius. We can, however, be sure that about 1418 there was nothing Leonardo Bruni needed except a manuscript to enable him to appreciate the importance of Polybius as a historian. The present *Londiniensis* 11728 may already have been in Florence at that time.

Bruni himself tells us in his *Commentaria rerum suo tempore gestarum* how at the turn of the century the war between Giangaleazzo Visconti and Florence had represented a revolution in the intellectual life of Italy—the rediscovery of Greek language and literature. . . . Hans Baron's admirable work on Leonardo Bruni and his time [*The Crisis of the Early Italian Renaissance,* 1966] can be said to be an extensive commentary on this theme formulated by Bruni himself. The young man, who, about 1403, had modelled his *Laudatio Florentinae Urbis* on Aristides' *Panathenaicus,* was a mature statesman and historian fifteen years later. He had come back to Florence in 1415 after long and disappointing service in the papal Curia. He was more than ever certain that Florence belonged to the line of direct descent from the ancient republics of Greece and Rome. He had started the *Historiae Florentini populi.* More or less together with the *Commentaria tria de Primo Bello Punico* he wrote in 1419 the preface to the new Statute of the *Parte Guelfa* in which he reasserted the idea of republican liberty. Even more significantly he composed in 1421 the pamphlet *De militia.* It is the merit of the edition and commentary by C. C. Bayley in 1961 to have revived interest in this little work. Criticisms of this edition have not always been fair. Professor Bayley did understand that *militia, miles* meant to Bruni 'cavalry, knight'. He did not interpret the pamphlet as an attack against mercenaries on behalf of civic armies—as if Bruni were Machiavelli. Bruni of course intended to glorify the equestrian order and to trace it back to ancient—and therefore honourable—origins. In such a context the Polybius Bruni knew could be of little use, since Bruni was certainly not acquainted with Book VI. Yet it is not an accident that the man who discovered Polybius as a historian was also especially interested in military problems. In various forms and situations the combination of admiration for Polybius as a historian and the interest in military problems was to remain characteristic of the whole debate on Polybius from Machiavelli to Justus Lipsius and Casaubon, not to mention the later Montesquieu.

Contemporaries sensed that Bruni was producing something important in his *Commentaria de Primo Bello Punico.* While he was still writing it in or about 1419, Ambrogio Traversari wrote to Francesco Barbaro: *Leonardus Arretinus commentaria scribere de primo bello poenico ex Polybio coepit, opus, ut audio, egregium; nam ipse non vidi.* We must bear in mind that Bruni did not intend his work as a simple translation of Books I-II, 35 by Polybius. He intended to

write history, more precisely that history of the first Punic War and of the Gallic War 225-222 B.C. which was missing in Livy. It must have given Bruni and his Florentine readers enormous pleasure to end with the occupation and humiliation of Milan by the Romans. Bruni paraphrased and freely supplemented his Polybius to make him look like Livy. The Sallustian component in Bruni's historical style which Antonio La Penna so acutely recognized in Bruni's *Historiae Florentini populi* and elsewhere does not seem to figure— at least to my untutored eye—in the history of the Punic War. Bruni's success in Livianizing Polybius may be indicated by a story we owe to Gianni Gervasoni (he published it in 1925). According to this story in 1783 Lorenzo Mascheroni, 'insigne matematico, leggiadro poeta e ottimo cittadino' (as Vincenzo Monti later defined him), thought he had discovered in an old MS. Livy's account of the first Punic War. After having transcribed the greater part of the MS. he revealed its contents to his fellow-citizen of Bergamo, the learned Canonico Conte Camillo Agliardi. Agliardi immediately recognized the nature of the text: Leonardo Bruni's *De Primo Bello Punico,* of course. Mascheroni turned to his Muse for consolation:

> Mio venerato Monsignor Canonico,
> Affè, m'avete fatto il bel servizio
> Da farmi per un anno malinconico.
> Che v'è venuto in cor di darmi indizio
> Di quel volume, ch'io non voglio dire,
> Che allegro io mi copiava a precipizio?

Two points are relevant in Bruni's historical method. First of all he thought that there were only two ways of writing history: one was to observe and recount contemporary facts, the other to discover new sources and to present their accounts in one's own appropriate language. As he wrote in his preface to his translation of Plutarch's life of Marc Antony—perhaps before 1405: *In historia vero, in qua nulla est inventio, non video equidem, quid intersit, an ut facta, an ut ab alio dicta, scribas. In utroque enim par labor est, aut etiam maior in secundo.* In perfect accord with these principles, he went on producing, as his own histories, what we would treat as translations or paraphrases of ancient texts: his *Commentaria rerum graecarum* of 1439 are a paraphrase of Xenophon's *Hellenica,* and the *De bello Italico adversus Gothicos libri IV* of 1441, his last big work, are almost undiluted Procopius. He never concealed his sources: Polybius is mentioned specifically in the introduction to his history of the Punic War. But he thought he had done the day's work if he put his sources into his own prose. At the same time (and this is my second point) he was well aware that ancient writers contradicted each other because they followed different sources. He thought he was imitating the ancients in so far as the ancients themselves blindly followed their sources; he knew that this situation created difficulties, but as far as I am aware he never formulated any general principle about the solution of such difficulties. He came very near to the root of the problem in a letter to Cardinal Colonna who had asked questions about a contradiction between Livy and Polybius concerning *de legione illa quae Regium occupavit:* the references must be Polybius, I, 7 *versus* Livy, XXVIII, 28, 2 and XXXI, 31, 6. Bruni admits of course the existence of this contradiction between ancient authorities and appeals to the authority of Polybius as justification for the version he had preferred:. . . . Having translated Polybius' Book I, Bruni knew what Polybius thought about the bias of Fabius Pictor and Philinus. In fact he deduced rather perversely from his author that Livy had followed Fabius Pictor, but Polybius had preferred Philinus as his source. If he, Bruni, had followed Polybius, and therefore by implication Philinus, the explanation was simple: Livy's account was lost. . . .

This mixture of uncritical repetition of ancient sources and of very critical awareness that the ancient authorities themselves were conditioned by their own sources is the real beginning of historical criticism. Thus Bruni had discovered a missing chapter of Republican Roman history and had suddenly presented Polybius as an authority on Republican Rome. This was very little compared to what he gave his contemporaries with his translation of Aristotle's *Politics*. From Aristotle he derived the interpretation of the Florentine constitution as a mixed constitution, which he was able to present in Greek to his Greek friends about 1438 in [a pamphlet]. But the link between Polybius and Aristotle was to become clear later with the rediscovery of Book VI. In 1437 Sicco Polenton had concluded in Padua the second edition of his *Scriptorum Illustrium Latinae Linguae libri XVIII*. There (but not in the first draft of 1426 which is preserved in *Cod. Ricc.* 121), Polybius is taken for granted as the authority for the first Punic War. He is also specifically mentioned as one of the Greek authors whom the Italians have lately made accessible. . . . Bruni had started his Greek studies with a translation of Basilius. Plutarch and Polybius were his authors. The allusion of Sicco Polenton to him is obvious: Ptolemy had been translated by one of Bruni's fellow students under Chrysoloras, Giacomo da Scarparia.

The new status of Polybius was recognized by Pope Nicholas V, about 1450, when Polybius was included among the Greek historians to be translated into Latin. Niccolò Perotti, who was chosen for the translation, was in the service of Bessarion, and there can be little doubt that his name was suggested by Bessarion and that he used one of the manuscripts owned by his protector. As *Marcianus Graecus* 369 was written later in 1470, *Marcianus* 371 is a strong candidate for identification with the codex used by Perotti. But as one of his letters to the Pope's librarian Giovanni Tortelli shows, he found it a difficult MS. to work on and

asked to see *Polybium summi pontificis qui olim d. episcopi Coronensis fuit*. The allusion, as so much else concerning Perotti, was clarified by Cardinal Mercati, who recognized in it MS. *Vat. Gr.* 1005 of the fourteenth century originally owned by Cristoforo Garatone, Bishop of Corone, who died in 1448.

Perotti finished the translation of Book V, the last available to him, in the summer of 1454. Besides 'interim' rewards, he received five hundred golden 'ducati', for which he expressed gratitude in an epigram. In the next century the translation was found to be incompetent and it was finally denounced by Casaubon in words which ruined Perotti's reputation. But for the rest of the fifteenth century—and indeed even in the sixteenth century—Perotti's translation was the vehicle by means of which Polybius circulated in Europe. Unlike Bruni, Perotti did not believe that Polybius was useful only where Livy was missing. A passage of one of his letters to Tortelli contradicts Bruni's opinion. . . .

What the almost simultaneous translation of the greatest Greek historians under Pope Nicholas V meant to European historiography is a point beyond our terms of reference today. We are still left with the curiosity to know what was happening to the rest of the preserved text of Polybius while the first five books were circulating in Latin. Hans Baron has repeatedly stated that when Leonardo Bruni in one of his letters (8, 4) distinguishes between panegyric and history . . . he follows Polybius X, 21, 8 who opposes *encomium* to history. This would imply knowledge of the *Excerpta antiqua* and make it necessary to ask why Bruni seems to be unaware of Book VI with its discussion of the Roman constitution. But the distinction between *encomium* and history is in Cicero. It may have been reinforced by the teaching of Chrysoloras, with or without any specific reference to Polybius. I should like, however, to leave the question open, because we know at present too little about the circulation of the materials contained in the *Excerpta antiqua*.

What is now the main MS. for the *Excerpta,* F, *Vat. Urbinas Gr.* 102 of the tenth or eleventh century, was in the library of Urbino at least from 1482 onwards. Copies circulated in Italy during the early sixteenth century. More precisely, F2, *Vaticanus Gr.* 1647, which was derived from F, belonged to Andrea Navagero at the beginning of the sixteenth century.

The first clear sign of acquaintance with the excerpts of Book VI was discovered not long ago by Carlo Dionisotti in one of those obvious printed texts to which few turn. Bernardo Rucellai who died in 1514 refers to Polybius' sixth Book in his *Liber de urbe Roma* first printed in Florence in the eighteenth century. We know in fact that the *Liber de urbe Roma* was written before 1505 because it is mentioned in the *De honesta disciplina* by Pietro Crinito who died in 1505. . . .

Thus in the first years of the sixteenth century Polybius' Book VI was discussed in Florence though no formal Latin translation of it was as yet in circulation. Machiavelli did not have to go far to learn about the cycle of the constitutions. There is no need to suppose that he had to wait for Janus Lascaris or anybody else to come to Florence to translate for him the Greek he was unable to read. The substance of Book VI had been known in Florence for several years when, to all appearances in 1513, he started writing his *Discorsi*. Seldom has so much ingenuity been misused as in J. H. Hexter's paper *Seyssel, Machiavelli and Polybius VI: the mystery of the missing translation* (*Studies in the Renaissance* 3, 1956, pp. 75-96). What remains memorable is that Machiavelli was the first to appreciate Polybius as a political thinker. Machiavelli also availed himself of Polybius in the *Arte della Guerra* about 1520 and was certainly confirmed by him in his admiration for the Roman military model, but his actual use of Polybius' texts (never explicitly quoted) is very restricted.

As we have seen, it was in Florence that Polybius was rediscovered, first by Leonardo Bruni as a historian, then by Machiavelli and his contemporaries as a political thinker. It was probably also in Florence that Polybius was first studied philologically. Politian not only made extracts from Polybius (which are preserved in the famous MS. of the Bibliothèque Nationale, MS. Gr. 3069, and perhaps in the Turin MS. I, III, 13$^{1-2}$); he also used Polybius critically in his *Miscellaneorum Centuria Secunda* recently published by Vittore Branca and Manlio Pastore Stocchi. At no. 38 of the new *Centuria* Politian discusses the meaning of *Catorthoma* and leaves an empty space to be filled by quotations of the relevant Greek texts. In the margin he adds: *ex Thucydide aliquid et Polybio*. He intended to turn to Thucydides and Polybius for examples. . . . The excellent editors have failed to notice, if I am not mistaken, that Polybius did not appear in Politian's *Centuria Prima*. His appearance in the second *Centuria* is therefore an event. But we must remember that Polybius was by then read in some universities. Rudolphus Agricola may have become acquainted with Polybius in Ferrara about 1475.

II

After Machiavelli translations of the military chapters of Book VI multiply. There are at least four between 1525 and 1550. One was made by Machiavelli's admirer and disciple, Bartolomeo Cavalcanti, an exile from Florence. From 1537 to 1548, he served the Duke of Ferrara, Ercole II, who was not interested in republics, but was very ready to improve his army. For him Cavalcanti translated from Polybius a *Discorso circa la milizia romana* in 1539. In the following year Cavalcanti translated from Polybius XVIII, ch. 28-33, *La comparazione tra l'armadura e l'ordinanza de' Ro-*

mani e de' Macedoni. Finally, he wrote a dissertation on the Roman Camp, *Calculo della castrametatione*, which was printed, together with the *Comparazione*, in 1552 in a collection of pamphlets *Del modo dell' accampare*. Later, perhaps when he was old and poor in Padua about 1560, Cavalcanti went back to Polybius in the context of his *Trattati sopra gli ottimi reggimenti delle repubbliche antiche e moderne*. Here he used Polybius to support Aristotle on the mixed constitution, though he remarked drily that Polybius did not know Aristotle's *Politics* 'perchè nei tempi di Polibio, i libri di Aristotele non erano ancora stati trovati, nè i Romani ne potevano aver notizia'. Cavalcanti had obtained a complete transcription of the *Excerpta antiqua* of the *Cod. Urbinas* 102. His letters, which were made accessible by Mrs Christina Roaf in 1967, contain many details, new to me, about plans to publish the *Excerpta antiqua* in Italy. In a letter of 1540 to Pier Vettori he speaks of a projected publication by Paolo Manuzio. He also explains by implication why he did not go on with the complete translation of the *Excerpta* which he had promised. 'Giorgio greco', that is, Giorgio Balsamone who used to check Cavalcanti's translations of Polybius word by word, died about that time. Certainly no one was in any hurry to print the Greek text of Polybius. Aldus Manutius significantly did not handle him. When in 1529 Janus Lascaris at last edited in Venice a fragment of Book VI, the Latin preceded the Greek and the publisher Joannes Antonius de Sabio felt obliged to explain: *Graeco libro ut omnia conferri possint adiuncto*.

> [It] was in Florence that Polybius was rediscovered, first by Leonardo Bruni as a historian, then by Machiavelli and his contemporaries as a political thinker.
>
> — *Arnaldo Momigliano*

Meanwhile, in accordance with the general trend, Polybius was being edited in Greek outside Italy. The text of Books I-V was first published at Haguenau in 1530 by Vincentius Opsopaeus (Heidnecker) who used a MS. sent to him by Jacobus Ottonis Aetzelius of Nuremberg. The MS. was the present *Monacensis Gr.* 157 (C), a fourteenth-century MS. brought from Constantinople after 1453 which for a while was in the library of Matthias Corvinus, King of Hungary. Later, in 1577, we find this MS. in the hands of Joachim Camerarius who gave it as a present to Albrecht V of Bavaria—hence its present location in the Bayerische Staatsbibliothek. Opsopaeus' introduction is important for its eulogy of Aldo Manuzio, its attack on the Thomist theologians and its high appreciation of Polybius himself. . . . In 1549 Johannes Hervagius published in

Basle the *editio princeps* of the *Excerpta antiqua*. The text of the *Excerpta antiqua* came from a MS. in the possession of Don Diego Hurtado de Mendoza which was later burned in the fire of the Escorial in 1671. The translation into Latin was by Wolfgang Musculus.

Translations into modern languages were meanwhile in demand: L. Maigret published a French translation of Books I-V in 1545(?) and of Book VI in 1546(?). The Italian translation by L. Domenichi, notoriously incompetent, belongs to the same year, 1546. The English came a bad third in 1568 with a meagre translation of Book I by Christopher Watson of St John's College, Cambridge. The arrival of Polybius in England was, however, celebrated in a poem by R. W. which ends thus:

> Then Vertue learne
> That thou mayst earne
> Such glorie for to have
> As Momus sect
> Can not reject
> When thou arte closde in grave.

In 1574 Guil. Xylander published his German translation which Casaubon considered good. In 1582 Fulvio Orsini published in Antwerp the Polybius contained in the *Excerpta de legationibus* on a MS. sent to him by the great Antonius Augustinus, Bishop of Tarragona, the present U, now split between *Vat. Gr.* 1418 and *Neapolitanus Gr.* III, B, 15, which is a copy by Andreas Darmarius of a lost MS. of the Escorial. Another edition of the *Eclogae legationum* by D. Hoeschel was published in Augsburg in 1603. They were the texts which paved the way for Casaubon's Paris edition of 1609. Casaubon, however, benefited from the acquaintance with other MSS. and especially from the readings communicated to him by Andreas Schottus from a MS. in his possession of the *Excerpta de legationibus,* the present *Bruxellensis* 11301/16.

The removal of the centre of the classical scene to France, Germany and the Low Countries only served to increase the interest in Polybius as a historian and as a theoretician of political and military organization. The humanistic national history which the Italians had diffused throughout Europe (Polydorus Virgilius, Paulus Aemilius, etc.) was beginning to lose favour. History was becoming the repository of prudence and wisdom in an age of religious conflicts and political absolutism. *Historia si adsit ex pueris facit senes: sin absit, ex senibus pueros.* These words by Juan Luis Vives, *De tradendis disciplinis* (*Opera,* I, 1555, p. 505) are echoed in endless variations by all sixteenth-century writers on history and the art of history writing. Prudence, direct experience, travels, geography, technical expertise and a general respect for truth were the virtues required of the historian; and Polybius seemed to have all of them. He lacked

style, but translation into Latin would improve him. About 1550 Benedetto Varchi declared in the 'Proemio' to the *Storia Fiorentina:* 'Polibio, il quale de' Greci avemo preso a dover imitare, siccome Cornelio Tacito fra' Latini'. In 1552 Roger Ascham rather improbably associated Polybius with Commynes in his praise: they 'have done the duties of wise and worthy writers'. In 1566 Bodin thought that Paolo Giovio could not compete with Polybius in direct experience of military and political affairs. . . .

Francescus Balduinus saw in Polybius the ideal combination of the historian and of the lawyer. . . . Not by chance had Marcus Brutus . . . chosen to read him before the battle of Pharsalus. Francesco Patrizi and many others repeated with Polybius that the eye is better than the ear as a historical organ. Uberto Folietta in his *De similitudine normae Polybianae* could play with the sophistic question: if Polybius is right in asserting that the true historian tells only the truth, why is it possible to have good stories (such as Homer's account of the Trojan war) which are not entirely true? What is the difference, if any, between *historicus verax* and *historicus verus?* Patrizi was indeed inclined to believe that Polybius had crossed the border between history and philosophy, but had to allow one of the speakers in his *Della Historia Diece Dialoghi,* 1560, to interrupt him: 'E io vorrei . . . che tutti gli historici fossero cosí misti di filosofo et d'historico, come si è Polibio.'

One of the reasons why Polybius became so authoritative was that he offered the best alternative to the obsession with Tacitus which was typical of the intellectual climate about 1585, especially in Italy and Spain. In more than one sense, Tacitus had become irresistible. He offered exactly that mixture of Machiavellianism, moralism, epigrammatic acuteness and pathos which the age liked. But the cooler minds turned to Polybius with relief, as he obviously knew more about war and politics and spoke about a better historical period. Justus Lipsius, the greatest student of Tacitus—but never a vulgar 'Tacitista'—was the most exacting interpreter of Polybius as a military historian.

Interest in Polybius as a military historian is noticeable everywhere in the sixteenth century. For instance, Guillaume du Bellay, lieutenant de Roy à Turin, prepared a volume of *Instructions sur le faict de la guerre extraictes des livres de Polybe, Frontin, Vegèce, Cornazan, Machiavel et plusieurs autres bons autheurs* which appeared posthumously in Paris in 1549, if they were his. His concern was the creation of a national militia to replace mercenaries. But in 1594 Lipsius recognized only one real predecessor to his *De militia Romana libri quinque. Commentarius ad Polybium,* namely *La militia Romana di Polibio di Tito Livio e di Dionigi Alicarnaseo* by Francesco Patrizi, 1583.

The acknowledgement is significant. Patrizi, as we have seen, was not a blind admirer of Polybius. Even in his *La militia Romana* he shares the reservations expressed by Dionysius of Halicarnassus about Polybius. Yet Patrizi—an ignorant man in comparison with the massive erudition of Lipsius—may truly be described as Lipsius' predecessor because he believed that Polybius could provide a decisive contribution to the improvement of military organization, both in technique and in morale. In his dedication to Alfonso II d'Este Patrizi states that Roman military institutions were the only ones which could cope with the Turks; they would not be essentially affected by the 'nuova inventione della artigliaria'. The mention of the artillery was especially necessary in addressing a duke of Ferrara, since the Estensi had pioneered the use of the new weapon.

Lipsius was not concerned with the rise of national militias. He observes that they are unsuitable for monarchic states and that even a republic like Venice does not use its own citizens as soldiers. But the Turks show that a careful system of recruitment is required:. . . . The Romans have something to teach about recruitment, too, but it is in battle order and military discipline that they are the best masters. Roman superiority in battle order is clear:. . . . Even the Scythians were better disciplined than modern armies. . . .

It is not necessary to illustrate here the enormous success of the military commentary on Polybius prepared by Lipsius. Though he published it as a professor in the Catholic University of Louvain, after having run away from the Protestant University of Leiden, his work was used as a military handbook by the Protestants even more than by the Catholics. He was the spiritual and technical guide behind the military reforms of Maurice of Orange, who had been his pupil in Leiden. Wilhelm Ludwig of Nassau was equally an admirer of Lipsius. One of the problems these military reformers had to face was the creation of an educated class of officers who would be able to lead and control their troops. Lipsius provided not only technical principles derived from Polybius, but also moral principles derived from Stoic philosophy. The notion that the Romans of the Republic, having been victorious for so long, held the secrets of military success, was so deeprooted and widespread that Claudius Salmasius' *De re militari Romanorum,* written originally for Prince Frederick Henry of Orange, was left unpublished on purpose until 1657. Wilhelm Ludwig of Nassau made a thorough study of Polybius' account of the battle of Cannae. He recognized that Perotti's translation of that section of Polybius was unreliable and had another translation made by Volrat von Plessen.

Approved as a pragmatic historian of the highest competence by Bodin, presented to the ruling classes as an authority on war by Lipsius, Polybius was read and studied about 1600 as perhaps never before or after. His difficult and unclassical language was no longer an obstacle to Western readers who had attained new levels of knowledge of Greek and were particularly interested (as were Salmasius and Grotius) in Late Greek. Casaubon never published the monumental commentary he had planned, but his edition and translation of 1609 offered the best guide to interpretation and was a pleasure to the eye. In the introduction he summarized all the contemporary motives for admiring Polybius. He extolled his mastery of the military and diplomatic arts and his ability to understand the causes of events; he maintained that he was a religious man and even praised his style; he compared him advantageously with Thucydides, Xenophon, Sallust, Livy, etc., and finished by preferring him to Tacitus. . . .

Casaubon may well have contributed to the popularity of Polybius in England when he moved to London in 1610. But William Camden needed little encouragement from Casaubon to take Polybius as his mentor for the *Annales rerum Anglicarum et Hibernicarum regnante Elizabetha,* 1615.

The abundant erudite work of the seventeenth century on and around Polybius (such as the edition of the *Excerpta Peiresciana* by H. Valesius, 1634, and the commentary by Jacobus Gronovius, 1670) was supported by this warm feeling for the master of historical pragmatism. In 1615 H. Grotius included Plutarch and Polybius in his plan of studies, but left Thucydides out of it. Gerardus Ioannes Vossius expressed common opinion in making Polybius the central figure of his *Ars historica,* 1623 and in praising him in *De historicis graecis* (2nd ed., 1651). . . .

Casaubon's influence is easily recognized in later compilations. For instance, John Dryden composed a 'character' of Polybius which appeared as a preface to the translation of Polybius by Sir H. S[hears] in 1693. Dryden, like Casaubon, is still concerned with the question whether Polybius or Tacitus is the better historian. He has, however, some curious notions of his own, not necessarily inspired by better scholarship. He believes that Constantine the Great collected the 'negotiations' of Polybius as an ambassador. As he assumes Constantine the Great to have been English, he can conclude: 'I congratulate my country, that a prince of our extraction (as was Constantine) has the honour of obliging the Christian World by these remainders of our great historian.'

But if one had to follow seriously the course of Polybius' reputation during the seventeenth century, one would probably have to account for a change of emphasis in his fame. This change ultimately emerged very clearly in England in the early eighteenth century. It was now Polybius' picture of the mixed government which attracted attention. The balance of power in England was compared with the balance of power in Rome. As England was also a state where religion was controlled by the civil power, any reference in Polybius—or indeed in any other writer—to the place of religion in Rome was treated with interest. Even the debate on early parliaments involved Polybius. This makes a very different story, which I hope to tell elsewhere.

I shall conclude by summarizing the story I have been able to put together for today. Polybius was rediscovered in Florence as a historian of the first Punic War by Leonardo Bruni about 1420. Though he had been translated into Latin by the middle of the fifteenth century, his reputation as a historian and as a political thinker does not seem to have been widely diffused. It was in republican Florence, too, that the importance of his Book VI was recognized for the first time by Machiavelli and others at the beginning of the sixteenth century. Even the first philological work on him seems to have been done in Florence, by Politian. The idea of printing the Greek text does not appear to have interested the Italians until it was too late. The publication of Polybius in Germany coincided with the opening of a new stage in Greek studies—and with the new didactic and pragmatic mood of European historiography. Polybius' reputation soared rapidly in the second part of the sixteenth century. His fame was based on his expertise as a military and diplomatic historian. The Dutch republicans took his lessons to heart, though paradoxically the lesson was spelled out by Justus Lipsius after he had preferred Catholicism and monarchy to Protestantism and republic. Finally, Polybius and his Protestant editor, Casaubon, took refuge in England, and the Dutch had a better reason for remaining faithful to both. . . .

A. M. Eckstein (essay date 1985)

SOURCE: "Polybius, Syracuse, and the Politics of Accommodation," in *Greek and Byzantine Studies,* Vol. 26, No. 3, Autumn, 1985, pp. 265-82.

[*In the following excerpt, Eckstein discusses Polybius's attitude towards the political hegemony exercised by Rome, arguing that the historian "was a political realist from beginning to end."*]

Polybius' intended audience was made up of political men; his avowed purpose was to prepare such men for political action in the real world; his theme was the expansion of Roman power. Despite the simplicity of these basic principles of the *Histories,* there remains considerable disagreement about Polybius' attitude towards Rome. This is the result partly of the fragmentary nature of the extant text, partly of the obscurity of some of Polybius' own remarks. There is particular debate over whether Polybius' view of Rome gradual-

ly became more accommodating over time. Walbank strongly favors this hypothesis, while others (Musti, Shimron) have recently asserted that Polybius always remained "a loyal Greek." Any new material would be useful in this dispute. There is in fact evidence that has not yet been brought to bear.

In the surviving text of the *Histories* there are four encomia of 'good kings' of the third and second centuries B.C.: Hiero II of Syracuse (in Books 1 and 7); Attalus I of Pergamum (Book 18); Eumenes II of Pergamum (Book 32); and Massinissa of Numidia (Book 36). Their very names indicate immediately a certain underlying direction in Polybius' thought, for an enduring cornerstone of the foreign policy of all four of these 'good kings' was cooperation with Rome. Conversely, all those kings who opposed Rome militarily (Hieronymus of Syracuse, Philip V, Antiochus III, Perseus, Andriscus the Pseudo-Philip) come in for heavy criticism: they are foolish and mostly tyrannical, not 'good kings'.

The encomium of Hiero II is particularly instructive, because Hiero's policies were so closely bound up with those of Rome and the encomium occurs so early in the *Histories*. Moreover, Polybius' explicit contrast in Book 7 between the achievements of Hiero and the troubles caused by his anti-Roman successor Hieronymus provides an early and precise model of the famous condemnations of anti-Roman politicians that characterize the last books of the work. While these latter condemnations have led Walbank to argue that Polybius' attitude towards Rome became increasingly accommodating as the *Histories* drew to a close, it may well be that Polybius was a political realist from beginning to end.

Our understanding of Polybius' attitude towards kings and kingship has been greatly enhanced by K.-W. Welwei's re-examination of the assumption that Polybius, who grew up under a republican form of government in Achaea, hated monarchy *per se*. Welwei has shown that the situation was far more complex: while Polybius clearly disliked oppressive personal despotism, he also made a distinction between raw tyranny and true kingship. The true king possessed innate personal excellence. . . and greatness of spirit . . . , best reinforced by education and training; his basic task was the care of his subjects' welfare, and he should seek to engage in benevolent actions . . . both on their behalf and, out of his general concern for mankind . . . , on behalf of others as well. The true king's maturity of character was expressed by moderation . . . in all his actions, including a restrained style of life and a mild internal régime; moreover, he devoted a large portion of his energy to securing personally the protection of his community and its interests against all external dangers. A successful king, therefore, was so outstanding an individual that he found his subjects obeying him more or less voluntarily, out of a sense of respect and even awe.

Polybius did not, of course, invent this concept of the true king. He drew upon an intellectual tradition, reaching back as far as Isocrates, Xenophon, and Plato, that formed the common inheritance of Hellenistic political thought on kingship. The traits of Polybius' true king appear in summary form in Book 6, where in a general examination of systems of government we find a contrast between monarchy and its degenerate twin, tyranny (6.6f). But these concepts of kingship are applied consistently in Polybius' discussion of individual rulers throughout the *Histories*: specifically, in the four encomia we have already mentioned, beginning with Hiero of Syracuse.

As we have noted, Polybius discusses Hiero in detail twice. In 1.8.3-17.1 Hiero figures prominently in the events surrounding the outbreak of the First Punic War. In 7.8.1-8 Polybius offers a general evaluation of Hiero and his rule, now looking back over a reign of more than fifty years. In both sections Polybius presents Hiero as an ideal ruler. Even as a young man Hiero was a natural statesman worthy of being a king (1.8.3); he rose to power in Syracuse without any initial advantages beyond his outstanding character (7.8.1f). Polybius passes quickly over Hiero's original coup d'état, emphasizing instead the mild nature of his early régime (1.8.4). The mildness of Hiero's government is stressed again in Book 7, where Polybius even claims that the king, throughout his long reign, never exiled, executed, or even injured a single Syracusan citizen (7.8.2). Hiero was similarly restrained in his personal style of life, though he was eventually surrounded by great prosperity; Polybius says that in this way the king preserved his physical and mental vigor past the age of ninety (7.8.7f), while at the same time avoiding envy (7.8.3). Within his own family, Hiero was able to inspire intense loyalty (7.8.9). As a result, popular in Syracuse from the beginning (1.8.5), Hiero remained immensely and universally popular to the end of his reign (7.8.5-7).

There is no reason to doubt that Hiero was basically a 'good' ruler. On the other hand, Berve has suggested that Polybius' edifying picture of Hiero's character and régime may in some respects be overdrawn. The Roman governor at Lilybaeum, for example, felt it necessary in 215 to send a strong Roman naval force to Syracuse upon hearing a (false) rumor of Hiero's death, in order to ensure that power remained in the hands of Hiero's family (7.3.5-7). This hardly suggests that the family, or the monarchy, was universally popular. It is also difficult to believe that Hiero's extensive and very efficient system of taxation contributed to his popularity. But if Polybius' picture of an idyllic Syracuse under Hiero is somewhat exaggerated, this only emphasizes that behind Polybius' ardent praise of Hiero lay an

ideological commitment. Some elements of this commitment should already be obvious from his conception of the true king; there are others.

The primary characteristic of Hiero's reign, according to Polybius, was peace. . . . As Welwei puts it, Hiero appears to Polybius as an "Idealherrscher und Friedensfürst." The reference is partly to internal peace, but it is also an obvious reference to Syracusan foreign relations. Here the crucial event was Hiero's decision in 263 to come to terms with Roman power, a decision on which Polybius comments at some length.

In 264 war had broken out, between Rome on the one side and Carthage and Syracuse on the other, over Roman protection of Messana and its Mamertine rulers. The combined Carthaginian-Syracusan siege of Messana eventually failed, and in 263 the armies of Rome overran all of northeastern Sicily. In Polybius' account Hiero now re-evaluated the general situation and his own position, and rationally calculated that the Romans were far more powerful than Carthage (1.16.4). This conviction impelled him to make peace with Rome, a peace he successfully negotiated with the Roman commanders in Sicily, the consuls M'. Valerius Maximus and M'. Otacilius Crassus. Hiero agreed to pay Rome a war indemnity and to restrict himself to the southeastern corner of Sicily (1.16.5-9: Hiero's ambitions in the northeast had been one of the causes of the war). Polybius continues (1.16.10f):

> King Hiero, having placed himself under the protection of the Romans, always furnished them with resources according to the necessities of the situation. Henceforth he ruled over Syracuse in security and treated the Greeks in such a way as to win from them crowns and honors. We may, indeed, regard him as the most illustrious of rulers, and the one who reaped for the longest time the fruits of his own wisdom, both in particular cases and in general policy.

Polybius' judgment on Hiero's decision to go over to the Roman side seems wholly positive, and it leads to a general encomium emphasizing Hiero's wisdom. . . . Indeed, this evaluation is so startlingly 'pro-Roman' that scholars since Gelzer have assumed that it derives ultimately not from Polybius himself, but from Fabius Pictor.

Even if this were certain, it would not diminish in the least the significance of the passage. Polybius was no mindless copier, and he was well aware of Fabius Pictor's political bias (*cf.* 1.14f); if in Fabius he found sentiments such as these concerning Hiero and chose to include them in the *Histories,* it was because they contributed to some intellectual purpose of his own. In any case, we cannot be certain that the thinking of 1.16.10f is not Polybius' own. Gelzer's original argument was very brief: merely that the depiction of Hiero in 1.16.10f is so pro-Roman as to be un-Polybian. But this begs the question; moreover, whatever its origin, Polybius chose to include this passage without the slightest caveat to his readers. In favor of direct Polybian authorship is the consistency of tone in 1.6.10f with that of the final encomium of Hiero in 7.8, which seems to express Polybius' own evaluation of the king. Moreover, the reference in 1.16.10f to Hiero's benefactions after 263 to the wider Greek world would hardly derive from Fabius Pictor (why should he care?), while, on the other hand, we know that this is precisely the benevolent behavior Polybius expected of the true king. In fact, in his final encomium Polybius once again praises Hiero's benefactions to the Greeks and comments on the great reputation they won for him in the Greek world (7.8.6).

There is good reason, therefore, to conclude that the highly positive judgment of Hiero at 1.16.10f represents Polybius' thinking, and not that of Fabius Pictor. Even more important for our purpose, Polybius consciously allowed this depiction of Hiero to suggest to his readers a favorable response to the first decision by a Greek statesman in the **Histories** to seek an accommodation with Roman power. And if there is perhaps some exaggeration in Polybius' representation of Hiero's decision as a model of rational political decision-making (1.16.4), this only serves to strengthen the proposition that in 1.16 Polybius was seeking to make a didactic point to his readers.

One may add that Hiero's agreement with the Romans in 263 was probably simply a treaty of peace, and not a military alliance with stipulated requirements for concrete Syracusan military aid to Rome. This, in turn, would suggest that Polybius, in noting that Hiero "always furnished [the Romans] with resources according to the necessities of the situation" (1.16.10), meant to indicate that Hiero, wise to make a political accommodation with Rome in 263, continued to show political wisdom throughout his reign by always cooperating voluntarily with the Romans and supporting them in their various projects.

There may well be a similar didactic point in Polybius' final encomium of Hiero at 7.8. The passage is introduced by belittling comments on Hiero's anti-Roman successor, Hieronymus, and continues with the remark that it would be more useful for his readers to reflect upon the career of Hiero instead (7.7.1-7). The positive evaluation of Hiero's régime and character that follows is set in the perspective of the chaos and disaster that are about to engulf Syracuse after the half-century of peace and prosperity that resulted from Hiero's policies. This is clear from the position of the encomium of Hiero in the early fragments of Book 7, where it is the culmination of (and a strong contrast to) the main story of Hieronymus' wanton destruction of the friendly relations between Syracuse and Rome that

Hiero had carefully constructed (7.2-7). We also know that the encomium of Hiero was followed, later in Book 7, by an account of how the anti-Roman policies of Hieronymus led, after his own death, to outright war with Rome. The consequence of that war, of course, was the end of Syracuse as an independent state.

We need not conclude, however, that Polybius was a pro-Roman sycophant, or that he consciously advocated sycophancy in others. The best argument against such an interpretation may be found in Polybius' comments on the policies of Hiero after the end of the First Punic War (1.83.2-4). He says that from the start of Carthage's deadly war with the Mercenaries (241 B.C.), Hiero had been glad to comply with every Carthaginian request for aid. This probably took the form of grain shipments. Polybius adds that Hiero gladly helped Carthage because he was convinced that the physical survival of Carthage was in his own interest, both in regard to his Sicilian dominions and his friendship with Rome; in this way, no one power (*i.e.,* Rome) would completely and easily dominate the western Mediterranean. Polybius concludes that in so doing Hiero acted very wisely and intelligently . . . , for one should never contribute to the attainment by one state of a power so proponderant that none dare dispute it even on the basis of acknowledged treaty-rights.

In contrast to the 'pro-Roman' implications of the judgment of Hiero presented in 1.16, Gelzer and others have claimed that in 1.83 we see the 'real' Polybius. But in fact there is no true contradiction between the sentiments. In the former passage Polybius praises Hiero for his intelligence in originally bending to the reality of Roman power, and thus accepting Roman hegemony; in the latter, Polybius praises him for seeking to preserve the objective conditions that allow Syracuse to retain a relative independence *within* an acknowledged Roman hegemony. Indeed, the aim of Hiero's maneuvers at 1.83, as Polybius presents them, is not to destroy Roman hegemony, or even to escape from it, but precisely to *maintain* the current conditions of his friendship with Rome (1.83.3), conditions made abundantly clear in 1.16.

H. H. Schmitt has argued that in 1.83.2-4 Polybius is in fact presenting Hiero with approval as a classic practitioner of balance of power theory. No doubt there is an element of such thinking in the passage, for the preservation of Carthage would naturally impede complete Roman domination (and thus eventual oppression) of the states of the western Mediterranean. But Polybius' aim here is much broader and less focused than the illustration of a balance of power theory *per se*—which, in the form elucidated by Schmitt (the searching out and steadfast support of an external counter-weight to a hegemonic power) is inapplicable to the foreign policy of Hiero. Rather, the comments in 1.83 on Hiero's actions articulate one of Polybius' general principles concerning the interaction of a weak state directly with a hegemonic one: the weak state, if it can avoid it, should not by its own behavior abet the strengthening of that hegemony. This explains why Polybius' remark here is in the present tense, a usage that greatly puzzled Schmitt, for by the time Polybius was writing, there *was* no power in the Mediterranean capable of acting as a counter-weight to Rome. Moreover, if the basis of Hiero's foreign policy had been the concept of preserving an international balance of power, Hiero would naturally have moved to support the weaker party during the Second Punic War (Carthage), or would at least have tried to remain *de facto* neutral: in this way, there would have been a better chance of redressing the balance of power, then greatly in favor of Rome. But Polybius was well aware, and told his readers, that Hiero strongly supported Rome in the Second Punic War—just as he was aware, and told his readers, that the heart of Hiero's foreign policy from 263 onwards had been cooperation with Rome. In fact, there was no other alternative.

Thus, Polybius' description in 1.16 of a stateman's rational acceptance of the reality of an unfavorable military-political situation stands in close relationship to that in 1.83, which describes the statesman's attempt to maneuver *within* that unfavorable situation to maintain whatever advantage is still possible both for himself and for his community. Perhaps Polybius' sensitivity to such problems stems from his background as a citizen not of a great power, but of a state that had always been relatively weak even within the Greek context.

In short, Polybius in Book 1 indicates his approval of two modes of political behavior: he accepts cooperation with Rome out of practical necessity (and perhaps even for local advantage), combining this with a countervailing stress on avoiding unnecessary capitulation to Roman power. Both these principles will receive more famous expression much later in the ***Histories***. What is striking, and important for our understanding of the development of Polybius' thought, is that we find both principles made explicit so early. But if both are already important in Polybius' thinking about Rome in Book 1, the warning about unnecessary capitulation to Roman power (1.83.4) only comes into play because Polybius already assumes that a policy of general cooperation with Rome will so often be the only politically intelligent policy for Greek states to follow. Syracuse is the first example.

If Polybius presents Hiero as the archetype of the practical, intelligent, and successful statesman, the opposite is the case with Hiero's grandson. Hieronymus was only fifteen when he came to the throne of Syracuse (Liv. 24.5.9); in Polybius' judgment, he soon proved himself an immature and incompetent ruler. He fell under the influence of various poor advisors; to-

gether, they steered Syracuse away from Rome, eventually concluding an alliance with Carthage. Meanwhile, the régime was continually rent by bitter factional strife that led to occasional executions and, after thirteen months, to the murder of Hieronymus himself. Polybius consistently refers to Hieronymus with contempt as "the boy." The new king was "naturally of highly unstable character," a situation made worse by his evil advisors (7.4.6). He was drawn to Carthage by misleadingly positive accounts of Hannibal's campaign in Italy (7.4.4). He not only rejected Roman envoys who had come to renew Hiero's old treaty, but wantonly insulted them (7.3.4-9), disregarding their dignified warning that he was acting against both justice and his own best interests (7.4.4). Highly susceptible to flattery, Hieronymus began to take too seriously his descent from Pyrrhus, and his ambitions grew irrational: he was originally willing to conclude an alliance with Carthage in return for Syracusan control over the eastern half of Sicily, but was soon demanding the whole island (7.4.2-9). The Carthaginian government, for its part, perceived "the boy's complete instability and mental derangement" . . . , but they also saw that it was in their immediate interests to agree to everything he demanded (7.4.8f). When the new treaty subsequently came up for discussion among Hieronymus' advisors, those who opposed it (the native Syracusans) remained silent, fearing the king's lack of self-control (7.5.3).

Polybius' general conclusion is that Hieronymus' character was "exceedingly capricious and violent" (7.7.5), and that he was worthless as a subject for serious study; as we have noted, Polybius comments that it would be far more agreeable, and also far more useful to the serious student of politics, to consider at length the career of Hiero instead (7.7.8).

Polybius' account of the reign of Hieronymus has received little attention; while Hiero is discussed in detail in Welwei's catalogue of Polybian depictions of good and bad rulers, Hieronymus is missing entirely. But despite Polybius' strictures in 7.7.8, it is clear from the fragments surviving from the early part of Book 7 that Polybius discussed the politics of Hieronymus' régime at length. Moreover, what does survive of this account (in 7.2-7) provides further evidence for Polybius' general ideology of kingship, for Hieronymus' régime is presented as in every respect the opposite of Hiero's. Instead of an internal stability lasting decades, we see instability of such severity that it soon destroyed the ruler himself; instead of constant mildness of government, we see increasing cruelty; instead of habitual self-restraint amid the temptations of great luxury, we see growing megalomania; instead of careful analysis of the realities of the geopolitical situation of Syracuse and the construction of an equally careful foreign policy, we see a ruler easily and fatally misled about the true balance of power in the world; finally, instead of decades of peace and prosperity, we see Syracuse brought to the brink of a disastrous war with Rome. Thus, it is hardly surprising that for Polybius, the arbitrary and self-absorbed Hieronymus is not an exemplar of true kingship (as his wise grandfather Hiero so obviously is), but represents the degenerate twin of kingship: Polybius places Hieronymus squarely among the ranks of the tyrants.

But if Hieronymus appears to Polybius as a ruler actually more foolish than truly evil, it is a foolishness that expresses itself not only in chaotic internal politics, but more importantly in foreign policy. Childishly enthralled by stories of Hannibal's victories in Italy, carried away by an irrational vision of rule over all Sicily, Hieronymus allowed himself to be drawn over to the side of Carthage. Indeed, it is precisely in the context of Hieronymus' irrational ambitions that Polybius concentrates his criticism of the young king's personality, put into the mouths of the Carthaginians themselves (7.4.8f). Now, such wide ambitions among rulers are not, for Polybius, foolish *per se,* nor are they the invariable sign of a tyrant: their wisdom depends upon the political context in which they are conceived and the means by which they are carried out. Thus, Philip II of Macedon receives only the highest praise for the vision, energy, and skill with which he extended his hegemony over Greece. But his approval of Philip II only serves to bring Polybius' condemnation of Hieronymus' dreams into sharper relief: Philip was a king of the far past, and Polybius' criticism of Hieronymus is based on his failure to see that he was living in an age of *Roman* power that imposed severe restraints upon Syracusan policy. The price of Syracusan peace and prosperity had been (and had to be) the abandonment of traditional ambitions to dominate the island. Polybius praises Hiero in 1.16 for realising this; he condemns Hieronymus as "mentally deranged" for failing to do so.

It may be that Polybius' view of Hieronymus is somewhat unfair. After all, Hieronymus had come to the Syracusan throne in the year after the Roman catastrophe at Cannae and had no personal experience of Roman steadfastness in adversity: in 215 it was possible to believe that Roman hegemony in Sicily was on the wane. As for claiming the entire island, one may argue that it was intelligent policy for Hieronymus to exact from Carthage as high a price as possible in return for his military cooperation. But if Polybius has (once again) simplified the actual political situation at Syracuse, this only reveals (once again) his desire to make a didactic point: in this case, that statesmen who chose to oppose Rome militarily were making a very foolish miscalculation, no matter what the immediate situation.

Finally, it is important to note that Polybius' condemnation of the personality and policy of Hieronymus in

Book 7 is an early model of those more famous Polybian condemnations of the 'irrational' personalities and policies of anti-Roman politicians that appear later in the *Histories*. Hieronymus is called immature, highly unstable, and even mentally deranged. Similarly, in Book 23 Polybius takes the (alleged) preparations of Philip V for a war of revenge against Rome as evidence—along with his increasing tyranny—that in the 180's Philip, too, had gone insane. Again, those Macedonians who supported the disastrous attempt to resurrect the Antigonid monarchy (149/8) appear to Polybius to have been struck by madness sent from heaven (36.17.13-15). And shortly thereafter, the Achaean leaders who went to war with Rome over the issue of possible Roman liberation of Sparta from the Achaean League also are depicted by Polybius as stupid or even insane. There are common themes in Book 7 and the later Books 23, 36, and 38: (1) policies flow from personalities, and (2) behind all these destructive attempts to break free of Roman hegemony lie seriously flawed, irrational politicians. Moreover, if Polybius' discussion of the events in Achaea in the 140's is explicitly intended as a warning to his readers to avoid such disastrous (and even ridiculous) mistakes in the future (38.4.8), surely the same holds true for Polybius' condemnation of Hieronymus in Book 7. Clearly, the 'fully developed' Polybian view of the necessity of cooperation with Rome was already a prominent feature of his work early in the text, and is not merely a characteristic of the later books of the *Histories,* especially the last decade.

Polybius' attitude towards Hiero and Hieronymus can further be used to help date more precisely Polybius' own intellectual development, as well as to clarify what he hoped would be the impact of his *Histories* among the Greeks. First, Polybius' consistent reference in Books 1-15 to Carthage as an existing state is a strong indication that this part of the *Histories* (*i.e.,* down to the end of the Second Punic War) was already written by 150 B.C., while Polybius was still an exile in Rome. This means, in turn, that Polybius' understanding of the limits imposed on the political behavior of communities confronting Roman power was fully developed before the disasters of 149-146 in Greece; therefore, Polybius' ideology of 'the political art of the possible' cannot be viewed simply as a result of those events. Second, there are good reasons for believing that all of Books 1-15 had actually been published by 150. Thus, Polybius' advice, explicit and implied, on the necessity and benefits of cooperation with Rome was advanced publicly to the Greek world before the collapse of the Achaean League. This may further explain the special bitterness in Polybius' later depiction of the 'irrational' anti-Roman politicians of the 140's, especially in Achaea itself.

In fact, we should not be surprised to find an explicit attitude of political 'realism' towards Roman power so early in Polybius' work. From his own description, this was precisely the view he had taken as a young politician during the period 170-168. The Achaean political situation at this time is well known. Polybius himself was an adherent of the faction centered around Philopoemen, and, after the latter's death, around Archon and Polybius' own father, Lycortas. These men advocated asserting the letter of Achaean rights under the League's equal treaty of alliance with Rome—although they also seem increasingly to have conceded the necessity of ultimate obedience to any really persistent Roman request, as well as the wisdom of supporting Rome in any major Roman project. The Archon-Lycortas group was opposed by a faction centered around Callicrates that advocated much more whole-hearted cooperation with the Romans. In the late 170's, when Roman relations with Perseus of Macedon became strained, there were various Roman expressions of concern about Achaean loyalty, based specifically on the attitudes of the men around Archon and Lycortas.

At the time, these Roman suspicions were hotly denied; and indeed, when war actually broke out between Rome and Macedon (spring 171), Archon, as *strategos* of the Achaean League for 172/1, immediately complied with a Roman request for direct military assistance. Yet when his faction assembled in the autumn of 170 to consider its position on the war, now that Archon was running again for *strategos* (for 170/69), there was in fact a considerable difference of opinion. Some advocated a direct confrontation with Callicrates and his supporters on the grounds that they were too pro-Roman (Polyb. 28.6.6); Lycortas himself urged that they aid neither Macedon nor Rome (28.6.3-5). But Archon advised the group to "obey circumstances" . . . and not give their enemies any excuse to denounce them as anti-Roman (28.6.7). Some modern scholars hold that Archon was merely proposing a policy of 'waiting on events', nothing more. But one should remember that the Lycortas-Archon group was under considerable pressure in the autumn of 170 to adopt an overtly pro-Roman stance, if only for the sake of self-preservation: there had been rumors that they would be publicly accused by the Romans themselves of taking an anti-Roman attitude (28.3.7f). Polybius has Archon now say that the group must not allow themselves to suffer the fate of the Aetolian politician Nicander and his friends, already deported to Italy for anti-Roman behavior (28.6.7). Moreover, in a neglected passage that serves as Polybius' direct gloss on Archon's policy as re-elected *strategos,* we are told that Archon and his followers were in favor of "working with the Romans" and their friends . . . (28.7.1). In other words, at the meeting in autumn 170 what Archon advocated was full Achaean cooperation with Rome against Perseus; this had been his policy as *strategos* in 172/1, and this was his position now. Further, it is important to note that Polybius says he *supported*

Archon (28.6.8), in effect publicly parting company with his father, who advocated neutrality (cf. 28.6.3-5). It may be that Polybius took this remarkable step because he himself was about to run for hipparch (28.6.9) and felt he had to adopt a more 'responsible' position on the great issue of Achaean cooperation with Rome. Even so, the incident reveals much about Polybius' thinking concerning 'the political art of the possible' long before the *Histories* came to be written.

One can follow this attitude further in the actions of Archon and Polybius once they were elected and took office for 170/69. Polybius' first act was to advocate restoring certain Achaean honors to the pro-Roman Eumenes II of Pergamum. Shortly thereafter, Archon carried a proposal that the Achaean League spontaneously offer the services of the full Achaean military levy to Q. Marcius Philippus, the new Roman commander in Greece; and it was Polybius who personally headed the Achaean delegation sent to make this offer (28.12.4f). The offer was declined, but Polybius stayed on voluntarily with the Romans, taking part in Philippus' campaign against Perseus in 169 (28.13.1-7). After returning to Achaea, Polybius advocated the dispatch of a small Achaean military force to aid Ptolemaic Egypt, now threatened by Antiochus IV (29.23-25: winter 169/8). But he immediately dropped this proposal when Philippus by letter urged the League to support the Roman policy of mediation of this conflict; and indeed, the Achaean embassy of mediation sent out in response to Philippus' letter included Archon himself (29.25.6).

None of this prevented Polybius and other Achaean politicians from being deported to Italy after Pydna, on Callicrates' denunciation of their anti-Roman views: the Lycortas-Archon group had been under suspicion too long (one reason why Archon, in autumn 170, had advocated full cooperation with Rome). Polybius himself condemns as false all Callicrates' specific allegations (30.13.9f); and his account of his own conduct as hipparch in 170/69—a narrative there seems little reason to question—seems to bear this out. To accept Polybius' narrative is not a naïve act of faith. First, Polybius' public behavior makes sense given the difficult political circumstances of the men around Lycortas and Archon, the Roman pressures on them, and Archon's conscious policy of attempting to turn aside Roman suspicion from the group. Second, it is clear that in his account of this period Polybius is not simply engaging in propaganda aimed at endearing himself and his friends to Rome at all costs: he makes no secret of the hostility to Rome of some of his close associates, including his own father (28.6.3-6). He also indicates that he personally delayed making Archon's offer of Achaean troops to Philippus until the time was most suitable for *Achaean* interests, *i.e.,* not those of Rome (28.13.1-4). And he claims that he advocated restoring some, but not the most extravagant, of the

Achaean honors to the pro-Roman Eumenes II (28.7). This is not a whitewash. In the absence of contrary evidence, as Walbank observes [in *Polybius,* 1972], we should assume that Polybius is essentially telling the truth about his own public acts.

This reconstruction of Polybius' political behavior in 170-168 tells us much, in turn, about the younger Polybius. He believed that in the crisis of the Roman war with Perseus, the Achaean League (and especially his own political faction) had no rational choice but to adopt a policy of basic cooperation with Rome. On the other hand, he did what he could to avoid complete sycophancy and the sacrifice of Achaean interests. Thus, it makes sense that someone with Polybius' principles of political 'realism' with regard to Rome—apparent in his actions in 170-168—would, while composing the earlier books of his *Histories,* find the political behavior of Hiero rational, attractive, and even exemplary, and that of Hieronymus immature, irrational, and deranged.

Given the implications of Polybius' evaluation of Hiero and Hieronymus, as well as the reconstruction offered above of Polybius' own political behavior in 170-168, we seem once more to be faced with the questions: did Polybius then care nothing for 'Greek freedom' *per se*? Was he merely a cold and unfeeling advocate of *Machtpolitik* who bowed to the will of the stronger, or (worse) a quisling? The issue is more complex than this. In the Hellenistic age, political hegemony was even more prevalent than in the Classical period, and it had also become more acceptable intellectually, its forms often more polite. Thus, Polybius grew up in a world where the political hegemony of great states was a long-acknowledged fact of life. No one knew the situation better than Achaean politicians: the Achaean League had long had an accommodation with Macedon and (later) with Rome, while Aratus' efforts to gain full independence of action for the League had led to near disaster in the 220's at the hands of Cleomenes of Sparta. Similarly, it may have seemed to many Greeks in 170-168 that the issue was not Greek freedom or Greek enslavement to Rome, but rather a choice between the loose hegemony over Greece exercised by the Romans or a much tighter control over Greece that might be exercised by Perseus from nearby Macedon. In any event, Polybius believed that the options available to most statesmen were quite limited, and he took submission to some sort of hegemony to be the natural condition of all but the most powerful states. In this situation, it was certainly the duty of the weaker state to preserve its interests and its autonomy as best it could; but submission even to a marginally satisfactory relationship of hegemony was preferable to hopeless and destructive rebellion. Nevertheless, the issue of how to behave in relation to a stronger state was only one element in Polybius' central focus, which was not simply upon

freedom *versus* submission to hegemony, but rather upon rational *versus* irrational decision-making. The latter emphasis on 'rationality' was what was most important, and it was on this basis that Polybius wrote the *Histories* as a guide to politicians. These considerations explain much about his attitudes, from the beginning of the work, towards those Greek statesmen who had to deal with the overwhelming fact of Roman power.

Wesley E. Thompson   (essay date 1985)

SOURCE: "Fragments of the Preserved Historians—Especially Polybius," in *The Greek Historians: Literature and History— Papers Presented to A. E. Raubitschek,* Anma Libri, 1985, pp. 119-39.

[*In the following excerpt, Thompson examines ways in which the fragmentary state of the remains of Polybius's* Histories *may have affected historians' views of his work.*]

There is a romantic allure to collecting and interpreting fragments of lost works. What could be more pleasurable than reconstructing the plot of *Prometheus Unbound*? And Toni Raubitschek certainly enjoyed himself studying what Theopompus and Theophrastus said about ostracism. But the same interest does not extend to quotations from works which are preserved in their entirety. We know, for instance, who cites Androtion and what sort of information they gain from him, whether it be facts from Athenian history, details of cult, or merely unusual words. But we do not know who quotes Xenophon, nor whether the *Hellenica,* the *Anabasis,* or the *Memorabilia* was the most influential work, nor whether he was cited as the final authority or merely quoted in comparison with Diodorus for fourth century history, Plato for the life of Socrates, and Herodotus for Persian ethnography. Likewise, you can find the fragments of Isaeus without much trouble, but it would be very difficult to find out who saw fit to quote the speeches which have survived and whether they were used as historical sources or literary models. Occasionally it is possible to make some progress along these lines. Hude's *editio maior* contains a full collection of citations from Thucydides, but very little has been done with it.

In the call to the meeting we are asked "what direction research and explanation should take in the coming decades." It seems to me that one useful project for the future would be to collect the "fragments" of Herodotus and Xenophon—and, for that matter, those of the extant orations—and then to exploit this material and the evidence gathered by Hude for Thucydides.

Even now, without the collection process, it is still possible to learn a great deal about one of the major historians—Polybius—by studying the fragments of those books of his which have come down to us complete. Our text of the remaining, fragmentary books is derived almost entirely from two sources, the so-called *Excerpta Antiqua* from the first eighteen books, and the collection of Excerpts taken from the whole work, compiled at the command of the Emperor Constantine Porphyrogenitus. The latter is arranged according to subject matter, such as material to illustrate diplomatic embassies, military stratagems, and plots against kings, subjects which no doubt interested the Emperor Constantine greatly. The rationale for the choice of the *Excerpta Antiqua* has not been adequately determined.

The last half of Polybius' history, as we have it, consists largely of diplomatic history and the internal politics of the Greek cities. One would hardly guess that Polybius was also, perhaps even primarily, a military historian. The reason for this misleading impression is obvious. Most of the text is derived from the Constantinian collection devoted to embassies, and Polybius regularly explains the factional disputes that lead to, or result from, diplomatic missions. Even when there is a war on, our texts of Polybius tell us more about the diplomatic maneuverings than about actual fighting. It's something like preserving Book 5 of Thucydides while throwing away Books 6 and 7. The Third Macedonian War, for example, occupies some fifty-five pages in the Teubner edition. Of these, thirty-three pages are derived from the collection of excerpts *De Legationibus*.

For the same reason we learn very little about *res Asiae* from Polybius. Since the Seleucids were further removed geographically and less dependent politically than mainland Greece, there was much less diplomatic intercourse between them and the Romans, and thus much less material to interest the compiler of the *De Legationibus*. And, of course, he had no concern at all for the fighting which the Seleucids waged. Let us take as our test case this time the Sixth Syrian War, where all but three excerpts are from the *De Legationibus*. Thus we learn how Antiochus Epiphanes justified his declaration of war (28.20), how the Achaens rejected the call of Lycortas' faction to send troops to the Ptolemies and chose instead to honor the Roman request to mediate a settlement to the conflict (29.23-25), and finally how the Romans ended the war through aggressive diplomacy and their threat to intervene on the side of Egypt (29.27). But we learn nothing at all about how Antiochus came within a whisker of capturing all of Egypt. The closest we come to putting on armor is a fragment preserved by Athenaeus in which Polybius describes Antiochus' victory parade (30.25).

For the purposes of history the selection process of the Constantinian Excerpts is not such a serious matter: we can, after all, obtain a lot of information from Livy and Diodorus about the events which the excerptors omitted. But for the purposes of historiography this method of selection has led to a great distortion, even deformation, of the scope and nature of Polybius' work. It helps to create the impression of a monomaniac, hammering away constantly at the same topic, the Roman manipulation of Greek internal discord, with only an occasional so-called "methodological" digression, in which the author complains mercilessly about the shortcomings of other historians and preaches the need for learning from his own brand of writing history.

In his recent essay, "On Historical Fragments and Epitomes" [in *CQ* 74 (1980)], Brunt says that "even excerpts [as opposed to mere fragments], unless they are very numerous, substantial, and representative, cannot reveal the *scope* of an author's work. For instance the Constantinian excerpts from Arrian's *Anabasis* come chiefly from the volumes on *Virtue and Vice* and on *Gnomai* and overweight its moralizing and sententious elements." As I have indicated, the main contributor to our version of the second half of Polybius is the *De Legationibus*. The next two major sources are these same collections on *Virtue and Vice,* and on *Gnomai*. The effect of their contribution to the text of Polybius is the same as Brunt describes in the case of Arrian. The difference is that nobody has to depend on these compilations of extracts for his text of Arrian: he can read it straight. But we can have only the kind of Polybius that the Byzantine anthologists chose to preserve.

Brunt adds, "Epitomators in general seem to have aimed not at producing faithful resumés but at recording, sometimes at length, what they thought of most interest, and their principles of selection are at times impenetrable. They do not necessarily offer a faithful miniature of the original as a whole." He cites the summary of Arrain's *Anabasis* made by Bishop Photius. "It occupies," he says, "about a hundred lines of the Teubner text, of which nineteen suffice for the first three books; there is not even a mention of the siege of Tyre. By contrast Photius can list almost all the brides and bridegrooms at the Susa weddings. He distorts the whole economy of the work." Brunt concludes that "'Fragments' and even epitomes reflect the interests of the authors who cite or summarize lost works as much as or more than the characteristics of the works concerned."

Once this is said, it all seems obvious enough, and surely Polybius scholars must be aware of the problem and react accordingly. But I would agree with Brunt that "scholars have often been too precipitate in characterizing and evaluating lost histories on the basis of evidence that is irremediably insufficient, and that in particular too little account is commonly taken of the relevant characteristics of the authors who preserve the 'reliquiae', their reliability in quoting or summarizing, and their own interests and purposes." Even our greatest authority on Polybius, a man who is not only learned but also very perceptive, has not been able to avoid this mistake. At a conference like this one Professor Walbank was asked "whether we have a clear notion of the criteria according to which the excerpts were made: we cannot assume *a priori* that the tenth century excerptors were interested in the problem of Roman imperialism." Walbank simply replied, "These are important points and the answers are not easy. The interests of the excerptors can, I suppose, be deduced from the actual content of the surviving excerpts." In response, Momigliano suggested a much better way to proceed: to make "a comparison between the excerpts from books I-V and the full text. This, as far as I know, has never been properly done."

This is an excellent idea, to which I return shortly, but first I want to argue that Momigliano has fallen into the same trap which he himself pointed out. In a piece written for *The New York Review of Books* [reprinted in his *Essays in Ancient and Modern Historiography,* 1977] he says that "there are at least two basic facts which [Polybius] underrates. One is the Roman conquest of Spain and the other is the Roman organization of Italy. In either case we may suspect that he was misled by his Greek preoccupations and prejudices." In discussing his first contention he observes, "The decision to remain in Spain and to control it was a compound of economic considerations (mines to explore and lands to colonize) and of instinctive pleasure in power . . . But if there was inducement to plunder and massacre at pleasure, there was also a danger of demoralization of which the Romans themselves soon became aware. It was to fight corruption in dealing with the Spanish provinces that they first instituted special tribunals for malversation in 149 B.C., and there are other signs that they became uneasy about the behaviour of their generals in the Peninsula. Unless we are misled by the lacunas in Polybius' text, he appears to be insensitive to the problems presented to Rome by its conquest of Spain. There is no sign that he realized that the destruction of Numantia by his friend Scipio raised the same moral problems as the destruction of Corinth and Carthage."

Even if the lay reader actually notices the proviso, "Unless we are misled by the lacunas in Polybius' text . . . ," he will surely ignore it. Clearly Momigliano himself does not believe that in the missing portions of his history Polybius actually did comment on the importance of Spain. He ascribes "Greek preoccupations and prejudices" to Polybius without allowing for the possibility that these are the faults of the epitomators. The military historian M.J.V. Bell [in *CQ* 66 (1972)] also assures the reader that Polybius "was a Greek, not particularly interested in Spain as the balance of his work shows." But is this really the case? In Book 3

Polybius comments on the significance of Spain to the Carthaginians (10.5-6; cf. 35.5-6) and describes some of Hannibal's fighting there (13.5-14.10 and 17). And in his second preface he announces that, following his exposition of the Roman constitution, he will show how it made possible the reconquest of Italy and Sicily and the subjugation of the Spaniards and Celts (3.2.6). He also promises "an account of the subsequent policy of the conquerors and their method of universal rule, as well as of the various opinions and appreciations of their rulers entertained by the subjects, and finally I must describe what were the prevailing and dominant tendencies and ambitions of the various peoples in their private and public life." Surely this proves that Polybius had an interest in Spain which the excerptors did not share. He goes on to say (3.5.1) that he will describe the Roman war against the Celtiberians and Vaccaei, but once again the compiler of the *De Legationibus* has omitted this conflict since his task was to record negotiating, not fighting.

To summarize, then, when Oswyn Murray says, [in *CQ* 66 (1972)], "Certainly Polybius is the greatest surviving political historian of the period, and our accounts [of Hellenistic historiography] will always to some extent be biased towards his preoccupations," I would quarrel with the word "his." Certainly you cannot excerpt what the author himself did not include, and surely Greece was more important than Spain to Polybius, but the almost total purgation of Spain from the text of Polybius shows that our accounts of Hellenistic history writing are biased toward the prejudices and preoccupations of the men who chopped and whittled Polybius down to manageable size.

When we ask "what direction research and explanation should take in the coming decades," I would answer that we should put first things first. Before anyone undertakes an analysis of Polybius similar to the studies of Herodotus and Thucydides which have appeared lately, we need to determine the nature of the bias that underlies our text of Polybius, along the lines suggested by Momigliano. It is necessary to study what the compiler of the *Excerpta Antiqua,* for instance, chose from the first five books and more importantly—what he omitted from his collection. This should provide a clear indication of what he has omitted from Books 6-18. One must then compare what he did retain from those books to see whether his standards change in the course of his work. One would do the same for the various volumes of the Constantinian Excerpts to discover on what basis items were chosen for the *De Legationibus, On Virtue and Vice, Gnomai,* and the rest.

This would be a vast undertaking, for the Constantinian Excerpts contain huge chunks of other historians besides Polybius, running to over 1500 pages. Ideally, to understand the mentality of the excerptors one should know his Herodotus so well that in reading through the Constantinian Excerpts of that author he will know what is missing and comprehend the full extent of the loss. And he will know his Thucydides too, and also his Xenophon. The task requires a tremendous power of imagination, for it is one thing to analyze the texts we have before us, but something altogether different to appreciate the significance of what has been lost.

As an example of the sort of research I have in mind, the remainder of my paper will be given over to an analysis of the way the *Excerpta Antiqua* were chosen. Since we are concerned today with the direction of future research, it seems more appropriate to present an ongoing project rather than a completed one. Even better, this is not a topic where the answer was known in advance and merely needed to be documented: at the beginning of this line of inquiry I had not the slightest idea of what I would find.

First it would be standard procedure to outline current ideas on the subject, but in this case I have only found one scholar who even addresses the question of how the *Excerpta Antiqua* were compiled. John Moore, who has studied the manuscript tradition of Polybius, asked himself [in *Greek Roman and Byzantine Studies* 12 (1971)] why the *Excerpta Antiqua* are drawn only from the first eighteen books. "No satisfactory hypothesis has so far been advanced as to why they should have ended at this point, but consideration of content suggests the following as a possibility. By the end of XVIII the excerpts had not merely covered the history to the end of the Second Punic War, but had also dealt with the conflict with Philip V which was an almost inevitable result of relations between Rome and Philip during the Second Punic War, and had brought the narrative down to a suitable climax with the battle of Cynoscephalae and the Isthmus declaration of 196 B.C. The presence of some material dealing with other areas would be natural, granted Polybius' method of writing history." That is, he assumes that the *Excerpta Antiqua* constitute, in Brunt's words, "a faithful miniature" of the first half of the **Histories**. The inadequacy of such an explanation will be apparent as soon as one realizes that it is the *De Legationibus,* not the *Excerpta Antiqua,* which preserves the *senatus consultum* on the freedom of the Greeks and the joyous celebration of it at the Isthmian Games.

To give some idea of the type of material which the selector of the Excerpts omits I have surveyed Book 3, where the events are well known. He does not include Polybius' introduction (1), which is pretty much a repetition of what he has already copied from the beginning of Book 1 (1.1-3.5), nor does he transcribe the list of wars and other topics which Polybius proposes to treat (2-5). He ignores the theoretical discussion of what constitutes the causes of wars as distinct from the

pretexts (6-7), and Polybius' specific application of his doctrine to the Second Punic War (8-15). Thus—a point of some significance for Momigliano's case—the excerptor does not notice the growth of Carthaginian power in Spain (13-15.1), which Polybius regards as one of the causes of the war (10.6). The compiler then skips over the *dikaiologia,* in which Polybius presents the arguments about where guilt for the war lies (20-21) and offers his own interpretation of the three treaties between Rome and Carthage (22-30). The selector also omits Polybius' argument for the value of studying cause and effect (31) and his *apologia* for the enormous length of his work (32).

When the historian finally reaches the military portion of Book 3, the compiler ignores Hannibal's preparations, including campaigns to secure Carthage's hold on Spain (33.5-35). Nor does he copy Polybius' account of Hannibal's troop strength (35.7-8; 56.4), which—the historian proudly informs the reader (33.17-18)—is based on an inscription set up by Hannibal himself. Likewise he ignores the distances of Hannibal's route, much of which Polybius painstakingly calculated and retraced in person (39; 48.12). He skips over most of the crossing of the Rhone (42-46) and the Alps (50-56).

Once Hannibal reaches Italy, the compiler ignores the basic strategy of the war, including Hannibal's decision to move away from friendly territory and fight the war on hostile ground (78.5), his instigation of revolt throughout Italy, and—in particular—the motive and significance of his attack on the plain of Capua (90.10-12). The excerptor also overlooks the counter-strategy devised by Fabius Maximus (89.2-90.5) and Roman attempts to take the offensive outside Italy (76; 96-99). We search in vain for Polybius' judgment that the cause of Rome's ultimate victory was its *politeia* (118.7-9).

We also miss some of the particulars of the action, including the first battle in Italy (65), the Roman retreat to the Trebia (66-68), and Hannibal's various marches through the peninsula, especially the grueling three and one-half day passage of the swamp lying before Trasimene (79).

As you can see, the excerptor has badly defaced Polybius' narrative, and we can expect that the result will be the same in those books where the *Excerpta Antiqua* constitute the main source for our texts.

What, then, has he included? Only matters military and geographical. He transcribes Polybius' discussion of the three continents and their boundaries (36.6-38.5), as well as his geography of the Rhone and the Alps (47.2-4). His military excerpts include the great battles of the Trebia (70.1-75.4), Trasimene (80.1-85.4), and Cannae (108.2-117.6), which might indicate that his work was directed to the general reader who wanted to know the most significant events of the war, without the burden of superfluous detail and the vast quantity of turgid prose Polybius serves up. But in reading the excerpts from Book 3, I developed the suspicion that our man was really more interested in military stratagems than famous battles, and that suspicion was confirmed in studying the other books.

In the very first excerpt from Book 3, Polybius describes the Roman attack on the island of Pharos, in which they first put men ashore at an uninhabited spot and then sail brazenly into the main harbor. When the defenders sally out to meet the ships, the commandoes ambush them. Or take the crossings of the Rhone and the Alps. The excerptor omits all the fighting at the Rhone (42-43) and simply copies out Hannibal's device for transporting the elephants by tying rafts together (45.6-46.7). He does not even include the actual crossing of the panic stricken animals (46.8-12); he is solely interested in the *mechane*. It took Hannibal fifteen days to cross the Alps, but the compiler has preserved the activity of a single day (50.1-51.11). Hannibal sends troops ahead during the night to seize the peaks above a certain pass. This first discourages the natives from attacking, but when they see the baggage train in difficulty, they make their assault. Hannibal is then able to attack them in turn from the high ground. Other obvious stratagems by the Carthaginian are his staging of a gladiatorial contest between two prisoners of war to demonstrate to his own men that it is better to die fighting than to submit to slavery, and his trick of attaching torches to the horns of cattle so that Fabius Maximus follows the animals while Hannibal's troops escape in the opposite direction.

Hannibal wins many of his victories by ambush, and the excerptor includes two such stratagems based on the principle of knowing the personality of the opposing general. Chapter 81, included in the *Excerpta,* contains Polybius' reflections on the subject in general: "For there is no denying that he who thinks that there is anything more essential to a general than the knowledge of his opponent's principles and character, is both ignorant and foolish." One must see "what are the weak spots that can be discovered in [the opponent's] mind," and exploit such faults as sloth, drinking, lust, cowardice, and stupidity. "Rashness . . . and undue boldness and blind anger, as well as vaingloriousness and conceit, are easy to be taken advantage of by his enemy and are most dangerous to his friends; for such a general is the easy victim of all manner of plots, ambushes, and cheatery. Therefore the leader who will soonest gain a decisive victory, is he who is able to perceive the faults of others and to choose that manner and means of attacking the enemy which will take full advantage of the weaknesses of their commander."

Hannibal puts these precepts into practice by learning the character of Flaminius and Marcus Minucius. In a passage from the *Excerpta* which calls to mind Thucydides' description of Cleon at Amphipolis, Polybius says that Hannibal found out that "Flaminius was a thorough mob-courtier and demagogue, with no talent for the practical conduct of war and exceedingly self-confident withal. [Thus] he calculated that if he passed by the Roman army and advanced into the country in his front, the Consul would on the one hand never look on while he laid it waste for fear of being jeered at by his soldiery; and on the other hand he would be so grieved that he would be ready to follow anywhere, in his anxiety to gain the coming victory himself without waiting for the arrival of his colleague." Flaminius then follows Hannibal into the trap at Trasimene, a passage which the selector transcribed in full. He also chose to include a relatively minor affair in which "Hannibal . . . was aware of the rivalry [between the two dictators Fabius and Minucius] and of Marcus' impulsiveness and ambition." Now Minucius was also puffed up by a minor victory, so Hannibal devised a plan to take advantage of his over-confidence. He placed men in ambush during the night and the next day began to fortify a hill that lay between his position and the Roman camp, "well knowing that owing to his previous achievement Minucius would instantly advance to frustrate this project." When the Romans came out to dispute possession of the hill, Hannibal unleashed his men from the hiding-place.

Even though some of the excerpts from Book 3 are quite colorful and might interest the general reader, the evidence is strong that the excerptor was preparing a book with a fairly narrow focus for those concerned with military tactics rather than simply a condensed version of an overly long historical classic. In university terms, he was compiling a text for a course in military science, not ancient history.

In the other books where our text is complete, the epitomator is more catholic in his taste. Once again we find the geographical passages: descriptions of Italy (2.14.4-17.8), Byzantium and the Black Sea (4.38.1-45.8), and Media (5.44.3-11). In addition, we find selections that seem to correspond in type to the material which appears in the Constantinian Excerpts. We have character sketches of Aratus (4.8.1-12) and Philip V (4.24.4-7; 5.9.1-12.8), the sort of thing that appears in the collection *On Virtue and Vice,* and about a dozen general observations that could be classified as *gnomai,* such as, "So great is the difference both to individuals and to states between carefulness and wisdom on the one hand, and folly with negligence on the other, that in the latter case good fortune actually inflicts damage, while in the former disaster is the cause of profit."

We have the military excerpts, of course, including two set pieces, Sellasia (2.65.6-69.11) and Raphia, and a trio of lesser encounters, which—at first sight—seem to illustrate different types of fighting that a general must master. One is the battle of Caphyae (4.11.1-13.2), where Polybius stresses the importance of terrain, criticizing Aratus for his failure to use his heavy infantry against the Aetolian light infantry in the plain, where he would have had the advantage. In another excerpt (2.25.1-31.7) the Gauls are caught between two Roman armies and accordingly line up with one half of their army facing one way, and the other half facing the opposite direction. Finally, a battle between Philip V and the Spartans (5.22.1-23.6) seems to be about breaking through a strong defensive position.

The selector has also chosen two stratagems devised by Hamilcar Barca (1.75.5-76.9). Noticing that the Bagradas River, which blocked his advance, became very shallow at its mouth when the wind blew strongly upon it at certain times, Hamilcar was able to lead his army across at just the right spot and just the right moment. Thereupon he defeated his opponents, who attacked from two sides, by feigning retreat and—once the enemy broke ranks to pursue—by wheeling around into battle formation.

There are three passages of general historical interest: the preface to Book 1 (1.1-3.5), Polybius' summary of the growth of Roman power up to the First Punic War (1.6.1-7.11), and a *gnome* emphasizing the importance and difficulty of writing a universal history (5.32.1-33.8). Finally, we have a seemingly inexplicable choice about the arrival of a Numidian defector to the camp of Hamilcar (1.77.6-78.15).

Despite exceptions, it is clear that we have a military, not a political, compendium. The compiler has no interest in the history of the Achaean League, the tyrants of Sparta, or the social question in Greece. Even the military selections are not representative, as they favor tactics over strategy. The selector entirely omits the First Punic War in favor of the attack on Pharos, includes nothing to explain the Mercenary War of which the battle of the Bagradas is part, and has no interest in long marches, such as Hannibal's great treks or the lightning campaigns of Philip V through the Peloponnese which drew the admiration of Polybius. His prime concern is what Polybius calls "plots, ambushes, and cheatery," and this interest grows more pronounced in the remaining books.

Instead of going through the whole of the *Excerpta Antiqua*, I have chosen to compare the selections from Books 7-11 with those from the first pentad. We find once again extracts about geography and observations on the character of such men as Aratus (8.12), Antiochus the Great (11.34), and Hasdrubal (11.1.2-3.6). The excerptor is especially interested in the character of Scipio Africanus, how he relies on planning and does not trust to luck (10.2-17), and how he wins the

support of his troops by his own moderation in the treatment of women prisoners (10.18-19) and his refusal of kingship (10.40). There is one major battle, Philopoemen's victory at Mantinea (11.11-18), one document, Hannibal's treaty with Philip (7.9), and at least one embassy speech (11.4-6). We also find a number of *gnomai,* including two historiographical passages. In one Polybius again emphasizes the need for universal history (8.1-2); in the other (9.1-2) he justifies his omission of the entertaining in favor of the useful, which is, of course, the excerptor's own creed.

By far the most prominent feature of the second pentad is the large number of stratagems. Their importance to the excerptor is best demonstrated by his inclusion of stratagems which are almost identical to those which he copied from Books 1-5. A campaign of Antiochus corresponds to that portion of Hannibal's crossing of the Alps which the selector included in his book. Hannibal learned that the natives guarded the passes by day and returned home at night, and thus was able to seize the peaks in their absence. Antiochus twice found barbarians guarding passes and by occupying the peaks was able to drive them out with a shower of missiles (10.29.3-31.3). Later in his journey, hearing that some other natives guarded a river crossing during the day but went home at night, he rode ahead and seized the spot when they had retired for the evening. Then he bravely fought off their counter-attacks (10.49). Antiochus' Anabasis lasted some six years, but apart from the capture of a fortified town (10.31.6-13) these exploits of the king are the only actions that caught the selector's eye.

Again in the first pentad the Romans at Pharos, and Hannibal in his duel with Marcus Minucius, first set an ambush and then lured the enemy out of a protected position by provocatively dispatching troops in plain sight. So the *Excerpta Antiqua* from Book 8 contain a story of how Philip V caused his own men to suffer a defeat in the open field so that the garrison left the Acrolissus in quest of booty, only to fall into his ambush. And the excerptor chose to preserve a battle in which Scipio lured the Spaniards into a meadow by placing cattle there as bait. Just as Hamilcar noticed that the winds made the Bagradas shallow at a certain spot, so Scipio observed that low tide exposed a land bridge to a place from which the citadel of New Carthage could be climbed. He told his men that Neptune promised him in a dream to help the Romans, and the dream seemed to come true when (just on schedule) the waters receded, opening the fortress to attack (10.8.6-7; 11.7, 14).

After taking the trouble to record Hannibal's device of joining rafts together to ferry elephants, the excerptor now copies Polybius' account of how the Romans tied ships together at the siege of Syracuse in order to support giant war machines. He also preserved Polybius' detailed description of these implements as well as the ingenious devices which Archimedes prepared for the defense. He also included the description of Philip's war machine at Echinus, a kind of moving scaffolding with troops stationed on three floors (9.41).

And there are new stratagems. Polybius himself uses the word (11.22.1) in connection with Scipio's two tricks that won the battle of Ilipa (11.20-24): first he brought his army out to fight before the Carthaginians had a chance to eat and then stationed his best men on the wings with the unreliable Spaniards in the middle. The excerptor also transcribed the battle of Baecula, in which Scipio again attacked on the wings while holding his center in reserve (10.33).

In another selection Polybius recounts Hannibal's march on Rome aimed at drawing off the Roman army besieging Capua, and compares it with Epaminondas' march on Sparta, which forced the defenders of Mantinea to leave it unguarded (9.3-9).

One of the collections of Constantinian. Excerpta consisted of stratagems. Although it has not survived, we do know that one of the items was a passage in which Polybius describes how Philopoemen trained his men in all the various cavalry maneuvers. This selection also appears in the *Excerpta Antiqua* (10.23), as does a passage in which Scipio trains his forces at New Carthage (10.20).

Hannibal's assault on Tarentum (8.24.4-34.13) involves a series of stratagems: the way the traitors arrange to come and go at will by pretending to hunt or pillage (24.9-13; 25.4-11); Hannibal's secret march on the city from a distance of three days, which he capped off by arresting everyone outside the town to prevent detection (26); and his device of hauling ships overland from the harbor to the outer sea in order to blockade the Roman garrison (34).

Finally, the capture of Sardes, based—like many of these stratagems—on the principle of hitting the enemy when and where he least expects it. Buried in Polybius' account of the battle of the Trebia is an observation (3.71.2-3) that teaches this lesson: "the Romans, while very suspicious of thickly-wooded ground, which the Celts usually chose for their ambuscades, were not at all afraid of flat and treeless places, not being aware that they are better adapted than woods for the concealment and security of an ambush." Three times, then, in the second pentad the excerptor found material to illustrate that a citadel can be taken at its strongest point, where no one would expect an attack. Philip took the Acrolissus because, relying on its natural strength, the enemy set only a few men to guard

it (8.13.9) and the king was able to fool them. At New Carthage Scipio attacked at a spot which was usually under water and so left unguarded (10.14.13-14). And Sardes was taken when one of Antiochus' men saw that vultures and other birds alighted on a portion of the wall of the citadel. He inferred that the defenders were not standing guard there, relying instead on the sheerness of the rock wall. That, of course, is where the attackers scaled the heights and entered the city (7.15-18).

The key to the selection process of the *Excerpta Antiqua* comes, I think, in a passage from Book 9: "The accidents attendant on military projects require much circumspection, but success is in every case possible if the steps we take to carry out our plans are soundly reasoned out. That in military operations what is achieved openly and by force is much less than what is done by stratagem and the use of opportunity, can easily be learnt from the history of former wars" (12.1-2). So victory in war is won by the general who—like Scipio—relies on planning and does not trust to luck and knows how to employ stratagems. But the successful leader must master other elements of war, for the quotation continues (12.3-5), "And it is no less easy to be convinced by facts that in those actions depending on the choice of opportunity failure is far more frequent than success. Nor can anyone doubt that most of the failures are due either to error or to negligence on the part of the commander. We must therefore inquire in what such faults consist."

He then proceeds to show the practical importance of astronomy and geometry to a commander, noting, for instance, that Philip V and Cleomenes missed a rendezvous with men who planned to betray their own cities, because each king neglected to figure the time of nightfall according to the season (9.18). Throughout his collection from 7-11 the excerptor has made sure to include other admonitions to would-be leaders. One of the *gnomai* which he copied from Book 1 says, in effect, that being a soldier is one thing, but being a general is another. Thus he also records Polybius' advice not to become involved in minor skirmishes, such as led to the death of the consul Marcellus (10.32-33.7), but to manage the broader concerns of a campaign, as exemplified in the excerpt on how Philopoemen rode sometimes bravely at the head of the cavalry, but then wisely dropped to the rear or inspected the center of the corps in order to gain a view of the whole situation (10.24). When Scipio fights at New Carthage he has three shieldbearers to ward off missiles (10.13.1-5). The Excerpts also include Polybius' teaching that a general should not rashly entrust himself to his enemies, illustrated by the fates of Ti. Sempronius Gracchus and Achaeus. And while some might prefer to view the episode as an indicator of Scipio's character, I would cite as an example of how to avoid danger the excerpt (11.25-30) in which he puts down a mutiny among his troops through a combination of rhetoric and ruthlessness.

The excerptor includes a long discussion of the Roman method of dividing booty, which Polybius recommends as a safety measure (10.16-17.5). Since under the Greek method, "most of the men start pillaging, commanders cannot maintain any control and run the risk of disaster, and indeed many who have been successful in their object have, after capturing the enemy's camp or a town, not only been driven out but have met with complete disaster simply for the above reason." The selector clearly shares the historian's didactic purposes, for the passage ends, "Commanders should therefore excercise the utmost care and foresight about this matter, so that as far as is possible the hope of equal participation in the booty . . . may be common to all."

One final selection shows clearly that we are dealing with a military handbook and not a faithful miniature, viz., Polybius' comparison of his own system of fire signals with the one recommended by Aeneas Tacticus (10.43-47). The excerptor allotted almost as much space to this item as to the famous description of the Roman constitution in Book 6 (11.11-18.8).

Is it credible, then, that during the tenth century someone would compile a series of excerpts from Polybius to serve as a textbook of tactics? The answer is clearly, yes, for the great textual critic A. Dain has observed that the common Byzantine practice of reworking classical literature (*retractatio*) was a response "to the need to adapt an ancient work to new conditions." The Emperor Constantine himself writes that he regularly took certain books with him on campaign: books on generalship, weaponry, and history, especially Polyaenus and Syrianus. Five abridgments of Polyaenus were available during this period, and his stratagems were rearranged according to type to make them more useful. The *Excerpta Antiqua* are the result of reworking Polybius in the same way.

The topics chosen from Polybius are not merely useful, they are the main concerns of Byzantine commanders. According to Toynbee's excellent analysis of military handbooks of the tenth century [*Constantine Porphyrogenitus and His World,* 1973], the primary Byzantine tactic was to follow marauding invaders and cut them off at the pass, seizing the heights with light-armed troops who would rain missiles (especially arrows) down on the enemy. This is why the only excerpt from the crossing of the Alps is Hannibal's occupation of the heights, and why the selector recorded Antiochus' seizure of mountain peaks and a river crossing. When the Byzantines raided Muslim lands, says Toynbee, "The most difficult and dangerous of all contingencies for an East Roman Army is to find that a kleisoúra on the Army's line of retreat from enemy

territory has been occupied by the enemy. Keep away from any occupied kleisoúra. It is the terrain, not the enemy himself, that creates the danger. Terrain can enable a weaker force to defeat a stronger. If you can, compel the enemy to evacuate the kleisoúra by sending infantry through other kleisoúrai, that he has not occupied, to take him in the rear. If the enemy cannot be forced or tempted to evacuate, and if his position is impregnable, take one of the side-roads." This would explain the excerptor's interest in Hannibal's escape from the plain of Capua with his trick of attaching torches to the horns of cattle. It would also explain why he included a description of Philip V's victory over the Spartans (5.22.1-23.6). The King was returning north after ravaging Laconia (5.19) and found his way blocked since Sparta lay on his left and the Eurotas and some hills on his right. The forces within the city could attack his flank as he marched past, and Lycurgus had occupied the hills. Since there were no side roads, Philip had to force the position, driving his opponents from the heights.

I originally thought that the selector included the battle in which the Romans attack the Gauls from the front and the rear (2.25.1-31.7) as an example of how to manage fighting on two fronts, but now we can see the real reason for this excerpt: the Gauls were heading home with an enormous haul of booty when a second Roman army unexpectedly arrived by sea at Pisa and then seized the pass through which the Gauls had to proceed.

Sir Charles Oman says [in *The History of the Art of War in the Hiddle Ages, Vol. 1,* 1924], "Of the spirit of chivalry there was not a spark in the Byzantine . . . [He] was equally remote from the haughty contempt for sleights and tricks which had inspired the ancient Romans, and from the chivalrous ideals which grew to be at once the strength and the weakness of the Teutonic West . . . They considered it absurd to expend stores, money, and the valuable lives of veteran soldiers in achieving by force an end that could equally well be obtained by skill." It is in this tradition that our excerptor copied down Polybius' observation (9.12.2) that "in military operations what is achieved openly and by force is much less than what is done by stratagem and the use of opportunity." The Byzantine, according to Sir Charles, "had a strong predilection for stratagems, ambushes, and simulated retreats." We have already seen the selector's great interest in ambushes and in Hamilcar's feigned retreat at the Bagradas. A favorite device of the Byzantine handbooks, and one actually used against the pretender John Bryennius, is to send out a small force to attack the enemy or to ravage his territory. When they encounter resistance, they flee pell-mell, and lead their pursuers into an ambush. The *Excerpta Antiqua* include two battles (3.104-105; 8.13-14) in which commanders use their men as bait.

One of the main themes of the handbooks is the need to exercise troops in military maneuvers and discipline well before heading off to meet the foe, and Leo the Deacon on at least half a dozen occasions mentions that a general prepared his forces this way. This interest accounts for the preservation of 10.23, where Philopoemen exercises his men. The Byzantine use of fire signals explains the selection of Polybius' discussion of this device. Another passage which only begins to reveal its meaning in the light of Byzantine *tactica* is Polybius' account of Hamilcar's conduct in the Mercenary War (1.77.6-78.15), beginning with the arrival at his camp of an African noble seeking to defect. As Toynbee puts it, "The interrogation of prisoners and deserters is also considered to be indispensable," and Polybius shows Hamilcar examining the young man who wants to become his helper, as well as Antiochus scrutinizing the Cretan who offers to betray Achaeus (8.17.2). Finally, we notice the similarity between Hannibal's march on Rome, intended to relieve Capua, and "a brilliantly successful diversionary raid into Cilicia that was made by Nikêphóros Phokás the elder" which forced "the Cilician Moslems to raise their siege of the East Roman fortress Místheia."

It is easy to believe that the *Excerpta Antiqua* were chosen for their similarity to Byzantine military practices. That in itself does not mean that a Byzantine commander was consciously following Polybius whenever he outfoxed the enemy, but it does mean that the study of Polybius, Polyaenus, and handbooks which go back to the Roman Empire helped shape the overall outlook of a tenth century general.

There are a few topics remaining to complete this research project. We need to examine the character sketches in the *Excerpta Antiqua* more closely to see whether they correspond to those portions of Byzantine manuals which discuss the qualities of a good general. Professor Pearson, I am sure, will want to know what attracted the compiler to preserve part of the historiographical Book 12. Perhaps the largest problem of all is Book 6. I always used to wonder why anyone would be interested in that tedious description of the Roman camp. Now I know: Byzantine handbooks are filled with similar descriptions which go back—by the process of *retractatio*—to Polybius. Now, paradoxically, I wonder why the man who showed so little interest in politics chose to preserve Polybius' discussion of constitutional cycles and his description of the Roman *politeia*.

FURTHER READING

Baronowski, Donald Walter. "Polybius on the Causes of the Third Punic War." *Classical Philology* 90, No. 1 (January 1995): 6-31.

Examines Polybius's analysis of the causes of the war in order to clarify the historian's view of the war and his attitude towards the Roman empire.

Derow, P. S. "Polybius, Rome, and the East." *The Journal of Roman Studies* 69 (1979): 1-5.

A close examination of the evidence Polybius provides of Roman imperial aims and his analysis of this evidence.

Dixon, Suzanne. "Polybius on Roman Women and Property." *American Journal of Philology* 106, No. 2 (Summer 1985): 147-70.

Looks at passages in the *Histories* for evidence regarding the property rights of Roman women in the second century B.C.

Eckstein, A[rthur] M. "Polybius, the Achaeans, and the 'Freedom of the Greeks.'" *Greek Roman and Byzantine Studies* 31, No. 1 (Spring 1990): 45-71.

Scrutinizes Polybius's discussion of Roman policy in Greece at the beginning of the second century B.C. and the historian's emphasis on Achaean contributions to the development of that policy.

————. "Josephus and Polybius: A Reconsideration." *Classical Antiquity* 9, No. 2 (October 1990): 175-208.

Examines the possible influence of the writings of Polybius on the Jewish historian Josephus (c. 37-100 A.D.).

Eckstein, Arthur M. *Moral Vision in* The Histories *of Polybius*. Berkeley: University of California Press, 1995, 331 p.

Disputes the view that Polybius judged human conduct on strictly pragmatic grounds, arguing that his writings reflect a consistent concern for ethical standards of behavior.

Momigliano, Arnaldo. "The Historian's Skin." In *Essays in Ancient and Modern Historiography*, pp. 67-77. Middletown, CT: Wesleyan University Press: 1977.

provides an overview and evaluation of Polybius' life and writings.

Usher, Stephen. "Polybius and His Predecessors." In *The Historians of Greece and Rome*, pp. 100-24. New York: Taplinger, 1970.

An overview of Polybius' writings that places them in historical and historiographical context.

Walbank, F. W. *A Historical Commentary on Polybius*. 3 vols. Oxford at the Clarendon Press, 1957-79.

A detailed, book-by-book study of the remaining fragments of the *Histories*, by the leading modern authority on Polybius. The introduction to Vol. I is excerpted above.

————. "Polemic in Polybius." *The Journal of Roman Studies* 52 (1962): 1-12.

Identifies possible political and personal motives for Polybius's criticisms of earlier historians.

————. "Polybius and Rome's Eastern Policy." *The Journal of Roman Studies* 53 (1963): 1-13.
Weighs the substance, origins, and credibility of Polybius's explanation for the rise of Rome.

————. *Polybius*. Berkeley: University of California Press, 1972, 201 p.
A general study of Polybius, covering in particular his theories of history and of history-writing and his views on Roman government, military practices, and imperial policies.

Thucydides

c. 455/460 B.C.-*c.* 399 B.C.

Greek historian.

INTRODUCTION

Thucydides' reputation as a primary historian of the ancient world derives from his one work, the *History of the Peloponnesian War*. Thucydides began compiling his work at the onset of the war in 431 B.C., becoming one of the earliest historians to write contemporary history, and he continued to record the events of the war as it unfolded. The work chronicles most of the war, although Thucydides died before its conclusion; his account ends at 411 B.C., seven years before the war ended in 404. His dedication to an accurate and impartial presentation sets him apart from his contemporaries, in whose works supernatural events and moral purpose typically play a greater role. He attempted to eschew "fable" and bias in his work, as he explained: "Of the events of war I have not ventured to speak from any chance information, nor according to any notion of my own; I have described nothing but what I either saw myself or learnt from others, of whom I made the most careful and particular inquiry." His method became known as "scientific" history because Thucydides drew on developing scientific knowledge in his environment—such as Hippocrates' then novel treatises on medicine—and applied it to the study of history. This fact also caused subsequent historians to claim him as the father of modern history. In the mid-eighteenth century, philosopher David Hume declared that "the first page of Thucydides is the commencement of real history."

Biographical Information

Thucydides was the son of an Athenian, Olorus, who was most likely a grandson to the Thracian King Olorus. Thucydides may also have been related to Cimon, another grandson to the king, and a leading Athenian statesman. Judging from the breadth of knowledge displayed in the *History*, historians surmise that Thucydides received his education in Athens, although he held property including gold mines in Thrace. In 424 B.C. he was elected as a general to protect the region; however, when he failed to defend the coveted Athenian colony of Amphipolis from Sparta, he was sent to trial, convicted, and subsequently exiled from Athens until the war ended in 404 B.C. While in exile he traveled extensively, making connections with sympathizers from both sides of the conflict and collecting eyewitness accounts of the war. He also did most of his writing at this time, having

begun at the war's onset in 431 B.C., before his exile, and apparently leaving the work unfinished on his death in 399 B.C. He died shortly after his return to Athens and was buried in Cimon's family vault.

Major Works

The *History of the Peloponnesian War*, comprised of eight books, presents the war's duration through accounts of events and speeches, a device Thucydides adopted from the Greek historian Herodotus. In Book 1 Thucydides stated as his objective to give an accurate account of the war he deemed the most consequential in human history, and to provide knowledge that he hoped would instruct and guide future readers. In a preamble to the Athenian conflict with Sparta, he briefly summarized early Greek history and described the key military incidents that provided an environment for the growth of Athenian power. Books 2-4 chronicle the main events in the first part of the Peloponnesian War known as the Archidamian War, including the Plague and the Funeral Oration (Book 2), the revolt of Lesbos (Book 3), the Athenian victory at Sphacteria, and the fall of Amphipolis to Brasidas (Book 4). Book 5 tells of the deaths of Brasidas and Cleon, the Peace of Nicias, and Mantinean War, and the subjugation of Melos. Books 6 and 7 describe Nicias' ill-fated expedition to Sicily, and the unfinished eighth book describes the revolt led by the Athenian allies and the naval warfare near Asia Minor. Scholars consider the last book unfinished since it both lacks the speeches found in the first seven books and stops at the year 411 B.C., well before the end of the war in 404 B.C. Not only do speeches constitute a sizable portion of the preceding books, but the *History* generally treats speeches as an intregal part of the political scene; the Funeral Oration by Pericles, in which Thucydides recalled an idealized Athens, has received considerable critical attention as an important text in itself. The *History* is also studied for its portraits of certain key players in the historical events, including Pericles, a highly influential Athenian statesman; Cleon, the statesman who inherited Pericles' position of influence; and two Athenian generals, Nicias and Alcibiades.

Textual History

While critics generally agree that Thucydides must have collected the material for and composed his history throughout the duration of the war, dating the various portions of the work has produced considerable debate. Efforts at dating must proceed largely from the *Histo-*

ry's internal evidence, since the earliest known manuscript dates to the tenth century. Fifty such manuscripts exist in libraries across Europe, many dating from the eleventh and twelth centuries. Translations into English proliferated in the nineteenth century, the most authoritative generally thought to be Benjamin Jowett's 1881 edition.

Critical Reception

Thucydides was largely unknown as a historian during his lifetime, possibly due in part to his lengthy exile. Substantial appreciation first came in the second century B.C. from the Greek historian Polybius and in the first century A.D. from Roman authors Caesar and Sallust. He also wielded a significant influence on subsequent Greek historians, including Dexippus (third century), Procopius (sixth century), and Critobulus (fifteenth century). Later political philosophers Niccolò Machiavelli, the Italian statesman, and Thomas Hobbes, the English writer, admired his analytical methods, and Thomas Jefferson mentioned him favorably in an 1812 letter to John Adams. Nineteenth-century classicists have also admired his work, praising both his methods of composition and his apparently impartial approach to history; their studies generally consisted of painstaking, line-by-line analyses, often for the purpose of determining when Thucydides wrote each part of the history, an issue about which there has been much debate.

Twentieth-century classicists have moved away from this kind of analysis to more broad-based concerns, especially embracing the *History* during the major military conflicts of the century. In general, their theses about Thucydides range between two extreme positions, one of which finds the historian a wholly objective and accurate recorder of facts, while the other views him as a politically engaged man who necessarily conveys the biases of his own age and viewpoint. In an essay that dubs Thucydides "The Modern Spirit," G. F. Abbott has characterized the historian as a "student who cares for historical facts and who knows that historical facts can only be ascertained, if at all, by sceptical inquiry—by that close and cold scrutiny which nips like a frost the fables dictated by ignorance or interest and fostered by credulity."

The common characterization of Thucydides as the precursor of modern history is based on his significant differences from other historians of his age, as demonstrated in the work of Charles Norris Cochrane. Cochrane maintains that while the supernatural—specifically the will of the gods—plays a central role in most ancient histories, Thucydides keeps an unusually persistent eye on the natural, precisely in the "scientific" manner Hippocrates was developing in his medical treatises. Cochrane and like-minded critics have studied Thucydides's portraits of individuals and groups (nations, armies, etc.) for their unusually modern, psychological analyses of human nature, which ultimately suggest that Thucydides attributes historical events not to the gods but to human nature.

Counter to the approach Abbott and Cochrane typify stands a line of thought initiated in 1907 by Francis MacDonald Cornford's *Thucydides Mythistoricus*, in which the author argues that Thucydides, despite his intentions, embedded his own ideas about history in general and specifically about the war through which he lived in his chronicle. W. P. Wallace's 1964 essay represents the culmination of this extreme; the critic not only argues that Thucydides invested the *History* with his own perspective, but also concludes that "it is somehow not quite respectable to give one's reader's as little choice as Thucydides gives his."

Most criticism falls somewhere between these two poles. Some schoalars have suggested, for example, that Thucydides's notion of history may itself have allowed for a sense of accuracy not at odds with bias. Along these lines, most critics agree that Thucydides presents his readers with two causes of the Peloponnesian war, one of which he considers superficial and the other, "real." While there were a series of diplomatic exchanges between Athens and Sparta regarding the allegiance of certain city-states that led up to the conflict, Thucydides suggests that the larger force at work was Sparta's fear of Athens' imperial expansion. Much of his analytical method and his careful accuracy is aimed, as most critics agree, toward uncovering this underlying cause, so that the image of a "scientific" Thucydides is often synonymous with the image of a Thucydides committed to a particular view of history. Moreover, some scholars contend that Thucydides' objectivity necessarily had certain viewpoints built into it, since the very definition of "history" in his era is based on certain assumptions about which there is still debate.

PRINCIPAL ENGLISH TRANSLATIONS

Thucydides (the Loeb edition, translated by Charles Forster Smith) 1930-35
Thucydides (translated by Benjamin Jowett) 1881
The History of the Peloponnesian War (translated by Rex Warner) 1972

CRITICISM

Dionysius of Halicarnassus (essay date 8 B.C.?)

SOURCE: "Translation of Usener-Radermacher Text

of *De Thucydide,*" in *Dionysius of Halicarnassus: On Thucydides,* translated by W. Kendrick Pritchett, University of California Press, 1975, pp. 1-46.

[*A Greek who taught rhetoric in Rome, Dionysius was a prominent literary figure and the author of* Roman Antiquities, *a history of Rome from its origins to the First Punic War, and* Scripta rhetorica, *a collection of letters and essays on literary criticism valued for its thorough analysis and comparative method. In the following excerpt from his* On Thucydides, *Dionysius comments on what he views as some positive and negative attributes of the historian's style. Since the exact date of composition for this piece is unknown, Dionysius's death date has been used as the essay date.*]

[Thucydides] was unwilling either to confine his history to a single region as did Hellanicus, or to elaborate into a single work the achievements of Greeks and barbarians in every land, as did Herodotus; but scorning the former as trifling and petty and of little value to the readers, and rejecting the latter as too comprehensive to fall within the purview of the human mind, if one would be very exact, he selected a single war, the war that was waged between the Athenians and Peloponnesians, and gave his attention to writing about this. Since he was physically robust and sound of mind, living through the duration of the war, he put together his narrative not from chance rumors but on the basis of personal experience, in cases where he was present himself, and on information from the most knowledgeable people, where he was in the dark as a result of his exile. In this way, then, he differed from the historians before him, and I say this since he chose a subject which neither consists entirely of one member (monokolon) nor is divided into many irreconcilable parts. Moreover, he did not insert anything of the mythical into his history, and he refused to divert his history to practice deception and magic upon the masses, as all the historians before him had done, telling of Lamias issuing from the earth in woods and glens, and of amphibious nymphs arising from Tartarus and swimming through the seas, partly shaped like beasts, and having intercourse with human beings; telling also about demi-gods, the offspring of mortals and gods, and many other stories that seem incredible and very foolish to our times.

. . . . .

I have not been led to say these things by the desire to censure those writers, since, on the contrary, I have much indulgence towards them for mentioning the fictions of myths when writing national and local history. For among all men alike there are preserved some records of both national and local traditions . . . which children have received from their parents and have taken care to hand down to their children in turn and

they have insisted that those who wished to publish them should record them as they have received them from their elders. These historians, then, were compelled to embellish their local histories by such mythical digressions. On the other hand, it was not suitable for Thucydides, who chose just one subject in which he participated, to mix theatrical enticements with the narrative, or to practice the deceit against readers which those compilations customarily exhibited, but to be useful. . . .

. . . . .

Philosophers and rhetoricians, if not all of them, yet most of them, bear witness to Thucydides that he has been most careful of the truth, the high-priestess of which we desire history to be. He adds nothing to the facts that should not be added, and takes nothing therefrom, nor does he take advantage of his position as a writer, but he adheres to his purpose without wavering, leaving no room for criticism, and abstaining from envy and flattery of every kind, particularly in his appreciation of men of merit. For in the first book, when he makes mention of Themistocles, he unstintingly mentions all of his good qualities, and in the second book in the discussion of the statesmanship of Pericles, he pronounces a eulogy such as was worthy of a man whose reputation has penetrated everywhere. Likewise, when he was compelled to speak about Demosthenes the general, Nicias the son of Niceratus, Alcibiades the son of Clinias, and other generals and speakers, he has spoken so as to give each man his due. To cite examples is unnecessary to readers of his history. This then is what may be said about the historian's success in connection with the treatment of his subject-matter—points that are good and worthy of imitation.

. . . . .

The defects of Thucydidean workmanship and the features that are criticized by some persons relate to the more technical side of his subject matter, what is called the economy of the discourse, something that is desirable in all kinds of writing, whether one chooses philosophical or oratorical subjects. The matter in question has to do with the division (diairesis), order (taxis) and development (exergasia). . . .

. . . . .

There are many . . . portions throughout the whole history that one may find either to have been worked out with the most consummate elaboration and that admit of neither addition nor subtraction, or else to have been carelessly skimmed over and to present not the slightest suggestion of . . . skill, and this is especially true of his harangues and dialogues and other pieces of oratory. In his anxiety for these, he seems to

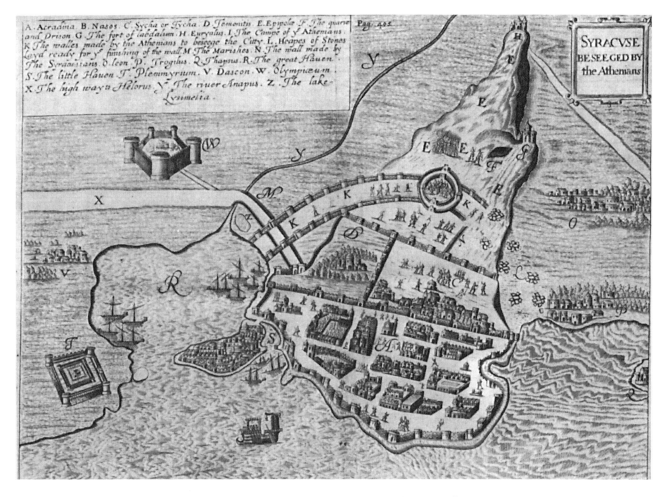

Map of Syracuse from the 1634 edition of Hobbes's translation.

have left his history incomplete. Such, too, is the view of Cratippus, who flourished at the same time as he, and who collected the matter passed over by him, for he says that not only have the speeches been an impediment to the narrative, but they are also annoying to the hearers. At any rate he maintains that Thucydides noticed this and so put no speech in the closing portions of his history, though there were many events in Ionia and many events at Athens that called for the use of dialogues and harangues. Certainly, if one compares the first and eighth books with each other, they would not seem to form part of the same plan nor to be the work of the same genius. The one book comprising a few, small events is full of oratory, whereas the other embracing many great events shows a scarcity of public speeches.

. . . . .

I have even thought that in his very speeches the man has given evidence of the same failing, so much so that in dealing with the same subject and on the same occasion he writes some things that he ought not to have said, and omits others that he ought to have said, as, for example, he has done in regard to the city of the Mytilenaeans in the third book. After the capture of the city and the arrival of the captives, whom the general Paches had dispatched to Athens, though two meetings of the ecclesia were held at Athens (Thuc. III.36), our author has omitted as unnecessary the speeches that were made by the leaders of the people at the first of these meetings, in which the demos voted to kill the prisoners and the rest of the Mytilenaeans who had reached manhood, and to enslave the women and children; but the speeches (III.36-49) that dealt with the same subject and that were delivered by the same persons at the later meeting at which the majority experienced a sort of repentance, the historian has admitted as necessary.

. . . . .

And as for the much talked-of funeral speech (II.35-46), which Thucydides recounted in the second book, for what reason, pray, is it placed in this book rather than in another? For whether on the occasion of great disasters that had befallen the city when many brave Athenians had perished in battle it was befitting for the customary lamentations to be made over them, or, by reason of the great services which brought conspicuous renown to the city or added to its power, it was meet for the dead to be honored with the praises of funeral speeches, any book that one might choose would be a more suitable place for the funeral oration than this book. For, in this book, the Athenians who fell during this first invasion of the Peloponnesians were very few in number, and not even these performed any illustrious deeds, as Thucydides himself writes (II.22): After first saying of Pericles that "he watched the city and kept it as quiet as possible, but he continually sent out small numbers of horsemen to keep patrols of the <hostile> army from sallying forth into the farms near the city and doing damage," he says that a brief cavalry conflict took place "at Phrygia between a single squad of Athenian cavalry accompanied by Thessalians and the Boetian horsemen. In this engagement the Thessalians and Athenians were not worsted until the hoplites came to the assistance of the Boeotians and so they were put to flight and a few of the Thessalians and Athenians were killed. But the dead were recovered on the same day without a truce. And the Peloponnesians erected a trophy on the following day." But in the fourth book (cf. Thuc. IV.9-23, 26-40) the men who fought with Demosthenes at Pylos against a force of the Lacedaemonians, attacking them by land and from the sea and conquering them in both the battles, and who thereby filled the city with boasting, were far superior in numbers and worth to the above-mentioned soldiers. Why then, pray, in the case of the few horsemen who brought neither reputation nor additional power to the city, does the historian open the public graves and introduce the most distinguished leader of the people, Pericles, in the act of reciting that lofty tragic composition; whereas, in honor of the larger number and more valiant who caused the people who declared war against the Athenians to surrender to them, and who were more worthy of obtaining such an honor, he did not compose a funeral oration? To dismiss all the other battles on land and on sea, in which many perished who much more deserved to be honored with the funeral eulogy than those frontier guardsmen of Attica, amounting to about ten or fifteen horsemen, how much more worthy of the funeral lamentations and eulogies were those of the Athenians and allies who met their death in Sicily along with Nicias and Demosthenes in the naval engagements and in the land battles and lastly in that wretched flight, who numbered no less than forty thousand and who were not even able to obtain the customary mode of burial? But the historian was so neglectful of these men that he has even omitted to state that the city went into public mourning and duly made the customary offerings to the shades of those who had died in foreign lands, and appointed as the orator of the occasion the man who was the most competent speaker of the orators of that time. For it was not likely that the Athenians would go into public mourning for the fifteen horsemen, but would not deem worthy of any honor the men that fell in Sicily, among whom . . . [lacuna] and of the muster-roll of citizens those that perished were more in number than five thousand. But it seems that the historian (for I shall say what I think), desiring to use the personality of Pericles and to put in his mouth the funeral eulogy that he had composed, since the man died in the second year of the war and did not live at the time of any of the disasters that subsequently befell the city, bestowed upon that small and insignificant deed a praise that went far beyond the real worth of the matter. . . .

. . . . .

I am now going to speak about his style (to lektikon) in which the individuality of the author is most clearly seen. Perhaps it may be necessary in connection with this topic (idea) also, to state in advance into how many parts diction (lexis) is divided and what are the qualities it embraces; then to show without concealing anything what was the state of literary expression when Thucydides received it from his predecessors, and what parts of it were due to his innovations, whether for better or for worse.

. . . . .

That all diction (lexis) is divided into two primary divisions, (1), the choice of the words by which things are designated, and, (2), the composition <of these> into larger and smaller groups (lit. parts), and that each of these is subdivided into still other divisions, the choice of the elementary parts of speech (nominal, verbal, and conjunctive, I mean) into literal (kyria) and figurative (tropike) expression, and composition into phrases (kommata), clauses (kola), and periods (periodoi); and that both of these classes (I mean simple and uncompounded words and the combination of these) happen to be capable of assuming certain figures (schemata); and that of the so-called virtues (aretai) some are essential and must be found in every kind of discourse, whilst others are accessory (epithetoi) and receive their peculiar force only when the former are present as a foundation, <all those matters> have been stated by many before. Hence I need not now speak about them, nor state the considerations and rules which are many in number, upon which each of these qualities is based. For these matters also have been most carefully worked out.

. . . . .

Which of these features all of Thucydides' predecessors used and which of them they used but slightly, taking up from the beginning as I promised, I shall summarize. For thus one will more accurately recognize the individual style (charakter) of our author. Now I have no means of conjecturing what was the language used by the very ancient writers who are known only by their names, whether they used a style that was plain (lite), unadorned (akosmetos), and had nothing superfluous (perittos), but only what was useful and indispensable, or whether they employed a style that was stately (pompike), dignified (axiomatike) and elaborate (egkataskeuos) and provided with accessory embellishments (kosmoi). For neither have the writings of the majority of them been preserved up to our times, nor are those that have been preserved believed by everybody to belong to those men, among others the works of Cadmus of Miletus and Aristaeus of Proconnesus, and the like. But the authors who lived before the Peloponnesian war and survived up to the time of Thucydides, all of them as a rule followed the same plan, both those who chose the Ionic dialect which flourished more than the others at those times, and those writers who chose the old Attic dialect which showed only a few slight differences from the Ionic. For all these writers . . . were more concerned about the literal meaning of the words than about their figurative use, and they admitted the latter only to impart flavor (hedysma), as it were, to their style; and as to their composition all of them used the same kind, the plain and unstudied, and in the framing of their words and their thoughts they did not deviate to any considerable extent from the everyday (tetrimmene), current (koine) and familiar manner of diction (dialektos). Now the diction (lexis) of all of these writers possesses the necessary virtues—it is pure (kathara), clear (saphes), and fairly concise (syntomos), each preserving the peculiar idiom (charakter) of the language; but the accessory virtues, which to the largest extent reveal the power of the orator, are not found in their entirety nor in their highest state of development, but only in small numbers and in a slightly developed stage,—I refer to such qualities as sublimity (hypsos), elegance (kalliremosyne), solemnity (semnologia), and splendor (megaloprepeia). Nor does their diction reveal intensity (tonos), nor gravity (baros) nor sentiment (pathos) that arouses the mind, nor a vigorous (erromenon) and combative (enagonion) spirit, which are productive of so-called eloquence (deinotes). <This is true of all> with the single exception of Herodotus. This author in the choice of words, in his composition, and in the variety (poikilia) of his figures far surpassed all the others, and made his prose utterance resemble the best kind of poetry, by reason of his persuasiveness (peitho), graces of style (charites), and great charm (hedone). In the greatest and most conspicuous qualities <he was second to none.> . . . [Text defective] . . . Only the qualities of a forensic nature seem to be lacking, whether he was not naturally gifted with these, or, whether in pursuance of a certain design he voluntarily rejected them as unsuited to history.

For the author has not made use of many deliberative or forensic speeches, nor does his strength (alke) consist in imparting the elements of passion (pathainein) and forcefulness (deinopoiein) to his narrative.

. . . . .

Following this author and the others whom I previously mentioned, and recognizing the qualities that each of these authors possessed, Thucydides was the first man to endeavor to introduce into historical composition a certain peculiar style (charakter) and one that had been disregarded by all others. In the choice of his words he preferred a diction that was figurative (tropike), obscure (glottematike), archaic (aperchaiomene), and foreign (xene) in the place of that which was in common use and familiar to the men of his time; in the composition of the smaller and larger divisions <of the sentence> he used the dignified (axiomatike), austere (austera), sturdy (stibara), and stable (bebekuia), and one that by the harsh sound of the letters grates roughly on the ears instead of the clear (liguros), soft (malaka), and polished (synexesmene) kind, and one in which there is no clashing of sounds. On the use of figures, in which he desired to differ as far as possible from his predecessors, he bestowed the greatest effort. . . .

The most conspicuous and characteristic features of the author are his efforts to express the largest number of things in the smallest number of words, and to compress a number of thoughts into one, and his tendency to leave his hearer still expecting to hear something more, all of which things produce a brevity that lacks clearness. To sum it up, there are four instruments, as it were, of Thucydidean diction (lexis): poetical vocabulary (to poietikon ton onomaton), great variety of figures (to polyeides ton schematon), harshness of sound combination (to trachy tes harmonias), and swiftness in saying what he has to say (to tachos ton semasion). Its qualities (chromata) are solidity (striphnon) and compactness (pyknon), pungency (pikron) and harshness (austeron), gravity (embrithes), tendency to inspire awe and fear (deinon kai phoberon), and above all these the power of stirring the emotions (pathetikon). That is about the kind of author Thucydides is as regards the characteristics of his diction (lexis), in which he differed from all the other authors. Now when the author's powers keep pace with his purpose, the success is perfect and marvelous; but when the ability lags behind and the tension (tonos) is not maintained throughout, the rapidity of the narrative makes the diction obscure, and introduces other ugly blemishes. For the author does not throughout his history observe the proper use of foreign and coined words nor the limit to which he may go before he stops, though there are principles regulating their use that are good and binding in every kind of writing.

Thomas Hobbes (essay date 1629)

SOURCE: "To The Readers," in *Hobbes's Thucydides,* edited by Richard Schlatter, Rutgers University Press, 1975, pp. 6-9.

[*Hobbes was an eminent English philosopher best known for his* Leviathan, or the Matter, Form, and Power of a Commonwealth, Ecclesiastical and Civil *(1651), in which he presented his theory of social contract. In the following preface to his 1629 translation of Thucydides's* History, *Hobbes praises the historian's objectiveness and vivid, descriptive style.*]

It hath been noted by divers, that Homer in poesy, Aristotle in philosophy, Demosthenes in eloquence, and others of the ancients in other knowledge, do still maintain their primacy: none of them exceeded, some not approached, by any in these later ages. And in the number of these is justly ranked also our Thucydides; a workman no less perfect in his work, than any of the former; and in whom (I believe with many others) the faculty of writing history is at the highest. For the principal and proper work of history being to instruct and enable men, by the knowledge of actions past, to bear themselves prudently in the present and providently towards the future: there is not extant any other (merely human) that doth more naturally and fully perform it, than this of my author. It is true, that there be many excellent and profitable histories written since: and in some of them there be inserted very wise discourses, both of manners and policy. But being discourses inserted, and not of the contexture of the narration, they indeed commend the knowledge of the writer, but not the history itself: the nature whereof is merely narrative. In others, there be subtle conjectures at the secret aims and inward cogitations of such as fall under their pen; which is also none of the least virtues in a history, where conjecture is thoroughly grounded, not forced to serve the purpose of the writer in adorning his style, or manifesting his subtlety in conjecturing. But these conjectures cannot often be certain, unless withal so evident, that the narration itself may be sufficient to suggest the same also to the reader. But Thucydides is one, who, though he never digress to read a lecture, moral or political, upon his own text, nor enter into men's hearts further than the acts themselves evidently guide him: is yet accounted the most politic historiographer that ever writ. The reason whereof I take to be this. He filleth his narrations with that choice of matter, and ordereth them with that judgment, and with such perspicuity and efficacy expresseth himself, that, as Plutarch saith, he maketh his auditor a spectator. For he setteth his reader in the assemblies of the people and in the senate, at their debating; in the streets, at their seditions; and in the field, at their battles. So that look how much a man of understanding might have added to his experience, if he had then lived a beholder of their proceedings, and familiar with the men and business of the time: so much almost may he profit now, by attentive reading of the same here written. He may from the narrations draw out lessons to himself, and of himself be able to trace the drifts and counsels of the actors to their seat.

These virtues of my author did so take my affection, that they begat in me a desire to communicate him further: which was the first occasion that moved me to translate him. For it is an error we easily fall into, to believe that whatsoever pleaseth us, will be in like manner and degree acceptable to all: and to esteem of one another's judgment, as we agree in the liking or dislike of the same things. And in this error peradventure was I, when I thought, that as many of the more judicious as I should communicate him to, would affect him as much as I myself did. I considered also, that he was exceedingly esteemed of the Italians and French in their own tongues: notwithstanding that he be not very much beholden for it to his interpreters. Of whom (to speak no more than becomes a candidate of your good opinion in the same kind) I may say this: that whereas the author himself so carrieth with him his own light throughout, that the reader may continually see his way before him, and by that which goeth before expect what is to follow; I found it not so in them. The cause whereof, and their excuse, may be this: they followed the Latin of Laurentius Valla, which was not without some errors; and he a Greek copy not so correct as now is extant. Out of French he was done into English (for I need not dissemble to have seen him in English) in the time of King Edward the Sixth: but so, as by multiplication of error he became at length traduced, rather than translated into our language. Hereupon I resolved to take him immediately from the Greek, according to the edition of Æmilius Porta: not refusing or neglecting any version, comment, or other help I could come by. Knowing that when with diligence and leisure I should have done it, though some error might remain, yet they would be errors but of one descent; of which nevertheless I can discover none, and hope they be not many. After I had finished it, it lay long by me: and other reasons taking place, my desire to communicate it ceased.

For I saw that, for the greatest part, men came to the reading of history with an affection much like that of the people in Rome: who came to the spectacle of the gladiators with more delight to behold their blood, than their skill in fencing. For they be far more in number, that love to read of great armies, bloody battles, and many thousands slain at once, than that mind the art by which the affairs both of armies and cities be conducted to their ends. I observed likewise, that there were not many whose ears were well accustomed to the names of the places they shall meet with in this history; without the knowledge whereof it can neither patiently be read over, perfectly understood, nor easily remembered: especially being many, as here it falleth out. Because in that age almost every city both in Greece and Sicily, the two main scenes of this war, was a distinct commonwealth by itself, and a party in the quarrel.

Nevertheless I have thought since, that the former of these considerations ought not to be of any weight at all, to him that can content himself with the few and better sort of readers: who, as they only judge, so is their approbation only considerable. And for the difficulty arising from the ignorance of places, I thought it not so insuperable, but that with convenient pictures of the countries it might be removed. To which purpose, I saw there would be necessary especially two: a general map of Greece, and a general map of Sicily. The latter of these I found already extant, exactly done by Philip Cluverius; which I have caused to be cut, and you have it at the beginning of the sixth book. But for maps of Greece, sufficient for this purpose, I could light on none. For neither are the tables of Ptolemy, and descriptions of those that follow him, accommodate to the time of Thucydides; and therefore few of the places by him mentioned, therein described: nor are those that be, agreeing always with the truth of history. Wherefore I was constrained to draw one as well as I could myself. Which to do, I was to rely for the main figure of the country on the modern description now in reputation: and in that, to set down those places especially (as many as the volume was capable of) which occur in the reading of this author, and to assign them that situation, which, by travel in Strabo, Pausanias, Herodotus, and some other good authors, I saw belonged unto them. And to shew you that I have not played the mountebank in it, putting down exactly some few of the principal, and the rest at adventure, without care and without reason, I have joined with the map an index, that pointeth to the authors which will justify me where I differ from others. With these maps, and those few brief notes in the margin upon such passages as I thought most required them, I supposed the history might be read with very much benefit by all men of good judgment and education, (for whom also it was intended from the beginning by Thucydides), and have therefore at length made my labour public, not without hope to have it accepted. Which if I obtain, though no otherwise than in virtue of the author's excellent matter, it is sufficient.

Richard Jebb (essay date 1880)

SOURCE: "The Speeches of Thucydides," in *Essays and Addresses,* Cambridge at the University Press, 1907, pp. 359-443.

[*Jebb was a Scottish-born classicist, translator, and author of numerous works on ancient literature, and the founder of the Cambridge Philological Society, the Society for the Promotion of Hellenic Studies, and the British School of Archeology in Athens. In the essay excerpted below, originally published in 1880 in* Hellenica: a Collection of Essays on Greek Poetry, Philosophy, History, and Religion, *Jebb approaches the speeches as a vital part of the* History *for their "light on the inner workings of the Greek political mind, . . . on the whole play of feeling and opinion which lay behind the facts." He further applauds Thucydides's ability to balance the accuracy of the speeches with dramatic presentation.*]

The famous phrase in which Thucydides claims a lasting value for his work has had the fate of many striking expressions: it is often quoted apart from the words which explain it. "A possession for ever," not "the rhetorical triumph of an hour": taken by itself this has a ring of exultation, noble perhaps, yet personal, as if the grave self-mastery of the historian had permitted this one utterance in the tone of the Roman poet's confident retrospect or the English poet's loftier hope, speaking of a monument more enduring than brass, of things so written that men should not willingly let them die. It is the context that reduces the meaning to a passionless precision. "The absence of fable in the *History*," he says, "will perhaps make it less attractive to hearers; but it will be enough if it is found profitable by those who desire an exact knowledge of the past as a key to the future, which in all human probability will repeat or resemble the past. The work is meant to be a possession for ever, not the rhetorical triumph of an hour." That the intention of Thucydides has been fulfilled in his own sense is due largely to the speeches which form between a fourth and fifth of the whole work. It is chiefly by these that the facts of the Peloponnesian war are transformed into typical examples of universal laws and illuminated with a practical significance for the students of politics in every age and country. The scope of the speeches is seen best if we consider what the *History* would be without them. The narrative would remain, with a few brief comments on great characters or events, and those two passages in which Thucydides describes the moral effects of pestilence and of party-strife. But there would be little or no light on the inner workings of the Greek political mind, on the courses of reasoning which determined the action, on the whole play of feeling and opinion which lay behind the facts. . . .

Thucydides has stated the general principles on which he composed the speeches in his *History*. The precise interpretation of that statement depends, however, partly on the question—How far is it probable that Thucydides is there instituting a tacit comparison between his own method and that of Herodotus? So far as we know, the work of Herodotus was the only prose work in which Thucydides could have found a precedent for dramatic treatment applied to history. If Thucydides knew that work, it would naturally be present to his mind at the moment when he was stating the rules of

Title page for Thomas Hobbes's translation of Thucydides's History.

his own practice. It can be shown almost certainly that a period of at least twenty years must have elapsed between the time at which Herodotus ceased to write and the time at which the *History* of Thucydides received the form in which it has come down to us. It was possible, then, for Thucydides to know the work of Herodotus; that he actually knew it, and that he pointedly alludes to it in several places, cannot be doubted by any one who weighs the whole evidence.

In the view of Thucydides there had hitherto been two classes of writers concerned with the recording of events. First, there were the poets, especially the epic poets, of whom Homer is the type, whose characteristic tendency, in the eyes of Thucydides, is to exaggerate the greatness or splendour of things past. Secondly, there were the prose writers whom he calls chroniclers . . . ; and these he characterises by saying that they "compiled" their works with a view to attracting audiences at a recitation, rather than to truth; dealing largely, as they did, with traditions which could no longer be verified, but had passed into the region of myth. Now with such chroniclers Herodotus was undoubtedly classed by Thucydides. The traits common to Herodotus and the other chroniclers, as Thucydides viewed them, were I the omission of really accurate research— the tendency to take what lay ready to the writer's hand . . . ; 2 the mixture of a fabulous element with history; 3 the pursuit of effect in the first place, and of truth only in the second. Probably Thucydides would have said that Herodotus was more critically painstaking and less indiscriminately tolerant of fable than most of the other chroniclers, but that his study of effect was more systematic and more ambitious. The imaginary dialogues and speeches in Herodotus would be the most conspicuous illustrations of this desire for effect. If they were not absolute novelties in the chronicler's art, at least we may be sure that they had never before been used in such large measure, or with such success.

The first aim of Thucydides in his introduction is to show that the Peloponnesian war is more important than any event of which the Greeks have record. He then states the principles on which his *History of the War* has been composed. "As to the various speeches made on the eve of the war, or in its course, I have found it difficult to retain a memory of the precise words which I had heard spoken; and so it was with those who brought me reports. But I have made the persons say what it seemed to me most opportune for them to say in view of each situation; at the same time, I have adhered as closely as possible to the general sense of what was actually said. As to the deeds done in the war, I have not thought myself at liberty to record them on hearsay from the first informant, or on arbitrary conjecture. My account rests either on personal knowledge, or on the closest possible scrutiny of each statement made by others. The process of research

was laborious, because conflicting accounts were given by those who had witnessed the several events, as partiality swayed or memory served them."

The phenomena of the war, then, as materials for history, are classed by Thucydides under two heads— . . . things said, and . . . , things done. These are the two elements of human agency. As regards . . . the deeds, he is evidently contrasting his own practice with that of the chroniclers generally. He has not taken his facts, as they did, without careful sifting . . . : he had formed a higher conception of his task. . . . In regard to the words . . . , he is tacitly contrasting his own practice with that of Herodotus, the only conspicuous example in this department. If his statement were developed in this light, it might be paraphrased thus:—Thucydides says: (I) I have not introduced a speech except when I had reason to know that a speech was actually made: unlike Herodotus, when he reports the conversation between Croesus and Solon, the debate of the Persian conspirators, the discussion in the cabinet of Xerxes. (2) I do not pretend to give the exact form of the speeches made: as a writer implies that he does when, without warning the reader, he introduces a speech with the formula, "He said these things," . . . instead of "He spoke to this effect". . . . (3) On the other hand, I have faithfully reproduced the speaker's general line of argument, the purport and substance of his speech, so far as it could be ascertained. Herodotus disregards this principle when he makes Otanes, Megabyzus and Dareius support democracy, oligarchy and monarchy by arguments which no Persian could have used. And in filling up such outlines, my aim has been to make the speaker say what, under the circumstances, seemed most opportune. . . .

The last phrase is noticeable as marking a limit of dramatic purpose. According to the regular usage of the words . . . in Thucydides, it can mean only "what the occasion required"—not necessarily what was most suitable to the character of the speaker. The latter idea would have been expressed by a different phrase. . . . That is, in filling up the framework supplied by the reported "general sense" of a speech, Thucydides has freely exercised his own judgment on the situation. Suppose a report to have reached him in this shape: "Hermocrates spoke in the congress at Gela, urging the Sicilian cities to lay aside their feuds and unite against Athens." In composing on this theme, the first thought of Thucydides would be, "What were the best arguments available?" rather than, "What arguments would Hermocrates have used?" This general rule would, of course, be liable to various degrees of modification in cases where the speaker was well known to the historian as having marked traits of character, opinion or style.

"Set speeches," says Voltaire, "are a sort of oratorical lie, which the historian used to allow himself in old times. He used to make his heroes say what they might have said. . . . At the present day these fictions are no longer tolerated. If one put into the mouth of a prince a speech which he had never made, the historian would be regarded as a rhetorician." How did it happen that Thucydides allowed himself this "oratorical lie,"—Thucydides, whose strongest characteristic is devotion to the truth, impatience of every inroad which fiction makes into the province of history, laborious persistence in the task of separating fact from fable; Thucydides, who was not constrained, like later writers of the old world, by an established literary tradition; who had no Greek predecessors in the field of history, except those chroniclers whom he despised precisely because they sacrificed truth to effect? Thucydides might rather have been expected to express himself on this wise: "The chroniclers have sometimes pleased their hearers by reporting the very words spoken. But, as I could not give the words, I have been content to give the substance, when I could learn it."

In order to find the point of view at which Thucydides stood, we must remember, first of all, the power which epic poetry had then for centuries exercised over the Greek mind. The same love of the concrete and comprehensible which moved the early Greeks to clothe abstract conceptions of a superhuman power in the forms of men and women, "strangers to death and old age for ever," led them also to represent the energy of the human spirit as much as possible in the form of speech. The Homeric ideal of excellence is the man of brave deeds and wise words. The Homeric debates are not merely brilliant, but also thoroughly dramatic in their way of characterising the speakers. The *Iliad* and *Odyssey* accustomed the Greeks to expect two elements in every vivid presentation of an action—first, the proofs of bodily prowess, the account of what men did; and then, as the image of their minds, a report of what they said. Political causes strengthened this feeling. Public speech played a much larger part in the affairs of States than it now does. Envoys spoke before an assembly or a council on business which would now be transacted by the written correspondence of statesmen or diplomatists. Every adult citizen of a Greek democracy had his vote in the assembly which finally decided great issues. To such a citizen the written history of political events would appear strangely insipid if it did not give at least some image of those debates which imparted the chief zest to civic life and by which political events were chiefly controlled. He was one who (in modern phrase) had held a safe seat in Parliament from the time when he came of age; who had lived in the atmosphere of political debate until it had become to him an almost indispensable excitement; and who would feel comparatively little interest in hearing the result of a Parliamentary division unless he was enabled to form some idea of the process by which the result had been reached. Such a man would not have been satisfied with the meagre information that

the Athenian Ecclesia had discussed the fate of Mitylene, that Cleon had advocated a massacre, that Diodotus had opposed it, and that the view of Diodotus had prevailed by a narrow majority. His imagination would at once transport him to the scene of the parliamentary combat. He would listen in fancy, as he had so often listened in reality, to the eloquence of antagonistic orators, he would balance the possible arguments for severity or clemency, he would conceive himself present at the moment when one uplifted hand might incline the scale of life or death, and he would feel the thrill of relief with which those who supported Diodotus found that Athens was saved at the eleventh hour—saved, if the bearers of the respite, rowing night and day, could reach Lesbos in time—from the infamy of devoting a population to the sword. When Thucydides gave in full the speeches made by Cleon and Diodotus, he was helping his reader, the average citizen of a Greek republic, to do on more accurate lines that which the reader would otherwise have tried to do for himself. Thucydides was writing for men who knew Greek politics from within, and he knew that, if they were to follow him with satisfied attention, he must place them at their accustomed point of view. The literary influences of the age set in the same direction. At the beginning of the war the Attic drama had been in vigour for more than forty years. The fame of Aeschylus was a youthful memory to men who had passed middle life; Sophocles was sixty-four, Euripides was forty-nine. Each had given great works to Athens, and was yet to give more. An age of vivid energy had found the poetry most congenial to it in the noblest type of tragedy, and this, in turn, fed the Greek desire to know character through deed and word. In the hands of Euripides tragedy further became the vehicle of dialectical subtleties and the dramatic mirror of public debate. At the same time Attic oratory was being prepared by two currents of influence which converged on Athens—the practical culture of Ionia, represented by the Sophists, and the Sicilian art of rhetoric.

If the speeches in Thucydides were brought under a technical classification, the Funeral Oration would be the only example of the "panegyrical" or epideictic class; the pleading of the Plataeans and Thebans before the Spartan Commissioners might possibly be called "forensic"; and all the other speeches would be in some sense "deliberative." But such a classification, besides being rather forced, does not correspond to any real differences of structure or form. If the speeches are to be viewed in their literary relation to the *History,* it is enough to observe that the addresses of leaders to their troops may be regarded as practically forming a class apart.

The right of an adult citizen to attend the debates of the Ecclesia must have been acquired by Thucydides many years before the war began. From its very commencement, as he says, he had formed the purpose of writing its history. There is every probability that he had heard most or all of the important discussions which took place in the Ecclesia between 433 and 424 B.C. It was in 423 B.C., or at the end of the year before, that his exile of twenty years from Athens began. Thence we can name some at least of the speeches to which he probably refers as heard by himself . . . and not merely reported to him. Such would be the addresses of the Corcyrean and Corinthian envoys, when they were rival suitors for the Athenian alliance in 433 B.C.; the speeches of Pericles; the debate on Mitylene in 427 B.C.; and the speech of the Lacedaemonian envoys in 425 B.C., making overtures of peace to Athens. If he was not present on all these occasions, still, as a resident citizen, he would have exceptional facilities for obtaining a full and accurate account. Taking this group of speeches first, then, we may consider how far they are apparently historical in substance, or show traces of artificial treatment.

After giving the addresses of the envoys from Corcyra and Corinth in 433 B.C., Thucydides notices the course of the debate in the Ecclesia. Two sittings were held. At the first, he says, the Athenians inclined to the arguments of the Corcyreans, and were disposed to conclude an alliance both offensive and defensive; at the second they repented of this, but decided to conclude a defensive alliance. The considerations which prevailed with them were, that war was unavoidable in any case; that the Corcyrean navy must not be allowed to pass into the hands of the Corinthians; and that Corcyra was a useful station for coasting voyages. These three arguments are just those on which the Corcyrean speech, as given by Thucydides, chiefly turns. The circumstantial account of the debate in the Ecclesia cannot be treated as fictitious. Either, then, Thucydides has given the substance of the arguments really used by the Corcyreans, or he has ascribed to them arguments used on their side by Athenian speakers in the Ecclesia. Now the speech of the Corinthian envoys has at least one mark of substantial authenticity: the references to benefits conferred on Athens by Corinth in the matters of Samos and Aegina would certainly have occurred to a Corinthian envoy more readily than to an Athenian writer. In both the Corcyrean and the Corinthian speech it seems probable that Thucydides has given the substance of what was really said, though he may have added touches from his recollections of the subsequent debate in the assembly. Similar is the case of the speech made by the Lacedaemonian envoys at Athens in 425 B.C. The historian's comment on it is as follows: "The Lacedaemonians spoke at such length [*i.e.* for Spartans], in the belief that the Athenians had previously desired a truce, and had been hindered only by Spartan opposition; so that, when peace was offered, they would gladly accept it, and restore the men." This clearly implies that the speech ascribed to the envoys—which Thucydides may well have heard—is historical in substance.

The Thucydidean speeches of Pericles raise three distinct questions:—How far do they preserve the form and style of the statesman's oratory? how far do they express the ruling ideas of his policy? and how far do they severally represent what he said on the several occasions?

As Thucydides must have repeatedly heard Pericles—whom he describes as the first of Athenians, most powerful in action and in speech,—it would be strange if he had not endeavoured to give at least some traits of the eloquence which so uniquely impressed contemporaries. Pericles is said to have left nothing written: but Aristotle and Plutarch have preserved a few of the bold images or striking phrases which tradition attributed to him. Several examples of such bold imagery occur in the Thucydidean speeches of Pericles, and it can hardly be doubted that they are phrases which have lived in the historian's memory. But the echo is not heard in single phrases only. Every reader of the Funeral Oration must be aware of a majesty in the rhythm of the whole, a certain union of impetuous movement with lofty grandeur, which Thucydides has given to Pericles alone. There is a large alloy, doubtless, of rhetorical ornament in the new manner of overstrained antithesis: but the voice of the Olympian Pericles is not wholly lost in it. There can be no question, again, that the speeches of Pericles in the Ecclesia accurately represent the characteristic features of his policy at the time. But how far do they severally represent what Pericles said on the several occasions? Thucydides makes Pericles use different topics of encouragement at three successive stages.

In 432 B.C. Pericles emboldens the Athenians to reject the Peloponnesian demands by a general comparison of the resources and prospects on either side. In 431 B.C., when Archidamus is about to invade Attica, Pericles repeats his former exhortations, but supplements them by a detailed exposition of Athenian resources, financial and military. In 430 B.C., after the second invasion of Attica, when the land had been devastated and while the plague was raging, Pericles convened a special meeting of the Ecclesia, with the twofold purpose of reassuring his countrymen and of allaying their resentment against himself. "As to the prospects of the war, you may rest satisfied," he says, "with the arguments by which I have proved to you on many other occasions that you have no cause of uneasiness. But I must notice a special advantage which the scale of your empire confers,—one, I think, which has never occurred to you,—which I have not mentioned in addressing you before, and which I should not have noticed now—as the claim implied might seem too arrogant—did I not see you unreasonably dejected. You think that you rule your allies alone. I tell you that of the two fields open to human action, land and sea, the latter is under your absolute dominion, not merely to the extent of your actual empire, but as much further as you please. While you hold the sea in your present naval strength, you cannot be resisted by the Persian king, or by any nation on earth." Thus, as the pressure on the Athenian spirit becomes more and more severe, the exhortations of Pericles go on from strength to strength, until, at the darkest hour of all, they culminate in a triumphant avowal that the naval empire of Athens is not relative but absolute, is not an empire over a limited confederacy but a boundless supremacy on the sea. If this ascending scale, so fitly graduated, was due to the invention or arrangement of Thucydides, it was a dramatic conception. But it seems more probable that the topics really used by Pericles on these three occasions were substantially those given by the historian. It is difficult otherwise to justify the emphatic clearness with which the special theme of the second speech is distinguished from that of the first, and that of the third, again, from both. On the other hand, the first speech of Pericles betrays some remarkable traces of manipulation by the writer. Earlier in the same year the Corinthian envoy at the Peloponnesian congress had given several reasons for believing that the Peloponnesians were likely to prevail in the war. With help from the sacred treasuries of Delphi and Olympia, he had said, they might lure away the foreign seamen of Athens by offering higher pay. They could acquire naval skill by practice. And among the possibilities of the war he suggests the occupation of a fortress in the enemy's country. The speech of Pericles answers these arguments point by point. But the correspondence is not merely in the topics. The very phrases of the Corinthian speech are repeated by Pericles in his reply. Similar parallelisms may be traced between the Corinthian speech and that delivered by the Spartan Archidamus on the occasion of the former congress: one with which the Corinthians cannot be supposed to be acquainted in detail, since it was made to the Spartans only, after strangers had withdrawn. The fact is that the eight speeches recorded by Thucydides as delivered at Athens or Sparta before the commencement of the war form, for his purpose, a group by themselves. In these he has worked up the chief arguments and calculations which were current on either side. Collectively, they are his dramatic presentation of the motives at work, the grievances on each side, the hopes and fears, based on a comparison of resources, with which the combatants entered on the struggle. At the end of his first speech Pericles says: "I have many other reasons to give for hoping that we shall prevail; but these shall be given hereafter as the events arise . . ."—thus foreshadowing the speech of which an abstract is given on a subsequent occasion. In this particular case, as we have seen, the disposition of topics may well be authentic in the main. But the composer's phrase is significant. It suggests the habit of selecting from a certain stock of available material and disposing the extracts with something of a dramatist's freedom.

In the Funeral Oration there is nothing, apart from the diction, which distinctly shows the invention of Thucydides. At first sight there is some plausibility in the view that such an oration would probably have contained allusions to the heroic legends of Attica, and that the mind of Thucydides is to be traced in their suppression. But the argument may be turned the other way. The very absence of mythical embellishment, it might be urged, is rather a proof of the fidelity with which Thucydides has reported a speaker who, regardless of the vulgar taste, was resolved to treat a well-worn theme in a new and higher strain. One or two passages, indeed, have been supposed to hint at the moral deterioration of the Athenian democracy in the years which followed the death of Pericles; but the supposition seems gratuitous.

It remains to notice the debate in the Ecclesia on the punishment of Mitylene. Cleon urges a massacre, Diodotus opposes it. "These views," says Thucydides, "having been stated with nearly balanced effect, the assembly came after all to a division; and on a show of hands the parties proved nearly equal, but the view of Diodotus prevailed." The words can only mean that, in the speeches of Cleon and Diodotus, Thucydides has given the real substance of the arguments which were found to be so "nearly balanced," and which led to so close a division. Cleon's speech has one striking characteristic. In several places it echoes phrases which occur in the speeches of Pericles. But, with these verbal parallelisms, there is a pointed contrast of spirit. As Pericles describes the good side of the intellectual Athenian nature, Cleon brings out its weak side. As Pericles insists on the Athenian combination of intelligence with courage, Cleon declares that this intelligence leads men to despise the laws, and prefers ignorance combined with moderation. Pericles is gone: Cleon echoes the words of the statesman as whose successor he poses, at the very moment when he is contradicting his principles. It may be observed that when Thucydides reports the speech of the Syracusan demagogue Athenagoras, he marks his manner by a certain violence of expression. Cleon, whom Thucydides calls "most violent," has no violence of expression. Probably this abstention from vehemence of the demagogic type, this superficial imitation of Pericles, are traits in which the Cleon of Thucydides is historical.

This closes the series of those seven speeches, delivered at Athens, for which Thucydides probably derived the "general sense" either from his own recollection or from the sources accessible to a resident citizen. The only one of these which exhibits distinct traces of artificial dealing with subject matter is the first speech of Pericles. And in this the only traces are, first, a certain adjustment of the language to that of the Corinthian speech made earlier in the same year; and, secondly, a phrase by which the composer prepares the reader for a subsequent speech of Pericles. . . .

The expression of character in the Thucydidean speeches has the same kind of limitation which was generally observed in Attic tragedy. It is rather typical than individual. Thucydides seizes the broad and essential characteristics of the speaker, and is content with marking these. We are sometimes reminded of the direct simplicity with which the epic or tragic heroes introduce themselves: "I am Odysseus, the marvel of men for all wiles, and my fame goes up to heaven." "I am pious Aeneas, renowned above the stars." "You voted for war," says Pericles, "and now you are angry with me,—a man who deems himself second to none in discerning and expounding the right course,—a man devoted to his country and proof against corruption." These were salient points in the public character of Pericles as conceived by the historian, and accordingly Pericles is made to say so. The fate of Nicias seemed to Thucydides a signal example of unmerited misfortune, since Nicias had been remarkable throughout life for the practice of orthodox virtue. And so, in his speech before the retreat from Syracuse, Nicias says, "The tenor of my life has been loyal to the gods, just and without offence among men." In the debate at Athens on the Sicilian expedition Alcibiades is introduced by a prefatory sketch of his position and character. Thucydides notices his ambition, his magnificence, especially in the matter of horses and chariots, the licence of his private life, his insolence, his public efficiency, his personal unpopularity. Then Alcibiades speaks, and begins by saying in so many words that he has a better right than others to high command; he boasts of having entered seven chariots at Olympia; he avows that he does not regard his fellow-citizens as his equals; he asks whether his personal unpopularity interferes with his administrative capacity. The speech is merely the sketch developed. It is the character of Alcibiades, as Thucydides saw its salient points, condensed in a dramatic form; but it is not such a speech as Alcibiades could conceivably have made on this occasion, or indeed on any. Thucydides has given us distinct portraits of the chief actors in the Peloponnesian war, but these portraits are to be found in the clearly narrated actions of the men; the words ascribed to them rarely do more than mark the stronger lines of character; they seldom reveal new traits of a subtler kind. The tendency of Thucydides was less to analyse individual character than to study human nature in its general or typical phenomena. His observation was directed, first, towards motives and passions which may be considered, in regard to practical politics, as universal influences: next, towards the collective attributes which distinguish whole communities from each other. Thus the normal Spartan character is exhibited in its merits and its defects. The political character of the Athenians is arraigned and defended; their intellectual character is illustrated in its strength and its weakness. And Thucydides shows a desire to comprehend these conceptions of national character in formulas, which he gives as epigrams to his speakers. The Spartan disposition, says

an Athenian, might be described as one which regards everything that is pleasant as honourable, and everything that is expedient as just. The Athenians, says a Corinthian, are, in brief, men who will neither rest nor allow others to rest. Athens, says Pericles, might be described as the school of Greece, and the Athenian nature as the most gracefully versatile in the world.

Those cases in which Thucydides gives merely a brief summary of a speech or debate suggest how slight the materials may often have been which he worked up in the oratorical form. The political or ethical reflections with which the meagre outlines were filled up were doubtless supplied in large measure by Thucydides himself. The speeches, taken altogether, are pervaded by certain general conceptions, expressed in formulas more or less constant, which indicate unity of authorship. But it cannot be said, in the same sense, that they bear the stamp of one mind. They do, indeed, suggest certain intellectual habits, but it is seldom possible to distinguish between opinions or modes of thought which were in the air, and such as may have been proper to Thucydides. Nor would much be gained if we could. The real interest of the speeches in this aspect is something more than biographical; it is their interest as a contribution to the intellectual history of a transitional period in an age of singular mental energy. The age of faith was passing by, and a rational basis for ethics—which were then included in politics—was only in process of being sought.

Thucydides is here the representative of a time which, for the most part, could no longer believe with Herodotus, but which had not yet learned to bring a Socratic method to bear on generalisations. He appears—so far as he is revealed at all—as a thinker of intense earnestness, with a firm and subtle apprehension of his chosen subject, alike in its widest bearings and in its minutest details; and of profound sensibility in regard to the larger practical aspects, that is the political aspects, of human destiny. He has neither a dogmatic religion nor a system of ethics. He cleaves to positive fact; his generalisations rarely involve a speculative element, but are usually confined to registering the aggregate results of observation upon human conduct in given circumstances. In the spirit of a sceptical age he makes his speakers debate questions of political or personal morality to which no definite answer is offered. In Plato's *Gorgias* Callicles distinguishes between "natural" and "conventional" justice, contending that "natural justice" entitles the strong to oppress the weak, and that "conventional justice" is merely a device of the weak for their own protection. In the *Republic* Thrasymachus defends a similar doctrine, namely, that "justice is another's good and the interest of the stronger, and that injustice is a man's own profit and interest, though injurious to the weaker."

The sophist Hippias, in Xenophon's *Memorabilia,* argues in a like strain that justice and law are merely arbitrary and conventional. This, no doubt, was one of the commonplaces of sophistical dialectic in the time of Thucydides. The Athenian speakers in his History defend the aggressive policy of Athens by arguments which rest on substantially the same basis as those of the Platonic Callicles and Thrasymachus. But the historian is content to state their case from their own point of view; he does not challenge the doctrine—as the Platonic Socrates does—by comments of his own. The victims of aggression, indeed, the Plataeans or Melians, appeal to a higher justice than the right of might, and Thucydides hints that his sympathies are with them; but that is all. The abstention is characteristic. On the whole, it may be said that he evinces a personal liking for moral nobleness, but refrains from delivering moral judgments, as if these would imply laws which he was not prepared to affirm or deny. But he insists on discovering a rational basis for action. If a man or a State pursues a certain line of policy, there must be some intelligible reasons, he feels, which can be urged for it.

This desire to enter into the mind of the actors—to find the motive behind the deed, and to state it with all possible logical force—is the mainspring of the oratory in Thucydides, in so far as this is his own creation. It is an element of dramatic vividness; sometimes also of dramatic untruth, when the reasonings supplied by the historian to his actors are subtler than would probably have occurred to the speakers or commended themselves to the hearers. Thucydides is a philosophical historian, in the sense that he wishes to record the exact truth, in a form which may be serviceable for the political instruction of mankind. But he has not, in the sense of Plato or Aristotle, a theory of ethics or politics. Thucydides groups the observed facts of practical politics, but without attempting to analyse their ultimate laws. It might be possible to piece together Thucydidean texts and, by filling up a few gaps, to form a tolerably coherent system of doctrine; but the process would be artificial and delusive.

Possibly a Shakespeare might re-create Thucydides from the fragments of his personal thought, but the breath of life would be the poet's gift; the broken lights are all that really remain. The paradoxes of one age are said to be the truisms of the next, but the violent contrast suggested by the epigram is hardly the important point to seize if we desire to trace the growth of opinion. There was a moment when the so-called paradoxes were neither paradoxes nor as yet truisms, but only rather new and intelligent opinions, seen to be such against the foil of notions which were decaying, but had not quite gone out. For instance, when Thucydides makes his speakers say, as he so often does, that the future is uncertain, we do more justice to the originality of the remark if we remember that in the time of Thucydides there were those who thought that the future was very frequently indicated, at great moments, by

signs from the gods. Herodotus, for example, would have disputed the statement that the future is uncertain, if it had been placed before him as an unlimited proposition covering such crises as the Peloponnesian war.

The same consideration applies to many of the political or moral aphorisms, which may be regarded as those of Thucydides himself. They are in silent controversy with some unexpressed dissidence of contemporaries. The principle of tacit contrast pervades the whole *History,* as in the Funeral Oration the picture of Athens requires to be supplemented by a mental picture of the Sparta to which it is opposed. This was of the inmost nature of Thucydides: the reluctance "to speak at superfluous length" was deep in him. His general views must be measured both by the credulity and by the higher scepticism of a naïve age; so gauged, they are never commonplaces, but, at the least, hints for a part of the history which he has not told in words, because he did not distinctly conceive that it could ever need to be told. "Fortune" . . . is the name by which he usually designates the incalculable element in human life; but this "fortune" is no blind chance; it is, as he once explains it, "the fortune given by heaven" . . . , the inscrutable dispensation of a divine Providence. The course of this fortune not only baffles prediction, but is sometimes directly opposed to the reasonable beliefs of men concerning the source which dispenses it. Thrice only in the long tragedy of the war, as Thucydides unfolds it, do men appeal expressly to the gods, invoking the name of religion, in their agony, against tyrannous strength; thrice the power behind the veil is deaf, thrice the hand of the avenger is withheld, and the miserable suppliant is struck down by the secure malignity of man. The Plataeans appeal to the altars which had witnessed the consecration of Greek liberty, and the Spartans kill them in cold blood. The Melians are confident against the Athenians as the righteous against the unjust; their city is sacked, their men are slain, their women and children enslaved. Nicias, after the great defeat at Syracuse, believes that the jealousy of the gods must now be exhausted, and has a firm hope, based on a good life, for himself and his followers; but the wretched remnant of his defeated army are in great part butchered as they slake their thirst with the bloody water of the Assinarus; he himself is put to death lest he should tell tales under torture, and the survivors pass into a horrible slavery. Thucydides feels that the ways of Heaven are hard to understand, but he does not complain of them; they are matters not for reasoning but for resignation. He regards the fear of the gods as a potent check on the bad impulses of men, and notices the loss of this fear as a grave symptom of moral anarchy. As to omens, oracles, and similar modes of seeking miraculous light or aid, he nowhere denies the possibility of such light or aid being occasionally given, though his contempt is excited by the frequency of imposture; this, however, he would affirm—that such resources are not to be tried until all resources within human control have been tried in vain. There is one way only, Thucydides holds, by which man can certainly influence his own destiny, and that is by bringing an intelligent judgment . . . to bear on facts. Some have traced the influence of Anaxagoras in the prominence which Thucydides gives to the intellectual principle; but no such prompting was needed by a strong understanding of sceptical bent, and it may be observed that Thucydides has at least not adopted the language of Anaxagoras. It is the peculiar merit of the Athenian character, as portrayed in Thucydides, to recognise intelligence as the true basis of action and the true root of courage, instead of regarding mental culture as adverse to civic loyalty and warlike spirit. If soothsayers cannot give us prescience, reason well used can enable such a man as Themistocles at least to conjecture the future. In a trial of human forces the chances baffle prediction, but superiority in ideas . . . is a sure ground of confidence. Yet the man of sound judgment will not presume on this confidence, for he will remember that the other element, "fortune," is beyond his control. Justice, rightly understood, is the "common good," and is identical with true self-interest. As the remorseless exaction of an extreme penalty, "justice" may be opposed to "equity"; or as a moral standard, it may be opposed to "self-interest" in the lower sense. And self-interest, when thus opposed to justice, can appeal to "the immemorial usage," believed to obtain among the gods, and so certainly established among men that it may plausibly be called a sort of natural necessity,—that the stronger shall rule the weaker. No speaker in Thucydides goes quite so far as Callicles in the *Gorgias,* or proclaims this to be "natural" as distinguished from "conventional" justice. It is not said to be just, but only natural and not unreasonable. The argument against capital punishment, which is put into the mouth of Diodotus, rests on the observation that no restraints have yet been devised which can be trusted to keep human passions in check. Legislators have gone through the whole list of possible penalties, and even the prospect of death is found insufficient to deter those who are goaded by want or ambition, and tempted by opportunity. The friendship of men and of communities must be founded in the first place on a persuasion of mutual benevolence, and on some congeniality of character; but in the long-run the only sure bond between States is identity of interests. The Peloponnesian league is loose just because the interests diverge. In default of a common interest, the only guarantee for an alliance is balanced fear. Similarly, in the relation of the citizen to the State, patriotism is enforced by the dependence of private on public welfare. Pericles even says that no fair or just legislation can be expected from citizens who have not such a stake in the country as is represented by the lives of children. The distinctive merits of an oligarchy—always provided that it is constitutional, and not of the narrow type which Thucydides

calls a "dynasty"—are fairly recognised in the *History*. Archidamus and Brasidas claim stability, moderation and disciplined loyalty for the Spartan State. A true democracy is pictured as one in which three elements work together for the common good: the rich are the guardians of property, the able men offer counsel, and the mass of the citizens decide on the opinions laid before them. Democracy was the form of government under which Athens had been greatest and most free: and the best phase of the Athenian democracy in his recollection, Thucydides says, was just after the Revolution of the Four Hundred, since then the oligarchic and popular elements were judiciously tempered. Destiny may alter the part which a State is called upon to perform, and its institutions may require to be modified accordingly. Thus the Corinthians say to the Spartans, "Your system is out of date if you are to cope with Athens. In politics, as in art, improvements must prevail. Fixed institutions are best for a city at peace. But the call to manifold enterprise imposes the need of manifold development. Hence—owing to their varied experience—the Athenians have been greater innovators than you." The analogy suggested here between politics and a progressive art is the more significant when it is remembered what the historian's age had seen accomplished in sculpture, architecture and drama. It is also worthy of remark that the only unqualified censures of democracy which occur in Thucydides, and the only protests against change as such, are ascribed to the "violent" Cleon and the "licentious" Alcibiades.

The choice of moments for the introduction of speeches is not, with Thucydides, a matter of rhetorical caprice, but has an intelligible relation to the general plan of his work. A speech or debate reported in the direct form always signalises a noteworthy point in the inner or mental history of the war, as distinguished from the narrative of its external facts: it announces thoughts and arguments which exercised an important influence, and which therefore require to be apprehended with the utmost possible distinctness. The event which furnishes the occasion for inserting a speech need not be of first-rate importance in itself, if only it is typical of its kind, and therefore suitable for the dramatic exhibition of reasonings which applied to several similar cases. The destruction of Plataea by Sparta was an impressive event; but its effect on the general course of the war would scarcely have warranted the amount of space devoted to the Plataean and Theban pleadings, if the occasion had not been a typical illustration of Spartan and Theban policy. Such, again, is the case of Mitylene, viewed as exemplifying the relation between Athens and her subject allies; and the dramatic form is given accordingly, not merely to the Athenian debate on Mitylene, but also to the appeal of the Mityleneans at Olympia. The speech of Brasidas at Acanthus is given in the direct form as a specimen of his persuasive diplomacy in dealing with the cities of the Chalcidic peninsula. The rival overtures of Athens and Syracuse to Camarina have a similarly representative character in relation to the wavering neutrality of the Sicilian cities, and accordingly the direct form is given to the arguments of Euphemus and of Hermocrates. The absence of speeches in the Eighth Book has been reckoned among the proofs that this book had not received the author's last touches. There can be no doubt that Thucydides was prevented by death from completing or revising the Eighth Book: but if his general practice is considered, the argument from the absence of speeches will appear questionable. Much of the Eighth Book is occupied with negotiations, either clandestine or indecisive, or both; and in a period of similar character which fills the greater part of the Fifth Book Thucydides nowhere employs the dramatic form. It cannot surprise us that Thucydides has not given a dramatic emphasis to the mere misrepresentations by which Alcibiades and Chalcideus prevailed on the Chians to revolt. The Revolution of the Four Hundred certainly afforded opportunities for the insertion of speeches made in debate. But that Revolution was primarily concerned with the form of the Athenian constitution; its special importance for the history of the war lay in the use which Alcibiades was making of it to procure his own recall. This is perhaps the only point in the extant part of the Eighth Book at which the usual practice of Thucydides would lead us to expect the dramatic emphasis; and just here it is found. Peisander brings his opponents to admit that the case of Athens is desperate without the help of Persia. "This, then," he says, "we cannot get, unless we adopt a more temperate policy, and concentrate the administration in fewer hands, so as to secure the confidence of the king, . . . and recall Alcibiades, the only man living who can gain our end." In a revision of the book Thucydides would possibly have worked up the speech of Peisander at greater length.

As regards the language of the speeches, Thucydides plainly avows that it is chiefly or wholly his own. The dramatic truth, so far as it goes, is in the matter, not in the form. He may sometimes indicate such broad characteristics as the curt bluntness of the ephor Sthenelaidas or the insolent vehemence of Alcibiades. But, as a rule, there is little discrimination of style. In all that concerns expression, the speeches are essentially the oratorical essays of the historian himself. At the end of the war, when he composed or revised them, the art of Rhetoric was thoroughly established at Athens. The popular dialectic of the Sophists had been combined with lessons in the minute proprieties of language. Protagoras taught correctness in grammatical forms, Prodicus in the use of synonyms. The Sicilian Rhetoric had familiarised Athenian speakers with principles of division and arrangement. Gorgias, with his brilliant gift of expression, had for a while set the fashion of strained antithesis and tawdry splendour. It might have been expected from the character of his mind that

Thucydides would be keenly alive to what was hollow and false in the new rhetoric. Several touches in the *History* show that he was so. Citizens in grave debate are contrasted with men who play audience to the empty displays of sophists. A contempt for rhetorical commonplace is frequently indicated. Thus Pericles declines to dilate on the legendary glories of Athens or on the advantages of patriotic fortitude, and Hermocrates begs to be excused from enlarging on the hardships of war or the blessings of peace. On the technical side, however, Thucydides shows the influence of the new art. This often appears in his method of marshalling topics and in his organisation of the more elaborate speeches. It is seen still more clearly if his style is compared with that of the orator Antiphon. The extant work of Antiphon as a writer of speeches for the law-courts falls in the years 421-411 B.C. The warmth of the terms in which Thucydides describes him as "a master of device and of expression,"—a phase identical with that which is ascribed, as a definition of statesman-like ability, to Pericles—testifies at least to an intellectual sympathy. There is, however, no evidence for the ancient tradition that the historian was the pupil of the orator. Thucydides and Antiphon belong to the same rhetorical school, and represent the same early stage in the development of Attic prose. Both writers admit words of an antique or a decidedly poetical cast. Both delight in verbal contrasts, pointed by insisting on the precise difference between terms of similar import. Both use metaphors rather bolder than Greek prose easily tolerated in its riper age. On the other hand, there are three respects in which the composition of Thucydides may be contrasted with that of Antiphon. First, Thucydides has a pregnant brevity which would not have been possible in such measure for a practical orator, since no ordinary hearer could have followed his meaning with full comprehension. Secondly, Thucydides often departs not only from the natural but from the rhetorical order of words, in order to throw a stronger emphasis on the word which is the key-note to the thought; and in this again he is seen to be writing for readers, not for hearers. Thirdly, the strings of clauses, forming periods of a somewhat loose and inartistic kind, are longer with Thucydides than with Antiphon, and this because Thucydides is striving to express ideas of a more complex nature. The originality and the striking interest of the historian's style consists, in fact, in this, that we see a vigorous mind in the very act of struggling to mould a language of magnificent but immature capabilities. Sometimes the direction of the thought changes in the moment that it is being uttered. Then arise obscurities which have their source in the intense effort of Thucydides to be clear at each successive moment—to say exactly what he means at that moment. The strong consciousness of logical coherence then makes him heedless of formal coherence. The student of Thucydides has one consolation which is not always present to the student of a difficult writer. He knows that he is not engaged in the hopeless or thankless task of unravelling a mere rhetorical tangle. Every new light on the thought is sure to be a new light on the words. . . .

Thucydides set the first great example of making historical persons say what they might have said. The basis of his conception was common to the whole ancient world: it was the sovereign importance of speech in political and civic life. But in Thucydides the use of the licence is dramatic—that is, conducive to the truthful and vivid presentment of action. In most of the later Greek and Roman historians it is either rhetorical—that is, subservient to the display of the writer's style—or partly dramatic and partly rhetorical. The art of rhetoric passed through two stages of educational significance in the ancient world. In the first stage, with which Thucydides was contemporary, rhetoric meant a training for real debate in the assembly or the law-courts. Then, as Greek political life died down, rhetoric came to mean the art of writing or declaiming. The speeches in Thucydides have the dramatic spirit, and not the rhetorical, because, although the art of rhetoric has helped to make them, they are in direct relation with real action and real life. The rhetorical historians of the ancient world represent the second stage of rhetoric: their speeches are only more or less possible declamations. The modern writers who attempted to revive the practice were in a lower deep still, since for them rhetoric was not even a living element of culture. But it may be well to consider a little more closely how far and in what sense Thucydides can be called dramatic. The epithet "dramatic" is sometimes applied to narrative when no more is apparently meant than that it is vivid or graphic. In the proper sense, however, a narrative is dramatic only when it elicits the inherent eloquence of facts. Thucydides is dramatic, for instance, when he places the Melian dialogue immediately before the Sicilian expedition. The simple juxtaposition of insolence and ruin is more effective than comment. The bare recital, thus ordered, makes the same kind of impression which the actions themselves would have made if one had immediately succeeded the other before our eyes. It might not be difficult, with a little adroitness, to represent Thucydides as a conscious dramatic artist throughout his work; and an ingenious writer has actually shown how his *History* may be conceived as a tragedy cast into five acts. But it would perhaps be truer to say that the war itself presented striking contrasts, analogous to those which a dramatic poet contrives: the dullest writer could not have wholly missed these contrasts; and if Diodorus had been the historian, his work, too, might have revealed the five acts; but Thucydides was peculiarly well fitted to bring out these contrasts with the most complete effect. He was so, because he felt the whole moment and pathos of the events themselves; because he saw them with the distinctness of intense concentration; and because, partly under the influence of language, he had even more than the ordinary Greek

love of antithesis. It is obvious that the Peloponnesian war, as a subject for history, may be said to have dramatic unity in the sense that it is a single great action: as, by an analogous metaphor, the subject of Herodotus may be said to have epic unity, because the various parts, though they cannot be brought within the compass of one action, can be brought within the compass of one narrative. And, apart from this rudimentary dramatic unity, the Peloponnesian war has a further analogy to a drama in presenting a definite moment at which the cardinal situation is decisively reversed—as it is reversed in the *Oedipus Tyrannus,* for instance, when the king discovers that he is an incestuous parricide. That moment is the Sicilian expedition. The supreme test of "dramatic" quality in a history of the Peloponnesian war must be the power with which the historian has marked the significance of the Sicilian expedition as the tragic "revolution" (*peripeteia*), the climax of pity and terror, the decisive reversal. Thucydides has devoted the whole of his Sixth and Seventh Books to the events of those two years, thus at once marking the significance of the expedition as the turning point of the war. And every reader knows with what tremendous effect he has traced its course, from the moment when the whole population of Athens was gathered at the Peiraeus in the early midsummer morning to see the splendid fleet sail for Sicily, and the trumpet commanded silence while the whole multitude joined in prayer, and wine was poured from vessels of silver and gold as the paean arose, down to that overthrow of which he writes that they were destroyed with utter destruction, and that few out of many came home. Here, at the point in his story which supplies the crucial test, Thucydides shows that he possesses true dramatic power. By the direct presentment of the facts, not by reflections upon them, he makes us feel all that is tragic in the Sicilian disaster itself, and also all that it means in relation to the larger tragedy of the war. The same power is seen in many particular episodes of the *History*: for example, in the self restrained majesty of Pericles, the great protagonist of the opening war, whose courage, amidst havoc and pestilence, ever rises as the Athenian courage declines; or in the first appearance of Alcibiades on the scene, with his brilliant versatility and his profound lack of loyalty, with his unmeasured possibilities for good or evil, just when the Sicilian project is trembling in the balance. Without pressing the parallel between the *History* and a work of dramatic art to any fanciful length, it may be said with a definite meaning that Thucydides has not merely the inspiration of action, but often also the spirit of the noblest tragic drama.

It is natural to regret his silence in regard to the social and intellectual life of his age. The simplest explanation of it is that he did not conceive such details as requisite for the illustration of his purely political subject. The art and poetry of the day, the philosophy and the society, were perhaps in his view merely the decorations of the theatre in which the great tragedy of the war was being played. Though he wrote for all time, he did not conceive of an audience who would have to reconstruct this theatre before they could fully comprehend his drama. No writer has ever been at once so anxiously careful and so haughtily improvident of the future. His characteristic dislike of superfluous detail seems to have been allied with a certain hardness of temperament, such as is indicated by the tone of his reference to the poets. His banishment may also have infused something of bitterness into his recollections of the Athenian life, with all its gracious surroundings, with all its social and intellectual delights, from which he was suddenly cut off, so that he should know them no more until he came back in his old age and found them changed. No one can tell now how the memories of early sympathies may have grouped themselves in his mind as he looked out in later years from his home in Thrace on the sea over which he had sailed on the long past day when he failed to save Amphipolis; but at least there is a twofold suggestiveness in those passages which touch on the glories of Athens. There is the feeling of the man who has never lost his love and admiration for the Athenian ideal; and there is also a certain reluctance to translate this ideal into concrete images, as if, in the words of Oedipus after his ruin, it were sweet for thought to dwell beyond the sphere of griefs. Perhaps in this very reticence the modern world may find a gain when it views his work from the artistic side. Thucydides must always hold his fame by a double right; not only as a thinker who, in an age of transitional scepticism, clearly apprehended the value of disciplined intelligence as a permanent force in practical politics, but also as a writer who knew how to make great events tell their own story greatly; and the dramatic power of the immortal **History** is heightened by its dramatic reserve.

Frank Byron Jevons (essay date 1886)

SOURCE: "Thucydides," in *A History of Greek Literature: From the Earliest Period to the Death of Demosthenes,* Charles Scribner's Sons, 1900, pp. 327-48.

[*In the following excerpt from his monograph written in 1886, Jevons maintains that Thucydides sought "to give a strict and faithful account of the facts" of the Peloponnesian War and demonstrates the importance of the War to Western history.*]

"Thucydides, an Athenian, wrote the history of the war in which the Peloponnesians and the Athenians fought against one another. He began to write when they first took up arms, believing that it would be great and memorable above any previous war. For he argued that both states were then at the full height of their military power, and he saw the rest of the Hellenes either siding or intending to side with one or other of

them. No movement ever stirred Hellas more deeply than this; it was shared by many of the barbarians, and might be said event to affect the world at large." These are the words with which Thucydides begins his history. He was born in the Athenian deme Halimus, belonging to the tribe Leontis, on the coast between Phalerum and Colias. His father, Olorus, was related, though in what degree we do not know, to the Thracian Olorus, whose daughter married the famous Miltiades, and was mother of Cimon. At the outbreak of the Peloponnesian war in B.C. 432, when Thucydides, as he himself says, began to write, he was probably about forty years of age. The first twenty years of his life were spent under the administration of his great relative Cimon, and the next twenty under that of the man for whom Thucydides had such admiration, Pericles. About Thucydides' early life and education we have no direct information. We may, however, fairly assume that he met and learned from all the great men who at this time lived in or found their way to Athens. The philosopher Anaxagoras, who has left traces of his influence even on Herodotus, may be credited with having contributed to the formation of the mind of Thucydides, whose views on natural science and on religion are more closely connected with those of Anaxagoras than are even those of Herodotus. The orator Antiphon, whose style resembles that of Thucydides—both are classed by Dionysius as belonging to the "severe style"—may have been Thucydides' literary model, and was certainly in other relations known to and studied by Thucydides, as is shown by the manner in which he speaks of Antiphon. The sophist Protagoras, Gorgias the rhetorician, and Prodicus, have all left marks of their influence on the style of Thucydides. At Athens, though not at Olympia, he in all probability, when about twenty-five years of age, heard Herodotus read portions of his history. Æschylus he may well have seen; Sophocles, Euripides, Aristophanes, and Phidias he must have met. Poetry, architecture, science, philosophy, and rhetoric all found in Athens, or sent there their best exponents; all helped to shape the citizens of Athens, and to make it right for one of her sons to say, "We are lovers of the beautiful, yet simple in our tastes, and we cultivate the mind without loss of manliness. Wealth we employ, not for talk and ostentation, but when there is a real use for it. To avow poverty with us is no disgrace; the true disgrace is in doing nothing to avoid it. An Athenian citizen does not neglect the state because he takes care of his own household; and even those of us who are engaged in business have a very fair idea of politics. We alone regard a man who takes no interest in public affairs, not as a harmless, but a useless character; and if few of us are originators, we are all sound judges of a policy." With these convictions Thucydides could not but "fix his eyes upon the greatness of Athens, until he became filled with the love of her, and impressed with the spectacle of her glory."

Educated in this city and by these means, and endowed with an originality and energy of mind which have elevated him to the level of the greatest minds the world has produced, Thucydides began in B.C. 432 to write the history of the Peloponnessian war, then commencing. Possessing extensive property and the right of working gold-mines in Thrace, and being consequently one of the leading men in Thrace, Thucydides must have spent a certain part of every year there. But the larger part of his time he passed in Athens. The speeches of Pericles he certainly heard; his admiration for Pericles' statesmanship is shown by what he says of it; and he may have been among the personal friends of Pericles. In B.C. 430 the plague, which wrought great harm to Athens, nearly deprived the world of Thucydides' history. He was, he says, himself attacked, and witnessed the sufferings of others. The celebrated debates on the fate of the Mitylenæans in B.C. 427, and the Spartan proposals for peace in B.C. 425, in consequence of the affair of Pylos, he was present at; and he may have taken part in some of the military operations of the earlier years of the war. At any rate, in B.C. 424 he acted as strategus, being one of the two Athenian generals intrusted with the protection of Thrace. He allowed, however, the Spartan Brasidas to occupy Amphipolis, the key to the whole of that country; the result of this serious disaster being that Thucydides was an exile from Athens for twenty years. That this was a heavy punishment to him it is impossible to doubt; but so far from its injuring the prosecution of his work, it had the opposite effect. It set him free from other claims on his time and attention; his work probably became the sole palliative to the exile's grief; and his enforced absence from Athens gave him the opportunity he could not have otherwise enjoyed of visiting the Peloponnese, and seeing the war from both sides. He says, "For twenty years I was banished from my country after I held the command at Amphipolis, and associating with both sides, with the Peloponnesians quite as much as the Athenians, because of my exile, I was thus enabled to watch quietly the course of events." He seems to have visited the places affected by the war not only in Greece, but, as his acquaintance with the topography and early history of Sicily shows, in Sicily and Italy; and everywhere he sought out eyewitnesses, "of whom," he says, "I made the most careful and particular inquiry." At length, in B.C. 404, he returned after his protracted exile to his country, six months after the destruction of the walls of Athens by Lysander. How long he lived after this is uncertain. He perhaps died before B.C. 396, for he says, when mentioning the eruption of Etna, which took place in B.C. 426, that only three eruptions were known to have taken place "since the Hellenes first settled in Sicily." and this statement was not true after the eruption of B.C. 396. But he may have lived after B.C. 396 and not revised the passage in question. Nor will a passage, in which he is supposed to imply that Archidamas at the time of writing was dead, bear much pressing. In fine,

we do not know when he died, or where or how, though tradition says he was killed by a robber in Thrace. He lived long enough after the end of the war to put into shape most of the history which he began to write at the beginning of the war, as is shown by various passages, such as the reference in the first book to the destruction of the walls of Athens by Lysander, or the analysis in the second book of the causes which led to the final defeat of Athens, passages which can only have been written at the end of the war. On the other hand, he did not live long enough to complete his history, for the last book does not seem to have received the author's final revision, and instead of coming down to the end of the war, brings us only down to B.C. 411, the twenty-first year of this seven-and-twenty years' war.

Thucydides began to write the history of the Peloponnesian war, "believing that it would be great and memorable above any previous war." "No movement," he says, "stirred Hellas more deeply than this." The importance of the war, long as it was, and great as the sufferings it caused, is not to be measured by its length or destructiveness. It was, on the whole, a struggle between the two great Greek races, the Ionians and the Dorians, and between oligarchy and democracy. On the issue of the war it depended whether Athens, which was in possession of the intellectual supremacy of Greece, was also to hold the political; or whether the Spartans, who knew how to fight but not how to live, were to be at liberty to plant rapacious and irresponsible oligarchies in the cities that they conquered. These issues, and they were momentous enough, Thucydides saw; one other consequence, and that an inevitable one, Thucydides must have seen, though he could not know how soon it was to become in its turn a cause and produce other consequences—the necessary exhaustion of Greece, after so long a struggle, that led to the ruin of Greece. Two generations after the end of the Peloponnesian war, Greece lost her political liberty, and with it her literary genius, for want of the strength which had been wasted in the war of which Thucydides wrote.

If these, the political, results were all that is to be learnt from the story of the Peloponnesian war, it would have perhaps an interest for the students of history only. But for those who view the history of Greece from the standpoint of Athens—and erroneous as, for the purposes of history, this view may be, it is the view which gratitude for the art and literature we have inherited from Athens inclines most of us to take—the tale of this war must have, independent of its consequences, something of the fascination which the war itself had for such an onlooker as Thucydides. The hopes and fears with which such a spectator witnessed the successes and disasters of Athens as they followed on one another we who read of them do not feel, for we know from the beginning the result. But notwithstanding, as we read, our hearts are stirred by admiration for the courage with which the Athenians rose above each new disaster, and by regret that so much courage should be doomed only to aggravate their suffering. Still, as we read of each new chance of peace offering itself, now after the success at Pylos, now at the one year's truce, now when Cleon and Brasidas, the two obstacles to peace, are gone, we sigh that the opportunity should be lost, that Athens should persist in treading or be forced along the path of destruction. We watch her with a regret more intense than that with which we watch, impotent to help where we fain would save, the errors of some hero of fiction or the drama; for this is truth and that is fiction; the one is the story of a single imaginary sufferer, the other of the very sufferings of a nation.

Were this the only hold which the history of the Peloponnesian war has upon our interest, it would be enough to earn eager readers for Thucydides in all ages. But this is not all. The losses in wealth and blood, the material disasters and the political humiliation of Athens, which at first sight seem to make up the cost of the war, though they constitute claims on our sympathy for Athens, are not the whole price which Greece or Athens paid for this great and memorable war, as they are not that in the war which touches us most deeply. What touches us most closely is not the sufferings—great as they were—bravely borne by the Athenian people, but Athens' moral fall. That the Athenians, who abandoned hearth and home to the Persian invader for the common good, whose self-sacrificing devotion to the national cause of Hellas put them far above, not merely the craven Greeks who joined the Persians, but far above the selfish indifference of the Peloponnesians to anything but the safety of the Peloponnese; that the Athenians who saved Hellas should have grasped at empire, should have become a menace to Greece, and brought about the war which two generations after gave the independence of Hellas over into the hands of the Macedonian conqueror— this we feel is "the pity of it." As we trace in the pages of Thucydides the course and causes of this falling off, we begin to understand that the fear and pity which it is the function of tragedy to inspire may be excited by the historian as well as the poet, by the actual events of history when told by a great historian, as well as by the creations of a poet's mind. The story of Œdipus, as Sophocles, the contemporary of Thucydides, tells it, fills us with pity for the man "more sinned against than sinning," and with fear for ourselves when, seeing how every step which Œdipus takes to avoid the crimes he is fated to commit only leads him inevitably to commit them, we become possessed with a sense of the ruthless power of Heaven, and the fearful catastrophes to which the slightest deviations from the paths of righteousness may lead. The same sentiments are aroused by the history of the Peloponnesian war as Thucydides tells it. It was her very patriotism and self-

sacrifice which led to the moral fall of Athens. Not only of our vices, but of our virtues do the gods make whips to scourge us. The services of Athens to the national cause made the Greeks look up to her as their leader; she was placed by them at the head of the confederacy of Delos; her energy in prosecuting the war, and the indolence of the allies who allowed her to do the fighting against the Persians, converted her leadership practically into empire. "That empire," as the Athenians said to the Lacedæmonians in B.C. 432, shortly before the outbreak of the war, "was not acquired by force; but you (the Lacedæmonians) would not stay and make an end of the barbarians and the allies came of their own accord and asked us to be their leaders. The subsequent development of our power was originally forced upon us by circumstances." And the Athenians go on to say, "An empire was offered to us; can you wonder that, acting as human nature always will, we accepted it, and refused to give it up again?" The excuse may be accepted, but excuses, even when accepted, cannot prevent our actions from producing their consequences; and the consequence of the Athenian acceptance of empire was the Peloponnesian war. Thucydides says, "The real though unavowed cause [of the war] I believe to have been the growth of the Athenian power, which terrified the Lacedæmonians and forced them into war." The war once begun, the next result of empire was the impossibility of withdrawing from the war. When the Athenians, overwhelmed by the unexpected disaster of the plague, were inclined to peace, Pericles put before them, in B.C. 430, the simple truth, which admitted of no reply: "Once more, you are bound to maintain the imperial dignity of your city, in which you all take pride, for you should not covet the glory unless you will endure the toil. And do not imagine that you are fighting about a simple issue, freedom or slavery; you have an empire to lose, and there is the danger to which the hatred of your imperial rule has exposed you. Neither can you resign your power, if, at this crisis, any timorous or inactive spirit is for thus playing the honest man. For by this time your empire has become a tyranny which, in the opinion of mankind, may have been unjustly gained, but which cannot be safely surrendered. The men of whom I was speaking, if they could find followers, would soon ruin a city, and if they were to go and found a state of their own, would equally ruin that." The principle which Pericles thus laid down, Cleon, in B.C. 427, proceeded to put into application. The Mitylenæans, who had originally joined the confederacy of Delos, and now found themselves belonging to the Athenian empire, withdrew. They were, however, attacked as rebels, and conquered by the Athenians; and the Athenians decreed that every man in Mitylene should be killed and the women and children enslaved. As Cleon said to the Athenians, "If they were right in revolting, you must be wrong in maintaining your empire. But if, right or wrong, you are resolved to rule, then rightly or wrongly they must be chastised for your good. Otherwise, you must give up your empire, and, when virtue is no longer dangerous, you may be as virtuous as you please." The same year as that in which the Mitylenæans suffered was to show that the consequences of our actions cannot be limited to ourselves, and that the innocent pay the penalty as well as the authors of a misdeed; for in this year the Platæans, who had stood a rigorous siege with remarkable bravery, succumbed, and thus the war brought it about that the Spartans, who had defeated the Persians at Platæa with the aid of the Platæans, were about to slaughter the Platæans, and raze to the ground their city, memorable for the defeat of the common foe of Hellas. The pity of it is summed up in one sentence of the Platæans' appeal to the Spartans. "The Platæans, who were zealous in the cause of Hellas even beyond their strength, are now friendless, spurned, and rejected by all. None of our old allies will help us, and we fear that you, O Lacedæmonians, our only hope, are not to be depended upon." The imperial position of Athens, which in this year necessitated the slaughter of a thousand Mitylenæans, whose offence was struggling for their freedom, produced more fruit eleven years later; for as the necessities of empire made it impossible for Athens to retire, so they offered her every inducement to advance. "The Melians," says Thucydides, "were colonists of the Lacedæmonians, who would not submit to Athens like the other islanders. At first they were neutral, and would take no part; but when the Athenians tried to coerce them by ravaging their lands, they were driven into open hostilities." The Melians, therefore, being weak, were to be crushed, and the conscience of Athens, having adapted itself to its imperial position, felt no need of excuses. "We Athenians," said they to the Melians, "will use no fine words; we will not go out of our way to prove at length that we have a right to rule because we overthrew the Persian, or that we attack you now because we are suffering any injury at your hands. We should not convince you if we did. . . . You and we should say what we really think, and aim only at what is possible, for we both alike know that into the discussion of human affairs the question of justice only enters where the pressure of necessity is equal, and that the powerful exact what they can, and the weak grant what they must." Melos was annexed, and Athens continued to advance, whereby she not merely left the question of justice behind, but also neglected the advice which Pericles had given her twenty years before, "Not to seek to enlarge her dominion while the war was going on." Sicily was next attacked. "They virtuously professed that they were going to assist their own kinsmen and their newly-acquired allies, but the simple truth was that they aspired to the empire of Sicily," says Thucydides, an Athenian. The Sicilian expedition failed disastrously, and contributed more than any other error on the part of Athens to her fall. And it, too, was recommended by arguments drawn from the imperial position of Athens. "We cannot," said Alcibiades, "cut down an empire as we might a household; but having once gained our present position, we must keep a firm hold upon some, and contrive occasion against others; for if we are not rulers, we shall be subjects."

It is this tale told in detail, with no striving after effect, but with a calm and cold veracity which imprints the story with painful distinctness on the imagination and the mind, that makes Thucydides as interesting as Sophocles, and the fate of Athens a moral study as absorbing as that of Œdipus. One difference, however, will strike those who read both authors. Destiny, which is the eventual source of all Œdipus' actions, plays no part in Thucydides. How universally useful destiny might be to the historian, Herodotus had already shown. It was a key to which no lock could fail to open. If a storm wrecked Persian ships, this was "in order that" the Persian fleet might not be larger than the Greek fleet. If Xerxes made a mistake in his campaign, this was because destiny had decreed his defeat. But this crude use of destiny could have as little attraction for Thucydides when applied to the solution of historical problems, as for Sophocles when applied to moral problems. Sophocles uses it more sparingly and more effectively. As far as Œdipus is concerned, fate only interposes directly once; in the oracle warning him of the crimes he will commit—and granted but this one interposition, all the actions of Œdipus flow naturally and inevitably. But Thucydides knows not even this refined form of destiny. To Thucydides, a man's own actions are his fate; they are a man's destiny, which decrees what he shall do and what he shall be. The absence of any other kind of destiny from the history of Thucydides does not prove that Thucydides had no belief in destiny. Its absence is satisfactorily accounted for by its being no part of Thucydides' design to entertain theological considerations. His object was to set down only facts, which admit of closer proof than destiny is susceptible of. It will help to the understanding of this and other points to read his own words:—

"Of the events of the war I have not ventured to speak from any chance information, nor according to any notion of my own; I have described nothing but what I either saw myself or learnt from others, of whom I made the most careful and particular inquiry. The task was a laborious one, because eye-witnesses of the same occurrences gave different accounts of them, as they remembered or were interested in the actions of one side or the other. And very likely the strictly historical character of my narrative may be disappointing to the car. But if he who desires to have before his eyes a true picture of the events which have happened, and of the like events which may be expected to happen hereafter in the order of human things, shall pronounce what I have written to be useful, then I shall be satisfied. My history is an everlasting possession, not a prize composition which is heard and forgotten."

The object of Thucydides, then, was to give a strict and faithful account of facts. He had no preconceived theory to prove, no "notion of his own" which his history was to establish. The actual facts, free from the distortions of inaccurate memories or of prejudiced eyes, once established, his history would be an everlasting possession for the guidance of future generations. To the actual facts, then, he confines himself, without moralising and without theorising. For instance, in his great description of the plague he says: "No human art was of any avail, and as to supplications in temples, inquiries of oracles, and the like, they were utterly useless, and at last men were overpowered by the calamity and gave them all up." What he himself thinks on the objective utility of prayer he does not say; he simply notes the fact that in this case supplications were useless, with the same abstention from theorising as he notes, in the next chapter, that the disease after attacking the throat moved down to the chest. Moral disorders he treats in the same positive way as he describes the plague; he notes that a symptom of extreme demoralisation is disregard of law, human and divine. In the same way he records both that Brasidas thought that he captured Lecythus by supernatural aid, and that when Lecythus was attacked the walls happened to be accidentally deserted. So, too, he notes that the Spartans celebrated their religious festivals regardless of the military situation, and that their enemies profited by the fact. The Lacedæmonians, in accordance with their tradition, consulted oracles, but did not guide their policy by them—*e.g.* they consulted Delphi at the beginning of the war as to whether they should declare war or not, but they left the decision to the general meeting of their allies; and the Corinthians used the oracle to silence scruples as to the justice of the war, but trusted to grounds of policy as the means of convincing their hearers. The Spartans also employed the imputed "pollution" of Pericles, not from religious motives, but for purposes of policy; as they and other Greeks regularly appealed to the gods rather from wont than conviction. Amongst the Athenians the religion of their forefathers was held in no better esteem. They purified Delos conventionally. The celebrated affair of the Hermæ was a religious offence, but was converted into political capital. Even for their unjustifiable attack on the Melians, the Athenians count on the approval of the gods. And Thucydides recounts all these things with no comment and no expression of his own opinion: he gives the facts. With regard to oracles and portents he is equally reserved. He observes that in times of excitement everything of the nature of a portent is curiously noted; and he records that after the failure of the Sicilian expedition the Athenians were furious "with the soothsayers and prophets, and all who by the influence of religion had at the time inspired them with the belief that they would conquer Sicily." He is aware that ambiguity is of much virtue in an oracle: he says of the Athenians during the plague, "In their troubles they naturally

called to mind a verse which the elder men among them declared to have been current long ago:—'A Dorian war will come and a plague with it.' There was a dispute about the precise expression; some saying that *limos*, a famine, and not *loimos*, a plague, was the original word. Nevertheless, as might have been expected—for men's memories reflected their sufferings—the argument in favour of *loimos* prevailed at the time. But if ever in future years another Dorian war arises which happens to be accompanied by a famine, they will probably repeat the verse in the other form." The vagueness of another oracle—"Better the Pelasgian ground left waste"—allows him to say for it, "The oracle, without mentioning the war, foresaw that the place would be inhabited some day for no good." Though whether the foresight of the oracle is to be regarded as human or divine, he does not say. When an oracle is fulfilled he notes the fact; in estimating the length of the war he says, "He who reckons up the actual periods of time will find that I have rightly given the exact number of years. He will also find that this was the solitary instance in which those who put their faith in oracles were justified by the event. For I well remember how, from the beginning to the end of the war, there was a common and often-repeated saying that it was to last thrice nine years. I lived through the whole of it, and was of mature years and judgment, and I took great pains to make out the exact truth." This being so, the Athenians had grounds, therefore, it would seem—whether the fulfilment of this solitary oracle was supernatural or casual—for advising the Melians not to have recourse "to prophecies and oracles and the like, which ruin men by the hopes which they inspire in them."

In the same way as he thus prefers to record historical facts without having recourse to any theory, whether of destiny or divine intervention, he records such natural phenomena as were considered portentous, and what was known about them. Thus he duly narrates how when the Athenians were about to leave Sicily, the occurrence of an eclipse of the moon terrified them into delaying their departure, and thus brought about the destruction of them all. But he also notes elsewhere, with regard to solar eclipses, that it is apparently only at the beginning of the lunar month that they are possible. In one place he observes that during a battle in Sicily, "as is often the case in the fall of the year, there came on a storm of rain and thunder, whereby the Athenians were yet more disheartened, for they thought that everything was conspiring to their destruction." Of another engagement he says, "During the battle there came on thunder and lightning and a deluge of rain; these added to the terror of the inexperienced who were fighting for the first time, but experienced soldiers ascribed the storm to the time of the year, and were much more alarmed at the stubborn resistance of the enemy." The plague was considered by many people to be a fulfilment of the promise of

Apollo to assist the Spartans. Thucydides says, "The disease certainly did set in immediately after the invasion of the Peloponnesians, and did not spread into the Peloponnesus in any degree worth speaking of, while Athens felt its ravages most severely, and next to Athens the places which were most populous." But he had a few chapters before said, "The disease is said to have begun south of Egypt in Æthiopia; thence it descended into Egypt and Libya, and after spreading over the greater part of the Persian empire, suddenly fell upon Athens." He records all the facts, but does not express "any notion of his own."

The determined resolution of Thucydides to adhere to the facts of the war has materially influenced the form of his work. Having no preconceived theory of his own, no philosophy of history from which to deduce the facts of the war *a priori,* Thucydides follows, not a logical, but a strictly chronological order. The events of each year are ranged under that year. The story of a siege, for instance, such as that of Platæa, which lasted three years, is not told in one continuous section, but what happened in each year is told under the head of that year, and thus the story of the siege is twice dropped and twice picked up again. The adoption of this annalistic method by Thucydides is the more noteworthy because there were no annalists in Greece. The materials out of which annals sprang in the Middle Ages, lists of magistrates, festivals, &c., and family records, existed in Greece; but before annals could be developed out of them, Thucydides produced history. To us this chronological method of Thucydides seems, as it is, somewhat clumsy. It fetters the historian without apparently affording any compensation. But it must be remembered that in the time of Thucydides there was no uniform system of chronology current throughout Greece. Later, the method of reckoning years by Olympiads, *i.e.* by the recurrence of the Olympic games every four years, was universally adopted by the Greeks. But in the time of Thucydides each state had its own mode of reckoning, and commenced its civil year, not on the same day as any other state, but when its own chief magistrate entered on office, or on some other such principle. This latter difficulty Thucydides evaded by disregarding the civil year and following the natural year, which he divides into summer and winter. This procedure had this advantage, that it suited admirably a record of military operations, which, in the case of the Greeks, ceased in the winter and were carried on only in the summer. The other difficulty which arose in the absence of a uniform chronology, that of specifying the year, Thucydides got over as best he could by counting from the date of some well-known event, and by reference to the chronological system of various states. This, for instance, is his way of specifying the year in which the Peloponnesian war began: "For fourteen years the thirty years' peace which was concluded after the recovery of Eubæa remained un-

broken; but in the fifteenth year, when Chrysis the high-priestess of Argos was in the forty-eighth year of her priesthood, Ænesias being the Ephor at Sparta, and at Athens Pythodorus having two months of his archonship to run, in the sixth month after the engagement at Potidæa, and at the beginning of spring," &c. We, with our fixed system of chronology, say "in B.C. 431." Modern historians, who can specify the date of an event with three strokes of the pen, may arrange events in any order they think most lucid; but Thucydides, having once specified his year, had good reason for adhering to the chronological order of events. The annalistic method might fetter the historian, but it secured his chronology, which other wise might have fluctuated.

Beyond this division into summers, winters, and years, no other seems to have been designed by Thucydides. The division into eight books, as we have his work, though made early, was not made by Thucydides. There are traces in the scholiasts of a division into thirteen books, and Diodorus mentions a division into nine books. But these divisions are probably later even than the one we have. Thucydides, however, does sometimes speak of "the first war" or "the ten years' war," and of "the Sicilian war," and the "Ionic war"; and so it has been conjectured that he intended a division into five parts—the introduction, the ten years' war, the period before the Sicilian expedition, the Sicilian war, and the Ionic war. But the narrative flows on without regard to the subdivisions; the references which Thucydides makes to them are few, and they exercise no influence on the form or matter of his work. Indeed, he seems to have neglected any attempt to break up his work into sections possessing balance, symmetry, proportion, or form, with as much contempt as he disclaims any design of making his history pleasing to the car. The division into years is "strictly historical." Nothing more is aimed at. At any rate, the notion that Thucydides' history is composed on the analogy of a drama, and is arranged in a prologue and five acts, is purely fanciful, and as grotesquely incongruous with Thucydides' conception of the functions of the historian as any piece of "subjectivity" could be. Of all manifestations of power, self-restraint impresses men most, partly because it is the form which power least often takes; and there is scarcely a page of Thucydides that does not exemplify his strength in this respect. Where strong expression seems justifiable, where even it seems demanded, Thucydides contents himself with a sober statement. Events which call aloud for some expression of pity or of horror he leaves to speak for themselves, without a word from him. Where the temptation to any other writer to comment or to moralise would be irresistible, Thucydides resists it. He places before the reader the agonies of a nation, as in his account of the Sicilian expedition, or the presence of death, as in his description of the plague, with grave silence.

Problems of political morality, which he had studied for years and in which his keen intellect took the profoundest interest, he states so far as they were debated or exemplified in the war; but he is not betrayed into speculation; he confines himself to facts. On the great problems of life it is sometimes said that it is impossible for a man to hold his judgment in perpetual suspense; but Thucydides seems to have had them perpetually present to his mind, and to have perpetually regarded the material before him as inadequate for the formation of a decision. It is this habit of never going beyond his facts, of never losing sight of his purpose to ascertain and record facts, this self-restraint which never relaxes, that makes the reader respect and marvel at the power of Thucydides. It creates absolute confidence in him, in his will and his power to record the plain truth. It makes his very silence eloquent, and his least word weighty beyond the superlatives, the exclamations, or asseverations of other writers. This, however, is only the negative side of his power. His silent self-restraint prepares us to be impressed by his words, but his words also impress us. His facts are more valuable than others' comments, and for this there is a reason. In Thucydides' history we have the facts of the war as Thucydides saw them; and the difference between his work and that, say, of Xenophon, who continued Thucydides' incomplete work, is much the same as that between what a geologist and a navvy see in a railway cutting, or a botanist and a ploughboy see in a hedge-bottom, or between what Shelley and a farm-labourer hear in a skylark's song. That is to say, Thucydides had a knowledge of what happened in the war comparable to the geologist's or botanist's knowledge of his science, and he further had, like Shelley, the genius to transmute what he heard into words more precious than gold. Beyond this, in the way of analysis, it is not possible to go far. The intimate acquaintance which he gives us with the Peloponnesian war is proof of the clearness and grasp with which he realised all the details and the whole significance of the war; but to ask how this clear sight was acquired or conveyed is folly. It is better to try and profit by than spy into genius.

The genius of Thucydides is seen in the way in which he not only conveys to the reader his own clear perception of the facts and the course of the war, but also arouses in the reader the emotions with which he himself followed the various incidents of the struggle. In other words, Thucydides' literary genius is as great as his historical genius. Over the literary as well as the historical difficulties involved by his chronological method of relating facts he rides triumphant. It is said that his work is without a plan, and this is true; there is no more plot or plan in his annals than there would be in a diary of the war. But this defect is rather apparent than real. Every incident is viewed by Thucydides in the light thrown on it by the whole war, and thus its importance and position is assigned to it as

unerringly and as clearly as though all the other events narrated by Thucydides had been grouped with the purpose of giving this one incident its proper literary value. But although Thucydides disdains to strive after the external balance and harmony which he might have obtained by articulating his history, and by grouping his facts so as to reach the consummation of a culmination, still this is, from a literary point of view, even more than compensated for by the internal proportions of his work, in virtue of which each incident receives its proper amount of attention and receives light from and throws light on every other incident and the whole course of the war. But although everything which belongs to the narrative of the war fits in with the narrative harmoniously, there are various digressions having nothing to do with the war, *e.g.* that about Harmodius and Aristogiton, which, however valuable in themselves, absolutely spoil the form of the work, as they also constitute an undeniable exception to the strictness with which Thucydides otherwise excludes all matter which does not bear directly on his subject. Whether this is due to simple neglect, or to absolute contempt for literary form, may be doubted. Errors of taste are to be found in Thucydides—they occur precisely when, abandoning his general principle, he strives after effect—and these digressions may have been inserted by him under the impression that a history to possess literary form must have episodes, since they were to be found in Herodotus and the logographers. At the same time, though his annalistic method involves literary disadvantages, it also brings with it some compensating advantages. The system of dropping one thread of the narrative when the end of a year is reached, and then taking up the narrative of the other events of the year, though it sometimes, as in the case of the Sicilian expedition, interrupts with foreign matter the main narrative, yet elsewhere and more generally affords a welcome relief, and a variety such as is attained in a drama by means of a secondary plot.

But it is in the matter, not in the manner, of his work that Thucydides' literary greatness makes itself most felt. And here it is difficult to determine what department and what quality in his work claims our greatest admiration. For the political philosopher of all ages, and for the student of Greek thought, the speeches will ever rank as the greatest work of "the greatest historian that ever lived" [*Life of Lord Macauley*]. And it is a pardonable error if, in the luminous profundity of the thought contained in them, we lose sight of "the antitheses, the climaxes, the plays of words, the point which is no point," that mar the speeches as literature. It is rather to the narrative that we must look for the literary perfection of Thucydides; and there we must turn, not to the philosophical disquisition—great and justly famous as it is—on the effects of civil war, but to the description of the plague, which has had many and able imitators, from Lucretius onwards, but none to approach Thucydides; or to the seventh book, the retreat from Syracuse, of which Macaulay said, "There is no prose composition in the world, not even the *De Corona,* which I place so high," and Gray, "Is it or is it not the finest thing you ever read in your life?" Macaulay speaks of the "intense interest," the "magnificent light and the terrible shade of Thucydides;" and these words apply not only to the Sicilian expedition, but to the whole narrative. In some instances they apply also to the speeches. The speeches are not in all instances devoted wholly to political wisdom. Characters are drawn, as, *e.g.* in the speeches of Alcibiades, Nicias, Archidamus, and Pericles. While in other speeches, *e.g.* the funeral oration, the appeal of the Platæans, the final speech of Nicias to his men, the light is as magnificent and the shade as terrible as in any part of the narrative.

The language of Thucydides is often considered obscure and difficult. Obscure, in the sense that he does not quite know what he wishes to express, he certainly is not. With regard to the difficulty of his style, it is necessary to draw a distinction. When he is narrating events, his style is simple, powerful, and beautiful. When he begins to philosophise and to generalise, he begins to be difficult to understand. But here again we must distinguish. The philosophical reflections of Thucydides are contained mostly in the speeches, and it is in the speeches that he most conspicuously departs from his resolve to describe the simple facts of the war without any attempt to please the ear. It is in the speeches that Thucydides deliberately makes an attempt at form, and whereas when he makes no effort he does attain form, he as signally fails when he is faithless to his principle of not seeking after effect. Doubtless, in throwing his own recollections or the reports of others into the form of direct speeches, Thucydides was practically obeying necessity. To the Greek, in whose life, from the time of Homer, public speaking occupied a large place, to the Athenian above all, whose main occupation in time of peace was the making and hearing of political speeches, a history which contained no speeches would have been no faithful reflection of political life. Thus Thucydides felt himself to a certain extent constrained by his desire to write a faithful history to introduce direct oration; and thus he was constrained to strive after form; for to merely reproduce by an act of memory the original form in which the speeches were delivered was, as he tells us, impossible. In this attempt at form Thucydides allowed himself to be guided by the precept and the example of the early rhetoricians, who, though they helped to lay the foundations of Greek oratory, were immeasurably removed from even the natural ease and grace of Lysias, much more from the perfection of Demosthenes. Thus the mistakes of Thucydides are the mistakes of his masters, not his own, and their mistakes were incidental to and inevitable in the earliest attempts to form artistic prose. The florid rhetoric of Gorgias appears in bad taste to us, but to the Athenians of his time it was

a revelation. It showed that beauty was possible in prose as well as in verse. Its principal defect—that it ignored the difference between poetry and prose—we, who have great prose-writings to compare with it, can readily see. But Thucydides, who had to create prose, may be excused for joining the rest of Athens in admiration of the rhetoricians. Thus the conceits of Thucydides, to which his difficulty is partly due, are owing to the early stage of development to which prose and oratory in his time had reached.

A second cause is to be found in the undeveloped stage of the language. Although there seems no reason to doubt that thought is to a limited extent possible without language, no considerable or continuous advance of thought is so possible. An idea, once captured and imprisoned, so to speak, in a word, is thenceforward available to succeeding generations. Thus the child in learning the meanings of words is storing its mind with ideas. By means of language the child, as with seven-leagued boots, traverses large spaces in the realm of thought, which its ancestors took years to subjugate by means of language, and which are still firmly held by the words they planted there. We at the present day inherit a language the total number of whose words is several times greater than the number any single one of us uses; while though there are many words—technical ones—which the majority of us do not even know the meaning of, we can, when necessary, acquire that knowledge by a reference to a dictionary. It is, therefore, hard for us to realise a stage of language in which there were more ideas than there were words to express them, and in which there was not only no dictionary to explain the meaning of words, but the very idea that it was possible to define the meaning of a word was a new and startling conception, which was used by Socrates, the originator thereof, as long as he had a monopoly of it, to the utter discomfiture of all who came in argument against him. Yet this was the state of the language by means of which Thucydides had to convey ideas that the world had yet never conceived of. Further, at the present day our linguistic conscience permits us to take a word wherever we find it if we want it, or, indeed, if we do not much want it. From naked savages on opposite sides of the world we take the words "palaver" and "taboo," as readily as we appropriate a technicality from languages that are dead. But Thucydides borrowed neither ideas nor the words to clothe them in. He writes pure Attic.

Hitherto we have spoken as though the lack of a vocabulary were the only difficulty with which Thucydides had to contend; but a still more serious difficulty was that the language had as yet no settled or recognised grammar. By this is meant not merely that some centuries had yet to elapse before Dionysius Thrax was to make the first attempt to throw together a body of rules which may be regarded as the beginning of

Greek grammar. People may and must speak grammatically before the principles on which they—or those best worth attention—speak can be observed and noted in a grammar. But Thucydides belongs to a time when people did not, even unconsciously, systematically follow the same analogies or the same principles under similar circumstances. It is not, therefore, to be wondered at if, in the absence of grammatical moulds to receive it, the thought of Thucydides should overflow in some sentences, or solidify into some shape for which later literature has no parallel or only a distant analogy. Nor is it strange if, under the weight of Thucydides' thought, which would have strained the strength of a more developed language, Attic in its then cartilaginous and plastic condition should have sometimes yielded, and have sometimes betrayed the weight thrown on it.

It has been the custom to institute comparisons between Thucydides and other historians, mainly, one would suppose, because Thucydides is by far the greatest of historians. Between him and Herodotus or Xenophon the comparison must be one of contrast, and is one which the reader may be left to draw out for himself; but on the comparison between him and Roman historians a word must be said. In the first place, in any such comparison it should be noticed that Herodotus, Thucydides, and Xenophon, whatever the differences between them, all belong to a literature which is essentially original and creative; whereas the Roman historians belong to a literature which is not original or creative. In the next place, the three Greek historians belong to the best period of Greek literature, but the Roman historians do not belong to the golden age of Latin literature. As to the comparison between Thucydides and Sallust, what resemblance imitation could produce there is; but genius cannot—certainly that of Thucydides cannot—be imitated. Between Thucydides and Tacitus there are some points of resemblance. Both are great historians; both have a profound knowledge of human nature; and both take somewhat pessimistic views of human nature and of life. As to style, both possess great power; both are difficult at times to understand, and brevity is one of the characteristics of each. But to imagine that to Thucydides in his own line it is possible to compare Tacitus, great as he is, is a mistake. The first quality demanded of a historian is credibility; and whatever conclusion we may come to about the credibility of Tacitus, it is impossible to maintain that his reputation stands as high as that of Thucydides in this respect. Thucydides laid the foundations of scientific history, but Tacitus has built elsewhere. Both historians draw largely on oral testimony; but whereas Thucydides understood that the historian should go only to witnesses of the events he wished to record, and that their evidence, and even his own recollection of what he has himself seen, require testing and corroborating, Tacitus was content with hearsay evidence at third or fourth hand. When

Thucydides had recourse to documentary evidence, it was, as far as we can discover, to official documents that he went; or, if he has occasion to refer to other histories, it is in a way which shows that he criticised them closely. Tacitus, on the other hand, has as little notion of criticising documentary as oral testimony, and relies on partisan memoirs as though they were wholly true.

We expect in a historian not only capacity to ascertain facts, but impartiality in stating them; and this quality no historian possesses so eminently as Thucydides. He writes an impartial history of a struggle in which he himself was one of the combatants. Tacitus writes a partial history of events from which he was so far removed in time that we might have reasonably expected from him an unbiased history. Thucydides' love for his native country—and it was great—never leads him to exaggerate the successes or minimise the defeats or the defects of Athens. Tacitus shares the weak amiability of Livy in never admitting a Roman defeat if it is possible to close his eyes to it. In politics there is the same distance between the two historians. Thucydides had political views, but he was a moderate politician, and his views were such that they rather assisted him than prevented him from comprehending the standpoint of others. Tacitus, on the other hand, shared the yearning of his order after a state of things which it was impossible to restore—yearnings which the nobility of Rome expressed the more virulently because they were conscious that they had not the energy or the courage to do anything to get what they sighed for. Tacitus was, on the whole, hostile to the political régime which he undertook to portray.

Let us now consider Tacitus and Thucydides, not as historians, but from the literary point of view. Both suffer from the inconveniences entailed by their following the annalistic method; but these inconveniences are felt much more strongly in Tacitus than in Thucydides. It is no depreciation of Tacitus to say that, great as is the interest with which we read him, it is not the intense interest which Thucydides inspires. The power of Tacitus as a writer is great and undeniable, and he is a master of light and shade, but it is not the magnificent light and the terrible shade of Thucydides. Both writers have the power of brevity, and this is frequently considered to constitute a great resemblance between them; but there is no difference between them so great and so characteristic as this supposed point of resemblance. Where the sentences of Thucydides are brief, it is because they are surcharged with thought; they are weighty with wisdom, and they sink into the mind. The sentences of Tacitus are brief because ejaculatory, exclamatory, abjurgatory. The one is the brevity of condensation, the other of amputation. Thucydides' is the brevity of dignity, Tacitus' the brevity of breathlessness. In fine, Tacitus is a "stylist," Thucydides is none. Thucydides is a perpetual demonstration that there is a higher art than that of concealing art—the art of dispensing with it.

Francis MacDonald Cornford (essay date 1907)

SOURCE: "Mythistoria and the Drama," in *Thucydides Mythistoricus,* 1907. Reprint by Routledge and Kegan Paul, 1965, pp. 129-52.

[*Cornford was an English classicist whose books include* From Religion to Philosophy *(1912),* Greek Religious Thought *(1923), and* Before and after Socrates *(1932). In the following excerpt from a work originally published in 1907, Cornford argues that— despite the historian's intentions to "exclude the mythical"—Thucydides "unconciously" fitted his* History *to the structure of Greek drama.*]

MYTHISTORIA AND THE DRAMA

The epithet 'dramatic' has often been applied to Thucydides' work; but usually nothing more is meant than that he allows his persons to speak for themselves, and presents their character with vividness. The dramatization which we have pointed out in the treatment of Cleon is a very different thing; it is a principle of construction which, wherever it operates, determines the selection of incidents to be recorded, and the proportions and perspective assigned them. In this chapter we shall attempt to describe and analyse the type of drama that we have to do with, and to trace the literary influence under which Thucydides worked.

We ought first, perhaps, to meet a possible objection. It may be urged that Thucydides in his preface expressly excludes anything of the nature of poetical construction from his literal record of what was said and what was done. He criticizes the methods of poets and story-writers, and warns us that, at the cost of making his story 'somewhat unattractive', he intends to exclude 'the mythical'. . . .

He cannot, therefore, it might be inferred, have done what we have thought we found him doing. But we would ask for a careful examination of the passage in question. What was in Thucydides' thoughts when he wrote it, and above all, what precisely did he mean to exclude when he banished 'the mythical'?

The words occur towards the end of the introduction, which is designed to establish Thucydides' belief that the Peloponnesian war was the most memorable of all that had ever been in Greece. The possible rivals, he points out, are the Trojan war and the Persian invasion. For the first of these events the only literary evidence we have is that of the epic poets, and chiefly of Homer, whose record cannot be checked by direct observation, while much of his theme through the lapse

of time has passed, or 'won over', into the region of the mythical and incredible. The only tests we have are certain indications in the existing condition of Greece which seem inconsistent with the past state of things as represented by the literary authorities. With these indications we must be content; and they suffice to show that the epic poets embellished their tale by exaggeration. The story-writers, again, on whom we depend for the history of the Persian wars, were not bent upon accurate statement of truth;—witness the carelessness of Herodotus about points of detail. Their object was rather to make their recitations attractive and amusing to their audience; and if we discount their evidence accordingly, we shall find, going by ascertained facts alone, that the Peloponnesian war was the greatest ever seen.

Thucydides next passes abruptly to the formulation of his own method; he intends to record what was said and what was done as accurately and literally as possible. The result, he then remarks, will probably be somewhat unattractive to an audience at a recitation, because the facts recorded will have nothing 'mythical' about them; he will be content, however, if they are judged useful by people who wish to know the plain truth of what happened.

The phrase 'winning over into the mythical' is illuminating. It suggests the transformation which begins to steal over all events from the moment of their occurrence, unless they are arrested and pinned down in writing by an alert and trained observer. Even then some selection cannot be avoided—a selection, moreover, determined by irrelevant psychological factors, by the accidents of interest and attention. Moment by moment the whole fabric of events dissolves in ruins and melts into the past; and all that survives of the thing done passes into the custody of a shifting, capricious, imperfect, human memory. Nor is the mutilated fragment allowed to rest there, as on a shelf in a museum; imagination seizes on it and builds it with other fragments into some ideal construction, which may have a plan and outline laid out long before this fresh bit of material came to the craftsman's hand to be worked into it, as the drums of fallen columns are built into the rampart of an Acropolis. Add to this the cumulative effects of oral tradition. One ideal edifice falls into ruin; pieces of it, conglomerates of those ill-assorted and haphazard fragments, are carried to another site and worked into a structure of, perhaps, a quite different model. Thus fact shifts into legend, and legend into myth. The facts *work loose;* they are detached from their roots in time and space and shaped into a story. The story is moulded and remoulded by imagination, by passion and prejudice, by religious preconception or aesthetic instinct, by the delight in the marvellous, by the itch for a moral, by the love of a good story; and the thing becomes a legend. A few irreducible facts will remain; no more, perhaps, than the names of persons and places—Arthur, Caerleon, Camelot; but even these may at last drop out or be turned by a poet into symbols. 'By Arthur,' said Tennyson, 'I always meant the soul, and by the Round Table the passions and capacities of man.' The history has now all but won over into the mythical. Change the names, and every trace of literal fact will have vanished; the story will have escaped from time into eternity.

When we study this process, we seem to make out two phases of it, which, for the criticism of Thucydides, it is necessary to distinguish. The more important and pervasive of the two is the moulding of fact into types of myth contributed by traditional habits of thought. This process of *infiguration* if we may coin the word may be carried to any degree. Sometimes the facts happen to fit the mould, and require hardly any modification; mere unconscious selection is enough. In other cases they have to be stretched a little here, and patted down there, and given a twist before they will fit. In extreme instances, where a piece is missing, it is supplied by mythological inference from the interrupted portions which call for completion; and here we reach the other phase of the process, namely *invention*. This is no longer a matter of imparting a form to raw material; it is the creation of fresh material when the supply of fact is not sufficient to fill the mould. It leads further to the embroidery of fabulous anecdote, which not only has no basis in fact, but is a superfluous addition, related to fact as illustrations in a book are related to the text.

The process, in both its phases, can be illustrated from the version preserved by Thucydides of the legend of Harmodius and Aristogeiton, the tyrant-slayers. Harmodius' sister, whom the tyrant insults, makes her first appearance in this account. She is superfluous, since the murderers had already a sufficient private motive arising out of the love-quarrel. That is not in itself an argument against her historical character, for superfluous people sometimes do exist; but other circumstances make it not improbable that she owes her existence to the mythical type which normally appears in legend when tyrants have to be slain. The two brothers, or lovers, and the injured sister, or wife—the relationships vary—are the standing *dramatis personae* on such occasions. Collatinus, Brutus, and Lucretia are another example from legend; while the purely mythical type which shapes such legends is seen in the Dioscuri and Helen. The suggestion is that Harmodius and Aristogeiton were identified with the Heavenly Twins. If there is any truth in the story of how Peisistratus was conducted back to Athens by a woman dressed as Athena and accepted by the citizens as the goddess in person, it is not surprising that the next generation of Athenians should have recognized the Dioscuri in Harmodius and his friend. Given that identification, the injured sister is felt to be a desirable, if not indis-

pensable, accessory; she is filled in by inference, and she becomes a candidate for the place of 'basket-bearer' in the Panathenaic procession, at which the murder took place. Thus, the legend of Harmodius illustrates both the phases of the process we described: first, it is moulded on the mythical type of the Heavenly Twins, and then invention supplies the missing third figure.

Mythical types of this sort can be discovered and classified only after a wide survey of comparative Mythistoria; for we all take our own habits of thought for granted, and we cannot perceive their bias except by contrast. The Greek who knew only Greek legend could not possibly disengage the substance from the form; all he could do was to prune away the fabulous and supernatural overgrowths, and cut down poetry into prose. It is thus that Thucydides treats myths like the story of Tereus, Procne, and Philomela; he rationalizes them, thinking that he has reduced them to history when he has removed unattested and improbable accretions, such as the transformation of Tereus into a hoopoe. But history cannot be made by this process (which is still in use); all that we get is, not the original facts, but a mutilated legend; and this may very well be so mutilated that it is no longer possible to distinguish the informing element of fiction, which was discernible till we effaced the clues.

The phenomenon that especially concerns us now is something much wider than the mythical infiguration of a single incident here or there, such as the legend of the Tyrantslayers. It is the moulding of a long series of events into a plan determined by an *art form*. When we set the *Persians* of Aeschylus beside the history of Herodotus, we see at once that the tragedian in dramatizing the events of Xerxes' invasion, some of which he had personally witnessed, has also worked them into a theological scheme, preconceived and contributed by his own mind. Further we remark that Herodotus, although he is operating in a different medium and writing a saga about the glory of Athens, uses the same theological train of thought as a groundwork, and falls in with the dramatic conception of Aeschylus. This is a case of the infiguration of a whole train of events by a form which is mythical, in so far as it involves a theological theory of sinful pride punished by jealous divinity, and is also an art form, by which the action is shaped on dramatic principles of construction, involving such features as climax, reversal, catastrophe. The theory and the form together provide the setting of the whole story—the element which makes it a work of art. This element is so structural that it cannot be removed without the whole fabric falling to pieces, and at the same time so latent and pervasive, as not to be perceptible until the entire work is reviewed in its large outline. Even then it can be detected only by a critic who is on his guard and has not the same scheme inwrought into the substance of his own mind; for if he is himself disposed to see the events in conformity with the scheme, then the story will answer his expectation and look to him perfectly natural.

When Thucydides speaks of 'the mythical', it seems probable from the context that he is thinking chiefly of *inventive* 'embellishment'. The accretions of fabulous anecdote are comparatively easy to detect; they often bring in the supernatural in the forms of vulgar superstition, and being for this reason improbable, they require better evidence than is forthcoming. Also, poets tend to *magnify* their theme for purposes of panegyric, flattering to their audience; they will, for instance, represent Agamemnon's expedition as much larger than it probably was. It is on these grounds that Thucydides objects to the evidence of Ionian Epos and Herodotean story-telling. He warns us against the faults which struck his notice; and he was on his guard against them, even more than against the popular superstition and dogmatic philosophy of the day, which he tacitly repudiates. But there was one thing against which he does not warn us, precisely because it was the framework of his own thought, not one among the objects of reflection,—a scheme contributed, like the Kantian categories of space and time, by the mind itself to whatever was presented from outside. Thucydides, like Descartes, thought he had stripped himself bare of every preconception; but, as happened also with Descartes, his work shows that there was after all a residuum wrought into the substance of his mind and ineradicable because unperceived. This residuum was his philosophy of human nature, as it is set forth in the speech of Diodotus,—a theory of the passions and of their working which carried with it a principle of dramatic construction presently to be described. That he was not forearmed against this, he himself shows when, in attacking Herodotus, he accuses him of trivial errors of fact, and does not bring the one sweeping and valid indictment which is perfectly relevant to his own point about the embellishment of the Persian War. The dramatic construction of Herodotus' work, which stares a modern reader in the face, apparently escaped the observation of his severest ancient critic.

Another proof can be drawn from Thucydides' own account of a series of events which he evidently believed to be historical, the closing incidents, namely, of Pausanias' career. He shows us the Spartan king intriguing with the Persian, and 'bent upon the empire of Hellas'. Pausanias commits certain treacherous acts; boasts of his power to the Great King; 'intends, if the king please, to marry his daughter'; is so 'uplifted' by the king's answer that he can no longer live like ordinary men; behaves like an oriental; cannot keep silence about his larger designs; makes himself difficult of access, and displays a harsh temper. We know all these symptoms well enough, and we foresee the end. Pausanias is recalled, but the evidence against him is insufficient. He writes a letter betraying his designs and ending with an order for the execution of the bear-

er. The messenger, whose suspicions are aroused, opens the letter and shows it to the authorities at Sparta. The ephors arrange that they shall be concealed behind a partition and overhear a conversation between the king and his treacherous messenger, who contrives to draw from Pausanias a full and damning avowal. The end follows in the Brazen House.

This is not the sort of thing that Thucydides objects to as 'mythical'; it is not 'fabulous', not the embroidery of mere poetical invention; and so he reports it all in perfect good faith. What does not strike him, and what does strike us, is that the story is a drama, framed on familiar lines, and ready to be transferred to the stage without the alteration of a detail. The earlier part is a complete presentation of the 'insolent' type of character. The climax is reached by a perfect example of 'Recoil' . . . , where the hero gives the fatal letter to the messenger, and thus by his own action precipitates the catastrophe. The last scene is staged by means of a theatrical property now so cheapened by use as to be barely respectable—a screen! The manner of the hero's death involved sacrilege, and was believed to bring a curse upon his executioners. Could we have better proof that Thucydides was not on his guard against dramatic construction, and was predisposed to see in the working of events a train of 'causes' which tragedy had made familiar?

When we are alive to the dramatic setting, we can infer with some certainty the stages through which the Thucydidean story of Pausanias has passed. The original stratum of fact must have been that Pausanias somehow misconducted himself, was recalled, and put to death in circumstances which were capable of being used by superstition and policy against the ephors. These facts worked loose into a legend, shaped by imagination on the model of preconceived morality and views of human nature. The mould is supplied by drama; and meanwhile fabulous invention is busy in many minds, embroidering the tale with illustrative anecdotes. Thucydides brushes away these extravagant and unattested accretions, and reduces the legend again to what seemed to him a natural series of events. It is only we who can perceive that what he has left is the dramatized legend, not the historical facts out of which it was worked up. It is not wildly paradoxical to think that the historian who accepted the legend of Pausanias might frame on the same pattern the legend of Cleon. Not that Thucydides invented anything; all that was needed was to select, half unconsciously, those parts of his life which of themselves composed the pattern.

We must now come to closer quarters with the epithet 'dramatic'. It is worth noting, at the outset, that in the mere matter of external form, the history seems to show the influence of tragedy,—a fact which need not surprise us, if we remember that Thucydides had no model for historical writing. The brief abstract of the annalist was a scaffold, not a building; and Thucydides was an architect, not a carpenter. Chroniclers and story-writers like Herodotus had chosen the lax form of epic, congenial to ramblers; but whatever the history was to be, it was not to be like Herodotus, and it was to draw no inspiration from the tradition of Ionian Epos. So Thucydides turned to drama—the only other developed form of literature then existing which could furnish a hint for the new type to be created. The severe outline and scrupulous limitations of this form satisfied his instinct for self-suppression. The epic poet stands before his audience and tells his own tale; but the dramatist never appears at all: the 'thing done' . . . works itself out before the spectators' eyes; the thing said comes straight from the lips of the actors.

Best of all, to Thucydides' thinking, if we, of after times, could ourselves have watched every battle as it was won and lost, and ourselves have heard every speech of envoy and statesman; we should then have known all, and much more than all, this history was designed to tell. But as this cannot be, we are to have the next thing to it; we shall sit as in a theatre, where the historian will erect his mimic stage and hold the mirror up to Nature. Himself will play the part of 'messenger' and narrate 'what was actually done' with just so much of vividness as the extent of his own information warrants. For the rest, the actors shall tell their own tale, as near as may be, in the very words they used, 'as I heard them myself, or as others reported them.'

Speeches are much more prominent in Thucydides' history than they are in that of Herodotus. The change seems partly due to the later historian's preference for setting forth motives in the form of 'pretexts', instead of giving his own opinion; but it is also due to his being an Athenian. Plato similarly chose to cast his speculations in the dramatic form of dialogue, allowing various points of view to be expressed by typical representatives, without committing himself to any of them. Even oratory at Athens was dramatically conceived; the speech-writer did not appear as advocate in court; he wrote speeches in character to be delivered by his clients. It has often been remarked that the debates in Thucydides resemble in some points of technique the debates in a Euripidean play. There is moreover in one respect an intellectual kinship between Thucydides and the dramatist who was contemporaneously moulding the form of tragedy to the strange uses of realism, and working away from Aeschylus as Thucydides had to work away from Herodotus. The two men are of very different temperaments; but in both we seem to find the same sombre spirit of renunciation, the same conscious resolve nowhere to overstep the actual, but to present the naked thoughts and actions of humanity, just as they saw them. No matter how crude the light, how harsh the outline, so that the thing done and the thing said shall stand out as they were, in isolated sharpness, though

> Mist is under and mist above, . . .
> And we drift on legends for ever.

These considerations, however, touch only the question of external form: they show why so much that we should state directly is stated indirectly by Thucydides, in speeches. The choice of this form is consistent with a complete absence of *plot* or of dramatic construction: otherwise Thucydides could not have chosen it at starting; for at that moment the plot lay in the unknown future. We mention the point only because evidently it was somewhat easier for an historian who consciously borrowed the outward form of tragedy, to take unconsciously the further step, and fall in with its inward form and principle of design. It is this which we now wish to define more closely. The type of drama we have detected in the history is not the Euripidean type; it will be found, on examination, to show an analogy with the older form existing in the tragedies of Aeschylus.

The resemblances are reducible to two main points. The first is an analogy of technical construction, seen in the use and correlation of different parts of the work. The second is a community of psychological conceptions: a mode of presenting character, and also a theory of the passions which has a place not only in psychology, but in ethics. We shall begin by studying the structure; but we may bear in mind that this structure is closely involved with the psychological theory.

An art form, such as the Aeschylean drama, shapes itself as a sort of crust over certain beliefs which harden into that outline. When this has happened, the beliefs themselves—the content of the mould—may gradually be modified and transmuted in many ways. Finally, they may melt and almost fade away, leaving the type, which is preserved as a traditional form of art. This survival of an element of technical construction may be illustrated by the instance of 'reversal'. . . . A 'reversal of fortune' is the cardinal point of primitive tragedy; and it originally means an overthrow caused by an *external* supernatural agency—Fate or an angry god. When the belief in such agencies fades, 'reversal' remains as a feature in drama; but the change of situation is now caused by the hero's own act. The notion of 'recoil' comes in: that is to say, the fatal action itself produces results just the opposite of those intended—a perfectly natural occurrence. In this way a piece of technique outlasts the belief which gave rise to it.

The Aeschylean drama appears to us to have gone through a process of this kind. The structure, as we find it, seems to imply an original content of beliefs in some respects more primitive than those explicitly held by Aeschylus himself, but surviving in his mind with sufficient strength to influence his work. Similarly, as we hope to show, in transmission from Aeschylus to Thucydides, the dramatic type has again outlasted much of the belief which informed it in the Aeschylean stage. It is the artistic structure which is permanent; the content changes with the advance of thought. Hence, if we point to Aeschylean technique in Thucydides, we are not necessarily attributing to him the creed of Aeschylus.

We must first attempt to describe the structure of Aeschylean tragedy. In order to understand it we must try to imagine a yet more primitive stage in the development of the drama than any represented in extant Greek literature, a stage which the earliest of Aeschylus' plays has already left some way behind. A glance at the development of modern drama may help us.

Certain features which survived in Greek tragedy suggest that we should look back to a type somewhat resembling the mediaeval mystery and some of the earliest modern dramas, such as *Everyman,* which are like the mystery in being religious performances and in the element of allegorical abstraction. Their effect, due in part to each of these features, may be described as *symbolic. Everyman* is a sermon made visible. To watch it is like watching the pastime called 'living chess', in which the pieces are men and women, but the man who is dressed like a bishop is nothing more than a chessman who happens to be automatic. He has not the episcopal character; his dress is a disguise with nothing behind it; his words, if he spoke, would be the speech of a parrot. And so it is with *Everyman.* The persons are not persons at all, but *personae,* masks, symbols, the vehicles of abstract ideas. They do not exist, and could not be conceived as existing, in real space and time. They have no human characters, no inward motives, no life of their own. Everyman, as his name is meant to show, is in fact not *a* man, but Man, the universal.

The main development of modern drama shows, in one of its aspects, the process by which this symbolic method gives way to the realistic. The process consists in the gradual filling in of the human being behind the mask, till the humanity is sufficiently concrete and vital to burst the shell and step forth in solid flesh and blood. The symbol comes to contain a type of character; the type is particularized into a unique individual. The creature now has an independent status and behaviour of its own. Every gesture and every word must be such as would be used by an ordinary human being with the given character in the given situation. Once created, the personality is an original centre; it cannot be made to do what we please or to utter our thoughts. In some such terms as these a modern novelist or playwright will speak of his characters; and it is thus that they appear to us.

Now we can observe a certain intermediate stage in which these two methods, the symbolic and the realistic, are balanced in antagonism, so as to produce a curious effect of tension and incoherency. A good instance is Marlowe's *Faustus.* Faustus himself occupies the central plane; he is a living man, but still imprisoned in a symbolical type. The intrusion of humanity has gone far enough to disturb the abstract effect, and it reacts on some of the persons in the play who ought to be purely symbolic. Lucifer, it is true, is kept apart and remains non-human; but Mephistophilis oscillates in our imagination between the ideal and reality, with a distressing result. Again, on a lower level than Faustus there is yet another grade of persons, in contrast with whom he shows up as heroic and ideal. These are the vintner, the horse-courser, and other pieces of common clay picked out of a London alley; they belong to a different world, and we feel that they could no more communicate with the tragic characters than men can talk with angels. Thus there are in this one play four sets or orders of persons: (1) the purely abstract and *symbolic,* such as Lucifer, who only appears on an upper stage at certain moments, and takes no part in the action; (2) the *intermediate,* for instance Mephistophilis, who ought to be symbolic, but treads the lower stage, a cowled enigma, horrible because at moments he ceases to be symbolic without becoming human; (3) the *heroic* or tragic: Faustus, who is an ideal half realized, hanging together on its own plane; (4) the *real*: common mortals who would attract no attention in Fleet Street.

The Greek drama, although in the detail of historical development it started at a different point from the modern, and followed another course, seems, nevertheless, to pass through a phase analogous to that which we have just described. The original substance of the drama was the choral lyric; the actors as they afterwards became began as an excrescence. At a certain stage the actors are assimilated to the chorus and move in the same atmosphere. Thus in the earliest play of Aeschylus, the *Suppliants,* we find that the chorus of Danaids are actually the heroines of the action, which centres round them, so that they are not merely on the same plane with the actors, but themselves a complex actor, and the effect is simple, coherent, and uniform. In the *Prometheus,* again, the chorus belong to the same ideal world as the Titan hero, a world in which abstract symbols like Mastery and Violence can move without showing as unreal against the other persons. The whole drama is on the symbolic plane, the life in it being due to anthropomorphic imagination, not to the intrusion of realism.

But in the latest plays of Aeschylus, the beginning of a change is clearly marked: the actors are becoming human, while the lyric is rising above them, or else remains suspended in a rarer atmosphere from which they are sinking. This is a natural stage in the passage from pure symbolism to realism. The advance shows itself externally in the *drifting apart* of the lyrical element from the dialogue,—a separation which, of course, widens in the later tragedians, till the choral ode, though still an indispensable and very beautiful feature, becomes in point of construction little more than an interlude, which relieves the concentrated intensity of the action. This change is commonly taken as a phenomenon which needs no explanation; but really it is caused inevitably by the *coming to life* of the persons in the drama. In proportion as these become more real, the lyric becomes more ideal and further removed from the action.

In the stage observable in Aeschylus' latest plays, the choral part is still *dramatic,* and of equal importance with the dialogue. The two elements are evenly balanced; but at the same time they have begun to occupy different worlds, so that we are sensible of the transition from one to the other. The result is a curious duplication of the drama which now has two aspects, the one universal and timeless, the other particular and temporal.

The nature of this phenomenon will, we hope, become clear, if we take as an illustration the *Agamemnon.* In this play, the visible presentation shows how the conqueror of Troy came home and was murdered by the queen. The events that go forward on the stage are *particular* events, located at a point of legendary time and of real space. The characters are certain individuals, legendary or historic—there is to Aeschylus no difference here—who lived at that moment and trod that sport of earth. But in the choral odes the action is lifted out of time and place on to the plane of the universal. When the stage is clear and the visible presentation is for the time suspended, then, above and beyond the transient spectacle of a few suffering mortals caught, just there and then, in the net of crime, loom up in majestic distance and awful outline the truths established, more unchangeably than the mountains, in the eternal counsels of Zeus. The pulse of momentary passion dies down; the clash and conflict of human wills, which just now had held us in breathless concentration, sink and dwindle to the scale of a puppet-show; while the enduring song of Destiny unrolls the theme of blood-haunted Insolence lured by insistent Temptation into the toils of Doom. As though on a higher stage, uncurtained in the choral part, another company of actors concurrently plays out a more majestic and symbolic drama. On this invisible scene walk the figures of Hybris and Peitho, of Nemesis and Ate—not the bloodless abstractions of later allegory, but still clothed in the glowing lineaments of supernatural reality. The curtain lifts for a timeless moment on the spectacle of human life in an aspect known to the all-seeing eyes of Zeus; and when it drops again, we turn back to the mortal tragedy of Agamemnon and Clytemnestra, enlightened, purified, uplifted, calm.

Thus we find in Aeschylus something analogous to the hierarchy of persons we noted in *Faustus*; although, for various reasons, there is not the same crude effect of incoherency and tension. The supernatural characters—Zeus, supreme above all, and the demonic figures of Hybris, Nemesis, Ate, and the rest, are not *seen,* as Lucifer is seen on the upper stage of the Elizabethan theatre, but remain in the spiritual world to which lyrical emotion exalts the inward eye—the world where metaphor (as we call it) is the very stuff of reality, where Cassandra quickens and breathes, and whence she strays among mortal men like a fallen spirit, sweet-voiced, mad, and broken-winged. Hence the effect is far more awful and solemn than the actual apparition of Lucifer; and when Apollo and Athene and the spirits of vengeance take human shape in the *Eumenides,* a spell is broken, a veil rent, an impression shattered, for which not the most splendid symphony of poetical language can atone.

Here, however, we would confine our attention to the *Agamemnon.* At the lower end of the scale we find a further advance of realism in some minor characters, the watchman and the herald; the nurse in the *Choephori* is of the same order. These are allowed some wonderful touches of common humanity, below the heroic level; for they are not directly concerned in the central action, and a little irrelevant naturalism does no harm, if it is not carried far. But they are only just below the heroic standard, and are certainly not the sort of people you would have met in a walk to the Piraeus.

Thus, the two planes in the *Agamemnon* are divided by an interval less wide and less abrupt than the divisions in *Faustus.* In psychological conception also the union is very close, since the heroic characters are still so abstract and symbolic that they are barely distinguishable from the pure abstractions of the lyrical world. Agamemnon, for instance, is simply Hybris typified in a legendary person. He is a hero flown with 'insolence' (the pride and elation of victory), and that is all that can be said of him. He is not, like a character in Ibsen, a complete human being with a complex personality,—a centre from which relations radiate to innumerable points of contact in a universe of indifferent fact. He has not a continuous history: nothing has ever happened to him except the conquest of Troy and the sacrifice of Iphigenia; nothing ever could happen to him except Pride's fall and the stroke of the axe. As we see him, he is not a man, but a single state of mind, which has never been preceded by other states of mind (except one, at the sacrifice in Aulis), but is isolated, without context, margin, or atmosphere. Every word he says, in so far as he speaks for himself and not for the poet, comes straight out of that state of mind and expresses some phase of it. He has a definite relation to Cassandra, a definite relation to Clytemnestra; but no relation to anything else. If he can be said to have a *character* at all, it consists solely of certain defects which make him liable to Insolence; if he has any *circumstances,* they are only those which prompt him to his besetting passion.

Now it is in some such way as this that Thucydides presents his principal characters. Cleon is a good instance. He is allowed no individuality, no past history, no atmosphere, no irrelevant relations. He enters the story abruptly from nowhere. A single phrase fixes his type, as though on a play-bill: 'Cleon, the most violent of the citizens and first in the people's confidence'; that is all we know of him. There follows a speech in which the type reveals itself in a state of mind,—Violence in its several phases. Then he vanishes, to reappear, before Sphacteria, as Violence with one of its aspects ('covetousness') emphasized, and a sudden passion of ambitious self-confidence . . . added thereto. Finally, we see him wrecked by this passion at Amphipolis. Pericles is introduced in the same way, with a single epithet: 'Pericles, the son of Xanthippos, a man at that time first among the Athenians, and *most powerful . . .* in action and in speech.' His characteristic quality is wise foresight (. . . —the opening word of his first speech); and he stands also, in the Funeral Oration, for the glory . . . of Athens. Alcibiades we shall study later. In every case the principal characters are nearly as far removed from realism, nearly as abstract and impersonal as the heroic characters in Aeschylus. Thucydides, in fact, learnt his psychology from the drama, just as we moderns (whether historians or not) learn ours, not by direct observation, but from the drama and the novel.

But we can carry the analogy further; it extends to minor points of Aeschylean technical construction, which follow naturally upon the drifting apart of lyric and dialogue. In the *Agamemnon* we note that the separation of the two planes has gone far enough to make it impossible for the members of the chorus to interfere with the action at its crisis. The elders, when they hear the death-cry, cannot enter the palace; not because the door is locked, nor yet because they are feeble old men. Rather they are old men because an impassable barrier of convention is forming between chorus and actors, and their age gives colour to their powerlessness. The need of a separate stage for the actors, though tradition may cling to the old orchestra, is already felt. The poet is half aware of the imaginative separation, and he bridges it by links of two kinds—formal links of technical device, and internal connexions of a psychological sort, which will occupy us in the next chapter.

The formal links are provided by what is called 'tragic irony'. The dialogue is so contrived that, instructed by the lyric, we can catch in it allusions to grander themes than any of which the speakers are conscious, and follow the action with eyes opened to a universal sig-

nificance, hidden from the agents themselves. Tragic irony, however, is not a deliberately invented artifice; it arises of itself in the advance from the purely symbolic stage of drama. In that earliest stage the whole dialogue might be called 'ironical', in the sense that it is the poet's message to the audience, not the expression of the persons' characters, for they have none. But it becomes ironical in the strict sense only when the persons begin to have elementary characters and minds, and so to be conscious of one meaning of their words, which is not the whole meaning or the most important. The effect is now no longer merely symbolic, but *hypnotic;* the speaker on the stage is like a somnambulist—alive, but controlled and occupied by an external personality, the playwright.

Tragic irony is used by Aeschylus with great freedom; because his persons are still so near to the symbolic, they have so little character and psychology of their own, that they do not mind serving as mouthpieces. Here and there we find instances of perfect irony, where the speaker's words bear both constructions equally well, and are at once the natural expression of the appropriate state of mind and also a message from the poet to the spectator, applying one of the lyrical themes. This is the only sort of irony admitted by Sophocles, whose characters have become so human that they will not speak merely for another. In Aeschylus, however, there are whole speeches which are hypnotic, and hardly in character at all. The effect is so unfamiliar to readers schooled in realism that it is often missed.

The first two speeches of Clytemnestra, for instance, seem to be of this kind; notably, the beacon speech. If we try to interpret this as a realistic revelation of Clytemnestra's character and thoughts, we shall not find that it helps us to much insight, because its main function has nothing to do with her character. The poet is speaking through her, and the thoughts are his. The early part of the play, down to the entrance of Agamemnon, is an overture, in which Aeschylus musters and marshals the abstract themes which are to be the framework of the trilogy. One of them is expressed in the beacon speech; and it is this. The fire of Idaean Zeus has fallen upon Troy, 'neither before its season nor striking as an idle glancing shaft beyond the stars'; but that *same* fire, the symbol of Justice, speeds now to 'strike the roof of the Atreidae'. From mountain top it leaps and hastens across the sea to mountain top; and like the torch passed from hand to hand in the race, it is itself a runner and the only one which 'running first and last reaches the goal'. This description of the symbolic fire conducted along the beacon chain is given to Clytemnestra because it can be given to no one else, not because it is the best means of illustrating her psychology. The speech, by the way, also exhibits another artifice employed to link the two planes—the allusive verbal echo between dialogue and lyric. The symbol of the fire, in a slightly varied form, recurs at

Two soldiers in combat, c. 600-590 B.C.

the beginning of the next chorus, and the keyword . . . is reiterated to mark the correspondence.

Now the speeches in Thucydides can be roughly classed under four heads. There are, first, a few realistic speeches by minor characters; for instance, the short, sharp utterance of the Spartan ephor, which has the trick of the laconic practical man. Next, there are idealistic speeches, designed as direct expressions of character or of national ideals; the Funeral Oration will serve as an example. These shade off, through a class in which sketches of national character are introduced indirectly, with some strain upon dramatic probability, into a class where irony is openly employed in the tragic manner. Cleon's Mytilenean speech, for instance, is nearly all of the character-revealing sort, but it contains a passage about the evil results of exceptional prosperity which is without any true application to the position of Lesbos or to the history of the revolt. It runs as follows:

> Conceiving a reckless confidence in the future, and hopes that outran their strength though they fell short of their desires, they went to war; and they thought fit to prefer might to right, for where they thought they saw a chance of success, they set upon us when we were doing them no wrong. It is always so: when exceptional prosperity comes sudden and unexpected to a city, it turns to insolence: and, in general, good fortune is safer for mankind when it answers to calculation than when it surpasses expectation, and one might almost say that men find it easier to drive away adversity than to preserve prosperity. We were wrong from the first. We ought never to have put the Mytileneans above the rest by exceptional treatment; then their insolence would not have come to this height. It is a general rule that human nature despises flattery, and respects unyielding strength.

These words are patently inapplicable to the revolted island, whose exceptional position was notoriously a survival of the status originally enjoyed by every one of the allies, but now forfeited by all but a few; to speak of it as a sudden access of prosperity is simply meaningless. We are driven to see in the passage a use of tragic irony; Thucydides puts into Cleon's mouth the very moral which his own career is to illustrate. The device is unskilfully employed, since dramatic probability is too completely sacrificed. Sophocles would not have passed these sentences, which on the speaker's lips have not even a plausible meaning; but Aeschylus would have passed them, and after all Thucydides was only an amateur tragedian.

A fourth use of speeches is illustrated by the Spartan envoys' homily before Sphacteria. This is still further removed from realism, and resembles the beacon speech, which is but one degree below the lyric plane. The historian, reluctant to break silence in his own person, sets forth the theme and framework of his drama in the form of a solemn warning. He has already described the Athenians at Pylos as 'wishing to follow up their present good fortune to the furthest point'. This is a dangerous frame of mind, against which Themistocles had warned the Athenians after Salamis, when they wished to press forward and destroy the Persians' bridges over the Hellespont. 'I have often,' says Themistocles, 'myself witnessed occasions, and I have heard of many from others, where men who had been conquered by an enemy, having been driven quite to desperation, have renewed the fight and retrieved their former disasters. We have now had the great good luck . . . to save both ourselves and all Greece by the repulse of this vast cloud of men; let us then be content and not press them too hard, now that they have begun to fly. Be sure that we have not done this by our own might. It is the work of gods and heroes, who were jealous that one man should be king at once of Europe and Asia. . . . At present all is well with us—let us then abide in Greece, and look to ourselves and to our families.'

The warning of the Spartan envoys is conceived in the same spirit; but it is unheeded and unanswered. No answer, indeed, was possible; the speech is not an argument, but a prophecy. A reply from Cleon, a statement of the war party's policy, such as modern critics desiderate, would be as inappropriate as a reply from Clytemnestra to the Second Chorus in the *Agamemnon*. The stage is clear while this prophecy, addressed not to the actors but to the spectators, passes unheard by those who, could they have heard it, might have been saved.

One further point of formal resemblance between Aeschylus and Thucydides is the allusive echoing of significant phrases, which sustain the moral motive dominant in the plot. We have seen an instance of this device in the repetition of the words 'coveting more' . . . , which reappear at critical moments after the use of them in the envoys' speech; and we shall note other examples later. This completes the analogy with Aeschylean form, so far as concerns external peculiarities.

Charles Norris Cochrane (essay date 1929)

SOURCE: "Thucydides," in *Thucydides and the Sci-* *ence of History,* Oxford University Press, 1929, pp. 14-34.

[*In the following excerpt, Cochrane identifies Thucydides as a "scientific" historian, demonstrating that "Thucydides adapted the principles and methods of Hippocratic medicine to the interpretation of history" and further asserting that therein lies his "power and originality."*]

Ideas such as those enunciated by the Hippocratic school were unquestionably floating about in the Hellenic world as early as the middle of the fifth century B.C. Herodotus, for example, was well aware of the requirements of a genuinely scientific hypothesis, as he showed by his refusal to accept the theory of a 'stream of ocean', or any other figment of the poetic imagination, as an adequate explanation of the periodic rise and fall of the waters of the Nile. He also displayed familiarity with the theory that physical conditions determine human character, when he remarked, in his concluding chapter, as though to point the moral of his history, that 'soft countries are wont to produce soft inhabitants. It is impossible that the same land should yield an excellent harvest and men who are good in war'. Now if Herodotus had consistently made use of these principles as canons of historical interpretation, instead of introducing the religious or metaphysical principles which he actually employed, he might still have produced a great work, but it would have been an anticipation of Thucydides rather than the work which we actually possess. As it was, he frequently employed scientific standards both in the examination of fact . . . and in its interpretation. . . . The interpretation, for instance, of the Persian defeat at Plataea (ix. 62) as being the result of inferiority not in brains or strength, but in equipment and in the science of warfare, is quite 'scientific'. But it is when Herodotus comes to the ultimate questions of human history that he reaches an impasse; the reason being that he is unable to determine whether it is ultimately God or man who pulls the strings. This difficulty is illustrated by the passage (vii. 1-19) in which he discusses the causes of the Persian invasion. The physical causes having been expounded with great vigour and perspicacity, he finally turns from them as inadequate, and imports God in the shape of a nocturnal vision, to account for the act which Thucydides would have unquestionably referred to the love of domination and the prospect of power. If then, in the judgement, of moderns, Herodotus is inferior to Thucydides, it is not because he is a 'romancer'. That theory should long ago have been discarded. If we praise Thucydides and decry Herodotus at the present day, it is because our spiritual affiliations are with 'science' rather than with 'philosophy'; for Thucydides is the most scientific, as Herodotus is the most philosophic of Greek historians.

It has been thought necessary to depict at some length

the background of Thucydides' thought for two reasons. Firstly, Cornford, in his brilliant and powerful argument, has referred the **Histories** to quite another setting. Secondly, the critics of Cornford, while they have put their fingers on what are without doubt the genuine characteristics of Thucydides, do not seem to have accounted adequately for the fact that those characteristics emerge in his work. Thus, in their hands, Thucydides himself appears as a portent, an 'uncaused' phenomenon in the stream of European thought. [J. B.] Bury, for instance, speaks of his 'powerful and original mind'; and a recent writer [G.F. Abbott, in *Thucydides, A Study in Historical Reality*, 1925] says: 'It is all the more to the credit of Thucydides that, living in an age when scientists still occupied themselves with problems altogether beyond the reach of scientific investigation, he did not allow his mind to wander into barren speculations, but kept it with unswerving steadfastness to those lines of thought upon which experience or deduction from experience could be brought to bear profitably. Upon these lines he concentrates his whole attention; and for the rest he has nothing to do but to take the universe as he finds it.' These critics go too far. In the fifth century B.C., at least in the one department of medicine, genuine science had emerged among the Greeks; and the power and originality of Thucydides lies in his having attempted to adapt the principles and methods of that science to the study of society.

There is no doubt that Thucydides, through his well-known connexion with the Thrace-ward regions, had at least the opportunity of meeting the Father of Medicine and becoming familiar with his work. That he actually did so is a probable inference from the close and, in some cases, startling analogies of style between the **Histories** and the *Corpus Hippocraticum*. These analogies have been noticed by most thoughtful students. Forbes, for instance, in his introduction to Thucydides i, recalls the penetrating observation of Littré [in *Œuvres d' Hippocrate*]: 'Thucydides lived and wrote at the same time as the physician of Cos; the more I have reflected on the style of the two, and sought to penetrate into its processes, its form, and its feeling, the more fully I am convinced that a close affinity existed between these writers. . . . It is to Thucydides that Hippocrates must be compared; in both we have a grave way of speaking, a style full of vigour, a choice of phrases full of meaning, and a use of the Greek language, which, although great pains have been taken with it, is nevertheless less flowing than that of Plato.' He then cites the *Airs, Waters, Places* (ch. xvi) as exhibiting these analogies of style.

It is our contention, however, that the analogy goes much deeper than mere style: that, in fact, Thucydides adapted the principles and methods of Hippocratic medicine to the interpretation of history; and to the demonstration of this the rest of this chapter must be devoted.

The commentators have noted that Thucydides was keenly interested in natural phenomena, and have collected examples of his observations, e.g. of eclipses, tidal waves, the whirlpool of Charybdis, the silting up of the Acheloüs mouth, volcanic action at Stromboli and Aetna, forest fires, and the effects of the plague on flora and fauna at Athens. They have further observed that in each and every case he sought a natural explanation of the phenomenon in question. But Herodotus had already, in his disquisition on the topography of the Thessalian plain, provided a model for the rational explanation of natural phenomena, when he remarked (vii. 129) that the gap at the mouth of the Peneius river is the work of an earthquake and consequently that those who like to call earthquakes the work of Poseidon may do so. Thucydides, therefore, cannot be credited with originality in this field; although one may notice in passing that his grip on the principle of the uniformity of nature is firmer than that of his predecessor. Herodotus, in default of a plausible natural explanation, may sometimes be tempted to take refuge in supernaturalism. Thucydides never yields to superstition. Ignorant, for example, though he be of the real causes of the solar eclipse, he is content to state the observable facts, that this phenomenon occurs only at the beginning of the lunar month; confident that the eclipse has no supernatural significance, and that in due course will be made the generalization which will explain the phenomenon to the satisfaction of scientific minds (ii. 28).

The originality of Thucydides lies rather in his attempt to bring *all human action* within the realm of natural causes. In this connexion should be noticed the peculiar word πρόφασις which he uses to designate a 'natural cause'. This word, which in Homer, Herodotus, and later writers unquestionably connotes 'formulated reason' or 'pretext', means in Thucydides 'exciting cause' or the 'physical antecedent of a physical state'. To Cornford πρόφασις has proved a stumbling-block; it is one of the foundation stones upon which he builds his theory of Thucydides *Myth*-historicus. Other commentators, impressed with its apparently obvious meaning in Thucydides, have argued that, in this as in other cases, etymology must give way to common sense. The fact is that the word, as used by the historian, is in the highest degree technical. It is uniformly used by Hippocrates in the sense of 'exciting cause', and has been taken over directly by Thucydides in his attempt to apply the methods of medicine to history; the adaptation of methods involving, as is usual, the adoption of terminology.

In Thucydides, then, as in Hippocrates, it is assumed that all human actions and sufferings are subject to natural causes, and by these are meant the causes that are proper to human nature. In other words, both writers accept *men* no less than *things* as ultimates for the purposes of historical as of medical science. To Cornford this appears as a grave defect. He says: 'If we would understand Thucydides we must not regard a human action as partly caused by innumerable influences of environment, and by events that happened before the agent was born, right back into an immeasurable past. . . . The world upon which the Greek looked presented no such spectacle as this. Human affairs—the subject-matter of history—were not to him a single strand in the illimitable web of natural evolution; their course was shaped solely by one or both of two factors: immediate human motives and the will of gods and spirits, of Fortune, or of Fate. The rationalist who rejected the second class was left with the first alone—the original and uncaused acts of human wills.' The modern passion for reducing history to mechanics could hardly go farther than this. But surely Hippocrates and Thucydides are entitled, for the purposes of their science, to lay down their own postulates; and to admit if they so desire, specifically 'psychical' alongside of 'material' causes as ultimate factors for history. Again Cornford appears to go too far when he remarks that the ancients 'looked simply and solely to the feelings, motives, characters of individuals or of cities. These and (apart from supernatural agencies) these only, appeared to them to shape the course of human history.' The observations, quoted above from *Airs, Waters, Places* effectually dispose of such a view. To Hippocrates the ultimate factors were human motives in relation to environment, institutional as well as geographical. In his study of the evolution of Greek society at the beginning of the first book, Thucydides takes the cue and applies the Hippocratean principle to the elucidation of past as well as present, with such brilliance that the passage may truly be described as one of the greatest, as it is one of the earliest studies in human geography to be found in European literature.

To embark on a detailed examination of Thucydides' psychology would take us too far afield. It is sufficient to say that, like Hippocrates, Thucydides regards human nature as a relatively uniform and stable entity, in which, for purposes of analysis, one may distinguish . . . the intelligence which affords direction to the activities of the organism, and the various potentialities . . . which unfold in response to their respective stimuli, and result in various changes . . . which make for the well-being of the organism or otherwise. Here may be noted how modern is the psychology of Thucydides in contrast with the classical or 'faculty' psychology which was derived from Platonism, in that he stresses the unity of the organism in the response which it makes to any particular stimulus (iii. 45. 7). 'In a word then, it is impossible and absurd to suppose that, when human nature is subjected to a powerful urge in any direction, it can be diverted either by force of law, or by any other terror.' Again (iii. 45. 1), 'Yet carried away by hope, they take the risk of [rebelling against Athens]. No one ever condemns

himself to death in advance, when he embarks on a dangerous enterprise'. This last passage illustrates how, according to Thucydidean psychology, judgement tends to reinforce desire, so that the resultant act is an act of the whole personality.

Thus personality counts as a factor in human history, and has to be taken into account in the explanation of events. Spontaneous combustion may account for forest fires (ii. 77. 4), but to explain the downfall of the Athenian Empire are needed the personalities of Cleon, Nicias, and Alcibiades, each of whom, in his own way, made his unwitting contribution to that catastrophe. Thucydides therefore parades them across the stage, not in order to abuse them or praise them, still less to gratify the idle curiosity of the casual reader with a mirror of statesmen, but simply in order that he may bring out the facts and ideas connected with them which are relevant to the analysis upon which his eye is steadily fixed.

On the other hand, the growth of society is no more spontaneous than its destruction. As Hippocrates had said, growth is the result of shock which stimulates the mind and awakens it from stagnation. Such shocks, Thucydides observes, as though developing the Hippocratean thesis, are those that come from the struggle for control of the valleys, resulting in the successive organizations of power which culminate in the *polis*, or the clash of cultures resulting from invasion, or the fusion of immigrant with native as in the case of Thesean Athens. No less significant are the accumulations of capital, which suggest to their possessors all sorts of possibilities hitherto undreamed of; and the invention of ships and the art of navigation, which constitute the foundations of historical Greece. In all cases, where new ideas are involved, it is assumed that these ideas were born in somebody's brain. Thus Ameinocles of Corinth appears as the man who invented the trireme and later introduced it into Samos. Similarly with the idea of consolidation. . . . In Athens this did not come about spontaneously, but was the work of Theseus, a man of power as well as wisdom. Theseus, stimulated by the existence of perils which arose not merely from foreign incursions but also from mutual quarrels among the village communities in Attica, and working by means of persuasion mingled with force, imposed on the inhabitants of the peninsula a unitary organization which afterwards got the sanction of religion; and deserved it, because indeed it saved the Athenians not only from foreigners but also from themselves. One is reminded of the observation of Hippocrates, quoted above, that there is an element of compulsion connected with *nomos,* but that *nature* ultimately comes in to reinforce it, so that it becomes indeed a sort of second nature itself. And one may suppose that consolidation, which was in Athens brought about as the response to certain conditions, came about in Argos and elsewhere, if not in response to the same conditions, at least to conditions equally compelling, or was introduced according to the self-same law of imitation which led the Samians to copy the naval architecture of the people of Corinth, and which to this day prompts progressive individuals and nations to import and adopt the advanced ideas of their rivals.

The power of innovation or 'invention' is one of the subjects which most engage the attention of Thucydides, and one which he discusses in various passages. In their speech at Sparta (i. 68-71), the Corinthians charge the Spartans with apathy and stagnation, and apparently attribute these defects of character to the peculiarity of the environment of Lycurgan institutions. On the other hand (70. 2) the Athenians are represented as innovators, quick to conceive an idea and to execute the plans which they conceive, beyond their powers daring, prepared to gamble beyond their judgment, in the moment of peril sustained by hope, venturing fearlessly abroad, etc.; so that (§9) in short, if one said that they were born neither to take any rest themselves or to allow it to other men, one would speak the mere truth. These characteristics, which constituted such a menace to the conservative states of Greece, are (71. 2) referred to the atmosphere and institutions of Athens. 'Your institutions,' the Corinthians say, 'compared with those of the Athenians, are out of date.'

The nature and purpose of the speeches in Thucydides must be reserved for later treatment. Meanwhile, it may be noted that Thucydides either shared with Pericles or was prepared to attribute to him a point of view substantially the same as that which he puts into the mouth of the Corinthians in the passage just quoted. In the *Funeral Speech* Pericles accounts for the unique qualities of his fellow citizens in precisely the same way, viz. as a result of the spiritual atmosphere created in Athens by the great generation to which Themistocles belonged, and maintained in ever increasing power and volume by their successors. The specific points which he makes, reminding one again of *Airs, Waters, Places,* are worth noting:

(1) The Athenians are autochthonous, and the natural product of the peculiar geographical conditions in the Attic peninsula.

(2) The shock of the Persian War gave Athens the first great impulse towards her imperial destiny. While Sparta and other conservative Greek states failed to rise to the occasion, and to effect those adaptations necessary to meet the new conditions created by the war, the empire-builders of Athens seized their opportunity and created the empire, which not without toil and stress they handed on to the succeeding generation.

(3) The empire, as they possessed it, was the consequence of the atmosphere, social and political, of Athens.

With regard to the question of innovation—the capacity for conceiving and applying new ideas in human life—Thucydides in two passages, speaking in his own person, reveals his opinion. The first passage is in the estimate of Themistocles (i. 138. 3-6), the second, in the estimate of Pericles (ii. 65); and, of these, the former is the more significant. In the *Funeral Speech* also (ii. 37) it is argued that the spirit of equality in Athens is not inimical to distinction, that, in fact, so far from implying a cult of mediocrity, it actually makes provision for the employment of talent . . . wherever it may be found. The existence of talent—special endowment—Thucydides was prepared to recognize; whether it was the peculiar abilities of an Antiphon, or an Alcibiades, or even a Cleon, or the more normal qualities of a Demosthenes or a Brasidas, each of whom played his part in weaving the web of history, so that account has to be taken of him by the judicious historian. Accordingly, in the contribution of formative ideas to the life of the community, some men, such as Pericles and Themistocles, stood preeminently above their fellows. The latter, in whose fertile brain the idea of empire was first conceived, seems to have fascinated Thucydides. In estimating his contribution to Athenian life, he protested against the somewhat unfavourable verdict of Herodotus. Employing the current formulae of sophistic analysis, nature and nurture . . . , he reveals his belief that while nurture may save men from mediocrity, it can never account for genius. For the significance of Themistocles lay precisely in the revelation which he gave of the strength of natural genius. Without the advantages of a protracted education, but by the sheer force of his genius, he was in fact supreme in his ability to extemporize expedients to meet the necessities of the day. This is the answer which Thucydides makes to those (like Cornford) who complain that he makes too much of the 'uncaused actions of human will'. For history, talent—especially insight and penetration . . . —is, like human nature itself, original and ultimately inexplicable, a postulate in fact necessary to the science. Thus did Thucydides dispose of the question of mind in evolution; and his authority survived to create the psychological interpretation of history common to the greatest of subsequent classical historians. For us in our day it has remained to essay the task of dehumanizing the history of humanity.

Thucydides was a child of Periclean Athens, and the intense individualism of the age in which he lived made it natural for him, perhaps, to consider the problem of society and of history from the point of view of the relationship of individuals to the group. Accordingly, Thucydides is never tempted to conceive of society itself as an organism—and so far his point of view would meet with acceptance by 'realistic' sociologists of the present day. On the other hand, he was evidently impressed with the attempt in Periclean Athens to unify the interests and sentiments of the individual and the group, and he was no less impressed with the fatal failure to do so in the case, not merely of Alcibiades, but of the less spectacular conservative and ultra-reactionary landed classes with which he himself was connected. In one respect his individualistic prepossessions seem to have exposed him to the just criticism of the commentators, that is, in his account of the evolution of society in primitive Greece. The canons of interpretation which he employs in this field are exactly the same as he employs in his analysis of current history; and so he seems to have accepted the historicity of legendary figures like Agamemnon and Minos, the latter of whom, say How and Wells [in *Herodotus*], he makes into a prehistoric Pericles. We may note in passing that he guards himself from dogmatism by referring constantly to the merely traditional character of his authorities. Nevertheless, in his reconstruction of early Greek history it is probable that Thucydides allowed himself to be carried away to some extent by the experience of his own day. A fifth-century Athenian could hardly have imagined a society like that of medieval Europe. He failed equally to appreciate the strength of the religious motive in the still undifferentiated society of primitive Greece. However, this at least is clear, that, in his treatment of prehistoric Greece, Thucydides fell victim to the formulation of an induction on too narrow a foundation of fact; for the individualism of the fifth century B.C. cannot be regarded as in any degree universal, though perhaps it is normal in developed societies. But it was not his method, so much as the inadequacy of the facts at his disposal, which was at fault.

The reconstruction of a past, remote whether in time or, more significantly, in spirit, may seem at best a hopeless task; and, as the real triumph of Thucydides lay in contemporary history, we gladly turn to his work in that field. The view of human motivation, which he appears to have held in common with Hippocrates, has already been examined. Beyond this, all belongs for the historian to the realm of τύχη or chance. Philosophy may, but science cannot know of 'any cause' capable of bringing to pass the plague in Athens at a critical moment in her history, or of any 'cause' capable of producing that fatal eclipse of the moon which completely immobilized the already terrified men of Athens at the last moment when escape was still possible from the hands of a vengeful and relentless foe. For history these are and must remain mere coincidences. Therefore, to those who accept the self-denying ordinance of history they must be relegated to the realm of . . . the incalculable. It is important to notice that in these, as in other cases, it is the coincidence itself which does not yield to any form of prognostication. Hippocrates (*Airs,* ii) had already remarked that the contribution of astronomy to medicine was anything but insignificant, on account of the effect which

celestial events have on the *diseases* and the *digestive organs* of mankind. Similarly, the effect of the plague at Athens upon the morale of the Athenians is a proper subject of scientific investigation; and at the same time the plague itself is traced to a natural cause, in contagion, through the Piraeus from Egypt. The coincidence of events, however, remains inexplicable. Accordingly, while theologians and philosophers may dispute regarding the ultimate meaning of such coincidence, as Polybius does about the coincidences that in his day laid the Mediterranean world at the feet of Rome, or Sallust (in his letter to Caesar *de Ordinanda Republica*) about the coincidences that in their turn brought the Roman world beneath the heel of the dictator, the truly scientific historian, limited by his self-imposed method, can do nothing but hold his peace.

Scientific history, as Thucydides argues (i. 20-2), has nothing in common with imaginative literature, but consists in the diligent and unremitting search for truth, and it has its own standards of evidence . . . similar to the evidences of medicine, which are under favourable conditions adequate. . . . The truths of history like those of medicine consist first in the actual transactions which have taken place . . . ; and these, even if they are subjects of first-hand knowledge, should be accepted only after most careful check with the results of independent observations. Next come the λόγοι, or formulations—summaries and at the same time interpretations—in so far as these entered into and affected the course of events. With regard to the transactions themselves, Thucydides notes in true scientific fashion the common dangers to which the historian is exposed, the psychological perils arising from moral bias, defective recollection, as well as the carelessness and lack of observation characteristic of mankind. In the case of the λόγοι the difficulties of the historian are more acute.

For in the λόγοι, the permanently valuable elements of his work, Thucydides faced the problem, not merely of reporting correctly what was actually said on each occasion, but of amplifying and developing these statements in a manner appropriate to the occasion. To the modern historian, this may seem a strange kind of realism; actually in the hands of Thucydides this quaint literary convention, which Herodotus had carried over from the epic or the drama, affords an admirable vehicle for the expression of those points of view, always partial, frequently conflicting, which determined the transactions—the great issues, in short, of the war and the mainsprings of human action in relation thereto. The ***Funeral Speech*** then, and all the other speeches, represent the thought of Thucydides just as they are expressed in language which is unquestionably his own. But in another sense they are genuinely objective, in so far as each of them constitutes an analysis conveying to the reader the attitude of representative individuals or groups in relation to the facts which came up for discussion. To state the facts and formulate the issues, this appears to have been the aim of Thucydides. Thus he was almost always enabled to avoid dogmatic judgements in his own person. And if the facts are well authenticated and the points of view are fairly and adequately represented, the device enables the historian to withdraw from the picture, leaving the reader to judge for himself. If this was Thucydides' aim, he appears amply to have achieved it, as witness the controversies which in modern times the commentators have waged regarding the significance of the war.

The λόγοι, therefore, represent the attempt of Thucydides to do for history what Hippocrates was at the same time trying to do for medicine—the attempt, that is, to establish such classifications or formulations (τὰ ϵζδη) as would raise history from the level of mere chronicle, characteristic of the annalists just as in medicine the same formulations were needed if medical science was to escape from the mere empiricism of the Cnidian school. Through the symptoms to arrive at a general description and thence to penetrate, if possible, to the true classification of the malady, this is the procedure which Hippocrates advocates and which he designates by the words *semeiology* and *prognosis*. But this was the very process which Thucydides sought to apply to history, which thus for him becomes the semeiology and prognosis of human life.

The unforgettable picture of the plague at Athens, copied by Lucretius and imitated by Procopius in ancient, as it was by Gibbon in modern times, has always been accepted as one of the best illustrations of Thucydides' temperament, the keenness with which he observed concrete fact, the cold detachment with which he reported the symptoms of a malady to which he himself had fallen victim, the precise analytical power with which he portrayed the changes, not merely bodily but also mental, of the disease. For the commentators generally the account of the plague has illustrated these characteristics. For us it does more; it constitutes the most intimate link between Thucydides and Hippocrates, and seems indeed to be the bridge between the two.

In his account of the plague Thucydides follows precisely the Hippocratic procedure. After the general introduction (ii. 47-8), in which he describes the outbreak and its gravity, he begins (49) by what in Hippocratic terminology is a κατά στασις—a general description of the conditions, climatic and otherwise, prevailing during the summer in which the plague broke out. Then follows the general description of symptoms, including a reference (§6) to the fact that the 'crisis' occurred as a rule on the seventh or ninth day. Now there is no feature of Hippocratic theory more striking than this notion that every malady tends to run a normal course up to a crisis, which once surmounted, the patient normally recovers. So Thucydides, having dealt with the course of the disease up to its crisis, goes on (§6-7) to describe what may be called the complications attending recovery. Such, he concludes, is the general description or semeiology of the epidemic. With regard to its classification or prognosis, unfortunately no rational account can be given. For, contrary to normal experience, the affliction spread to beast and bird, and also (51. 2) there was no specific remedy, so to speak, the application of which assured relief. Then, too, it smote all alike (51. 3) whatever had been their medical history or their regimen of life. Thus this epidemic eluded rational classification from every point of view. The passage incidentally throws light on the Thucydidean conception of πρόγνωσς what is 'classification' and how is it possible?

Hippocratean prognosis, after the general description of symptoms, usually includes an account of psychical reactions. In his attempt, indeed, to relate psychical manifestations to the physical constitution, Hippocrates is generally credited with having developed the theory of the four primary humours, of health as a blending of these in due proportions relative to the organism, and of disease as a disturbance, normally resulting from a failure in the process of assimilation. Accordingly, Thucydides proceeds to record the depression and hopelessness that settle down on the patient, when the presence of the disease is detected, as well as his vain elation when the crisis is successfully passed, and the hope, scientifically groundless, that he would never perish of any other disease. He notices also the effect of the situation upon those who, themselves not having as yet fallen victims, either feared to approach the sufferers, or if they did so, paid the penalty of their unselfish idealism (51. 5) with their lives.

In the Hippocratean sense, the plague was an unparalleled shock, and *likely* therefore to be the occasion of derangements equally unparalleled. Such was indeed the case, and (53) Thucydides goes on to describe the general outbreak of social anarchy and demoralization which was its result—an outbreak in which the most evil passions of human nature were released, and which human law proved as powerless as divine authority to check. Thus neither Hellenic religion nor Periclean statesmanship sufficed to provide safeguards adequate to meet the shock (§4).

The canons of interpretation employed for the prognosis of the plague seem to us to be the canons employed also in the interpretation of Greek history generally. For Thucydides, the evolution of society is determined by a principle which, in contradistinction, on the one hand to materialism, and on the other to idealism, we venture to designate as that of 'physical determinism' ('Physical', following the usage of Hippocrates and Thucydides. Modern usage perversely seeks to restrict the meaning of this word to that of 'the world with man left out'.). Logically, perhaps, following the classification of Aristotle, causes may be distinguished as 'material', 'formal', 'efficient', and 'final'; but it should be remembered that these distinctions had not yet been made when Thucydides wrote; and it may be questioned whether, from the point of view of historical interpretation, they were or are of any great value. For, from the standpoint of science, the kind of 'formal' and 'final' causes which have been employed have proved useless; because such causes are not susceptible of observation and verification by scientific procedure. But, in any case, science does not raise itself by its own bootstraps; and there is no possible demonstration, scientifically speaking, of the existence either of nature or of God. *Natural causes* there are, unless man is a madman living in a madhouse; and these are at one and the same time 'material' and 'efficient'. For example, when Thucydides attributes the beginnings of the city state to the accumulation of capital, he does not mean to imply that the 'material', whether it be land, cattle, slaves, or hard cash, is what determines the course of evolution. These things, to him, constitute capital in so far as their meaning and significance are appreciated by their possessors. In other words, he is thinking in terms analogous to those employed in the parable of the Talents. The man without a sense of the value of his possession buries it in the earth. His fellow, conscious of what may be done with his, puts it to work and makes it bear fruit. The just sense of value, which enables the prudent speculator to size up the situation and to manipulate with profit the forces at his disposal, is the same sense of value which Thucydides attributes to personalities like Themistocles and Pericles. Carlyle, exaggerating no doubt the significance of great personalities, turns history itself into the biographies of its great men. Thucydides is perhaps more judicious, and never forgets to relate genius to the circumstances which give it an opportunity for free play. Thus in another age Nicias, with his conventional morality, might have exercised a salutary influence on the fortunes of his country. As a politician, however, in democratic and imperialist Athens, and as the reluctant leader of her forces in an enterprise which he loathed, his very virtues proved pernicious and contributed to the disaster which he had sought so studiously to avoid. This is not to say that in politics there is no morality; yet it does imply that political situations may arise in which a man can be *too moral,* or rather that in certain situations the rules of conventional morality can with difficulty be applied. In such situations, the advice of Plato is, characteristically, that the 'good' man should take refuge under the wall. In this connexion, the function of the scientist is to state the observable facts; while once more theologian and philosopher may speculate regarding the mysterious ways of Providence or Fate.

Thus, while Fate or Providence rewards each man according to his desert, the only 'moral' which the historian can draw is that it is necessary to cultivate that mysterious power of insight, which science postulates as a natural endowment of individuals and peoples. Thus the problem of the social physician becomes a problem of finding appropriate nourishment, we shall not say for the soul, but for the constitution of man; and we shall see in the following chapter how the problem of doing so is faced, as Thucydides sees it, by Sparta and Athens, and in each case with what observable results.

George Cornewall Lewis asserts Thucydides's ultimate practicality:

For close, cogent, and appropriate reasoning upon practical political questions, the speeches of Thucydides have never been surpassed; and, indeed, they may be considered as having reached the highest excellence of which the human mind is capable in this department. The understanding of Thucydides, however, was essentially practical; it had been trained in the school of practical politics; and though his comments on actual events are generally conceived in a philosophical spirit (as those on the plague of Athens, and on the Corcyræan sedition); yet they are strictly historical, and are suggested by his subject. . . .

George Cornewall Lewis, in On the Methods of Observation and Reasoning in Politics, *1852. Reprint by Arno Press, 1974.*

For it is noteworthy that in both cases the problem is faced, and that both the system of liberty and the system of authority are represented as positive prescriptions of a definite and intelligible regimen of life. Athenian liberalism, no less than Spartan authoritarianism, is far removed in spirit and in practice from the optimistic liberalism or anarchism of modern times. Neither Hippocrates nor, presumably, Thucydides ever supposed that 'nature', if left to herself, could work the miracle of cure.

He, however, who looks for a positive statement of Thucydides' own views on this subject, will look in vain; for the pages of Thucydides contain no ready-made system of social therapeutics. Hippocrates had divided the work of the physician into three parts: semeiology, prognosis, and therapeutics. Semeiology and prognosis are really two aspects of the same process. They include at one and the same time the accurate observation and the intelligent appreciation of data. Thus the mechanical notion of 'induction', by which one is supposed first to collect the data and then to generalize from them, is not Hippocratic, and whoever of the moderns may desire to have the credit of discovering 'induction' may do so. To Hippocrates, as to Thucydides, it is obvious that if you set about collecting pebbles in order to make a generalization from them, you must have in your mind the rough idea of a pebble to start with, otherwise it may turn out that after all you have been collecting eggs or apples instead of pebbles. Thus the function of semeiology, and prognosis is simply to widen the connotation of the class or, in other words, it is not a mechanical and passive, but an active mental process, and this is what makes it a capacity which few in the highest degree enjoy, so that, exemplified in a Themistocles, it is a subject for admiration. Thus scientific history makes no attempt to rob life of its great mystery. It accepts the fact of natural endowment as an essential condition of well-being and progress; at the same time noting the comparative rarity of its occurrence in any very full measure; and the consequence for mankind of those great inventions which spring from the brains of its possessors.

The scientific historian, as such, limits himself to the semeiology and prognosis of society; leaving to the political philosopher the task of constructing, on the basis of this prognosis, an adequate system of social therapeutics. This, then, is the real reason for many of the peculiarities of Thucydides which the commentators have noted and for which they have tried to account. His 'objectivity' and 'detachment' are results of the scientific method which he consciously adopts, and seeks conscientiously to apply. This, rather than the circumstances of his birth and life—his mixed descent, his affiliation with the conservatives, his exile by the democrats—enables him to characterize his native country, and put his finger with unerring precision on both the strength and weakness of imperial democracy. Moreover, his reticence is the reticence of relevancy. His duty is to consider the significance of personalities and events, in strict relation to his purpose. Hence those silences in regard to what happened, if the events had no bearing on the particular issue under discussion, which after all distinguish history from annals. Hence also those partial portraits or sketches of personalities, so vivid as far as they go, but yet so irritating to the modern, with his habit of discursive reading and of discursive writing. These, also, are in strict keeping with scientific method, and serve to distinguish history from biography. Finally, it is vain to look in the pages of Thucydides for any systematic statement of his beliefs. The good social physician will, in prognosis, keep strictly to the task of writing the 'history' of his patients, and he will reserve his schemes of social therapeutics for special treatment later, if he himself essays the task of treatment.

Yet, to all who accept the method of science, i.e. the view that life itself is the real teacher of mankind, so that it is necessary to consider how men do as a fact behave, before considering how they should, the one task is the necessary preliminary of the other. Such a conviction may without doubt be attributed to Thucydides; therein lies for him and for those who think with him the usefulness of history.

If this point of view be accepted, it limits decisively the scope and nature of social science. Sociologists, as such, should cease to look in history for anything except observable physical causes; and they should no longer attempt to extract from the study of society any *general* law of progress, as they have long since ceased to find in history any general law of decline, and as, in modern times, few or none of them profess to discover in it evidence for a law of cycles. To do otherwise is to violate the first principle of scientific method, as laid down by the author of *Ancient Medicine,* and applied by Thucydides to sociology—to confuse the 'is' with the 'ought'—in short, to disguise what is really philosophy in the gown of science. For it was against the general hypothesis that the author of *Ancient Medicine* had levelled the full weight of his artillery, seeking to demolish this citadel as the necessary preliminary to genuine science. It is both the right and the duty of science to speak in terms of limited and concrete ends. History, for instance, may properly consider the 'progress' of Rome under the principate in the direction of centralized and bureaucratic autocracy; or it may consider the decline of the city state from a condition of independence and self-sufficiency to that of a mere municipality under the imperialism of Alexander or of Rome. But to the questions: 'what constitutes progress or decline in general, how do these come about, and how may they be measured?' history returns no answer. These are general hypotheses, utterly unverifiable by observation; that is, they belong to the realm of philosophy, and not to the field of history and social science.

The word 'history' is full of ambiguity, and this is not surprising, because of the various senses in which the word is commonly used. We shall not speak of those to whom the record of the past is quite without meaning, although there is perhaps an increasing number of such. Apart from them, there are many people who regard history as a record once and for all delivered to the saints. For them, this record is sacred, and no considerations of truth are allowed to disturb the source from which they draw nourishment to feed their favourite prejudices. To others, history is merely material for propaganda. Unconscious, perhaps, of the sharp distinction between 'historical' and 'imaginative' literature, or, it may be, despairing of the possibility of an accurate interpretation of the past, they do not hesitate to 'reconstruct' history by the suppression of features which are unpleasant or disagreeable to them; and thus Clio is prostituted to the cause of world-peace, or progress, or whatever worthy or unworthy cause they desire to foster. There are, however, still others who follow Thucydides in regarding history as the diligent and unremitting search for truth, and who combine the most profound respect for the 'facts', in so far as these can be discovered, with the attempt to interpret these facts, as the physician endeavours to interpret the symptoms of his patient. To these history is really the equivalent of political science. In the present chapter we have endeavoured to set forth the method of this science as Thucydides saw it. In subsequent chapters we shall attempt to illustrate the fruits of the method, as he uses it for (*a*) the prognosis of power (social welfare as realized in state and empire), and (*b*) the prognosis of weakness, or the pathology of society. Besides illustrating certain results which the scientific method yields, this survey will perhaps serve to demonstrate its limitations, especially in relation to what may be described as the philosophical method of approaching the same profound questions.

John H. Finley Jr. (essay date 1942)

SOURCE: "The Plan and Methods of the *History*," in *Thucydides,* The University of Michigan Press, 1963, pp. 74-110.

[*Focusing on the opening chapters or "archeology" of the* History *in the following excerpt from his 1942 monograph, Finley asserts that the material reveals Thucydides' "belief that history is both useful and scientific."*]

[The] transition from Thucydides' age to his work is necessarily abrupt, because it is impossible to follow his development step by step as Plato's, for instance, can to some extent be followed. Thus one is confronted, on the one hand, with many facts of his life and many tendencies of his age which have an obvious bearing on his completed work and, on the other hand, with the complicated and impersonal work itself. But to see exactly how the one set of facts concerning his life and age grew into the other fact which is his *History* is impossible, because the agent effecting the change, the mind of Thucydides, stands aloof and distant. Hence, if one analyze too much the thought of his age, one neglects the *History* as an organic whole. But if one be concerned with the *History* alone, it will seem to exist, as the works of Aristotle long seemed, as something apart from all else, born fully grown. But since this inescapable gulf exists, it must be recognized. . . .

Like the opening lines of other Greek writings—the swift, majestic introductions to the *Iliad* and *Odyssey* or the wonderfully lucent scene at the start of the *Republic*—[the first sentences of the *History*] tell much of the work. It will be recalled that after giving his name Thucydides says that he undertook his *History* because he foresaw, even at the outbreak, that the war would exceed any earlier conflict in importance. It was, he says, the greatest upheaval ever to afflict the Greek world. But it is characteristic of him that, instead of turning at once to the background and causes of the war, he pauses at the beginning to substantiate this first statement by an elaborate study of the remote past.

He does so ostensibly because of the enormous fame of the Trojan War, and the next eighteen sections comprising the so-called Archaeology constitute, so far as form is concerned, not so much an introduction as a digression designed to support his view that the present war was vastly more serious. Such digressions occur frequently in the *History,* being the one means by which, in the absence of notes or appendices, a mind as sensitive as his to the demands of proof could substantiate its claims. Actually, however, the Archaeology expounds with such sweep and clarity what were to him the basic forces in the development of Greece that it forms an indispensable beginning to the *History*.

But before turning to the Archaeology it is necessary to say a word or two more of these first sentences. It will be remarked that Thucydides fails to say here that the war which he is about to describe lasted twenty-seven years and included not only the so-called Archidamian War, which came to an end in 421 with the delusive Peace of Nicias, but all the further hostilities down to the final surrender of Athens in 404. He first states this fact in so many words in the so-called second introduction prefaced to the narrative after the Peace of Nicias. The passage begins as follows: "The same Thucydides of Athens set down these events also in order as they occurred, by summers and winters, up to the time when the Lacedaemonians and their allies made an end to the empire of the Athenians and dismantled the long walls and the Piraeus." He then goes on to defend the view that all the hostilities of this twenty-seven year period constituted one war, to reckon exactly how long the war lasted, and to state, in the sentences quoted earlier, that he had lived through it all.

Now his failure to say as much at the start has given rise, in the century that has elapsed since the writings of the Hamburg scholar, F. W. Ullrich [*Beiträge zur Erklärung des Thukydides,* Hamburg, 1846], to an extended, though (in the opinion of the present writer) largely mistaken, controversy in regard to the composition of the *History*. The view of Ullrich, revised and restated in a thousand ways by his successors, was that Thucydides wrote the first four and a quarter books of the *History* in the belief that the war had ended in 421 with the Peace of Nicias, but that he later realized his mistake and, after the end of the war in 404, altered much of what he had written, appending the second introduction in the fifth book to justify his treatment of the whole conflict as one war. Nevertheless, the view continues, he died before completing his revision, and the work that we have contains many early passages harshly and inconsistently juxtaposed beside later passages. To attempt to refute this view in detail, as has been attempted elsewhere, would be a long and perhaps not over-profitable task. Suffice it to say that the main reason for believing that the *History* was composed not at widely scattered times but essentially at one time after 404 when the outcome of events had become clear, is to be found in its tight, organic development not only of certain leading ideas but of many minor themes as well. That fact, it is to be hoped, will be evident as we go on. That is not to say that Thucydides failed to make use of earlier notes; he inevitably did, and some of these notes may not tally in detail with his final opinions. Moreover, he evidently wrote with some difficulty, perhaps going back at times to insert new passages beside those already written, and he died without completing his work or even fully revising what we have of it. It is generally assumed that the main part of the fifth book and all the eighth book, both of which lack speeches, are particularly incomplete, and the view may be correct, especially for the eighth book, although it seems not impossible that Thucydides may have intended to treat certain years in this unemphatic way, reserving his fullest emphasis for what were to him the great symptomatic events of the war. But in spite of these marks of incompleteness, it nevertheless seems inconceivable that he could have given so searching and so consistent a picture of how and why all the parties to the war (and Athens particularly) acted from first to last as they did, unless he was viewing the war clearly and as a whole. One instinctively assumes so brilliant and closely knit a work to be the product of one period of intense creation, but that assumption appears inescapable when a man's very opinions postulate a full knowledge of events. Would an historian writing, for instance, of Napoleon and Napoleonic France in 1800 at the time of Marengo have seen in the subject exactly what he saw in 1815, after Waterloo? Similarly, could Thucydides, after the Peace of Nicias in 421, have written in such a way of the strength and weakness of Athens that what he wrote then would have tallied exactly with what he wrote seventeen years later? The answer gives the basic grounds for believing in the unity of the *History*.

But there is another and minor argument to the same effect, which brings us back to the opening sections of the *History*. It was observed above that the Archaeology is not, properly speaking, an introduction but a digression designed to support Thucydides' initial statements regarding the magnitude of the war. The second introduction is likewise a digression on the idea, tacitly assumed from the first, that all the wars of the period comprised, in fact, a single struggle, and on how long in years, months, and days the struggle lasted. It follows that one need not expect Thucydides to have treated the unity and length of the war at the outset, as he might have, had he been writing a formal introduction. Given his rigorous methods, he would have had to go into these matters in some detail, as is clear from the second introduction, and the place where they properly and conveniently came up was after peace had seemingly been made. Readers who had just lived through the war would meanwhile hardly be uncertain what war he was referring to, and the second introduc-

tion cannot have broached an unfamiliar idea. But at the start he was not chiefly concerned with the length of the war as such, which he alludes to merely in passing (for instance, in the aorist of the second sentence—"this *was* in fact the greatest upheaval," and again in section 23). Absorbed with his initial train of thought and forced by his self-imposed standards to demonstrate its truth exactly, he allows the first three sentences to suffice as an introduction, and plunges at once into the argument, demanded alike by these sentences and by the work as a whole, that the magnitude of any war depends on the contemporary state of material civilization. It may be that, as the rhetorician Dionysius observed, he should have begun by tracing the history of Greece from the remote past to the present, instead of, as he does, dividing the subject between the Archaeology and the Pentecontaëtia, the latter of which, like the former, is simply a confirmatory digression. Had he done so, he would certainly have made a more conventional beginning and might also have described the subject of his work, that is, the twenty-seven years of war, more explicitly. As it was, his pressing analytical mind set itself more searching goals, and these opening sentences stand witness to the fact not that he was ignorant of the length of the war when he wrote them but that the pressure of his thought dictated a procedure which had other merits than simple clarity. Since on any theory much of the first book was written after 404, one might after all assume that he would have revised this opening passage first of all, had he known that it did not phrase his view of the whole struggle.

These remarks do scant justice to the long-standing dispute on the composition of the *History,* which nevertheless will now be left on one side except as it comes up in passing. What has been said, however, may at least have cast some further light on the mind of Thucydides, as it reveals itself in these first sentences. The pressing succession of clauses, the breadth of the inferences made, the haste with which, having stated his concept of the war, he proceeds to verify it—all bespeak a mind, austere, swift, imperious, absorbed with the causal relation of events. These traits are the more evident if one compare the introduction of Herodotus, "Here are set forth the inquiries of Herodotus of Halicarnassus, [undertaken] in order that the deeds of men should not grow dim with time and that the great and wondrous monuments both of the Hellenes and of the barbarians should not become unrenowned, and also [to narrate] why they fought one another." Herodotus, like Homer, looks to the past, seeking to preserve great deeds from oblivion. He even goes further and, like his predecessor, the geographer Hecataeus, would celebrate also the monuments of men's skill. There is little here of proof, though he later says that he feels obliged to report what he has heard, whether he believes it or not. Thucydides, on the other hand, turns to the past, not (as we have seen) for its own sake, but in order to confirm his views on the present. He does not think of himself as a commemorator; he is not even, like Herodotus, wholly concerned with great events in themselves, but almost equally with their social and political causes. One could go on to contrast the quite different feeling for proof in the two introductions and their dissimilar pace and intensity. But what is perhaps more worth observing is the size, so to speak, of the canvas sketched by the two men. Herodotus will set forth not only a longer past but, geographically, a far wider world. In these reaches, his work may be said to resemble that of Aeschylus, as it does also in its emphasis on the religious and moral import of the events described. Thucydides, on the other hand, gives all but a few pages to the far narrower scene and briefer period of the Peloponnesian War and, even when he digresses, does so to illustrate forces then at work. His breadth is not that of time or space but of representative action and lasting tendency. Thus his work resembles the bounded but intense plays of Sophocles, which take an action at its height and illuminate in swift succession the latent natures of all who are involved in it. Just so, Thucydides takes the states of Greece and, particularly, Athens at their height and reveals in the responses of each to the fierce demands of these twenty years the potentialities long inherent in their ways of life and government.

Something has been said already concerning both the occasion for the Archaeology and the reasoning on which it is based. Formally, this analysis of the weakness of Greece in earlier times justifies Thucydides' claims concerning the magnitude of the present war. His method is to postulate the kind of society that would have been appropriate to men's habits and standards in earlier times, as these were known either by tradition or from surviving literary works. These facts constituted confirmatory pieces of evidence, called by him τεκμήρια or σημεῖα, but his basic reasoning follows the pattern of what is likely or natural. Like the Old Oligarch, he assumes that certain social characteristics necessarily imply a certain form of government.

But more important is the idea of progress to which the Archaeology gives expression. The idea is often said to be foreign to antiquity and was in fact less common than two other attitudes: on the one hand, the sense of decline from a happier past (an attitude natural to such troubled periods as those of Hesiod or of the youthful Horace and Virgil) and, on the other hand, the concept, best expressed by Plato, that societies rise and decline cyclically, as they approximate or depart from the norms of just government. But that Athenians generally should have believed in progress through the great creative period of the mid fifth century is both natural in itself and well attested by our sources. Indeed, as will be discussed later, an optimistic faith in man's developing powers inevitably accompanied the

rise of democracy then, as it has in modern times. The tragedians are all concerned with the idea. Aeschylus' *Prometheus* and *Eumenides,* Sophocles' great ode on the triumphs of man in the *Antigone,* the speech of Theseus in Euripides' *Suppliants,* the lost *Palamedes* of each of the three dramatists, and the *Sisyphus* of Critias, all in one way or another betray the sense that modern times surpass all times before. Plato represents the sophist protagoras as discussing the rise of civilization, and the tract *On Ancient Medicine* traces the slow growth in the art of healing in a critical and even a patronizing spirit. Thucydide's accuracy will therefore hardly be doubted when in the **History** Pericles too speaks of Athens' achievements as beyond anything ever known, and when Diodotus, in a passage quoted in the last chapter, sketches the evolution of law in much the same spirit as that of the tract **On Ancient Medicine**. The attitude which Thucydides imputes to these men corresponds exactly to his own in the Archaeology, and there can be no doubt that it reflects the general sense of great contemporary progress that surrounded him in his youth. But when he states a little later that his work will be valuable to future generations because history repeats itself, it is clear that he finally adopted a cyclical view of history very much like Plato's. He had seen the brilliant material progress of Athens checked and squandered, in the course of the war, by a social instability bred of that very progress, and he traces the process of eclipse with an insight which originates, one could almost say, in surprise. The cyclical view of history was virtually forced upon him by events. On both historical and literary grounds, it is therefore extraordinarily apt that, at the very outset of his work when he is about to recreate the state of Greece at the start of the war, he should thus conjure up the idea of progress. The Archaeology explains why, as a young man, he foresaw the magnitude of the war and, by some unconscious process of reversion, may well express much of his earlier reasoning. At least it conveys quite purely that confident admiration for the present which breathes through the Funeral Oration and in contrast to which the later narrative is even darker than it otherwise would be.

The argument of the Archaeology is, in brief, as follows:

> In very early times no settled life existed. Men fought over the better land, and since it was not adequately fortified, the weak were constantly forced out. Attica, where the soil was poor, provides the exception proving the rule. For the same people were able to maintain themselves there permanently. In this purely tribal stage, there existed as yet no sense of common Greek nationality. The period came to an end only when Minos, by creating a navy, enforced the conditions of settled life. (That piracy had been extremely common is shown by the fact that in Homer it involves no stigma. In western

Greece, where men still carry arms, one sees a living remnant of a way of life once quite general. Indeed, it is not many generations since Athenians gave up carrying arms and assumed luxurious habits of dress and adornment. The Spartans, on the other hand, early adopted the soberer dress common at the present, as well as the fashion of exercising stript. The earlier Greek habits in this connection more resemble the barbarian habits of the present.)

With the naval domination of Minos, men were for the first time sufficiently peaceful to acquire wealth. Instead of living inland through fear of piracy, they now built walls and occupied advantageous positions by the sea. These new foundations, by fostering commerce, further raised the level of civilization, the weak meanwhile submitting to the strong, not only through force but for the sake of profit. Similar financial authority and naval power (not, as has been said, the oaths of the suitors) enabled Agamemnon later to muster the Trojan expedition. Nevertheless, from Homer's catalogue of ships it is evident that this expedition, representing as it did the full power of Greece, fell far below the standard of the present war. (It has, indeed, been assumed from the small remains of Mycenae that Agamemnon's power must have been small, but the inference is incorrect, since the small remains of Sparta would give no indication of her actual power.) The real difficulty of the Trojan expedition was the relative poverty of the times. The Greek force could not be adequately provisioned, and hence a part of it was always foraging away from Troy.

After the Trojan War fell the troubled period of invasions, followed in turn by that of colonization in Ionia and the west, and only gradually were the conditions of settled life restored. With the increase of trade, great advances were made once more, particularly at Corinth, which was very powerful commercially (the trireme was invented there). Somewhat later Samos likewise acquired naval power, and later still the Phocaeans of Massilia, the Syracusans, Corcyreans, and Athenians. These successive navies continued the main source of dominion in Greece, military undertakings being for the most part brief and local. Nevertheless, even these earlier naval developments did not totally fulfil their promise, having been checked, in the case of Corinth, by the rise of the somewhat unadventurous tyrants and, in the case of Samos, by the Persians. Only in Sicily occurred any considerable development of power. Eventually, however, largely through Sparta's efforts, the strength of the tyrants was broken. (Sparta alone maintained her normal form of government continuously and owed her position to that fact.) Finally, after the Persian wars, the naval state of Athens and the military state of Sparta emerged as the dominating forces in Greece. Athens created an empire and Sparta a league of oligarchic cities subordinate, if not tributary, to herself. Whether against each other or their rebellious allies, both states gained great experience in arms during the fifty years before the war.

Such is the argument of the Archaeology, and its insight must strike one as most remarkable. The scheme of historical development is in all essentials that followed today (the chief exception being that Thucydides seems to connect the period of invasions with the somewhat later period of colonization). More striking still is the understanding of, earlier society that it reveals. Only very recently has the way of life underlying the early epic poetry of Greece and of modern Europe been looked at with a similar realism. And that Thucydides reached these conclusions from very broken evidence and states them with trenchancy and breadth is doubly remarkable when one considers how glorious the tradition of the Homeric world remained even among his contemporaries. But these merits of the archaeology concern us less than the formative ideas of the *History* which are first expressed here.

First, there is the concept that settled life and material progress are possible only through political unification, which in practice meant forcible control by some central authority. As Minos and Agamemnon in earlier times delivered Greece from a state of extreme localism and thus created the settled conditions necessary for commerce and the arts of peace, so, it is implied, has Athens, and to an even higher degree. Before Minos only transitory and shifting settlements had existed, but, when he made navigation safe, strong communities grew up in places convenient for trade, and, though this meant that the weak must accept dominion by the strong, they were glad to do so for the higher standard of living which resulted. The expedition that Agamemnon led against Troy was of a size of which only a settled and therefore a centralized society would be capable. Now, in the present war, Sparta pictured herself as the liberator of Greece, that is, the restorer of local independence to the many cities controlled or menaced by Athens. The characteristically Greek desire for autonomy is often and sympathetically portrayed by Thucydides, but the Archaeology, like many following passages, shows that this simple question of independence versus subjection was not, to him, all that was at stake in the war. The great material progress of his time was inconceivable to him as apart from Athens' control of the subject cities. For the Athenian empire, rather than the backward land-states led by Sparta, was the progressive force in the period—how much so appears in his confident belief, to be discussed in the next chapter, that Athens should have won the war easily. In short, in the Archaeology he reads back into the time of Minos and Agamemnon that crucial problem which bewitched all Greek history: how the full sovereignty of smaller states was compatible with unification and progress.

It might be objected that, in assuming that unification could be had only when one strong state exerts its control over others, Thucydides neglects the possibilities of voluntary coöperation. But that issue, to his

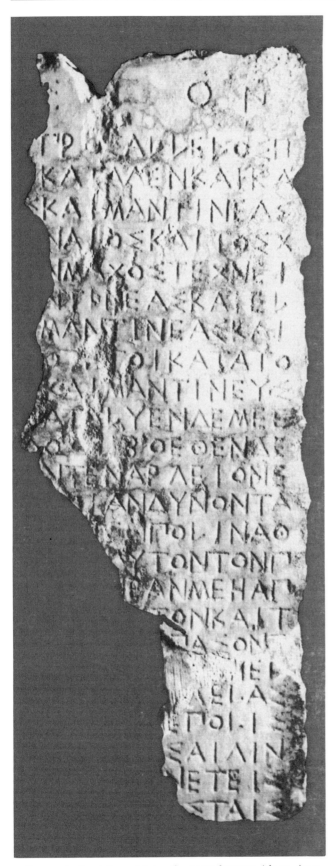

Fragment of a stele containing the treaty between Athens, Argos, Mantineia, and Elis of 420 B.C., quoted by Thucydides.

mind, was dead, at least so far as the Delian League was concerned, since he notes with some bitterness in the Pentacontaëtia that the Ionian states through their own sloth and weakness early surrendered complete leadership to Athens. This disparity in vigor between the Ionians and the Athenians is a crucial and tragic fact of the period. The living issue to Thucydides was, therefore, not the presence or absence of control by Athens, but rather the mildness or despotism of her control, and, as we shall see, one of the central themes of the *History* concerns exactly this transition from the doctrines of generous leadership enunciated in the Funeral Oration to those of naked absolutism expressed in the Melian Dialogue. Thucydides has often been compared with Machiavelli in his detached and, in some respects, amoral attitude towards power. But he is not Machiavellian in the ordinary sense of the word: that is, he is not solely concerned with the acquisition and the use of power but rather, as the Archaeology shows, with its significance in the history of civilization. For to him power meant unification and unification material progress, and if therefore Athens was in one sense a tyrant city, as her enemies alleged, she was equally the teacher and guide of Greece.

A second idea propounded in the Archaeology which has a vast bearing on the work as a whole concerns the part played by naval power in Greek history. Its early development by Minos and Agamemnon gave rise to the first marked advances in civilization, and it was of equal moment for the rebirth of Greek culture following the period of the invasions. In listing the great navies of Greece in section fourteen Thucydides concludes with the Athenian, mentioning the well-known fact that Themistocles was its originator. Later in the first book he says in so many words that Themistocles, by fortifying the Piraeus and making Athens primarily a naval state, laid the foundations of the empire. It need hardly be said that Pericles continued the work of his predecessor. His strategy in the war was a naval strategy, and his whole policy in transforming Athens into a commercial democracy was based on control of the sea. It follows, therefore, that, to the historian, Themistocles had rediscovered and Pericles reapplied the ancient secret of empire in Greece. But to speak of naval power to any Greek of Thucydides' time was to speak of the lower classes, . . . and therefore of democracy. "To begin with," says the Old Oligarch [or Pseudo-Xenophon, in his *Constitution of Athens,*], "I say that the poorer classes and the demos rightly possess more authority than the well-born and the rich, because it is the demos that rows the ships and makes the city powerful. The pilots, the boatswains, the captains of penteconters, the prowmen, the shipbuilders, these strengthen the city far more than the hoplites, the nobles, and the well-bred." And in fact, of course, Themistocles and Pericles, the proponents of the navy, were likewise the leaders of the popular party. The Old Oligarch is right when he says that the lower classes were politically important in Athens because the empire was based on them. To Thucydides, therefore, the idea of naval supremacy was inevitably associated with that of democracy. He remarks, it will be recalled, that Corinth had earlier failed to fulfil her promise as a naval power because of the cramping policy of the tyrants. One concludes that one reason, to his mind, why Athens had achieved more fully than any earlier state the political and material advances which had always followed from the possession of naval power was to be found in her developed democracy. This line of thought attains its fullest expression in the Funeral Oration, where Pericles finds the key to Athens enormous achievements in the liberated energy of her citizens. More will be said of that later. The important point here is that, in the Archaeology, Thucydides sets the strength of Athens in the perspective of Greek history, and by giving its cause a naval supremacy which in turn implied democracy, raises the fundamental question of his work: namely, how strong the democracy of Athens, the source of her power, was to prove politically.

This point leads to the last of the leading ideas adumbrated in the Archaeology. Thucydides remarks that Sparta, though not a naval state, had nevertheless been extremely strong because of her stable institutions. He notes, however, the old-fashioned simplicity both of Spartan life and of the actual town of Sparta, and over and over again this picture of the city as a stalwart but antiquated force in the Greek world returns. "Your ways are old-fashioned as compared with theirs," say the Corinthians at the assembly of the Peloponnesian League. "But in politics, as in mechanics, the new inevitably displaces the old." It follows from the great importance which Thucydides attached to material progress that he thought Sparta outmoded as a power and no longer fitted for her ancient position of leadership. Indeed, never having been a naval state, she had been strong, to his mind, for no positive reason but for the negative reason that she was well governed when the rest of Greece was under the fettering control of the tyrants. For he expressly says that, in Greek experience, no great empire had ever been founded on landpower. One returns, therefore, to the conclusion reached in the last paragraph, that Athens, whose dominion rested on a basis justified by the whole course of Greek history, should not only have defeated Sparta but have displaced her as the mistress of the Greek world. Nevertheless, he identifies in the Archaeology the one element which was Sparta's strength and was to prove the weakness of Athens: namely, stability of government. As we have seen, the greatness of Athens was, to him, dependent on her being a democracy, not only or chiefly because the poorer classes were the backbone of the fleet but because freedom alone could supply men individually with the self-confidence and vigor which were necessary for the maintenance of Athens' far-flung interests. He was not blind, however, to the weaknesses which could develop in a democracy through popular pressure and under the strain of war. When, therefore, he later finds the cause of Athens' defeat, neither in the strength of her enemies nor in her own lack of resources, but in the mistakes of Pericles' more violent successors, he returns to the same factor to which he had pointed in the Archaeology as the source of Sparta's strength.

The connection between political unity and material progress, the significance in Greek history of naval power (a power best achieved by a democracy), and the importance of stable government, these are the nerves of the *History* as a whole first revealed in the Archaeology. As a study of the remote past, it is undoubtedly colored by the author's attitude to the present, as all historiography probably is to some extent. Nevertheless, Thucydides transcends the more obvious vices of such an attitude both by the rigor of his methods and by the largeness of the principles which he invokes. There can be little doubt that these principles form part of what he refers to just beyond as the recurrent teachings of history.

We pass now to the famous section which follows on the method and purpose of the work. Just before it, Thucydides restates his belief in the supreme magnitude of the present war and his confidence in the essential picture which he has given of early Greece. This affirmation prompts him to glance, with amusing and quite characteristic irony, at those who easily accept all tradition, even such local and verifiable tradition as that Harmodius and Aristogeiton killed Hippias rather than Hipparchus, or who believe "the poets' gilding songs or what the logographers have written less for the sake of truth than to lend charm to their recitations." This last remark evidently applies to Herodotus, two of whose statements had just been singled out for criticism. "While a war is going on," Thucydides adds, "people always think it the greatest ever to have been fought, but, when it is over, they go back to admiring the past." The scholiast on the digression on the conspiracy of Cylon later in the first book somewhat mysteriously observes, "here the lion laughed," and the remark comes to mind at this and a few other passages where Thucydides finds a dry amusement, not unmixed with annoyance, in the follies of mankind. But whether his strictures of his contemporaries are wholly just may be doubted. At least, Pericles too is made to speak, no doubt authentically, of the supreme brilliance of the present as compared with the past, and even Thucydides' careful methods were by no means alien to the spirit of the time.

The actual statement of his method falls into two parts: first, on what basis he has composed his speeches, and then what evidence underlies his narrative. He concludes by stating the purpose of the *History*. Something has been said of the passage already, but because of its extreme importance we may here look into it in some detail.

It begins as follows: "As for the speeches delivered by the several statesmen before and during the war, it proved difficult for me to report the exact substance of what was said, whether I heard the speeches myself or learned of them from others. I have therefore made the speakers express primarily what in my own opinion was called for under the successive circumstances, at the same time keeping as close as possible to the general import of what was actually said."

The first thing perhaps that strikes one in these sentences is Thucydides' fundamental desire for accuracy, the same desire which he had expressed in the section preceding and, indeed, from the outset. Nevertheless, because it proved impossible to report the exact substance of what was said . . . he makes no claim to do so. What he has failed to report seems not entirely clear; presumably, the wording and structure of the originals. It has been suggested [by A. Grosskinsky in his *Das Programm des Thukydides* (1936)] that he sometimes gives as one speech what was originally two or three speeches, though that may be stretching his words too far. But at least he has given himself a good deal of latitude. For he goes on to say that, though he has kept as close as possible to the general import of what was said (the clause, it should be noted, has a purely secondary, limiting force), he has caused his speakers to say primarily what he himself thought called for at each stage of events. In the phrase "what was called for" (literally "the things necessary," . . .), one obviously reaches the crux of the passage, since this is what the speeches chiefly contain. Unfortunately the connotation of the words is somewhat difficult to fix. Most commentators have given them an entirely political meaning. Speaking later of Themistocles, the historian calls him supremely able to conceive "what was called for" . . . and, from the context, he is evidently thinking of Themistocles' ability to see the decisive elements in any practical situation. Hence the words presumably have the same meaning here. Thucydides therefore means that he has set forth in any given speech those broad considerations, political, social, historical or even psychological in character, on which, to his mind, the choice of policy at a given moment depended. In other words, the speeches contain an analysis of the principal factors in the war, as these appeared at different times to the leaders of the several states or to opposing leaders in any one state. The speeches, therefore, are in no sense detailed copies of actual speeches; for, if they had been, they would not have contained Thucydides' own estimate of a situation. On the other hand, neither do they set forth his personal views; otherwise they would not have been limited to the standpoint of the actual speakers. They may be described as expounding what Thucydides thought would have seemed to him the factors in a given situation, had he stood in the place of his speakers.

But a further point of interpretation remains which does not alter so much as clarify the meaning of the passage: namely, the rhetorical connotation which the words "what was called for," . . . had for him. In speaking of Themistocles in the passage just cited, he expresses his amazement at the sheer genius whereby, without any formal training and on the spur of the moment, he could see and expound "what was called for," . . . that is, as we have seen, the decisive elements in a situation (which are further defined just before as having to do with the probable future course of events). Thucydides' astonishment is the more striking because both Pericles and Antiphon are later said to have had the same ability. Thucydides uses virtually the same words of the three men, except that in the case of the latter two he expresses no surprise. Antiphon the professional rhetorician and Pericles the friend of sophists and philosophers were clearly not untrained as speakers, and their powers of estimating and expounding the elements of a situation were therefore admirable but not astonishing, whereas Themistocles' similar powers seemed almost incredible. A few other passages bear on the question. Gorgias in the *Helen* appears to use τό δεον to describe a speaker's reasoning, and in Plato's Phaedrus, where Socrates is about to analyze the speech just read to him, he clearly refers to its argumentation as opposed to its language in Thucydides' manner by the words τὰ δεοντα. But a final passage from the *History* is more informative, that at the end of the present paragraph where he says that his work will set forth the nature of coming events. Now the untutored Themistocles is said to have seen just that. "He was," says the historian, "a supreme judge of present policies and supremely able to conjecture what would ensue even in the distant future." And Pericles, it has already been said, is expressly praised for his foresight; indeed, the *History* largely concerns how correct that foresight was. When therefore, on the one hand, both these men are said to have had foresight and to have expounded ["what was called for"] and, on the other hand, the *History* as a whole is to set forth the nature of future events and the speeches to contain [the term "what was called for"], it follows that [the words "what was called for"] are the instruments of conveying the tendencies of society and human nature on which alone foresight can be based. But, as we saw, it seemed in the highest degree surprising that Themistocles should have been aware of these deep recurrent elements in experience which permit foreknowledge. Therefore knowledge of them must have been gained after his time, and, since that knowledge is used in speaking, it can hardly be dissociated from the sophistic movement. Accordingly, it seems clear, [the words "what was called for"] have a partly rhetorical connotation.

Here it is necessary to recall what was said in the last chapter: namely, that the sophistic arguments from likelihood, from expedience, and from the law of nature were more than mere tools of persuasion. They seemed to provide a searching (one had almost said, a scientific) insight into human nature. The grip of the sophists on the thought of the later fifth century is hardly to be explained on any other assumption. These arguments, moreover, appeared the more valuable because they were wholly directed to the practical tasks of speaking and hence of government. Sophistic rhetoric had arisen because, in the changed conditions of the time, it seemed to furnish speakers with the means of estimating human conduct and calculating the probable course of events. It was not, therefore, as we tend to think that rhetoric is, an art of adornment unconnected with thought; it was as much concerned with thought as with expression, uniting both into an effective, practical instrument. When, therefore, Thucydides says that he has caused his speakers to say "what was called for," using the term in a half-rhetorical sense to signify the main lines of reasoning possible under various circumstances, that does not mean that he is not also using the words in the political sense described above. So completely was rhetoric the vehicle of political thought. The fact that the term ["what was called for"] had to him only one meaning, whereas we can detect two, shows rather how exclusive an instrument of political analysis the argumentation of his time seemed to him to be.

This profound validity which he felt that argumentation to possess in many ways gives the key to his speeches. One can say that they are in purpose something like the *Tetralogies* of Antiphon: that is, compressed examples of the reasoning to be followed under different circumstances, though they are at the same time more than that, because they both convey the point of view of actual speakers and are the main means of presenting the compelling forces in the history of the time. It is as if Thucydides had made a virtue of a necessity by saying that, if his speeches could not have the merit of exact truth, they would at least have the merit of clarifying the main reasons for events. And since his work as a whole is to acquaint men with the recurrent forces in history, then the speeches became to him the main means to that end. It is in this way that he effects the union between the specific and the generic which was referred to in the last chapter as vital to his thought. Doubtless such other passages as the Archaeology or the description of the revolutionary mind likewise do so; doubtless also the prognostic value of the book lies to some extent in the mere pattern of the events which it describes. Nevertheless, the arguments of the speeches, precisely because they embody that searching and realistic estimate of human behavior introduced by the sophists, must have been to Thucydides the primary link between his narrative and what he considered its deeper teachings.

A few final deductions concerning the speeches thus become possible. In the first place, because they embody arguments of a fundamental character, they may be expected to play an organic, even an interrelated, part in the work as a whole. It will appear in the following chapters that many speeches look to one another and that in some Thucydides even violates reality by ascribing to one speaker a knowledge of what another was even then saying some distance away. The fact should not be surprising, since, granted the searching nature of the arguments, the speeches naturally possess a significance in some sense transcending their immediate circumstances. At the same time, many speeches appear in pairs, partly because they reflect actual debates, but partly also because the coupling of arguments more clearly reveals their contrasting implications. As we saw, this form of antithetical debate had a strong influence on fifth-century thought from the time of Protagoras on. But if these tendencies inherent in the nature of Thucydides' arguments seem to rob the speeches of veracity, there are other and strong considerations to the contrary. For if the sophistic arguments were in any sense as widely known as has been represented, then they constitute in themselves strong proof of his veracity. The many correspondences between the speeches and the actual writings of the years in question prove, if they prove anything, that his concept of oratory was formed in the very period of which he wrote and thus, in the main, well represents the manner of speaking then common. That may not be the case, to be sure, of speeches delivered by Spartans, Corinthians, Syracusans, and others. These men actually spoke in their own dialects and, though we know little on the subject, were presumably less versed than Athenians in the contemporary forms of argument. But, as will appear in a later chapter, Athenians at least probably did not vary enormously in their manner of oratory. Lysias had not as yet evolved his concept that the style should be suited to the speaker, nor had Plato and Isocrates advanced their more complex theories of style and argumentation. Rather, these men thought of the oratory that preceded them as rigid and uniform. If, then, the speeches do occasionally violate reality and fulfil a larger function of contrast and interpretation in the work as a whole, they can be fundamentally veracious, at least in the case of Athenians. That is merely to say that we are dealing here with two kinds of veracity: the one of circumstance, the other of outlook and attitude. The former Thucydides sometimes violated, though even here one must remember that he kept to the import of what was actually said. The latter he maintained, because he could not by his nature be unveracious but, even more, because he was raised in the same tradition of oratory as his Athenian speakers.

Finally, the speeches have a value quite relative to the speakers and the circumstances, and their deeper meaning (so Thucydides seems to suggest) will be apparent only to readers gifted with political insight. The first point is obvious, though sometimes neglected. For when he expressly limits himself to the points of view actually advanced by the several speakers, he is evidently committed to giving their judgment, not his own. Thus it is incorrect to read his approval into all the opinions advanced in the *History*; in fact, it is impossible, since the frequent pairing of speeches means that they convey opposite opinions. How, then, may one penetrate this enigmatic surface and find what Thucydides considered the core of truth beneath? The answer is not easy; for one must remember that, whatever their deeper meaning, the speeches always and primarily recreate an actual dilemma which confronted statesmen at a given time and of which none of them could know the solution. Quite as much as the characters of tragedy, Thucydides' speakers face an uncertain future and reveal their wisdom or their folly by the course which they advocate. This plan, strange to our conception of history, undoubtedly seemed natural to him (he probably imagined no other), precisely because he wished to reconstruct the actual course of events, believing that only from reality could any permanent lesson be drawn. The reader, then, is much in the position of the speakers, since he too must decide at any given moment which course is desirable. Yet, needless to say, he is more fortunate; for the later narrative quickly shows the result of earlier decisions, and Thucydides also does not entirely withhold his own judgment. Such passages as the Archaeology, the statement of the causes of the war, the appraisal of Pericles, and the description of the war's brutalizing effect, definitely express the historian's own views and, by so doing, offer a standard by which to interpret the speeches. For instance, we have already seen that, in the Archaeology, Thucydides states the prime importance both of empire and of naval power in Greek history and also that the latter idea is inseparable from his concept of democracy as the energizing force which made Attic naval power possible. When therefore Pericles, held up as an example of foresight, explains the function both of the Athenian navy and of democracy, one is justified in believing that his views coincide with the historian's. Or conversely, after Thucydides has sketched the brutalizing effect of war, it is incorrect to conclude that the doctrine of naked power advanced in the Melian Dialogue represents his views. It merely pictures views then actually held by the speakers. But such interpretations of the meaning of the *History* must be reserved for the next chapters. Here it is merely necessary to see that the speeches have a value relative to the speakers and to the stage of the conflict which they represent, and that only the course of the war, coupled with Thucydides' direct statements, can show which speeches convey his own judgment. But in this fact probably inheres what he considered the usefulness of his book. He himself analyzes some of the forces at work in the war, concurs in the judgment of certain of his speakers, but in all cases, whether he considered his speak-ers wise or foolish, shows the larger reasons on which their policies were based. He expects that his readers will be men of political interests faced with analogous problems in the future, and he leaves a manual of statecraft for their use.

It remains, then, to speak of the final sentences in the paragraph on his method. Having described the speeches and stated that detailed accuracy cannot be expected in them, he goes on to say that in his narrative, on the other hand, he has spared no effort to achieve complete fidelity. "As for the events of the war, I did not consider it proper to report them on the information of any chance witness, but [I have reported] only what I myself saw or learned from others, after testing their information in detail with the greatest possible care. The truth was hard to discover because reports of the same event by different witnesses were not identical but varied with the observer's memory or bias."

In the narrative then, if not in the speeches, Thucydides has maintained an ideal of absolute and rigidly tested truth. It is interesting to observe his method as he expresses it here. Negatively, he has avoided Herodotus' practice of reporting any chance story. Positively, he relies either on his own personal observation or on the tested reports of witnesses, presumably several in each case, since the variation in their reports much impressed him. These informants were men from both sides. So much appears from his previously mentioned statement in the fifth book to the effect that his exile had the advantage of enabling him to talk with the enemy. His difficulties as well as the resource with which he met them are illustrated in another passage of the fifth book, where, after telling how the Spartans with characteristic secretiveness concealed their numbers at the battle of Mantinea, he goes on to analyze the organization of the Spartan army and thus to achieve a fairly exact reckoning.

His extraordinary care in gathering less important details could be illustrated from many passages such as the following from the account of the Ambracian army in the second book: "Their barbarian contingents consisted of a thousand Chaonians who, being a people without kings, were lead by Photius and Nicanor, the members of the ruling house who enjoyed the magistracy for that year. With them came the Thesprotians, also a kingless people. The Molossians and Atitanians were commanded by Sabylinthus, the guardian of the King Tharyps who was still a child, and the Parauaeans by their King Oroedus." Another type of passage shows his interest in geographical facts learned presumably either by his own efforts or from works on the subject: for instance, the following on the army of the Thracian King Sitalces: "His rule extended, in the direction of the independent Paeonians, as far as the Paeonic Laeaeans and the Strymon river, which flows from Mount Scombrus through the territory of the

Laeaeans and the Agriani. In the direction of the Triballi, likewise independent, the boundary is formed by the Treres and Tiltari who live to the north of Mount Scombrus extending westward as far as the river Oscius. The latter rises in the same mountains as the Nestus and the Hebrus, a huge deserted range adjoining Rhodope." When one reflects how constantly such details are given and what care was demanded in acquiring them, their unobtrusive presence in the *History* inspires unfailing amazement. Like the more important facts, such as the names of generals and the number of troops at crucial engagements or the exact wording of treaties, they reveal how seriously the preceding statement on the accuracy of the narrative was meant.

But one other point of some importance for his narrative must be mentioned in this connection, namely, his system of chronology. Confronted as he was with a variety of calendars in use in the various Greek states (the official Attic year beginning in midsummer, the Spartan in the autumn, and so on) and with the additional difficulty that these calendars, being based on lunar months, varied markedly from year to year, he abandoned them entirely. Or rather, he used them just once to fix the outbreak of the war with reference to the official Attic and Spartan years and to the list of priestesses in the temple of Hera at Argos. Thereafter he calculated by years of the war, which he subdivided in turn into a winter and a summer season. Within these subdivisions he is often more precise, dating events as near the beginning or end, at the early harvest or late vintage. On the other hand, his system precludes his giving exact dates, forcing him to fix events primarily by their sequence. It need hardly be said that such a system hampers his narrative. The description of the long siege of Plataea, for instance, thus falls under three separate years. But he adopted it consciously and doubtless with a full understanding of its limitations. Thus when he finds fault with the chronology of Hellanicus, it is quite evident that he thinks his own standards far superior. At the same time, when he confesses in the final sentence of the present section that his work will be less attractive, because less fabulous, than those of his predecessors, one concludes that he realized well how cramping these same standards were, even as they revealed themselves in his chronology. Nevertheless, his satisfaction in his system is very great. He several times points out that it enabled him to achieve more reliable reckonings than any which might have been based on official calendars. In short, his chronology reflects the same ideal of accuracy that is expressed in this whole section and revealed in great and small ways throughout the book. And if such details, whether of fact or of chronology, sometimes break the thread of important happenings, they supplied, he undoubtedly felt, the sole basis for any larger estimate of the war. They also reveal a side of his mind which was concerned not with judgment but with fact alone.

The section concludes with words as famous as any in the *History:* "The absence of the fabulous will, I fear, detract from the charm of my work. But if it be found useful by those who wish to know the exact nature of events that once took place and, by reason of human nature, will take place again in similar or analogous form, that is enough. My work has been composed, not for the applause of today's hearing, but as a possession forever." The first sentence repeats his passionate contempt for those who found fable easier than truth and the past greater, because more golden, than the present. The second states his belief that history is both useful and scientific: useful, because posterity will find in the experience of the past some indication of the forces at work in their own day; scientific, because those forces are implicit in human nature and, as such, can be studied and recorded as something quite permanent.

This view, as we have seen, reflects a characteristic attitude of the Greek mind, an attitude which found truth neither in divine revelation nor in the purely material aspects of nature but rather in the observed traits of human character and the lasting tendencies of society. More particularly, the statement embodies a new sense which came into being in the latter half of the fifth century that conduct is predictable, that men of a certain sort tend to act in a certain way, that certain conditions will always produce certain results; in sum, that human nature too is subject to almost mechanistic laws. What those laws are can perhaps hardly be defined exactly. In reading the *History,* one feels that Thucydides was constantly trying to reduce the movements of society to some clear, orderly pattern, but that this pattern, suggested over and over again by recurrent themes and repeated situations, in the end always eluded him. That is not to say that he does not state what were to him the compulsive forces in the war. We have already observed in connection with the Archaeology what he considered some of these forces to be, and others will emerge in coming chapters. But over and above these specific tendencies, there is the sense that the social, as much as the individual, organism acts as a unit following the laws of its being, and perhaps the subtlest charm of Thucydides is constantly to suggest, if not to define, these laws. Especially do the speeches, as has been said, serve this end. The searching commentaries which they give on social and individual conduct seem to lay bare the guiding nerves beneath events. That the thought and oratory of the time had, generally speaking, a similar object has already been argued. There can at least be no doubt that Thucydides, imbued as he was with the new teachings of the sophists, rested his work squarely on his estimate of human nature . . . , and predicted eternal usefulness for it because human nature in its cyclical course would forever bring back similar situations. At the same time, to his view, his work could not fulfil this function were it not absolutely truthful. Accuracy, congenial to him in itself, ultimately subserved this long-term object. Conscious then of these two merits, fidelity and depth, he makes the single boast of the *History,* a boast as Olympian as his usual reticence, that he has composed his work not for a day, but forever.

A. W. Gomme (essay date 1945)

SOURCE: "What Thucydides Takes for Granted" and "Thucydides' Self-Imposed Limitations," in *A Historical Commentary on Thucydides,* Oxford at the Clarendon Press, 1945, pp. 1-25, 25-29.

[*Gomme, a scholar of Greek letters, was the author of* Essays in Greek History and Literature *(1937). In the following excerpt, he first describes the economic, military, and political contexts and assumptions of Thucydides' work and then documents what the historian elected to exclude.*]

GENERAL ECONOMIC CONDITIONS

Thucydides was well aware of the importance of the economic factor in history. In his sketch of the early development of the Greek states in his opening chapters he lays more stress on it than on anything else, both in general (e.g. 2. 2-4, 7. 1) and for particular states, as Athens (2. 5) and Corinth (13. 5), and particular events, as the Trojan war (II). But he does not give a general survey of economic conditions in Greece in the last third of the fifth century, because it would be familiar to his readers (it is a little absurd to complain, as we do by implication, that he did not foresee his modern readers, that he did not foresee the course which European history was to take after the conquests of Alexander and the Romans as one result of which he was to become a 'classical writer' in the modern sense); he does not describe the importance of the independent small-farmer class in nearly every Greek state, especially in Athens, most of the Peloponnese, and Boeotia; of the large land-owners in Thessaly; of the presence of an indigenous serf-class in Lakonia, Argos, and Thessaly, and its absence in Athens; of the commercial and industrial development in Corinth, Athens, and Syracuse, and the consequent great increase in the non-indigenous slave population and in the number of foreign free men, nor the apparently peculiar conditions in a few states such as Chios and Kerkyra with their large numbers of slaves—not serfs—working on the land. He understood such things, and frequently mentions economic factors which directly affected the conduct of the war (and which are so closely bound up with strategy that they will be best dealt with in the next section). But he gives no survey of the whole such as *we* should have welcomed. How much we should have welcomed it can be seen by one instance. Many modern scholars have thought that the

economic factor was an important, or the principal, cause of the Peloponnesian war itself; Thucydides did not—he supposed a political cause. The moderns may be right and Thucydides wrong, though it is quite a mistake to suppose that he misunderstood the matter because he knew nothing of economic factors in history; but how much more intelligently we should have been able to discuss the question, if Thucydides had himself supplied us with the data. We have not, however, any right to claim that he ought to have done: the general conditions of Greek economy were simple and known to his readers.

CONDITIONS OF WARFARE

In practically all land-wars between Greek states previous to the Peloponnesian war, and in most of them after it, victory and defeat depended on the issue of a battle on level ground between two armies of hoplites, with occasionally some cavalry to play a minor, defensive part—to hinder an outflanking movement and to cover a retreat. This is at once a paradox in a land so mountainous as Greece, where level ground is hard to get at, a land one would have thought made for mountain-fighting by quick-moving light-armed infantry. The Aitolians, who in the greater part of their lands had no plains, were masters of this kind of warfare, which was completely effective against hoplites, as the Athenians on one occasion discovered; just as, at the other extreme, the Thessalians knew how to defend their wide plains with cavalry, which was almost as effective. But the great majority of states relied almost exclusively on a hoplite army, large or small according to the size of the state, and fought in the small plains. Hoplites, with good defensive armour and with offensive weapons for hand-to-hand fighting only, must fight in close formation, must maintain their cohesion; the best trained of them preserved best a kind of parade-ground stiffness; hence they could only fight on level ground. Attempts at more open fighting by hoplites were generally failures (cf. Thuc. iv. 129; Polyb. xi. 15. 7-16. 5, a notable instance); even a small break in the level could disturb their ranks . . . so they chose the plain. But that does not explain why no state with a plain to defend developed a light-armed force to attack enemy hoplites in the hills before they reached the plain. Demosthenes, after his defeat in Aitolia, made good use of his experience when he fought the Spartans on Sphakteria with his light-armed troops; but this had little effect on the military organization of Athens or of any other state. Even after the spectacular success of Iphikrates in the fourth century, the old methods in essentials were continued.

[G. B] Grundy, in the ninth and tenth chapters of his *Thucydides,* has discussed the problem at length. He points out that the immediate cause of the preference for hoplite-fighting in the plains was economic. In the ordinary warfare between neighbouring states, waged in spring and early summer, the essential thing for the invaded state was to defend its crops, particularly its corn, on which it depended for the ensuing year. Every state, even every inland state, was not necessarily self-supporting in its food-supply (cf. i. 120. 2); but it depended to a large extent on its own crops. Hence the battle to protect them; hence also the decisive nature of the one battle—if the defending state won it, it had saved its means of life, and the war was over unless it wished to retaliate. If the invading state won it, it could, more or less, dictate terms; for its army could quickly destroy or carry off the enemy's corn. The problem for the invading state was to destroy the enemy's harvest without losing a large part of its own through taking away the farmers from their fields for the invasion; hence generally an invasion before harvest time with a view to the destruction rather than the capture of the enemy's crops, and the necessity for a quick decision so that the men can get back in time for their own harvest. That was one of the causes of the superiority of the Spartan army. Sparta possessed—for Greece—abundant and very fertile land; but her citizens did not have to farm it themselves; that was done for them by the helots, and the citizens were free to indulge not only in a more intensive military training than was possible for others, but in warfare in seasons that were very inconvenient for the enemy, and for longer periods. Only the contingent of Perioikoi in her army consisted of men who were normally employed in productive work. Athens equally with Sparta was capable of conducting prolonged campaigns, but for a different reason. The Peloponnesians would be able to invade Attica and destroy the crops, even perhaps at their leisure vines and olive-trees and buildings—a much more serious matter, for they represented capital, and would take years to replace—but the Athenians were not dependent on these for food; the country people could withdraw every year within the walls, and so long as they controlled the sea they could import what they wished—not food only, but timber for the fleet with which to control the sea—so long also as they had money to buy the food and timber, or goods to give in exchange for them. Hence the importance to Athens of her accumulated capital and her manufacturing industry. This ability of both Sparta and Athens to wage a long war (though Sparta was badly handicapped by her allies . . .), and the very different causes of this ability are the principal matter of difference between the Peloponnesian and all previous Greek wars, as Thucydides, always alive to the economic factor, brings out clearly in the first book, in the speeches at the conferences at Sparta and in that of Perikles. His contemporary, the Old Oligarch, in his superficial way, or in spite of it, also shows appreciation of the good economic position of Athens, and of its effects in a war against a Greek land-power.

The above explanation, however, of the ordinary Greek preference for hoplite warfare, correct enough as far as it goes, does not really solve the problem. It explains why Tegea or Elis or Argos must defend her plains against the Spartan invader, and cannot, like the Athenians, retire behind impregnable walls; but it does not answer the question, why were not the strategy and the tactics of mountain warfare by light-armed troops developed in order to prevent the invasion reaching the plains? Almost every state had a mountain barrier easily (one would have thought) defensible against hoplites, if we bear in mind the vulnerability of hoplites on rough ground. It is not that the passes are in themselves very difficult to cross, from spring to autumn: those over Täygetos and into Arkadia from north and east are the most difficult in the Peloponnese; but they are no ground for hoplites against active light-armed, and in many of them there are long distances in which marching must be in single file. Nor do any passes in Greece (except in the north-west over the Pindus) stand alone—they can be turned by not-distant alternative routes; but again, light-armed men can change direction quicker than hoplites. Yet we hardly ever hear in Greek history of a defensive use of mountain country to prevent invasion. Lamachos, in the *Acharnians* (1073-7), is ordered to the hills, and in winter, but to stay a border-raid, not an army; hence the order was necessary in winter as well as in summer; Lamachos' force was to act in the same way as cavalry in the plains when the enemy was in Attica. Thucydides tells us that in 457 the Spartan army in Boeotia could not get home because an Athenian fleet patrolled the gulf of Corinth (across which they had arrived in central Greece) and Athenian forces held Megara and Pegai, δύσοδός τε γὰρ ἡ Γεράνεια καὶ ἐφρουρεῖτο αἰεὶ ὑπό Ἀθηναίων (i. 107. 3). This looks like a sensible defensive policy, which could be used against the Peloponnesians coming from the south as from the north. This particular line was lost when Megara was lost; but the next, that between Megara and Eleusis, was almost as defensible, yet was never defended, not even, as far as we know, used to harry and delay, if not to stop, an invading force. Argos has a fine natural barrier against Sparta both on the south-west and on the west (if the Spartans advanced through Arkadia); but in the many wars between these two states the battles were all fought by hoplites in the plains. The classic example of the use of a narrow pass by the Greeks, Thermopylai, is the exception which proves the rule. This was narrow, so that a small army could defend it with no danger of being outflanked, or surrounded, provided the sea was safe and the mountains on the south adequately guarded; but it was level, and had room enough for hoplites to move, and a wall across it, like the Isthmus at Corinth, which hoplites could defend; it was not defended by light-armed mountaineers. The pass at Parapotamioi between Phokis and Boeotia was another of the same kind, though nothing like so easily defensible; so was the position at Mantineia in 362, and that at Chaironeia taken by the Greeks in 338. But when the Greeks were driven out of Thermopylai and had to retreat to Attica, they did not defend the passes over Kithairon and Parnes; they relied on their fleet. In the fourth century, and to some degree in the fifth, Athens had an elaborate system of frontier forts, from Eleusis to Rhamnous; but they were not intended to stop, hardly even to delay, an invading hoplite army.

I believe that the reason for the failure to develop a true mountain strategy was social and political rather than economic. Light-armed troops, able to fight in more open formation than hoplites, every man therefore more independent of his fellows, and to move rapidly from one threatened pass to another, if they were to be generally effective and not only in special circumstances, in Aitolia or Sphakteria or pursuing the dispirited Athenian hoplites retreating from Syracuse, needed a more prolonged and thorough training than the Greek states, other than Sparta, wished for their citizens; they must be almost a professional army, or rather there must be at least a cadre of professional officers, and so an officer class (corresponding both to our commissioned and our non-commissioned officers), a thing no Greek state (except Sparta in her own way) wanted or thought of. I am not among those who think the hoplite armies only half-trained militia. For their own purposes, that is, tactically in pitched battles, as heavy-armed, slow-moving troops, fighting in close formation, they were most of them admirably trained, as they showed on many occasions, against foreign troops, Persian, Macedonian, or Keltic, as well as in Greek wars; and against the weapons of the light-armed, arrows, javelins, and stones, they were, on their own ground, invincible. But the Greeks were not strategically well trained; for that professional officers are necessary. For ordinary hoplite fighting the Greeks, especially the farmer class, were prepared to undergo the training that was necessary, and to fight for their country when invaded. In spite of their many wars, they never regarded warfare as anything but a tragic interruption of ordinary life; it was not something permanent, a continuous activity, and so did not require a professional skill and a hierarchy of officers (contrast Sparta, v. 66. 3). Moreover, the hoplite system was in all states, for the hoplite class, a thoroughly democratic one; and the fact that every man could supply his own armour and weapons—for sword, shield, and buckler are not rapidly consumed like arrows and javelins, shells and bullets, and each man has his own, whereas guns and tanks must belong to an army—helped the Greek view of the relationship of the citizen to the State: a citizen contributed to the needs of the state when called upon, he was not taxed by a superior government; and there was no need for the state to possess a large store of arms which might fall into the hands of ambitious men and be as dangerous to normal well-ordered public life as (it was felt) would be a professional military class. So no well-organized light-armed force was ever formed by any Greek state:

in those in which the hoplite class was predominant, light-armed fighting, such as it was, was left to the very poor, landless men, despised and neglected; in Athens, after the hoplites and the poorer classes had been merged politically into one demos and when the navy was organized, it was the poor who served as rowers—partly no doubt at first because, before the new naval tactics were developed, rowing was despised (and was never very desirable), partly because the poor could not contribute their own weapons and the state (of course) must supply the ships and their oars; and even in Athens, after the complete triumph of the radical democracy, both the social and the military distinction between the hoplite and the thetic classes survived. Sparta, with the leisure for a professional army, could doubtless have trained a light-armed corps had she wished; but so long as her rivals were content with hoplites, she had but little need for them. With her strong hoplite force she was in little danger of invasion; and there were no enemy light-armed to prevent her crossing her own mountain frontiers whenever she liked.

Nor did the Greeks in Thucydides' day possess a *cavalry* technique. This, however, is not surprising when we consider the nature of the country, unsuitable most of it both to the breeding of horses—of cavalry horses at least—and to their use. Most states, including Sparta before 424 (iv. 55. 2), had no cavalry; Athens and Boeotia had small forces. These were used at home to prevent raiding beyond the enemy's armed camp (i. 111. 1, ii. 22. 2, iii. 1. 2), in enemy country to make a raid; in pitched battles they were present on the wings, to harry an outflanking movement (especially against the left wing) and to hinder pursuit (v. 67. 1, 2, 73. 1), seldom for a decisive action (iv. 93. 4, 94. 1, 96. 5 with n.). Even in Thessaly, with its fine horses and its knightly ruling class, the cavalry, good as it was, could not defeat infantry: they could only confine it to narrow quarters, though for defensive purposes this might be decisive, for it could prevent raiding for supplies (i. 111. 1; cf. Xen. *Hell.* iv. 3. 3-8). Alexander the Great was the first to develop effective cavalry tactics. We must remember as well that in Greece the cavalry too was, within its class, democratic: officers and men were alike gentlemen.

Of this matter of supplies for an army we hear little in Greek historians. Campaigns were normally expected to be short; an invading army took a few days' rations with them, and for the rest expected to get their food either from a friendly city used as a base or by raiding the enemy. The Plataia campaign of 479, in which we hear of a supply convoy from the Peloponnese (Hdt. ix. 39. 2, 50), was exceptional: not only was the Greek army many times larger than the average, but their position on the northern slopes of Kithairon, with the enemy in possession of Boeotia, allowed them no supplies on the spot, and the country immediately behind them, Attica, had been denuded. When an elaborate campaign like that to Sicily was planned, arrangements for supplies were made both by the state and by private individuals (vi. 44. 1; cf. 31. 5); and doubtless similar things were done for other less important but distant expeditions. Even so, not only purchase and requisition, but foraging and raiding by the soldiers themselves were necessary, with fatal consequences often not only to the raiders but to the discipline of the main forces. The classical example of such ill consequences is Aigospotamoi; where we must blame the generals, not for letting the crews on shore—that was necessary—nor for the foraging as such—some forces must go for supplies—but for keeping no proper watch and neglecting discipline.

There is another apparent paradox in Greek warfare in the fifth century—the primitive nature of their methods of siege; but in this case the paradox is more easily explained. It was due to two causes. The first was the immense superiority of the defensive weapon, the wall whether of stone or mud-brick, over the offensive—javelins, arrows, or hand-worked battering-rams. Even in the fourth and third centuries when engines of attack had been elaborated, such as high towers from which men could shoot at the defenders, and a sort of artillery—cross-bows that fired iron bolts and large stones—the defensive was uppermost; for the 'firing' was all at short range and the engines and towers, to be movable, must be of wood, and an energetic defence could set them on fire. Mining was used to sap foundations; but counter-mining was as easy. Neither Philip nor Demetrios Poliorketes was successful in assaults on well-defended towns, Perinthos, Byzantion, Rhodes; and neither Philip nor Alexander, neither Demetrios nor his son Antigonos, tried to take Athens by assault. There was only one effective method of taking a walled town, properly defended, by assault—a reckless expenditure of human life. Apart from the use of such siege-engines as were available, walls could be scaled by ladders; but here the defence had a great advantage—it could concentrate on the points of attack, and a handful could resist a large number; unless the attack had a great superiority in numbers and was prepared for heavy losses, it could not succeed against resolute men. This was the method successfully used by the Carthaginians in Sicily at the end of the fifth century; and it succeeded largely by its novelty; it took the Greeks entirely by surprise. We are reminded of the success of the Japanese in the Russian war of 1904: it had been supposed that the machine-gun had established the superiority of the defence over attack once more; and the Russians had not calculated on the reckless disregard of life by the Japanese. This method was not available to the Greek states with their small populations; success would have been much too dearly bought—we must remember what a large proportion of citizens were in the fighting line. This is the

second cause for the Greek failure in siege operations. So that a defence properly organized was always successful so long as food and water lasted (no large supply of munitions was necessary when men fought mainly with swords); occasionally a place was taken by a sudden surprise attack; but the only sure way of taking a walled town was by a long siege which reduced it by hunger. A proper defence could be managed by but a small body of men (the siege of Plataia, described in detail by Thucydides, is the extreme instance in Greek history), or by the older and less active or inexperienced citizens (i. 93. 6, ii. 13. 7). All this is easily to be understood; and the only matter for wonder is on occasion the very great disproportion of numbers, as at Plataia, and the fact that surprise was not more often attempted—for example, why did not the Athenians, under the command of Alkibiades, ever try on some fine winter's night to capture Dekeleia? One can imagine Demosthenes making the attempt.

A walled city therefore with access to the sea and to supplies from the sea was practically impregnable, as Athens proved to be throughout her history from the building of the long walls to 262 B.C. so long as she or her allies could use the sea; and Megara and Patrai were similarly made impregnable while they were allied with Athens (i. 103. 4, v. 52. 2). If the state attacking a coastal city itself commanded the sea, it would demand that the wall on the sea side be destroyed or in its permanent possession, as the Athenians at Poteidaia (i. 56. 2, n.) and Demetrios at Athens in 294, to avoid the necessity of a siege; the wall on the land side would be preserved for defence, as by the Athenians at Teos (viii. 16. 3).

To reduce a town by hunger, however, would in most cases take many months and even years; and the Greeks were as little reckless of time as of lives; to have a great part of the citizen population away for long periods meant too great a loss of production at home. This difficulty, however, could be largely overcome. The besieging army built a wall round itself (of earth or stone according to circumstances), between its lines and the city-wall; behind this it could defend itself as effectively against sorties by the besieged as the latter could against assault by the besiegers. Hence but a small number of men could be left to hold this besieging wall, and it was the regular practice for the main part of the attacking army to leave after this wall had been built (Poteidaia, i. 65. 3; Plataia, ii. 77. I, 78. 2; Skione, iv. 133.4; cf. Dekeleia, vii. 27. 3). This helps to explain why in 458 the Athenians could only send their reserve forces against Corinth when they had just commenced the siege of Aigina and had their main army there and in Egypt, while in the next summer, though Aigina had not yet fallen, they could send such large forces to fight at Tanagra and Oinophyta (i. 105. 3-4, 107. 5-108. 4; cf. also nn. on 110. I, 4). If the besieging army was in danger of attack from without as well as from the besieged city, it would build a double wall and encamp within it; if the enemy secured something like command of the surrounding country the besiegers became literally the besieged (the Athenians before Syracuse, vii. II. 4).

If the siege was by both land and sea, conditions were only slightly altered: the land force of the besiegers built their wall round the land side of the town, and the fleet had or could have a palisade on or near the shore behind which the ships could retire as well as one round its camp on land as a protection against raids (Mytilene, Syracuse); the only difference lay in the fact that the section of the fleet which was actually patrolling the sea had necessarily no external protection (Samos, i. 116. 2-3, 117. I).

Of naval warfare there is less to be said. Of the general principles of naval strategy, the advantages of sea-power, the ability for example of the state which holds it to attack where it will, and at a distance from home, Thucydides gives no systematic account, though he mentions much by the way. In tactics, on the other hand, development had been so rapid and so recent that he everywhere explains them fully; and for general conditions we need to keep in mind but two things, which I have illustrated elsewhere: that the trireme was a lightly built vessel, designed primarily for manœuvre in battle, not for voyages, and for drawing up on shore; and that with its total complement of nearly two hundred men, it was not possible to provide much storage space for food and drink nor sleeping quarters. In the ordinary way, therefore, except on journeys of extreme urgency, the trireme, unlike the merchant vessel, must put in to shore every evening; only a day or two's supply of food could be carried, and men must sleep and find water to drink. That meant not only that a trireme must more or less hug the shore, as on the long voyage to Sicily, vi. 42, 44 (and because it must anyhow, for these reasons, hug the shore, the builders were enabled to construct it so lightly), but that the shore must be friendly or neutral; and that if a fleet is taking part in the siege of a city, it must have a camp on land near by (iii. 6. 2, iv. 27. I, &c.). This explains much of the detail in the history of the Peloponnesian war.

The trireme could be rowed at some 4 to 5 knots, and for a short burst—that is, when making an attack in battle—it might reach 7 or 8; under sail it would also travel at some 5 knots with favourable winds. This means it would normally cover from 35 to 45 miles in a day, in a calm sea (for men cannot row more than 8-10 hours a day, except in a very urgent case), 80-90 at most under sail. Bad weather, especially the choppy seas of the Mediterranean, would check considerably the lightly built trireme, with an upper deck not more than 16 feet above the water. This made a voyage difficult and slow in the winter months (and often in the summer); but it must not be supposed that this stopped winter voyages altogether, as is often stated. Ambassadors sailed to Sicily, cavalry were conveyed to Methone in Macedonia, in the winter of 416-415 (vi. 7. 1, 3); communications were regular with Poteidaia and Syracuse during the siege-operations; there was much winter sailing in the Ionian war, from 412. . . .

Such were the general conditions, economic, social, and technical, determining Greek strategy and tactics, which Thucydides took for granted; the application of them in detail he abundantly illustrates. But there are other strategical factors particular to this war of which we should have expected a general survey, but he does not give it. For example, we expect an account of the principal routes by which the all-important supplies of food and timber must reach Athens, and which must be defended at all costs. It is not that he is unconscious of the importance of such factors; he often mentions them in the course of his narrative: food supplies, vii. 27. 4-28. 1 (Dekeleia), ii. 69, viii. 35. 2 (ships from Egypt); timber, iv. 108. 1, vii. 25. 2, viii. 1. 3. But there is no general explanation. . . . Why did Perikles not add: 'and especially guard the food-routes from the Pontos and from Egypt (via Rhodes), and the timber-routes from Thrace and Macedonia, and above all Euboea'? Nor does Thucydides explain the strategic importance of Megara to Athens, nor tell us anything of such problems on the Peloponnesian side, except in general terms, i. 120. 2, ii. 69; nothing for example of Corinthian interests west of the Adriatic, and Peloponnesian dependence on them. He is silent as well on the purely military side of strategy; he gives particulars when they are significant for his narrative, as the strategic value of Herakleia Trachinia, iii. 92, and of Amphipolis, iv. 108. 1, but no survey, no account, for example, of the means of communication, and so of joint action, between the Peloponnese and Boeotia and hence of the strategic importance of Plataia, and between the Peloponnese, via Amphissa and Doris, and Thessaly (note his very brief reference, iii. 92. 4); nor of the immediate strategical problems of Demosthenes in Aitolia and Akarnania, nor of Naupaktos and the Athenian position in the Gulf of Corinth. These are matters, of geography and elementary economics, of which he assumes a knowledge in his readers; but it is a somewhat rash assumption.

It is the same with the topography of a campaign: except for a few cases such as Amphipolis and Pylos, he contents himself with the briefest description, as of the Epirus coast between Acheron and Sybota (i. 46-54: see below, p. 179), or with none, as of Memphis, Prosopitis, and in Egypt (i. 104. 2, 109-10). Did he take these last to be known, from Herodotos . . . or are they just from his notes, never explained, like Derdas, Pausanias, and Philippos in i. 56-65? Or is it from literary principle, as Jacoby suggests? . . .

CONSTITUTIONAL PRACTICE

By this I mean the actual working of the constitution in the different states. If we compare the Athenian with the Roman constitution of the century between c. 250 and 150 B.C., on paper they appear to be very similar: each with a council or senate, annual magistrates elected by the people, and an assembly of the people whose assent was necessary to new laws and to certain vital executive actions such as alliances and war and peace. We know that in practice they were very different; and Polybios is at some pains to explain the working of the Roman constitution to his readers. Thucydides felt no such need to explain Athenian practice; not only because his readers were familiar with the principal facts, but because his narrative illustrates these facts very fully throughout. We should know from his work even if we had no other evidence that the ekklesia did in fact control affairs, and control them directly; a wise statesman might guide it, a foolish or dishonest one mislead it, but it could never be ignored; neither a powerful magistracy nor a powerful council directed policy. Similarly we know from him that the apella at Sparta had a decisive voice in the decision of war and peace; so too had the general body of Statemembers of the Peloponnesian League; Sparta was not all-powerful in the League, nor any magistrates or the gerousia in Sparta. We might well, however, have been given a fuller description of the League, especially of Sparta's position within it once war had been declared. We learn something of that from the introductory first book, from Archidamos' speech and the Corinthians' at the second congress, as well as in the course of the narrative (the peace negotiations after the capture of Pylos and towards the end of the Ten Years' War); but we would have welcomed something more explicit. Still more should we have welcomed an account of the organization of the Athenian empire, particularly of the garrisons in the cities, the cleruchies, the constitutional changes effected by Athens, and the recruitment of land-troops and crews for the fleet from the subject states; but in this case Thucydides would perhaps have given such an account if he had ever completed his survey of the development of the empire out of the Delian League, for he appears to promise it.

· · · · ·

Apart from these omissions, there are others (or so they seem to us) due to Thucydides' conception of his task, to the limits which he imposed upon himself. In the first place, he was writing a ***History of the Peloponnesian War,*** not a *History of Greece* (or *of Athens*) *from 431 to 404,* still less a political or cultural history of Athens from 479 to 404. He confined himself to the war. We may regret this, and wish that he had written of the glory that was Athens or some

such noble theme; but we must recognize it. More than this: he interpreted his task as one with narrow limits. He not only omitted the cultural and economic history which would be proper to a *History of Athens,* or *of Greece,* but also political history where it did not seem to him to have a direct bearing on the war, directly to affect its course, as did the rivalry between Kleon and Nikias and between Nikias and Alkibiades, or to be caused by it, as were the *stasis* in Kerkyra and the revolution of the Four Hundred in Athens. *They* were part of the . . . the great disturbance that was the war; but ordinary party strife or rival ambitions were to be ignored. "Thucydides reviews the mass of events and chooses by his own insight the part that is worthy of recital. This part he undertakes to describe while it is actually happening; he works to that end and what lies outside his theme does not interest him." It interests him, as witness his digressions; but he will not let them divert him from his main purpose, as Herodotos did. Owing to this austerity we have lost much.

It is not (once again) that he did not understand cultural history, that he had no eye for a fine building, no ear for poetry, or no feeling for that combination of freedom and order which was the Greek aim in politics and almost their achievement; the Epitaphios, to which he gives so prominent a place in his work, is itself one of the finest tributes ever paid to Athens. This was indeed one of the chief problems of which he was conscious: was this ideal Athens worth the risk of a great and destructive war? It was the central theme: it was this civilization, of which Athens was the head, which was in danger of destruction by the war. But he did not feel it his duty to describe its development, either before or during the war. Nor, as we have seen, did he undervalue economic forces; but he does not describe their particular effects. He does not, for example, tell us to what extent, if at all, the campaigns abroad restricted the Peloponnesian harvest or the Athenian fleet restricted Peloponnesian imports (cf. iii. 86. 4); not even the effect of the blockade on Megara (cf. iv. 66. 1)—of that we learn more from Aristophanes; nor what proportion of the Athenian fleet was engaged in the defence of the trade-routes for *their* imports, or what was the effect on Athenian finances of the increased import of food from abroad made necessary by the annual invasions of the Peloponnesians. In the matter of finance indeed we can unhesitatingly find fault. Thucydides knew its importance (i. 80. 3-4, 83. 2, 141. 3-5; iii. 13. 6; vi. 34. 2), and gives in detail some of Athens' financial resources (ii. 13. 2-5); but as he does not give the whole of the state's revenue nor—what is more important—the expenditure for any one year or over a series of years, the true value of these resources remains unknown. He occasionally mentions particular expenditure (the siege of Poteidaia: ii. 70. 2; cf. also iii. 17 with nn.); but he does not relate current expenditure with current income. He is content with generalizations, brief summaries, and hints (cp. especially vi. 31. 5: this partly because he had not trustworthy figures and would not guess). Nor does he tell us consistently how the money was raised: he tells us that the special property tax was imposed for the first time in 428 and produced 200 talents (iii. 19. 1), but after that there is silence. We do not know from him by how much the allies' tribute varied from year to year, nor—and this is the most remarkable ommission in his narrative—of the doubling or trebling of the tribute in 425. And in consequence of this we do not know from him either the economic or the political consequences of the different taxes—the effects on men's minds as well as on their pockets both at Athens and in 'the cities'. For this, or for some of it, we turn to Aristophanes.

We can understand Thucydides' temper best, however, by observing his treatment of another element in history—the biographical. He clearly had a liking for biography, a keen sense of personality, as is shown by his account of Perikles, Nikias, Kleon, Alkibiades, and Brasidas, and above all by his long, and for his purpose quite unnecessary, excursus on Pausanias and Themistokles; where he goes out of his way to describe the fortunes and characters of the two men who λαμπρότατοι εγενοντο τῶν κμθ᾽ἑαυτοὺς. But except for this he excludes all biographical detail from his narrative—not because he thought individuals had little effect on events—he emphasizes the importance of Perikles, Brasidas, and Alkibiades—, but partly because the detail is untrustworthy, chiefly because it is trivial: attractive, but in itself unimportant in the midst of great political events. It is in this more than in anything else that he shows his determination not to write like Herodotos, not to allow himself to be beguiled and to beguile others by what is simply attractive (cf. i. 22. 4, n.). His superb silence on the anecdotes and gossip and the scandals about Perikles at the beginning of the war is the principal case in point. It proves not only that he regarded the stories themselves as too puerile to need refuting, but that he did not believe either that Perikles was guided in his policy by personal motives, or that his political position was shaken by the outbreak of the war. If we turn from Thucydides to Ephoros' account of the origins of the war, as reflected in Diodors, or to the fairer-minded but not more critical Plutarch, we seem to pass from a world of adults to a world of children. Yet we lose much from Thucydides' silence, and would have lost more if Aristophanes (who also wrote for adults) had not been preserved. For the gossip and the scandal are historical in this sense, that they did exist at the time; attacks were made on Perikles, though they left his supremacy undisturbed; stories were spread abroad and his friends prosecuted by men who were afraid to prosecute him himself. These all help to show the temper of the time; they throw light on the events and on the

"critical and ungenerous" side of the Athenian character; and the Olympian silence of Thucydides would have left these currents and eddies of opinion unrecorded. An equally clear, if not quite so important, a case is that of Alkibiades. Thucydides mentions the general lawlessness of his private life, and its effect on men's attitudes towards him (vi. 15. 3-4, 28. 2)—a matter of great importance for the history of the war, for Alkibiades, unlike Perikles, was overthrown and his overthrow had disastrous consequences for Athens; but he gives no details of it, because he will not tell anecdotes, and it would remain vague for us, lacking its proper significance, if we had not the invaluable Plutarch. It matters not whether the anecdotes told by Plutarch are true, provided they were told at the time and believed by many (provided, that is, that Plutarch faithfully reports contemporary gossip); for it was these anecdotes, true or false in themselves but true to Alkibiades' character, that affected the minds of his fellow-countrymen. But Thucydides will not gossip; he will not give personal details. He refuses even to tell us that the famous Gorgias was one of the ambassadors from Leontioi in 427 and made a great, if temporary, impression upon his hearers. It need not be added that autobiography is even farther from his purpose, farther still any attempt at an apologia for his own failure.

For all these things that he omits, some because he will not mention them, some because he thought it unnecessary, others perhaps because he did not understand their significance, we must go to other sources. . . . A word needs to be said about Thucydides' own methods of obtaining information; for that is another matter on which he is silent. He tells us that he began making notes of events from the first, and that he got information from both camps and especially, after his exile, from the enemy's; that he himself witnessed some events and heard some speeches, but about others had to collect his information from elsewhere. But he does not specify; he never says which speech he heard or at which event he was present, nor what in any one case his other sources of information were, how long after the event he was able to make inquiries, what care he took to test what was told him, what battlefields he visited. There is only one event at which we know he was present—when he was in command, and there are a large number which we know he did not witness; but that is all. We are in his hands; we can only judge him by the result, by our own sentiments as we read him and by the testimony of others. That testimony is indeed as silent about Thucydides as he was about himself; but their silence is as eloquent as his: Ephoros, for all his efforts, varied from him but little (and always for the worse), and added less; Xenophon, Kratippos, and Theopompos began their histories where he left off; Philistos wrote of the siege from the Syracusan point of view, but could find little apparently to add to Thucydides. Aristophanes supplements his narrative admirably; contemporary official documents nearly everywhere confirm it. All who have written of the Peloponnesian war since Ephoros have had the same experience: they can only translate and abridge; Thucydides has imposed his will, as no other historian has ever done. Yet in very few cases can we test the truth of his narrative.

G. B. Grundy (essay date 1948)

SOURCE: "Thucydides and the Philosophy of History," in *Thucydides and the History of His Age, Vol. II,* Basil Blackwell, 1948, pp. 28-80.

[*In the following excerpt, Grundy suggests that Thucydides imbued the* History *with his own philosophical perspective—an "essentially practical" or cynical viewpoint—despite his claims to objectivity.*]

THE PHILOSOPHIC ELEMENT IN THUCYDIDES

Any student or any reader who is interested in Thucydides will require as full a proof as possible of his aim as an author. In the case of his philosophy the difficulty of acquiring a comprehensive knowledge of it is due to the fact that Thucydides associated, not merely each section, but each item of it with that event in his narrative which suggested it.

The result is not an ordered treatise, but a mass of material scattered, it might almost be said at random, through his work. Thus the collection of it is a somewhat laborious business, a labour which may be taken once and for all by one man and need not be repeated again and again by those who are interested in the study of the subject.

This section is therefore devoted to the collection of such passages in his work under rather comprehensive headings, with notes attached to those passages which seem to require some explanation.

That does not apply to all his views. Some of them require no explanation, as they are founded on elements in human nature which are innate in man and quite independent of the circumstances under which he lives. Still there are many elements in human life which result from the circumstances in which those lives are lived, and sometimes the actions and ideas of an age have to be interpreted in the light of what is known of the spirit of that age.

General Philosophy of Life

Thucydides' philosophy is essentially practical, not speculative, for, though it deals with the future, it is only with that part of the future which, as he believes, can be deduced from the facts of the past. His belief in that future has been very largely justified by the facts of history.

> (I. 22.) The absence of romance in my history will, I fear, detract somewhat from its interest; but if it be judged useful by those inquirers who desire an exact knowledge of the past as an aid to the interpretation of the future, which in the course of things must resemble, if it does not reflect it, I shall be content.

Many of his philosophical dicta bear on ordinary social life, and, though it is necessary to quote them as part of his philosophy, they do not call for comment at the present day, as they deal with matters which come within the ordinary experience of men of the present world, and are an expression of truths which have been stated again in the voluminous literature of later times. But at the time at which Thucydides wrote there was no voluminous literature, and the only literature from which he could borrow anything he did borrow, were the philosophical writings of the sophists, and perhaps here and there a brief passage from the dramatists. It is not of course possible to say in every case where Thucydides is stating his own conclusions from the facts of life, but it is probable that he does so in the vast majority of instances, while some passages may be novel renderings of ideas which may have been previously existent in some vague form in the minds of his readers. But the passages must be quoted here as they appear in various parts of his work. They show his views on the philosophy of life, which must always be a large part of the philosophy of history.

> (I. 42.) To abstain from wronging others who are your equals affords a surer basis for power than a dangerous pursuit of gain incited by an apparent temporary advantage.

This is a truth which Germany would have done well to realise before the first World War and, to a certain extent, before the last war.

> (I. 76.) The truth is that those who use force do not need law.

This is almost certainly suggested by the dictum of the sophists in its crude form 'might is right', that dictum which Plato attacked so violently in the Republic without taking into account the fact that those same sophists also stated the solution of the unpleasant fact—concession made by the stronger to the weaker which mitigates in the only way possible the working of this brutal truth. The words, which Thucydides puts into the mouths of the Athenians, are, so far as he is concerned, an unpleasant fact; and it is with facts alone that his philosophy deals. This is shown in another sentence later in the same chapter: 'but it seems that men are less angered by injustice than by constraint'.

He does not moralise on such facts. As is his way he leaves the moral conclusions from them to his readers. Some commentators on his work have remarked on the absence from it of moral conclusions. As far as expression goes that is true; but as far as moral implication goes it is very misleading. His work is full of them.

> (I. 71.) You fail to see that peace stays longest with those who are more careful to use their power justly than to show their determination not to submit to injustice.

This is the position of the Spartans as described by the Corinthians.

It is admittedly difficult to see how these words apply to the situation at the moment at which they are said to have been uttered, the time when Corinth was urging Sparta to take the lead of the Peloponnesian League in war with Athens. It is not a very satisfactory suggestion, that it is better to attack a power which shows the intention to be aggressive than to wait till the aggression actually takes place.

> (I. 71.) Improvements ever prevail.

An obvious truth; but one truth which had to be impressed on an age in which many of the Greek race were staunch upholders of ancient customs and ideas.

> (II. 35., *Funeral Oration*.) For men can endure to hear others praised only so long as they can severally persuade themselves of their own ability to equal the actions recounted. When this point is passed envy comes in and with it incredulity.

A cynical remark, but very true.

> (II. 40., *Funeral Oration*.) Usually daring results from ignorance, caution from reflection.

Emphasises the necessity of thought before action.

> (II. 43., *Funeral Oration*.) Heroes have the whole world for their tomb.

This is a very fine translation of one of the finest epigrams in history. There lie behind it certain ideas which editors and translators of Thucydides seem to have overlooked.

Whatever doubt there may be as to whether the Funeral Oration is of Thucydides' own composition or a report of the actual speech made by Pericles, there cannot be much doubt that this is a quotation from what Pericles actually said, and he said it with a very practical purpose—to dispel from the minds of his hearers a feeling which would cause them the greatest

unhappiness. That feeling would be caused by certain beliefs associated, not with the Greek state religion, but with that family religion which seems to have had more influence on the Greek mind, that ancestor worship which was equally strong in both the Greek and the early Roman world. It is based on the idea that the living were guarded in life by the spirits of their deceased ancestors, and that those spirits watched over them and had some power to alleviate the ills and misfortunes of life. Associated with this was the further idea that the body of the deceased ancestor must be buried amid the scenes which had been familiar to him in life—that otherwise his spirit could not be happy, and that consequently his descendants must see that his body was laid near his old home. Hence the living sought by every means in their power to carry out this religious duty, and it became a recognised principle in Greek international law that victors in a battle should surrender the bodies of those of the defeated who had fallen in the fight. It was a rule any infraction of which shocked the Greek mind intensely, as Thucydides shows in his reference to the refusal of the Boeotians to surrender the bodies of the Athenian slain at Delium, and the still more striking example of the trial and punishment of the victorious generals after Arginusae for not picking up after the battle the bodies of the drowned and such as survived on the wrecks.

Marathon, where the Athenian dead were buried in the mound, was acknowledged to be an exception justified, as it was thought, by the exceptional glory won by those who took part in the victory, and the consequent idea that the spirits of the dead might be happy on the scene of their great triumph.

> (II. 44.) For honour never grows old; and honour it is, not gain, as some would have it, that rejoices the heart of age and helplessness.

> (II. 52., Psychology of the period of the plague.) Bodies lay on one another in the agonies of thirst, and half-dead creatures reeled about the streets and round all the fountains in their longing for water. The sacred places also in which they had quartered themselves were full of the corpses of persons who had died there just as they were, for the disaster passed all bounds, and men, not knowing what might become of them, became utterly careless of everything whether sacred or profane. All the burial rites before in use were entirely upset, and they buried the bodies as best they could. Many from want of the proper appliances, through so many of their friends having died already, had recourse to the most shameless sepultures. Sometimes getting the start of those who had raised a pile, they threw their own dead body on the stranger's pyre and ignited it. Sometimes they tossed the corpse which they were carrying on the top of another that was burning and went off. Nor was this the only form of lawless extravagance which owed its origin to the plague. Men coolly ventured on what they had

formerly done in a corner and not just as they pleased, seeing the rapid transitions produced by persons in prosperity suddenly dying and those who before had nothing succeeding to their property. So they resolved to spend quickly and enjoy themselves, regarding their lives and riches alike as things of a day. Perseverance in what men called honour was popular with none, it was so uncertain whether they would be spared to attain an object; but present enjoyment, and all that contributed to it, was laid down as both honourable and useful. Fear of gods or law of man, there was none to restrain them. As for the first, they judged it to be the same whether they worshipped them or not, as they saw all alike perishing; and, for the last, no one expected to live to be brought to trial for his offences, but felt that a far severer sentence had been passed on them and hung ever over their heads, and before this fell it was only reasonable to enjoy life a little.

The psychology here described was repeated again in the middle ages when plague fell on large towns.

The strict and scrupulous formality of Greek funeral ceremonial is very clearly implied here.

It has been stated in modern histories that the Greeks employed both inhumation and cremation in burial of the dead.

It seems possible that this is too wide a statement. The belief in the spirit of the dead residing with the body in the grave, would tend to promote inhumation as the method of disposal of the bodies of the deceased, just as the belief in the literal resurrection of the body led the early Christians to resort to inhumation in place of the practice of cremation which prevailed in the pagan world. They may have been forced to adopt cremation in the case of those who died at some great distance from their homes, and may also have done so in the case of those who died of plague lest the bodies might infect the living.

(II. 61.) For the judgment of mankind is relentless to the weakness that falls short of a recognised renown, as it is jealous of the arrogance that aspires higher than its due.

(II. 64.) Besides the hand of heaven must be borne with resignation, that of the enemy with fortitude.

(II. 64.) Decay is a law of nature. . . .

This may have been a commonplace of Thucydides' day, but one of which idealists have to be reminded. Applied to human institutions its truth is due to the fact that governments and free peoples, especially democracies, have, owing maybe to a desire to promote the interests of some particular class in the population, or to follow through ignorance the lead of an ambi-

tious demagogue, failed to recognise those factors in their political institutions which have in the past promoted the attainable happiness of the community as a whole, and have substituted for them innovations which are eventually destructive of welfare and happiness. If a state were realisable which, like that of the Romans under the early Roman Empire, had a constitution which worked well in the interests of its whole population, and had also rulers who were capable of seeing clearly what modifications were necessary to meet changes due to changing external circumstances, then human nature would have to be treated as an exception to this 'law of nature', for it might attain to the highest practical ideal in a world where the good cannot be maintained without active resistance to the evil. Ideals to be durable must be backed by force.

(III. 64.) He who faces odium for great ends is right in his determination.

(III. 64.) They whose minds are least depressed by calamity and are most capable of meeting it are the greatest men and the greatest communities.

Illustrated by the British people in the first disastrous years of the late war.

Thucydides uses every opportunity for the insertion of some item of political philosophy, even of the philosophy of the violent and ruthless imperialist, a type with which he had no real sympathy.

(III. 39., *Cleon's Speech.*)

The philosophy laid down in the passages cannot for the most part be taken to represent the views of Thucydides. It is really of a negative character, a warning of the type of argument which may be expected from a violent extremist. But there are passages in the speech which are no doubt really expressive of the historian's own political philosophy.

(III. 39.) The truth is that nothing so tends to make a people insolent as sudden and unlooked-for good fortune. In most cases it is safer for mankind to have success in reason than out of reason, and it is easier for them, one may say, to stave off adversity than to preserve prosperity.

Probably a consideration added to the speech by Thucydides. No race has reason to know the truth of it better than the British in view of their experience after the war of 1914-18.

(III. 39.) Men are by nature generally inclined to treat the subservient with contempt, and the unyielding with respect.

(III. 40.) It is they who wrong their neighbour

without a cause who pursue their victim to the death on account of the danger which they foresee in letting the enemy survive.

The wholesale murders by the Germans during the recent war illustrate this dictum. But communist tendency before the war also illustrated it.

> (III. 45., *Speech of Diodotus*.) Individuals, when acting in masses, irrationally magnify the objects for which they strive.

> (IV. 62., *Speech of Hermocrates at Gela*.) The incalculable element of the future exercises the widest influence and is the most treacherous, and yet in fact the most useful of all things, as it frightens us all equally, and makes us consider before attacking each other.

This is not a dictum which could have claimed much originality at the time at which it was written, for the Greeks seem to have always had a profound fear of the chances of life. What is emphasised is the part it plays as a deterrent of action, backed by a powerful element in human psychology.

Much the same sentiment is expressed in IV. 65.

> (IV. 61. *Speech of Hermocrates at Gela*.) I do not blame those who wish to rule, but those who are ready to serve; for it is ever natural to man to rule those who yield to him, as it is to resist those who molest him. One is not less invariable than the other. Meanwhile those who see dangers and refuse to provide for them properly, or have come here without having made up their minds that our first duty is to unite to get rid of the common peril, are mistaken.

Probably Thucydides knew that some such view had been expressed in the original speech. It is a curious and rather unexpected deduction for the doctrine 'might is right'.

> (IV. 62. *Hermocrates' Speech at Gela*.) Vengeance is not necessarily successful because it is just, that is to say because a wrong has been done, nor strength sure because it is confident. The incalculability of the future is the prevalent factor, and while it is the most uncertain, would nevertheless seem to be the most useful because, as all alike fear it, we think twice before attacking one another.

Here is the familiar emphasis on the incalculability of the future, a fact the Athenians were most inclined to forget, and of which those who advised them were equally inclined to remind them.

> (IV. 86. *Speech of Brasidas*.) I am not come here

to help this party or that; and the freedom which I pretend to offer is not of so dubious a kind that I should think of disregarding your constitution and of enslaving the many to the few or the few to the many. That would be heavier than a foreign yoke.

These may be words spoken by Brasidas, or at any rate a reproduction of the general sense of what he said. The words are applicable to the present time (Jan. 1945) when England has interfered in Greece to prevent a well-armed communist element from dominating the government of the country.

> (IV. 92. *Speech of Pagondas before Delium*.) As between neighbours generally freedom means simply a determination to hold one's own; and with neighbours like these, who are trying to enslave near and far alike, there is nothing for it but to fight it out to the last.

> (IV. 108. *Narrative Text*.) It being the habit of mankind to give to careless hope what they long for, and to use sovereign reason to thrust aside what they do not fancy.

A reflection of Thucydides' own.

> (V. 86-111. *Extracts from the Melian Dialogue*.)

> (V. 89.) You know as well as we do that right, as the world goes, is only a question between equals in power, while the strong do what they can, and the weak suffer what they must.

> (V. 103.) Hope, danger's comforter, may be indulged in by those who have enough and to spare, if not without loss, at all events without ruin. But its nature is to be extravagant, and those who go so far as to put their all upon the venture see it in its true colours when they are ruined.

> (V. 103.) Nor be like the generality of mankind who, when salvation is, humanly speaking, theirs, when what seemed obvious hopes fail them, when things go wrong, have recourse to blind hope founded on prophecies and oracles and suchlike things as lead men to their destruction.

In so far as philosophy is concerned the whole dialogue is by implication an attack on the doctrine that might is right, that doctrine which Thucydides, as is shown by other passages in his history, abominated, and against that trust in hope for the future which he attacks again and again as an example of human folly. In a sense the whole dialogue might be quoted; but further quotation would be little more than a repetition of the philosophical doctrines which the passages quoted exemplify.

It is rather curious that, though Thucydides attacks, not the truth of the doctrine of the sophists, but its inapplicability to good social life, he never mentions the remedy for it which the sophists suggested as the only remedy, if social life was to be peaceful and happy, the concession of the stronger to the weaker. He accepted doctrine as a natural but not a moral law. He felt that for the happiness of human societies the strong must make concessions to the weak, and he probably felt that neither could be happy in social life unless such concessions were made.

He himself puts the natural law so crudely in the dialogue that there cannot be much doubt that he set out to write the dialogue in order to condemn by implication the doctrine itself and the appeal made to it by the Athenian ultra-democrats. It is one of the passages in his history that makes the assumption that he himself was an ultra-democrat irrational and impossible.

It is also a unique example of the dialogue form in his history.

> (VI. 11. *Nicias' Speech on the proposed Sicilian Expedition.*) We all know that that which is farthest off and the reputation of which can least be tested is most admired.

Seems like an anticipation of Tacitus' 'Omne ignotum pro magnifico'.

> (VI. 89. *Speech of Alcibiades at Sparta.*) As for democracy, we men of sense know what it is—and no one better than I who have every reason for cursing it. But there is nothing new to be said about a patent absurdity.

This can hardly represent Thucydides' view of every species of democracy; but it is a true statement of the view taken of it by the oligarchs of his time.

The Greek idea of patriotism was not that which the word implies in literature of the present day. In Greece in the historic period there was more sympathy between the oligarchs of different states and the democrats of different states than between the oligarchs and democrats of the same state.

The position normal at the time in Greek politics did not prevail in Athens because the existence of the Empire made it possible to find economic support for the proletariat from the tribute and, during this time of war, by employment in the fleet; and the oligarchs were too few in number to dare to move a finger without the prospect of immediate and enduring support from Sparta, that which the national party then in power at Sparta was not disposed to give.

But no Greek expected an oligarch to be loyal to his state when it was under a democracy, nor a Greek democrat, when his state was ruled by an oligarchy. How far a dissatisfied party might go is illustrated by the connivance of the Athenian democrats with Persia at the time of Marathon.

Alcibiades goes on to say 'So much for the prejudice with which I am regarded', which shows that the Spartans suspected his bona fides until they saw that he had good reason to be hostile to the Athenian democracy. They regarded his antipathy to democracy as being, under the circumstances, quite natural, and were therefore prepared to take and follow his advice in certain important respects. Also the language put into the mouth of Alcibiades by Thucydides assumes that under the circumstances he may be trusted to act in their interest.

This sympathy between extremist parties in different countries, and their tendency to let it override national patriotism, has become very noticeable in the states of Europe since the beginning of this century. The feeling was also strong at the time of the great French revolution, and remained more or less so till 1848. But in the later half of the Nineteenth Century it seems to have died away. The communist rising in Paris in 1870-71 attracted very little open sympathy in other countries.

> (VII. 14. *Nicias' Dispatch from Syracuse.*) Besides I know that you have a characteristic love of being told the best side of things, and then to blame the speaker if the expectations which he raised in your minds are not justified by the result; and therefore I thought it safest to declare to you the truth.

This is a difficulty which statesmen dependent for their position on popular support have often had to face.

> (VII. 67. *Speech of Gylippus.*) Where there is the greatest hope there is also the greatest ardour for action.

> (VII. 68. *Speech of Gylippus.*) The rarest dangers are those in which failure brings little loss and success the greatest advantage.

POLITICAL PHILOSOPHY

In the previous section the quotations aim at giving Thucydides' philosophy of general life. In what follows they deal with political life. The boundary between the two is somewhat vague and largely dependent on the individual who happens to be drawing it; so the reader may think that some of the quotations which appear in each of these sections ought to appear in the other.

It has been necessary to speak of Thucydides' personal views in reference to certain passages which have been already discussed. He never discloses their nature in any express words, a policy in accordance with that suppression of his own personality which is so noticeable in his history. His comments on facts, for example, in the passage in which he speaks so strongly of the effects of revolution on the psychology of the Greeks of his day, do not take the form of explicit expressions of his own opinions. But that they are so implicitly is quite clear.

It has been stated that Thucydides was a moderate democrat. Of tyranny he says nothing which could give any clue as to his feelings with regard to it, except that he says of the tyranny of the Peisistratids that it became unpopular towards its end, which may imply that he had nothing to say against it as it was during the lifetime of Peisistratus. He mentions of course more than once the suspicion entertained by the Athenians that Alcibiades was aiming at tyranny; but he does not blame Alcibiades for so doing. It is possible that he thought that a tyranny under him would have been better than the political position in Athens in the last phase of the war, for he expresses the opinion that, had Athens entrusted the management of the war to him, she might have been spared the disaster which overtook her. He speaks frequently of oligarchs and oligarchies; but of oligarchy as an institution he has practically nothing to say.

Thucydides was however an imperialist, but of the moderate type represented by the moderate democrats. They felt obliged to maintain the empire for reasons put by Thucydides in the mouths of the Athenians at the conference preceding the outbreak of the war. He did not approve of harsh and violent treatment of any ally who showed a determination to retire from membership of the League. The speech which he attributes to Diodotus in the Mytilenian debate expresses probably his own views. Judging by his remarks on the subjugation of Naxos in 466 or 467 he seems to have regarded it as an injustice and a mistake that punishment for revolt should take the form of deprivation of local freedom. How Thucydides proposed to reconcile the political independence of the members of the League with the absolute necessity of maintaining it as an individual force against Persia, he neither says nor implies.

PHILOSOPHY OF POLITICS

(I. 34. *Speech of the Corcyraeans.*) Every colony that is well treated honours its parent state, but becomes estranged from it by injustice. For colonists are not sent forth on the understanding that they are to be the slaves of those who remain behind, but that they are to be their equals.

It is of course well known that Greek colonisation differed from that of modern times in that the colony, from the time of its founding, had political independence. In modern times colonies have progressed gradually towards such independence, and that has led to the degree of independence attained becoming at times a matter of dispute between them and the mother country. Cf. the case of England's American colonies at the time of the War of Independence.

Still the remark attributed to the Corcyraeans by Thucydides is just as true in the present as in his day.

(I. 42. *Corinthian Speech at Athens.*) Abstention from all injustice to other first-rate powers is a greater tower of strength than anything which can be gained by the sacrifice of permanent tranquillity for an apparent temporary advantage.

(I. 75. *Speech of the Athenians at Lacedaemon.*) And at last when almost all hated us, when some had already revolted and had been subdued, when you had ceased to be the friends you once were, and had become objects of suspicion and dislike, it seemed no longer safe to give up our empire, as all who left it would fall to you.

It has been seen throughout history, that in nearly every alliance or coalition between different states constraint has had to be exercised either by the mass of the confederacy or by a dominant state under one of two sets of circumstances—when some of the members fail to make their contribution to the forces, military, naval, or financial of the alliance, and secondly, when some members wish to leave the coalition before the end for which it was formed is attained.

If the constraining power be a single state then, when the alliance is dissolved, it is heir to a very hostile feeling on the part of the powers on whom this constraint has had to be exercised.

In the case of the anti-Persian League, of which Athens was the leader, the period in its existence, after the Eurymedon, when the work of the League seemed to be done, and Athens nevertheless refused to dissolve it, fell within the time when the moderate democrats dominated in Athenian politics.

(I. 76. *Athenian Speech at Sparta.*) It has always been the law that the weaker should be controlled by the stronger.

An assertion of the natural law that might is right. It is somewhat strange that Thucydides, who had no sympathy with this law, inserts this passage in a speech made by an Athenian delegate at a time when Athens was under the control of Pericles. Various explanations of it are possible, but no one of them is convincing.

> (I. 76. *Athenian Speech at Sparta.*) Calculations of interest have made you take up the cry of justice, a consideration which no one ever yet brought forward to hinder his own ambition when he had a chance of gaining anything by might.

The cynical character of this and the previous quotation from this speech make it possible that Thucydides wishes to indicate that the speaker is an ultra-democrat. His reports of the language of the members of the party in other parts of his work seem designed to express the cynicism of the views of political extremists.

> (I. 77. *Athenian Speech at Sparta.*) When force can be used, law does not come in.

The same cynicism as in the previous quotations from the speech.

> (I. 123. *Corinthian Speech at the Second Congress at Sparta.*) Treaties are broken not by resistance, but by aggression.

> (I. 141. *Pericles' Speech*). For in a single battle the Peloponnesians and their allies can face the rest of Greece, but they cannot carry on war against a power with equipment so different from their own because, not having one governing body, they cannot do anything with quick promptitude; since all of those states have equal votes and are of different races each seeks to forward its own interest. Hence, as is usual under such circumstances, what is done is only half done, for some wish to wreak some private revenge while others are by no means anxious to waste their own resources, and, being slow in coming together, they give but little time to the affairs of the alliance as a whole, but a much longer time to the management of their own individual interests.

This tendency in alliances and leagues has often been illustrated in history. A noticeable instance of it is the difficulties with the continental allies of England in the period preceding the battle of Blenheim. It was also strikingly illustrated when the recent League of Nations attempted to make Italy refrain from an attack on Abyssinia.

> (II. 63. *Speech of Pericles.*) Prosperity is never safe unless combined with readiness to act.

> (III. 12. *Mytilenian Speech at Olympia.*) What then was this friendship, or what substantial freedom could there be when we accepted each other against

our inclination; where fear made them court us in war, and us them in peace; where sympathy, the ordinary basis of confidence, had its place supplied by terror, fear having more part than friendship in keeping us in the alliance: and where the first of us who was encouraged by impunity was certain to break faith with the other? (III. 37. *Speech of Cleon.*) Bad laws which are never changed are better for a state than good laws which have no authority.

Whether this is a dictum with which Thucydides would agree is doubtful. But it must be remembered that there is a philosophy of the bad and the worse as well as of the good and the bad.

ALLIANCE

> (I. 32. *Corcyraean Speech at Athens.*) (A state) which never in the past formed a voluntary alliance with anyone has now to ask alliance of others, and owing to this policy we have isolated ourselves for the present war with Corinth, and what aforetime seemed prudence to us, the avoidance of risk involved in any foreign alliance due to the danger involved in the policy of a neighbour, this isolation now seems folly and weakness.

As to the cases in history in which some states have followed a policy of isolation, its wisdom or unwisdom has depended on the circumstances of the time. But generally speaking, there is danger in such a policy when it involves the refusal to help other states which are assailed by an aggressor, since their subjugation may lead to a new geographical situation in which the aggressive state is brought nearer to the isolated state, and that state has to appeal for help to those states to which it has in the past refused it.

> (I. 39. *Corinthian Speech.*) They should have shared their power with you before they asked you to share their fortunes.

The results of isolation are indicated in the preceding comment on the passage from the Corcyraean speech.

THE PHILOSOPHY OF WAR

Thucydides' philosophy of war includes much which has become commonplace in the centuries that have passed since he wrote. But his remarks have a truth which is wonderful, considering that they were not drawn from centuries of past military experience embracing a large mass of literature, but are the conclusions which a very able man drew from a very meagre supply of facts, and drew correctly, owing to his capacity for seeing which were the permanent and which were the incidental elements in the making of events. It is a distinction which only the highest intellect can make successfully.

The attitude to war shown by mankind at all ages of the world is remarkable for much backsight, if a word may be used in a new application, and very little foresight. Soldiers, especially those of armies with a great past history, are intensely conservative of those military principles which have led them to victory in the past, regardless of developments, however significant, which have rendered those principles out of date. The Spartans at the beginning of the Ten Years' War were, in spite of the warnings of Archidamus, quite convinced that the hoplite phalanx would be just as effective in that war as it had been in the wars of the past.

It was the same with the Romans in the days of Rutilius Rufus. For a hundred years they had been blind to the lessons which the Second Punic War ought to have taught them. The English in the Boer War were still using close order in attack, though its ineffectiveness against the modern rifle had been conclusively shown at Plevna twenty-three years before.

It will not be necessary to comment on the passages in Thucydides which state principles in the art of war. They will merely be quoted. Many other examples in medieval and modern warfare might be quoted in reference to the principle which has just been discussed.

As Thucydides was writing the history of a war, his references to the major and minor principles of war are naturally numerous.

(I. 34. *Speech of Corcyraeans at Athens*.) It is our policy to be beforehand with her . . . We ought to form plans against her instead of waiting to defeat her designs.

(I. 34. *Speech of Corcyraeans at Athens*.) Since he who has least cause to repent the fact that he has given way to opponents will be the safest in the end.

This would be applicable to Munich, had not the criminal laxity of previous years made any other course impossible.

(I. 36. *Speech of the Corcyraeans*.) You must remember on the one hand that your strength will be formidable to your antagonists; and on the other, that whatever the confidence you derive from refusing to receive us, your weakness will have no terrors for a strong enemy.

Largely applicable to the situation just before the outbreak of the war of 1914-18, when Britain seemed to hesitate about entering the war in case of the invasion of Belgium.

(III. 30. *Speech of Teutiaplus the Elean on the Revolt*

of Mytilene.) Let us not shrink from the risk, but let us remember that this is just one of the surprises of war that we have all heard of; and that to be able to guard against these in one's own case, and to have the eye to see them when they can be used against an enemy is what makes a successful general.

(I. 69. *Corinthian Speech at Sparta*.) For it is not he who reduces a people to subjection, but he who could prevent that being done, but ignores it, who is more truly the doer of the deed.

(I. 78. *Speech of the Athenians at Sparta*.) As to war, do not wait till you are engaged in it to be convinced of the great incalculability of its nature. It is wont, if prolonged, to become an affair of chance from which neither of us will be exempt, and its issue is an unseen risk. Men on entering into a war resort first to action which is that which they ought to postpone; but, when disaster overtakes them, resort to deliberation.

(I. 42. *Pericles' Speech*.) For the times and tides of war wait for no man.

Cf. Runstedt's recent attack (December 1944) on the allies in the Ardennes.

(I. 82. *Speech of Archidamus*.) War undertaken by a coalition for sectional interests, whose progress there is no means of foreseeing, does not easily admit of creditable settlement.

(I. 81. *Speech of Archidamus*.) For let us not be elated by the fatal hope of the war being ended by the devastation of their lands.

(I. 83. *Speech of Archidamus*.) War is a matter not so much of arms as of money, which makes arms of use.

(I. 84. *Speech of Archidamus*.) We are warlike owing to our being well-disciplined—warlike, because the main element in it is a sense of one's own measure, as in courage the main element is a feeling which makes us shun disgrace.

(I. 85. *Speech of Archidamus*.) We always in practice base our preparations against an enemy on the assumption that his plans are good.

There have been many subsequent occasions in history on which successful generals have attributed much of their success to this assumption.

(I. 120. *Corinthian Speech at the Second Congress at Sparta*.) If wise men remain quiet while they are not injured, brave men abandon peace for war when they are injured, returning to an understanding on a favourable opportunity: in fact they are neither intoxicated by their success in war, nor disposed to take an injury for the sake of the delightful tranquillity of peace. Indeed to falter for the sake of such delights is, if he fail to act, the quickest way of losing the sweets of repose which make you shun war, while to conceive extravagant pretensions from success in war is to forget how hollow is the confidence by which you are elated. For if many ill-conceived plans have succeeded through the still greater fatuity of an opponent, many more, apparently well-laid, have on the contrary ended in disgrace. For there is never an exact correspondence between the promise of deliberation and the performance of execution; but speculation may be carried on in safety, while fear causes failure in action.

Strongly applicable to the states of Western Europe in the years preceding the second world war.

(I. 122. *Speech of Corinthians*.) For war of all things proceeds least on definite rules, but draws principally on itself for contrivances to meet an emergency.

It is difficult to see clearly in what application this statement is made. Taking the history of war as a whole, there have been occasions which have illustrated its truth; but success, even under these circumstances, depends on adherence to general rules of war established by long experience.

(I. 140. *Speech of Pericles.*) I know that the spirit with which men are persuaded to go to war is not that with which they actually engage in it, and that their opinions vary with the variations of events.

(I. 140. *Speech of Pericles*.) If you give way, you will instantly have to meet some greater demand, as having been frightened into concession; while a firm refusal will make them clearly understand that they must treat you more as equals.

In some ways correspondent to the position at the time of Munich.

(I. 140. *Speech of Pericles*.) For sometimes the course of things is as arbitrary as the plans of Man; indeed this is why we usually blame chance for whatever does not happen as we expected.

(I. 141. *Speech of Pericles*.) Farmers are a class that are always more ready to serve in person than in purse.

(I. 143. *Speech of Pericles*.) Seamanship, like everything else, is a matter of art, and will not permit of being taken as a by-play, and picked up at odd times. On the contrary, it is so exacting as almost to exclude by-play altogether.

(II. 63. *Speech of Pericles*.) You cannot decline the burden of empire and still expect to share its honours . . , For what you hold is, to speak somewhat plainly, tyranny. To take it perhaps was wrong; but to let it go is unsafe.

Thucydides' moral attitude towards these statements cannot be judged. They may merely give a general idea of what Pericles actually said. He leaves the moral situation on one side; but he does believe that these things are true, though they are the outcome of a morally doubtful situation. It may be seen that these truths are to a certain extent applicable to the present relations between Britain and India. (1945).

(II. 64. *Speech of Pericles*.) Unambition is never secure without vigour at its side.

It is possible that Pericles was referring to that movement towards a negotiated peace, which existed in Athens in these early years of the war. Its existence is known from certain passages in Aristophanes.

(IV. 17. *Speech of Lacedaemonian envoys at Athens after the disaster on Sphacteria*.) You can avoid the mistake of those who meet with an extraordinary piece of good fortune, and are led on by hope to grasp continually at something further, through having already succeeded without expecting it. Those who have known most vicissitudes of good and bad have justly lost faith in their prosperity. And your state and ours have had the experience which might teach them this lesson.

(VI. 91. *Speech of Alcibiades at Sparta*.) The surest method of harming an enemy is to find out what he most fears, and to choose this means of attacking him, since everyone naturally knows best his own weak points.

Illustrated in the recent war by the attacks which the allies have made from the air on German manufacturing centres, especially in the Ruhr.

DEMOCRACY

(III. 37. *Speech of Cleon*.) Often before now and on other occasions have I been convinced that democracy is incapable of empire, and never more than by your present change of mind with regard to the Mytilenians.

This is in nowise an expression of Thucydides' own view, but one of the various passages which illustrates the psychology of the ultra-democrats.

RHETORIC

(III. 38. *Speech of Cleon.*) In such contests the state gives the rewards to others and takes the danger for herself. The persons to blame are you who are so foolish as to institute these contests; who go to see an oration as you would go to see a sight, take your facts on hearsay, judge of the practicability of a project by the wit of its advocates, and, as far as the past is concerned, you do not accept what you have actually seen as more trustworthy than what you have heard in specious verbal criticisms. The easy victims of new-fangled arguments, unwilling to follow the conclusions of experience, slaves to every new paradox, contemptuous of everyday experience; the first wish of every man being that he could speak himself, the next to rival those who can speak by seeming to be quite *au fait* with their ideas, by applauding every hit almost before it is made, and by being as quick in catching an argument as you are slow in foreseeing its consequences; asking, so to speak, for something different from the conditions under which we live, and yet comprehending inadequately those very conditions; very slaves to the pleasure of the ear, and more like the audience of a rhetorician than the council of a state.

As a picture of real life in a democracy this is one of the most remarkable passages in Thucydides. The same thing might be said with truth of political audiences at the present day and in modern times.

It is rather remarkable that Thucydides puts the words into the mouth of Cleon. But Cleon was condemning, not his own ultra-democrats, but those of the moderate party who had doubtless flocked into the city with the express intention of getting the decision of the day before, condemning the whole male population of Mytilene to death, revoked.

The Athenian Assembly suffered from the same weakness as the assemblies of other city states, namely that it was inconvenient and difficult for the rural population to attend its meetings at the city centre of the state, so that at Athens the town population was assured of a majority, unless any important or exciting proposal was to come before the meeting.

In Attica the rural population, chiefly small farmers, was mainly of the middle or moderate conservative party, whereas the town population of Athens and Piraeus was mainly ultra-democratic. Thucydides says that at the beginning of the Peloponnesian War the rural outnumbered the urban population.

REVOLUTION

(III. 82-4.) Later the whole Greek world so to speak was convulsed in forms varying in various places, the democratic leaders seeking to introduce the Athenians, and the oligarchs the Lacedaemonians.

In peace they would not have had an excuse for calling them in, nor would they have been willing to do so, but in war it was different, and each having an alliance with which they could both harm their opponents and benefit themselves, helpers from outside were easily introduced by would-be revolutionaries. And many grievous things befell the states by way of revolution, such as do occur and always will occur so long as human nature remains the same, but in a more or less violent measure, and differing in form with the variety of circumstances which accompany them. For in peace and prosperity states and individuals display better dispositions, owing to their not falling under imperious necessities.

But war, which takes away the supply of daily bread, is a hard schoolmaster, and assimilates the temper of the masses to the circumstances of the time. Revolution therefore ran its course from city to city, and those at which it arrived latest, having heard what had previously happened elsewhere, carried matters much further in respect to innovation of design, elaboration in attack, and the brutality of their acts of revenge. And they changed the ordinary meanings of terms as applied to acts, owing to the way in which they thought right to regard them. For senseless audacity was called manly *esprit de corps,* and caution was called specious cowardice, and moderation a coward's excuse, and a wise caution in everything useless inaction. And an impulsive rashness was ascribed to a manly nature, and considerations of safety a plausible excuse for changing sides. The harsh and violent man was always to be trusted, and anyone who opposed him was untrustworthy. A successful plotter was a shrewd fellow, and he who saw through it shrewder still. But one who took measures to render neither of these things necessary was one who broke up his party and was afraid of his adversaries. Speaking plainly, he who forestalled one likely to injure the party was praised, so also one who brought in one who had had no intention of joining it. So, too, relationship was regarded as less binding than partisanship, owing to the latter making a man more ready to take blind risks; such associations not having in view the blessings derivable from the law as established, but the promotion of their own interests in contravention of the established laws; while the confidence of their members in each other rests less on any divine sanction than on complicity in crime. The fair speeches of adversaries were received with active precautions by the stronger of the two, and not with a generous confidence. Revenge was held of more account than self-preservation. Oaths of reconciliation, if proffered on either side to meet a momentary difficulty, held good so long as those who swore them had no other resource; but when opportunity offered, he who first ventured to seize it and to take his enemy off his guard thought that vengeance sweeter which was due to the trustfulness of the other side than if taken openly, and he took into account the safety of it, and further, having won a victory by deceit, he had won the prize of intelligence. Indeed criminals are more often called clever than simpletons are called honest, and men are ashamed of being the one, but proud of being the other. The cause of all these evils was the lust for power due to greed and ambition. Out of this came the zeal of contending parties. For the leaders in the states, each side under a specious name, the political equality of the proletariat, and the prestige of a wise aristocracy, whilst nominally managing the public interests, made them prizes, and trying in every way to get the better of one another, ventured on the most terrible deeds, and proceeded to reprisals still more terrible, not inflicting punishment in accordance with justice and the interests of the state, but limiting it only at their own pleasure. They were ready to glut the animosity of the moment either by condemnation on an unjust verdict or by forcible seizure of power. Thus neither party paid attention to religion; but the use of fair names to arrive at guilty ends was in high reputation. The moderates were destroyed by both sides, either because they did not join either, or because they were grudged their chance of survival.

Thus every form of wickedness arose in the Hellenic world by way of revolution, and the old simplicity in which nobility had so large a place was ridiculed and disappeared. Being arrayed against one another in ideas, antagonistic parties prevailed with resulting widespread distrust, for there was no regard for a promise or oath such as might have brought about a reconciliation, but all when they held the upper hand, not reckoning on any hope of security, could provide against danger rather than cherish confidence. And intellectual inferiors were usually the survivors. For from fear of their own inferiority and the cleverness of their opponents, they feared to be worsted in debate and caught off their guard by the versatility in design of opponents who plotted against them. And so they took bold action. So their opponents with a contemptuous confidence that they would see through them and that there was no need to take action where strategy would be effective, were caught unawares and perished.

In Corcyra men ventured on most of these acts, and did all that might be perpetrated by men who had been governed with tyranny rather than tolerance by those who now offered them an opportunity for revenge, some wishing to get rid of their wonted poverty and above all, owing to what they had suffered, to get hold of their neighbours' property, gave false verdicts in the courts, and some, not with a view to gain the better of rivals but of men on an equality with themselves, carried away by ungovernable passion, made cruel and pitiless attacks on them. For the time being all order in civic life ceased, and human nature always rebelling against the law and now its master, readily showed itself to be of an unbridled temper superior to justice and hostile to all superiority, for otherwise it would not have put gain before moral right, had not envy had

an evil influence. Men claim, when revenging themselves on others, to set aside the accepted laws on matters on which depends the hope of salvation for those in trouble, and not to leave those laws in existence against the day when the man in trouble needs their help.

Before dealing with the matter of this passage there are certain things which must be said with regard to its form. Grammatically involved passages are found scattered through the speeches in Thucydides; but there is no passage in his history in which the confused nature of Thucydides' Greek is so difficult to unravel by grammatical analysis. Thucydides was aiming at exploiting the new style to the full, but, owing to his exile, he had to work alone.

There are two features of this passage in Thucydides which render it unique from a linguistic point of view. In the first place, it is the only passage in the actual narrative of his history in which he adopts the style he has used in the speeches. Secondly, so far as grammatical peculiarities are concerned, they are far more frequent, and in some cases present greater difficulties, than the language of the speeches. When he wrote the speeches he had made some advance at any rate in his writing of Greek on the new lines.

So much for the form of the passage. Of the matter it may be said that it is perhaps the most remarkable of his contributions to mass psychology. There is hardly an item in it which cannot be paralleled in the history of modern revolutions, and especially in the revolutions of the last thirty years. Yet these forecasts were made on premises very restricted in number and in respect to the period which provided them. Thucydides seems to have been as it were a psychological anatomist, who dissected the human mind with results just as scientific as the results of the dissection of the human body.

It would be superfluous to cite from the histories of modern revolutions parallels to the various characteristics of revolution which Thucydides cites. They are easily recognisable to anyone who has even a moderate knowledge of modern history.

Those who after reading the passages quoted in this chapter remain unconvinced of Thucydides' aim to be not merely a historian but also a historical philosopher, will not be convinced by anything that an editor of his work may say. But they may be reminded that it would have been strange if a man of his ability had claimed that his work was to be a 'possession for ever' on the basis merely of his narrative of the events of the war.

This philosophical element in his work cannot be paralleled in the work of any other ancient historian, and does not play any noticeable part in any work of a modern writer.

A soldier leaving for battle, c. 430 B.C.

One of the greatest losses the literary world has experienced is the fact that he did not live to continue it by insertions of speeches in the narrative of the fifth and eighth books, and in a history of the last years of the war which he never lived to write. It seems strange that he left his work incomplete, since it contains evidence that he lived at least till 398 or 399. One surmise is possible. The writing of history on a large scale leaves the writer a sadder if not a wiser man. He had to write the history of his own country, beginning at the time of the Periclean democracy and ending with the disaster of Aegospotami and its aftermath. The contrast between those last tragic years and the position at the time of the opening of the war may have broken his heart and led him to carry on reluctantly and slowly the task of telling the story of the bitter end, so slowly that death overtook him before he finished it.

David Grene (essay date 1950)

SOURCE: "Chance and Pity" and "Beyond Necessity," in *Man in His Pride,* University of Chicago Press, 1950, pp. 70-79, 80-92.

[*In the excerpt that follows, Grene endeavors to answer the question, "in the true domain of politics . . . where does Thucydides find his highest value?" In order to find an answer, he explores Thucydides's notion of primary historical forces—particularly necessity and chance—and examines those instances where Thucydides deems it appropriate to insert moral commentary on individual behavior.*]

Chance and Pity

Everybody who reads Thucydides has been struck by the sparseness of any personal moral comment on the men and the happenings which he describes. But few seem to have noticed how curiously the moral comment, such as it is, has been directed. There are, in particular, three passages of this kind, each embodying some personal judgment of the historian and at first sight quite separated in the nature and variety of comment, yet which on closer scrutiny show a similar kind of detached humanity.

a) The first is the story of the destruction of the Boeotian town of Mycalessus. Mycalessus was far inland, its walls ineffective and in parts dilapidated; it was quite remote from the war or any concern in it. Unfortunately it happened that the Athenians had hired a body of Thracian mercenaries who were supposed to go with Demosthenes to Sicily. They came too late to join the expedition and proved too expensive to keep on foot without a specifically allocated military task. So the Athenians ordered them sent home and put them, for their return journey, under the command of an

Athenian officer. Since the state was paying them a drachma a day per man, as long as they were under Athenian orders, and the journey home by land would take a considerable time, Deitrephes, their general, was instructed to employ them to do all possible harm to the enemy on the way back. It was under these circumstances that they marched through part of Boeotia and made their foray on this sleepy little country town of Mycalessus. Then Thucydides says: "They stormed Mycalessus and sacked its houses and its temples, killing every human being. They spared neither young nor old but killed everyone they met, women and children alike and even the pack animals and every living thing they saw. For these Thracians, like most other barbarians, are most bloodthirsty when they are confident. There was there, then, a terrible confusion and every form of death: in particular, they attacked a school—the largest in the town—where the children had just come in and butchered every one of them. This whole city suffered a catastrophe second to no other in its unexpectedness and horror." At the end of the passage he writes: "This is what happened to Mycalessus, a thing which is as much worth our tears as anything that occurred in this war, considering the small size of the town."

b) At the end of the Sicilian campaign Nicias surrendered to the Sicilian troops, though, as Thucydides tells us, because he trusted their Spartan general, Gylippus, rather than the Sicilians themselves. He and the other Athenian general, Demosthenes, were held for a while by the Sicilians at the request of Gylippus, but eventually they were both executed. According to Thucydides, the Syracusans among the Sicilians were afraid to spare Nicias lest under torture he should reveal the names of the considerable party within Syracuse itself which had tried to open negotiations with the Athenians. The total failure of the expedition and the loss of close to forty thousand men, killed, wounded, and prisoners, is very largely attributable to the stupidity, timidity, and incompetence of Nicias. Demosthenes had repeatedly tried to save the army, and his plans for this end were sound and their success probable. Nicias consistently balked them. These facts are vouched for by Thucydides himself in the seventh book. His comment on the end of Nicias is as follows: "On this charge, then, or one like it, Nicias died, being the least worthy of all the Greeks of my time to come to such a depth of misfortune, since he had lived all his life in accordance with what is popularly called virtue." Of Demosthenes he says nothing.

c) In 412-411 the democracy of Athens was overthrown by a conspiracy of oligarchs who had long been discontented with the prospects both of war and of peace if Athens remained democratic. The hope of enlisting Alcibiades and with him perhaps the help of Persia, which he was reputed to be able to deliver, weighed with some of this party. But the roots of the oligarchic attitude to the war, the democracy, and Sparta go back much further, as we saw in an earlier chapter. There were two wings of the oligarchic clique—a violent faction whose aim was a strong administration of a very few and a moderate constitutional party who wanted a restriction of the franchise and a remodeling of the constitution to bring it nearer to what Aristotle later calls a *politeia,* a mixture of democratic and oligarchic elements. The chief planner among the extreme oligarchs was a man named Antiphon; that of the moderates, Theramenes.

The extremists made the initial moves in the revolution and administered the city for a while by secret-police methods when, as Thucydides puts it, "no one of the rest of the citizens spoke against these measures, being afraid and seeing the size of the conspiracy; and if anyone did he was immediately killed in some convenient manner, and there was no search for the doers of the deed or justice to be had against them if suspected, but the multitude kept quiet and were so terror-stricken that each man who had no violence done him, even though he kept his mouth shut, thought it a gain." The terror did not last long, and the moderates among the oligarchs took control and drafted a new constitution which was to limit the franchise to five thousand. The extreme oligarchs had already formally suggested this, but, according to Thucydides, this was a mere pretense to make the transition from the democracy easier; they had no intention of making the five thousand a working political unity. Theramenes, however, the leader of the moderates, wanted the five thousand in good faith, and of the constitution set up in the name of the five thousand Thucydides says: "For now for the first time in my lifetime the Athenians seem to have enjoyed an excellent government; for there was a blend in it of the few and the many, and this was the first thing which lifted the city out of its ill condition."

Now if we look at these passages, first in their contexts and then in conjunction with one another, something of their strangeness becomes apparent. In the first place, none of the three constitutes what one might call remarkably merited comment—on a comparative basis. Is it not strange that the man who records the total destruction of Melos conducted in the most cold-blooded fashion, and the almost complete destruction of the city of Mitylene, and the execution of the Plataeans who surrendered after the siege should have had not one word of pity for the victims or blame for the executioners and reserve this pity and blame for the murder of a few hundred villagers and a schoolhouse of children in Boeotia? Is it not strange that the man who notes the end of Antiphon (described as "second to none among his day in virtue") and the end of Demosthenes, who had won the Pylos campaign so brilliantly, who had even almost rescued the Sicilian expedition from the failure to which Nicias' leadership

doomed it, without even a single phrase or comment, should have delivered so complete and comprehensive a verdict of praise on Nicias, who had lost the decisive battles of the war? And is it not strange that the man who had seen Periclean Athens and acknowledged its enormous power, resilience, and vitality should have reserved his praise of the "best government" for the rather dim academic experiment of Theramenes, which lasted a couple of months and was really hardly ever alive, as a functioning unit, at all?

One way to remove the sense of strangeness in these comments is to explain them individually and piecemeal. Each of them is, of course, susceptible of an individual explanation. We can say that, after all, Thucydides is human, like any other man; that the devastated village and the murdered school children appealed to his sense of pity as greater and more terrible events had somehow failed to do. Or we might force ourselves to see the emphasis on the size of Mycalessus as the important matter. Other cities greater than this had fallen but none more completely, considering its smallness. And we can explain away the comment on Nicias by assuming a personal friendship between Thucydides and Nicias and a personal hostility between Thucydides and Demosthenes. And we can explain away the statement on the constitution of Theramenes by saying that, after all, Thucydides is a moderate oligarch, by preference, that he has never approved of the democratic empire, and that his word of praise for the polity of Theramenes is his personal voice as a fifth-century politician. The common thread which runs through all such individual explanations is a separation of Thucydides the historian and Thucydides the man. We picture to ourselves a Thucydides austerely bent on his task of recording the Peloponnesian War yet at times revealing a sort of private humanity which he shares with all of us.

When a historian is primarily a philosopher of history and secondly a historian, as in the case of Hegel or Spengler, such a bifurcation of the professional and the personal is conceivable. Because the pattern is conceived first, born of the impact of some set of facts on the individual artist before the set of facts has taken artistic form. When this takes place, the particular foibles of the philosopher-historian can, at moments, crack the mold he has created. But when, as is true of Thucydides, the concrete particular, in its completeness, is both the form and the totality of the philosophy, the personal cannot intrude. What he has seen, detail by detail, is the story, and the story has major implications; but the implications spring from the story, not the story from a theory. The personal, in such a case, enters only when the historian selects his subject in the first place; it does not appear as an addendum or an interruption in the treatment of the subject.

More than this. If we look again at the three passages

quoted, we *can* see a common link in the moral comment. All three passages deal with men or events which are peculiarly within the realm of chance rather than in that of necessity.

In the case of Mycalessus, Thucydides stresses this. The soldiers who did the deed were mercenaries who came late for the operation to which they were assigned; it was a mere casual chance that they were sent back by way of Boeotia and that the instructions they received—to do all the harm to the enemy that they could en route—led them in the most accidental way upon this wretched Boeotian village. Mycalessus itself, witness its fallen and crumbling walls and its sense of utter security, was a place in no sense suited to play a role in this war. Melos might and naturally did become a bone of contention between Athens and Sparta; an island inhabited by Dorians siding with neither Athens nor Sparta is bound in terms of the logic of the war to suffer. But Mycalessus need not have, as far as this same logic went, and it is for that reason that Thucydides pities it.

The same sort of pattern is discernible in the story of Nicias and his relation to the Sicilian expedition. He did not want such an expedition at all and least of all wanted to command it, as we learn from Book vi. Being, in spite of his own intentions, elected general, he is, then, in a purely fortuitous way, deprived of the two assistants who could have made it a success: of Lamachus by death and of Alcibiades by desertion. He makes another desperate effort to get rid of the command following on his first failure, when he demands reinforcements so large that he assumes the Athenians will refuse and a successor to himself because of his incapacitation through illness. He succeeds in neither request. Fatally, the Athenians sent another army so large that he had no excuse left for failure; and they affirm their confidence in him by insisting on his retention of office. Finally, when beaten in the battle in the harbor, he might still have withdrawn his forces relatively intact, but the eclipse of the moon intervening found his superstitious weak spot, and the result of his enforced delay is the complete destruction of the army and himself.

The peculiar poignancy of Nicias' position is further emphasized when we bear in mind that he was, in his own esteem and in that of the Athenians, a very lucky general. He comes before us time and again with his uneasy reliance upon good fortune. Thucydides tells us that he was especially anxious to negotiate the peace of 421 which bears his name, because so far his good luck in generalship had been unbroken and he wished to have the record of a general never defeated. He had "lived all his life in accordance with what is popularly considered virtue" and with the timid caution of one who has been lucky and knows that luck can change. And the result of his "popular virtue" and his caution

about luck is to be involved himself and involve his country in the most prodigious catastrophe she had ever experienced.

There is, I believe, in these two passages the sense of Thucydides' awe in the face of chance. Thucydides was not a superstitious man; he plainly did not believe that chance was our name for God's contrivances or that the area which Diodotus labeled "chance" is really the pattern of destiny. But, I think, the peculiar ironies of chance inspired him with a kind of horror, and in these two instances, that of a well-meaning, decent, and incompetent man, meaninglessly enmeshed in a task demanding enormous skill, and the simple little country town with its men and women, children and animals, senselessly slaughtered by a hired mercenary army for no conceivable military purpose, the disproportion between the people and their fate awakened a human pity which is nonetheless explicable according to his own theory of history and its development.

The last instance—that of the comment on the Constitution of the Five Thousand—is much harder to place. The Constitution of the Five Thousand is certainly not peculiarly the product of chance, nor does chance in connection with it exhibit the irony which is remarkable in the case of Nicias and the village of Mycalessus. On the other hand, there is perhaps another way of seeing the Constitution of the Five Thousand as a thing not directly growing out of the necessity of history—thus explaining Thucydides' comment on it. In the chapter on *stasis* Thucydides says: "In peace and good times both states and individuals show better judgment because they do not fall into necessities which are too strong for will or intention." The "better" here probably indicates the same kind of moral comment as the "best" applied to the government of the Five Thousand: that is to say, in both cases "better" and "best" refer to some sort of moral excellence which is no longer possible when the stress of circumstances "likens the temper of most men to their circumstances."

This is further supported if we seek for a definition of "better" in the chapters on *stasis* and for "best" in that section dealing with the Constitution of the Five Thousand. The gist of the chapter on *stasis* is that the proper qualities of man in a state of normalcy—courage, caution, decency, and intelligence—become superseded by peculiar distortions in fact, such as insensate daring, ruthlessness, and universal suspicion, and that the use of the moral terms also changes. The distorted extremes received the moral titles due to their normal counterparts. In the chapter on the Constitution of the Five Thousand, Thucydides *cannot* mean that the "best government" is best in the sense that it will help Athens win the war, for the first actions of this government are directed toward a peace with Sparta. The reason he gives himself for the attribution of "best" is true and significant. "For it was a blend of the few and the many, and this was the first thing that lifted the city out of its ill condition." The conflict of the few and the many is the basis of *stasis,* and *stasis* Thucydides stamps as the peculiar internal condition resulting from external war.

In other words, allowing for the basic drives of human nature which lead to the potentiality of war between states and the potentialities of war within the society between the few who have and the many who have not, the actualization of human aggressiveness in war and in faction represents the hysterical condition at which point moral comment is no longer significant, since man's capacity is now entirely limited by circumstances, and neither his will nor his intention has any free play. At such a time the art of politics finds its proper exercise, since it is pre-eminently the art of understanding necessity and operating within the possibilities afforded by necessity. But the area where *moral* comment is in order is only that in which human beings can be regarded as in some sense operating with freedom to choose between one alternative and another without the direct force of necessity constraining them.

This latter is the case with the Constitution of the Five Thousand. It was, in a way, an academic experiment, since it tried to cure, in a root-and-branch fashion, the basic disease of the Athenian state, the conflict of the few and the many. It did this in preference to setting the winning of the war first, as the democrats would have it, or the establishment of a stable government, by fiat, as the extreme oligarchs wanted. It belongs in one of the rare breathing spaces between the compulsive assaults of necessity and embodies an effort by men consciously and freely to choose, theoretically, a better state. And it is in this spirit that Thucydides comments on it.

Summing up the three passages, we can state the result like this. Thucydides saw a struggle between good and bad in an individual man or a situation as worthy of comment only when the man or the situation belongs in the region which lies outside the direct control of necessity. Thus the chance destruction of Mycalessus and the chance which carried Nicias to be commander of the disastrous Sicilian expedition show, briefly, a piece of history which might have been different. In the light of its hypothetical difference the historian may and will comment morally. Again when an action can actually be consummated with the true possibility of choice—that is, when it proceeds from men's freedom of decision rather than the compulsion of necessity—a moral comment can be significant. But moral comment is out of place in the discussion of the war and the empire, for here are only the final and natural responses to a continuous process of circumstances, and what men ought to do in regard to the war and the empire *should* be dictated only by the necessity of coping with the existing situation.

Beyond Necessity

Though the comments we have last discussed are probably to be integrated in this theory of history as I have shown, they do not reveal the most significant attitude of Thucydides as a historian. In a sense this is quite evident in the light of the manner in which they have been traditionally explained. Had there not existed a very marked contradiction between these passages and the general spirit of the rest of the narrative, so many scholars would not have tried to see them as sentimental inserts or taken them at their face value as sarcastic comment. The analysis we have pursued so far does in fact show why there is this discrepancy of tone. In the passages on Nicias, Mycalessus, and the Constitution of the Five Thousand, Thucydides is remarking on phenomena which in a special way belong outside the realm of necessity. The *Archaeology* and the *Fifty Years* combined with certain of the speeches indicate to us what he considered the necessity of history to be and the qualities required by statesmen who would be true statesmen in the light of this necessity. What we must try to do now is to discuss where within this area—the necessity of history—the highest praise is given—to statesman and to state. When men's free will is effectually curbed by circumstances, and when chance does not obviously confuse the issue—in other words, in the true domain of politics—where does Thucydides find his highest value?

We can start from a passage which is puzzling enough in itself, unless we find the explanation we are seeking. Antiphon, according to Thucydides, was the intellect that dominated the extreme party of the oligarchs, the party, that is, that installed and maintained the reign of terror in 411. Here are the historian's own words: "The man who brought forward the proposal and to all outward appearance was the most energetic in destroying the democracy was Peisander; but the one who engineered the whole business and the manner in which it was brought to this pass and had thought most deeply about its contrivance was Antiphon, a man among the Athenians of his day second to none in virtue."

The word "virtue," unqualified, stands in the sharpest contrast to that in the verdict on Nicias, "what is considered virtue." A little research into the deeds chronicled of each figure amplifies what our conception of the two virtues should be. The violence of the oligarchs of Antiphon's party is quite clearly noted by Thucydides. There was a reign of terror in which order was maintained by judiciously selected secret executions. Thucydides' cool words of this demand attention: "And they killed certain men, though not very many, *who seemed to be suitable ones to remove,* and threw others into prison and banished others." In a sense, the whole record of Nicias, with his hesitation and irresolution and general tendency not to do the effective and ruthless thing, stands in the strongest contrast to this; but it is capped, as it were, by the pathetic note in his last speech to his soldiers: "I am in the same danger and hazard as the lowliest of you; I am no stronger than any of you—indeed you can see how my sickness prostrates me. Yet in my private life and otherwise I think my good fortune has previously been second to none. I have lived with much devotion to the gods and much justice in the sight of men and have merited no man's grudge."

It is hazardous, of course, to take a man's own judgment on himself as the historian's, but when the narrative, the historian's verdict, and the general's own speech all jibe, there can be little reason for rejecting the total portrait of Nicias as the presentation of a well-meaning incompetence, just as surely as Thucydides' comments on Antiphon and his party lead us to form a picture of ruthless efficiency. In other words, "conventional virtue" and the virtue of the statesman according to necessity are at opposite poles. We might notice too that the phrase in the general description of Antiphon, "the ablest in forming conceptions and in giving them voice," recalls another similar passage. This is Pericles' description of the duties of statesmen, in which the emphasis falls exactly on these two qualities with the same words: the need for forming conceptions and being able to express them. We might remember also the passage on Themistocles:

"Themistocles was a man who showed most certainly the strength of a native talent and for this is more worth our admiration than any other. By virtue of his peculiar understanding, without previous study to better or supplement it, he was the shrewdest judge of those crises that admit of virtually no deliberation and the best guesser at the future to its utmost limit. *That which he had in hand he was always able to give an account of* and was not incompetent to judge sufficiently well even that of which he was inexperienced. The future he foresaw, both for better and worse, to a remarkable extent. In a word, by brilliant natural gifts with the minimum of application he was the ablest man at improvising necessary measures."

The negative part of an inference from the use of "virtue" in the Antiphon passage is thus established. It is clear that the virtue Thucydides is praising in Antiphon has essentially nothing to do with mercy or humanity. We can also be sure of this in regard to Pericles, whose words on the empire we would do well to remember: "To acquire the empire may have been unjust: it is dangerous to let it go. You must remember that you hold a tyrant power." Is there any other attribute which can be exercised from the blanket definition of Antiphon's virtue which will help us to understand Thucydides' comment in a more general way?

Yes. Surely, according to Thucydides, the virtue of the statesman need not carry with it success. Neither Themistocles, Pericles, nor Antiphon was successful—personally successful, at least. That is to say, each of them achieved an enormous political task, the one the building of the long walls and the fleet to make the new empire, the second the extension of the empire and its preparation for the war, and the third the destruction of the democracy. But, in each case, the judgment of the multitude at some point intervened to wreck the purely personal satisfaction in achievement. Themistocles died in exile, a guest of the Persian king he had helped to defeat; Pericles at the end of his life was disgraced by the democracy he had led so long, even though in the last few months of his life he was reinstated; Antiphon was finally tried and executed by the people. Yet Thucydides tells us that Themistocles was "more worthy of our admiration than any other man in history," that Pericles was a single statesman of unique caliber in Athens' record, and that Antiphon was second to none of the Athenians in his day in virtue. Personal success, then, cannot be a necessary factor in the attributes of greatness, according to Thucydides. This is the more noteworthy, since, for him, foresight and efficiency are the prerequisites of a good statesman.

What do we find, then, positively, on the side of the statesman who commands Thucydides' admiration and the attribution of admiration? The achievement of a deed notable in terms of his own *History,* be that deed good or bad according to conventional Greek morality. More than that. The achievement must rise to the stature of uniqueness. As Thucydides felt that the historical significance of his time with its clash of these two great empires was unique, so uniqueness is for him, in a way, a guaranty of the importance of a given event. The fleet and the long walls; Athens' extraordinary endurance in the war; the destruction of the Athenian liberties of a hundred years' duration—all these have, for Thucydides, the stamp of singleness and the stamp of greatness. This is perhaps the very key to the personal failure of the statesmen, for the multitude cannot be taken along as a willing partner in the achievement of unique greatness. They constitute the difficulties to be overcome, the barrier that tests the strength of the assailant. And so, when the task is done, the many and the one relapse into their natural condition of antagonism, and, when the conflict becomes personal, the one must be beaten. But in the strange impersonality of self-sacrifice, in the desperate power and will to create something greater than the reach of a single man's ambition or benevolence, Thucydides found that which he called "virtue."

The life of nations for Thucydides is all of a piece in the early stages: the struggle for existence and then the struggle for supremacy. The object of interest for the nation in its historical development is *dynamis,* power, and this means dominion over others. Fear and greed are the driving motives on the road to imperialism, and there is no turning back. Yet in the course of the development there is a moment when these two factors are not the only ones. There is, as the Athenian envoys state it, honor. In the greatness of the thing created, the empire, there is a quality different from the qualities which created it; it is great in itself and for itself, and honor is its due from all.

The historical moment cannot, perhaps, last long; yet its greatness and dignity is the magnet of the historian's attention, and its decline the most penetrating exhibition of political motives, failures, and successes that can be offered him. Here is the significant recurring thing for Thucydides. That men struggle to live and then to dominate one another individually and nationally is a recurrent theme but does not attain any precision of form until their concerted and collective efforts have built a great monument to their individual greed and fear. In the hour that they honor that monument not only as the source of their own material well-being but as something apart from them, greater than them and worthy of their sacrifice, the greatest development of man, as Thucydides saw him, greatest politically and socially, has been attained. And, correspondingly, as the moment has called forth the most subtle and sophisticated sentiments of man living in a political society, its balance is rare and precarious. Overnight it dissolves again into an association of men, fearful and greedy.

History would be, then, for Thucydides, a series of significant mountains, the peaks rising at intervals in the endless chain. And, for the historian, the greatness and symmetrical proportions of the great thing that was made became valuable for their own sake, though, of course, the very appreciation of the greatness and the proportions implies a historian's emphasis. It is not hard to put this aspect of Thucydides' study together with his avoidance of conventional moral judgments, both on men and on the corporate political entities which they constitute and, more important still, with the inclusion of the few rather strange judgments we possess. The conventional moral judgment is, from his point of view, a failure on the level of significance. The ordinarily denominated virtues of man are not significant, in Thucydides' eyes, since they are not for him the genuinely predisposing factor in the creation of power; and only in power, in the building of something bigger than himself, is the peculiar excellence of the pressure of truly compulsive forces, fear and greed and their occasions—and the ability to transcend them within limits.

Yet the transcendence has no object; it must be its own object. This will hold good for the statesman and the state and the historian alike. The great statesman is the man who governs, not for his own advantage or nec-

essarily for the good of the governed (which would be the classical statement), but for the continued dignity and survival of the state which in Athens has its characteristic expression in power, wealth, and extent. The great state, like Athens, will seek no models but in itself be the object of imitation, living in the radiance of its own beauty and magnitude. The greatness of the history is in its truth and its significance; that it serves no man's delight or vanity or affiliation; that thus the events were and thus they will be again, since they are truly described and of the order that will recur.

Among statesmen a unique position in the history is occupied by Pericles, and it is to Pericles and Periclean Athens that we must look for the most significant expression of Thucydides' admiration.

There are only three speeches of Pericles reported in the *History*. They are the speech in which he advocates the declaration of war, the famous Funeral Speech, delivered over those that had fallen, and the speech in which he defends himself against the people's dissatisfaction with his conduct of the war. These three speeches peculiarly express the spirit of the city of Athens as she entered on her long struggle, and, apart from their significance inside Thucydides' *History,* they probably constitute the most extraordinary document we possess revealing the relation between the leading statesman and his people in a naked and unqualified democracy.

The first aspect of all three speeches that may surprise us is their frankness. It is not often that before a democratic electorate a politician can reveal his hopes and fears almost exactly as they must appear to himself, though perhaps in this there are signs of what Thucydides describes as Pericles' odd attitude to the people: "He dominated them, but in a spirit of freedom." For instance, in the first speech—that in which he urges the declaration of war—he warns the assembly that they may be inclined to feel quite different about the war when they are in it than when they are contemplating it as a future possibility. This, he tells us, is the wrong thing to do. "For it is possible for the outcome of events to proceed no less stupidly than the plans of men: that is why we are used to blame chance for whatever happens to us unexpectedly."

In the last speech in the *History,* where Pericles is forced to defend himself against unjust resentment in the early years of the war, he unhesitatingly lays the blame where it belongs: on the plague and the people's suffering under it which makes them unfair in their estimate of himself. He then proceeds to try to make them realize the true possibilities of success temporarily concealed from them by their immediate defection. Yet, as he does so, he cheerfully reveals to them that there is a *secret* in mastering them; that he is not handling them as man to man.

"As to your fears of your sufferings in this war, lest it grow so great that we can no longer surmount it—let suffice for you what I have told you before on the many occasions when I proved that your suspicions about the war were incorrect: yet I will add this one further matter on the greatness of your empire, something I am sure you have not thought of before yourselves nor have I made mention of it in my former speeches to you. Even now I would not have introduced this thing; for its presentation is somewhat too imposing—but that I see that you are unreasonably depressed. You think that your empire is over the allies alone; but I will show you this: there are two elements of the world for use, land and sea, and of the one you are total masters for as far as you now exercise that mastery and further if you please. No one, neither the Great King nor any other people on earth at present, will successfully repel you if you sail against them with the fleet you have now."

Here we are not concerned for the moment with the calm arrogance of the speech—that will be important later—but with the frankness it exhibits toward his audience. There is so clearly the implication that he is managing them, as of right of character and talent; that he knows the correct parts of the case to put now and at another time. And he tells them just this: *I would not have thought it advisable to produce an argument that is so arrogant in fact but that I see you irrationally depressed, and so I find that a little more of the naked truth than usual is necessary to restore you to a sensible frame of mind.* Here is the note of complete personal responsibility, without the blessing of divine sanction or hereditary legitimacy; and here is equally the undeviating openness of one who informs those whom he controls that his judgment is better than theirs and that only exceptional circumstances such as the present make it necessary for him to show them the deepest factors in his calculations.

But the frankness of these speeches is only one side of their basic character, and that may be summed up by saying that they are concerned with man and nothing but man. It is extraordinary in such speeches as these— one contemplating the city's engagement in a long war, one spoken in praise of the dead, one defending a leader suspected because of what was accidental mischance— that, with the exception of one insignificant and quite colorless reference, there should be no mention of divine guidance, divine blessing, or even, in a merely sentimental allusion, fatherland's gods.

That this is no general Greek practice, if we need convincing on the matter, we can see from Thucydides' own observations on the last speech of Nicias to his troops before their final battles in Sicily: "He said other things which men in such a contingency are apt to say, not guarding against appearing to anyone to talk platitudes, about women and children and gods of our country, things continually brought forward in the same form on behalf of all causes, yet in the presence of an existing emergency men judge them useful and urge them." But Pericles even in crisis will guard against seeming to talk platitudes. He shares with his hearers—knows it and draws his power from it—the knowledge that he and they are not like those of another age or another state who will bolster their hopes or their fears or even their sorrow by reference to beliefs outworn and dead. The city which is committed to the war, the city whose lovers the dead were over whom Pericles made his speech, was a manmade thing and existed only by the will and sacrifice of its men.

Here is the explanation of the strength of the materialistic appeal of Pericles to the citizens of Athens. They enjoy the products of the ends of the earth as natively as those of Attica. They may live their lives as they please, and no one may interfere. They are not harried by the demands of a harsh and continuous military service. Because, in a certain sense, the city is theirs and from beginning to end exhibits the immediate choice of its inhabitants, not the influence of tradition or sanctions imposed from outside. And in his final assessment of the city's chances against Sparta, Pericles, in the spirit of his city, describes the world as something essentially *for use:* earth and sea are for use, either in war or peace. In such a statement there is nothing of a reverence or an awe before something greater than man or even merely alien to him; nor is there any hesitation involved in balancing various intricate factors, some subject to human control and some not, which can go to the resolution of a military dilemma. There is the starkly bare statement of basic determining areas of conflict and power. Athens is master, absolute master, of one element. She is therefore virtually bound to win the war, in a land like Greece where in war or in peace the sea is the source of power. These speeches are exceedingly direct, and man is the center of the universe in the mouth of the speaker and the minds of the hearers.

Yet there is a very remarkable impersonality in the man-made object, the city for which the human sacrifice is demanded. The fathers and mothers who have lost their sons are urged to have more children: "For as far as you are concerned as individuals the children that are successors to those that are gone shall be a forgetfulness of these, and, for the state, this will profit her doubly, since she will not be left empty of men and shall be safer besides; for there is no giving of just or even counsel on the part of those who risk their children on the consequences of their advice and those who do not: these two parties are not on the same footing." Here we see that the reason for new children is largely at least to preserve the city and not only in respect to numbers but, subtly, because only those who have their most precious human possessions to lose will take sufficient thought for the considerations of state policy! The more one thinks of this, the more one sees that the city, "the praises of which, as I have spoken of them, are such in virtue of the fair deeds of her sons," is not only man-made; she has attained an independent existence such that her preservation means more than the happiness or misery of all her inhabitants.

This position is still considerably removed from the forms of state worship we have come to know later, because, in the first place, it is a state the total scope of which is itself—it does not, for Pericles, embody an ideal that is greater than it; and, in the second place, he contemplates its destruction at some future day, when the glory of it will be the only thing left.

"You must realize that your city has the greatest renown among all mankind for not yielding to misfortune, that it has spent more men's bodies and pains on war than any other, and that it has obtained the greatest power that the world has yet seen up to now. Even if we shall one day in this time come to disaster—and this we may, for everything that is born decays too— the memory of that power shall be everlasting: that we were Greeks and ruled more Greeks than any others had; that in the greatest wars we held our own against them all and individually; and that our city was the greatest and the most abundant in everything." You must disregard the hatred of your subjects, he says, for "hatred does not abide for long, but the brilliance you have now and the repute hereafter are all that are left for everlasting memory."

The bareness of this, in all its abstractness, is terrible enough. Glory is all that remains, yet the glory is not of the victory of a principle, a faith, or a civilization; it is glory that attaches ultimately to defeat as well as to victory, a memory held in awe, in which the blackest deeds against Greek morality have their place as truly as the love of beauty and wisdom, the story of a city whose greatness is lovely and untouchable, created by man but not responsible to him, knowing no God and no life beyond itself.

And Thucydides' conception of his own worth as a writer is closely linked with the value he saw in the war and its political setting. Slowly and painfully he left behind the values of the poets and the logographers. He did not want to entertain nor did he wish to record great and glorious events, "that their memory might not be lost from among men . . . or fail of their due distinction." That which is true and that which is permanent are what he wanted to record, and what was true and permanent in the nature of man reflected in the deeds of fifth-century Greece was rarely entertaining and hardly ever glorious. Harsh, brutal, and bloody as the deeds were, he must face them with no comforting possibility of moralizing them away against a prospect of a necessarily brighter future or a universal good

design of divine origin. To realize them in their true meaning, to divest himself of hope of things different and of unmeaning resentment at things as they were, to cling bitterly and doggedly to explaining the cold-bloodedness and brutality in terms that could at least be verified after the fashion of his world, became the whole duty of the historian. As his work attained its peculiar austere perfection, perhaps Thucydides felt a kinship with Pericles, who sought no glory and no reward except in the creation of something greater than himself, yet a something rooted in the brutal truths of the life around him.

Pericles is great because, though he rose on the fear and greed of his countrymen, though the empire he built was built on fear and greed, he and perhaps it transcended this fear and greed. He feared nothing and was greedy for nothing. He cowed the people when they were overconfident and heartened them when they were downcast. Everyone knew that money could not tempt him. And it is because of this that he stood above all his fellows, and it is through the defect of this quality of disinterestedness that his successors reduced all again to the level of their fears and greeds and ruined both the state and themselves.

And the city of Athens, the national equivalent of Pericles among individuals? Is she not the school of Greece? However she may have robbed the allies to build the Parthenon and robbed the Greek city-states of the freedom they treasured, she had become, as the Funeral Speech indicates, something greater than all this. She had become a model of human society, tolerant and gracious, now that the days of conquering were over. In the Athens of Pericles Thucydides saw something great and admirable which compelled his intellectual homage and his emotional acceptance as nothing else did. If one believed that the history of man politically is a story of greed, strife, and fear, and their working in the society created by them, there was still a time when these passions had for a historical moment been immobilized in a balanced beauty and strength, and Periclean Athens was this historical moment. The enormous wealth which the commercial democracy alone could create—as Thucydides so well knew—was here to set off dramatically the symbols of Athenian rule: The Athenian can eat at his table the fruits of the ends of the earth as commonly as the olives of neighboring Attica.

Yet the democracy whose dynamic was greed and fear and whose might was the offspring of that greed and fear was held in check by a single autocrat whose rule it accepted because he was not as other men were. In this voluntary acquiescence of the vulgar, in this submission to the statesman who neither flattered nor feared them but who put heart into them or made them tremble with the witchcraft of his own aloof certainty, Thucydides may have seen the transcendence of the materialism in which he believed. Here was power as it truthfully was, based on fear, pride, and greed, yet it touched something too magical for measurement.

F. E. Adcock (essay date 1963)

SOURCE: in *Thucydides and His History,* Cambridge at the University Press, 1963, pp. 27-57.

[*In the following excerpt, Adcock first analyses Thucydides' manner of presentation: he contends that the speeches present a dialectical movement through argument and persuasion, proceeding indirectly towards the final purpose. Adcock posits that purpose second: the history makes an ethical argument about the primacy of civic life over private life.*]

THE SPEECHES

Thucydides has told his readers what they are to think about the content of the speeches either in the first part or the whole of his work. When he wrote the sentence is not known for certain, whether it was before he began to write the narrative which follows, or after he had written his account of the antecedents of the war that broke out in 431 or at some later date after he had had a quorum of experience in writing the **History** or, perhaps more probably, when he had written his account of the Ten Years War or, even conceivably, at the end of the twenty-seven years that began in 431 B.C. and went on until the fall of Athens. It is wise to suppose that he meant what he said and was at pains to say what he meant.

If this is so, then his readers have been warned that the speeches are not, and could not be for reasons stated, the *ipsissima verba* of the speakers.

This does not imply that, if he had before him a complete record of what was actually said, he would have decided to reproduce it, even after a sort of translation of the words into his own style and dialect, and so give the actual text of what was said. We are told, indeed, that, in composing his speeches, the historian kept as closely as possible to 'the overall purport or purpose of what was actually said', written in such a way as to coincide with his opinion of what the several speakers would most likely have presented to their hearers as being 'what the situation required'. The reference to his own opinion presents a limiting factor one way, as his reference to the 'overall purport or purpose of what was actually said' is a limiting factor in another way. Thus, when the procedure has been applied, the reader will know something at least of what the historian regarded as what the situation required and an approximation at least to what was actually said. Thucydides limits his knowledge in terms of the difficulty (or even impossibility) of remembering precisely what was said.

The speeches to which this *caveat* applies are speeches which he heard himself or of which he received reports from others who were present when and where speeches were made. Frailty of memory would only concern him where he inserts a speech in his history, and it is natural to assume that he does not in fact insert speeches of which he cannot have had at any rate some information. So far as this procedure is applied, it seems to preclude the insertion of speeches when he does not know something at least of what was actually said. This means that, where this procedure applies, all the speeches we have are based upon some knowledge. Under this procedure no speech would appear where no speech was made, for no one can have any knowledge of a speech which never existed.

To insert speeches with no knowledge at all of their actual content would be so notable a departure from this procedure that it is very difficult to believe that he would not have warned his readers that such a departure has been made. A very heavy burden of proof rests upon those who assert that this happened, and a study of the relevant circumstances strongly suggests that Thucydides did not insert in his history speeches which are wholly fictitious in the sense that they have no basis whatever of ascertained fact. And it is very difficult to escape from the conclusion that at whatever time he announced this procedure he intended it to apply to the whole work in which it occurs.

It may be possible to suppose that, at times, he took more freedom in the interpretation of what material he had, but hardly possible to suppose that this freedom extended to the insertion of speeches which are wholly imaginary and without any basis of ascertained fact. There may be differences between the closeness to reality of different speeches varying with Thucydides' sources of information.

For example, as regards the speech of Sthenelaidas at Sparta, if Thucydides was informed of the exceptional voting procedure applied by the ephor, he would presumably also be informed of 'the overall purport and purpose of what was actually said' by him. Here and there, it is just possible that Thucydides assumed that a general encouraged his troops before battle, as Nicias is said to do before the first engagement against the Syracusan levies, and that he felt himself on firm ground when he attributed to Nicias the encouragement of saying that his army was more experienced than the Syracusan levies, as became almost apparent by the course of the battle. It was so much what the situation required that he might conceivably have taken it for granted. But this ought not to apply to deliberative speeches on policy.

It is often asserted that such a deliberative speech could not have taken its present form because no Assembly could have followed the arguments as they listened to the orator declaiming them. But the speeches we possess are not so unintelligible as that, even if they require the reader to give close attention to what he read. What Thucydides wrote is for his readers to peruse at their leisure with the text before them, and with the custom of reading aloud, so that they could study their meaning with knowledge of where their study was difficult. The writer may diverge from the *ipsissima verba* of the speeches, but does his best 'to come as nearly as possible' to what matters most, 'the overall purport or purpose of what was actually said'. It is not enough to say that he restricted himself to what the speakers were convinced was *true,* for now and again he makes a speaker say something which he knows the speaker cannot have believed to be true or something which he himself cannot have believed to be true in fact. He is well aware that speakers making a case for some policy or action may say things which neither the historian nor the speaker believe to be true. The simplest and most certain example of this is the false statement attributed to Brasidas about the identity of his army before Acanthus with his army before Megara some months before. Brasidas must have known that it was false, and Thucydides in a later passage says that it was, and this could not be due to information not yet at his disposal when he wrote the speech he attributes to Brasidas. Brasidas, too, knew at the time that it was false, although his Acanthian hearers did not. Where there was a difference between what appears in a speech and what has appeared in the narrative we must suppose that the truth as Thucydides sees it is to be found in the narrative, which is directed to the statement of what happened in a way the words of an orator may not be. It is a fault in method to treat these statements otherwise, and not to admit that a speech may contain a statement at variance with the facts, but 'an approximation to the purport or purpose of what was in fact said', and that is all.

These considerations do not greatly diminish the value to a historian of what appears in a speech: what is needed is a critical and careful evaluation of what the reader reads, after the warning which he has received. A speaker may therefore fail to give the truth, the whole truth and nothing but the truth, but what is given deserves close attention within the limits which Thucydides has set himself after giving the reader warning of what he is doing.

As a rule, the circumstances of speeches, when carefully studied, reveal a *possibility* of this required quota of knowledge. This possibility applies to speeches which scholars have declared to possess no such basis of knowledge as gives to them an element at least of authenticity. It may be illustrated by three instances of speeches in which any element of authenticity has often been denied.

Take first the speech of Athenian envoys at the first Conference at Sparta. That Athenian envoys were present and were allowed to intervene is stated as a fact of equal authority with other events which are being described. It is *a priori* probable that Pericles would wish to know what was being said at Sparta. It was not alien from Greek procedure to admit their presence and to allow them to speak. If they were not present and so did not speak, the statement that they were would be known to be false by the time at which he may have expected to publish his account of the war to which they were a preamble: whatever we may think of the suitability of the speech, it is very rash to deny that a speech was made by Athenian envoys.

Secondly, we may consider the Plataean and Theban speeches after the surrender of the city. That speeches were made is beyond serious doubt. But how could Thucydides have any direct knowledge about their content and general purport or purpose? As for the Plataean speech, Thucydides, in a way that is an exception to his usual practice, names the speakers. One of them was Lacon, *proxenos* of Sparta, who could very properly have been in favour of capitulation on terms which included a fair judgment by the Spartans. If that was so, he could affirm that he had done Sparta a service, for the capitulation was in Sparta's interests. And if he did, his life would be spared and so the historians could discover at first or second hand the gist of his plea. As for what the Thebans said in reply, this could be known to him at least as soon as the armistice of 423-422 enabled the historian to make inquiries about it, at Thebes or elsewhere. It need not be just a fictitious refutation of what the Plataeans said.

Finally, we reach the Melian Dialogue (V, 85-113). The occasion is not just a fiction. That there were negotiations is beyond doubt. It was the duty of the Athenian generals to secure, if possible, the surrender of the city without recourse to a siege. And the Dialogue is highly realistic and to the point for that purpose. The general trend of the arguments on either side was known to the Athenian negotiators, who would report to Athens, not, of course, in a *procès-verbal* of the discussions but their general character, if only to show they had done their best for their purpose.

The same would be true of the report which the Melian representatives must have made to their fellow citizens, some of whom, if only those who betrayed the city, were spared. We must also suppose that the first thing the Melians did before the Athenian lines were drawn round their city was to send to Sparta to ask for help, reporting at least the trend of the negotiations. If so, this could reach Thucydides, who, if he was not at Sparta at the time could find out what was known there from whatever source. If this is so, and the possibility seems to be beyond doubt, Thucydides *could* procure the knowledge that he needed in order to recount, in the form of a dialogue, the general course of the discussion.

These are important instances of speeches, or of a dialogue as a substitute for set speeches, which scholars have too hastily regarded as going wholly beyond the historian's knowledge. He could know enough for his purpose, which was to assist his readers to study 'the plain reality of what happened'.

Granted that in all, or practically all, the speeches there is an authentic element, there is to be found also a stylistic character which is uniform throughout them all. This is immediately apparent, and does not require justification. It is assumed that his readers are familiar with the old-fashioned Attic which is used for the narrative. There is no attempt at the *vraisemblance* that might be suggested by a variation between the vocabulary and syntactical usage of Pericles or any other Athenian of the day and the laconic Doric in which we assume the kings or ephors would address the Spartan Apella. The army which Archidamus addressed at the Isthmus before the invasion of Attica contained officers who spoke in the dialects of their cities; the troops of Brasidas were in part helots, in part men from Peloponnesian states, but it would not occur to a Greek reader that they might not all equally well understand what their commander was saying. What mattered was the reader. This diction was not an absolute rule, or a literary convention from which Thucydides could not free himself, as he does when it comes to the citation of a treaty written in Doric in v, 77 and 79. It was convenient, the more as the argumentation used by the historian was conceived of in his own speech as well as thought.

This argumentation proceeds throughout in much the same manner with the use of gnomic generalizations to assist the deployment of the dialectic which is uniform throughout as is the addiction to antitheses, above all between 'word' and 'act'. The vulgarian Cleon can echo what Pericles had been made to say with the same forcible dignity. Now and again, in some terse and bold, almost contemptuous, aphorism, we may seem to hear Alcibiades, or Nicias in the words of his conventional piety. If the style may be the man, the man may use the style, but with economical delicacy of touch. To the dialectical force of a Pericles Cleon may add his natural violence, the partner of his persuasiveness. The moral is that Thucydides is the master of his own style and not the slave of any literary convention.

One hint of his masterful way is a liking for paradox, which, as it were, calls to attention the hearers of the speeches by a sharp emphasis which challenges normality. The historian had taken with him into exile a formed and consistent style which, indurated by constant use, stayed with him to the end of his work.

There is one apparent change in the historian's practice which it is not easy to explain. In Book v between Brasidas' speech before the battle of Amphipolis and the Melian Dialogue, and throughout the whole of Book VIII, no set speeches occur. It has been thought that Book VIII was unfinished and would have contained speeches had it received its final form. But when its diction is examined, it does not appear to be less finished than some other of the books. Some scholars have stressed a pronouncement attributed to Cratippus that the historian decided to abandon the use of set speeches because they hampered the pace of the narrative and presented difficulties to the readers [Dionysius of Halicarnassus]. There is no agreement whether Cratippus was a younger contemporary of Thucydides and so might have been in his counsels, or whether he was a later writer who was just giving his own deduction from the absence of set speeches, a deduction which is no more than his own. The most probable explanation is that Book VIII contains no debate of the first importance and that if Thucydides had thought of introducing such a debate at the time of the oligarchical revolution of 411 B.C. he might have preferred to wait until he could obtain more information on his hoped-for return to Athens. For whatever reason he did not carry out this intention: there is no sign that he introduced into his work matter to be discovered later at Athens, such as is cited in Aristotle's *Constitution of Athens* (29 ff.).

The oligarchic revolution was shortlived and transient in its effects, and Thucydides may have been content with what is found in Book VIII as we have it. In that book we find more of Thucydides' judgment of the personalities and of their policies than elsewhere in the works, and this, taken in conjunction with some reports of speeches in *Oratio Obliqua,* may have seemed to give what was required. And if no more seemed needed, Thucydides may have spared himself the labour of composing set speeches.

It may be that this explanation may apply to a part of Book v after the Peace of Nicias if Thucydides wrote those chapters before he came to believe that they were an integral part of his whole work, so that he wrote with less *élan* and intensity of purpose than in earlier books. There are twelve set speeches in Books VI and VII, but these were written as belonging to a theme notable in its own right and then as part of a *crescendo* of emphasis as the expedition proceeded.

There is one speech, the *Epitaphios* of Pericles, which on one theory was written after the fall of Athens in protest against a movement that belittled Pericles and Periclean Athens with him. This theory gives to the speech a dramatic effect, partly as a contrast between the bright hopes of 431 B.C. and the dark shadow of the Plague in the next year, and partly as a contrast between the high hopes with which the war began and the disaster which overtook Athens at the end of the whole period of twenty-seven years. There may be discovered an elegiac note in the passage in which it is hinted that sacrifices it commemorates may be in vain. Years ago I accepted this thesis [*Cambridge Ancient History*], but it now seems to me that I was mistaken in following what, at that time, was the dominant view, supported as it was by great names such as Eduard Meyer. It now appears to me that it was written in 431 B.C., while the voice of Pericles still sounded in the historian's ears—the authentic echo of what was demanded of the citizens in that hour. It is then, as other speeches are, closely linked to the situation of the moment, when the first year of the war had appeared to justify Periclean strategy. The fact that few Athenians had fallen in the cavalry skirmishes of that summer does not make it less worthy of record. Athens still stood splendid and united in love for the city, and this, together with the character of Athenian society, is celebrated at that very moment as it deserved. The moral declension that was to be described in the third book was still in the future.

There is one more point that deserves mention in this context. The almost amateurish courage of the Athenians is proclaimed as a match for the long-studied discipline of Sparta and her army. It is not easy to believe that this claim would have been made after the indiscipline and folly of Aegospotami had thrown away Athens' last hope of survival. Would not a speech so confident and so proud have seemed bitter irony to the historian if it was then that he wrote the speech? Thus, difficult as it is to be sure, it now seems to me that the picture of the high summer of Athenian power and warlike confidence was written at the moment when it was true. That bravery and self-devotion cannot command success is part of the historian's philosophy of war, and praise is due to those who meet the dangers of the moment, whatever the ultimate outcome may prove to be among the paradoxes and vicissitudes from which no war is exempt.

Whatever our conclusion may be about the date at which the Funeral Speech was written, it does not resolve a question which is perhaps beyond solution. This is how far the speech is dictated by Thucydides' own view of Athens and how far by his admiration for Pericles which led him to allow Pericles to think for him, so that we may only find in the speech praise of a community of which Pericles had been the spiritual and intellectual begetter. What may come nearest to the truth may be the conclusion that what Thucydides admired and what Pericles accepted with pride was 'in name a democracy, in deed rule exercised by the first citizen'. More will be said about this in a later chapter.

We may now turn to a group of speeches which may be considered by themselves. A battle, and a hoplite battle in particular, often began with generals' speech-es on both sides. In a hoplite battle the speech is, as it were, part of the battle-cry which started the charge. Thucydides at Mantinea in 418 B.C. notes that the Spartans do not need this tonic and it is their business to keep their heads so as to be able to swing inwards and not merely rush at the enemy. The object of the speech before such a battle is to give the troops confidence in themselves, their cause and, incidentally, their general. It may go back to the Homeric practice of a man launching a phrase before he launches his spear or his close-quarters attack. But it has a more practical effect. In a naval battle, where signalling is difficult, it is desirable for the captains on ships to know the general's plan for the battle. It is also encouragement to discipline and obedience to orders or to dispel some cause of discouragement. But in smaller encounters Thucydides does not provide a general's speech, and hardly ever a pair of speeches, one to each side. In the two speeches of the Peloponnesian admirals and of Phormio in the Corinthian Gulf, the Peloponnesians are told to trust to their courage to make up for lack of trained skill, the Athenians to trust to discipline and trained skill to make up for their inferior numbers. The speech of Demosthenes at Pylos is answered not by a formal speech before the Spartan attack but by the vehement call of Brasidas to force a landing at all costs. Before Delium the speech of Pagondas is about why they should fight, of Hippocrates why they should hope to win. Before Trafalgar Nelson's signal in effect reminds the crews of their long acquired obedience to orders and of their reputation. It in a way combines the effect of both sets of speeches in the Corinthian Gulf.

Sometimes there is only one speech, that of the general who is about to win a victory or achieve a military success. The account of the battle is made more intelligible by the knowledge of what the general wanted to do. Sometimes there may be no speech because the general has not grasped the situation or because it changes after the operations have begun. For example, Demosthenes in Aetolia is not given a speech because he did not make one or anticipate the course of the fighting. At Sphacteria there are no speeches. Demosthenes does not explain beforehand how he proposes to achieve his purpose for no such speech is needed or could do good. Before Amphipolis Brasidas makes a speech, but Cleon, who was not expecting to fight, did not for he hardly directs the course of the battle. The two battle speeches, in Illyria and before Amphipolis, of Brasidas help to indicate his psychological appreciation of the enemy and of his own troops, and the speech of Phormio underlines the reason for Athenian naval supremacy and does not explain the course of the engagement that followed because this is not yet known. The speech of the Peloponnesian admirals before the battle underlines the theme of natural courage, rather than of the tactics which were going to be used. The speech of Demosthenes underlines the value of hope, when it is the only thing that helps. 'Hope is not a good guide, but is a good companion on the way.' It sets a determined Athenian against a determined Spartan. The speech of Nicias before the first engagement with the Syracusans states the fact that the experienced Athenian army can expect to be superior to a levy *en masse* of Syracusans. There is no Syracusan speech (perhaps because Thucydides did not know what they said, perhaps because there was no time for it to be made). Pagondas before Delium underlines his will to fight, and suggests that the Athenians had perhaps underrated the Boeotians' determination, so that the attack, of itself, would produce a psychological effect on the Athenians.

Sometimes the purpose of the speech is to underline the importance of the battle and the tactical chances of either side, as in the speeches before the battle in the Great Harbour. One might have expected a speech by Demosthenes before the night attack on Epipolae, but that was not a battle that really went according to plan and it is of course possible that Demosthenes in order to make sure of the advantage of surprise did not make a speech but concerted his plan secretly with the separate commanders. The speech of Nicias before the retreat (VII, 77) is part of the characterization of Nicias and stresses the gravity and indeed tragedy of the retreat.

Where battle is not actually joined there are no general's speeches. The letter of Nicias to the Athenians is not so much a speech as the Thucydidean account of the situation as Nicias saw it. The two speeches of Pericles which discuss the strategical balance of the sides in a future war are concerned with policy and overall strategy and not with battle tactics. It looks as if Thucydides felt he needed to know something of what was said to put his speech in the frame of an immediate operation. In general, Greek battles depended more on morale than on tactics, and the morale of troops is one branch of that psychological observation of human nature and behaviour that was Thucydides' constant study. In particular he makes the generals' speeches fit the psychology of the general and that of his troops. He underlines the awareness that Athenian troops have a quality of *élan* which may be brittle if anything happened to upset them. He has a valuation of the military quality of troops of different cities. The tactical conduct of the battle is not anticipated but is left to be revealed by the course of the engagement which follows, and this is true of the speeches of Brasidas to his troops before the battle in Illyria and the battle before Amphipolis.

THUCIDIDEAN DIALECTIC

Thucydides had grown up in a period in which men were prone to think by way of argument, by the shock of one thesis colliding with another. The notion that there are two sides to every question was an assump-

tion preached by Protagoras, and illustrated in the *Clouds of Aristophanes*. It is obvious that statesmen in a community where decisions are reached by persuading a concourse of citizens to vote one way or another must prevail by argument which appeals to them. A general must make his troops so think and feel that their action will match the purpose of their commander. In most battles a vehement self-confidence, however induced, gives the best chance of victory. The Orders of the Day of the Emperor Napoleon or Field-Marshal Montgomery aim at achieving this. An army that lost heart had lost the battle. In the deliberations led by statemen something based more on intellectual calculation was required and dialectic was here the art of magnifying the advantages and minimizing the disadvantages of any particular policy or course of action. To achieve this result any argument that could persuade was the right argument, and veracity, the servant and not the master of argument, is a weapon among others, a means and not an end.

At the time when Thucydides was learning his trade, a most potent argument was the argument from probability, which, as Aristotle was to say in his *Rhetoric,* relies upon the confusion of a general with a particular probability. More and more, the Greeks had become vulnerable to the lures of this argument which was now practised in the courts. Hence we may expect to find, as we do, that speeches often begin with a generalizing maxim, of which the present thesis is asserted to be an instance. Prone to believe that what is often true is always true, a Greek Assembly might be attuned to an orator's purpose. A skilful use of this dialectical argument may flatter, while it deceives, the hearer's intelligence. The converse of this, an apparent paradox, appeals to the quick-witted, for it suggests that the hearer is cleverer than his neighbours. It is thus asserted that a man who allows something to happen is as responsible as a man who takes positive action to bring it about. This is not always so in real life, but it is tempting to believe it with an uncritical readiness. It is what Bacon might have called an *idolum fori.* A sharp distinction between what is said and what is actual fact is an argument in itself, and this distinction had to Thucydides an especial appeal, for the opposition is highly intelligible. So is the distinction drawn between what is expedient and what is just; each of the two is persuasive and each is governed by its own *rationale,* and where they can be allied, their strength is great. Where their force is unequal, either may be stressed and prove decisive.

There is one oratorical device which is not often found in speeches because of the economy of the work. The speeches are concerned with particular situations which have been described in the narrative of the events that led up to them. As a rule, the veracity of the narrative is to be assumed and what it contains can be taken as read so as to predispose the hearer to accept the speaker's arguments. There may be exceptions to this general rule if the ignorance of the audience can be practised upon. Brasidas, in his speech at Acanthus (IV, 86-7), is represented as making a false statement about the size of his army because, as Grote observed, [in his *History of Greece*], its falsity cannot be discovered before the decision is taken. To judge from the speech attributed to Brasidas before the battle of Amphipolis, this mendacity would appear to him to be a legitimate *ruse de guerre,* such as befits the skill of a shrewd general.

It has been argued that the historian sets himself to make his speakers say what they in their heart of hearts believe. But to do that might be to injure their case, and this injury is something they must avoid at all costs.

It has also been argued that the historian's dialectic is used to indicate what he himself believed, so as to correct his narrative. If this be so, it belies what he says has been his practice. When he refers to his own opinion it is not his opinion of what was true but what the situation would have required a speaker to say, and these need not be identical. Themistocles is said to have had a singular capacity for improvising what the situation required of him, but that might often be a lie, from which he, of all men, would least shrink.

The dialectical methods of Thucydides are at the disposal of either side in a debate, and so are used impartially to reinforce either. All is fair in war, and, proverbially, 'war is impartial', favouring neither one side nor the other. A speech is like a missile which has one single purpose, to hit its target. The man who throws the spear should be able to see his mark, and Thucydides gives him eyes to see it. The dialectical skill put at the disposal of a speaker will raise his actual arguments to a higher power. Thus the reader will best judge the case for either side, and so appreciate the validity of either thesis. Hence the validity or wisdom of whatever case prevailed. Thucydides is aware that the right thing may be done for the wrong reason, but his readers will be the wiser if they are given the arguments in their most cogent and persuasive form.

But set speeches are not the only way to illuminate the *rationale* of actions. It is apparent that in the narrative of events it is rare for Thucydides to commend or to condemn. The plain and intelligible record of events leaves the reader to use his own judgment, but, now and again, narrative is so phrased as to indicate a judgment, when an action succeeds or fails according to the actors' view of what was required. Demosthenes' adventure in Aetolia appears to fail because he would not wait to secure the help of troops who would be best fitted to bring it to success. The dialectic of action or inaction illuminates the situation.

The fortune of war, in its paradoxical way, may make good plans fail and bed plans succeed, but it belongs

to the clear story of what happened to indicate at times whether the plans were good or bad. The Spartans on Sphacteria are killed or captured within twenty days, but the promise to achieve this is condemned as 'lunatic'. Herein, it is argued that success is not the one criterion of military skill and insight. This judgment of Cleon's promise may be inspired by malice, but that may not make it any less cogent or less instructive to the future general, who will learn his trade by studying what happened in the past and how it happened. In the account of the night attack on Epipolae, the plain tale of what happened will teach, what the history of war has so often taught, that few operations are so hazardous and unpromising as night attacks, even if in war 'bad may be the best'. All this is the application of the historian's own study of what happened.

This illumination may be provided by the historian's choice of what to emphasize and what to leave unrecorded. In the first year of the War the Athenians invaded the Megarid, and this is fully described, for it is part of the counter-offensive which will raise Athenian morale. Thucydides came to know that something of this kind happened in each of the next six years and he says so, but in no one of these years does he mention it, for the effect was progressively smaller. You cannot cut down the same olive tree twice. What matters is what matters. The light falls where there is something worth seeing, something worth notice, and of that the historian is the judge.

Here and there, evidence from other sources shows that Thucydides has failed to mention events of which he may be presumed to have some knowledge. The reasons for this are matters of legitimate conjecture, and where a probable reason can be found it deserves consideration in judging how Thucydides argued to himself what he would present to his readers for their future study. He was a highly autonomous man, who made his own rules for himself and must not be too readily assumed to be dominated by the literary conventions of his successors in the field of history.

Those who assert that Thucydides was precluded from citing the text of a treaty by a stylistic rule must have regard to the fact that he sometimes does so. He might, in a final revision, have preferred to put things otherwise, but that would be his second thoughts or even his third. We can only surmise that what we have was not always his last word. The assumption that his readers would be wholly baffled by the sight of the original text of a treaty in the Doric dialect is refuted by what appears in the *Acharnians* and the *Lysistrata* of Aristophanes.

The upshot of all this is that Thucydides' practice was, as it would naturally be, to describe things as he saw them and thought it best to say them, subject to a strong intention not to allow himself to be deceived by the frailties of others. An interesting contrast is to be found in the description of the attack on Sphacteria, which shows no sign of being described so as to attribute its success either to chance, or to Demosthenes as distinct from Cleon. In the dictum that follows his condemnation of Cleon's promise, namely that men of judgment welcomed the alternatives of securing the prisoners or of being rid of Cleon, Thucydides indulges his disapproval of Cleon at a point where he was not inhibited by his duty to his narrative of operations.

In the narrative, then, he seeks to be precise, to avoid in himself the faults he observes in others. His facts are caught up and preserved in a fine web of thought. For he is writing, not to satisfy what seems to him irrelevant curiosity, but to assist by his own judgment and presentation 'the study of those who will give their minds to understand how it actually happened', which may be 'why it happened at all'. And he sees events as one great dialectical argument in which human intelligence is the final arbiter in the seat of judgment. *Securus iudicat.*

THUCYDIDEAN ETHICS AND POLITICS

Thucydides was a rich man of good birth and aristocratic connections, an Athenian citizen. His normal ethical standards may be assumed to be those of his class, and there is nothing in his work to prove they were not. In politics—How should a city's governors be chosen? Pericles in the Funeral Speech approves of equality of opportunity in state affairs. But only 'of opportunity'. Men of talent are not excluded from office by poverty, but they are chosen to have authority only if they seem worthy of it. It is possible this is what Pericles said without its being what Thucydides himself thought. But it seems Thucydidean: to him the city comes first, the individual citizen second, and, as the city needs talent wherever it can find it among the citizens, he would not wish to see its area of choice limited. Without 'disparity of esteem' the right men might not be chosen. It was true that, for various purposes, citizens were treated as equal, whether they were or not, especially in membership of the Council or the jury courts. But with these Thucydides is hardly concerned. What matters in a war is the quality of generals, in the field and at home, and those are not chosen by lot. For special missions also men are chosen by direct choice.

The Assembly is, at least in theory, sovereign and it has the last word. The Demos meeting in Assembly has its faults: it is mutable, excitable and, as a body, it may be gullible. 'It is easier to mislead many men than one' [Herodotus, V, 97, 2]. But it was persuadable by skilful argument, of which it was a good judge, and might be obedient to authority based on personal ascendancy and the courageous use of it. Without such guidance it may go astray. Remove its guide and what

is left may be false lights, and this cannot be denied. So democracy might be foolish, unthinking, and, as is said in Alcibiades' speech at Sparta, there is nothing new to say about it. Its salvation is to be persuaded into right decisions by the wise, by men who think of the city first and their own material advantage second, if at all. Of Pericles, whom Thucydides admired, it is said that his patriotism and his incorruptibility reinforced his eloquence, his foresight and his courage.

To possess these qualities is the mark of a true statesman, the kind of man for whom Thucydides' history was written; without these qualities, the cleverest of men may be suspect and so not be followed, however wise their policies may be. What was wrong with Alcibiades is that he was not like Pericles, though, when at a crisis he put the city first, he is praised for what, in that moment, he was.

The city comes first: the interests of the city come first, and whatever does not serve these interests is a bad thing and not a good. The practice of private virtue, inhibited by private scruples, if it limits the city's power or disregards its interests, is dismissed with an ironical, contemptuous phrase. When private virtues—courage, self-abnegation, honesty, a simple-mindedness that has a large ingredient of nobility, serve the community, they are highly praised: but only then. In great affairs of state, civic virtue—courage and devotion—is the one virtue that claims pre-eminence. When the war has begun, this is what Athens can claim to inspire in all her citizens, above all a passionate devotion which goes over all.

To turn from the citizen to the city: the city embodies power, and power grows from power and from nothing else. No other interests may prevail against it; no other criterion is in place. The ancient mythical past of Athens was full of stories of generosity, the protection of the weak, but in the present the exhibition of these qualities is limited by the immediate interests of the state. If moderation is politic, a means to create a more lasting power, it is a virtue, but only then.

To be admired is a legitimate ambition, but as the spring of courage, the spur of action, in the public interest. The virtue of a citizen is aristocratic virtue, democratically used if your state is democratic. That was true of Athens in its bright day, and much of it survived in its dark day. When men are attuned to it, it produces greatness in a city and it becomes human nature on the highest plane. This is not an ethical ideal, to be inculcated for its own sake, but as an ingredient in Athens' greatness. The sharing of it unites a state: what divides a state, above all civil strife, is its enemy. Thus civic virtue is easiest preserved in peace; it is endangered by the compulsions of war. But if the security and interests of the city lead to war, this danger must be endured.

Thucydides observes a progressive decline in ethical standards as war and civil strife continue. This appears to be inevitable, so that it becomes a reasonable expectation that men will behave worse and worse both in public and private—private ambition, partisan passion, disloyalty to the state become common, and new standards of behaviour, even new words of praise or blame, reflect this decline.

Intellectual force on this lower plane may still exist, effective for its own purposes. Courage retains its value and extorts admiration from the historian, and so does the subordination of personal ambition and party feeling to the interests of the city in war. A compromise government that helps Athenian resistance for a time is highly praised. But this spirit of compromise is rare and short-lived and throughout the history it becomes rare and rarer. Having observed the degeneration of civic ethics set out in phase after phase, he has shown the true meaning of what has happened and so the historian has done his task. We are told of the symptoms and effect of this great *malaise* as we are told the same of the great plague, where, too, there is praise for self-denying patriotic courage of those who rose above the demoralization that the plague induced.

The historian has an intellectual distaste for professions belied by acts and he explains Spartan bad faith to the Plataeans by regarding it as an unworthy surrender to the Thebans, who are made as hateful as the Plataeans are made, at least, pitiable. But it is to be observed he does not hesitate to make a Spartan say what is untrue if that is what his case requires. His diligent desire to reach and speak the truth about events did not make him subordinate the needs of war, in which all is fair, to the cause of veracity.

There is a sense in which Thucydides may justly be described as a student of ethics of communities, but this does not deny his firm belief that great states will pursue greatness with the profoundest egotism: for that is the nature of cities, comparable with the nature of men.

It is not plain to see that Thucydides, throughout all his history, has any declared preference for this or that form of constitution. He observes, almost without comment, the hostility of the many to the few and of the few to the many, assumed by the author of the pseudo-Xenophontic *Constitution of Athens* and, later, elevated to a dogma by Aristotle.

In general, Thucydides judges men by their purposes, rather than by the means, however unscrupulous, they use to attain them, and as the process of ethical decline continues he becomes apt to take for granted a personal egotism which matches community or party egotism. In place of men subordinating their interests to the city he expects that they will subordinate the city to their interests, or to their hostility to men they dis-

trust or dislike. The failure to use the abilities of Alcibiades as a director of warlike resources is made responsible for Athenian defeats and in the end to the final overthrow of Athens. Democracy without Pericles, once it is filled with jealous rivalries, does not deserve to survive, but oligarchy is not the cure; it is another form of the disease. Thucydides may have agreed with Pope:

> For forms of government let fools contest;
> Whate'er is best administered, is best.

The one criterion that has validity in war is the effective management of the war. The one consolation for defeat is past greatness and courage in adversity. Greatness, the domination and exploitation of others, cannot be forgone. It is better to have ruled and lost, than never to have ruled at all.

Some scholars have hoped to find in Thucydides a Panhellenic patriotism, a search for national unity and sympathy of Greek for Greek. But of this it is hard to find a clear trace. There is pride in the Athenian share of the defence of Greece against the Persians, but that is above all a pride in warlike resolution and resource, the act, not the cause. And the great possession of Athens that could not be taken away was the memory that she had ruled over more Greeks than any other city and had fought more wars to bring it about and preserve it. Old traditions of benevolence and generosity on the part of Athens are silent. What remains and lasts for ever is the memory of courage, resilience in adversity, and resolution and 'what is else not to be overcome'.

To all seeming, Thucydides never supposed that the gods intervened in human affairs or, if they ever did, their action, as that of Chance, was unpredictable. He valued conformity with the state religion as a social bond, a kind of preservative of traditional ethics, which, moulded by the community, had value for the state. When Nicias perished, his end was the more lamentable, not because he was not to blame for it, but because his faith in Heaven had been misplaced. The historian's strong conviction that human events are guided by human wits and will preserved him from substituting a predestined Nemesis for the study of what happened and why. Men should not blind themselves; and he did not blind himself either. Things are what they are, and men have made them so.

This realism does not mean that his heart did not ever stir within him. When the Athenians decreed the massacre of the Mityleneans, he described the decree as 'savage and monstrous', not arguing that it was so, but simply describing it as any sensible or civilized man would have described it. To him needless cruelty was odious, the more because anger darkens the mind. Though, when it comes to that, Cleon's decree is refuted by cool dispassionate *raison d' État,* in which the plea of pity is disclaimed. Thucydides is not silent about the Athenian repentance, for he knew that without its presence and effect the Athenians might well have committed what he believed to be at once a crime and a blunder. His native way of thinking was to avoid emotional excess, and an excess of passion is the enemy of reason, which is the path of wisdom. When he spoke of one other odious act it was the massacre at Mycalessus, and the destruction of the barbarous Thracians was the penalty executed not by Heaven but by men. He has human sympathy for Nicias, hoping against hope for help from Heaven, as he has for the tumult of hopes and fears of the Athenians watching their ships sinking in the Great Harbour at Syracuse.

We may surmise that in the days of the plague he would not have been frightened to help his fellow citizens, for it was a part of aristocratic ethics not to be afraid in a good cause.

The first of crimes was passionate folly. Those who ruled over others incurred hatred, but that was its price and the price was worth paying. He seems to respect the Spartans' usual adherence to a code of conduct, but when at Hysiae the Spartans massacred the inhabitants, he has no word of blame for it, any more than for what happened at Scione and Melos. For war is 'a violent preceptor', and its pupils cannot evade its teaching.

De Ste. Croix describes the *History* as a tool for the active citizen:

Thucydides surely wanted his History to be of practical use to the citizen (not just the politician, of course, if particularly to him), in very much the same way as the author of *Epidemics I & III* designed his work to be used by the practising physician. The History of Thucydides would provide the citizen with a series of political case-histories, complete with all the relevant facts—above all, the motives from which the men concerned had acted—brought out as fully and accurately as possible. Government in Greek cities was direct rather than representative: instead of electing men every few years, as we do, to make all the major decisions for them, those Greek citizens who had political rights constantly had to take decisions in person, on small matters and great. So I believe that Thucydides, like the author of the Hippocratic *Epidemics,* intended the *knowledge* gained from his case-histories to issue in informed and intelligent *action.* His readers would have to make their own decisions, based on knowledge of which he could supply only a part. . . .

G. E. M. de Ste. Croix, in The Origins of the Peloponnesian War, *Duckworth, 1972.*

Michael Grant (essay date 1970)

SOURCE: "Speeches and Personalities in Thucydides," in *The Ancient Historians,* Charles Scribner's Sons, 1970, pp. 88-101.

[*In the following excerpt, Grant defends the "accuracy" of Thucydides's speeches, basing his argument on an examination of contemporary Greek notions of the purpose of public speech. He speculates that Thucydides believed that individuals in history were "there to reveal underlying causes" of the course of history; therefore, their speeches are not only vital to written history, but also are accurate inasmuch as they articulate those underlying causes.*]

Thucydides' history would not have been at all the same without the speeches. This device, which seems so strange to us in a historical work, had been adapted by Herodotus from Homer, and Thucydides—who after all came from Athens, where talk was a fine art—carried its employment a good deal further. Twenty-four per cent of his whole work consists of such orations, which number no less than forty, and, like his other digressions, are carefully and ingeniously spaced. Phoenix, in the *Iliad,* had instructed Achilles to be a speaker of words as well as a doer of deeds, and Thucydides couples words and deeds together as the materials of history.

It is very clear to him that the two forms of activity are closely linked. Diodotus, offering moderate counsel about Mytilene is made to say that 'anyone who denies that words can be a guide to action must either be a fool or have some personal interest at stake'. For one thing, speeches *create* action—good or evil, for Diodotus' opponent Cleon is chosen to show how disastrous the gift of the gab can be. Besides, Thucydides holds the very Greek opinion that no one will get anywhere at all unless he is articulate. 'Someone', Pericles is made to say, 'who has the knowledge, but lacks the power clearly to express it, is no better off than if he never had any ideas at all.'

Man, that is to say, is a rational being whose actions are based on decisions, and these can only be the outcome of verbal formulations. Speech is the root of all political life, and the point had never been so evident as it was at this time. For professional rhetoricians were intensely active, and the practical fruit of their efforts, formal speech-making, also underwent far-reaching developments. Pericles, whose orations play such a leading role in Thucydides' work, was said to have been the first to deliver a written speech in court—and the fact that he had learnt philosophy from Anaxagoras (who was also Thucydides' teacher) inspired Plato to describe him as the greatest of orators. The earliest Greek speech which has come down to us—relating to the murder of a certain

Herodes—likewise belongs to the period of the Peloponnesian War (*c.* 417). It was delivered by the rhetorician Antiphon of Rhamnus, whose style has a good deal in common with Thucydides; and indeed it was from him that the historian was reported to have learnt his rhetorical skills.

Apparently Thucydides recited parts of his work; and surely these recitations included some of the speeches which were so appropriate to such a medium. Moreover, these orations form a perfect illustration of his view that the whole of history is based on articulateness—on words as well as deeds. A historian, therefore, must take pains to record what people said. The method he himself uses is a carefully calculated one.

> In this history I have made use of set speeches, some of which were delivered just before and others during the war. I have found it difficult to remember the precise words used in the speeches which I listened to myself, and my various informants have experienced the same difficulty. So my method has been, while keeping as closely as possible to the general sense of the words that were actually used, to make the speakers say what, in my opinion, was called for by each situation.

Perhaps Herodotus had been criticised for inventing speeches; and that may be why Thucydides felt it incumbent on himself to explain how he is going to proceed. He admits that his speeches do not set out to represent the exact words of the speakers, for this, as he reasonably says, would have been impossible. He aims, instead, at conveying a general impression—the essence rather than the substance.

The additional indication that he included 'what was called for' might be held to mean that he tells us what the speakers 'had to' say, and therefore what they *did* say. But the phrase seems more likely to signify 'what the various occasions demanded'. If that is so, he is admitting that scope has been given to his imagination. Such a criterion could clash with the requirement that the general sense of what had actually been said should always be reproduced. And indeed, just as Herodotus had included purely mythical orations, it is pretty clear that Thucydides very often pays more attention to what a situation seems to him to 'call for' than to any texts of actual discourses that could have been available to him.

His speeches make little attempt to reproduce speakers' individual characteristics or probable styles. Like a simple nurse in Aeschylus, and a policeman in Sophocles, the speakers talk the language not of themselves but of their author. Their orations are closer in structure to rhetorical textbooks than to any genuine extant speech. They are also much shorter than the sort of harangues that were actually delivered on public occa-

sions—as we can tell from those that have survived. Moreover, some of Thucydides' speeches are singularly out of place, indeed tactless, in relation to their occasion. For example the admiral Phormio's address to his sailors could not possibly have been delivered to any crowd of mariners in such a form, though it is apt enough as an explanation of Athenian policy for the benefit of the reader. And the Assembly meeting to discuss Mytilene surely cannot have proceeded as Thucydides said it did. Moreover, Attic oratorical style had been moving rapidly during the war, but the style of Thucydides does nothing of the kind; quite apart from the question of whether their substance is authentic, the speeches in later books such as VI and VII must have been, stylistically, far removed from any possible originals. But some of the speeches quoted in Thucydides may never have been delivered at all.

If they were delivered, the fact that he does not exactly reproduce them does not necessarily mean that he was ignorant of what had been said. He may sometimes, it is true, have written down a version while his memory was vivid. But even then, like other ancient historians, he felt free to select, add and elaborate before transcribing the oration for his history. The fact that a speech may have been known, so that any alterations he introduced could be detected, constituted no objection. For verbatim inclusion would have been artistically damaging.

He had quite other purposes in mind; and they were purposes which entirely overrode and overruled the criterion of mere fidelity to what had actually been said. In his view, the speakers are not just there in their own right. To a certain extent, they are mouthpieces of the historian, in that they provide the medium for a substantial part of his huge contribution to the development of abstract and rational thinking. But they are much more than merely his mouthpieces. They are there to reveal underlying causes; to display the characters and tempers and motives of individuals and nations; to penetrate to general truths which might not have emerged from the details of the narrative; to get the participants in events, political or military, to speak for themselves; and to bring out, by methods impossible for a mere chronicle, subjective elements that are indispensable to our understanding.

We shall win, and why, explain typical speakers. And then subsequent developments show whether their calculations were good or bad—ostensibly without the historian intervening, so that the reader is given the illusion of independence. In this way, for example, we are introduced to the essence of Athenian power and to its gradual deterioration from the Periclean ideal. The clashes of opinion at Sparta before the war, and the reactions to these various views expressed by Pericles on the Athenian side, show an interlocking arrangement of one point answering another, often at a distance of time and place: and in reporting one oration the historian sometimes shows foreknowledge of a later one.

The influence of contemporary sophists—described by one of their number, Prodicus of Ceos, as men half-way between philosophers and political scientists—is clearly detectable in the manner in which close concentration is focused upon a single argument. The method used is often that of 'ring' or 'loop' composition: statement, proof, restatement. By these means, unarguable truth being so elusive, the attempt is made to achieve the 'probability' stressed by the sophist-rhetorician Gorgias, like philosophers before him, as the best attainable ideal. The potentialities and powers of the spoken and written word were now appreciated as never before. And so colliding intellectual theses are stated, by Thucydides, in extreme forms—corresponding with the antithetical tastes of this age in which Protagoras of Abdera (an Ionian town in Thrace) (485-415) was admitting the possibility of opposite views on any and every question. Consequently, Thucydides' speeches often occur in pairs. But sometimes, for example when Pericles is speaking, or the able Syracusan Hermocrates, the cogency of what they say is implied by the omission of any riposte from another orator. The same expository technique, without reply or antitheses, is adopted for additional set-pieces of special significance, for which, although speeches are not involved, the technique of speeches is used: such as the plague at Athens, and civil strife in Corcyra, and the dispatch sent by the Athenian general Nicias from Sicily.

To identify the historian's speeches with the choral odes of tragedy would be going too far. Yet they do owe many features to the tragic dramatists. They, too, for several decades past, had been introducing imaginary forensic speeches into their plays. The whole procedure of Thucydides is theatrical, bringing the past vividly before the reader like a drama on the stage, with the intention of revealing character and not just recording events. The whole depiction of national and personal psychologies in these speeches is analogous to the practice of the tragedians. In particular, on a great many occasions, we are strongly reminded of Euripides (*c.* 485-406 BC), who was essentially the dramatist of the Peloponnesian War. Thoroughly Euripidean, for example, is Thucydides' debate on the doom of rebellious Melos, in which sophisticated arguments are put forward in a dramatic dialogue form. Reminiscent of tragedy, also, is the historian's unmodern tendency to generalise, to seek the eternal in every event, often coining abstract terms for the purpose, again in the manner of Euripides. The reputation of Thucydides throughout the ages has scarcely fallen short of the tragedians, with whom he has so much in common; and this reputation has largely been due to the impact of his speeches.

Moreover, there is a strong poetic, tragic tinge about his actual language, and this feature, too, is particularly accentuated in the speeches; their precision and passion are those of poetry. Gorgias observed that the effects of orally delivered poetry upon audiences included 'fearful anxiety, tears and lamentation, and grief-stricken yearning'. His own success owed a lot to poetical effects; and so did the emotional highlights of Thucydides' story.

And yet this style is archaic and harsh. Crammed with meaning and overtone, sentence after sentence possesses the astringent conciseness of a gnomic utterance. The order of words is unnatural, and diction is contorted almost to the breaking-point of the language—and the translator. These elaborate, twisted antithetical rhythms are very different from the loose and easy fluency of Herodotus. They breathe the spirit of an age of rhetoricians and sophists which had only dawned at Athens after Herodotus wrote. Gorgias was the first to speak of 'figures of speech', and Thucydides noted and adapted not only his methods of argument but his diction. The historian's aim, says H. C. Baldry, 'was to master the new-fangled game of abstract thought'.

And yet his response was entirely his own. For example, he characteristically avoided the normal symmetry of the antithetical style, breaking up its formal balance. The whole effect is one of estrangement, individual and wilful. This surprising method has even inspired conjecture that Thucydides, whose father had a Thracian name, only learnt Greek as a second language. That is unlikely, but it does so happen that two antithetical and epigrammatic writers who influenced him, Protagoras and Democritus, were fellow-Thracians, both from the city of Abdera. And, without accusing Thucydides of writing pidgin Greek, it is possible to suppose that his insistence on a curiously old-fashioned idiom—the feature that particularly struck ancient critics—reflects the geographical and spiritual isolation of his banishment from Athens. Exile had not affected Herodotus, or at least not in this way—it had broadened and not soured him. The experience has seldom failed to leave its stamp, in one way or another, on any writer; and it marked Thucydides with an alienation that is reflected in his peculiar, unnatural Greek.

His narrative style possesses the same characteristics as his speeches and set-pieces, but to a far less extreme degree. The language is still compact, but not so much contorted as succinct. His writing was also famous for its speed, a quality likewise attributed to Democritus. Severe, grave, and terrifyingly intense, Thucydides presses on with inexorable rapidity. Occasionally, if the dramatic requirements of the narrative demand it, there is instead a slow and halting march. But when he has something terrible to write about, such as the final destruction of the Athenian expeditionary force in the Sicilian river Assinarus, the tale rushes ahead.

> When day came Nicias led his army on, and the Syracusans and their allies pressed them hard in the same way as before, showering missiles and hurling javelins in upon them from every side. The Athenians hurried towards the river Assinarus.

> Once they reached the river, they rushed down into it, and now all discipline was at an end. Every man wanted to be the first to get across, and, as the enemy persisted in his attacks, the crossing now became a difficult matter. Forced to crowd in close together, they fell upon each other, trampled each other underfoot. Some were killed immediately by their own spears, others got entangled among themselves and among the baggage and were swept away by the river.

> Syracusan troops were stationed on the opposite bank, which was a steep one. They hurled down their weapons from above on the Athenians, most of whom, in a disordered mass, were greedily drinking in the deep river-bed. And the Peloponnesians came down and slaughtered them, especially those who were in the river. The water immediately became foul, but nevertheless they went on drinking it, all muddy as it was and stained with blood. Indeed, most of them were fighting among themselves to have it.

In his account of the Sicilian expedition the historian deploys all his talents, because the Syracusans were the only people in whom Athens met its match. Full of tragedies and dramatic ironies, this account of an utter catastrophe which wisdom could have avoided was the climax of Book VII. Macaulay described the book as the summit of human art.

Thucydides' way of telling the story is cerebral, the product of an exceptionally powerful mind. It conveys the intellectual effort which had given birth to the work.

For his history, throughout, is a glorification of intelligence. Its purpose is not only to enable people to know. That is not enough, being a mere meaningless accumulation. The aim is also to make readers understand. In keeping with Gorgias' teaching that full, total knowledge is beyond attainment, the task must be tackled in a humble spirit. When, therefore, Thucydides has general laws in mind, he does not lay them down dogmatically, but only suggests what is likely. Thucydides agreed with Democritus' assertion that to understand the cause of any one thing was worth more to him than the whole kingdom of the Persians—and another contemporary, Socrates, was reported to have expressed similar sentiments.

For these men lived in an epoch when the Ionian spirit

of investigation had finally taken deep rots in the fertile soil of Athens. People were prepared to investigate everything; and the comparatively few years that had elapsed since Herodotus composed his work had established great gains in the efficiency of their techniques. And so, just as Thucydides probes incessantly to comprehend events, this capacity to understand is also the quality he admires most in the characters of his history. Protagoras was now asserting that man is the measure of all things, but his fellow-townsman Democritus added that no one is likely to prevail by native qualities alone without training. Thucydides, however, believed that even an untutored person could succeed if only his intellect was powerful enough. The career of Themistocles, for example, seemed to him to show how mind, granted perseverance and subtlety, is capable of rising even above the disadvantage of a deficient education.

But it is far better to have the opportunity to learn, and Thucydides above all wants his readers, whether students or statesmen, to be given the greatest possible opportunities of comprehending what is going on. For all attendant circumstances are merely subordinate, or should be made subordinate, to the minds of man. Thucydides, says Antony Andrewes, 'sees events as one great dialectical argument in which human intelligence is the final arbiter in the seat of judgment'. His insistence on reason as the ideal anticipates Aristotle's emphasis both on wisdom and on practical intelligence. The distinction was a refinement that came after Thucydides; he is content to stress the cerebral quality in general as the criterion by which people and causes must be judged.

All his important personages, therefore, are shrewd planners and calculators, and the word for 'understand' or 'judgment' (*gnomai, gnome*) occurs 305 times in his work. The Greeks admired the middle course so much because they found it hard to achieve; and similarly Thucydides appreciated intelligence because he knew that even in his own city, crammed with intelligent people, it did not by any means always prevail. Instead he felt, as Cornford says, that 'human affairs move along a narrow path lit by a few dim rays of foresight (*gnome*) or the false, wandering fires of hope'. Most of all was this true of politics, the sphere which Thucydides had chosen for his analysis of the applications of human reason.

To understand the successes and failures of this power, it was obviously necessary to study psychology. Earlier philosophers had concentrated on physics and metaphysics, but now Socrates and Democritus and the sophists had turned the eyes of the Greek world on to human behaviour. We have the former's views filtered through (or invented by) Plato, and Democritus' ethical and psychological works survive in fragments, which, although numerous, are not numerous enough to enable us to reconstruct his system. As for Thucydides, this interest in the human personality is deficient in a certain necessary quality of variegated untidiness, because his pursuit of this aspect is subordinated to other aims. He likes biography; his delineations of famous men contributed to the formation of that literary genre. But everything judged to be irrelevant and trivial is rigorously excluded. For what the historian wants to do is to elucidate, through his characters, the *types* of person who react to given sets of circumstances, who fix the characters of states, who decide the features which oppose Athens to Sparta. This is to say, we are far, deliberately far, from Herodotus' preference for more personal and private factors. Thucydides judges men not as individuals but as politicians.

That, for example, is how he sees Pericles. Only two years after the beginning of the Peloponnesian War, Pericles was already dead. Yet he is the central figure of the work, and in a sense its hero. There is no knowing what Thucydides thought of the earlier, pre-war Pericles, the young, demagogic, imperialist on the make; for he does not choose to tell us. But about his conduct of the initial period of the war we are told a good deal; and the background of these events is described in the speeches attributed to him. Two of these orations, it seems, only reached their present form many years after his death. Yet it is difficult to read the Funeral Speech without feeling that Thucydides had to some extent, later if not sooner, become infected with the glory of the imperial state. The ideal may not have been perfect, but it was magnificent; and, looked at in retrospect, it provided a dramatic foil to the disastrous present.

Admiration of the departed order implied respect for the man who had brought it into being. And indeed, when we come to the actual subject of the history, namely the war, its outbreak is not regarded as Pericles' fault. There is no suggestion that he could have avoided it, and the gossip that he started hostilities from private motives of his own is dismissed with contempt. As regards the actual conduct of the military operations, the verdict of Thucydides, at whatever date or by whatever stages it was reached, again spoke unequivocally in favour of Pericles. 'During the whole period of time when Pericles was at the head of affairs the state was widely led and firmly guarded, and it was under him that Athens was at her greatest. And when the war broke out, here also he appears to have accurately estimated what the power of Athens was.' In the end the Athenians lost the war, it is true. But they only lost it many years after Pericles' death. And, although his calculations had admittedly been turned awry by the plague, it was not because of him that they failed. On the contrary, if he had continued to be in charge, they would have won. They lost because his successors did everything he had told them not to do. He had

counselled them to look after the navy, but to refrain from imperial expansion during the war (though perhaps he was less purely defensive than Thucydides made out). He also advised them to avoid taking any action which might risk the safety of Athens itself. But they did the exact opposite, in all respects. *They,* not Pericles, pursued private motives; and they fell fatally into civil strife. Pericles, with his 'position, intelligence and human integrity', had been able to respect their liberty and yet lead them at the same time. Those who followed him could not.

Of these successors to Pericles we know very little. Except for some caricatures by the comic dramatist Aristophanes, there is scant information except from Thucydides himself—and his pictures merely consist of a few malevolent flashes. After Pericles' death, the leading politician for some years was Cleon. Thucydides brings him to our notice in three episodes. He was the man who, in 427, proposed the decree to execute the rebellious Mytileneans, which was passed but rescinded the next day. In 425 it was he who won a considerable victory at Pylos on the western coast of the Peloponnese, when members of the Spartan military *élite* were (exceptionally) taken prisoner on the island of Sphacteria. And in 422-421 it was again Cleon who proceeded to Macedonia to win Amphipolis back from the Spartan Brasidas. But on this occasion he failed, and the enemy killed him.

Like the conservative Aristophanes, who treated Cleon as a lamentable and violent demagogue, Thucydides has the lowest possible opinion of the man, and says so in lethal asides. He is degraded to the status of a clown unworthy of the dignity of history—someone who throve in an atmosphere of disturbance, because 'in a time of peace and quiet, people would be more likely to notice his evil doings and less likely to believe his slander of others'.

In regard to Mytilene, Cleon was unnecessarily brutal and revengeful—which was an unwise way of treating allies. He also proclaimed a deplorable desire to prevent his fellow Athenians from engaging in free discussion. At Pylos he was grasping and arrogant, and made a 'mad' promise (though it came off). And thereafter, when we learn of his sordid end in Macedonia, it is hard to forget that Amphipolis, which Cleon had failed to recover, was the very same place which Thucydides himself had lost. The recovery of the town might have meant his return from the exile his failure had earned him. Moreover, the circumstances that had led to the city's loss and Thucydides' disgrace could reasonably be ascribed to Cleon's overbearing measures against the allies. These were all reasons for regarding Cleon acrimoniously.

Coarse fellow though he may have been, he was able, particularly as a financier—and he earned respect from orators in the following century. However, his merits were of no concern to the purpose of Thucydides. His point was that Cleon displayed a dramatic antithesis, a debased perversion, of Pericles: vulgarian contrasted with man of culture, second-rate with first-rate, inferior demagogue with enlightened guide. Cleon's savagery towards the allies was a typical example of how he did everything Pericles told his successors not to do. The violence of his domestic and foreign policy over a period of years could, in the view of the historian, be partially blamed for the lapse into civil strife which was really what cost Athens the war. And the same sort of censure was merited by his successor Hyperbolus, another butt of comic poets, who was exiled (ostracised) in 417, 'not from any fear of his power and influence, but for his villainy, and because the city was ashamed of him'.

Thucydides' characterisation of two other leading Athenian figures in the war is more subtle. One is Nicias, who was responsible for the Peace of 421 but met with utter disaster in the expedition to Sicily, and was executed by the Syracusans (413). The historian's verdict is an unexpected and cryptic one: 'Nicias was a man who, of all the Hellenes in my time, least deserved to come to so miserable an end, since the whole of his life had been devoted to the study and practice of virtue.' Not a word, here, about the usual political and military subjects, or about his gifts in those spheres—gifts which were adequate but not brilliant, and earned him a reputation of respectable timidity from Aristophanes. The comment of Thucydides, as far as it goes, is accurate enough. But its omissions and implications are significant. First of all, there is a tragic contrast between his pious, conventional virtues and his appalling end. But, above all, it is implied, with a grim and ironical clearsightedness, that these qualities, excellent though they are in their way, will not guarantee the intelligent and effective conduct of affairs. The Sicilian catastrophe had proved as much, with terrifying finality. 'Thucydides' epitaph on Nicias', remarks C.M. Bowra, 'is the verdict of a man who knew that, in the destinies of peoples, goodness is not enough.'

All the same, even if not enough, it is a useful thing to have. For example, the absence of these standard, solid merits in Nicias' young opponent Alcibiades was a serious political handicap both to himself and to Athens. Before the Sicilian expedition, says the historian, Alcibiades had not been given important commands because of his debauched personal habits. Obviously these were bound to intensify his estrangement from the very proper Nicias, and so they contributed to dangerous dissension in the State. And the radicals disliked his extravagances quite as much as Nicias did.

Unlike Herodotus, Thucydides does not usually go into a man's private life. But in this case he had to, since it affected Alcibiades' career and consequently exercised a direct influence on the war. For when, in 415, Alcibiades was withdrawn from the Sicilian expedition and took refuge with the enemies of Athens, it was again suspicion of his lack of principles which had turned his fellow-citizens against him. Ostensibly, the charge was impiety, but what really inspired his opponents was the generally unreliable unsolidity of his character. However, after Alcibiades had come back to an Athenian command (411), he deserved well of his fellow-countrymen. For when the fleet at Samos wanted to attack their own city of Athens—temporarily under an oligarchic dictatorship—he refused to let them. Politically unprincipled though he was, by this intervention, says Thucydides, 'he rendered as eminent a service to the state as any man ever did'. This exceptionally high praise prepares us for the conclusion that, in spite of the flaws in his private life, his rejection and dismissal by his own people (repeated all over again in 406) was ruinous to Athens. And the historian is probably thinking of Alcibiades (and deliberately speaking in warmer terms than Herodotus) when he praises Themistocles, that equally brilliant and unsound figure of the earlier war. Here was another man whose unreliable, hazardous character and conduct had likewise helped to drive him into the arms of Athens' enemies. And yet, when not hampered by this defect, he too had performed splendid actions.

How had Themistocles managed to achieve these things? Not because of his background, because he had none, but because of his intellect, foresight and ability to make quick decisions. This continual emphasis on brain-power sometimes makes Thucydides' verdicts rather disconcerting. The standard translation of *arete* is 'virtue'. But the term is applied not only to the devout Nicias, but also to Antiphon, who, whatever the merits of his prose style, was a sanguinary, treacherous plotter, the leading oligarchic extremist of 411. The surprising attribution of virtue to such a man is intended, as Bury pointed out, 'to express the intelligence, dexterity and will power of a competent statesman, in sharp contradistinction to the conventional *arete* of the popular conception'. This was not virtue as most people understood it, but something more closely comparable to the *virtù* which Machiavelli saw in tough, skilful Sforzas and Borgias of his own day. Thucydides liked men who concentrated their energy on the tasks at hand. There is not much talk of natural benevolence. Instead, speeches prefer to harp on action-enhancing qualities such as courage.

Courage operates in the mass as well as in individuals. The psychology of masses and groups is a field in which Thucydides achieved extraordinary pioneer advances. With the acutest perceptiveness he analysed and expressed the changing attitudes of states, factions, councils, assemblies, and above all armies. Generals' speeches are skilfully adapted to the thoughts and feelings of their various contingents—unless it suits his purpose to do otherwise. The results of Greek battles depended on morale rather than tactics, and here we see the mentality of the soldiers, their excitements and exaltations and despairs. As the Sicilian expedition draws towards its calamitous close in a decisive sea-battle in Syracuse harbour, there is an unforgettable picture of the agonised Athenian troops looking on, their fears for the future like nothing they had ever experienced before, their bodies agonisedly swaying this way and that to match the vicissitudes of their ships, on which everything depended.

W. den Boer (essay date 1977)

SOURCE: "Thucydides," in *Progress in the Greece of Thucydides,* North Holland Publishing, 1977, pp. 21-38.

[*In the excerpt that follows, den Boer enters the debate over Thucydides' views on progress as a necessary part of history—that is, whether events in time necessarily "progress" toward some higher condition. He concludes, through an examination of the opening chapters of the* History *and contemporary Greek thought in general, that such a notion of history did not exist for Thucydides.*]

One author who was not impressed by the accomplishments of man was Thucydides. Nevertheless, in the eyes of many scholars he is one of the champions of progress. "More important is the idea of progress to which the Archaeology gives expression"—[J. H. Finley] pronounces. Let us now try to determine what Thucydides really said. We are entitled to do so because scholars of repute oppose the views of Mme [Jacqueline] de Romilly and J. H. Finley. I mention Hans-Peter Stahl's book, *Thukydides, Die Stellung des Menschen im geschichtlichen Prozess,* which was published in 1966, as an example of such opposition. [Stahl writes,] "it seems that Thucydides himself sees the importance of what was the development of human knowledge not in change (Fortschritt) but in the determinant factor of *might,* which remains the same".

To discover who is right it is necessary to deal carefully with chapters 1-19 of Book I. I hope that my *paraphrases* of passages from this famous introduction will give a preliminary answer.

Chapter I. Thucydides writes about a unique event— a great war—the greatest disturbance in the history of the Greeks. His studies led him to the conclusion that the history of the preceding period, compared to his own, indicated no greatness, either in warfare or in anything else.

Chapter II. In ancient times, the country which is now called Hellas had no settled population. There was a series of migrations of various tribes who were constantly under the pressure of invaders stronger than they were: there was no commerce, no safe communication routes, either by land or by sea, and because of these factors the tribes were always prepared to abandon their territory.

From these two chapters alone it already becomes clear that we have to enlarge upon the statements of Stahl. The historian is anxious to prove that the Peloponnesian war holds more importance than any other event before it. Such digressions are familiar and are called αὐξήσεις, additions to show how important the subject is. For this purpose the writer has τεχμήρια, which he will emphasise in the following chapters. These 'signs' will demand our attention: in chapter 2 some such signs are already evident, *viz.* invasions, no settled population, no commerce, no safe communication. It is important therefore, for us to be sceptical from the first of the idea set out by Romilly in her important article. She tries to persuade us that the problem of whether 'progress' occurs in I. 1-21, is a simple one. As is to be expected, her answer is in the affirmative, although she has to admit that the exposition deals with the importance of wars and states, the extension of political groups and the size of their means with which to determine the scale of warfare. But, so it is alleged, this is only the framework. The historian's tenet or doctrine is of a clear affirmation, coherent and outspoken, of progress. In my opinion this statement is misconceived and stems from prejudice.

However, Thucydides does give 'signs' for his own view that before the Peloponnesian war there had been no great military achievement in Hellas. The underlying causes for this were:

1. No settled population.

2. Inhabitants always prepared to abandon their own territory.

3. No commerce.

4. No safe communication by land or sea.

5. No surplus left over for capital.

6. Production only of necessities.

7. No regular system of agriculture.

8. This all culminated in lack of protection by fortifications.

9. Invasions at any moment.

10. No reluctance of the population in moving from their homes.

Point 10 brings us back to point 1.

And all these statements are combined by two other signs which on the surface appear to oppose each other, but which in fact do corroborate the passage as a whole:

> 11. The most frequent changes of population occurred where the soil was most fertile (e.g. Thessaly, Boeotia and most of the Peloponnese).

> 12. Attica was remarkably free from political disunity because of the poverty of her soil.

In the conclusions of chapters I and II the 'sign' of Attica is an important and excellent example of the historian's theory "that it was because of migration that there was an uneven development elsewhere; for when people were driven out of other areas of Greece by war or other disturbances, the most powerful of them first took refuge in Athens which was a stable society, finally becoming citizens of Athens. The influx of people created such an increase in the population that it resulted in Attica becoming too small for its inhabitants and so colonies of people were sent out to Ionia".

It should be emphasized again, that in general the author's aim was only to explain how this great war could have occurred. This point is sometimes forgotten by modern commentators. During the course of time there was a development of circumstances which brought about the possibility of war. The purpose of Thucydides in the Archaeology was to elucidate the conditions which led to 'the greatest war', and there is no passage, not even a sentence, which does not serve this purpose. There is no need for detail, and the author does not dwell on it; he merely gives the main outline of the theme by the use of brief 'signs' rather than by the use of particulars.

Chapter III. The lack of unity among the inhabitants of early Greece can be confirmed by yet another observation, from Homeric poetry. The words 'Hellas' and 'Hellenes' as a common name for land and population are late in appearing. There is no record of action in any form being taken by Hellas as a whole before the event of the Trojan War. Even the poet Homer, who lived many years after this war, refers only to the population of a very restricted area—the inhabitants of Phthiotis—when using the name Hellenes. It was the followers of Achilles who came from Phthiotis. Neither does Homer use the word 'barbarians', which proves that the people who were later known as 'Hellenes' did not see themselves as a united whole, as distinguishable from foreign outsiders. "In any case these various Hellenic states, weak in themselves and lacking in communications with one another, took no kind of collective action before the time of

the Trojan War. And they could not have united even for the Trojan expedition unless they had previously acquired a greater knowledge of seafaring".

Chapter IV. The end of the previous chapter opens the way for the next 'sign': the first Thalassocracy of Minos, Lord of the Cyclades islands, in which he founded most of the colonies. One of the results of his power was security for seafaring people. "It is reasonable to suppose that he did his best to put down piracy in order to secure his own revenues".

Chapter V. This chapter takes the reader back to the remote past, piracy and the social position of the pirate. Piracy was practised by all the inhabitants of the coastal areas, and success in it was a reason for pride. A similar form of robbery was also prevalent on land.

Chapter VI. (Even now there are still people who live by these means). Personal security demanded the carrying of weapons and people were hesitant to discontinue this practice. In spite of their way of life being filled with menace and danger the Athenians were among the first to lay aside their arms and to adopt a more relaxed and luxurious form of living. A case in point here concerns clothing, and there are two stages to be discerned. In the first stage it was customary for the older members to wear costly clothes, and this was also the fashion among their kinsmen in Ionia. Later came a less pretentious way of dressing—more after the present-day fashion—which was first adopted by the Lacedaemonians. The custom of nakedness when playing games also comes from the Lacedaemonians. Formerly, Greek athletes wore loin cloths, even at the Olympic Games, and this is still the custom among some of the barbarians. "And one could show that the early Hellenes had many other similar customs to those of the present-day barbarians".

An additional observation may not be out of place here. "Human (=Greek) Progress" is not emphasized in this chapter. Its main content concerns the disappearance of violence,—the wearing of arms in ordinary life being no longer necessary, the change in people's manners, and an easier mode of life, illustrated by the trend towards a more simple form of clothing.

Chapter VII. After discussing the conditions of living in the previous chapter Thucydides returns to the question of navigation and its consequences. The art of navigation had been developed at a relatively late stage. A 'sign' of that part of the reconstruction of the past is that older settlements were founded inland, whereas the cities founded in recent times, when navigation had become safer, were built in coastal areas. The geographic position of these settlements protected the newly built harbours.

Chapter VIII. It was because of this protection that

attacks from the sea became less profitable and regular commerce began to flourish: it also became possible for Minos to organize a navy and to improve the sea communication routes.

The introduction of this passage in particular confirms the widespread piracy (which was checked by Minos). According to tradition the islands of the Aegean were originally inhabited by the Carians. When Delos was purified by the Athenians all the graves on the island were opened up, and it was discovered that over half the bodies were those of Carians. This could be recognised by the types of weapons buried with the bodies, as well as by the method of burial. It is important to remember that this, and other archaeological remarks have no direct relation to the central theme—the accumulation of power; he does not say that the Carians exerted their military power over an extensive area. In this connection we should bear in mind von Fritz' observation that the opening of the graves bore out the traditional tales. We are therefore confronted here with one of the first attempts, if not the first, to combine . . . the 'signs', with archaeological evidence. The successful organisation of Minos drove out the pirates and brought prosperity to the coastal regions. The results of this prosperity brought with them differences of wealth and power. Minos' measures brought about possibilities for power so that a situation arose in which the coastal areas were able to acquire wealth and their population to lead a more settled way of life. Some areas were more prosperous than others. Differences occurred. Through the acquisition of capital resources the more powerful cities were able to subject the people of the weaker cities. Hellas had already developed along these lines to a certain degree at the time of the expedition to Troy.

Chapters IX-XI. The Trojan War will occupy us only briefly. The appreciation of Thucydides' argument, and in particular the question of history *contra* legend, can be omitted. According to Thucydides the war was the result of one of the concentrations of power, the development of which he had traced in the preceding chapter. In modern literature the evaluation of these chapters, which are filled with names from myths and legends, is not always favourable towards Thucydides. However, this is of no concern to us at the moment. The sensible middle course favoured by K. von Fritz seems to me highly preferable to the hyper-criticisms of Ed. Schwartz and the apologetics of Gomme. If nevertheless I had to make a choice between the interpretations of Schwartz and Gomme, I would side with the latter because of his awareness of the tremendous difficulties in treating this subject from a remote past. To have seen the history in mythology as a central problem, is of great merit. Thucydides perceived this, as he did also in the case of the early history of Attica (II 15-17). In my opinion there is no value in discussing the problem of whether or not we should blame

him for mentioning Agamemnon and Pelops. The most important point is that the idea of progress is not mentioned in his account. His impressive treatment of the difficult problems in the early history of Greece has been the reason why scholars have repeatedly made the mistake of comparing him with his predecessors in this respect and seeing progress within the evaluation of the past. This, though, is not the progress of human society as such. Here is the point at which scholars part company. It does, of course, depend upon the lens through which we are compelled to look. I, for one, do not think that the following quotations have any bearing on progress.

1-1: "all the evidence leads me to conclude that these periods (sc. the remote past) were not great periods either in warfare or in anything else".

3-1: "the weakness of the early inhabitants" (before the Trojan War).

3-4: "these various Hellenic states . . . took no kind of collective action before the time of the Trojan War".

10-5: "not a large number went on the expedition" (against Troy).

11-1: "the cause (of this small number) was lack of money and want of supplies".

11-3: "as it was, just as lack of money was the reason why previous expeditions were not really considerable, so in the course of this one (the Trojan War), we shall find . . . that it was inferior to its fame".

In all these quotations Thucydides attempts to put forward his own subject as being greater than the events of the more distant past. He does not speak about human misery ('misère') but about military 'weakness'. Before the time of the Trojan War the things lacking were the necessary equipment, and the shortage of materials, but not the needs of the population.

When we look at Thuc. I 1-11 as a whole we can see that, from a modern point of view, the most vulnerable parts of the exposition are those which draw attention to the most important historical problems.

(a) How did the Greeks become conscious of their unity, opposed to the Barbarians? His answer is that Hellen, the son of Deucalion, when he became strong, was invited to the aid of other cities. I see this act as military aid, and cannot endorse von Fritz who draws the conclusion that the fact that Hellen and his sons were invited to other cities shows an awareness of cultural unity, not a unity of language or of race. Neither the first nor the two others are even remotely connected with the passage as I see it. The other states invite them as allies in a military enterprise. So Thucydides proclaims military reasons for the unity of the Greeks.

(b) Commerce and economic growth are only possible when the sea is free from piracy. That means also that one state has to possess the maritime power to impose its peace on the others.

(c) The origin of power in the Greek world. It started with Mycenae, which nobody nowadays will deny.

(d) The Trojan War. The historicity was never doubted in ancient times. Thucydides scrutinizes the circumstances under which such an enterprise could take place.

We must agree with von Fritz that to put these four problems clearly before his audience is 'eine grossartige Leistung'. Might is proclaimed without any moral commentary. H.-P. Stahl's statements seem to be the most satisfactory.

There are still eight more chapters to be treated and these deal with the more recent past. Here especially, there is the temptation to glorify one's own time. This temptation is sometimes irresistible to the human mind. Did Thucydides have the intellectual power to resist this popular view? The question is worth our consideration.

Chapter XII deals with the period after the Trojan War. The summary is very brief and it is not possible for any ancient or modern historian to do more until rather more progress has been made with recent archaeological research. We might safely say that in this chapter Thucydides sketched the *decline of power* only "very superficially". But, we can ask, who has done it better over the centuries? And in any case his purpose was to produce no more than a superficial sketch. A superficial sketch of this type left the way clear for him to deal with the new concentrations of power and with the question of how such concentrations of power could arise. He alludes briefly to the period of colonization, because this was yet another means of gaining power. Even making allowance for brevity, the words "Ionia and most of the islands were colonized by the Athenians, the Peloponnesians founded most of the colonies in Italy and Sicily", are very unsatisfactory. They should be understood as meaning only that colonization was one of the great causes of enhancement of power which led to the war, and be taken as a hint as to what would occur much later.

Chapters XIII-XIV. It is often said that this passage lacks coherence, but I am not convinced of this. Thucydides makes himself perfectly clear. He demonstrates the differences between monarchy and tyranny from the position the economy holds in both forms of gov-

ernment. The patriarchal kings get their 'share', their "gifts of honour"—I insist on giving the original meaning to γέρατα mentioned in this chapter. However with the introduction of new forms of wealth the old aristocracy—which inherited its power from the kings—was no longer master of the situation. As Hellas grew more powerful and continued to acquire still more wealth than before, tyrannies began to be established in most of the cities, along with the increase of their revenue, whereas before that there had been hereditary kingships based on fixed prerogatives.

A shift of power follows, and a city organised along this pattern of tyranny and based upon the higher and lower levels of its citizens, requires centres of power. One such centre of power was the navy.

When Thucydides' account is reconstructed in this way much of what appears strange and 'unfinished' becomes clear. He does not speak about the oligarchies which proceed tyranny, because they were not essential to his purpose—the development of the state and the powers of the state. He does not touch upon all possible centres of power, but only upon maritime power, for he knows that it is precisely this which will explain the military conflict. Corinth and Athens rise from the shadows of time. It comes as no surprise that Thucydides places maritime history at the centre of the stage, so to speak, for he had already done so in chapter X, when discussing the partners of Mycenae in the Trojan War. He does the same again in chapter XIII, first with Corinth, when he mentions shipbuilding, the types of ships, and the construction of harbours and docks.

Here also I am disinclined to follow those scholars who accuse Thucydides of a passing and superficial treatment of his subject matter. In my opinion his report is remarkably to the point. Once again H.-P. Stahl's characterization of the 'Archaeology' of Thucydides proves to be the right one. All Thucydides' observations are centered around the development of power, which means that he needs no more than a minimum of material for his sketch. This is where the master reveals himself. He reveals himself as being not only master but also as an unbiased judge of persons and events. It does not seem accidental that this passage ends with the end of the naval history of Greece, at it were, through the achievements of Themistocles. Thucydides praises Themistocles elsewhere in what is, for him, unusual eulogy.

The particular mention given to the enormous achievements of the Phocaeans could be based on the oral tradition, or it might be due to the influence of other authors, among whom Hecataeus is likely to have been the first. I believe Thucydides was right to mention the founders of Massilia who, before they built their settlements there, had defeated the Carthaginians. After all, he could hardly have found a better illustration of such successful Greek initiative at sea.

Chapters XV and XVI are the counterparts of the two previous chapters. They are not so brilliantly worked to a climax, but nevertheless they serve the author's purpose well in his efforts to elucidate the development of power on land. The author himself explains the reasons for the impression of their being less satisfactory and lacking the depth of chapters XIII and XIV, when he states: "There was no warfare on land that resulted in any considerable accession of power". One might reproach him for viewing the wars on land only as important skirmishes between neighbours, for omitting the expansion of Argos and the power of its king Pheidon. But I repeat my earlier statement that Thucydides' intention was not to give a brief survey of history—he chose historical landmarks only for his main thesis, which was the development of concentrated power. I think that perhaps he was right in not considering the Messenian war as a part of the development of concentrated power. After all, in spite of the success of the wars, Sparta was, in the early stages, isolated from the mainstream of *Greek* development of power. So far as Thucydides was concerned, *Greek* development of power was connected with ephemeral alliances between states more than with the formation of leagues, and so far as archaic Sparta was concerned such alliances were not so evident.

The nearest approach to collective action was the ancient war between Chalcis and Eretria (the Lelantine war). During this war the rest of the Hellenic world sided with one or the other of the two combatants (end of Ch. XV). The counterpart to this conclusion is the fact that the different states which were isolated from the others suffered all sorts of obstacles to their continuous growth. The Ionian cities suffered greatly from their lack of alliances with each other. The Persian Empire stands as the great example of unity, subduing Lydia and the Greek cities in Asia and, "strong in the possession of the Phoenician navy", conquering the islands as well.

Chapter XVII. In the same perspective it is necessary to try to understand the failure of the tyrannies—even those which succeeded in maintaining themselves over shorter period: "since they had regard for their own interests only". The exceptions amongst these were the tyrants in Sicily who (as we have to interpret their being mentioned by the author) went beyond their immediate local interests. Indeed, the menace of Carthage and of the Siculi sometimes forced the Greek settlements to unite their forces.

From this we must conclude that in almost every case a concentration of power was lacking. This was the reason for so many states falling victims to the great powers, the Persians and the Lacedaemonians. Thucy-dides does not explain why these two forces were the exceptions. However much one would have liked to have the opinion of Thucydides about the Persian Empire, it did not concern him. His aim was the situation in his own time and an explanation of the predominant position of Sparta, which is given in the next chapter. Here, though, he does have to make some remarks on the glorious war against Persia.

Chapter XVIII and XIX. The conclusion of the former chapters is summarized in the last passage of chapter XVIII: "So for a long time the state of affairs everywhere in Hellas was such that nothing very remarkable could be done by any combination of powers and that even the individual cities were lacking in enterprise".

Now *chapter XVIII* brings forward another factor in the remarkable report of Thucydides: the stability of Sparta was based on the stability of its constitution. This idea was also present in the preceding chapter, if we bear in mind that the possibility for tyranny was made easier because of the lack of unity amongst the victims. Tyranny is always a product of political instability. Sparta had never been under tyranny and so continued as a politically stable society. This development was all the more remarkable since Thucydides knew that "from the time when the Dorians first settled in Sparta there had been a particularly long period of political disunity".

By taking Sparta as an example it can be seen that it is possible for a land state with no strong economic basis for power to be powerful as the result of a good and stable constitution. Such power, however, has its limits, and there are dangers which threaten its existence. Although there are great risks involved when there are numerous concentrations of rather weaker power: these are sometimes more dangerous than confrontations between two strong centres of power, because these provoke pockets of resistance. This phenomenon can be seen from chapters I-XVII, and is further confirmed in chapters XVIII-XIX; sometimes explicit statements on it are made, and sometimes it can be deduced by implication.

The Persian Wars demonstrate the creation of two different concentrations of power on mainland Greece—Athens and Sparta. This is shown in Chapter XVIII by the facts of Marathon, the naval preparation, and Sparta's command ten years later. Rivalry arose in spite of the common effort, and the war-time alliance was short-lived.

Chapter XIX underlines the significance of the two concentrations of power. Sparta and her allies, who did *not* have to pay tribute, Athens and her allies (whose fleets had been taken over in the course of time by Athens, with the exception of the fleets of Chios and Lesbos) who did have to pay contributions of money.

This then was the situation within the concentrations of power, and the purpose of Thucydides was to illustrate it in the chapters mentioned.

At the end of Thucydides' survey two things became clear. He works by the method of tekmèria—'signs'—. These 'signs' prove the importance of concentrations of power. Moreover, the economic factors are given more importance than was ever given by a Greek historian. Throughout the whole course of Greek historiography economic factors were never accorded much importance. As with so many great innovators, there were no successors to Thucydides, nor even imitators. When attention was given to economic factors during the new developments of historical research in modern times, Thucydides was not represented as a forerunner. The inspiration of these researchers was derived from (modern) social and economic sciences and not from antiquity. In antiquity all that was written about the influence of social and economic data was mostly too theoretical to be of any importance to the practical work of the historian, or it was limited to one or two observations about a restricted problem in a restricted period. Aristotle is a case in point here, and some data from Xenophon can illustrate it.

On the basis of the foregoing treatment of Thucydides' Archaeology, it is my intention to emphasize that a similar development can be traced concerning 'progress'. Thucydides does indeed give some examples of the improvement in the relationship between the human race and its environment, but these remarks are merely used as background for his main purpose, which was the exposition of the development of 'power'. It is therefore understandable that Lovejoy and Boas should have paid little attention to his work in general. One of the texts in G. H. Hildebrand's revised edition of F. J. Teggart, *The Idea of Progress* (1949), is taken from the Archaeology, but the great champions of Thucydides as a proponent of the idea of progress are Mme de Romilly and E. R. Dodds. A single quotation from Dodds is probably sufficient to illustrate their point of view: "Thucydides saw the past history of Greece as pursuing a gradual upward course". Others must judge between these words and my treatment. I must confess that I cannot find in Thucydides what Dodds states here in general terms.

W. Robert Connor (essay date 1985)

SOURCE: "Narrative Discourse in Thucydides," in *The Greek Historians: Literature and History—Papers Presented to A. E. Raubitschek,* Anma Libri, 1985, pp. 1-17.

[*In the following excerpt, Connor argues that the predominant critical examination of Thucydides as a political scientist and a historical scientist neglects the* strength of his narrative technique—and consequently misses "the pleasure of reading" his History.]

There are today many signs of a sea change in our understanding of the relationship between literature and history and hence in our understanding of the historians of the past and of historical writing in the present. Lawrence Stone drew attention to some of these signs a few years ago in an essay entitled "The Revival of Narrative" [*Past and Present* 85 (Nov. 1979)]. Stone argued that there was a "noticeable shift of content, method and style among a very tiny, but disproportionately prominent, section of the historical profession." The change was from what he called "structural" history to "narrative" history, that is to historical writing that is descriptive rather than analytical and whose central focus is on man and not on circumstances. He was not referring, of course, to the writing of antiquarians, or annalists, but to the shift from quantitative or "scientific" history toward another set of questions, especially those about the role of power and of the individual in history and also to the effort "to discover what was going on inside people's heads in the past, and what it was like to live in the past, questions which inevitably lead back to the use of narrative." Eric Hobsbawn in reply challenged many of Stone's conclusions but conceded "there is evidence that the old historical avant-garde no longer rejects, despises and combats the old fashioned 'history of events' or even biographical history, as some of it used to" [*Past and Present* 86 (1980)].

I suspect there is more of a change than Hobsbawn, and perhaps even than Stone, admitted. The signs multiply that a major change is under way, one with important implications for all who are concerned with history. We are witnessing, I believe, not just a resurgent academic appreciation of some traditional techniques of historical scholarship, nor a recognition that narrative theory affects historical writing as much as it does the novel, but a rethinking of some of the fundamental modes whereby our culture relates to the past. The issue, if I am correct, is not just the revival of narrative but a new and more experiential mode of historical understanding. This large claim is not to be argued in short compass. My aim here is more modest, to look at one author from antiquity, writing in what I believe was a period similar in one respect to our own— its rethinking of its relationship to the past and of the problem of writing about the past. Studying narrative discourse in Thucydides will not by itself clarify what is happening in our own culture, but it may contain a few hidden analogies to some of the changes going on right now.

We have now almost stopped talking about Thucydides as a "scientific historian." That analogy, borrowed from the enthusiasms of an earlier generation, had a long life in Thucydidean studies and caused much belief. It encouraged the notion that Thucydides was not so much a writer as a proto-political scientist and sent readers scurrying about to find in his work "laws" comparable to those found by natural scientists. Much attention was thus paid to passages that generalized about human nature or that expounded the so-called Law of the Stronger. Little attention was paid to the fact that these passages are almost always found in the speeches of the work, and that the structure of the debates and their setting within the narrative often subvert or modify the generalizations advanced by individual speakers. The search for the laws of a political science in Thucydides made him into a hard line Cold Warrior, teaching the lesson of the tough-minded pursuit of self interest and national interest. The attempt to make Thucydides into a "scientific historian," in other words, narrowed and distorted our understanding of the literary richness of the work. Still, the analogy did help us become aware of certain important features of the text, even if it did not go far toward explaining them. It drew attention to the restraint and austerity of Thucydides, the comparative infrequency of authorial interventions, and the avoidance of explicit judgments and evaluations. To be sure, it also tempted us to mistake these features for an attempt to write a purely "objective" or "value-free" history and to neglect the frequent and powerful indications of *implicit* value judgments throughout the *Histories*. The analogy to scientific history, in other words, did what analogies usually do—it opened our eyes to some features of the text and obscured some other features, equally important for a full and balanced appreciation.

Now that we have swung away from the view that Thucydides was a cold and detached observer and have begun to emphasize the elements of feeling, involvement, judgment, and pathos in his work, it is easy to be scornful of the old belief in a "scientific" Thucydides. But we learned a lot in that school, including the great debt Thucydides owed to the intellectual revolution of the mid fifth century B.C., especially to Hippocratic medicine and the early Sophists. Thucydides' work, we agree, was profoundly influenced—not molded or determined—but influenced by the thinking about myth, persuasion, and psychology that was going on during his childhood and youth. Out of that revolution Thucydides drew some of the elements that were to prove most important for his work. He combined a realistic, tough-minded psychology, the Hippocratics' insistence on careful testing of observations and reported facts, and the argumentative techniques of the Sophists into a powerful machine for historical analysis.

We can best see this engine at work in the opening chapters of the *Histories,* the so-called "Archaeology," where it is applied to the legends of early Greece. If we look closely, we note a surprising contrast between Thucydides and the supposedly more credulous Hero-

dotus. Thucydides turns out to be willing to accept a considerable amount of this legendary material, but only after it has come through his analytical engine. Along the way the variants in the stories are studied, the alleged motives of the actors are tested against his "modern" psychology and an interpretation is presented that is grounded in analogies from primitive cultures and arguments from probability.

Consider one example. Herodotus begins his history of the Persian wars by telling some legends about early hostilities between Greeks and barbarians. He includes two versions of the story of Paris' abduction of Helen, but then dismisses both: "Which of these two accounts is true I shall not trouble to decide. I shall proceed at once to point out the person who first within my own knowledge commenced aggressions on the Greeks, after which I shall go forward with my history . . ." (Herodotus 1.5, trans. G. Rawlinson). Soon we are studying the expansions of the Persian empire in the sixth century B.C.

Thucydides, by contrast, refines and then accepts legends about early Greece. The opening of *his* history, the "Archaeology," accepts the reality of the Greek expedition against Troy. But he drastically reinterprets traditional legends: "Agamemnon," he says, "seems to me to have assembled his expedition not so much because of the oaths which Tyndareus imposed upon the suitors of Helen [that is, that they should assist the successful suitor if anyone ever abducted Helen] but because he was the most powerful man of his day" (1.9.1). He leaves no room here for story-telling about the power of oaths or the chivalric loyalty of unsuccessful suitors. Power counts and Agamemnon had it; naturally then, others followed when he gave the order. If we look through the *Histories* we find that Thucydides accepts a surprising amount of legendary material but accepts it only after his new historical method has separated plausible versions from myth, sentimentality and downright falsehood.

This method, Thucydides' new historical engine, is one of the boldest and most powerful inventions of the intellectual revolution of the fifth century. We understand it and appreciate it thanks in large part to the phase of our own past that emphasized the "scientific" nature of Thucydides' work. But that emphasis did little to help us understand how this historical method functions within the text. For that we must turn to the aspect of Thucydides that has attracted so much attention in recent years—the nature of narrative discourse. Much interesting work has been or is being done in this rich field, but I shall concentrate on a very specific question, and a very difficult one: Why do we believe Thucydides' account? What makes him seem so persuasive and compelling? To phrase the question in this way is not to imply that all historians believe Thucydides all the time—far from it. But those critics who have challenged Thucydides most sharply will be the first to point out the extraordinary hold he has upon our thinking about the Peloponnesian War. Even when his account has received repeated and serious criticism, historians and laymen alike are reluctant to repudiate it. To be sure we try to utilize *all* our sources about antiquity, especially those by contemporary writers, but Thucydides enjoys, rightly or wrongly, an esteem not accorded to Ctesias, Xenophon, Appian, Suetonius, or even Herodotus, Polybius, Livy and Tacitus. Why is this? The reason is not that Thucydides' account has been tested against a large number of independently verifiable facts and found consistently reliable. Only rarely can his work be compared to contemporary documents, and when it is compared, as when we have an inscription, there is almost always a problem. The problems do not *refute* Thucydides; we simply lack solid, independent verification. It is then something else that causes the intensity of belief engendered by Thucydides.

What is this something? Surely it is in part the recognition that Thucydides, whatever his biases and faults, is a highly intelligent observer. But how do we know that? And how can we test that impression? There is no sufficient outside authority to which we can appeal. We have only the words of the text to rely upon. In other words, the narrative discourse of Thucydides itself establishes the authority of the writer and persuades us to listen with respect, if not total assent.

It achieves this hold, moreover, without using many of the conventions of scholarly history. Obviously no one would expect to find in his work the apparatus of modern historical research, but the contrast between Thucydides and Herodotus indicates how rarely Thucydides uses the devices by which Herodotus presented to his readers the problems of finding out about the past. Herodotus will commonly identify the places where he finds a serious difficulty; he will report alternative versions or views; he will cite the consideration that leads him to prefer one version to another and he will state his conclusion in language that expresses the degree of confidence he feels. He may make mistakes of fact or logic; he may even be quite silly, but the problematic of history is always before our eyes. As [R. W.] Macan said in his appreciation of Herodotus in the *Cambridge Ancient History,* "Where there is a variant, he will not suppress alternatives, or impose his own judgment upon posterity. Even when his own mind is made up, he will allow his informants, and his public, the benefit of the doubt." The historian and his reader are colleagues, sharing the problems and engaged in dialogue about their solution.

Thucydides' practice is quite the opposite. Through most of his work, he avoids discussing the problems of history and presents a finished product. As Macan says, "The results of his method, which is to extract for his readers, to all generations, a clear and chronologized narrative, the precise sources of which are seldom even indicated, must be taken or left on his authority, and on his authority alone." Reader and author stand in a different relationship. They are not colleagues, but performer and audience, the writer who knows how to produce a polished work and the audience who appreciates its craftsmanship and reacts to its quality.

To Thucydides' detractors this is sufficient to condemn him for "brain-washing" or manipulation. We expect to be colleagues, especially if we are professional historians (not that Thucydides ever was), and feel cheated if we are not allowed to look over his shoulder at the reports and documents he is using. Thucydides' defenders, on the other hand, wax eloquent. Gomme, following Gilbert Murray, for example, wrote that Thucydides was "determined to do all the work himself and to present only the finished product to the public, as the artist does. Wren showed St. Paul's Cathedral to the world, not his plans for it; so does the painter his picture; so did Pheidias his sculpture" [*The Greek Attitude to Poetry and History,* 1954].

If we step aside for a moment from the speeches for the prosecution and the defense, we notice something that seems to me more important than praise or blame. Thucydides' avoidance or rejection of the conventions of historical argument make it all the more difficult to give a satisfactory answer to our original question: Why do we believe Thucydides? We do not believe him because he has identified and clarified the problems, cited his sources, gathered the evidence and established his conclusions with such plausibility that we are forced to assent. Perhaps we believe him for precisely the opposite reason—because he writes not as the scribes and Pharisees do, but with authority.

That authority derives, I believe, from three sources. To one I have already alluded: it is the demonstration of historical method in the "Archaeology." The opening twenty-three chapters are a short, highly selective inquiry into some aspects of the past and constitute an *epideixis,* a demonstration piece, showing what Thucydides' method can do. They constitute an implicit *a fortiori* argument. If Thucydides' powerful engine can extract such a compelling interpretation of the remote past, *a fortiori* it should be able to attain important results in interpreting and analyzing the recent past. That, I believe, is what Thucydides implies when, after the investigation of early Greece, he points out the difficulties of finding out about the remote past but goes on to affirm that anyone who accepts the approximations he has derived from the indicators (*tekma ria*) he has mentioned will not go astray (1.21.1). He then turns to the problems of reconstructing the events of the Peloponnesian War. The famous "programmatic" or "methodological chapter" (1.22) is not a comprehensive statement of his historical principles but an affirmation of difficulties overcome and hence of the enduring utility of his work.

The first source of Thucydides' authority then is the demonstration of his historical method. But once the engine has been displayed, it is locked up again. We may hear it rumbling away in the background somewhere; we are reminded of its existence from time to time. But we do not regularly see it collecting, analyzing, testing and selecting reports and data about events and turning them into finished historical narrative.

Thus for much of the work the historical method of Thucydides is out of sight, if not entirely out of mind. In these portions its effects are reinforced by two further sources of authority. One is Thucydidean "style," that formidable, overwhelming complexity that can shatter all the neat antilogies and balances of Greek and strain the language to its limit.

Once again it is important to ask the simple but fundamental question. Why is Thucydides' style so difficult? Is it, as Collingwood thought [in his *The Idea of History,* 1956], the result of Thucydides' bad conscience, his uneasiness at pretending to write history when he was really writing political science or theory? Or is the more conventional answer correct—that it is the result of the originality and subtlety of his ideas. Is there some gnostic message concealed in the complexity of his expression? If we look closely, we find, I believe, that neither of these answers is correct. The difficulties derive not from the author's psychic disquiet nor from hidden subtleties, but from a desire to affirm his respect for the complexity of historical events and human motives. In Thucydides we discover not an arcane philosophy but a style that replicates the intractability of historical experience. It assures the reader that the author will not oversimplify or reduce events to cliché, antithesis, or dogma.

This assurance is conveyed by, and much of the difficulty arises from, Thucydides' use of multiple viewpoints in narrating events. He will begin from one point of view, and switch, usually without warning or marker, to quite a different perspective. Often we end by viewing a single event from two or three different viewpoints. In the account of the third year of the war, for example, Thucydides tells of the consternation that swept through Athens when a Peloponnesian fleet appeared in the Saronic Gulf. The Peloponnesians had almost defeated the Athenian ships in the Corinthian Gulf. Then, at the end of the campaigning season, the Peloponnesian commanders decide to undertake one more operation. They will march their sailors overland, each carrying his oarlock and seat cushion, to Megara where forty ships are drawn up in their ally's dockyards. With these ships, they plan to make a surprise attack on the Piraeus.

Up to this point the narrative is straightforward, perfectly clear, even relatively easy Greek. Then follows a sentence of such contorted phraseology—not to mention its nine negatives in 35 words—that the critics have tried to emend it or delete it. Crawley's translation smooths out some of the difficulties but catches the main idea:

> There was no fleet on the look out in the harbor [of the Piraeus] and no one had the least idea of the enemy attempting a surprise: while an open attack would, it was thought, never be deliberately ventured on, or if in contemplation would be speedily known at Athens. (2.93.3)

Crawley has added a crucial phrase to the Greek: "while an open attack would, *it was thought,* never be deliberately ventured upon . . ." . Why did Crawley add this phrase? He recognized and marked for his reader what is implicit and hence a source of obscurity in the Greek: that Thucydides has shifted from reporting the attitude of the Peloponnesians to conveying the psychology of the Athenians. In the next sentence, when Thucydides shifts back to the plans of the Peloponnesians, the reader understands, thanks to this contorted sentence, both the Peloponnesians' feeling that their original plan was terribly risky, and the ironic fact that precisely because of that risk it might well have worked:

> . . . arriving at night and launching their vessels from Nisaea, they sailed, not to Piraeus as they originally intended, being afraid of the risk, besides which there was some talk of a wind having stopped them, but to the point of Salamis . . .

The rest of the account of the operation continues this alternation between Peloponnesian and Athenian viewpoints. The effect is consistently ironic: by the time we hear of the Peloponnesian decision to abandon their original plan we know that from the Athenian point of view it might have worked; by the time we hear of the panic in Athens, we know that from the Peloponnesian point of view the plan was too risky to carry through. The irony is characteristic of Thucydides and so are the rapid changes of viewpoint, a major component of his style and an important contributor to this second source of his authority.

The richness of Thucydides' account comes sharply into focus if we compare this passage to the smooth and nicely balanced version of the episode supplied by Diodorus of Sicily. Diodorus reduces all to a single viewpoint, that of one Peloponnesian commander; he omits the vivid detail of the march overland with each rower carrying his oarlock and seat cushion, and by failing to mention the growing fears of the Peloponnesian commanders leaves his reader without explanation for the outcome of the operation, an attack on Salamis not Piraeus:

In this year, Cnemus, the Lacedaemonian admiral, who was inactive in Corinth, decided to seize the Piraeus. He had received information that no ships in the harbour had been put into the water for duty and no soldiers had been detailed to guard the port; for the Athenians, as he had learned, had become negligent about guarding it because they by no means expected any enemy would have the audacity to seize the place. Consequently Cnemus, launching forty triremes which had been hauled up on the beach at Megara, sailed by night to Salamis, and falling unexpectedly on the fortrees on Salamis called Boudorium, he towed away three ships and overran the entire island. (Diodorus 12.49.2-3, trans. C.H. Oldfather)

No one needs corroboration from contemporary documents or even a knowledge of the chronological and historiographical relationship between Thucydides and Diodorus to know which of these two accounts to prefer.

A third source of authority, however, may prove even more important. To call this the "experiential" or "participatory" aspect of Thucydides' work would be cumbersome, but the terms for all their awkwardness call attention to a feature often neglected in the work. We do not usually think of Thucydides as a writer who keeps drawing his readers into the narrative of events until they feel they are themselves present, actually experiencing them. But Thucydides achieves this implication of the reader to an extraordinary degree. We do not often let ourselves be caught up in the vicarious experience of the actions he describes, but we should. For every minute we spend searching for laws or theory or gnostic insights, we might well allot equal time and attention to Thucydides' ability to recreate events and moods.

To achieve this end Thucydides has many techniques, chief among them the dramatic interplay between abstraction and sudden flashes of vividness. His style aspires to a level of generality that brings out the similarity of one episode to another. It often verges on the formulaic. But darting through it are words, phrases, sometimes whole episodes whose extraordinary vividness creates the illusion that we are ourselves present, witnessing events. In the passage we have just examined, for example, Thucydides notes that each sailor carried with him on the march his oarlock and cushion. In recounting the initial attack on Plataea, he focusses on the spear point jammed into the lock of the gate to prevent escape (2.4.3). At the siege of Plataea we observe the careful planning of the escape, the counting of the bricks (3.20.3), the removal of the sandal from the right foot (3.22.2), the armament and name of the leader of those who first climbed the ladders (3.22.3). In the account of the battle near Naupactus we watch an Athenian ship wheel rapidly about an anchored merchantman and ram its Leucadian pursuer

amidship and sink it (2.91.3); on Sphacteria we experience the dust, the headgear pierced by arrows, the broken spears (4.34.3). Every attentive reader of Thucydides could expand the list and note the close bond between visual detail and the mood of the scene and the feelings of the participants. Vision in Thucydides is the privileged sense, most commonly invoked and most directly linked to the emotions.

Yet modern critics have said far less about the vivid side of Thucydides' style than about the complexities of his moral and political beliefs. In this respect, for all their obvious faults, the ancient critics are closer to the mark. Plutarch, for example, stressed Thucydides' use of *enargeia,* vividness, in his comments on Thucydides.

> The most effective historian is the one who makes his narrative like a painting by giving a visual quality to the sufferings and characters. Thucydides certainly always strives after this vividness in his writing, eagerly trying to transform his reader into a spectator and to let the sufferings that were so dazzling and upsetting to those who beheld them have a similar effect on those who read about them. (Plutarch *On the Fame of the Athenians,* ch. 3 [*Moralia* 347A])

Hobbes [in his Preface to a translation of Thucydides, 1629] made a similar observation, but set it in a more provocative context. He praised Thucydides as "the most politic historiographer that ever writ. The reason wherefore I take to be this . . . he maketh his auditor a spectator." And how did Thucydides attain this most politic result? "The narrative," Hobbes says, "doth secretly instruct the reader and more effectively than can be done by precept." The political lessons and the utility of the ***Histories,*** in other words, derive not from Thucydides' explicit comments or implicit theorizing, but from the reader's own involvement in the work.

Once we recognize this, many features of the work become far more intelligible. We can worry less about the author's hidden theories and more about our own reactions to the text. And as we become more active participants in the events described, we can dispense with the narrator's guidance and explicit comments. The narrator can become self-effacing, speak in the third person, intervene only rarely with his own judgments and evaluations and let the reader do, in Henry James' phrase, "quite half the labor." He may pretend that the war itself is the narrator which reveals its own greatness to those who scrutinize events closely enough (1.21.2).

We recognize, of course, that this is pretense, or a game in which reader and author engage. History is not chronicle, and Thucydides was certainly not a modest registering machine duly recording each event in colorless exactitude. He is present, selecting, shaping, coloring, at every episode, every phrase, every subscript. We ancient historians and philologists have reached the age of discretion at which we can reasonably be expected to recognize that the shaping of the text by the author, even as the author pretends to remove himself from his story, is not a bad habit, unprofessional conduct on the part of the writer. It is one way a writer can accomplish an essential part of his purpose—the involvement of the reader in the events and the activation of the reader's own evaluative capacities.

The illusion created by Thucydides, then, is one of immediate presence, of our own participation in the events described. That illusion, in Thucydides' view at least, excludes another one, and a very near and dear one to our historical hearts. Thucydides avoids letting his reader think that he is in the archive selecting the documents, or in the author's study participating in the choice of one version over another. We are not his colleague. Instead, the documents have been gathered, the informants interrogated, the selection of alternative versions has been completed. This much of the work is done and the reader is presented with the final product and asked to respond to it.

In this respect Thucydides' practice contrasts very sharply with that of Herodotus. To many modern readers Herodotus is much more congenial. As we read his work we are constantly reminded of the difficulties he encountered in assembling and shaping his material—the legends and biased accounts presented to him as fact, the leg-pulling, the gaps and the polemics he encountered. We are at his side, sharing the decisions with him, and enjoying the process. By contrast Thucydides may seem to us, as he does to Truesdale Brown [in *Historia* 31 (1982)], to underestimate our intelligence:

> . . . while breaking new ground in his scrupulous use of sources, he underestimated the intelligence of his readers. Having arrived at his own conclusions by a critical examination of the evidence he does not share the materials he rejects with the reader. Herodotus was less critical . . . he could not bear to omit anything which he felt might appeal to his readers.

Brown's comments call attention to a major contrast between the two writers. But his explanation leaves out of sight the possibility that there are different principles at work. Thucydides imposes a different division of labor between author and reader. The historian's job is to investigate, compile, select, edit and present. The reader's half, the greater half, is to react, to assess, and thereby to learn.

This feature of Thucydides' technique has several important consequences for our understanding of the

Histories, two of which call for special comment. The first concerns the ease with which description of mood is confused with statement of fact. The second returns to the major topic of this paper, the establishment of Thucydides' authority.

First, mood. One of Thucydides' goals, we have suggested, was to create in his reader the illusion that he is himself present at events. Sometimes this goal leads to descriptions not of the event itself but of the reactions and feelings of those who were present at the event. The most famous of these passages is the description of the great naval battle in the harbor at Syracuse. The main portion of the description of the battle contains passages such as this:

> . . . while the naval battle was hanging in the balance, the land army of each side experienced a great conflict and convergence of reactions. The group from the immediate area were eager to win, with a view to even greater glory; those who had invaded feared lest they should experience even worse than their present state. Since for the Athenians everything depended on the ships, their fear of the future was beyond any comparison and thanks to the uncertainty of the naval battle, uncertain too had to be the vision of it from the land. Since one could see only a small portion of the action, nor did all look at the same spot, those who saw in one engagement their own forces succeeding were encouraged and would turn to invocations of the gods not to deprive them of their safety. But those who looked at a defeat raised a ritual lament even while they were shouting and from the sight of what had happened lost their spirit even more than those who were in the engagement. . . . (7.71.1-3)

The passage is an excellent example of several Thucydidean techniques—shifting viewpoints, the emphasis on vision, the creation of mood. But William Scott Ferguson deplored this approach:

> . . . Thucydides fails even to suggest the factors that determined the outcome. Instead, he dwells on certain typical incidents in the confused fighting that followed, and then turns our attention to the spectators on the shore, and leaves us to infer the manifold vicissitudes of the protracted struggle from the agony of fear, joy, anxiety. . . .

True enough. Thucydides' concern, however, was not to recover the tactics, such as they were, of this confused battle, but to record the changes in the morale of the Athenians, the crucial factor in the next stage of the operations. We have in this passage another kind of *enargeia,* a vividness not of precise details but of mood.

For the reader passages such as this pose special problems. One can, for example, mistake mood for fact. Again, Thucydides does not always stop to distinguish and to mark important differences. Sometimes it is not entirely clear whether he is telling us what the situation was or how it seemed to contemporary observers. At the beginning of book eight, for example, Thucydides discusses the situation in Athens when news came of the loss of the expedition in Sicily:

> All things on all sides grieved them and there surrounded them in this situation fear and dismay of the very greatest sort. For since they had lost, both individually and as a city, many heavy-armed soldiers and cavalry and crack troops of a quality the match of which they did not see to be available, they were depressed. Likewise since they did not see sufficient ships in their dockyards nor money in their treasury, nor crews for their ships, they despaired of any salvation in the present situation. They believed that the enemies from Sicily would immediately sail with their fleets against the Piraeus, especially since they had conquered so decisively, and that their own more immediate enemies at that very time had made double efforts in full force and would bear down upon them from land and sea and that their own allies would revolt and join them. (8.1.2-3)

The passage tells us how the Athenians looked upon their situation in the bleak moments when the news about Sicily arrived. It is full of descriptions of feelings—how they saw things, what they *believed* would happen. But many excellent commentators take the passage as Thucydides' assertion of *facts,* and then point out, using evidence from other passages in Thucydides, that the situation was by no means as hopeless as this passage suggests. Meiggs, for example [in *The Athenian Empire* (1972)], writes "the empire, meanwhile, according to Thucydides, threatened collapse as the allies competed fiercely to be the first to revolt, now that Athens' power was broken. His detailed narrative does not fully bear out this gloomy analysis." And Andrewes in the new Oxford commentary on book eight (p.6), noting that Athenian despair about their navy, concludes, "clearly the decree of 431 (ii.24.2) had not been maintained to keep a reserve of a hundred triremes, the best of each year, in readiness with their trierarchs." Perhaps not, but as Andrewes points out, their despair about their finances makes no mention of the reserve fund of one thousand talents also established in 431 and still available for use in the post-Sicilian emergency (8.15.1). Thucydides says that the Athenians did not see the resources to deal with the present situation; he does not say there were no resources to see.

As we read on in book eight the facts gradually become clear and the mood of the Athenians gradually changes: there *is* a reserve fund; not *all* allies revolt; those that do revolt often act prematurely; Sparta is not

effective in exploiting the situation and the Syracusans are not swift or decisive in their intervention. At Cynossema Athens wins a major victory. In the eighth book we trace an irregular movement from despair to growing confidence, from apparent defeat to the renewed efforts of the Athenians in a final, and even greater, struggle. If we understand Thucydides' emphasis on changing moods, this book becomes more intelligible and we are far less likely, here or elsewhere, to mistake description of moods for statements about facts.

In a second way too we can now better understand Thucydides' technique and why it has produced such intense conviction. At certain points the narrative creates in the reader the feeling of being directly present at an episode in the war. We are as far from the historians' study as we can possibly be; we are in the war itself. We see; we hear; we even know the plans and thoughts of the participants. The crucial elements are before us, not in pictorial fullness, as one might find in a Hellenistic historian, but through highly selective detail. As Lawrence Stone has said of Peter Brown, "The deliberate vagueness, the pictorial approach, . . . the concern for what was going on inside people's heads, are all characteristic of a fresh way of writing history." And like a *pointilliste* painting it draws us in, involves our minds in the process of creation, and wins our assent. Seeing is, after all, believing.

Those who have learned what history is from professional scholars and who know a good footnote when they see one, may find this a paradoxical conclusion. How can one believe a writer who, after a few opening chapters, simply bypasses the whole problematic of history and writes as if he knew precisely what went on in the war, and even in the participants' heads? If we had been weaned on Macaulay and Carlyle, things might look different. Those writers remind us that in History's house there are many rooms and many passageways. We lose something if we block off too many parts of the mansion or condemn too much of it too soon.

And what is it, precisely, we risk if we close the chambers Thucydides occupied? The loss of vicarious experience and of the sense of participating in a reality far different from our daily life, the very thing that makes the study of history so important for the growth of the mind and imagination. "But surely," one might object, "this vicarious experience can be obtained without sacrificing the constant gestures of respect for the problematic of history which are the marks of modern scholarly history." Perhaps, but one should not underestimate the difficulty. For many readers any pause over the problems of historical evidence and reconstruction, any worry about conflicting sources or assessments, any entry into the historian's study, shatters the illusion of participating in the past. The problematic of history impedes its experiential power. To talk about the problems of historical analysis imposes a chasm between reader and past event. Even when it produces conviction, a residue of doubt remains. For historical analysis is always based on the calculation of probabilities. We read the arguments and assent, but our language reminds us of the uncertainty. We say we are "almost one hundred percent sure" or that we are "half-way convinced" or that we have "found the preponderance of evidence" on one side of the matter.

The division of labor we have noted in Thucydides bypasses this problem. Thucydides may have his doubts and unresolved problems. But he keeps them to himself and lets the reader transcend them. The conviction which attends the reading of Thucydides' work is thus not related to the calculation of probabilities or the careful assessment of plausible solutions. We feel we have been there. The world Thucydides has described, the patterns of power and human conduct, are so consistent, so real, that we have no choice but to assent. We are moved by the greater logic that derives its power not from accumulated evidence or carefully constructed syllogisms but from the evocation of a coherent world. At length we feel, not that we have deduced the nature of that world, but that we have temporarily become part of it. Of course we then believe—not despite, but because of the fact that Thucydides does not write as the scribes and Pharisees do, but as one with authority.

What shall we then conclude about Thucydides' authority? Why *do* we believe him? We have seen three sources of it in the work, the first the powerful engine of historical analysis whose workings are best to be seen in the "Archaeology." The second is a style that affirms the author's respect for the complexity of historical events and that views the past from multiple perspectives. The third source, perhaps the most important, is the reader's feeling of experiencing the events described.

The sources do not all cohabit in blissful harmony. Indeed between the second and the third there is an inevitable tension—the rapid shifting of viewpoints risks a shattering of the experiential quality of the work. But Thucydides' style not only contributes to his authority but sustains the tension and transforms it into the uniquely powerful result we have all experienced in reading Thucydides. It accounts for something scholars of Thucydides experience but often fail to mention—Thucydides' appeal as a writer and the pleasure of reading him. If we concentrate too much on the scientist or philosopher, we lose sight of the vividness of his writing and the rich, demanding but rewarding experience of reading a great writer. Expecting profundity we can miss the color, the swift-paced action, the detail, the opportunity to see, to experience, to understand. To say this is not to make Thucydides into

a simple writer, not to minimize the efforts he expects from his readers. But it is a reminder of the ability of this work to avoid the eventual emptiness of an exclusively analytical method and to resist with equal determination the tendency so evident in Hellenistic historiography to report anything that is sufficiently lurid and sensational. What makes Thucydides' work what it is—one of the unsurpassed and enduring achievements of prose narrative—is precisely this tension and interaction among different modes of narrative discourse.

FURTHER READING

Abbott, G. F. *Thucydides: A Study in Historical Reality*, George Routledge & Sons, 1925.
    Argues that Thucydides' approach to historical writing breaks from the conventions of classical history and anticipates modern styles.

Connor, W. R. "A Post Modernist Thucydides?" *The Classical Journal* 72, No. 4 (April-May 1977): 289-98.
    Reviews modern criticism on Thucydides's *History*, remarking in particular on recent pronounced shifts in critical opinion.

De Romilly, Jacqueline. *Thucydides and Athenian Imperialism*. Oxford: Basil Blackwell, 1963, 400 p.
    Analyzes Thucydides' attitude toward the expansion of Athens as a political and military power.

Dover, K. J. *Thucydides*. New Surveys in the Classics No. 7. Oxford: Oxford University Press, 1973, 44 p.
    Provides an overview of issues relevant to the study of the *History*, including Thucydides' prose style, his use of speeches, and his expression of personal opinions.

Edmunds, Lowell. *Chance and Intelligence in Thucydides*. Cambridge, Mass.: Harvard University Press, 1975, 243 p.
    Examines the antithetical Greek concepts of intelligence and chance and their function in Thucydides' *History*.

Gomme, A. W. "Thucydides" and "Thucydides (*Continued*)." In *The Greek Attitude to Poetry and History*, pp. 116-38, 139-64. Berkeley: University of California Press, 1954.
    Explores Thucydides's ideas regarding history in social and cultural context.

Hunter, Virginia J. *Thucydides: The Artful Reporter*. Toronto: A. M. Hakkert, 1973, 210 p.
    Demonstrates that the *History* was shaped by Thucydides' interest in the motives and purposes of statesmen.

————. *Past and Process in Herodotus and Thucydides.* Princeton: Princeton University Press, 1982, 371 p.

Analyzes Thucydides' perception of history and what it means to record history, based on the theories of Ferdinand Braudel and Michel Foucault.

Lord, Louis E. *Thucydides and the World War.* Martin Classical Lectures Vol. XII. 1945. Reprint. New York: Russell and Russell, 1967, 304 p.

Offers an extensive overview of Thucydides's *History,* including historical background and a summary of the content of the work.

Mahaffy, J. P. "Thycidides—Andocides, Critias." In *A History of Classical Greek Literature,* pp. 98-133. New York: Harper & Brothers, 1880.

Praises Thucydides for his "trustworthiness" and lucidity.

Parry, Adam. "Thucydides' Use of Abstract Language." *Yale French Studies* 45 (1970): 3-20.

Discusses Thucydides in the context of the development of abstract expression in the Greek language.

Pouncey, Peter R. *The Necessities of War: A Study of Thucydides' Pessimism.* New York: Columbia University Press, 1980, 195 p.

Asserts that Thucydides believed human nature to be grounded in fear and self-interest, and that these were the primary factors that led to the Peloponnesian war.

Wallace, W. P. "Thucydides." *Pheonix: The Journal of the Classical Association of Canada* XVIII, no. 4 (Winter 1964): 251-61.

Provides a review of some of the critical material on Thucydides in order to substantiate the author's view that "it is somehow not quite respectable to give one's readers as little choice as Thucydides gives his."

Westlake, H. D. *Individuals in Thucydides.* Cambridge, England: Cambridge University Press, 1968, 324 p.

Traces the evolution of Thucydides' approach in presenting important individuals.

————. *Essays on the Greek Historians and Greek History.* Manchester: Manchester University Press, 1969, 332 p.

Contains several essays on various topics in Thucydides studies.

Woodhead, A. Geoffrey. *Thucydides on the Nature of Power.* Martin Classical Lectures Vol. XXIV. Cambridge, Mass.: Harvard University Press, 1970, 222 p.

Explores Thucydides' attitude toward power and the exercise of power by the individuals and institutions of his era.

Xenophon

c. 430 B.C.-c. 354 B.C.

Creek historian and philosopher.

INTRODUCTION

Xenophon was a fourth-century Greek historian best known for his *Hellenica*, which began where Thucydides's *History of the Peloponnesian War* had stopped, and for the semi-historical, semi-novelistic *Cyropaedia*. While he often appears alongside Herodotus and Thucydides in major studies of Greek historiography, he is not always included with enthusiasm. Critics have regularly remarked on his limitations as a historian, finding his presentation of historical material selective and biased. He is also found wanting as a philosopher: critics brand his dialogues, such as the *Oeconomicus* and the *Symposium*, derivative, weak on comprehension and original insight, and unsuccessful in the attempt to capture socratic thought. Such critical condemnations, however, are relatively recent: his reputation in the centuries following his own age was very high and remained so through the Renaissance. Since the height of the Roman Empire, Xenophon has won praise for his detailed and reliable information on military matters, for his style, which is simple, straightforward, and concise, and for his aptitude as a story-teller. By the nineteenth century, his *Anabasis*, an account of a Greek army's travails in Persia, became a common textbook for young people studying Greek because of its accessibility and narrative pull. Overall, however, he was by this time often named only to be criticized. Nonetheless, his works have received extensive critical attention, both for their documentation of Greek life and ancient history and for their rhetorical strategies.

Biographical Information

Xenophon was born in Ercheia, a rural district outside of Athens; his father, Gryllus, was probably an upper-class Athenian citizen. Biographer J. K. Anderson surmised from Xenophon's environment and writings that his upbringing and personal opinions were generally conservative—invested in preserving the class structure into which he was born. He grew up during the Peloponnesian War (431-404 B.C.) and appears to have had his first military experience as a cavalryman close to the end of the war. When the war ended, the preceding era of Athenian democracy also came to a close, replaced by the oligarchic rule of thirty men, later known as the Thirty Tyrants. Initially, many men of Xenophon's class supported this change, since, accord-

ing to authorities on Greek history, many believed that Greek democracy had become excessive during the war and had possibly harmed the Greek cause. Ultimately, however, the Thirty lost the support of the upper classes; when they were overthrown, democracy reemerged.

Despite an unremarkable intellect, Xenophon met and became a disciple of Socrates, the most influential thinker of his age and many others. According to Xenophantic legend, the young man was traversing a passage in Athens when the philosopher barred his way and began asking him questions about where one could find various kinds of goods, to which Xenophon replied with the names of various kinds of vendors. When Socrates asked him, "And where do men find virtue?" Xenophon had no answer, at which Socrates invited the young man to follow and learn from him. Ultimately, however, military experience appears to have been of greater value to Xenophon than intellectual training. In approximately 402 B.C. Xenophon's friend Proxenus invited him on a military expedition: they would fight in Persia, on a mercenary basis, for Cyrus the Younger, who was challenging his brother Aratxerxes' claim to the Persian throne. It was a politically risky move, since he would be selling his military loyalty outside of Greece and to a man viewed as an enemy by Athenian authorities. Xenophon, on Socrates's advice, sought the counsel of the oracle at Delphi, but rather than asking the oracle if he should fight for Cyrus, he asked to which god he should make a sacrifice to ensure success. His determination may have been motivated, as several historians have speculated, by the need to make up losses suffered by his family estate under the demands of the Thirty Tyrants.

In Cyrus's service the next year, Xenophon was affiliated with a Greek army of 10,000 soldiers. He became one of their leaders after Cyrus's defeat and the execution of most of the Greek commanders, when the column needed to make its way back home. The account of that expedition, known as the March of the 10,000, became one of Xenophon's most popular works, the *Anabasis*. Xenophon followed his Persian military career with a similar position for Agesilaus, a Spartan king, in 396-394 B.C. Here he risked his political position at home even further, since Sparta was a traditional enemy of Athens. In 394 B.C., this association brought him directly into battle with Athenian forces, after which the Athenian authorities formally exiled him and confiscated his property. His reputation in Athens had endured earlier blows when Socrates was tried and executed in 399 B.C., with suspicion cast on many of his followers.

Deprived of his home in Athens, Xenophon acquired an estate at Scillus in Elis, in Spartan territory, where he pursued his writing in earnest and raised a family. He remained at Scillus for two decades, roughly from 390-370 B.C., until Sparta lost Scillus to Thebes, and then relocated to Corinth. When Spartan-Athenian relations improved in c. 365 B.C., Xenophon was able to return to Athens; some historians have located him back in Athens after that date, but most have described him remaining in Corinth until his death.

Major Works

Xenophon was a prolific writer, producing many works from the end of the fifth century to his death, all of which appear to have survived in some form or another. Critics generally group his works into three categories—histories, philosophical works, and technical works—although many of the pieces defy easy categorization. His status as a historian derives mainly from the *Hellenica*, the *Anabasis*, and the *Cyropaedia*. He may have begun the *Hellenica*, his most ambitious historical work, as early as 411 B.C., thereby matching his intial writing date with the opening of the history. The seven books trace the history of Greece from 411 B.C.-362 B.C. The *Hellenica* also fields the most fire from critical scholars, since it appears to fail the standard criteria of historical accuracy and impartiality. The *Anabasis* has earned more favor and has been praised for its narrative style and apparently more solid historical detail. Although the author refers to himself in the third person throughout, the work, probably written in 379 B.C., is largely autobiographical, relating Xenophon's own experiences and observations during the March of the 10,000. The *Anabasis* and the *Cyropaedia*, on the other hand, have been appreciated for the new territories they appeared to explore: a kind of proto-novelistic storytelling and experiment in biography and autobiography. The *Cyropaedia*, c. 365 B.C., combines Persian history and biography in a narrative presentation of the life of Cyrus the Elder, who founded the Persian monarchy. Scholars have hotly debated its value as history, many asserting that the picture of Persia Xenophon presents is too romantic and that Xenophon marred his objectivity with his desire to make the text a lesson in good citizenship and good leadership. Critics agree, however, that it has had a major influence on later generations, both contributing to the development of the novel and, in the words of Moses Hadas, having "an appreciable effect in shaping European ideas of what a gentleman should be." Xenophon also apparently completed one other biography in 365 B.C., the *Agesilaus*, an encomium, or laudatory biography, of the Spartan king Agesilaus, for whom Xenophon fought.

Like his historical works, Xenophon's philosophical works have also come under attack. Some critics have suggested that they be classified as a kind of memoir, since almost all present Socrates as a central character. The most famous of these are in fact called "memoirs"—the *Memorabilia* possibly begun in c. 384 B.C. and completed in c. 356 B.C.—Xenophon's memories presented for the specific purpose of depicting Socrates. The earliest portion of the *Memorabilia* may have been the *Apology*, Xenophon's rendition of Socrates' trial, meant as a defense of his teacher. The accuracy of the *Memorabilia* is considered doubtful and suggests that Xenophon failed to reproduce Socrates's doctrines very clearly. The other socratic dialogues, however, receive even more criticism, sometimes fielding the charge that Xenophon's Socrates appears simply as the mouthpiece for Xenophon's own thoughts. These works include the *Apology*; the *Oeconomicus (On Household Management)*, c. 362 B.C., in which Ischomachus, a young husband, consults Socrates about how best to manage his estate economy and, specifically, his new wife; and the *Symposium*, a philosophical dialogue set during an imaginary dinner party, formally much like Plato's work of the same name, praised for its unusually strong structure and consistency. One other philosophical work, the *Hiero*, also c. 365 B.C., presented a dialogue, between King Hiero I of Syracuse and the poet Simonides, on the nature of rule. Xenophon also produced quite a few technical manuals, ranging across his favorite topics. Sometimes the *Oeconomicus* is included among them because of its detailed information about a typical Greek estate of the era. Other technical manuals present similarly valuable information on different topics, including the highly valued *On the Spartan Constitution* (c. 388 B.C.) and *On Horsemanship* (c. 380 B.C.).

Textual History

Many critics and editors have suggested that the centrality of Xenophon's name in the study of Greek historiography has less to do with the quality of his work than with the extent to which it has been preserved. It appears that most, if not all, of his writings survive in some form, usually in Medieval or Renaissance transcriptions or translations. The absence of original and even ancient manuscripts has led to considerable debate over dating Xenophon's writings, especially regarding the different books of the *Hellenica*; consequently, most works are placed either in the author's twenty years in Elis or in the period after his exile was revoked. Extant manuscripts that are housed in libraries in the Middle East and throughout Europe, with the earliest dating from 1166 A.D.

Critical Reception

Although Xenophon's reputation appeared to be that of a minor author in his own age, he became a favorite of Roman readers including Cato the Elder, Cicero, Julius Ceaser, and Mark Antony, all of whom favored his military expertise and simple prose style. In the second century B.C., Lucian classed Xenophon with his two notable predecessors, Herodotus and Thucydides, and commented that in his own age "everyone wanted to be a Xenophon." His currency remained high with European readers through the Middle Ages and Renaissance. The fifteenth century saw many Latin translations of his works, and the sixteenth century, many translations into modern tongues. By the the nineteenth century, however, his reputation had fallen. His later style, which retained the simplicity of his earlier works but became ever more colloquial, carried little weight with the century's scholars of Greek literature and his historical works came under fire for their evident partiality and errors. The judgement trailed through into the twentieth century, captured in M. I. Finley's remark in 1959 that the *Hellenica* "is very unreliable, tendentious, dishonest, dreary to read, and rarely illuminating on broader issues." Ironically, while Western scholars have tended to discount Xenophon's histo-

riographic skills and, specifically, to regard his depiction of Persia in the *Cyropaedia* as wholly romantic, Orientalists have long considered Xenophon a reliable source on the history of Persia. Only recently have these two currents pulled together enough for Orientalists to assure Western critics that Xenophon's knowledge appears to be reliable.

The late twentieth century has seen something of a revival in Xenophon's popularity, especially as his texts are studied as more than historical tracts. Classicist Leo Strauss has been instrumental in creating a resurgance of interest with his translation and study of the *Hiero*, or *On Tyranny*, in 1948, and J. K. Anderson's 1974 biographical study marked a groundswell in renewed appreciation. The bulk of this recent critical attention has focused on the *Cyropaedia*, since this text best allows critics to re-examine the issue of Xenophon's reliability as a historian. Emphasizing the necessary artifice of any literary production, Steven Hirsch and James Tatum have studied the book using the tools of literary analysis rather than historiography. From this perspective, the *Cyropaedia* becomes not only a rich text, but a central progenitor in the development of the Western novel. In a similar vein, Arnaldo Momigliano has recognized Xenophon as integral to the development of both biography and autobiography in Western literature, including him among the fourth-century Socratics who "moved to that zone between truth and fiction which is so bewildering to the professional historian."

PRINCIPAL ENGLISH TRANSLATIONS

The School of Cyrus (translated by William Barker) 1567
The Works of Xenophon (translated by H. G. Dakyns) 1890-97
The Art of Horsemanship (translated by Morris H. Morgan) 1893
Cyropaedia (translated by Walter Miller) 1914
The March up Country (Anabasis) (translated by W. H. D. Rouse) 1948
The Persian Expedition (translated by R. Warner) 1949
Recollections of Socrates, and Socrates Defense Before the Jury (translated by A. S. Benjamin) 1965
Hiero (translated by Leo Strauss) 1968
Xenophon's Socratic Discourse: An Interpretation of the Oeconomicus (translated by Carnes Lord) 1970
History of My Times (Hellenica) (translated by R. Warner) 1978
Memorabilia (translated by Amy L. Bonnette) 1994

CRITICISM

William Barker   (essay date 1567)

SOURCE: A preface to *The School of Cyrus,* by Xenophon, translated by William Barker, 1567. Reprint by Garland Publishing, Inc., 1987, pp. 1-8.

[*Barker, a fellow at Oxford University, completed the first known English translation of Xenophon's* Cyropaedia *in 1567. In the preface that follows, Barker dedicates the work to the Earls of Pembroke and Surrey, stressing the volume's educational value.*]

A Preface to the Right Honorable William, Earl of Pembroke, Lord Harbert of Cardife, knight of the honorable order of the Garter, and President of the King's Highness Council in the marches of Wales, William Bercker wishes health and honor.

Those authors be chiefly to heard, which have not only by finess of wit and diligence of study attained to an excellency, but also have had the experience of manners of men, and diversity of places, and have with wisdom and eloquence joined those two together. For as general things and order of nature can not be perceived, but by them whose natural sharpness of wit is helped with earnest and continual pain, fullness of study so the private doings and dispositions of men only known by daily use and trial of them. And there be many skillful in the one, that be in the other kind very simple, and say much of generalities, but in particularities be utterly ignorant, and other again, who can talk well and wisely in singular points wherein they be experienced, but in the other kind they be in a manner without understanding. Or they who have been brought up in study, and know no more than they have attained unto by reading, be in general things, labored in by other, and found out by much debating of common reason skillfuller than the common sort, and therefore called better learned, and they who have whet the fine edge of their wit, and peered their doings and inclinations of other, with diligent making of the seen, and remembering the marked, be called witty and wise men, and have good praise of their sayings and doings in common life. And hereby happeneth that which is commonly said, the best learned men be not the wisest. Either for that they can not tell particular things, which be in daily and common use of life, or else for cause, although their reason be well furnished with reading and understanding what is best, yet their affections and moods be not hardened enough, nor strengthened with experience and trial of things, and therefore be in their doings many times unadvised and simple. And because each of these things require a whole man's life to grow to any perfectness therein, and it seldom chanceth and once in a man's age, that perfect study and perfect experience meet together in one man, and

few painful wits be good, and fewer good wits be painful, therefore cometh it seldom to pass that there be many thoroughly wise men at one time and be more commonly talked of than seen and more looked for than found, and wished for rather than had. And this maketh that in all the course of learning and experience there be very few who satisfy goodly and well judging wits, and whom they would, that seek the price of fame, labor to follow in their writings, whole wits they marvel at in writing.

Some there be, who by diligence and nature have goodly understanding of praiseworthy things, and can find out well what is best to be done, and wittiest to be reasoned, but they lack the stream of eloquence, which floweth with delight to please the dainty ears and can roughly hew the matter to serve for good purpose, but yet lack the swift violence of sweet running talk, to carry away the indifferent mind to their intented purpose.

Other there be, whose wit melteth words sufficient to serve, and gusheth with abundance when they turn their cock, but it is muddy and troubled for lack of fined reason, and so serveth not the purpose well, although it be plentiful, but better unoccupied than spent in weighty causes. Thus Nature playeth well where she purposeth her show, and showeth what she liketh to open her diversity, and is fruitful to weeds if they lie untilled, and overgroweth her self with her own plenty, and by fruitfulness is unfruitful, except her fruitfulness be ordered, and wisom rules Nature, and pares away her excess wherewith she is overcharged, when she is unordered. The barren ground sometime with diligence is tilled, and bringeth forth such fruit, as such a ground can serve for, and what cunning can do where nature will not help, she showeth by her burden, and telleth us this lesson: That nature's want is helped where good husbandry is used, and if grounds well looked to, be of like value to the good grounds ill ordered and overgrown by sloth. Such hardness is it for good things well made to meet all in one man, and matchly to be copied, for nature and diligence to serve experience and study, all which things lightly fall not well together, except some godly grace from some diligent nature, which being well brought up and well disposed to, do furnish nature's beauty with the favor of good learning, and mark well in travail the common doings of men, and apply well together his learning and experience, and labor there unto join wisdom in talk by following of the wise and raising out his words of the nature of the matter, and driving to the end the order of his reason, and measuring by direction the affection of the hearer and draw him to the matter by cunning in conveyance, and not the matter unto him to serve his desire.

But Xenophon this Philosopher hath not only travailed in the general knowledge of true reason to have right understanding what is good and bad in life, and what is true and false in nature, but also travailed by experience to see the diversities of men's manners, and to acquaint himself with right order of civil government, and thereby hath attained to a great estimation of worthiness among the wise and learned, and judged a man most worthy, whose writings should be read with diligence, and travailed in for the fruits of wisdom. For he was Socrates' scholar, out of whose school came first the excellent philosophers, who were afterwards divided into certain sects, and filled all Greece with manifold knowledge, and being joined with the most notable men in schoolfellowship, got equal praise with the chieffest, and hath learnedly intricated the sum of well doings, in his book that he wrote of Socrates' worthy remembrances. For government and order of policy, he first travailed through not only Greece, but also remained with great estimation in the King of Persia's court, and understood not only the nature's of men, the usages of orders, the devices of council, the engines of war, but also the sports and pastimes most convenient for a leisureful life, and hath sorted with skill, that was engrossed by experience, and hath given rules of peace and war no learned man more, and furnisheth a gentleman with much goodly knowledge so much more to be commended than the other, that his rules be in practice for common life and not sought out of the depth of nature, whose perfectness as it is most commendable. So can it not best agree with the common use of life. But what is there that a wise man can with honesty desire, whereof not only the sparkles be scattered in him but also the great beams be largely set, that in such variety and plentifulness of good things, as it is not hard to choose the good, so is it very hard to choose the best. If knowledge of war be sought for, is there any that giveth truer and wiser rules, both for the captain to govern by and the soldier to be ruled after? Did not Scipio, as Tully citeth out of Polybius, think the books of Cyrus bringing up, so full of good instructions and warlike wisdom, that a good captain should never go without them? Was not Cyrus so well taught himself, that he learned not only obedience like a soldier, but government like a captain, and afterwards was fulfilled with all the noble virtues that may be wished with excellency in any ruler? And all those good lessons that either Cyrus learned, or Scipio praised, be contained in this treatise, and fit to be known at this time, not of that the kinds of war be not changed, but for cause those precepts which he gathered out of the everlasting and unchangable right of Nature's laws, do serve all men at all times, and come amiss to no country. The miseries and misfortunes of war, the shifts and escapes from the enemies, the forsight of dangers and avoiding of perils, be they anywhere more grievous or more manifold than in younger Cyrus going up against the King and in Xenophon's return again to Greece? If peace and quietness be looked for, can there be any better rules given for every man's private life, than the worthy remembrances of Socrates? which

books contain a sum of manners and life, and what is to be followed as good, and avoided as well, and what honesty and philosophy doth look for, and what nature uncorrupted can naturally require, and which is the right and easy way to the true and reasonable happiness. If government and order of common wealth be sought, can we have a perfecter example of a good ruler, than the praise of Agesilaus is? Which hath prescribed all the worthy virtues that a man can praisably desire, to funish a ruler, which hath not hereon all the incommodities that longeth to governers, and plain demonstrations how in seeking for pleasures, they be furthest from pleasures, and last to attain that wherin they labor first. Be not these books like true glasses, that will show none other favor and beauty of conditions, than be the owners in deed? Nor will not by flattery make mean things great, and great vices small, but according to the true proportion of the qualities, show the visage of the fame? If hunting, riding, and other chosen pastimes be fit to learned of Gentlemen, and taught of skillful men, who did experience them more naturally, and write of them more cunningly than Xenophon hath done? The matters whereof be neither unpleasant to be known, nor unhandsome to be practiced. And yet the chief ground works of riding be so naturally said by him, that he is at this day counted the best horseman that keepeth his orders in riding best, and goeth nighest that true way, which he by wisdom hath of long time prescribed. All these things which severally be scattered and sparse in other, be almost all in one gathered together in this book of Cyrus bringing up and going forth under this title, is indeed a pathway to wisdom, and for matter most fit to be read and known of all Gentlemen, and for fineness of style, most pleasant and perfect in his own tongue. And although herein I have a goodly occasion to commend the writer, that in the most eloquent and excellent tongue hath written most purely, yet because it carrieth the matter whole into another tongue, and keepeth his own fineness still in his own tongue, and our gross tongue is a rude and a barren tongue, when it is compared with so flourishing and plentiful a tongue. I will pass over this praise, with touching only the remembrance of it, and leave so large a matter until a better time, lest in commending his writing I might dispraise mine own, or else in an unneedful matter spend too many words. But shortly to conclude of all books which philosophers have written with judgement, and other hath translated with labor, no book there is which containeth better matter for life, order for war lines, policy for courtliness, wisdom for government, temperance for subjects, obedience for all states. I seem to praise this book too much; to the ignorant I may do, who can not judge, and therefore I pardon him, and yet least worthy pardon to rule over that he knoweth not, and be most busy where he hath lest skill, but to the wise I cannot, who weighing the matter and judging the examples, and examining the rules, shall find as much as plentiful wisdom wittily framed in this short treatise, and in other great volumes, having as express-ly every part of wisdom as well set together, as a little tablet containeth the lively face by cunning of work-manship, which the great table for want of cunning sometime doth miss. But because I thought it praise-worthy, I thought it labor worthy also and began my travail of this good opinion, supposing that which of reason contented me, might by the same reason con-tent others too. And besides the honest contenting which must needs be in well minded men, if any man learn anything that he is the better for, I trust he will yield me some thanks, by whose means he hath met with a good councellor, and learned plainly that he might long else have sought for, and therefore thank me for my pains herein at the least, if he further require me not to go on with the like. Therefore in devising to whom I might offer this honest travail of mine, well I trust bestowed, although of every noble man well, yet of no man better than of your good Lordship, whose virtues be better know unto me, than you yourself are, and therefore thought it fit to offer written virtues, where lively virtues dwell, to be better accepted where they see report of their ancient fame, and honor much es-teemed. And if the thing is welcomed not, yet another might: your children whom you love and bring them up in learning, and have chosen them of late a good schoolmaster, as I hear, whose diligence and discretion hath much always commended the good learning he hath, and other good qualities. The reading hereof to them may double profit them, both to learn the matter which is good and pleasant, and also to learn to turn Latin out of English, which way although it seem tri-fling to some, yet is it the readiest exercise that ever I could find, to make a child easily to attain to that profit, which else with labor they shall not (hit) at all. These things make me bold, although not much ac-quainted, to present to your Lordship the honor of my pains, most humbly desiring you to accept my bold-ness, moved yet with reason, and where the goodness of the matter, your Lordship's noble virtues, your chil-dren's bringing up, hath moved me here unto, you will for these causes accept well my good will, and I shall hereby think my self so bound to you, as other must to me, that hereby profiteth oughts, and desire the living LORD, whose rule goeth through all, to increase your Lordship's honor and nobleness always.

To the right honorable, my singular good lord, Philip, Earl of Surrey, son and heir to my lord and master the Duke of Norfolk's grace, William Bercker wishes fur-therance in forwardance of learning with continuance of virtue and honor.

When Alexander the Great did pass by the place where Achilles was buried, he said these words: "O happy Achilles, that had such a trumpet as Homer, to sound thy glory to the world." Of this saying did grow a disputation: whether the valiant captain, that by cour-age and policy attained fame, or the skillful writer, that by learning and cunning makes report thereof, is more worthy of commendation. For as the doer of noble deeds gives matter to the writer of goodly books, so those deeds should soon die, if they did not live by writ. When Zopyrus, a noble man of Persia, had dis-figured his body, and thereby won the city of Babylon, Darius, the king of that country, said: "I had rather have one such faithful subject as Zopyrus was, that ten such cities as Babylon is." Of which sentence rises this question: whether the mighty prince that commands what he will have done, or the worthy subject that executes the prince's pleasure, deserves greater praise. I will leave the matter in suspense, and suffer by si-lence to be given where it ought. And to your Lord-ship this I have to say: There is no gentleman alive has more occasion to be stirred by his ancestors' virtues, than you. For if I may remember unto you the noble acts that they have done, and singular services that they have showed, then must I say, that even from my Lords your great great grandfathers, to my Lord's grace your father, you have to receive examples of rare vir-tue, as well of warlike affairs done abroad, as of royal wisdom showed at home: whose steps to follow, you have two ways. The one is by learning, whereunto I rejoice to see you so well given. For by it, shall you receive such lessons in your youth, as the fame shall be instructions to your at more years. The other is experience, to the which I hope your will give yourself when time shall come. For as the one without the other hath a want, so both being joined together, makes a marvelous perfection. In the first you are yet to be trained with as good inducements as may be, and bet-ter can there none be than the reading of such authors as for the matter be most worthy, and for the manner be most skillful. Which being granted, I dare affirm, this Xenophon, whom I now present unto you, to be most fit for you. For he treateth of a prince that in his time exceeded all others, and in him he showeth a model of perfect and princely education. The handling of it is such, as for the excellency both in learning and experience can not be amended. For this Xenophon was scholar to Socrates, and proved so singular, as he was accompted concurrent with his schoolfellow Pla-to, who for his knowledge was surnamed Divine. This Xenophon was he, that after Cyrus the younger was slain in the expedition he made into Asia, brought home the Greeks that served in that voyage, amidst so many fierce enemies, over so many huge mountains, and through so many dangerous passages. And this was that Xenophon, whom Scipio the singular Roman, that overcame the valiant Hannibal of Carthage, had ever at his pillow, to receive instructions by night that he would practice by day. So as for both considerations, few or none have been found the like. Which although it be true, yet is there one thing that hath a while withdrawn me, from that I now am doing. And it is, that for your Lordship's further furtherance in learn-ing, and for mine own poor estimation, I should rather have exhibited unto you something in Latin than in

English, but as a forlorn scholar, not able to keep credit in learning, I do yet entertain myself studies not altogether devoid of learning, which I offer unto you. Indeed I must confess this translation to be done before I went into Italy, finding six books of the same enprinted when I did return, not by my desire, but only by the courtesy and good will of the printer, a furtherer of good learning. For these two later books I have often times been spoken to of diverse of my learned friends, whose requests at length I have satisfied. And because the only intent of the book is to show what a noble man by good education may prove unto, I have both by duty and skill made election of your Lordship, to be the last patron of it, as I made by very good Lord, the Earl of Penbroke, the first. To your Lordship the reading of such matter is convenient, to his Lordship, the judgement is to be referred. Your Lordship must talk of your book, his Lordship of his experience. For the which, joining him with you, as it were in commission, for the good will he hath born to my lord your grandfather, and for the friendship he beareth to my Lord your father, I dare say he will be both a father and a grandfather to you, if cause should require. I shall desire your Lordship, when you read, it to think the time will come, when you shall be called of your prince to take such journies as you shall see that Cyrus appointeth to such as you are, and to do such services as your most noble progenitors have done by the commandment of their princes, whose great glory shall ever so shine before your eyes, as you must needs forsee yourself to follow the same to the contentation of your prince, the benefit of your country, the joy of your parents, comfort of all your friends and servants: the which I among the rest do wish and trust to see. And so most humbly I take my leave of your Lordship. From my chamber at Howard house, the eighth day of this new year, 1567.

Alfred Pretor (essay date 1881)

SOURCE: "On the Peculiarities of Xenophon's Style," in *The Anabasis of Xenophon, Vol. I*, edited and translated by Alfred Pretor, Cambridge of the University Press, 1881, pp. 17-26.

[*In the following excerpt, Pretor prefaces his translation of Xenophon's* Anabasis *with comments on the author's limitations, including a tendency to be dry and "slovenly."*]

In the subject of his history Xenophon is fortunate beyond the majority of authors. The interest excited by the circumstances of the expedition and the desire to learn something of the unknown land through which the travellers made their way: above all, the dangers consequent upon the undertaking and the unparalleled bravery by which they were surmounted would have made the work acceptable, even if the shortcomings of

the historian had been of a more decided kind. It is true that to one class of readers the *Anabasis* will present but few attractions, and the student who expects to find in its records the brilliant descriptions of life and scenery which illustrate the path of modern exploration will inevitably be disappointed. It was the Fortunes of the Ten Thousand which Xenophon had undertaken to describe, and he has confined himself even too literally within the limits of his task. Of the physical characteristics of the countries through which he passed and of the tribes by which they were inhabited the information he affords us is of the scantiest and most meagre kind: indeed, if it were not for the frequent recurrence of barbaric names, the reader might easily persuade himself that the course of the Expedition had never passed beyond the shores of Greece.

Of the grand and beautiful in nature Xenophon shews not the faintest appreciation. It is true that he shares this failing—if failing it be—in common with most of the historians of antiquity. We must remember, however, that few, if any, can have had the same opportunities of witnessing Nature in all her moods, and it is at least remarkable that our author should allow no word to escape him of surprise or admiration at the scenes with which he must necessarily have become acquainted.

The best characteristic of the *Anabasis* is unquestionably the simplicity and truth with which the tale is told; and simplicity, when it is not made the excuse for negligence and want of taste, is perhaps the very highest merit that can be looked for in a style. But with Xenophon simplicity too often degenerates into baldness, and an unartificial style becomes a slovenly one.

John Pentland Mahaffey (essay date 1905)

SOURCE: "Xenophon the Precursor of Hellenism," in *The Progress of Hellenism in Alexander's Empire*, The University of Chicago Press, 1905, pp. 1-27.

[*In the following excerpt, Mahaffey uses Xenophon as a "case study" in his discussion of the transition from "Hellendom" to Hellenism in ancient Greece; he finds Xenophon exemplary of the period in both style and content.*]

. . . [By] "Hellenism" I mean that so-called "silver age" of Greek art and literature, when they became cosmopolitan, and not parochial; and by "Hellenistic," not only what *was* Greek, but what desired and assumed to be Greek, from the highest and noblest imitation down to the poorest travesty. The pigeon English of the Solomon islander is as far removed from the prose of Ruskin or of Froude as is the rudest Hellenistic epitaph or letter from the music of Plato's diction, but both are clear evidence of the imperial quality in that language which sways the life of millions of men far beyond the limits of its original domain. Yet it must needs be that as the matchless idiom of Aristophanes passed out to Macedonian noble, to Persian grandee, to Syrian trader, to Egyptian priest, each and all of these added somewhat of their national flavour, and so produced an idiom and a culture uniform indeed in application, though by no means uniform in construction.

It is customary to date the origin of this Hellenism from the reign of Alexander, whose house had adopted Greek culture, and whose arms carried it into the far East; but this is to my mind a superficial view, and it is the object of my first lecture to show you that Hellenism was a thing of older growth, and that it began from the moment that Athens ceased to be the dominant centre of Greece in politics as well as in letters.

The end of the long Peloponnesian war threw out of Greece a crowd of active and ambitious men—some exiled from their homes, some voluntary absentees—in search of employment. Neighbouring nationalities—Macedonians, Persians, Egyptians—were coming into nearer view, and becoming the possible homes of expatriated Greeks. All these countries had long since sought and found mercenaries, not only among the poor mountaineers of Achæa and Arcadia, but among the aristocrats of Lesbos and Rhodes, nay even of Athens and Sparta. And now mercenary service not only became more frequent and more respectable, but the relations between the employers and the employed began to change. Earlier Persian kings and satraps had regarded their Greek mercenaries as they regarded their Indian elephants—mere tools to win victories. The relations of the younger Cyrus with the Greeks were of a wholly different kind. He endeavoured to make them friends, and to reconcile them to Persian ideas of state and of sovereignty. How well he succeeded I will proceed to show in the case of Xenophon.

But not only in the case of active men and travellers but among the stay-at-home and purely literary, there grew up in this generation a feeling that culture was more than race, and wealth better than nobility. We have Isocrates, the rhetorician and schoolmaster, saying in a passage of which he probably did not himself apprehend the deep meaning, that to be an Athenian meant, not to be born in Attica, but to have attained to Attic culture. Socrates, the most undeniable of Athenians, had already by his teaching loosened the bonds of city patriotism. He had taught wider views, and laid larger issues before men; and so we have a typical pupil, Xenophon, using the Delphic oracle, not for Hellenic, but Hellenistic purposes, compelling its assent to his schemes of ambition, and looking forward to eastern war and travel as the obvious resource for a man without a fixed position at home.

It is an exceptional good fortune for the modern historian that this figure of Xenophon, furnished with all the books he ever wrote (and some which he never wrote), stands out so clearly at this momentous epoch, when constant petty wars and rumours of wars at home were preparing Greece for the coming change. He begins his life a pure Athenian, and to the end remained entitled by his style to the name of the Attic bee. But where did that bee not gather honey? Not merely from the thyme of Attica and the cistus of the Peloponnese, but from the rose gardens of Persia and the sunflowers of Babylonia. And so in every successive work there is some new flavour in the diction and the tone of thought, till we come in the *Cyropædia* to that extraordinary panegyric on the methods of the Persian monarchy, even including the employment of eunuchs to take charge of the king's household.

But generalities or metaphors are not sufficient to prove my case. Let us descend into details. I say that in the main features of his life and teaching Xenophon represents the first step in the transition from Hellenedom to Hellenism. It is apparent, first, in his language; for though he writes excellent Attic Greek, he discards the niceties of style which were then invading Attic prose, and which made the essays of his contemporary Isocrates, and the orations of Demosthenes, the most artificial of all the great prose writing the world has seen. Still more he allows himself the use of stray and strange words provincial in the sense of not being Attic, picked up in his travels at Sinope or Samos or Byzantium, and often appearing but once in his works. Thus his language distinctly approximates to that *common dialect* which was the *lingua franca* of all the Hellenistic world. Hence he remained always popular, while the writers in dialect—Sappho, Theocritus, nay even Herodotus—were well-nigh unintelligible to the Hellenistic child. There is, moreover, a great diminution in his use of particles, as compared, *e. g.,* with the prose of Plato. These delicate spices, which gave flavour to every page of Plato, very soon lost their perfume; they became as unintelligible to the later Greeks as they are to our scholars; that is to say, grammarians could still talk about them, but no man knew how to use them. And so the simpler prose of Xenophon became the highest ideal of their aspirations.

But if in this respect his life became simpler and plainer, in others it followed a contrary course. In his Socratic dialogues he had given a very complete analysis of all that could be attained in Attic life. His Socrates is not only a perfect man of high intellectual endowments, who discusses all the problems of life, but the pupils he has trained, men of high birth and independent fortune, are represented as putting his theory into practice. Ischomachus, in the dialogue or tract *On Household Economy,* not only gives us a famous picture of the educating of his own wife, after her marriage, but tells of the whole course of the work and the amusements of an Attic country gentleman. None of us questions that it was in this Socratic education that Xenophon laid the foundation of his all-around capacities both for intellectual and for practical life. He was not a deep philosopher, and he cared not to be; but, as Tacitus says of Agricola, another practical man, *retinuit, quod est difficillimum, in philosophia modum*. He had not the tastes or the ambitions of a college Don. When he had graduated, so to speak, under Socrates, he went out into the world. And there he found other nations which could do some things better than the Greeks, and could attain great happiness denied to them.

There are several blind spots in the ideal prospects of Ischomachus—the Attic gentleman. In the first place, field sports were impossible in Attica. In a land so thickly populated, and so carefully cultivated, large properties were scarce, and preservation impossible. So game was long since extirpated from Attica. But no sooner did Xenophon go to visit the younger Cyrus in Asia Minor than he woke up to the dignities and delights of hunting. This taste he kept up all his life. After his return with the Ten Thousand, he was attached to the Spartans in their campaigns against the Persian satraps, and so he had frequently the chance of poaching their splendid preserves. In later life, when Sparta desired to reward him, he obtained a sporting estate on the Arcadian side of Olympia, which he turns aside to describe (in his *Anabasis* V, 3) with evident delight. He writes tracts on hunting, and says that the pursuit of the hare is so fascinating as to make a man forget that he ever was in love with anything else. Now, all this side of his life he learned not from Socrates or at Athens, but from his intercourse with Persian grandees.

In another place, when speaking of order in the keeping of a household, he quotes no Greek example, but rather the great Phœnician merchantman he had seen at Corinth, where all the tackle and the freight were packed away with such neatness and economy as to make it a sight for the Greeks to visit. And so he adds that the planting of a paradise belonging to his patron Cyrus was not only far superior to anything in Greece, but, what was more astonishing, that great prince had deigned to occupy his own hands with this planting. In the laying out, therefore, of orchards and parks he found that the Greeks had everything to learn from a race of men whom they had been brought up to hate and despise. I notice, by the way, that in one point both the Attic and the Persian gardens were still undeveloped. In all his descriptions of them Xenophon is silent on the culture of flowers. Nor does he ever speak of the beauty of his fruit trees in flower. When we hear of Alexandria, in the next century, that it produced beautiful flowers at every season in its greenhouses, we see that the Hellenism of Xenophon was only incipient. Queen Cleopatra had been taught many luxuries unknown even to the younger Cyrus.

Still the very changes of residence in Xenophon's life could not but broaden his views and enlarge his tastes beyond those of the cultivated Athenian. Consider for a moment how much of the world he had seen. Starting from Sardis with the army of Cyrus, and being free from discipline as a volunteer, he travelled all through southern Asia Minor into Babylonia, where he tells us of the strange and new aspect of the country, with its wide rivers, its great deserts, its dense cultivation, and its fauna and flora so much more tropical than anything known in Greece. Then comes the battle of Kunaxa and the disastrous death of his great patron, Cyrus. The famous retreat of the Ten Thousand is what has made Xenophon's name immortal, and though, as I gravely suspect, he has much exaggerated his own importance in that arduous affair, he must certainly have had the experience of a journey over the high passes of Armenia in deep snow and arctic temperature, to contrast with the burning plains of Babylonia. He returns along the north coast of Asia Minor, encountering many strange savage tribes, whose manners and customs he notes with curious interest. Then from Byzantium he makes a tour among the barbarians of European Thrace, and thence returns to Greece, only to revert again to Asia Minor, and this time to campaign in its central provinces. He next comes home with his second patron, King Agesilaus of Sparta, through Bæotia, where the famous battle of Koronea gives him a foretaste of Bæotian supremacy. Yet of all the Greeks none were so distasteful to him as these hardy vulgarians. Not even the great and refined Epaminondas earns from him more than rare and unwilling praise, and presently our travelled Athenian departs in exile to the Peloponnese, where he seems to have spent the rest of his long life.

Thus Xenophon had studied not only all Greece, but all the borders of the Greek world in Asia Minor and Thrace; he had penetrated the great Persian empire and learned its splendour and its weakness. In fact, the whole sphere of early Hellenism was under his ken. The West only—Sicily and southern Italy—he neglects, and this is quite characteristic of the rise of Hellenism in the next generation. All the desires, the ambitions, the prospects of the Greeks of the fourth and third centuries before Christ lay eastward, not westward. To them the Romans were yet unknown and unnoticed barbarians, and the Greek West no land of large promise like the East; for apart from the tough mountaineers of Calabria and Sicily, dangerous neighbours on land, there was the Carthaginian sea-power which took care to close the avenues of trade to the fabulous isles and coasts, that loomed against the setting sun. But in the armies he commanded there were not wanting many mercenaries hailing from the far West; there must also have been many who had served in Egypt; and it was from these that he derived his great respect and admiration for that ancient civilisation. The Egyptians who fight against the great Cyrus in Xenophon's romance, who are ultimately settled by him as a colony in Asia Minor, are the bravest and best of oriental nations. Such, then, being this man's wide experience, it is well worth seeking from his writings his general views regarding the Greek world, his estimate of its strength and of its weakness, and above all, what he has said—or would have said, had we asked him—of the future prospects of the complex of states around him.

The first and most important point I notice is his firm belief in the expansion of the Hellenic race. He has before him constantly the feasibility of settling colonies of Greeks anywhere through Asia. When the Ten Thousand reach the Black Sea, and the next problem is how to occupy or provide for them, one of the ideas always recurring, and one which makes Xenophon suspected by all those who are longing for their homes in Greece, is his supposed ambition to be the founder of a new Greek city on the Euxine, where by trade, and by intermarriage with the natives, his companions might acquire a new and a wealthy home. Had not Olbia and Apollonia and Trapezus and many other Greek colonies of earlier days fared splendidly in these remote but most profitable regions, where sea and land, river and plain, combined to produce their natural wealth for the enterprising stranger? The Thracian king, who calls in his services, quite naturally makes similar offers. Xenophon is to possess a castle, marry a Thracian princess, and settle down as a magnate who brings about him Greeks for the purposes of trade and of mercenary service. Every ambitious Greek had therefore this prospect dangling before his eyes. And this gave him a new, a practical, interest in learning to appreciate the qualities of the neighbour races, hitherto set down in the lump as barbarians. The Persian grandees on their side must have found both pleasure and profit in bringing Greeks about their courts. If so far back as the days of Sappho we hear that one of the girls she had educated in charms went to exercise them in Lydian Sardis, is it not to be assumed that also this Greek influence upon the East was still waxing? The profession of Greek mercenary was not confined to men-at-arms, and among the booty brought home by the Ten Thousand there were so many women that their outcry was quite a feature in the camp in moments of excitement. It is highly improbable that many of these had followed the army from Hellenic lands in their upward march, and if not, here was an eastern element affecting the next generation of the profession of arms. The fusion of races, therefore, though slow and sporadic, was distinctly on its increase. The campaigns of the Spartan king Agesilaus in Asia Minor, where he was attended, and no doubt advised, by Xenophon, pointed to a large invasion of the East; and had he not been recalled by the miserable dissensions and quarrels of Greece, the conquest, partial if not total, of the Persian empire was in near prospect. Isocrates in more than one public letter implores the leaders of his nationality to compose their parochial dis-

putes, and unite for the great object of becoming lords of the East.

The result he regarded as certain; but who was to accomplish this great Hellenic league for the subjugation of the East? On this question Xenophon's opinions and his forecast are not the less clear because we have to gather them indirectly from many stray indications in his works. He had had large practical experiences, besides the theoretical opinions of his master Socrates, to afford him materials for a sound judgment. In the first place, he had made essay of democracy, both the best and the worst that Greece could afford. He had lived an Athenian during the latter half of the great war which deprived his city of her supremacy, and he had seen his great master gradually alienating the majority by his trenchant criticism, till that master's life was sacrificed to the vulgar prejudices of a democratic jury. Yet Athens was the most refined and cultivated democracy that ever existed. The bitter and satirical tract *On the Polity of the Athenians,* still printed among the works of Xenophon, is now generally recognised as the work of an older writer, living at Athens when Xenophon was a child. But it would not have attained its place, or kept it so long, had not the readers of Xenophon felt that it expressed the opinions he was likely to hold. It is certain that the school of Socrates, even before his shameful prosecution and condemnation, were no friends of democracy. They all regarded the opinion of the majority, as such, worth nothing, and thought that the masses should be guided by the enlightened judgment of the select one or the select few. What they would have said or thought, had they made experience of the democracies of our day, is another question. They had before them a sovereign assembly which by a bare majority at a single meeting might abrogate a law or take away a human life without further penalty than the contrition and the shame which sometimes followed upon calmer reflection. There were no higher courts of appeal from the sovereign assembly, no rehearing by a second and smaller House; the Athenian demos was recognised as a tyrant, above the laws which itself had sanctioned. That such a state should carry out a large policy of conquest, based upon a confederation of friendly states, was clearly impossible. Apart from other difficulties, the conduct of military affairs by a political assembly was absurd. When a general could be appointed or dismissed by a mere civilian vote of ordinary citizens, was any prompt or elaborate campaign possible? The generals were all playing a political as well as a strategic game, and looking to their supporters at home more than to their troops abroad for support. There are not wanting parallels for all this in modern times. Great foreign conquests both then and now require something very different from the leading of a democratic assembly.

But Xenophon had other and far worse experiences of

Greek democracy. As a leader of importance, selected by the majority to command an army of Greek mercenaries, he found himself in an impromptu military republic, whose city was its camp, and whose laws the resolutions of armed men swayed by the momentary gusts of passion, of panic, or of pride. At the same time, they were no mere random adventures, who regarded the camp as their only home, but men of whom the majority had not gone out from poverty, but because they had heard so high a character of Cyrus. Some brought men, some money, with them; some had run away from home, or left wife and children behind them, with the hope and intention of coming back rich men. Yet such men, though obedient enough to discipline on the march or in action, were constantly breaking out into riots in camp; officers were deposed, innocent men hunted to death in the fury of the moment. To live among such people, still more to be responsible for the leading of them, was a life of imminent daily risk. Such was the wilder democracy which Xenophon experienced, and here he had not the resource, which he strongly recommends to the cavalry general in his tract, that above all things he must "square" the governing council of his city, and have on his side a leading politician to defend him. Xenophon therefore saw very plainly what hampered and weakened the Athens of Demosthenes in the next generation, and handed over Greece to Philip of Macedon—that a democracy which exposes its executive government to constant criticism, and which constantly discusses and changes its military plans, is wholly unfit to make foreign conquests and to rule an extended empire.

There was evidently far more hope from the side of Sparta, which at this very moment—I mean during Xenophon's youth and his campaigning days—held supremacy in Greece, commanded considerable armies, and was under monarchical government. More especially under an able king like Agesilaus, Xenophon must have felt his hopes of invading the East within reach of their fulfilment. But a closer survey of the far-famed Spartan constitution showed him that here, too, there were flaws and faults which made Sparta unfit to hold empire. He has left us a tract *On the Lacedæmonian Polity,* in which he details to us with admiration the strict discipline of that state and especially the thorough organisation of its education of boys and men for war. The order, the respect for authority, the simplicity of life, the subordination of even the most sacred family rights to the service of the state—all these aristocratic features fascinated every cultivated Greek who lived under the sway of that most capricious tyrant, a popular assembly. But they did not appreciate the compensating advantages which democracy, however dangerous and turbulent, afforded them.

As Grote has expounded to us with complacent insistence, no Spartan would have been so fitted to take a lead suddenly in public affairs, civil or military, as the cultivated pupil of Socrates from Athens, who jumps in a moment from an amateur into a general. When Sparta obtained her empire, she had no competent civil service to manage her dependencies. Her harmosts, as they were called, were but rude and overbearing soldiers, not above venality and other corruption, but wholly unable to maintain the imperial dignity which is the only justification of a ruler from without, the only counterpoising boon for those who find their liberties impaired. And even if there had been competent rulers among the Spartan aristocracy, the method of appointment was radically vicious. For though Sparta was in name a dual monarchy, the real power lay with the five ephors—so far as we know them, narrow and bigoted men—who were more anxious to keep the kings in subjection than to appoint fit men as governors in the subject cities. Xenophon's experiences when the Ten Thousand returned to Byzantium show us how arbitrary and cruel was the rule of these governors, how absurd their mutual jealousies, how incompetent their handling of great public interests. Yet there was no remedy while the ephors appointed their personal friends, against whose crimes it was well nigh impossible to obtain redress.

With all these various experiences before him, Xenophon wrote his largest and most elaborate treatise, doubtless that on which he staked his reputation—the book *On the Education of Cyrus.* The fate that mocks so many human efforts has not spared the Attic bee. This voluminous book, in which the many speeches and curious digressions seem to suggest the garrulity of advancing age, has been neglected from the author's own day till now, while the *Anabasis* has been inflicted on every schoolboy for two millenniums. The wonder is that so little-heeded a treatise ever survived the neglect of ages. Yet no Greek book should have excited greater likes and dislikes than this. Its theme is the vindication, both theoretically and practically, of absolute monarchy, as shown in the organisation of the Persian empire. In many other of his writings—as, for example, in the *Æconomicus,* he sets forth the Socratic idea that if you can find the man with a ruling soul, the *archic* man, you had better put him in control, and trust to his wisdom rather than to the counsels of many. But now he takes as his ideal the far-off figure of the first Cyrus, whose gigantic deeds impress alike the Hebrew prophet and the Greek philosopher, and, amplifying his picture with many romantic details, gives us in the form of a historical novel a monarch's handbook for the gaining and the administration of a great empire. We never hear that Alexander the Great read this treatise. Most probably his tutor Aristotle hid it from him with jealous care. For what teaching could be more odious to the Hellenic mind? Nevertheless, in all Greek literature there was hardly a book which would prove more interesting to Alexander, or more useful to him in justifying his adoption of oriental ideas.

What is even more striking is this, that after Alexander's magnificent display of what the "archic man" could do if he possessed an acknowledged monarchy, the whole Hellenistic world acquiesced in monarchy as the best and most practical form of government. The seventh and eighth books of the *Cyropædia* were in spirit but the earliest of the many tracts composed by Stoic and Peripatetic philosophers about monarchy . . ., and it was marvellous how even the democrats of Athens outbid their neighbours in their servile adulation of such a king as Demetrius, whose father had founded a new dynasty. Before a century had elapsed since Xenophon's treatise appeared, hardly a Greek city existed which was not directly or indirectly under the control of a king. Even the Rhodian confederacy lasted only because the surrounding kings found their finances more manageable in a neutral banking centre with vast credit, and therefore with vast capital secured in a place of safety. And so when a great earthquake ruined the city, it was all the kings of the Hellenistic world who sent contributions to restore it— kings at war or at variance one with the other, but all bound to support the financial credit of Rhodes and avert a commercial crash.

I will but notice one more feature in this monarchy which overspread the Hellenistic world, which Xenophon saw in his day and admired, though he did not fully comprehend its strange nature. It is this, that hereditary monarchy develops in its subjects a loyalty to the sovereign almost unintelligible to the modern republican. The notion that it was the highest honour not only to die for the king, but to live in his personal service, was as foreign to the old Hellenic societies as it is to the modern American. And yet among the great and proud nobility of Persia, as among that of the French monarchy, and even now in England, men and women of the greatest pride and the largest wealth are "lords-in-waiting," "women of the bed chamber," "mistresses of the robes," "chamberlains," and "maids of honour." Xenophon saw this kind of devotion at the very outset of the *Anabasis* (I, 5). If Clearchus, the Lacedæmonian general, saw anyone slothful or lagging behind, he struck him with his stick, but set to the work himself, in order that he might turn public opinion to his side. How different the position of Cyrus! He sees a lot of carts stuck in the deep mud of a pass, and the men set to extricate them shirking the work. Whereupon he calls upon his retinue of lords to show them an example. These, without a word, throwing off their purple headdress, dash into the mud with their costly tunics, their coloured trousers, with torcs of gold around their necks, and bracelets on their wrists, and, setting to work with a will drag out the carts forthwith. Xenophon wonders at this instance of discipline . . . in these young nobles. It was nothing of the kind. It was that loyalty that holds the personal service of the prince by divine right to be the noblest self-sacrifice. These Persians were proud to do the work of asses and of mules when called upon by their prince, and yet they were far greater gentlemen than the Greeks who would have been highly offended at such an order.

Starting, then, with Macedon and Persia, whose kings, like the Spartan kings, professed a descent from the gods, the whole Hellenistic world learned to regard a Ptolemy, a Seleucus, even an Attalus, as something superhuman in authority. This was the change which Xenophon foresaw as highly expedient, if not necessary to the management of a great empire.

It is, I think, well worth observing that this problem of monarchy did not occupy Xenophon merely in his old age. If the *Cyropædia* shows in its style, as I am convinced, something of the prolixity of age, the *Hiero,* or dialogue between that tyrant and Simonides, shows much of the exuberance of youth, and accordingly it has by general consent been classed among Xenophon's earliest works. In the former part of this most interesting tract Hiero sets forth the dangers and miseries of the Greek tyrant's life, surrounded as he was by flattery concealing hatred and mistrust, regarded as he was by all a public enemy, whose murder would be regarded an act of patriotism. Hiero details the circumstances which he regards essential to a tyrant's safety, and therefore certain to entail his unpopularity and its consequent miseries. A tyrant must keep up a mercenary force; he must therefore levy taxes for its support; he cannot possibly travel or see the world, for fear of a revolution in his absence, and so on, through the catalogue of difficulties, which were a commonplace of Greek literature. But when all is said on that side, Simonides reposts that it is not by reason of their external circumstances, but of their own characters, that Greek tyrants have earned the mistrust and hatred of men. He goes on to show how even a monarch not hereditary, who has risen from a private station, could earn the esteem and gratitude of his subjects, and, by identifying his own interests with those of his city, make himself the acknowledged benefactor of all around him. Even the keeping of a mercenary force is justified by good practical reasons, as the protection of frontiers was always a great burden to a citizen population, and as the readiness and discipline of professional soldiers must be superior to a sudden levy of amateurs in war, if such unwilling recruits can indeed be called amateurs. With such arguments Xenophon justifies the fact that most ambitious Greeks regarded the attaining to a tyranny as the very acme of their desires. However, if this fact was known to the Ten Thousand, it justifies not a little of their suspicions that Xenophon dreamt of being not only the founder but the autocrat of a new city on the Euxine. The picture of the benevolent tyrant, shown in the *Hiero,* would hardly be a sufficient guarantee to them that Xenophon, as a monarch, would indeed depart so widely from the ordinary and hateful traditions of a Greek tyranny. We need only here insist that the idea of monarchy had already occupied the early attention of the author of the *Cyropædia,* and that he had probably found the arguments in its favour an ordinary topic among the young aristocrats in the school of Socrates.

I confess that the extremes to which he carries his defence of the *imperii instrumenta* employed by the kings of Persia must be distasteful to any reasonable critic, most of all to any democrat, ancient or modern. The way in which he describes the great king absorbing all the interests and ambitions of his subjects, and making every man in the state look to the sovran as the fountain of honour and of promotion— all this savours of a Napoleonic centralisation and a Napoleonic tyranny, which, as it saps all individual independence, so it kills the growth and nurture of the highest qualities in human nature. This unpleasant side of the book may afford one reason for its systematic neglect. It is so far like one of those artificial school-exercises, so common in the next generation, where the speaker made it his glory to vindicate some villain or justify some crime. And perhaps Xenophon was infected with this "sophistic" more than his readers imagine. Nevertheless, I for one have no doubt that real convictions in favour of monarchy underlie all his semisophistical arguments.

Grote, the great historian of Greece, who was the first to inspire me, and perhaps many of you, with the love of Greek history and Greek literature, looks upon this momentous change as the death-knell of his favourite country. "'Tis Greece, but living Greece no more." And yet at no time did the Greeks do more for the letters, the commerce, the civility of all the ancient world. And hence it is that I have chosen this somewhat neglected period as the topic of my discourses.

J. B. Bury (essay date 1908)

SOURCE: "The Development of Greek Historiography after Thucydides," in *The Ancient Greek Historians,* 1908. Reprint by Dover Publications, 1958, pp. 150-90.

[In the excerpt that follows, Bury assesses Xenophon as one of the primary historians to follow Thucydides's career. Of the three that he examines, he finds Xenophon the "least meritorious," but influential nonetheless.]

Thucydides had set up a new standard and proposed a new model for historical investigation. He taught the Greeks to write contemporary political history; this was the permanent result of his work. But the secret of his critical methods may be said to have perished with him; it has been reserved for modern students fully to appreciate his critical acumen, and to estimate the immense labours which underlay the construction of his history but are carefully concealed like the foundation stones of a building. Influences came into play in the fourth century which drove history along other paths than those which he marked out; the best of the principles which his work had inculcated did not become canonical; and his historical treatment was not sympathetic under the new intellectual constellations.

The age succeeding his death was perhaps not favourable to the composition of political history. The engrossing intellectual interest was then political science, and the historical method had not been invented. The men who might otherwise have shone as historians were engaged in speculations on the nature of the state. They were eagerly seeking an answer to the speculative question: What is the best constitution? Only three historians of note arose in this period; they were more or less under the influence of Thucydides, but at long intervals behind.

Of these the only name familiar to posterity is Xenophon, who was probably the least meritorious of the three. To the circumstance that he is one of the very few classical Greek historians whose work has survived, he owes a prominence to which his qualities do not entitle him. In history as in philosophy he was a dilettante; he was as far from understanding the methods of Thucydides as he was from apprehending the ideas of Socrates. He had a happy literary talent, and his multifarious writings, taken together, render him an interesting figure in Greek literature. But his mind was essentially mediocre, incapable of penetrating beneath the surface of things. If he had lived in modern days, he would have been a high-class journalist and pamphleteer; he would have made his fortune as a war-correspondent; and would have written the life of some mediocre hero of the stamp of Agesilaus. So far as history is concerned, his true vocation was to write memoirs. The *Anabasis* is a memoir, and it is the most successful of his works. It has the defects which memoirs usually have, but it has the merits, the freshness, the human interest of a personal document. The adventures of the Ten Thousand are alive for ever in Xenophon's pages.

He took up the story of the Peloponnesian war where Thucydides had left it, and he carried down the history of Greece from that date to the fall of the Theban supremacy, in the work which we know as the *Hellenica.* By this work his powers as a historian must be judged. Some of its characteristics are due to the superficial lessons which the author learned from the founder of political history. In the first portion of the book he employed strictly the annalistic plan of Thucydides. He adopted the device of introducing speeches, and the objective method of allowing the actors to reveal themselves in their acts and words. He does not himself pourtray their characters, as he pourtrays Cyrus and the generals in the *Anabasis*. But he never goes down below the surface of events; he never analyses the deeper motives; and he writes with little disguise of his own predilections. His history is an apotheosis of Agesilaus; he does not conceal his strong philo-Laconian leanings or his hatred of Thebes; he pointedly ignores Epaminondas. His ideas about historical happenings were those of the average, conventional Athenian; and he ascribes the fall of the Spartan supremacy to divine nemesis, avenging the treacherous occupation of the Theban citadel. He cannot resist the commonplace attraction of commonplace moralising; he tells anecdotes which his austere predecessor would have disdained; but he has learned from Thucydides to keep to the matter in hand.

Other works of Xenophon had more influence than the *Hellenica,* on subsequent historiography; or, as it would probably be safer to say, reflected an interest which was to become not only permanent in literature but a conspicuous feature in history. I am referring to biography. Interest, deliberate and serious interest, in individual personalities, had been awakened by the sophistic illumination; and Euripides probably did as much as any single man to heighten and deepen it. A new branch of literature, biography, emerged; and the word [*bios*] life, acquired a new meaning, charged with the whole contents of a man's actions and character. Biography was founded by Isocrates and the pupils of Socrates. The earliest biography we possess is the *Evagoras* of Isocrates, and it is to this model that we owe the second, the *Agesilaus* of Xenophon. In other works of Isocrates also there are biographical sketches, and perhaps the portraits in the *Anabasis* were due to his influence. We can see too that the original personality of Socrates, which made a deep impression on his disciples, was effective in helping to establish this kind of literature; most of them used their pens; and the incidental portraiture of Plato, and the *Memoirs* of Xenophon, which are not a Life, have their significance for the rise of biography. I have not to follow its further development or to show how it was stimulated by the Peripatetic school. As a literary art ancient biography reached its highest perfection in Plutarch's gallery of great men. That series is invaluable to us, because the author consulted many books which are now lost; but he was not a historian; his interest was ethical. What we are here concerned to note is that, after Xenophon and Isocrates, historians generally considered sketches of character and biographical facts to be part of their business. It was a feature which was flagrantly liable to abuse, and often led to irrelevancies, which would have shocked Thucydides. But although, in practice, ancient character-portraits tended to be conventional and uninstructive, it was in principle an important advance to recognise that the analysis of character and personality has historical value, and cannot be confined within the limits which Thucydides had allowed.

Samuel James Pease (essay date 1934)

SOURCE: "Xenophon's *Cyropaedia,* 'The Compleat General'," in *The Classical Journal,* Vol. 29, no. 6, March, 1934, pp. 436-40.

[*In the essay that follows, Pease advocates for the historical value of the* Cyropaedia, *claiming it as thorough documentation of ancient Greek military strategy; he ultimately dubs it "the first general military treatise ever written."*]

Colonel Oliver L. Spaulding, Jr., in the June number of the *Classical Journal,* (XXVIII, 657-69), gives a list of ancient military writings, with a valuable appreciation of most of them. But Xenophon's *Cyropaedia* is very much more than "the amusement of his later years, the vehicle for his military fancies." Actually, the *Cyropaedia* is a work of unique military importance; it is in fact not only the earliest but the most exhaustive of all ancient military treatises; but its character has not been fully realized, because of the importance assigned to the character of Cyrus and because of certain romantic additions.

First, we may consider the outline of the various portions. The standard *ecphrasis* or detailed description of a war, centering in a single climactic battle, is given among the προγυμνάσματα of Hermogenes, many centuries after Xenophon. This includes every detail of antecedents, engagement, and consequents, and reads as follows:

> First we shall speak of what precedes the war, the gathering of the armies, the expenses, the fears; then the clashes, the slaughter, the deaths; then the trophy, then the paeans of the victors, the tears and the slavery of the others.

It will be worth while to compare in detail the outline of Thymbrara, the climactic battle of the *Cyropaedia*:—

A. Antecedents:

(Topography and date not included, as the discussion is theoretical.)

Securing of information: prisoners VI, 3, 5, spies VI, 3, 5, spies VI, 3, 15, etc.

Numbers: enemy VI, 2, 9; Cyrus' army in full VI, 2, 7-8.

Arrangement: of enemy given with numbers, of Cyrus VI, 3, 21.

Sacrifices, prayer, libation, breakfast VI, 4, 1, VII, 1.

Omens VII, 1, 2.

Formation: VII, 1, 5; paean 9, watchword 10.

B. Engagement:

Signal, advance VII, 1, 23, silence, paean, shout 25-26.

Vicissitudes: preliminary skirmish, successful maneuvers, flight of enemy, partial success 27.

Retreat of Abradates to tower, chariots 34.

Relief by Cyrus' rear attack on the enemy 36.

The mêlée 38.

C. Consequents:

Rewards and citations, military conclusions 46.

Treatment of prisoners, settlement of Egyptians 41.

General results 45-49 and in various later chapters.

It will be seen that Xenophon here uses the general outline, as does Syrianus, but omits much of the rhetoric; he substitutes morale for all, but a hint of fears; military results, for the joy of success and the sorrows of slavery; even the psychology is purely military, except for the one romantic touch to be described lat-

er. In other battles he makes use of all the other elements given by Syrianus, including the detailed rhetorical treatment of feelings.

Second, the work goes into exhaustive detail on almost every point. A partial list of the preparations for this one battle will suffice to show the minuteness and thoroughness of treatment. Cyrus provides for everything: high class and low class spies; details of new scythe chariots and wheeled turrets; encouragement of morale by discussions, hunting, special favors; camel archers; prisoners; incipient mutiny; formal battle speech fifteen days before the battle; necessity for immediate action; twenty days' provisions for a fifteen days' desert march; gradual substitution of water for wine to moisten bread or meal, beginning with the omission of wine after supper; omission of beds; securing of sour, bitter, salty appetizers; hand mills; medical supplies; extra straps; tools; wood for repairs; food for man and beast; road makers, smiths, carpenters, shoemakers; sutlers to sell nothing for fifteen days, but after that a special reward to the one who furnishes the best market (VI, 2). Mere fancy surely does not content itself with giving every detail of physical and psychological equipment for an exhausting march with a decisive battle at the end of fifteen days. And the immediate preparations for the battle, the battle itself, the capture of Sardis together with Croesus, the disposition of prisoners and booty after the battle are given with almost the same detail—forty-five pages for the one battle, over eighty for the different battles, a quarter of the whole volume.

Third, there is a variety of battle types. Just as Thymbrara is the typical field battle, so Babylon VII, 5) is the typical instance of a siege, the foray of the Assyrian crown prince is the typical border raid (I, 4), the establishing of the border is typical mountain fighting (III, 2), the capture of the Assyrian camp is a typical night surprise (III, 3-IV, 2). Such constant attention to detailed and varied outline, present even in the least of Xenophon's descriptions, indicates a definitely established rhetorical form. This is borne out by descriptions in other books of Xenophon and occurs frequently even in the great battle descriptions of Thucydides.

Fourth, the variety of detailed discussions of military topics is found both in and outside of the battle descriptions. Book I is largely taken up with the training of the young soldier. He is taught to deceive no one but the enemy; his training must embrace actual experience in fighting; in his play he must fight with clods and sticks. The description of the battle in III, 3, 55-70 is mainly a study in ideal morale as illustrative of the qualities listed in section 59 of that chapter. The description of an Assyrian camp at night is a technical excursus (III, 3, 26-28); the value of training is discussed in VI, 4, 10; the value of harangues in III, 3, 49-55.

Fifth, Xenophon undoubtedly intended the *Cyropaedia* to be a definite link in his chain of military works. The others belong each to a different type. Rhetorically speaking, the *Agesilaus* is a biography, almost purely epideictic; Book I of the *Anabasis* is a narrative, but with much biography of the same type; Books II-VII of the *Anabasis* combine autobiography with a *suasoria*, almost as if personally addressed to Alexander of Macedon; those portions of the *Hellenica* which deal with Agesilaus, his relatives, or opponents, closely resemble the *Agesilaus,* though the work as a whole is intended as a historical monograph.

The two difficulties in the way of understanding the true nature of the *Cyropaedia* have been the romantic element and the importance assigned to the character of Cyrus himself. But the romantic additions in Books VI-VII only partly conceal the really exhaustive nature of the treatise. We must remember that it is the first general military treatise ever written. As such, it partakes of the nature of early history writing; for as Herodotus has many suggestions from epic and tragedy, so this portion of the *Cyropaedia* has a double romance *motif* modeled on the *Iliad*. In the *Iliad* the wrath . . . results in the separation of Achilles and Briseis, who after the double testing are happily reunited; the wrath also brings about the separation of Hector and Andromache, who are reunited only in death. Similarly the refusal of Abradatas to yield to Cyrus brings about separation from his queen Pantheia, with a most startling result as Cyrus tries to console her after her husband's heroic death at Thymbrara (VII, 3, 8); while in contrast, at the distribution of awards at the close of the campaign (VIII, 4, 24), Tigranes of Armenia receives a "best dress" . . . for his wife, who has accompanied him on the campaign. While there are many parallels with the *Iliad,* even to the gleaming golden suit of armor given to Abradatas by Pantheia before the battle, the heart of both works is the orderly development of the war as a unit—with enormous digressions in the *Iliad,* with many very detailed discussions in the *Cyropaedia*.

In the minds of many readers the character of Cyrus absorbs the chief interest; but closer study shows that practically every concern of Cyrus in this work is military. Xenophon's admiration for Cyrus is based on the three qualities of reverence, justice, and self-control . . . , as Marchant points out in the *Praefatio* to his *Agesilaus* text; these are shared by Xenophon's other heroes, Socrates and Agesilaus. So on the advice of Polybius, a master of physical and psychological military engineering, the *Cyropaedia,* together with the *Memorabilia,* was carried by the younger Scipio on all his campaigns. If the importance of the *Memorabilia* in the minds of Polybius and Scipio may be represented—with due apologies to Izaak Walton—by the title, "The Compleat Gentleman," the *Cyropaedia* might be called "The Compleat General."

Leo Strauss (essay date 1948)

SOURCE: "The Teaching Concerning Tyranny," in *On Tyranny: An Interpretation of Xenophon's "Hiero,"* Political Science Classics, 1948, pp. 50-62.

[*Strauss published his book on tyranny in Xenophon's "Hiero" in 1948, only three years after the end of World War II. With that recent history as his context, Strauss attempts to determine what concept of tyranny the* Hiero, *a dialogue between a tyrannical ruler and a philosopher, presents. In the excerpt that follows, Strauss also considers how Xenophon's own political context may have influenced the form in which he presented his ideas.*]

Since tyranny is essentially a faulty political order, the teaching concerning tyranny necessarily consists of two parts. The first part has to make manifest the specific shortcomings of tyranny ("pathology"), and the second part has to show how these shortcomings can be mitigated ("therapeutics"). The bipartition of the *Hiero* reflects the bipartition of the "tyrannical" teaching itself. Now, Xenophon chose to present that teaching in the form of a dialogue, and he had therefore to choose a particular conversational setting. However sound, and even compelling, his reasons may have been, they certainly lead to the result that he has not given us his "tyrannical" teaching in its pure, scientific form, in the form of a treatise. The reader has to add to, and to subtract from, Hiero's and Simonides' speeches in order to lay hold of Xenophon's teaching. That addition and subtraction is not left to the reader's arbitrary decision. It is guided by the author's indications, some of which have been discussed in the preceding chapters. Nevertheless, a certain ambiguity remains, an ambiguity ultimately due, not to the unsolved riddles implied in many individual passages of the *Hiero,* but to the fact that a perfectly lucid and unambiguous connection between content and form, between a general teaching and a contingent event (e.g., a conversation between two individuals) is impossible.

Considering the primarily practical character of the "tyrannical" teaching as a political teaching, it is necessary that one interlocutor, the pupil, should be a tyrant. It is equally necessary that he should be an actual tyrant, not a potential tyrant. If the pupil were only become a potential tyrant, the teacher would have to show him how to become a tyrant, and in so doing he would have to teach him injustice, whereas in the case of an actual tyrant the teacher has the much less odious task of showing him a way toward lesser injustice. Seeing that a tyrant (Periander of Corinth) was said to have instituted most of the common devices for preserving tyranny, one might think that the natural teacher of the tyrannical art would be a great tyrant; but preservation of tyranny and correction of tyranny are two different things. Xenophon evidently felt that only a wise man could teach what he considered the tyrannical art, i.e., the art of ruling well as a tyrant, and that a tyrant would not be wise. This leads to the consequence that the wise man who teaches the tyrannical art cannot have learned that art from a tyrant as Socrates, who teaches the economic art, has learned it from an economist. In other words, the wise teacher of the tyrannical art has to teach it by himself, without any assistance, or he has to discover it by himself. Now, the wise man might transmit to his pupil the whole "tyrannical" teaching, i.e., both the indictment of tyranny and the correction of tyranny; but Xenophon apparently thought that a tyrant's indictment of tyranny would be more impressive for the average reader. Finally, the tyrant might start the conversation by complaining to a wise man about a tyrant's sad lot, in order to elicit his advice. This, however, would presuppose that the tyrant would have a wise friend whom he trusts, and that he would consider himself in need of advice. To sum up, the more one considers alternatives to the conversational setting chosen by Xenophon, the more one becomes convinced that his choice was sound.

Yet this choice, however sound and even necessary, leads to the result that Xenophon's indictment of tyranny is presented by a man who is not wise and who has a selfish interest in disparaging tyranny, whereas his praise of tyranny is presented by a wise man who argues in favor of tyranny without an apparent selfish interest. Besides, since the indictment of tyranny precedes the praise of tyranny, the indictment is presented on the basis of insufficient evidence—for Hiero does not take into account the facts or possibilities set forth by Simonides in the latter part of the *Hiero*—whereas the praise of tyranny seems to be voiced *en pleine connaissance de cause*. That is to say, Xenophon could not help being led to giving a greater weight, at least apparently, to the praise of tyranny than to the indictment of tyranny. The question arises whether this is merely the inevitable result of considerations such as those sketched before, or whether it is directly intended.

One might think for a moment that the ambiguity under consideration was caused merely by Xenophon's decision to treat at all in a dialogue the question of the improvement of tyrannical rule: every ambiguity would have been avoided if he had limited himself to indicting tyranny. A comparison of his conversational treatment of tyranny with Plato's, however, shows that this suggestion does not go to the root of the matter. Plato refrained from teaching the tyrannical art and he entrusted his indictment of tyranny to Socrates. The price which he had to pay for this choice was that he had to entrust his praise of tyranny to men who were not wise (Polos, Callicles, and Thrasymachus) and who therefore were openly praising the very injustice of tyranny. To avoid the latter inconvenience, Xenophon had

to pay the price of burdening a wise man with the task of praising tyranny. An effective conversational treatment of tyranny which is free from inconveniences is impossible. For there are only two possibilities apart from those chosen by Xenophon and Plato: the praise of tyranny by the wise might be succeeded by the indictment of tyranny by the unwise, and the indictment of tyranny by the wise might be succeeded by the praise of tyranny by the unwise; these alternatives are ruled out by the consideration that the wise man ought to have the last word.

It is more appropriate to say that the bearing of Xenophon's praise of tyranny is sufficiently limited, not only by the conversational setting, but above all by the fact that his wise man who praises tyranny makes sufficiently clear the essential shortcomings of tyranny. He describes tyranny at its best, but he lets it be understood that tyranny even at its best suffers from serious defects. This implied criticism of tyranny is much more convincing than Hiero's passionate indictment which serves a selfish purpose and which would be literally true only of the very worst kind of tyranny. To see the broad outline of Simonides' criticism of tyranny at its best, one has only to consider the result of his suggested correction of tyranny in the light of Xenophon's, or Socrates', definition of tyranny. Tyranny is defined in contradistinction to kingship: kingship is such rule as is exercised over willing subjects and is in accordance with the laws of the cities; tyranny is such rule as is exercised over unwilling subjects and accords, not with laws, but with the will of the ruler. This definition covers the common form of tyranny, but not tyranny at its best. Tyranny at its best, tyranny as corrected according to Simonides' suggestions, is no longer rule over unwilling subjects. It is most certainly rule over willing subjects. But it remains rule "not according to laws," i.e., it is absolute government. Simonides, who extols tyranny at its best, refrains from using the very term "law." Tyranny is essentially rule without laws, or more precisely, monarchic rule without laws.

Before considering the shortcomings of tyranny thus understood, we may dwell for a moment on its positive qualities. As regards the tyrant himself, Simonides asserts without hesitation that he may be perfectly happy. Furthermore, he leaves no doubt that the tyrant may be virtuous, and in fact of outstanding virtue. The correction of tyranny consists in nothing else than the transformation of the unjust or vicious tyrant who is more or less unhappy into a virtuous tyrant who is happy. As for the tyrant's subjects, or his city, Simonides makes it clear that it may be very happy. The tyrant and his subjects may be united by the bonds of mutual kindness. The subjects of the virtuous tyrant are treated, not like little children, but like comrades or companions. They are not deprived by him of honors. They are not disarmed; their military spirit is encouraged. Nor are the mercenaries, without whom tyranny is impossible, undesirable from the point of view of the city: they enable the city to wage war vigorously. When Simonides recommends that the tyrant should make a most ample use of prizes and that he should promote agriculture and commerce, if agriculture to a higher degree than commerce, he simply seems to approve of policies which Xenophon considered to befit a well-ordered commonwealth. He thus creates the impression that according to Xenophon tyrannical government can live up to the highest political standards.

Simonides' praise of beneficent tyranny, which at first sight seems to be boundless and rhetorically vague, proves on closer examination to be most carefully worded and to remain within very precise limits. Just as Simonides avoids in it the term "law," he avoids in it the term "freedom." The practical consequence of the absence of laws, he gives us to understand, is the absence of freedom: no laws, no liberty. All specific suggestions made by Simonides flow from this implied axiom, or reveal their political meaning in its light. For instance, when recommending to the tyrant that he consider the citizens as companions or comrades, he does not mean that the tyrant should treat the citizens as his equals, or even as freemen. For slaves may be companions as well as freemen. Furthermore, Simonides advises the tyrant that he consider the citizens as companions, and his friends as his own children: if his very friends are then in every respect his subordinates, the citizens will be his subordinates in a still more far-reaching sense. The advice just referred to shows in addition that Simonides does not go so far in his praise of beneficent tyranny as to call it "paternal" rule. It is true, the subjects of the beneficent tyrant are not disarmed; but in time of peace at least they do not protect themselves against the slaves and evildoers as the citizens of free commonwealths do; they are protected by the tyrant's bodyguard. They are literally at the mercy of the tyrant and his mercenaries, and they can only wish or pray that the tyrant will become, or remain, beneficent. The true character of tyranny even at its best is clearly indicated by Simonides' "Machiavellian" suggestion that the tyrant should do the gratifying things (such as the awarding of prizes) himself, while entrusting to others the punitive actions. It is hardly necessary to say that the tyrant's refraining from openly taking responsibility for punitive action does not bespeak a particular mildness of his rule: Non-tyrannical rulers take that responsibility without any concealment because their authority, deriving from law, is secure. Similarly, the extraordinarily ample use of prizes, especially for the promotion of agriculture, seems to serve the "tyrannical" purpose of keeping the subjects busy with their private concerns rather than with public affairs. At the same time it compensates for the lack of the natural incentives to increase one's wealth, a lack due to the precarious character of property rights under a tyrant. The best tyrant would con-

sider his fatherland his estate. This may be preferable to his impoverishing his fatherland in order to increase his private estate; yet it certainly implies that the best tyrant would consider his fatherland his private property which he would naturally administer according to his own discretion. Thus no subject of a tyrant could have any property rights against the tyrant. The subjects would pay as much as he deems necessary in the form of gifts or voluntary contributions. Nor can the tyrant be said to honor the citizens because he awards prizes or distinctions to some of them; he may be able and willing to enrich his subjects: he cannot accord to them the "equality of honor" which is irreconcilable with tyrannical rule and from the lack of which they may be presumed always to suffer.

These shortcomings of tyranny at its best are not, however, necessarily decisive. How Simonides, and Xenophon, judged of the value of tyranny at its best depends on what they thought of the importance of freedom. As for Simonides, he seems to esteem nothing as highly as honor or praise; and of praise he says that it will be the more pleasant the freer are those who bestow it. This leads to the consequence that the demands of honor or praise cannot be satisfied by tyranny however perfect. The tyrant will not enjoy honor of the highest kind because his subjects lack freedom, and on the other hand the tyrant's subjects will not enjoy full honor for the reason mentioned before. As for Xenophon himself, we have to start from the facts that freedom was considered the aim of democracy, as particularly distinguished from aristocracy, the aim of which was said to be virtue; and that Xenophon was not a democrat. Xenophon's view is reflected in Hiero's implicit assertion that the wise are not concerned with freedom. To establish Xenophon's attitude towards tyranny at its best as characterized by Simonides, we have to consider the relation of tyranny at its best, not to freedom, but to virtue. Only if virtue were impossible without freedom, would the demand for freedom be absolutely justified from Xenophon's point of view.

The term "virtue" occurs five times in the *Hiero*. In only two out of the five cases is it applied to human beings. Only once is it applied to the tyrant. Never is it applied to the tyrant's subjects. Simonides advises the tyrant to be proud of "the happiness of his city" rather than of "the virtue of his chariot horses": he does not mention the virtue of the city as a possible goal of tyrannical rule. It is safe to say that a city ruled by a tyrant is not supposed by him to "practice gentlemanliness as a matter of public concern." But, as has been proved by Socrates' life, there are virtuous men in cities which do not "practise gentlemanliness as a matter of public concern." It is therefore an open question whether and how far virtue is possible under a tyrant. The beneficent tyrant would award prizes for "prowess in war" and for "justice in contractual relations": he would not be concerned with fostering prowess simply and justice simply. This confirms Hiero's assertion that the brave and the just are not desirable as subjects of a tyrant. Only a qualified, or reduced, form of courage and justice befits the subjects of a tyrant. For prowess simply is closely akin to freedom, or love of freedom, and justice simply is obedience to laws. The justice befitting the subjects of a tyrant is the least political form of justice, or that form of justice which is most remote from public-spiritedness: the justice to be observed in contractual, private relations.

But how can a virtuous man—and Simonides' beneficent tyrant would seem to be a virtuous man—rest satisfied with the necessity of preventing his subjects from reaching the summit of virtue? Let us then reconsider the facts mentioned in the preceding paragraph. As regards the fact that Simonides ascribes to the tyrant's subjects a qualified form of prowess only, and fails to ascribe courage to them, we have to remember that in Xenophon's two lists of the virtues of Socrates, courage does not occur. As regards Simonides' failure to ascribe to the tyrant's subjects justice simply, we have to remember that justice can be understood as a part of moderation and that, according to an explicit statement of Simonides, the tyrant's subjects may very well possess moderation. As regards Simonides' failure to ascribe to the tyrant's subjects virtue as such, we have to remember that virtue is not necessarily a generic term, but may indicate a specific virtue distinguished from justice in particular. However this may be, the question of what Simonides thought about the possibility of virtue under tyrannical rule seems to be definitely settled by an explicit statement of his according to which "gentlemen" may live, and live happily, under a beneficent tyrant. In order not to misinterpret Simonides' ascribing to the tyrant's subjects only qualified forms of courage and justice, we have to compare it with Xenophon's failure, in his *Lacedaemoniorum respublica,* to ascribe justice in any sense to the Spartans themselves. The utmost one is entitled to say is that the virtue possible under a tyrant will have a specific color, a color different from that of republican virtue. It may tentatively be suggested that the place occupied within republican virtue by courage is occupied within the virtue befitting the subjects of the excellent tyrant by moderation which is produced by fear. But one has no right to assume that the virtue befitting the subjects of a good tyrant is meant to be inferior in dignity to republican virtue. How little Xenophon believed that virtue is impossible without freedom is shown most strikingly by his admiration for the younger Cyrus whom he does not hesitate to describe as a "slave."

If gentlemen can live happily under a beneficent tyrant, tyranny as corrected according to Simonides' suggestions might seem to live up to Xenophon's highest political standard. To see at once that this is the case, one merely has to measure Simonides' excellent tyrant by the criterion set forth in Xenophon's, or Socrates', definition of the good ruler. The virtue of the good ruler consists in making happy those whom he rules. The aim of the good ruler can be achieved by means of laws—this was done, according to Xenophon, in the most remarkable manner in Lycurgus' city—or by rule without laws, i.e., by tyranny: the beneficent tyrant as described by Simonides makes his city happy. It is certainly most significant that, as regards the happiness achieved by means of laws, Xenophon can adduce an actual example (Sparta), whereas as regards the happiness achieved by tyranny, he offers no other evidence than the promise of a poet. In other words, it is of very great importance that, according to Xenophon, the aim of the good ruler is much more likely to be achieved by means of laws than by means of absolute rule. This does not do away, however, with the admission that, as a matter of principle, rule of laws is not essential for good government.

Xenophon does not make this admission in so many words. He presents Simonides as describing tyranny at its best and as declaring that the tyrant can make his city happy. Considering the situation in which Simonides expounds his views of tyranny, the objection is justified that what he says serves the purpose of comforting a somewhat disturbed tyrant or at any rate is said *ad hominem* and ought not to be taken as expressing directly Xenophon's own views. We have therefore to consider whether the thesis that tyranny can live up to the highest political standard is defensible on the basis of Xenophon's, or Socrates', political philosophy.

To begin with, it must appear most paradoxical that Xenophon should have had any liking whatsoever for tyranny however good. Tyranny at its best is still rule without laws and, according to Socrates' definition, justice is identical with legality or obedience to laws. Thus tyranny in any form seems to be irreconcilable with the requirement of justice. On the other hand, tyranny would become morally possible if the identification of "just" and "legal" were not absolutely correct, or if "everything according to law were (only) *somehow* . . . just." The laws which determine what is legal are the rules of conduct upon which the citizens have agreed. "The citizens" may be "the multitude" or "the few"; "the few" may be the rich or the virtuous. That is to say, the laws, and hence what is legal, depend on the political order of the community for which they are given. Should Xenophon or his Socrates have believed that the difference between laws depending on a faulty political order and laws depending on a good political order is wholly irrelevant as far as justice is concerned? Should they have believed that rules prescribed by a monarch, i.e., not by "the citizens," cannot be laws? Besides, is it wholly irrelevant for justice whether what the laws prescribe is reasonable or unreasonable, good or bad? Finally, is it wholly irrelevant for justice whether the laws enacted by the legislator (the many, the few, the monarch) are forcibly imposed on, or voluntarily agreed to by, the other members of the community? Questions such as these are not raised by Xenophon, or his Socrates, but only by Xenophon's young and rash Alcibiades who, however, was a pupil of Socrates at the time when he raised those questions; only Alcibiades, and not Socrates, is presented by Xenophon as raising the Socratic question, "What is law?" Socrates' doubt of the unqualified identification of justice and legality is intimated, however, by the facts that, on the one hand, he considers an enactment of the "legislator" Critias and his fellows a "law" which, he says, he is prepared to obey; and that, on the other hand, he actually disobeys it because it is "against the laws." But apart from the consideration that the identification of "just" and "legal" would make impossible the evidently necessary distinction between just and unjust laws, there are elements of justice which necessarily transcend the dimension of the legal. Ingratitude, e.g., while not being illegal, is unjust. The justice in business dealings—Aristotle's commutative justice proper—which is possible under a tyrant, is for this very reason not essentially dependent on law. Xenophon is thus led to suggest another definition, a more adequate definition, of justice. According to it, the just man is a man who does not hurt anyone, but helps everyone who has dealings with him. To be just, in other words, simply means to be beneficent. If justice is then essentially trans-legal, rule without laws may very well be just: beneficent absolute rule is just. Absolute rule of a man who knows how to rule, who is a born ruler, is actually superior to the rule of laws, in so far as the good ruler is "a seeing law," and laws do not "see," or legal justice is blind. Whereas a good ruler is necessarily beneficent, laws are not necessarily beneficent. To say nothing of laws which are actually bad and harmful, even good laws suffer from the fact that they cannot "see." Now, tyranny is absolute monarchic rule. Hence the rule of an excellent tyrant is superior to, or more just than, rule of laws. Xenophon's realization of the problem of law, his understanding of the essence of law, his having raised and answered the Socratic question, "What is law?" enables and compels him to grant that tyranny may live up to the highest political standard. His giving, in the *Hiero,* a greater weight to the praise of tyranny than to the indictment of tyranny is then more than an accidental consequence of his decision to present the teaching concerning tyranny in the form of a dialogue.

Yet Simonides goes much beyond praising beneficent tyranny: he praises in the strongest terms the hoped-for beneficent rule of a tyrant who previously had committed a considerable number of crimes. By implication he admits that the praiseworthy character of tyranny at its best is not impaired by the unjust manner in which the tyrant originally acquired his power or in which he ruled prior to his conversion. Xenophon would have been prevented from fully agreeing with his Simonides regarding tyranny if he had been a legitimist or constitutionalist. Xenophon's Socrates makes it clear that there is only one sufficient title to rule: only knowledge, and not force and fraud or election, or, we may add, inheritance makes a man a king or ruler. If this is the case, "constitutional" rule, rule derived from elections in particular, is not essentially more legitimate than tyrannical rule, rule derived from force or fraud. Tyrannical rule as well as "constitutional" rule will be legitimate to the extent to which the tyrant or the "constitutional" rulers will listen to the counsels of him who "speaks well" because he "thinks well." At any rate, the rule of a tyrant who, after having come to power by means of force and fraud, or after having committed any number of crimes, listens to the suggestions of reasonable men, is essentially more legitimate than the rule of elected magistrates who refuse to listen to such suggestions, i.e., than the rule of elected magistrates as such. Xenophon's Socrates is so little committed to the cause of "constitutionalism" that he can describe the sensible men who advise the tyrant as the tyrant's "allies." That is to say, he conceives of the relation of the wise to the wise to the tyrant in almost exactly the same way as does Simonides.

While Xenophon seems to have believed that beneficent tyranny or the rule of a tyrant who listens to the counsels of the wise is, as a matter of principle, preferable to the rule of laws or to the rule of elected magistrates as such, he seems to have thought that tyranny at its best could hardly, if ever, be realized. This is shown most clearly by the absence of any reference to beneficent and happy tyrants who actually existed, not only from the *Hiero,* but from the *Corpus Xenophonteum* as a whole. It is true, in the **Education of Cyrus** he occasionally refers to a tyrant who was apparently happy; he does not say, however, that he was beneficent or virtuous. Above all, the monarch in question was not a Greek: the chances of tyranny at its best seem to be particularly small among Greeks. The reason why Xenophon was so sceptical regarding the prospects of tyranny at its best is indicated by a feature common to the two thematic treatments of tyranny at its best which occur in his works. In the **Hiero** as well as in the **Memorabilia,** the tyrant is presented as a ruler who needs guidance by another man in order to become a good ruler: even the best tyrant is, as such, an imperfect, an inefficient ruler. Being a tyrant, being called a tyrant and not a king, means having been unable to transform tyranny into kingship, or to transform a title which is generally considered defective into a title which is generally considered valid. The ensuing lack of unquestioned authority leads to the consequence that tyrannical government is essentially more oppressive and hence less stable than non-tyrannical government. Thus no tyrant can dispense with a bodyguard which is more loyal to him than to the city and which enables him to maintain his power against the wishes of the city. Reasons such as these explain why Xenophon, or his Socrates, preferred, for all practical purposes, at least as far as Greeks were concerned, the rule of laws to tyranny, and why they identified, for all practical purposes, the just with the legal.

The "tyrannical" teaching—the teaching which expounds the view that a case can be made for beneficent tyranny, and even for a beneficent tyranny which was originally established by force or fraud—has then a purely theoretical meaning. It is not more than a most forceful expression of the problem of law and legitimacy. When Socrates was charged with teaching his pupils to be "tyrannical," this doubtless was due to the popular misunderstanding of a theoretical thesis as a practical proposal. Yet the theoretical thesis by itself necessarily prevented its holders from being unqualifiedly loyal to Athenian democracy, e.g., for it prevented them from believing that democracy is simply the best political order. It prevented them from being "good citizens" (in the precise sense of the term) under a democracy. Xenophon does not even attempt to defend Socrates against the charge that he led the young to look down with contempt on the political order established in Athens. It goes without saying that the theoretical thesis in question might have become embarrassing for its holder in any city not ruled by a tyrant, i.e., in almost every city. Socrates' and Xenophon's acceptance of the "tyrannical" teaching would then explain why they became suspect to their fellow-citizens, and, therefore, to a considerable extent, why Socrates was condemned to death and Xenophon was condemned to exile.

It is one thing to accept the theoretical thesis concerning tyranny; it is another thing to expound it publicly. Every written exposition is to a smaller or larger degree a public exposition. The *Hiero* does not expound the "tyrannical" teaching. But it enables, and even compels, its reader to disentangle that teaching from the writings in which Xenophon speaks in his own name or presents the views of Socrates. Only if read in the light of the question posed by the *Hiero* do the relevant passages of Xenophon's other writings reveal their full meaning. The *Hiero* reveals, however, if only indirectly, the conditions under which the "tyrannical" teaching may be expounded. If the city is essentially the community kept together and ruled by law, the "tyrannical" teaching cannot exist for the citizen as citizen. The ultimate reason why the very tyrant Hiero strongly indicts tyranny is precisely that he is at bottom a citizen. Accordingly, Xenophon entrusted the only explicit praise of tyranny which he ever wrote to a "stranger," a man who does not have citizen responsibilities and who, in addition, voices the praise of tyranny not publicly but in a strictly private conversation with a tyrant, and for a purpose which supplies

him with an almost perfect excuse. Socrates did not consider it good that the wise man should be simply a stranger; Socrates was a citizen-philosopher. He could not, therefore, with propriety be presented as praising tyranny under any circumstances. There is no fundamental difference in this respect between Xenophon and Plato. Plato entrusted his discussion of the problematic character of the "rule of laws" to a stranger: Plato's Socrates is as silent about this grave, not to say awe-inspiring, subject as is Xenophon's Socrates. Simonides fulfills in the *Corpus Xenophonteum* a function comparable to that fulfilled in the *Corpus Platonicum* by the stranger from Elea.

Arnaldo Momigliano (essay date 1971)

SOURCE: "The Fourth Century," in *The Development of Greek Biography,* revised edition, Cambridge, Mass.: Harvard University Press, 1993, 43-64.

[In the following excerpt, originally published in 1971, Momigliano locates Xenophon at the forefront of fourth-century experiments in biography, which he claims occupied "that zone between truth and fiction."]

In the fourth century individual politicians found themselves in a position of power very different from that of their predecessors in the previous century. In the fifth century Miltiades, Themistocles, Leonidas, even Pericles and Cleon, had been the servants of the state to which they belonged. The tyrants of Sicily had been the exception, which disappeared in the course of the century. In the fourth century the initiative passes to states which built up their new power under the guidance of individual leaders. The conservative states, such as Sparta and Athens, have to adapt themselves to the new situation. Hence the new power of professional military commanders; hence ultimately the emergence of a professional politician like Demosthenes who cannot rely on the steady support of his city as Pericles had done, but has to establish or re-establish his authority in a succession of crises within his own city. In the fourth century Lysander, Conon, Agesilaus, Dionysius the Elder, Epaminondas, Philip of Macedon, and ultimately Demosthenes and Alexander the Great have a personal political line. They represent, as individuals, a greater source of hope and fear than the Athenian and Spartan politicians of the fifth century.

The new trends in philosophy and rhetoric emphasized the importance of individual education, performance, self-control. We have denied that the origins of biography are to be exclusively connected with Socrates and the Socratics. We have tried to show that the most ancient evidence for Greek biographical and autobiographical work is earlier than Socrates. This has thrown doubt also on F. Leo's thesis that Hellenistic biography is a product of the Aristotelian school and therefore in some sense a Socratic product. But this does not mean denying the obvious—namely that the Socratics were the leaders in biographical experiments in the fourth century.

The Socratics were infuriating in their own time. They are still infuriating in our time. They are never so infuriating as when approached from the point of view of biography. We like biography to be true or false, honest or dishonest. Who can use such terminology for Plato's *Phaedo* or *Apology,* or even for Xenophon's *Memorabilia*? We should all like to dismiss Plato, who cared too much about the bigger truth to be concerned with the smaller factual accuracy. We should like to save Xenophon the honest mediocre historian, who told the facts as he knew them best, by damning Xenophon the Socratic memorialist, who lost interest in historical correctness. But the fact we have to face is that biography acquired a new meaning when the Socratics moved to that zone between truth and fiction which is so bewildering to the professional historian. We shall not understand what biography was in the fourth century if we do not recognize that it came to occupy an ambiguous position between fact and imagination. Let us be in no doubt. With a man like Plato, and even with a smaller but by no means simpler man like Xenophon, this is a consciously chosen ambiguity. The Socratics experimented in biography, and the experiments were directed towards capturing the potentialities rather than the realities of individual lives. Socrates, the main subject of their considerations (there were other subjects, such as Cyrus), was not so much the real Socrates as the potential Socrates. He was not a dead man whose life could be recounted. He was the guide to territories as yet unexplored. Remember Phaedo's words: "I thought that in going to the other world he could not be without a divine call, and that he would be happy, if any man ever was, when he arrived there; and therefore I did not pity him as might have seemed natural at such an hour" (transl. B. Jowett). In Socratic biography we meet for the first time that conflict between the superior and the inferior truth which has remained a major problem for the student of the Gospels or of the lives of Saints. Nor is this the only type of ambiguity we discover in fourth-century biography. If philosophy introduced the search for the soul, rhetoric introduced the search for the improving word: anything can appear better or more than it is, if the right word is used. Plato sensed his enemy in Isocrates and the enmity was cordially reciprocated.

The fourth century is a time of strong, self-willed personalities which offer plenty of good opportunities to biographers. But it is also a time of divergent and conflicting explorations of the limits of human life, in terms of philosophy or in terms of rhetoric.

Both Plato and Xenophon apparently created new types of biographical and autobiographical narration: Xeno-

phon especially must be regarded as a pioneer experimenter in biographical forms. Behind them there is the problematic personality of Antisthenes—an older man who, if we knew him better, might easily appear an original and powerful contributor to biography. Apart from writing two dialogues on Cyrus, which may have influenced Xenophon's **Cyropaedia,** Antisthenes composed a book (perhaps a dialogue) on Alcibiades. This book certainly discussed details of Alcibiades' life, especially his relation to Socrates. It is going too far to describe it as a biography of Alcibiades, as Mullach did in the *Fragmenta Philosophorum Graecorum;* but it contributed to Alcibiades' biography. Antisthenes also wrote an attack against Athenian politicians in general, which was inevitably full of biographical details. Nor must we forget that Theopompus, the first historian to give a large place to biography, was an admirer of Antisthenes, whose skill he praised and whom he declared capable of winning over whomever he wanted by means of agreeable discourse.

Yet Theopompus was also, and even more, a pupil of Isocrates; and Isocrates has his part in the history of biography. In his turn Isocrates cannot be separated from the general trends of rhetorical and forensic eloquence which contributed more than is usually admitted to the technique of biographical and autobiographical accounts. I hope I am not surprising anyone if I say that I shall later treat Demosthenes' *De corona* as an autobiographical document. The technique for winning lawsuits and making political propaganda relied generally on the ability to present one's own and somebody else's life in a suitable light. The earliest extant biography of Alcibiades is in the speech Isocrates wrote for Alcibiades' son about 397 B.C.: the speech "On the Team of Horses." Later Isocrates added something of his own. He proposed a system of education which selected pupils according to inborn qualities and trained them according to a precise ideal of intellectual and moral perfection. He made it clear that eloquence was in itself productive of moral excellence. He also claimed for eloquence the old prerogative of poetry, which was to confer immortality by discovering and praising virtue. He defended this ideal in an autobiographical speech, "About the Exchange."

Isocrates' περὶ ἀντιδόσεως was never uttered before a court of law: it was a rhetorical exercise. But neither were the speeches which Plato and Xenophon put into the mouth of Socrates in self-defense ever uttered, at least not in that form. A conventional form of eloquence was used for new experiments. Being conventional, it set certain clear limits to the experiments. The biographic and autobiographic experiments of the fourth century see a man in relation to his profession, to his political community, to his school: they are portraits of public figures, not of private lives. The transitional character of these compositions is undeniable. The picture becomes even more complex if we

Xenophon and Socrates as depicted in a 1703 edition of Xenophon's Works.

remember that Isocrates was conscious of turning into prose that art of encomium for which Pindar had been richly paid. Xenophon, on the other hand, must have had the portraits by Euripides, *Suppliants*, in his mind when he wrote the portraits of the dead generals in the *Anabasis*. The interplay between new political and social ideals and old forms is an essential feature of fourth-century writing. At the same time the search for rules of life had to reckon with the new power of words. Plato's fear of being overpowered by rhetoric is as real as Isocrates' fear of having his words controlled by philosophers.

Isocrates' *Euagoras* was written about 370 B.C. Isocrates was not new to biographical sketches in speeches. I have already referred to the portrait of Alcibiades he drew in the speech "On the Team of Horses" about 397 B.C. But the *Euagoras* was something more ambitious. He considered it to be the first attempt at a prose encomium by a contemporary. Aristotle apparently did not accept this claim. In the first book of his *Rhetorics* he implicitly claimed priority for an obscure encomium for the Thessalian Hippolochus who, as Wilamowitz said in one of his most temperamental *Lesefrüchte,* was the boy for whom the courtesan Lais lost her life at the beginning of the fourth century (Plutarch *Amatorius*. But Isocrates may not have been conversant with this Thessalian product. Isocrates described Euagoras as an enquiring mind, a man who never thought of injustice and gained friends by generosity. The encomium is organized in chronological order but cannot properly be described as a biography of Euagoras from birth to death. While the reactions of Conon, of the king of Persia, and of the Spartans to Euagoras' achievements are told at some length, there is hardly one episode of Euagoras' life that can be said to be narrated. Isocrates combines rather ineffectually a static description of Euagoras' character with a chronological account of what other people did to Euagoras.

A few years later, about 360, Xenophon took *Euagoras* as a model for his *Agesilaus*. He had known Agesilaus personally; he had written or was going to write about him in his Hellenic History: the relation between the encomium of Agesilaus and the relevant sections of the *Hellenica* is notoriously a matter of dispute. The very fact that he wrote twice on Agesilaus shows that he made a distinction between the historical account of the *Hellenica* and the encomiastic (I do not say biographical) account of the pamphlet. He described the latter as an ἔπαινος and an encomium, namely an appreciation of the virtues and glory of the dead king. He therefore did for Agesilaus what Isocrates had done for the dead Euagoras. Like Isocrates before him, he must have been conscious of turning into prose the traditional poetic eulogy of a dead man; and he must also have shared Isocrates' belief or illusion that there was no clear link between his encomium and the prose funeral speeches for dead men of earlier times.

Xenophon, however, was not the man to follow Isocrates blindly. To begin with, he was much more interested in Agesilaus' actual achievements than Isocrates had been in Euagoras' deeds. He also had greater historical sense and experience than Isocrates. He knew, for instance, that notable sayings were normally not considered worth presenting in a book of history (*Hellenica* 2.3.56). We shall later see that he may have experimented with character drawing in the *Anabasis*. The untidy mixture of static eulogy and chronological account was not easily acceptable to the historian of the *Anabasis* and of the *Hellenica*. He therefore divided the encomium of Agesilaus into two parts. The first was written in the chronological order suggested by Isocrates, but was more factual. We can even say that it was much nearer to what later became a conventional biography. The second part was a nonchronological, systematic review of Agesilaus' virtues. As Xenophon explains at the beginning of chapter 3, after having given the record of the king's deeds he is now attempting to show the virtue that was in his soul. In arranging the praise of Agesilaus' virtues—"piety, justice, self-control, courage, wisdom, patriotism, urbanity"— he follows a scheme going back to Gorgias and adopted by other Socratics. There were also contingent reasons for such a systematic review of Greek virtues as typified by Agesilaus. Around 360 B.C. Xenophon was anxious to give an anti-Persian slant to his characterization of the Greek king: "I will next say how his behaviour contrasted with the *alazoneia*—the vainboasting—of the Persian king." But the dichotomy between the chronological survey of events and the systematic analysis of inherent qualities was an attempt to solve one of the most difficult problems facing a biographer: how to define a character without sacrificing the variety of events of an individual life. When we talk of *Life and Works* or of *The Man and his Work* we are still within the borders of Xenophon's dichotomy.

The same Xenophon wrote character sketches of contemporaries in his *Anabasis*. This work was certainly composed before the *Agesilaus,* but its relation to the *Euagoras* is much more difficult to define. The portraits of Proxenus and Meno appear to be written in the antithetic style dear to Isocrates (*Anabasis* 2.6.16-29), whereas the other two portraits of Cyrus (1.9) and of Clearchus (2.6.1-15) are stylistically independent. Ivo Bruns, who called attention to this difference, suggested that Xenophon had just written the portrait of Clearchus when Isocrates' *Euagoras* came into his hands: he hastened to imitate Isocrates in the portraits of Proxenus and Meno which follow that of Clearchus. This is too good to be true. It would of course imply a date for the *Anabasis* later than the publication of the *Euagoras*—that is, a terminus post quem of about 370 B.C. But even apart from the fact that there are more solid arguments for believing the contrary—namely that Isocrates had read the *Anabasis* when he published the *Panegyricus* in 380 B.C. (*Anabasis* 2.4.4 ~ *Panegyricus* 149)—I am not convinced that the influence of Isocrates' *Euagoras* on the *Anabasis* exists. These portraits are not *encomia*. If anything, the portrait of Meno is a ψόγος, a censure. Taken together, the four portraits represent four different types of men. Cyrus is more complex: a loyal friend and a ruthless enemy, brave in war, skilful in administration. His chief quality is loyalty and generosity towards friends. The typological interest is directly emphasized in the case of Clearchus: "Now such a conduct as this, in my opinion, reveals a man fond of war." Proxenus is the ambitious man in a good sense, Meno in the bad sense. It is worth noticing that even in the brief portrait of Cyrus great importance is attributed to his education. There is here a clear indication of the interest which Xenophon was to develop later in writing about the education of the other Cyrus, *Cyropaedia*. My tentative conclusion is that Xenophon had already shown an independent inclination to draw character before he came across Isocrates' *Euagoras*. The portraits of the *Anabasis* are Xenophon's own, and the influence of Isocrates on the *Agesilaus* is secondary.

Xenophon made a third experiment in biographical writing with his *Apomnemoneumata*. We call them *Memorabilia*, the arbitrary title given to them by Johannes Leonclavius in 1569. The correct translation of *Apomnemoneumata* is *Commentarii*, which is the title given to Xenophon's work by Aulus Gellius: "libros quos dictorum atque factorum Socratis commentarios composuit." The unity of the work, which was disputed in the past, is now hardly in doubt. H. Erbse made it clear that the whole work, not only the first two chapters of the first book, is a defense of Socrates in a legal style, which has its parallels in Lysias 16. Xenophon probably had in mind not the real accusers of Socrates, but the sophist Polycrates, who in about 393 B.C. had attacked Socrates' memory. Polycrates had produced an imaginary judicial speech against Socrates, and Xenophon answers in a judicially acceptable form. After having concluded the defense in the first two chapters of book I, he says at the beginning of chapter 3: "I propose to show how Socrates helped his companions both by his deeds and his words, and in order to do so, I shall relate all that I remember about them." This corresponds to the rule enunciated by Lysias: "In the *dokimasiai* one is justified in giving an account of the whole life." But in taking advantage of a legal device, Xenophon exploits it to an extent which makes it impossible to call his work an apology for Socrates. The report, the *Memorabilia* or *Commentarii*, became far more important than the apology.

Two questions interest us: whether Xenophon created the new literary genre of the *Memorabilia* and whether he intended to preserve real conversations of Socrates for posterity. We do not know of any *Memorabilia* before Xenophon. The fact that they combine a defense of Socrates with recollections of Socrates seems to speak for their originality.

Collections of sayings of philosophers and wise men had undoubtedly circulated in the fifth century. . . . [Sayings] of the Seven Wise Men were known before Socrates. Herodotus quotes some of them and knows that there were variants in the tradition. The popular wisdom of Aesop was known in the fifth century. It is also possible that written collections of Pythagorean sayings existed before Aristoxenus. But a collection of philosophical conversations as given by Xenophon is another matter, for which I cannot quote an exact parallel in Greece. What we can say is that Xenophon became a model for later compilations. Zeno collected *Memorabilia* of Crates. Persaeus similarly tried to preserve recollections of Zeno and Stilpo in convivial dialogues which were apparently also called *Memorabilia*. This tradition has given us Epictetus' speeches, *Memorabilia*, or, as Stobaeus called them, *Apomnemoneumata Epictetou*.

It is even more difficult to decide whether Xenophon intended to present real speeches. The question of Xenophon's intention is of course different from the question of whether Xenophon, even if he had intended to give the substance of real conversations in which Socrates had a leading part, was in a condition to fulfil his intention. The more one looks at the speeches, the less one can believe that Xenophon really intended to preserve the memory of the real Socrates. We may stretch our belief to accept that Socrates was waiting for the arrival of Xenophon to lecture his own son Lamprocles on his duties towards his mother (2.2). But the conversation between Socrates and Pericles the Younger is placed in the year in which the latter was a strategos (407 B.C.), though it reflects the situation of the Theban hegemony about 370 B.C. (3.5). The best research from K. Joël to O. Gigon has shown that what Xenophon does is to discuss topics which had been the subject of debate by other Socratics before him. If Xenophon was not exactly the cynic Joël envisaged in his classic book, he learned perhaps more from Antisthenes' writings than from Socrates by word of mouth. All the Socratics were involved in elaborate developments of Socrates' thought which bore little resemblance to the original. The paradoxical conclusion from our point of view is that in the so-called *Memorabilia* Xenophon created or perfected a biographical form—the report of conversations preceded by a general introduction to the character of the main speaker—but in actual fact used this form for what amounted to fiction.

This brings us to a point which becomes even more evident in Xenophon's greatest contribution to biography, the *Cyropaedia*. The *Cyropaedia* is indeed the most accomplished biography we have in classical Greek literature. It is a presentation of the life of a man from beginning to end and gives pride of place to his education and moral character. Nevertheless it is a paedagogical novel. The *Cyropaedia* was not, and probably never claimed to be, a true account of the life of a real person. Like Ctesias before him, Xenophon took advantage of his oriental subject to disregard historical truth. He was not the first of the Socratics to do so, if we may assume that Antisthenes' *Cyrus* preceded Xenophon's *Cyropaedia* in the same direction. The existence of previous Socratic writings of the same type may explain why Xenophon felt no need to warn his readers about the fictitious character of his biography: this was understood. But we shall never be able to tell exactly—even less than in the cases of Ctesias and Theopompus—how much is conscious fabrication of details and how much is elaboration of a tradition already rich in fictional elements. Xenophon had personal knowledge of the Persian state and of Persian institutions, and especially of the Persian army. He had Greek sources to supplement his information. He obviously tried to look plausible and well-informed. The last chapter of the *Cyropaedia* shows that he was concerned with the decline of the power of Persia just as in the *Constitution of Sparta* he had shown his concern for the decline of Sparta.

The papyri have definitely shown that erotic oriental romances existed in the first century after Christ, the date of the three extant fragments of the Ninus romance. The Ninus romance itself must be earlier than the date of the earliest papyri and goes back to 100 B.C. at least. We have therefore good reason to believe in the existence of a Hellenistic novel of oriental character. What interests us is that it claimed Xenophon's *Cyropaedia* as its model. It was remarked long ago that the *Suda* lexicon knows three Xenophons as authors of erotic romances, of which the alleged author of the extant story *Habrocomas and Anthia* is one. It seems probable that the name Xenophon in all these cases is a pseudonym or *nom de plume,* which shows the popularity of the writer of the *Cyropaedia* among writers and readers of novels. The *Cyropaedia* included the episode of Abradatas and Panthea, the classic example of a love story. Xenophon himself would have been surprised to know that he had become the great master and model of erotic stories: his *Cyropaedia* was highly moral. But this was the price he had to pay for producing the first biography, which was no biography at all, being a mixture of facts and fancies to communicate a philosophic message.

The *Cyropaedia* confirms a suspicion which the *Memorabilia* had already suggested: namely that true biography was preceded or at least inspiringly accompanied by fiction. The suspicion is reinforced when we think of Herodotus and even more of Ctesias. If Herodotus had honestly tried to separate what he could vouch for from what he could not, Ctesias had none of these preoccupations. He represented an uneasy compromise

between history and historical novel which influenced Xenophon. We might easily extend this consideration to Theopompus, who included in the *Philippica* a long excursus on θαυμάσια, on wondrous happenings, which gave a great deal of novelistic detail about religious prophets—Zoroaster, Epimenides, Silenus, Bakis. Theopompus was resolved to outbid Ctesias and perhaps Xenophon.

This point is important for the understanding of ancient biography at large even after the fourth century B.C. The borderline between fiction and reality was thinner in biography than in ordinary historiography. What readers expected in biography was probably different from what they expected in political history. They wanted information about the education, the love affairs, and the character of their heroes. But these things are less easily documented than wars and political reforms. If biographers wanted to keep their public, they had to resort to fiction. Socratic philosophy and Isocratean rhetoric joined hands in encouraging the introduction of fiction into biography.

I purposely refrain from probing into this matter more deeply, and turn from biography to autobiography.

The first name we meet in connection with fourth-century autobiography is again that of Xenophon. His *Anabasis* is for us the prototype of commentaries on a campaign written by one of the leading generals. He may have been preceded by his colleague Sophaenetus of Stymphalus, whose *Anabasis* is quoted by Stephanus Byzantius: but our ignorance of Sophaenetus is complete. E. Schwartz and F. Jacoby think of Sophaenetus' *Anabasis* as possibly a later forgery. A satisfactory analysis of Xenophon's work in historiographical terms does not appear to exist. His *Anabasis* is under the influence of fifth-century travel literature in its geographical sections: we have seen that travel literature inevitably had an autobiographical character. In the matter of military campaigns Xenophon has learned something from Thucydides and perhaps also from Ctesias. But he describes military campaigns with a strongly subjective approach and a clearly apologetic tone: he had his enemies. To redress the balance he writes in the third person. He apparently also uses the device of attributing his book to a non-existent Themistogenes. The *Anabasis* became a model both for its autobiographical character and for the effort to disguise it. The memorialistic literature of later times, to begin with Caesar, owes much to this double, partly contradictory, approach.

A very different kind of autobiographical production is the apologetic speech before a court of law. The famous model was the speech by Antiphon which Thucydides admired so much. It is all lost but for a fragment in a Geneva papyrus. What an authentic apology of this kind could be like is shown by Demosthenes' *De corona,* admittedly a later development of this genre: it was produced eighty years after Antiphon's speech in 330 B.C. Demosthenes chose the occasion for a complete apology for his anti-Macedonian policy. Part of the speech is inevitably nothing more than a personal attack by Demosthenes on his rival and accuser Aeschines. The rest is an attempt to make the audience realize under what conditions he, Demosthenes, had acted. Demosthenes never allows himself or his audience to forget that they have been defeated. But by placing his decisions in the proper context, he presents them as the only ones compatible with the honour of Athens and of himself. As he explains, it was inconceivable that Athens "should sink to such cowardice as by a spontaneous, voluntary act to surrender her liberty to Philip . . . The only remaining and the necessary policy was to resist with justice all his unjust designs." Thus Demosthenes provides fragments of his autobiography against the background of the Athenian resistance to Macedon. He searches his own past. He has to defend himself and therefore the results of his search are predetermined. Yet one feels that his question— whether an alternative conduct was morally possible— is not a rhetorical one. The fascination of the *De corona* lies in its basic sincerity. The speech is autobiographical not only because it deals with episodes of Demosthenes' life but because it is unified by a strange, powerful, tantalizing examination of the whole of his past.

The real apologetic speech was bound to produce the artificial apology, the speech written not for a trial but for home reading in defense either of somebody else or of oneself. Neither Plato's nor Xenophon's Apologies of Socrates were ever uttered. Though presented as having been composed and pronounced by Socrates, they were in fact written by his pupils long after Socrates' death. They are biographical sketches disguised as autobiographical sketches. They show Socrates aware of what either Plato or Xenophon knew. We shall never know the exact relation of these two documents to Socrates' true speeches. Of course Plato's picture does not agree with that of Xenophon and is incomparably more profound; but both pictures have their limits fixed by the true terms of the indictment against Socrates. The fiction is anchored to truth: the pseudo-autobiography must be true biography to a certain extent.

J. K. Anderson (essay date 1974)

SOURCE: "Religion and Politics," in *Xenophon,* Charles Scribner's Sons, 1974, pp. 34-45.

[*Working from Xenophon's writings and the little biographical material available, Anderson here reconstructs Xenophon's religious and political attitudes, which he characterizes as largely conservative.*]

I. RELIGION

Xenophon's education in religion and politics, whatever it may have owed to Socrates, was, like his moral instruction, not complicated by abstract speculations. Throughout his life, Xenophon remained the sort of conservative whose acceptance of the doctrines and principles that he has inherited seems either unintelligent, or dishonest, or both, to those who do not share them. Xenophon repeatedly represents himself as sacrificing before military operations, in order to determine, from the entrails of the victims, whether a projected operation would succeed or fail. At least once (*Anabasis* vi. 4.12ff.) he repeatedly delayed what seems to have been an absolutely necessary movement because the sacrifices had not turned out well, and noted that those who acted without waiting for the proper omens encountered misfortune, while after a favourable sacrifice was at length vouchsafed everything went splendidly. The episode bears some resemblance to one which he recounts of the campaign of 397 B.C. in Asia Minor (*Hellenica* iii. 1.17) when the Spartan Dercylidas lay inactive for four days outside the town of Cebron, 'much against his will', for want of favourable omens. The Persian satrap Pharnabazus was expected to appear at the head of a relieving force, and the delay seemed inexcusable to the professional officers in Dercylidas's army, one of whom attempted to act on his own initiative and was duly repulsed with loss. But, sure enough, the omens changed in time, and, just as the besiegers were being led to the assault, the gates were flung open and the governor surrendered, his hand forced by a mutiny of his Greek mercenaries. One cannot help suspecting that Dercylidas (nicknamed Sisyphus for his cunning) had been arranging the mutiny during the four days' delay, and used the 'omens' as an excuse to keep the soldiers quiet. But if so, did he really hoodwink Xenophon?

It is perhaps too easy to suppose that nobody can be sincere in professing belief in things which we do not believe ourselves, and the present tendency, even among writers not wholly unsympathetic to Xenophon, is to regard his religion as the vain repetition of empty formalities, at the best. At the worst, he is charged with dishonesty, not merely towards the gods but to his comrades in arms. It is more charitable to suppose that Xenophon's acceptance of the gods and religious practices of his ancestors was sincere, and at least one of his stories suggests a genuine, if uncritical, belief in the power of sacrifice. After the remnant of Cyrus's army had been transferred to the Spartan service, Xenophon was forced to sell his favourite horse to pay for his passage home. At this point he encountered a seer, Euclides of Phlius, who, after inspecting the entrails of a sacrifice that Xenophon had just made to Apollo, told him that to change his luck he must sacrifice, after the manner of his ancestors, to Zeus Meilichios, whom he had neglected since leaving home. On the next day Xenophon followed this advice, and obtained good omens, which were immediately followed by the arrival of agents, who not only retained him in the Spartan service, but gave him back his horse and refused to take any of the fifty gold pieces that he had received for it (*Anabasis* vii. 8.1-6). Here, if anyone was being fooled, it was Xenophon himself, and the seer's motive, if he was deceiving, is not obvious. Xenophon can only have thought the story worth telling as an instance of the power of sacrifice, both to make the gods' will known and to turn aside their displeasure. It would seem that he really did believe in Zeus Meilichios, and in Apollo, and in the other gods whom the city held lawful, but that his belief did not prompt him to speculate about their nature.

That the earth and its fulness, sun, moon and stars, day and night, and the changing seasons, had all been created by the gods for the express benefit of mankind, Xenophon makes Socrates affirm to the young scholar Euthydemus. The objection that not only man but the brute creation profited from these blessings was met by the assertion that the animals also were created for man's sake (*Memorabilia* iv. 3.2ff.). To prove the existence of the gods, Xenophon's Socrates relied upon the argument from design (*Memorabilia* i. 4.2ff.). Xenophon reports a dialogue that he heard on religious matters between him and Aristodemus, called 'the Little', who, as Socrates had learned, 'neither sacrificed to the gods nor used divination, but ridiculed those who did these things'. Socrates first asked whether Aristodemus admired any men for their wisdom, and received in reply the names of Homer, Melanippides the dithyrambic poet, Sophocles, Polyclitus the sculptor and Zeuxis the painter. He then asked whether those who made lifeless idols were more to be admired than the makers of intelligent and active living creatures. Aristodemus allowed the superiority of the latter, 'if, of course, they do not come about by mere chance but by design', and Socrates now drew from him the admission that things that plainly served some purpose were the work of design, and argued that eyes, ears, and the other parts of the body, each so evidently fitted to its purpose, 'were like the contrivances of some craftsman, wise and a lover of living creatures'. What of the natural instincts for child-rearing and self-preservation? These also looked like the contrivances of One who had purposed that living things should exist. But Aristodemus said that he could not see the heavenly powers, as he could see the craftsmen who created works of art. But, said Socrates, could he see his own soul, which controlled his body? By his argument, all his own actions were by chance, not by design. Socrates then dealt with other objections, as that the gods had no need of human worship, or that they took no thought for mankind. Aristodemus would believe that they cared for him when they sent him counsellors to advise him in his conduct, as Socrates said they did. But, replied Socrates, they made their will

known by divination and portents to the Athenians, to all Greece, to all mankind. Why did Aristodemus regard himself as the sole exception? Did he not know that the oldest and wisest human institutions were also the most pious? Let him reflect that his own eyes could see for a great distance, and his own mind consider simultaneously the affairs of Sicily and Egypt. Why should not God's eye see, and his mind consider, everything? Let him make trial of the gods by worshipping them, and see if they did not repay him by advising him about the unseen.

'And to me,' concludes Xenophon, 'he seemed by saying this to make his associates refrain from impious, unjust and shameful conduct not only when they were seen by men, but when they were in solitude, since they thought that not one of their actions would ever be unseen by the gods.'

Though Xenophon believed that the gods watched over, rewarded and punished the actions of men in this life, he shows (unlike Plato) little concern for the possibility of life after death. Xenophon's Socrates (it must be remembered that Xenophon was not present at the trial, as Plato was) faces death after his condemnation with courage and cheerfulness, but looks forward to surviving through the permanence of his beneficial and honourable actions (*Apology* 29) rather than through his own continued existence. Men still sang the praises of Palamedes, the Greek hero who, like Socrates, had been unjustly condemned to death, with more honour than those of his judicial murderer, Ulysses. He would testify to Socrates's innocence—but before what ghostly judges Xenophon does not make clear. Xenophon considered that the fate of Socrates was a blessing from the gods, not because he was translated to paradise, but because he escaped the hardest part of life, did not outlive his own mental and physical powers, and enjoyed the easiest of deaths (*Apology* 26, 32; cf. *Memorabilia* iv. 8, where Xenophon gives as his source for Socrates's last days a certain Hermogenes, son of Hipponicus).

This need not mean that Xenophon rejected the conventional belief—supported by Homer, though even the Homeric tradition was inconsistent—in the immortality of the soul. But he seems to have given the matter little thought, until his own old age turned him to consider his latter end. In the *Cyropaedia* (viii. 7), Cyrus's peaceful death at a ripe old age is carefully described. A superhuman being appeared to him in a dream as he lay sleeping in his palace, and warned him to prepare to depart to the gods. On awakening, he realized that the end of his life was approaching, and sacrificed 'to Ancestral Zeus and the Sun and the other gods', for the accomplishment of many noble actions, and in thanks for their divine guidance. On his return home, he took to his bed, and after three days, during which he refused food, he summoned his sons and his friends to his bedside. In his dying speech he spoke of his own uninterrupted prosperity, which he had never dared to count complete until now, for fear it should be cut short (compare Solon's speech to Croesus: Herodotus i. 32); bequeathed his empire to his elder son Cambyses, and to the younger the rule of great provinces: advised them on their conduct, and begged them to honour each other, if they had any thought of still pleasing him (*Cyropaedia* viii. 7.17ff.). 'For you do not, of course, suppose that you know clearly that I shall no longer exist, when I finish my human life. For you do not now see my soul, but from its achievements you infer its existence' (the same argument that Socrates had used to Aristodemus). 'Have you never perceived what terrors the souls of those who suffer unjustly inflict upon their murderers, or with what remorse they visit the ungodly? Do you think that the honours paid to the departed would persist, if their souls had no power over any of them? My sons, I have never yet been persuaded that the soul, as long as it is in the mortal body, lives, but when it departs from the body, it is dead. For I see that even mortal bodies, for as long as the soul is in them, are rendered alive by it.' (This seems to be a faint echo of the argument worked out in detail by Plato in the *Phaedo* that the soul, being the vital principle, cannot admit death.) 'Nor' (continues Cyrus) 'have I been persuaded that the soul will become senseless, when it is separated from the senseless body, but that when the mind is set apart, unmixed and pure, then it will naturally be most rational. At a man's dissolution, each part of him can be seen to return to its like, except the soul. For it alone is seen neither when it is present not when it departs. And consider, that of all mortal activities none is closer to death than sleep. But the soul of man is then indeed revealed at its most divine, and then foresees something of the future. For then, it seems, it is most free. If, then, these matters are as I think, and the soul departs from the body, bear reverence to my soul also and do as I request.'

Xenophon does not make clear—no doubt he was not clear himself—where he supposed the soul would go. Cyrus was to prepare to depart to the gods, but no doubt he was a hero, a special case for whom no ordinary fate was reserved. What did Xenophon hope for himself? He mentions the Eleusinian Mysteries more than once in his history—the bold stroke by which Alcibiades led out the whole Athenian army in 407 B.C. and conducted the procession to Eleusis by land for the first time since the Spartan occupation of Decelea; the beautiful voice in which Cleocritus, the herald of the mysteries, called upon the Athenians to end their civil war; the speech in which Callias the torchbearer rebuked the Spartans for ravaging the land 'where Triptolemus our ancestor is said to have revealed to Hercules your leader, and the Dioscuri, your fellow-citizens, before all other strangers, the secret rites of Demeter and the Maiden, and to have given the

seed of Demeter's harvest to the Peloponnese before all lands' (*Hellenica* i. 4.20; ii. 4.20-2; vi. 3.2-6). None of this proves, or even suggests, that he was himself an initiate, though we may be sure that he would have been careful, if he was one, to say nothing that might be construed as revealing the sacred mysteries.

Perhaps Xenophon's real hopes of immortality were those which Virtue holds out to Hercules as the reward of her followers (*Memorabilia* ii. 1.33). 'When their appointed end has come, they do not lie dishonoured in oblivion, but flourish in remembrance, and their praises are told for ever.'

> 'Only the actions of the just
> Smell sweet, and blossom in the dust.'

II. POLITICS

Xenophon's political views were also based on 'sound' inherited conservatism. There is a hint of up-to-date political theorizing in Xenophon's characterization of Critias, 'in the oligarchy the most ambitious and violent of all', and Alcibiades, 'in the democracy the most incontinent and insolent of all' (*Memorabilia* i. 2.12). But Xenophon, though he discusses the actual conduct of these two men at some length, in order to clear Socrates from blame for the misdeeds committed by his supposed former pupils, does not develop the view that every different constitutional form produces its own typical man, or attempt to characterize fully the abstractions 'oligarchic' man and 'democratic man', as Plato does in the *Republic*.

His political ideas reflect the inherited traditions and prejudices of his class, rather than advanced critical theory. A century earlier, the tyrants had been driven out of Athens and a new republican constitution drawn up by Cleisthenes. Under this the landowning class, consisting mostly of small farmers who worked their own land and were able to equip themselves for service in the ranks of the infantry, were politically and perhaps also numerically the most important part of the citizens. Special privileges, including the right to hold certain important offices and to serve in the cavalry upon their own horses, were reserved to the proprietors of larger estates, among whom we may suppose Xenophon's ancestors to have been included. It was a fundamental principle, and one that Xenophon seems to have accepted without question, that political rights went hand in hand with obligation to serve the state in person and with one's property.

By the second half of the fifth century B.C., though the basic 'Constitution of Cleisthenes' had only been modified in details, affecting chiefly the powers and manner of election of the magistrates, the balance of political power had shifted from the countryside to the city, and in favour of the landless poor. This was, in large part, the result of the Persian Wars and the development of Athenian seapower. The poor man, who could not pay for his own shield and spear, was at least able to pull an oar in the war-galleys, and so had a vital part to play in the armed services. At the same time, by driving the Persians from the islands and the rich Greek cities on the coast of Asia Minor, the Athenians had built up an empire of dependent allies and acquired large revenues which could be devoted not only to the upkeep of the fleet, but to public works like the buildings on the Acropolis. This of course created employment for the craftsmen of the city—'smiths and carpenters, moulders, founders and braziers, stone-cutters, dyers, goldsmiths, ivory-workers, painters, embroiderers, turners'—together with the men who transported their goods—'merchants and mariners and shipmasters by sea, and by land, cartwrights, cattle-breeders, waggoners, rope-makers, flax-workers, shoe-makers and leather-dressers, road-makers, miners' (Plutarch, *Pericles* 12.6-7, in 'Dryden's' translation). This public works programme was continued, by the building of the Erechtheum, even in the later years of the war.

Pay for attendance at the assembly and for jury-service helped to support the poor, especially the elderly, who were not kept away from the courts by other employment. The dependent allied cities were even bound by treaty each to supply an ox for sacrifice at the Great Panathenaic festival, so that whoever wanted to might carry away the meat. In this way the Athenian poor were provided at the allies' expense with a meat meal, a luxury that most of them probably had few other opportunities to enjoy.

Among Xenophon's writings is preserved a so-called *Constitution of the Athenians,* a clever, bitter political pamphlet upon the dealings between the Athenian democracy and its allies. Xenophon was certainly not the author, if for no other reason, because this work must have been composed in his childhood, before the Athenian power was ruined by the disasters in Sicily, the Spartans established a fixed base in Attica, and the Athenian confederation began to break up, when the revolts of the allies could no longer be contained. But Xenophon, like, it would seem, most of the young men of his age and social background, was brought up in the doctrines which the unknown writer expresses. Democracy had gone too far; the respectable classes, who served the state in person and with their purses, must be restored to their rightful position. The grievances of the allies must be redressed (that is, their revenues must no longer be used to subsidize an Athenian welfare state).

The war with Sparta and the expansionist maritime and commercial policy that had precipitated it, by bringing Athens into conflict with Sparta's allies Corinth and Megara, were to be deplored for many reasons. The war ruined the farmers, whose olive trees were cut down and barley fields flattened by invading armies, and drove the population of the countryside into the town. Defeat cost the Athenians their overseas possessions. Xenophon must often have met impoverished gentlemen, like Eutherus (*Memorabilia* ii. 8.1ff.). He had lost his property abroad (many Athenians in the days of the city's greatness had been settled on the lands of allies who had been reduced to subjection after trying to secede from the Athenian confederacy). His father had left him nothing in Athens. He must now work as a labourer while his strength lasted, and look forward to a poverty-stricken old age. Critobulus, in the *Oeconomicus,* was still a rich man, with estates in Attica, but his expenses outran his income, especially as so many relatives—ladies too well brought-up to help support themselves—were left on his hands. Other Athenians put the best face they could on things, like Charmides (*Symposium* 4.29ff.). In the days of his prosperity, what with the fear of burglars and the reality of taxation, he had been no better than a slave. Now he had lost his foreign investments and could no longer cultivate his estates, and the fine furniture had been sold up, and he could sleep secure. Better than that, he no longer had to abase himself before popular leaders; it was his own turn to be feared and courted by the rich, who rose from their seats at his approach and stepped aside for him in the street.

The war—fought by Athens defensively on land, offensively at sea—increased the importance of the rowers on the benches and decreased that of the hoplites, close-ordered spearmen who made up the bulk of the army (though by this time this list of those able to equip themselves, and so liable, for hoplite service included not only yeomen, but craftsmen, like Socrates, a sculptor by trade, and resident aliens). The war destroyed the unity of the Greek world. Sparta and Athens should pull together as 'yoke-fellows', as they had done at the time of the Persian wars. Moreover the Spartan State, at least if one did not examine it too critically, embodied much of the aristocratic ideal. It stood for government by gentlemen, trained from childhood to set service above self-interest, not for mobs misguided by ambitious politicians. Of course, even in the heroic times of the Persian invasions there had been highly-placed Spartans who disgraced their upbringing, like the Regent Pausanias who would have betrayed Greece to gratify his ambition. But the Spartans had themselves punished these regrettable deviates. Again, it was true that, if civilization were to be judged by creative achievement in literature and the arts, Sparta stood very low. But even that could be turned into a virtue by determined admirers. If Sparta had no fine public buildings, at least the Spartans had not bedizened their city like a courtesan at their allies' expense (cf. Plutarch, *Pericles* 12.2 on the Athenian building programme).

When Sparta finally got the upper hand the reality proved to be very different from what her admirers had expected. But perhaps this also was the consequence of the war, and the Spartans of 431 B.C., slow to anger against Athens but bowing to necessity and the will of their allies, would have been shocked to find that the result of a generation's fighting was not a Greece secure under a system of aristocratic alliances but a network of petty tyrannies supported by the bullying strength of the Spartan army.

However illusory the vision of Sparta may have been, it was shared by many of Xenophon's contemporaries, and of course any young man who displayed admiration for the Spartan system was suspected by good democrats. But it was one thing to wear one's hair long in the Spartan manner, quite another to betray one's country (cf. Lysias xvi. 18—a speech composed shortly after 394 B.C. for a young man of the cavalry class).

Unfortunately, while most of the upper classes were no doubt honest patriots, some of the advocates for peace and constitutional reform were in fact ready to commit treason, as appeared when an attempt was made in 411 B.C. to bring back the good old days by 'restoring the laws of Draco and Solon', as the party propagandists expressed it. The absence of the fleet, based on Samos because the main theatre of operations was now the eastern Aegean, allowed the 'reformers' to gain control of Athens for a time, but they proved incapable of either conducting the war or concluding a reasonable peace, and some of their leaders would have betrayed the defences of the Piraeus to Sparta. The fleet would not recognize the authority either of the Four Hundred who were supposed to be drawing up the new roll of Five Thousand fully-enfranchised citizens, or of the Five Thousand, even when it was allowed by common consent after the collapse of the Four Hundred that all who were qualified to serve as hoplites also qualified for the assembly. The sailors, who had not abandoned the struggle with Sparta to engage in civil war, had every reason to feel that their own patriotic service was far more deserving.

Xenophon represents Socrates as sharing the view that privilege should be the reward of service, though he is careful to give the sentiment a democratic twist (*Memorabilia* i. 2.58-9). He says that 'the accuser' alleged that Socrates frequently quoted Homer's description (*Iliad* ii. 188ff.), of how Odysseus restored order in the Achaean assembly by courteously requesting the kings and nobles to resume their seats, but striking the commons with his staff, and telling them to sit quiet and listen to their betters. 'For you are unwarlike and without valour, and count for nothing either in battle or in council.' Xenophon is careful to explain that Socrates was not urging his friends to strike the poor and the common people, for this would have amounted to ac-

knowledging that he himself should be struck. 'But he meant that men who are useless in word and deed, who are incapable of giving assistance in time of need either to an army or to the city, or to the people itself, and especially if they add impudence to uselessness, are to be restrained by all means, even if they happen to be very rich.' Despite this last saving clause, we may suppose that it was usually the poor whom Xenophon and his friends regarded as 'useless', especially in the military sense. In the *Symposium* (2.11ff.) after a dancing-girl has given a display of somersaults into and out of a circle of sword-blades, Socrates calls out that the spectators will not now deny that courage can be taught, since the performer, though a mere woman, has been trained to go so boldly among the sword-blades. This gives occasion for various remarks by the other members of the party, including a sneer by Philippus, a gate-crasher who makes his living by playing the buffoon at rich men's parties: 'I would like to see Pisander the demagogue taught to somersault among the swords, the man who refuses to join the army because he can't bear the sight of spear-points.'

To sum up, one cannot claim for Xenophon any profound moral or political insights. But piety, self-discipline and the ideal of service are not bad guides, and if Xenophon's own best service was not to be to Athens, the cause was not so much want of patriotism on his part as bad judgment and plain bad luck.

Christopher Grayson (essay date 1975)

SOURCE: "Did Xenophon Intend to Write History?," in *The Ancient Historian and His Materials,* edited by Barbara Levick, Gregg International, 1975, pp. 31-43.

[*In the following essay, Grayson offers a qualification to the general opinion that Xenophon was a poor historian by suggesting that the* Hellenica, *his most "historical" text, has a moral intent that overrides its function as history.*]

Xenophon as a historian stands condemned. His intellectual honesty is impugned as his abilities are questioned. For the history of the first half of the fourth century he is frequently ignored in favour of the unknown author of the *Hellenica Oxyrhynchia* fragments, in favour of parochial *Atthides,* hardly less fragmentary, in favour of orators, the bias of whose speeches is at the same time universally recognised, and also in favour of Ephorus, intuitively read between the lines of a third-rate first-century hack, Diodorus.

I have no defence to offer; nor should I venture here any ingenious thesis of systematic misrepresentation. Such is the undisputed prerogative of that master of the art [C. E. Steven] to whom this essay is with affection, and respect, dedicated. Instead I shall ask the simple question: did Xenophon intend to write history? There are I believe serious grounds for doubting this.

Criticism of the **Hellenica** as a historical work is general and well-known. The major faults are omissions (of minor details, as the patronymics of four of the seven generals at 6.3.2, but also of important and well-known historical events, as the Second Athenian Confederacy or Epaminondas' presence at Leuctra), elliptic writing . . . , delayed order (as Agesilaos' reaction to, and involvement in the aftermath of, Phoebidas' seizure of the Cadmeia, which is most revealingly noted at 5.4.13), and inaccuracies (in so far as these can be checked from the other sources, as for example that the Thebans were for provoking war with Phocis and made the alliance with Athens at 3.5.7 whereas the Boeotians as a whole are indicated both by *Hell. Oxy.* 18(13) and the inscription, Tod *GHI* 101). Full examples can be found in most commentators. A more interesting criticism, recently well analysed by [E. M.] Soulis, is the fictional character of Xenophon's way of writing: the presentation of information in personalised terms, the addition of literary frills or psychological observations, the introduction of anecdotes as if they were fairy-tales, constant reference to the truth or falsity of prophecies, interruption of narrative for comment upon it, use of vague terms of exaggeration, the generally anecdotal structure of the narrative, and the totally fictitious character and content of many speeches.

Criticism of Xenophon's historicity on these three grounds (broadly of omissions, inaccuracies, and fictional presentation) is valid and could be pressed further. I shall not do that here. It is however important to recognise that it was in *explaining* these weaknesses that critics found Xenophon's bias and attacked his intellectual capabilities (respectively his slipshod memory, his use of untrustworthy sources, his inadequate research, and his lack of dedication). But these interpretations are very much harder to sustain than the basic criticisms. Thus, for example, it is difficult to maintain that Xenophon carefully avoided mention of the Second Athenian Confederacy in order not to embarrass Sparta or in order to avoid praising Athens when the Confederacy was a well-known contemporary fact and must anyway be assumed for the activity of Athens in the 370's as described in the **Hellenica** itself. Furthermore, did not Thucydides equally omit significant events: the Peace of Callias, and Persian affairs? Is an incomplete final sentence the sole acceptable evidence of unfinished composition? Turning to the criticisms of lack of research and inaccuracy on the other hand we can point to many examples of careful composition in Xenophon. Clearly it is wrong to suppose all omissions and faults can be explained by a single line of interpretation, but to multiply interpretations of bias and connect them to an ingenious reconstruction of Xenophon's life and composition is as plainly absurd as the premiss that a *single* reconstruction may be found to accommodate *all* bias.

However the point that I wish to stress here is that these interpretations need not be justified at the outset. They are, it is true, needed to explain *historical* weaknesses in the **Hellenica;** but this assumption, that the work is historical, remains to be justified.

It is impossible of course to overlook the form of the **Hellenica:** a narrative account of Greek history, in roughly chronological order, apparently a straight continuation of Thucydides' account, and itself also anticipating further continuation. . . . However this is far from enough to establish that Xenophon's work was meant to be history, or even that it was meant to be as historical as Thucydides'.

The continuation from the end of Thucydides to Xenophon's **Hellenica** is awkward. Discrepancies have been noted in style, in chronology, in cross- and backward-references. They need not be repeated here, but add up to the conclusion that the 'continuation' is *purely* formal. If the most striking discrepancy, the syntactical break between the last sentence of Thucydides and the first of Xenophon, is pressed as it should be, it becomes possible to doubt whether Xenophon's work even formally was a continuation of Thucydides'. Possibly more attractive than the explanation that a sentence has been lost from either work, is that Xenophon may have rewritten someone else's continuation of Thucydides. Candidates are not hard to find: Cratippos' *Hellenica* and, if this was not the same work, the Oxyrhynchus *Hellenica* were both written early in the fourth century and there may have been others. Xenophon's **Hellenica** might therefore on this argument be regarded as much a rehearsal of a recognised literary theme (and later Theopompos repeated the exercise) as a continuation of an uncompleted history.

Further, whatever the relation of the *beginning* of Xenophon's **Hellenica** to Thucydides' history, there is good reason to dissociate the bulk of it from this beginning. Scholars have offered a bewildering array of possible reconstructions of the composition of the work, and little consensus exists. Virtually all however would agree on a break of some significance after 2.3.9. The most objective criterion available, that of statistical style analysis, has shown further that a considerable interval elapsed between the writing of this first part and that of the remainder. For a number of other reasons I should place the first part in the early 380's (or late 390's) and believe that the remainder was written, with interruptions for certain other works, in the last years of Xenophon's life in the 350's. This particular position is not perhaps so vital, as once the major break at 2.3.9 is recognised then it ceases to be possible to regard the **Hellenica** as a work conceived as a (historical) unity.

If Xenophon wrote with some idea of continuing Thucydides, a position that I feel should not be entirely abandoned, he nevertheless adjusted considerably his predecessor's whole perspective. Thucydides at 5.26.1 clearly marked what he considered to be the end of his account of the war: the dismantling of the Long Walls. Xenophon went on beyond this point (reached at **Hell.** 2.2.23) to add another few months before ending the war at 2.3.9. But more importantly Xenophon's extension was deliberate, as is clear from his marking the earlier point as where people *thought* that peace (or rather freedom) had come. This is heavy irony, as the subsequent events, described in Xenophon's **Hellenica,** but already obvious by the later 390's, would clearly show. The very end of the **Hellenica** can be compared here. The battle of Mantinea solved no problems, settled no differences, yet Xenophon concluded by inviting further continuation. To Xenophon might therefore I believe be ascribed the view that the affairs of Greece formed a continuum. This might be seen further as a reaction to the belief of Thucydides that events, as his Peloponnesian War, could be isolated as case histories. However, that Xenophon had a view about history, albeit a valid and interesting one, does not imply that he intended to write it.

Stronger in Xenophon than the idea of the continuity of the Greek struggle is the pessimism that accompanied such a realisation. Mantinea solved no problems, indeed Greece was more unsettled after the battle than before it (7.5.27). In other words, Xenophon's **Hellenica** has progressed from the idealisation of City-state conflict, from the virtues brought out on the battlefield, from the great men of his narrative, into an unsatisfactory reality. I feel it can be no accident that precisely the same approach can be found in the conclusions to other works of Xenophon. The **Anabasis** ends (at 7.8) with a somewhat sordid, and unrelated, campaign to win Xenophon a fortune: contrast his earlier idealistic dream to found a colony on the shores of the Black Sea, or his assertion of sharing all he possessed with his men, or even his pious and careful dedication to Artemis. In the final part of the **Cyropedia** (8.8) the glorious (and idealised) past of Persia is contrasted with its despicable present. Again the fourteenth, and plausibly the last proper, chapter of the **Lacedaemoniorum Respublica** contains critical comment on the real situation in Sparta, despite the excellence of the system described in the earlier theoretical chapters. Both these latter passages are of course notorious hunting grounds for those who seek changes in Xenophon's political attitudes, and who either regard the passages as spurious or as 'palinodes'. At the expense of much further argument, I shall simply note here that each passage represents a *different* change of opinion by Xenophon on a *different* subject: the moral fibre of Persia and the effectiveness of the Lycurgan régime. More impressive is the fact that all four books cited end with pessimistic

evaluation of realities in contrast to earlier (theoretical) potentialities. This conclusion must throw doubt upon the historical intent behind the works concerned: is this simply less obvious in the **Hellenica** because of its form and subject-matter than in say the **Lac. Resp.** or **Cyropedia?**

Apart from form and subject-matter some indication of Xenophon's historical intent in the **Hellenica** might also be sought in conscious reference to historical method or aim. There are however no passages which on examination show this, and certainly none comparable with Thucydides' statements at 1.22 or 2.35.2, for example.

Three passages can be considered. In the first, 7.2.1, Xenophon writes in detail about Phlius, 'for if one of the great powers does some fine and noble action all historians write about it; but it seems to me that if a state which is only a small one has done numbers of great and glorious things, there is all the more reason for letting people know about them.' These statements are all vague; no great states or historians are mentioned or even indicated. The remark is simply to introduce a digression on something 'fine and noble'— on how the Phliasians adhered to their alliance and remained loyal to their friends.

In the second passage, 2.3.56, Xenophon gives Theramenes' last words—the joke about a libation to his prosecutor Critias. This Xenophon says is 'not worthy of note', but then goes on to use it to make an observation about Theramenes' character, that even at death he did not cease being φρόνιμος or lose his sense of humour. We might infer that this observation was therefore more properly 'worthy of note'. I suspect however a literary device to introduce Xenophon's comment on Theramenes (which he wished to make for other reasons). It is clear that this passage (2.3.56) cannot be used to show that Xenophon had any historical criterion in mind.

4.8.1 is the last, and also most explicit, of the three passages. After his mainland narrative has reached 388/7, Xenophon turns to events overseas that have happened in the meantime and describes his method of selection: 'I shall pass over those actions that are not worth mentioning, dealing only with what deserves to be remembered'. What follows however hardly gives due space to matters of historical importance. Instead we read of Derkyllidas and the loyalty of Abydos, of Thibron's lack of discipline, of the contrasted fates of Thrasyboulos and Anaxibios (a moral fable), of Teleutias' control of his troops (balance and contrast to the earlier Thibron episode). These details moreover greatly overshadow in the **Hellenica** the battle of Cnidus and negotiations with Persia, to mention only the most obvious significant historical events of the period.

In historical terms these three passages are excessively general, irrelevant or simple-minded elaboration of the immediate context. However they do hang together in referring to what was worth mention, and in each case properly describe what Xenophon has done—namely to concentrate on *moral* points. I think it is perverse to insist upon a *historical* reference for 'worthy of mention' and then to criticise Xenophon for not living up to his own statement of intent.

Other intrusions by Xenophon into his narrative follow the same pattern as these passages that explicitly refer to his method. Apart from simple references to the date of writing (as 6.4.37 Tisiphonus still ruling) or to the fact of a digression (as 6.1.19 or 7.2.1), Xenophon invariably intervenes in order to point a lesson. Thus, often, he praises or criticises a military stratagem: 7.2.27-8 Iphicrates' rowing practice; 6.5.51 Iphicrates' delayed entry into the Peloponnese; 7.5.8 Epaminondas' camp; 3.4.16-18 observations on the morale at the Ephesus games; 4.3.16 the uniqueness of the battle of Coronea. Xenophon may also comment directly on individuals: 7.5.8 Epaminondas; 4.8.31 Thrasyboulos; or 2.3.56 Theramenes, as already discussed above. Similarly he may pass a moral judgement on events being described: 5.4.1 the downfall of Sparta attributed to $\dot{\alpha}\sigma\epsilon\beta\epsilon\iota\alpha$; 5.4.24 the unjustness of Sphodrias' trial. These passages could be supplemented by many more. It is by contrast extremely difficult to find an explicit *historical* judgement in Xenophon's *Hellenica* that it not itself some sort of moralistic comment. In 4.8.24 Teleutias (campaigning against Athens and Persia) captures Philocrates (an Athenian sent to help Euagoras against Persia); Xenophon brings out this very contradiction. Similarly, 7.5.26-27, the statement that Mantinea solved no problems, cannot but be read as a comment on the futility of the Peloponnesian struggles.

One seeks in vain evidence of concern on Xenophon's part for a properly historical approach equally to chronology, to causation, or to motivation. The vagaries of his chronology are notorious: the vacuous connections . . . ; the lack of absolute dates; the superficiality of the Thucydidean system imposed on the first part; the confusion of frequent flashbacks. Causation and motivation on the other hand were complicated subjects for all Greek writers of this period. Thucydides shows signs of changed positions on the latter, motivation, in his growing recognition of the relevance of the individual to his original city-state calculus; and the theory was being closely studied by fourth-century philosophers. In allowing a greater part for individuals in the *Hellenica* Xenophon certainly goes further than Thucydides. It is difficult however to feel that the motives and characters of Xenophon's individuals ever form an integral part of his historical narrative. On causation Xenophon can be more seriously criticised for presenting pretexts and for ignoring real causes: thus at 6.3.1

he describes the Athenian initiative for peace in a way that contrasts with the sort of planning for the mastery of Greece ascribed to the Thebans at 7.1.33. More often however he simply juxtaposes events, and in the later books especially falls back on divine intervention.

Again I shall not pursue these points further here. The historical criticisms are valid. My argument however is that they do not amount to any sound reason for considering that the *Hellenica* was written as history. Equally I have shown in this part that there is no positive evidence of historical intent behind the work. Its form and subject-matter amount only to a superficial indication; there are no explicit statements of intent, or of method; there is no evidence of concern for a historical approach to causation or motivation.

The traditional critical approach of Xenophon is therefore misguided as it assumes, wrongly, that Xenophon's *Hellenica* was written as history. In fact by collecting the elements of non-historicity contained in this traditional criticism a very plausible and more positive account of the work emerges: the strong fictional element in an ostensible historical form; the concentration upon Xenophon's personal interests, upon military stratagem, anecdote, and above all moral judgement; the positive advocacy of a particular way of life and attitude to politics.

If regarded as primarily didactic, the *Hellenica* fits well into the context of Xenophon's other works. This interpretation can further be fully supported by references in them. At *Anab.* 5.8.26 Xenophon defines what is worth remembering as the good *rather than* the bad. The vocabulary and the sentiment recall the three passages from the *Hellenica* considered above: 7.2.1, 2.3.56, 4.8.1. More explicitly didactic is the purpose of the Agesilaos (10.2). . . . The *Agesilaos* was an admitted encomium, but much of Agesilaos' career is also described in the *Hellenica,* and often word for word with the *Agesilaos*. Xenophon's views on education should be pursued in **Memorabilia,** where Socrates is represented by Xenophon as standing to teach $\kappa\alpha\lambda o\kappa\dot{\alpha}\gamma\alpha\theta\dot{\iota}\alpha$ at *Mem.* 1.2.12. The uniqueness of Sparta (we read elsewhere) lay in the fact that she was the only Greek state to make $\kappa\alpha\lambda o\kappa\dot{\alpha}\gamma\alpha\theta\dot{\iota}\alpha$ a public duty . . . (*Lac, Resp.* 10.4).

I do not think this view of Xenophon is necessarily very far from the position reached at present by modern critics of his supposedly historical writings. To take three examples: Soulis constantly and successfully criticises Xenophon's historical abilities; he wonders briefly whether Xenophon should be regarded as a historian at all; but then slips back into the traditional view of Xenophon's 'hypocrisy', called by Soulis, because of Xenophon's lack of consistency and patency, 'simple-minded'. [In *Historiographische Anschauungsformen Xenophons,* 1950, H. R.] Breitenbach has pursued the idea that Xenophon was primarily interested in leadership in the **Anabasis,** the **Agesilaos,** and the **Cyropedia;** the thesis should now, I suggest, be extended to the **Hellenica** and be broadened to wider issues. Finally [in *The Ten Thousand,* 1967, G. B.] Nussbaum has subjected the **Anabasis** to a detailed analysis of social organisation and of leadership, in theory and practice; not surprisingly he finds the work most suitable for such study, but he fails to make the further point, not a great one, that this was what Xenophon wrote it as.

My position need not be tied down to regarding the **Hellenica** as didactic and *not in any sense* historical. There is room for uncertainty as to what in the early fourth century counts as historical. The border-line between real and unreal, fact and fiction, was confused; that fact is most clearly seen in the biographical developments of the early part of the century (and Xenophon wrote biography); it is no less true of philosophical writing (the notorious Socratics, of which Xenophon was of course one); and of the pseudo-history of rhetoric (Isocrates, but again no less Xenophon). There was at this period considerable uncertainty about the function of history, and individual writers went different ways. Thucydides' approach has gained modern recognition, but was not necessarily acceptable to (nor understood by?) his contemporaries. The number of different 'histories' that were written to continue his account well illustrates the uncertainty. Ephorus and Theopompus show the predominantly moralistic approach that was ultimately established.

Theopompus abandoned his *Hellenica* at the battle of Cnidus and turned to Philip of Macedon. We might ask why, and one answer could well be that Theopompus recognised the historical importance of Philip. However, this does not explain his failure to complete the *Hellenica,* and, secondly, it is clear from the fragments that Theopompus' interest in Philip, his fascination for Philip, was not historical but moral. Whether Philip be hero or anti-hero, he clearly presented a more interesting subject than the continued bickering of Greek states. As Xenophon had written this, in the long run, went nowhere. If history is approached from a moralistic angle, it is clearly important to find suitable subjects. . . . This was what Theopompus found, and preferred, in Philip. It remains therefore briefly to consider here Xenophon's παραδείγματα, and to criticise his use of them. I can do little more however than indicate the shape of the problem.

First must be isolated the central themes in Xenophon's teaching. These I take to be Panhellenism (in the sense of a war against Persia to encourage some sort of unity between the states of Greece and closely akin, in effect, to Isocrates' final position) and the Peloponnesian way of life (distinct from the Spartan, which was only for Spartiates, but equally distinct from the polit-

ically charged outlook of most non-neutral city-states). Alongside these elements can be added instruction on military matters, and general moral issues (piety, observance of law, continence). These themes are deployed in the general παράδειγμα Xenophon chose— the Spartan alternative to Thucydides' Athenian Empire. The inadequacy in reality of this παράδειγμα explains much that is omitted from the **Hellenica** as also its extraordinary unevenness. But criticism should now follow, and I do not wish to give the impression of not being critical.

First Xenophon can be faulted on his understanding of some military details, especially Theban tactics. Second I find naïve his view that in inter-state politics all depended upon the καλοκἀγαθία of state leaders (the same criticism of course applies to the parallel philosopher-kings of Plato). Third his social outlook was unbelievably insular and one-sided, and his judgement in practice blinded by personal feelings. Finally I do not consider as at all realistic the Panhellenic ideal that rested on a campaign against the barbarian.

Such judgement naturally must be subjective, but I cannot accept Xenophon's use of his παράδειγμα any more than I can approve the distortion of history that has resulted. The final problem however remains: how are we to use Xenophon's **Hellenica** as historical evidence? I suggest that we can rely on it only marginally more happily than we resort to his **Cyropedia** for early Persian history or to the **Agesilaos** for Spartan policy. Issues touching the central didactic themes have been distorted considerably where we can check them. For example Agesilaos' plan to march ἀνωτάτω in Asia Minor is transposed to the end of his campaign there and left unfinished. In this case the reason for distortion could be a wish to leave open the possibility of a Panhellenic crusade, or it could be an attempt to conceal the extent of Agesilaos' failure, or it could be a literary device to contrast the potential of a united Greece with the unprofitable reality of disunion. No simple key exists to resolve such distortions, and the negative conclusion seems inevitable: given a fundamental break with historical fact in the total concept of the work there is no real reason to suppose any particular part of it accurate. Our estimation of Xenophon's imaginative powers may perhaps limit the extent of the fictitious element, but it cannot define it.

I should like to end by citing a passage from the treatise 'On Hunting' (**Cyneg.** 13.7). Doubts have been raised about the authorship of the whole, but this passage is certainly contemporary with Xenophon and I should like to believe it was in fact written by him. It is a conscious reflection of Thucydides 1.22; the author defends his account and explains his aim: 'My aim in writing has been to produce sound work that will make men not wiseacres . . . but wise and good. . . . For I wish my work not to *seem* useful . . . , but to be so, that it may stand for all time unrefuted. . . . If one accepts that Xenophon's *Hellenica* continued, but perverted, the purpose of Thucydides' histories, then this passage is confirmation. Moreover it points to precisely the reason for Xenophon's being read and liked in antiquity, and indeed right down to modern attempts to suppose him to be a Thucydides-type historian, which he most certainly was not. In the first century of this era Dio Chrysostom wrote that 'Xenophon, and he alone of the ancients, can satisfy all the requirements of a man in public life'.

Sir Philip Sidney claims Xenophon as a poet (c. 1582)

[There] have been many most excellent poets that never versified, and now swarm many versifiers that need never answer to the name of poets. For Xenophon, who did imitate so excellently as to give us *effigiem justi imperii,* 'the portraiture of a just Empire,' under name of Cyrus (as Cicero saith of him), made therein an absolute heroical poem. So did Heliodorus in his sugared invention of that picture of love in Theagenes and Chariclea; and yet both these writ in prose: which I speak to show that it is not rhyming and versing that maketh a poet, no more than a long gown maketh an advocate, who though he pleaded in armour should be an advocate and no soldier. But it is that feigning notable images of virtues, vices, or what else, with that delightful teaching, which must be the right describing note to know a poet by . . . .

Sir Philip Sidney, "Defence of Poesie," quoted in The Literature of Renaissance England, *edited by John Hollander and Frank Kermode, Oxford University Press, 1973.*

Arthur Heiserman (essay date 1977)

SOURCE: "Erotic Suffering," in *The Novel before the Novel,* The University of Chicago Press, 1977, pp. 3-10.

[*In the excerpt that follows, Heiserman briefly summarizes the* Cyropaedia, *stressing the elements that later authors of early romances could imitate; in this way, Heiserman argues, despite Xenophon's clearly didactic purposes, his work could be the "First Romance in the West."*]

One candidate for the role of "First Romance in the West" is the *Cyropaedia,* written by Xenophon, the spartanophile admirer of Socrates, about 400 B.C. More particularly, it is the story of Panthea and Abradatas, woven through books 5, 6, and 7 of the *Cyropaedia,* that is clearly romantic. This story is indeed exactly the kind of arcane, serious tale that Parthenius would have called an *erōtikon pathos:* its early date supports its candidacy—though similar stories in Herodotus, and the *Odyssey* itself, would win on this score; and its fame was apparently such that later romances sometimes adopted the name Xenophon—as though nineteenth-century English novelists had habitually signed their works "Richardson." But the story as Xenophon tells it is designed to reveal the virtues of Cyrus; for Cyrus himself, along with his career, is fashioned to show that "to rule men might be a task neither impossible nor even difficult, if one would only go about it in an intelligent manner." That is, Xenophon molds the conventions of the biography, the adventure, and the story of erotic suffering, already ancient in his time, to didactic ends.

In book 5, when Cyrus captures Susa, he wins Panthea, wife of Abradatas, as one of his many lovely prizes, and he asks his young friend Araspas to guard her until he, Cyrus, has time for women. Though Panthea disguises herself as a slave girl, Araspas can immediately identify her because her stature, her "grace," and her tears (which fall "even to her feet") evince her superiority; and this superiority, dramatized when she rends her garments upon hearing that Cyrus is to have her, signals that we are to take her predicament seriously. Already we recognize a convention of romance: the extraordinary and admirable character whose dominant value, marital fidelity, is jeopardized by fate. Xenophon might now have employed another convention: Araspas could here be struck by Eros and fall in love at first sight. But Xenophon chooses to make Araspas a conventional Scorner of Love so that he may return to Cyrus and work through still another convention: the Debate on Love. Many a courtly lover conducts this debate within himself; but Xenophon has Cyrus take part in it (as he could not if his minion were already in love with one of his women) to show how a prudent empire-builder deals with the conventional topics of these debates—Reason and Passion. Cooled by experience, Cyrus argues the right cause of reason and attacks erotic passion with ancient figures of speech: love is a disease, love enslaves even the gods, and so forth: Young Araspas mistakenly insists that love *is* rational—and trivial: "Everyone loves what suits his taste, as he does his clothes or shoes" (5. 1. 11). Later, in book 6, we learn that of course Cyrus is right. Araspas is suddenly brought to his king in chains because he has in the interval fallen so passionately in love with Panthea that he has attempted to rape her. Paternal Cyrus laughs at "the man who had claimed to be superior to the passion of love" (6. 1. 34) and demonstrates his compassionate wisdom by forgiving his squire, who confesses that he has learned "in the school of that crooked sophist Eros" that the soul's bad part leads us to betray our king, while the good part strives to obey him (6. 1. 41). But the psychodynamics inherent in all "courtly love" triangles—especially potent here because the lady has *two* kingly possessors, her husband and her conqueror—hardly interest Xenophon.

He uses the situation to enhance our admiration of Cyrus' strategic wit. Since the squire now seems to be his lord's enemy, Cyrus commands him to feign terror, pretend to defect, and return with the enemy's battle plan. When this is accomplished, we appreciate how Cyrus' mercy and intelligence bear political fruit.

But Xenophon has not yet extracted from this story of *erōtika pathēmata* all of its didactic potential. Cyrus rewards Panthea's chastity by permitting her to summon her husband to the camp. Grateful, and urged on by his grateful wife, the man volunteers to lead the van and charges to his death, winning the battle and illustrating how Cyrus' intelligence enables him to rule men. Even the story's final tableau celebrates Cyrus' virtues. In book 7, when he finds Panthea embracing her husband's corpse, Cyrus weeps. But his noble *sententia*—that it is glorious to die a brave victor—fails to console the admirable wife, who stabs herself. This pathetic scene is given a baroque twist when the corpse's hand, shaken by the conqueror, comes off at the wrist; but the conventions of horror soon give way to those of myth: three passing eunuchs who have observed Panthea's suicide stab themselves in frustrated emulation, and the great Cyrus, marveling and weeping, orders the erection of four great stones, one to commemorate the love of Panthea and Abradatas, the other three to memorialize the eunuchs; and these monuments, we are told, stand there to the present day. The intelligence of this wise ruler is crowned by the compassion that can honor passion; it sets an example for those who would rule men and makes the myths by which fame conquers death.

These conventional themes, characters, and predicaments are used in many later romances, tragedies, comedies, epics, and histories, both didactic and non-didactic.

W. E. Higgins (essay date 1977)

SOURCE: "The Active Life," in *Xenophon the Athenian: The Problem of the Individual and the Society of the "Polis,"* State University of New York Press, 1977, pp. 76-98.

[*In the following excerpt, Higgins delineates Xenophon's notion of the individual and his ideal relationship between individual and society; using the* Agesilaos *and* Anabasis *as examples, Higgins determines that "the claims of family and city regulate individual desire" and leadership, "if genuine, is not founded upon license but limit."*]

The Spartan king Agesilaos was lame in one leg and walked with a limp. Xenophon's encomium in his honor, however, never mentions this, just as it passes over in silence the oracle against a limping monarchy

current at his accession. Such reticence, which extends to the king's mental imperfections as well, suits the *Agesilaos'* thoroughly delicate nature. Here, by contrast with the more forthright *Hellenika,* physical flaws and flaws of character and policy are forgotten, criticism is eschewed, and every rhetorical device is fully employed to make deeds more illustrious which, if viewed impartially, might seem less worthy of praise. Xenophon in thus consciously improving his own historical record cannot be imagined to have expressed most completely in the encomium his own thoughts either about Agesilaos himself or about the kind of life Agesilaos pursued so energetically.

The *Agesilaos* is, moreover, the work of a friend acknowledging the very friendliness which so often animated the Spartan king. It was to Agesilaos that Xenophon owed his estate in Skillous, where he lived out so much of his exile from Athens; and it was with Agesilaos that a chance acquaintance, formed in Asia Minor, strengthened to an abiding bond which Xenophon must have appreciated all the more if, as is probable, his own city had already officially banished him. Xenophon's sense of gratitude was great; but it was a debt owed to his friend, not to his friend's city. As Agesilaos once told the Persian satrap Pharnabazos, friends from different cities will fight for their fatherlands against one another and even kill one another, if that is needed. So Xenophon admired Agesilaos the individual who was a Spartan, not Agesilaos *the* Spartan individual; and so in his old age, restored to his native home he came to write, upon the death of the king, words of praise which also illuminate those qualities of royal character on which he so often mediated.

It is Agesilaos' noble blood, fittingly enough, which Xenophon emphasizes first. He is, of course, following the standard procedure of an encomium when he begins with the Spartan king's lineage, but his treatment is more than perfunctory. For Xenophon wishes to make clear that his friend was not a man out of nowhere but that he was an individual who was part of a past and a past whose special lustre, though deserving of praise, was not an excuse for complacence but a model for action. Sparta's kings had always acted in the interests not of themselves but of their city, and never did they attempt to obtain greater powers (*meizonōn ōrhekhthēsan*) than they had received originally. The individual king, his family, and his *polis* form, in other words, a unit in which every member reinforces the other to the advantage of each and the detriment of none. In this way the city and the monarchy endured as the most stable polity in Greece, for stability was possible only through the absence of self-seeking ambition and the lust for more. Xenophon thus sees in Agesilaos a man defined by city and family, who is inevitably imbued with a sense of limit, the sense that his actions are directed by other than his own desires and aimed at something besides his own satisfaction. As Xenophon remarks later, nothing Agesilaos did failed to reveal that he was a lover of his city.

This sense of limit underlies all that Xenophon sees in his friend and unifies all the diversity of the king's deeds and virtues. Agesilaos never engages in wars of imperialist aggression. His campaigns in Asia Minor are undertaken to free the Greeks from the Persians; and his return home, highlighted by the battle of Koroneia, is seen as a loyal response to the orders of the Spartan government. In financial dealings he has a reputation for being not only fair but also absolutely uninterested in venal gain, for the prefers nobly to have less (*meionektein*) than unjustly to have more (*pleon ekhein*). The only thing he is content to have more of (*pleonektōn*) is not wealth or power, but hard work, while the charm which pervades his entire character is the manifestation of a contentment with the simple and an aversion from the excessive and extravagant. Agesilaos is a man who is constantly concerned to do exactly what is required of him, either as general, king, or servant of the gods. His trustworthiness and fidelity to compacts further illustrate, therefore, his passion for the proper and particular. He does not mean as king "to monarchize, be feared, and kill with looks":

> for though honor and power were his, and sovereignty in addition to these, . . . one did not see in him boastfulness but could have recognized, without seeking, a familial affection (*to philostorgon*) and desire to help friends.

This comparison of Agesilaos' rule to a family relationship is not an idle piece of warm praise. It reaffirms Xenophon's fundamental insight into Agesilaos' character, where the claims of family and city regulate individual desire. Agesilaos, in Xenophon's eyes, does not guide his actions according to a principle of self-aggrandizement but in the spirit of openness, trust, and mutual aid and protection which can prevail in the relationship of parent and child. The analogy is important, finally, because it makes clear just that insistence on simplicity, the avoidance of the grandly majestic, which paradoxically rendered the Spartan king's success so impressive. Because Agesilaos did not hold himself aloof, he was, as Xenophon remarks, longed after when he left Asia Minor not only as a good leader but also as a friend and father.

The sense of limit underlying Agesilaos' rule, its close and, as it were, familial rather than distant quality, also characterizes Agesilaos' justice. Always faithful to oaths sworn by the gods, he does not permit his victorious army to work injustice by violating his defeated foes' rights of sanctuary. By the same token, he does not allow captured enemies to be treated as men who are unjust but as men who are human beings. He is always glad when the just are rewarded more than the unjust, a thought befitting not only a moral man but also one who considers every action in terms of what it requires and not with a view to the gain it may bring at the expense of others. Indeed he regulates his life so carefully even in financial matters that "he was never compelled for money's sake to do anything unjust." But most important of all, and what Xenophon finds most praiseworthy about him, is his constancy of character when confronted with enormous wealth and power. Agesilaos does not embark on a personal quest for glory but continues to adhere to the commands of his city. His kingship is as great as it is because he is still king of himself. He returns to Greece showing clearly:

> how he would not take the whole world in place of his fatherland, nor new friends in place of old, nor shameful and easy gains instead of noble and just ones, even if they involved dangers.

After the battle at Koroneia, Agesilaos reveals how he has chosen

> instead of being the greatest man in Asia, at home to have the customary ways rule and to have them rule him.

Once again, therefore, the city, this time by its laws and decrees, even as it puts a check on the king's actions, enables him to realize all the more the true nature of his royalty.

It is this kind of royalty in limits which men might tend to dismiss as being unremunerative in power or wealth or as being downright shabby. Xenophon therefore consciously opposes to the frugal excellence of Agesilaos the sumptuous splendor of the Persian king in order to show up the latter as a sham and a mockery, as the mere appearance of monarchy and not its substance. Unlike Agesilaos, the Great King flees the cold and the hot, "through weakness of soul imitating the life not of good men but of the weakest animals." He hides himself from others and is difficult of access, as if to strengthen his claims to power, and although the Persian is always seen in the *Agesilaos* as an enslaver, there is a clear suggestion that the weak and effeminate eastern ruler is no less a slave than his own subjects, because he himself is in thrall to pleasure and to a bogus sense of his own might. The Spartan king, on the other hand, can endure all toils and is subject to no vainglory. He is a free man, whose characteristic deed in the encomium is to defeat the Persians and to bring freedom to the Greeks they sought to master. Ever the Socratic, Xenophon seeks in the *Agesilaos* to define "what is a king" and to suggest that royalty, if genuine, is not founded upon license but limit. The Persian, for all his appearance of power, is an *alazōn*, which is to say, an imposter who claims to be greater than he really is.

It thus gradually becomes clear that the **Agesilaos** is not concerned merely to preserve the memory of one man's deeds and virtues. While it is, of course, true that the events of Agesilaos' life explain in one way Xenophon's inclusion of his encounters with the Persians, it would nevertheless be an incomplete vision of the work which failed to see how it operates simultaneously on a level which transcends the simply chronological. Xenophon seems intent on trying to understand what lies behind an action when he remarks that Agesilaos' character will best become clear from his deeds, while his virtues, when examined, will reveal what inspired all that he did. Neither inner nor outer reality are by themselves sufficient for an understanding of the Spartan king; the two facets must be appreciated together. Xenophon is paying more than a personal debt or private homage in writing his encomium; for not only does he see in Agesilaos an individual embodiment of various abstractions like justice, piety, wisdom, and patriotism, but also an exemplar, a kind of standard according to which other men may direct their action no less than they do according to the demands of justice and fidelity:

> The excellence of Agesilaos would seem to me to be a noble model (*kalon . . . paradeigma*) for those wishing to practice nobility.

The **Agesilaos** thus constantly operates on two levels, the chronological and the timeless, the literal and the emblematic.

In seeking to praise his friend, therefore, Xenophon has also managed to find what is praiseworthy in a life devoted to *arete* and *doxa,* exploits of excellence and fame, and to find an inherent antagonism between this kind of heroism and the claims of the self, between true heroism and the heady trappings of power. In genuine nobility, as he sees it, there is something essentially Greek which the Persian can only ape but never achieve, if only because the Greek is free. Excellence to be real must be willed; and it is fitting that in Agesilaos' life Xenophon sees little that results from the domination of passion or chance. Luck does not make a man essentially better as a general or an economist even if it may win him an occasional fight or find him an occasional treasure. So too before describing Koroneia, Xenophon explicitly says he does not praise Agesilaos for being a man who engaged in a glorious but otherwise senseless battle against vastly superior numbers. The forces were, on the contrary, evenly matched; it was Agesilaos' planning and ability to command that merit honor, and anything else is foolishness.

It is also shortly after Koroneia, at Corinth, that Age-

silaos expresses his sorrow over the fratricidal warfare of the Greeks, how the numbers of fallen could better have fought against the Persians. Though this remark and Xenophon's juxtaposing elsewhere the Greek and Persian monarchy might suggest a political slant, propaganda is not Xenophon's aim. He has in mind something larger and more noble. Xenophon the encomiast is interested in something more abiding than time's encomium; like a Socratic he praises what is eternally memorable, what will live forever. The **Agesilaos** does not urge men to an assault on Persia so much as it urges them, if bent on renown, to consider the self-mastery of the Spartan king. This alone can bring that lasting personal glory some might have thought possible only apart from the city, perhaps even outside Greece in Persia itself.

It may well be wondered what Agesilaos would have thought of his friend's tribute; he might barely have recognized himself. He was a man of deeds, not thoughts, and it is precisely in a "thoughtful" way that Xenophon chooses to assess him. It may be, after all, that the deception of an encomium, as apparent and expected as it is, can not fully conceal the difference between friend and friend, between one kind of *arete* and another. Agesilaos idealized is the perfect man of affairs, but he is not necessarily the best man. For Xenophon does not suggest that his actions flow from first principles rigorously examined, nor does he ever allow to intrude the problem posed by obedience to the demands of a *polis* when those demands are unjust. He does not mean to denigrate Agesilaos' glory; indeed it is thanks to Xenophon that Agesilaos will always outshine the Persian. Yet Xenophon finds fidelity to the city and benefaction to others most fully realized not in a king of royal birth but in a man of lesser station, whose only exploit is to bear witness to the ancient laws of Athens and to reveal their subversion by others through his constant inquiries into the truth. Though sharing much in common with Agesilaos in Xenophon's mind, Socrates nevertheless stands apart from him because he is endowed with an understanding of heroic renown and patriotism which goes beyond the deceits of an encomium, however mild.

. . . . .

Like Agesilaos, Xenophon had personal knowledge of the Persians; but unlike the king, his encounter with them did not reveal his perfect citizenship or even necessarily his good sense. He reports in the **Anabasis** that he makes up his mind to serve with the younger Cyrus after a friend, Proxenos, has enticed him to join by promising that he can make Cyrus Xenophon's friend, the Cyrus whom Proxenos thinks "more important for himself than his fatherland." When Xenophon seeks Socrates' advice, his teacher cautions him about the dangers of offending his fellow Athenians, whom Cyrus has helped to defeat in the Peloponnesian War.

Yet when Xenophon inquires of the Oracle, the question he puts—how will things turn out best on the journey—shows that he is determined to go. He has little hesitation, and even Socrates can not break his resolve. Xenophon's account of the results of the decision, the *Anabasis,* may thus be taken as the most important of his non-Socratic works, since it shows the consequences of an imprudent personal rejection of Socrates and of the city which nurtured them both. As a resolute, vigorous, and headstrong young man he seeks out a life of adventure, away from the city, in the company of another friend, who is, as Xenophon makes clear, a student of the sophist Gorgias of Leontinoi, and eager "to do great things."

Cyrus is just the sort to appeal to such men. As his obituary reveals, he was an extravagant and dashing man who searched for the dangerous and grappled with it hand-to-hand. It is said to his credit that he was lavish with his wealth, sharing it liberally amongst others, who became his fast friends and who were encouraged to make more money on their own. Nor was he an unjust man, since he always rewarded those who did right and so further insured men's observance of what was proper. It is not surprising, therefore, that everyone who knew him considered him, of all the Persians after his great namesake, the most royal and most deserving of empire.

Yet his regal nature has a more chilling side. Those not won over to his justice and authority are punished with an extravagant severity which must have repelled as well as warned his Hellenic comrades as they saw people along the highways blind or lacking hands or feet. Open and friendly as Cyrus may be, his largesse never seems to rise above the aims of simple self-advancement. He is the center and the circumference, who is all and contains all but who never seems to win to himself men who think of more than money. Cyrus is the ultimate mercenary, and it is mercenaries he attracts to his service. Though most royal of Persians, he is not inevitably most royal of men. So enamoured of the material and its uses as he is, it is not surprising that he should yearn for the throne of another, that this prince, for all his apparent justice, can yet become a rebel and seek to take his own brother's life.

There is, then, in Cyrus a certain deceptiveness, beneath the swashbuckling bravery a designing aloofness. Not for nothing does he keep his truest thoughts to himself and effect a masterpiece of deceit by enlisting his army of Greeks and gaining men like Proxenos and the young Xenophon. They do not know where they are really going until they have gone too many stathmoi and parasangs to turn back. Geography has mastered them; demands for more money help ease their entrapment. Most of them, Xenophon says, did not join Cyrus out of poverty but because they were attracted by reports of Cyrus' excellence; they hoped to profit by his generosity and return home with riches, "hearing that the others with Cyrus were doing quite well for themselves." They saw the allure of *arete* and did not think twice before succumbing to it. But allure was all it was, and for many it was fatal.

It is remarkable how much guile and how much deceitful speech occur in the narrative of the march to Kounaxa. Klearkhos, Cyrus' confidant, resorts to tears and protestations of devotion for his men in an effort to win their favor and to keep them on the campaign against Artaxerxes, although they should know him to be a rough and war-loving man who strikes his men unreasonably. Cyrus himself is an expert at cozening, of course. When two Greeks actually desert him, causing some of their forsaken comrades to wish them captured as cowards and some to pity them if apprehended, Cyrus proclaims his goodwill toward those who left, thereby increasing for himself the goodwill of those who remained. Yet earlier a Greek has realized that to leave Cyrus, even with his prior consent, is a risky business; for he can sink their transports with his triremes, and any guide he provides for a land march can well lead them to where there is no return.

A small incident in Babylonia, where Xenophon sees fit to recall an example of Persian discipline, should also have prompted doubts in more minds than it did about Cyrus as a commander, once all knew his purpose. One day some wagons become stuck in mud, halting the forward march, which has to proceed swiftly if Artaxerxes is to be taken by surprise and his defeat rendered easy. Cyrus and his best and wealthiest men investigate the situation, then Cyrus despatches some soldiers to remedy the problem. But Cyrus thinks they are working too slowly and "as in anger" (*hōsper orgēi*) he orders his companions, finery and all, to jump in the mud and help get the wagons out. There may be more than a little humor in the scene of these begrimed dandies sloshing in the mud, while Cyrus remains apart, ever the Persian prince. How different the action of Klearkhos the Greek general, who thinks nothing of getting down into the dirt with the men subordinate to him, or, later, of Xenophon who dismounts from his horse to walk like an infantryman or is seen by his men half-naked in the cold, chopping wood. Cyrus at no time seems to mix with his men, to be available to them; never is he called, like the ideal commander of the *Agesilaos,* a father to them. He was not that kind of man; he did not fraternize, as Artaxerxes could affirm.

But the scene suggests more. When the Persian nobles rush off headlong to obey their leader, running as if they were in a race, Xenophon calls it an example of *eutaxia.* Does he mean that he admires their immediate response to the order, or is he perhaps being slightly sarcastic in calling their racing from all sides "good formation"? For it is precisely good formation that Cyrus' Persian troops lack at the crucial battle, Kounaxa, and the same impatience which causes Cyrus' angry command about the stuck wagons finally causes his undoing. When Artaxerxes does not appear to fight at the time Cyrus thinks he will, Cyrus becomes careless and marches with his defenses down and his troops in disarray (*anatetaragmenon*). When battle is finally joined, the scene in his army is one of utter confusion:

> Then indeed there was much confusion; for the Greeks and everyone were thinking that the King would fall upon them straightway, when they were out of order.

Cyrus himself, as soon as he sees close up his long-awaited brother, cannot control himself, shouting out excitedly, "I see the man," and protected by only a few, he charges off against him. And there Cyrus and his retinue perish.

It is curious that in relating Cyrus' death Xenophon should pause to describe, in a narrative otherwise remarkably swift, the scimitar and other finery belonging to a loyal servant of the prince, who died with him. Xenophon leaves one final and lasting image of the wealth of the dashing and seemingly heroic Persian rebel and of the way he could use it to reward even a faithful attendant, let alone a noble. But at the same time Cyrus and his Persians have lost, their fine garb and gorgeous weaponry count for nothing. At Kounaxa a truth finally emerges from the preceding deceit; only the Greek mercenaries, unpaid but disciplined, achieve victory. Cyrus earlier admires them for their freedom and sees that it has nothing to do with money:

> Be therefore men worthy of the freedom you possess and for which I count you fortunate. For know well that I would prefer freedom to all the things I own, many times over.

It is fitting, too, that Xenophon should close his obituary of Cyrus with the notice that Ariaios, a companion of Cyrus, flees the battle as soon as he sees the prince is dead. He and his force become thereafter minions of Artaxerxes, when before they had been "most loyal to Cyrus." Doubtless they reckon it is time to look for a new donor of gifts. Their action reveals that profound slavery to things from which not even the most royal Persian is free.

Kounaxa makes clear to the Greeks the value of their discipline and freedom, but they do not yet correctly apprehend the true nature of their situation. Appeals to them from Artaxerxes to surrender their arms only elicit in response gnomic truths such as "rule is the prerogative of those who conquer in battle" or "conquerors do not surrender." The deceit of earlier days has taken

on a new character, as the Greeks now attempt to fool themselves, confident in their own excellence. When a Greek in Artaxerxes' employ, Phalinos, informs them of their real predicament, deep as they are in Persian territory, lost, without supplies, greatly outnumbered, he factually rebuts the mildly intellectual but totally pointless queries of Gorgias' student Proxenos about the workings of the King's mind. He also disappoints Klearkhos' hope that he, a Greek who knows the King, will advise the Greeks to disregard Artaxeres. One other interlocutor, an Athenian named Theopompos, perhaps voices best the heady heroism of the army, for which the emissary has only scorn. On arms and *aretē*) alone did the Greeks rely, and with them, Theopompos proclaims, they can fight for the possessions of the Persians. Phalinos laughs:

> You seem like a philosopher, young man, and you speak not without charm. Yet know that you are a fool if you can imagine that your excellence could ever vanquish the might of the King.

Only gradually do the Greeks come to appreciate their situation and the need for sensible action. But even so, they express their understanding with a swagger; the King must be attacked, they insist to Klearkhos:

> for he will not willingly desire us, having got back to Greece, to announce how we, the number that we are, conquered the King at his very doors and got away having made him a laughingstock.

Klearkhos knows the more sober realities yet seems incapable of developing a successful plan of withdrawal. In fact his position as commander is something he obtained only because no one else had any experience. As Xenophon shows in his character sketches, the Greek generals lack some essential qualities of leadership; and the misfortunes and uncertainty of the Greeks after Kounaxa are the result not only of their own bravado but also of the poor direction they received. None of the commanders can accurately assess the situation and get the force out, neither the naive Proxenos nor the unsubtle Klearkhos. The latter turns to the gods, hoping for answers better sought in deliberation. When a stranger, who turns out subsequently to have been suborned by the enemy, reveals some seemingly disastrous news, the Spartan is "thrown into terrible confusion" (*etarakhthē sphodra*) and becomes afraid. His last address to Tissaphernes is a masterpiece of quandary and pious doubletalk; at his poor wit's end he seeks support in bogus faith. In accepting the satrap's ominous invitation to a parley, he merely acquiesces to a greater master in deceit. For Tissaphernes' final speech to Klearkhos and the Greeks before the slaughter of the captains and arrest of the generals is irony perfected to vengeance; his passions to be trusted by them, he assures the Greeks, is what has kept him from destroying them.

Tissaphernes' assault upon the Greek commanders is considered and astute. It is only when deprived of so many leaders that the Greeks finally understand fully their predicament, going over in their minds the very things Phalinos and Klearkhos have told them before. But what impresses them most in their despair is the thought that they will never again look upon their fatherlands, parents, wives, and children. The very things they have so blithely left behind in the pursuit of adventure and fortune are now the very ones that will inspire them to acts of heroism which monetary reward could not induce. Now they begin to realize their nature as Greeks, and they expel from their midst anyone who dishonors his fatherland with counsels of submission. New leaders take over, Xenophon among them, elected, not appointed by fiat; and plans are discussed in assembly, not kept secret or delivered by generals from on high.

The army, in other words, discovers its hope in its freedom and begins to act in accord with it. At this time, too, deception begins to vanish; the inspiring speeches of Xenophon, designed to lift flagging spirits, are the first in the *Anabasis,* for all their rhetoric, to be free of mendacity or uncertainty. Though he may minimize the dangers confronting him and his fellows, he never lies; and once he has succeeded in giving them a sense of direction, persuasive haragues become less frequent and less long. Speech, once the vehicle of deceit, gives way to action, the quest for glory to the quest for the simple goal of home and homeland. A sense of direction has been achieved.

Xenophon considers the essential requirement of the retreat to be good leadership, and from the beginning he displays a concern that competent commanders be put in charge. His first act, even before addressing the despairing troops, is to rouse the surviving officers and to arrange for the replacement of those arrested or dead. As he tells them, nothing honorable or good can ever happen without a commander, especially in war. In good order (*eutaxia*) is salvation; lack of discipline has already destroyed many. When addressing the rank and file he urges them to be more orderly and obedient to their officers than they have been before. He shows himself from the first as a man confident in the success which structure and organization bring and consequently as a man devoted to preserving this ordered system.

Many have observed how the retreating army resembles a *polis,* and its operation lends itself to valuable sociological study. Nor can there be any doubt that its cohesiveness as a group aided it in its successful march to the sea. It is fascinating also to observe how different abilities are used: Cretans make good archers, and Rhodians good slingers. All work together for the common good under the guidance of commanders who can push forward no matter what, like the Spartan Kheirisophos, or who can quickly contrive stratagems

to surmount special hindrances, like the Athenian Xenophon. It is, in fact, remarkable that Xenophon reports only one real falling out between him and the chief commander, for they were very dissimilar men.

But it is Xenophon himself who, more than any other, seems to embody the highest purpose of the force. Though only a rearguard officer, he gives the impression that he was everywhere. He is the man who keeps the army together in the snows of Armenia, who is always available to them for conversation day or night, who is called "father" and "benefactor." Above all he is the man who will not let them forget their goal like the men of Odysseus who ate the lotus.

But if Xenophon saves them from the Persians and the elements, he can not save them from themselves. Their joy at reaching the sea makes them forget that the sea was not their true goal. Thinking all their troubles are over, they celebrate games as though they have made a conquest. Kheirisophos is greeted joyously when he proposes to go to his friend, the Spartan admiral Anaxibios, for ships to carry the army back to their fatherland. One man from the rank and file, tired of walking and carrying, expresses the happy thoughts of all:

> I yearn, now that I have finished with those toils, since we have reached the sea, to sail the rest of the way and stretched out like Odysseus to arrive in Greece.

Xenophon now confronts a folly (*aphrosune*) which becomes more and more destructive to that very structure he has worked so hard to preserve. His first proposals about taking necessary precautions while they wait for Kheirisophos' return the men greet with a bored response that Xenophon captures in the dully repeated phrase *edoxe kai tauta* (motion passed), a sharp contrast to their joyous and enthusiastic reception of Kheirisophos shortly before. More and more the men look to their own private interests, and the army's discipline falls apart. On one occasion they are even surprised by an enemy and routed into a disorderly retreat, which only gives the foe added encouragement. This, as Xenophon quietly observes, had never happened before. Envoys and messengers are no longer immune from the physical assault of disgruntled individuals who act only on their own authority. The men have become like rabid dogs, and Xenophon's insistence on reason only makes him the object of their attacks. His fellow officers turn on him as well, as each vies with the other for supreme command. In search of popular favor, one of them tries to please his men by irresponsibly giving them everything they want.

The structure thus crumbles both at the top and the bottom; and the army antagonizes the local population, even attempting to take Greek cities by storm. Such brigandage costs them almost three thousand lives in the end. What is the cause? The divided army's re-union after Xenophon's group has helped another unit out of difficulty is suggestive. Then the men "were glad to see each other and welcomed each other like brothers." The *Anabasis* implies that only adversity is enough to keep these men together; without danger they go their own way. In fact even on the march to the sea some men were out to get an advantage over their comrades, as Xenophon reveals when justifying some disciplinary actions he took. The breakdown of the army is only the natural outcome of its own nature. It begins as a chance assemblage of men, with no strong ties of city or family among them. They are all out for profit, and this is apparent as soon as the men feel safe from mortal danger. It is a fitting conclusion that, far from returning home to Greece, these mercenaries once again march up-country against their old foe Tissa-phernes. To have imagined they were a *polis* in any real sense was a delusion, and therefore the *Anabasis* does not so much present a record of the mutability of things as it does the tendency of all things to manifest finally their genuine selves.

What is truly remarkable, however, is Xenophon's reaction. Constantly trying to work against the disrup-tion of the force, he is ever more on the defensive before it. He gets next to nothing as reward for his labors and yet seems convinced that he can make an enduring polity out of this clearly temporary grouping of men. He can even conceive, almost pathetically, of establishing a colony on a particularly favorable site, only to be jeered at by an army still insisting it wants to get to Greece. What he thinks is revealing:

> he thought it would be a glorious thing to increase the territory and power of Greece if the men established a city. And it seemed to him it would be a great city as he thought over the number of the men and the people living in the Pontic area.

Xenophon still has a mind set on glorious exploit. Like the men's, his nature has not changed from the time he first joined Cyrus' expedition. Later on he can comment on how hard it will be when the actions of some deprive all of the praise and honor (*epainou kai timēs*) they thought to get in Greece and cause them to be considered the inferior of their country-men. Not surprisingly when he is offered the post of supreme commander, he desires to accept, for he thinks of the greater honor he will have before his friends and the greater name he will have before the city; last of all he thinks he may be capable of doing some good for the army.

Xenophon is the victim of his own delusion. The army he helped form into a successfully functioning unit he misconstrues as something lasting that can bring him renown. In trying to keep it together he is attempting the impossible. It is even doubtful if he fully appreci-ates what a city is. In his calculations for his colony he only adds up the numbers who will inhabit it, all sol-diers, while his eagerness to march with Cyrus in the first place seems to suggest that he considers his native city both as a place he can lightly leave and the place where his own glory may shine. There is no notion of the intricacies of civic justice and civic life. It all seems so easy. He has not yet learned to understand the les-son of Socrates, who stays in the city through radical democracy and radical oligarchy, trying always to be true to its ancient laws and seeking to discover and elucidate through conversation and reason what are the basic principles which give the *polis* life.

This is not to say, however, that Xenophon is no better than the men around him, that he is just some sort of glorified mercenary. His poverty proves that money did not ultimately matter; and, as he tells Seuthes, he considers no possession more honorable for a man, especially a leader, than excellence, justice, and nobil-ity. The difficulty lies in his slowness to learn that the way in which he pursues these virtues is one of toil fraught with reversals. Although his defense of his actions before Seuthes and the army rings true, it re-veals his failure to comprehend how the men could turn on him or Seuthes betray him. He sarcastically calls his fellow Greeks "most gifted with memory of everything" when he rails at their present ingratitude after all he has done for them; on another occasion he expresses surprise (*thaumazō*) that people seem only to remember the few harsh things he had to do and not the saving assistance he often rendered:

> But it is an honorable thing, surely, and just and holy and more pleasant to remember the good things rather than the bad.

Only very gradually does the awareness grow in him that he cannot keep everything as perfect as he wants it and that his excellence does not insure permanence. He turns down the supreme command because he con-siders "that it is unclear to every man what the future will bring and therefore there is also a danger of losing the reputation one has already achieved." He begins to think more and more of leaving the army and returning home to Athens. But he is always drawn back to the army in its need, even though he gets nothing for his efforts:

> Well, it is necessary, I suppose, for a man to expect everything when even I am now accused by you just when I imagine to myself that I have exerted the greatest zeal on your behalf.

The headstrong Xenophon who dropped everything to travel with Proxenos is not ignorant, let alone incom-petent; he is merely too easily deceived, deceived about the nature and actions of others, deceived about his own nature and desires. He is his own worst enemy.

As a seer tells him, even if money is about to come Xenophon's way, some obstacle will always appear, not the least being the obstacle he is to himself.

Xenophon's personality dominates most of the *Anabasis,* so clearly any attempt to explain the work must be made in terms of this. It cannot be forgotten, furthermore, that the record of the Ten Thousand Xenophon preserves is very much his own view. As [Félix] Dürrbach pointed out in a classic study ["L'Apologie de Xénophon," *Revue des Études Grecques,* 1893], Diodoros' account makes no mention of Xenophon; and it is evident that Diodoros did not use the *Anabasis* as a source for events like Kounaxa. Since Xenophon published it under the pseudonym Themistogenes of Syracuse, he speaks of himself as a separate, different person, making it possible, as Plutarch long ago observed, to lend a greater air of verisimilitude to what he says about his own deeds. It looks as though Xenophon had an apologetic purpose in mind, therefore, when he undertook the composition; and this may be what prompted Ephoros, Diodoros' source, to avoid it as a reliable record of what occurred on the march up-country.

Most commentary on the *Anabasis* has, in fact, been concerned with its alleged *Tendenz,* seeking explanations outside the work for those which it ought to contain within itself. Why must Xenophon have necessarily had an immediately practical purpose in mind when writing the *Anabasis* or any other work? What was Xenophon writing an apology for? Was it a response to the account of the campaign written by one of his colleagues in command, Sophainetos? In the absence of significant portions of Sophainetos' work this must remain a gratuitous assumption. Was it to respond to the charges made against him by others of the expedition or even to charges made against the men themselves by hostile Greeks in Asia Minor or in the fatherland? This, too, is unconvincing, for even if the earliest conceivable publication date is accepted, it remains obscure why Xenophon, at his ease in Skillous, waited more than a decade to defend himself or his army. And even if it is assumed that he could have blown the dust off issues and events long past, why does he spend so much time in the *Anabasis* about so many things unrelated to *apologia,* like the character study of Cyrus, the different kinds of native dances, descriptions of foreign food and foreign customs, strategic devices like winter leggings, various kinds of bows, and ways to cut glare from the sunlit snow? What has *apologia* got to do with men chasing ostriches and wild donkeys or getting sick on honey? A work of defense, moreover, implies a certain method of operation by which evidence is sifted and selected for biased ends. Yet Xenophon seems free of such prejudice: he records both the folly and the heroism of the men prior to and after Kounaxa, he never displays partiality to one group over another, is content to call a man good or bad on his own personal merits, and, what is most important, his defenses of his own actions ultimately reveal his own folly.

To seek to explain the *Anabasis* in terms of a *Tendenz* is too narrow a view at best. The conflicts between Diodorus' source and Xenophon do not have to be explained by assuming that Xenophon had an ulterior motive which caused him to distort artfully what really happened. If Ephoros neglected Xenophon, it need not be the result of a superior historical understanding which led him to prefer Sophainetos, Ktesias, or whomever. Perhaps as a student of Isokrates he deliberately avoided the work of a known Socratic. Or perhaps Ephoros found another account more suitable for his purposes, not because it was more accurate but because it was more straightforward, lacking all those details which give point and life to Xenophon's narrative. For the reader of Diodoros, even bearing in mind Diodoros is only providing a summary for inclusion within a much larger and different framework, would hardly get the idea that the march of the Ten Thousand was anything more than a series of military and geographical obstacles overcome.

The *Anabasis,* to be sure, does record the actions of historical men in a definite time and place; but perhaps Xenophon never had historical precision uppermost in his mind as his chief aim. Thus even though he admits knowing Ktesias' account of Kounaxa, he does not follow it, despite the fact that Ktesias was closer to the center of action than Xenophon was. Xenophon is more concerned with the heroic action of Cyrus, to show that his death was the sort to be expected from a man of his kind, to show that this death was indicative of the man's whole life. By the same token Xenophon may err in the geography of the army's route, but this is less an indication of Xenophon's sloppiness or his failure to consult even his own diaries (if they ever existed) than it is another indication that he was interested in something else which need not, moreover, have had anything to do with *apologia.* He records the numbers of stathmoi and parasangs traversed by the army of Cyrus not just to give his book an air of authenticity but to suggest quietly the ever deepening ensnarement of the Greeks within Persian territory. When the retreating force comes across some ruined cities of the Persian past, once again Xenophon records this not so much because the army did in reality pass by them but because they testify to the weakness of the Persians from whom the army is fleeing; for the ancient Persians conquered none of these places by force of arms but only owing to chance acts of nature. Finally is it for accuracy's sake that Xenophon narrates how the Greeks, who thought they were home free once they had reached the sea, got sick on the local sweet, encountered in this region the most barbarian people they had ever seen, and found olives nonexistent amongst

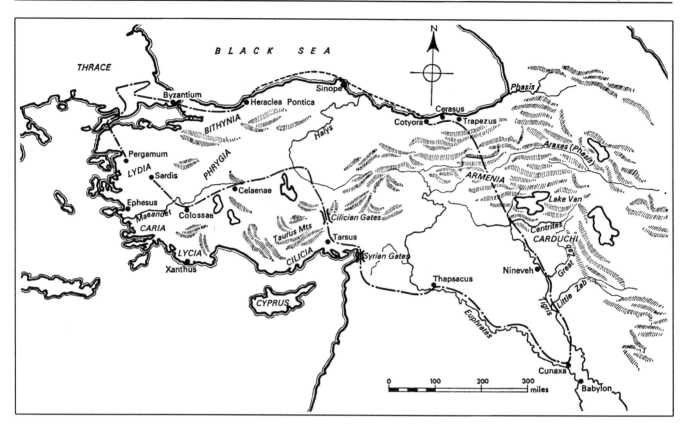

A map showing the march of the 10,000.

the regional produce? Doubtless all these things happened, or things like them; but within Xenophon's context they seem to have a resonance which transcends the purely reportorial, suggesting a truth about the army beyond its simple passage.

It would be better, therefore, to realize that the *Anabasis,* though dealing in a narrative and unfictionalized way with a historical event, is clearly one man's obviously idiosyncratic vision of that event, and that it was clearly meant to be understood as such. The *Anabasis* differs in its own angle of view from straightforward history, from the *Hellenika,* for example, just as the *Agesilaos* differs in its fashion. Most simply put, the Anabasis records a young man's journey away from home and the experiences he had while traveling. But Xenophon also sees something more to it, that the desire to be away from his city was the desire of a personality infatuated with heroic champions like Cyrus who did not always observe the duties of custom and law and that the very life of travel he embarked upon for the chance to display his own *aretē* became a snare and a delusion when he blindly tried to effect something permanent. In this ability to preserve a perfect tension between the concrete events of a journey and the suggestion of a larger dimension behind them, the *Anabasis* recalls its ultimate literary forebear, the *Odyssey* of Homer; and Xenophon's explicit allusions

to that poem perhaps best indicate his understanding of the nature of his own literary endeavor.

Xenophon figures so much in the *Anabasis,* therefore, because it is about him and his life; it is avowedly, not deceitfully or apologetically, one-sided. But this prominence is also revealing, for it contrasts so markedly with Xenophon's retiring presence in most of his other works. It is in itself a further indication of that young spirit which went forth to seek its own fame and its own glory, which sought its own honor and failed to heed the voice of teacher or to respect the god.

The final remark of the *Anabasis* reports the arrival of Thibron and Xenophon's release from command, as the remnant of the Ten Thousand march against Tissaphernes. What is on the mind of these men who before have thought only of Greece? What must that man have been thinking who imagined he would return to his fatherland stretched out like Odysseus? Doubtless the promises of pay and the new prospects for fortune and adventure make them forget. Fools that they are, they lose their day of homecoming.

Xenophon's own fate is similar. Desire as he may to leave the army, the gods will not permit it. When eventually he returns to Greece, it is to a life in exile from Athens on an estate at Skillous. The god he tried to evade at Delphi has been vindicated. Even in his dream the night he rouses the army, he sees that there may be no escape:

> but on the other hand, because the dream came from Zeus the Great King and because the fire seemed to blaze in a circle, he was afraid lest he be unable to get out of the King's territory, but should be closed in on all sides by obstacles.

How revealing it is, therefore, to find him so concerned at Skillous with the due observance of divine ritual and so aware of the danger of its neglect. Even more revealing, however, is the simplicity and quiet of his life there. Family, farming, the hunt, it all seems somehow far removed from the adventures of an earlier day. He seems to have come to a new understanding about the nature of *philotimia,* the love of glory and fame, to have reduced the scope of his past ambitions to a contentment with place and the stability of the definite which he could not find while addicted to travel.

How far removed, as well, this is from Isokrates' panhellenic propaganda, with which the *Anabasis* is frequently associated. It is even thought that Isokrates in his *Panegyrikos* quotes from Xenophon, although the alleged echo is only of a common word, not a passage, and the context and character of the remarks differ one from the other. There is no denying that the experience of the Ten Thousand soon became famous, and men of affairs both Greek and Persian often surmised what it boded for the future of barbarian and Hellenic conflict. By 380 it is hardly surprising that a rhetorical pundit could see in it a living witness to the superiority of a united Hellas over the effete East, a rallying cry to rouse his countrymen from internal strife to a foreign holy war. But Xenophon knew more about Persia than most of his contemporaries and was only too well aware that its power was not easily toppled. As he himself put it, an intelligent observer recognized that the King's empire was strong in the extent of its territory and the number of its people, and weak only if attack was swift. The *Anabasis* could not make more clear, either, how difficult leaving Persia could be and, more crucial still, how difficult and finally impossible it was to keep an army of Greeks united. It is not that Xenophon did not appreciate Persian weakness for what it was or that he did not harbor in his heart panhellenic hopes or desires. He may well have done so. But he seems to have known better than the vacuous nestorizings of Isokrates the difference between dream and reality.

For it is finally with this awareness that the *Anabasis* deals. Many have observed how misleading its title is; only the first book is a march up-country, the rest being a journey down to the sea. But perhaps the title itself indicates that literalism is a poor guide to the book's meaning and that misapprehension and deception are

its recurring concerns. The *Anabasis* is not merely about a geographic ascent or the trick played by Cyrus on the Greeks. Rather it concerns the deeper deception many men play on themselves as they pursue what they think most important in life and what they think most gives it meaning, namely, *philotimia,* kingdom, power, and glory. Nothing better intimates a late date for the composition of the *Anabasis* than Xenophon's mature perception of this delusion, especially as it applies to himself, or the detachment with which he can examine his own actions as though he were writing about someone else, a certain "Xenophon" whom Themistogenes of Syracuse describes and who did not fully heed Socrates. But this also holds true for the Xenophon who lived at Skillous; for the life he led there was still deficient: it was not the life of a citizen of Athens. That is to say, the *Anabasis* may not have been possible until its author saw the contented peace of the estate shattered by Elean incursions, which compelled him to wander again. Perhaps he realized only when back in Athens, an exile no more, that only there could he genuinely pursue that quest to which Socrates might have continually invited him had he not foolishly gone after Cyrus: . . .

> Not only for Cyrus' sake did Xenophon march up towards the Persians
> But in search of a road which led up to Zeus.

Steven W. Hirsch (essay date 1985)

SOURCE: "1001 Iranian Nights: History and Fiction in Xenophon's *Cyropaedia,*" in *The Greek Historians: Literature and History,* Anma Libri, 1985, pp. 65-85.

[*Arguing that Classical scholars have usually treated Persia as a negligible detail of setting in the* Cyropaedia, *Hirsch makes its presence central in the essay that follows in order to vindicate Xenophon's knowledge of Persian culture.*]

This paper, which concerns itself with one of the more curious pieces of literature which have come down to us from classical antiquity—the *Cyropaedia* of Xenophon—is written in that spirit of respect for the intelligence and integrity of the ancient authors which has always characterized the writing and teaching of Toni Raubitschek, to whom this volume is dedicated.

Xenophon, as is well known, was an Athenian of aristocratic family whose adult life spanned the first half of the fourth century B.C. Student of Socrates, participant in the unsuccessful revolt of the Persian prince Cyrus, mercenary commander, exile, friend of the Spartan king Agesilaus, gentleman farmer and litterateur, he experienced more of the world than is granted to most men.

Xenophon nevertheless is a much maligned figure who has been out of favor with students of Greek literature and history in recent times. Somewhere it has been said that he was "a better philosopher than Thucydides, a better historian than Plato," by which it was meant that he was thoroughly mediocre in all his endeavors. Certainly, no one would presume to claim that he was the equal of such intellectual giants as Thucydides and Plato. But Xenophon was a more interesting and creative personality than is usually allowed. Indeed, in certain respects he shows greater enlightenment than his more brilliant and famous contemporaries. For one thing, he had overcome typical Greek prejudices towards barbarians and had developed a balanced and respectful attitude towards Persia, that vast empire whose power and pretensions cast a shadow across the Greek consciousness throughout the classical era. In his political theorizing Xenophon is able to do what Plato and Aristotle cannot—to envision a stage of political development beyond the independent Greek *polis*. In this, as in other respects, he foreshadows the Hellenistic age ushered in by Alexander the Great a quarter century after his death. Finally, he wrote books on a wide range of topics, historical, philosophical and technical. Here he was an innovator who was not afraid to cross traditional genre lines, and who created, or participated in the early development of, several new literary genres—memoir in the *Anabasis,* philosophic dialogue in the *Memorabilia,* biography in the *Agesilaus.*

Perhaps the most difficult to categorize of all his works is the *Cyropaedia*. The title, Κύρου παιδεία, means "The Education of Cyrus," and is nominally the story of Cyrus the Great, the Iranian king who founded the Persian Empire in the mid-sixth century B.C. But the eight books of the *Cyropaedia* amount to far more than the education of Cyrus, unless education is taken in its widest sense as the experience and knowledge gathered during a lifetime. The work begins with the ancestry and birth of Cyrus, and gives ample coverage to his boyhood and education. Glossing over his years as a teenager and young adult, it concentrates on his conquests and the initial provisions which he made for administration of the new empire which he had won. It then skips over the rest of his reign until it reaches his last days and his deathbed political testament to friends and heirs.

In the preface Xenophon makes the following claim:

> Thus, as we meditated on this analogy, we were inclined to conclude that for man, as he is constituted, it is easier to rule over any and all other creatures than to rule over men. But when we reflected that there was one Cyrus, the Persian, who reduced to obedience a vast number of men and cities and nations, we were then compelled to change our opinion and decide that to rule men might be a task neither impossible nor even difficult, if one

should only go about it in an intelligent manner . . . . Believing this man to be deserving of all admiration, we have therefore investigated who he was in his origin, what natural endowments he possessed, and what sort of education he had enjoyed, that he so greatly excelled in governing men. Accordingly, what we have found out or think we know concerning him we shall now endeavor to present. (*Cyropaedia* 1.1.3; 1.1.6)

The reader is urged to keep in mind that, on Xenophon's own testimony, the *Cyropaedia* is an investigation of how Cyrus conquered and ruled his empire.

Despite Xenophon's explicit statement of purpose, there has never been a consensus on the question—"What is the *Cyropaedia?*" There are almost as many opinions as there are commentators on such fundamental issues as the genre of the work, its purpose and its inspiration. This is because it does not fit neatly into any established literary genre, ancient or modern.

What can be said, however, is that the majority of classical scholars have never been able to give any serious regard to the historical setting of the *Cyropaedia,* that is, the Old Persia of Cyrus the Great. To quote a recent study of Xenophon:

> Xenophon's choice of subject need not, therefore, be taken as an indication of some new cosmopolitanism, nor a reflection of his own travels abroad, especially since a Persian ingredient in the *Kyroupaideia* is little more than a flavoring. [W.E. Higgins, *Xenophon the Athenian,* 1977]

For most classicists, the Persian context of the *Cyropaedia* is mere exotic decoration and of no real significance. They prefer to see it as a thoroughly Greek work which has been transferred to a fairy-tale "Persian" setting. Moreover, they imply that Xenophon simply invented most of the alleged "events" in the career of his Cyrus. It follows that, for them, the work is worth little as a source of information on Persian history, culture or institutions, nor can one gain from it any insights into the attitude of fourth century Greeks towards Persia. On the other hand, many Orientalists who are concerned with the civilization of ancient Iran have taken a very different view. For them the *Cyropaedia* has long been a major source of information concerning the history and institutions of the Persian Empire.

In light of these two fundamentally antithetical approaches to the work, it is a matter of obvious importance to determine the nature of the *Cyropaedia.* Is it history, is it fiction, or is it something in between? The answer to this question will dictate the extent to which, and the way in which, the historian is entitled to make use of the *Cyropaedia.* And insofar as the *Cyropaedia* was widely read in antiquity and had considerable impact on the evolution of a number of literary genres, it should be a matter of interest, not just to the historian of ancient Persia, but also to the intellectual historian who is concerned with the development of Greek thought.

To understand the nature of the *Cyropaedia* and the purposes of the author, it is essential to grasp the role of Persia in the work. Herein lies the key to the *Cyropaedia*. The traditional view of classicists, as has been said, is to minimize the significance of the Persian historical and cultural context. But there are a number of reasons for questioning this traditional view. In the first place, it begs the question to assert that Xenophon's choice of a Persian setting is of no particular importance. This issue deserves to be examined with an open mind. One must ask why Xenophon has chosen a Persian king and allegedly Persian models of education, ethics, leadership and administration to express his ideals. The question takes on added interest if the Greeks of the fourth century were really as contemptuous of Persian "barbarians" as is commonly maintained, for these same Greeks were the audience for whom Xenophon wrote.

In the second place, those who insist that the authentically Persian features in the *Cyropaedia* are few and inconsequential are simply mistaken. Indeed, the *Cyropaedia* contains numerous facts about the Persian Empire, its history, culture, institutions and peoples. Some can be confirmed elsewhere in Greek and Oriental sources, while others are at least quite plausible. Xenophon claims that many of the customs and institutions of the elder Cyrus' day are still in force in Persia in his own time. He also claims to have done research and to have had access to Oriental songs and legends. Moreover, Orientalists have detected stories and motifs in the *Cyropaedia* which recur in different contexts in the *Shahnama* and other Persian literature based on early oral tradition. Consequently, the investigator of the *Cyropaedia* must ask himself why Xenophon has gone to the trouble of discovering and reporting this wealth of data about Persia.

In the third place, it must be realized that the *Cyropaedia* is about the acquisition and administration, not of a *polis,* but of an empire. Some commentators explain that Xenophon was deeply disturbed by the instability of city-state governments and the incessant warfare within and between the Greek communities during his lifetime, and that this prompted him to a discourse on government in the *Cyropaedia.* Thus, the *Cyropaedia* is supposed to be seen as prescribing some sort of solution to the problems of the Greek *polis.* Once again, those who espouse this view seem to be proceeding from a set of *a priori* assumptions about what the attitude and interests of Xenophon, as a patriotic fourth century Greek, ought to have been.

Indeed, many of Xenophon's contemporaries were concerned with the problems of the Greek city-state. Plato in the *Republic* and the *Laws* and Aristotle in the *Politics* gave much deep thought to the nature of the *polis,* and each offered his vision of the ideal community. In both cases the emphasis is on the structure of the state. However, the comparison with Plato and Aristotle only serves to point up the differences in Xenophon's approach. Not only is Xenophon talking about a much larger and more complex political entity, that is, an empire extending over vast distances and comprising many different peoples, with all the problems of administration that this must entail, but he also focuses not so much on political structures as on the character of the individual ruler. Could he really have been prompted to this meditation by a desire to solve the problems of (for the sake of example) the contemporary Athenian democracy?

In fact, things had not been going entirely well for the Persian Empire either in the fourth century, what with the secession of Egypt, the attempted coup d'état of Cyrus the younger, and revolts of Cypriots, Phoenicians and disaffected Persian satraps. One should not dismiss out of hand the possibility that Xenophon has been prompted to these reflections by the problems of contemporary Persia. At any rate, one must ask—"Why has Xenophon concerned himself with the problems facing an *individual* who seeks to rule, not a city-state, but an *empire*?"

The foregoing consideration raise doubts about the prevailing assumption that the Persian context and the authentically Persian elements of the *Cyropaedia* are superficial and of little real moment. Xenophon obviously had a keen interest in, and ample knowledge about, Persia. It is my contention that the *Cyropaedia* is much more "Persian" in inspiration than is usually conceded. In order to establish this contention, it will be necessary to consider, first, the character of the *Cyropaedia,* by which I mean its genre, the sources to which Xenophon had access and the way in which he used them. Then we will take up the problem of the Persian setting, and I will suggest a number of reasons why Xenophon may have chosen to set his account in the Old Persia of Cyrus the Great. Finally, we will briefly take up the question of how reliable the *Cyropaedia* is as a source of information on the history, culture, and institutions of ancient Persia. Only from the vantage point provided by such a survey can one fairly evaluate the true position of the *Cyropaedia* on that elusive boundary between history and fiction.

There is, has been said, little agreement among commentators about the genre of the *Cyropaedia*. Perhaps there is no single, simple answer, since here, as elsewhere, Xenophon was apparently willing to cross traditional genre lines. Nevertheless, certain things can be said. The starting point must be Xenophon's own prefatory statement that he is concerned with the question of how one may govern that most problematic of creatures—Man—and that Cyrus' success in this enterprise makes him a fruitful subject for investigation. On Xenophon's own testimony, the *Cyropaedia* is to be an investigation of how Cyrus conquered and ruled his empire. In accordance with this design, Xenophon focuses on certain episodes in Cyrus' life—youth, conquests, initial consolidation of power and last moments—and virtually ignores the rest of a long life. Events from the past have been selected, and segments of Cyrus' life emphasized, largely because they illuminate the matter of what kind of ruler Cyrus had been. This selection allows Xenophon to expatiate upon the early signs of Cyrus' outstanding nature, the program of education which molded his character, the manner in which he carried out his conquests, his initial provisions for administration of the new empire, and his death-bed political testament. Thus, while it may contain much historical and biographical material, the *Cyropaedia* is neither history nor biography. A comprehensive and continuous treatment of the full career of Cyrus, such as would be expected in either a history of Old Persia or a biography of Cyrus, is not attempted and was surely never contemplated.

In light of Xenophon's statement of purpose and the contents of the work, it can, perhaps, be characterized as a didactic work on the subjects of education, values, military science, and political administration, drawing upon the example of Cyrus for its paradigmatic value and in order to provide a cohesive and entertaining framework for the instructional material. Such a formulation is safe enough and would probably win general approbation, but it does not tackle the fundamental issue of historicity. As was seen earlier, many classical scholars regard the framework of plot and setting as largely, or entirely, fictional, and believe that Xenophon invented most of the story line and drew his intellectual inspiration from Greek societies such as Sparta. To assert this is to ignore Xenophon's twin claims that he means to examine the career of the historical Cyrus for the illumination which it may provide on the problem of good government and that he is going to relate what he had discovered as a result of his researches.

At this juncture, we need to consider the sources of information on Old Persia which were available to Xenophon. They fall into three major categories. First, Greek books. Although he does not cite Herodotus by name anywhere, it is highly probable that he was familiar with Herodotus' *Histories*. There are strong similarities between Xenophon's and Herodotus' accounts of Cyrus' capture of Sardis and Babylon. Furthermore, Xenophon's story of the interview between Cyrus and Croesus, the captured king of Lydia, virtually proves his familiarity with the Herodotean version, for his

alteration of the Herodotean account of these events amounts to an implicit criticism of Herodotus' treatment of the role of Delphi (*Cyropaedia* 7.2.9-28). That he had read Ctesias' *Persica* is proven by his citation of it in the *Anabasis* (1.8.26). It is reasonable to assume that he made some use of Ctesias for the *Cyropaedia*. As will be seen later, there are strong similarities between his and Ctesias' accounts of the death of Cyrus. Xenophon probably also made use of other Greek historical works which have not survived, or whose remains are too fragmentary to permit a firm connection to be established.

Barbarian oral tradition constitutes a second category of source material. Xenophon occasionally cites the stories and songs about Cyrus to be found among the barbarians. Clearly Cyrus had become a figure of legend among the peoples of the Near East. Herodotus claimed to be aware of four different versions of the birth of Cyrus and many tales of his death, and this process of mythifying will have gone that much further by Xenophon's time. Xenophon presumably picked up such stories in the course of his travels in the Persian Empire, first as a member of the entourage of the younger Cyrus and later as a commander of Greek mercenaries.

Xenophon's experiences in the Persian Empire are also integral to the third category of evidence. Obviously he could draw upon what he had seen and learned first-hand in the course of his travels. There is ample evidence that Xenophon tended to read back into the past certain Persian practices of his own day. He frequently marks this by employing some variant of the phrase ἔτι καὶ νῦν—"and still today . . ."

Thus Xenophon claims to have done research and he had access to a variety of sources. We may have our doubts about the historicity of Herodotus' and Ctesias' accounts of the career of Cyrus and about the veracity of the oral traditions circulating among the barbarians. And, in some cases, Xenophon may be mistaken in assuming that a contemporary Persian institution or custom was in existence already in Cyrus' day. But what is most important, for present purposes, is that Xenophon drew upon sources of information which he considered, and had every reason to consider, to be of some value.

It is fair to assume that Xenophon, like Herodotus before him, often had a number of versions of a story from which to choose, especially in the case of a now-legendary figure such as Cyrus. Sometimes he takes over a version which we know to be derived from Herodotus or Ctesias. In theses cases there is no problem. At other times he gives a different account which is not attested elsewhere. Critics tend to point to these cases as examples of how Xenophon is prone to fabricate stories at will. However, later in this paper we will examine several instances in which the chance survival of outside evidence guarantees that the authority of Xenophon is to be preferred to that of Herodotus. It is, therefore, methodologically unsound simply to presume that Xenophon has invented any story for which independent confirmation has not chanced to survive into modern times.

Why does Xenophon choose the particular version which he reports in a given case? This brings us back to the problem of genre and purpose. If the *Cyropaedia* is a didactic work, them his principle of selection is most likely the suitability of a given version to his didactic purposes. With numerous traditions about Cyrus in circulation, Xenophon was in a position to choose the ones which best enabled him to illustrate those qualities of character and intellect which he felt were most important in a leader and ruler. There is no indication that he has submitted the material which he gathered to the kind of rigorous critical scrutiny which a Thucydides would have demanded. After all, a precise reconstruction of the past is not Xenophon's avowed goal. However, there is a meaningful difference between spontaneous invention of stories, of which Xenophon is so frequently accused, and the selective use of authentic traditions about the past.

To this point I have been arguing that we should take Xenophon at his word when he claims to have drawn upon authentic traditions about Cyrus and Old Persia in order to explore the problem of government. But how are we to account for the fact that Xenophon has chosen a Persian setting for the framework of his didactic treatise? It is a choice that is, in many ways, surprising, especially if one accepts the standard pronouncements about the hostility towards Persia of Xenophon and his Greek contemporaries. Some scholars dodge the apparent paradox by claiming that the Persian setting is a matter of little real significance— a literary fancy and nothing more—and need not be taken seriously. They confidently explain that the distance in space and time of Cyrus' Old Persia removed it from the realm of the "historical." It served as a convenient stage on which Xenophon could produce his own didactic fairy tale, while disregarding the inconvenient realities of history. Others assure us that Xenophon is merely following a well-established Greek tradition about Cyrus which can be seen in Aeschylus, Herodotus, Plato and Antisthenes. These commentators may be right about the advantages offered by a chronologically and spatially distant setting and about the prior existence of a favorable Greek tradition about Cyrus. But they are wrong to imply that these considerations make Xenophon's choice less meaningful. He could have chosen, as he did in the *Hiero,* a setting from the Greek past, or, as Plato did in the *Republic,* a hypothetical situation. But he did not. He chose a Persian setting. I believe that, at the very least, Xenophon should be credited with the

capacity for making a deliberate and meaningful choice.

Several factors may help to account for Xenophon's choice of a Persian setting. In the first place, the situation begins to simplify itself if only one accepts Xenophon's own claims about the work. He said that he was exercised by the question—"How may one rule Mankind successfully?" If, in search of an answer to this question, he looked to Cyrus the Great and Old Persia, this ought not to occasion much surprise. Indeed, for an open-minded Greek of the fourth century it really should have been the obvious place to look. The greatness and capacity of Cyrus and the Persians as builders and rulers of a vast empire spoke for itself. Cyrus and his immediate successors had rapidly conquered an empire of unprecedented type and dimensions, encompassing a multitude of different peoples and extending (in modern geographical terms) from Turkey to India, from Russia to the Sudan. For almost two hundred years the Persian Empire had dominated most of the world as the Greeks knew it. For one who was in search of a solution to the problem of administering an empire, the authentic historical experience of Persia would clearly be of the utmost instructional value.

Any reasonable Greek might have reached this conclusion, but Xenophon had an advantage over most other reasonable Greeks—his own familiarity with the Persian Empire and its ruling people. To my mind, a large part of the inspiration for Xenophon's choice of a Persian setting is to be found in his contacts with the Persian prince Cyrus and other Persians in Cyrus' retinue during the march up-country to Babylonian Cunaxa in the year 401 B.C. These events, which he so eloquently described in the *Anabasis,* undoubtedly made a deep impression on the young Xenophon, and there are more than a few indications that he was captivated by the dashing young Persian prince with the famous name.

Many commentators have remarked upon the similarities between the younger Cyrus of the *Anabasis* and the elder Cyrus of the *Cyropaedia.* Xenophon himself makes the connection in the encomium which he inserts after his account of the heroic death in battle of the prince at Cunaxa (*Anabasis* 1.9). The encomium opens with a suggestive evaluation of Cyrus:

> He was a man who, of all the Persians who have lived since that ancient Cyrus, was both the most kingly and the most worthy to rule.

I wish to argue that the comparison was suggested to Xenophon by the younger Cyrus himself. When Cyrus set out to organize a rebellion against his brother, the Persian king Artaxerxes II, he must have known that he would need some sort of a propaganda theme which he could employ both to attract support for his cause and to justify his usurpation of the throne. It appears that he took advantage of his famous name and summoned up memories of a former period of greatness, the Old Persia of Cyrus the Great. Plutarch preserves a remark of the younger Cyrus to the effect that Artaxerxes, because of his faintheartedness and softness, could neither keep his horse on the hunt nor his throne in a crisis. Cyrus may have argued that Artaxerxes was not worthy of the Persian throne. The famous Cyrus of the past had won an empire on account of his excellence, and the new Cyrus, who, as Xenophon says, was most like his namesake in kingliness and worthiness to rule, deserved to sit on the throne of empire and promised to revive the customs and qualities that had made Persia great.

Admittedly, this reconstruction of Cyrus' propaganda campaign is conjectural, but it can be confirmed by the counter-propaganda which issued from Artaxerxes' camp. If the rebel prince Cyrus was invoking the legendary Cyrus, it was to Artaxerxes' advantage to belittle this claim. One can detect this process at work in the *Persica* of Ctesias, a Greek who served as physician to Artaxerxes' family and lived at the Persian court at the time of the younger Cyrus' rebellion. Whereas Herodotus and Xenophon agree that the elder Cyrus was the son of Cambyses, Ctesias makes him a commoner, son of a low-born cut-throat named Atradates and his goatherd wife Argoste, who began his career as a servant at the Median court. This is tantamount to a denial that Cyrus was an Achaemenid, a member of the legitimate line of Persian kings.

Cyrus was also removed from the official genealogy of the royal family. A pair of Old Persian inscriptions on gold tablets which were found at Ecbatana carry the names of Ariaramnes and Arsames, addressing each as "the great King, King of Kings, King in Persia." Ariaramnes and Arsames were the great-grandfather and grandfather of Darius I, a member of a junior branch of the Achaemenid clan, who wrested power from the line of Cyrus in the 520s. These two shadowy figures had not been kings of Persia, and the terminology used in these inscriptions—"King of Kings"—is wrong for the period of vassalage to Media. Orientalists feel that the orthography of these inscriptions is appropriate to the time of Artaxerxes II, and Kent has suggested that they may have been part of an anti-Cyrus propaganda campaign related to the revolt of Cyrus the younger. By erecting these inscriptions, Artaxerxes is claiming that the legitimate royal line is that of Darius. Cyrus the founder is being ousted from the royal line, and in this way Artaxerxes hopes to counter his brother's pretensions to revive the Old Persia of Cyrus the Great.

Xenophon will have been exposed to the propaganda of the younger Cyrus while he was traveling with the prince, for this propaganda was directed primarily at the Persians in Cyrus' camp. It thus appears that the comparison of the two Cyruses was an idea which Xenophon derived from his Persian patron. But he took over more than this. The package of propaganda being disseminated by the rebel prince presumably incorporated a picture of Cyrus the founder which the new Cyrus undertook to emulate and a concept of Old Persia which he promised to restore. I would therefore go so far as to say that Xenophon received a very particular vision of Cyrus the Great and Old Persia from the younger Cyrus himself.

So powerful was the impression which this made on Xenophon that he could not easily disassociate the younger Cyrus from the ancestor whom he claimed to imitate and, in a sense, reincarnate. There are a fair number of passages in the *Cyropaedia* in which Xenophon remarks upon a trait or habit of the elder Cyrus in terms similar or identical to those used for the younger Cyrus in the *Anabasis*. They undergo comparable educations, show a remarkable aptitude and enthusiasm for its basic features—riding, shooting, hunting—and excel over all other boys in their age-group. Each is susceptible, as a youth, to reckless daring. Each has the habit of exercising before meals, each sends food to friends as a gesture of affection, and each proclaims his desire to outdo friends and enemies at doing good and harm respectively. Finally, there are multiple correspondences, sometimes in virtually identical phraseology, between Xenophon's description of the younger Cyrus' conduct as satrap in Asia Minor and his account of the elder Cyrus' efforts to guarantee the security of his person by winning popularity among friends, potential rivals and subjects. It is hard to resist the conclusion that, insofar as Xenophon paints a portrait of the character, conduct and personal relations of the elder Cyrus, it is based largely on the personality of his one-time patron, Cyrus the prince.

If, as has been maintained here, Xenophon modeled the figure of Cyrus the Great on the personality of the younger Cyrus, and he derived a vision of Old Persia in the time of the founder from the hopes, dreams and self-serving claims of the younger Cyrus, this does not constitute grounds for accusing Xenophon of lack of concern for historical accuracy or willful distortion of truth. The personality of Cyrus, dead now for one hundred and fifty years and encrusted with layer upon layer of legend, was irrecoverable. Where was Xenophon to turn for an accurate picture of conditions in sixth century Iran? Thucydides had complained of the insurmountable difficulties facing one who tried to reconstruct the history of the remote past and he was not even thinking about the additional barriers which had to be faced in dealing with an alien culture. Xenophon worked with what he had. The fullest and most vivid picture of Cyrus and Old Persia available to him came from the camp of the younger Cyrus. To the extent that the *Cyropaedia* violates history, this is at least partially due, not to bald invention on Xenophon's part, but to the fact that he had to rely on his sources, written and oral, with the younger Cyrus prominent among the latter.

How historically reliable is the *Cyropaedia*? The *communis opinio,* as has been seen, holds that Xenophon indulged in free invention of allegedly historical events. Critics are especially quick to pounce whenever Xenophon contradicts the "historical" tradition found in Herodotus. Yet there are occasions when it can be confirmed from Oriental evidence that Xenophon is correct where Herodotus is wrong or lacks information. A case in point involves the ancestry of Cyrus. Herodotus had accepted the folklore motif of Cyrus' exposure as a baby and made his father Cambyses "well born and of a quiet temper . . . much lower than a Mede of middle estate." Xenophon, on the other hand, correctly reports that Cyrus was the son of Cambyses, King of Persia, a principality within the Median Empire (*Cyropaedia* 1.2.1). This is confirmed by the so-called Cyrus Cylinder, a propaganda tract in Akkadian cuneiform composed after the capture of Babylon, presumably at the behest of Cyrus, which gives his lineage as:

> . . . son of Cambyses, great king, king of Anshan
> . . . of a family which always (exercised) kingship
> . . .

As Xenophon's Cyrus is poised to attack Assyria (by which name Xenophon refers to the neo-Babylonian kingdom), he gains the allegiance of the Assyrian vassal Gobryas, who later plays an important part in the capture of Babylon (*Cyropaedia* 4.6.1; 7.5.24-30). This time confirmation comes from the Nabonidus Chronicle, a contemporary cuneiform document which describes, among other events of the reigns of Nabonidus and Cyrus, the fall of Babylon. One Ugbaru, the Babylonian governor of Gutium, accompanied Cyrus when he took Babylon and helped with the initial administrative reorganization. Nothing of this individual and his role is known to Herodotus.

Such examples provide a salutary warning that it is rash to see Xenophon as invariably mistaken or guilty of a fabrication whenever he disagrees with Herodotus or reports an incident or detail which has not chanced to be confirmed elsewhere. Let me emphasize this point with a final substantial example.

Xenophon's account of the death of Cyrus is regularly cited as a blatant example of the liberties which Xenophon takes with the established "history" of Cyrus. It is assumed that he simply invented his version because it suited his literary and didactic purposes, that is, the glorification and idealization of Cyrus, although he knew the truth full well from reading Herodotus.

In Herodotus' pages Cyrus dies a sudden and violent death in battle against the Massagetae. His body is captured, and the bloodthirsty nomad queen sticks his head in a sack of blood and taunts him. All too often it is forgotten that Herodotus goes on to say:

> Many stories are related of Cyrus' death; this, that
> I have told, is the worthiest of credence.

A very different account is found in the waning pages of the *Cyropaedia* (8.7). Cyrus, now far advanced in years, has returned to the Persian homeland. A dream informs him that he is soon to die, and shortly thereafter he becomes weak and bedridden. Summoning his sons, his friends and the Persian officials, he proclaims his last will and testament. Cambyses, the elder son, is to be king, while Tanaoxares is to receive the satrapies of Media, Armenia and Cadusia. Both are urged to love each other and to treat all men fairly. Cyrus also gives instructions for his burial.

Much of the content of Cyrus' deathbed oration is invented by Xenophon. Cyrus' declaration that he has always avoided *hubris,* knowing that misfortune could strike at any time and that no man can be accounted truly blessed until he is dead, is a thoroughly Greek sentiment which immediately calls to mind the lecture of Solon to Croesus in Herodotus' pages. Cyrus' discourse on the immortality of the soul is reminiscent of the speeches of Socrates as he prepares to die in Plato's *Apology* and *Phaedo.*

However, the historical framework of the scene is manifestly not the invention of Xenophon. For there is a strikingly similar account of the last moments of Cyrus in the earlier *Persica* of Ctesias. Here Cyrus is wounded in battle against the Derbici, an obscure central Asian people. He is carried back to his camp, where he lingers for several days. Before dying he must have summoned his friends and family, for he appoints Cambyses to succeed him as king, while making the younger son, Tanyoxarkes, master of Bactria, Choramnia, Parthia and Carmania. He urges his friends and family to show love for one another, praying for blessings on those who abide in mutual good fellowship and cursing those who initiate evil.

One can readily discern that Xenophon has drawn upon either Ctesias or the tradition from which Ctesias derived. Both have a deathbed scene in which the moribund monarch summons his family and associates in order to deliver his last will and testament. In both versions the younger son is called Tanaoxares/Tanyoxarkes, whereas he is known in our other sources by some variant of Persian Bardiya, and he is given a command comprising several regions in central Asia. In both versions Cyrus urges concord upon those who survive him, and he dies in the presence of family and friends. If the full text of Ctesias' account of this event had survived, rather than Photius' brief epitome, it might be possible to point to even more correspondences.

Any consideration of which version is to be preferred must take into account an additional factor—the tomb of Cyrus. In Xenophon's dramatic deathbed scene, Cyrus discusses arrangements for his own burial. It is known that Cyrus was buried in a stately tomb at Pasargadae. This tomb was visited and restored by Alexander the Great, and is described by the historians of that era. From their reports one can be certain that it was no cenotaph, but rather housed the body of Cyrus. This fact can easily be accounted for by the versions of the death of Cyrus given by Xenophon and Ctesias, for Xenophon has him expire in Persia and Ctesias maintains that Cambyses had the body of Cyrus returned from the land of the Derbici to Persia, where it was buried. But it is hard to reconcile the tomb of Cyrus at Pasargadae with Herodotus' account, in which Cyrus' body is captured and dismembered by the vengeful Massagetae.

Finally, as [Arthur E.] Christensen has shown [in *Les gestes des rois dans les traditions de l'Iran antique,* 1936], Xenophon's overall conception of the death of Cyrus is firmly rooted in Iranian tradition. In the *Shahnama* of Ferdowsi, which preserves the cultural concepts and story patterns of ancient Iranian oral tradition, the life of the ideal king ends with a scene in which the dying king summons family, friends and advisers, arranges the succession, makes known his last wishes, and communicates to his successors a political testament. The conclusion of the *Cyropaedia* fits precisely into this mold.

It must be emphasized that no attempt is being made here to argue for the historicity of the *Cyropaedia* as a whole. Numerous episodes, conversations, speeches and private encounters must have been invented by Xenophon, for there could have been no possible source for such material. And it is precisely in these scenes, the didactic and philosophical core of the *Cyropaedia,* that the patently Greek elements of thought, speech and values are strongest. However, it should now be acknowledged that this core is set into a historical and cultural framework, and that, for the construction of this framework, Xenophon had access to credible sources—Greek written sources, Greek and barbarian oral tradition, and the example of Persian customs and institutions of his own day. As a result, the *Cyropaedia* contains a greater quantity of valuable information about Persian history, culture and institutions than is generally recognized, and even where one is inclined to doubt the historicity of a given event, it should be conceded that Xenophon may have preserved an authentic Greek or barbarian tradition—however false or distorted—about Persian history. The student of ancient Iran would be foolish to neglect the *Cyropaedia* or reject it out of hand.

I have argued above that Xenophon received a particularly vivid picture of Cyrus the Great and Old Persia from the entourage of the younger Cyrus. Obviously this vision of the Persian past is not likely to be correct in all essentials. After all, not only was it part of a campaign of political propaganda meant to justify Cyrus' ambition, but there is no reason to believe that there existed, in ancient Iran, a critical historical tradition which would have made possible an accurate recreation of the events, personalities and conditions of the sixth century. But the traditions embodied in the *Cyropaedia* may, in some degree, represent a different sort of truth. It may reflect the Persians' own conceptions about their past, and would thereby provide us with precious insights into the traditions and values of the aristocracy in fourth century Persia. As such, it would be analogous to the early books of Livy, which, if they preserve little that is historically accurate about Rome in the era of the Kings and the earliest days of the Republic, do constitute a priceless treasury of conceptions about the past held by Romans in the late Republic and early Empire.

One last consideration is in order. How did Xenophon conceive of his achievement in writing the *Cyropaedia*? We in the modern world tend to treat the boundary between truth and fiction as absolute, as clearly separating two different and irreconcilable orders of things. But it is, I suppose, now widely recognized that this boundary was a shifting and permeable one for the people of classical antiquity. Of course, any formulation of Xenophon's own conception of his mission must inevitably remain tentative, but I suspect that his situation might profitably be compared to that of a pair of modern writers who are usually classified as authors of "historical fiction." Robert Graves and Gore Vidal have both written stories set in the ancient world, and both have, on occasion, issued revealing protests against the classification of their works as "fiction." Each insists in his own way that, though he is not a professional historian, his work is based on historical research and represents a reconstruction of the past. If it be permitted to recast their claims in Aristotle's terms, the implication is that their works are valuable, not only for the general truths about human affairs which fiction seeks to convey, but also for the particular truths which derive from knowledge of the actual events and conditions of the past.

Xenophon probably lacked the self-awareness of these modern writers, and the relevant categories of history and novel were only in process of formation in his time. But I wonder whether he would not have been himself in a similar light, and have claimed that the *Cyropaedia* offered both particular truths to be garnered from the record of the past and the higher truths which he superimposed by artistic license.

V. J. Gray (essay date 1989)

SOURCE: "Xenophon's *Defence of Socrates*: The Rhetorical Background to the Socratic Problem," in *Classical Quarterly,* Vol. XXXIX, no. 1, 1989, pp. 136-40.

[*In the following essay, Gray asserts that the form and even the ideas of Xenophon's* Defence of Socrates *were shaped by rhetorical requirements, specifically the "rule of propriety"—that a speaker's words in a dialogue must be appropriate to his character.*]

The death of Socrates gave birth to an industry of biographical literature which often took the form of a defence (*apologia*) or prosecution (*katēgoria*), sometimes purporting to be the actual defence or prosecution conducted at his trial. Plato and Xenophon wrote works in his defence. Among his critics, one Polycrates had a certain notoriety. Lysias, Theodectes and Demetrius of Phalerum, orators and rhetoricians like Polycrates, were credited with further works of apology. There were doubtless many others. The aim of this paper is to show that Xenophon wrote his *Defence* in the light of the rhetorical theory that required that a speaker utter words and thoughts appropriate . . . to his character.

The *Defence* deals with a specific aspect of the character Socrates revealed at his trial: his high-mindedness (*megalēgoria*). It begins,

> It is also worthwhile to recall the way in which Socrates deliberated on his defence and the end of his life when he was called to trial. Others have also offered written reports about this, and all have captured his high-mindedness (*megalēgorian*). So it is clear that Socrates really did speak in this way. But they have not made this feature clear: that he had already decided that death was for him preferable to life. So that his high-mindedness appears to be something rather ill considered (*aphronestera*).

Xenophon attributes the explanation of his high-mindedness to the information given him by Hermogenes, another associate of Socrates. This is where he brings in 'propriety' or 'appropriateness'.

> Hermogenes the son of Hipponicus was a friend of Socrates and gave such reports of him as make his high mindedness appear appropriate to his intellect. . . .

Thus the controversy turns on the issue of propriety. Hermogenes made his high-mindedness appropriate, previous written accounts had not.

Xenophon saw *megalēgoria* (lit. 'big talk') as a fault of character associated with self praise, the antithesis of the good grace he so admired in Agesilaus of Sparta. Yet even he recognised that on certain occasions it could be appropriate. This must be such an occasion, for Socrates talks very big in the *Defence*. He refuses to admit the charges against him. On the charge of impiety, he counter claims that he is favoured by a god, an unrestrained piece of self praise that alienates the jury: those who did not disbelieve him felt jealous of his favour (10-13). He informs them that the god said that none was more just, prudent or free than Socrates, and he drives the point home with proofs (14-18). On the charge of corruption, he counter claims that he is in fact a very excellent teacher deserving of honour (19-21). After the verdict, he grandly compares himself to Palamedes, another victim of injustice, but of heroic status (26). Xenophon frankly admits that this 'big talk' contributed to his condemnation (32). It is understandable that some thought Socrates was mad to have run the risk of alienating a jury that held his life in its hands. Xenophon's concern is equally understandable. No Socratic could tolerate a view of the master that denied him plain common sense.

By the end of the fourth century B.C. the Greeks had developed a considerable body of psychological theory in association with the theory of rhetoric, and the virtue of 'propriety' was central to it. Aristotle considered rhetoric a branch of knowledge requiring a high degree of what we would call psychological insight. It involved three kinds of 'proofs' designed to persuade, the first depending on the character projected by the speaker, the second on the emotions aroused in the audience, the third on the actual arguments of the speech (*Rhet.* 1.2.3). The key to the first and second proofs was propriety. To be persuasive, the language and sentiments of the speaker had to be appropriate to the character he wished to project, the emotion he sought to arouse, and the general circumstances of the speech. Aristotle says of style in particular:

> Propriety of style . . . will be obtained by the expression of emotion and character and by proportion to the subject matter. Style is proportionate to the subject matter when weighty

matters are not treated off-hand, nor trifling matters with dignity.

Historians too, who had long observed propriety in their speeches, had acknowledged the theory by the end of the fourth century.

But propriety was already an issue in Xenophon's time. His contemporary, Isocrates, probably writing in the 380s, says,

> Speeches cannot be successful unless they fit the occasion and are written with propriety . . . , it requires a great deal of application not to miss the occasion, but to adorn the whole speech with appropriate thoughts.

So that when Xenophon sets out to improve on previous accounts by making Socrates' high-mindedness appear *appropriate,* he seems to be applying rhetorical theory to the Socratic controversy. When he applies the rhetorical concept of propriety to the particular problem of Socrates' *megalēgoria,* which previous writers had failed to explain, he is emphasisting his particular contribution in this area. There is a clear criticism of Plato's *Apology* here, if it is the earlier work, as commonly supposed.

Dionysius of Halicarnassus confirms that trials like those of Socrates had at any rate by his day become subjects for discussion in these rhetorical terms. In what seems to be an echo of the kind of debate of which Xenophon's **Defence** formed a part, he criticises Thucydides for crediting Pericles with inappropriate high-mindedness in his speech to the demoralised Athenians after the first invasion of Attica and the onset of plague, when they threatened to depose him. Socrates had been on trial for his life. According to Dionysius, Pericles was also virtually on trial for his life. Socrates' speech was literally an *apologia.* Pericles' speech is called an *apologia.* The criticism seems to be a *topos.*

Thucydides had Pericles reproach the Athenians for their lack of resolution instead of making concessions to their anger. Dionysius says these could have been *appropriate* words for the historian to utter in his own person, but in the mouth of a man on trial for his life, they were utterly *inappropriate.* His reproaches inflamed the Athenians instead of appeasing them (44). He also praised himself in the highest terms as a policy maker, a patriot, and a man above corruption (45). All this recalls the *megalēgoria* of Socrates. Indeed, Dionysius uses almost the same words of Pericles as Xenophon does of Socrates when he describes the impropriety of his high-mindedness . . .

> It was not this attitude of reproach, but the attitude of request that was the attitude most appropriate to his intellect.

Xenophon's πρεπουσαν . . . τῆ διανοία seems to refer to Socrates' 'intellect', and Dionysius takes the same point of reference for his own imputation of impropriety. Though he uses *dianoia* to mean mere 'thought' elsewhere in the section, he makes its connexion with 'intellect' clear later when he says,

> It would be remarkable if Pericles, the greatest orator of his day, had not known *what any even moderately intelligent man would have known,* that while in all orations speakers who praise their own virtues without restraint invariably exasperate their audiences, this is especially so when they are on trial in the lawcourts or in the assembly, where they face the prospect not of loss of prestige, but of actual punishment.

Dionysius and Xenophon part company on only one point. Dionysius finds it impossible to believe that Pericles really spoke so inappropriately. His opinion is that Thucydides had created the impropriety, by composing a speech without consideration for the basic rule:

> The invention of the most cogent arguments is not to be admired for its own sake, unless they be appropriate to the events, the characters, the situation and all other factors . . . as a defendant, Pericles should have been made to speak humbly and in such a manner as to turn away the jury's anger. This would have been the proper procedure for a historian who sought to imitate real life.

Xenophon could not accept this solution, because it was agreed by all that Socrates did display the quality of high-mindedness. He was therefore forced to search for other explanations of the apparent implausibility of a man on trial for his life who had failed to appeal to his judges. He found the answer in Hemogenes' reports. Socrates did not conform to the accepted psychology of a man on trial for his life. He preferred to die by *megalēgoria* than live by appeasement. His reasoning is spelled out (3-9). He had lived a life of perfection so far, an object of admiration to himself and his friends. The future held only the prospect of old age, decay of the senses and the intellect, loss of admiration, lack of repute. If he died easily by hemlock, his reputation would be untarnished in his own eyes and those of his friends, and they would miss him. He decided therefore to use the trial to advertise his perfection and secure that reputation forever. Anytus would endure an evil reputation in life and death for what he did, but Socrates would live on as the Socrates of the trial, glorious in memory (31-2). His reputation was assured (7, 26, 29, 34).

The existence of the Socratic literature validates his reasoning and vindicates the propriety of his *megalēgoria.* He did live on in the 'Memories' of friends like Xenophon, at the peak of his powers, his death preserving and adding lustre to his memory, untarnished as he intended.

> In contemplating the man's wisdom and nobility, I cannot fail to remember him, nor to praise his memory. If a man who seeks virtue had met anyone more helpful than Socrates, I judge him covered with the greatest blessing.

The tribute that ends the *Defence* is the ultimate answer to the charge of impropriety, clear proof that his *megal goria* was well considered.

The *Defence* offers, as further proof of his attitude to death, his lightness of heart even after the verdict. Xenophon appears to use this section to suggest that Socrates had indeed adopted the unpleasant trait of *megalēgoria* only as a deliberate expedient for the trial, and that it was not his natural way with his friends. His reply to those who advised escape was to ask jokingly where he could find a place inaccessible to death (23). He told those who wept that they should have begun weeping long ago, since nature had condemned him to death from the moment of his very birth (27). When Apollodorus lamented the injustice of the sentence, Socrates stroked his head, and inquired whether Apollodorus would prefer him to deserve his death, and he smiled as he said it (28). He went to his death cheerful in his looks, his movements and his gait, 'very much in agreement with his words (27), an extension of the rule of propriety to physical description, which also confirmed his characteristic good humour.

The rhetorical theory behind the *Defence* leaves the historicity of Xenophon's Socrates open to question. The rule of propriety was meant to create the impression of truth to life, which allowed for a rhetorical kind of truth that took the audience as its only measure. The Socrates of literature might need to be different from the Socrates of real life if he were to convince the audience. The Socrates of the *Defence* does have eminently acceptable reasons for courting death. The poets had long agreed on the merits of an easy death over the miseries of old age. The expectation of immortality through the afterlife of the memory was conventional wisdom, endorsed by Xenophon elsewhere. The truth might have been different. Socrates' alleged belief in the afterlife of the soul might be relevant, if it could be established, but Plato's evidence is difficult to control because it is overlaid with his own beliefs. This may apply to Xenophon as well. He attributes the doctrine of the immortality of the soul to Cyrus at the end of the *Cyropaidia,* but not to Socrates. It is natural to suppose from the silence of the Defence that Xenophon did not believe that hope of immortality explained Socrates' *megalēgoria* in any way. If he was aware that others believed so, but did not agree with them, his silence may be eloquent. Even

if he did believe it, it is just possible that the demands of propriety precluded his mentioning it. Belief in individual immortality might not convince his readers even as a part of the explanation if they did not share the belief.

The *Defence* indicates that the Socratic problem was being discussed in the light of the rule of propriety, which was to become the basis of the Peripatetic tradition of rhetorical theory. Xenophon cannot have been the first to apply the rule in general. Lysias, the master of *mimēsis,* who was supremely able to convey the character and emotion and circumstances of the speaker by the use of appropriate sentiment and style, must have applied it to the speech of defence he wrote for Socrates. Xenophon might still have been the first, nevertheless, as his *Defence* implies, to explain the propriety of Socratic *megalēgoria* in particular. Diogenes Laertius says that when Lysias presented Socrates with his speech, Socrates rejected it on the grounds that it was *not appropriate* for him. This is meant as a paradox. Diogenes interprets the rejection to mean that it was forensic rather than philosophical, but the point may be that Lysias failed to portray the *megalēgoria* Socrates considered appropriate. Lysias had a special skill in portraying the ordinary man, and, as we have seen, the ordinary man on trial for his life did not use *megalēgoria*. The story may therefore emphasise both the unusual nature of the Socratic *megalēgoria* and its important place in any account of Socrates' defence. Xenophon acknowledges both in his *Defence*. It certainly confirms that individual authors of Socratic defence speeches had their own individual assessments of the type of speech appropriate for the character involved and the circumstances facing him. Rhetorical theory was well on the way to producing the Socratic problem.

Vivienne Gray (essay date 1989)

SOURCE: An introduction to *The Character of Xenophon's "Hellenica,"* Gerald Duckworth & Co. Ltd., 1989, pp. 1-9.

[*In her introduction, an excerpt from which follows, Gray states her desire to correct previous condemnations of Xenophon's text as a poor history, arguing that critics must acknowledge Xenophon as a philosophical writer with moral purposes before they can judge the text properly.*]

The attempt to understand the nature of Xenophon's *Hellenica* has a long history. Part of the problem is that Xenophon makes no prefatory statement of the programme of the history. It begins *in medias res* as a continuation of Thucydides' unfinished history of the Peloponnesian War and there is no indication in the text even of the identity of the author, let alone his intended theme, purpose or method. As it happens the identity of the author is no problem, but the theme and purpose and method remain unclear. The incidental comments he makes on such matters in the body of the work are by no means programmatic for the whole, nor are they necessarily complete statements in themselves. Whatever the reason for the lack of a preface, and there have been several theories, this feature of the *Hellenica* creates problems for the reader, who is given no idea of what to expect nor any guide to assess what is offered, apart from what is suggested by the fact of the continuation of Thucydides.

In view of the lack of preface there has been a natural tendency to try to understand the *Hellenica* in the light of its antecedents. This is in line with the tendency of most ancient literature to imitate what is best in a tradition and innovate in that context. Xenophon shows that tendency over a wide range of his other works. Naturally enough too, since the *Hellenica* is a continuation of Thucydides, the tradition in which Xenophon is assumed to be writing is the tradition of Thucydides.

Xenophon was one of several who completed Thucydides' history of the Peloponnesian War, left unfinished in the middle of the account of the events of 411 BC. Admittedly, the greater part of the work concerned events subsequent to that war: the installation of the Thirty Tyrants and the civil war at Athens they provoked and the reconciliation, and then the history of Greek affairs in general right down to the battle of Mantinea in 362 BC. Nevertheless, the fact of the continuation suggested to many that at least the early part of the work should be an imitation of Thucydides, as well as a continuation. They emphasised Thucydidean and other features that seemed to distinguish this section from the rest as one inspired by Thucydidean historiography.

Yet it falls so manifestly short of Thucydides' standards that a serious imitation seems out of the question. It is on a far smaller scale for the most part, does not exhibit that particularly Thucydidean concern for accuracy and analysis and is not written in his kind of language. Even its use of his seasonal chronology is unsystematic, and the differences between the continuation and the rest are now thought to have been exaggerated.

Continuations are not obliged to be imitations of what they continue. There is no expectation that the other historians who completed Thucydides' account also imitated him. Only the abruptness of this particular continuation and the lack of a preface really encourage the belief in Xenophon's case. Xenophon ended his own *Hellenica* with the hope that he would find a continuator: 'Let this be the limit of my account. The events that follow will perhaps be the concern of another historian.' It is hard to believe that he expected this continuator to share his view of history, or his particular themes and interests. Xenophon was obliged to make his continuation more abrupt since Thucydides had not completed what he wanted to say and had left events in mid-stream, but there was no compulsion on him to write in the manner of his predecessor.

If Xenophon is not writing in the manner of Thucydides, the problem of the nature of the continuation remains unsolved. Negative characterisations of the work, based on the expectation that he should be writing like Thucydides but is not are all too easy. Positive characterisations are more difficult. It is equally difficult to characterise the rest of the work, after the continuation is complete. Some style a great deal of it *memoir,* especially the account of the Spartan war in Asia in the third and fourth books, and this is used to explain the state of the narrative, not only what is included and what is omitted, but also the way in which episodes are presented, for example in the way of conversations. Yet the theory has proven quite defective. Some progress has been made toward a typically Xenophontic characterisation of the whole in recognising the tendency to portray good military leadership and select and present many episodes to that end, but even the principal exponent of this refuses to allow that it is the key to the whole. Many episodes do not conform to the tendency. His tendency to make moralising comments has been noted, and his alleged irony, but again these are at best partial and incomplete characterisations. There is a need for more characterisation. The more there is and the more consistent it is through all parts of the *Hellenica,* the more chance there is of understanding what Xenophon was trying to achieve. The more chance there is too of settling the long debated question of whether it is a unified composition, exhibiting a continuity of interest, method and style, or a disparate series of sections composed at different times, or a basic kernel of memoir that grew gradually into a full-scale history of Greek affairs, as various traditions of criticism have at various times supposed.

Dionysius of Halicarnassus, an important literary critic of the first century BC, believed that Xenophon's historical works, the *Cyropaidia,* the *Anabasis* and the *Hellenica,* were inspired by the historical writing of Herodotus rather than Thucydides, and he included the continuation of the Peloponnesian War in this. He summarised the principal features of Xenophon's historical writing and compared them with those of Herodotus and Thucydides and others in his *On Imitation,* now no longer fully extant, and in his letter to Gnaeus Pompeius Geminus.

Dionysius judges his authors by criteria of style and subject matter. He treats historians slightly differently from the writers of speeches, who are his principal interest. He includes under the category of subject matter the nobility of the theme chosen by the historian, the propriety of the beginning and end points of the history, the use of digressions, the internal organisation, and the ethical characteristics displayed. Herodotus, he said, had chosen the fine and impressive theme of the success of the Greeks against the Persians, taking the story down to the expulsion of the Persians from Greece. Xenophon had also chosen themes 'fine and impressive and fit for a philosopher'. His *Cyropaidia* was the 'image of a good and successful king', his *Anabasis* contains a 'grand encomium of those Greeks who went with Cyrus', and his *Hellenica* has the overthrow of the Thirty Tyrants at Athens and the rebuilding of the Athenian Walls. The quality of the themes revealed the quality of the man, his choice of subject reflecting his character. On the other hand, Thucydides had chosen the theme of the Peloponnesian War, a far less fine and impressive affair, a great misfortune for Greece, and the end of her prosperity. Dionysius particularly criticised Thucydides for his envisaged end point, suggesting that it would have been far better to go on to describe the return of the exiles from Phyle and the beginning of the recovery of Athenian freedom after the end of the Athenian civil war that followed on the main war. When he comes to discuss the theme of Xenophon's *Hellenica,* he specifically commends him for taking the story of the Peloponnesian War right down to the recovery of Athens symbolised by the rebuilding of her defensive walls in the fourth book.

The modern explanations of why Xenophon took the story of the Peloponnesian War further than Thucydides envisaged are really no better than this, nor do they offer a better explanation of why he devoted almost two thirds of the second book of the *Hellenica,* a very large section of his work as a whole, to the recovery of Athenian freedom. Dionysius may be right in giving an ethical explanation.

Dionysius presents Xenophon's choice of subject matter as well as his historical themes as a reflection of the good moral character he also attributes to Herodotus. Herodotus is generous throughout, showing pleasure in success and pain in misfortune, whereas Thucydides is outspoken and bitter, particularly toward his own city of Athens, 'remembering the harm it did him', a reference to his exile at the city's hands. Xenophon's works reflect a character that is throughout 'pious, just, enduring and affable'. These are qualities that cannot be restricted to what is revealed in his choice of themes and subject matter, but must extend beyond that to the manner and style of the account.

Dionysius characterised Xenophon's historical works as imitations of Herodotus rather than Thucydides because of the character they revealed. Harodotus

chose a theme that was the mark of a great and noble soul, and was gentle and understanding, Thucydides chose a theme that was the mark of a mean and ignoble soul, and was harsh and bitter. Xenophon chose themes of a quality fit for a philosopher, that is, a man of moral worth, and he revealed a character, as Dionysius says, 'adorned with all the virtues'. This ethical characterisation of historical works may be quite invalid, or Dionysius may be too fond of the theme of literary imitation of one author by another, but the view that Xenophon leans more to Herodotus than he does to Thucydides in this respect is at least interesting, and at best, in the light of modern belief, rather revolutionary.

Dionysius characterises other areas of Xenophon's historical works as Herodotean, for instance the organisation. He likens him to Herodotus and sets him apart from Thucydides in his preference for a natural organisation where one story is followed through to its conclusion or at least to a natural break before another is begun. Thucydides broke up even the most tightly unified story into its seasonal parts. What Dionysius says is certainly true of Xenophon's interweaving of the narrative of the Spartan campaign against Asia with events in Greece in the years following the Peloponnesian War, and the separate treatment of the narrative of the Corinthian War first by land and then by sea, in two unconnected blocks. Oddly, Dionysius seems unconcerned about Xenophon's use of seasonal organisation for some of his continuation.

Dionysius also likens Xenophon to Herodotus and sets him apart from Thucydides in his use of digressions to give relief from the tedium of speeches and military engagements that made up the core of written history. It is not all that easy to decide what constitutes a digression in the *Hellenica,* but it is certain that the story of the rise and fall of Jason of Pherae is one such (6.1, 4.27-37), as well as the story of the trial of the killers of Euphron (7.3.4-11), and the account of the achievements of the men of Phlius (7.2). Thucydides had few such digressions.

Dionysius seems to believe that Xenophon tried to imitate the linguistic style of Herodotus as well, but did not measure up. He says that both shared a pure and suitable vocabulary, and both exhibited charm in their writing, but Xenophon lacked the beauty of the linguistic expression of Herodotus. He also found him deficient in adapting his expression to his subject matter in the writing of speeches for characters in his history. This type of comment reflects the belief held by the tradition of Peripatetic literary criticism Dionysius practised, that the principal stylistic virtue was the virtue of propriety, in which both sentiment and expression were made appropriate to the character of the speaker and the nature of the subject matter in hand. Yet though

Xenophon failed to match Herodotus, he certainly departed from Thucydidean stylistic practice. Dionysius commented that Thucydides had no charm of the Herodotean sort and that he completely failed to adapt the expression of his speeches to the character of his speakers. His speeches were all in the one style and therefore all of the one character. This made for tedium and lack of variety. Other critics, such as Demetrius and Longinus, restrict their analysis of Xenophon's works, including his historical works, purely to stylistic matters like these.

Herodotean influence on Xenophon's *Hellenica* is a subject well worth pursuing. It was always unwise to insist on Thucydides as the only model for imitation. There is the earlier tradition of historical writing to consider and it is chiefly represented by Herodotus. Current understanding of the *Hellenica* allows Xenophon no contact with this earlier tradition, nor indeed with the contemporary tradition, represented for example by Ctesias, and it fails to set him in the context of the nature of historical writing in his times. Thucydides had far less influence on historians contemporary with Xenophon than Herodotus did. His most obvious influence was his style of storytelling, but it did not stop there.

Ctesias, who was Xenophon's contemporary, wrote a history of Persia that set out to correct alleged errors in Herodotus and fill gaps in his record. At the same time he told stories that owed a direct debt to Herodotus, like the one about Queen Semiramis turning into a bird and flying off with the flock, or the truly inspired account of the stratagem of the dummy elephants preserved by Diodorus Siculus. His stories of court intrigue owe a debt to Herodotus too. There are passages in which the debt is one of linguistic expression. The letter Ctesias writes for Stryangaeus to his beloved is in the tradition of the speech Herodotus wrote for Queen Tomyris against Cyrus.

The historian Theopompus, who wrote a continuation of the Peloponnesian War as well as a history of Philip of Macedon, openly declared his competition with Herodotus in the matter of storytelling: 'I shall tell stories better than Hellanicus or Herodotus or Ctesias.' He offers an ancient version of Rip van Winkel who slept for many years and woke to find the world changed, as well as a version of the famous meeting of Midas and Silenus previously told by Herodotus himself, and a story about Pherecydes previously told of Pythagoras. His account of the Persian King's preparations for an expedition against Egypt is modelled in tone and language on Herodotus' account of Xerxes' preparations for Greece.

At the beginning of the third century Duris of Samus recast whole episodes from Herodotus, evidently hoping to outdo him in some way, perhaps by using his plainer linguistic style to bring his events down to earth. Against all this, the influence of Thucydides seems meagre. It was virtually restricted to the anonymous author of the *Hellenica Oxyrhynchia.*

The argument that Herodotus has influenced Xenophon's account in some serious way requires considerable substantiation, but given the influence he had on quite a few other fourth-century historians, it does not seems an altogether surprising or ingenious argument to advance. I have already expressed the view that Herodotus has influenced his *Hiero,* where the shape of the dialogue, which represents a meeting between a wise man and a tyrant who discuss the nature of happiness, is attested in Herodotus in the stories of the meetings between Solon and Croesus and Croesus and Cyrus in his first book. Xenophon takes this essentially Herodotean narrative pattern and experiments with it, casting it in Socratic dialogue to create an effective vehicle for the expression of his own ideas about the nature of the happiness of the tyrant. His *Cyropaidia* recasts whole episodes from Herodotus.

There is another ancient characterisation of the *Hellenica* that is also worth the pursuit. The *Hiero* shows that some of Herodotus' material, like his meetings between wise men and tyrants, could be a vehicle for philosophy. Diogenes Laertius included Xenophon in his lives of the philosophers. He considered his historical writing an offshoot of his philosophic activity, 'First of the philosophers, he also wrote history.' Dionysius of Halicarnassus, as we have seen, thought that Xenophon revealed the character of a philosopher, 'adorned with all the virtues', in his historical writing. The ancient tradition saw Xenophon as a philosopher first and foremost, an historian second. His historical works were ultimately philosophic. This was because he was a pupil of the philosopher Socrates and the writer of numerous Socratic works: the *Memorabilia,* in which he depicted the moral goodness of Socrates through reports of his conversations and speeches, the *Apologia Socratis,* in which he discussed the quality of high-mindedness Socrates showed at his trial, the *Oeconomicus,* in which Socrates learned the art of estate management from Ischomachus, and the *Hiero,* in which the poet Simonides and the tyrant Hiero discussed tyranny in the Socratic manner.

Xenophon's own definition of philosophy was the pursuit of moral excellence and his ideal philosopher was Socrates, a man himself possessed of all the virtues and adept at leading his companions towards the same goals, by dialectic and other forms of conversation and by offering himself as a model for imitation. His contemporary Isocrates also defined philosophy as the pursuit of moral excellence, but not according to Socratic methods. He believed that the study of the art of rhetoric was the way, and wrote his essays in his typical grand rhetorical style on his typically grand

and uplifting themes at least partly for the education of his companions in philosophy. Theopompus the historian of Philip, who was alleged to be a pupil of Isocrates, was known for his revelation of vice and virtue, best seen in his moralising comments on the court of Philip.

Almost all of Xenophon's works are in some way touched by this moral and philosophic purpose. There are clear examples in the Socratic works. His *Hiero* is a straight philosophical dialogue on the nature of the happiness of the ruler. His *Agesilaus* offers the picture of a military leader possessed of all the virtues as a model for imitation. The *Cyropaidia* seeks to explain the success of Cyrus in moral terms by investigating his background and his education. Even his technical works have a generally moral purpose, including the preface and the epilogue to the *Cynegeticus*. It would be surprising if the *Hellenica* did not show a similar purpose, and not only in the way of direct moralising.

Ancient Greek history had always to some extent offered examples of virtue. This gave the genre the potential for philosophy. Herodotus was congenial to those who wished to present and investigate such qualities because his history was firmly fixed on instances of achievement that included the moral dimension. He says in his preface:

> This is the achievement of the inquiry of Herodotus of Halicarnassus designed to ensure that what men have done is not obliterated by the passing of time, and that the great and astonishing works achieved by men both Greek and barbarian do not go unglorified, particularly the causes of their mutual wars.

His description of the battle of Thermopylae (7.202-33) is a good illustration of this focus on ethical achievement, for it is almost totally devoted to examples of Spartan courage. This is the point of the story of the visit of the Persian scout to the Spartan camp and his report of the men there exercising and combing their hair, which Demaratus interprets as proof of their calm courage in the face of overwhelming odds. The preliminaries to the main battle commemorate the courage of the seer Megistias and the king Leonidas in refusing to leave their positions. The final struggle vividly commemorates Spartan courage, fighting to the last with their bare hands and teeth(!). There is a separate story of the exchange between the Spartan Dieneces and the man from Trachis in which Dieneces revealed his courage in words rather than deeds; when he was told that the Persian arrows would fly so thickly they would block out the sun, Dieneces welcomed the news on the grounds that they would fight in the shade. Herodotus offers his speech as a *memorial* to his courage, just as solid as the epitaphs he cites from the battlefield. The section ends with the contrasting

stories of the two Spartans suffering from eye disease, one of whom played the coward and returned to Sparta to endure a life of disgrace until he redeemed his life in death at Plataea, the other being led blindly into battle by his servant to die gloriously. There is a further contrast between courage and cowardice in the story of the Thebans who surrendered to Xerxes, only to be branded for their action by the Persians themselves.

Xenophon's few statements of intent in his *Hellenica* reveal that same firm focus on the moral achievement. At the beginning of the fifth book, he describes the enthusiastic farewell given Teleutias by the men under his command when he left them on the expiry of his term of office (5.1.4):

> I know that in this description I am recounting no expenditure danger or stratagem worthy of report, but it seems to me that this is worthy of a man's consideration, what it was that Teleutias did to produce such a disposition in his men. That is a human achievement most worthy of report, more than great wealth or many dangers.

The focus on moral achievement is explicit. What is defined as worthy of report is the winning of enthusiastic support from those one leads, an important quality of the good commander in Xenophon's well known theory. The qualities of the leader were food for philosophical thought. Xenophon has Socrates discuss the problem of how to win willing obedience in the *Memorabilia* and the *Oeconomicus,* and the problem is the focus of the *Cyropaidia* and the *Hiero*. Moreover, Xenophon is here going out of his way to find moral achievement where it is not at first evident. He says that the scene of farewell for Teleutias itself reveals no great achievement, but he encourages the reader to look below the surface of the scene to discover a very great achievement indeed, one of the greatest in his view.

In discussing the many fine achievements of the small city of Phlius (7.2.1), he produces a further example of a firm focus

> If any of the large cities has a single fine achievement to its credit, all the historians record it. But it seems to me that if a small city has many fine achievements to its credit, that is even more worthy of revelation.

He goes on to explain that these many fine achievements were the deeds of courage and endurance the men of Phlius accomplished in their stalwart attempt to remain loyal to their ally Sparta in her time of misfortune after the defeat at Leuctra. He contrasts their loyalty with the treachery of her fair-weather friends. Thus their achievements have a strong moral overtone. Friendship was one of the particular concerns of the Xenophontic philosopher.

Loyalty in misfortune is the focus of another of Xenophon's comments. In describing his plans for the account of the Corinthian War (4.8.1), he comments:

> I shall record those events worthy of recall and pass over those not worthy of report.

An early incident demonstrates what this means. The Spartan Dercylidas is portrayed keeping the men of Abydus loyal to Sparta in a speech. Part of what he says is that their loyalty will be 'remembered for all time' because it is loyalty in misfortune (4.8.4). It was indeed rare loyalty to remain with Sparta though she no longer had a fleet on the seas and the enemy fleet was virtually at the gates.

Dionysius and other ancient critics suggest various avenues of approach to the *Hellenica.* My own characterisation proceeds from a close reading of the text. I believe the text is often misread because modern readers, even scholarly ones, do not have sufficient command of the moral values Xenophon takes for granted in his audience, or the forms of historical discourse he prefers, or his structuring of episodes and his use of language. I beg the reader's indulgence for a highly detailed investigation of relatively short passages but make no apology, since they are necessary. What I am presenting amounts to a literary characterisation of the *Hellenica,* but one which has serious consequences for the use of the *Hellenica* as history. I would argue that this literary characterisation is in fact a necessary preliminary to any such use.

James Tatum   (essay date 1989)

SOURCE: "Revision," in *Xenophon's Imperial Fiction: On "The Education of Cyrus,"* Princeton University Press, 1989, pp. 215-39.

[*The following excerpt from Tatum's book treats the "epilogue" of the* Cyropaedia, *which, Tatum argues, "turns a work of idealistic fiction into a narrative of disillusionment." Tatum further asserts that Xenophon understood this disjunction and, therefore, anticipated later critiques, most notably Plato's in* The Laws.]

Like Cyrus and his empire, Xenophon's achievement should ultimately be measured not by what he created, but by how he created it. [In *The Philosophy of Literary Form,* 1967] Kenneth Burke has described the circumstances which obtain for many kinds of writing; what he says is especially relevant to readers of this imperial fiction:

> Critical and imaginative works are answers to

questions posed by the situation in which they arose. They are not merely answers, they are *strategic* answers, *stylized* answers.

The *Cyropaedia*'s romance of model fathers and obedient sons ends with Cyrus's death (8.7.28), so that we may say that all the questions posed by the prologue are answered by then. These are the answers Burke means, answers whose formulation and purpose are already determined by the questions Xenophon first asked. The symmetry of 1.1 and 8.7 is obvious and satisfying—if you like symmetry.

It seems that Xenophon did not. He disrupts the very harmonies he had labored to create. The strategic and stylized answer to the question he posed at the beginning of the *Cyropaedia* becomes itself a question, but with this important difference: through his invention of the romantic world that is Cyrus's education, he creates yet another question for himself, and it is one he does not so much answer, as complain about. For the end of *The Education of Cyrus* is neither strategic nor stylized in Burke's sense of those words. It is a return to the questioning mode of the prologue, and not a graceful one; it is filled with anger and exasperation. History and experience intrude at the end of the *Cyropaedia,* so that what was the inspiration of its fictions becomes the negation of those fictions. This is the burden of the last chapter of the *Cyropaedia:* it turns a work of idealistic fiction into a narrative of disillusionment.

Xenophon's rival, Socratic Plato also saw this incoherence, and his comments on it are very substantial. As always in Plato, they are indirect, appearing in the "divinations" of a certain Athenian in Book 3 of *The Laws.* The Athenian aims to discredit the example of Cyrus and his *paideia.* I shall argue that he is aided in his task by the disillusioned comments of Xenophon himself. The Athenian spells out the implications of Xenophon's final chapter for the rest of the *Cyropaedia,* in essence rewriting it so that the exemplary education of Cyrus is perceived as altogether inadequate, something that would naturally culminate in the disillusionment of Xenophon's final chapter.

In the process of exposing the inadequacies of Cyrus as a manager of his own household, however, Plato also offers us a brilliant dissection of the poetics of the *Cyropaedia,* a poetics which he proceeds to deconstruct with lethal effect. For the account of the *oikos* of Cyrus in *The Laws* is a parody of *The Education of Cyrus.* If you read what the Athenian says and then reread the *Cyropaedia,* you will find all the artistry . . . very hard to take seriously. Such may be the immediate effect of any parody. But in the process, Plato also points toward an issue larger than the integrity of just one text. He and Xenophon together— Xenophon by inventing these fictions, Plato by attacking them—bring into focus the crucial question of the artistic and political limitations of what Xenophon created.

To see how Xenophon himself perceived the limits of his own writing, we need to return for a moment to the last words of Cyrus.

I

For an instant, Xenophon's text and his hero Cyrus seem to be in perfect harmony. Cyrus has no more to say, Cyrus dies, and the text of the *Cyropaedia* looks as if it will expire with him:

> "Remember this last word of mine," he said. "If you do good to your friends, you will also be able to punish your enemies. And now, farewell, dear sons; say farewell to your mother as from me. And to all my friends both present and absent, farewell." With these words he shook hands with all of them, covered himself over, and so he died. (8.7.28)

Even as he dies Cyrus has managed to make the thoughtful gesture. It is not easy to envision what better alternative Xenophon could have devised for ending the project he conceived in Book 1. Yet harmony promptly turns into dissonance. The death of Cyrus was not enough to silence Xenophon after all. He says immediately afterwards:

> That Cyrus's empire was the fairest and the greatest of all kingdoms in Asia, it is its own witness. For it was bounded on the east by the Indian Ocean, on the north by the Black Sea, on the west by Cyprus and Egypt, and on the south by Ethiopia. And although it was of this magnitude, it was governed by the single will of Cyrus; and he honored his subjects and cared for them as if they were his own children, and for their part they revered Cyrus as a father. (8.8.1)

This description of Cyrus's empire repeats a recent passage in Book 8, with little variation:

> From that time on Cyrus bounded his empire on the east by the Indian Ocean, on the north by the Black Sea, on the west by Cyprus and Egypt, and on the south by Ethiopia. (8.6.21)

The sequel to Cyrus's death does more than echo this passage; it recalls the entire *Cyropaedia*, through a rapid and impressionistic overview. The description of Cyrus's empire, previously elaborated with some care (1.1, 8.6.21-23), is now reduced to a pair of superlative adjectives (*kallistê* and *megistê,* "the fairest" and "the biggest"). The complex art of government Cyrus devised is summed up by the phrase, "it was governed by the single will of Cyrus." This is not an inaccurate

summary; Cyrus cared for those he ruled as if they were his *paides* (children), and they in turn regarded him as their *patêr* (father). But Xenophon is rushing through what was good about Cyrus's empire, only so that he may get to his real theme, which is to tell what was bad:

> As soon as Cyrus was dead, however, his children fell at once into dissension, states and notions began to revolt, and everything began to deteriorate. (8.8.2)

With this brief transition out of the way, Xenophon briskly advances his criticisms. They are crude and vigorous. Everything has gone from bad to worse after Cyrus's death. The principles of the Persians (*gnômai*) are all changed from those Cyrus knew. Now Persians are irreligious and no longer cultivate the gods, they are wicked to friends and relations alike, they are dishonest with anything that has to do with money (8.8.2-7). Nor are they any better in the care of their bodies or cultivation of their physical strength. They neglect everything that would make them good warriors and good citizens. They shun any kind of labor; they are greedy, they drink too much, they go on marches rarely and then not for long. They neglect hunting, both for its own sake and as a training for war; and they do not teach their children horsemanship (8.8.8-14). These are capital crimes for the author of treatises on hunting and horsemanship. There has also been a genetic regression, to the model of only one of the two national characters Cyrus united in his person; instead of old-fashioned Persian rigor (*karteria*), the present-day Persians exhibit only the softness of the Medes (*malakia*) (8.8.15). They have expensive bedding, extravagant tastes in food and dress, they load down their horses with rich trappings, and they no longer employ the scythe-bearing chariots Cyrus invented. These are the reasons why the Persians have made themselves unfit for war. They make soldiers out of everyone, and expect that men who have been raised in luxury will be fit for war. But they no longer fight at close range, either as footsoldiers or as charioteers. Instead they let mercenaries do their fighting for them, and Greek mercenaries at that (8.8.20-26).

This polemic runs straight through to the end of the *Cyropaedia*. What began as an ironic and convoluted reflection (*ennoia*) in Book 1 now ends like a Cynic diatribe, or a piece of invective from an Attic orator, or a Roman satire. Everything is fair game, even the Persians' habits of dining:

> In former times it was their custom also to eat but once so that they might devote the whole day to business and hard work. Now, to be sure, the custom of eating but once a day still prevails—but they begin to eat at the hour when those who breakfast earliest begin their morning meal, and they keep on eating and drinking until the hour when those who stay up latest go to bed. (8.8.9)

The decline and fall can be measured by their use of chamberpots:

> They once had the custom of not bringing pots into their banquets, obviously because they thought that if one did not drink to excess, both mind and body would be less uncertain. So even now the custom of not bringing in the pots still obtains, but they drink so much that, instead of carrying anything in, they are themselves carried out when they are no longer able to stand straight enough to walk out. (8.8.10)

The effectiveness of this palpable hit is enhanced by the wordplay of chamberpots not carried in (*eispheresthai*), as opposed to the bodies of Persians who are carried out dead drunk (*ekpherontai*): *tosouton de pinousin hôste anti tou eispherein autoi ekpherontai.* There is a Juvenalian touch to the education of the Persian young, where the *paideia* of Persian *paides* is reduced to learning the art of poisoning:

> The boys of that time used also to learn the properties of the products of the earth, so as to avail themselves of the useful ones and keep away from those that were harmful. But now it looks as if they learned them only in order to do as much harm as possible. At any rate, there is no place where more people die or lose their lives from poisons than there. (8.8.14)

To the extent that the *Cyropaedia* shows how an ideal prince may fashion an empire and then run it well, this attack could be said to be a criticism of it. But the focus here is really more on Cyrus's descendants and contemporary Persia than on the text of the *Cyropaedia*. And the decline of Persia should be no surprise to anyone who knows anything about the course of political institutions. In Greece there would be first and foremost the example of Athens itself, a decline clearly foreseen by Pericles at the end of the second book of Thucydides—to say nothing again here about Xenophon's own *Hellenica*. The question of the rightness or wrongness of Xenophon's ending, if indeed there is such a question, is not one that would likely detain a politically engaged reader of *The Education of Cyrus* for very long. It was first raised as a more narrowly conceived problem in textual criticism.

2

For most of its history—say, from the time Xenophon published until the middle of the nineteenth century—the last chapter was read as a continuation of the *Cyropaedia* after Cyrus's death. It was not read as a recantation, but as a recital of an all too familiar theme in history. Its point was simple and, to anyone who knew the course of empires, unexceptionable. What Cyrus created was admirable, but it did not last. Thus the last chapter brings us back full circle, not so much

to where we began, the program outlined in the prologue, as to the social and political conditions that inspired Xenophon to write the *Cyropaedia* in the first place: the uniformly unhappy experience of all kinds of government, including empires and monarchies. There is no such thing as an empire that lasts, and the one that Cyrus created was no exception. Only those innocent of this fact of political life could be surprised.

Then came readers who were surprised, and they thought themselves far from innocent. It is all very well to say that the epilogue faithfully reflects what eventually happens to any empire if it lasts long enough. Was this Xenophon's point, to say something obvious to anyone who knows Herodotus or Thucydides? It requires no elaborate learning, ancient or modern, to grasp the idea that empires fade away. German philology passed by that truism and focused on Xenophon's Greek text with a single-mindedness that no previous commentators or translators had been prepared or willing to give it. The end of the *Cyropaedia* became strictly a problem of philology: how does this epilogue fit with the text that precedes it? This was an abiding question as modern critical editions of Xenophon began to take shape, roughly by 1857 and the publication of Dindorf's Oxford edition of Xenophon. It was observed that the last chapter—styled variously an epilogue, palinode, or recantation—was in no way prepared for by either the prologue or the main narrative. While the last chapter did not challenge the *Cyropaedia* directly, its attack on the degeneracy of Xenophon's Persia (roughly of the 360s B.C.) does implicitly question the efficacy of the education of Cyrus.

Translators of the Renaissance like Poggio, Vasque de Lucène, or William Barker did not register this problem, but textual critics did. They had their own agenda, and it was one as particular as that of any tutor to any prince. With a strong if sometimes unexamined determination to achieve harmony of ideas and symmetry of design, they discerned many obstacles in the way of the unquestioning acceptance of the epilogue. Previous commentators and translators as well as ancient and medieval scribes now all seemed guilty of an inattentive reading of the last chapter of the *Cyropaedia*. Here in brief was their objection.

First, the epilogue rendered the entire purpose of Cyrus's exemplary education irrelevant. What was the efficacy of having written about such ideals if they culminated in such miserable results? Secondly, the epilogue shifts from the most positive view of Persia in Greek literature, to one of the most negative, anti-Persian diatribes Greek literature has to offer. It was not clear how so divergent a statement could be reconciled with the text that precedes it. Beyond these substantive issues, there was the scarcely less important consideration of the epilogue's language and style: the last chapter seemed childish in its polemic, different in every way from the placid narrative of the *Cyropaedia,* and most especially its prologue (1.1). Closely read, the epilogue became an enigma, with no good reason to be where it is. Since German philology was raising even sharper questions about Homer, it is not surprising the debate would turn on questions of authenticity. One was inclined to look for discrepancies, and if necessary, to invent them where none had existed before.

These skeptical readings led to radical conclusions about what to do with the last chapter. Every proposal was designed to distance it as much as possible from the rest of the *Cyropaedia.* The best that could be said in favor of its authenticity was that Xenophon changed his mind and dashed off these afterthoughts, with no effort to make them harmonize with his prior text. He does not say what it was in contemporary Persia that so excited him, except its vices. These are enumerated with vigor and in some detail, yet they remain vices in a generalized sense, the way vices often are portrayed in political satire and lampoon. Thus a more attractive solution was to conclude that a classic stylist like Xenophon had had nothing to do with the epilogue. Someone else added it later, for his own purposes. By attributing the epilogue to a nameless interpolator, we could close the hermeneutic circle, more or less, by making the end of the *Cyropaedia* coincide with its hero's death. As we have seen, while this ending is not predicted in the prologue, Cyrus's final speech is so moving that no one seemed to notice the temporal leaps at the end. Thus the Loeb editor William Miller's comment in 1914: "It spoils the perfect unity of the work up to this chapter. . . . The chapter is included here in accord with all the manuscripts and editions. But the reader is recommended to close the book and read no further." Instead of the epilogue the Renaissance had read, the last chapter could be taken as merely a footnote to fourth-century history that had nothing to do with an otherwise perfected life of Cyrus. If the rest of the *Cyropaedia* were dull, so be it. At least one could say it was a dullness well composed.

Such was one consequence of the desire to have a finished text. If Xenophon's earlier readers had been guilty of overlooking the difficulties the nineteenth century would expose, however, these later disbelievers were themselves all too philological, too much in love with Xenophon's words to the exclusion of other considerations that are just as relevant.

An enduring characteristic of those of us engaged in philology and literary criticism is our ability to discover solutions to the problems we ourselves have invented. In an inaugural dissertation of 1880, Gustav Eichler demonstrated that the alternatives need not be conceived as a simple yes or no to the question of authen-

ticity. He was a scrupulous reader of Xenophon's text; using the same method as his analytical colleagues, he came to rather different conclusions. He exposed the hidden assumptions of his predecessors by referring to *Cyropaedia* 8.8 as the last chapter (*caput extremum*) of the *Cyropaedia,* rather than its "epilogue." He agreed that it did not fit well with the text that preceded it; it is for this reason that he resists dignifying the last chapter with the formal term "epilogue." This reasonableness was disarming enough. But then, in a detailed analysis of all aspects of its rhetoric (language, style, arguments), he also demonstrated that if Xenophon did not write the last chapter, its author was someone who knew Xenophon's style instinctively, often even by heart. No summary of Eichler's analysis can do justice to what he demonstrated, since the force of his argument depends on its accumulation of detail. You will need to examine it for yourself to see if you agree. To summarize, Xenophon's stylistic markers can be traced at every level of the last chapter's Greek, from choice of words, to use of particles, to characteristic ways of introducing and concluding the points of an argument. Eichler ends by confessing that he can find no persuasive reason why Xenophon was moved to add such a coda. He urges that we refrain from speculating about why Xenophon added the last chapter. He can find no single historical event that would explain it. The wisdom of his restraint has been confirmed by later attempts to do otherwise. Analytical criticism had its answer, and on its own terms.

In support of Eichler's analyses we might bring forward again a point already implicit in Chapter 2. For Xenophon, the gap between the political and historical world he lived in and the romantically successful but fictional world of the *Cyropaedia* finally outweighed his authorial desire to preserve the integrity of the text he had created. Contradictory strategies and mutually exclusive points of view exist side by side at many places in his writings. The final sentence of the *Cyropaedia* is characteristic of his tendency to revise:

> If anyone finds that he holds an opinion contrary to mine, let him examine their deeds and he will find that these testify to the truth of what I say. (8.8.27)

Elsewhere he poses a similar rhetorical challenge to someone or other (*tis*) as a way of validating his argument or anticipating a possible objection. It is not surprising for Xenophon to conclude with some such twist as this.

Sometimes cited, more often not, the work of Gustav Eichler has had less effect than it should have on subsequent readers of the *Cyropaedia.* So far as I can tell, his argument has made no impression even on the conscientious few who do cite him. But Eichler is important precisely because his conclusions leave us with more than a little ambivalence about the last chapter. This is where we should be: not so very different in our view of the text from Xenophon himself. What follows will amplify Eichler's point and extend it beyond the philological debate over the end of the *Cyropaedia*. The issue to address now is not its authenticity, but what this ending reveals about the connections between what Xenophon had created and actual political experience, both in Xenophon's time, and more generally.

3

The unrelievedly negative conclusion to the *Cyropaedia* puts down Xenophon's Persian contemporaries. This move may have been a self-serving one on Xenophon's part, a rhetorical ploy calculated to make what he had written more attractive to a Greek audience. By attacking contemporary Persia for its abuse of the legacy and example of Cyrus the Great, Xenophon is not only able to come down from utopian ideals to historical reality; he is also able to come back to present-day Greece itself. A return to the contemporary world would enable a Greek audience to deal with this Persian model for good government in a particular way. The last chapter brings **The Education of Cyrus** to the here and now, where it would be, surely, an irrelevant model for the Persians, but where it might yet be a possible model for the Greeks. In the main, however, Xenophon's personal reasons for turning so sharply away from the fictions he had created are now something we can only speculate about. The irony of history is that no Athenian or Spartan was ever able to exploit the model he had created nearly so well as Alexander and his Macedonians.

Not quite so much a matter for speculation is what the end of the *Cyropaedia* can teach us about the poetics of **The Education of Cyrus,** which is the issue with which we have been concerned from the beginning; namely, how it was that Xenophon managed to intertwine the fictional and the political in a single text. For this purpose Plato's critique of the *Cyropaedia* is of critical importance. As we observed in Chapter 2, the comment in passing by the Athenian in Book 3 of *The Laws* inspired the notion that there was a rivalry between Plato and Xenophon. This comment, along with Cicero's *imago iusti imperii* in his letter to his brother Quintus, is an influential testimony that has been replayed from Diogenes Laertius and Aulus Gellius to the present.

> Now I divine that Cyrus, though in other respects a good general and a friend to his city, failed completely to grasp what is a correct education [*orthê paideia*], and didn't direct his mind at all to household management [*oikonomia*]. (*Laws*)

Recall that this sideswipe at the *paideia* of the *Cyro-*

paedia was actually only a point of departure for Diogenes and Aulus Gellius, a way of introducing speculations about the *Cyropaedia* as a response to the *Republic*. As we also saw, if such a rivalry actually existed, it was a powerfully inefficient one. The *Cyropaedia* expounds views that Xenophon professes everywhere in his work; Plato might have provoked him to reply, but we cannot know this for certain. Later readers like Sidney or Milton in the *Aereopagitica* perceived such a rivalry, but mainly because they preferred the example of Cyrus to what Milton calls the "airey burgomasters" of the *Republic*. Xenophon seemed to them more practical about the problems of government; his ideal prince was a natural mirror in which they could see a reflection of their own concerns. The rivalry of the *Republic* and the *Cyropaedia* was mainly a contest in the eye of later beholders.

With this passage from *The Laws,* however, we have to deal with an obvious response to the *Cyropaedia,* and it is much more than a sideswipe. It is a fundamental critique of **The Education of Cyrus,** because it goes far beyond the simple observation of this often quoted passage, that the *Kyrou paideia* was not an *orthê paideia*. The Athenian begins by focusing on what Xenophon does not tell us about Cyrus: his conduct as a father to his own sons, and the way he neglected the *oikonomia* or household management of his own family. Throughout this "divination" of the Athenian, Plato writes with an extreme sensitivity to the text of the *Cyropaedia,* and with no little regard for what Cyrus and his descendants actually did in history as reported in the first and third books of Herodotus. The gap between what Xenophon says about the education of Cyrus and what he does not say about the education of Cyrus's sons permits the opening wedge of a critique that turns the poetics of the *Cyropaedia* against itself.

The Athenian's comments in *The Laws* are essentially a dialectical response to all of the *Cyropaedia*. We should not be surprised that Plato would reply to Xenophon; it is part of his own program to explore possible answers to the question, What is a correct education, an *orthê paideia*? The Athenian is committed to defining what education is from the beginning of *The Laws,* because education plays a critical role in the *nomoi* of the city he seeks to found.

> Athenian: What we mean by education [*paideia*] is not yet defined. When we at present blame or praise the upbringings [*trophai*] of different persons, we say that one of us is "educated" [*pepaideumenos*] and another is "uneducated" [*apaideutos*], sometimes applying the latter characterization to human beings who are very well educated [*mala pepaideumenoi*] in trade or merchant shipping or some other such things. So it's appropriate that in our present discussion we do not consider these sorts of things

to be education; we mean rather the education from childhood [*ek paidôn paideia*] in virtue [*aretê*] that makes one desire and love to become a perfect citizen who knows how to rule and be ruled with justice [*archein te kai archesthai meta dikês*]. It is this upbringing alone, it appears to me, that this discussion would wish to isolate and to proclaim as education. (*Laws*)

This passage should be as disturbing to a reader of the **Cyropaedia** as the familiar tag about Cyrus's misunderstanding of *orthê paideia* in Book 3. Xenophon does not examine the basic theme of his own work in this way, either in the prologue or anywhere later in the course of the education into which that prologue leads. It might be objected that this charge is not altogether fair. Xenophon starts with a problem in history and actual experience, not in philosophy; he turns to the specific example of Cyrus and his education as a way of solving that problem. Nevertheless, by comparison to this enquiry—and we must remember it is a preliminary consideration that comes in the first of twelve books of *The Laws*—the **Cyropaedia** seems to move blithely forward, examining none of the critical issues the Athenian argues must be examined before one undertakes to educate the young.

Furthermore, the Athenian conceives of education in terms identical to the project of the **Cyropaedia**. Xenophon narrates the deeds (*praxeis*) of Cyrus *apo paidos*, from childhood onwards, describing an ideal ruler who excelled all others in the art of ruling and being ruled, *archein te kai archesthai*. Cyrus draws a sharp distinction between the educated and the uneducated, but these are *pepaideumenoi* and *apaideutoi* in the comparatively narrow sense which the Athenian is most determined to avoid. Training in the arts of war is an activity desirable in citizens, but it is also training on the same level as trade or merchant shipping or other such things, because it is not concerned with the formation of those virtues that make a good person. As the Athenian concludes,

> As for an upbringing [*trophê*] that aims at money, or some sort of strength, or some other sort of wisdom without intelligence and justice, the argument proclaims it to be vulgar, illiberal, and wholly unworthy to be called education. But let's not get into a dispute with each other over the name. Let's simply hold fast to the argument now being agreed to by us, the argument that states: "Those who are correctly educated [*orthôs pepaideumenoi*] usually become good [*agathoi*], and nowhere should education be dishonored, as it is first among the noblest things for the best men. If it ever goes astray, and if it is possible to set it right, everyone ought always to do so as much as he can, throughout the whole of life." (*Laws*)

By this reasoning, **The Education of Cyrus** may be said to create a romantic vision of *paideia* that is finally contradicted by actual experience, because it was an education prematurely conceived, one focused on the creation of political power by one individual before the true nature and purpose of such an education had been adequately examined. Such is the Athenian's general consideration of the question, well before he turns to the specific example of Cyrus and his successors.

Cyrus and his education are then taken up in Book 3, in the course of a discussion of the comparative virtues of the Athenian and Persian systems of government. Each nation best exemplifies, respectively, democracy and its antithesis, monarchy. The best kind of government is one that weaves together elements from both. The good empire that Cyrus created enjoyed something like this mixture, yet it was destroyed under Cambyses his son and then almost restored by his grandson Darius. The Athenian offers to figure out how this happened by divination (*manteia*). The offer of a "divination" by the Athenian is a significant move, because by prophesizing (the denominative verb from *mantis*, "prophet," is *manteuomai*), he is not explaining what happened by an account from history, but by the art of prophecy which links him with the oldest tradition in Greece of wisdom and wisdom literature, beginning with the portrait of the *mantis* Calchas in the *Iliad*. It is an art that will enjoy an important place within the city which *The Laws* aims to found. Diviners of laws will there have the same status as the *nomophylakes* or guardians of the laws in the city to come.

But the *mantis* the Athenian describes is not merely a neutral intermediary revealing truths by divine inspiration. He could be like Calchas, whom Agamemnon calls a *mantis kakôn*, a prophet of evils, full of guile and trickery. For this reason the diviners of the city founded by *The Laws* will occupy a clearly defined place in the function of their office. The divination of the Athenian is in pointed contrast to the *ennoia* or reflection of the author of the **Cyropaedia**. Reflections or inner thoughts are the product of personal experience recollected and reexamined. Xenophon's reflections at the opening of the **Cyropaedia** were cast in general terms, as we observed, but at the same time these were general views that had clear resonance in actual political experience. While the source of the prologue's wisdom was history and reflection about the lessons it seemed to teach, the source of the Athenian's wisdom is fundamentally different. It is a revelation or a prophecy, not, he avers, anything to be represented as known fact.

Of course this is disingenuous, and the conclusion of the conversation about Cyrus and the Persians proves it. The Athenian is claiming less for himself than he could if he cared to.

Clinias: These things are said to have happened, and it is likely that they happened more or less this way.

The Athenian "divines" that what he says was true, but his interlocutor Clinias concludes that it is *said* to have happened (*legetai*), and that it is *likely* that it happened (*eoiken . . . gegonênai*). This is the same realm of probability of knowledge about the past that Cyrus recommends his sons study, if they cannot learn from the example of Cyrus himself:

> then learn from the things that happened in the past; for these things are the best kind of instruction (*tôn progegenêmenôn manthanete; hautê gar aristê didaskalia*). (8.7.24)

What the Athenian says can be confirmed the same way Cyrus's teachings are confirmed. But the things that have happened, "history" in a general sense rather than in the original Herodotean meaning of "inquiries," are also the source of everything that will contradict the example set by Cyrus. Things that happen in history after Cyrus's death are what mark the limits of Xenophon's fiction.

4

For all but the final scene of the *Cyropaedia,* Cyrus is without children, and the education of his sons is perforce nothing the *Cyropaedia* could describe. But as Xenophon says in the last chapter, it was the rivalry between Cambyses his elder son and the younger Tanaoxares that caused the breakup of the empire Cyrus created (8.8.2). He passed over the education of Cyrus's sons, as he passed over most of Cyrus's life, because the romance he had conceived did not require such completeness. One writer's economy of design thereby becomes in another's view an oversight to be corrected. Xenophon had given Plato all the opening he needed.

While Cyrus himself was a disciplined person, the Athenian says, he failed to give his own sons the same education he enjoyed. He neglected them because he probably "spent his whole life, from youth onwards [*ek neou*], preoccupied with military matters, and turned his children over to the women to be brought up." The result was that they were reared as if already blessed by fortune (*eudaimones*), in what the Athenian terms a *gynaikeia trophê,* a "feminine upbringing." They lacked nothing from the moment they were born, were opposed by no one about anything, and praised by everyone for whatever they did or said. While Xenophon's Cyrus lacks none of these good things, much of his education depended on his success in resisting such temptations. The children of the Persian royal family led the *bios kakos* or evil life children of exceptionally rich and tyrannical men often lead. They were nur-

tured by the very things *The Education of Cyrus* shows us Cyrus avoided.

Cyrus's alleged neglect of the education of his own sons thus undercuts a central metaphor of the *Cyropaedia,* which is that of the "father" (*patêr*) to the army and all the nations he governs. Cyrus appears to the Athenian to have achieved this status of father to nations by denying his own children what he readily offered everyone else. Nor is that all. The concept of *oikonomia,* in both its strict and its more expansive, Xenophontic sense, also comes under attack. As the father failed, so fails his household management: not the economy of his empire, but the economy of the household that was the model for the larger *oikos* of his empire. Cyrus clearly knew nothing about how his own house should be run.

With the *patêr* and *oikonomia* of Xenophon's imperial fiction under this kind of review, it is not surprising that the paradigm of the shepherd of men (*poimên*) does not escape the Athenian's notice. Recall the prologue of the *Cyropaedia* and its droll analogy between the arts of governing men and the arts of animal husbandry: as Xenophon moves back and forth, from successful herdsmen, shepherds, and cowherds and their obedient "subjects," to the less successful rulers of human beings, there is created the impression that the arts of an ideal ruler like Cyrus might be viewed as, in a sense, a variety of human husbandry; a ruler's subjects can be treated with the same detachment with which a herdsman and shepherd treat the flocks in their charge. The force of this analogy in the prologue extends forward to Cyrus's later conduct with his subjects; compare his detachment about such troublesome people as the sophist of Armenia, Panthea, or Cyaxares. Now that metaphor of the shepherd of the people, and its literal counterpart, the actual shepherd who tends flocks of sheep, are both subjected to this "divination" by Plato's deconstructionist Athenian:

> Their father, meanwhile, kept acquiring flocks and herds, including many droves of men along with many other animals, on their behalf; but he didn't know that they to whom he was going to give all this were not being educated in their father's art, which was Persian [*tên patrôian ou paideuomenous technên, ousan Persikên*], for the Persians are shepherds [*poimenes*] because of the rough country from which they originate. This art is a tough one, sufficient to make men very strong herdsmen, capable of living outdoors, able to keep watch without sleep, and ready to serve as soldiers whenever they have to. He failed to see that women and eunuchs had given his sons an education which had been corrupted by the so-called happiness of the Medes, and the sons turned out as one would expect, after having been brought up without any restraint.

The Athenian flattens out the *Cyropaedia*'s analogy linking shepherds and rulers together, as well as the implied lesson that one learn to cultivate the same attitude towards one's subjects that a shepherd has towards his flock. He puts Cyrus into the business of indiscriminately acquiring flocks and herds of animals and droves of men together (*poimnia, probata; agelai andrôn*). Sheer acquisition is the theme; there is nothing here about an epistemology of rule. Compared to the arts which Cyrus learned, education is here conceived in a much simpler way. The Persian art the Athenian speaks of is concerned with making men strong herdsmen who can be tough soldiers when they have to be. This was Cyrus's inheritance from his father, but he fails to teach even this much to his own children. The regression to the softness of the Medes (*malakia*) is precisely the same charge Xenophon levels against the Persians at 8.8.15.

Plato's version of Persian royal history is not at variance with Herodotus' account of the same persons and events, but the source of most of his "divination" about Cyrus and his successors is, evidently, the *Cyropaedia* itself. What the Athenian says is almost entirely a negative revision of Xenophon's positive project. Even so, he does not refrain from observing that those who do not remember the past are condemned to repeat it. Cambyses' son Darius fared much better, says the Athenian, because he was not the son of a king and was not brought up in this kind of luxurious education. He was as good a ruler as his father was bad, and he reestablished the empire that Cambyses had done so much to undo. But then Darius made the same mistake as his grandfather had; he allowed his son Xerxes to have a royal and luxurious education, with the same enervating results.

> "O Darius," it is perhaps very just to say, "you have failed to learn from the vice [*kakon*, "evil"] of Cyrus and have brought up Xerxes in the same habits as Cyrus did Cambyses!" Since he was an offspring of the same sorts of education [*tôn autôn paideiôn genomenos ekgonos*], he wound up suffering just about the same things as Cambyses.

The whole import of Cyrus's education in *The Education of Cyrus* is that one learn from his positive example. If Cyrus's sons could not learn from him, he says, then they should learn from the example of those who have lived before him, the *progegenêmenoi* mentioned at 8.7.24. This principle of following a good example is inculcated in us from the prologue to the end of Cyrus's life. It is one widely shared in much of Greek literature, beginning in Homer and continuing through Plutarch to the lives of Christian saints. One problem about following it is the value of the life to be imitated; the quality of one's paradigms can vary a good deal. Another is that this principle is often hard to

observe, even when there is a worthy model.

And this is the *coup de grâce* of the Athenian's divinations about Cyrus and Persia. The whole notion of learning from unexamined examples is called into question. It is a very typical move for Plato to make. There is not only nothing to be learned from Cyrus and his education; there is not even anything instructive about the fate of his successors in the art of ruling an empire. From the perspective of the *Laws,* the disillusionment of the final chapter of the *Cyropaedia* can come as no surprise. With a faulty conception of such basic things as education, household management, and the role of the father, none of which Xenophon examined the way the Athenian has examined them, what else could you expect?

5

Plato's criticism of Xenophon could be directed against any kind of fiction, whether novel, poem, or romance. Particularly vulnerable would be that point where the original vision of the author falters or transforms itself into something contrary to what he began with, as here. Yet this deconstruction of the *Cyropaedia,* while devastating in its completeness, has had little impact on Xenophon's later readers. The nature of political experience may account for this. Moments in which the laws of the world can be created the way *The Laws* prescribe are rare; its world is as remote and unreal in its own way as is the world of Cyrus and his education. It is far more typical that princes of a future empire, authors as they are of their own kinds of fiction, take the *nomoi* or customs and laws of the world as they find them and transform them in their imaginations. This invention is what links the kingdom of a poet's fancy with a prince's actual realm.

Beyond later rulers' inclination to ignore inconvenient or impractical analyses of the way to gain power, there remains the question of this closure as a literary phenomenon. Xenophon's discovery of the limits of fiction proved powerfully prophetic of things to come. Consider Cervantes' adroit solution to the problem of ending the first part of *Don Quixote* (Chapter 52), where the story of "the rest of Don Quixote's life" gets to be told only by a chance discovery worthy of Apuleius or Plato himself. An aged doctor is found with a lead box containing parchments of Castilian verses written in Gothic script. From these Cervantes says he was able to transcribe various tantalizing epitaphs, sonnets, and will about the knight errant, Sancho Panza, and Dulcinea.

> These were such verses as could be deciphered. The rest, as the characters were worm-eaten, were entrusted to a university scholar to guess out their meaning. We are informed that he has done so, at

the cost of many nights of study and much labour, and that he intends to publish them, which gives us hope of a third expedition of Don Quixote.

Spenser's open-ended ending of *The Faerie Queene* comes even closer to the experience of the author whom he claimed as his model. Like the *Cyropaedia,* The Faerie Queene changes course toward the end, becoming something other than what it first promised to be. Unlike Xenophon, and much more like Cervantes, Spenser is able to dramatize this shift in his poetry and give it voice. To begin with he may have had in mind Xenophon's Cyrus for his allegorical figure of Arthur, but his imitation of Xenophon may have made him a truer follower of the *Cyropaedia* than he expected to be. *The Faerie Queene* is incomplete, judged at least by the description of the project Spenser gives in his Letter of 23 January 1589 to Sir Walter Raleigh. It was to be a long epic poem in twelve books corresponding to "the twelve private morall vertues, as Aristotle hath devised." And the power that rules over this later change and incompleteness is Mutabilitie, a goddess who can put even Jove himself in his place.

> To whom, thus Mutability: "The things
>   Which we see not how they are moved
>   and swayd,
>   Ye may attribute to your selves as Kings,
>   And say they by your secret powre are
>   made:
>   But what we see not, who shall us
>   perswade?
>   But were they so, as ye them faine to be,
>   Moved by your might, and ordred by
>   your ayde;
>   Yet what if I can prove, that even yee
> Your selves are likewise changed, and subject
>   unto me?"
>
> (*Mutabilitie,* 7.49)

Spenser's conclusion to the poem consists of two stanzas reflecting on Mutabilitie's speech and her powers. The power of mutability is a familiar theme in English Renaissance poetry and thought. What I should like to stress here is simply the resonance this famous closure has with the problematic ending of *The Education of Cyrus.*

The final stanzas of *The Faerie Queene* comprehend our entire experience in reading the *Cyropaedia:* that *ennoia* or opening reflection that began the work (1.1), the speech of Cambyses about the all-seeing and all-powerful gods who may or may not take notice of human affairs (1.6), the final speech of Cyrus on the disposition of his soul and his empire (8.7), and the disillusionment of the last chapter, where everything Cyrus created seems to have come to naught (8.8).

> When I bethinke me on that speech whyleare
>   [earlier],
>   Of Mutability, and well it way [consider]:
>   Me seemes, that though she all unworthy
>   were
>   Of the Heav'ns Rule; yet very sooth to
>   say,
>   In all things else she beares the greatest
>   sway.
>   Which makes me loath this state of life
>   so tickle [uncertain],
>   And love of things so vaine to cast away;
>   Whose flowring pride, so fading and so
>   fickle,
> Short Time shall soon cut down with his
>   consuming sickle.
>
> Then gin I thinke on that which Nature sayd,
>   Of that same time when no more Change
>   shall be,
>   But stedfast rest of all things firmely
>   stayd
>   Upon the pillours of Eternity,
>   That is contrayr to Mutabilitie:
>   For, all that moveth, doth in Change
>   delight:
>   But thence-forth all shall rest eternally
>   With Him that is the God of Sabbaoth
>   hight:
> O that great Sabbaoth God, graunt me that
>   Sabaoths sight.
>
> *The VIII. Canto, unperfite.*

Mutabilitie imposes her own limits on a writer, no matter what the original project. To put it in terms of the twentieth century rather than of Spenser, Xenophon's imperial fiction turned into [Georg] Lukács's novel of disillusionment.

> Nature is alive inside man but, when it is lived as culture, it reduces man to the lowest, most mindless, most idea-forsaken conventionality. This is why the mood of the epilogue to *War and Peace,* with its nursery atmosphere where all passion has been spent and all seeking ended, is more profoundly disconsolate than the endings of the most problematic novels of disillusionment. Nothing is left of what was there before; as the sand of the desert covers pyramids, so every spiritual thing has been swamped, annihilated, by animal nature. [*The Theory of the Novel,* 1973]

The final chapter of *The Education of Cyrus* is disappointing in one way; in another these second thoughts are a useful comment on the relationship between fiction and poetry and the world of the poets and writers who create them. This relationship is fundamentally different from the contract that is established between fictional realism and the reader of the realistic novel— a perspective alien to the kind of fiction Xenophon sought to create.

6　　　　　　　　　　　　　　　**FURTHER READING**

Like Cyrus's achievements, Xenophon's text is therefore itself an artistic creation subject to revision, change and decline; it returns to history to confront the frustrations experience imposes on persons and institutions in actual history. As we have seen, when Xenophon begins his prologue with a cyclical view of Greek political institutions, it is a matter of indifference which government men choose. They can undo any of them willingly. His essential point is the innate disposition of men to resist those who attempt to rule over them. Now the grand vision and the transcendent theme of the art of *to archein anthrôpôn* have collapsed into particularity once again. This is the most basic response to the fictions of poetry and romance. The very pressures from the world that drew Xenophon toward writing fiction in the end impinge on the perfected world that he creates through Cyrus. The death of Cyrus the character brings about not only the end of the *Cyropaedia,* but a dissolution of the romantic world he created. The gap between the perfections of Cyrus and the imperfections of present-day Persia is so great the fantasy cannot continue. The result is discordant; compared to Spenser, Cervantes, and Tolstoy, it is certainly not so beautifully done, or so artistic.

But Xenophon is not their kind of artist, nor is he a poet who can resist an ontologically privileged reality and counterpose his own supreme fiction. For him, the problems the *Cyropaedia* addresses are inescapably privileged by reality. Therein he discovers another kind of irony. Just as he records how Cyrus, Agesilaus, Epaminondas, and even he himself embarked on one project in life and ended up in ways none of them could foresee, so now he discovers that even the writing of fiction can be as much subject to revision as any other kind of text.

The difficulty for Xenophon was that although he had invented the imperial fiction of the *Cyropaedia,* he was himself far from being a romantic. Inescapable proof of the wisdom of his revisionist thoughts about what he had created lay no more than a generation away, in the career of Cyrus's first imitator, Alexander. With Xenophon an important inspiration, he made an empire by imposing a romantic fiction on the world about him; in life and even more in death he was the inspiration for romance. Yet his empire also failed to survive his passing. You might say that Alexander the Great followed the *Cyropaedia* to the letter, its final chapter as well as its prologue. The same career can be observed in later artists and princes who were inspired by the example of Cyrus. As they turned to the creation of their own fictional worlds, they also discovered similar ironies about themselves and their creations. I do not think Xenophon would have found these later developments in literature and politics at all surprising.

Gray, V. J. "Continuous History and Xenophon, *Hellenica.*" In *American Journal of Philology* 112, No. 2 (Summer 1991): 201-28.

　　Argues for an "essential unity" in the *Hellenica,* refuting critics who perceive the work to have been composed at largely disparate points in time.

Henry, W. P. *Greek Historical Writing: A Historiographical Essay Based on Xenophon's "Hellenica."* Chicago: Argonaut, 1966, 219 p.

　　A detailed analytical study of the *Hellenica,* often cited by later critics as the authority on the dating and composition of Xenophon's history.

Hirsch, Steven W. *The Friendship of the Barbarians.* Hanover and London: University Press of New England, 1985, 216 p.

　　Pursues the questions concerning Xenophon's knowledge of and attitudes about Persia beyond study of the *Cyropaedia* and into Xenophon's other writings.

Johnstone, Steven. "Virtuous Toil, Vicious Work: Xenophon on Aristocratic Style." *Classical Philology* 89, no. 3 (July 1994): 219-40.

　　Analyses passages from many of Xenophon's works, focusing especially on descriptions of individual self-control, in order to demonstrate "Xenophon's interests in constructing a style of living that would justify and enhance the power of elites."

Mahaffy, J. P. "Xenophon." In *A History of Classical Greek Literature, Vol. II: The Prose Writers* , pp. 252-91. New York: Harper & Brothers, 1880.

　　Offers a detailed overview of Xenophon, beginning with a biographical sketch, moving through all of the works, and concluding with a commentary on "Xenophon's Defects."

Sage, Paula Winsor. "Tradition, Genre, and Character Portrayal: *Cyropaedia* 8.7 and *Anabasis* 1.9." In *Greek, Roman and Byzantine Studies* 32, No. 1 (Spring 1991): 61-79.

　　Presents correspondances between death scenes in the *Cyropaedia* and the *Anabasis,* in the process determining some of Xenophon's characteristic rhetorical strategies.

Stadter, Philip A. "Fictional Narrative in the *Cyropaedia.*" In *American Journal of Philology* 112, No. 4 (Winter 1991): 461-91.

　　Claiming for the *Cyropaedia* the status of "the first extant novel," this article investigates its different narrative elements, with an extended study of the function of time.

Strauss, Leo. *Xenophon's Socratic Discourse: An*

Interpretation of the Oeconmicus. Ithaca and London: Cornell University Press, 1970, 211 p.

> Provides, alongside a "new, literal translation," a chapter-by-chapter commentary on the *Oeconomicus*.

———. *Xenophon's Socrates*. Ithaca and London: Cornell University Press, 1972, 181 p.

> Provides detailed commentary on Xenophon's Socratic writings, including the *Memorabilia, Apology of Socrates to the Jury*, and *Symposium*.

Usher, Stephen. "Xenophon." In *The Historians of Greece and Rome*, pp. 66-99. New York: Taplinger Publishing Co., 1969.

> Presents a general and accessible study of Xenophon's works, with an extended discussion of the *Hellenica*.

Westlake, H. D. "Individuals in Xenophon, *Hellenica*." In *Essays on the Greek Historians and Greek History*, pp. 203-25. Manchester, England: Manchester University Press, 1969.

> Examines the concept of the individual at work in Xenophon's *Hellenica*, with an overall emphasis on the military leader.

CLASSICAL AND MEDIEVAL LITERATURE CRITICISM

INDEXES

Literary Criticism Series
Cumulative Author Index

Literary Criticism Series
Cumulative Topic Index

CMLC Cumulative Nationality Index

CMLC Cumulative Title Index

CMLC Cumulative Critic Index

How to Use This Index

The main references

```
Calvino, Italo
  1923-1985.....CLC 5, 8, 11, 22, 33, 39,
                              73; SSC 3
```

list all author entries in the following Gale Literary Criticism series:

BLC = *Black Literature Criticism*
CLC = *Contemporary Literary Criticism*
CLR = *Children's Literature Review*
CMLC = *Classical and Medieval Literature Criticism*
DA = *DISCovering Authors*
DC = *Drama Criticism*
HLC = *Hispanic Literature Criticism*
LC = *Literature Criticism from 1400 to 1800*
NCLC = *Nineteenth-Century Literature Criticism*
PC = *Poetry Criticism*
SSC = *Short Story Criticism*
TCLC = *Twentieth-Century Literary Criticism*
WLC = *World Literature Criticism, 1500 to the Present*

The cross-references

```
See also CANR 23; CA 85-88;
  obituary CA 116
```

list all author entries in the following Gale biographical and literary sources:

AAYA = *Authors & Artists for Young Adults*
AITN = *Authors in the News*
BEST = *Bestsellers*
BW = *Black Writers*
CA = *Contemporary Authors*
CAAS = *Contemporary Authors Autobiography Series*
CABS = *Contemporary Authors Bibliographical Series*
CANR = *Contemporary Authors New Revision Series*
CAP = *Contemporary Authors Permanent Series*
CDALB = *Concise Dictionary of American Literary Biography*
CDBLB = *Concise Dictionary of British Literary Biography*
DLB = *Dictionary of Literary Biography*
DLBD = *Dictionary of Literary Biography Documentary Series*
DLBY = *Dictionary of Literary Biography Yearbook*
HW = *Hispanic Writers*
JRDA = *Junior DISCovering Authors*
MAICYA = *Major Authors and Illustrators for Children and Young Adults*
MTCW = *Major 20th-Century Writers*
NNAL = *Native North American Literature*
SAAS = *Something about the Author Autobiography Series*
SATA = *Something about the Author*
YABC = *Yesterday's Authors of Books for Children*

Literary Criticism Series
Cumulative Author Index

A. E. . . . . TCLC 3, 10
See also Russell, George William

Abasiyanik, Sait Faik   1906-1954
See Sait Faik
See also CA 123

Abbey, Edward   1927-1989 . . . . . . CLC 36, 59
See also CA 45-48; 128; CANR 2, 41

Abbott, Lee K(ittredge)   1947- . . . . . . CLC 48
See also CA 124; DLB 130

Abe, Kobo   1924-1993 . . . . . CLC 8, 22, 53, 81
See also CA 65-68; 140; CANR 24;
DAM NOV; MTCW

Abelard, Peter   c. 1079-c. 1142 . . . CMLC 11
See also DLB 115

Abell, Kjeld   1901-1961 . . . . CLC 15
See also CA 111

Abish, Walter   1931- . . . . CLC 22
See also CA 101; CANR 37; DLB 130

Abrahams, Peter (Henry)   1919- . . . . . CLC 4
See also BW 1; CA 57-60; CANR 26;
DLB 117; MTCW

Abrams, M(eyer) H(oward)   1912- . . . CLC 24
See also CA 57-60; CANR 13, 33; DLB 67

Abse, Dannie   1923- . . . . CLC 7, 29; DAB
See also CA 53-56; CAAS 1; CANR 4, 46;
DAM POET; DLB 27

Achebe, (Albert) Chinua(lumogu)
1930- . . . . . CLC 1, 3, 5, 7, 11, 26, 51, 75;
BLC; DA; DAB; DAC; WLC
See also AAYA 15; BW 2; CA 1-4R;
CANR 6, 26, 47; CLR 20; DAM MST,
MULT, NOV; DLB 117; MAICYA;
MTCW; SATA 40; SATA-Brief 38

Acker, Kathy   1948- . . . . CLC 45
See also CA 117; 122

Ackroyd, Peter   1949- . . . . CLC 34, 52
See also CA 123; 127; DLB 155; INT 127

Acorn, Milton   1923- . . . . CLC 15; DAC
See also CA 103; DLB 53; INT 103

Adamov, Arthur   1908-1970 . . . . . CLC 4, 25
See also CA 17-18; 25-28R; CAP 2;
DAM DRAM; MTCW

Adams, Alice (Boyd)   1926- . . . CLC 6, 13, 46
See also CA 81-84; CANR 26; DLBY 86;
INT CANR-26; MTCW

Adams, Andy   1859-1935 . . . . TCLC 56
See also YABC 1

Adams, Douglas (Noel)   1952- . . . CLC 27, 60
See also AAYA 4; BEST 89:3; CA 106;
CANR 34; DAM POP; DLBY 83; JRDA

Adams, Francis   1862-1893 . . . . NCLC 33

Adams, Henry (Brooks)
1838-1918 . . . . . . TCLC 4, 52; DA; DAB;
DAC
See also CA 104; 133; DAM MST; DLB 12,
47

Adams, Richard (George)
1920- . . . . CLC 4, 5, 18
See also AAYA 16; AITN 1, 2; CA 49-52;
CANR 3, 35; CLR 20; DAM NOV;
JRDA; MAICYA; MTCW; SATA 7, 69

Adamson, Joy(-Friederike Victoria)
1910-1980 . . . . CLC 17
See also CA 69-72; 93-96; CANR 22;
MTCW; SATA 11; SATA-Obit 22

Adcock, Fleur   1934- . . . . CLC 41
See also CA 25-28R; CANR 11, 34;
DLB 40

Addams, Charles (Samuel)
1912-1988 . . . . CLC 30
See also CA 61-64; 126; CANR 12

Addison, Joseph   1672-1719 . . . . LC 18
See also CDBLB 1660-1789; DLB 101

Adler, Alfred (F.)   1870-1937 . . . . . TCLC 61
See also CA 119

Adler, C(arole) S(chwerdtfeger)
1932- . . . . CLC 35
See also AAYA 4; CA 89-92; CANR 19,
40; JRDA; MAICYA; SAAS 15;
SATA 26, 63

Adler, Renata   1938- . . . . CLC 8, 31
See also CA 49-52; CANR 5, 22; MTCW

Ady, Endre   1877-1919 . . . . TCLC 11
See also CA 107

Aeschylus
525B.C.-456B.C. . . . . CMLC 11; DA;
DAB; DAC
See also DAM DRAM, MST

Afton, Effie
See Harper, Frances Ellen Watkins

Agapida, Fray Antonio
See Irving, Washington

Agee, James (Rufus)
1909-1955 . . . . TCLC 1, 19
See also AITN 1; CA 108; 148;
CDALB 1941-1968; DAM NOV; DLB 2,
26, 152

Aghill, Gordon
See Silverberg, Robert

Agnon, S(hmuel) Y(osef Halevi)
1888-1970 . . . . CLC 4, 8, 14
See also CA 17-18; 25-28R; CAP 2; MTCW

Agrippa von Nettesheim, Henry Cornelius
1486-1535 . . . . LC 27

Aherne, Owen
See Cassill, R(onald) V(erlin)

Ai   1947- . . . . CLC 4, 14, 69
See also CA 85-88; CAAS 13; DLB 120

Aickman, Robert (Fordyce)
1914-1981 . . . . CLC 57
See also CA 5-8R; CANR 3

Aiken, Conrad (Potter)
1889-1973 . . . CLC 1, 3, 5, 10, 52; SSC 9
See also CA 5-8R; 45-48; CANR 4;
CDALB 1929-1941; DAM NOV, POET;
DLB 9, 45, 102; MTCW; SATA 3, 30

Aiken, Joan (Delano)   1924- . . . . CLC 35
See also AAYA 1; CA 9-12R; CANR 4, 23,
34; CLR 1, 19; DLB 161; JRDA;
MAICYA; MTCW; SAAS 1; SATA 2,
30, 73

Ainsworth, William Harrison
1805-1882 . . . . NCLC 13
See also DLB 21; SATA 24

Aitmatov, Chingiz (Torekulovich)
1928- . . . . CLC 71
See also CA 103; CANR 38; MTCW;
SATA 56

Akers, Floyd
See Baum, L(yman) Frank

Akhmadulina, Bella Akhatovna
1937- . . . . CLC 53
See also CA 65-68; DAM POET

Akhmatova, Anna
1888-1966 . . . . CLC 11, 25, 64; PC 2
See also CA 19-20; 25-28R; CANR 35;
CAP 1; DAM POET; MTCW

Aksakov, Sergei Timofeyvich
1791-1859 . . . . NCLC 2

Aksenov, Vassily
See Aksyonov, Vassily (Pavlovich)

Aksyonov, Vassily (Pavlovich)
1932- . . . . CLC 22, 37
See also CA 53-56; CANR 12, 48

Akutagawa Ryunosuke
1892-1927 . . . . TCLC 16
See also CA 117

Alain   1868-1951 . . . . TCLC 41

Alain-Fournier . . . . TCLC 6
See also Fournier, Henri Alban
See also DLB 65

Alarcon, Pedro Antonio de
1833-1891 . . . . NCLC 1

Alas (y Urena), Leopoldo (Enrique Garcia)
1852-1901 . . . . TCLC 29
See also CA 113; 131; HW

Albee, Edward (Franklin III)
1928- . . . . . . CLC 1, 2, 3, 5, 9, 11, 13, 25,
53, 86; DA; DAB; DAC; WLC
See also AITN 1; CA 5-8R; CABS 3;
CANR 8; CDALB 1941-1968;
DAM DRAM, MST; DLB 7;
INT CANR-8; MTCW

Alberti, Rafael   1902- . . . . CLC 7
See also CA 85-88; DLB 108

Albert the Great   1200(?)-1280 . . . . CMLC 16
See also DLB 115

Alcala-Galiano, Juan Valera y
See Valera y Alcala-Galiano, Juan

Author Index

Bamdad, A.
See Shamlu, Ahmad

Banat, D. R.
See Bradbury, Ray (Douglas)

Bancroft, Laura
See Baum, L(yman) Frank

Banim, John 1798-1842 . . . . **NCLC 13**
See also DLB 116, 158, 159

Banim, Michael 1796-1874 . . . . . . **NCLC 13**
See also DLB 158, 159

Banks, Iain
See Banks, Iain M(enzies)

Banks, Iain M(enzies) 1954- . . . . **CLC 34**
See also CA 123; 128; INT 128

Banks, Lynne Reid . . . . **CLC 23**
See also Reid Banks, Lynne
See also AAYA 6

Banks, Russell 1940- . . . . **CLC 37, 72**
See also CA 65-68; CAAS 15; CANR 19;
DLB 130

Banville, John 1945- . . . . **CLC 46**
See also CA 117; 128; DLB 14; INT 128

Banville, Theodore (Faullain) de
1832-1891 . . . . **NCLC 9**

Baraka, Amiri
1934- . . . . **CLC 1, 2, 3, 5, 10, 14, 33;**
BLC; DA; DAC; DC 6; PC 4
See also Jones, LeRoi
See also BW 2; CA 21-24R; CABS 3;
CANR 27, 38; CDALB 1941-1968;
DAM MST, MULT, POET, POP;
DLB 5, 7, 16, 38; DLBD 8; MTCW

Barbauld, Anna Laetitia
1743-1825 . . . . **NCLC 50**
See also DLB 107, 109, 142, 158

Barbellion, W. N. P. . . . . **TCLC 24**
See also Cummings, Bruce F(rederick)

Barbera, Jack (Vincent) 1945- . . . . . . **CLC 44**
See also CA 110; CANR 45

Barbey d'Aurevilly, Jules Amedee
1808-1889 . . . . **NCLC 1; SSC 17**
See also DLB 119

Barbusse, Henri 1873-1935 . . . . **TCLC 5**
See also CA 105; DLB 65

Barclay, Bill
See Moorcock, Michael (John)

Barclay, William Ewert
See Moorcock, Michael (John)

Barea, Arturo 1897-1957 . . . . **TCLC 14**
See also CA 111

Barfoot, Joan 1946- . . . . **CLC 18**
See also CA 105

Baring, Maurice 1874-1945 . . . . **TCLC 8**
See also CA 105; DLB 34

Barker, Clive 1952- . . . . **CLC 52**
See also AAYA 10; BEST 90:3; CA 121;
129; DAM POP; INT 129; MTCW

Barker, George Granville
1913-1991 . . . . **CLC 8, 48**
See also CA 9-12R; 135; CANR 7, 38;
DAM POET; DLB 20; MTCW

Barker, Harley Granville
See Granville-Barker, Harley
See also DLB 10

Barker, Howard 1946- . . . . **CLC 37**
See also CA 102; DLB 13

Barker, Pat(ricia) 1943- . . . . **CLC 32**
See also CA 117; 122; CANR 50; INT 122

Barlow, Joel 1754-1812 . . . . **NCLC 23**
See also DLB 37

Barnard, Mary (Ethel) 1909- . . . . . . **CLC 48**
See also CA 21-22; CAP 2

Barnes, Djuna
1892-1982 . . . **CLC 3, 4, 8, 11, 29; SSC 3**
See also CA 9-12R; 107; CANR 16; DLB 4,
9, 45; MTCW

Barnes, Julian 1946- . . . . **CLC 42; DAB**
See also CA 102; CANR 19; DLBY 93

Barnes, Peter 1931- . . . . **CLC 5, 56**
See also CA 65-68; CAAS 12; CANR 33,
34; DLB 13; MTCW

Baroja (y Nessi), Pio
1872-1956 . . . . **TCLC 8; HLC**
See also CA 104

Baron, David
See Pinter, Harold

Baron Corvo
See Rolfe, Frederick (William Serafino
Austin Lewis Mary)

Barondess, Sue K(aufman)
1926-1977 . . . . **CLC 8**
See also Kaufman, Sue
See also CA 1-4R; 69-72; CANR 1

Baron de Teive
See Pessoa, Fernando (Antonio Nogueira)

Barres, Maurice 1862-1923 . . . . . . **TCLC 47**
See also DLB 123

Barreto, Afonso Henrique de Lima
See Lima Barreto, Afonso Henrique de

Barrett, (Roger) Syd 1946- . . . . **CLC 35**

Barrett, William (Christopher)
1913-1992 . . . . **CLC 27**
See also CA 13-16R; 139; CANR 11;
INT CANR-11

Barrie, J(ames) M(atthew)
1860-1937 . . . . **TCLC 2; DAB**
See also CA 104; 136; CDBLB 1890-1914;
CLR 16; DAM DRAM; DLB 10, 141,
156; MAICYA; YABC 1

Barrington, Michael
See Moorcock, Michael (John)

Barrol, Grady
See Bograd, Larry

Barry, Mike
See Malzberg, Barry N(athaniel)

Barry, Philip 1896-1949 . . . . **TCLC 11**
See also CA 109; DLB 7

Bart, Andre Schwarz
See Schwarz-Bart, Andre

Barth, John (Simmons)
1930- . . . . . . **CLC 1, 2, 3, 5, 7, 9, 10, 14,**
27, 51, 89; SSC 10
See also AITN 1, 2; CA 1-4R; CABS 1;
CANR 5, 23, 49; DAM NOV; DLB 2;
MTCW

Barthelme, Donald
1931-1989 . . . . . . **CLC 1, 2, 3, 5, 6, 8, 13,**
23, 46, 59; SSC 2
See also CA 21-24R; 129; CANR 20;
DAM NOV; DLB 2; DLBY 80, 89;
MTCW; SATA 7; SATA-Obit 62

Barthelme, Frederick 1943- . . . . **CLC 36**
See also CA 114; 122; DLBY 85; INT 122

Barthes, Roland (Gerard)
1915-1980 . . . . **CLC 24, 83**
See also CA 130; 97-100; MTCW

Barzun, Jacques (Martin) 1907- . . . . **CLC 51**
See also CA 61-64; CANR 22

Bashevis, Isaac
See Singer, Isaac Bashevis

Bashkirtseff, Marie 1859-1884 . . . **NCLC 27**

Basho
See Matsuo Basho

Bass, Kingsley B., Jr.
See Bullins, Ed

Bass, Rick 1958- . . . . **CLC 79**
See also CA 126

Bassani, Giorgio 1916- . . . . **CLC 9**
See also CA 65-68; CANR 33; DLB 128;
MTCW

Bastos, Augusto (Antonio) Roa
See Roa Bastos, Augusto (Antonio)

Bataille, Georges 1897-1962 . . . . **CLC 29**
See also CA 101; 89-92

Bates, H(erbert) E(rnest)
1905-1974 . . . . . . **CLC 46; DAB; SSC 10**
See also CA 93-96; 45-48; CANR 34;
DAM POP; MTCW

Bauchart
See Camus, Albert

Baudelaire, Charles
1821-1867 . . . . . **NCLC 6, 29; DA; DAB;**
DAC; PC 1; SSC 18; WLC
See also DAM MST, POET

Baudrillard, Jean 1929- . . . . **CLC 60**

Baum, L(yman) Frank 1856-1919 . . . **TCLC 7**
See also CA 108; 133; CLR 15; DLB 22;
JRDA; MAICYA; MTCW; SATA 18

Baum, Louis F.
See Baum, L(yman) Frank

Baumbach, Jonathan 1933- . . . . . . **CLC 6, 23**
See also CA 13-16R; CAAS 5; CANR 12;
DLBY 80; INT CANR-12; MTCW

Bausch, Richard (Carl) 1945- . . . . . . **CLC 51**
See also CA 101; CAAS 14; CANR 43;
DLB 130

Baxter, Charles 1947- . . . . **CLC 45, 78**
See also CA 57-60; CANR 40; DAM POP;
DLB 130

Baxter, George Owen
See Faust, Frederick (Schiller)

Baxter, James K(eir) 1926-1972 . . . . **CLC 14**
See also CA 77-80

Baxter, John
See Hunt, E(verette) Howard, (Jr.)

Bayer, Sylvia
See Glassco, John

Baynton, Barbara 1857-1929 . . . . . . **TCLC 57**

Beagle, Peter S(oyer) 1939- .... **CLC 7**
See also CA 9-12R; CANR 4; DLBY 80;
INT CANR-4; SATA 60

Bean, Normal
See Burroughs, Edgar Rice

Beard, Charles A(ustin)
1874-1948 .... **TCLC 15**
See also CA 115; DLB 17; SATA 18

Beardsley, Aubrey 1872-1898 ..... **NCLC 6**

Beattie, Ann
1947- .... **CLC 8, 13, 18, 40, 63; SSC 11**
See also BEST 90:2; CA 81-84; DAM NOV,
POP; DLBY 82; MTCW

Beattie, James 1735-1803 .... **NCLC 25**
See also DLB 109

Beauchamp, Kathleen Mansfield 1888-1923
See Mansfield, Katherine
See also CA 104; 134; DA; DAC;
DAM MST

Beaumarchais, Pierre-Augustin Caron de
1732-1799 .... **DC 4**
See also DAM DRAM

Beaumont, Francis 1584(?)-1616 ...... **DC 6**
See also CDBLB Before 1660; DLB 58, 121

**Beauvoir, Simone (Lucie Ernestine Marie
Bertrand) de**
1908-1986 .... **CLC 1, 2, 4, 8, 14, 31, 44,
50, 71; DA; DAB; DAC; WLC**
See also CA 9-12R; 118; CANR 28;
DAM MST, NOV; DLB 72; DLBY 86;
MTCW

Becker, Jurek 1937- .... **CLC 7, 19**
See also CA 85-88; DLB 75

Becker, Walter 1950- .... **CLC 26**

Beckett, Samuel (Barclay)
1906-1989 ...... **CLC 1, 2, 3, 4, 6, 9, 10,
11, 14, 18, 29, 57, 59, 83; DA; DAB;
DAC; SSC 16; WLC**
See also CA 5-8R; 130; CANR 33;
CDBLB 1945-1960; DAM DRAM, MST,
NOV; DLB 13, 15; DLBY 90; MTCW

Beckford, William 1760-1844 .... **NCLC 16**
See also DLB 39

Beckman, Gunnel 1910- .... **CLC 26**
See also CA 33-36R; CANR 15; CLR 25;
MAICYA; SAAS 9; SATA 6

Becque, Henri 1837-1899 .... **NCLC 3**

Beddoes, Thomas Lovell
1803-1849 .... **NCLC 3**
See also DLB 96

Bedford, Donald F.
See Fearing, Kenneth (Flexner)

Beecher, Catharine Esther
1800-1878 .... **NCLC 30**
See also DLB 1

Beecher, John 1904-1980 .... **CLC 6**
See also AITN 1; CA 5-8R; 105; CANR 8

Beer, Johann 1655-1700 .... **LC 5**

Beer, Patricia 1924- .... **CLC 58**
See also CA 61-64; CANR 13, 46; DLB 40

Beerbohm, Henry Maximilian
1872-1956 .... **TCLC 1, 24**
See also CA 104; DLB 34, 100

Beerbohm, Max
See Beerbohm, Henry Maximilian

Beer-Hofmann, Richard
1866-1945 .... **TCLC 60**
See also DLB 81

Begiebing, Robert J(ohn) 1946- ..... **CLC 70**
See also CA 122; CANR 40

Behan, Brendan
1923-1964 .... **CLC 1, 8, 11, 15, 79**
See also CA 73-76; CANR 33;
CDBLB 1945-1960; DAM DRAM;
DLB 13; MTCW

Behn, Aphra
1640(?)-1689 ...... **LC 1, 30; DA; DAB;
DAC; DC 4; PC 13; WLC**
See also DAM DRAM, MST, NOV, POET;
DLB 39, 80, 131

Behrman, S(amuel) N(athaniel)
1893-1973 .... **CLC 40**
See also CA 13-16; 45-48; CAP 1; DLB 7,
44

Belasco, David 1853-1931 .... **TCLC 3**
See also CA 104; DLB 7

Belcheva, Elisaveta 1893- .... **CLC 10**
See also Bagryana, Elisaveta

Beldone, Phil "Cheech"
See Ellison, Harlan (Jay)

Beleno
See Azuela, Mariano

Belinski, Vissarion Grigoryevich
1811-1848 .... **NCLC 5**

Belitt, Ben 1911- .... **CLC 22**
See also CA 13-16R; CAAS 4; CANR 7;
DLB 5

Bell, James Madison
1826-1902 .... **TCLC 43; BLC**
See also BW 1; CA 122; 124; DAM MULT;
DLB 50

Bell, Madison (Smartt) 1957- ...... **CLC 41**
See also CA 111; CANR 28

Bell, Marvin (Hartley) 1937- ..... **CLC 8, 31**
See also CA 21-24R; CAAS 14;
DAM POET; DLB 5; MTCW

Bell, W. L. D.
See Mencken, H(enry) L(ouis)

Bellamy, Atwood C.
See Mencken, H(enry) L(ouis)

Bellamy, Edward 1850-1898 ...... **NCLC 4**
See also DLB 12

Bellin, Edward J.
See Kuttner, Henry

Belloc, (Joseph) Hilaire (Pierre)
1870-1953 .... **TCLC 7, 18**
See also CA 106; DAM POET; DLB 19,
100, 141; YABC 1

Belloc, Joseph Peter Rene Hilaire
See Belloc, (Joseph) Hilaire (Pierre)

Belloc, Joseph Pierre Hilaire
See Belloc, (Joseph) Hilaire (Pierre)

Belloc, M. A.
See Lowndes, Marie Adelaide (Belloc)

Bellow, Saul
1915- ...... **CLC 1, 2, 3, 6, 8, 10, 13, 15,
25, 33, 34, 63, 79; DA; DAB; DAC;
SSC 14; WLC**
See also AITN 2; BEST 89:3; CA 5-8R;
CABS 1; CANR 29; CDALB 1941-1968;
DAM MST, NOV, POP; DLB 2, 28;
DLBD 3; DLBY 82; MTCW

Belser, Reimond Karel Maria de
See Ruyslinck, Ward

Bely, Andrey .... **TCLC 7; PC 11**
See also Bugayev, Boris Nikolayevich

Benary, Margot
See Benary-Isbert, Margot

Benary-Isbert, Margot 1889-1979 ... **CLC 12**
See also CA 5-8R; 89-92; CANR 4;
CLR 12; MAICYA; SATA 2;
SATA-Obit 21

Benavente (y Martinez), Jacinto
1866-1954 .... **TCLC 3**
See also CA 106; 131; DAM DRAM,
MULT; HW; MTCW

Benchley, Peter (Bradford)
1940- .... **CLC 4, 8**
See also AAYA 14; AITN 2; CA 17-20R;
CANR 12, 35; DAM NOV, POP;
MTCW; SATA 3

Benchley, Robert (Charles)
1889-1945 .... **TCLC 1, 55**
See also CA 105; DLB 11

Benda, Julien 1867-1956 .... **TCLC 60**
See also CA 120

Benedict, Ruth 1887-1948 .... **TCLC 60**

Benedikt, Michael 1935- .... **CLC 4, 14**
See also CA 13-16R; CANR 7; DLB 5

Benet, Juan 1927- .... **CLC 28**
See also CA 143

Benet, Stephen Vincent
1898-1943 .... **TCLC 7; SSC 10**
See also CA 104; DAM POET; DLB 4, 48,
102; YABC 1

Benet, William Rose 1886-1950 ... **TCLC 28**
See also CA 118; DAM POET; DLB 45

Benford, Gregory (Albert) 1941- .... **CLC 52**
See also CA 69-72; CANR 12, 24, 49;
DLBY 82

Bengtsson, Frans (Gunnar)
1894-1954 .... **TCLC 48**

Benjamin, David
See Slavitt, David R(ytman)

Benjamin, Lois
See Gould, Lois

Benjamin, Walter 1892-1940 ..... **TCLC 39**

Benn, Gottfried 1886-1956 .... **TCLC 3**
See also CA 106; DLB 56

Bennett, Alan 1934- ..... **CLC 45, 77; DAB**
See also CA 103; CANR 35; DAM MST;
MTCW

Bennett, (Enoch) Arnold
1867-1931 .... **TCLC 5, 20**
See also CA 106; CDBLB 1890-1914;
DLB 10, 34, 98, 135

Bennett, Elizabeth
See Mitchell, Margaret (Munnerlyn)

Bennett, George Harold 1930-
　　See Bennett, Hal
　　See also BW 1; CA 97-100

Bennett, Hal . . . . CLC 5
　　See also Bennett, George Harold
　　See also DLB 33

Bennett, Jay 1912- . . . . CLC 35
　　See also AAYA 10; CA 69-72; CANR 11,
　　42; JRDA; SAAS 4; SATA 41;
　　SATA-Brief 27

Bennett, Louise (Simone)
　　1919- . . . . CLC 28; BLC
　　See also BW 2; DAM MULT; DLB 117

Benson, E(dward) F(rederic)
　　1867-1940 . . . . TCLC 27
　　See also CA 114; DLB 135, 153

Benson, Jackson J. 1930- . . . . CLC 34
　　See also CA 25-28R; DLB 111

Benson, Sally 1900-1972 . . . . CLC 17
　　See also CA 19-20; 37-40R; CAP 1;
　　SATA 1, 35; SATA-Obit 27

Benson, Stella 1892-1933 . . . . TCLC 17
　　See also CA 117; DLB 36

Bentham, Jeremy 1748-1832 . . . . . NCLC 38
　　See also DLB 107, 158

Bentley, E(dmund) C(lerihew)
　　1875-1956 . . . . TCLC 12
　　See also CA 108; DLB 70

Bentley, Eric (Russell) 1916- . . . . CLC 24
　　See also CA 5-8R; CANR 6; INT CANR-6

Beranger, Pierre Jean de
　　1780-1857 . . . . NCLC 34

Berendt, John (Lawrence) 1939- . . . . CLC 86
　　See also CA 146

Berger, Colonel
　　See Malraux, (Georges-)Andre

Berger, John (Peter) 1926- . . . . . . CLC 2, 19
　　See also CA 81-84; DLB 14

Berger, Melvin H. 1927- . . . . CLC 12
　　See also CA 5-8R; CANR 4; CLR 32;
　　SAAS 2; SATA 5

Berger, Thomas (Louis)
　　1924- . . . . CLC 3, 5, 8, 11, 18, 38
　　See also CA 1-4R; CANR 5, 28;
　　DAM NOV; DLB 2; DLBY 80;
　　INT CANR-28; MTCW

Bergman, (Ernst) Ingmar
　　1918- . . . . CLC 16, 72
　　See also CA 81-84; CANR 33

Bergson, Henri 1859-1941 . . . . TCLC 32

Bergstein, Eleanor 1938- . . . . CLC 4
　　See also CA 53-56; CANR 5

Berkoff, Steven 1937- . . . . CLC 56
　　See also CA 104

Bermant, Chaim (Icyk) 1929- . . . . . . CLC 40
　　See also CA 57-60; CANR 6, 31

Bern, Victoria
　　See Fisher, M(ary) F(rances) K(ennedy)

Bernanos, (Paul Louis) Georges
　　1888-1948 . . . . TCLC 3
　　See also CA 104; 130; DLB 72

Bernard, April 1956- . . . . CLC 59
　　See also CA 131

Berne, Victoria
　　See Fisher, M(ary) F(rances) K(ennedy)

Bernhard, Thomas
　　1931-1989 . . . . CLC 3, 32, 61
　　See also CA 85-88; 127; CANR 32;
　　DLB 85, 124; MTCW

Berriault, Gina 1926- . . . . CLC 54
　　See also CA 116; 129; DLB 130

Berrigan, Daniel 1921- . . . . CLC 4
　　See also CA 33-36R; CAAS 1; CANR 11,
　　43; DLB 5

Berrigan, Edmund Joseph Michael, Jr.
　　1934-1983
　　See Berrigan, Ted
　　See also CA 61-64; 110; CANR 14

Berrigan, Ted . . . . CLC 37
　　See also Berrigan, Edmund Joseph Michael,
　　Jr.
　　See also DLB 5

Berry, Charles Edward Anderson 1931-
　　See Berry, Chuck
　　See also CA 115

Berry, Chuck . . . . CLC 17
　　See also Berry, Charles Edward Anderson

Berry, Jonas
　　See Ashbery, John (Lawrence)

Berry, Wendell (Erdman)
　　1934- . . . . CLC 4, 6, 8, 27, 46
　　See also AITN 1; CA 73-76; CANR 50;
　　DAM POET; DLB 5, 6

Berryman, John
　　1914-1972 . . . . . . CLC 1, 2, 3, 4, 6, 8, 10,
　　　　　　　　　　　　　　　　　　　13, 25, 62
　　See also CA 13-16; 33-36R; CABS 2;
　　CANR 35; CAP 1; CDALB 1941-1968;
　　DAM POET; DLB 48; MTCW

Bertolucci, Bernardo 1940- . . . . CLC 16
　　See also CA 106

Bertrand, Aloysius 1807-1841 . . . . NCLC 31

Bertran de Born c. 1140-1215 . . . . . CMLC 5

Besant, Annie (Wood) 1847-1933 . . . TCLC 9
　　See also CA 105

Bessie, Alvah 1904-1985 . . . . CLC 23
　　See also CA 5-8R; 116; CANR 2; DLB 26

Bethlen, T. D.
　　See Silverberg, Robert

Beti, Mongo . . . . CLC 27; BLC
　　See also Biyidi, Alexandre
　　See also DAM MULT

Betjeman, John
　　1906-1984 . . . CLC 2, 6, 10, 34, 43; DAB
　　See also CA 9-12R; 112; CANR 33;
　　CDBLB 1945-1960; DAM MST, POET;
　　DLB 20; DLBY 84; MTCW

Bettelheim, Bruno 1903-1990 . . . . . . CLC 79
　　See also CA 81-84; 131; CANR 23; MTCW

Betti, Ugo 1892-1953 . . . . TCLC 5
　　See also CA 104

Betts, Doris (Waugh) 1932- . . . . CLC 3, 6, 28
　　See also CA 13-16R; CANR 9; DLBY 82;
　　INT CANR-9

Bevan, Alistair
　　See Roberts, Keith (John Kingston)

Bialik, Chaim Nachman
　　1873-1934 . . . . TCLC 25

Bickerstaff, Isaac
　　See Swift, Jonathan

Bidart, Frank 1939- . . . . CLC 33
　　See also CA 140

Bienek, Horst 1930- . . . . CLC 7, 11
　　See also CA 73-76; DLB 75

Bierce, Ambrose (Gwinett)
　　1842-1914(?) . . . . TCLC 1, 7, 44; DA;
　　　　　　　　　　　　　　　DAC; SSC 9; WLC
　　See also CA 104; 139; CDALB 1865-1917;
　　DAM MST; DLB 11, 12, 23, 71, 74

Billings, Josh
　　See Shaw, Henry Wheeler

Billington, (Lady) Rachel (Mary)
　　1942- . . . . CLC 43
　　See also AITN 2; CA 33-36R; CANR 44

Binyon, T(imothy) J(ohn) 1936- . . . . CLC 34
　　See also CA 111; CANR 28

Bioy Casares, Adolfo
　　1914- . . . CLC 4, 8, 13, 88; HLC; SSC 17
　　See also CA 29-32R; CANR 19, 43;
　　DAM MULT; DLB 113; HW; MTCW

Bird, Cordwainer
　　See Ellison, Harlan (Jay)

Bird, Robert Montgomery
　　1806-1854 . . . . NCLC 1

Birney, (Alfred) Earle
　　1904- . . . . CLC 1, 4, 6, 11; DAC
　　See also CA 1-4R; CANR 5, 20;
　　DAM MST, POET; DLB 88; MTCW

Bishop, Elizabeth
　　1911-1979 . . . . . . CLC 1, 4, 9, 13, 15, 32;
　　　　　　　　　　　　　　　　DA; DAC; PC 3
　　See also CA 5-8R; 89-92; CABS 2;
　　CANR 26; CDALB 1968-1988;
　　DAM MST, POET; DLB 5; MTCW;
　　SATA-Obit 24

Bishop, John 1935- . . . . CLC 10
　　See also CA 105

Bissett, Bill 1939- . . . . CLC 18; PC 14
　　See also CA 69-72; CAAS 19; CANR 15;
　　DLB 53; MTCW

Bitov, Andrei (Georgievich) 1937- . . . CLC 57
　　See also CA 142

Biyidi, Alexandre 1932-
　　See Beti, Mongo
　　See also BW 1; CA 114; 124; MTCW

Bjarme, Brynjolf
　　See Ibsen, Henrik (Johan)

Bjornson, Bjornstjerne (Martinius)
　　1832-1910 . . . . TCLC 7, 37
　　See also CA 104

Black, Robert
　　See Holdstock, Robert P.

Blackburn, Paul 1926-1971 . . . . . . CLC 9, 43
　　See also CA 81-84; 33-36R; CANR 34;
　　DLB 16; DLBY 81

Black Elk 1863-1950 . . . . TCLC 33
　　See also CA 144; DAM MULT; NNAL

Black Hobart
　　See Sanders, (James) Ed(ward)

Blacklin, Malcolm
　　See Chambers, Aidan

Blackmore, R(ichard) D(oddridge)
1825-1900 . . . . TCLC 27
See also CA 120; DLB 18

Blackmur, R(ichard) P(almer)
1904-1965 . . . . CLC 2, 24
See also CA 11-12; 25-28R; CAP 1; DLB 63

Black Tarantula, The
See Acker, Kathy

Blackwood, Algernon (Henry)
1869-1951 . . . . TCLC 5
See also CA 105; DLB 153, 156

Blackwood, Caroline 1931- . . . . CLC 6, 9
See also CA 85-88; CANR 32; DLB 14;
MTCW

Blade, Alexander
See Hamilton, Edmond; Silverberg, Robert

Blaga, Lucian 1895-1961 . . . . CLC 75

Blair, Eric (Arthur) 1903-1950
See Orwell, George
See also CA 104; 132; DA; DAB; DAC;
DAM MST, NOV; MTCW; SATA 29

Blais, Marie-Claire
1939- . . . . CLC 2, 4, 6, 13, 22; DAC
See also CA 21-24R; CAAS 4; CANR 38;
DAM MST; DLB 53; MTCW

Blaise, Clark 1940- . . . . CLC 29
See also AITN 2; CA 53-56; CAAS 3;
CANR 5; DLB 53

Blake, Nicholas
See Day Lewis, C(ecil)
See also DLB 77

Blake, William
1757-1827 . . . . NCLC 13, 37; DA; DAB;
DAC; PC 12; WLC
See also CDBLB 1789-1832; DAM MST,
POET; DLB 93; MAICYA; SATA 30

Blake, William J(ames) 1894-1969 . . . PC 12
See also CA 5-8R; 25-28R

Blasco Ibanez, Vicente
1867-1928 . . . . TCLC 12
See also CA 110; 131; DAM NOV; HW;
MTCW

Blatty, William Peter 1928- . . . . CLC 2
See also CA 5-8R; CANR 9; DAM POP

Bleeck, Oliver
See Thomas, Ross (Elmore)

Blessing, Lee 1949- . . . . CLC 54

Blish, James (Benjamin)
1921-1975 . . . . CLC 14
See also CA 1-4R; 57-60; CANR 3; DLB 8;
MTCW; SATA 66

Bliss, Reginald
See Wells, H(erbert) G(eorge)

Blixen, Karen (Christentze Dinesen)
1885-1962
See Dinesen, Isak
See also CA 25-28; CANR 22, 50; CAP 2;
MTCW; SATA 44

Bloch, Robert (Albert) 1917-1994 . . . CLC 33
See also CA 5-8R; 146; CAAS 20; CANR 5;
DLB 44; INT CANR-5; SATA 12;
SATA-Obit 82

Blok, Alexander (Alexandrovich)
1880-1921 . . . . TCLC 5
See also CA 104

Blom, Jan
See Breytenbach, Breyten

Bloom, Harold 1930- . . . . CLC 24
See also CA 13-16R; CANR 39; DLB 67

Bloomfield, Aurelius
See Bourne, Randolph S(illiman)

Blount, Roy (Alton), Jr. 1941- . . . . . CLC 38
See also CA 53-56; CANR 10, 28;
INT CANR-28; MTCW

Bloy, Leon 1846-1917 . . . . TCLC 22
See also CA 121; DLB 123

Blume, Judy (Sussman) 1938- . . . CLC 12, 30
See also AAYA 3; CA 29-32R; CANR 13,
37; CLR 2, 15; DAM NOV, POP;
DLB 52; JRDA; MAICYA; MTCW;
SATA 2, 31, 79

Blunden, Edmund (Charles)
1896-1974 . . . . CLC 2, 56
See also CA 17-18; 45-48; CAP 2; DLB 20,
100, 155; MTCW

Bly, Robert (Elwood)
1926- . . . . CLC 1, 2, 5, 10, 15, 38
See also CA 5-8R; CANR 41; DAM POET;
DLB 5; MTCW

Boas, Franz 1858-1942 . . . . TCLC 56
See also CA 115

Bobette
See Simenon, Georges (Jacques Christian)

Boccaccio, Giovanni
1313-1375 . . . . CMLC 13; SSC 10

Bochco, Steven 1943- . . . . CLC 35
See also AAYA 11; CA 124; 138

Bodenheim, Maxwell 1892-1954 . . . TCLC 44
See also CA 110; DLB 9, 45

Bodker, Cecil 1927- . . . . CLC 21
See also CA 73-76; CANR 13, 44; CLR 23;
MAICYA; SATA 14

Boell, Heinrich (Theodor)
1917-1985 . . . . CLC 2, 3, 6, 9, 11, 15, 27,
32, 72; DA; DAB; DAC; WLC
See also CA 21-24R; 116; CANR 24;
DAM MST, NOV; DLB 69; DLBY 85;
MTCW

Boerne, Alfred
See Doeblin, Alfred

Boethius 480(?)-524(?) . . . . CMLC 15
See also DLB 115

Bogan, Louise
1897-1970 . . . . CLC 4, 39, 46; PC 12
See also CA 73-76; 25-28R; CANR 33;
DAM POET; DLB 45; MTCW

Bogarde, Dirk . . . . CLC 19
See also Van Den Bogarde, Derek Jules
Gaspard Ulric Niven
See also DLB 14

Bogosian, Eric 1953- . . . . CLC 45
See also CA 138

Bograd, Larry 1953- . . . . CLC 35
See also CA 93-96; SAAS 21; SATA 33

Boiardo, Matteo Maria 1441-1494 . . . . LC 6

Boileau-Despreaux, Nicolas
1636-1711 . . . . LC 3

Boland, Eavan (Aisling) 1944- . . . CLC 40, 67
See also CA 143; DAM POET; DLB 40

Bolt, Lee
See Faust, Frederick (Schiller)

Bolt, Robert (Oxton) 1924-1995 . . . . CLC 14
See also CA 17-20R; 147; CANR 35;
DAM DRAM; DLB 13; MTCW

Bombet, Louis-Alexandre-Cesar
See Stendhal

Bomkauf
See Kaufman, Bob (Garnell)

Bonaventura . . . . NCLC 35
See also DLB 90

Bond, Edward 1934- . . . . CLC 4, 6, 13, 23
See also CA 25-28R; CANR 38;
DAM DRAM; DLB 13; MTCW

Bonham, Frank 1914-1989 . . . . CLC 12
See also AAYA 1; CA 9-12R; CANR 4, 36;
JRDA; MAICYA; SAAS 3; SATA 1, 49;
SATA-Obit 62

Bonnefoy, Yves 1923- . . . . CLC 9, 15, 58
See also CA 85-88; CANR 33; DAM MST,
POET; MTCW

Bontemps, Arna(ud Wendell)
1902-1973 . . . . CLC 1, 18; BLC
See also BW 1; CA 1-4R; 41-44R; CANR 4,
35; CLR 6; DAM MULT, NOV, POET;
DLB 48, 51; JRDA; MAICYA; MTCW;
SATA 2, 44; SATA-Obit 24

Booth, Martin 1944- . . . . CLC 13
See also CA 93-96; CAAS 2

Booth, Philip 1925- . . . . CLC 23
See also CA 5-8R; CANR 5; DLBY 82

Booth, Wayne C(layson) 1921- . . . . . CLC 24
See also CA 1-4R; CAAS 5; CANR 3, 43;
DLB 67

Borchert, Wolfgang 1921-1947 . . . . . TCLC 5
See also CA 104; DLB 69, 124

Borel, Petrus 1809-1859 . . . . NCLC 41

Borges, Jorge Luis
1899-1986 . . . CLC 1, 2, 3, 4, 6, 8, 9, 10,
13, 19, 44, 48, 83; DA; DAB; DAC;
HLC; SSC 4; WLC
See also CA 21-24R; CANR 19, 33;
DAM MST, MULT; DLB 113; DLBY 86;
HW; MTCW

Borowski, Tadeusz 1922-1951 . . . . . . TCLC 9
See also CA 106

Borrow, George (Henry)
1803-1881 . . . . NCLC 9
See also DLB 21, 55

Bosman, Herman Charles
1905-1951 . . . . TCLC 49

Bosschere, Jean de 1878(?)-1953 . . . TCLC 19
See also CA 115

Boswell, James
1740-1795 . . . . . . LC 4; DA; DAB; DAC;
WLC
See also CDBLB 1660-1789; DAM MST;
DLB 104, 142

Bottoms, David 1949- . . . . CLC 53
See also CA 105; CANR 22; DLB 120;
DLBY 83

Boucicault, Dion 1820-1890 . . . . . . NCLC 41

Boucolon, Maryse 1937-
See Conde, Maryse
See also CA 110; CANR 30

Bourget, Paul (Charles Joseph)
1852-1935 .... TCLC **12**
See also CA 107; DLB 123

Bourjaily, Vance (Nye) 1922- .... CLC **8, 62**
See also CA 1-4R; CAAS 1; CANR 2;
DLB 2, 143

Bourne, Randolph S(illiman)
1886-1918 .... TCLC **16**
See also CA 117; DLB 63

Bova, Ben(jamin William) 1932- .... CLC **45**
See also AAYA 16; CA 5-8R; CAAS 18;
CANR 11; CLR 3; DLBY 81;
INT CANR-11; MAICYA; MTCW;
SATA 6, 68

Bowen, Elizabeth (Dorothea Cole)
1899-1973 ...... CLC **1, 3, 6, 11, 15, 22;**
SSC 3
See also CA 17-18; 41-44R; CANR 35;
CAP 2; CDBLB 1945-1960; DAM NOV;
DLB 15; MTCW

Bowering, George 1935- .... CLC **15, 47**
See also CA 21-24R; CAAS 16; CANR 10;
DLB 53

Bowering, Marilyn R(uthe) 1949- ... CLC **32**
See also CA 101; CANR 49

Bowers, Edgar 1924- .... CLC **9**
See also CA 5-8R; CANR 24; DLB 5

Bowie, David .... CLC **17**
See also Jones, David Robert

Bowles, Jane (Sydney)
1917-1973 .... CLC **3, 68**
See also CA 19-20; 41-44R; CAP 2

Bowles, Paul (Frederick)
1910- .... CLC **1, 2, 19, 53; SSC 3**
See also CA 1-4R; CAAS 1; CANR 1, 19,
50; DLB 5, 6; MTCW

Box, Edgar
See Vidal, Gore

Boyd, Nancy
See Millay, Edna St. Vincent

Boyd, William 1952- .... CLC **28, 53, 70**
See also CA 114; 120

Boyle, Kay
1902-1992 ..... CLC **1, 5, 19, 58; SSC 5**
See also CA 13-16R; 140; CAAS 1;
CANR 29; DLB 4, 9, 48, 86; DLBY 93;
MTCW

Boyle, Mark
See Kienzle, William X(avier)

Boyle, Patrick 1905-1982......... CLC **19**
See also CA 127

Boyle, T. C. 1948-
See Boyle, T(homas) Coraghessan

Boyle, T(homas) Coraghessan
1948- .... CLC **36, 55, 90; SSC 16**
See also BEST 90:4; CA 120; CANR 44;
DAM POP; DLBY 86

Boz
See Dickens, Charles (John Huffam)

Brackenridge, Hugh Henry
1748-1816 .... NCLC **7**
See also DLB 11, 37

Bradbury, Edward P.
See Moorcock, Michael (John)

Bradbury, Malcolm (Stanley)
1932- .... CLC **32, 61**
See also CA 1-4R; CANR 1, 33;
DAM NOV; DLB 14; MTCW

Bradbury, Ray (Douglas)
1920- .... CLC **1, 3, 10, 15, 42; DA;**
DAB; DAC; WLC
See also AAYA 15; AITN 1, 2; CA 1-4R;
CANR 2, 30; CDALB 1968-1988;
DAM MST, NOV, POP; DLB 2, 8;
INT CANR-30; MTCW; SATA 11, 64

Bradford, Gamaliel 1863-1932..... TCLC **36**
See also DLB 17

Bradley, David (Henry, Jr.)
1950- .... CLC **23; BLC**
See also BW 1; CA 104; CANR 26;
DAM MULT; DLB 33

Bradley, John Ed(mund, Jr.)
1958- .... CLC **55**
See also CA 139

Bradley, Marion Zimmer 1930-..... CLC **30**
See also AAYA 9; CA 57-60; CAAS 10;
CANR 7, 31; DAM POP; DLB 8;
MTCW

Bradstreet, Anne
1612(?)-1672 ...... LC **4, 30; DA; DAC;**
PC 10
See also CDALB 1640-1865; DAM MST,
POET; DLB 24

Brady, Joan 1939- .... CLC **86**
See also CA 141

Bragg, Melvyn 1939- .... CLC **10**
See also BEST 89:3; CA 57-60; CANR 10,
48; DLB 14

Braine, John (Gerard)
1922-1986 .... CLC **1, 3, 41**
See also CA 1-4R; 120; CANR 1, 33;
CDBLB 1945-1960; DLB 15; DLBY 86;
MTCW

Brammer, William 1930(?)-1978 .... CLC **31**
See also CA 77-80

Brancati, Vitaliano 1907-1954..... TCLC **12**
See also CA 109

Brancato, Robin F(idler) 1936- ..... CLC **35**
See also AAYA 9; CA 69-72; CANR 11,
45; CLR 32; JRDA; SAAS 9; SATA 23

Brand, Max
See Faust, Frederick (Schiller)

Brand, Millen 1906-1980.......... CLC **7**
See also CA 21-24R; 97-100

Branden, Barbara .... CLC **44**
See also CA 148

Brandes, Georg (Morris Cohen)
1842-1927 .... TCLC **10**
See also CA 105

Brandys, Kazimierz 1916- .... CLC **62**

Branley, Franklyn M(ansfield)
1915- .... CLC **21**
See also CA 33-36R; CANR 14, 39;
CLR 13; MAICYA; SAAS 16; SATA 4,
68

Brathwaite, Edward Kamau 1930-... CLC **11**
See also BW 2; CA 25-28R; CANR 11, 26,
47; DLB 125

Brautigan, Richard (Gary)
1935-1984 .... CLC **1, 3, 5, 9, 12, 34, 42**
See also CA 53-56; 113; CANR 34;
DAM NOV; DLB 2, 5; DLBY 80, 84;
MTCW; SATA 56

Braverman, Kate 1950- .... CLC **67**
See also CA 89-92

Brecht, Bertolt
1898-1956 ...... TCLC **1, 6, 13, 35; DA;**
DAB; DAC; DC 3; WLC
See also CA 104; 133; DAM DRAM, MST;
DLB 56, 124; MTCW

Brecht, Eugen Berthold Friedrich
See Brecht, Bertolt

Bremer, Fredrika 1801-1865 ..... NCLC **11**

Brennan, Christopher John
1870-1932 .... TCLC **17**
See also CA 117

Brennan, Maeve 1917-............. CLC **5**
See also CA 81-84

Brentano, Clemens (Maria)
1778-1842 .... NCLC **1**
See also DLB 90

Brent of Bin Bin
See Franklin, (Stella Maraia Sarah) Miles

Brenton, Howard 1942- .... CLC **31**
See also CA 69-72; CANR 33; DLB 13;
MTCW

Breslin, James 1930-
See Breslin, Jimmy
See also CA 73-76; CANR 31; DAM NOV;
MTCW

Breslin, Jimmy .... CLC **4, 43**
See also Breslin, James
See also AITN 1

Bresson, Robert 1901- .... CLC **16**
See also CA 110; CANR 49

Breton, Andre 1896-1966... CLC **2, 9, 15, 54**
See also CA 19-20; 25-28R; CANR 40;
CAP 2; DLB 65; MTCW

Breytenbach, Breyten 1939(?)- .. CLC **23, 37**
See also CA 113; 129; DAM POET

Bridgers, Sue Ellen 1942- .... CLC **26**
See also AAYA 8; CA 65-68; CANR 11,
36; CLR 18; DLB 52; JRDA; MAICYA;
SAAS 1; SATA 22

Bridges, Robert (Seymour)
1844-1930 .... TCLC **1**
See also CA 104; CDBLB 1890-1914;
DAM POET; DLB 19, 98

Bridie, James.................... TCLC **3**
See also Mavor, Osborne Henry
See also DLB 10

Brin, David 1950-................ CLC **34**
See also CA 102; CANR 24;
INT CANR-24; SATA 65

Brink, Andre (Philippus)
1935- .... CLC **18, 36**
See also CA 104; CANR 39; INT 103;
MTCW

Brinsmead, H(esba) F(ay) 1922- .... CLC **21**
See also CA 21-24R; CANR 10; MAICYA;
SAAS 5; SATA 18, 78

Brittain, Vera (Mary)
1893(?)-1970 . . . . CLC 23
See also CA 13-16; 25-28R; CAP 1; MTCW

Broch, Hermann 1886-1951 . . . . . . TCLC 20
See also CA 117; DLB 85, 124

Brock, Rose
See Hansen, Joseph

Brodkey, Harold 1930- . . . . CLC 56
See also CA 111; DLB 130

Brodsky, Iosif Alexandrovich 1940-
See Brodsky, Joseph
See also AITN 1; CA 41-44R; CANR 37;
DAM POET; MTCW

Brodsky, Joseph . . CLC 4, 6, 13, 36, 50; PC 9
See also Brodsky, Iosif Alexandrovich

Brodsky, Michael Mark 1948- . . . . . CLC 19
See also CA 102; CANR 18, 41

Bromell, Henry 1947- . . . . CLC 5
See also CA 53-56; CANR 9

Bromfield, Louis (Brucker)
1896-1956 . . . . TCLC 11
See also CA 107; DLB 4, 9, 86

Broner, E(sther) M(asserman)
1930- . . . . CLC 19
See also CA 17-20R; CANR 8, 25; DLB 28

Bronk, William 1918- . . . . CLC 10
See also CA 89-92; CANR 23

Bronstein, Lev Davidovich
See Trotsky, Leon

Bronte, Anne 1820-1849 . . . . NCLC 4
See also DLB 21

Bronte, Charlotte
1816-1855 . . . . NCLC 3, 8, 33; DA;
DAB; DAC; WLC
See also AAYA 17; CDBLB 1832-1890;
DAM MST, NOV; DLB 21, 159

Bronte, Emily (Jane)
1818-1848 . . . . NCLC 16, 35; DA; DAB;
DAC; PC 8; WLC
See also AAYA 17; CDBLB 1832-1890;
DAM MST, NOV, POET; DLB 21, 32

Brooke, Frances 1724-1789 . . . . LC 6
See also DLB 39, 99

Brooke, Henry 1703(?)-1783 . . . . LC 1
See also DLB 39

Brooke, Rupert (Chawner)
1887-1915 . . . . . . TCLC 2, 7; DA; DAB;
DAC; WLC
See also CA 104; 132; CDBLB 1914-1945;
DAM MST, POET; DLB 19; MTCW

Brooke-Haven, P.
See Wodehouse, P(elham) G(renville)

Brooke-Rose, Christine 1926- . . . . . . CLC 40
See also CA 13-16R; DLB 14

Brookner, Anita
1928- . . . . CLC 32, 34, 51; DAB
See also CA 114; 120; CANR 37;
DAM POP; DLBY 87; MTCW

Brooks, Cleanth 1906-1994 . . . . . CLC 24, 86
See also CA 17-20R; 145; CANR 33, 35;
DLB 63; DLBY 94; INT CANR-35;
MTCW

Brooks, George
See Baum, L(yman) Frank

Brooks, Gwendolyn
1917- . . . . . . CLC 1, 2, 4, 5, 15, 49; BLC;
DA; DAC; PC 7; WLC
See also AITN 1; BW 2; CA 1-4R;
CANR 1, 27; CDALB 1941-1968;
CLR 27; DAM MST, MULT, POET;
DLB 5, 76; MTCW; SATA 6

Brooks, Mel . . . . CLC 12
See also Kaminsky, Melvin
See also AAYA 13; DLB 26

Brooks, Peter 1938- . . . . CLC 34
See also CA 45-48; CANR 1

Brooks, Van Wyck 1886-1963 . . . . . . CLC 29
See also CA 1-4R; CANR 6; DLB 45, 63,
103

Brophy, Brigid (Antonia)
1929- . . . . CLC 6, 11, 29
See also CA 5-8R; CAAS 4; CANR 25;
DLB 14; MTCW

Brosman, Catharine Savage 1934- . . . . CLC 9
See also CA 61-64; CANR 21, 46

Brother Antoninus
See Everson, William (Oliver)

Broughton, T(homas) Alan 1936- . . . CLC 19
See also CA 45-48; CANR 2, 23, 48

Broumas, Olga 1949- . . . . CLC 10, 73
See also CA 85-88; CANR 20

Brown, Charles Brockden
1771-1810 . . . . NCLC 22
See also CDALB 1640-1865; DLB 37, 59,
73

Brown, Christy 1932-1981 . . . . CLC 63
See also CA 105; 104; DLB 14

Brown, Claude 1937- . . . . CLC 30; BLC
See also AAYA 7; BW 1; CA 73-76;
DAM MULT

Brown, Dee (Alexander) 1908- . . CLC 18, 47
See also CA 13-16R; CAAS 6; CANR 11,
45; DAM POP; DLBY 80; MTCW;
SATA 5

Brown, George
See Wertmueller, Lina

Brown, George Douglas
1869-1902 . . . . TCLC 28

Brown, George Mackay 1921- . . . . CLC 5, 48
See also CA 21-24R; CAAS 6; CANR 12,
37; DLB 14, 27, 139; MTCW; SATA 35

Brown, (William) Larry 1951- . . . . . . CLC 73
See also CA 130; 134; INT 133

Brown, Moses
See Barrett, William (Christopher)

Brown, Rita Mae 1944- . . . . . CLC 18, 43, 79
See also CA 45-48; CANR 2, 11, 35;
DAM NOV, POP; INT CANR-11;
MTCW

Brown, Roderick (Langmere) Haig-
See Haig-Brown, Roderick (Langmere)

Brown, Rosellen 1939- . . . . CLC 32
See also CA 77-80; CAAS 10; CANR 14, 44

Brown, Sterling Allen
1901-1989 . . . . CLC 1, 23, 59; BLC
See also BW 1; CA 85-88; 127; CANR 26;
DAM MULT, POET; DLB 48, 51, 63;
MTCW

Brown, Will
See Ainsworth, William Harrison

Brown, William Wells
1813-1884 . . . . NCLC 2; BLC; DC 1
See also DAM MULT; DLB 3, 50

Browne, (Clyde) Jackson 1948(?)- . . . CLC 21
See also CA 120

Browning, Elizabeth Barrett
1806-1861 . . . . . NCLC 1, 16; DA; DAB;
DAC; PC 6; WLC
See also CDBLB 1832-1890; DAM MST,
POET; DLB 32

Browning, Robert
1812-1889 . . . . NCLC 19; DA; DAB;
DAC; PC 2
See also CDBLB 1832-1890; DAM MST,
POET; DLB 32; YABC 1

Browning, Tod 1882-1962 . . . . CLC 16
See also CA 141; 117

Brownson, Orestes (Augustus)
1803-1876 . . . . NCLC 50

Bruccoli, Matthew J(oseph) 1931- . . CLC 34
See also CA 9-12R; CANR 7; DLB 103

Bruce, Lenny . . . . CLC 21
See also Schneider, Leonard Alfred

Bruin, John
See Brutus, Dennis

Brulard, Henri
See Stendhal

Brulls, Christian
See Simenon, Georges (Jacques Christian)

Brunner, John (Kilian Houston)
1934- . . . . CLC 8, 10
See also CA 1-4R; CAAS 8; CANR 2, 37;
DAM POP; MTCW

Bruno, Giordano 1548-1600 . . . . LC 27

Brutus, Dennis 1924- . . . . CLC 43; BLC
See also BW 2; CA 49-52; CAAS 14;
CANR 2, 27, 42; DAM MULT, POET;
DLB 117

Bryan, C(ourtlandt) D(ixon) B(arnes)
1936- . . . . CLC 29
See also CA 73-76; CANR 13;
INT CANR-13

Bryan, Michael
See Moore, Brian

Bryant, William Cullen
1794-1878 . . . . . NCLC 6, 46; DA; DAB;
DAC
See also CDALB 1640-1865; DAM MST,
POET; DLB 3, 43, 59

Bryusov, Valery Yakovlevich
1873-1924 . . . . TCLC 10
See also CA 107

Buchan, John 1875-1940 . . . TCLC 41; DAB
See also CA 108; 145; DAM POP; DLB 34,
70, 156; YABC 2

Buchanan, George 1506-1582 . . . . LC 4

Buchheim, Lothar-Guenther 1918- . . . CLC 6
See also CA 85-88

Buchner, (Karl) Georg
1813-1837 . . . . NCLC 26

Buchwald, Art(hur) 1925- . . . . CLC 33
See also AITN 1; CA 5-8R; CANR 21;
MTCW; SATA 10

Cary, (Arthur) Joyce (Lunel)
1888-1957 .... TCLC 1, 29
See also CA 104; CDBLB 1914-1945;
DLB 15, 100

Casanova de Seingalt, Giovanni Jacopo
1725-1798 .... LC 13

Casares, Adolfo Bioy
See Bioy Casares, Adolfo

Casely-Hayford, J(oseph) E(phraim)
1866-1930 .... TCLC 24; BLC
See also BW 2; CA 123; DAM MULT

Casey, John (Dudley) 1939- .... CLC 59
See also BEST 90:2; CA 69-72; CANR 23

Casey, Michael 1947- .... CLC 2
See also CA 65-68; DLB 5

Casey, Patrick
See Thurman, Wallace (Henry)

Casey, Warren (Peter) 1935-1988 ... CLC 12
See also CA 101; 127; INT 101

Casona, Alejandro .... CLC 49
See also Alvarez, Alejandro Rodriguez

Cassavetes, John 1929-1989 .... CLC 20
See also CA 85-88; 127

Cassill, R(onald) V(erlin) 1919- ... CLC 4, 23
See also CA 9-12R; CAAS 1; CANR 7, 45;
DLB 6

Cassirer, Ernst 1874-1945 .... TCLC 61

Cassity, (Allen) Turner 1929- .... CLC 6, 42
See also CA 17-20R; CAAS 8; CANR 11;
DLB 105

Castaneda, Carlos 1931(?)- .... CLC 12
See also CA 25-28R; CANR 32; HW;
MTCW

Castedo, Elena 1937- .... CLC 65
See also CA 132

Castedo-Ellerman, Elena
See Castedo, Elena

Castellanos, Rosario
1925-1974 .... CLC 66; HLC
See also CA 131; 53-56; DAM MULT;
DLB 113; HW

Castelvetro, Lodovico 1505-1571 ..... LC 12

Castiglione, Baldassare 1478-1529 ... LC 12

Castle, Robert
See Hamilton, Edmond

Castro, Guillen de 1569-1631 .... LC 19

Castro, Rosalia de 1837-1885 ..... NCLC 3
See also DAM MULT

Cather, Willa
See Cather, Willa Sibert

Cather, Willa Sibert
1873-1947 .... TCLC 1, 11, 31; DA;
DAB; DAC; SSC 2; WLC
See also CA 104; 128; CDALB 1865-1917;
DAM MST, NOV; DLB 9, 54, 78;
DLBD 1; MTCW; SATA 30

Catton, (Charles) Bruce
1899-1978 .... CLC 35
See also AITN 1; CA 5-8R; 81-84;
CANR 7; DLB 17; SATA 2;
SATA-Obit 24

Cauldwell, Frank
See King, Francis (Henry)

Caunitz, William J. 1933- .... CLC 34
See also BEST 89:3; CA 125; 130; INT 130

Causley, Charles (Stanley) 1917- ..... CLC 7
See also CA 9-12R; CANR 5, 35; CLR 30;
DLB 27; MTCW; SATA 3, 66

Caute, David 1936- .... CLC 29
See also CA 1-4R; CAAS 4; CANR 1, 33;
DAM NOV; DLB 14

Cavafy, C(onstantine) P(eter)
1863-1933 .... TCLC 2, 7
See also Kavafis, Konstantinos Petrou
See also CA 148; DAM POET

Cavallo, Evelyn
See Spark, Muriel (Sarah)

Cavanna, Betty .... CLC 12
See also Harrison, Elizabeth Cavanna
See also JRDA; MAICYA; SAAS 4;
SATA 1, 30

Cavendish, Margaret Lucas
1623-1673 .... LC 30
See also DLB 131

Caxton, William 1421(?)-1491(?) ..... LC 17

Cayrol, Jean 1911- .... CLC 11
See also CA 89-92; DLB 83

Cela, Camilo Jose
1916- .... CLC 4, 13, 59; HLC
See also BEST 90:2; CA 21-24R; CAAS 10;
CANR 21, 32; DAM MULT; DLBY 89;
HW; MTCW

Celan, Paul ...... CLC 10, 19, 53, 82; PC 10
See also Antschel, Paul
See also DLB 69

Celine, Louis-Ferdinand
.... CLC 1, 3, 4, 7, 9, 15, 47
See also Destouches, Louis-Ferdinand
See also DLB 72

Cellini, Benvenuto 1500-1571 .... LC 7

Cendrars, Blaise .... CLC 18
See also Sauser-Hall, Frederic

Cernuda (y Bidon), Luis
1902-1963 .... CLC 54
See also CA 131; 89-92; DAM POET;
DLB 134; HW

Cervantes (Saavedra), Miguel de
1547-1616 .... LC 6, 23; DA; DAB;
DAC; SSC 12; WLC
See also DAM MST, NOV

Cesaire, Aime (Fernand)
1913- .... CLC 19, 32; BLC
See also BW 2; CA 65-68; CANR 24, 43;
DAM MULT, POET; MTCW

Chabon, Michael 1965(?)- .... CLC 55
See also CA 139

Chabrol, Claude 1930- .... CLC 16
See also CA 110

Challans, Mary 1905-1983
See Renault, Mary
See also CA 81-84; 111; SATA 23;
SATA-Obit 36

Challis, George
See Faust, Frederick (Schiller)

Chambers, Aidan 1934- .... CLC 35
See also CA 25-28R; CANR 12, 31; JRDA;
MAICYA; SAAS 12; SATA 1, 69

Chambers, James 1948-
See Cliff, Jimmy
See also CA 124

Chambers, Jessie
See Lawrence, D(avid) H(erbert Richards)

Chambers, Robert W. 1865-1933... TCLC 41

Chandler, Raymond (Thornton)
1888-1959 .... TCLC 1, 7
See also CA 104; 129; CDALB 1929-1941;
DLBD 6; MTCW

Chang, Jung 1952- .... CLC 71
See also CA 142

Channing, William Ellery
1780-1842 .... NCLC 17
See also DLB 1, 59

Chaplin, Charles Spencer
1889-1977 .... CLC 16
See also Chaplin, Charlie
See also CA 81-84; 73-76

Chaplin, Charlie
See Chaplin, Charles Spencer
See also DLB 44

Chapman, George 1559(?)-1634...... LC 22
See also DAM DRAM; DLB 62, 121

Chapman, Graham 1941-1989 ...... CLC 21
See also Monty Python
See also CA 116; 129; CANR 35

Chapman, John Jay 1862-1933 ..... TCLC 7
See also CA 104

Chapman, Walker
See Silverberg, Robert

Chappell, Fred (Davis) 1936- .... CLC 40, 78
See also CA 5-8R; CAAS 4; CANR 8, 33;
DLB 6, 105

Char, Rene(-Emile)
1907-1988 .... CLC 9, 11, 14, 55
See also CA 13-16R; 124; CANR 32;
DAM POET; MTCW

Charby, Jay
See Ellison, Harlan (Jay)

Chardin, Pierre Teilhard de
See Teilhard de Chardin, (Marie Joseph)
Pierre

Charles I 1600-1649 .... LC 13

Charyn, Jerome 1937- .... CLC 5, 8, 18
See also CA 5-8R; CAAS 1; CANR 7;
DLBY 83; MTCW

Chase, Mary (Coyle) 1907-1981 ...... DC 1
See also CA 77-80; 105; SATA 17;
SATA-Obit 29

Chase, Mary Ellen 1887-1973 .... CLC 2
See also CA 13-16; 41-44R; CAP 1;
SATA 10

Chase, Nicholas
See Hyde, Anthony

Chateaubriand, Francois Rene de
1768-1848 .... NCLC 3
See also DLB 119

Chatterje, Sarat Chandra 1876-1936(?)
See Chatterji, Saratchandra
See also CA 109

Chatterji, Bankim Chandra
1838-1894 .... NCLC 19

Chatterji, Saratchandra .... TCLC 13
See also Chatterje, Sarat Chandra

Chatterton, Thomas 1752-1770 .... LC 3
See also DAM POET; DLB 109

Chatwin, (Charles) Bruce
1940-1989 .... CLC 28, 57, 59
See also AAYA 4; BEST 90:1; CA 85-88;
127; DAM POP

Chaucer, Daniel
See Ford, Ford Madox

Chaucer, Geoffrey
1340(?)-1400 ... LC 17; DA; DAB; DAC
See also CDBLB Before 1660; DAM MST,
POET; DLB 146

Chaviaras, Strates 1935-
See Haviaras, Stratis
See also CA 105

Chayefsky, Paddy .... CLC 23
See also Chayefsky, Sidney
See also DLB 7, 44; DLBY 81

Chayefsky, Sidney 1923-1981
See Chayefsky, Paddy
See also CA 9-12R; 104; CANR 18;
DAM DRAM

Chedid, Andree 1920- .... CLC 47
See also CA 145

Cheever, John
1912-1982 ...... CLC 3, 7, 8, 11, 15, 25,
64; DA; DAB; DAC; SSC 1; WLC
See also CA 5-8R; 106; CABS 1; CANR 5,
27; CDALB 1941-1968; DAM MST,
NOV, POP; DLB 2, 102; DLBY 80, 82;
INT CANR-5; MTCW

Cheever, Susan 1943- .... CLC 18, 48
See also CA 103; CANR 27; DLBY 82;
INT CANR-27

Chekhonte, Antosha
See Chekhov, Anton (Pavlovich)

Chekhov, Anton (Pavlovich)
1860-1904 ..... TCLC 3, 10, 31, 55; DA;
DAB; DAC; SSC 2; WLC
See also CA 104; 124; DAM DRAM, MST

Chernyshevsky, Nikolay Gavrilovich
1828-1889 .... NCLC 1

Cherry, Carolyn Janice 1942-
See Cherryh, C. J.
See also CA 65-68; CANR 10

Cherryh, C. J. .... CLC 35
See also Cherry, Carolyn Janice
See also DLBY 80

Chesnutt, Charles W(addell)
1858-1932 .... TCLC 5, 39; BLC; SSC 7
See also BW 1; CA 106; 125; DAM MULT;
DLB 12, 50, 78; MTCW

Chester, Alfred 1929(?)-1971 .... CLC 49
See also CA 33-36R; DLB 130

Chesterton, G(ilbert) K(eith)
1874-1936 .... TCLC 1, 6; SSC 1
See also CA 104; 132; CDBLB 1914-1945;
DAM NOV, POET; DLB 10, 19, 34, 70,
98, 149; MTCW; SATA 27

Chiang Pin-chin 1904-1986
See Ding Ling
See also CA 118

Ch'ien Chung-shu 1910- .... CLC 22
See also CA 130; MTCW

Child, L. Maria
See Child, Lydia Maria

Child, Lydia Maria 1802-1880 .... NCLC 6
See also DLB 1, 74; SATA 67

Child, Mrs.
See Child, Lydia Maria

Child, Philip 1898-1978 .... CLC 19, 68
See also CA 13-14; CAP 1; SATA 47

Childress, Alice
1920-1994 .. CLC 12, 15, 86; BLC; DC 4
See also AAYA 8; BW 2; CA 45-48; 146;
CANR 3, 27, 50; CLR 14; DAM DRAM,
MULT, NOV; DLB 7, 38; JRDA;
MAICYA; MTCW; SATA 7, 48, 81

Chislett, (Margaret) Anne 1943- .... CLC 34

Chitty, Thomas Willes 1926- .... CLC 11
See also Hinde, Thomas
See also CA 5-8R

Chivers, Thomas Holley
1809-1858 .... NCLC 49
See also DLB 3

Chomette, Rene Lucien 1898-1981
See Clair, Rene
See also CA 103

Chopin, Kate
.... TCLC 5, 14; DA; DAB; SSC 8
See also Chopin, Katherine
See also CDALB 1865-1917; DLB 12, 78

Chopin, Katherine 1851-1904
See Chopin, Kate
See also CA 104; 122; DAC; DAM MST,
NOV

Chretien de Troyes
c. 12th cent. - .... CMLC 10

Christie
See Ichikawa, Kon

Christie, Agatha (Mary Clarissa)
1890-1976 ...... CLC 1, 6, 8, 12, 39, 48;
DAB; DAC
See also AAYA 9; AITN 1, 2; CA 17-20R;
61-64; CANR 10, 37; CDBLB 1914-1945;
DAM NOV; DLB 13, 77; MTCW;
SATA 36

Christie, (Ann) Philippa
See Pearce, Philippa
See also CA 5-8R; CANR 4

Christine de Pizan 1365(?)-1431(?) .... LC 9

Chubb, Elmer
See Masters, Edgar Lee

Chulkov, Mikhail Dmitrievich
1743-1792 .... LC 2
See also DLB 150

Churchill, Caryl 1938- ... CLC 31, 55; DC 5
See also CA 102; CANR 22, 46; DLB 13;
MTCW

Churchill, Charles 1731-1764 .... LC 3
See also DLB 109

Chute, Carolyn 1947- .... CLC 39
See also CA 123

Ciardi, John (Anthony)
1916-1986 .... CLC 10, 40, 44
See also CA 5-8R; 118; CAAS 2; CANR 5,
33; CLR 19; DAM POET; DLB 5;
DLBY 86; INT CANR-5; MAICYA;
MTCW; SATA 1, 65; SATA-Obit 46

Cicero, Marcus Tullius
106B.C.-43B.C. .... CMLC 3

Cimino, Michael 1943- .... CLC 16
See also CA 105

Cioran, E(mil) M. 1911- .... CLC 64
See also CA 25-28R

Cisneros, Sandra 1954- ...... CLC 69; HLC
See also AAYA 9; CA 131; DAM MULT;
DLB 122, 152; HW

Clair, Rene .... CLC 20
See also Chomette, Rene Lucien

Clampitt, Amy 1920-1994 .... CLC 32
See also CA 110; 146; CANR 29; DLB 105

Clancy, Thomas L., Jr. 1947-
See Clancy, Tom
See also CA 125; 131; INT 131; MTCW

Clancy, Tom .... CLC 45
See also Clancy, Thomas L., Jr.
See also AAYA 9; BEST 89:1, 90:1;
DAM NOV, POP

Clare, John 1793-1864 ...... NCLC 9; DAB
See also DAM POET; DLB 55, 96

Clarin
See Alas (y Urena), Leopoldo (Enrique
Garcia)

Clark, Al C.
See Goines, Donald

Clark, (Robert) Brian 1932- .... CLC 29
See also CA 41-44R

Clark, Curt
See Westlake, Donald E(dwin)

Clark, Eleanor 1913- .... CLC 5, 19
See also CA 9-12R; CANR 41; DLB 6

Clark, J. P.
See Clark, John Pepper
See also DLB 117

Clark, John Pepper
1935- .... CLC 38; BLC; DC 5
See also Clark, J. P.
See also BW 1; CA 65-68; CANR 16;
DAM DRAM, MULT

Clark, M. R.
See Clark, Mavis Thorpe

Clark, Mavis Thorpe 1909- .... CLC 12
See also CA 57-60; CANR 8, 37; CLR 30;
MAICYA; SAAS 5; SATA 8, 74

Clark, Walter Van Tilburg
1909-1971 .... CLC 28
See also CA 9-12R; 33-36R; DLB 9;
SATA 8

Clarke, Arthur C(harles)
1917- ..... CLC 1, 4, 13, 18, 35; SSC 3
See also AAYA 4; CA 1-4R; CANR 2, 28;
DAM POP; JRDA; MAICYA; MTCW;
SATA 13, 70

Clarke, Austin 1896-1974 .... CLC 6, 9
See also CA 29-32; 49-52; CAP 2;
DAM POET; DLB 10, 20

Clarke, Austin C(hesterfield)
1934- .... CLC 8, 53; BLC; DAC
See also BW 1; CA 25-28R; CAAS 16;
CANR 14, 32; DAM MULT; DLB 53,
125

Clarke, Gillian 1937- .... CLC 61
See also CA 106; DLB 40

Clarke, Marcus (Andrew Hislop)
    1846-1881 . . . . **NCLC 19**

Clarke, Shirley   1925- . . . . **CLC 16**

Clash, The
    See Headon, (Nicky) Topper; Jones, Mick;
    Simonon, Paul; Strummer, Joe

Claudel, Paul (Louis Charles Marie)
    1868-1955 . . . . **TCLC 2, 10**
    See also CA 104

Clavell, James (duMaresq)
    1925-1994 . . . . **CLC 6, 25, 87**
    See also CA 25-28R; 146; CANR 26, 48;
    DAM NOV, POP; MTCW

Cleaver, (Leroy) Eldridge
    1935- . . . . **CLC 30; BLC**
    See also BW 1; CA 21-24R; CANR 16;
    DAM MULT

Cleese, John (Marwood)   1939- . . . . . **CLC 21**
    See also Monty Python
    See also CA 112; 116; CANR 35; MTCW

Cleishbotham, Jebediah
    See Scott, Walter

Cleland, John   1710-1789 . . . . **LC 2**
    See also DLB 39

Clemens, Samuel Langhorne   1835-1910
    See Twain, Mark
    See also CA 104; 135; CDALB 1865-1917;
    DA; DAB; DAC; DAM MST, NOV;
    DLB 11, 12, 23, 64, 74; JRDA;
    MAICYA; YABC 2

Cleophil
    See Congreve, William

Clerihew, E.
    See Bentley, E(dmund) C(lerihew)

Clerk, N. W.
    See Lewis, C(live) S(taples)

Cliff, Jimmy . . . . **CLC 21**
    See also Chambers, James

Clifton, (Thelma) Lucille
    1936- . . . . **CLC 19, 66; BLC**
    See also BW 2; CA 49-52; CANR 2, 24, 42;
    CLR 5; DAM MULT, POET; DLB 5, 41;
    MAICYA; MTCW; SATA 20, 69

Clinton, Dirk
    See Silverberg, Robert

Clough, Arthur Hugh   1819-1861 . . **NCLC 27**
    See also DLB 32

Clutha, Janet Paterson Frame   1924-
    See Frame, Janet
    See also CA 1-4R; CANR 2, 36; MTCW

Clyne, Terence
    See Blatty, William Peter

Cobalt, Martin
    See Mayne, William (James Carter)

Cobbett, William   1763-1835 . . . . . **NCLC 49**
    See also DLB 43, 107, 158

Coburn, D(onald) L(ee)   1938- . . . . . . **CLC 10**
    See also CA 89-92

Cocteau, Jean (Maurice Eugene Clement)
    1889-1963 . . . . **CLC 1, 8, 15, 16, 43; DA;
                         DAB; DAC; WLC**
    See also CA 25-28; CANR 40; CAP 2;
    DAM DRAM, MST, NOV; DLB 65;
    MTCW

Codrescu, Andrei   1946- . . . . **CLC 46**
    See also CA 33-36R; CAAS 19; CANR 13,
    34; DAM POET

Coe, Max
    See Bourne, Randolph S(illiman)

Coe, Tucker
    See Westlake, Donald E(dwin)

Coetzee, J(ohn) M(ichael)
    1940- . . . . **CLC 23, 33, 66**
    See also CA 77-80; CANR 41; DAM NOV;
    MTCW

Coffey, Brian
    See Koontz, Dean R(ay)

Cohan, George M.   1878-1942 . . . . . **TCLC 60**

Cohen, Arthur A(llen)
    1928-1986 . . . . **CLC 7, 31**
    See also CA 1-4R; 120; CANR 1, 17, 42;
    DLB 28

Cohen, Leonard (Norman)
    1934- . . . . **CLC 3, 38; DAC**
    See also CA 21-24R; CANR 14;
    DAM MST; DLB 53; MTCW

Cohen, Matt   1942- . . . . **CLC 19; DAC**
    See also CA 61-64; CAAS 18; CANR 40;
    DLB 53

Cohen-Solal, Annie   19(?)- . . . . **CLC 50**

Colegate, Isabel   1931- . . . . **CLC 36**
    See also CA 17-20R; CANR 8, 22; DLB 14;
    INT CANR-22; MTCW

Coleman, Emmett
    See Reed, Ishmael

Coleridge, Samuel Taylor
    1772-1834 . . . . **NCLC 9; DA; DAB;
                              DAC; PC 11; WLC**
    See also CDBLB 1789-1832; DAM MST,
    POET; DLB 93, 107

Coleridge, Sara   1802-1852 . . . . **NCLC 31**

Coles, Don   1928- . . . . **CLC 46**
    See also CA 115; CANR 38

Colette, (Sidonie-Gabrielle)
    1873-1954 . . . . . . **TCLC 1, 5, 16; SSC 10**
    See also CA 104; 131; DAM NOV; DLB 65;
    MTCW

Collett, (Jacobine) Camilla (Wergeland)
    1813-1895 . . . . **NCLC 22**

Collier, Christopher   1930- . . . . **CLC 30**
    See also AAYA 13; CA 33-36R; CANR 13,
    33; JRDA; MAICYA; SATA 16, 70

Collier, James L(incoln)   1928- . . . . . **CLC 30**
    See also AAYA 13; CA 9-12R; CANR 4,
    33; CLR 3; DAM POP; JRDA;
    MAICYA; SAAS 21; SATA 8, 70

Collier, Jeremy   1650-1726 . . . . **LC 6**

Collier, John   1901-1980 . . . . **SSC 19**
    See also CA 65-68; 97-100; CANR 10;
    DLB 77

Collins, Hunt
    See Hunter, Evan

Collins, Linda   1931- . . . . **CLC 44**
    See also CA 125

Collins, (William) Wilkie
    1824-1889 . . . . **NCLC 1, 18**
    See also CDBLB 1832-1890; DLB 18, 70,
    159

Collins, William   1721-1759 . . . . **LC 4**
    See also DAM POET; DLB 109

Colman, George
    See Glassco, John

Colt, Winchester Remington
    See Hubbard, L(afayette) Ron(ald)

Colter, Cyrus   1910- . . . . **CLC 58**
    See also BW 1; CA 65-68; CANR 10;
    DLB 33

Colton, James
    See Hansen, Joseph

Colum, Padraic   1881-1972 . . . . **CLC 28**
    See also CA 73-76; 33-36R; CANR 35;
    CLR 36; MAICYA; MTCW; SATA 15

Colvin, James
    See Moorcock, Michael (John)

Colwin, Laurie (E.)
    1944-1992 . . . . **CLC 5, 13, 23, 84**
    See also CA 89-92; 139; CANR 20, 46;
    DLBY 80; MTCW

Comfort, Alex(ander)   1920- . . . . **CLC 7**
    See also CA 1-4R; CANR 1, 45; DAM POP

Comfort, Montgomery
    See Campbell, (John) Ramsey

Compton-Burnett, I(vy)
    1884(?)-1969 . . . . . . **CLC 1, 3, 10, 15, 34**
    See also CA 1-4R; 25-28R; CANR 4;
    DAM NOV; DLB 36; MTCW

Comstock, Anthony   1844-1915 . . . . **TCLC 13**
    See also CA 110

Conan Doyle, Arthur
    See Doyle, Arthur Conan

Conde, Maryse   1937- . . . . **CLC 52**
    See also Boucolon, Maryse
    See also BW 2; DAM MULT

Condillac, Etienne Bonnot de
    1714-1780 . . . . **LC 26**

Condon, Richard (Thomas)
    1915- . . . . **CLC 4, 6, 8, 10, 45**
    See also BEST 90:3; CA 1-4R; CAAS 1;
    CANR 2, 23; DAM NOV;
    INT CANR-23; MTCW

Congreve, William
    1670-1729 . . . . **LC 5, 21; DA; DAB;
                              DAC; DC 2; WLC**
    See also CDBLB 1660-1789; DAM DRAM,
    MST, POET; DLB 39, 84

Connell, Evan S(helby), Jr.
    1924- . . . . **CLC 4, 6, 45**
    See also AAYA 7; CA 1-4R; CAAS 2;
    CANR 2, 39; DAM NOV; DLB 2;
    DLBY 81; MTCW

Connelly, Marc(us Cook)
    1890-1980 . . . . **CLC 7**
    See also CA 85-88; 102; CANR 30; DLB 7;
    DLBY 80; SATA-Obit 25

Connor, Ralph . . . . **TCLC 31**
    See also Gordon, Charles William
    See also DLB 92

Conrad, Joseph
    1857-1924 . . . . **TCLC 1, 6, 13, 25, 43, 57;
                        DA; DAB; DAC; SSC 9; WLC**
    See also CA 104; 131; CDBLB 1890-1914;
    DAM MST, NOV; DLB 10, 34, 98, 156;
    MTCW; SATA 27

Conrad, Robert Arnold
See Hart, Moss

Conroy, Pat 1945-............ **CLC 30, 74**
See also AAYA 8; AITN 1; CA 85-88;
CANR 24; DAM NOV, POP; DLB 6;
MTCW

Constant (de Rebecque), (Henri) Benjamin
1767-1830 .... **NCLC 6**
See also DLB 119

Conybeare, Charles Augustus
See Eliot, T(homas) S(tearns)

Cook, Michael 1933- .... **CLC 58**
See also CA 93-96; DLB 53

Cook, Robin 1940- .... **CLC 14**
See also BEST 90:2; CA 108; 111;
CANR 41; DAM POP; INT 111

Cook, Roy
See Silverberg, Robert

Cooke, Elizabeth 1948- .... **CLC 55**
See also CA 129

Cooke, John Esten 1830-1886..... **NCLC 5**
See also DLB 3

Cooke, John Estes
See Baum, L(yman) Frank

Cooke, M. E.
See Creasey, John

Cooke, Margaret
See Creasey, John

Cooney, Ray .... **CLC 62**

Cooper, Douglas 1960-........... **CLC 86**

Cooper, Henry St. John
See Creasey, John

Cooper, J. California.............. **CLC 56**
See also AAYA 12; BW 1; CA 125;
DAM MULT

Cooper, James Fenimore
1789-1851 .... **NCLC 1, 27**
See also CDALB 1640-1865; DLB 3;
SATA 19

Coover, Robert (Lowell)
1932- .. CLC 3, 7, 15, 32, 46, 87; SSC 15
See also CA 45-48; CANR 3, 37;
DAM NOV; DLB 2; DLBY 81; MTCW

Copeland, Stewart (Armstrong)
1952- .... **CLC 26**

Coppard, A(lfred) E(dgar)
1878-1957 .... **TCLC 5; SSC 21**
See also CA 114; YABC 1

Coppee, Francois 1842-1908 ...... **TCLC 25**

Coppola, Francis Ford 1939-....... **CLC 16**
See also CA 77-80; CANR 40; DLB 44

Corbiere, Tristan 1845-1875 ..... **NCLC 43**

Corcoran, Barbara 1911-......... **CLC 17**
See also AAYA 14; CA 21-24R; CAAS 2;
CANR 11, 28, 48; DLB 52; JRDA;
SAAS 20; SATA 3, 77

Cordelier, Maurice
See Giraudoux, (Hippolyte) Jean

Corelli, Marie 1855-1924........ **TCLC 51**
See also Mackay, Mary
See also DLB 34, 156

Corman, Cid.................... **CLC 9**
See also Corman, Sidney
See also CAAS 2; DLB 5

Corman, Sidney 1924-
See Corman, Cid
See also CA 85-88; CANR 44; DAM POET

Cormier, Robert (Edmund)
1925- ..... CLC 12, 30; DA; DAB; DAC
See also AAYA 3; CA 1-4R; CANR 5, 23;
CDALB 1968-1988; CLR 12; DAM MST,
NOV; DLB 52; INT CANR-23; JRDA;
MAICYA; MTCW; SATA 10, 45, 83

Corn, Alfred (DeWitt III) 1943-.... **CLC 33**
See also CA 104; CANR 44; DLB 120;
DLBY 80

Corneille, Pierre 1606-1684.... **LC 28; DAB**
See also DAM MST

Cornwell, David (John Moore)
1931- .... **CLC 9, 15**
See also le Carre, John
See also CA 5-8R; CANR 13, 33;
DAM POP; MTCW

Corso, (Nunzio) Gregory 1930-... **CLC 1, 11**
See also CA 5-8R; CANR 41; DLB 5, 16;
MTCW

Cortazar, Julio
1914-1984 ...... CLC 2, 3, 5, 10, 13, 15,
33, 34; HLC; SSC 7
See also CA 21-24R; CANR 12, 32;
DAM MULT, NOV; DLB 113; HW;
MTCW

CORTES, HERNAN 1484-1547..... **LC 31**

Corwin, Cecil
See Kornbluth, C(yril) M.

Cosic, Dobrica 1921- .... **CLC 14**
See also CA 122; 138

Costain, Thomas B(ertram)
1885-1965 .... **CLC 30**
See also CA 5-8R; 25-28R; DLB 9

Costantini, Humberto
1924(?)-1987 .... **CLC 49**
See also CA 131; 122; HW

Costello, Elvis 1955-.............. **CLC 21**

Cotter, Joseph Seamon Sr.
1861-1949 .... **TCLC 28; BLC**
See also BW 1; CA 124; DAM MULT;
DLB 50

Couch, Arthur Thomas Quiller
See Quiller-Couch, Arthur Thomas

Coulton, James
See Hansen, Joseph

Couperus, Louis (Marie Anne)
1863-1923 .... **TCLC 15**
See also CA 115

Coupland, Douglas 1961-..... **CLC 85; DAC**
See also CA 142; DAM POP

Court, Wesli
See Turco, Lewis (Putnam)

Courtenay, Bryce 1933-........... **CLC 59**
See also CA 138

Courtney, Robert
See Ellison, Harlan (Jay)

Cousteau, Jacques-Yves 1910-...... **CLC 30**
See also CA 65-68; CANR 15; MTCW;
SATA 38

Coward, Noel (Peirce)
1899-1973 .... **CLC 1, 9, 29, 51**
See also AITN 1; CA 17-18; 41-44R;
CANR 35; CAP 2; CDBLB 1914-1945;
DAM DRAM; DLB 10; MTCW

Cowley, Malcolm 1898-1989 .... **CLC 39**
See also CA 5-8R; 128; CANR 3; DLB 4,
48; DLBY 81, 89; MTCW

Cowper, William 1731-1800....... **NCLC 8**
See also DAM POET; DLB 104, 109

Cox, William Trevor 1928- ... **CLC 9, 14, 71**
See also Trevor, William
See also CA 9-12R; CANR 4, 37;
DAM NOV; DLB 14; INT CANR-37;
MTCW

Coyne, P. J.
See Masters, Hilary

Cozzens, James Gould
1903-1978 .... **CLC 1, 4, 11**
See also CA 9-12R; 81-84; CANR 19;
CDALB 1941-1968; DLB 9; DLBD 2;
DLBY 84; MTCW

Crabbe, George 1754-1832....... **NCLC 26**
See also DLB 93

Craig, A. A.
See Anderson, Poul (William)

Craik, Dinah Maria (Mulock)
1826-1887 .... **NCLC 38**
See also DLB 35; MAICYA; SATA 34

Cram, Ralph Adams 1863-1942.... **TCLC 45**

Crane, (Harold) Hart
1899-1932 .... **TCLC 2, 5; DA; DAB;**
DAC; PC 3; WLC
See also CA 104; 127; CDALB 1917-1929;
DAM MST, POET; DLB 4, 48; MTCW

Crane, R(onald) S(almon)
1886-1967 .... **CLC 27**
See also CA 85-88; DLB 63

Crane, Stephen (Townley)
1871-1900 .... **TCLC 11, 17, 32; DA;**
DAB; DAC; SSC 7; WLC
See also CA 109; 140; CDALB 1865-1917;
DAM MST, NOV, POET; DLB 12, 54,
78; YABC 2

Crase, Douglas 1944-............. **CLC 58**
See also CA 106

Crashaw, Richard 1612(?)-1649...... **LC 24**
See also DLB 126

Craven, Margaret
1901-1980 .... **CLC 17; DAC**
See also CA 103

Crawford, F(rancis) Marion
1854-1909 .... **TCLC 10**
See also CA 107; DLB 71

Crawford, Isabella Valancy
1850-1887 .... **NCLC 12**
See also DLB 92

Crayon, Geoffrey
See Irving, Washington

Creasey, John 1908-1973 .... **CLC 11**
See also CA 5-8R; 41-44R; CANR 8;
DLB 77; MTCW

Crebillon, Claude Prosper Jolyot de (fils)
1707-1777 .... **LC 28**

Credo
  See Creasey, John

Creeley, Robert (White)
  1926- ..... **CLC 1, 2, 4, 8, 11, 15, 36, 78**
  See also CA 1-4R; CAAS 10; CANR 23, 43;
  DAM POET; DLB 5, 16; MTCW

Crews, Harry (Eugene)
  1935- .... **CLC 6, 23, 49**
  See also AITN 1; CA 25-28R; CANR 20;
  DLB 6, 143; MTCW

Crichton, (John) Michael
  1942- .... **CLC 2, 6, 54, 90**
  See also AAYA 10; AITN 2; CA 25-28R;
  CANR 13, 40; DAM NOV, POP;
  DLBY 81; INT CANR-13; JRDA;
  MTCW; SATA 9

Crispin, Edmund .... **CLC 22**
  See also Montgomery, (Robert) Bruce
  See also DLB 87

Cristofer, Michael 1945(?)- .... **CLC 28**
  See also CA 110; DAM DRAM; DLB 7

Croce, Benedetto 1866-1952 ...... **TCLC 37**
  See also CA 120

Crockett, David 1786-1836 .... **NCLC 8**
  See also DLB 3, 11

Crockett, Davy
  See Crockett, David

Crofts, Freeman Wills
  1879-1957 .... **TCLC 55**
  See also CA 115; DLB 77

Croker, John Wilson 1780-1857 .. **NCLC 10**
  See also DLB 110

Crommelynck, Fernand 1885-1970 .. **CLC 75**
  See also CA 89-92

Cronin, A(rchibald) J(oseph)
  1896-1981 .... **CLC 32**
  See also CA 1-4R; 102; CANR 5; SATA 47;
  SATA-Obit 25

Cross, Amanda
  See Heilbrun, Carolyn G(old)

Crothers, Rachel 1878(?)-1958..... **TCLC 19**
  See also CA 113; DLB 7

Croves, Hal
  See Traven, B.

Crowfield, Christopher
  See Stowe, Harriet (Elizabeth) Beecher

Crowley, Aleister.................. **TCLC 7**
  See also Crowley, Edward Alexander

Crowley, Edward Alexander 1875-1947
  See Crowley, Aleister
  See also CA 104

Crowley, John 1942-.............. **CLC 57**
  See also CA 61-64; CANR 43; DLBY 82;
  SATA 65

Crud
  See Crumb, R(obert)

Crumarums
  See Crumb, R(obert)

Crumb, R(obert) 1943-............ **CLC 17**
  See also CA 106

Crumbum
  See Crumb, R(obert)

Crumski
  See Crumb, R(obert)

Crum the Bum
  See Crumb, R(obert)

Crunk
  See Crumb, R(obert)

Crustt
  See Crumb, R(obert)

Cryer, Gretchen (Kiger) 1935-...... **CLC 21**
  See also CA 114; 123

Csath, Geza 1887-1919.......... **TCLC 13**
  See also CA 111

Cudlip, David 1933- .... **CLC 34**

Cullen, Countee
  1903-1946 ...... **TCLC 4, 37; BLC; DA;**
                                                DAC
  See also BW 1; CA 108; 124;
  CDALB 1917-1929; DAM MST, MULT,
  POET; DLB 4, 48, 51; MTCW; SATA 18

Cum, R.
  See Crumb, R(obert)

Cummings, Bruce F(rederick) 1889-1919
  See Barbellion, W. N. P.
  See also CA 123

Cummings, E(dward) E(stlin)
  1894-1962 ...... **CLC 1, 3, 8, 12, 15, 68;**
                                    DA; DAB; DAC; PC 5; WLC 2
  See also CA 73-76; CANR 31;
  CDALB 1929-1941; DAM MST, POET;
  DLB 4, 48; MTCW

Cunha, Euclides (Rodrigues Pimenta) da
  1866-1909 .... **TCLC 24**
  See also CA 123

Cunningham, E. V.
  See Fast, Howard (Melvin)

Cunningham, J(ames) V(incent)
  1911-1985 .... **CLC 3, 31**
  See also CA 1-4R; 115; CANR 1; DLB 5

Cunningham, Julia (Woolfolk)
  1916- .... **CLC 12**
  See also CA 9-12R; CANR 4, 19, 36;
  JRDA; MAICYA; SAAS 2; SATA 1, 26

Cunningham, Michael 1952- .... **CLC 34**
  See also CA 136

Cunninghame Graham, R(obert) B(ontine)
  1852-1936 .... **TCLC 19**
  See also Graham, R(obert) B(ontine)
  Cunninghame
  See also CA 119; DLB 98

Currie, Ellen 19(?)-............... **CLC 44**

Curtin, Philip
  See Lowndes, Marie Adelaide (Belloc)

Curtis, Price
  See Ellison, Harlan (Jay)

Cutrate, Joe
  See Spiegelman, Art

Czaczkes, Shmuel Yosef
  See Agnon, S(hmuel) Y(osef Halevi)

Dabrowska, Maria (Szumska)
  1889-1965 .... **CLC 15**
  See also CA 106

Dabydeen, David 1955- .... **CLC 34**
  See also BW 1; CA 125

Dacey, Philip 1939- .... **CLC 51**
  See also CA 37-40R; CAAS 17; CANR 14,
  32; DLB 105

Dagerman, Stig (Halvard)
  1923-1954 .... **TCLC 17**
  See also CA 117

Dahl, Roald
  1916-1990 ...... **CLC 1, 6, 18, 79; DAB;**
                                                                DAC
  See also AAYA 15; CA 1-4R; 133;
  CANR 6, 32, 37; CLR 1, 7; DAM MST,
  NOV, POP; DLB 139; JRDA; MAICYA;
  MTCW; SATA 1, 26, 73; SATA-Obit 65

Dahlberg, Edward 1900-1977... **CLC 1, 7, 14**
  See also CA 9-12R; 69-72; CANR 31;
  DLB 48; MTCW

Dale, Colin..................... **TCLC 18**
  See also Lawrence, T(homas) E(dward)

Dale, George E.
  See Asimov, Isaac

Daly, Elizabeth 1878-1967........ **CLC 52**
  See also CA 23-24; 25-28R; CAP 2

Daly, Maureen 1921-............. **CLC 17**
  See also AAYA 5; CANR 37; JRDA;
  MAICYA; SAAS 1; SATA 2

Damas, Leon-Gontran 1912-1978 ... **CLC 84**
  See also BW 1; CA 125; 73-76

Dana, Richard Henry Sr.
  1787-1879 .... **NCLC 53**

Daniel, Samuel 1562(?)-1619........ **LC 24**
  See also DLB 62

Daniels, Brett
  See Adler, Renata

Dannay, Frederic 1905-1982 .... **CLC 11**
  See also Queen, Ellery
  See also CA 1-4R; 107; CANR 1, 39;
  DAM POP; DLB 137; MTCW

D'Annunzio, Gabriele
  1863-1938 .... **TCLC 6, 40**
  See also CA 104

d'Antibes, Germain
  See Simenon, Georges (Jacques Christian)

Danvers, Dennis 1947-............ **CLC 70**

Danziger, Paula 1944- .... **CLC 21**
  See also AAYA 4; CA 112; 115; CANR 37;
  CLR 20; JRDA; MAICYA; SATA 36,
  63; SATA-Brief 30

Da Ponte, Lorenzo 1749-1838.... **NCLC 50**

Dario, Ruben 1867-1916 .... **TCLC 4; HLC**
  See also CA 131; DAM MULT; HW;
  MTCW

Darley, George 1795-1846 .... **NCLC 2**
  See also DLB 96

Daryush, Elizabeth 1887-1977.... **CLC 6, 19**
  See also CA 49-52; CANR 3; DLB 20

Dashwood, Edmee Elizabeth Monica de la
  Pasture 1890-1943
  See Delafield, E. M.
  See also CA 119

Daudet, (Louis Marie) Alphonse
  1840-1897 .... **NCLC 1**
  See also DLB 123

Daumal, Rene 1908-1944........ **TCLC 14**
  See also CA 114

Davenport, Guy (Mattison, Jr.)
  1927- .... **CLC 6, 14, 38; SSC 16**
  See also CA 33-36R; CANR 23; DLB 130

Davidson, Avram 1923-
See Queen, Ellery
See also CA 101; CANR 26; DLB 8

Davidson, Donald (Grady)
1893-1968 . . . . **CLC 2, 13, 19**
See also CA 5-8R; 25-28R; CANR 4;
DLB 45

Davidson, Hugh
See Hamilton, Edmond

Davidson, John 1857-1909 . . . . **TCLC 24**
See also CA 118; DLB 19

Davidson, Sara 1943- . . . . **CLC 9**
See also CA 81-84; CANR 44

Davie, Donald (Alfred)
1922- . . . . **CLC 5, 8, 10, 31**
See also CA 1-4R; CAAS 3; CANR 1, 44;
DLB 27; MTCW

Davies, Ray(mond Douglas) 1944- . . **CLC 21**
See also CA 116; 146

Davies, Rhys 1903-1978 . . . . **CLC 23**
See also CA 9-12R; 81-84; CANR 4;
DLB 139

Davies, (William) Robertson
1913- . . . . . **CLC 2, 7, 13, 25, 42, 75; DA;**
DAB; DAC; WLC
See also BEST 89:2; CA 33-36R; CANR 17,
42; DAM MST, NOV, POP; DLB 68;
INT CANR-17; MTCW

Davies, W(illiam) H(enry)
1871-1940 . . . . **TCLC 5**
See also CA 104; DLB 19

Davies, Walter C.
See Kornbluth, C(yril) M.

Davis, Angela (Yvonne) 1944- . . . . . . **CLC 77**
See also BW 2; CA 57-60; CANR 10;
DAM MULT

Davis, B. Lynch
See Bioy Casares, Adolfo; Borges, Jorge
Luis

Davis, Gordon
See Hunt, E(verette) Howard, (Jr.)

Davis, Harold Lenoir 1896-1960 . . . . **CLC 49**
See also CA 89-92; DLB 9

Davis, Rebecca (Blaine) Harding
1831-1910 . . . . **TCLC 6**
See also CA 104; DLB 74

Davis, Richard Harding
1864-1916 . . . . **TCLC 24**
See also CA 114; DLB 12, 23, 78, 79;
DLBD 13

Davison, Frank Dalby 1893-1970 . . . **CLC 15**
See also CA 116

Davison, Lawrence H.
See Lawrence, D(avid) H(erbert Richards)

Davison, Peter (Hubert) 1928- . . . . . **CLC 28**
See also CA 9-12R; CAAS 4; CANR 3, 43;
DLB 5

Davys, Mary 1674-1732 . . . . **LC 1**
See also DLB 39

Dawson, Fielding 1930- . . . . **CLC 6**
See also CA 85-88; DLB 130

Dawson, Peter
See Faust, Frederick (Schiller)

Day, Clarence (Shepard, Jr.)
1874-1935 . . . . **TCLC 25**
See also CA 108; DLB 11

Day, Thomas 1748-1789 . . . . **LC 1**
See also DLB 39; YABC 1

Day Lewis, C(ecil)
1904-1972 . . . . **CLC 1, 6, 10; PC 11**
See also Blake, Nicholas
See also CA 13-16; 33-36R; CANR 34;
CAP 1; DAM POET; DLB 15, 20;
MTCW

Dazai, Osamu . . . . **TCLC 11**
See also Tsushima, Shuji

de Andrade, Carlos Drummond
See Drummond de Andrade, Carlos

Deane, Norman
See Creasey, John

de Beauvoir, Simone (Lucie Ernestine Marie
Bertrand)
See Beauvoir, Simone (Lucie Ernestine
Marie Bertrand) de

de Brissac, Malcolm
See Dickinson, Peter (Malcolm)

de Chardin, Pierre Teilhard
See Teilhard de Chardin, (Marie Joseph)
Pierre

Dee, John 1527-1608 . . . . **LC 20**

Deer, Sandra 1940- . . . . **CLC 45**

De Ferrari, Gabriella 1941- . . . . **CLC 65**
See also CA 146

Defoe, Daniel
1660(?)-1731 . . . . **LC 1; DA; DAB; DAC;**
WLC
See also CDBLB 1660-1789; DAM MST,
NOV; DLB 39, 95, 101; JRDA;
MAICYA; SATA 22

de Gourmont, Remy
See Gourmont, Remy de

de Hartog, Jan 1914- . . . . **CLC 19**
See also CA 1-4R; CANR 1

de Hostos, E. M.
See Hostos (y Bonilla), Eugenio Maria de

de Hostos, Eugenio M.
See Hostos (y Bonilla), Eugenio Maria de

Deighton, Len . . . . **CLC 4, 7, 22, 46**
See also Deighton, Leonard Cyril
See also AAYA 6; BEST 89:2;
CDBLB 1960 to Present; DLB 87

Deighton, Leonard Cyril 1929-
See Deighton, Len
See also CA 9-12R; CANR 19, 33;
DAM NOV, POP; MTCW

Dekker, Thomas 1572(?)-1632 . . . . . . **LC 22**
See also CDBLB Before 1660;
DAM DRAM; DLB 62

Delafield, E. M. 1890-1943 . . . . **TCLC 61**
See also Dashwood, Edmee Elizabeth
Monica de la Pasture
See also DLB 34

de la Mare, Walter (John)
1873-1956 . . . . **TCLC 4, 53; DAB; DAC;**
SSC 14; WLC
See also CDBLB 1914-1945; CLR 23;
DAM MST, POET; DLB 19, 153;
SATA 16

Delaney, Franey
See O'Hara, John (Henry)

Delaney, Shelagh 1939- . . . . **CLC 29**
See also CA 17-20R; CANR 30;
CDBLB 1960 to Present; DAM DRAM;
DLB 13; MTCW

Delany, Mary (Granville Pendarves)
1700-1788 . . . . **LC 12**

Delany, Samuel R(ay, Jr.)
1942- . . . . **CLC 8, 14, 38; BLC**
See also BW 2; CA 81-84; CANR 27, 43;
DAM MULT; DLB 8, 33; MTCW

De La Ramee, (Marie) Louise 1839-1908
See Ouida
See also SATA 20

de la Roche, Mazo 1879-1961 . . . . . . **CLC 14**
See also CA 85-88; CANR 30; DLB 68;
SATA 64

Delbanco, Nicholas (Franklin)
1942- . . . . **CLC 6, 13**
See also CA 17-20R; CAAS 2; CANR 29;
DLB 6

del Castillo, Michel 1933- . . . . **CLC 38**
See also CA 109

Deledda, Grazia (Cosima)
1875(?)-1936 . . . . **TCLC 23**
See also CA 123

Delibes, Miguel . . . . **CLC 8, 18**
See also Delibes Setien, Miguel

Delibes Setien, Miguel 1920-
See Delibes, Miguel
See also CA 45-48; CANR 1, 32; HW;
MTCW

DeLillo, Don
1936- . . . . . **CLC 8, 10, 13, 27, 39, 54, 76**
See also BEST 89:1; CA 81-84; CANR 21;
DAM NOV, POP; DLB 6; MTCW

de Lisser, H. G.
See De Lisser, Herbert George
See also DLB 117

De Lisser, Herbert George
1878-1944 . . . . **TCLC 12**
See also de Lisser, H. G.
See also BW 2; CA 109

Deloria, Vine (Victor), Jr. 1933- . . . . **CLC 21**
See also CA 53-56; CANR 5, 20, 48;
DAM MULT; MTCW; NNAL; SATA 21

Del Vecchio, John M(ichael)
1947- . . . . **CLC 29**
See also CA 110; DLBD 9

de Man, Paul (Adolph Michel)
1919-1983 . . . . **CLC 55**
See also CA 128; 111; DLB 67; MTCW

De Marinis, Rick 1934- . . . . **CLC 54**
See also CA 57-60; CANR 9, 25, 50

Demby, William 1922- . . . . **CLC 53; BLC**
See also BW 1; CA 81-84; DAM MULT;
DLB 33

Demijohn, Thom
See Disch, Thomas M(ichael)

de Montherlant, Henry (Milon)
See Montherlant, Henry (Milon) de

Demosthenes 384B.C.-322B.C. . . . . **CMLC 13**

de Natale, Francine
See Malzberg, Barry N(athaniel)

Denby, Edwin (Orr) 1903-1983 . . . . . **CLC 48**
See also CA 138; 110

Denis, Julio
See Cortazar, Julio

Denmark, Harrison
See Zelazny, Roger (Joseph)

Dennis, John 1658-1734 . . . . **LC 11**
See also DLB 101

Dennis, Nigel (Forbes) 1912-1989 . . . . **CLC 8**
See also CA 25-28R; 129; DLB 13, 15;
MTCW

De Palma, Brian (Russell) 1940- . . . . **CLC 20**
See also CA 109

De Quincey, Thomas 1785-1859 . . . **NCLC 4**
See also CDBLB 1789-1832; DLB 110; 144

Deren, Eleanora 1908(?)-1961
See Deren, Maya
See also CA 111

Deren, Maya . . . . **CLC 16**
See also Deren, Eleanora

Derleth, August (William)
1909-1971 . . . . **CLC 31**
See also CA 1-4R; 29-32R; CANR 4;
DLB 9; SATA 5

Der Nister 1884-1950 . . . . **TCLC 56**

de Routisie, Albert
See Aragon, Louis

Derrida, Jacques 1930- . . . . **CLC 24, 87**
See also CA 124; 127

Derry Down Derry
See Lear, Edward

Dersonnes, Jacques
See Simenon, Georges (Jacques Christian)

Desai, Anita 1937- . . . . . . **CLC 19, 37; DAB**
See also CA 81-84; CANR 33; DAM NOV;
MTCW; SATA 63

de Saint-Luc, Jean
See Glassco, John

de Saint Roman, Arnaud
See Aragon, Louis

Descartes, Rene 1596-1650 . . . . **LC 20**

De Sica, Vittorio 1901(?)-1974 . . . . . **CLC 20**
See also CA 117

Desnos, Robert 1900-1945 . . . . **TCLC 22**
See also CA 121

Destouches, Louis-Ferdinand
1894-1961 . . . . **CLC 9, 15**
See also Celine, Louis-Ferdinand
See also CA 85-88; CANR 28; MTCW

Deutsch, Babette 1895-1982 . . . . **CLC 18**
See also CA 1-4R; 108; CANR 4; DLB 45;
SATA 1; SATA-Obit 33

Devenant, William 1606-1649 . . . . . . **LC 13**

Devkota, Laxmiprasad
1909-1959 . . . . **TCLC 23**
See also CA 123

De Voto, Bernard (Augustine)
1897-1955 . . . . **TCLC 29**
See also CA 113; DLB 9

De Vries, Peter
1910-1993 . . . . **CLC 1, 2, 3, 7, 10, 28, 46**
See also CA 17-20R; 142; CANR 41;
DAM NOV; DLB 6; DLBY 82; MTCW

Dexter, Martin
See Faust, Frederick (Schiller)

Dexter, Pete 1943- . . . . **CLC 34, 55**
See also BEST 89:2; CA 127; 131;
DAM POP; INT 131; MTCW

Diamano, Silmang
See Senghor, Leopold Sedar

Diamond, Neil 1941- . . . . **CLC 30**
See also CA 108

Diaz del Castillo, Bernal 1496-1584 . . **LC 31**

di Bassetto, Corno
See Shaw, George Bernard

Dick, Philip K(indred)
1928-1982 . . . . **CLC 10, 30, 72**
See also CA 49-52; 106; CANR 2, 16;
DAM NOV, POP; DLB 8; MTCW

Dickens, Charles (John Huffam)
1812-1870 . . . . . . **NCLC 3, 8, 18, 26, 37,**
50; DA; DAB; DAC; SSC 17; WLC
See also CDBLB 1832-1890; DAM MST,
NOV; DLB 21, 55, 70, 159; JRDA;
MAICYA; SATA 15

Dickey, James (Lafayette)
1923- . . . . **CLC 1, 2, 4, 7, 10, 15, 47**
See also AITN 1, 2; CA 9-12R; CABS 2;
CANR 10, 48; CDALB 1968-1988;
DAM NOV, POET, POP; DLB 5;
DLBD 7; DLBY 82, 93; INT CANR-10;
MTCW

Dickey, William 1928-1994 . . . . . . **CLC 3, 28**
See also CA 9-12R; 145; CANR 24; DLB 5

Dickinson, Charles 1951- . . . . **CLC 49**
See also CA 128

Dickinson, Emily (Elizabeth)
1830-1886 . . . . **NCLC 21; DA; DAB;**
DAC; PC 1; WLC
See also CDALB 1865-1917; DAM MST,
POET; DLB 1; SATA 29

Dickinson, Peter (Malcolm)
1927- . . . . **CLC 12, 35**
See also AAYA 9; CA 41-44R; CANR 31;
CLR 29; DLB 87, 161; JRDA; MAICYA;
SATA 5, 62

Dickson, Carr
See Carr, John Dickson

Dickson, Carter
See Carr, John Dickson

Diderot, Denis 1713-1784 . . . . **LC 26**

Didion, Joan 1934- . . . . . **CLC 1, 3, 8, 14, 32**
See also AITN 1; CA 5-8R; CANR 14;
CDALB 1968-1988; DAM NOV; DLB 2;
DLBY 81, 86; MTCW

Dietrich, Robert
See Hunt, E(verette) Howard, (Jr.)

Dillard, Annie 1945- . . . . **CLC 9, 60**
See also AAYA 6; CA 49-52; CANR 3, 43;
DAM NOV; DLBY 80; MTCW;
SATA 10

Dillard, R(ichard) H(enry) W(ilde)
1937- . . . . **CLC 5**
See also CA 21-24R; CAAS 7; CANR 10;
DLB 5

Dillon, Eilis 1920-1994 . . . . **CLC 17**
See also CA 9-12R; 147; CAAS 3; CANR 4,
38; CLR 26; MAICYA; SATA 2, 74;
SATA-Obit 83

Dimont, Penelope
See Mortimer, Penelope (Ruth)

Dinesen, Isak . . . . **CLC 10, 29; SSC 7**
See also Blixen, Karen (Christentze
Dinesen)

Ding Ling . . . . **CLC 68**
See also Chiang Pin-chin

Disch, Thomas M(ichael) 1940- . . . **CLC 7, 36**
See also AAYA 17; CA 21-24R; CAAS 4;
CANR 17, 36; CLR 18; DLB 8;
MAICYA; MTCW; SAAS 15; SATA 54

Disch, Tom
See Disch, Thomas M(ichael)

d'Isly, Georges
See Simenon, Georges (Jacques Christian)

Disraeli, Benjamin 1804-1881 . . **NCLC 2, 39**
See also DLB 21, 55

Ditcum, Steve
See Crumb, R(obert)

Dixon, Paige
See Corcoran, Barbara

Dixon, Stephen 1936- . . . . . **CLC 52; SSC 16**
See also CA 89-92; CANR 17, 40; DLB 130

Dobell, Sydney Thompson
1824-1874 . . . . **NCLC 43**
See also DLB 32

Doblin, Alfred . . . . **TCLC 13**
See also Doeblin, Alfred

Dobrolyubov, Nikolai Alexandrovich
1836-1861 . . . . **NCLC 5**

Dobyns, Stephen 1941- . . . . **CLC 37**
See also CA 45-48; CANR 2, 18

Doctorow, E(dgar) L(aurence)
1931- . . . . . **CLC 6, 11, 15, 18, 37, 44, 65**
See also AITN 2; BEST 89:3; CA 45-48;
CANR 2, 33; CDALB 1968-1988;
DAM NOV, POP; DLB 2, 28; DLBY 80;
MTCW

Dodgson, Charles Lutwidge 1832-1898
See Carroll, Lewis
See also CLR 2; DA; DAB; DAC;
DAM MST, NOV, POET; MAICYA;
YABC 2

Dodson, Owen (Vincent)
1914-1983 . . . . **CLC 79; BLC**
See also BW 1; CA 65-68; 110; CANR 24;
DAM MULT; DLB 76

Doeblin, Alfred 1878-1957 . . . . **TCLC 13**
See also Doblin, Alfred
See also CA 110; 141; DLB 66

Doerr, Harriet 1910- . . . . **CLC 34**
See also CA 117; 122; CANR 47; INT 122

Domecq, H(onorio) Bustos
See Bioy Casares, Adolfo; Borges, Jorge
Luis

Domini, Rey
See Lorde, Audre (Geraldine)

Dominique
See Proust, (Valentin-Louis-George-Eugene-)
Marcel

Don, A
See Stephen, Leslie

Donaldson, Stephen R. 1947- . . . . **CLC 46**
See also CA 89-92; CANR 13; DAM POP;
INT CANR-13

Donleavy, J(ames) P(atrick)
1926- . . . . CLC **1, 4, 6, 10, 45**
See also AITN 2; CA 9-12R; CANR 24, 49;
DLB 6; INT CANR-24; MTCW

Donne, John
1572-1631 . . . . LC **10, 24; DA; DAB;**
DAC; PC 1
See also CDBLB Before 1660; DAM MST,
POET; DLB 121, 151

Donnell, David 1939(?)- . . . . CLC **34**

Donoghue, P. S.
See Hunt, E(verette) Howard, (Jr.)

Donoso (Yanez), Jose
1924- . . . . CLC **4, 8, 11, 32; HLC**
See also CA 81-84; CANR 32;
DAM MULT; DLB 113; HW; MTCW

Donovan, John 1928-1992 . . . . CLC **35**
See also CA 97-100; 137; CLR 3;
MAICYA; SATA 72; SATA-Brief 29

Don Roberto
See Cunninghame Graham, R(obert)
B(ontine)

Doolittle, Hilda
1886-1961 . . . . . CLC **3, 8, 14, 31, 34, 73;**
DA; DAC; PC 5; WLC
See also H. D.
See also CA 97-100; CANR 35; DAM MST,
POET; DLB 4, 45; MTCW

Dorfman, Ariel 1942- . . . . CLC **48, 77; HLC**
See also CA 124; 130; DAM MULT; HW;
INT 130

Dorn, Edward (Merton) 1929- . . . CLC **10, 18**
See also CA 93-96; CANR 42; DLB 5;
INT 93-96

Dorsan, Luc
See Simenon, Georges (Jacques Christian)

Dorsange, Jean
See Simenon, Georges (Jacques Christian)

Dos Passos, John (Roderigo)
1896-1970 . . . . . . CLC **1, 4, 8, 11, 15, 25,**
34, 82; DA; DAB; DAC; WLC
See also CA 1-4R; 29-32R; CANR 3;
CDALB 1929-1941; DAM MST, NOV;
DLB 4, 9; DLBD 1; MTCW

Dossage, Jean
See Simenon, Georges (Jacques Christian)

Dostoevsky, Fedor Mikhailovich
1821-1881 . . . . . . NCLC **2, 7, 21, 33, 43;**
DA; DAB; DAC; SSC 2; WLC
See also DAM MST, NOV

Doughty, Charles M(ontagu)
1843-1926 . . . . TCLC **27**
See also CA 115; DLB 19, 57

Douglas, Ellen . . . . CLC **73**
See also Haxton, Josephine Ayres;
Williamson, Ellen Douglas

Douglas, Gavin 1475(?)-1522 . . . . LC **20**

Douglas, Keith 1920-1944 . . . . TCLC **40**
See also DLB 27

Douglas, Leonard
See Bradbury, Ray (Douglas)

Douglas, Michael
See Crichton, (John) Michael

Douglass, Frederick
1817(?)-1895 . . . . . . NCLC **7; BLC; DA;**
DAC; WLC
See also CDALB 1640-1865; DAM MST,
MULT; DLB 1, 43, 50, 79; SATA 29

Dourado, (Waldomiro Freitas) Autran
1926- . . . . CLC **23, 60**
See also CA 25-28R; CANR 34

Dourado, Waldomiro Autran
See Dourado, (Waldomiro Freitas) Autran

Dove, Rita (Frances)
1952- . . . . CLC **50, 81; PC 6**
See also BW 2; CA 109; CAAS 19;
CANR 27, 42; DAM MULT, POET;
DLB 120

Dowell, Coleman 1925-1985 . . . . CLC **60**
See also CA 25-28R; 117; CANR 10;
DLB 130

Dowson, Ernest Christopher
1867-1900 . . . . TCLC **4**
See also CA 105; DLB 19, 135

Doyle, A. Conan
See Doyle, Arthur Conan

Doyle, Arthur Conan
1859-1930 . . . . TCLC **7; DA; DAB;**
DAC; SSC 12; WLC
See also AAYA 14; CA 104; 122;
CDBLB 1890-1914; DAM MST, NOV;
DLB 18, 70, 156; MTCW; SATA 24

Doyle, Conan
See Doyle, Arthur Conan

Doyle, John
See Graves, Robert (von Ranke)

Doyle, Roddy 1958(?)- . . . . CLC **81**
See also AAYA 14; CA 143

Doyle, Sir A. Conan
See Doyle, Arthur Conan

Doyle, Sir Arthur Conan
See Doyle, Arthur Conan

Dr. A
See Asimov, Isaac; Silverstein, Alvin

Drabble, Margaret
1939- . . . . CLC **2, 3, 5, 8, 10, 22, 53;**
DAB; DAC
See also CA 13-16R; CANR 18, 35;
CDBLB 1960 to Present; DAM MST,
NOV, POP; DLB 14, 155; MTCW;
SATA 48

Drapier, M. B.
See Swift, Jonathan

Drayham, James
See Mencken, H(enry) L(ouis)

Drayton, Michael 1563-1631 . . . . LC **8**

Dreadstone, Carl
See Campbell, (John) Ramsey

Dreiser, Theodore (Herman Albert)
1871-1945 . . . . . . TCLC **10, 18, 35; DA;**
DAC; WLC
See also CA 106; 132; CDALB 1865-1917;
DAM MST, NOV; DLB 9, 12, 102, 137;
DLBD 1; MTCW

Drexler, Rosalyn 1926- . . . . CLC **2, 6**
See also CA 81-84

Dreyer, Carl Theodor 1889-1968 . . . . CLC **16**
See also CA 116

Drieu la Rochelle, Pierre(-Eugene)
1893-1945 . . . . TCLC **21**
See also CA 117; DLB 72

Drinkwater, John 1882-1937 . . . . . TCLC **57**
See also CA 109; 149; DLB 10, 19, 149

Drop Shot
See Cable, George Washington

Droste-Hulshoff, Annette Freiin von
1797-1848 . . . . NCLC **3**
See also DLB 133

Drummond, Walter
See Silverberg, Robert

Drummond, William Henry
1854-1907 . . . . TCLC **25**
See also DLB 92

Drummond de Andrade, Carlos
1902-1987 . . . . CLC **18**
See also Andrade, Carlos Drummond de
See also CA 132; 123

Drury, Allen (Stuart) 1918- . . . . CLC **37**
See also CA 57-60; CANR 18;
INT CANR-18

Dryden, John
1631-1700 . . . . LC **3, 21; DA; DAB;**
DAC; DC 3; WLC
See also CDBLB 1660-1789; DAM DRAM,
MST, POET; DLB 80, 101, 131

Duberman, Martin 1930- . . . . CLC **8**
See also CA 1-4R; CANR 2

Dubie, Norman (Evans) 1945- . . . . . . CLC **36**
See also CA 69-72; CANR 12; DLB 120

Du Bois, W(illiam) E(dward) B(urghardt)
1868-1963 . . . . . . CLC **1, 2, 13, 64; BLC;**
DA; DAC; WLC
See also BW 1; CA 85-88; CANR 34;
CDALB 1865-1917; DAM MST, MULT,
NOV; DLB 47, 50, 91; MTCW; SATA 42

Dubus, Andre 1936- . . . CLC **13, 36; SSC 15**
See also CA 21-24R; CANR 17; DLB 130;
INT CANR-17

Duca Minimo
See D'Annunzio, Gabriele

Ducharme, Rejean 1941- . . . . CLC **74**
See also DLB 60

Duclos, Charles Pinot 1704-1772 . . . . . LC **1**

Dudek, Louis 1918- . . . . CLC **11, 19**
See also CA 45-48; CAAS 14; CANR 1;
DLB 88

Duerrenmatt, Friedrich
1921-1990 . . . . . . CLC **1, 4, 8, 11, 15, 43**
See also CA 17-20R; CANR 33;
DAM DRAM; DLB 69, 124; MTCW

Duffy, Bruce (?)- . . . . CLC **50**

Duffy, Maureen 1933- . . . . CLC **37**
See also CA 25-28R; CANR 33; DLB 14;
MTCW

Dugan, Alan 1923- . . . . CLC **2, 6**
See also CA 81-84; DLB 5

du Gard, Roger Martin
See Martin du Gard, Roger

Duhamel, Georges 1884-1966 . . . . CLC **8**
See also CA 81-84; 25-28R; CANR 35;
DLB 65; MTCW

Dujardin, Edouard (Emile Louis)
1861-1949 . . . . **TCLC 13**
See also CA 109; DLB 123

Dumas, Alexandre (Davy de la Pailleterie)
1802-1870 . . . . . . **NCLC 11; DA; DAB;**
DAC; WLC
See also DAM MST, NOV; DLB 119;
SATA 18

Dumas, Alexandre
1824-1895 . . . . **NCLC 9; DC 1**

Dumas, Claudine
See Malzberg, Barry N(athaniel)

Dumas, Henry L. 1934-1968 . . . . . **CLC 6, 62**
See also BW 1; CA 85-88; DLB 41

du Maurier, Daphne
1907-1989 . . . . **CLC 6, 11, 59; DAB;**
DAC; SSC 18
See also CA 5-8R; 128; CANR 6;
DAM MST, POP; MTCW; SATA 27;
SATA-Obit 60

Dunbar, Paul Laurence
1872-1906 . . . . . . **TCLC 2, 12; BLC; DA;**
DAC; PC 5; SSC 8; WLC
See also BW 1; CA 104; 124;
CDALB 1865-1917; DAM MST, MULT,
POET; DLB 50, 54, 78; SATA 34

Dunbar, William 1460(?)-1530(?) . . . . **LC 20**
See also DLB 132, 146

Duncan, Lois 1934- . . . . **CLC 26**
See also AAYA 4; CA 1-4R; CANR 2, 23,
36; CLR 29; JRDA; MAICYA; SAAS 2;
SATA 1, 36, 75

Duncan, Robert (Edward)
1919-1988 . . . . **CLC 1, 2, 4, 7, 15, 41, 55;**
PC 2
See also CA 9-12R; 124; CANR 28;
DAM POET; DLB 5, 16; MTCW

Duncan, Sara Jeannette
1861-1922 . . . . **TCLC 60**
See also DLB 92

Dunlap, William 1766-1839 . . . . **NCLC 2**
See also DLB 30, 37, 59

Dunn, Douglas (Eaglesham)
1942- . . . . **CLC 6, 40**
See also CA 45-48; CANR 2, 33; DLB 40;
MTCW

Dunn, Katherine (Karen) 1945- . . . . . **CLC 71**
See also CA 33-36R

Dunn, Stephen 1939- . . . . **CLC 36**
See also CA 33-36R; CANR 12, 48;
DLB 105

Dunne, Finley Peter 1867-1936 . . . . **TCLC 28**
See also CA 108; DLB 11, 23

Dunne, John Gregory 1932- . . . . **CLC 28**
See also CA 25-28R; CANR 14, 50;
DLBY 80

Dunsany, Edward John Moreton Drax
Plunkett 1878-1957
See Dunsany, Lord
See also CA 104; 148; DLB 10

Dunsany, Lord . . . . **TCLC 2, 59**
See also Dunsany, Edward John Moreton
Drax Plunkett
See also DLB 77, 153, 156

du Perry, Jean
See Simenon, Georges (Jacques Christian)

Durang, Christopher (Ferdinand)
1949- . . . . **CLC 27, 38**
See also CA 105; CANR 50

Duras, Marguerite
1914- . . . . . **CLC 3, 6, 11, 20, 34, 40, 68**
See also CA 25-28R; CANR 50; DLB 83;
MTCW

Durban, (Rosa) Pam 1947- . . . . **CLC 39**
See also CA 123

Durcan, Paul 1944- . . . . **CLC 43, 70**
See also CA 134; DAM POET

Durkheim, Emile 1858-1917 . . . . . . **TCLC 55**

Durrell, Lawrence (George)
1912-1990 . . . . **CLC 1, 4, 6, 8, 13, 27, 41**
See also CA 9-12R; 132; CANR 40;
CDBLB 1945-1960; DAM NOV; DLB 15,
27; DLBY 90; MTCW

Durrenmatt, Friedrich
See Duerrenmatt, Friedrich

Dutt, Toru 1856-1877 . . . . **NCLC 29**

Dwight, Timothy 1752-1817 . . . . . . **NCLC 13**
See also DLB 37

Dworkin, Andrea 1946- . . . . **CLC 43**
See also CA 77-80; CAAS 21; CANR 16,
39; INT CNAR-16; MTCW

Dwyer, Deanna
See Koontz, Dean R(ay)

Dwyer, K. R.
See Koontz, Dean R(ay)

Dylan, Bob 1941- . . . . . . **CLC 3, 4, 6, 12, 77**
See also CA 41-44R; DLB 16

Eagleton, Terence (Francis) 1943-
See Eagleton, Terry
See also CA 57-60; CANR 7, 23; MTCW

Eagleton, Terry . . . . **CLC 63**
See also Eagleton, Terence (Francis)

Early, Jack
See Scoppettone, Sandra

East, Michael
See West, Morris L(anglo)

Eastaway, Edward
See Thomas, (Philip) Edward

Eastlake, William (Derry) 1917- . . . . . **CLC 8**
See also CA 5-8R; CAAS 1; CANR 5;
DLB 6; INT CANR-5

Eastman, Charles A(lexander)
1858-1939 . . . . **TCLC 55**
See also DAM MULT; NNAL; YABC 1

Eberhart, Richard (Ghormley)
1904- . . . . **CLC 3, 11, 19, 56**
See also CA 1-4R; CANR 2;
CDALB 1941-1968; DAM POET;
DLB 48; MTCW

Eberstadt, Fernanda 1960- . . . . **CLC 39**
See also CA 136

Echegaray (y Eizaguirre), Jose (Maria Waldo)
1832-1916 . . . . **TCLC 4**
See also CA 104; CANR 32; HW; MTCW

Echeverria, (Jose) Esteban (Antonino)
1805-1851 . . . . **NCLC 18**

Echo
See Proust, (Valentin-Louis-George-Eugene-)
Marcel

Eckert, Allan W. 1931- . . . . **CLC 17**
See also CA 13-16R; CANR 14, 45;
INT CANR-14; SAAS 21; SATA 29;
SATA-Brief 27

Eckhart, Meister 1260(?)-1328(?) . . **CMLC 9**
See also DLB 115

Eckmar, F. R.
See de Hartog, Jan

Eco, Umberto 1932- . . . . **CLC 28, 60**
See also BEST 90:1; CA 77-80; CANR 12,
33; DAM NOV, POP; MTCW

Eddison, E(ric) R(ucker)
1882-1945 . . . . **TCLC 15**
See also CA 109

Edel, (Joseph) Leon 1907- . . . . . . **CLC 29, 34**
See also CA 1-4R; CANR 1, 22; DLB 103;
INT CANR-22

Eden, Emily 1797-1869 . . . . **NCLC 10**

Edgar, David 1948- . . . . **CLC 42**
See also CA 57-60; CANR 12;
DAM DRAM; DLB 13; MTCW

Edgerton, Clyde (Carlyle) 1944- . . . . **CLC 39**
See also AAYA 17; CA 118; 134; INT 134

Edgeworth, Maria 1768-1849 . . . **NCLC 1, 51**
See also DLB 116, 159; SATA 21

Edmonds, Paul
See Kuttner, Henry

Edmonds, Walter D(umaux) 1903- . . **CLC 35**
See also CA 5-8R; CANR 2; DLB 9;
MAICYA; SAAS 4; SATA 1, 27

Edmondson, Wallace
See Ellison, Harlan (Jay)

Edson, Russell . . . . **CLC 13**
See also CA 33-36R

Edwards, Bronwen Elizabeth
See Rose, Wendy

Edwards, G(erald) B(asil)
1899-1976 . . . . **CLC 25**
See also CA 110

Edwards, Gus 1939- . . . . **CLC 43**
See also CA 108; INT 108

Edwards, Jonathan
1703-1758 . . . . **LC 7; DA; DAC**
See also DAM MST; DLB 24

Efron, Marina Ivanovna Tsvetaeva
See Tsvetaeva (Efron), Marina (Ivanovna)

Ehle, John (Marsden, Jr.) 1925- . . . . **CLC 27**
See also CA 9-12R

Ehrenbourg, Ilya (Grigoryevich)
See Ehrenburg, Ilya (Grigoryevich)

Ehrenburg, Ilya (Grigoryevich)
1891-1967 . . . . **CLC 18, 34, 62**
See also CA 102; 25-28R

Ehrenburg, Ilyo (Grigoryevich)
See Ehrenburg, Ilya (Grigoryevich)

Eich, Guenter 1907-1972 . . . . **CLC 15**
See also CA 111; 93-96; DLB 69, 124

Eichendorff, Joseph Freiherr von
1788-1857 . . . . **NCLC 8**
See also DLB 90

Eigner, Larry . . . . **CLC 9**
See also Eigner, Laurence (Joel)
See also DLB 5

Espriella, Don Manuel Alvarez
See Southey, Robert

Espriu, Salvador 1913-1985........ **CLC 9**
See also CA 115; DLB 134

Espronceda, Jose de 1808-1842... **NCLC 39**

Esse, James
See Stephens, James

Esterbrook, Tom
See Hubbard, L(afayette) Ron(ald)

Estleman, Loren D. 1952-......... **CLC 48**
See also CA 85-88; CANR 27; DAM NOV,
POP; INT CANR-27; MTCW

Eugenides, Jeffrey 1960(?)-........ **CLC 81**
See also CA 144

Euripides c. 485B.C.-406B.C......... **DC 4**
See also DA; DAB; DAC; DAM DRAM,
MST

Evan, Evin
See Faust, Frederick (Schiller)

Evans, Evan
See Faust, Frederick (Schiller)

Evans, Marian
See Eliot, George

Evans, Mary Ann
See Eliot, George

Evarts, Esther
See Benson, Sally

Everett, Percival L. 1956-......... **CLC 57**
See also BW 2; CA 129

Everson, R(onald) G(ilmour)
1903-....................... **CLC 27**
See also CA 17-20R; DLB 88

Everson, William (Oliver)
1912-1994 .... **CLC 1, 5, 14**
See also CA 9-12R; 145; CANR 20; DLB 5,
16; MTCW

Evtushenko, Evgenii Aleksandrovich
See Yevtushenko, Yevgeny (Alexandrovich)

Ewart, Gavin (Buchanan)
1916-.................... **CLC 13, 46**
See also CA 89-92; CANR 17, 46; DLB 40;
MTCW

Ewers, Hanns Heinz 1871-1943 ... **TCLC 12**
See also CA 109; 149

Ewing, Frederick R.
See Sturgeon, Theodore (Hamilton)

Exley, Frederick (Earl)
1929-1992 .... **CLC 6, 11**
See also AITN 2; CA 81-84; 138; DLB 143;
DLBY 81

Eynhardt, Guillermo
See Quiroga, Horacio (Sylvestre)

Ezekiel, Nissim 1924-............. **CLC 61**
See also CA 61-64

Ezekiel, Tish O'Dowd 1943-....... **CLC 34**
See also CA 129

Fadeyev, A.
See Bulgya, Alexander Alexandrovich

Fadeyev, Alexander............... TCLC 53
See also Bulgya, Alexander Alexandrovich

Fagen, Donald 1948-............. **CLC 26**

Fainzilberg, Ilya Arnoldovich 1897-1937
See Ilf, Ilya
See also CA 120

Fair, Ronald L. 1932-............. **CLC 18**
See also BW 1; CA 69-72; CANR 25;
DLB 33

Fairbairns, Zoe (Ann) 1948-....... **CLC 32**
See also CA 103; CANR 21

Falco, Gian
See Papini, Giovanni

Falconer, James
See Kirkup, James

Falconer, Kenneth
See Kornbluth, C(yril) M.

Falkland, Samuel
See Heijermans, Herman

Fallaci, Oriana 1930-............. **CLC 11**
See also CA 77-80; CANR 15; MTCW

Faludy, George 1913-............. **CLC 42**
See also CA 21-24R

Faludy, Gyoergy
See Faludy, George

Fanon, Frantz 1925-1961..... **CLC 74; BLC**
See also BW 1; CA 116; 89-92;
DAM MULT

Fanshawe, Ann 1625-1680.......... **LC 11**

Fante, John (Thomas) 1911-1983 ... **CLC 60**
See also CA 69-72; 109; CANR 23;
DLB 130; DLBY 83

Farah, Nuruddin 1945-....... **CLC 53; BLC**
See also BW 2; CA 106; DAM MULT;
DLB 125

Fargue, Leon-Paul 1876(?)-1947... **TCLC 11**
See also CA 109

Farigoule, Louis
See Romains, Jules

Farina, Richard 1936(?)-1966 .... **CLC 9**
See also CA 81-84; 25-28R

Farley, Walter (Lorimer)
1915-1989 .... **CLC 17**
See also CA 17-20R; CANR 8, 29; DLB 22;
JRDA; MAICYA; SATA 2, 43

Farmer, Philip Jose 1918-....... **CLC 1, 19**
See also CA 1-4R; CANR 4, 35; DLB 8;
MTCW

Farquhar, George 1677-1707........ **LC 21**
See also DAM DRAM; DLB 84

Farrell, J(ames) G(ordon)
1935-1979 .... **CLC 6**
See also CA 73-76; 89-92; CANR 36;
DLB 14; MTCW

Farrell, James T(homas)
1904-1979 .... **CLC 1, 4, 8, 11, 66**
See also CA 5-8R; 89-92; CANR 9; DLB 4,
9, 86; DLBD 2; MTCW

Farren, Richard J.
See Betjeman, John

Farren, Richard M.
See Betjeman, John

Fassbinder, Rainer Werner
1946-1982 .... **CLC 20**
See also CA 93-96; 106; CANR 31

Fast, Howard (Melvin) 1914-...... **CLC 23**
See also AAYA 16; CA 1-4R; CAAS 18;
CANR 1, 33; DAM NOV; DLB 9;
INT CANR-33; SATA 7

Faulcon, Robert
See Holdstock, Robert P.

Faulkner, William (Cuthbert)
1897-1962 ..... **CLC 1, 3, 6, 8, 9, 11, 14,
18, 28, 52, 68; DA; DAB; DAC; SSC 1;
WLC**
See also AAYA 7; CA 81-84; CANR 33;
CDALB 1929-1941; DAM MST, NOV;
DLB 9, 11, 44, 102; DLBD 2; DLBY 86;
MTCW

Fauset, Jessie Redmon
1884(?)-1961 .... **CLC 19, 54; BLC**
See also BW 1; CA 109; DAM MULT;
DLB 51

Faust, Frederick (Schiller)
1892-1944(?) .... **TCLC 49**
See also CA 108; DAM POP

Faust, Irvin 1924-................. **CLC 8**
See also CA 33-36R; CANR 28; DLB 2, 28;
DLBY 80

Fawkes, Guy
See Benchley, Robert (Charles)

Fearing, Kenneth (Flexner)
1902-1961 .... **CLC 51**
See also CA 93-96; DLB 9

Fecamps, Elise
See Creasey, John

Federman, Raymond 1928-...... **CLC 6, 47**
See also CA 17-20R; CAAS 8; CANR 10,
43; DLBY 80

Federspiel, J(uerg) F. 1931-........ **CLC 42**
See also CA 146

Feiffer, Jules (Ralph) 1929-.... **CLC 2, 8, 64**
See also AAYA 3; CA 17-20R; CANR 30;
DAM DRAM; DLB 7, 44;
INT CANR-30; MTCW; SATA 8, 61

Feige, Hermann Albert Otto Maximilian
See Traven, B.

Feinberg, David B. 1956-1994...... **CLC 59**
See also CA 135; 147

Feinstein, Elaine 1930-............ **CLC 36**
See also CA 69-72; CAAS 1; CANR 31;
DLB 14, 40; MTCW

Feldman, Irving (Mordecai) 1928-.... **CLC 7**
See also CA 1-4R; CANR 1

Fellini, Federico 1920-1993 ..... **CLC 16, 85**
See also CA 65-68; 143; CANR 33

Felsen, Henry Gregor 1916- .... **CLC 17**
See also CA 1-4R; CANR 1; SAAS 2;
SATA 1

Fenton, James Martin 1949-....... **CLC 32**
See also CA 102; DLB 40

Ferber, Edna 1887-1968........... **CLC 18**
See also AITN 1; CA 5-8R; 25-28R; DLB 9,
28, 86; MTCW; SATA 7

Ferguson, Helen
See Kavan, Anna

Ferguson, Samuel 1810-1886..... **NCLC 33**
See also DLB 32

Fergusson, Robert 1750-1774 .... **LC 29**
See also DLB 109

Forster, E(dward) M(organ)
1879-1970 . . . . . CLC 1, 2, 3, 4, 9, 10, 13,
15, 22, 45, 77; DA; DAB; DAC; WLC
See also AAYA 2; CA 13-14; 25-28R;
CANR 45; CAP 1; CDBLB 1914-1945;
DAM MST, NOV; DLB 34, 98;
DLBD 10; MTCW; SATA 57

Forster, John   1812-1876 . . . . NCLC 11
See also DLB 144

Forsyth, Frederick   1938- . . . . . . CLC 2, 5, 36
See also BEST 89:4; CA 85-88; CANR 38;
DAM NOV, POP; DLB 87; MTCW

Forten, Charlotte L. . . . . TCLC 16; BLC
See also Grimke, Charlotte L(ottie) Forten
See also DLB 50

Foscolo, Ugo   1778-1827 . . . . NCLC 8

Fosse, Bob . . . . CLC 20
See also Fosse, Robert Louis

Fosse, Robert Louis   1927-1987
See Fosse, Bob
See also CA 110; 123

Foster, Stephen Collins
1826-1864 . . . . NCLC 26

Foucault, Michel
1926-1984 . . . . CLC 31, 34, 69
See also CA 105; 113; CANR 34; MTCW

Fouque, Friedrich (Heinrich Karl) de la Motte
1777-1843 . . . . NCLC 2
See also DLB 90

Fourier, Charles   1772-1837 . . . . . . NCLC 51

Fournier, Henri Alban   1886-1914
See Alain-Fournier
See also CA 104

Fournier, Pierre   1916- . . . . CLC 11
See also Gascar, Pierre
See also CA 89-92; CANR 16, 40

Fowles, John
1926- . . . . . . CLC 1, 2, 3, 4, 6, 9, 10, 15,
33, 87; DAB; DAC
See also CA 5-8R; CANR 25; CDBLB 1960
to Present; DAM MST; DLB 14, 139;
MTCW; SATA 22

Fox, Paula   1923- . . . . CLC 2, 8
See also AAYA 3; CA 73-76; CANR 20,
36; CLR 1; DLB 52; JRDA; MAICYA;
MTCW; SATA 17, 60

Fox, William Price (Jr.)   1926- . . . . . CLC 22
See also CA 17-20R; CAAS 19; CANR 11;
DLB 2; DLBY 81

Foxe, John   1516(?)-1587 . . . . LC 14

Frame, Janet . . . . CLC 2, 3, 6, 22, 66
See also Clutha, Janet Paterson Frame

France, Anatole . . . . TCLC 9
See also Thibault, Jacques Anatole Francois
See also DLB 123

Francis, Claude   19(?)- . . . . CLC 50

Francis, Dick   1920- . . . . CLC 2, 22, 42
See also AAYA 5; BEST 89:3; CA 5-8R;
CANR 9, 42; CDBLB 1960 to Present;
DAM POP; DLB 87; INT CANR-9;
MTCW

Francis, Robert (Churchill)
1901-1987 . . . . CLC 15
See also CA 1-4R; 123; CANR 1

Frank, Anne(lies Marie)
1929-1945 . . . . TCLC 17; DA; DAB;
DAC; WLC
See also AAYA 12; CA 113; 133;
DAM MST; MTCW; SATA-Brief 42

Frank, Elizabeth   1945- . . . . CLC 39
See also CA 121; 126; INT 126

Franklin, Benjamin
See Hasek, Jaroslav (Matej Frantisek)

Franklin, Benjamin
1706-1790 . . . . . LC 25; DA; DAB; DAC
See also CDALB 1640-1865; DAM MST;
DLB 24, 43, 73

Franklin, (Stella Maraia Sarah) Miles
1879-1954 . . . . TCLC 7
See also CA 104

Fraser, (Lady) Antonia (Pakenham)
1932- . . . . CLC 32
See also CA 85-88; CANR 44; MTCW;
SATA-Brief 32

Fraser, George MacDonald   1925- . . . . CLC 7
See also CA 45-48; CANR 2, 48

Fraser, Sylvia   1935- . . . . CLC 64
See also CA 45-48; CANR 1, 16

Frayn, Michael   1933- . . . . . . CLC 3, 7, 31, 47
See also CA 5-8R; CANR 30;
DAM DRAM, NOV; DLB 13, 14;
MTCW

Fraze, Candida (Merrill)   1945- . . . . . CLC 50
See also CA 126

Frazer, J(ames) G(eorge)
1854-1941 . . . . TCLC 32
See also CA 118

Frazer, Robert Caine
See Creasey, John

Frazer, Sir James George
See Frazer, J(ames) G(eorge)

Frazier, Ian   1951- . . . . CLC 46
See also CA 130

Frederic, Harold   1856-1898 . . . . . . NCLC 10
See also DLB 12, 23; DLBD 13

Frederick, John
See Faust, Frederick (Schiller)

Frederick the Great   1712-1786 . . . . . . LC 14

Fredro, Aleksander   1793-1876 . . . . . NCLC 8

Freeling, Nicolas   1927- . . . . CLC 38
See also CA 49-52; CAAS 12; CANR 1, 17,
50; DLB 87

Freeman, Douglas Southall
1886-1953 . . . . TCLC 11
See also CA 109; DLB 17

Freeman, Judith   1946- . . . . CLC 55
See also CA 148

Freeman, Mary Eleanor Wilkins
1852-1930 . . . . TCLC 9; SSC 1
See also CA 106; DLB 12, 78

Freeman, R(ichard) Austin
1862-1943 . . . . TCLC 21
See also CA 113; DLB 70

French, Albert   1943- . . . . CLC 86

French, Marilyn   1929- . . . . . . CLC 10, 18, 60
See also CA 69-72; CANR 3, 31;
DAM DRAM, NOV, POP;
INT CANR-31; MTCW

French, Paul
See Asimov, Isaac

Freneau, Philip Morin   1752-1832 . . NCLC 1
See also DLB 37, 43

Freud, Sigmund   1856-1939 . . . . TCLC 52
See also CA 115; 133; MTCW

Friedan, Betty (Naomi)   1921- . . . . . . CLC 74
See also CA 65-68; CANR 18, 45; MTCW

Friedlaender, Saul   1932- . . . . CLC 90
See also CA 117; 130

Friedman, B(ernard) H(arper)
1926- . . . . CLC 7
See also CA 1-4R; CANR 3, 48

Friedman, Bruce Jay   1930- . . . . CLC 3, 5, 56
See also CA 9-12R; CANR 25; DLB 2, 28;
INT CANR-25

Friel, Brian   1929- . . . . CLC 5, 42, 59
See also CA 21-24R; CANR 33; DLB 13;
MTCW

Friis-Baastad, Babbis Ellinor
1921-1970 . . . . CLC 12
See also CA 17-20R; 134; SATA 7

Frisch, Max (Rudolf)
1911-1991 . . . . . CLC 3, 9, 14, 18, 32, 44
See also CA 85-88; 134; CANR 32;
DAM DRAM, NOV; DLB 69, 124;
MTCW

Fromentin, Eugene (Samuel Auguste)
1820-1876 . . . . NCLC 10
See also DLB 123

Frost, Frederick
See Faust, Frederick (Schiller)

Frost, Robert (Lee)
1874-1963 . . . . CLC 1, 3, 4, 9, 10, 13, 15,
26, 34, 44; DA; DAB; DAC; PC 1; WLC
See also CA 89-92; CANR 33;
CDALB 1917-1929; DAM MST, POET;
DLB 54; DLBD 7; MTCW; SATA 14

Froude, James Anthony
1818-1894 . . . . NCLC 43
See also DLB 18, 57, 144

Froy, Herald
See Waterhouse, Keith (Spencer)

Fry, Christopher   1907- . . . . CLC 2, 10, 14
See also CA 17-20R; CANR 9, 30;
DAM DRAM; DLB 13; MTCW;
SATA 66

Frye, (Herman) Northrop
1912-1991 . . . . CLC 24, 70
See also CA 5-8R; 133; CANR 8, 37;
DLB 67, 68; MTCW

Fuchs, Daniel   1909-1993 . . . . CLC 8, 22
See also CA 81-84; 142; CAAS 5;
CANR 40; DLB 9, 26, 28; DLBY 93

Fuchs, Daniel   1934- . . . . CLC 34
See also CA 37-40R; CANR 14, 48

Fuentes, Carlos
1928- . . . . . . CLC 3, 8, 10, 13, 22, 41, 60;
DA; DAB; DAC; HLC; WLC
See also AAYA 4; AITN 2; CA 69-72;
CANR 10, 32; DAM MST, MULT,
NOV; DLB 113; HW; MTCW

Fuentes, Gregorio Lopez y
See Lopez y Fuentes, Gregorio

Gee, Maurice (Gough) 1931-....... **CLC 29**
See also CA 97-100; SATA 46

Gelbart, Larry (Simon) 1923-... **CLC 21, 61**
See also CA 73-76; CANR 45

Gelber, Jack 1932-....... **CLC 1, 6, 14, 79**
See also CA 1-4R; CANR 2; DLB 7

Gellhorn, Martha (Ellis) 1908-.. **CLC 14, 60**
See also CA 77-80; CANR 44; DLBY 82

Genet, Jean
    1910-1986 ... **CLC 1, 2, 5, 10, 14, 44, 46**
See also CA 13-16R; CANR 18;
    DAM DRAM; DLB 72; DLBY 86;
    MTCW

Gent, Peter 1942-................ **CLC 29**
See also AITN 1; CA 89-92; DLBY 82

Gentlewoman in New England, A
See Bradstreet, Anne

Gentlewoman in Those Parts, A
See Bradstreet, Anne

George, Jean Craighead 1919-...... **CLC 35**
See also AAYA 8; CA 5-8R; CANR 25;
    CLR 1; DLB 52; JRDA; MAICYA;
    SATA 2, 68

George, Stefan (Anton)
    1868-1933 .... **TCLC 2, 14**
See also CA 104

Georges, Georges Martin
See Simenon, Georges (Jacques Christian)

Gerhardi, William Alexander
See Gerhardie, William Alexander

Gerhardie, William Alexander
    1895-1977 .... **CLC 5**
See also CA 25-28R; 73-76; CANR 18;
    DLB 36

Gerstler, Amy 1956-.............. **CLC 70**
See also CA 146

Gertler, T. .... **CLC 34**
See also CA 116; 121; INT 121

Ghalib 1797-1869 .... **NCLC 39**

Ghelderode, Michel de
    1898-1962 .... **CLC 6, 11**
See also CA 85-88; CANR 40;
    DAM DRAM

Ghiselin, Brewster 1903-.......... **CLC 23**
See also CA 13-16R; CAAS 10; CANR 13

Ghose, Zulfikar 1935-............. **CLC 42**
See also CA 65-68

Ghosh, Amitav 1956- .... **CLC 44**
See also CA 147

Giacosa, Giuseppe 1847-1906 ...... **TCLC 7**
See also CA 104

Gibb, Lee
See Waterhouse, Keith (Spencer)

Gibbon, Lewis Grassic .... **TCLC 4**
See also Mitchell, James Leslie

Gibbons, Kaye 1960- .... **CLC 50, 88**
See also DAM POP

Gibran, Kahlil
    1883-1931 .... **TCLC 1, 9; PC 9**
See also CA 104; DAM POET, POP

Gibson, William
    1914- .... **CLC 23; DA; DAB; DAC**
See also CA 9-12R; CANR 9, 42;
    DAM DRAM, MST; DLB 7; SATA 66

Gibson, William (Ford) 1948-... **CLC 39, 63**
See also AAYA 12; CA 126; 133;
    DAM POP

Gide, Andre (Paul Guillaume)
    1869-1951 .... **TCLC 5, 12, 36; DA;**
        DAB; DAC; SSC 13; WLC
See also CA 104; 124; DAM MST, NOV;
    DLB 65; MTCW

Gifford, Barry (Colby) 1946-....... **CLC 34**
See also CA 65-68; CANR 9, 30, 40

Gilbert, W(illiam) S(chwenck)
    1836-1911 .... **TCLC 3**
See also CA 104; DAM DRAM, POET;
    SATA 36

Gilbreth, Frank B., Jr. 1911-....... **CLC 17**
See also CA 9-12R; SATA 2

Gilchrist, Ellen 1935-.. **CLC 34, 48; SSC 14**
See also CA 113; 116; CANR 41;
    DAM POP; DLB 130; MTCW

Giles, Molly 1942- .... **CLC 39**
See also CA 126

Gill, Patrick
See Creasey, John

Gilliam, Terry (Vance) 1940-....... **CLC 21**
See also Monty Python
See also CA 108; 113; CANR 35; INT 113

Gillian, Jerry
See Gilliam, Terry (Vance)

Gilliatt, Penelope (Ann Douglass)
    1932-1993 .... **CLC 2, 10, 13, 53**
See also AITN 2; CA 13-16R; 141;
    CANR 49; DLB 14

Gilman, Charlotte (Anna) Perkins (Stetson)
    1860-1935 .... **TCLC 9, 37; SSC 13**
See also CA 106

Gilmour, David 1949-............. **CLC 35**
See also CA 138, 147

Gilpin, William 1724-1804....... **NCLC 30**

Gilray, J. D.
See Mencken, H(enry) L(ouis)

Gilroy, Frank D(aniel) 1925-........ **CLC 2**
See also CA 81-84; CANR 32; DLB 7

Ginsberg, Allen
    1926- ...... **CLC 1, 2, 3, 4, 6, 13, 36, 69;**
        DA; DAB; DAC; PC 4; WLC 3
See also AITN 1; CA 1-4R; CANR 2, 41;
    CDALB 1941-1968; DAM MST, POET;
    DLB 5, 16; MTCW

Ginzburg, Natalia
    1916-1991 .... **CLC 5, 11, 54, 70**
See also CA 85-88; 135; CANR 33; MTCW

Giono, Jean 1895-1970......... **CLC 4, 11**
See also CA 45-48; 29-32R; CANR 2, 35;
    DLB 72; MTCW

Giovanni, Nikki
    1943- ...... **CLC 2, 4, 19, 64; BLC; DA;**
        DAB; DAC
See also AITN 1; BW 2; CA 29-32R;
    CAAS 6; CANR 18, 41; CLR 6;
    DAM MST, MULT, POET; DLB 5, 41;
    INT CANR-18; MAICYA; MTCW;
    SATA 24

Giovene, Andrea 1904-............. **CLC 7**
See also CA 85-88

Gippius, Zinaida (Nikolayevna) 1869-1945
See Hippius, Zinaida
See also CA 106

Giraudoux, (Hippolyte) Jean
    1882-1944 .... **TCLC 2, 7**
See also CA 104; DAM DRAM; DLB 65

Gironella, Jose Maria 1917-....... **CLC 11**
See also CA 101

Gissing, George (Robert)
    1857-1903 .... **TCLC 3, 24, 47**
See also CA 105; DLB 18, 135

Giurlani, Aldo
See Palazzeschi, Aldo

Gladkov, Fyodor (Vasilyevich)
    1883-1958 .... **TCLC 27**

Glanville, Brian (Lester) 1931-...... **CLC 6**
See also CA 5-8R; CAAS 9; CANR 3;
    DLB 15, 139; SATA 42

Glasgow, Ellen (Anderson Gholson)
    1873(?)-1945 .... **TCLC 2, 7**
See also CA 104; DLB 9, 12

Glaspell, Susan (Keating)
    1882(?)-1948 .... **TCLC 55**
See also CA 110; DLB 7, 9, 78; YABC 2

Glassco, John 1909-1981 .... **CLC 9**
See also CA 13-16R; 102; CANR 15;
    DLB 68

Glasscock, Amnesia
See Steinbeck, John (Ernst)

Glasser, Ronald J. 1940(?)-........ **CLC 37**

Glassman, Joyce
See Johnson, Joyce

Glendinning, Victoria 1937-........ **CLC 50**
See also CA 120; 127; DLB 155

Glissant, Edouard 1928-........ **CLC 10, 68**
See also DAM MULT

Gloag, Julian 1930- .... **CLC 40**
See also AITN 1; CA 65-68; CANR 10

Glowacki, Aleksander
See Prus, Boleslaw

Glueck, Louise (Elisabeth)
    1943-............... **CLC 7, 22, 44, 81**
See also CA 33-36R; CANR 40;
    DAM POET; DLB 5

Gobineau, Joseph Arthur (Comte) de
    1816-1882 .... **NCLC 17**
See also DLB 123

Godard, Jean-Luc 1930-........... **CLC 20**
See also CA 93-96

Godden, (Margaret) Rumer 1907-... **CLC 53**
See also AAYA 6; CA 5-8R; CANR 4, 27,
    36; CLR 20; DLB 161; MAICYA;
    SAAS 12; SATA 3, 36

Godoy Alcayaga, Lucila 1889-1957
See Mistral, Gabriela
See also BW 2; CA 104; 131; DAM MULT;
    HW; MTCW

Godwin, Gail (Kathleen)
    1937-............ **CLC 5, 8, 22, 31, 69**
See also CA 29-32R; CANR 15, 43;
    DAM POP; DLB 6; INT CANR-15;
    MTCW

Godwin, William 1756-1836...... **NCLC 14**
See also CDBLB 1789-1832; DLB 39, 104,
    142, 158

Goethe, Johann Wolfgang von
1749-1832 .... **NCLC 4, 22, 34; DA;**
DAB; DAC; PC 5; WLC 3
See also DAM DRAM, MST, POET;
DLB 94

Gogarty, Oliver St. John
1878-1957 .... **TCLC 15**
See also CA 109; DLB 15, 19

Gogol, Nikolai (Vasilyevich)
1809-1852 .... **NCLC 5, 15, 31; DA;**
DAB; DAC; DC 1; SSC 4; WLC
See also DAM DRAM, MST

Goines, Donald
1937(?)-1974 .... **CLC 80; BLC**
See also AITN 1; BW 1; CA 124; 114;
DAM MULT, POP; DLB 33

Gold, Herbert 1924-....... **CLC 4, 7, 14, 42**
See also CA 9-12R; CANR 17, 45; DLB 2;
DLBY 81

Goldbarth, Albert 1948-........ **CLC 5, 38**
See also CA 53-56; CANR 6, 40; DLB 120

Goldberg, Anatol 1910-1982 .... **CLC 34**
See also CA 131; 117

Goldemberg, Isaac 1945-.......... **CLC 52**
See also CA 69-72; CAAS 12; CANR 11,
32; HW

Golding, William (Gerald)
1911-1993 .... **CLC 1, 2, 3, 8, 10, 17, 27,**
58, 81; DA; DAB; DAC; WLC
See also AAYA 5; CA 5-8R; 141;
CANR 13, 33; CDBLB 1945-1960;
DAM MST, NOV; DLB 15, 100; MTCW

Goldman, Emma 1869-1940 ...... **TCLC 13**
See also CA 110

Goldman, Francisco 1955-......... **CLC 76**

Goldman, William (W.) 1931-.... **CLC 1, 48**
See also CA 9-12R; CANR 29; DLB 44

Goldmann, Lucien 1913-1970 ...... **CLC 24**
See also CA 25-28; CAP 2

Goldoni, Carlo 1707-1793 .... **LC 4**
See also DAM DRAM

Goldsberry, Steven 1949-.......... **CLC 34**
See also CA 131

Goldsmith, Oliver
1728-1774 ...... **LC 2; DA; DAB; DAC;**
WLC
See also CDBLB 1660-1789; DAM DRAM,
MST, NOV, POET; DLB 39, 89, 104,
109, 142; SATA 26

Goldsmith, Peter
See Priestley, J(ohn) B(oynton)

Gombrowicz, Witold
1904-1969 .... **CLC 4, 7, 11, 49**
See also CA 19-20; 25-28R; CAP 2;
DAM DRAM

Gomez de la Serna, Ramon
1888-1963 .... **CLC 9**
See also CA 116; HW

Goncharov, Ivan Alexandrovich
1812-1891 .... **NCLC 1**

Goncourt, Edmond (Louis Antoine Huot) de
1822-1896 .... **NCLC 7**
See also DLB 123

Goncourt, Jules (Alfred Huot) de
1830-1870 .... **NCLC 7**
See also DLB 123

Gontier, Fernande 19(?)- .... **CLC 50**

Goodman, Paul 1911-1972.... **CLC 1, 2, 4, 7**
See also CA 19-20; 37-40R; CANR 34;
CAP 2; DLB 130; MTCW

Gordimer, Nadine
1923- .... **CLC 3, 5, 7, 10, 18, 33, 51, 70;**
DA; DAB; DAC; SSC 17
See also CA 5-8R; CANR 3, 28;
DAM MST, NOV; INT CANR-28;
MTCW

Gordon, Adam Lindsay
1833-1870 .... **NCLC 21**

Gordon, Caroline
1895-1981 ... **CLC 6, 13, 29, 83; SSC 15**
See also CA 11-12; 103; CANR 36; CAP 1;
DLB 4, 9, 102; DLBY 81; MTCW

Gordon, Charles William 1860-1937
See Connor, Ralph
See also CA 109

Gordon, Mary (Catherine)
1949- .... **CLC 13, 22**
See also CA 102; CANR 44; DLB 6;
DLBY 81; INT 102; MTCW

Gordon, Sol 1923-................ **CLC 26**
See also CA 53-56; CANR 4; SATA 11

Gordone, Charles 1925-.......... **CLC 1, 4**
See also BW 1; CA 93-96; DAM DRAM;
DLB 7; INT 93-96; MTCW

Gorenko, Anna Andreevna
See Akhmatova, Anna

Gorky, Maxim........ **TCLC 8; DAB; WLC**
See also Peshkov, Alexei Maximovich

Goryan, Sirak
See Saroyan, William

Gosse, Edmund (William)
1849-1928 .... **TCLC 28**
See also CA 117; DLB 57, 144

Gotlieb, Phyllis Fay (Bloom)
1926- .... **CLC 18**
See also CA 13-16R; CANR 7; DLB 88

Gottesman, S. D.
See Kornbluth, C(yril) M.; Pohl, Frederik

Gottfried von Strassburg
fl. c. 1210-................. **CMLC 10**
See also DLB 138

Gould, Lois .... **CLC 4, 10**
See also CA 77-80; CANR 29; MTCW

Gourmont, Remy de 1858-1915.... **TCLC 17**
See also CA 109

Govier, Katherine 1948-.......... **CLC 51**
See also CA 101; CANR 18, 40

Goyen, (Charles) William
1915-1983 .... **CLC 5, 8, 14, 40**
See also AITN 2; CA 5-8R; 110; CANR 6;
DLB 2; DLBY 83; INT CANR-6

Goytisolo, Juan
1931-............ **CLC 5, 10, 23; HLC**
See also CA 85-88; CANR 32;
DAM MULT; HW; MTCW

Gozzano, Guido 1883-1916 .... **PC 10**
See also DLB 114

Gozzi, (Conte) Carlo 1720-1806 .. **NCLC 23**

Grabbe, Christian Dietrich
1801-1836 .... **NCLC 2**
See also DLB 133

Grace, Patricia 1937-............. **CLC 56**

Gracian y Morales, Baltasar
1601-1658 .... **LC 15**

Gracq, Julien................. **CLC 11, 48**
See also Poirier, Louis
See also DLB 83

Grade, Chaim 1910-1982 .... **CLC 10**
See also CA 93-96; 107

Graduate of Oxford, A
See Ruskin, John

Graham, John
See Phillips, David Graham

Graham, Jorie 1951-............. **CLC 48**
See also CA 111; DLB 120

Graham, R(obert) B(ontine) Cunninghame
See Cunninghame Graham, R(obert)
B(ontine)
See also DLB 98, 135

Graham, Robert
See Haldeman, Joe (William)

Graham, Tom
See Lewis, (Harry) Sinclair

Graham, W(illiam) S(ydney)
1918-1986 .... **CLC 29**
See also CA 73-76; 118; DLB 20

Graham, Winston (Mawdsley)
1910-..................... **CLC 23**
See also CA 49-52; CANR 2, 22, 45;
DLB 77

Grant, Skeeter
See Spiegelman, Art

Granville-Barker, Harley
1877-1946 .... **TCLC 2**
See also Barker, Harley Granville
See also CA 104; DAM DRAM

Grass, Guenter (Wilhelm)
1927-..... **CLC 1, 2, 4, 6, 11, 15, 22, 32,**
49, 88; DA; DAB; DAC; WLC
See also CA 13-16R; CANR 20;
DAM MST, NOV; DLB 75, 124; MTCW

Gratton, Thomas
See Hulme, T(homas) E(rnest)

Grau, Shirley Ann
1929-.............. **CLC 4, 9; SSC 15**
See also CA 89-92; CANR 22; DLB 2;
INT CANR-22; MTCW

Gravel, Fern
See Hall, James Norman

Graver, Elizabeth 1964-.......... **CLC 70**
See also CA 135

Graves, Richard Perceval 1945- .... **CLC 44**
See also CA 65-68; CANR 9, 26

Graves, Robert (von Ranke)
1895-1985 ...... **CLC 1, 2, 6, 11, 39, 44,**
45; DAB; DAC; PC 6
See also CA 5-8R; 117; CANR 5, 36;
CDBLB 1914-1945; DAM MST, POET;
DLB 20, 100; DLBY 85; MTCW;
SATA 45

Gray, Alasdair (James) 1934- ...... **CLC 41**
See also CA 126; CANR 47; INT 126;
MTCW

Gray, Amlin 1946- . . . . CLC 29
See also CA 138

Gray, Francine du Plessix 1930- . . . . CLC 22
See also BEST 90:3; CA 61-64; CAAS 2;
CANR 11, 33; DAM NOV;
INT CANR-11; MTCW

Gray, John (Henry) 1866-1934 . . . . TCLC 19
See also CA 119

Gray, Simon (James Holliday)
1936- . . . . CLC 9, 14, 36
See also AITN 1; CA 21-24R; CAAS 3;
CANR 32; DLB 13; MTCW

Gray, Spalding 1941- . . . . CLC 49
See also CA 128; DAM POP

Gray, Thomas
1716-1771 . . . . . . LC 4; DA; DAB; DAC;
PC 2; WLC
See also CDBLB 1660-1789; DAM MST;
DLB 109

Grayson, David
See Baker, Ray Stannard

Grayson, Richard (A.) 1951- . . . . CLC 38
See also CA 85-88; CANR 14, 31

Greeley, Andrew M(oran) 1928- . . . . CLC 28
See also CA 5-8R; CAAS 7; CANR 7, 43;
DAM POP; MTCW

Green, Brian
See Card, Orson Scott

Green, Hannah
See Greenberg, Joanne (Goldenberg)

Green, Hannah . . . . CLC 3
See also CA 73-76

Green, Henry . . . . CLC 2, 13
See also Yorke, Henry Vincent
See also DLB 15

Green, Julian (Hartridge) 1900-
See Green, Julien
See also CA 21-24R; CANR 33; DLB 4, 72;
MTCW

Green, Julien . . . . CLC 3, 11, 77
See also Green, Julian (Hartridge)

Green, Paul (Eliot) 1894-1981 . . . . . . CLC 25
See also AITN 1; CA 5-8R; 103; CANR 3;
DAM DRAM; DLB 7, 9; DLBY 81

Greenberg, Ivan 1908-1973
See Rahv, Philip
See also CA 85-88

Greenberg, Joanne (Goldenberg)
1932- . . . . CLC 7, 30
See also AAYA 12; CA 5-8R; CANR 14,
32; SATA 25

Greenberg, Richard 1959(?)- . . . . CLC 57
See also CA 138

Greene, Bette 1934- . . . . CLC 30
See also AAYA 7; CA 53-56; CANR 4;
CLR 2; JRDA; MAICYA; SAAS 16;
SATA 8

Greene, Gael . . . . CLC 8
See also CA 13-16R; CANR 10

Greene, Graham
1904-1991 . . . . CLC 1, 3, 6, 9, 14, 18, 27,
37, 70, 72; DA; DAB; DAC; WLC
See also AITN 2; CA 13-16R; 133;
CANR 35; CDBLB 1945-1960;
DAM MST, NOV; DLB 13, 15, 77, 100;
DLBY 91; MTCW; SATA 20

Greer, Richard
See Silverberg, Robert

Gregor, Arthur 1923- . . . . CLC 9
See also CA 25-28R; CAAS 10; CANR 11;
SATA 36

Gregor, Lee
See Pohl, Frederik

Gregory, Isabella Augusta (Persse)
1852-1932 . . . . TCLC 1
See also CA 104; DLB 10

Gregory, J. Dennis
See Williams, John A(lfred)

Grendon, Stephen
See Derleth, August (William)

Grenville, Kate 1950- . . . . CLC 61
See also CA 118

Grenville, Pelham
See Wodehouse, P(elham) G(renville)

Greve, Felix Paul (Berthold Friedrich)
1879-1948
See Grove, Frederick Philip
See also CA 104; 141; DAC; DAM MST

Grey, Zane 1872-1939 . . . . TCLC 6
See also CA 104; 132; DAM POP; DLB 9;
MTCW

Grieg, (Johan) Nordahl (Brun)
1902-1943 . . . . TCLC 10
See also CA 107

Grieve, C(hristopher) M(urray)
1892-1978 . . . . CLC 11, 19
See also MacDiarmid, Hugh; Pteleon
See also CA 5-8R; 85-88; CANR 33;
DAM POET; MTCW

Griffin, Gerald 1803-1840 . . . . NCLC 7
See also DLB 159

Griffin, John Howard 1920-1980 . . . . CLC 68
See also AITN 1; CA 1-4R; 101; CANR 2

Griffin, Peter 1942- . . . . CLC 39
See also CA 136

Griffiths, Trevor 1935- . . . . CLC 13, 52
See also CA 97-100; CANR 45; DLB 13

Grigson, Geoffrey (Edward Harvey)
1905-1985 . . . . CLC 7, 39
See also CA 25-28R; 118; CANR 20, 33;
DLB 27; MTCW

Grillparzer, Franz 1791-1872 . . . . . . NCLC 1
See also DLB 133

Grimble, Reverend Charles James
See Eliot, T(homas) S(tearns)

Grimke, Charlotte L(ottie) Forten
1837(?)-1914
See Forten, Charlotte L.
See also BW 1; CA 117; 124; DAM MULT,
POET

Grimm, Jacob Ludwig Karl
1785-1863 . . . . NCLC 3
See also DLB 90; MAICYA; SATA 22

Grimm, Wilhelm Karl 1786-1859 . . NCLC 3
See also DLB 90; MAICYA; SATA 22

**Grimmelshausen, Johann Jakob Christoffel
von** 1621-1676 . . . . LC 6

Grindel, Eugene 1895-1952
See Eluard, Paul
See also CA 104

Grisham, John 1955- . . . . CLC 84
See also AAYA 14; CA 138; CANR 47;
DAM POP

Grossman, David 1954- . . . . CLC 67
See also CA 138

Grossman, Vasily (Semenovich)
1905-1964 . . . . CLC 41
See also CA 124; 130; MTCW

Grove, Frederick Philip . . . . TCLC 4
See also Greve, Felix Paul (Berthold
Friedrich)
See also DLB 92

Grubb
See Crumb, R(obert)

Grumbach, Doris (Isaac)
1918- . . . . CLC 13, 22, 64
See also CA 5-8R; CAAS 2; CANR 9, 42;
INT CANR-9

Grundtvig, Nicolai Frederik Severin
1783-1872 . . . . NCLC 1

Grunge
See Crumb, R(obert)

Grunwald, Lisa 1959- . . . . CLC 44
See also CA 120

Guare, John 1938- . . . . CLC 8, 14, 29, 67
See also CA 73-76; CANR 21;
DAM DRAM; DLB 7; MTCW

Gudjonsson, Halldor Kiljan 1902-
See Laxness, Halldor
See also CA 103

Guenter, Erich
See Eich, Guenter

Guest, Barbara 1920- . . . . CLC 34
See also CA 25-28R; CANR 11, 44; DLB 5

Guest, Judith (Ann) 1936- . . . . CLC 8, 30
See also AAYA 7; CA 77-80; CANR 15;
DAM NOV, POP; INT CANR-15;
MTCW

Guevara, Che . . . . CLC 87; HLC
See also Guevara (Serna), Ernesto

Guevara (Serna), Ernesto 1928-1967
See Guevara, Che
See also CA 127; 111; DAM MULT; HW

Guild, Nicholas M. 1944- . . . . CLC 33
See also CA 93-96

Guillemin, Jacques
See Sartre, Jean-Paul

Guillen, Jorge 1893-1984 . . . . CLC 11
See also CA 89-92; 112; DAM MULT,
POET; DLB 108; HW

Guillen (y Batista), Nicolas (Cristobal)
1902-1989 . . . . . CLC 48, 79; BLC; HLC
See also BW 2; CA 116; 125; 129;
DAM MST, MULT, POET; HW

Guillevic, (Eugene) 1907- . . . . CLC 33
See also CA 93-96

Guillois
See Desnos, Robert

Guiney, Louise Imogen
1861-1920 . . . . TCLC 41
See also DLB 54

Guiraldes, Ricardo (Guillermo)
1886-1927 . . . . TCLC 39
See also CA 131; HW; MTCW

Gumilev, Nikolai Stephanovich
1886-1921 . . . . TCLC 60

Gunn, Bill . . . . CLC 5
See also Gunn, William Harrison
See also DLB 38

Gunn, Thom(son William)
1929- . . . . CLC 3, 6, 18, 32, 81
See also CA 17-20R; CANR 9, 33;
CDBLB 1960 to Present; DAM POET;
DLB 27; INT CANR-33; MTCW

Gunn, William Harrison 1934(?)-1989
See Gunn, Bill
See also AITN 1; BW 1; CA 13-16R; 128;
CANR 12, 25

Gunnars, Kristjana 1948- . . . . CLC 69
See also CA 113; DLB 60

Gurganus, Allan 1947- . . . . CLC 70
See also BEST 90:1; CA 135; DAM POP

Gurney, A(lbert) R(amsdell), Jr.
1930- . . . . CLC 32, 50, 54
See also CA 77-80; CANR 32;
DAM DRAM

Gurney, Ivor (Bertie) 1890-1937 . . . TCLC 33

Gurney, Peter
See Gurney, A(lbert) R(amsdell), Jr.

Guro, Elena 1877-1913 . . . . TCLC 56

Gustafson, Ralph (Barker) 1909- . . . . CLC 36
See also CA 21-24R; CANR 8, 45; DLB 88

Gut, Gom
See Simenon, Georges (Jacques Christian)

Guthrie, A(lfred) B(ertram), Jr.
1901-1991 . . . . CLC 23
See also CA 57-60; 134; CANR 24; DLB 6;
SATA 62; SATA-Obit 67

Guthrie, Isobel
See Grieve, C(hristopher) M(urray)

Guthrie, Woodrow Wilson 1912-1967
See Guthrie, Woody
See also CA 113; 93-96

Guthrie, Woody . . . . CLC 35
See also Guthrie, Woodrow Wilson

Guy, Rosa (Cuthbert) 1928- . . . . CLC 26
See also AAYA 4; BW 2; CA 17-20R;
CANR 14, 34; CLR 13; DLB 33; JRDA;
MAICYA; SATA 14, 62

Gwendolyn
See Bennett, (Enoch) Arnold

H. D. . . . . CLC 3, 8, 14, 31, 34, 73; PC 5
See also Doolittle, Hilda

H. de V.
See Buchan, John

Haavikko, Paavo Juhani
1931- . . . . CLC 18, 34
See also CA 106

Habbema, Koos
See Heijermans, Herman

Hacker, Marilyn 1942- . . . . CLC 5, 9, 23, 72
See also CA 77-80; DAM POET; DLB 120

Haggard, H(enry) Rider
1856-1925 . . . . TCLC 11
See also CA 108; 148; DLB 70, 156;
SATA 16

Hagiwara Sakutaro 1886-1942 . . . . TCLC 60

Haig, Fenil
See Ford, Ford Madox

Haig-Brown, Roderick (Langmere)
1908-1976 . . . . CLC 21
See also CA 5-8R; 69-72; CANR 4, 38;
CLR 31; DLB 88; MAICYA; SATA 12

Hailey, Arthur 1920- . . . . CLC 5
See also AITN 2; BEST 90:3; CA 1-4R;
CANR 2, 36; DAM NOV, POP; DLB 88;
DLBY 82; MTCW

Hailey, Elizabeth Forsythe 1938- . . . CLC 40
See also CA 93-96; CAAS 1; CANR 15, 48;
INT CANR-15

Haines, John (Meade) 1924- . . . . CLC 58
See also CA 17-20R; CANR 13, 34; DLB 5

Hakluyt, Richard 1552-1616 . . . . LC 31

Haldeman, Joe (William) 1943- . . . . . CLC 61
See also CA 53-56; CANR 6; DLB 8;
INT CANR-6

Haley, Alex(ander Murray Palmer)
1921-1992 . . . . CLC 8, 12, 76; BLC; DA;
DAB; DAC
See also BW 2; CA 77-80; 136; DAM MST,
MULT, POP; DLB 38; MTCW

Haliburton, Thomas Chandler
1796-1865 . . . . NCLC 15
See also DLB 11, 99

Hall, Donald (Andrew, Jr.)
1928- . . . . CLC 1, 13, 37, 59
See also CA 5-8R; CAAS 7; CANR 2, 44;
DAM POET; DLB 5; SATA 23

Hall, Frederic Sauser
See Sauser-Hall, Frederic

Hall, James
See Kuttner, Henry

Hall, James Norman 1887-1951 . . . TCLC 23
See also CA 123; SATA 21

Hall, (Marguerite) Radclyffe
1886(?)-1943 . . . . TCLC 12
See also CA 110

Hall, Rodney 1935- . . . . CLC 51
See also CA 109

Halleck, Fitz-Greene 1790-1867 . . NCLC 47
See also DLB 3

Halliday, Michael
See Creasey, John

Halpern, Daniel 1945- . . . . CLC 14
See also CA 33-36R

Hamburger, Michael (Peter Leopold)
1924- . . . . CLC 5, 14
See also CA 5-8R; CAAS 4; CANR 2, 47;
DLB 27

Hamill, Pete 1935- . . . . CLC 10
See also CA 25-28R; CANR 18

Hamilton, Alexander
1755(?)-1804 . . . . NCLC 49
See also DLB 37

Hamilton, Clive
See Lewis, C(live) S(taples)

Hamilton, Edmond 1904-1977 . . . . . . CLC 1
See also CA 1-4R; CANR 3; DLB 8

Hamilton, Eugene (Jacob) Lee
See Lee-Hamilton, Eugene (Jacob)

Hamilton, Franklin
See Silverberg, Robert

Hamilton, Gail
See Corcoran, Barbara

Hamilton, Mollie
See Kaye, M(ary) M(argaret)

Hamilton, (Anthony Walter) Patrick
1904-1962 . . . . CLC 51
See also CA 113; DLB 10

Hamilton, Virginia 1936- . . . . CLC 26
See also AAYA 2; BW 2; CA 25-28R;
CANR 20, 37; CLR 1, 11; DAM MULT;
DLB 33, 52; INT CANR-20; JRDA;
MAICYA; MTCW; SATA 4, 56, 79

Hammett, (Samuel) Dashiell
1894-1961 . . . . CLC 3, 5, 10, 19, 47;
SSC 17
See also AITN 1; CA 81-84; CANR 42;
CDALB 1929-1941; DLBD 6; MTCW

Hammon, Jupiter
1711(?)-1800(?) . . . . NCLC 5; BLC
See also DAM MULT, POET; DLB 31, 50

Hammond, Keith
See Kuttner, Henry

Hamner, Earl (Henry), Jr. 1923- . . . CLC 12
See also AITN 2; CA 73-76; DLB 6

Hampton, Christopher (James)
1946- . . . . CLC 4
See also CA 25-28R; DLB 13; MTCW

Hamsun, Knut . . . . TCLC 2, 14, 49
See also Pedersen, Knut

Handke, Peter 1942- . . CLC 5, 8, 10, 15, 38
See also CA 77-80; CANR 33;
DAM DRAM, NOV; DLB 85, 124;
MTCW

Hanley, James 1901-1985 . . . CLC 3, 5, 8, 13
See also CA 73-76; 117; CANR 36; MTCW

Hannah, Barry 1942- . . . . CLC 23, 38, 90
See also CA 108; 110; CANR 43; DLB 6;
INT 110; MTCW

Hannon, Ezra
See Hunter, Evan

Hansberry, Lorraine (Vivian)
1930-1965 . . . . . . CLC 17, 62; BLC; DA;
DAB; DAC; DC 2
See also BW 1; CA 109; 25-28R; CABS 3;
CDALB 1941-1968; DAM DRAM, MST,
MULT; DLB 7, 38; MTCW

Hansen, Joseph 1923- . . . . CLC 38
See also CA 29-32R; CAAS 17; CANR 16,
44; INT CANR-16

Hansen, Martin A. 1909-1955 . . . . . TCLC 32

Hanson, Kenneth O(stlin) 1922- . . . . CLC 13
See also CA 53-56; CANR 7

Hardwick, Elizabeth 1916- . . . . CLC 13
See also CA 5-8R; CANR 3, 32;
DAM NOV; DLB 6; MTCW

Hardy, Thomas
1840-1928 . . . . . . **TCLC 4, 10, 18, 32, 48,**
53; DA; DAB; DAC; PC 8; SSC 2; WLC
See also CA 104; 123; CDBLB 1890-1914;
DAM MST, NOV, POET; DLB 18, 19,
135; MTCW

Hare, David 1947- . . . . **CLC 29, 58**
See also CA 97-100; CANR 39; DLB 13;
MTCW

Harford, Henry
See Hudson, W(illiam) H(enry)

Hargrave, Leonie
See Disch, Thomas M(ichael)

Harjo, Joy 1951- . . . . **CLC 83**
See also CA 114; CANR 35; DAM MULT;
DLB 120; NNAL

Harlan, Louis R(udolph) 1922- . . . . . **CLC 34**
See also CA 21-24R; CANR 25

Harling, Robert 1951(?)- . . . . **CLC 53**
See also CA 147

Harmon, William (Ruth) 1938- . . . . . **CLC 38**
See also CA 33-36R; CANR 14, 32, 35;
SATA 65

Harper, F. E. W.
See Harper, Frances Ellen Watkins

Harper, Frances E. W.
See Harper, Frances Ellen Watkins

Harper, Frances E. Watkins
See Harper, Frances Ellen Watkins

Harper, Frances Ellen
See Harper, Frances Ellen Watkins

Harper, Frances Ellen Watkins
1825-1911 . . . . **TCLC 14; BLC**
See also BW 1; CA 111; 125; DAM MULT,
POET; DLB 50

Harper, Michael S(teven) 1938- . . **CLC 7, 22**
See also BW 1; CA 33-36R; CANR 24;
DLB 41

Harper, Mrs. F. E. W.
See Harper, Frances Ellen Watkins

Harris, Christie (Lucy) Irwin
1907- . . . . **CLC 12**
See also CA 5-8R; CANR 6; DLB 88;
JRDA; MAICYA; SAAS 10; SATA 6, 74

Harris, Frank 1856(?)-1931 . . . . **TCLC 24**
See also CA 109; DLB 156

Harris, George Washington
1814-1869 . . . . **NCLC 23**
See also DLB 3, 11

Harris, Joel Chandler
1848-1908 . . . . **TCLC 2; SSC 19**
See also CA 104; 137; DLB 11, 23, 42, 78,
91; MAICYA; YABC 1

Harris, John (Wyndham Parkes Lucas)
Beynon 1903-1969
See Wyndham, John
See also CA 102; 89-92

Harris, MacDonald . . . . **CLC 9**
See also Heiney, Donald (William)

Harris, Mark 1922- . . . . **CLC 19**
See also CA 5-8R; CAAS 3; CANR 2;
DLB 2; DLBY 80

Harris, (Theodore) Wilson 1921-. . . . **CLC 25**
See also BW 2; CA 65-68; CAAS 16;
CANR 11, 27; DLB 117; MTCW

Harrison, Elizabeth Cavanna 1909-
See Cavanna, Betty
See also CA 9-12R; CANR 6, 27

Harrison, Harry (Max) 1925- . . . . . . **CLC 42**
See also CA 1-4R; CANR 5, 21; DLB 8;
SATA 4

Harrison, James (Thomas)
1937- . . . . **CLC 6, 14, 33, 66; SSC 19**
See also CA 13-16R; CANR 8; DLBY 82;
INT CANR-8

Harrison, Jim
See Harrison, James (Thomas)

Harrison, Kathryn 1961- . . . . **CLC 70**
See also CA 144

Harrison, Tony 1937-. . . . . **CLC 43**
See also CA 65-68; CANR 44; DLB 40;
MTCW

Harriss, Will(ard Irvin) 1922- . . . . . . **CLC 34**
See also CA 111

Harson, Sley
See Ellison, Harlan (Jay)

Hart, Ellis
See Ellison, Harlan (Jay)

Hart, Josephine 1942(?)- . . . . **CLC 70**
See also CA 138; DAM POP

Hart, Moss 1904-1961 . . . . **CLC 66**
See also CA 109; 89-92; DAM DRAM;
DLB 7

Harte, (Francis) Bret(t)
1836(?)-1902 . . . . **TCLC 1, 25; DA; DAC;**
SSC 8; WLC
See also CA 104; 140; CDALB 1865-1917;
DAM MST; DLB 12, 64, 74, 79;
SATA 26

Hartley, L(eslie) P(oles)
1895-1972 . . . . **CLC 2, 22**
See also CA 45-48; 37-40R; CANR 33;
DLB 15, 139; MTCW

Hartman, Geoffrey H. 1929-. . . . . . . **CLC 27**
See also CA 117; 125; DLB 67

Hartmann von Aue
c. 1160-c. 1205 . . . . **CMLC 15**
See also DLB 138

Hartmann von Aue 1170-1210. . . . **CMLC 15**

Haruf, Kent 1943- . . . . **CLC 34**
See also CA 149

Harwood, Ronald 1934-. . . . . **CLC 32**
See also CA 1-4R; CANR 4; DAM DRAM,
MST; DLB 13

Hasek, Jaroslav (Matej Frantisek)
1883-1923 . . . . **TCLC 4**
See also CA 104; 129; MTCW

Hass, Robert 1941-. . . . . **CLC 18, 39**
See also CA 111; CANR 30, 50; DLB 105

Hastings, Hudson
See Kuttner, Henry

Hastings, Selina. . . . . **CLC 44**

Hatteras, Amelia
See Mencken, H(enry) L(ouis)

Hatteras, Owen. . . . . **TCLC 18**
See also Mencken, H(enry) L(ouis); Nathan,
George Jean

Hauptmann, Gerhart (Johann Robert)
1862-1946 . . . . **TCLC 4**
See also CA 104; DAM DRAM; DLB 66,
118

Havel, Vaclav
1936- . . . . **CLC 25, 58, 65; DC 6**
See also CA 104; CANR 36; DAM DRAM;
MTCW

Haviaras, Stratis . . . . **CLC 33**
See also Chaviaras, Strates

Hawes, Stephen 1475(?)-1523(?) . . . . . **LC 17**

Hawkes, John (Clendennin Burne, Jr.)
1925- . . . . . . **CLC 1, 2, 3, 4, 7, 9, 14, 15,**
27, 49
See also CA 1-4R; CANR 2, 47; DLB 2, 7;
DLBY 80; MTCW

Hawking, S. W.
See Hawking, Stephen W(illiam)

Hawking, Stephen W(illiam)
1942- . . . . **CLC 63**
See also AAYA 13; BEST 89:1; CA 126;
129; CANR 48

Hawthorne, Julian 1846-1934 . . . . . **TCLC 25**

Hawthorne, Nathaniel
1804-1864 . . . . **NCLC 39; DA; DAB;**
DAC; SSC 3; WLC
See also CDALB 1640-1865; DAM MST,
NOV; DLB 1, 74; YABC 2

Haxton, Josephine Ayres 1921-
See Douglas, Ellen
See also CA 115; CANR 41

Hayaseca y Eizaguirre, Jorge
See Echegaray (y Eizaguirre), Jose (Maria
Waldo)

Hayashi Fumiko 1904-1951. . . . . . . **TCLC 27**

Haycraft, Anna
See Ellis, Alice Thomas
See also CA 122

Hayden, Robert E(arl)
1913-1980 . . . . . . **CLC 5, 9, 14, 37; BLC;**
DA; DAC; PC 6
See also BW 1; CA 69-72; 97-100; CABS 2;
CANR 24; CDALB 1941-1968;
DAM MST, MULT, POET; DLB 5, 76;
MTCW; SATA 19; SATA-Obit 26

Hayford, J(oseph) E(phraim) Casely
See Casely-Hayford, J(oseph) E(phraim)

Hayman, Ronald 1932-. . . . . **CLC 44**
See also CA 25-28R; CANR 18, 50;
DLB 155

Haywood, Eliza (Fowler)
1693(?)-1756 . . . . **LC 1**

Hazlitt, William 1778-1830 . . . . . . **NCLC 29**
See also DLB 110, 158

Hazzard, Shirley 1931- . . . . **CLC 18**
See also CA 9-12R; CANR 4; DLBY 82;
MTCW

Head, Bessie 1937-1986. . . **CLC 25, 67; BLC**
See also BW 2; CA 29-32R; 119; CANR 25;
DAM MULT; DLB 117; MTCW

Headon, (Nicky) Topper 1956(?)- . . . **CLC 30**

Holmes, Oliver Wendell
1809-1894 .... **NCLC 14**
See also CDALB 1640-1865; DLB 1;
SATA 34

Holmes, Raymond
See Souster, (Holmes) Raymond

Holt, Victoria
See Hibbert, Eleanor Alice Burford

Holub, Miroslav 1923- .... **CLC 4**
See also CA 21-24R; CANR 10

Homer
c. 8th cent. B.C.- ..... **CMLC 1, 16; DA;**
DAB; DAC
See also DAM MST, POET

Honig, Edwin 1919- .... **CLC 33**
See also CA 5-8R; CAAS 8; CANR 4, 45;
DLB 5

Hood, Hugh (John Blagdon)
1928- .... **CLC 15, 28**
See also CA 49-52; CAAS 17; CANR 1, 33;
DLB 53

Hood, Thomas 1799-1845 .... **NCLC 16**
See also DLB 96

Hooker, (Peter) Jeremy 1941- ...... **CLC 43**
See also CA 77-80; CANR 22; DLB 40

Hope, A(lec) D(erwent) 1907- .... **CLC 3, 51**
See also CA 21-24R; CANR 33; MTCW

Hope, Brian
See Creasey, John

Hope, Christopher (David Tully)
1944- .... **CLC 52**
See also CA 106; CANR 47; SATA 62

Hopkins, Gerard Manley
1844-1889 .... **NCLC 17; DA; DAB;**
DAC; WLC
See also CDBLB 1890-1914; DAM MST,
POET; DLB 35, 57

Hopkins, John (Richard) 1931- ...... **CLC 4**
See also CA 85-88

Hopkins, Pauline Elizabeth
1859-1930 .... **TCLC 28; BLC**
See also BW 2; CA 141; DAM MULT;
DLB 50

Hopkinson, Francis 1737-1791 ...... **LC 25**
See also DLB 31

Hopley-Woolrich, Cornell George 1903-1968
See Woolrich, Cornell
See also CA 13-14; CAP 1

Horatio
See Proust, (Valentin-Louis-George-Eugene-)
Marcel

Horgan, Paul (George Vincent O'Shaughnessy)
1903-1995 .... **CLC 9, 53**
See also CA 13-16R; 147; CANR 9, 35;
DAM NOV; DLB 102; DLBY 85;
INT CANR-9; MTCW; SATA 13;
SATA-Obit 84

Horn, Peter
See Kuttner, Henry

Hornem, Horace Esq.
See Byron, George Gordon (Noel)

Hornung, E(rnest) W(illiam)
1866-1921 .... **TCLC 59**
See also CA 108; DLB 70

Horovitz, Israel (Arthur) 1939- ..... **CLC 56**
See also CA 33-36R; CANR 46;
DAM DRAM; DLB 7

Horvath, Odon von
See Horvath, Oedoen von
See also DLB 85, 124

Horvath, Oedoen von 1901-1938 ... **TCLC 45**
See also Horvath, Odon von
See also CA 118

Horwitz, Julius 1920-1986 .... **CLC 14**
See also CA 9-12R; 119; CANR 12

Hospital, Janette Turner 1942- ..... **CLC 42**
See also CA 108; CANR 48

Hostos, E. M. de
See Hostos (y Bonilla), Eugenio Maria de

Hostos, Eugenio M. de
See Hostos (y Bonilla), Eugenio Maria de

Hostos, Eugenio Maria
See Hostos (y Bonilla), Eugenio Maria de

Hostos (y Bonilla), Eugenio Maria de
1839-1903 .... **TCLC 24**
See also CA 123; 131; HW

Houdini
See Lovecraft, H(oward) P(hillips)

Hougan, Carolyn 1943- .... **CLC 34**
See also CA 139

Household, Geoffrey (Edward West)
1900-1988 .... **CLC 11**
See also CA 77-80; 126; DLB 87; SATA 14;
SATA-Obit 59

Housman, A(lfred) E(dward)
1859-1936 ...... **TCLC 1, 10; DA; DAB;**
DAC; PC 2
See also CA 104; 125; DAM MST, POET;
DLB 19; MTCW

Housman, Laurence 1865-1959 ..... **TCLC 7**
See also CA 106; DLB 10; SATA 25

Howard, Elizabeth Jane 1923- ... **CLC 7, 29**
See also CA 5-8R; CANR 8

Howard, Maureen 1930- ..... **CLC 5, 14, 46**
See also CA 53-56; CANR 31; DLBY 83;
INT CANR-31; MTCW

Howard, Richard 1929- ...... **CLC 7, 10, 47**
See also AITN 1; CA 85-88; CANR 25;
DLB 5; INT CANR-25

Howard, Robert Ervin 1906-1936 ... **TCLC 8**
See also CA 105

Howard, Warren F.
See Pohl, Frederik

Howe, Fanny 1940- .... **CLC 47**
See also CA 117; SATA-Brief 52

Howe, Irving 1920-1993 .... **CLC 85**
See also CA 9-12R; 141; CANR 21, 50;
DLB 67; MTCW

Howe, Julia Ward 1819-1910 ..... **TCLC 21**
See also CA 117; DLB 1

Howe, Susan 1937- .... **CLC 72**
See also DLB 120

Howe, Tina 1937- .... **CLC 48**
See also CA 109

Howell, James 1594(?)-1666 .... **LC 13**
See also DLB 151

Howells, W. D.
See Howells, William Dean

Howells, William D.
See Howells, William Dean

Howells, William Dean
1837-1920 .... **TCLC 7, 17, 41**
See also CA 104; 134; CDALB 1865-1917;
DLB 12, 64, 74, 79

Howes, Barbara 1914- .... **CLC 15**
See also CA 9-12R; CAAS 3; SATA 5

Hrabal, Bohumil 1914- .... **CLC 13, 67**
See also CA 106; CAAS 12

Hsun, Lu
See Lu Hsun

Hubbard, L(afayette) Ron(ald)
1911-1986 .... **CLC 43**
See also CA 77-80; 118; CANR 22;
DAM POP

Huch, Ricarda (Octavia)
1864-1947 .... **TCLC 13**
See also CA 111; DLB 66

Huddle, David 1942- .... **CLC 49**
See also CA 57-60; CAAS 20; DLB 130

Hudson, Jeffrey
See Crichton, (John) Michael

Hudson, W(illiam) H(enry)
1841-1922 .... **TCLC 29**
See also CA 115; DLB 98, 153; SATA 35

Hueffer, Ford Madox
See Ford, Ford Madox

Hughart, Barry 1934- .... **CLC 39**
See also CA 137

Hughes, Colin
See Creasey, John

Hughes, David (John) 1930- .... **CLC 48**
See also CA 116; 129; DLB 14

Hughes, (James) Langston
1902-1967 ..... **CLC 1, 5, 10, 15, 35, 44;**
BLC; DA; DAB; DAC; DC 3; PC 1;
SSC 6; WLC
See also AAYA 12; BW 1; CA 1-4R;
25-28R; CANR 1, 34; CDALB 1929-1941;
CLR 17; DAM DRAM, MST, MULT,
POET; DLB 4, 7, 48, 51, 86; JRDA;
MAICYA; MTCW; SATA 4, 33

Hughes, Richard (Arthur Warren)
1900-1976 .... **CLC 1, 11**
See also CA 5-8R; 65-68; CANR 4;
DAM NOV; DLB 15, 161; MTCW;
SATA 8; SATA-Obit 25

Hughes, Ted
1930- .... **CLC 2, 4, 9, 14, 37; DAB;**
DAC; PC 7
See also CA 1-4R; CANR 1, 33; CLR 3;
DLB 40, 161; MAICYA; MTCW;
SATA 49; SATA-Brief 27

Hugo, Richard F(ranklin)
1923-1982 .... **CLC 6, 18, 32**
See also CA 49-52; 108; CANR 3;
DAM POET; DLB 5

Hugo, Victor (Marie)
1802-1885 .... **NCLC 3, 10, 21; DA;**
DAB; DAC; WLC
See also DAM DRAM, MST, NOV, POET;
DLB 119; SATA 47

Huidobro, Vicente
See Huidobro Fernandez, Vicente Garcia

Jacobs, Jim 1942-................ **CLC 12**
See also CA 97-100; INT 97-100

Jacobs, W(illiam) W(ymark)
1863-1943 .... **TCLC 22**
See also CA 121; DLB 135

Jacobsen, Jens Peter 1847-1885 .. **NCLC 34**

Jacobsen, Josephine 1908-......... **CLC 48**
See also CA 33-36R; CAAS 18; CANR 23, 48

Jacobson, Dan 1929- .... **CLC 4, 14**
See also CA 1-4R; CANR 2, 25; DLB 14; MTCW

Jacqueline
See Carpentier (y Valmont), Alejo

Jagger, Mick 1944-.............. **CLC 17**

Jakes, John (William) 1932-....... **CLC 29**
See also BEST 89:4; CA 57-60; CANR 10, 43; DAM NOV, POP; DLBY 83; INT CANR-10; MTCW; SATA 62

James, Andrew
See Kirkup, James

James, C(yril) L(ionel) R(obert)
1901-1989 .... **CLC 33**
See also BW 2; CA 117; 125; 128; DLB 125; MTCW

James, Daniel (Lewis) 1911-1988
See Santiago, Danny
See also CA 125

James, Dynely
See Mayne, William (James Carter)

James, Henry Sr. 1811-1882..... **NCLC 53**

James, Henry
1843-1916 ...... **TCLC 2, 11, 24, 40, 47;**
DA; DAB; DAC; SSC 8; WLC
See also CA 104; 132; CDALB 1865-1917; DAM MST, NOV; DLB 12, 71, 74; DLBD 13; MTCW

James, M. R.
See James, Montague (Rhodes)
See also DLB 156

James, Montague (Rhodes)
1862-1936 .... **TCLC 6; SSC 16**
See also CA 104

James, P. D. .... **CLC 18, 46**
See also White, Phyllis Dorothy James
See also BEST 90:2; CDBLB 1960 to Present; DLB 87

James, Philip
See Moorcock, Michael (John)

James, William 1842-1910..... **TCLC 15, 32**
See also CA 109

James I 1394-1437 .... **LC 20**

Jameson, Anna 1794-1860 .... **NCLC 43**
See also DLB 99

Jami, Nur al-Din 'Abd al-Rahman
1414-1492 .... **LC 9**

Jandl, Ernst 1925- .... **CLC 34**

Janowitz, Tama 1957- .... **CLC 43**
See also CA 106; DAM POP

Japrisot, Sebastien 1931-......... **CLC 90**

Jarrell, Randall
1914-1965 ...... **CLC 1, 2, 6, 9, 13, 49**
See also CA 5-8R; 25-28R; CABS 2; CANR 6, 34; CDALB 1941-1968; CLR 6; DAM POET; DLB 48, 52; MAICYA; MTCW; SATA 7

Jarry, Alfred
1873-1907 .... **TCLC 2, 14; SSC 20**
See also CA 104; DAM DRAM

Jarvis, E. K.
See Bloch, Robert (Albert); Ellison, Harlan (Jay); Silverberg, Robert

Jeake, Samuel, Jr.
See Aiken, Conrad (Potter)

Jean Paul 1763-1825 .... **NCLC 7**

Jefferies, (John) Richard
1848-1887 .... **NCLC 47**
See also DLB 98, 141; SATA 16

Jeffers, (John) Robinson
1887-1962 .... **CLC 2, 3, 11, 15, 54; DA;**
DAC; WLC
See also CA 85-88; CANR 35; CDALB 1917-1929; DAM MST, POET; DLB 45; MTCW

Jefferson, Janet
See Mencken, H(enry) L(ouis)

Jefferson, Thomas 1743-1826 .... **NCLC 11**
See also CDALB 1640-1865; DLB 31

Jeffrey, Francis 1773-1850...... **NCLC 33**
See also DLB 107

Jelakowitch, Ivan
See Heijermans, Herman

Jellicoe, (Patricia) Ann 1927-...... **CLC 27**
See also CA 85-88; DLB 13

Jen, Gish .... **CLC 70**
See also Jen, Lillian

Jen, Lillian 1956(?)-
See Jen, Gish
See also CA 135

Jenkins, (John) Robin 1912-....... **CLC 52**
See also CA 1-4R; CANR 1; DLB 14

Jennings, Elizabeth (Joan)
1926- .... **CLC 5, 14**
See also CA 61-64; CAAS 5; CANR 8, 39; DLB 27; MTCW; SATA 66

Jennings, Waylon 1937-........... **CLC 21**

Jensen, Johannes V. 1873-1950.... **TCLC 41**

Jensen, Laura (Linnea) 1948- ...... **CLC 37**
See also CA 103

Jerome, Jerome K(lapka)
1859-1927 .... **TCLC 23**
See also CA 119; DLB 10, 34, 135

Jerrold, Douglas William
1803-1857 .... **NCLC 2**
See also DLB 158, 159

Jewett, (Theodora) Sarah Orne
1849-1909 ...... **TCLC 1, 22; SSC 6**
See also CA 108; 127; DLB 12, 74; SATA 15

Jewsbury, Geraldine (Endsor)
1812-1880 .... **NCLC 22**
See also DLB 21

Jhabvala, Ruth Prawer
1927- .... **CLC 4, 8, 29; DAB**
See also CA 1-4R; CANR 2, 29; DAM NOV; DLB 139; INT CANR-29; MTCW

Jiles, Paulette 1943-.......... **CLC 13, 58**
See also CA 101

Jimenez (Mantecon), Juan Ramon
1881-1958 .... **TCLC 4; HLC; PC 7**
See also CA 104; 131; DAM MULT, POET; DLB 134; HW; MTCW

Jimenez, Ramon
See Jimenez (Mantecon), Juan Ramon

Jimenez Mantecon, Juan
See Jimenez (Mantecon), Juan Ramon

Joel, Billy .... **CLC 26**
See also Joel, William Martin

Joel, William Martin 1949-
See Joel, Billy
See also CA 108

John of the Cross, St. 1542-1591 .... **LC 18**

Johnson, B(ryan) S(tanley William)
1933-1973 .... **CLC 6, 9**
See also CA 9-12R; 53-56; CANR 9; DLB 14, 40

Johnson, Benj. F. of Boo
See Riley, James Whitcomb

Johnson, Benjamin F. of Boo
See Riley, James Whitcomb

Johnson, Charles (Richard)
1948- .... **CLC 7, 51, 65; BLC**
See also BW 2; CA 116; CAAS 18; CANR 42; DAM MULT; DLB 33

Johnson, Denis 1949-............. **CLC 52**
See also CA 117; 121; DLB 120

Johnson, Diane 1934-........ **CLC 5, 13, 48**
See also CA 41-44R; CANR 17, 40; DLBY 80; INT CANR-17; MTCW

Johnson, Eyvind (Olof Verner)
1900-1976 .... **CLC 14**
See also CA 73-76; 69-72; CANR 34

Johnson, J. R.
See James, C(yril) L(ionel) R(obert)

Johnson, James Weldon
1871-1938 .... **TCLC 3, 19; BLC**
See also BW 1; CA 104; 125; CDALB 1917-1929; CLR 32; DAM MULT, POET; DLB 51; MTCW; SATA 31

Johnson, Joyce 1935-............. **CLC 58**
See also CA 125; 129

Johnson, Lionel (Pigot)
1867-1902 .... **TCLC 19**
See also CA 117; DLB 19

Johnson, Mel
See Malzberg, Barry N(athaniel)

Johnson, Pamela Hansford
1912-1981 .... **CLC 1, 7, 27**
See also CA 1-4R; 104; CANR 2, 28; DLB 15; MTCW

Johnson, Samuel
1709-1784 ..... **LC 15; DA; DAB; DAC;**
WLC
See also CDBLB 1660-1789; DAM MST; DLB 39, 95, 104, 142

Johnson, Uwe
1934-1984 . . . . **CLC 5, 10, 15, 40**
See also CA 1-4R; 112; CANR 1, 39;
DLB 75; MTCW

Johnston, George (Benson) 1913- . . . **CLC 51**
See also CA 1-4R; CANR 5, 20; DLB 88

Johnston, Jennifer 1930- . . . . **CLC 7**
See also CA 85-88; DLB 14

Jolley, (Monica) Elizabeth
1923- . . . . **CLC 46; SSC 19**
See also CA 127; CAAS 13

Jones, Arthur Llewellyn 1863-1947
See Machen, Arthur
See also CA 104

Jones, D(ouglas) G(ordon) 1929- . . . . **CLC 10**
See also CA 29-32R; CANR 13; DLB 53

Jones, David (Michael)
1895-1974 . . . . **CLC 2, 4, 7, 13, 42**
See also CA 9-12R; 53-56; CANR 28;
CDBLB 1945-1960; DLB 20, 100; MTCW

Jones, David Robert 1947-
See Bowie, David
See also CA 103

Jones, Diana Wynne 1934- . . . . **CLC 26**
See also AAYA 12; CA 49-52; CANR 4,
26; CLR 23; DLB 161; JRDA; MAICYA;
SAAS 7; SATA 9, 70

Jones, Edward P. 1950- . . . . **CLC 76**
See also BW 2; CA 142

Jones, Gayl 1949- . . . . **CLC 6, 9; BLC**
See also BW 2; CA 77-80; CANR 27;
DAM MULT; DLB 33; MTCW

Jones, James 1921-1977 . . . . **CLC 1, 3, 10, 39**
See also AITN 1, 2; CA 1-4R; 69-72;
CANR 6; DLB 2, 143; MTCW

Jones, John J.
See Lovecraft, H(oward) P(hillips)

Jones, LeRoi . . . . **CLC 1, 2, 3, 5, 10, 14**
See also Baraka, Amiri

Jones, Louis B. . . . . **CLC 65**
See also CA 141

Jones, Madison (Percy, Jr.) 1925- . . . **CLC 4**
See also CA 13-16R; CAAS 11; CANR 7;
DLB 152

Jones, Mervyn 1922- . . . . **CLC 10, 52**
See also CA 45-48; CAAS 5; CANR 1;
MTCW

Jones, Mick 1956(?)- . . . . **CLC 30**

Jones, Nettie (Pearl) 1941- . . . . **CLC 34**
See also BW 2; CA 137; CAAS 20

Jones, Preston 1936-1979 . . . . **CLC 10**
See also CA 73-76; 89-92; DLB 7

Jones, Robert F(rancis) 1934- . . . . **CLC 7**
See also CA 49-52; CANR 2

Jones, Rod 1953- . . . . **CLC 50**
See also CA 128

Jones, Terence Graham Parry
1942- . . . . **CLC 21**
See also Jones, Terry; Monty Python
See also CA 112; 116; CANR 35; INT 116

Jones, Terry
See Jones, Terence Graham Parry
See also SATA 67; SATA-Brief 51

Jones, Thom 1945(?)- . . . . **CLC 81**

Jong, Erica 1942- . . . . . . **CLC 4, 6, 8, 18, 83**
See also AITN 1; BEST 90:2; CA 73-76;
CANR 26; DAM NOV, POP; DLB 2, 5,
28, 152; INT CANR-26; MTCW

Jonson, Ben(jamin)
1572(?)-1637 . . . . **LC 6; DA; DAB; DAC;
DC 4; WLC**
See also CDBLB Before 1660;
DAM DRAM, MST, POET; DLB 62,
121

Jordan, June 1936- . . . . **CLC 5, 11, 23**
See also AAYA 2; BW 2; CA 33-36R;
CANR 25; CLR 10; DAM MULT,
POET; DLB 38; MAICYA; MTCW;
SATA 4

Jordan, Pat(rick M.) 1941- . . . . **CLC 37**
See also CA 33-36R

Jorgensen, Ivar
See Ellison, Harlan (Jay)

Jorgenson, Ivar
See Silverberg, Robert

Josephus, Flavius c. 37-100 . . . . . **CMLC 13**

Josipovici, Gabriel 1940- . . . . **CLC 6, 43**
See also CA 37-40R; CAAS 8; CANR 47;
DLB 14

Joubert, Joseph 1754-1824 . . . . **NCLC 9**

Jouve, Pierre Jean 1887-1976 . . . . . . **CLC 47**
See also CA 65-68

Joyce, James (Augustine Aloysius)
1882-1941 . . . . **TCLC 3, 8, 16, 35, 52;
DA; DAB; DAC; SSC 3; WLC**
See also CA 104; 126; CDBLB 1914-1945;
DAM MST, NOV, POET; DLB 10, 19,
36; MTCW

Jozsef, Attila 1905-1937 . . . . **TCLC 22**
See also CA 116

Juana Ines de la Cruz 1651(?)-1695 . . . **LC 5**

Judd, Cyril
See Kornbluth, C(yril) M.; Pohl, Frederik

Julian of Norwich 1342(?)-1416(?) . . . . **LC 6**
See also DLB 146

Juniper, Alex
See Hospital, Janette Turner

Just, Ward (Swift) 1935- . . . . **CLC 4, 27**
See also CA 25-28R; CANR 32;
INT CANR-32

Justice, Donald (Rodney) 1925- . . **CLC 6, 19**
See also CA 5-8R; CANR 26; DAM POET;
DLBY 83; INT CANR-26

Juvenal c. 55-c. 127 . . . . **CMLC 8**

Juvenis
See Bourne, Randolph S(illiman)

Kacew, Romain 1914-1980
See Gary, Romain
See also CA 108; 102

Kadare, Ismail 1936- . . . . **CLC 52**

Kadohata, Cynthia . . . . **CLC 59**
See also CA 140

Kafka, Franz
1883-1924 . . . . **TCLC 2, 6, 13, 29, 47, 53;
DA; DAB; DAC; SSC 5; WLC**
See also CA 105; 126; DAM MST, NOV;
DLB 81; MTCW

Kahanovitsch, Pinkhes
See Der Nister

Kahn, Roger 1927- . . . . **CLC 30**
See also CA 25-28R; CANR 44; SATA 37

Kain, Saul
See Sassoon, Siegfried (Lorraine)

Kaiser, Georg 1878-1945 . . . . **TCLC 9**
See also CA 106; DLB 124

Kaletski, Alexander 1946- . . . . **CLC 39**
See also CA 118; 143

Kalidasa fl. c. 400- . . . . **CMLC 9**

Kallman, Chester (Simon)
1921-1975 . . . . **CLC 2**
See also CA 45-48; 53-56; CANR 3

Kaminsky, Melvin 1926-
See Brooks, Mel
See also CA 65-68; CANR 16

Kaminsky, Stuart M(elvin) 1934- . . . **CLC 59**
See also CA 73-76; CANR 29

Kane, Paul
See Simon, Paul

Kane, Wilson
See Bloch, Robert (Albert)

Kanin, Garson 1912- . . . . **CLC 22**
See also AITN 1; CA 5-8R; CANR 7;
DLB 7

Kaniuk, Yoram 1930- . . . . **CLC 19**
See also CA 134

Kant, Immanuel 1724-1804 . . . . . . **NCLC 27**
See also DLB 94

Kantor, MacKinlay 1904-1977 . . . . . . **CLC 7**
See also CA 61-64; 73-76; DLB 9, 102

Kaplan, David Michael 1946- . . . . . . **CLC 50**

Kaplan, James 1951- . . . . **CLC 59**
See also CA 135

Karageorge, Michael
See Anderson, Poul (William)

Karamzin, Nikolai Mikhailovich
1766-1826 . . . . **NCLC 3**
See also DLB 150

Karapanou, Margarita 1946- . . . . **CLC 13**
See also CA 101

Karinthy, Frigyes 1887-1938 . . . . . . **TCLC 47**

Karl, Frederick R(obert) 1927- . . . . . **CLC 34**
See also CA 5-8R; CANR 3, 44

Kastel, Warren
See Silverberg, Robert

Kataev, Evgeny Petrovich 1903-1942
See Petrov, Evgeny
See also CA 120

Kataphusin
See Ruskin, John

Katz, Steve 1935- . . . . **CLC 47**
See also CA 25-28R; CAAS 14; CANR 12;
DLBY 83

Kauffman, Janet 1945- . . . . **CLC 42**
See also CA 117; CANR 43; DLBY 86

Kaufman, Bob (Garnell)
1925-1986 . . . . **CLC 49**
See also BW 1; CA 41-44R; 118; CANR 22;
DLB 16, 41

Kaufman, George S. 1889-1961..... **CLC 38**
See also CA 108; 93-96; DAM DRAM;
DLB 7; INT 108

Kaufman, Sue .... **CLC 3, 8**
See also Barondess, Sue K(aufman)

Kavafis, Konstantinos Petrou 1863-1933
See Cavafy, C(onstantine) P(eter)
See also CA 104

Kavan, Anna 1901-1968...... **CLC 5, 13, 82**
See also CA 5-8R; CANR 6; MTCW

Kavanagh, Dan
See Barnes, Julian

Kavanagh, Patrick (Joseph)
1904-1967 .... **CLC 22**
See also CA 123; 25-28R; DLB 15, 20;
MTCW

Kawabata, Yasunari
1899-1972 ..... **CLC 2, 5, 9, 18; SSC 17**
See also CA 93-96; 33-36R; DAM MULT

Kaye, M(ary) M(argaret) 1909-..... **CLC 28**
See also CA 89-92; CANR 24; MTCW;
SATA 62

Kaye, Mollie
See Kaye, M(ary) M(argaret)

Kaye-Smith, Sheila 1887-1956..... **TCLC 20**
See also CA 118; DLB 36

Kaymor, Patrice Maguilene
See Senghor, Leopold Sedar

Kazan, Elia 1909-........... **CLC 6, 16, 63**
See also CA 21-24R; CANR 32

Kazantzakis, Nikos
1883(?)-1957 .... **TCLC 2, 5, 33**
See also CA 105; 132; MTCW

Kazin, Alfred 1915- .... **CLC 34, 38**
See also CA 1-4R; CAAS 7; CANR 1, 45;
DLB 67

Keane, Mary Nesta (Skrine) 1904-
See Keane, Molly
See also CA 108; 114

Keane, Molly.................... **CLC 31**
See also Keane, Mary Nesta (Skrine)
See also INT 114

Keates, Jonathan 19(?)-........... **CLC 34**

Keaton, Buster 1895-1966........ **CLC 20**

Keats, John
1795-1821 .... **NCLC 8; DA; DAB;**
DAC; PC 1; WLC
See also CDBLB 1789-1832; DAM MST,
POET; DLB 96, 110

Keene, Donald 1922- .... **CLC 34**
See also CA 1-4R; CANR 5

Keillor, Garrison.................. **CLC 40**
See also Keillor, Gary (Edward)
See also AAYA 2; BEST 89:3; DLBY 87;
SATA 58

Keillor, Gary (Edward) 1942-
See Keillor, Garrison
See also CA 111; 117; CANR 36;
DAM POP; MTCW

Keith, Michael
See Hubbard, L(afayette) Ron(ald)

Keller, Gottfried 1819-1890....... **NCLC 2**
See also DLB 129

Kellerman, Jonathan 1949- .... **CLC 44**
See also BEST 90:1; CA 106; CANR 29;
DAM POP; INT CANR-29

Kelley, William Melvin 1937-...... **CLC 22**
See also BW 1; CA 77-80; CANR 27;
DLB 33

Kellogg, Marjorie 1922-............ **CLC 2**
See also CA 81-84

Kellow, Kathleen
See Hibbert, Eleanor Alice Burford

Kelly, M(ilton) T(erry) 1947-....... **CLC 55**
See also CA 97-100; CAAS 22; CANR 19,
43

Kelman, James 1946-.......... **CLC 58, 86**
See also CA 148

Kemal, Yashar 1923- .... **CLC 14, 29**
See also CA 89-92; CANR 44

Kemble, Fanny 1809-1893 .... **NCLC 18**
See also DLB 32

Kemelman, Harry 1908-........... **CLC 2**
See also AITN 1; CA 9-12R; CANR 6;
DLB 28

Kempe, Margery 1373(?)-1440(?) ..... **LC 6**
See also DLB 146

Kempis, Thomas a 1380-1471 .... **LC 11**

Kendall, Henry 1839-1882....... **NCLC 12**

Keneally, Thomas (Michael)
1935- ...... **CLC 5, 8, 10, 14, 19, 27, 43**
See also CA 85-88; CANR 10, 50;
DAM NOV; MTCW

Kennedy, Adrienne (Lita)
1931- .... **CLC 66; BLC; DC 5**
See also BW 2; CA 103; CAAS 20; CABS 3;
CANR 26; DAM MULT; DLB 38

Kennedy, John Pendleton
1795-1870 .... **NCLC 2**
See also DLB 3

Kennedy, Joseph Charles 1929-
See Kennedy, X. J.
See also CA 1-4R; CANR 4, 30, 40;
SATA 14

Kennedy, William 1928-... **CLC 6, 28, 34, 53**
See also AAYA 1; CA 85-88; CANR 14,
31; DAM NOV; DLB 143; DLBY 85;
INT CANR-31; MTCW; SATA 57

Kennedy, X. J................... **CLC 8, 42**
See also Kennedy, Joseph Charles
See also CAAS 9; CLR 27; DLB 5

Kenny, Maurice (Francis) 1929- .... **CLC 87**
See also CA 144; CAAS 22; DAM MULT;
NNAL

Kent, Kelvin
See Kuttner, Henry

Kenton, Maxwell
See Southern, Terry

Kenyon, Robert O.
See Kuttner, Henry

Kerouac, Jack ..... **CLC 1, 2, 3, 5, 14, 29, 61**
See also Kerouac, Jean-Louis Lebris de
See also CDALB 1941-1968; DLB 2, 16;
DLBD 3

Kerouac, Jean-Louis Lebris de 1922-1969
See Kerouac, Jack
See also AITN 1; CA 5-8R; 25-28R;
CANR 26; DA; DAB; DAC; DAM MST,
NOV, POET, POP; MTCW; WLC

Kerr, Jean 1923-................. **CLC 22**
See also CA 5-8R; CANR 7; INT CANR-7

Kerr, M. E. .... **CLC 12, 35**
See also Meaker, Marijane (Agnes)
See also AAYA 2; CLR 29; SAAS 1

Kerr, Robert .... **CLC 55**

Kerrigan, (Thomas) Anthony
1918- .... **CLC 4, 6**
See also CA 49-52; CAAS 11; CANR 4

Kerry, Lois
See Duncan, Lois

Kesey, Ken (Elton)
1935- ...... **CLC 1, 3, 6, 11, 46, 64; DA;**
DAB; DAC; WLC
See also CA 1-4R; CANR 22, 38;
CDALB 1968-1988; DAM MST, NOV,
POP; DLB 2, 16; MTCW; SATA 66

Kesselring, Joseph (Otto)
1902-1967 .... **CLC 45**
See also DAM DRAM, MST

Kessler, Jascha (Frederick) 1929-.... **CLC 4**
See also CA 17-20R; CANR 8, 48

Kettelkamp, Larry (Dale) 1933- .... **CLC 12**
See also CA 29-32R; CANR 16; SAAS 3;
SATA 2

Keyber, Conny
See Fielding, Henry

Keyes, Daniel 1927-.... **CLC 80; DA; DAC**
See also CA 17-20R; CANR 10, 26;
DAM MST, NOV; SATA 37

Khanshendel, Chiron
See Rose, Wendy

Khayyam, Omar
1048-1131 .... **CMLC 11; PC 8**
See also DAM POET

Kherdian, David 1931-........... **CLC 6, 9**
See also CA 21-24R; CAAS 2; CANR 39;
CLR 24; JRDA; MAICYA; SATA 16, 74

Khlebnikov, Velimir .... **TCLC 20**
See also Khlebnikov, Viktor Vladimirovich

Khlebnikov, Viktor Vladimirovich 1885-1922
See Khlebnikov, Velimir
See also CA 117

Khodasevich, Vladislav (Felitsianovich)
1886-1939 .... **TCLC 15**
See also CA 115

Kielland, Alexander Lange
1849-1906 .... **TCLC 5**
See also CA 104

Kiely, Benedict 1919-.......... **CLC 23, 43**
See also CA 1-4R; CANR 2; DLB 15

Kienzle, William X(avier) 1928- .... **CLC 25**
See also CA 93-96; CAAS 1; CANR 9, 31;
DAM POP; INT CANR-31; MTCW

Kierkegaard, Soren 1813-1855.... **NCLC 34**

Killens, John Oliver 1916-1987..... **CLC 10**
See also BW 2; CA 77-80; 123; CAAS 2;
CANR 26; DLB 33

Killigrew, Anne 1660-1685.......... **LC 4**
See also DLB 131

Kim
See Simenon, Georges (Jacques Christian)

Kincaid, Jamaica 1949- . . . **CLC 43, 68; BLC**
See also AAYA 13; BW 2; CA 125;
CANR 47; DAM MULT, NOV;
DLB 157

King, Francis (Henry) 1923- . . . . . **CLC 8, 53**
See also CA 1-4R; CANR 1, 33;
DAM NOV; DLB 15, 139; MTCW

King, Martin Luther, Jr.
1929-1968 . . . . **CLC 83; BLC; DA; DAB;
DAC**
See also BW 2; CA 25-28; CANR 27, 44;
CAP 2; DAM MST, MULT; MTCW;
SATA 14

King, Stephen (Edwin)
1947- . . . . . . **CLC 12, 26, 37, 61; SSC 17**
See also AAYA 1, 17; BEST 90:1;
CA 61-64; CANR 1, 30; DAM NOV,
POP; DLB 143; DLBY 80; JRDA;
MTCW; SATA 9, 55

King, Steve
See King, Stephen (Edwin)

King, Thomas 1943- . . . . **CLC 89; DAC**
See also CA 144; DAM MULT; NNAL

Kingman, Lee. . . . . **CLC 17**
See also Natti, (Mary) Lee
See also SAAS 3; SATA 1, 67

Kingsley, Charles 1819-1875 . . . . . **NCLC 35**
See also DLB 21, 32; YABC 2

Kingsley, Sidney 1906-1995. . . . . . . **CLC 44**
See also CA 85-88; 147; DLB 7

Kingsolver, Barbara 1955- . . . . . . **CLC 55, 81**
See also AAYA 15; CA 129; 134;
DAM POP; INT 134

Kingston, Maxine (Ting Ting) Hong
1940- . . . . **CLC 12, 19, 58**
See also AAYA 8; CA 69-72; CANR 13,
38; DAM MULT, NOV; DLBY 80;
INT CANR-13; MTCW; SATA 53

Kinnell, Galway
1927- . . . . **CLC 1, 2, 3, 5, 13, 29**
See also CA 9-12R; CANR 10, 34; DLB 5;
DLBY 87; INT CANR-34; MTCW

Kinsella, Thomas 1928- . . . . **CLC 4, 19**
See also CA 17-20R; CANR 15; DLB 27;
MTCW

Kinsella, W(illiam) P(atrick)
1935- . . . . **CLC 27, 43; DAC**
See also AAYA 7; CA 97-100; CAAS 7;
CANR 21, 35; DAM NOV, POP;
INT CANR-21; MTCW

Kipling, (Joseph) Rudyard
1865-1936 . . . . . **TCLC 8, 17; DA; DAB;
DAC; PC 3; SSC 5; WLC**
See also CA 105; 120; CANR 33;
CDBLB 1890-1914; CLR 39; DAM MST,
POET; DLB 19, 34, 141, 156; MAICYA;
MTCW; YABC 2

Kirkup, James 1918- . . . . **CLC 1**
See also CA 1-4R; CAAS 4; CANR 2;
DLB 27; SATA 12

Kirkwood, James 1930(?)-1989 . . . . . . **CLC 9**
See also AITN 2; CA 1-4R; 128; CANR 6,
40

Kirshner, Sidney
See Kingsley, Sidney

Kis, Danilo 1935-1989 . . . . **CLC 57**
See also CA 109; 118; 129; MTCW

Kivi, Aleksis 1834-1872 . . . . **NCLC 30**

Kizer, Carolyn (Ashley)
1925- . . . . **CLC 15, 39, 80**
See also CA 65-68; CAAS 5; CANR 24;
DAM POET; DLB 5

Klabund 1890-1928. . . . . **TCLC 44**
See also DLB 66

Klappert, Peter 1942- . . . . **CLC 57**
See also CA 33-36R; DLB 5

Klein, A(braham) M(oses)
1909-1972 . . . . **CLC 19; DAB; DAC**
See also CA 101; 37-40R; DAM MST;
DLB 68

Klein, Norma 1938-1989 . . . . **CLC 30**
See also AAYA 2; CA 41-44R; 128;
CANR 15, 37; CLR 2, 19;
INT CANR-15; JRDA; MAICYA;
SAAS 1; SATA 7, 57

Klein, T(heodore) E(ibon) D(onald)
1947- . . . . **CLC 34**
See also CA 119; CANR 44

Kleist, Heinrich von
1777-1811 . . . . **NCLC 2, 37**
See also DAM DRAM; DLB 90

Klima, Ivan 1931- . . . . **CLC 56**
See also CA 25-28R; CANR 17, 50;
DAM NOV

Klimentov, Andrei Platonovich 1899-1951
See Platonov, Andrei
See also CA 108

Klinger, Friedrich Maximilian von
1752-1831 . . . . **NCLC 1**
See also DLB 94

Klopstock, Friedrich Gottlieb
1724-1803 . . . . **NCLC 11**
See also DLB 97

Knebel, Fletcher 1911-1993. . . . . **CLC 14**
See also AITN 1; CA 1-4R; 140; CAAS 3;
CANR 1, 36; SATA 36; SATA-Obit 75

Knickerbocker, Diedrich
See Irving, Washington

Knight, Etheridge
1931-1991 . . . . **CLC 40; BLC; PC 14**
See also BW 1; CA 21-24R; 133; CANR 23;
DAM POET; DLB 41

Knight, Sarah Kemble 1666-1727 . . . . . **LC 7**
See also DLB 24

Knister, Raymond 1899-1932. . . . . . **TCLC 56**
See also DLB 68

Knowles, John
1926- . . . . . . **CLC 1, 4, 10, 26; DA; DAC**
See also AAYA 10; CA 17-20R; CANR 40;
CDALB 1968-1988; DAM MST, NOV;
DLB 6; MTCW; SATA 8

Knox, Calvin M.
See Silverberg, Robert

Knye, Cassandra
See Disch, Thomas M(ichael)

Koch, C(hristopher) J(ohn) 1932- . . . **CLC 42**
See also CA 127

Koch, Christopher
See Koch, C(hristopher) J(ohn)

Koch, Kenneth 1925- . . . . **CLC 5, 8, 44**
See also CA 1-4R; CANR 6, 36;
DAM POET; DLB 5; INT CANR-36;
SATA 65

Kochanowski, Jan 1530-1584. . . . . . . **LC 10**

Kock, Charles Paul de
1794-1871 . . . . **NCLC 16**

Koda Shigeyuki 1867-1947
See Rohan, Koda
See also CA 121

Koestler, Arthur
1905-1983 . . . . **CLC 1, 3, 6, 8, 15, 33**
See also CA 1-4R; 109; CANR 1, 33;
CDBLB 1945-1960; DLBY 83; MTCW

Kogawa, Joy Nozomi 1935- . . . **CLC 78; DAC**
See also CA 101; CANR 19; DAM MST,
MULT

Kohout, Pavel 1928- . . . . **CLC 13**
See also CA 45-48; CANR 3

Koizumi, Yakumo
See Hearn, (Patricio) Lafcadio (Tessima
Carlos)

Kolmar, Gertrud 1894-1943. . . . . . . **TCLC 40**

Komunyakaa, Yusef 1947- . . . . **CLC 86**
See also CA 147; DLB 120

Konrad, George
See Konrad, Gyoergy

Konrad, Gyoergy 1933- . . . . . . **CLC 4, 10, 73**
See also CA 85-88

Konwicki, Tadeusz 1926- . . . . . **CLC 8, 28, 54**
See also CA 101; CAAS 9; CANR 39;
MTCW

Koontz, Dean R(ay) 1945- . . . . **CLC 78**
See also AAYA 9; BEST 89:3, 90:2;
CA 108; CANR 19, 36; DAM NOV,
POP; MTCW

Kopit, Arthur (Lee) 1937- . . . . **CLC 1, 18, 33**
See also AITN 1; CA 81-84; CABS 3;
DAM DRAM; DLB 7; MTCW

Kops, Bernard 1926- . . . . **CLC 4**
See also CA 5-8R; DLB 13

Kornbluth, C(yril) M. 1923-1958. . . . **TCLC 8**
See also CA 105; DLB 8

Korolenko, V. G.
See Korolenko, Vladimir Galaktionovich

Korolenko, Vladimir
See Korolenko, Vladimir Galaktionovich

Korolenko, Vladimir G.
See Korolenko, Vladimir Galaktionovich

Korolenko, Vladimir Galaktionovich
1853-1921 . . . . **TCLC 22**
See also CA 121

Korzybski, Alfred (Habdank Skarbek)
1879-1950 . . . . **TCLC 61**
See also CA 123

Kosinski, Jerzy (Nikodem)
1933-1991 . . . . **CLC 1, 2, 3, 6, 10, 15, 53,
70**
See also CA 17-20R; 134; CANR 9, 46;
DAM NOV; DLB 2; DLBY 82; MTCW

Kostelanetz, Richard (Cory) 1940- . . **CLC 28**
See also CA 13-16R; CAAS 8; CANR 38

Kostrowitzki, Wilhelm Apollinaris de
   1880-1918
   See Apollinaire, Guillaume
   See also CA 104

Kotlowitz, Robert 1924-........... **CLC 4**
   See also CA 33-36R; CANR 36

Kotzebue, August (Friedrich Ferdinand) von
   1761-1819 .... **NCLC 25**
   See also DLB 94

Kotzwinkle, William 1938- ... **CLC 5, 14, 35**
   See also CA 45-48; CANR 3, 44; CLR 6;
   MAICYA; SATA 24, 70

Kozol, Jonathan 1936-........... **CLC 17**
   See also CA 61-64; CANR 16, 45

Kozoll, Michael 1940(?)-......... **CLC 35**

Kramer, Kathryn 19(?)-.......... **CLC 34**

Kramer, Larry 1935- .... **CLC 42**
   See also CA 124; 126; DAM POP

Krasicki, Ignacy 1735-1801 ...... **NCLC 8**

Krasinski, Zygmunt 1812-1859 .... **NCLC 4**

Kraus, Karl 1874-1936........... **TCLC 5**
   See also CA 104; DLB 118

Kreve (Mickevicius), Vincas
   1882-1954 .... **TCLC 27**

Kristeva, Julia 1941- .... **CLC 77**

Kristofferson, Kris 1936-......... **CLC 26**
   See also CA 104

Krizanc, John 1956-.............. **CLC 57**

Krleza, Miroslav 1893-1981........ **CLC 8**
   See also CA 97-100; 105; CANR 50;
   DLB 147

Kroetsch, Robert
   1927-........... **CLC 5, 23, 57; DAC**
   See also CA 17-20R; CANR 8, 38;
   DAM POET; DLB 53; MTCW

Kroetz, Franz
   See Kroetz, Franz Xaver

Kroetz, Franz Xaver 1946- .... **CLC 41**
   See also CA 130

Kroker, Arthur 1945-.............. **CLC 77**

Kropotkin, Peter (Aleksieevich)
   1842-1921 .... **TCLC 36**
   See also CA 119

Krotkov, Yuri 1917-.............. **CLC 19**
   See also CA 102

Krumb
   See Crumb, R(obert)

Krumgold, Joseph (Quincy)
   1908-1980 .... **CLC 12**
   See also CA 9-12R; 101; CANR 7;
   MAICYA; SATA 1, 48; SATA-Obit 23

Krumwitz
   See Crumb, R(obert)

Krutch, Joseph Wood 1893-1970.... **CLC 24**
   See also CA 1-4R; 25-28R; CANR 4;
   DLB 63

Krutzch, Gus
   See Eliot, T(homas) S(tearns)

Krylov, Ivan Andreevich
   1768(?)-1844 .... **NCLC 1**
   See also DLB 150

Kubin, Alfred (Leopold Isidor)
   1877-1959 .... **TCLC 23**
   See also CA 112; 149; DLB 81

Kubrick, Stanley 1928-............ **CLC 16**
   See also CA 81-84; CANR 33; DLB 26

Kumin, Maxine (Winokur)
   1925- .... **CLC 5, 13, 28**
   See also AITN 2; CA 1-4R; CAAS 8;
   CANR 1, 21; DAM POET; DLB 5;
   MTCW; SATA 12

Kundera, Milan
   1929-........... **CLC 4, 9, 19, 32, 68**
   See also AAYA 2; CA 85-88; CANR 19;
   DAM NOV; MTCW

Kunene, Mazisi (Raymond) 1930-... **CLC 85**
   See also BW 1; CA 125; DLB 117

Kunitz, Stanley (Jasspon)
   1905- .... **CLC 6, 11, 14**
   See also CA 41-44R; CANR 26; DLB 48;
   INT CANR-26; MTCW

Kunze, Reiner 1933-.............. **CLC 10**
   See also CA 93-96; DLB 75

Kuprin, Aleksandr Ivanovich
   1870-1938 .... **TCLC 5**
   See also CA 104

Kureishi, Hanif 1954(?)-........... **CLC 64**
   See also CA 139

Kurosawa, Akira 1910-............ **CLC 16**
   See also AAYA 11; CA 101; CANR 46;
   DAM MULT

Kushner, Tony 1957(?)- .... **CLC 81**
   See also CA 144; DAM DRAM

Kuttner, Henry 1915-1958....... **TCLC 10**
   See also CA 107; DLB 8

Kuzma, Greg 1944-............... **CLC 7**
   See also CA 33-36R

Kuzmin, Mikhail 1872(?)-1936 .... **TCLC 40**

Kyd, Thomas 1558-1594...... **LC 22; DC 3**
   See also DAM DRAM; DLB 62

Kyprianos, Iossif
   See Samarakis, Antonis

La Bruyere, Jean de 1645-1696...... **LC 17**

Lacan, Jacques (Marie Emile)
   1901-1981 .... **CLC 75**
   See also CA 121; 104

**Laclos, Pierre Ambroise Francois Choderlos
   de** 1741-1803 .... **NCLC 4**

La Colere, Francois
   See Aragon, Louis

Lacolere, Francois
   See Aragon, Louis

La Deshabilleuse
   See Simenon, Georges (Jacques Christian)

Lady Gregory
   See Gregory, Isabella Augusta (Persse)

Lady of Quality, A
   See Bagnold, Enid

**La Fayette, Marie (Madelaine Pioche de la
   Vergne Comtes** 1634-1693....... **LC 2**

Lafayette, Rene
   See Hubbard, L(afayette) Ron(ald)

Laforgue, Jules
   1860-1887 .... **NCLC 5, 53; PC 14;
                                        SSC 20**

Lagerkvist, Paer (Fabian)
   1891-1974 .... **CLC 7, 10, 13, 54**
   See also Lagerkvist, Par
   See also CA 85-88; 49-52; DAM DRAM,
   NOV; MTCW

Lagerkvist, Par .... **SSC 12**
   See also Lagerkvist, Paer (Fabian)

Lagerloef, Selma (Ottiliana Lovisa)
   1858-1940 .... **TCLC 4, 36**
   See also Lagerlof, Selma (Ottiliana Lovisa)
   See also CA 108; SATA 15

Lagerlof, Selma (Ottiliana Lovisa)
   See Lagerloef, Selma (Ottiliana Lovisa)
   See also CLR 7; SATA 15

La Guma, (Justin) Alex(ander)
   1925-1985 .... **CLC 19**
   See also BW 1; CA 49-52; 118; CANR 25;
   DAM NOV; DLB 117; MTCW

Laidlaw, A. K.
   See Grieve, C(hristopher) M(urray)

Lainez, Manuel Mujica
   See Mujica Lainez, Manuel
   See also HW

Lamartine, Alphonse (Marie Louis Prat) de
   1790-1869 .... **NCLC 11**
   See also DAM POET

Lamb, Charles
   1775-1834 .... **NCLC 10; DA; DAB;
                                       DAC; WLC**
   See also CDBLB 1789-1832; DAM MST;
   DLB 93, 107; SATA 17

Lamb, Lady Caroline 1785-1828.. **NCLC 38**
   See also DLB 116

Lamming, George (William)
   1927- .... **CLC 2, 4, 66; BLC**
   See also BW 2; CA 85-88; CANR 26;
   DAM MULT; DLB 125; MTCW

L'Amour, Louis (Dearborn)
   1908-1988 .... **CLC 25, 55**
   See also AAYA 16; AITN 2; BEST 89:2;
   CA 1-4R; 125; CANR 3, 25, 40;
   DLBY 80; MTCW

Lampedusa, Giuseppe (Tomasi) di ... **TCLC 13**
   See also Tomasi di Lampedusa, Giuseppe

Lampman, Archibald 1861-1899 .. **NCLC 25**
   See also DLB 92

Lancaster, Bruce 1896-1963........ **CLC 36**
   See also CA 9-10; CAP 1; SATA 9

Landau, Mark Alexandrovich
   See Aldanov, Mark (Alexandrovich)

Landau-Aldanov, Mark Alexandrovich
   See Aldanov, Mark (Alexandrovich)

Landis, John 1950-............... **CLC 26**
   See also CA 112; 122

Landolfi, Tommaso 1908-1979... **CLC 11, 49**
   See also CA 127; 117

Landon, Letitia Elizabeth
   1802-1838 .... **NCLC 15**
   See also DLB 96

Landor, Walter Savage
   1775-1864 .... **NCLC 14**
   See also DLB 93, 107

Landwirth, Heinz 1927-
   See Lind, Jakov
   See also CA 9-12R; CANR 7

Lane, Patrick 1939- . . . . **CLC 25**
   See also CA 97-100; DAM POET; DLB 53;
   INT 97-100

Lang, Andrew 1844-1912 . . . . **TCLC 16**
   See also CA 114; 137; DLB 98, 141;
   MAICYA; SATA 16

Lang, Fritz 1890-1976 . . . . **CLC 20**
   See also CA 77-80; 69-72; CANR 30

Lange, John
   See Crichton, (John) Michael

Langer, Elinor 1939- . . . . **CLC 34**
   See also CA 121

Langland, William
   1330(?)-1400(?) . . . . . . **LC 19; DA; DAB;
                                                   DAC**
   See also DAM MST, POET; DLB 146

Langstaff, Launcelot
   See Irving, Washington

Lanier, Sidney 1842-1881 . . . . **NCLC 6**
   See also DAM POET; DLB 64; DLBD 13;
   MAICYA; SATA 18

Lanyer, Aemilia 1569-1645 . . . . . . **LC 10, 30**
   See also DLB 121

Lao Tzu . . . . **CMLC 7**

Lapine, James (Elliot) 1949- . . . . **CLC 39**
   See also CA 123; 130; INT 130

Larbaud, Valery (Nicolas)
   1881-1957 . . . . **TCLC 9**
   See also CA 106

Lardner, Ring
   See Lardner, Ring(gold) W(ilmer)

Lardner, Ring W., Jr.
   See Lardner, Ring(gold) W(ilmer)

Lardner, Ring(gold) W(ilmer)
   1885-1933 . . . . **TCLC 2, 14**
   See also CA 104; 131; CDALB 1917-1929;
   DLB 11, 25, 86; MTCW

Laredo, Betty
   See Codrescu, Andrei

Larkin, Maia
   See Wojciechowska, Maia (Teresa)

Larkin, Philip (Arthur)
   1922-1985 . . . . **CLC 3, 5, 8, 9, 13, 18, 33,
                                              39, 64; DAB**
   See also CA 5-8R; 117; CANR ;
   CDBLB 1960 to Present; DAM MST,
   POET; DLB 27; MTCW

Larra (y Sanchez de Castro), Mariano Jose de
   1809-1837 . . . . **NCLC 17**

Larsen, Eric 1941- . . . . **CLC 55**
   See also CA 132

Larsen, Nella 1891-1964 . . . . . **CLC 37; BLC**
   See also BW 1; CA 125; DAM MULT;
   DLB 51

Larson, Charles R(aymond) 1938- . . . **CLC 31**
   See also CA 53-56; CANR 4

Las Casas, Bartolome de 1474-1566 . . **LC 31**

Lasker-Schueler, Else 1869-1945 . . **TCLC 57**
   See also DLB 66, 124

Latham, Jean Lee 1902- . . . . **CLC 12**
   See also AITN 1; CA 5-8R; CANR 7;
   MAICYA; SATA 2, 68

Latham, Mavis
   See Clark, Mavis Thorpe

Lathen, Emma . . . . **CLC 2**
   See also Hennissart, Martha; Latsis, Mary
   J(ane)

Lathrop, Francis
   See Leiber, Fritz (Reuter, Jr.)

Latsis, Mary J(ane)
   See Lathen, Emma
   See also CA 85-88

Lattimore, Richmond (Alexander)
   1906-1984 . . . . **CLC 3**
   See also CA 1-4R; 112; CANR 1

Laughlin, James 1914- . . . . **CLC 49**
   See also CA 21-24R; CAAS 22; CANR 9,
   47; DLB 48

Laurence, (Jean) Margaret (Wemyss)
   1926-1987 . . . . **CLC 3, 6, 13, 50, 62;
                                                 DAC; SSC 7**
   See also CA 5-8R; 121; CANR 33;
   DAM MST; DLB 53; MTCW;
   SATA-Obit 50

Laurent, Antoine 1952- . . . . **CLC 50**

Lauscher, Hermann
   See Hesse, Hermann

Lautreamont, Comte de
   1846-1870 . . . . **NCLC 12; SSC 14**

Laverty, Donald
   See Blish, James (Benjamin)

Lavin, Mary 1912- . . . . . . **CLC 4, 18; SSC 4**
   See also CA 9-12R; CANR 33; DLB 15;
   MTCW

Lavond, Paul Dennis
   See Kornbluth, C(yril) M.; Pohl, Frederik

Lawler, Raymond Evenor 1922- . . . . **CLC 58**
   See also CA 103

Lawrence, D(avid) H(erbert Richards)
   1885-1930 . . . . **TCLC 2, 9, 16, 33, 48, 61;
                                   DA; DAB; DAC; SSC 4, 19; WLC**
   See also CA 104; 121; CDBLB 1914-1945;
   DAM MST, NOV, POET; DLB 10, 19,
   36, 98; MTCW

Lawrence, T(homas) E(dward)
   1888-1935 . . . . **TCLC 18**
   See also Dale, Colin
   See also CA 115

Lawrence of Arabia
   See Lawrence, T(homas) E(dward)

Lawson, Henry (Archibald Hertzberg)
   1867-1922 . . . . **TCLC 27; SSC 18**
   See also CA 120

Lawton, Dennis
   See Faust, Frederick (Schiller)

Laxness, Halldor . . . . **CLC 25**
   See also Gudjonsson, Halldor Kiljan

Layamon fl. c. 1200- . . . . **CMLC 10**
   See also DLB 146

Laye, Camara 1928-1980 . . . **CLC 4, 38; BLC**
   See also BW 1; CA 85-88; 97-100;
   CANR 25; DAM MULT; MTCW

Layton, Irving (Peter)
   1912- . . . . **CLC 2, 15; DAC**
   See also CA 1-4R; CANR 2, 33, 43;
   DAM MST, POET; DLB 88; MTCW

Lazarus, Emma 1849-1887 . . . . **NCLC 8**

Lazarus, Felix
   See Cable, George Washington

Lazarus, Henry
   See Slavitt, David R(ytman)

Lea, Joan
   See Neufeld, John (Arthur)

Leacock, Stephen (Butler)
   1869-1944 . . . . **TCLC 2; DAC**
   See also CA 104; 141; DAM MST; DLB 92

Lear, Edward 1812-1888 . . . . **NCLC 3**
   See also CLR 1; DLB 32; MAICYA;
   SATA 18

Lear, Norman (Milton) 1922- . . . . . . **CLC 12**
   See also CA 73-76

Leavis, F(rank) R(aymond)
   1895-1978 . . . . **CLC 24**
   See also CA 21-24R; 77-80; CANR 44;
   MTCW

Leavitt, David 1961- . . . . **CLC 34**
   See also CA 116; 122; CANR 50;
   DAM POP; DLB 130; INT 122

Leblanc, Maurice (Marie Emile)
   1864-1941 . . . . **TCLC 49**
   See also CA 110

Lebowitz, Fran(ces Ann)
   1951(?)- . . . . **CLC 11, 36**
   See also CA 81-84; CANR 14;
   INT CANR-14; MTCW

Lebrecht, Peter
   See Tieck, (Johann) Ludwig

le Carre, John . . . . **CLC 3, 5, 9, 15, 28**
   See also Cornwell, David (John Moore)
   See also BEST 89:4; CDBLB 1960 to
   Present; DLB 87

Le Clezio, J(ean) M(arie) G(ustave)
   1940- . . . . **CLC 31**
   See also CA 116; 128; DLB 83

Leconte de Lisle, Charles-Marie-Rene
   1818-1894 . . . . **NCLC 29**

Le Coq, Monsieur
   See Simenon, Georges (Jacques Christian)

Leduc, Violette 1907-1972 . . . . **CLC 22**
   See also CA 13-14; 33-36R; CAP 1

Ledwidge, Francis 1887(?)-1917 . . . **TCLC 23**
   See also CA 123; DLB 20

Lee, Andrea 1953- . . . . **CLC 36; BLC**
   See also BW 1; CA 125; DAM MULT

Lee, Andrew
   See Auchincloss, Louis (Stanton)

Lee, Don L. . . . . **CLC 2**
   See also Madhubuti, Haki R.

Lee, George W(ashington)
   1894-1976 . . . . **CLC 52; BLC**
   See also BW 1; CA 125; DAM MULT;
   DLB 51

Lee, (Nelle) Harper
   1926- . . . . **CLC 12, 60; DA; DAB; DAC;
                                                           WLC**
   See also AAYA 13; CA 13-16R;
   CDALB 1941-1968; DAM MST, NOV;
   DLB 6; MTCW; SATA 11

Lee, Helen Elaine 1959(?)- . . . . **CLC 86**
   See also CA 148

Lee, Julian
   See Latham, Jean Lee

Lee, Larry
   See Lee, Lawrence

Lewis, Matthew Gregory
1775-1818 .... **NCLC 11**
See also DLB 39, 158

Lewis, (Harry) Sinclair
1885-1951 ..... **TCLC 4, 13, 23, 39; DA;**
DAB; DAC; WLC
See also CA 104; 133; CDALB 1917-1929;
DAM MST, NOV; DLB 9, 102; DLBD 1;
MTCW

Lewis, (Percy) Wyndham
1884(?)-1957 .... **TCLC 2, 9**
See also CA 104; DLB 15

Lewisohn, Ludwig 1883-1955...... **TCLC 19**
See also CA 107; DLB 4, 9, 28, 102

Lezama Lima, Jose 1910-1976 ... **CLC 4, 10**
See also CA 77-80; DAM MULT;
DLB 113; HW

L'Heureux, John (Clarke) 1934-.... **CLC 52**
See also CA 13-16R; CANR 23, 45

Liddell, C. H.
See Kuttner, Henry

Lie, Jonas (Lauritz Idemil)
1833-1908(?) .... **TCLC 5**
See also CA 115

Lieber, Joel 1937-1971............ **CLC 6**
See also CA 73-76; 29-32R

Lieber, Stanley Martin
See Lee, Stan

Lieberman, Laurence (James)
1935- .... **CLC 4, 36**
See also CA 17-20R; CANR 8, 36

Lieksman, Anders
See Haavikko, Paavo Juhani

Li Fei-kan 1904-
See Pa Chin
See also CA 105

Lifton, Robert Jay 1926-.......... **CLC 67**
See also CA 17-20R; CANR 27;
INT CANR-27; SATA 66

Lightfoot, Gordon 1938-.......... **CLC 26**
See also CA 109

Lightman, Alan P. 1948- .... **CLC 81**
See also CA 141

Ligotti, Thomas (Robert)
1953- .... **CLC 44; SSC 16**
See also CA 123; CANR 49

Li Ho 791-817.................... **PC 13**

Liliencron, (Friedrich Adolf Axel) Detlev von
1844-1909 .... **TCLC 18**
See also CA 117

Lilly, William 1602-1681.......... **LC 27**

Lima, Jose Lezama
See Lezama Lima, Jose

Lima Barreto, Afonso Henrique de
1881-1922 .... **TCLC 23**
See also CA 117

Limonov, Edward 1944-.......... **CLC 67**
See also CA 137

Lin, Frank
See Atherton, Gertrude (Franklin Horn)

Lincoln, Abraham 1809-1865..... **NCLC 18**

Lind, Jakov .... **CLC 1, 2, 4, 27, 82**
See also Landwirth, Heinz
See also CAAS 4

Lindbergh, Anne (Spencer) Morrow
1906- .... **CLC 82**
See also CA 17-20R; CANR 16;
DAM NOV; MTCW; SATA 33

Lindsay, David 1878-1945 .... **TCLC 15**
See also CA 113

Lindsay, (Nicholas) Vachel
1879-1931 ... **TCLC 17; DA; DAC; WLC**
See also CA 114; 135; CDALB 1865-1917;
DAM MST, POET; DLB 54; SATA 40

Linke-Poot
See Doeblin, Alfred

Linney, Romulus 1930- .... **CLC 51**
See also CA 1-4R; CANR 40, 44

Linton, Eliza Lynn 1822-1898.... **NCLC 41**
See also DLB 18

Li Po 701-763.................. **CMLC 2**

Lipsius, Justus 1547-1606 .... **LC 16**

Lipsyte, Robert (Michael)
1938- .... **CLC 21; DA; DAC**
See also AAYA 7; CA 17-20R; CANR 8;
CLR 23; DAM MST, NOV; JRDA;
MAICYA; SATA 5, 68

Lish, Gordon (Jay) 1934-.. **CLC 45; SSC 18**
See also CA 113; 117; DLB 130; INT 117

Lispector, Clarice 1925-1977...... **CLC 43**
See also CA 139; 116; DLB 113

Littell, Robert 1935(?)- .... **CLC 42**
See also CA 109; 112

Little, Malcolm 1925-1965
See Malcolm X
See also BW 1; CA 125; 111; DA; DAB;
DAC; DAM MST, MULT; MTCW

Littlewit, Humphrey Gent.
See Lovecraft, H(oward) P(hillips)

Litwos
See Sienkiewicz, Henryk (Adam Alexander
Pius)

Liu E 1857-1909................ **TCLC 15**
See also CA 115

Lively, Penelope (Margaret)
1933- .... **CLC 32, 50**
See also CA 41-44R; CANR 29; CLR 7;
DAM NOV; DLB 14, 161; JRDA;
MAICYA; MTCW; SATA 7, 60

Livesay, Dorothy (Kathleen)
1909- .... **CLC 4, 15, 79; DAC**
See also AITN 2; CA 25-28R; CAAS 8;
CANR 36; DAM MST, POET; DLB 68;
MTCW

Livy c. 59B.C.-c. 17 .... **CMLC 11**

Lizardi, Jose Joaquin Fernandez de
1776-1827 .... **NCLC 30**

Llewellyn, Richard
See Llewellyn Lloyd, Richard Dafydd
Vivian
See also DLB 15

Llewellyn Lloyd, Richard Dafydd Vivian
1906-1983 .... **CLC 7, 80**
See also Llewellyn, Richard
See also CA 53-56; 111; CANR 7;
SATA 11; SATA-Obit 37

Llosa, (Jorge) Mario (Pedro) Vargas
See Vargas Llosa, (Jorge) Mario (Pedro)

Lloyd Webber, Andrew 1948-
See Webber, Andrew Lloyd
See also AAYA 1; CA 116; 149;
DAM DRAM; SATA 56

Llull, Ramon c. 1235-c. 1316..... **CMLC 12**

Locke, Alain (Le Roy)
1886-1954 .... **TCLC 43**
See also BW 1; CA 106; 124; DLB 51

Locke, John 1632-1704 .... **LC 7**
See also DLB 101

Locke-Elliott, Sumner
See Elliott, Sumner Locke

Lockhart, John Gibson
1794-1854 .... **NCLC 6**
See also DLB 110, 116, 144

Lodge, David (John) 1935-........ **CLC 36**
See also BEST 90:1; CA 17-20R; CANR 19;
DAM POP; DLB 14; INT CANR-19;
MTCW

Loennbohm, Armas Eino Leopold 1878-1926
See Leino, Eino
See also CA 123

Loewinsohn, Ron(ald William)
1937- .... **CLC 52**
See also CA 25-28R

Logan, Jake
See Smith, Martin Cruz

Logan, John (Burton) 1923-1987..... **CLC 5**
See also CA 77-80; 124; CANR 45; DLB 5

Lo Kuan-chung 1330(?)-1400(?)...... **LC 12**

Lombard, Nap
See Johnson, Pamela Hansford

London, Jack.. **TCLC 9, 15, 39; SSC 4; WLC**
See also London, John Griffith
See also AAYA 13; AITN 2;
CDALB 1865-1917; DLB 8, 12, 78;
SATA 18

London, John Griffith 1876-1916
See London, Jack
See also CA 110; 119; DA; DAB; DAC;
DAM MST, NOV; JRDA; MAICYA;
MTCW

Long, Emmett
See Leonard, Elmore (John, Jr.)

Longbaugh, Harry
See Goldman, William (W.)

Longfellow, Henry Wadsworth
1807-1882 ..... **NCLC 2, 45; DA; DAB;**
DAC
See also CDALB 1640-1865; DAM MST,
POET; DLB 1, 59; SATA 19

Longley, Michael 1939-.......... **CLC 29**
See also CA 102; DLB 40

Longus fl. c. 2nd cent. - .... **CMLC 7**

Longway, A. Hugh
See Lang, Andrew

Lonnrot, Elias 1802-1884........ **NCLC 53**

Lopate, Phillip 1943- .... **CLC 29**
See also CA 97-100; DLBY 80; INT 97-100

Lopez Portillo (y Pacheco), Jose
1920- .... **CLC 46**
See also CA 129; HW

Lopez y Fuentes, Gregorio
1897(?)-1966 . . . . **CLC 32**
See also CA 131; HW

Lorca, Federico Garcia
See Garcia Lorca, Federico

Lord, Bette Bao 1938- . . . . **CLC 23**
See also BEST 90:3; CA 107; CANR 41;
INT 107; SATA 58

Lord Auch
See Bataille, Georges

Lord Byron
See Byron, George Gordon (Noel)

Lorde, Audre (Geraldine)
1934-1992 . . . . **CLC 18, 71; BLC; PC 12**
See also BW 1; CA 25-28R; 142; CANR 16,
26, 46; DAM MULT, POET; DLB 41;
MTCW

Lord Jeffrey
See Jeffrey, Francis

Lorenzo, Heberto Padilla
See Padilla (Lorenzo), Heberto

Loris
See Hofmannsthal, Hugo von

Loti, Pierre . . . . **TCLC 11**
See also Viaud, (Louis Marie) Julien
See also DLB 123

Louie, David Wong 1954- . . . . **CLC 70**
See also CA 139

Louis, Father M.
See Merton, Thomas

Lovecraft, H(oward) P(hillips)
1890-1937 . . . . **TCLC 4, 22; SSC 3**
See also AAYA 14; CA 104; 133;
DAM POP; MTCW

Lovelace, Earl 1935- . . . . **CLC 51**
See also BW 2; CA 77-80; CANR 41;
DLB 125; MTCW

Lovelace, Richard 1618-1657 . . . . **LC 24**
See also DLB 131

Lowell, Amy 1874-1925 . . **TCLC 1, 8; PC 13**
See also CA 104; DAM POET; DLB 54,
140

Lowell, James Russell 1819-1891 . . **NCLC 2**
See also CDALB 1640-1865; DLB 1, 11, 64,
79

Lowell, Robert (Traill Spence, Jr.)
1917-1977 . . . **CLC 1, 2, 3, 4, 5, 8, 9, 11,
15, 37; DA; DAB; DAC; PC 3; WLC**
See also CA 9-12R; 73-76; CABS 2;
CANR 26; DAM MST, NOV; DLB 5;
MTCW

Lowndes, Marie Adelaide (Belloc)
1868-1947 . . . . **TCLC 12**
See also CA 107; DLB 70

Lowry, (Clarence) Malcolm
1909-1957 . . . . **TCLC 6, 40**
See also CA 105; 131; CDBLB 1945-1960;
DLB 15; MTCW

Lowry, Mina Gertrude 1882-1966
See Loy, Mina
See also CA 113

Loxsmith, John
See Brunner, John (Kilian Houston)

Loy, Mina . . . . **CLC 28**
See also Lowry, Mina Gertrude
See also DAM POET; DLB 4, 54

Loyson-Bridet
See Schwob, (Mayer Andre) Marcel

Lucas, Craig 1951- . . . . **CLC 64**
See also CA 137

Lucas, George 1944- . . . . **CLC 16**
See also AAYA 1; CA 77-80; CANR 30;
SATA 56

Lucas, Hans
See Godard, Jean-Luc

Lucas, Victoria
See Plath, Sylvia

Ludlam, Charles 1943-1987 . . . . . **CLC 46, 50**
See also CA 85-88; 122

Ludlum, Robert 1927- . . . . **CLC 22, 43**
See also AAYA 10; BEST 89:1, 90:3;
CA 33-36R; CANR 25, 41; DAM NOV,
POP; DLBY 82; MTCW

Ludwig, Ken . . . . **CLC 60**

Ludwig, Otto 1813-1865 . . . . **NCLC 4**
See also DLB 129

Lugones, Leopoldo 1874-1938 . . . . . **TCLC 15**
See also CA 116; 131; HW

Lu Hsun 1881-1936 . . . . . . **TCLC 3; SSC 20**
See also Shu-Jen, Chou

Lukacs, George . . . . **CLC 24**
See also Lukacs, Gyorgy (Szegeny von)

Lukacs, Gyorgy (Szegeny von) 1885-1971
See Lukacs, George
See also CA 101; 29-32R

Luke, Peter (Ambrose Cyprian)
1919-1995 . . . . **CLC 38**
See also CA 81-84; 147; DLB 13

Lunar, Dennis
See Mungo, Raymond

Lurie, Alison 1926- . . . . **CLC 4, 5, 18, 39**
See also CA 1-4R; CANR 2, 17, 50; DLB 2;
MTCW; SATA 46

Lustig, Arnost 1926- . . . . **CLC 56**
See also AAYA 3; CA 69-72; CANR 47;
SATA 56

Luther, Martin 1483-1546 . . . . **LC 9**

Luzi, Mario 1914- . . . . **CLC 13**
See also CA 61-64; CANR 9; DLB 128

Lynch, B. Suarez
See Bioy Casares, Adolfo; Borges, Jorge
Luis

Lynch, David (K.) 1946- . . . . **CLC 66**
See also CA 124; 129

Lynch, James
See Andreyev, Leonid (Nikolaevich)

Lynch Davis, B.
See Bioy Casares, Adolfo; Borges, Jorge
Luis

Lyndsay, Sir David 1490-1555 . . . . . . **LC 20**

Lynn, Kenneth S(chuyler) 1923- . . . . **CLC 50**
See also CA 1-4R; CANR 3, 27

Lynx
See West, Rebecca

Lyons, Marcus
See Blish, James (Benjamin)

Lyre, Pinchbeck
See Sassoon, Siegfried (Lorraine)

Lytle, Andrew (Nelson) 1902- . . . . . . **CLC 22**
See also CA 9-12R; DLB 6

Lyttelton, George 1709-1773 . . . . **LC 10**

Maas, Peter 1929- . . . . **CLC 29**
See also CA 93-96; INT 93-96

Macaulay, Rose 1881-1958 . . . . . **TCLC 7, 44**
See also CA 104; DLB 36

Macaulay, Thomas Babington
1800-1859 . . . . **NCLC 42**
See also CDBLB 1832-1890; DLB 32, 55

MacBeth, George (Mann)
1932-1992 . . . . **CLC 2, 5, 9**
See also CA 25-28R; 136; DLB 40; MTCW;
SATA 4; SATA-Obit 70

MacCaig, Norman (Alexander)
1910- . . . . **CLC 36; DAB**
See also CA 9-12R; CANR 3, 34;
DAM POET; DLB 27

MacCarthy, (Sir Charles Otto) Desmond
1877-1952 . . . . **TCLC 36**

MacDiarmid, Hugh
. . . . **CLC 2, 4, 11, 19, 63; PC 9**
See also Grieve, C(hristopher) M(urray)
See also CDBLB 1945-1960; DLB 20

MacDonald, Anson
See Heinlein, Robert A(nson)

Macdonald, Cynthia 1928- . . . . . . **CLC 13, 19**
See also CA 49-52; CANR 4, 44; DLB 105

MacDonald, George 1824-1905 . . . . . **TCLC 9**
See also CA 106; 137; DLB 18; MAICYA;
SATA 33

Macdonald, John
See Millar, Kenneth

MacDonald, John D(ann)
1916-1986 . . . . **CLC 3, 27, 44**
See also CA 1-4R; 121; CANR 1, 19;
DAM NOV, POP; DLB 8; DLBY 86;
MTCW

Macdonald, John Ross
See Millar, Kenneth

Macdonald, Ross . . . . . **CLC 1, 2, 3, 14, 34, 41**
See also Millar, Kenneth
See also DLBD 6

MacDougal, John
See Blish, James (Benjamin)

MacEwen, Gwendolyn (Margaret)
1941-1987 . . . . **CLC 13, 55**
See also CA 9-12R; 124; CANR 7, 22;
DLB 53; SATA 50; SATA-Obit 55

Macha, Karel Hynek 1810-1846 . . **NCLC 46**

Machado (y Ruiz), Antonio
1875-1939 . . . . **TCLC 3**
See also CA 104; DLB 108

Machado de Assis, Joaquim Maria
1839-1908 . . . . **TCLC 10; BLC**
See also CA 107

Machen, Arthur . . . . **TCLC 4; SSC 20**
See also Jones, Arthur Llewellyn
See also DLB 36, 156

Machiavelli, Niccolo
1469-1527 . . . . . . **LC 8; DA; DAB; DAC**
See also DAM MST

MacInnes, Colin 1914-1976...... CLC **4, 23**
See also CA 69-72; 65-68; CANR 21;
DLB 14; MTCW

MacInnes, Helen (Clark)
1907-1985 .... CLC **27, 39**
See also CA 1-4R; 117; CANR 1, 28;
DAM POP; DLB 87; MTCW; SATA 22;
SATA-Obit 44

Mackay, Mary 1855-1924
See Corelli, Marie
See also CA 118

Mackenzie, Compton (Edward Montague)
1883-1972 .... CLC **18**
See also CA 21-22; 37-40R; CAP 2;
DLB 34, 100

Mackenzie, Henry 1745-1831 .... NCLC **41**
See also DLB 39

Mackintosh, Elizabeth 1896(?)-1952
See Tey, Josephine
See also CA 110

MacLaren, James
See Grieve, C(hristopher) M(urray)

Mac Laverty, Bernard 1942-....... CLC **31**
See also CA 116; 118; CANR 43; INT 118

MacLean, Alistair (Stuart)
1922-1987 .... CLC **3, 13, 50, 63**
See also CA 57-60; 121; CANR 28;
DAM POP; MTCW; SATA 23;
SATA-Obit 50

Maclean, Norman (Fitzroy)
1902-1990 .... CLC **78; SSC 13**
See also CA 102; 132; CANR 49;
DAM POP

MacLeish, Archibald
1892-1982 .... CLC **3, 8, 14, 68**
See also CA 9-12R; 106; CANR 33;
DAM POET; DLB 4, 7, 45; DLBY 82;
MTCW

MacLennan, (John) Hugh
1907-1990 .... CLC **2, 14; DAC**
See also CA 5-8R; 142; CANR 33;
DAM MST; DLB 68; MTCW

MacLeod, Alistair 1936- ..... CLC **56; DAC**
See also CA 123; DAM MST; DLB 60

MacNeice, (Frederick) Louis
1907-1963 ...... CLC **1, 4, 10, 53; DAB**
See also CA 85-88; DAM POET; DLB 10,
20; MTCW

MacNeill, Dand
See Fraser, George MacDonald

Macpherson, James 1736-1796 ...... LC **29**
See also DLB 109

Macpherson, (Jean) Jay 1931-...... CLC **14**
See also CA 5-8R; DLB 53

MacShane, Frank 1927-.......... CLC **39**
See also CA 9-12R; CANR 3, 33; DLB 111

Macumber, Mari
See Sandoz, Mari(e Susette)

Madach, Imre 1823-1864........ NCLC **19**

Madden, (Jerry) David 1933- .... CLC **5, 15**
See also CA 1-4R; CAAS 3; CANR 4, 45;
DLB 6; MTCW

Maddern, Al(an)
See Ellison, Harlan (Jay)

Madhubuti, Haki R.
1942- .... CLC **6, 73; BLC; PC 5**
See also Lee, Don L.
See also BW 2; CA 73-76; CANR 24;
DAM MULT, POET; DLB 5, 41;
DLBD 8

Maepenn, Hugh
See Kuttner, Henry

Maepenn, K. H.
See Kuttner, Henry

Maeterlinck, Maurice 1862-1949 ... TCLC **3**
See also CA 104; 136; DAM DRAM;
SATA 66

Maginn, William 1794-1842...... NCLC **8**
See also DLB 110, 159

Mahapatra, Jayanta 1928-......... CLC **33**
See also CA 73-76; CAAS 9; CANR 15, 33;
DAM MULT

Mahfouz, Naguib (Abdel Aziz Al-Sabilgi)
1911(?)-
See Mahfuz, Najib
See also BEST 89:2; CA 128; DAM NOV;
MTCW

Mahfuz, Najib................. CLC **52, 55**
See also Mahfouz, Naguib (Abdel Aziz
Al-Sabilgi)
See also DLBY 88

Mahon, Derek 1941-.............. CLC **27**
See also CA 113; 128; DLB 40

Mailer, Norman
1923- ...... CLC **1, 2, 3, 4, 5, 8, 11, 14,
28, 39, 74; DA; DAB; DAC**
See also AITN 2; CA 9-12R; CABS 1;
CANR 28; CDALB 1968-1988;
DAM MST, NOV, POP; DLB 2, 16, 28;
DLBD 3; DLBY 80, 83; MTCW

Maillet, Antonine 1929-...... CLC **54; DAC**
See also CA 115; 120; CANR 46; DLB 60;
INT 120

Mais, Roger 1905-1955 .... TCLC **8**
See also BW 1; CA 105; 124; DLB 125;
MTCW

Maistre, Joseph de 1753-1821.... NCLC **37**

Maitland, Sara (Louise) 1950-...... CLC **49**
See also CA 69-72; CANR 13

Major, Clarence
1936- .... CLC **3, 19, 48; BLC**
See also BW 2; CA 21-24R; CAAS 6;
CANR 13, 25; DAM MULT; DLB 33

Major, Kevin (Gerald)
1949- .... CLC **26; DAC**
See also AAYA 16; CA 97-100; CANR 21,
38; CLR 11; DLB 60; INT CANR-21;
JRDA; MAICYA; SATA 32, 82

Maki, James
See Ozu, Yasujiro

Malabaila, Damiano
See Levi, Primo

Malamud, Bernard
1914-1986 ...... CLC **1, 2, 3, 5, 8, 9, 11,
18, 27, 44, 78, 85; DA; DAB; DAC;
SSC 15; WLC**
See also AAYA 16; CA 5-8R; 118; CABS 1;
CANR 28; CDALB 1941-1968;
DAM MST, NOV, POP; DLB 2, 28, 152;
DLBY 80, 86; MTCW

Malaparte, Curzio 1898-1957 ..... TCLC **52**

Malcolm, Dan
See Silverberg, Robert

Malcolm X.................. CLC **82; BLC**
See also Little, Malcolm

Malherbe, Francois de 1555-1628..... LC **5**

Mallarme, Stephane
1842-1898 .... NCLC **4, 41; PC 4**
See also DAM POET

Mallet-Joris, Francoise 1930-...... CLC **11**
See also CA 65-68; CANR 17; DLB 83

Malley, Ern
See McAuley, James Phillip

Mallowan, Agatha Christie
See Christie, Agatha (Mary Clarissa)

Maloff, Saul 1922-................ CLC **5**
See also CA 33-36R

Malone, Louis
See MacNeice, (Frederick) Louis

Malone, Michael (Christopher)
1942- .... CLC **43**
See also CA 77-80; CANR 14, 32

Malory, (Sir) Thomas
1410(?)-1471(?) ...... LC **11; DA; DAB;
DAC**
See also CDBLB Before 1660; DAM MST;
DLB 146; SATA 59; SATA-Brief 33

Malouf, (George Joseph) David
1934- .... CLC **28, 86**
See also CA 124; CANR 50

Malraux, (Georges-)Andre
1901-1976 ...... CLC **1, 4, 9, 13, 15, 57**
See also CA 21-22; 69-72; CANR 34;
CAP 2; DAM NOV; DLB 72; MTCW

Malzberg, Barry N(athaniel) 1939-... CLC **7**
See also CA 61-64; CAAS 4; CANR 16;
DLB 8

Mamet, David (Alan)
1947- .... CLC **9, 15, 34, 46; DC 4**
See also AAYA 3; CA 81-84; CABS 3;
CANR 15, 41; DAM DRAM; DLB 7;
MTCW

Mamoulian, Rouben (Zachary)
1897-1987 .... CLC **16**
See also CA 25-28R; 124

Mandelstam, Osip (Emilievich)
1891(?)-1938(?) ...... TCLC **2, 6; PC 14**
See also CA 104

Mander, (Mary) Jane 1877-1949... TCLC **31**

Mandiargues, Andre Pieyre de....... CLC **41**
See also Pieyre de Mandiargues, Andre
See also DLB 83

Mandrake, Ethel Belle
See Thurman, Wallace (Henry)

Mangan, James Clarence
1803-1849 .... NCLC **27**

Maniere, J.-E.
See Giraudoux, (Hippolyte) Jean

Manley, (Mary) Delariviere
1672(?)-1724 .... LC **1**
See also DLB 39, 80

Mann, Abel
See Creasey, John

Matheson, Richard Burton   1926- . . . **CLC 37**
See also CA 97-100; DLB 8, 44; INT 97-100

Mathews, Harry   1930-. . . . . **CLC 6, 52**
See also CA 21-24R; CAAS 6; CANR 18, 40

Mathews, John Joseph   1894-1979. . . **CLC 84**
See also CA 19-20; 142; CANR 45; CAP 2; DAM MULT; NNAL

Mathias, Roland (Glyn)   1915-. . . . . . **CLC 45**
See also CA 97-100; CANR 19, 41; DLB 27

Matsuo Basho   1644-1694. . . . . **PC 3**
See also DAM POET

Mattheson, Rodney
See Creasey, John

Matthews, Greg   1949- . . . . **CLC 45**
See also CA 135

Matthews, William   1942-. . . . . **CLC 40**
See also CA 29-32R; CAAS 18; CANR 12; DLB 5

Matthias, John (Edward)   1941-. . . . . . **CLC 9**
See also CA 33-36R

Matthiessen, Peter
1927- . . . . **CLC 5, 7, 11, 32, 64**
See also AAYA 6; BEST 90:4; CA 9-12R; CANR 21, 50; DAM NOV; DLB 6; MTCW; SATA 27

Maturin, Charles Robert
1780(?)-1824 . . . . **NCLC 6**

Matute (Ausejo), Ana Maria
1925- . . . . **CLC 11**
See also CA 89-92; MTCW

Maugham, W. S.
See Maugham, W(illiam) Somerset

Maugham, W(illiam) Somerset
1874-1965 . . . . . . **CLC 1, 11, 15, 67; DA; DAB; DAC; SSC 8; WLC**
See also CA 5-8R; 25-28R; CANR 40; CDBLB 1914-1945; DAM DRAM, MST, NOV; DLB 10, 36, 77, 100; MTCW; SATA 54

Maugham, William Somerset
See Maugham, W(illiam) Somerset

Maupassant, (Henri Rene Albert) Guy de
1850-1893 . . . . . **NCLC 1, 42; DA; DAB; DAC; SSC 1; WLC**
See also DAM MST; DLB 123

Maurhut, Richard
See Traven, B.

Mauriac, Claude   1914-. . . . . **CLC 9**
See also CA 89-92; DLB 83

Mauriac, Francois (Charles)
1885-1970 . . . . **CLC 4, 9, 56**
See also CA 25-28; CAP 2; DLB 65; MTCW

Mavor, Osborne Henry   1888-1951
See Bridie, James
See also CA 104

Maxwell, William (Keepers, Jr.)
1908- . . . . **CLC 19**
See also CA 93-96; DLBY 80; INT 93-96

May, Elaine   1932- . . . . **CLC 16**
See also CA 124; 142; DLB 44

Mayakovski, Vladimir (Vladimirovich)
1893-1930 . . . . **TCLC 4, 18**
See also CA 104

Mayhew, Henry   1812-1887 . . . . . . **NCLC 31**
See also DLB 18, 55

Mayle, Peter   1939(?)-. . . . . **CLC 89**
See also CA 139

Maynard, Joyce   1953-. . . . . **CLC 23**
See also CA 111; 129

Mayne, William (James Carter)
1928- . . . . **CLC 12**
See also CA 9-12R; CANR 37; CLR 25; JRDA; MAICYA; SAAS 11; SATA 6, 68

Mayo, Jim
See L'Amour, Louis (Dearborn)

Maysles, Albert   1926- . . . . **CLC 16**
See also CA 29-32R

Maysles, David   1932-. . . . . **CLC 16**

Mazer, Norma Fox   1931- . . . . **CLC 26**
See also AAYA 5; CA 69-72; CANR 12, 32; CLR 23; JRDA; MAICYA; SAAS 1; SATA 24, 67

Mazzini, Guiseppe   1805-1872 . . . . **NCLC 34**

McAuley, James Phillip
1917-1976 . . . . **CLC 45**
See also CA 97-100

McBain, Ed
See Hunter, Evan

McBrien, William Augustine
1930- . . . . **CLC 44**
See also CA 107

McCaffrey, Anne (Inez)   1926-. . . . . . **CLC 17**
See also AAYA 6; AITN 2; BEST 89:2; CA 25-28R; CANR 15, 35; DAM NOV, POP; DLB 8; JRDA; MAICYA; MTCW; SAAS 11; SATA 8, 70

McCall, Nathan   1955(?)-. . . . . **CLC 86**
See also CA 146

McCann, Arthur
See Campbell, John W(ood, Jr.)

McCann, Edson
See Pohl, Frederik

McCarthy, Charles, Jr.   1933-
See McCarthy, Cormac
See also CANR 42; DAM POP

McCarthy, Cormac   1933-. . . . . . **CLC 4, 57, 59**
See also McCarthy, Charles, Jr.
See also DLB 6, 143

McCarthy, Mary (Therese)
1912-1989 . . . **CLC 1, 3, 5, 14, 24, 39, 59**
See also CA 5-8R; 129; CANR 16, 50; DLB 2; DLBY 81; INT CANR-16; MTCW

McCartney, (James) Paul
1942- . . . . **CLC 12, 35**
See also CA 146

McCauley, Stephen (D.)   1955- . . . . . **CLC 50**
See also CA 141

McClure, Michael (Thomas)
1932- . . . . **CLC 6, 10**
See also CA 21-24R; CANR 17, 46; DLB 16

McCorkle, Jill (Collins)   1958-. . . . . . **CLC 51**
See also CA 121; DLBY 87

McCourt, James   1941-. . . . . **CLC 5**
See also CA 57-60

McCoy, Horace (Stanley)
1897-1955 . . . . **TCLC 28**
See also CA 108; DLB 9

McCrae, John   1872-1918. . . . . **TCLC 12**
See also CA 109; DLB 92

McCreigh, James
See Pohl, Frederik

McCullers, (Lula) Carson (Smith)
1917-1967 . . . . **CLC 1, 4, 10, 12, 48; DA; DAB; DAC; SSC 9; WLC**
See also CA 5-8R; 25-28R; CABS 1, 3; CANR 18; CDALB 1941-1968; DAM MST, NOV; DLB 2, 7; MTCW; SATA 27

McCulloch, John Tyler
See Burroughs, Edgar Rice

McCullough, Colleen   1938(?)-. . . . . . **CLC 27**
See also CA 81-84; CANR 17, 46; DAM NOV, POP; MTCW

McDermott, Alice   1953- . . . . **CLC 90**
See also CA 109; CANR 40

McElroy, Joseph   1930- . . . . **CLC 5, 47**
See also CA 17-20R

McEwan, Ian (Russell)   1948- . . . **CLC 13, 66**
See also BEST 90:4; CA 61-64; CANR 14, 41; DAM NOV; DLB 14; MTCW

McFadden, David   1940-. . . . . **CLC 48**
See also CA 104; DLB 60; INT 104

McFarland, Dennis   1950- . . . . **CLC 65**

McGahern, John
1934- . . . . **CLC 5, 9, 48; SSC 17**
See also CA 17-20R; CANR 29; DLB 14; MTCW

McGinley, Patrick (Anthony)
1937- . . . . **CLC 41**
See also CA 120; 127; INT 127

McGinley, Phyllis   1905-1978 . . . . . . **CLC 14**
See also CA 9-12R; 77-80; CANR 19; DLB 11, 48; SATA 2, 44; SATA-Obit 24

McGinniss, Joe   1942-. . . . . **CLC 32**
See also AITN 2; BEST 89:2; CA 25-28R; CANR 26; INT CANR-26

McGivern, Maureen Daly
See Daly, Maureen

McGrath, Patrick   1950-. . . . . **CLC 55**
See also CA 136

McGrath, Thomas (Matthew)
1916-1990 . . . . **CLC 28, 59**
See also CA 9-12R; 132; CANR 6, 33; DAM POET; MTCW; SATA 41; SATA-Obit 66

McGuane, Thomas (Francis III)
1939- . . . . **CLC 3, 7, 18, 45**
See also AITN 2; CA 49-52; CANR 5, 24, 49; DLB 2; DLBY 80; INT CANR-24; MTCW

McGuckian, Medbh   1950-. . . . . **CLC 48**
See also CA 143; DAM POET; DLB 40

McHale, Tom   1942(?)-1982. . . . . . . **CLC 3, 5**
See also AITN 1; CA 77-80; 106

McIlvanney, William   1936-. . . . . **CLC 42**
See also CA 25-28R; DLB 14

McIlwraith, Maureen Mollie Hunter
See Hunter, Mollie
See also SATA 2

McInerney, Jay 1955- . . . . CLC 34
See also CA 116; 123; CANR 45;
DAM POP; INT 123

McIntyre, Vonda N(eel) 1948- . . . . . CLC 18
See also CA 81-84; CANR 17, 34; MTCW

McKay, Claude
. . . . TCLC 7, 41; BLC; DAB; PC 2
See also McKay, Festus Claudius
See also DLB 4, 45, 51, 117

McKay, Festus Claudius 1889-1948
See McKay, Claude
See also BW 1; CA 104; 124; DA; DAC;
DAM MST, MULT, NOV, POET;
MTCW; WLC

McKuen, Rod 1933- . . . . CLC 1, 3
See also AITN 1; CA 41-44R; CANR 40

McLoughlin, R. B.
See Mencken, H(enry) L(ouis)

McLuhan, (Herbert) Marshall
1911-1980 . . . . CLC 37, 83
See also CA 9-12R; 102; CANR 12, 34;
DLB 88; INT CANR-12; MTCW

McMillan, Terry (L.) 1951- . . . . . CLC 50, 61
See also BW 2; CA 140; DAM MULT,
NOV, POP

McMurtry, Larry (Jeff)
1936- . . . . CLC 2, 3, 7, 11, 27, 44
See also AAYA 15; AITN 2; BEST 89:2;
CA 5-8R; CANR 19, 43;
CDALB 1968-1988; DAM NOV, POP;
DLB 2, 143; DLBY 80, 87; MTCW

McNally, T. M. 1961- . . . . CLC 82

McNally, Terrence 1939- . . . . . . CLC 4, 7, 41
See also CA 45-48; CANR 2;
DAM DRAM; DLB 7

McNamer, Deirdre 1950- . . . . CLC 70

McNeile, Herman Cyril 1888-1937
See Sapper
See also DLB 77

McNickle, (William) D'Arcy
1904-1977 . . . . CLC 89
See also CA 9-12R; 85-88; CANR 5, 45;
DAM MULT; NNAL; SATA-Obit 22

McPhee, John (Angus) 1931- . . . . . . CLC 36
See also BEST 90:1; CA 65-68; CANR 20,
46; MTCW

McPherson, James Alan
1943- . . . . CLC 19, 77
See also BW 1; CA 25-28R; CAAS 17;
CANR 24; DLB 38; MTCW

McPherson, William (Alexander)
1933- . . . . CLC 34
See also CA 69-72; CANR 28;
INT CANR-28

Mead, Margaret 1901-1978 . . . . CLC 37
See also AITN 1; CA 1-4R; 81-84;
CANR 4; MTCW; SATA-Obit 20

Meaker, Marijane (Agnes) 1927-
See Kerr, M. E.
See also CA 107; CANR 37; INT 107;
JRDA; MAICYA; MTCW; SATA 20, 61

Medoff, Mark (Howard) 1940- . . . CLC 6, 23
See also AITN 1; CA 53-56; CANR 5;
DAM DRAM; DLB 7; INT CANR-5

Medvedev, P. N.
See Bakhtin, Mikhail Mikhailovich

Meged, Aharon
See Megged, Aharon

Meged, Aron
See Megged, Aharon

Megged, Aharon 1920- . . . . CLC 9
See also CA 49-52; CAAS 13; CANR 1

Mehta, Ved (Parkash) 1934- . . . . CLC 37
See also CA 1-4R; CANR 2, 23; MTCW

Melanter
See Blackmore, R(ichard) D(oddridge)

Melikow, Loris
See Hofmannsthal, Hugo von

Melmoth, Sebastian
See Wilde, Oscar (Fingal O'Flahertie Wills)

Meltzer, Milton 1915- . . . . CLC 26
See also AAYA 8; CA 13-16R; CANR 38;
CLR 13; DLB 61; JRDA; MAICYA;
SAAS 1; SATA 1, 50, 80

Melville, Herman
1819-1891 . . . . . NCLC 3, 12, 29, 45, 49;
DA; DAB; DAC; SSC 1, 17; WLC
See also CDALB 1640-1865; DAM MST,
NOV; DLB 3, 74; SATA 59

Menander
c. 342B.C.-c. 292B.C. . . . . CMLC 9; DC 3
See also DAM DRAM

Mencken, H(enry) L(ouis)
1880-1956 . . . . TCLC 13
See also CA 105; 125; CDALB 1917-1929;
DLB 11, 29, 63, 137; MTCW

Mercer, David 1928-1980 . . . . CLC 5
See also CA 9-12R; 102; CANR 23;
DAM DRAM; DLB 13; MTCW

Merchant, Paul
See Ellison, Harlan (Jay)

Meredith, George 1828-1909 . . . TCLC 17, 43
See also CA 117; CDBLB 1832-1890;
DAM POET; DLB 18, 35, 57, 159

Meredith, William (Morris)
1919- . . . . CLC 4, 13, 22, 55
See also CA 9-12R; CAAS 14; CANR 6, 40;
DAM POET; DLB 5

Merezhkovsky, Dmitry Sergeyevich
1865-1941 . . . . TCLC 29

Merimee, Prosper
1803-1870 . . . . NCLC 6; SSC 7
See also DLB 119

Merkin, Daphne 1954- . . . . CLC 44
See also CA 123

Merlin, Arthur
See Blish, James (Benjamin)

Merrill, James (Ingram)
1926-1995 . . . . CLC 2, 3, 6, 8, 13, 18, 34
See also CA 13-16R; 147; CANR 10, 49;
DAM POET; DLB 5; DLBY 85;
INT CANR-10; MTCW

Merriman, Alex
See Silverberg, Robert

Merritt, E. B.
See Waddington, Miriam

Merton, Thomas
1915-1968 . . CLC 1, 3, 11, 34, 83; PC 10
See also CA 5-8R; 25-28R; CANR 22;
DLB 48; DLBY 81; MTCW

Merwin, W(illiam) S(tanley)
1927- . . . CLC 1, 2, 3, 5, 8, 13, 18, 45, 88
See also CA 13-16R; CANR 15;
DAM POET; DLB 5; INT CANR-15;
MTCW

Metcalf, John 1938- . . . . CLC 37
See also CA 113; DLB 60

Metcalf, Suzanne
See Baum, L(yman) Frank

Mew, Charlotte (Mary)
1870-1928 . . . . TCLC 8
See also CA 105; DLB 19, 135

Mewshaw, Michael 1943- . . . . CLC 9
See also CA 53-56; CANR 7, 47; DLBY 80

Meyer, June
See Jordan, June

Meyer, Lynn
See Slavitt, David R(ytman)

Meyer-Meyrink, Gustav 1868-1932
See Meyrink, Gustav
See also CA 117

Meyers, Jeffrey 1939- . . . . CLC 39
See also CA 73-76; DLB 111

Meynell, Alice (Christina Gertrude Thompson)
1847-1922 . . . . TCLC 6
See also CA 104; DLB 19, 98

Meyrink, Gustav . . . . TCLC 21
See also Meyer-Meyrink, Gustav
See also DLB 81

Michaels, Leonard
1933- . . . . CLC 6, 25; SSC 16
See also CA 61-64; CANR 21; DLB 130;
MTCW

Michaux, Henri 1899-1984 . . . . . . CLC 8, 19
See also CA 85-88; 114

Michelangelo 1475-1564 . . . . LC 12

Michelet, Jules 1798-1874 . . . . NCLC 31

Michener, James A(lbert)
1907(?)- . . . . CLC 1, 5, 11, 29, 60
See also AITN 1; BEST 90:1; CA 5-8R;
CANR 21, 45; DAM NOV, POP; DLB 6;
MTCW

Mickiewicz, Adam 1798-1855 . . . . . NCLC 3

Middleton, Christopher 1926- . . . . . . CLC 13
See also CA 13-16R; CANR 29; DLB 40

Middleton, Richard (Barham)
1882-1911 . . . . TCLC 56
See also DLB 156

Middleton, Stanley 1919- . . . . CLC 7, 38
See also CA 25-28R; CANR 21, 46;
DLB 14

Middleton, Thomas 1580-1627 . . . . DC 5
See also DAM DRAM, MST; DLB 58

Migueis, Jose Rodrigues 1901- . . . . . CLC 10

Mikszath, Kalman 1847-1910 . . . . . TCLC 31

Miles, Josephine
1911-1985 . . . . CLC 1, 2, 14, 34, 39
See also CA 1-4R; 116; CANR 2;
DAM POET; DLB 48

Militant
See Sandburg, Carl (August)

Mill, John Stuart 1806-1873 . . . . . NCLC 11
See also CDBLB 1832-1890; DLB 55

Millar, Kenneth 1915-1983 . . . . **CLC 14**
See also Macdonald, Ross
See also CA 9-12R; 110; CANR 16;
DAM POP; DLB 2; DLBD 6; DLBY 83;
MTCW

Millay, E. Vincent
See Millay, Edna St. Vincent

Millay, Edna St. Vincent
1892-1950 . . . . . . **TCLC 4, 49; DA; DAB;
DAC; PC 6**
See also CA 104; 130; CDALB 1917-1929;
DAM MST, POET; DLB 45; MTCW

Miller, Arthur
1915- . . . . **CLC 1, 2, 6, 10, 15, 26, 47, 78;
DA; DAB; DAC; DC 1; WLC**
See also AAYA 15; AITN 1; CA 1-4R;
CABS 3; CANR 2, 30;
CDALB 1941-1968; DAM DRAM, MST;
DLB 7; MTCW

Miller, Henry (Valentine)
1891-1980 . . . . **CLC 1, 2, 4, 9, 14, 43, 84;
DA; DAB; DAC; WLC**
See also CA 9-12R; 97-100; CANR 33;
CDALB 1929-1941; DAM MST, NOV;
DLB 4, 9; DLBY 80; MTCW

Miller, Jason 1939(?)- . . . . **CLC 2**
See also AITN 1; CA 73-76; DLB 7

Miller, Sue 1943- . . . . **CLC 44**
See also BEST 90:3; CA 139; DAM POP;
DLB 143

Miller, Walter M(ichael, Jr.)
1923- . . . . **CLC 4, 30**
See also CA 85-88; DLB 8

Millett, Kate 1934- . . . . **CLC 67**
See also AITN 1; CA 73-76; CANR 32;
MTCW

Millhauser, Steven 1943- . . . . **CLC 21, 54**
See also CA 110; 111; DLB 2; INT 111

Millin, Sarah Gertrude 1889-1968 . . **CLC 49**
See also CA 102; 93-96

Milne, A(lan) A(lexander)
1882-1956 . . . . **TCLC 6; DAB; DAC**
See also CA 104; 133; CLR 1, 26;
DAM MST; DLB 10, 77, 100, 160;
MAICYA; MTCW; YABC 1

Milner, Ron(ald) 1938- . . . . **CLC 56; BLC**
See also AITN 1; BW 1; CA 73-76;
CANR 24; DAM MULT; DLB 38;
MTCW

Milosz, Czeslaw
1911- . . . **CLC 5, 11, 22, 31, 56, 82; PC 8**
See also CA 81-84; CANR 23; DAM MST,
POET; MTCW

Milton, John
1608-1674 . . . . . . **LC 9; DA; DAB; DAC;
WLC**
See also CDBLB 1660-1789; DAM MST,
POET; DLB 131, 151

Min, Anchee 1957- . . . . **CLC 86**
See also CA 146

Minehaha, Cornelius
See Wedekind, (Benjamin) Frank(lin)

Miner, Valerie 1947- . . . . **CLC 40**
See also CA 97-100

Minimo, Duca
See D'Annunzio, Gabriele

Minot, Susan 1956- . . . . **CLC 44**
See also CA 134

Minus, Ed 1938- . . . . **CLC 39**

Miranda, Javier
See Bioy Casares, Adolfo

Mirbeau, Octave 1848-1917 . . . . . . **TCLC 55**
See also DLB 123

Miro (Ferrer), Gabriel (Francisco Victor)
1879-1930 . . . . **TCLC 5**
See also CA 104

Mishima, Yukio
. . . . . . **CLC 2, 4, 6, 9, 27; DC 1; SSC 4**
See also Hiraoka, Kimitake

Mistral, Frederic 1830-1914 . . . . . . **TCLC 51**
See also CA 122

Mistral, Gabriela . . . . **TCLC 2; HLC**
See also Godoy Alcayaga, Lucila

Mistry, Rohinton 1952- . . . . . . **CLC 71; DAC**
See also CA 141

Mitchell, Clyde
See Ellison, Harlan (Jay); Silverberg, Robert

Mitchell, James Leslie 1901-1935
See Gibbon, Lewis Grassic
See also CA 104; DLB 15

Mitchell, Joni 1943- . . . . **CLC 12**
See also CA 112

Mitchell, Margaret (Munnerlyn)
1900-1949 . . . . **TCLC 11**
See also CA 109; 125; DAM NOV, POP;
DLB 9; MTCW

Mitchell, Peggy
See Mitchell, Margaret (Munnerlyn)

Mitchell, S(ilas) Weir 1829-1914 . . **TCLC 36**

Mitchell, W(illiam) O(rmond)
1914- . . . . **CLC 25; DAC**
See also CA 77-80; CANR 15, 43;
DAM MST; DLB 88

Mitford, Mary Russell 1787-1855 . . **NCLC 4**
See also DLB 110, 116

Mitford, Nancy 1904-1973 . . . . **CLC 44**
See also CA 9-12R

Miyamoto, Yuriko 1899-1951 . . . . . **TCLC 37**

Mo, Timothy (Peter) 1950(?)- . . . . . . **CLC 46**
See also CA 117; MTCW

Modarressi, Taghi (M.) 1931- . . . . . . **CLC 44**
See also CA 121; 134; INT 134

Modiano, Patrick (Jean) 1945- . . . . . **CLC 18**
See also CA 85-88; CANR 17, 40; DLB 83

Moerck, Paal
See Roelvaag, O(le) E(dvart)

Mofolo, Thomas (Mokopu)
1875(?)-1948 . . . . **TCLC 22; BLC**
See also CA 121; DAM MULT

Mohr, Nicholasa 1935- . . . . . . **CLC 12; HLC**
See also AAYA 8; CA 49-52; CANR 1, 32;
CLR 22; DAM MULT; DLB 145; HW;
JRDA; SAAS 8; SATA 8

Mojtabai, A(nn) G(race)
1938- . . . . **CLC 5, 9, 15, 29**
See also CA 85-88

Moliere
1622-1673 . . . . . **LC 28; DA; DAB; DAC;
WLC**
See also DAM DRAM, MST

Molin, Charles
See Mayne, William (James Carter)

Molnar, Ferenc 1878-1952 . . . . **TCLC 20**
See also CA 109; DAM DRAM

Momaday, N(avarre) Scott
1934- . . . **CLC 2, 19, 85; DA; DAB; DAC**
See also AAYA 11; CA 25-28R; CANR 14,
34; DAM MST, MULT, NOV, POP;
DLB 143; INT CANR-14; MTCW;
NNAL; SATA 48; SATA-Brief 30

Monette, Paul 1945-1995 . . . . **CLC 82**
See also CA 139; 147

Monroe, Harriet 1860-1936 . . . . **TCLC 12**
See also CA 109; DLB 54, 91

Monroe, Lyle
See Heinlein, Robert A(nson)

Montagu, Elizabeth 1917- . . . . **NCLC 7**
See also CA 9-12R

Montagu, Mary (Pierrepont) Wortley
1689-1762 . . . . **LC 9**
See also DLB 95, 101

Montagu, W. H.
See Coleridge, Samuel Taylor

Montague, John (Patrick)
1929- . . . . **CLC 13, 46**
See also CA 9-12R; CANR 9; DLB 40;
MTCW

Montaigne, Michel (Eyquem) de
1533-1592 . . . . . . **LC 8; DA; DAB; DAC;
WLC**
See also DAM MST

Montale, Eugenio
1896-1981 . . . . **CLC 7, 9, 18; PC 13**
See also CA 17-20R; 104; CANR 30;
DLB 114; MTCW

Montesquieu, Charles-Louis de Secondat
1689-1755 . . . . **LC 7**

Montgomery, (Robert) Bruce 1921-1978
See Crispin, Edmund
See also CA 104

Montgomery, L(ucy) M(aud)
1874-1942 . . . . **TCLC 51; DAC**
See also AAYA 12; CA 108; 137; CLR 8;
DAM MST; DLB 92; JRDA; MAICYA;
YABC 1

Montgomery, Marion H., Jr. 1925- . . **CLC 7**
See also AITN 1; CA 1-4R; CANR 3, 48;
DLB 6

Montgomery, Max
See Davenport, Guy (Mattison, Jr.)

Montherlant, Henry (Milon) de
1896-1972 . . . . **CLC 8, 19**
See also CA 85-88; 37-40R; DAM DRAM;
DLB 72; MTCW

Monty Python
See Chapman, Graham; Cleese, John
(Marwood); Gilliam, Terry (Vance); Idle,
Eric; Jones, Terence Graham Parry; Palin,
Michael (Edward)
See also AAYA 7

Moodie, Susanna (Strickland)
1803-1885 . . . . **NCLC 14**
See also DLB 99

Mooney, Edward 1951-
See Mooney, Ted
See also CA 130

Nichols, John (Treadwell) 1940- .... **CLC 38**
See also CA 9-12R; CAAS 2; CANR 6;
DLBY 82

Nichols, Leigh
See Koontz, Dean R(ay)

Nichols, Peter (Richard)
1927- .... **CLC 5, 36, 65**
See also CA 104; CANR 33; DLB 13;
MTCW

Nicolas, F. R. E.
See Freeling, Nicolas

Niedecker, Lorine 1903-1970.... **CLC 10, 42**
See also CA 25-28; CAP 2; DAM POET;
DLB 48

Nietzsche, Friedrich (Wilhelm)
1844-1900 .... **TCLC 10, 18, 55**
See also CA 107; 121; DLB 129

Nievo, Ippolito 1831-1861 .... **NCLC 22**

Nightingale, Anne Redmon 1943-
See Redmon, Anne
See also CA 103

Nik. T. O.
See Annensky, Innokenty Fyodorovich

Nin, Anais
1903-1977 ...... **CLC 1, 4, 8, 11, 14, 60;**
SSC 10
See also AITN 2; CA 13-16R; 69-72;
CANR 22; DAM NOV, POP; DLB 2, 4,
152; MTCW

Nissenson, Hugh 1933- .... **CLC 4, 9**
See also CA 17-20R; CANR 27; DLB 28

Niven, Larry .... **CLC 8**
See also Niven, Laurence Van Cott
See also DLB 8

Niven, Laurence Van Cott 1938-
See Niven, Larry
See also CA 21-24R; CAAS 12; CANR 14,
44; DAM POP; MTCW

Nixon, Agnes Eckhardt 1927- ...... **CLC 21**
See also CA 110

Nizan, Paul 1905-1940 .... **TCLC 40**
See also DLB 72

Nkosi, Lewis 1936- .... **CLC 45; BLC**
See also BW 1; CA 65-68; CANR 27;
DAM MULT; DLB 157

Nodier, (Jean) Charles (Emmanuel)
1780-1844 .... **NCLC 19**
See also DLB 119

Nolan, Christopher 1965- .... **CLC 58**
See also CA 111

Norden, Charles
See Durrell, Lawrence (George)

Nordhoff, Charles (Bernard)
1887-1947 .... **TCLC 23**
See also CA 108; DLB 9; SATA 23

Norfolk, Lawrence 1963- .... **CLC 76**
See also CA 144

Norman, Marsha 1947- .... **CLC 28**
See also CA 105; CABS 3; CANR 41;
DAM DRAM; DLBY 84

Norris, Benjamin Franklin, Jr.
1870-1902 .... **TCLC 24**
See also Norris, Frank
See also CA 110

Norris, Frank
See Norris, Benjamin Franklin, Jr.
See also CDALB 1865-1917; DLB 12, 71

Norris, Leslie 1921- .... **CLC 14**
See also CA 11-12; CANR 14; CAP 1;
DLB 27

North, Andrew
See Norton, Andre

North, Anthony
See Koontz, Dean R(ay)

North, Captain George
See Stevenson, Robert Louis (Balfour)

North, Milou
See Erdrich, Louise

Northrup, B. A.
See Hubbard, L(afayette) Ron(ald)

North Staffs
See Hulme, T(homas) E(rnest)

Norton, Alice Mary
See Norton, Andre
See also MAICYA; SATA 1, 43

Norton, Andre 1912- .... **CLC 12**
See also Norton, Alice Mary
See also AAYA 14; CA 1-4R; CANR 2, 31;
DLB 8, 52; JRDA; MTCW

Norton, Caroline 1808-1877 ...... **NCLC 47**
See also DLB 21, 159

Norway, Nevil Shute 1899-1960
See Shute, Nevil
See also CA 102; 93-96

Norwid, Cyprian Kamil
1821-1883 .... **NCLC 17**

Nosille, Nabrah
See Ellison, Harlan (Jay)

Nossack, Hans Erich 1901-1978 ..... **CLC 6**
See also CA 93-96; 85-88; DLB 69

Nostradamus 1503-1566 .... **LC 27**

Nosu, Chuji
See Ozu, Yasujiro

Notenburg, Eleanora (Genrikhovna) von
See Guro, Elena

Nova, Craig 1945- .... **CLC 7, 31**
See also CA 45-48; CANR 2

Novak, Joseph
See Kosinski, Jerzy (Nikodem)

Novalis 1772-1801 .... **NCLC 13**
See also DLB 90

Nowlan, Alden (Albert)
1933-1983 .... **CLC 15; DAC**
See also CA 9-12R; CANR 5; DAM MST;
DLB 53

Noyes, Alfred 1880-1958 .... **TCLC 7**
See also CA 104; DLB 20

Nunn, Kem 19(?)- .... **CLC 34**

Nye, Robert 1939- .... **CLC 13, 42**
See also CA 33-36R; CANR 29;
DAM NOV; DLB 14; MTCW; SATA 6

Nyro, Laura 1947- .... **CLC 17**

Oates, Joyce Carol
1938- ...... **CLC 1, 2, 3, 6, 9, 11, 15, 19,**
33, 52; DA; DAB; DAC; SSC 6; WLC
See also AAYA 15; AITN 1; BEST 89:2;
CA 5-8R; CANR 25, 45;
CDALB 1968-1988; DAM MST, NOV,
POP; DLB 2, 5, 130; DLBY 81;
INT CANR-25; MTCW

O'Brien, Darcy 1939- .... **CLC 11**
See also CA 21-24R; CANR 8

O'Brien, E. G.
See Clarke, Arthur C(harles)

O'Brien, Edna
1936- ... **CLC 3, 5, 8, 13, 36, 65; SSC 10**
See also CA 1-4R; CANR 6, 41;
CDBLB 1960 to Present; DAM NOV;
DLB 14; MTCW

O'Brien, Fitz-James 1828-1862... **NCLC 21**
See also DLB 74

O'Brien, Flann........ **CLC 1, 4, 5, 7, 10, 47**
See also O Nuallain, Brian

O'Brien, Richard 1942- .... **CLC 17**
See also CA 124

O'Brien, Tim 1946- .... **CLC 7, 19, 40**
See also AAYA 16; CA 85-88; CANR 40;
DAM POP; DLB 152; DLBD 9;
DLBY 80

Obstfelder, Sigbjoern 1866-1900... **TCLC 23**
See also CA 123

O'Casey, Sean
1880-1964 ...... **CLC 1, 5, 9, 11, 15, 88;**
DAB; DAC
See also CA 89-92; CDBLB 1914-1945;
DAM DRAM, MST; DLB 10; MTCW

O'Cathasaigh, Sean
See O'Casey, Sean

Ochs, Phil 1940-1976 .... **CLC 17**
See also CA 65-68

O'Connor, Edwin (Greene)
1918-1968 .... **CLC 14**
See also CA 93-96; 25-28R

O'Connor, (Mary) Flannery
1925-1964 .... **CLC 1, 2, 3, 6, 10, 13, 15,**
21, 66; DA; DAB; DAC; SSC 1; WLC
See also AAYA 7; CA 1-4R; CANR 3, 41;
CDALB 1941-1968; DAM MST, NOV;
DLB 2, 152; DLBD 12; DLBY 80;
MTCW

O'Connor, Frank.......... **CLC 23; SSC 5**
See also O'Donovan, Michael John

O'Dell, Scott 1898-1989.......... **CLC 30**
See also AAYA 3; CA 61-64; 129;
CANR 12, 30; CLR 1, 16; DLB 52;
JRDA; MAICYA; SATA 12, 60

Odets, Clifford
1906-1963 .... **CLC 2, 28; DC 6**
See also CA 85-88; DAM DRAM; DLB 7,
26; MTCW

O'Doherty, Brian 1934- .... **CLC 76**
See also CA 105

O'Donnell, K. M.
See Malzberg, Barry N(athaniel)

O'Donnell, Lawrence
See Kuttner, Henry

Page, Louise 1955- . . . . **CLC 40**
See also CA 140

Page, P(atricia) K(athleen)
1916- . . . . **CLC 7, 18; DAC; PC 12**
See also CA 53-56; CANR 4, 22;
DAM MST; DLB 68; MTCW

Paget, Violet 1856-1935
See Lee, Vernon
See also CA 104

Paget-Lowe, Henry
See Lovecraft, H(oward) P(hillips)

Paglia, Camille (Anna) 1947- . . . . **CLC 68**
See also CA 140

Paige, Richard
See Koontz, Dean R(ay)

Pakenham, Antonia
See Fraser, (Lady) Antonia (Pakenham)

Palamas, Kostes 1859-1943 . . . . **TCLC 5**
See also CA 105

Palazzeschi, Aldo 1885-1974 . . . . **CLC 11**
See also CA 89-92; 53-56; DLB 114

Paley, Grace 1922- . . . . **CLC 4, 6, 37; SSC 8**
See also CA 25-28R; CANR 13, 46;
DAM POP; DLB 28; INT CANR-13;
MTCW

Palin, Michael (Edward) 1943- . . . . . **CLC 21**
See also Monty Python
See also CA 107; CANR 35; SATA 67

Palliser, Charles 1947- . . . . **CLC 65**
See also CA 136

Palma, Ricardo 1833-1919 . . . . **TCLC 29**

Pancake, Breece Dexter 1952-1979
See Pancake, Breece D'J
See also CA 123; 109

Pancake, Breece D'J . . . . **CLC 29**
See also Pancake, Breece Dexter
See also DLB 130

Panko, Rudy
See Gogol, Nikolai (Vasilyevich)

Papadiamantis, Alexandros
1851-1911 . . . . **TCLC 29**

Papadiamantopoulos, Johannes 1856-1910
See Moreas, Jean
See also CA 117

Papini, Giovanni 1881-1956 . . . . **TCLC 22**
See also CA 121

Paracelsus 1493-1541 . . . . **LC 14**

Parasol, Peter
See Stevens, Wallace

Parfenie, Maria
See Codrescu, Andrei

Parini, Jay (Lee) 1948- . . . . **CLC 54**
See also CA 97-100; CAAS 16; CANR 32

Park, Jordan
See Kornbluth, C(yril) M.; Pohl, Frederik

Parker, Bert
See Ellison, Harlan (Jay)

Parker, Dorothy (Rothschild)
1893-1967 . . . . **CLC 15, 68; SSC 2**
See also CA 19-20; 25-28R; CAP 2;
DAM POET; DLB 11, 45, 86; MTCW

Parker, Robert B(rown) 1932- . . . . . . **CLC 27**
See also BEST 89:4; CA 49-52; CANR 1,
26; DAM NOV, POP; INT CANR-26;
MTCW

Parkin, Frank 1940- . . . . **CLC 43**
See also CA 147

Parkman, Francis, Jr.
1823-1893 . . . . **NCLC 12**
See also DLB 1, 30

Parks, Gordon (Alexander Buchanan)
1912- . . . . **CLC 1, 16; BLC**
See also AITN 2; BW 2; CA 41-44R;
CANR 26; DAM MULT; DLB 33;
SATA 8

Parnell, Thomas 1679-1718 . . . . **LC 3**
See also DLB 94

Parra, Nicanor 1914- . . . . **CLC 2; HLC**
See also CA 85-88; CANR 32;
DAM MULT; HW; MTCW

Parrish, Mary Frances
See Fisher, M(ary) F(rances) K(ennedy)

Parson
See Coleridge, Samuel Taylor

Parson Lot
See Kingsley, Charles

Partridge, Anthony
See Oppenheim, E(dward) Phillips

Pascoli, Giovanni 1855-1912 . . . . . . **TCLC 45**

Pasolini, Pier Paolo
1922-1975 . . . . **CLC 20, 37**
See also CA 93-96; 61-64; DLB 128;
MTCW

Pasquini
See Silone, Ignazio

Pastan, Linda (Olenik) 1932- . . . . . . **CLC 27**
See also CA 61-64; CANR 18, 40;
DAM POET; DLB 5

Pasternak, Boris (Leonidovich)
1890-1960 . . . . . . **CLC 7, 10, 18, 63; DA;**
DAB; DAC; PC 6; WLC
See also CA 127; 116; DAM MST, NOV,
POET; MTCW

Patchen, Kenneth 1911-1972 . . . **CLC 1, 2, 18**
See also CA 1-4R; 33-36R; CANR 3, 35;
DAM POET; DLB 16, 48; MTCW

Pater, Walter (Horatio)
1839-1894 . . . . **NCLC 7**
See also CDBLB 1832-1890; DLB 57, 156

Paterson, A(ndrew) B(arton)
1864-1941 . . . . **TCLC 32**

Paterson, Katherine (Womeldorf)
1932- . . . . **CLC 12, 30**
See also AAYA 1; CA 21-24R; CANR 28;
CLR 7; DLB 52; JRDA; MAICYA;
MTCW; SATA 13, 53

Patmore, Coventry Kersey Dighton
1823-1896 . . . . **NCLC 9**
See also DLB 35, 98

Paton, Alan (Stewart)
1903-1988 . . . . . . **CLC 4, 10, 25, 55; DA;**
DAB; DAC; WLC
See also CA 13-16; 125; CANR 22; CAP 1;
DAM MST, NOV; MTCW; SATA 11;
SATA-Obit 56

Paton Walsh, Gillian 1937-
See Walsh, Jill Paton
See also CANR 38; JRDA; MAICYA;
SAAS 3; SATA 4, 72

Paulding, James Kirke 1778-1860 . . **NCLC 2**
See also DLB 3, 59, 74

Paulin, Thomas Neilson 1949-
See Paulin, Tom
See also CA 123; 128

Paulin, Tom . . . . **CLC 37**
See also Paulin, Thomas Neilson
See also DLB 40

Paustovsky, Konstantin (Georgievich)
1892-1968 . . . . **CLC 40**
See also CA 93-96; 25-28R

Pavese, Cesare
1908-1950 . . . . . **TCLC 3; PC 13; SSC 19**
See also CA 104; DLB 128

Pavic, Milorad 1929- . . . . **CLC 60**
See also CA 136

Payne, Alan
See Jakes, John (William)

Paz, Gil
See Lugones, Leopoldo

Paz, Octavio
1914- . . . . **CLC 3, 4, 6, 10, 19, 51, 65;**
DA; DAB; DAC; HLC; PC 1; WLC
See also CA 73-76; CANR 32; DAM MST,
MULT, POET; DLBY 90; HW; MTCW

Peacock, Molly 1947- . . . . **CLC 60**
See also CA 103; CAAS 21; DLB 120

Peacock, Thomas Love
1785-1866 . . . . **NCLC 22**
See also DLB 96, 116

Peake, Mervyn 1911-1968 . . . . **CLC 7, 54**
See also CA 5-8R; 25-28R; CANR 3;
DLB 15, 160; MTCW; SATA 23

Pearce, Philippa . . . . **CLC 21**
See also Christie, (Ann) Philippa
See also CLR 9; DLB 161; MAICYA;
SATA 1, 67

Pearl, Eric
See Elman, Richard

Pearson, T(homas) R(eid) 1956- . . . . **CLC 39**
See also CA 120; 130; INT 130

Peck, Dale 1967- . . . . **CLC 81**
See also CA 146

Peck, John 1941- . . . . **CLC 3**
See also CA 49-52; CANR 3

Peck, Richard (Wayne) 1934- . . . . . . **CLC 21**
See also AAYA 1; CA 85-88; CANR 19,
38; CLR 15; INT CANR-19; JRDA;
MAICYA; SAAS 2; SATA 18, 55

Peck, Robert Newton
1928- . . . . **CLC 17; DA; DAC**
See also AAYA 3; CA 81-84; CANR 31;
DAM MST; JRDA; MAICYA; SAAS 1;
SATA 21, 62

Peckinpah, (David) Sam(uel)
1925-1984 . . . . **CLC 20**
See also CA 109; 114

Pedersen, Knut 1859-1952
See Hamsun, Knut
See also CA 104; 119; MTCW

Peeslake, Gaffer
See Durrell, Lawrence (George)

Peguy, Charles Pierre
1873-1914 .... TCLC 10
See also CA 107

Pena, Ramon del Valle y
See Valle-Inclan, Ramon (Maria) del

Pendennis, Arthur Esquir
See Thackeray, William Makepeace

Penn, William 1644-1718 .... LC 25
See also DLB 24

Pepys, Samuel
1633-1703 ..... LC 11; DA; DAB; DAC;
WLC
See also CDBLB 1660-1789; DAM MST;
DLB 101

Percy, Walker
1916-1990 .... CLC 2, 3, 6, 8, 14, 18, 47,
65
See also CA 1-4R; 131; CANR 1, 23;
DAM NOV, POP; DLB 2; DLBY 80, 90;
MTCW

Perec, Georges 1936-1982 .... CLC 56
See also CA 141; DLB 83

Pereda (y Sanchez de Porrua), Jose Maria de
1833-1906 .... TCLC 16
See also CA 117

Pereda y Porrua, Jose Maria de
See Pereda (y Sanchez de Porrua), Jose
Maria de

Peregoy, George Weems
See Mencken, H(enry) L(ouis)

Perelman, S(idney) J(oseph)
1904-1979 ... CLC 3, 5, 9, 15, 23, 44, 49
See also AITN 1, 2; CA 73-76; 89-92;
CANR 18; DAM DRAM; DLB 11, 44;
MTCW

Peret, Benjamin 1899-1959 .... TCLC 20
See also CA 117

Peretz, Isaac Loeb 1851(?)-1915 ... TCLC 16
See also CA 109

Peretz, Yitzkhok Leibush
See Peretz, Isaac Loeb

Perez Galdos, Benito 1843-1920 ... TCLC 27
See also CA 125; HW

Perrault, Charles 1628-1703 .... LC 2
See also MAICYA; SATA 25

Perry, Brighton
See Sherwood, Robert E(mmet)

Perse, St.-John .... CLC 4, 11, 46
See also Leger, (Marie-Rene Auguste) Alexis
Saint-Leger

Perutz, Leo 1882-1957 .... TCLC 60
See also DLB 81

Peseenz, Tulio F.
See Lopez y Fuentes, Gregorio

Pesetsky, Bette 1932- .... CLC 28
See also CA 133; DLB 130

Peshkov, Alexei Maximovich 1868-1936
See Gorky, Maxim
See also CA 105; 141; DA; DAC;
DAM DRAM, MST, NOV

Pessoa, Fernando (Antonio Nogueira)
1888-1935 .... TCLC 27; HLC
See also CA 125

Peterkin, Julia Mood 1880-1961 .... CLC 31
See also CA 102; DLB 9

Peters, Joan K. 1945- .... CLC 39

Peters, Robert L(ouis) 1924- .... CLC 7
See also CA 13-16R; CAAS 8; DLB 105

Petofi, Sandor 1823-1849 .... NCLC 21

Petrakis, Harry Mark 1923- .... CLC 3
See also CA 9-12R; CANR 4, 30

Petrarch 1304-1374 .... PC 8
See also DAM POET

Petrov, Evgeny .... TCLC 21
See also Kataev, Evgeny Petrovich

Petry, Ann (Lane) 1908- ...... CLC 1, 7, 18
See also BW 1; CA 5-8R; CAAS 6;
CANR 4, 46; CLR 12; DLB 76; JRDA;
MAICYA; MTCW; SATA 5

Petursson, Halligrimur 1614-1674 .... LC 8

Philips, Katherine 1632-1664 .... LC 30
See also DLB 131

Philipson, Morris H. 1926- .... CLC 53
See also CA 1-4R; CANR 4

Phillips, David Graham
1867-1911 .... TCLC 44
See also CA 108; DLB 9, 12

Phillips, Jack
See Sandburg, Carl (August)

Phillips, Jayne Anne
1952- .... CLC 15, 33; SSC 16
See also CA 101; CANR 24, 50; DLBY 80;
INT CANR-24; MTCW

Phillips, Richard
See Dick, Philip K(indred)

Phillips, Robert (Schaeffer) 1938- ... CLC 28
See also CA 17-20R; CAAS 13; CANR 8;
DLB 105

Phillips, Ward
See Lovecraft, H(oward) P(hillips)

Piccolo, Lucio 1901-1969 .... CLC 13
See also CA 97-100; DLB 114

Pickthall, Marjorie L(owry) C(hristie)
1883-1922 .... TCLC 21
See also CA 107; DLB 92

Pico della Mirandola, Giovanni
1463-1494 .... LC 15

Piercy, Marge
1936- .... CLC 3, 6, 14, 18, 27, 62
See also CA 21-24R; CAAS 1; CANR 13,
43; DLB 120; MTCW

Piers, Robert
See Anthony, Piers

Pieyre de Mandiargues, Andre 1909-1991
See Mandiargues, Andre Pieyre de
See also CA 103; 136; CANR 22

Pilnyak, Boris .... TCLC 23
See also Vogau, Boris Andreyevich

Pincherle, Alberto 1907-1990 ... CLC 11, 18
See also Moravia, Alberto
See also CA 25-28R; 132; CANR 33;
DAM NOV; MTCW

Pinckney, Darryl 1953- .... CLC 76
See also BW 2; CA 143

Pindar 518B.C.-446B.C. .... CMLC 12

Pineda, Cecile 1942- .... CLC 39
See also CA 118

Pinero, Arthur Wing 1855-1934 ... TCLC 32
See also CA 110; DAM DRAM; DLB 10

Pinero, Miguel (Antonio Gomez)
1946-1988 .... CLC 4, 55
See also CA 61-64; 125; CANR 29; HW

Pinget, Robert 1919- .... CLC 7, 13, 37
See also CA 85-88; DLB 83

Pink Floyd
See Barrett, (Roger) Syd; Gilmour, David;
Mason, Nick; Waters, Roger; Wright,
Rick

Pinkney, Edward 1802-1828 ..... NCLC 31

Pinkwater, Daniel Manus 1941- .... CLC 35
See also Pinkwater, Manus
See also AAYA 1; CA 29-32R; CANR 12,
38; CLR 4; JRDA; MAICYA; SAAS 3;
SATA 46, 76

Pinkwater, Manus
See Pinkwater, Daniel Manus
See also SATA 8

Pinsky, Robert 1940- .... CLC 9, 19, 38
See also CA 29-32R; CAAS 4;
DAM POET; DLBY 82

Pinta, Harold
See Pinter, Harold

Pinter, Harold
1930- ..... CLC 1, 3, 6, 9, 11, 15, 27, 58,
73; DA; DAB; DAC; WLC
See also CA 5-8R; CANR 33; CDBLB 1960
to Present; DAM DRAM, MST; DLB 13;
MTCW

Pirandello, Luigi
1867-1936 ...... TCLC 4, 29; DA; DAB;
DAC; DC 5; WLC
See also CA 104; DAM DRAM, MST

Pirsig, Robert M(aynard)
1928- .... CLC 4, 6, 73
See also CA 53-56; CANR 42; DAM POP;
MTCW; SATA 39

Pisarev, Dmitry Ivanovich
1840-1868 .... NCLC 25

Pix, Mary (Griffith) 1666-1709 .... LC 8
See also DLB 80

Pixerecourt, Guilbert de
1773-1844 .... NCLC 39

Plaidy, Jean
See Hibbert, Eleanor Alice Burford

Planche, James Robinson
1796-1880 .... NCLC 42

Plant, Robert 1948- .... CLC 12

Plante, David (Robert)
1940- .... CLC 7, 23, 38
See also CA 37-40R; CANR 12, 36;
DAM NOV; DLBY 83; INT CANR-12;
MTCW

Plath, Sylvia
1932-1963 ..... CLC 1, 2, 3, 5, 9, 11, 14,
17, 50, 51, 62; DA; DAB; DAC; PC 1;
WLC
See also AAYA 13; CA 19-20; CANR 34;
CAP 2; CDALB 1941-1968; DAM MST,
POET; DLB 5, 6, 152; MTCW

Pritchard, William H(arrison)
1932- .... **CLC 34**
See also CA 65-68; CANR 23; DLB 111

Pritchett, V(ictor) S(awdon)
1900- ...... **CLC 5, 13, 15, 41; SSC 14**
See also CA 61-64; CANR 31; DAM NOV;
DLB 15, 139; MTCW

Private 19022
See Manning, Frederic

Probst, Mark 1925- .... **CLC 59**
See also CA 130

Prokosch, Frederic 1908-1989.... **CLC 4, 48**
See also CA 73-76; 128; DLB 48

Prophet, The
See Dreiser, Theodore (Herman Albert)

Prose, Francine 1947-............. **CLC 45**
See also CA 109; 112; CANR 46

Proudhon
See Cunha, Euclides (Rodrigues Pimenta) da

Proulx, E. Annie 1935- .... **CLC 81**

Proust, (Valentin-Louis-George-Eugene-)
Marcel
1871-1922 .... **TCLC 7, 13, 33; DA;**
DAB; DAC; WLC
See also CA 104; 120; DAM MST, NOV;
DLB 65; MTCW

Prowler, Harley
See Masters, Edgar Lee

Prus, Boleslaw 1845-1912 .... **TCLC 48**

Pryor, Richard (Franklin Lenox Thomas)
1940- .... **CLC 26**
See also CA 122

Przybyszewski, Stanislaw
1868-1927 .... **TCLC 36**
See also DLB 66

Pteleon
See Grieve, C(hristopher) M(urray)
See also DAM POET

Puckett, Lute
See Masters, Edgar Lee

Puig, Manuel
1932-1990 ... **CLC 3, 5, 10, 28, 65; HLC**
See also CA 45-48; CANR 2, 32;
DAM MULT; DLB 113; HW; MTCW

Purdy, Al(fred Wellington)
1918- .... **CLC 3, 6, 14, 50; DAC**
See also CA 81-84; CAAS 17; CANR 42;
DAM MST, POET; DLB 88

Purdy, James (Amos)
1923- .... **CLC 2, 4, 10, 28, 52**
See also CA 33-36R; CAAS 1; CANR 19;
DLB 2; INT CANR-19; MTCW

Pure, Simon
See Swinnerton, Frank Arthur

Pushkin, Alexander (Sergeyevich)
1799-1837 ..... **NCLC 3, 27; DA; DAB;**
DAC; PC 10; WLC
See also DAM DRAM, MST, POET;
SATA 61

P'u Sung-ling 1640-1715 .... **LC 3**

Putnam, Arthur Lee
See Alger, Horatio, Jr.

Puzo, Mario 1920- .... **CLC 1, 2, 6, 36**
See also CA 65-68; CANR 4, 42;
DAM NOV, POP; DLB 6; MTCW

Pym, Barbara (Mary Crampton)
1913-1980 .... **CLC 13, 19, 37**
See also CA 13-14; 97-100; CANR 13, 34;
CAP 1; DLB 14; DLBY 87; MTCW

Pynchon, Thomas (Ruggles, Jr.)
1937- ..... **CLC 2, 3, 6, 9, 11, 18, 33, 62,**
72; DA; DAB; DAC; SSC 14; WLC
See also BEST 90:2; CA 17-20R; CANR 22,
46; DAM MST, NOV, POP; DLB 2;
MTCW

Qian Zhongshu
See Ch'ien Chung-shu

Qroll
See Dagerman, Stig (Halvard)

Quarrington, Paul (Lewis) 1953-.... **CLC 65**
See also CA 129

Quasimodo, Salvatore 1901-1968 ... **CLC 10**
See also CA 13-16; 25-28R; CAP 1;
DLB 114; MTCW

Queen, Ellery................... **CLC 3, 11**
See also Dannay, Frederic; Davidson,
Avram; Lee, Manfred B(ennington);
Sturgeon, Theodore (Hamilton); Vance,
John Holbrook

Queen, Ellery, Jr.
See Dannay, Frederic; Lee, Manfred
B(ennington)

Queneau, Raymond
1903-1976 .... **CLC 2, 5, 10, 42**
See also CA 77-80; 69-72; CANR 32;
DLB 72; MTCW

Quevedo, Francisco de 1580-1645.... **LC 23**

Quiller-Couch, Arthur Thomas
1863-1944 .... **TCLC 53**
See also CA 118; DLB 135, 153

Quin, Ann (Marie) 1936-1973 .... **CLC 6**
See also CA 9-12R; 45-48; DLB 14

Quinn, Martin
See Smith, Martin Cruz

Quinn, Simon
See Smith, Martin Cruz

Quiroga, Horacio (Sylvestre)
1878-1937 .... **TCLC 20; HLC**
See also CA 117; 131; DAM MULT; HW;
MTCW

Quoirez, Francoise 1935-........... **CLC 9**
See also Sagan, Francoise
See also CA 49-52; CANR 6, 39; MTCW

Raabe, Wilhelm 1831-1910 .... **TCLC 45**
See also DLB 129

Rabe, David (William) 1940-... **CLC 4, 8, 33**
See also CA 85-88; CABS 3; DAM DRAM;
DLB 7

Rabelais, Francois
1483-1553 ...... **LC 5; DA; DAB; DAC;**
WLC
See also DAM MST

Rabinovitch, Sholem 1859-1916
See Aleichem, Sholom
See also CA 104

Racine, Jean 1639-1699 .... **LC 28; DAB**
See also DAM MST

Radcliffe, Ann (Ward) 1764-1823 .. **NCLC 6**
See also DLB 39

Radiguet, Raymond 1903-1923 .... **TCLC 29**
See also DLB 65

Radnoti, Miklos 1909-1944 ...... **TCLC 16**
See also CA 118

Rado, James 1939-............... **CLC 17**
See also CA 105

Radvanyi, Netty 1900-1983
See Seghers, Anna
See also CA 85-88; 110

Rae, Ben
See Griffiths, Trevor

Raeburn, John (Hay) 1941-........ **CLC 34**
See also CA 57-60

Ragni, Gerome 1942-1991 .... **CLC 17**
See also CA 105; 134

Rahv, Philip 1908-1973 .... **CLC 24**
See also Greenberg, Ivan
See also DLB 137

Raine, Craig 1944-............... **CLC 32**
See also CA 108; CANR 29; DLB 40

Raine, Kathleen (Jessie) 1908- ... **CLC 7, 45**
See also CA 85-88; CANR 46; DLB 20;
MTCW

Rainis, Janis 1865-1929 .... **TCLC 29**

Rakosi, Carl..................... **CLC 47**
See also Rawley, Callman
See also CAAS 5

Raleigh, Richard
See Lovecraft, H(oward) P(hillips)

Raleigh, Sir Walter 1554(?)-1618 .... **LC 31**
See also CDBLB Before 1660

Rallentando, H. P.
See Sayers, Dorothy L(eigh)

Ramal, Walter
See de la Mare, Walter (John)

Ramon, Juan
See Jimenez (Mantecon), Juan Ramon

Ramos, Graciliano 1892-1953 ..... **TCLC 32**

Rampersad, Arnold 1941-.......... **CLC 44**
See also BW 2; CA 127; 133; DLB 111;
INT 133

Rampling, Anne
See Rice, Anne

Ramsay, Allan 1684(?)-1758 .... **LC 29**
See also DLB 95

Ramuz, Charles-Ferdinand
1878-1947 .... **TCLC 33**

Rand, Ayn
1905-1982 ...... **CLC 3, 30, 44, 79; DA;**
DAC; WLC
See also AAYA 10; CA 13-16R; 105;
CANR 27; DAM MST, NOV, POP;
MTCW

Randall, Dudley (Felker)
1914-................... **CLC 1; BLC**
See also BW 1; CA 25-28R; CANR 23;
DAM MULT; DLB 41

Randall, Robert
See Silverberg, Robert

Ranger, Ken
See Creasey, John

Ransom, John Crowe
1888-1974 . . . . **CLC 2, 4, 5, 11, 24**
See also CA 5-8R; 49-52; CANR 6, 34;
DAM POET; DLB 45, 63; MTCW

Rao, Raja 1909- . . . . **CLC 25, 56**
See also CA 73-76; DAM NOV; MTCW

Raphael, Frederic (Michael)
1931- . . . . **CLC 2, 14**
See also CA 1-4R; CANR 1; DLB 14

Ratcliffe, James P.
See Mencken, H(enry) L(ouis)

Rathbone, Julian 1935- . . . . **CLC 41**
See also CA 101; CANR 34

Rattigan, Terence (Mervyn)
1911-1977 . . . . **CLC 7**
See also CA 85-88; 73-76;
CDBLB 1945-1960; DAM DRAM;
DLB 13; MTCW

Ratushinskaya, Irina 1954- . . . . **CLC 54**
See also CA 129

Raven, Simon (Arthur Noel)
1927- . . . . **CLC 14**
See also CA 81-84

Rawley, Callman 1903-
See Rakosi, Carl
See also CA 21-24R; CANR 12, 32

Rawlings, Marjorie Kinnan
1896-1953 . . . . **TCLC 4**
See also CA 104; 137; DLB 9, 22, 102;
JRDA; MAICYA; YABC 1

Ray, Satyajit 1921-1992 . . . . **CLC 16, 76**
See also CA 114; 137; DAM MULT

Read, Herbert Edward 1893-1968 . . . . **CLC 4**
See also CA 85-88; 25-28R; DLB 20, 149

Read, Piers Paul 1941- . . . . . . **CLC 4, 10, 25**
See also CA 21-24R; CANR 38; DLB 14;
SATA 21

Reade, Charles 1814-1884 . . . . **NCLC 2**
See also DLB 21

Reade, Hamish
See Gray, Simon (James Holliday)

Reading, Peter 1946- . . . . **CLC 47**
See also CA 103; CANR 46; DLB 40

Reaney, James 1926- . . . . **CLC 13; DAC**
See also CA 41-44R; CAAS 15; CANR 42;
DAM MST; DLB 68; SATA 43

Rebreanu, Liviu 1885-1944 . . . . **TCLC 28**

Rechy, John (Francisco)
1934- . . . . **CLC 1, 7, 14, 18; HLC**
See also CA 5-8R; CAAS 4; CANR 6, 32;
DAM MULT; DLB 122; DLBY 82; HW;
INT CANR-6

Redcam, Tom 1870-1933 . . . . **TCLC 25**

Reddin, Keith . . . . **CLC 67**

Redgrove, Peter (William)
1932- . . . . **CLC 6, 41**
See also CA 1-4R; CANR 3, 39; DLB 40

Redmon, Anne . . . . **CLC 22**
See also Nightingale, Anne Redmon
See also DLBY 86

Reed, Eliot
See Ambler, Eric

Reed, Ishmael
1938- . . . **CLC 2, 3, 5, 6, 13, 32, 60; BLC**
See also BW 2; CA 21-24R; CANR 25, 48;
DAM MULT; DLB 2, 5, 33; DLBD 8;
MTCW

Reed, John (Silas) 1887-1920 . . . . . . **TCLC 9**
See also CA 106

Reed, Lou . . . . **CLC 21**
See also Firbank, Louis

Reeve, Clara 1729-1807 . . . . **NCLC 19**
See also DLB 39

Reich, Wilhelm 1897-1957 . . . . **TCLC 57**

Reid, Christopher (John) 1949- . . . . . **CLC 33**
See also CA 140; DLB 40

Reid, Desmond
See Moorcock, Michael (John)

Reid Banks, Lynne 1929-
See Banks, Lynne Reid
See also CA 1-4R; CANR 6, 22, 38;
CLR 24; JRDA; MAICYA; SATA 22, 75

Reilly, William K.
See Creasey, John

Reiner, Max
See Caldwell, (Janet Miriam) Taylor
(Holland)

Reis, Ricardo
See Pessoa, Fernando (Antonio Nogueira)

Remarque, Erich Maria
1898-1970 . . . . **CLC 21; DA; DAB; DAC**
See also CA 77-80; 29-32R; DAM MST,
NOV; DLB 56; MTCW

Remizov, A.
See Remizov, Aleksei (Mikhailovich)

Remizov, A. M.
See Remizov, Aleksei (Mikhailovich)

Remizov, Aleksei (Mikhailovich)
1877-1957 . . . . **TCLC 27**
See also CA 125; 133

Renan, Joseph Ernest
1823-1892 . . . . **NCLC 26**

Renard, Jules 1864-1910 . . . . **TCLC 17**
See also CA 117

Renault, Mary . . . . **CLC 3, 11, 17**
See also Challans, Mary
See also DLBY 83

Rendell, Ruth (Barbara) 1930- . . **CLC 28, 48**
See also Vine, Barbara
See also CA 109; CANR 32; DAM POP;
DLB 87; INT CANR-32; MTCW

Renoir, Jean 1894-1979 . . . . **CLC 20**
See also CA 129; 85-88

Resnais, Alain 1922- . . . . **CLC 16**

Reverdy, Pierre 1889-1960 . . . . **CLC 53**
See also CA 97-100; 89-92

Rexroth, Kenneth
1905-1982 . . . . . . **CLC 1, 2, 6, 11, 22, 49**
See also CA 5-8R; 107; CANR 14, 34;
CDALB 1941-1968; DAM POET;
DLB 16, 48; DLBY 82; INT CANR-14;
MTCW

Reyes, Alfonso 1889-1959 . . . . **TCLC 33**
See also CA 131; HW

Reyes y Basoalto, Ricardo Eliecer Neftali
See Neruda, Pablo

Reymont, Wladyslaw (Stanislaw)
1868(?)-1925 . . . . **TCLC 5**
See also CA 104

Reynolds, Jonathan 1942- . . . . **CLC 6, 38**
See also CA 65-68; CANR 28

Reynolds, Joshua 1723-1792 . . . . **LC 15**
See also DLB 104

Reynolds, Michael Shane 1937- . . . . **CLC 44**
See also CA 65-68; CANR 9

Reznikoff, Charles 1894-1976 . . . . **CLC 9**
See also CA 33-36; 61-64; CAP 2; DLB 28,
45

Rezzori (d'Arezzo), Gregor von
1914- . . . . **CLC 25**
See also CA 122; 136

Rhine, Richard
See Silverstein, Alvin

Rhodes, Eugene Manlove
1869-1934 . . . . **TCLC 53**

R'hoone
See Balzac, Honore de

Rhys, Jean
1890(?)-1979 . . . . **CLC 2, 4, 6, 14, 19, 51;**
SSC 21
See also CA 25-28R; 85-88; CANR 35;
CDBLB 1945-1960; DAM NOV; DLB 36,
117; MTCW

Ribeiro, Darcy 1922- . . . . **CLC 34**
See also CA 33-36R

Ribeiro, Joao Ubaldo (Osorio Pimentel)
1941- . . . . **CLC 10, 67**
See also CA 81-84

Ribman, Ronald (Burt) 1932- . . . . **CLC 7**
See also CA 21-24R; CANR 46

Ricci, Nino 1959- . . . . **CLC 70**
See also CA 137

Rice, Anne 1941- . . . . **CLC 41**
See also AAYA 9; BEST 89:2; CA 65-68;
CANR 12, 36; DAM POP

Rice, Elmer (Leopold)
1892-1967 . . . . **CLC 7, 49**
See also CA 21-22; 25-28R; CAP 2;
DAM DRAM; DLB 4, 7; MTCW

Rice, Tim(othy Miles Bindon)
1944- . . . . **CLC 21**
See also CA 103; CANR 46

Rich, Adrienne (Cecile)
1929- . . . . **CLC 3, 6, 7, 11, 18, 36, 73, 76;**
PC 5
See also CA 9-12R; CANR 20;
DAM POET; DLB 5, 67; MTCW

Rich, Barbara
See Graves, Robert (von Ranke)

Rich, Robert
See Trumbo, Dalton

Richard, Keith . . . . **CLC 17**
See also Richards, Keith

Richards, David Adams
1950- . . . . **CLC 59; DAC**
See also CA 93-96; DLB 53

Richards, I(vor) A(rmstrong)
1893-1979 . . . . **CLC 14, 24**
See also CA 41-44R; 89-92; CANR 34;
DLB 27

Richards, Keith 1943-
See Richard, Keith
See also CA 107

Richardson, Anne
See Roiphe, Anne (Richardson)

Richardson, Dorothy Miller
1873-1957 .... TCLC 3
See also CA 104; DLB 36

Richardson, Ethel Florence (Lindesay)
1870-1946
See Richardson, Henry Handel
See also CA 105

Richardson, Henry Handel......... TCLC 4
See also Richardson, Ethel Florence
(Lindesay)

Richardson, Samuel
1689-1761 ...... LC 1; DA; DAB; DAC;
WLC
See also CDBLB 1660-1789; DAM MST,
NOV; DLB 39

Richler, Mordecai
1931- .... CLC 3, 5, 9, 13, 18, 46, 70;
DAC
See also AITN 1; CA 65-68; CANR 31;
CLR 17; DAM MST, NOV; DLB 53;
MAICYA; MTCW; SATA 44;
SATA-Brief 27

Richter, Conrad (Michael)
1890-1968 .... CLC 30
See also CA 5-8R; 25-28R; CANR 23;
DLB 9; MTCW; SATA 3

Ricostranza, Tom
See Ellis, Trey

Riddell, J. H. 1832-1906 .... TCLC 40

Riding, Laura................... CLC 3, 7
See also Jackson, Laura (Riding)

Riefenstahl, Berta Helene Amalia 1902-
See Riefenstahl, Leni
See also CA 108

Riefenstahl, Leni................ CLC 16
See also Riefenstahl, Berta Helene Amalia

Riffe, Ernest
See Bergman, (Ernst) Ingmar

Riggs, (Rolla) Lynn 1899-1954 .... TCLC 56
See also CA 144; DAM MULT; NNAL

Riley, James Whitcomb
1849-1916 .... TCLC 51
See also CA 118; 137; DAM POET;
MAICYA; SATA 17

Riley, Tex
See Creasey, John

Rilke, Rainer Maria
1875-1926 .... TCLC 1, 6, 19; PC 2
See also CA 104; 132; DAM POET;
DLB 81; MTCW

Rimbaud, (Jean Nicolas) Arthur
1854-1891 ..... NCLC 4, 35; DA; DAB;
DAC; PC 3; WLC
See also DAM MST, POET

Rinehart, Mary Roberts
1876-1958 .... TCLC 52
See also CA 108

Ringmaster, The
See Mencken, H(enry) L(ouis)

Ringwood, Gwen(dolyn Margaret) Pharis
1910-1984 .... CLC 48
See also CA 148; 112; DLB 88

Rio, Michel 19(?)-................ CLC 43

Ritsos, Giannes
See Ritsos, Yannis

Ritsos, Yannis 1909-1990..... CLC 6, 13, 31
See also CA 77-80; 133; CANR 39; MTCW

Ritter, Erika 1948(?)-............. CLC 52

Rivera, Jose Eustasio 1889-1928... TCLC 35
See also HW

Rivers, Conrad Kent 1933-1968...... CLC 1
See also BW 1; CA 85-88; DLB 41

Rivers, Elfrida
See Bradley, Marion Zimmer

Riverside, John
See Heinlein, Robert A(nson)

Rizal, Jose 1861-1896.......... NCLC 27

Roa Bastos, Augusto (Antonio)
1917-................. CLC 45; HLC
See also CA 131; DAM MULT; DLB 113;
HW

Robbe-Grillet, Alain
1922- ...... CLC 1, 2, 4, 6, 8, 10, 14, 43
See also CA 9-12R; CANR 33; DLB 83;
MTCW

Robbins, Harold 1916-............. CLC 5
See also CA 73-76; CANR 26; DAM NOV;
MTCW

Robbins, Thomas Eugene 1936-
See Robbins, Tom
See also CA 81-84; CANR 29; DAM NOV,
POP; MTCW

Robbins, Tom................ CLC 9, 32, 64
See also Robbins, Thomas Eugene
See also BEST 90:3; DLBY 80

Robbins, Trina 1938- .... CLC 21
See also CA 128

Roberts, Charles G(eorge) D(ouglas)
1860-1943 .... TCLC 8
See also CA 105; CLR 33; DLB 92;
SATA-Brief 29

Roberts, Kate 1891-1985 .... CLC 15
See also CA 107; 116

Roberts, Keith (John Kingston)
1935- .... CLC 14
See also CA 25-28R; CANR 46

Roberts, Kenneth (Lewis)
1885-1957 .... TCLC 23
See also CA 109; DLB 9

Roberts, Michele (B.) 1949-........ CLC 48
See also CA 115

Robertson, Ellis
See Ellison, Harlan (Jay); Silverberg, Robert

Robertson, Thomas William
1829-1871 .... NCLC 35
See also DAM DRAM

Robinson, Edwin Arlington
1869-1935 .... TCLC 5; DA; DAC; PC 1
See also CA 104; 133; CDALB 1865-1917;
DAM MST, POET; DLB 54; MTCW

Robinson, Henry Crabb
1775-1867 .... NCLC 15
See also DLB 107

Robinson, Jill 1936-.............. CLC 10
See also CA 102; INT 102

Robinson, Kim Stanley 1952- ...... CLC 34
See also CA 126

Robinson, Lloyd
See Silverberg, Robert

Robinson, Marilynne 1944-........ CLC 25
See also CA 116

Robinson, Smokey................ CLC 21
See also Robinson, William, Jr.

Robinson, William, Jr. 1940-
See Robinson, Smokey
See also CA 116

Robison, Mary 1949-............. CLC 42
See also CA 113; 116; DLB 130; INT 116

Rod, Edouard 1857-1910 .... TCLC 52

Roddenberry, Eugene Wesley 1921-1991
See Roddenberry, Gene
See also CA 110; 135; CANR 37; SATA 45;
SATA-Obit 69

Roddenberry, Gene .... CLC 17
See also Roddenberry, Eugene Wesley
See also AAYA 5; SATA-Obit 69

Rodgers, Mary 1931-............. CLC 12
See also CA 49-52; CANR 8; CLR 20;
INT CANR-8; JRDA; MAICYA;
SATA 8

Rodgers, W(illiam) R(obert)
1909-1969 .... CLC 7
See also CA 85-88; DLB 20

Rodman, Eric
See Silverberg, Robert

Rodman, Howard 1920(?)-1985..... CLC 65
See also CA 118

Rodman, Maia
See Wojciechowska, Maia (Teresa)

Rodriguez, Claudio 1934-.......... CLC 10
See also DLB 134

Roelvaag, O(le) E(dvart)
1876-1931 .... TCLC 17
See also CA 117; DLB 9

Roethke, Theodore (Huebner)
1908-1963 ...... CLC 1, 3, 8, 11, 19, 46
See also CA 81-84; CABS 2;
CDALB 1941-1968; DAM POET; DLB 5;
MTCW

Rogers, Thomas Hunton 1927- ..... CLC 57
See also CA 89-92; INT 89-92

Rogers, Will(iam Penn Adair)
1879-1935 .... TCLC 8
See also CA 105; 144; DAM MULT;
DLB 11; NNAL

Rogin, Gilbert 1929-.............. CLC 18
See also CA 65-68; CANR 15

Rohan, Koda .... TCLC 22
See also Koda Shigeyuki

Rohmer, Eric.................... CLC 16
See also Scherer, Jean-Marie Maurice

Rohmer, Sax .... TCLC 28
See also Ward, Arthur Henry Sarsfield
See also DLB 70

Saba, Umberto 1883-1957 .... **TCLC 33**
See also CA 144; DLB 114

Sabatini, Rafael 1875-1950 ...... **TCLC 47**

Sabato, Ernesto (R.)
1911- .... **CLC 10, 23; HLC**
See also CA 97-100; CANR 32;
DAM MULT; DLB 145; HW; MTCW

Sacastru, Martin
See Bioy Casares, Adolfo

Sacher-Masoch, Leopold von
1836(?)-1895 .... **NCLC 31**

Sachs, Marilyn (Stickle) 1927- ..... **CLC 35**
See also AAYA 2; CA 17-20R; CANR 13,
47; CLR 2; JRDA; MAICYA; SAAS 2;
SATA 3, 68

Sachs, Nelly 1891-1970 .... **CLC 14**
See also CA 17-18; 25-28R; CAP 2

Sackler, Howard (Oliver)
1929-1982 .... **CLC 14**
See also CA 61-64; 108; CANR 30; DLB 7

Sacks, Oliver (Wolf) 1933- .... **CLC 67**
See also CA 53-56; CANR 28, 50;
INT CANR-28; MTCW

Sade, Donatien Alphonse Francois Comte
1740-1814 .... **NCLC 47**

Sadoff, Ira 1945-.................. **CLC 9**
See also CA 53-56; CANR 5, 21; DLB 120

Saetone
See Camus, Albert

Safire, William 1929-............. **CLC 10**
See also CA 17-20R; CANR 31

Sagan, Carl (Edward) 1934-........ **CLC 30**
See also AAYA 2; CA 25-28R; CANR 11,
36; MTCW; SATA 58

Sagan, Francoise .... **CLC 3, 6, 9, 17, 36**
See also Quoirez, Francoise
See also DLB 83

Sahgal, Nayantara (Pandit) 1927-... **CLC 41**
See also CA 9-12R; CANR 11

Saint, H(arry) F. 1941- .... **CLC 50**
See also CA 127

St. Aubin de Teran, Lisa 1953-
See Teran, Lisa St. Aubin de
See also CA 118; 126; INT 126

Sainte-Beuve, Charles Augustin
1804-1869 .... **NCLC 5**

Saint-Exupery, Antoine (Jean Baptiste Marie
Roger) de
1900-1944 .... **TCLC 2, 56; WLC**
See also CA 108; 132; CLR 10; DAM NOV;
DLB 72; MAICYA; MTCW; SATA 20

St. John, David
See Hunt, E(verette) Howard, (Jr.)

Saint-John Perse
See Leger, (Marie-Rene Auguste) Alexis
Saint-Leger

Saintsbury, George (Edward Bateman)
1845-1933 .... **TCLC 31**
See also DLB 57, 149

Sait Faik .... **TCLC 23**
See also Abasiyanik, Sait Faik

Saki .... **TCLC 3; SSC 12**
See also Munro, H(ector) H(ugh)

Sala, George Augustus .... **NCLC 46**

Salama, Hannu 1936-............. **CLC 18**

Salamanca, J(ack) R(ichard)
1922- .... **CLC 4, 15**
See also CA 25-28R

Sale, J. Kirkpatrick
See Sale, Kirkpatrick

Sale, Kirkpatrick 1937-.......... **CLC 68**
See also CA 13-16R; CANR 10

Salinas, Luis Omar 1937- ... **CLC 90; HLC**
See also CA 131; DAM MULT; DLB 82;
HW

Salinas (y Serrano), Pedro
1891(?)-1951 .... **TCLC 17**
See also CA 117; DLB 134

Salinger, J(erome) D(avid)
1919- ...... **CLC 1, 3, 8, 12, 55, 56; DA;**
DAB; DAC; SSC 2; WLC
See also AAYA 2; CA 5-8R; CANR 39;
CDALB 1941-1968; CLR 18; DAM MST,
NOV, POP; DLB 2, 102; MAICYA;
MTCW; SATA 67

Salisbury, John
See Caute, David

Salter, James 1925- .... **CLC 7, 52, 59**
See also CA 73-76; DLB 130

Saltus, Edgar (Everton)
1855-1921 .... **TCLC 8**
See also CA 105

Saltykov, Mikhail Evgrafovich
1826-1889 .... **NCLC 16**

Samarakis, Antonis 1919- .... **CLC 5**
See also CA 25-28R; CAAS 16; CANR 36

Sanchez, Florencio 1875-1910 ..... **TCLC 37**
See also HW

Sanchez, Luis Rafael 1936-........ **CLC 23**
See also CA 128; DLB 145; HW

Sanchez, Sonia 1934-... **CLC 5; BLC; PC 9**
See also BW 2; CA 33-36R; CANR 24, 49;
CLR 18; DAM MULT; DLB 41;
DLBD 8; MAICYA; MTCW; SATA 22

Sand, George
1804-1876 ..... **NCLC 2, 42; DA; DAB;**
DAC; WLC
See also DAM MST, NOV; DLB 119

Sandburg, Carl (August)
1878-1967 .... **CLC 1, 4, 10, 15, 35; DA;**
DAB; DAC; PC 2; WLC
See also CA 5-8R; 25-28R; CANR 35;
CDALB 1865-1917; DAM MST, POET;
DLB 17, 54; MAICYA; MTCW; SATA 8

Sandburg, Charles
See Sandburg, Carl (August)

Sandburg, Charles A.
See Sandburg, Carl (August)

Sanders, (James) Ed(ward) 1939- ... **CLC 53**
See also CA 13-16R; CAAS 21; CANR 13,
44; DLB 16

Sanders, Lawrence 1920-.......... **CLC 41**
See also BEST 89:4; CA 81-84; CANR 33;
DAM POP; MTCW

Sanders, Noah
See Blount, Roy (Alton), Jr.

Sanders, Winston P.
See Anderson, Poul (William)

Sandoz, Mari(e Susette)
1896-1966 .... **CLC 28**
See also CA 1-4R; 25-28R; CANR 17;
DLB 9; MTCW; SATA 5

Saner, Reg(inald Anthony) 1931- .... **CLC 9**
See also CA 65-68

Sannazaro, Jacopo 1456(?)-1530 ...... **LC 8**

Sansom, William
1912-1976 .... **CLC 2, 6; SSC 21**
See also CA 5-8R; 65-68; CANR 42;
DAM NOV; DLB 139; MTCW

Santayana, George 1863-1952 ..... **TCLC 40**
See also CA 115; DLB 54, 71; DLBD 13

Santiago, Danny .... **CLC 33**
See also James, Daniel (Lewis)
See also DLB 122

Santmyer, Helen Hoover
1895-1986 .... **CLC 33**
See also CA 1-4R; 118; CANR 15, 33;
DLBY 84; MTCW

Santos, Bienvenido N(uqui) 1911-... **CLC 22**
See also CA 101; CANR 19, 46;
DAM MULT

Sapper .... **TCLC 44**
See also McNeile, Herman Cyril

Sappho fl. 6th cent. B.C.-..... **CMLC 3; PC 5**
See also DAM POET

Sarduy, Severo 1937-1993 .... **CLC 6**
See also CA 89-92; 142; DLB 113; HW

Sargeson, Frank 1903-1982 .... **CLC 31**
See also CA 25-28R; 106; CANR 38

Sarmiento, Felix Ruben Garcia
See Dario, Ruben

Saroyan, William
1908-1981 ..... **CLC 1, 8, 10, 29, 34, 56;**
DA; DAB; DAC; SSC 21; WLC
See also CA 5-8R; 103; CANR 30;
DAM DRAM, MST, NOV; DLB 7, 9, 86;
DLBY 81; MTCW; SATA 23;
SATA-Obit 24

Sarraute, Nathalie
1900- .... **CLC 1, 2, 4, 8, 10, 31, 80**
See also CA 9-12R; CANR 23; DLB 83;
MTCW

Sarton, (Eleanor) May
1912- .... **CLC 4, 14, 49**
See also CA 1-4R; CANR 1, 34;
DAM POET; DLB 48; DLBY 81;
INT CANR-34; MTCW; SATA 36

Sartre, Jean-Paul
1905-1980 .... **CLC 1, 4, 7, 9, 13, 18, 24,**
44, 50, 52; DA; DAB; DAC; DC 3; WLC
See also CA 9-12R; 97-100; CANR 21;
DAM DRAM, MST, NOV; DLB 72;
MTCW

Sassoon, Siegfried (Lorraine)
1886-1967 .... **CLC 36; DAB; PC 12**
See also CA 104; 25-28R; CANR 36;
DAM MST, NOV, POET; DLB 20;
MTCW

Satterfield, Charles
See Pohl, Frederik

Saul, John (W. III) 1942- .... **CLC 46**
See also AAYA 10; BEST 90:4; CA 81-84;
CANR 16, 40; DAM NOV, POP

Seelye, John 1931-............... **CLC 7**

Seferiades, Giorgos Stylianou 1900-1971
See Seferis, George
See also CA 5-8R; 33-36R; CANR 5, 36;
MTCW

Seferis, George .... **CLC 5, 11**
See also Seferiades, Giorgos Stylianou

Segal, Erich (Wolf) 1937- .... **CLC 3, 10**
See also BEST 89:1; CA 25-28R; CANR 20,
36; DAM POP; DLBY 86;
INT CANR-20; MTCW

Seger, Bob 1945-................ **CLC 35**

Seghers, Anna .... **CLC 7**
See also Radvanyi, Netty
See also DLB 69

Seidel, Frederick (Lewis) 1936-..... **CLC 18**
See also CA 13-16R; CANR 8; DLBY 84

Seifert, Jaroslav 1901-1986..... **CLC 34, 44**
See also CA 127; MTCW

Sei Shonagon c. 966-1017(?) ...... **CMLC 6**

Selby, Hubert, Jr.
1928-......... **CLC 1, 2, 4, 8; SSC 20**
See also CA 13-16R; CANR 33; DLB 2

Selzer, Richard 1928-............ **CLC 74**
See also CA 65-68; CANR 14

Sembene, Ousmane
See Ousmane, Sembene

Senancour, Etienne Pivert de
1770-1846 .... **NCLC 16**
See also DLB 119

Sender, Ramon (Jose)
1902-1982 .... **CLC 8; HLC**
See also CA 5-8R; 105; CANR 8;
DAM MULT; HW; MTCW

Seneca, Lucius Annaeus
4B.C.-65............. **CMLC 6; DC 5**
See also DAM DRAM

Senghor, Leopold Sedar
1906-................. **CLC 54; BLC**
See also BW 2; CA 116; 125; CANR 47;
DAM MULT, POET; MTCW

Serling, (Edward) Rod(man)
1924-1975 .... **CLC 30**
See also AAYA 14; AITN 1; CA 65-68;
57-60; DLB 26

Serna, Ramon Gomez de la
See Gomez de la Serna, Ramon

Serpieres
See Guillevic, (Eugene)

Service, Robert
See Service, Robert W(illiam)
See also DAB; DLB 92

Service, Robert W(illiam)
1874(?)-1958 ...... **TCLC 15; DA; DAC;
WLC**
See also Service, Robert
See also CA 115; 140; DAM MST, POET;
SATA 20

Seth, Vikram 1952-............ **CLC 43, 90**
See also CA 121; 127; CANR 50;
DAM MULT; DLB 120; INT 127

Seton, Cynthia Propper
1926-1982 .... **CLC 27**
See also CA 5-8R; 108; CANR 7

Seton, Ernest (Evan) Thompson
1860-1946 .... **TCLC 31**
See also CA 109; DLB 92; DLBD 13;
JRDA; SATA 18

Seton-Thompson, Ernest
See Seton, Ernest (Evan) Thompson

Settle, Mary Lee 1918-........ **CLC 19, 61**
See also CA 89-92; CAAS 1; CANR 44;
DLB 6; INT 89-92

Seuphor, Michel
See Arp, Jean

Sevigne, Marie (de Rabutin-Chantal) Marquise
de 1626-1696 .... **LC 11**

Sexton, Anne (Harvey)
1928-1974 .... **CLC 2, 4, 6, 8, 10, 15, 53;
DA; DAB; DAC; PC 2; WLC**
See also CA 1-4R; 53-56; CABS 2;
CANR 3, 36; CDALB 1941-1968;
DAM MST, POET; DLB 5; MTCW;
SATA 10

Shaara, Michael (Joseph, Jr.)
1929-1988 .... **CLC 15**
See also AITN 1; CA 102; 125; DAM POP;
DLBY 83

Shackleton, C. C.
See Aldiss, Brian W(ilson)

Shacochis, Bob .... **CLC 39**
See also Shacochis, Robert G.

Shacochis, Robert G. 1951-
See Shacochis, Bob
See also CA 119; 124; INT 124

Shaffer, Anthony (Joshua) 1926-.... **CLC 19**
See also CA 110; 116; DAM DRAM;
DLB 13

Shaffer, Peter (Levin)
1926- ...... **CLC 5, 14, 18, 37, 60; DAB**
See also CA 25-28R; CANR 25, 47;
CDBLB 1960 to Present; DAM DRAM,
MST; DLB 13; MTCW

Shakey, Bernard
See Young, Neil

Shalamov, Varlam (Tikhonovich)
1907(?)-1982 .... **CLC 18**
See also CA 129; 105

Shamlu, Ahmad 1925- .... **CLC 10**

Shammas, Anton 1951-............ **CLC 55**

Shange, Ntozake
1948- .... **CLC 8, 25, 38, 74; BLC; DC 3**
See also AAYA 9; BW 2; CA 85-88;
CABS 3; CANR 27, 48; DAM DRAM,
MULT; DLB 38; MTCW

Shanley, John Patrick 1950-....... **CLC 75**
See also CA 128; 133

Shapcott, Thomas W(illiam) 1935- .. **CLC 38**
See also CA 69-72; CANR 49

Shapiro, Jane..................... **CLC 76**

Shapiro, Karl (Jay) 1913- .. **CLC 4, 8, 15, 53**
See also CA 1-4R; CAAS 6; CANR 1, 36;
DLB 48; MTCW

Sharp, William 1855-1905 .... **TCLC 39**
See also DLB 156

Sharpe, Thomas Ridley 1928-
See Sharpe, Tom
See also CA 114; 122; INT 122

Sharpe, Tom..................... **CLC 36**
See also Sharpe, Thomas Ridley
See also DLB 14

Shaw, Bernard.................... **TCLC 45**
See also Shaw, George Bernard
See also BW 1

Shaw, G. Bernard
See Shaw, George Bernard

Shaw, George Bernard
1856-1950 ... **TCLC 3, 9, 21; DA; DAB;
DAC; WLC**
See also Shaw, Bernard
See also CA 104; 128; CDBLB 1914-1945;
DAM DRAM, MST; DLB 10, 57;
MTCW

Shaw, Henry Wheeler
1818-1885 .... **NCLC 15**
See also DLB 11

Shaw, Irwin 1913-1984....... **CLC 7, 23, 34**
See also AITN 1; CA 13-16R; 112;
CANR 21; CDALB 1941-1968;
DAM DRAM, POP; DLB 6, 102;
DLBY 84; MTCW

Shaw, Robert 1927-1978 .... **CLC 5**
See also AITN 1; CA 1-4R; 81-84;
CANR 4; DLB 13, 14

Shaw, T. E.
See Lawrence, T(homas) E(dward)

Shawn, Wallace 1943- .... **CLC 41**
See also CA 112

Shea, Lisa 1953-................. **CLC 86**
See also CA 147

Sheed, Wilfrid (John Joseph)
1930- .... **CLC 2, 4, 10, 53**
See also CA 65-68; CANR 30; DLB 6;
MTCW

Sheldon, Alice Hastings Bradley
1915(?)-1987
See Tiptree, James, Jr.
See also CA 108; 122; CANR 34; INT 108;
MTCW

Sheldon, John
See Bloch, Robert (Albert)

Shelley, Mary Wollstonecraft (Godwin)
1797-1851 .... **NCLC 14; DA; DAB;
DAC; WLC**
See also CDBLB 1789-1832; DAM MST,
NOV; DLB 110, 116, 159; SATA 29

Shelley, Percy Bysshe
1792-1822 .... **NCLC 18; DA; DAB;
DAC; PC 14; WLC**
See also CDBLB 1789-1832; DAM MST,
POET; DLB 96, 110, 158

Shepard, Jim 1956-.............. **CLC 36**
See also CA 137

Shepard, Lucius 1947-............ **CLC 34**
See also CA 128; 141

Shepard, Sam
1943- .... **CLC 4, 6, 17, 34, 41, 44; DC 5**
See also AAYA 1; CA 69-72; CABS 3;
CANR 22; DAM DRAM; DLB 7;
MTCW

Shepherd, Michael
See Ludlum, Robert

Sherburne, Zoa (Morin) 1912-...... **CLC 30**
See also AAYA 13; CA 1-4R; CANR 3, 37;
MAICYA; SAAS 18; SATA 3

Sheridan, Frances 1724-1766........ **LC 7**
See also DLB 39, 84

Sheridan, Richard Brinsley
1751-1816 .... **NCLC 5; DA; DAB;**
DAC; DC 1; WLC
See also CDBLB 1660-1789; DAM DRAM,
MST; DLB 89

Sherman, Jonathan Marc.......... **CLC 55**

Sherman, Martin 1941(?)-........ **CLC 19**
See also CA 116; 123

Sherwin, Judith Johnson 1936-... **CLC 7, 15**
See also CA 25-28R; CANR 34

Sherwood, Frances 1940-......... **CLC 81**
See also CA 146

Sherwood, Robert E(mmet)
1896-1955 .... **TCLC 3**
See also CA 104; DAM DRAM; DLB 7, 26

Shestov, Lev 1866-1938......... **TCLC 56**

Shiel, M(atthew) P(hipps)
1865-1947 .... **TCLC 8**
See also CA 106; DLB 153

Shiga, Naoya 1883-1971.......... **CLC 33**
See also CA 101; 33-36R

Shilts, Randy 1951-1994 .... **CLC 85**
See also CA 115; 127; 144; CANR 45;
INT 127

Shimazaki Haruki 1872-1943
See Shimazaki Toson
See also CA 105; 134

Shimazaki Toson................. **TCLC 5**
See also Shimazaki Haruki

Sholokhov, Mikhail (Aleksandrovich)
1905-1984 .... **CLC 7, 15**
See also CA 101; 112; MTCW;
SATA-Obit 36

Shone, Patric
See Hanley, James

Shreve, Susan Richards 1939-...... **CLC 23**
See also CA 49-52; CAAS 5; CANR 5, 38;
MAICYA; SATA 46; SATA-Brief 41

Shue, Larry 1946-1985............ **CLC 52**
See also CA 145; 117; DAM DRAM

Shu-Jen, Chou 1881-1936
See Lu Hsun
See also CA 104

Shulman, Alix Kates 1932-...... **CLC 2, 10**
See also CA 29-32R; CANR 43; SATA 7

Shuster, Joe 1914-.............. **CLC 21**

Shute, Nevil.................... **CLC 30**
See also Norway, Nevil Shute

Shuttle, Penelope (Diane) 1947-..... **CLC 7**
See also CA 93-96; CANR 39; DLB 14, 40

Sidney, Mary 1561-1621 .... **LC 19**

Sidney, Sir Philip
1554-1586 ..... **LC 19; DA; DAB; DAC**
See also CDBLB Before 1660; DAM MST,
POET

Siegel, Jerome 1914- .... **CLC 21**
See also CA 116

Siegel, Jerry
See Siegel, Jerome

Sienkiewicz, Henryk (Adam Alexander Pius)
1846-1916 .... **TCLC 3**
See also CA 104; 134

Sierra, Gregorio Martinez
See Martinez Sierra, Gregorio

Sierra, Maria (de la O'LeJarraga) Martinez
See Martinez Sierra, Maria (de la
O'LeJarraga)

Sigal, Clancy 1926-.............. **CLC 7**
See also CA 1-4R

Sigourney, Lydia Howard (Huntley)
1791-1865 .... **NCLC 21**
See also DLB 1, 42, 73

Siguenza y Gongora, Carlos de
1645-1700 .... **LC 8**

Sigurjonsson, Johann 1880-1919... **TCLC 27**

Sikelianos, Angelos 1884-1951 .... **TCLC 39**

Silkin, Jon 1930- .... **CLC 2, 6, 43**
See also CA 5-8R; CAAS 5; DLB 27

Silko, Leslie (Marmon)
1948- .... **CLC 23, 74; DA; DAC**
See also AAYA 14; CA 115; 122;
CANR 45; DAM MST, MULT, POP;
DLB 143; NNAL

Sillanpaa, Frans Eemil 1888-1964... **CLC 19**
See also CA 129; 93-96; MTCW

Sillitoe, Alan
1928- .... **CLC 1, 3, 6, 10, 19, 57**
See also AITN 1; CA 9-12R; CAAS 2;
CANR 8, 26; CDBLB 1960 to Present;
DLB 14, 139; MTCW; SATA 61

Silone, Ignazio 1900-1978 .... **CLC 4**
See also CA 25-28; 81-84; CANR 34;
CAP 2; MTCW

Silver, Joan Micklin 1935- .... **CLC 20**
See also CA 114; 121; INT 121

Silver, Nicholas
See Faust, Frederick (Schiller)

Silverberg, Robert 1935- .... **CLC 7**
See also CA 1-4R; CAAS 3; CANR 1, 20,
36; DAM POP; DLB 8; INT CANR-20;
MAICYA; MTCW; SATA 13

Silverstein, Alvin 1933- .... **CLC 17**
See also CA 49-52; CANR 2; CLR 25;
JRDA; MAICYA; SATA 8, 69

Silverstein, Virginia B(arbara Opshelor)
1937- .... **CLC 17**
See also CA 49-52; CANR 2; CLR 25;
JRDA; MAICYA; SATA 8, 69

Sim, Georges
See Simenon, Georges (Jacques Christian)

Simak, Clifford D(onald)
1904-1988 .... **CLC 1, 55**
See also CA 1-4R; 125; CANR 1, 35;
DLB 8; MTCW; SATA-Obit 56

Simenon, Georges (Jacques Christian)
1903-1989 .... **CLC 1, 2, 3, 8, 18, 47**
See also CA 85-88; 129; CANR 35;
DAM POP; DLB 72; DLBY 89; MTCW

Simic, Charles 1938-... **CLC 6, 9, 22, 49, 68**
See also CA 29-32R; CAAS 4; CANR 12,
33; DAM POET; DLB 105

Simmons, Charles (Paul) 1924-..... **CLC 57**
See also CA 89-92; INT 89-92

Simmons, Dan 1948-.............. **CLC 44**
See also AAYA 16; CA 138; DAM POP

Simmons, James (Stewart Alexander)
1933-...................... **CLC 43**
See also CA 105; CAAS 21; DLB 40

Simms, William Gilmore
1806-1870 .... **NCLC 3**
See also DLB 3, 30, 59, 73

Simon, Carly 1945-.............. **CLC 26**
See also CA 105

Simon, Claude 1913-....... **CLC 4, 9, 15, 39**
See also CA 89-92; CANR 33; DAM NOV;
DLB 83; MTCW

Simon, (Marvin) Neil
1927- .... **CLC 6, 11, 31, 39, 70**
See also AITN 1; CA 21-24R; CANR 26;
DAM DRAM; DLB 7; MTCW

Simon, Paul 1942(?)- .... **CLC 17**
See also CA 116

Simonon, Paul 1956(?)- .... **CLC 30**

Simpson, Harriette
See Arnow, Harriette (Louisa) Simpson

Simpson, Louis (Aston Marantz)
1923- .... **CLC 4, 7, 9, 32**
See also CA 1-4R; CAAS 4; CANR 1;
DAM POET; DLB 5; MTCW

Simpson, Mona (Elizabeth) 1957-... **CLC 44**
See also CA 122; 135

Simpson, N(orman) F(rederick)
1919-...................... **CLC 29**
See also CA 13-16R; DLB 13

Sinclair, Andrew (Annandale)
1935-.................... **CLC 2, 14**
See also CA 9-12R; CAAS 5; CANR 14, 38;
DLB 14; MTCW

Sinclair, Emil
See Hesse, Hermann

Sinclair, Iain 1943-.............. **CLC 76**
See also CA 132

Sinclair, Iain MacGregor
See Sinclair, Iain

Sinclair, Mary Amelia St. Clair 1865(?)-1946
See Sinclair, May
See also CA 104

Sinclair, May.................. **TCLC 3, 11**
See also Sinclair, Mary Amelia St. Clair
See also DLB 36, 135

Sinclair, Upton (Beall)
1878-1968 ...... **CLC 1, 11, 15, 63; DA;**
DAB; DAC; WLC
See also CA 5-8R; 25-28R; CANR 7;
CDALB 1929-1941; DAM MST, NOV;
DLB 9; INT CANR-7; MTCW; SATA 9

Singer, Isaac
See Singer, Isaac Bashevis

Singer, Isaac Bashevis
1904-1991 .... **CLC 1, 3, 6, 9, 11, 15, 23,**
38, 69; DA; DAB; DAC; SSC 3; WLC
See also AITN 1, 2; CA 1-4R; 134;
CANR 1, 39; CDALB 1941-1968; CLR 1;
DAM MST, NOV; DLB 6, 28, 52;
DLBY 91; JRDA; MAICYA; MTCW;
SATA 3, 27; SATA-Obit 68

Singer, Israel Joshua 1893-1944... **TCLC 33**

Singh, Khushwant 1915-.......... CLC 11
    See also CA 9-12R; CAAS 9; CANR 6

Sinjohn, John
    See Galsworthy, John

Sinyavsky, Andrei (Donatevich)
    1925-...................... CLC 8
    See also CA 85-88

Sirin, V.
    See Nabokov, Vladimir (Vladimirovich)

Sissman, L(ouis) E(dward)
    1928-1976.............. CLC 9, 18
    See also CA 21-24R; 65-68; CANR 13;
    DLB 5

Sisson, C(harles) H(ubert) 1914-..... CLC 8
    See also CA 1-4R; CAAS 3; CANR 3, 48;
    DLB 27

Sitwell, Dame Edith
    1887-1964 .... CLC 2, 9, 67; PC 3
    See also CA 9-12R; CANR 35;
    CDBLB 1945-1960; DAM POET;
    DLB 20; MTCW

Sjoewall, Maj 1935-.............. CLC 7
    See also CA 65-68

Sjowall, Maj
    See Sjoewall, Maj

Skelton, Robin 1925-............. CLC 13
    See also AITN 2; CA 5-8R; CAAS 5;
    CANR 28; DLB 27, 53

Skolimowski, Jerzy 1938-......... CLC 20
    See also CA 128

Skram, Amalie (Bertha)
    1847-1905 .... TCLC 25

Skvorecky, Josef (Vaclav)
    1924-.......... CLC 15, 39, 69; DAC
    See also CA 61-64; CAAS 1; CANR 10, 34;
    DAM NOV; MTCW

Slade, Bernard................. CLC 11, 46
    See also Newbound, Bernard Slade
    See also CAAS 9; DLB 53

Slaughter, Carolyn 1946-......... CLC 56
    See also CA 85-88

Slaughter, Frank G(ill) 1908- ...... CLC 29
    See also AITN 2; CA 5-8R; CANR 5;
    INT CANR-5

Slavitt, David R(ytman) 1935-.... CLC 5, 14
    See also CA 21-24R; CAAS 3; CANR 41;
    DLB 5, 6

Slesinger, Tess 1905-1945 .... TCLC 10
    See also CA 107; DLB 102

Slessor, Kenneth 1901-1971........ CLC 14
    See also CA 102; 89-92

Slowacki, Juliusz 1809-1849 ..... NCLC 15

Smart, Christopher
    1722-1771 .... LC 3; PC 13
    See also DAM POET; DLB 109

Smart, Elizabeth 1913-1986........ CLC 54
    See also CA 81-84; 118; DLB 88

Smiley, Jane (Graves) 1949- .... CLC 53, 76
    See also CA 104; CANR 30, 50;
    DAM POP; INT CANR-30

Smith, A(rthur) J(ames) M(arshall)
    1902-1980 .... CLC 15; DAC
    See also CA 1-4R; 102; CANR 4; DLB 88

Smith, Anna Deavere 1950-........ CLC 86
    See also CA 133

Smith, Betty (Wehner) 1896-1972... CLC 19
    See also CA 5-8R; 33-36R; DLBY 82;
    SATA 6

Smith, Charlotte (Turner)
    1749-1806 .... NCLC 23
    See also DLB 39, 109

Smith, Clark Ashton 1893-1961 .... CLC 43
    See also CA 143

Smith, Dave.................. CLC 22, 42
    See also Smith, David (Jeddie)
    See also CAAS 7; DLB 5

Smith, David (Jeddie) 1942-
    See Smith, Dave
    See also CA 49-52; CANR 1; DAM POET

Smith, Florence Margaret 1902-1971
    See Smith, Stevie
    See also CA 17-18; 29-32R; CANR 35;
    CAP 2; DAM POET; MTCW

Smith, Iain Crichton 1928- .... CLC 64
    See also CA 21-24R; DLB 40, 139

Smith, John 1580(?)-1631 .... LC 9

Smith, Johnston
    See Crane, Stephen (Townley)

Smith, Joseph, Jr. 1805-1844 .... NCLC 53

Smith, Lee 1944-.............. CLC 25, 73
    See also CA 114; 119; CANR 46; DLB 143;
    DLBY 83; INT 119

Smith, Martin
    See Smith, Martin Cruz

Smith, Martin Cruz 1942-......... CLC 25
    See also BEST 89:4; CA 85-88; CANR 6,
    23, 43; DAM MULT, POP;
    INT CANR-23; NNAL

Smith, Mary-Ann Tirone 1944-..... CLC 39
    See also CA 118; 136

Smith, Patti 1946- .... CLC 12
    See also CA 93-96

Smith, Pauline (Urmson)
    1882-1959 .... TCLC 25

Smith, Rosamond
    See Oates, Joyce Carol

Smith, Sheila Kaye
    See Kaye-Smith, Sheila

Smith, Stevie ...... CLC 3, 8, 25, 44; PC 12
    See also Smith, Florence Margaret
    See also DLB 20

Smith, Wilbur (Addison) 1933-..... CLC 33
    See also CA 13-16R; CANR 7, 46; MTCW

Smith, William Jay 1918- .... CLC 6
    See also CA 5-8R; CANR 44; DLB 5;
    MAICYA; SATA 2, 68

Smith, Woodrow Wilson
    See Kuttner, Henry

Smolenskin, Peretz 1842-1885.... NCLC 30

Smollett, Tobias (George) 1721-1771 .. LC 2
    See also CDBLB 1660-1789; DLB 39, 104

Snodgrass, W(illiam) D(e Witt)
    1926-............. CLC 2, 6, 10, 18, 68
    See also CA 1-4R; CANR 6, 36;
    DAM POET; DLB 5; MTCW

Snow, C(harles) P(ercy)
    1905-1980 .... CLC 1, 4, 6, 9, 13, 19
    See also CA 5-8R; 101; CANR 28;
    CDBLB 1945-1960; DAM NOV; DLB 15,
    77; MTCW

Snow, Frances Compton
    See Adams, Henry (Brooks)

Snyder, Gary (Sherman)
    1930-.............. CLC 1, 2, 5, 9, 32
    See also CA 17-20R; CANR 30;
    DAM POET; DLB 5, 16

Snyder, Zilpha Keatley 1927-...... CLC 17
    See also AAYA 15; CA 9-12R; CANR 38;
    CLR 31; JRDA; MAICYA; SAAS 2;
    SATA 1, 28, 75

Soares, Bernardo
    See Pessoa, Fernando (Antonio Nogueira)

Sobh, A.
    See Shamlu, Ahmad

Sobol, Joshua..................... CLC 60

Soderberg, Hjalmar 1869-1941 .... TCLC 39

Sodergran, Edith (Irene)
    See Soedergran, Edith (Irene)

Soedergran, Edith (Irene)
    1892-1923 .... TCLC 31

Softly, Edgar
    See Lovecraft, H(oward) P(hillips)

Softly, Edward
    See Lovecraft, H(oward) P(hillips)

Sokolov, Raymond 1941-........... CLC 7
    See also CA 85-88

Solo, Jay
    See Ellison, Harlan (Jay)

Sologub, Fyodor .... TCLC 9
    See also Teternikov, Fyodor Kuzmich

Solomons, Ikey Esquir
    See Thackeray, William Makepeace

Solomos, Dionysios 1798-1857 ... NCLC 15

Solwoska, Mara
    See French, Marilyn

Solzhenitsyn, Aleksandr I(sayevich)
    1918- ...... CLC 1, 2, 4, 7, 9, 10, 18, 26,
                34, 78; DA; DAB; DAC; WLC
    See also AITN 1; CA 69-72; CANR 40;
    DAM MST, NOV; MTCW

Somers, Jane
    See Lessing, Doris (May)

Somerville, Edith 1858-1949 ...... TCLC 51
    See also DLB 135

Somerville & Ross
    See Martin, Violet Florence; Somerville,
    Edith

Sommer, Scott 1951- .... CLC 25
    See also CA 106

Sondheim, Stephen (Joshua)
    1930-................... CLC 30, 39
    See also AAYA 11; CA 103; CANR 47;
    DAM DRAM

Sontag, Susan 1933-... CLC 1, 2, 10, 13, 31
    See also CA 17-20R; CANR 25;
    DAM POP; DLB 2, 67; MTCW

Sophocles
496(?)B.C.-406(?)B.C..... **CMLC 2; DA;
DAB; DAC; DC 1**
See also DAM DRAM, MST

Sordello 1189-1269............ **CMLC 15**

Sorel, Julia
See Drexler, Rosalyn

Sorrentino, Gilbert
1929-........... **CLC 3, 7, 14, 22, 40**
See also CA 77-80; CANR 14, 33; DLB 5;
DLBY 80; INT CANR-14

Soto, Gary 1952-........ **CLC 32, 80; HLC**
See also AAYA 10; CA 119; 125;
CANR 50; CLR 38; DAM MULT;
DLB 82; HW; INT 125; JRDA; SATA 80

Soupault, Philippe 1897-1990 ...... **CLC 68**
See also CA 116; 147; 131

Souster, (Holmes) Raymond
1921-.............. **CLC 5, 14; DAC**
See also CA 13-16R; CAAS 14; CANR 13,
29; DAM POET; DLB 88; SATA 63

Southern, Terry 1926-............ **CLC 7**
See also CA 1-4R; CANR 1; DLB 2

Southey, Robert 1774-1843 .... **NCLC 8**
See also DLB 93, 107, 142; SATA 54

Southworth, Emma Dorothy Eliza Nevitte
1819-1899 .... **NCLC 26**

Souza, Ernest
See Scott, Evelyn

Soyinka, Wole
1934-....... **CLC 3, 5, 14, 36, 44; BLC;
DA; DAB; DAC; DC 2; WLC**
See also BW 2; CA 13-16R; CANR 27, 39;
DAM DRAM, MST, MULT; DLB 125;
MTCW

Spackman, W(illiam) M(ode)
1905-1990 .... **CLC 46**
See also CA 81-84; 132

Spacks, Barry 1931-.............. **CLC 14**
See also CA 29-32R; CANR 33; DLB 105

Spanidou, Irini 1946-............. **CLC 44**

Spark, Muriel (Sarah)
1918-....... **CLC 2, 3, 5, 8, 13, 18, 40;
DAB; DAC; SSC 10**
See also CA 5-8R; CANR 12, 36;
CDBLB 1945-1960; DAM MST, NOV;
DLB 15, 139; INT CANR-12; MTCW

Spaulding, Douglas
See Bradbury, Ray (Douglas)

Spaulding, Leonard
See Bradbury, Ray (Douglas)

Spence, J. A. D.
See Eliot, T(homas) S(tearns)

Spencer, Elizabeth 1921-......... **CLC 22**
See also CA 13-16R; CANR 32; DLB 6;
MTCW; SATA 14

Spencer, Leonard G.
See Silverberg, Robert

Spencer, Scott 1945-.............. **CLC 30**
See also CA 113; DLBY 86

Spender, Stephen (Harold)
1909-............. **CLC 1, 2, 5, 10, 41**
See also CA 9-12R; CANR 31;
CDBLB 1945-1960; DAM POET;
DLB 20; MTCW

Spengler, Oswald (Arnold Gottfried)
1880-1936 .... **TCLC 25**
See also CA 118

Spenser, Edmund
1552(?)-1599 .... **LC 5; DA; DAB; DAC;
PC 8; WLC**
See also CDBLB Before 1660; DAM MST,
POET

Spicer, Jack 1925-1965 ...... **CLC 8, 18, 72**
See also CA 85-88; DAM POET; DLB 5, 16

Spiegelman, Art 1948-............ **CLC 76**
See also AAYA 10; CA 125; CANR 41

Spielberg, Peter 1929-............. **CLC 6**
See also CA 5-8R; CANR 4, 48; DLBY 81

Spielberg, Steven 1947-........... **CLC 20**
See also AAYA 8; CA 77-80; CANR 32;
SATA 32

Spillane, Frank Morrison 1918-
See Spillane, Mickey
See also CA 25-28R; CANR 28; MTCW;
SATA 66

Spillane, Mickey .... **CLC 3, 13**
See also Spillane, Frank Morrison

Spinoza, Benedictus de 1632-1677 .... **LC 9**

Spinrad, Norman (Richard) 1940-... **CLC 46**
See also CA 37-40R; CAAS 19; CANR 20;
DLB 8; INT CANR-20

Spitteler, Carl (Friedrich Georg)
1845-1924 .... **TCLC 12**
See also CA 109; DLB 129

Spivack, Kathleen (Romola Drucker)
1938-........................ **CLC 6**
See also CA 49-52

Spoto, Donald 1941-............. **CLC 39**
See also CA 65-68; CANR 11

Springsteen, Bruce (F.) 1949-...... **CLC 17**
See also CA 111

Spurling, Hilary 1940-............ **CLC 34**
See also CA 104; CANR 25

Spyker, John Howland
See Elman, Richard

Squires, (James) Radcliffe
1917-1993 .... **CLC 51**
See also CA 1-4R; 140; CANR 6, 21

Srivastava, Dhanpat Rai 1880(?)-1936
See Premchand
See also CA 118

Stacy, Donald
See Pohl, Frederik

Stael, Germaine de
See Stael-Holstein, Anne Louise Germaine
Necker Baronn
See also DLB 119

Stael-Holstein, Anne Louise Germaine Necker
Baronn 1766-1817 .... **NCLC 3**
See also Stael, Germaine de

Stafford, Jean 1915-1979... **CLC 4, 7, 19, 68**
See also CA 1-4R; 85-88; CANR 3; DLB 2;
MTCW; SATA-Obit 22

Stafford, William (Edgar)
1914-1993 .... **CLC 4, 7, 29**
See also CA 5-8R; 142; CAAS 3; CANR 5,
22; DAM POET; DLB 5; INT CANR-22

Staines, Trevor
See Brunner, John (Kilian Houston)

Stairs, Gordon
See Austin, Mary (Hunter)

Stannard, Martin 1947-........... **CLC 44**
See also CA 142; DLB 155

Stanton, Maura 1946- .... **CLC 9**
See also CA 89-92; CANR 15; DLB 120

Stanton, Schuyler
See Baum, L(yman) Frank

Stapledon, (William) Olaf
1886-1950 .... **TCLC 22**
See also CA 111; DLB 15

Starbuck, George (Edwin) 1931-.... **CLC 53**
See also CA 21-24R; CANR 23;
DAM POET

Stark, Richard
See Westlake, Donald E(dwin)

Staunton, Schuyler
See Baum, L(yman) Frank

Stead, Christina (Ellen)
1902-1983 .... **CLC 2, 5, 8, 32, 80**
See also CA 13-16R; 109; CANR 33, 40;
MTCW

Stead, William Thomas
1849-1912 .... **TCLC 48**

Steele, Richard 1672-1729.......... **LC 18**
See also CDBLB 1660-1789; DLB 84, 101

Steele, Timothy (Reid) 1948-....... **CLC 45**
See also CA 93-96; CANR 16, 50; DLB 120

Steffens, (Joseph) Lincoln
1866-1936 .... **TCLC 20**
See also CA 117

Stegner, Wallace (Earle)
1909-1993 .... **CLC 9, 49, 81**
See also AITN 1; BEST 90:3; CA 1-4R;
141; CAAS 9; CANR 1, 21, 46;
DAM NOV; DLB 9; DLBY 93; MTCW

Stein, Gertrude
1874-1946 ...... **TCLC 1, 6, 28, 48; DA;
DAB; DAC; WLC**
See also CA 104; 132; CDALB 1917-1929;
DAM MST, NOV, POET; DLB 4, 54, 86;
MTCW

Steinbeck, John (Ernst)
1902-1968 ...... **CLC 1, 5, 9, 13, 21, 34,
45, 75; DA; DAB; DAC; SSC 11; WLC**
See also AAYA 12; CA 1-4R; 25-28R;
CANR 1, 35; CDALB 1929-1941;
DAM DRAM, MST, NOV; DLB 7, 9;
DLBD 2; MTCW; SATA 9

Steinem, Gloria 1934-............. **CLC 63**
See also CA 53-56; CANR 28; MTCW

Steiner, George 1929-............. **CLC 24**
See also CA 73-76; CANR 31; DAM NOV;
DLB 67; MTCW; SATA 62

Steiner, K. Leslie
See Delany, Samuel R(ay, Jr.)

Steiner, Rudolf 1861-1925........ **TCLC 13**
See also CA 107

Stendhal
1783-1842 .... **NCLC 23, 46; DA; DAB;
DAC; WLC**
See also DAM MST, NOV; DLB 119

Stephen, Leslie 1832-1904........ **TCLC 23**
See also CA 123; DLB 57, 144

Stephen, Sir Leslie
See Stephen, Leslie

Stephen, Virginia
See Woolf, (Adeline) Virginia

Stephens, James 1882(?)-1950 . . . . . **TCLC 4**
See also CA 104; DLB 19, 153

Stephens, Reed
See Donaldson, Stephen R.

Steptoe, Lydia
See Barnes, Djuna

Sterchi, Beat 1949- . . . . **CLC 65**

Sterling, Brett
See Bradbury, Ray (Douglas); Hamilton,
Edmond

Sterling, Bruce 1954- . . . . **CLC 72**
See also CA 119; CANR 44

Sterling, George 1869-1926 . . . . **TCLC 20**
See also CA 117; DLB 54

Stern, Gerald 1925- . . . . **CLC 40**
See also CA 81-84; CANR 28; DLB 105

Stern, Richard (Gustave) 1928- . . . **CLC 4, 39**
See also CA 1-4R; CANR 1, 25; DLBY 87;
INT CANR-25

Sternberg, Josef von 1894-1969 . . . . . **CLC 20**
See also CA 81-84

Sterne, Laurence
1713-1768 . . . . . . **LC 2; DA; DAB; DAC;**
WLC
See also CDBLB 1660-1789; DAM MST,
NOV; DLB 39

Sternheim, (William Adolf) Carl
1878-1942 . . . . **TCLC 8**
See also CA 105; DLB 56, 118

Stevens, Mark 1951- . . . . **CLC 34**
See also CA 122

Stevens, Wallace
1879-1955 . . . . **TCLC 3, 12, 45; DA;**
DAB; DAC; PC 6; WLC
See also CA 104; 124; CDALB 1929-1941;
DAM MST, POET; DLB 54; MTCW

Stevenson, Anne (Katharine)
1933- . . . . **CLC 7, 33**
See also CA 17-20R; CAAS 9; CANR 9, 33;
DLB 40; MTCW

Stevenson, Robert Louis (Balfour)
1850-1894 . . . . . **NCLC 5, 14; DA; DAB;**
DAC; SSC 11; WLC
See also CDBLB 1890-1914; CLR 10, 11;
DAM MST, NOV; DLB 18, 57, 141, 156;
DLBD 13; JRDA; MAICYA; YABC 2

Stewart, J(ohn) I(nnes) M(ackintosh)
1906-1994 . . . . **CLC 7, 14, 32**
See also CA 85-88; 147; CAAS 3;
CANR 47; MTCW

Stewart, Mary (Florence Elinor)
1916- . . . . **CLC 7, 35; DAB**
See also CA 1-4R; CANR 1; SATA 12

Stewart, Mary Rainbow
See Stewart, Mary (Florence Elinor)

Stifle, June
See Campbell, Maria

Stifter, Adalbert 1805-1868 . . . . . . **NCLC 41**
See also DLB 133

Still, James 1906- . . . . **CLC 49**
See also CA 65-68; CAAS 17; CANR 10,
26; DLB 9; SATA 29

Sting
See Sumner, Gordon Matthew

Stirling, Arthur
See Sinclair, Upton (Beall)

Stitt, Milan 1941- . . . . **CLC 29**
See also CA 69-72

Stockton, Francis Richard 1834-1902
See Stockton, Frank R.
See also CA 108; 137; MAICYA; SATA 44

Stockton, Frank R. . . . . **TCLC 47**
See also Stockton, Francis Richard
See also DLB 42, 74; DLBD 13;
SATA-Brief 32

Stoddard, Charles
See Kuttner, Henry

Stoker, Abraham 1847-1912
See Stoker, Bram
See also CA 105; DA; DAC; DAM MST,
NOV; SATA 29

Stoker, Bram . . . . **TCLC 8; DAB; WLC**
See also Stoker, Abraham
See also CDBLB 1890-1914; DLB 36, 70

Stolz, Mary (Slattery) 1920- . . . . **CLC 12**
See also AAYA 8; AITN 1; CA 5-8R;
CANR 13, 41; JRDA; MAICYA;
SAAS 3; SATA 10, 71

Stone, Irving 1903-1989 . . . . **CLC 7**
See also AITN 1; CA 1-4R; 129; CAAS 3;
CANR 1, 23; DAM POP;
INT CANR-23; MTCW; SATA 3;
SATA-Obit 64

Stone, Oliver 1946- . . . . **CLC 73**
See also AAYA 15; CA 110

Stone, Robert (Anthony)
1937- . . . . **CLC 5, 23, 42**
See also CA 85-88; CANR 23; DLB 152;
INT CANR-23; MTCW

Stone, Zachary
See Follett, Ken(neth Martin)

Stoppard, Tom
1937- . . . . . . **CLC 1, 3, 4, 5, 8, 15, 29, 34,**
63; DA; DAB; DAC; DC 6; WLC
See also CA 81-84; CANR 39;
CDBLB 1960 to Present; DAM DRAM,
MST; DLB 13; DLBY 85; MTCW

Storey, David (Malcolm)
1933- . . . . **CLC 2, 4, 5, 8**
See also CA 81-84; CANR 36;
DAM DRAM; DLB 13, 14; MTCW

Storm, Hyemeyohsts 1935- . . . . **CLC 3**
See also CA 81-84; CANR 45;
DAM MULT; NNAL

Storm, (Hans) Theodor (Woldsen)
1817-1888 . . . . **NCLC 1**

Storni, Alfonsina
1892-1938 . . . . **TCLC 5; HLC**
See also CA 104; 131; DAM MULT; HW

Stout, Rex (Todhunter) 1886-1975 . . . **CLC 3**
See also AITN 2; CA 61-64

Stow, (Julian) Randolph 1935- . . **CLC 23, 48**
See also CA 13-16R; CANR 33; MTCW

Stowe, Harriet (Elizabeth) Beecher
1811-1896 . . . . . **NCLC 3, 50; DA; DAB;**
DAC; WLC
See also CDALB 1865-1917; DAM MST,
NOV; DLB 1, 12, 42, 74; JRDA;
MAICYA; YABC 1

Strachey, (Giles) Lytton
1880-1932 . . . . **TCLC 12**
See also CA 110; DLB 149; DLBD 10

Strand, Mark 1934- . . . . . . **CLC 6, 18, 41, 71**
See also CA 21-24R; CANR 40;
DAM POET; DLB 5; SATA 41

Straub, Peter (Francis) 1943- . . . . . . **CLC 28**
See also BEST 89:1; CA 85-88; CANR 28;
DAM POP; DLBY 84; MTCW

Strauss, Botho 1944- . . . . **CLC 22**
See also DLB 124

Streatfeild, (Mary) Noel
1895(?)-1986 . . . . **CLC 21**
See also CA 81-84; 120; CANR 31;
CLR 17; DLB 160; MAICYA; SATA 20;
SATA-Obit 48

Stribling, T(homas) S(igismund)
1881-1965 . . . . **CLC 23**
See also CA 107; DLB 9

Strindberg, (Johan) August
1849-1912 . . . . . . **TCLC 1, 8, 21, 47; DA;**
DAB; DAC; WLC
See also CA 104; 135; DAM DRAM, MST

Stringer, Arthur 1874-1950 . . . . **TCLC 37**
See also DLB 92

Stringer, David
See Roberts, Keith (John Kingston)

Strugatskii, Arkadii (Natanovich)
1925-1991 . . . . **CLC 27**
See also CA 106; 135

Strugatskii, Boris (Natanovich)
1933- . . . . **CLC 27**
See also CA 106

Strummer, Joe 1953(?)- . . . . **CLC 30**

Stuart, Don A.
See Campbell, John W(ood, Jr.)

Stuart, Ian
See MacLean, Alistair (Stuart)

Stuart, Jesse (Hilton)
1906-1984 . . . . **CLC 1, 8, 11, 14, 34**
See also CA 5-8R; 112; CANR 31; DLB 9,
48, 102; DLBY 84; SATA 2;
SATA-Obit 36

Sturgeon, Theodore (Hamilton)
1918-1985 . . . . **CLC 22, 39**
See also Queen, Ellery
See also CA 81-84; 116; CANR 32; DLB 8;
DLBY 85; MTCW

Sturges, Preston 1898-1959 . . . . **TCLC 48**
See also CA 114; 149; DLB 26

Styron, William
1925- . . . . **CLC 1, 3, 5, 11, 15, 60**
See also BEST 90:4; CA 5-8R; CANR 6, 33;
CDALB 1968-1988; DAM NOV, POP;
DLB 2, 143; DLBY 80; INT CANR-6;
MTCW

Suarez Lynch, B.
See Bioy Casares, Adolfo; Borges, Jorge
Luis

Su Chien 1884-1918
See Su Man-shu
See also CA 123

Suckow, Ruth 1892-1960 . . . . **SSC 18**
See also CA 113; DLB 9, 102

Sudermann, Hermann 1857-1928 . . **TCLC 15**
See also CA 107; DLB 118

Sue, Eugene 1804-1857 . . . . **NCLC 1**
See also DLB 119

Sueskind, Patrick 1949- . . . . **CLC 44**
See also Suskind, Patrick

Sukenick, Ronald 1932- . . . . . **CLC 3, 4, 6, 48**
See also CA 25-28R; CAAS 8; CANR 32;
DLBY 81

Suknaski, Andrew 1942- . . . . **CLC 19**
See also CA 101; DLB 53

Sullivan, Vernon
See Vian, Boris

Sully Prudhomme 1839-1907 . . . . . . **TCLC 31**

Su Man-shu . . . . **TCLC 24**
See also Su Chien

Summerforest, Ivy B.
See Kirkup, James

Summers, Andrew James 1942- . . . . . **CLC 26**

Summers, Andy
See Summers, Andrew James

Summers, Hollis (Spurgeon, Jr.)
1916- . . . . **CLC 10**
See also CA 5-8R; CANR 3; DLB 6

Summers, (Alphonsus Joseph-Mary Augustus)
Montague 1880-1948 . . . . **TCLC 16**
See also CA 118

Sumner, Gordon Matthew 1951- . . . . **CLC 26**

Surtees, Robert Smith
1803-1864 . . . . **NCLC 14**
See also DLB 21

Susann, Jacqueline 1921-1974 . . . . . . **CLC 3**
See also AITN 1; CA 65-68; 53-56; MTCW

Su Shih 1036-1101 . . . . **CMLC 15**

Suskind, Patrick
See Sueskind, Patrick
See also CA 145

Sutcliff, Rosemary
1920-1992 . . . . **CLC 26; DAB; DAC**
See also AAYA 10; CA 5-8R; 139;
CANR 37; CLR 1, 37; DAM MST, POP;
JRDA; MAICYA; SATA 6, 44, 78;
SATA-Obit 73

Sutro, Alfred 1863-1933 . . . . **TCLC 6**
See also CA 105; DLB 10

Sutton, Henry
See Slavitt, David R(ytman)

Svevo, Italo . . . . **TCLC 2, 35**
See also Schmitz, Aron Hector

Swados, Elizabeth (A.) 1951- . . . . **CLC 12**
See also CA 97-100; CANR 49; INT 97-100

Swados, Harvey 1920-1972 . . . . **CLC 5**
See also CA 5-8R; 37-40R; CANR 6;
DLB 2

Swan, Gladys 1934- . . . . **CLC 69**
See also CA 101; CANR 17, 39

Swarthout, Glendon (Fred)
1918-1992 . . . . **CLC 35**
See also CA 1-4R; 139; CANR 1, 47;
SATA 26

Sweet, Sarah C.
See Jewett, (Theodora) Sarah Orne

Swenson, May
1919-1989 . . . . **CLC 4, 14, 61; DA; DAB;**
DAC; PC 14
See also CA 5-8R; 130; CANR 36;
DAM MST, POET; DLB 5; MTCW;
SATA 15

Swift, Augustus
See Lovecraft, H(oward) P(hillips)

Swift, Graham (Colin) 1949- . . . . **CLC 41, 88**
See also CA 117; 122; CANR 46

Swift, Jonathan
1667-1745 . . . . . . **LC 1; DA; DAB; DAC;**
PC 9; WLC
See also CDBLB 1660-1789; DAM MST,
NOV, POET; DLB 39, 95, 101; SATA 19

Swinburne, Algernon Charles
1837-1909 . . . . . . **TCLC 8, 36; DA; DAB;**
DAC; WLC
See also CA 105; 140; CDBLB 1832-1890;
DAM MST, POET; DLB 35, 57

Swinfen, Ann . . . . **CLC 34**

Swinnerton, Frank Arthur
1884-1982 . . . . **CLC 31**
See also CA 108; DLB 34

Swithen, John
See King, Stephen (Edwin)

Sylvia
See Ashton-Warner, Sylvia (Constance)

Symmes, Robert Edward
See Duncan, Robert (Edward)

Symonds, John Addington
1840-1893 . . . . **NCLC 34**
See also DLB 57, 144

Symons, Arthur 1865-1945 . . . . **TCLC 11**
See also CA 107; DLB 19, 57, 149

Symons, Julian (Gustave)
1912-1994 . . . . **CLC 2, 14, 32**
See also CA 49-52; 147; CAAS 3; CANR 3,
33; DLB 87, 155; DLBY 92; MTCW

Synge, (Edmund) J(ohn) M(illington)
1871-1909 . . . . **TCLC 6, 37; DC 2**
See also CA 104; 141; CDBLB 1890-1914;
DAM DRAM; DLB 10, 19

Syruc, J.
See Milosz, Czeslaw

Szirtes, George 1948- . . . . **CLC 46**
See also CA 109; CANR 27

Tabori, George 1914- . . . . **CLC 19**
See also CA 49-52; CANR 4

Tagore, Rabindranath
1861-1941 . . . . **TCLC 3, 53; PC 8**
See also CA 104; 120; DAM DRAM,
POET; MTCW

Taine, Hippolyte Adolphe
1828-1893 . . . . **NCLC 15**

Talese, Gay 1932- . . . . **CLC 37**
See also AITN 1; CA 1-4R; CANR 9;
INT CANR-9; MTCW

Tallent, Elizabeth (Ann) 1954- . . . . . **CLC 45**
See also CA 117; DLB 130

Tally, Ted 1952- . . . . **CLC 42**
See also CA 120; 124; INT 124

Tamayo y Baus, Manuel
1829-1898 . . . . **NCLC 1**

Tammsaare, A(nton) H(ansen)
1878-1940 . . . . **TCLC 27**

Tan, Amy 1952- . . . . **CLC 59**
See also AAYA 9; BEST 89:3; CA 136;
DAM MULT, NOV, POP; SATA 75

Tandem, Felix
See Spitteler, Carl (Friedrich Georg)

Tanizaki, Jun'ichiro
1886-1965 . . . . . . **CLC 8, 14, 28; SSC 21**
See also CA 93-96; 25-28R

Tanner, William
See Amis, Kingsley (William)

Tao Lao
See Storni, Alfonsina

Tarassoff, Lev
See Troyat, Henri

Tarbell, Ida M(inerva)
1857-1944 . . . . **TCLC 40**
See also CA 122; DLB 47

Tarkington, (Newton) Booth
1869-1946 . . . . **TCLC 9**
See also CA 110; 143; DLB 9, 102;
SATA 17

Tarkovsky, Andrei (Arsenyevich)
1932-1986 . . . . **CLC 75**
See also CA 127

Tartt, Donna 1964(?)- . . . . **CLC 76**
See also CA 142

Tasso, Torquato 1544-1595 . . . . **LC 5**

Tate, (John Orley) Allen
1899-1979 . . . **CLC 2, 4, 6, 9, 11, 14, 24**
See also CA 5-8R; 85-88; CANR 32;
DLB 4, 45, 63; MTCW

Tate, Ellalice
See Hibbert, Eleanor Alice Burford

Tate, James (Vincent) 1943- . . . **CLC 2, 6, 25**
See also CA 21-24R; CANR 29; DLB 5

Tavel, Ronald 1940- . . . . **CLC 6**
See also CA 21-24R; CANR 33

Taylor, C(ecil) P(hilip) 1929-1981 . . . **CLC 27**
See also CA 25-28R; 105; CANR 47

Taylor, Edward
1642(?)-1729 . . . **LC 11; DA; DAB; DAC**
See also DAM MST, POET; DLB 24

Taylor, Eleanor Ross 1920- . . . . **CLC 5**
See also CA 81-84

Taylor, Elizabeth 1912-1975 . . . **CLC 2, 4, 29**
See also CA 13-16R; CANR 9; DLB 139;
MTCW; SATA 13

Taylor, Henry (Splawn) 1942- . . . . . . **CLC 44**
See also CA 33-36R; CAAS 7; CANR 31;
DLB 5

Taylor, Kamala (Purnaiya) 1924-
See Markandaya, Kamala
See also CA 77-80

Taylor, Mildred D. . . . . CLC 21
　　See also AAYA 10; BW 1; CA 85-88;
　　CANR 25; CLR 9; DLB 52; JRDA;
　　MAICYA; SAAS 5; SATA 15, 70

Taylor, Peter (Hillsman)
　　1917-1994 . . . . . CLC 1, 4, 18, 37, 44, 50,
　　　　　　　　　　　　　　71; SSC 10
　　See also CA 13-16R; 147; CANR 9, 50;
　　DLBY 81, 94; INT CANR-9; MTCW

Taylor, Robert Lewis　1912- . . . . CLC 14
　　See also CA 1-4R; CANR 3; SATA 10

Tchekhov, Anton
　　See Chekhov, Anton (Pavlovich)

Teasdale, Sara　1884-1933. . . . . TCLC 4
　　See also CA 104; DLB 45; SATA 32

Tegner, Esaias　1782-1846. . . . . NCLC 2

Teilhard de Chardin, (Marie Joseph) Pierre
　　1881-1955 . . . . TCLC 9
　　See also CA 105

Temple, Ann
　　See Mortimer, Penelope (Ruth)

Tennant, Emma (Christina)
　　1937- . . . . CLC 13, 52
　　See also CA 65-68; CAAS 9; CANR 10, 38;
　　DLB 14

Tenneshaw, S. M.
　　See Silverberg, Robert

Tennyson, Alfred
　　1809-1892 . . . . NCLC 30; DA; DAB;
　　　　　　　　　　　　　　DAC; PC 6; WLC
　　See also CDBLB 1832-1890; DAM MST,
　　POET; DLB 32

Teran, Lisa St. Aubin de . . . . CLC 36
　　See also St. Aubin de Teran, Lisa

Terence　195(?)B.C.-159B.C. . . . . . . CMLC 14

Teresa de Jesus, St.　1515-1582 . . . . . . LC 18

Terkel, Louis　1912-
　　See Terkel, Studs
　　See also CA 57-60; CANR 18, 45; MTCW

Terkel, Studs . . . . CLC 38
　　See also Terkel, Louis
　　See also AITN 1

Terry, C. V.
　　See Slaughter, Frank G(ill)

Terry, Megan　1932- . . . . CLC 19
　　See also CA 77-80; CABS 3; CANR 43;
　　DLB 7

Tertz, Abram
　　See Sinyavsky, Andrei (Donatevich)

Tesich, Steve　1943(?)- . . . . CLC 40, 69
　　See also CA 105; DLBY 83

Teternikov, Fyodor Kuzmich　1863-1927
　　See Sologub, Fyodor
　　See also CA 104

Tevis, Walter　1928-1984 . . . . CLC 42
　　See also CA 113

Tey, Josephine . . . . TCLC 14
　　See also Mackintosh, Elizabeth
　　See also DLB 77

Thackeray, William Makepeace
　　1811-1863 . . . . NCLC 5, 14, 22, 43; DA;
　　　　　　　　　　　　DAB; DAC; WLC
　　See also CDBLB 1832-1890; DAM MST,
　　NOV; DLB 21, 55, 159; SATA 23

Thakura, Ravindranatha
　　See Tagore, Rabindranath

Tharoor, Shashi　1956- . . . . CLC 70
　　See also CA 141

Thelwell, Michael Miles　1939- . . . . . CLC 22
　　See also BW 2; CA 101

Theobald, Lewis, Jr.
　　See Lovecraft, H(oward) P(hillips)

Theodorescu, Ion N.　1880-1967
　　See Arghezi, Tudor
　　See also CA 116

Theriault, Yves　1915-1983 . . . . CLC 79; DAC
　　See also CA 102; DAM MST; DLB 88

Theroux, Alexander (Louis)
　　1939- . . . . CLC 2, 25
　　See also CA 85-88; CANR 20

Theroux, Paul (Edward)
　　1941- . . . . CLC 5, 8, 11, 15, 28, 46
　　See also BEST 89:4; CA 33-36R; CANR 20,
　　45; DAM POP; DLB 2; MTCW;
　　SATA 44

Thesen, Sharon　1946- . . . . CLC 56

Thevenin, Denis
　　See Duhamel, Georges

Thibault, Jacques Anatole Francois
　　1844-1924
　　See France, Anatole
　　See also CA 106; 127; DAM NOV; MTCW

Thiele, Colin (Milton)　1920- . . . . CLC 17
　　See also CA 29-32R; CANR 12, 28;
　　CLR 27; MAICYA; SAAS 2; SATA 14,
　　72

Thomas, Audrey (Callahan)
　　1935- . . . . CLC 7, 13, 37; SSC 20
　　See also AITN 2; CA 21-24R; CAAS 19;
　　CANR 36; DLB 60; MTCW

Thomas, D(onald) M(ichael)
　　1935- . . . . CLC 13, 22, 31
　　See also CA 61-64; CAAS 11; CANR 17,
　　45; CDBLB 1960 to Present; DLB 40;
　　INT CANR-17; MTCW

Thomas, Dylan (Marlais)
　　1914-1953 . . . TCLC 1, 8, 45; DA; DAB;
　　　　　　　　　　　　DAC; PC 2; SSC 3; WLC
　　See also CA 104; 120; CDBLB 1945-1960;
　　DAM DRAM, MST, POET; DLB 13, 20,
　　139; MTCW; SATA 60

Thomas, (Philip) Edward
　　1878-1917 . . . . TCLC 10
　　See also CA 106; DAM POET; DLB 19

Thomas, Joyce Carol　1938- . . . . CLC 35
　　See also AAYA 12; BW 2; CA 113; 116;
　　CANR 48; CLR 19; DLB 33; INT 116;
　　JRDA; MAICYA; MTCW; SAAS 7;
　　SATA 40, 78

Thomas, Lewis　1913-1993 . . . . CLC 35
　　See also CA 85-88; 143; CANR 38; MTCW

Thomas, Paul
　　See Mann, (Paul) Thomas

Thomas, Piri　1928- . . . . CLC 17
　　See also CA 73-76; HW

Thomas, R(onald) S(tuart)
　　1913- . . . . CLC 6, 13, 48; DAB
　　See also CA 89-92; CAAS 4; CANR 30;
　　CDBLB 1960 to Present; DAM POET;
　　DLB 27; MTCW

Thomas, Ross (Elmore)　1926- . . . . . . CLC 39
　　See also CA 33-36R; CANR 22

Thompson, Francis Clegg
　　See Mencken, H(enry) L(ouis)

Thompson, Francis Joseph
　　1859-1907 . . . . TCLC 4
　　See also CA 104; CDBLB 1890-1914;
　　DLB 19

Thompson, Hunter S(tockton)
　　1939- . . . . CLC 9, 17, 40
　　See also BEST 89:1; CA 17-20R; CANR 23,
　　46; DAM POP; MTCW

Thompson, James Myers
　　See Thompson, Jim (Myers)

Thompson, Jim (Myers)
　　1906-1977(?) . . . . CLC 69
　　See also CA 140

Thompson, Judith . . . . CLC 39

Thomson, James　1700-1748 . . . . . . LC 16, 29
　　See also DAM POET; DLB 95

Thomson, James　1834-1882 . . . . . . NCLC 18
　　See also DAM POET; DLB 35

Thoreau, Henry David
　　1817-1862 . . . . . NCLC 7, 21; DA; DAB;
　　　　　　　　　　　　　　DAC; WLC
　　See also CDALB 1640-1865; DAM MST;
　　DLB 1

Thornton, Hall
　　See Silverberg, Robert

Thucydides　c. 455B.C.-399B.C. . . . . CMLC 17

Thurber, James (Grover)
　　1894-1961 . . . . CLC 5, 11, 25; DA; DAB;
　　　　　　　　　　　　　　DAC; SSC 1
　　See also CA 73-76; CANR 17, 39;
　　CDALB 1929-1941; DAM DRAM, MST,
　　NOV; DLB 4, 11, 22, 102; MAICYA;
　　MTCW; SATA 13

Thurman, Wallace (Henry)
　　1902-1934 . . . . TCLC 6; BLC
　　See also BW 1; CA 104; 124; DAM MULT;
　　DLB 51

Ticheburn, Cheviot
　　See Ainsworth, William Harrison

Tieck, (Johann) Ludwig
　　1773-1853 . . . . NCLC 5, 46
　　See also DLB 90

Tiger, Derry
　　See Ellison, Harlan (Jay)

Tilghman, Christopher　1948(?)- . . . . . CLC 65

Tillinghast, Richard (Williford)
　　1940- . . . . CLC 29
　　See also CA 29-32R; CANR 26

Timrod, Henry　1828-1867 . . . . NCLC 25
　　See also DLB 3

Tindall, Gillian　1938- . . . . CLC 7
　　See also CA 21-24R; CANR 11

Tiptree, James, Jr. . . . . CLC 48, 50
　　See also Sheldon, Alice Hastings Bradley
　　See also DLB 8

Titmarsh, Michael Angelo
　　See Thackeray, William Makepeace

Tocqueville, Alexis (Charles Henri Maurice
　　Clerel Comte)　1805-1859 . . . . . NCLC 7

Tolkien, J(ohn) R(onald) R(euel)
1892-1973 . . . . . . **CLC 1, 2, 3, 8, 12, 38;**
DA; DAB; DAC; WLC
See also AAYA 10; AITN 1; CA 17-18;
45-48; CANR 36; CAP 2;
CDBLB 1914-1945; DAM MST, NOV,
POP; DLB 15, 160; JRDA; MAICYA;
MTCW; SATA 2, 32; SATA-Obit 24

Toller, Ernst 1893-1939 . . . . **TCLC 10**
See also CA 107; DLB 124

Tolson, M. B.
See Tolson, Melvin B(eaunorus)

Tolson, Melvin B(eaunorus)
1898(?)-1966 . . . . **CLC 36; BLC**
See also BW 1; CA 124; 89-92;
DAM MULT, POET; DLB 48, 76

Tolstoi, Aleksei Nikolaevich
See Tolstoy, Alexey Nikolaevich

Tolstoy, Alexey Nikolaevich
1882-1945 . . . . **TCLC 18**
See also CA 107

Tolstoy, Count Leo
See Tolstoy, Leo (Nikolaevich)

Tolstoy, Leo (Nikolaevich)
1828-1910 . . . . . . **TCLC 4, 11, 17, 28, 44;**
DA; DAB; DAC; SSC 9; WLC
See also CA 104; 123; DAM MST, NOV;
SATA 26

Tomasi di Lampedusa, Giuseppe 1896-1957
See Lampedusa, Giuseppe (Tomasi) di
See also CA 111

Tomlin, Lily . . . . **CLC 17**
See also Tomlin, Mary Jean

Tomlin, Mary Jean 1939(?)-
See Tomlin, Lily
See also CA 117

Tomlinson, (Alfred) Charles
1927- . . . . **CLC 2, 4, 6, 13, 45**
See also CA 5-8R; CANR 33; DAM POET;
DLB 40

Tonson, Jacob
See Bennett, (Enoch) Arnold

Toole, John Kennedy
1937-1969 . . . . **CLC 19, 64**
See also CA 104; DLBY 81

Toomer, Jean
1894-1967 . . . . . . **CLC 1, 4, 13, 22; BLC;**
PC 7; SSC 1
See also BW 1; CA 85-88;
CDALB 1917-1929; DAM MULT;
DLB 45, 51; MTCW

Torley, Luke
See Blish, James (Benjamin)

Tornimparte, Alessandra
See Ginzburg, Natalia

Torre, Raoul della
See Mencken, H(enry) L(ouis)

Torrey, E(dwin) Fuller 1937- . . . . **CLC 34**
See also CA 119

Torsvan, Ben Traven
See Traven, B.

Torsvan, Benno Traven
See Traven, B.

Torsvan, Berick Traven
See Traven, B.

Torsvan, Berwick Traven
See Traven, B.

Torsvan, Bruno Traven
See Traven, B.

Torsvan, Traven
See Traven, B.

Tournier, Michel (Edouard)
1924- . . . . **CLC 6, 23, 36**
See also CA 49-52; CANR 3, 36; DLB 83;
MTCW; SATA 23

Tournimparte, Alessandra
See Ginzburg, Natalia

Towers, Ivar
See Kornbluth, C(yril) M.

Towne, Robert (Burton) 1936(?)- . . . . **CLC 87**
See also CA 108; DLB 44

Townsend, Sue 1946- . . **CLC 61; DAB; DAC**
See also CA 119; 127; INT 127; MTCW;
SATA 55; SATA-Brief 48

Townshend, Peter (Dennis Blandford)
1945- . . . . **CLC 17, 42**
See also CA 107

Tozzi, Federigo 1883-1920 . . . . **TCLC 31**

Traill, Catharine Parr
1802-1899 . . . . **NCLC 31**
See also DLB 99

Trakl, Georg 1887-1914 . . . . **TCLC 5**
See also CA 104

Transtroemer, Tomas (Goesta)
1931- . . . . **CLC 52, 65**
See also CA 117; 129; CAAS 17;
DAM POET

Transtromer, Tomas Gosta
See Transtroemer, Tomas (Goesta)

Traven, B. (?)-1969 . . . . **CLC 8, 11**
See also CA 19-20; 25-28R; CAP 2; DLB 9,
56; MTCW

Treitel, Jonathan 1959- . . . . **CLC 70**

Tremain, Rose 1943- . . . . **CLC 42**
See also CA 97-100; CANR 44; DLB 14

Tremblay, Michel 1942- . . . . . . **CLC 29; DAC**
See also CA 116; 128; DAM MST; DLB 60;
MTCW

Trevanian . . . . **CLC 29**
See also Whitaker, Rod(ney)

Trevor, Glen
See Hilton, James

Trevor, William
1928- . . . . . **CLC 7, 9, 14, 25, 71; SSC 21**
See also Cox, William Trevor
See also DLB 14, 139

Trifonov, Yuri (Valentinovich)
1925-1981 . . . . **CLC 45**
See also CA 126; 103; MTCW

Trilling, Lionel 1905-1975 . . . . **CLC 9, 11, 24**
See also CA 9-12R; 61-64; CANR 10;
DLB 28, 63; INT CANR-10; MTCW

Trimball, W. H.
See Mencken, H(enry) L(ouis)

Tristan
See Gomez de la Serna, Ramon

Tristram
See Housman, A(lfred) E(dward)

Trogdon, William (Lewis) 1939-
See Heat-Moon, William Least
See also CA 115; 119; CANR 47; INT 119

Trollope, Anthony
1815-1882 . . . . . **NCLC 6, 33; DA; DAB;**
DAC; WLC
See also CDBLB 1832-1890; DAM MST,
NOV; DLB 21, 57, 159; SATA 22

Trollope, Frances 1779-1863 . . . . . **NCLC 30**
See also DLB 21

Trotsky, Leon 1879-1940 . . . . **TCLC 22**
See also CA 118

Trotter (Cockburn), Catharine
1679-1749 . . . . **LC 8**
See also DLB 84

Trout, Kilgore
See Farmer, Philip Jose

Trow, George W. S. 1943- . . . . **CLC 52**
See also CA 126

Troyat, Henri 1911- . . . . **CLC 23**
See also CA 45-48; CANR 2, 33; MTCW

Trudeau, G(arretson) B(eekman) 1948-
See Trudeau, Garry B.
See also CA 81-84; CANR 31; SATA 35

Trudeau, Garry B. . . . . **CLC 12**
See also Trudeau, G(arretson) B(eekman)
See also AAYA 10; AITN 2

Truffaut, Francois 1932-1984 . . . . . . **CLC 20**
See also CA 81-84; 113; CANR 34

Trumbo, Dalton 1905-1976 . . . . **CLC 19**
See also CA 21-24R; 69-72; CANR 10;
DLB 26

Trumbull, John 1750-1831 . . . . **NCLC 30**
See also DLB 31

Trundlett, Helen B.
See Eliot, T(homas) S(tearns)

Tryon, Thomas 1926-1991 . . . . **CLC 3, 11**
See also AITN 1; CA 29-32R; 135;
CANR 32; DAM POP; MTCW

Tryon, Tom
See Tryon, Thomas

Ts'ao Hsueh-ch'in 1715(?)-1763 . . . . **LC 1**

Tsushima, Shuji 1909-1948
See Dazai, Osamu
See also CA 107

Tsvetaeva (Efron), Marina (Ivanovna)
1892-1941 . . . . **TCLC 7, 35; PC 14**
See also CA 104; 128; MTCW

Tuck, Lily 1938- . . . . **CLC 70**
See also CA 139

Tu Fu 712-770 . . . . **PC 9**
See also DAM MULT

Tunis, John R(oberts) 1889-1975 . . . **CLC 12**
See also CA 61-64; DLB 22; JRDA;
MAICYA; SATA 37; SATA-Brief 30

Tuohy, Frank . . . . **CLC 37**
See also Tuohy, John Francis
See also DLB 14, 139

Tuohy, John Francis 1925-
See Tuohy, Frank
See also CA 5-8R; CANR 3, 47

Turco, Lewis (Putnam) 1934- . . . **CLC 11, 63**
See also CA 13-16R; CAAS 22; CANR 24;
DLBY 84

Vazov, Ivan (Minchov)
    1850-1921 .... TCLC 25
    See also CA 121; DLB 147

Veblen, Thorstein (Bunde)
    1857-1929 .... TCLC 31
    See also CA 115

Vega, Lope de 1562-1635 .... LC 23

Venison, Alfred
    See Pound, Ezra (Weston Loomis)

Verdi, Marie de
    See Mencken, H(enry) L(ouis)

Verdu, Matilde
    See Cela, Camilo Jose

Verga, Giovanni (Carmelo)
    1840-1922 .... TCLC 3; SSC 21
    See also CA 104; 123

Vergil
    70B.C.-19B.C. ..... CMLC 9; DA; DAB;
                                        DAC; PC 12
    See also DAM MST, POET

Verhaeren, Emile (Adolphe Gustave)
    1855-1916 .... TCLC 12
    See also CA 109

Verlaine, Paul (Marie)
    1844-1896 .... NCLC 2, 51; PC 2
    See also DAM POET

Verne, Jules (Gabriel)
    1828-1905 .... TCLC 6, 52
    See also AAYA 16; CA 110; 131; DLB 123;
    JRDA; MAICYA; SATA 21

Very, Jones 1813-1880 .... NCLC 9
    See also DLB 1

Vesaas, Tarjei 1897-1970 .... CLC 48
    See also CA 29-32R

Vialis, Gaston
    See Simenon, Georges (Jacques Christian)

Vian, Boris 1920-1959 .... TCLC 9
    See also CA 106; DLB 72

Viaud, (Louis Marie) Julien 1850-1923
    See Loti, Pierre
    See also CA 107

Vicar, Henry
    See Felsen, Henry Gregor

Vicker, Angus
    See Felsen, Henry Gregor

Vidal, Gore
    1925- ..... CLC 2, 4, 6, 8, 10, 22, 33, 72
    See also AITN 1; BEST 90:2; CA 5-8R;
    CANR 13, 45; DAM NOV, POP; DLB 6,
    152; INT CANR-13; MTCW

Viereck, Peter (Robert Edwin)
    1916- .... CLC 4
    See also CA 1-4R; CANR 1, 47; DLB 5

Vigny, Alfred (Victor) de
    1797-1863 .... NCLC 7
    See also DAM POET; DLB 119

Vilakazi, Benedict Wallet
    1906-1947 .... TCLC 37

Villiers de l'Isle Adam, Jean Marie Mathias
    Philippe Auguste Comte
    1838-1889 .... NCLC 3; SSC 14
    See also DLB 123

Villon, Francois 1431-1463(?) .... PC 13

Vinci, Leonardo da 1452-1519 ...... LC 12

Vine, Barbara .... CLC 50
    See also Rendell, Ruth (Barbara)
    See also BEST 90:4

Vinge, Joan D(ennison) 1948- ...... CLC 30
    See also CA 93-96; SATA 36

Violis, G.
    See Simenon, Georges (Jacques Christian)

Visconti, Luchino 1906-1976 .... CLC 16
    See also CA 81-84; 65-68; CANR 39

Vittorini, Elio 1908-1966 ...... CLC 6, 9, 14
    See also CA 133; 25-28R

Vizinczey, Stephen 1933- .... CLC 40
    See also CA 128; INT 128

Vliet, R(ussell) G(ordon)
    1929-1984 .... CLC 22
    See also CA 37-40R; 112; CANR 18

Vogau, Boris Andreyevich 1894-1937(?)
    See Pilnyak, Boris
    See also CA 123

Vogel, Paula A(nne) 1951- .... CLC 76
    See also CA 108

Voight, Ellen Bryant 1943- .... CLC 54
    See also CA 69-72; CANR 11, 29; DLB 120

Voigt, Cynthia 1942- .... CLC 30
    See also AAYA 3; CA 106; CANR 18, 37,
    40; CLR 13; INT CANR-18; JRDA;
    MAICYA; SATA 48, 79; SATA-Brief 33

Voinovich, Vladimir (Nikolaevich)
    1932- .... CLC 10, 49
    See also CA 81-84; CAAS 12; CANR 33;
    MTCW

Vollmann, William T. 1959- .... CLC 89
    See also CA 134; DAM NOV, POP

Voloshinov, V. N.
    See Bakhtin, Mikhail Mikhailovich

Voltaire
    1694-1778 ..... LC 14; DA; DAB; DAC;
                                        SSC 12; WLC
    See also DAM DRAM, MST

von Daeniken, Erich 1935- .... CLC 30
    See also AITN 1; CA 37-40R; CANR 17,
    44

von Daniken, Erich
    See von Daeniken, Erich

von Heidenstam, (Carl Gustaf) Verner
    See Heidenstam, (Carl Gustaf) Verner von

von Heyse, Paul (Johann Ludwig)
    See Heyse, Paul (Johann Ludwig von)

von Hofmannsthal, Hugo
    See Hofmannsthal, Hugo von

von Horvath, Odon
    See Horvath, Oedoen von

von Horvath, Oedoen
    See Horvath, Oedoen von

von Liliencron, (Friedrich Adolf Axel) Detlev
    See Liliencron, (Friedrich Adolf Axel)
    Detlev von

Vonnegut, Kurt, Jr.
    1922- ...... CLC 1, 2, 3, 4, 5, 8, 12, 22,
    40, 60; DA; DAB; DAC; SSC 8; WLC
    See also AAYA 6; AITN 1; BEST 90:4;
    CA 1-4R; CANR 1, 25, 49;
    CDALB 1968-1988; DAM MST, NOV,
    POP; DLB 2, 8, 152; DLBD 3; DLBY 80;
    MTCW

Von Rachen, Kurt
    See Hubbard, L(afayette) Ron(ald)

von Rezzori (d'Arezzo), Gregor
    See Rezzori (d'Arezzo), Gregor von

von Sternberg, Josef
    See Sternberg, Josef von

Vorster, Gordon 1924- .... CLC 34
    See also CA 133

Vosce, Trudie
    See Ozick, Cynthia

Voznesensky, Andrei (Andreievich)
    1933- .... CLC 1, 15, 57
    See also CA 89-92; CANR 37;
    DAM POET; MTCW

Waddington, Miriam 1917- .... CLC 28
    See also CA 21-24R; CANR 12, 30;
    DLB 68

Wagman, Fredrica 1937- .... CLC 7
    See also CA 97-100; INT 97-100

Wagner, Richard 1813-1883 .... NCLC 9
    See also DLB 129

Wagner-Martin, Linda 1936- .... CLC 50

Wagoner, David (Russell)
    1926- .... CLC 3, 5, 15
    See also CA 1-4R; CAAS 3; CANR 2;
    DLB 5; SATA 14

Wah, Fred(erick James) 1939- ...... CLC 44
    See also CA 107; 141; DLB 60

Wahloo, Per 1926-1975 .... CLC 7
    See also CA 61-64

Wahloo, Peter
    See Wahloo, Per

Wain, John (Barrington)
    1925-1994 .... CLC 2, 11, 15, 46
    See also CA 5-8R; 145; CAAS 4; CANR 23;
    CDBLB 1960 to Present; DLB 15, 27,
    139, 155; MTCW

Wajda, Andrzej 1926- .... CLC 16
    See also CA 102

Wakefield, Dan 1932- .... CLC 7
    See also CA 21-24R; CAAS 7

Wakoski, Diane
    1937- .... CLC 2, 4, 7, 9, 11, 40
    See also CA 13-16R; CAAS 1; CANR 9;
    DAM POET; DLB 5; INT CANR-9

Wakoski-Sherbell, Diane
    See Wakoski, Diane

Walcott, Derek (Alton)
    1930- .... CLC 2, 4, 9, 14, 25, 42, 67, 76;
                                        BLC; DAB; DAC
    See also BW 2; CA 89-92; CANR 26, 47;
    DAM MST, MULT, POET; DLB 117;
    DLBY 81; MTCW

Waldman, Anne 1945- .... CLC 7
    See also CA 37-40R; CAAS 17; CANR 34;
    DLB 16

Waldo, E. Hunter
    See Sturgeon, Theodore (Hamilton)

Waldo, Edward Hamilton
    See Sturgeon, Theodore (Hamilton)

Walker, Alice (Malsenior)
1944- .... CLC **5, 6, 9, 19, 27, 46, 58;**
BLC; DA; DAB; DAC; SSC **5**
See also AAYA 3; BEST 89:4; BW 2;
CA 37-40R; CANR 9, 27, 49;
CDALB 1968-1988; DAM MST, MULT,
NOV, POET, POP; DLB 6, 33, 143;
INT CANR-27; MTCW; SATA 31

Walker, David Harry 1911-1992.... CLC **14**
See also CA 1-4R; 137; CANR 1; SATA 8;
SATA-Obit 71

Walker, Edward Joseph 1934-
See Walker, Ted
See also CA 21-24R; CANR 12, 28

Walker, George F.
1947- .... CLC **44, 61; DAB; DAC**
See also CA 103; CANR 21, 43;
DAM MST; DLB 60

Walker, Joseph A. 1935- .... CLC **19**
See also BW 1; CA 89-92; CANR 26;
DAM DRAM, MST; DLB 38

Walker, Margaret (Abigail)
1915- .... CLC **1, 6; BLC**
See also BW 2; CA 73-76; CANR 26;
DAM MULT; DLB 76, 152; MTCW

Walker, Ted .... CLC **13**
See also Walker, Edward Joseph
See also DLB 40

Wallace, David Foster 1962- .... CLC **50**
See also CA 132

Wallace, Dexter
See Masters, Edgar Lee

Wallace, (Richard Horatio) Edgar
1875-1932 .... TCLC **57**
See also CA 115; DLB 70

Wallace, Irving 1916-1990 ...... CLC **7, 13**
See also AITN 1; CA 1-4R; 132; CAAS 1;
CANR 1, 27; DAM NOV, POP;
INT CANR-27; MTCW

Wallant, Edward Lewis
1926-1962 .... CLC **5, 10**
See also CA 1-4R; CANR 22; DLB 2, 28,
143; MTCW

Walley, Byron
See Card, Orson Scott

Walpole, Horace 1717-1797 .... LC **2**
See also DLB 39, 104

Walpole, Hugh (Seymour)
1884-1941 .... TCLC **5**
See also CA 104; DLB 34

Walser, Martin 1927- .... CLC **27**
See also CA 57-60; CANR 8, 46; DLB 75,
124

Walser, Robert
1878-1956 .... TCLC **18; SSC 20**
See also CA 118; DLB 66

Walsh, Jill Paton .... CLC **35**
See also Paton Walsh, Gillian
See also AAYA 11; CLR 2; DLB 161;
SAAS 3

Walter, Villiam Christian
See Andersen, Hans Christian

Wambaugh, Joseph (Aloysius, Jr.)
1937- .... CLC **3, 18**
See also AITN 1; BEST 89:3; CA 33-36R;
CANR 42; DAM NOV, POP; DLB 6;
DLBY 83; MTCW

Ward, Arthur Henry Sarsfield 1883-1959
See Rohmer, Sax
See also CA 108

Ward, Douglas Turner 1930- .... CLC **19**
See also BW 1; CA 81-84; CANR 27;
DLB 7, 38

Ward, Mary Augusta
See Ward, Mrs. Humphry

Ward, Mrs. Humphry
1851-1920 .... TCLC **55**
See also DLB 18

Ward, Peter
See Faust, Frederick (Schiller)

Warhol, Andy 1928(?)-1987 .... CLC **20**
See also AAYA 12; BEST 89:4; CA 89-92;
121; CANR 34

Warner, Francis (Robert le Plastrier)
1937- .... CLC **14**
See also CA 53-56; CANR 11

Warner, Marina 1946- .... CLC **59**
See also CA 65-68; CANR 21

Warner, Rex (Ernest) 1905-1986.... CLC **45**
See also CA 89-92; 119; DLB 15

Warner, Susan (Bogert)
1819-1885 .... NCLC **31**
See also DLB 3, 42

Warner, Sylvia (Constance) Ashton
See Ashton-Warner, Sylvia (Constance)

Warner, Sylvia Townsend
1893-1978 .... CLC **7, 19**
See also CA 61-64; 77-80; CANR 16;
DLB 34, 139; MTCW

Warren, Mercy Otis 1728-1814... NCLC **13**
See also DLB 31

Warren, Robert Penn
1905-1989 .... CLC **1, 4, 6, 8, 10, 13, 18,**
39, 53, 59; DA; DAB; DAC; SSC 4; WLC
See also AITN 1; CA 13-16R; 129;
CANR 10, 47; CDALB 1968-1988;
DAM MST, NOV, POET; DLB 2, 48,
152; DLBY 80, 89; INT CANR-10;
MTCW; SATA 46; SATA-Obit 63

Warshofsky, Isaac
See Singer, Isaac Bashevis

Warton, Thomas 1728-1790 .... LC **15**
See also DAM POET; DLB 104, 109

Waruk, Kona
See Harris, (Theodore) Wilson

Warung, Price 1855-1911 .... TCLC **45**

Warwick, Jarvis
See Garner, Hugh

Washington, Alex
See Harris, Mark

Washington, Booker T(aliaferro)
1856-1915 .... TCLC **10; BLC**
See also BW 1; CA 114; 125; DAM MULT;
SATA 28

Washington, George 1732-1799 ...... LC **25**
See also DLB 31

Wassermann, (Karl) Jakob
1873-1934 .... TCLC **6**
See also CA 104; DLB 66

Wasserstein, Wendy
1950- .... CLC **32, 59, 90; DC 4**
See also CA 121; 129; CABS 3;
DAM DRAM; INT 129

Waterhouse, Keith (Spencer)
1929- .... CLC **47**
See also CA 5-8R; CANR 38; DLB 13, 15;
MTCW

Waters, Frank (Joseph) 1902- ...... CLC **88**
See also CA 5-8R; CAAS 13; CANR 3, 18;
DLBY 86

Waters, Roger 1944- .... CLC **35**

Watkins, Frances Ellen
See Harper, Frances Ellen Watkins

Watkins, Gerrold
See Malzberg, Barry N(athaniel)

Watkins, Paul 1964- .... CLC **55**
See also CA 132

Watkins, Vernon Phillips
1906-1967 .... CLC **43**
See also CA 9-10; 25-28R; CAP 1; DLB 20

Watson, Irving S.
See Mencken, H(enry) L(ouis)

Watson, John H.
See Farmer, Philip Jose

Watson, Richard F.
See Silverberg, Robert

Waugh, Auberon (Alexander) 1939- .. CLC **7**
See also CA 45-48; CANR 6, 22; DLB 14

Waugh, Evelyn (Arthur St. John)
1903-1966 ...... CLC **1, 3, 8, 13, 19, 27,**
44; DA; DAB; DAC; WLC
See also CA 85-88; 25-28R; CANR 22;
CDBLB 1914-1945; DAM MST, NOV,
POP; DLB 15; MTCW

Waugh, Harriet 1944- .... CLC **6**
See also CA 85-88; CANR 22

Ways, C. R.
See Blount, Roy (Alton), Jr.

Waystaff, Simon
See Swift, Jonathan

Webb, (Martha) Beatrice (Potter)
1858-1943 .... TCLC **22**
See also Potter, Beatrice
See also CA 117

Webb, Charles (Richard) 1939- ...... CLC **7**
See also CA 25-28R

Webb, James H(enry), Jr. 1946- .... CLC **22**
See also CA 81-84

Webb, Mary (Gladys Meredith)
1881-1927 .... TCLC **24**
See also CA 123; DLB 34

Webb, Mrs. Sidney
See Webb, (Martha) Beatrice (Potter)

Webb, Phyllis 1927- .... CLC **18**
See also CA 104; CANR 23; DLB 53

Webb, Sidney (James)
1859-1947 .... TCLC **22**
See also CA 117

Webber, Andrew Lloyd .... CLC **21**
See also Lloyd Webber, Andrew

Weber, Lenora Mattingly
1895-1971 . . . . CLC 12
See also CA 19-20; 29-32R; CAP 1;
SATA 2; SATA-Obit 26

Webster, John 1579(?)-1634(?) . . . . DC 2
See also CDBLB Before 1660; DA; DAB;
DAC; DAM DRAM, MST; DLB 58;
WLC

Webster, Noah 1758-1843 . . . . NCLC 30

Wedekind, (Benjamin) Frank(lin)
1864-1918 . . . . TCLC 7
See also CA 104; DAM DRAM; DLB 118

Weidman, Jerome 1913- . . . . CLC 7
See also AITN 2; CA 1-4R; CANR 1;
DLB 28

Weil, Simone (Adolphine)
1909-1943 . . . . TCLC 23
See also CA 117

Weinstein, Nathan
See West, Nathanael

Weinstein, Nathan von Wallenstein
See West, Nathanael

Weir, Peter (Lindsay) 1944- . . . . CLC 20
See also CA 113; 123

Weiss, Peter (Ulrich)
1916-1982 . . . . CLC 3, 15, 51
See also CA 45-48; 106; CANR 3;
DAM DRAM; DLB 69, 124

Weiss, Theodore (Russell)
1916- . . . . CLC 3, 8, 14
See also CA 9-12R; CAAS 2; CANR 46;
DLB 5

Welch, (Maurice) Denton
1915-1948 . . . . TCLC 22
See also CA 121; 148

Welch, James 1940- . . . . CLC 6, 14, 52
See also CA 85-88; CANR 42;
DAM MULT, POP; NNAL

Weldon, Fay
1933- . . . . CLC 6, 9, 11, 19, 36, 59
See also CA 21-24R; CANR 16, 46;
CDBLB 1960 to Present; DAM POP;
DLB 14; INT CANR-16; MTCW

Wellek, Rene 1903- . . . . CLC 28
See also CA 5-8R; CAAS 7; CANR 8;
DLB 63; INT CANR-8

Weller, Michael 1942- . . . . CLC 10, 53
See also CA 85-88

Weller, Paul 1958- . . . . CLC 26

Wellershoff, Dieter 1925- . . . . CLC 46
See also CA 89-92; CANR 16, 37

Welles, (George) Orson
1915-1985 . . . . CLC 20, 80
See also CA 93-96; 117

Wellman, Mac 1945- . . . . CLC 65

Wellman, Manly Wade 1903-1986 . . CLC 49
See also CA 1-4R; 118; CANR 6, 16, 44;
SATA 6; SATA-Obit 47

Wells, Carolyn 1869(?)-1942 . . . . . . TCLC 35
See also CA 113; DLB 11

Wells, H(erbert) G(eorge)
1866-1946 . . . . TCLC 6, 12, 19; DA;
DAB; DAC; SSC 6; WLC
See also CA 110; 121; CDBLB 1914-1945;
DAM MST, NOV; DLB 34, 70, 156;
MTCW; SATA 20

Wells, Rosemary 1943- . . . . CLC 12
See also AAYA 13; CA 85-88; CANR 48;
CLR 16; MAICYA; SAAS 1; SATA 18,
69

Welty, Eudora
1909- . . . . . . CLC 1, 2, 5, 14, 22, 33; DA;
DAB; DAC; SSC 1; WLC
See also CA 9-12R; CABS 1; CANR 32;
CDALB 1941-1968; DAM MST, NOV;
DLB 2, 102, 143; DLBD 12; DLBY 87;
MTCW

Wen I-to 1899-1946 . . . . TCLC 28

Wentworth, Robert
See Hamilton, Edmond

Werfel, Franz (V.) 1890-1945 . . . . . . TCLC 8
See also CA 104; DLB 81, 124

Wergeland, Henrik Arnold
1808-1845 . . . . NCLC 5

Wersba, Barbara 1932- . . . . CLC 30
See also AAYA 2; CA 29-32R; CANR 16,
38; CLR 3; DLB 52; JRDA; MAICYA;
SAAS 2; SATA 1, 58

Wertmueller, Lina 1928- . . . . CLC 16
See also CA 97-100; CANR 39

Wescott, Glenway 1901-1987 . . . . CLC 13
See also CA 13-16R; 121; CANR 23;
DLB 4, 9, 102

Wesker, Arnold 1932- . . CLC 3, 5, 42; DAB
See also CA 1-4R; CAAS 7; CANR 1, 33;
CDBLB 1960 to Present; DAM DRAM;
DLB 13; MTCW

Wesley, Richard (Errol) 1945- . . . . CLC 7
See also BW 1; CA 57-60; CANR 27;
DLB 38

Wessel, Johan Herman 1742-1785 . . . . LC 7

West, Anthony (Panther)
1914-1987 . . . . CLC 50
See also CA 45-48; 124; CANR 3, 19;
DLB 15

West, C. P.
See Wodehouse, P(elham) G(renville)

West, (Mary) Jessamyn
1902-1984 . . . . CLC 7, 17
See also CA 9-12R; 112; CANR 27; DLB 6;
DLBY 84; MTCW; SATA-Obit 37

West, Morris L(anglo) 1916- . . . . . CLC 6, 33
See also CA 5-8R; CANR 24, 49; MTCW

West, Nathanael
1903-1940 . . . . . TCLC 1, 14, 44; SSC 16
See also CA 104; 125; CDALB 1929-1941;
DLB 4, 9, 28; MTCW

West, Owen
See Koontz, Dean R(ay)

West, Paul 1930- . . . . CLC 7, 14
See also CA 13-16R; CAAS 7; CANR 22;
DLB 14; INT CANR-22

West, Rebecca 1892-1983 . . CLC 7, 9, 31, 50
See also CA 5-8R; 109; CANR 19; DLB 36;
DLBY 83; MTCW

Westall, Robert (Atkinson)
1929-1993 . . . . CLC 17
See also AAYA 12; CA 69-72; 141;
CANR 18; CLR 13; JRDA; MAICYA;
SAAS 2; SATA 23, 69; SATA-Obit 75

Westlake, Donald E(dwin)
1933- . . . . CLC 7, 33
See also CA 17-20R; CAAS 13; CANR 16,
44; DAM POP; INT CANR-16

Westmacott, Mary
See Christie, Agatha (Mary Clarissa)

Weston, Allen
See Norton, Andre

Wetcheek, J. L.
See Feuchtwanger, Lion

Wetering, Janwillem van de
See van de Wetering, Janwillem

Wetherell, Elizabeth
See Warner, Susan (Bogert)

Whalen, Philip 1923- . . . . CLC 6, 29
See also CA 9-12R; CANR 5, 39; DLB 16

Wharton, Edith (Newbold Jones)
1862-1937 . . . . . . TCLC 3, 9, 27, 53; DA;
DAB; DAC; SSC 6; WLC
See also CA 104; 132; CDALB 1865-1917;
DAM MST, NOV; DLB 4, 9, 12, 78;
DLBD 13; MTCW

Wharton, James
See Mencken, H(enry) L(ouis)

Wharton, William (a pseudonym)
. . . . CLC 18, 37
See also CA 93-96; DLBY 80; INT 93-96

Wheatley (Peters), Phillis
1754(?)-1784 . . . . LC 3; BLC; DA; DAC;
PC 3; WLC
See also CDALB 1640-1865; DAM MST,
MULT, POET; DLB 31, 50

Wheelock, John Hall 1886-1978 . . . . CLC 14
See also CA 13-16R; 77-80; CANR 14;
DLB 45

White, E(lwyn) B(rooks)
1899-1985 . . . . CLC 10, 34, 39
See also AITN 2; CA 13-16R; 116;
CANR 16, 37; CLR 1, 21; DAM POP;
DLB 11, 22; MAICYA; MTCW;
SATA 2, 29; SATA-Obit 44

White, Edmund (Valentine III)
1940- . . . . CLC 27
See also AAYA 7; CA 45-48; CANR 3, 19,
36; DAM POP; MTCW

White, Patrick (Victor Martindale)
1912-1990 . . . CLC 3, 4, 5, 7, 9, 18, 65, 69
See also CA 81-84; 132; CANR 43; MTCW

White, Phyllis Dorothy James 1920-
See James, P. D.
See also CA 21-24R; CANR 17, 43;
DAM POP; MTCW

White, T(erence) H(anbury)
1906-1964 . . . . CLC 30
See also CA 73-76; CANR 37; DLB 160;
JRDA; MAICYA; SATA 12

White, Terence de Vere
1912-1994 . . . . CLC 49
See also CA 49-52; 145; CANR 3

White, Walter F(rancis)
1893-1955 .... **TCLC 15**
See also White, Walter
See also BW 1; CA 115; 124; DLB 51

White, William Hale 1831-1913
See Rutherford, Mark
See also CA 121

Whitehead, E(dward) A(nthony)
1933- .... **CLC 5**
See also CA 65-68

Whitemore, Hugh (John) 1936- ..... **CLC 37**
See also CA 132; INT 132

Whitman, Sarah Helen (Power)
1803-1878 .... **NCLC 19**
See also DLB 1

Whitman, Walt(er)
1819-1892 ..... **NCLC 4, 31; DA; DAB;
DAC; PC 3; WLC**
See also CDALB 1640-1865; DAM MST,
POET; DLB 3, 64; SATA 20

Whitney, Phyllis A(yame) 1903- .... **CLC 42**
See also AITN 2; BEST 90:3; CA 1-4R;
CANR 3, 25, 38; DAM POP; JRDA;
MAICYA; SATA 1, 30

Whittemore, (Edward) Reed (Jr.)
1919- .... **CLC 4**
See also CA 9-12R; CAAS 8; CANR 4;
DLB 5

Whittier, John Greenleaf
1807-1892 .... **NCLC 8**
See also CDALB 1640-1865; DAM POET;
DLB 1

Whittlebot, Hernia
See Coward, Noel (Peirce)

Wicker, Thomas Grey 1926-
See Wicker, Tom
See also CA 65-68; CANR 21, 46

Wicker, Tom .... **CLC 7**
See also Wicker, Thomas Grey

Wideman, John Edgar
1941- .... **CLC 5, 34, 36, 67; BLC**
See also BW 2; CA 85-88; CANR 14, 42;
DAM MULT; DLB 33, 143

Wiebe, Rudy (Henry)
1934- .... **CLC 6, 11, 14; DAC**
See also CA 37-40R; CANR 42;
DAM MST; DLB 60

Wieland, Christoph Martin
1733-1813 .... **NCLC 17**
See also DLB 97

Wiene, Robert 1881-1938........ **TCLC 56**

Wieners, John 1934- .... **CLC 7**
See also CA 13-16R; DLB 16

Wiesel, Elie(zer)
1928- ...... **CLC 3, 5, 11, 37; DA; DAB;
DAC**
See also AAYA 7; AITN 1; CA 5-8R;
CAAS 4; CANR 8, 40; DAM MST,
NOV; DLB 83; DLBY 87; INT CANR-8;
MTCW; SATA 56

Wiggins, Marianne 1947- .... **CLC 57**
See also BEST 89:3; CA 130

Wight, James Alfred 1916-
See Herriot, James
See also CA 77-80; SATA 55;
SATA-Brief 44

Wilbur, Richard (Purdy)
1921- ... **CLC 3, 6, 9, 14, 53; DA; DAB;
DAC**
See also CA 1-4R; CABS 2; CANR 2, 29;
DAM MST, POET; DLB 5;
INT CANR-29; MTCW; SATA 9

Wild, Peter 1940- .... **CLC 14**
See also CA 37-40R; DLB 5

Wilde, Oscar (Fingal O'Flahertie Wills)
1854(?)-1900 .... **TCLC 1, 8, 23, 41; DA;
DAB; DAC; SSC 11; WLC**
See also CA 104; 119; CDBLB 1890-1914;
DAM DRAM, MST, NOV; DLB 10, 19,
34, 57, 141, 156; SATA 24

Wilder, Billy .... **CLC 20**
See also Wilder, Samuel
See also DLB 26

Wilder, Samuel 1906-
See Wilder, Billy
See also CA 89-92

Wilder, Thornton (Niven)
1897-1975 ...... **CLC 1, 5, 6, 10, 15, 35,
82; DA; DAB; DAC; DC 1; WLC**
See also AITN 2; CA 13-16R; 61-64;
CANR 40; DAM DRAM, MST, NOV;
DLB 4, 7, 9; MTCW

Wilding, Michael 1942- .... **CLC 73**
See also CA 104; CANR 24, 49

Wiley, Richard 1944- .... **CLC 44**
See also CA 121; 129

Wilhelm, Kate .... **CLC 7**
See also Wilhelm, Katie Gertrude
See also CAAS 5; DLB 8; INT CANR-17

Wilhelm, Katie Gertrude 1928-
See Wilhelm, Kate
See also CA 37-40R; CANR 17, 36; MTCW

Wilkins, Mary
See Freeman, Mary Eleanor Wilkins

Willard, Nancy 1936- .... **CLC 7, 37**
See also CA 89-92; CANR 10, 39; CLR 5;
DLB 5, 52; MAICYA; MTCW;
SATA 37, 71; SATA-Brief 30

Williams, C(harles) K(enneth)
1936- .... **CLC 33, 56**
See also CA 37-40R; DAM POET; DLB 5

Williams, Charles
See Collier, James L(incoln)

Williams, Charles (Walter Stansby)
1886-1945 .... **TCLC 1, 11**
See also CA 104; DLB 100, 153

Williams, (George) Emlyn
1905-1987 .... **CLC 15**
See also CA 104; 123; CANR 36;
DAM DRAM; DLB 10, 77; MTCW

Williams, Hugo 1942- .... **CLC 42**
See also CA 17-20R; CANR 45; DLB 40

Williams, J. Walker
See Wodehouse, P(elham) G(renville)

Williams, John A(lfred)
1925- .... **CLC 5, 13; BLC**
See also BW 2; CA 53-56; CAAS 3;
CANR 6, 26; DAM MULT; DLB 2, 33;
INT CANR-6

Williams, Jonathan (Chamberlain)
1929- .... **CLC 13**
See also CA 9-12R; CAAS 12; CANR 8;
DLB 5

Williams, Joy 1944- .... **CLC 31**
See also CA 41-44R; CANR 22, 48

Williams, Norman 1952- .... **CLC 39**
See also CA 118

Williams, Sherley Anne
1944- .... **CLC 89; BLC**
See also BW 2; CA 73-76; CANR 25;
DAM MULT, POET; DLB 41;
INT CANR-25; SATA 78

Williams, Shirley
See Williams, Sherley Anne

Williams, Tennessee
1911-1983 ..... **CLC 1, 2, 5, 7, 8, 11, 15,
19, 30, 39, 45, 71; DA; DAB; DAC;
DC 4; WLC**
See also AITN 1, 2; CA 5-8R; 108;
CABS 3; CANR 31; CDALB 1941-1968;
DAM DRAM, MST; DLB 7; DLBD 4;
DLBY 83; MTCW

Williams, Thomas (Alonzo)
1926-1990 .... **CLC 14**
See also CA 1-4R; 132; CANR 2

Williams, William C.
See Williams, William Carlos

Williams, William Carlos
1883-1963 .... **CLC 1, 2, 5, 9, 13, 22, 42,
67; DA; DAB; DAC; PC 7**
See also CA 89-92; CANR 34;
CDALB 1917-1929; DAM MST, POET;
DLB 4, 16, 54, 86; MTCW

Williamson, David (Keith) 1942- .... **CLC 56**
See also CA 103; CANR 41

Williamson, Ellen Douglas 1905-1984
See Douglas, Ellen
See also CA 17-20R; 114; CANR 39

Williamson, Jack.................. **CLC 29**
See also Williamson, John Stewart
See also CAAS 8; DLB 8

Williamson, John Stewart 1908-
See Williamson, Jack
See also CA 17-20R; CANR 23

Willie, Frederick
See Lovecraft, H(oward) P(hillips)

Willingham, Calder (Baynard, Jr.)
1922-1995 .... **CLC 5, 51**
See also CA 5-8R; 147; CANR 3; DLB 2,
44; MTCW

Willis, Charles
See Clarke, Arthur C(harles)

Willy
See Colette, (Sidonie-Gabrielle)

Willy, Colette
See Colette, (Sidonie-Gabrielle)

Wilson, A(ndrew) N(orman) 1950- .. **CLC 33**
See also CA 112; 122; DLB 14, 155

Wilson, Angus (Frank Johnstone)
1913-1991 .. **CLC 2, 3, 5, 25, 34; SSC 21**
See also CA 5-8R; 134; CANR 21; DLB 15,
139, 155; MTCW

Wilson, August
1945- .... **CLC 39, 50, 63; BLC; DA;
DAB; DAC; DC 2**
See also AAYA 16; BW 2; CA 115; 122;
CANR 42; DAM DRAM, MST, MULT;
MTCW

Wilson, Brian   1942- .... **CLC 12**

Wilson, Colin   1931- .... **CLC 3, 14**
See also CA 1-4R; CAAS 5; CANR 1, 22,
33; DLB 14; MTCW

Wilson, Dirk
See Pohl, Frederik

Wilson, Edmund
1895-1972 .... **CLC 1, 2, 3, 8, 24**
See also CA 1-4R; 37-40R; CANR 1, 46;
DLB 63; MTCW

Wilson, Ethel Davis (Bryant)
1888(?)-1980 .... **CLC 13; DAC**
See also CA 102; DAM POET; DLB 68;
MTCW

Wilson, John   1785-1854 .... **NCLC 5**

Wilson, John (Anthony) Burgess   1917-1993
See Burgess, Anthony
See also CA 1-4R; 143; CANR 2, 46; DAC;
DAM NOV; MTCW

Wilson, Lanford   1937- .... **CLC 7, 14, 36**
See also CA 17-20R; CABS 3; CANR 45;
DAM DRAM; DLB 7

Wilson, Robert M.   1944- .... **CLC 7, 9**
See also CA 49-52; CANR 2, 41; MTCW

Wilson, Robert McLiam   1964- ..... **CLC 59**
See also CA 132

Wilson, Sloan   1920- .... **CLC 32**
See also CA 1-4R; CANR 1, 44

Wilson, Snoo   1948- .... **CLC 33**
See also CA 69-72

Wilson, William S(mith)   1932- ..... **CLC 49**
See also CA 81-84

Winchilsea, Anne (Kingsmill) Finch Counte
1661-1720 .... **LC 3**

Windham, Basil
See Wodehouse, P(elham) G(renville)

Wingrove, David (John)   1954- ...... **CLC 68**
See also CA 133

Winters, Janet Lewis .... **CLC 41**
See also Lewis, Janet
See also DLBY 87

Winters, (Arthur) Yvor
1900-1968 .... **CLC 4, 8, 32**
See also CA 11-12; 25-28R; CAP 1;
DLB 48; MTCW

Winterson, Jeanette   1959- .... **CLC 64**
See also CA 136; DAM POP

Winthrop, John   1588-1649 .... **LC 31**
See also DLB 24, 30

Wiseman, Frederick   1930- .... **CLC 20**

Wister, Owen   1860-1938 .... **TCLC 21**
See also CA 108; DLB 9, 78; SATA 62

Witkacy
See Witkiewicz, Stanislaw Ignacy

Witkiewicz, Stanislaw Ignacy
1885-1939 .... **TCLC 8**
See also CA 105

Wittgenstein, Ludwig (Josef Johann)
1889-1951 .... **TCLC 59**
See also CA 113

Wittig, Monique   1935(?)- .... **CLC 22**
See also CA 116; 135; DLB 83

Wittlin, Jozef   1896-1976 .... **CLC 25**
See also CA 49-52; 65-68; CANR 3

Wodehouse, P(elham) G(renville)
1881-1975 ... **CLC 1, 2, 5, 10, 22; DAB;
DAC; SSC 2**
See also AITN 2; CA 45-48; 57-60;
CANR 3, 33; CDBLB 1914-1945;
DAM NOV; DLB 34; MTCW; SATA 22

Woiwode, L.
See Woiwode, Larry (Alfred)

Woiwode, Larry (Alfred)   1941- ... **CLC 6, 10**
See also CA 73-76; CANR 16; DLB 6;
INT CANR-16

Wojciechowska, Maia (Teresa)
1927- .... **CLC 26**
See also AAYA 8; CA 9-12R; CANR 4, 41;
CLR 1; JRDA; MAICYA; SAAS 1;
SATA 1, 28, 83

Wolf, Christa   1929- .... **CLC 14, 29, 58**
See also CA 85-88; CANR 45; DLB 75;
MTCW

Wolfe, Gene (Rodman)   1931- .... **CLC 25**
See also CA 57-60; CAAS 9; CANR 6, 32;
DAM POP; DLB 8

Wolfe, George C.   1954- .... **CLC 49**
See also CA 149

Wolfe, Thomas (Clayton)
1900-1938 ..... **TCLC 4, 13, 29, 61; DA;
DAB; DAC; WLC**
See also CA 104; 132; CDALB 1929-1941;
DAM MST, NOV; DLB 9, 102; DLBD 2;
DLBY 85; MTCW

Wolfe, Thomas Kennerly, Jr.   1931-
See Wolfe, Tom
See also CA 13-16R; CANR 9, 33;
DAM POP; INT CANR-9; MTCW

Wolfe, Tom .... **CLC 1, 2, 9, 15, 35, 51**
See also Wolfe, Thomas Kennerly, Jr.
See also AAYA 8; AITN 2; BEST 89:1;
DLB 152

Wolff, Geoffrey (Ansell)   1937- ..... **CLC 41**
See also CA 29-32R; CANR 29, 43

Wolff, Sonia
See Levitin, Sonia (Wolff)

Wolff, Tobias (Jonathan Ansell)
1945- .... **CLC 39, 64**
See also AAYA 16; BEST 90:2; CA 114;
117; CAAS 22; DLB 130; INT 117

Wolfram von Eschenbach
c. 1170-c. 1220 .... **CMLC 5**
See also DLB 138

Wolitzer, Hilma   1930- .... **CLC 17**
See also CA 65-68; CANR 18, 40;
INT CANR-18; SATA 31

Wollstonecraft, Mary   1759-1797 ...... **LC 5**
See also CDBLB 1789-1832; DLB 39, 104,
158

Wonder, Stevie .... **CLC 12**
See also Morris, Steveland Judkins

Wong, Jade Snow   1922- .... **CLC 17**
See also CA 109

Woodcott, Keith
See Brunner, John (Kilian Houston)

Woodruff, Robert W.
See Mencken, H(enry) L(ouis)

Woolf, (Adeline) Virginia
1882-1941 .... **TCLC 1, 5, 20, 43, 56;
DA; DAB; DAC; SSC 7; WLC**
See also CA 104; 130; CDBLB 1914-1945;
DAM MST, NOV; DLB 36, 100;
DLBD 10; MTCW

Woollcott, Alexander (Humphreys)
1887-1943 .... **TCLC 5**
See also CA 105; DLB 29

Woolrich, Cornell   1903-1968 .... **CLC 77**
See also Hopley-Woolrich, Cornell George

Wordsworth, Dorothy
1771-1855 .... **NCLC 25**
See also DLB 107

Wordsworth, William
1770-1850 .... **NCLC 12, 38; DA; DAB;
DAC; PC 4; WLC**
See also CDBLB 1789-1832; DAM MST,
POET; DLB 93, 107

Wouk, Herman   1915- .... **CLC 1, 9, 38**
See also CA 5-8R; CANR 6, 33;
DAM NOV, POP; DLBY 82;
INT CANR-6; MTCW

Wright, Charles (Penzel, Jr.)
1935- .... **CLC 6, 13, 28**
See also CA 29-32R; CAAS 7; CANR 23,
36; DLBY 82; MTCW

Wright, Charles Stevenson
1932- .... **CLC 49; BLC 3**
See also BW 1; CA 9-12R; CANR 26;
DAM MULT, POET; DLB 33

Wright, Jack R.
See Harris, Mark

Wright, James (Arlington)
1927-1980 .... **CLC 3, 5, 10, 28**
See also AITN 2; CA 49-52; 97-100;
CANR 4, 34; DAM POET; DLB 5;
MTCW

Wright, Judith (Arandell)
1915- .... **CLC 11, 53; PC 14**
See also CA 13-16R; CANR 31; MTCW;
SATA 14

Wright, L(aurali) R.   1939- .... **CLC 44**
See also CA 138

Wright, Richard (Nathaniel)
1908-1960 .... **CLC 1, 3, 4, 9, 14, 21, 48,
74; BLC; DA; DAB; DAC; SSC 2; WLC**
See also AAYA 5; BW 1; CA 108;
CDALB 1929-1941; DAM MST, MULT,
NOV; DLB 76, 102; DLBD 2; MTCW

Wright, Richard B(ruce)   1937- ...... **CLC 6**
See also CA 85-88; DLB 53

Wright, Rick   1945- .... **CLC 35**

Wright, Rowland
See Wells, Carolyn

Wright, Stephen Caldwell   1946- .... **CLC 33**
See also BW 2

Wright, Willard Huntington   1888-1939
See Van Dine, S. S.
See also CA 115

Wright, William   1930- .... **CLC 44**
See also CA 53-56; CANR 7, 23

Wroth, LadyMary 1587-1653(?) ..... **LC 30**
See also DLB 121

Wu Ch'eng-en 1500(?)-1582(?)....... **LC 7**

Wu Ching-tzu 1701-1754 .... **LC 2**

Wurlitzer, Rudolph 1938(?)- ... **CLC 2, 4, 15**
See also CA 85-88

Wycherley, William 1641-1715 .... **LC 8, 21**
See also CDBLB 1660-1789; DAM DRAM;
DLB 80

Wylie, Elinor (Morton Hoyt)
1885-1928 .... **TCLC 8**
See also CA 105; DLB 9, 45

Wylie, Philip (Gordon) 1902-1971... **CLC 43**
See also CA 21-22; 33-36R; CAP 2; DLB 9

Wyndham, John.................. **CLC 19**
See also Harris, John (Wyndham Parkes
Lucas) Beynon

Wyss, Johann David Von
1743-1818 .... **NCLC 10**
See also JRDA; MAICYA; SATA 29;
SATA-Brief 27

Xenophon
c. 430B.C.-c. 354B.C........ **CMLC 17**

Yakumo Koizumi
See Hearn, (Patricio) Lafcadio (Tessima
Carlos)

Yanez, Jose Donoso
See Donoso (Yanez), Jose

Yanovsky, Basile S.
See Yanovsky, V(assily) S(emenovich)

Yanovsky, V(assily) S(emenovich)
1906-1989 .... **CLC 2, 18**
See also CA 97-100; 129

Yates, Richard 1926-1992 ..... **CLC 7, 8, 23**
See also CA 5-8R; 139; CANR 10, 43;
DLB 2; DLBY 81, 92; INT CANR-10

Yeats, W. B.
See Yeats, William Butler

Yeats, William Butler
1865-1939 ..... **TCLC 1, 11, 18, 31; DA;**
DAB; DAC; WLC
See also CA 104; 127; CANR 45;
CDBLB 1890-1914; DAM DRAM, MST,
POET; DLB 10, 19, 98, 156; MTCW

Yehoshua, A(braham) B.
1936- .... **CLC 13, 31**
See also CA 33-36R; CANR 43

Yep, Laurence Michael 1948- ...... **CLC 35**
See also AAYA 5; CA 49-52; CANR 1, 46;
CLR 3, 17; DLB 52; JRDA; MAICYA;
SATA 7, 69

Yerby, Frank G(arvin)
1916-1991 .... **CLC 1, 7, 22; BLC**
See also BW 1; CA 9-12R; 136; CANR 16;
DAM MULT; DLB 76; INT CANR-16;
MTCW

Yesenin, Sergei Alexandrovich
See Esenin, Sergei (Alexandrovich)

Yevtushenko, Yevgeny (Alexandrovich)
1933- .... **CLC 1, 3, 13, 26, 51**
See also CA 81-84; CANR 33;
DAM POET; MTCW

Yezierska, Anzia 1885(?)-1970 ..... **CLC 46**
See also CA 126; 89-92; DLB 28; MTCW

Yglesias, Helen 1915-.......... **CLC 7, 22**
See also CA 37-40R; CAAS 20; CANR 15;
INT CANR-15; MTCW

Yokomitsu Riichi 1898-1947 ..... **TCLC 47**

Yonge, Charlotte (Mary)
1823-1901 .... **TCLC 48**
See also CA 109; DLB 18; SATA 17

York, Jeremy
See Creasey, John

York, Simon
See Heinlein, Robert A(nson)

Yorke, Henry Vincent 1905-1974 ... **CLC 13**
See also Green, Henry
See also CA 85-88; 49-52

Yosano Akiko 1878-1942 .. **TCLC 59; PC 11**

Yoshimoto, Banana................ **CLC 84**
See also Yoshimoto, Mahoko

Yoshimoto, Mahoko 1964-
See Yoshimoto, Banana
See also CA 144

Young, Al(bert James)
1939- .... **CLC 19; BLC**
See also BW 2; CA 29-32R; CANR 26;
DAM MULT; DLB 33

Young, Andrew (John) 1885-1971.... **CLC 5**
See also CA 5-8R; CANR 7, 29

Young, Collier
See Bloch, Robert (Albert)

Young, Edward 1683-1765.......... **LC 3**
See also DLB 95

Young, Marguerite 1909-......... **CLC 82**
See also CA 13-16; CAP 1

Young, Neil 1945-............... **CLC 17**
See also CA 110

Yourcenar, Marguerite
1903-1987 .... **CLC 19, 38, 50, 87**
See also CA 69-72; CANR 23; DAM NOV;
DLB 72; DLBY 88; MTCW

Yurick, Sol 1925-................. **CLC 6**
See also CA 13-16R; CANR 25

Zabolotskii, Nikolai Alekseevich
1903-1958 .... **TCLC 52**
See also CA 116

Zamiatin, Yevgenii
See Zamyatin, Evgeny Ivanovich

Zamora, Bernice (B. Ortiz)
1938- .... **CLC 89; HLC**
See also DAM MULT; DLB 82; HW

Zamyatin, Evgeny Ivanovich
1884-1937 .... **TCLC 8, 37**
See also CA 105

Zangwill, Israel 1864-1926....... **TCLC 16**
See also CA 109; DLB 10, 135

Zappa, Francis Vincent, Jr. 1940-1993
See Zappa, Frank
See also CA 108; 143

Zappa, Frank.................... **CLC 17**
See also Zappa, Francis Vincent, Jr.

Zaturenska, Marya 1902-1982.... **CLC 6, 11**
See also CA 13-16R; 105; CANR 22

Zelazny, Roger (Joseph)
1937-1995 .... **CLC 21**
See also AAYA 7; CA 21-24R; 148;
CANR 26; DLB 8; MTCW; SATA 57;
SATA-Brief 39

Zhdanov, Andrei A(lexandrovich)
1896-1948 .... **TCLC 18**
See also CA 117

Zhukovsky, Vasily 1783-1852 .... **NCLC 35**

Ziegenhagen, Eric................. **CLC 55**

Zimmer, Jill Schary
See Robinson, Jill

Zimmerman, Robert
See Dylan, Bob

Zindel, Paul
1936- ..... **CLC 6, 26; DA; DAB; DAC;**
DC 5
See also AAYA 2; CA 73-76; CANR 31;
CLR 3; DAM DRAM, MST, NOV;
DLB 7, 52; JRDA; MAICYA; MTCW;
SATA 16, 58

Zinov'Ev, A. A.
See Zinoviev, Alexander (Aleksandrovich)

Zinoviev, Alexander (Aleksandrovich)
1922-...................... **CLC 19**
See also CA 116; 133; CAAS 10

Zoilus
See Lovecraft, H(oward) P(hillips)

Zola, Emile (Edouard Charles Antoine)
1840-1902 ...... **TCLC 1, 6, 21, 41; DA;**
DAB; DAC; WLC
See also CA 104; 138; DAM MST, NOV;
DLB 123

Zoline, Pamela 1941-............. **CLC 62**

Zorrilla y Moral, Jose 1817-1893.. **NCLC 6**

Zoshchenko, Mikhail (Mikhailovich)
1895-1958 .... **TCLC 15; SSC 15**
See also CA 115

Zuckmayer, Carl 1896-1977........ **CLC 18**
See also CA 69-72; DLB 56, 124

Zuk, Georges
See Skelton, Robin

Zukofsky, Louis
1904-1978 .... **CLC 1, 2, 4, 7, 11, 18;**
PC 11
See also CA 9-12R; 77-80; CANR 39;
DAM POET; DLB 5; MTCW

Zweig, Paul 1935-1984........ **CLC 34, 42**
See also CA 85-88; 113

Zweig, Stefan 1881-1942 .... **TCLC 17**
See also CA 112; DLB 81, 118

Literary Criticism Series
Cumulative Topic Index

This index lists all topic entries in Gale's *Classical and Medieval Literature Criticism, Contemporary Literary Criticism, Literature Criticism from 1400 to 1800, Nineteenth-Century Literature Criticism,* and *Twentieth-Century Literary Criticism.*

Age of Johnson LC 15: 1-87
  Johnson's London, 3-15
  aesthetics of neoclassicism, 15-36
  "age of prose and reason," 36-45
  clubmen and bluestockings, 45-56
  printing technology, 56-62
  periodicals: "a map of busy life," 62-74
  transition, 74-86

AIDS in Literature CLC 81: 365-416

American Abolitionism NCLC 44: 1-73
  overviews, 2-26
  abolitionist ideals, 26-46
  the literature of abolitionism, 46-72

American Black Humor Fiction TCLC 54: 1-85
  characteristics of black humor, 2-13
  origins and development, 13-38
  black humor distinguished from related literary trends, 38-60
  black humor and society, 60-75
  black humor reconsidered, 75-83

American Civil War in Literature NCLC 32: 1-109
  overviews, 2-20
  regional perspectives, 20-54
  fiction popular during the war, 54-79
  the historical novel, 79-108

American Frontier in Literature NCLC 28: 1-103
  definitions, 2-12
  development, 12-17
  nonfiction writing about the frontier, 17-30
  frontier fiction, 30-45
  frontier protagonists, 45-66
  portrayals of Native Americans, 66-86
  feminist readings, 86-98
  twentieth-century reaction against

frontier literature, 98-100

American Humor Writing NCLC 52: 1-59
  overviews, 2-12
  the Old Southwest, 12-42
  broader impacts, 42-45
  women humorists, 45-58

American Popular Song, Golden Age of TCLC 42: 1-49
  background and major figures, 2-34
  the lyrics of popular songs, 34-47

American Proletarian Literature TCLC 54: 86-175
  overviews, 87-95
  American proletarian literature and the American Communist Party, 95-111
  ideology and literary merit, 111-17
  novels, 117-36
  Gastonia, 136-48
  drama, 148-54
  journalism, 154-59
  proletarian literature in the United States, 159-74

American Romanticism NCLC 44: 74-138
  overviews, 74-84
  sociopolitical influences, 84-104
  Romanticism and the American frontier, 104-15
  thematic concerns, 115-37

American Western Literature TCLC 46: 1-100
  definition and development of American Western literature, 2-7
  characteristics of the Western novel, 8-23
  Westerns as history and fiction, 23-34
  critical reception of American Western

literature, 34-41
  the Western hero, 41-73
  women in Western fiction, 73-91
  later Western fiction, 91-99

Art and Literature TCLC 54: 176-248
  overviews, 176-93
  definitions, 193-219
  influence of visual arts on literature, 219-31
  spatial form in literature, 231-47

Arthurian Literature CMLC 10: 1-127
  historical context and literary beginnings, 2-27
  development of the legend through Malory, 27-64
  development of the legend from Malory to the Victorian Age, 65-81
  themes and motifs, 81-95
  principal characters, 95-125

Arthurian Revival NCLC 36: 1-77
  overviews, 2-12
  Tennyson and his influence, 12-43
  other leading figures, 43-73
  the Arthurian legend in the visual arts, 73-76

Australian Literature TCLC 50: 1-94
  origins and development, 2-21
  characteristics of Australian literature, 21-33
  historical and critical perspectives, 33-41
  poetry, 41-58
  fiction, 58-76
  drama, 76-82
  Aboriginal literature, 82-91

Beat Generation, Literature of the TCLC 42: 50-102
  overviews, 51-59

Topic Index

Topic Index

Topic Index

CMLC Cumulative Nationality Index

CMLC Cumulative Title Index

Title Index

Title Index

487

Title Index

CMLC Cumulative Critic Index

Abe Akio
Sei Shōnagon **6**:299

Abusch, Tzvi
Epic of Gilgamesh **3**:365

Adams, Charles Darwin
Demosthenes **13**:148

Adams, Henry
The Song of Roland **1**:166

Adcock, F. E.
Thucydides **17**:288

Addison, Joseph
Aeneid **9**:310
Iliad **1**:282
Ovid **7**:292
Sappho **3**:379
Sophocles **2**:293

Adler, Mortimer J.
Plato **8**:342

Adlington, William
Apuleius **1**:6

Aiken, Conrad
Murasaki, Lady **1**:423

Albert, S.M.
Albert the Great **16**:33

Alighieri, Dante
Aeneid **9**:297
Bertran de Born **5**:4
Seneca, Lucius Annaeus **6**:331

Sordello **15**:323

Ali-Shah, Omar
Khayyám **11**:288

Allen, Archibald W.
Livy **11**:334

Allen, Richard F.
Njáls saga **13**:358

Allinson, Francis G.
Menander **9**:204

Allison, Rev. William T.
The Book of Psalms **4**:371

Al-Nadīm
Arabian Nights **2**:3

Alphonso-Karkala, John B.
Kalevala **6**:259

Alter, Robert
The Book of Psalms **4**:451

Ambivius, Lucius
Terence **14**:302

Amis, Kingsley
Beowulf **1**:112

Anacker, Robert
Chrétien de Troyes **10**:144

Anderson, George K.
Beowulf **1**:98
The Dream of the Rood **14**:245

Anderson, J. K.
Xenophon **17**:342

Anderson, William S.
Juvenal **8**:59

Andersson, Theodore M.
Hrafnkel's Saga **2**:103

Apuleius, Lucius
Apuleius **1**:3

Aquinas, St. Thomas
Augustine, St. **6**:5
Averroës **7**:3
Plato **8**:217

Arendt, Hannah
Augustine, St. **6**:116

Aristophanes
Aeschylus **11**:73

Aristotle
Aeschylus **11**:73
Greek Historiography **17**:13
Hesiod **5**:69
Iliad **1**:273
Plato **8**:202
Sophocles **2**:291

Arnold, E. Vernon
Seneca, Lucius Annaeus **6**:362

Arnold, Edwin
Hesiod **5**:71
Iliad **1**:308
Odyssey **16**:208

Sappho **3**:384

Arnold, Mary
Poem of the Cid **4**:226

Arnold, Matthew
Aeneid **9**:316
Aristophanes **4**:54
Iliad **1**:300
Mabinogion **9**:146
The Song of Roland **1**:162
Sophocles **2**:311

Arnott, Geoffrey
Menander **9**:261

Arnott, W. G.
Menander **9**:253

Arnstein, Adolf
Meister Eckhart **9**:4

Arrowsmith, William
Aristophanes **4**:131

'Arùdì, Nizàmì-i-
Avicenna **16**:147

Ascham, Roger
Cicero, Marcus Tullius **3**:186

Ashe, Geoffrey
Arthurian Legend **10**:2

Asquith, Herbert Henry
Demosthenes **13**:135

Aston, W. G.

Critic Index

Critic Index

Critic Index

Critic Index

Critic Index

Critic Index

Critic Index

ISBN 0-8103-9301-8

90000